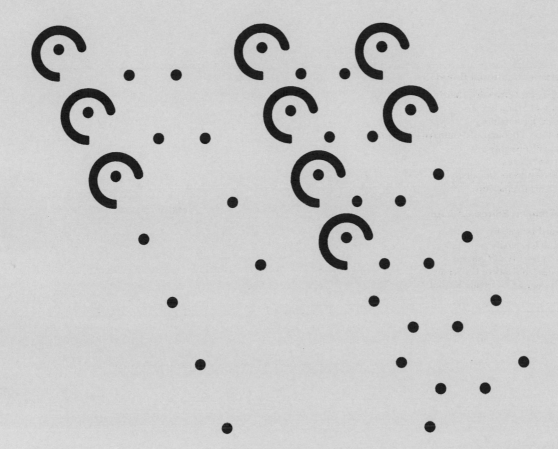

**Hermeneia
—A Critical
and Historical
Commentary
on the Bible**

Deutero-Isaiah

A Commentary on Isaiah 40–55
by Klaus Baltzer

Translated by
Margaret Kohl

Edited by
Peter Machinist

Fortress
Press

Minneapolis

Deutero-Isaiah
A Commentary on Isaiah 40–55

Cover and interior design by Kenneth Hiebert
Typesetting and page composition by
The HK Scriptorium

Library of Congress Cataloging-in-Publication Data

Baltzer, Klaus, date—
    Deutero-Isaiah : a commentary on Isaiah 40–55 /
by Klaus Baltzer ; edited by Peter Machinist ;
translated by Margaret Kohl.
        p.   cm. — (Hermeneia)
    Includes bibliographical references and indexes.
    ISBN 0-8006-6039-0 (alk. paper)
    1. Bible. O.T. Isaiah XL-LV—Commentaries.
I. Machinist, Peter. II. Title. III. Series:
Hermeneia—a critical and historical commentary
on the Bible.
    BS1515.3.B35   1999
    224'.1077—dc21   98-35306
                                    CIP

The paper used in this publication meets the mini-
mum requirements of American National Standard
for Information Sciences—Permanence of paper for
Printed Library Materials, ANSI Z329.48–1984.

Manufactured in the U.S.A.   AF 1-6039

05 04 03 02 01 1 2 3 4 5 6 7 8 9 10

For my dear wife, Jo

my companion —

with Deutero-Isaiah

Klaus Baltzer was born in 1928 and lives in Deisenhofen, Germany, where he and his late wife, Jo, raised four children. He received his education at the Kirchliche Hochschule in Wuppertal and at the universities of Tübingen, Bonn, and Heidelberg, where he developed his interests in form criticism, tradition history, and Old Testament theology. At Bonn, he was in Martin Noth's seminar; and at Heidelberg he studied with Gerhard von Rad, who supervised both his doctorate (1957) and his habilitation (1959). From 1958 to 1961 he was *Assistent* and then *Privatdozent* at Heidelberg.

After four decades of teaching, Baltzer is now emeritus Professor of Old Testament in the Protestant Faculty of the University of Munich, Germany. He has contributed significantly over the years to the study of the prophets through his many scholarly articles; and his major works prior to this commentary are *The Covenant Formulary: In Old Testament, Jewish, and Early Christian Writings* (Fortress Press, 1971), and *Die Biographie der Propheten* (Neukirchener, 1975). He is one of the original members of the Hermeneia Board.

Endpapers

The texts of Isaiah 40 (front endpapers) and 55 (back endpapers) are from the Isaiah Scroll discovered in Cave 1 at Qumran (1QIsa[a]). Isaiah 40 appears in cols. 32–33, and Isaiah 55 appears in cols. 45–46. The photos are from *Scrolls from Qumran Cave I,* ASOR Texts and Translations 2 (Jerusalem: Albright Institute of Archaeological Research, 1974). They were obtained with the kind help of professors Frank M. Cross and Philip J. King and are used with the permission of John C. Trever.

Contents

x

The name *Hermeneia,* Greek ἑρμηνεία, has been chosen as the title of the commentary series to which this volume belongs. The word *Hermeneia* has a rich background in the history of biblical interpretation as a term used in the ancient Greek-speaking world for the detailed, systematic exposition of a scriptural work. It is hoped that the series, like its name, will carry forward this old and venerable tradition. A second, entirely practical reason for selecting the name lies in the desire to avoid a long descriptive title and its inevitable acronym, or worse, an unpronounceable abbreviation.

The series is designed to be a critical and historical commentary to the Bible without arbitrary limits in size or scope. It will utilize the full range of philological and historical tools, including textual criticism (often slighted in modern commentaries), the methods of the history of tradition (including genre and prosodic analysis), and the history of religion.

Hermeneia is designed for the serious student of the Bible. It will make full use of ancient Semitic and classical languages; at the same time, English translations of all comparative materials—Greek, Latin, Canaanite, or Akkadian—will be supplied alongside the citation of the source in its original language. Insofar as possible, the aim is to provide the student or scholar with full critical discussion of each problem of interpretation and with the primary data upon which the discussion is based.

Hermeneia is designed to be international and interconfessional in the selection of authors; its editorial boards were formed with this end in view. Occasionally the series will offer translations of distinguished commentaries which originally appeared in languages other than English. Published volumes of the series will be revised continually, and eventually, new commentaries will replace older works in order to preserve the currency of the series. Commentaries are also being assigned for important literary works in the categories of apocryphal and pseudepigraphical works relating to the Old and New Testaments, including some of Essene or Gnostic authorship.

The editors of *Hermeneia* impose no systematic-theological perspective upon the series (directly, or indirectly by selection of authors). It is expected that authors will struggle to lay bare the ancient meaning of a biblical work or pericope. In this way the text's human relevance should become transparent, as is always the case in competent historical discourse. However, the series eschews for itself homiletical translation of the Bible.

The editors are heavily indebted to Augsburg Fortress for its energy and courage in taking up an expensive, long-term project, the rewards of which will accrue chiefly to the field of biblical scholarship.

The editor responsible for this volume is Peter Machinist of Harvard University.

Frank Moore Cross	*Helmut Koester*
For the Old Testament	For the New Testament
Editorial Board	Editorial Board

It must have been during the summer semester of 1950, in Heidelberg, that Gerhard von Rad set me as a subject for a seminar paper an exegesis of Isaiah 40. That was my first encounter with Deutero-Isaiah.

The beginnings of the commentary were bound up with the beginnings of *Hermeneia:* Helmut Koester and Frank M. Cross asked whether I would be willing to cooperate in working out plans for a commentary series, and whether I could myself write a commentary on Deutero-Isaiah. That was in 1962, in Evanston. Ever since then these two friends have accompanied the work with their advice and encouragement.

The actual work began in 1968, in Munich. The initial task was to take into account as far as possible the extensive interpretation history of Isaiah 40-55. I should like to name here three commentaries from which I learned particularly: Franz Delitzsch, *Biblischer Commentar über den Propheten Jesaja* (3d ed. Leipzig, 1879); James Muilenburg, "Isaiah 40-66," *Interpreter's Bible,* vol. 5 (Nashville, 1956) 381-773; W. A. M. Beuken, *Jesaja, deel II* (Nijkerk, 1979-83). Nevertheless, it soon became clear that I should have to strike out on my own path. The more Deutero-Isaiah became for me part of the far-off world of antiquity, the closer it also came to our own time. I hope that even those who are unable to assent to the fundamental theses I have put forward will find themselves able to profit from the commentary.

I am indebted to many people—some named here, some unnamed—for their help in the work. In seminars on texts and themes relating to Deutero-Isaiah, students challenged me through their interest, and contributed insights through their questions and observations.

Generations of student assistants helped especially in acquiring the necessary literature. Here I may name only Stefan Ark Nitsche, Ilona Clemens, Susanne Ehrich, Thomas Vogt, and Maren Leupolt.

The manuscript was typed by the secretaries of the Old Testament Institute of the Faculty for Protestant Theology: Rosemarie Wipfler, Gisela Böhme, and Anemone Körner. I should like to thank them here for the trouble they took over the far from easy text.

Throughout the years, my assistants Helmut Utzschneider, Thomas Krüger and Peter Marinković were my most important dialogue partners. In linguistic questions I was able to draw on the advice of Rüdiger Bartelmus.

I should also like to mention the pleasure and profit I derived from conversations "across the passage" with my colleague and friend Jörg Jeremias.

Thanks are due to the University of Munich for providing a unique opportunity for interdisciplinary work in fields connected with the eastern Mediterranean and the Middle East. This is precisely the area that Deutero-Isaiah designates as "islands" and "nations." In jointly held seminars I was able to work with, among others, Kai Brodersen, Peter Calmeyer, Johannes G. Deckers, Dieter Kessler, Manfred Görg, Regine Schulz, Astrid Nunn, and Manfred Krebernik. It was probably in these seminars that I learned most about the ancient world. Manfred

Krebernik and Kai Brodersen were in addition untiring in their response to questions and in their help with texts and literature. It is my most earnest hope that all concerned will strive to preserve the continued existence of interdisciplinary opportunities of this kind in Munich in the future too.

The work could not have been brought to a conclusion without the committed group of Micha Boerschmann, Daniela Fischer, Helge Frowein, Peter Kocher, and Kyu-Sang Yu, and above all not without the help and coordination of Peter Marinković.

I should like to thank my colleague Eckart Otto for his support in making the completion of the manuscript possible.

Peter Machinist was kind enough to act as my volume editor. Valerie Stein provided information about translations of German books and articles, and Mark Hamilton gave important help in editing the English translation.

Perce Lueders of Fortress Press accompanied the beginnings of the commentary; I remember him with gratitude. Marshall Johnson gave me the sometimes necessary encouragement to bring the work to a conclusion. That I was able to finish it owes much to K. C. Hanson's intensive labor.

Finally, I should like to express special thanks to Margaret Kohl. She was my first editorial reader. Her patient and precise questions throughout the translation enabled me to make a number of improvements to the whole. She gave the work its English dress. I should also like to thank her in the name of all those for whom English is the lingua franca, and for whom the translation may provide access to an understanding of the exegesis of Deutero-Isaiah.

Munich   *Klaus Baltzer*
1 October 1999

AASF	Annales Academiae Scientiarum Fennicae	AUSS	*Andrews University Seminary Studies*
ÄAT	Ägypten und Altes Testament	AVTRW	Aufsätze und Vorträge zur Theologie und Religionswissenschaft
AAWG	Abhandlungen der Akademie der Wissenschaften in Göttingen	BA	*Biblical Archaeologist*
AB	Anchor Bible	BAGD	W. Bauer, W. F. Arndt, F. W.
ABD	*Anchor Bible Dictionary*		Gingrich, and F. W. Danker, *A*
AcOr	*Acta orientalia*		*Greek-English Lexicon of the New*
ADPV	Abhandlungen des deutschen Palästina-Vereins	BASOR	*Testament*
ÄF	Ägyptologische Forschungen	BASOR	*Bulletin of the American Schools of Oriental Research*
AfO	*Archiv für Orientforschung*	BAW.GR	Bibliothek der Alten Welt—
AHw	W. von Soden, *Akkadisches Handwörterbuch*		Griechischen Reihe
AJBI	*Annual of the Japanese Biblical Institute*	BBB	Bonner biblische Beiträge
		BC	Biblischer Commentar über das Alte Testament (Keil & Delitzsch)
AJSL	*American Journal of Semitic Languages and Literature*	BDB	F. Brown, S. R. Driver, and C. A. Briggs, *Hebrew and English*
AK	*Antike Kunst, Lexikon Olten*		*Lexicon of the Old Testament*
ALGM	*Ausführliches Lexikon der griechischen und römischen Mythologie,* ed. Roscher	BEAT	Beiträge zur Erforschung des Alten Testaments und des antiken Judentums
ALUOS	*Annual of the Leeds University Oriental Society*	*BeO*	*Bibbia e oriente*
AMI	*Archäologische Mitteilungen aus Iran*	BETL	Bibliotheca ephemeridum theologicarum lovaniensium
AnBib	Analecta biblica	BFCTh	Beiträge zur Förderung christlicher Theologie
ANEP	J. B. Pritchard, ed., *Ancient Near Eastern Pictures*	BHH	B. Reicke and L. Rost, eds., *Biblisch-Historisches*
ANET	J. B. Pritchard, ed., *Ancient Near Eastern Texts*		*Handwörterbuch*
ANETS	Ancient Near Eastern Texts and Studies	BHK	R. Kittel, *Biblia hebraica*
		BHS	*Biblia hebraica stuttgartensia*
AnOr	Analecta orientalia	BHTh	Beiträge zur historischen Theologie
ANRW	*Aufstieg und Niedergang der römischen Welt*	*Bib*	*Biblica*
AnSt	*Anatolian Studies*	*BibLeb*	*Bibel und Leben*
AOAT	Alter Orient und Altes Testament	BibOr	Biblica et orientalia
AOB	*Altorientalische Bilder zum Alten Testament*	BibS(N)	Biblische Studien (Neukirchen, 1951–)
AOS	American Oriental Series	*Bijdr*	*Bijdragen* [Tijdschrift voor philosophie en theologie]
AOT	*Altorientalische Texte zum Alten Testament*	*BiOr*	*Bibliotheca orientalis*
ArOr	*Archiv orientální*	*BJRL*	*Bulletin of the John Rylands University Library of Manchester*
ARW	*Archiv für Religionswissenschaft*	*BK*	*Bibel und Kirche*
ASAE	*Annales du service des antiquités de l'Égypt*	BKAT	Biblischer Kommentar: Altes Testament
ASTI	*Annual of the Swedish Theological Institute*	*BLE*	*Bulletin de littérature ecclésiastique*
		BLit	*Bibel und Liturgie*
ATAbh	Alttestamentliche Abhandlungen	*BN*	*Biblische Notizen*
ATD	Das Alte Testament Deutsch	BOT	De Boeken van het Oude Testament
AThANT	Abhandlungen zur Theologie des Alten und Neuen Testaments	BPAA	Bibliotheca Pontificii Athenaei Antoniani
ATSAT	Arbeiten zu Text und Sprache im Alten Testament (St. Ottilien EOS Verlag)	*BR*	*Biblical Research*

BRGA	Beiträge zur Religionsgeschichte des Altertums
BRL	*Biblisches Reallexikon*
BSac	*Bibliotheca Sacra*
BT	*The Bible Translator*
BTB	*Biblical Theology Bulletin*
BTFT	*=Bijdragen* (see above)
BThSt	Biblisch-Theologische Studien
Burg.	*Burgense*
BVC	*Bible et vie chrétienne*
BVSAW.PH	Berichte über die Verhandlungen der Sächsischen Akademie der Wissenschaften zu Leipzig. Philologisch-historische Klasse
BWANT	Beiträge zur Wissenschaft vom Alten und Neuen Testament
BWZKM	Beihefte zur Wiener Zeitschrift für die Kunde des Morgenlandes
BZ	*Biblische Zeitschrift*
BZAW	Beihefte zur *ZAW*
CBFV	*Cahiers bibliques de foi et vie*
CBQ	*Catholic Biblical Quarterly*
CChrSL	Corpus Christianorum
ConBOT	Coniectanea biblica, Old Testament
CoTh	Collectanea Theologica
CPH	*Calwer Predigthilfen*
CTA	A. Herder, *Corpus des tablettes en cunéiformes alphabétiques*
CTh	Cahiers théologiques
CTM	Calwer theologische Monographien
CULGS	Cambridge University Library Genizah Series
CurTM	*Currents in Theology and Mission*
CV	*Communio Viatorum*. Prague
DAI	Deutsches Archäologisches Institut
DBAT	*Dielheimer Blätter zum Alten Testament*
DD	*Dor leDor*
Did(L)	*Didaskalia*. Lisbon
Div.	*Divinitas*. Roma, Pontificae Academiae Theologicae Romanae commentarii
DNL	Dissertationes Neerlandicae
DunRev	*Dunwoodie Review*
Ebib	Études bibliques
EdF	Erträge der Forschung
EHS.T	Europäische Hochschulschriften. Reihe 23: Theologie
EncJud	*Encyclopaedia judaica* (1971)
ErIsr	*Erets Israel*
EstEcl	*Estudios eclesiásticos*
ETL	*Ephemerides theologicae lovanienses*
EThR	*Études théologiques lovanienses*
ETS	Erfurter theologische Studien
EvQ	*Evangelical Quarterly*
EvT	*Evangelische Theologie*
Exp	*Expositor*
ExpT	*Expository Times*
FAT	Forschungen zum Alten Testament
FB	Forschung zur Bibel
FJB	Frankfurter judaistische Beiträge
FoiTe	*La foi et le temps*
FRLANT	Forschungen zur Religion und Literatur des Alten und Neuen Testaments
FThL	Forum theologiae linguisticae
FUR	*Freiburger Universitätsreden*
GAT	Grundrisse zum Alten Testament
GCS	Griechischen christlichen Schriftsteller
GKB	Gesenius-Kautzsch-Bergsträsser, *Hebräische Grammatik*
GKS	*Gesenius' Hebrew Grammar*, ed. E. Kautzsch, trans. A. E. Cowley
GPM	*Göttinger Predigtmeditationen*
GRBS	*Greek, Roman, and Byzantine Studies*
GTJ	*Grace Theological Journal*
GTS	Gettysburg Theological Studies
GThT	*Gereformeerd theologisch tijdschrift*
GuL	*Geist und Leben*
HALAT	W. Baumgartner et al., *Hebräisches und aramäisches Lexikon zum Alten Testament*
HALOT	W. Baumgartner et al., *Hebrew and Aramaic Lexicon of the Old Testament*
HAR	*Hebrew Annual Review*
HAT	Handbuch zum Alten Testament
HAW	Handbuch der Altertumswissenschaft
HBT	*Horizons in Biblical Theology*
HDSB	*Harvard Divinity School Bulletin*
Hesp.	*Hesperia*
HPR	*Homiletic and Pastoral Review*
HS	*Hebrew Studies*
HSAT	Die Heilige Schrift des Alten Testaments
HSM	Harvard Semitic Monographs
HTR	*Harvard Theological Review*
HTS	Harvard Theological Studies
HTS	*Hervormde teologiese studies*
HUCA	*Hebrew Union College Annual*
IB	*Interpreter's Bible*
IBS	*Irish Biblical Studies*
IDB	G. A. Buttrick, ed., *Interpreter's Dictionary of the Bible*
IEJ	*Israel Exploration Journal*
Imm.	*Immanuel*
Int	*Interpretation*
ISCP	Iowa Studies in Classical Philology
Itin.	*Itinerarium*
ITQ	*Irish Theological Quarterly*
JANESCU	*Journal of the Ancient Near Eastern Society of Columbia University*

JAOS	Journal of the American Oriental Society
JBC	R. E. Brown et al., eds., The Jerome Biblical Commentary
JBL	Journal of Biblical Literature
JbMiss	Jahrbuch für Mission
JBTh	Jahrbuch für Biblische Theologie
JDAI	Jahrbuch des Deutschen Archäologischen Instituts
JES	Journal of Ecumenical Studies
JETS	Journal of the Evangelical Theological Society
JJS	Journal of Jewish Studies
JLA	Jewish Law Annual
JNES	Journal of Near Eastern Studies
JNSL	Journal of Northwest Semitic Languages
JQR	Jewish Quarterly Review
JSHRZ	Jüdische Schriften aus hellenistisch-römischer Zeit
JSJ	Journal for the Study of Judaism in the Persian, Hellenistic, and Roman Period
JSOT	Journal for the Study of the Old Testament
JSOTSup	Journal for the Study of the Old Testament Supplement Series
JSS	Journal of Semitic Studies
JTS	Journal of Theological Studies
Judaica	Judaica: Beiträge zum Verständnis . . .
KAI	Kanaanäische und Aramäische Inschriften
KAR	Keilschrifttexte aus Assur religiösen Inhalts
KAT	E. Sellin, ed., Kommentar zum Alten Testament
KÄT	Kleine ägyptische Texte
KB	L. Koehler and W. Baumgartner, Lexikon in Veteris Testamenti libros
KD	Kerygma und Dogma
KEH	Kurzgefasstes-Exegetischer Handbuch
KEK	Kritisch-Exegetischer Kommentar über das Neue Testament
KHC	Kurzer Hand-Commentar zum Alten Testament
KlT	Kleine Texte für Vorlesungen und Übungen
KP	Der Kleine Pauly, Lexikon der Antike
LÄ	Lexikon der Ägyptologie
LavTP	Laval Théologique et Philosophique. Québec
LAW	Lexikon der Alten Welt
LB	Linguistica Biblica
LCL	Loeb Classical Library
LD	Lectio divina
Leš	Lešonénu
LoBAT	Leggere oggi la Bibbia. Antico Testamento
LOS	London Oriental Series
LUÅ	Lunds universitets årsskrift
MAOG	Mitteilungen der Altorientalischen Gesellschaft
MDAFA	Mémoires de la délégation archéologique française en Afghanistan
MDAIK	Mitteilungen des deutschen archäologischen Instituts. Cairo
MDOG	Mitteilungen der deutschen Orient-Gesellschaft
MIOF	Mitteilungen des Instituts für Orientforschung. Berlin
MoBi	Monde de la bible. Paris
MSAA.As	Marburger Studien zur Afrika- und Asienkundc, Scric B, Asicn
MThA	Münsteraner theologische Abhandlungen
MTZ	Münchener theologische Zeitschrift
MUSJ	Mélanges de l'université Saint-Joseph
MVAG	Mitteilungen der vorderasiatisch-ägyptischen Gesellschaft
NCB	New Century Bible
NedTT	Nederlands theologisch tijdschrift
NGTT	Nederduitse Gereformeerde Teologiese Tydskrif. Kaapstad
NRT	La nouvelle revue théologique
NRSV	New Revised Standard Version
NTOA	Novum Testamentum et Orbis Antiquus. Fribourg
NTT	Norsk Teologisk Tidsskrift
OBO	Orbis biblicus et orientalis
OLP	Orientalia lovaniensia periodica
OLZ	Orientalistische Literaturzeitung
Or	Orientalia (Rome)
OTE	Old Testament Essays. Pretoria
OTL	Old Testament Library
OTS	Oudtestamentische Studiën
OTStudies	Old Testament Studies
ParPass	Parola de passato
PEQ	Palestine Exploration Quarterly
PIASH	Proceedings of the Israel Academy of Sciences and Humanities
POS	Pretoria Oriental Series
POT	De Prediking van het Oude Testament
Proof	Prooftexts
PSB	Princeton Seminary Bulletin
PTMS	Pittsburgh (Princeton) Theological Monograph Series
PW	Pauly-Wissowa, Real-encyclopädie der classischen Altertumswissenschaft
QD	Questiones disputatae
RA	Revue d'assyriologie et d'archéologie orientale
RÄRG	Reallexikon der ägyptischen Religionsgeschichte, ed. H. Bonnet

RB	*Revue biblique*	SKG.G	Schriften der Königsberger
RBR	*Ricerche bibliche e religiose.* Milano		Gelehrten Gesellschaft
RechBib	Recherches bibliques		Geisteswissenschaftliche Klasse
RestQ	*Restoration Quarterly, Studies in*	SNTU	Studien zum Neuen Testament
	Christian Scholarship. Abilene,		und seiner Umwelt
	Tex.	SO	Symbolae Osloenses
RevB	*Revista bíblica*	SOTSMS	Society for Old Testament Study
RevQ	*Revue de Qumran*		Monograph Studies
RevScRel	*Revue des sciences religieuses*	SPAW	Sitzungsberichte der preussi-
RGG	*Religion in Geschichte und*		schen Akademie der
	Gegenwart		Wissenschaften
RHPhR	*Revue d'histoire et de philosophie*	SPIB	Scripta pontificii instituti biblici
	religieuses	*SSN*	*Studia Semitica Neerlandica*
RivB	*Rivista biblica*	STDJ	Studies on the Texts of the
RLA	*Reallexikon der Assyriologie*		Desert of Judah
RM	Ecclésiastiques Religionen der	*StGen*	*Studium Generale*
	Menschheit	*SThZ*	*Schweizerische theologische*
RSPT	*Revue des sciences philosophiques et*		*Zeitschrift*
	théologiques	STö	Sammlung Töpelmann
RSR	*Recherches de science religieuse*	*StTh*	*Studia Theologica*
RSV	*Revised Standard Version*	*SWJT*	*Southwestern Journal of Theology*
RTK	*Roczniki teologiczno-kanociczne.*	*TAik*	*Teologinen Aikakauskirja.* Helsinki
	Lublin	TBAW	Tübinger Beiträge zur Altertums-
RTP	*Revue de théologie et de philosophie*		wissenschaft
RTR	*Reformed Theological Review.*	TBC	Torch Biblical Commentary
	Melbourne	*TBT*	*The Bible Today*
RV	Religionsgeschichtliche	*TDNT*	G. Kittel and G. Friedrich, eds.,
	Volksbücher		*Theological Dictionary of the New*
RWTS	Religionswissenschaftliche Texte		*Testament*
	und Studien	*TDOT*	G. J. Botterweck and H.
SAÄK	Studien zur altägyptischen		Ringgren, eds., *Theological*
	Kultur. Hamburg		*Dictionary of the Old Testament*
SAHG	A. Falkenstein and W. von	TeT	Temi e testi. Roma
	Soden, *Sumerische und akkadische*	*TGI*	*Textbuch zur Geschichte Israels*
	Hymnen und Gebete	*THAT*	E. Jenni and C. Westermann,
SBB	Stuttgarter biblische Beiträge		eds., *Theologisches Handwörterbuch*
SBFLA	Studii biblici franciscani liber		*zum Alten Testament*
	annuus	*TBei*	*Theologische Beiträge*
SBLASP	Society of Biblical Literature	TBü	Theologische Bücherei
	Abstracts and Seminar Papers	*TGl*	*Theologie und Glaube*
SBLDS	SBL Dissertation Series	*ThEv*(SA)	*Theologia evangelica* (South
SBLMS	SBL Monograph Series		Africa)
SBLSCS	SBL Septuagint and Cognate	*ThPh*	*Theologie und Philosophie*
	Studies	ThSt(B)	Theologische Studien (ed. K.
SBLTT	SBL Texts and Translations		Barth)
SBS	Stuttgarter Bibelstudien	*ThViat*	*Theologia Viatorum,* Jahrbuch der
SBT	Studies in Biblical Theology		Kirchlichen Hochschule. Berlin
ScC	*Scuola cattolica*	TLOT	E. Jenni and C. Westermann,
ScEc	*Sciences Ecclésiastiques*		eds., *Theological Lexicon of the Old*
ScEs	*Science et esprit*		*Testament*
Schol.	*Scholastik*	TLZ	*Theologische Literaturzeitung*
SEÅ	*Svensk exegetisk årsbok*	TQ	*Theologische Quartalschrift*
Sem	*Semitica*	TRE	*Theologische Realenzyklopädie*
SHR	Studies in the History of	TRu	*Theologische Rundschau*
	Religion	*TTK*	*Tidsskrift for teologi og kirke.* Oslo
SIDIC	Series Internationale	TTZ	*Trierer theologische Zeitschrift*
	Documentation Judéo-	*TWAT*	G. J. Botterweck and H.
	chrétienne		Ringgren, eds., *Theologisches*
SJT	*Scottish Journal of Theology*		*Wörterbuch zum Alten Testament*

TWNT	G. Kittel and G. Friedrich, eds., *Theologisches Wörterbuch zum Neuen Testament*	WTJ	*Westminster Theological Journal*
		WuD	*Wort und Dienst*
		WVDOG	Wissenschaftliche Veröffentlichungen der Deutschen Orientgesellschaft
TynBul	*Tyndale Bulletin*		
TZ	*Theologische Zeitschrift*		
UF	*Ugarit-Forschungen*	WZ(L)	*Wissenschaftliche Zeitschrift der Karl-Marx-Universität Leipzig*
UGAÄ	Untersuchungen zur Geschichte und Altertumskunde Ägyptens. Leipzig.		
		YJS	Yale Judaic Studies
		ZA	*Zeitschrift für Assyriologie*
UL	C. Gordon, *Ugaritic Literature*	ZAH	*Zeitschrift für Althebraistik.* Stuttgart
UT	C. Gordon, *Ugaritic Textbook*		
UUÅ	Uppsala universitets årsskrift	ZAR	*Zeitschrift für altorientalische und biblische Rechtsgeschichte*
VAFLNW.G	Vorträge der Arbeitsgemeinschaft für Forschung des Landes Nordrhein-Westfalen— Geisteswissenschaftliche Reihe		
		ZÄS	*Zeitschrift für ägyptische Sprache und Altertumskunde.* Berlin
		ZAW	*Zeitschrift für die alttestamentliche Wissenschaft*
VD	*Verbum Domini*	ZBK	Zürcher Bibelkommentare
VF	*Verkündigung und Forschung*	ZDMG	*Zeitschrift der deutschen morgenländischen Gesellschaft*
VivPen	*Vivre et penser [=Revue biblique 50–52]*		
		ZDPV	*Zeitschrift des deutschen Palästina-Vereins*
VT	*Vetus Testamentum*		
VTSup	*Vetus Testamentum,* Supplements	ZLThK	*Zeitschrift für die lutherische Theologie und Kirche*
WBC	Word Biblical Commentary		
WCB	World Christian Books	ZNW	*Zeitschrift für die neutestamentliche Wissenschaft*
WeWa	*Western Watch.* Pittsburgh, Pa.		
WM	*Wörterbuch der Mythologie,* ed. H. W. Haussig, Stuttgart	ZRGG	*Zeitschrift für Religions- und Geistesgeschichte*
WMANT	Wissenschaftliche Monographien zum Alten und Neuen Testament	ZST	*Zeitschrift für systematische Theologie*
WO	*Die Welt des Orients*	ZThK	*Zeitschrift für Theologie und Kirche*
WSt	*Wiener Studien.* Zeitschrift für klassische Philologie und Patristik		

Deutero-Isaiah is the name given in research to the anonymous author of Isaiah 40–55 and to his work. The Greek *deuteros* (δεύτερος) means "the second"–hence the designation "Second Isaiah," which is also used. In the present commentary, however, the name Deutero-Isaiah (abbreviated to DtIsa) has been retained, in order to bring out the artificiality of the name given to the text.

In the canon of the Hebrew Bible, Isaiah 40–55 are chapters in the book that is named after the prophet Isaiah. The separate character of DtIsa was first described in detail by B. Duhm in his Isaiah commentary of 1892,[1] although some preliminary indications in this direction can already be found in J. C. Döderlein[2] and J. G. Eichhorn.[3] O. Eissfeldt, however, already points to "hints in Ibn Ezra (d.1167)."[4]

There are a number of reasons for distinguishing between DtIsa and Isaiah, but the different period of the historical events that form the background is particularly important. In Isaiah, Israel's enemies are the Assyrians. Their empire was destroyed by the Neo-Babylonians and the Medes at the end of the seventh century B.C.E. For DtIsa, the antagonist is Babylon. The exile (598/597 B.C.E.) and the fall of Jerusalem (587/586 B.C.E.) are the preceding events presupposed. In Isa 44:28 and 45:1 the Persian king Cyrus II (559–530 B.C.E.) is mentioned. In addition to this disparity in historical background, there are literary differences in style and genre. The thrust of Isaiah's theology is primarily judgment; DtIsa proclaims salvation and a new beginning.

It must be said, however, that the tripartite division of the book of Isaiah into Isaiah I (chaps. 1–39), Isaiah II or Deutero-Isaiah (chaps. 40–55) and Isaiah III or Trito-Isaiah (chaps. 56–66), is no longer unquestionably accepted in research.[5] The question of how the different parts of the book hang together is beginning to be raised once more. As H.-J. Kraus rightly puts it, this is probably not just a "bookbinding problem."[6]

What all three parts have in common is the theme of Zion/Jerusalem.[7] Common to them also is the entitling and concept of Israel's God as "the Holy One"[8] and "king."[9]

There are a number of possible ways of linking the different parts of the book of Isaiah, and these have continually been discussed. C. C. Torrey, for example, assumed that Isaiah 34–35 and 40–66 were connected.[10] C. R. Seitz has recently investigated chaps. 36–37, seeing them as a compositional link between Isaiah I and Deutero-Isaiah.[11] There are relationships in points of detail too. Isaiah 40 would seem to presuppose Isaiah 6 (the chapter describing the installation of the prophet Isaiah) or its tradition. The presupposition in both passages is the concept of the divine council.[12] The "oracles concerning Babylon" in Isa 13:1—14:23 and 21:1-10 play a part in the

1   B. Duhm, *Das Buch Jesaja* (1892; 4th ed., 1922).

2   J. C. Döderlein, *Esaias* (1775; 3d ed., 1789) XII–XV.

3   J. G. Eichhorn, *Einleitung in das AT* III (1783) 76–97.

4   O. Eissfeldt, *The Old Testament: An Introduction* (1965) 304. [*Einleitung in das AT* (3d ed., 1964), 408].

5   On the following see esp. C. R. Seitz, *Zion's Final Destiny* (1991), with a helpful account of the literature.

6   H.-J. Kraus, *Das Evangelium der unbekannten Propheten: Jesaja 40–66* (1990) 3.

7   Kraus (ibid., 4) points for the "Zion theology" to the following passages among others: Isa 1:27; 2:3; 4:5; 8:18; 12:6; 14:32; 18:7; 24:23; 28:16; 31:4; 35:10; 40:9; 46:13; 51:3, 16; 52:1, 7; 59:20; 60:14; 61:3; 62:1, 11.

8   Cf. Isa 1:4 (see also 5:19, 24; 30:11; 37:23); 5:16; 10:17, 20; 12:6; 17:7; 29:19, 23; 30:12 (see also 30:15; 45:11; 48:17); 31:1 (see 43:14); 40:25; 41:14 (43:14), 16, 20; 43:3, 15; 47:4; 49:7 (see 55:5); 54:5; 57:15; 60:9, 14.

9   Isa 6:5; 8:21; 24:23; 32:1; 33:17, 22; 41:21; 43:15; 52:7; cf. 57:15.

10   C. C. Torrey, *The Second Isaiah* (1928) 279–301. M. Pope followed this line ("Isaiah 34 in Relation to Isaiah 35, 40–66," *JBL* 71 [1952] 235–43). He observed "vocabulary affinities" between Isaiah 34–35 and 40–55. "The parallels in phraseology, ideology, and subject matter are also notable" (242). I could agree with these observations. I think also the genre of chaps. 34–35 is comparable to that of 40–55. But regarding the content, the position of these two texts is completely different. Isaiah 34–35 is very aggressive (see Pope, 243); Isaiah 40–55 is interested in a peaceful solution.

11   See Seitz, *Zion's Final Destiny* (1991) with its subtitle: *The Development of the Book of Isaiah: A Reassessment of Isaiah 36-39*.

12   See F. M. Cross, "The Council of Yahweh in Second Isaiah," *JNES* 12 (1953) 274–77. For the connections in content, cf. Seitz, "Return to the Divine Council," *Zion's Final Destiny*, 197–99.

description of Babylon's downfall in 46:1-2 and 47:1-15.[13] In DtIsa messianic expectations are transferred to Cyrus (45:1). The literary problem of the composition of Isaiah I must undoubtedly be seen in a more differentiated way than Duhm's formulation allows. This goes so far as to assume that the combination of Isaiah I and II had a subsequent influence on the text and structure of Isaiah I.[14] For example, I too believe that Isaiah's installation has been moved from the beginning of the prophet's biography (which is its proper place, according to the genre) to its present position in Isaiah 6.[15] Thus the "hardness of heart" (6:10) also no longer comes at the beginning; instead we have Isaiah chap. 1, the people's guilt and its consequences, and Isaiah chap. 2, the pilgrimage of the nations to Zion.[16]

Trito-Isaiah presents a special problem.[17] I myself no longer consider the sequence Deutero-Isaiah (40–55)—Trito-Isaiah (56–66) to be self-evident. Of course the two have much in common in language and tradition. But the differences should also be noted. Isaiah 60–62 presents a description of Yahweh's return to Zion that makes a more original, primary impression than 52:7-10, for example, whose theme is the same. In Trito-Isaiah the tone toward foreigners is clearly more hostile. The relationship to the cult is also different. And an assimilation of penitential and confessional liturgical fragments can be detected. Here further discussion is required.[18]

With regard to DtIsa itself, there is a wide measure of agreement among scholars about its demarcation, in the first place because of the correspondence between chaps. 40 and 55. The present commentary endorses this definition of the book's extent in light of its form and content.

The rest of the introduction will proceed in a series of methodical steps, and in so doing will trace the history of the research. The extensive literature shows that DtIsa's work has continually evoked new interest. Very different people have striven to understand the text, as well as its bearing on their faith. Their painstaking observations still stand, although the insights are subject to their time, as are ours. But in spite of this, new explanatory models must continually be developed in research. In the literature on DtIsa the frequency of diametrically opposing viewpoints is striking. For example, does the work consist of small units, or are we dealing with a single composition? The question of genres also has a bearing here. What is DtIsa's relationship to the cult? Are the Servant of God texts part of the whole, or additions? Is the individual interpretation of these texts more appropriate, or the collective one?

In the commentary I shall try to take up the opposing views, or at least to record the observations on which they are based.

I. Literary Questions

A. Textual Criticism

The Hebrew text of DtIsa is astonishingly well preserved.[19] This is true of the Masoretic text (MT), the reliability of which is confirmed by the Great Isaiah Scroll found in Qumran (1QIsaa).[20] The differences between MT and 1QIsaa are mainly orthographical. For

---

13 See below on the text.

14 See R. F. Melugin, *The Formation of Isaiah 40–55* (1976) 83, 176; R. Rendtorff, "Isaiah 6 in the Framework of the Composition of the Book," in *Canon and Theology* (1993) 170–80 ["Jes 6 im Rahmen der Komposition des Jesajabuches," in *The Book of Isaiah* (1989) 73–82].

15 See K. Baltzer, *Die Biographie der Propheten* (1975), esp. 108–13. For a different view see O. H. Steck, "Bemerkungen zu Jesaja 6," in *Wahrnehmungen Gottes im Alten Testament: Gesammelte Studien* (1982) 149–70.

16 Isa 54:14-17 contains a reference to 2:4, "swords into plowshares." See below on the text.

17 See K. Elliger, *Die Einheit des Tritojesaja* (1928); S. Sekine, *Die tritojesajanische Sammlung (Jes 56–66), redaktionsgeschichtlich untersucht* (1989), esp. 182–233.

18 A wealth of material from the aspect of the language is offered by A. L. H. M. van Wieringen's study, *Analogies in Isaiah*, vol. A: *Computerized Analysis of Parallel Text between Isaiah 56–66 and Isaiah 40–55;* vol. B: *Computerized Concordance of Analogies between Isaiah 56–66 and Isaiah 40–55* (1993).

19 See James Muilenburg's view (1956) 114: "The Hebrew text of Second Isaiah has been transmitted exceptionally well. Its superior value is shown by the way in which it has preserved parallelism and metrical construction and also by the fact that it generally yields a satisfactory sense. It is not flawless, but the number of corruptions is small" (with reference to C. C. Torrey, *Second Isaiah* [1928] 206–7).

20 As well as the textual apparatus in *BHS* (see, e.g., below under 55:13), it is worth drawing on the facsimile edition of 1QIsaa (e.g., *Scrolls from Qumran*

example, the repression of suffixes in MT may be due to a tendency to avoid a personalized interpretation of concepts ("*his* strength," "*his* glory"). My firm impression is that in the exegesis of individual passages 1QIsaᵃ is often preferable as probably preserving the original reading, although one must allow for the usual scribal and hearing errors.[21] The text's good state of preservation could, not least, suggest that the text of DtIsa was committed to writing at a relatively late date. Whether 1QIsaᵃ, in its structuring, paragraphing, and marginal marks, still permits the scenic division of the text of chaps. 40–55 to be detected is a question that requires examination.[22]

The Septuagint (LXX) version of the book of Isaiah has been preserved in an astonishingly large number of manuscripts. The different versions would require an investigation of their own.[23] The translation initially reflects the interpretation current in the Greek-speaking Jewish community in Alexandria from the third century B.C.E. onward.[24] We may assume that later Christian tradition influenced the history of the text. Eissfeldt's judgment in his *Introduction* was: "The translation of the Pentateuch is good, that of Isaiah of little use" (ET, p. 704). The rendering of Isaiah 40–55 shows no marked differences from the translation of the rest of the book.

The Greek translation ran into difficulty, however, over the wordplays that DtIsa so much enjoys and that extend even to deliberate ambiguities, as well as covert references to texts and traditions. Here the LXX presents its own unequivocal interpretation. It would be interesting to discover whether in so doing it gives preference to one particular interpretive level. The substitu-

tion by modern text critics of individual words and emendations on the basis of the LXX remains problematical. As far as we can see, the Greek version is no longer aware of the dramatic form of the DtIsa text. But certain individual manuscripts require further examination relative to this question.

The Targums, the Syriac translation, and the Vulgate are all part of the interpretive tradition and are consequently of interest, for example in the case of a text such as 52:13–53:12. K. Elliger made a noteworthy contribution to the textual criticism of DtIsa, and I should therefore like to draw particular attention to the text-critical notes in his commentary.[25] In some cases the premises of his interpretation of the text can no longer be shared, especially where the reconstruction of an *Ur*-text is concerned; but here a detailed discussion is required that would go outside the framework of the present commentary.[26] Where we are faced with a choice of readings, the decisions of Barthélemy, Lohfink, Rüger, and others are helpful.[27]

The ancient translations, then, were already interpretations, and the same must be said of modern translations too. Nevertheless, for the translation of Isaiah 40–55 one should draw on the various modern translations, for example, *La Bible de Jérusalem,* the

Cave I: The Great Isaiah Scroll . . . from photographs by J. C. Trever [ed. F. M. Cross, D. N. Freedman, and J. A. Sanders, 1976]). The German translation by W. Grimm and K. Dittert takes a number of readings from 1QIsaᵃ into account (*Das Trostbuch Gottes,* 1990). See also J. L. McKenzie, *Second Isaiah* (AB 20; 1973, with notes by D. N. Freedman).

21   E. Y. Kutscher has published an important study of 1QIsaᵃ, although I cannot always agree with his conclusions (*The Language and Linguistic Background of the Isaiah Scroll* [1QIsaᵃ] STDJ 6 [1974]). Kutscher claims that 1QIsaᵃ belongs to a group of "uncorrected texts (i.e., popular editions)" (83), whereas MT is "of a more archaic type" (77). Of interest are his observations regarding differences of language in Jerusalem and Judea (89, 95; see below on Isa 42:24; 49:20).

22   Thomas Krüger put this question to me.

23   See J. Ziegler, *Untersuchungen zur Septuaginta des Buches Isaias* (1934).

24   See here I. L. Seeligmann, *The Septuagint Version of Isaiah* (1948).

25   K. Elliger, *Jesaja II 40,1–45,7,* BKAT XI/1 (1978). Elliger's preliminary work on the text of Isa 45:8–55:13 has been incorporated in the continuation of his commentary made by H.-J. Hermisson (*Jesaja II* [fasc. 7-9] 45:8–45:25 [1991ff.]). See also H. W. Wolff's introduction to Elliger's own volume.

26   A good survey of the state of research, at least up to 1980, can be found in A. van der Kooij's study, *Die alten Textzeugen des Jesajabuches* (1981).

27   See D. Barthélemy, *Critique textuelle de l'Ancien Testament,* vol. 2: *Isaïe, Jérémie, Lamentations* (1986). See also E. Tov, *Textual Criticism of the Hebrew Bible*

Einheitsübersetzung, and the New Revised Standard
Version. For work with the present commentary, the
familiar translations, such as the Zurich Bible or the
revised Luther Bible, also have their usefulness.[28]

It is often not so much the Hebrew text as modern linguistic development that presents difficulty. Under the
influence of the various media, spoken language is
changing rapidly, and this presents a problem for any
translation.

The more we study DtIsa, the more we are struck by
the marvelous artistry and power of the language.
Differentiated means of expression are used. Every
translation has to create or arrive at clarity secondhand,
and in so doing pays the price of curtailing the full subtlety of the text.

The concern of the present commentary has been to
bring out the spectrum of what is said, even for readers
unfamiliar with the original language. Consequently I
have where necessary indicated the whole breadth of the
possible translations by using several alternative words,
divided by slashes.

The adequate translation of the ancient Hebrew tense
system into modern languages is a widely known difficulty. This fact is noted in several places in this commentary.[29] A special aspect of this problem is that, for the
purposes of the "liturgical drama," Deutero-Isaiah deliberately intertwines the past, present, and future tenses.

B. Literary Criticism

In OT exegesis literary criticism is an important instrument. It starts from the observation of discrepancies in
the text. Tensions in form and content, changes in language and style, repetitions—all these features are registered and explained on the basis of the text's literary
development, its revision, or redaction. These methods
have proved their worth in the case of the Pentateuch
and the prophetic writings, even though further critical
questions still have to be asked. It is understandable that
the same methods should also have been applied to
Deutero-Isaiah.[30] Even where the unity of Isaiah 40–55 is
presupposed, the differences between chaps. 40–48 and
49–55 have been explained by the methods of literary
criticism. The special position of the Cyrus texts has
raised literary questions, and the same is true above all
of the Servant of God texts. Attempts have been made to
work out the revision that the text has undergone and to
elicit strata that run right through it.[31] Exact and scrupu-
lous though the observations and reconstructions are,
the question is still whether the explanatory model
taken as the basis in each given case is adequate. It could
well be, for example, that the tensions between Isaiah
40–48 and Isaiah 49–55 are inherent in the content, not
in the supposition that one is redactionally later than
the other. The link between the Jacob-Israel tradition in
Isaiah 40–48 and the Zion/Jerusalem tradition in Isaiah

(1992), above all his "Index 1: Ancient Sources," s.v.
Isaiah 40–55 (420).

28 *La Bible de Jérusalem–La Sainte Bible traduite en
français sous la direction de l'École biblique de Jérusalem*
(1956; 2d ed. 1962); *Die Bibel, Einheitsübersetzung der
Heiligen Schrift* (1980); *Holy Bible, New Revised
Standard Version* (1989); *Die Heilige Schrift des Alten
und des Neuen Testaments, Zürcher Bibel* (1931, 1955,
1971); *Die Bibel oder Die ganze Heilige Schrift des Alten
und Neuen Testaments nach der Übersetzung Martin
Luthers,* revised text (1975).

29 In this commentary we use the traditional terms *perfect* and *imperfect* for the *qaṭal* and *yiqṭol* forms,
respectively, or the *afformative* and *preformative* con-
jugations. Concerning the problems of the aspects
in the Hebrew verbal system cf. P. Joüon and T.
Muraoka, *A Grammar of Biblical Hebrew,* vol. 2: *Part
Three: Syntax* (SubBi 14/II, 1991) 354ff.; R.
Bartelmus, *Einführung in das biblische Hebräisch*
(1994) esp. 70–71, 201–7. The ambiguity of the
imperfect and the polyvalence of the afformative
and preformative in general are treated by H.-P.
Müller, "*wa-, ha-* und das Imperfectum consecu-

tivum," *ZAH* 4 (1991) 144–60 (lit.!), and idem, "Das
Bedeutungspotential der Afformativkonjugation—
Zum sprachgeschichtlichen Hintergrund des
Althebräischen," *ZAH* 1 (1988) 74–98, 159–90. I
would like to thank R. Achenbach for valuable hints
concerning the recent discussion.

30 Cf. O. Kaiser's summing up in the 4th edition of his
Einleitung in das AT (1978) 240: "To be judged as
later additions, at least, are the polemics against the
production of idols and the cult of the gods in
40:19-20; 41:6-7; 42:17; 44:9-20; 45:16-17, 20b; 46:5-
8 and 48:22. We may also reckon with the insertion
of smaller additions in 40:7a?, b, 14bα, 16; 41:8b,
19a?, 20?; 42:16bβ, 19b, 21, 24bβγ; 43:5a, 7b*, 8?,
12b, 14bb, 21?, 28a; 44:5, 28b; 45:5b?, 9-10?, 14?,
18aα*, b?; 46:9bβ; 47:3a, 14b; 48:1bβ, 4, 5b, 8-10,
16aα*, b, 19b?, 22; 49:18bα*, 21bα*; 50:3?, 11?;
51:1-2, 4-8?, 11 and 52:4-6 [according to Fohrer and
Westermann]. But Elliger's doubts about 42:18-25;
48:17-19; 49:7*, 8bαβ, 22-26; 50:1-3; 51:10b-16 and
54–55 should not be pushed aside too hastily."

31 See, e.g., H.-C. Schmitt, "Prophetie und
Schultheologie im Deuterojesajabuch:

49–55 is programmatic for DtIsa's work as a whole. This is made clear in chap. 40, in the very first verses (vv. 1-2): "Comfort, comfort my people!—says your God. Speak to the heart of Jerusalem." Here we are already given the password to the unity. That the unity is disputed is reflected in the texts themselves.

Additions and redactional changes cannot in principle be excluded, but their share in the text as we have it is, in my view, very slight. Some of the rapid shifts of literary forms, persons and themes are connected with the genre to which DtIsa's work belongs. The date of the work (a point that we shall consider presently) must of course be taken into account as well.

C. Form and Genre Criticism

The application of form criticism meant a fundamental change in the exegesis of DtIsa.[32] The definition of the genres started from "the smallest units," and the result of this approach was to call into question the unity of these texts. The individual oracles listed varied in number from forty-nine in H. Gressmann to seventy in J. Begrich.[33] Is DtIsa merely a collection of individual oracles, or are we dealing with a conscious overall composition? That was the question under discussion.

In a further step, individual genres within DtIsa came to be described more precisely. J. Begrich's study of 1934 was a pioneer work. It established a connection between the "priestly salvation oracle" and the salvation oracles and oracles of assurance that a prayer has been heard, which we find in DtIsa.[34] C. Westermann then differentiated, within this genre, between an "assurance of salvation" (or "salvation oracle") and an "announcement of salvation."

J. Begrich termed a whole series of texts in DtIsa "judgment speeches." This description also came to be further differentiated by Westermann, A. Schoors, and R. F. Melugin, for example. "Judgment speeches" pronounced by Yahweh on Israel were now distinguished from those pronounced by Yahweh on "the peoples."

The "disputation sayings" are linked with the judgment speeches. But whether we can talk about a traditional genre here or whether the texts are DtIsa's own independent formulation is a question still under discussion.[35] Identifiable as genres, finally, are the hymnal sections in DtIsa's text. Here what Westermann calls "eschatological hymns of praise" can be distinguished from divine self-predications in hymnal form. The commentaries of J. Muilenburg and Westermann are examples showing that essential elements in the context of DtIsa's work can be elicited on the basis of a more penetrating definition of the genres. The same may be said of studies by Schoors and H. C. Spykerboer,[36] which develop this method further.

What has been too little studied and discussed, however, is the question about the composition as a whole.[37] This can also be seen as a question about genres, provided that we assume not merely "smallest units" and their *Sitz im Leben*, but also an integrating major or "umbrella" genre, which can absorb the different genres to which the smaller units belong. In the case of such a composite genre too, the question about the text's literary structure and function must be set in a social context. It is by deter-

Beobachtungen zur Redaktionsgeschichte von Jes 40–55," *ZAW* 91 (1979) 43–61; H.-J. Hermisson, "Einheit und Komplexität Deuterojesajas: Probleme der Redaktionsgeschichte von Jes 40–55," in *The Book of Isaiah* (1989) 287–312; O. H. Steck, *Gottesknecht und Zion. Gesammelte Aufsätze zu Deuterojesaja* (1992); R. G. Kratz, *Kyros im Deuterojesaja-Buch* (1991). Still of interest in the context of literary criticism is K. Elliger, *Deuterojesaja in seinem Verhältnis zu Tritojesaja* (1933).

32 See J. Muilenburg's survey of earlier research (1956) 384–92. A. Schoors, *I Am God Your Saviour, A Form-Critical Study of the Main Genres in Is. XL–LV* (1973) 1–31. Also D. Michel's summing up in "Deuterojesaja," *TRE* 8.510–30.

33 See the survey in Muilenburg (1956), 384.

34 J. Begrich, "Das priesterliche Heilsorakel," *ZAW* 11 (1934) 81–92; idem, *Studien zu Deuterojesaja* (1938,

reprint 1963) 25. On the following references (esp. the commentaries) see in each case the bibliography.

35 See H.-J. Hermisson, "Diskussionsworte bei Deuterojesaja. Zur theologischen Argumentation des Propheten," *EvTh* 31 (1971) 665–80.

36 H. C. Spykerboer, *The Structure and Composition of Deutero-Isaiah* (1976).

37 C. Westermann, for example, writes (*Sprache und Struktur der Prophetie Dtjes* [1981] 167): "Isa 40–55 is not a collection of single fragments belonging in each given case to different speech genres; it is a meaningful whole which has grown up out of these speech forms." Compare this with Schoors, *I Am God Your Saviour* (1973): "The collection itself is a problem. It seems indeed impossible to demonstrate that Is. xl–lv has been composed according to a certain design" (29).

mining the genre that we can open up the text's understanding of reality. The results also have consequences for the dating of the text. In DtIsa unity and diversity are in equilibrium. The texts make a consistent impression in their approach, their language, and their conceptual world. This being so, we can usefully and legitimately talk about DtIsa's theology. Nevertheless, the tensions that literary criticism has detected still remain.

Before developing an independent model for the genre of DtIsa's work, it may be useful to remind ourselves of some of the text's most striking features.

There is a large measure of agreement that chaps. 40 and 55 form a kind of frame for the book.[38] Chapter 40 announces the theme: comfort for Israel as God's people. The new exodus is promised, and it is with this promise that chap. 55 then ends (vv. 12-13). The decisive point is the reliability of the divine Word. Here 40:8 at the beginning corresponds to 55:11 at the end.

It can also be established that there are independent "mid-level" units (between smallest and major units) that can be understood on their own. The Servant of God texts are an example; they include a number of the smallest units that themselves vary in genre. These texts are linked through the person of the servant, but they are distributed throughout the composition. They could exist on their own, as many interpretations show; but DtIsa's book could also stand as a unity without the Servant of God texts. In the context of the book as we now have it, however, the Servant of God texts are obviously linked with the whole.

Something similar may also be said about the Cyrus texts. They too are relatively independent, so that C. C. Torrey, for example, could suggest seeing them as additions.[39]

Oracles concerning Babylon are for the most part restricted to chaps. 46 and 47. A definition of the genre of the whole would therefore have to take the mid-level units into account as well as the smallest ones.[40] So much, initially, for the composition of the work.

At first sight the speech sections and speech genres dominate the book.[41] It seems to be poorly provided with action. That there are different speakers is a point to be noted. Divine speech predominates. A speaker can occasionally comment on events, for example, "What shall I cry?" (40:6). The Servant of God himself speaks. Finally, we are told what the personifications Jacob/Israel or Zion/Jerusalem have to say.

Nevertheless, one should notice that the book contains action as well. The speeches describe what is happening, for example, what the artisans are doing as they manufacture the idols. Commands are given: "Get up upon a high mountain, messenger (of joy) Zion!" (40:9), or "Sit in (the) dust . . . Babylon!" (47:1). The texts having to do with judgment are not just judgment *speeches*. In this respect I would modify the genre definition. These are judgment *scenes*, in which differing standpoints are put forward. A judge comes on—the judge is Yahweh himself; witnesses are produced; there are defendants. The disputation sayings presuppose dialogue. In defining the genres we must find a place for these "action" elements.

What is striking, finally, is the pronounced "address" character of the book. Listeners (or readers) are drawn in. Their reaction is reported. Their agreement is sought. Arguments are put forward; opinion and behavior are supposed to change; directions for action are given. An indication of this bond with the audience are the many deictic particles ("see," "this one there," "that one," etc.).

As regards the time covered by the text, past (from creation onward), present, and future are intimately

38   Cf. e.g., Muilenburg, 385; C. R. North (1964) 71; C. Westermann (1966) 22; W. A. M. Beuken (1979) 15 and (1983) 306.

39   C. C. Torrey, *The Second Isaiah* (1928) 40–44. The most important recent investigation of the Cyrus texts is R. G. Kratz's study, *Kyros im Deuterojesaja-Buch* (1991), even though I am unable to agree with his literary-critical conclusions. He assigns to the Cyrus texts: 41:1-5a; 41:21-29; 44:28; 45:1-8; 45:9-13; 45:14-17; 46:9-13; 48:12-15. To these texts I would add 40:13, the first announcement of Cyrus in the prologue; see K. Baltzer, "Jes 40,13-14—ein Schlüssel zur Einheit Deutero-Jesajas?" in M. Görg, ed., *FS V.*

Hamp, BN 37 (1987) 7–10. The name of "Cyrus" is found only in 44:28 and 45:1.

40   The division into chaps. 40–48 and 49–55 is one of the themes of literary criticism. Consequently in his commentary, *Der Erste und der Letzte* (1981), R. P. Merendino could permit himself to investigate only chaps. 40–48.

41   See Y. Gitay, *Prophecy and Persuasion* (1981).

intertwined. The space envisaged is the whole world, from the heavenly to the earthly sphere.

This is a form of reality familiar to us from poetry especially; and the language of the text is a final indication that this is indeed poetry. A whole series of stylistic devices special to poetry are employed, in the choice of words and the use of images, in structure (e.g., *parallelismus membrorum*) and in the rhythms.[42]

D. Isaiah 40–55 as Liturgical Drama

1. A Comparison with Genres of This Kind in the Ancient World

A fundamental thesis of the present commentary is that DtIsa's work is a liturgical drama. The word *drama* can be used to designate an overall genre that is able to absorb other, very diverse separate genres. Although the individual parts are relatively independent, they are nonetheless all part of a whole. In our modern classification, and in the classical one too, this relation of the parts to the whole is expressed through the structure. Entrances of the dramatic personae, scenes, and acts are separate elements that together form the composition of the whole drama. The relationship between speech and action is constitutive. With regard to the content, in drama a single theme (or plot) is developed, or it may be several connected themes (or plots). These are put forward at the beginning and find their resolution at the end. The theme may be a familiar one, but in the drama it is newly interpreted against a wider or different horizon. The dramatic tension results from the diverse counteractions, interactions, and conflicts that are related to the topic. Emotional involvement and the understanding of the mind are the aim, the purpose being to achieve a certain reaction.

The drama is addressed to an audience. All those involved—author, players and audience—should agree on the rules of the game, an agreement that includes a common understanding of reality. The language is often (as here in DtIsa) the language of poetry, even if elements of everyday speech are also used. In calling the genre "drama" we have to be aware that when we use the term we initially associate it with our own ideas about the theater. As a heuristic construct this preconceived notion can even be useful. But we must bear in mind all the more constantly the differences between our ideas and those of DtIsa.

The term "*liturgical* drama" is intended to bring out the proximity to worship and the cult. The drama uses forms and subject matter already present in the liturgy, to the point when it itself may acquire a ritual function. This also implies that the performance can be repeated, and that the drama can be used at different places. This was not a matter of course in the case of Attic drama. One important assumption is the link between the liturgical drama and the feast-day calendar of a particular community.

More important than our modern ideas and concepts, however, is the comparison with the genres employed in the ancient world. This will be developed below, even if the account is of necessity only brief. Points of detail may be found in the body of the commentary.

For the OT, the information offered by the *Encyclopaedia Judaica* provides the starting point: "Neither biblical nor talmudic literature contains anything which can be described as 'theater' or 'drama' in the modern sense of these terms."[43] This impression depends in part on the texts that happen to have come down to us. In considering the drama of the ancient world in general, we have to remember how little of the literature is extant, if we except Attic drama. On the basis of what is available to us, we can indeed arrive at certain criteria, but there is neither a universally accepted definition of drama, nor is it possible fully to reconstruct its history.[44]

a. Babylonia

In the ancient Near Eastern world, there has been "drama" within the framework of the cult since time immemorial.[45] From the sphere of Babylonian influence

---

42 See J. J. Burden, "Poetic Texts," in *Words from Afar* (1986) 39–71; M. O'Connor, *Hebrew Verse Structure* (1980); J. L. Kugel, *The Idea of Biblical Poetry* (1981); see there also the index to DtIsa on p. 335.

43 L. Sowden, "Theater," *EncJud* 15 (1971) 1049.

44 T. H. Gaster, *Thespis: Ritual, Myth, and Drama in the Ancient Near East* (1950; 2d ed. 1966) has gathered together important texts on the subject, even if his

theses are individually problematic.

45 See here T. Jacobsen, "Religious Drama in Ancient Mesopotamia," in H. Goedicke and J. J. M. Roberts, eds., *Unity and Diversity: Essays in the History, Literature, and Religion of the Ancient Near East* (1975) 65–97.

scholars have drawn on the ritual of the New Year Festival (*akītu*) for comparison with DtIsa.[46] The body of this ritual describes the action that is carried out. What the priests have to recite is stated in each case. An interesting point is that although some of the extant texts date only from a relatively late period, they had undoubtedly been in use for a long time. An indication of the extent of the cultural exchange at this period is a text that contains a ritual corresponding to that of the Babylonian *akītu* festival. The possibility of such an exchange over space and time must therefore be taken into account. The very title of an article by R. C. Steiner shows the importance for DtIsa of the places named and the circumstances of the Persian period: "The Aramaic Text in Demotic Script: The Liturgy of a New Year's Festival Imported from Bethel to Syene by Exiles from Rash."[47] The text in question is contained in Papyrus Amherst 63. Syene (near Elephantine in southern Egypt) is mentioned in DtIsa under the name "the land of Sinim" (49:12; see below on the text and its significance). In the case of other texts, the Gilgamesh epic for example,[48] to ask whether they are open to dramatic presentation is not an impossible question.

b. Egypt

When we come to Egypt,[49] four texts are of special interest for an interpretation of DtIsa as a liturgical drama.[50] They date from the earliest and from the late periods. The extant versions are certainly not identical with the original texts. This suggests that they were used over a long time. These texts are connected with the major annual festivals.[51] The public could participate in them, and in this respect they differed from the daily temple ritual of the priesthoods. Feast, procession, and pilgrimage were closely connected. In this framework, dramatic performances were held at different places. Royal ideology and worship of the various deities correspond.

1) The Dramatic Ramesseum Papyrus[52]

This text probably dates from the early Egyptian period.[53] It has been preserved in a manuscript belonging to

46 F. Thureau-Dangin, *Rituels Accadiens* (1921) 127–54; *AOT* 215–303; *ANET* 331–35; *TUAT*, vol 2: *Religiöse Texte* (1986–91) 212–23; M. E. Cohen, *The Cultic Calendars of the Ancient Near East* (1993); B. Pongratz-Leisten, *INA ŠULMI ĪRUB: Die kulttopographische und ideologische Programmatik der akītu-Prozession in Babylonien und Assyrien im 1. Jahrtausend v. Chr.* (1994).

47 *JAOS* 111 (1991) 362–63. Now see the translation of the whole papyrus by Richard C. Steiner, "The Aramaic Text in Demotic Script (1.99)," in William W. Hallo and K. Lawson Younger Jr., eds., *The Context of Scripture*, vol. 1: *Canonical Compositions from the Biblical World* (1997) 309–27. I should like to express my thanks to M. Krebernik for drawing my attention to this text.

48 For part of this tradition see D. O. Edzard, "Gilgameš und Huwawa A," part I, *ZA* 80 (1990) 165–203; and part II, *ZA* 81 (1991) 165–233; idem, *"Gilgameš und Huwawa": Zwei Versionen der sumerischen Zedernwaldepisode nebst einer Edition von Version "B,"* Bayerische Akademie der Wissenschaften, Philosophisch-Historische Klasse, Sitzungsberichte, Jahrgang 1993, Heft 4 (1993).

49 I should like to express my thanks to D. Kessler, Munich, for our jointly held seminars on Israel and Egypt in the Persian period (winter semester 1989/90) and on temple and festival in Egypt and in the OT (winter semester 1992/93). These gave me essential impulses for the following comments.

50 On the history of research into the drama in Egypt see H. W. Fairman, *The Triumph of Horus: An Ancient Egyptian Sacred Drama* (1974) 1–13 (summary); E. Drioton, *Le théâtre égyptien* (1928) (but his theses are disputed); C. J. Becker, *Egyptian Festivals* (1967); J.-C. Goyon, "Dramatische Texte," *LÄ* 1 (1975) 1140–44 (with lit. and further texts); P. Derchain, "Kultspiele," *LÄ* 3 (1980) 856–59 (with lit.); R. Stadelmann, "Prozessionen," *LÄ* 4 (1982) 1160–64.

51 See J. Assmann, "Das ägyptische Prozessionsfest," in J. Assmann and T. Sundermeier, eds., *Das Fest und das Heilige: Religiöse Kontrapunkte zur Alltagswelt, Studien zum Verstehen fremder Religionen I* (1991) 105–22.

52 On the text see K. Sethe, *Dramatische Texte zu altägyptischen Mysterienspielen II: Der dramatische Ramesseumspapyrus: Ein Spiel zur Thronbesteigung des Königs* (1928) 83–264; S. Schott, *Mythe und Mythenbildung im Alten Ägypten* (1964, reprint 1945) 30–36 (important also for the relationship among cult, ritual and myth, and especially for his explanation of the detachment of the liturgical drama from ritual); Gaster, *Thespis,* 377–99; W. Helck, "Bemerkungen zum Ritual des dramatischen Ramesseumspapyrus," *Or* 23 (1954) 383–411; A. H. Gardiner, *The Ramesseum Papyri* (1955); J. Spiegel, "Göttergeschichten, Erzählungen, Märchen, Fabeln," *Handbuch der Orientalistik,* I/1, section 2 (2d ed. 1970) 148–49. See also H. Altenmüller, "Dramatischer Ramesseumspapyrus," *LÄ* 1 (1975) 1132–40.

the late Middle Kingdom. The festivities held at the coronation of Sesostris I (12th Dynasty, c. 1972–1928 B.C.E.) provided the occasion for the papyrus. The text consists of forty-six scenes. Each of them includes a narrative, which begins (in vertical lines) with "it happened" (ḫpr.n), followed by one or two short sentences, titlelike in form: "The doing of such and such a thing happened" (e.g., in the first scene: "It happened that the royal ship was made . . ."). The cultic action is narrated. The acting persons are called by their earthly titles, for example, the lector priest/master of the ceremony, the king.

Parallel to this an explanation follows, beginning "That is . . ." (pw). The mythological meaning of the narrated event is described. The lector priest becomes, for example, Thoth/Ibis, and the king becomes Horus. Actions that the god performs, or things that happen to him, are explained. But above all, divine speeches accompanying the scene are given word for word. The frequent use of wordplay is a striking feature, particularly in connection with cultic objects. In a horizontal series of pictures below the text, the scene in question is depicted once more, information about the place of the action also being given. The persons involved—onlookers, people with walk-on parts, witnesses, lector priest/master of the ceremony—all are named.

In this document, cult, myth and political action are linked.[54] It may give us an idea of what the "festal scroll" of a lector priest/master of the ceremony [Egyp. ḫry-ḥ(ȝ)b(w), literally "he who carries the festival scroll/ritual papyrus"] looked like.[55] The text is a "stage direction" for the performance. The recitation introduces the actors anew to their roles, to what they are supposed to do and say. The explanations give both actors and audience the necessary information about the meaning of what is being presented. The drama is part of the festival itself.[56]

2) The Memphite Theology[57]

The text has been preserved on what is known as the Shabaka Stone. According to the colophon, it is the copy of an ancient text made on the instructions of King Shabaka, the first ruler of the 25th Ethiopian Dynasty (713–698 B.C.E.).[58] His aim was no doubt to promote the unity of the kingdom, the restoration of Memphis as capital, and hence his own legitimation. The text itself was composed for the feast that took place on the first day of spring. It describes the struggle between the gods

---

53   The general assumption is a date at the end of the 2nd Dynasty (c. 2780–2635 B.C.E.); see Spiegel, "Göttergeschichten," 148.

54   See S. Schott, *Mythe und Mythenbildung im Alten Ägypten* (1964) 36: "The scene titles in the Ramesseum papyrus suggest that the main points of the action were that the king summons a ship, equips it and goes on board; that he is crowned, with the accompaniment of festivities and games symbolizing the battles that preceded the unification of the kingdom; and, finally, that he cares for and clothes his dead father." Important for an understanding of the institutional aspects of the action is the link between the installation of the new ruler and the apotheosis of his predecessor in the royal cult of the dead (cf. Ram. Pap. Scene 37 [114–16] - 38 [117–19]. See here J. C. Goyon, "Dramatische Texte," *LÄ* 1 (1975) 1140–44, 1142. For the political significance see also E. Hornung, *Geschichte als Fest* (1966).

55   Goyon describes the text as follows: "Substantially, it is conceived as a kind of aide-mémoire for the producer, drawn up functionally" (*LÄ* 1:1140–44, 1140).

56   See here J. Assmann, "Das ägyptische Prozessionsfest" (1991) 113–17.

57   H. Altenmüller, "Denkmal memphitischer Theologie," *LÄ* 1 (1975) 1065–69; W. Barta, "Der Epilog der Götterlehre von Memphis," *MDAIK* 28 (1972) 79ff.; J. von Beckerath, *Abriß der Geschichte des Alten Ägypten* (1971); J. H. Breasted, "The Philosophy of a Memphite Priest," *ZÄS* 39 (1901) 39-54; A. Erman, "Ein Denkmal memphitischer Theologie," SPAW 43 (1911) 916ff.; F. Junge, "Zur Fehldatierung des sogenannten Denkmals memphitischer Theologie oder Der Beitrag der ägyptischen Theologie zur Geistesgeschichte der Spätzeit," *MDAIK* 29/2 (1973) 195ff.; H. Junker, *Die Götterlehre von Memphis* (1939); K. Sethe, *Dramatische Texte in altägyptischen Mysterienspielen*, part 1: *Das Denkmal memphitischer Theologie, Die politische Lehre, Der Shabako-Stein des Britischen Museums*, UGAÄ X (1924, reprint 1964); Gaster, "The Egyptian Memphite Drama," in *Thespis*, 399–405; S. Schott, *Mythe und Mythenbildung im Alten Ägypten* (1964) 46–126.

58   The date of the text is disputed. Because of the archaic language it is often placed in the early period (Sethe: 1st Dynasty; Schott: 4th Dynasty, contemporary with the Pyramid Texts; Junker: 5th Dynasty, end of the Old Kingdom). According to Junge the language of both the text and the colophon of the stone is archaistic. He associates the whole text with the period of Shabaka. See also J. Leclant, "Schabaka," *LÄ* 5 (1984) 499–513.

Horus and Seth. The formerly divided country is reunited and assigned to Horus. He is crowned in Memphis. The fate of Osiris is narrated, with his burial in the "king's palace" in Memphis.

The text combines dramatic material and mythological narratives with a ritual in honor of the Memphite god Ptah, the chief god, who created the world through his word. Its content alone makes this text, too, of interest for DtIsa.

When we turn to the Ptolemaic period, two dramatic Egyptian texts must be mentioned, texts that at the same time signal the transition to the Hellenistic world. But though they themselves are late, these texts presuppose a long previous history, and that makes them of interest here.

3) The Dramatic Play in the Mammisi (Birth House) of Philae

The decoration of the north wall of the cell was studied by H. Goedicke, who published his findings under the title: *Die Darstellung des Horus, ein Mysterienspiel in Philae unter Ptolemäus VIII*[59] (The presentation of Horus. A mystery play in Philae in the reign of Ptolemy VIII). The title itself is an indication of Goedicke's basic theory.

4) The "Horus Myth" from Edfu[60]

The text is found on the wall enclosing the temple at Edfu, together with a "*bas* relief." It dates from the period of Ptolemy IX (or Ptolemy X?) c. 110 B.C.E. It describes Horus's fight with the enemy of the gods in the guise of a hippopotamus. What is remarkable about this text in its bearing on our present question (i.e., the genre and structure of the drama) is that it is distinctly divided, with a prologue and an epilogue. These frame three acts, each of them containing several scenes. According to D. Kessler in discussions, the schematic outline of the scenes can be reconstructed as follows:

- Scenic instruction for the master of the ceremony (*ḫry-ḥ(з)b(w)*, "the one who carries the festival scroll")
- Isis's invocation of Horus/Horus's song of victory (variable)
- Choric song for Horus
- Scenic directions for the master of the ceremony
- Invocation of Isis/Horus's song of victory (variable)
- Conclusion by the chorus.

The visual presentation in the relief and the text correspond. In act 1, for example, the scenery consists of two barks (small boats) on the sacred lake, with the king standing on the shore. The participants are Horus, Isis, the king, a demon as assistant in the hunt, the master of the ceremony [*ḫry-ḥ(з)b(w)*], dancers (as "harpoon throwers"), and finally the chorus.

If we take Egypt's long history into account, we have to say that only a small number of texts, fortuitously preserved, can be called "dramatic." These date from different eras, from the early down to the late period. They show a differentiated development. The unique character of these liturgical dramas can be seen in their original relation to the cult and, at the same time, their departure from the ritual. In the festival they link action, speech and dialogue with procession, music, and dance. The texts show that the performance took place beyond the inner space of the sanctuary, so that the public could take part. The people are drawn in as audience and to some extent as participants too.[61]

The texts themselves introduce the written form into the ordered progress of the festival.[62] This order no longer rests merely on oral tradition. The interpretation of ritual and myth is part of the subject matter of these

59 BWZKM 11 (1982). On Philae see also P. Derchain, "Kultspiele," *LÄ* 3 (1980) 856–59, who comments: "The festival of the return of the goddess, who had been far off, also gave an opportunity to act out the event in the appropriate reception temple (Hathor), although the main part of the performance consisted of dance and music, representing a ritualization of the outbreak of joy among the people at full moon" (857). He refers to Daumas in *ZÄS* 95 (1968) 1–17; and E. Brunner-Traut, *Der Tanz im alten Ägypten* (ÄF 6; 1937).

60 On the text see H. W. Fairman, *The Triumph of Horus: An Ancient Egyptian Sacred Drama* (1974),

with the account of an attempt at a performance of the drama. See P. Derchain, "Kultspiele," *LÄ* 3 (1980) 856–59, who remarks on our Edfu text: "Whole libretti, with scenery, are included there" (857 n. 14).

61 See H. Schlögl, "Schauspieler," *LÄ* 5 (1984) 545–46, with a reference to Herodotus's note mentioning that at the festival in Papremis over one thousand people participated, without their being priests (Herodotus 2.63).

62 See here J. Assmann, "Das ägyptische Prozessionsfest" (1991) 114–15: "The lector priest, on the other hand, had at his disposal the writings

dramas as indicated in the texts. In their unique character and form, and in their content too, the extant texts have to be understood as libretti or aides-mémoire for the festivals.[63] They give an impression of what the content of a festival scroll was. The texts are not the drama, but they do contain the most important directions for the performance, as regards both the action and the spoken word. In this respect we can perceive that the genre possesses characteristics that can be relevant for DtIsa too.

c. Attic Drama

For us, the best known dramatic texts belonging to the ancient world are those of Attic drama.[64] This has to do with European history, and the history of Western education especially. But we should be aware that here too we are dealing with a quite specific development.[65] For example, a particular feature of Attic drama is the strict separation of tragedy from comedy, both of them dramatic genres. In both cases the prehistory is disputed. Is the tragedy a genuine Attic development, or do outside influences also play a role, at least a contributory one? The relationship between drama and cult is also not unequivocally settled. There is a connection between the Dionysian cult and tragedy. Every year, at the beginning of March, the great Dionysian festivals were held in Athens, all free citizens participating. On this occasion tragedies were performed, the different poets vying with one another in their compositions.

The dithyramb was originally a song in honor of Dionysius. But the actors were not priests, nor was the chorus. The same can be said even more emphatically about comedy.

There is no doubt that the special character of Attic drama must be taken into account. It presupposes the city and its culture, and not least its democracy. The authors of the plays were citizens too, just as much as the artisans, and are known to us by name. They sacrificed to the gods and took part in discussions in the agora. At the festival, processions and theater were experiences shared by all. The public life of the city was their context. The theater was financed by various citizens, some of the promoters being known to us by name— today we should call them sponsors.

It would be worthwhile to trace the development of Attic drama, but that would take us too far afield. What is important, rather, to our study is the relevance of Attic drama for working out criteria of the genre "drama" in the ancient world. Two reasons impelled me to choose Attic drama as a paradigm outside the confines of the OT.

1. Hardly anywhere else do we possess so large a number of texts that have been accurately transmitted and well edited. When we think about the production, we must remember that even this wealth of material is no

---

containing the 'otherworldly' meaning that it was the purpose of the festival to actualize. . . . Between oral and written culture there is another widespread form: the culture of recitation, supported by written texts, which is still dependent on the festival as the most important means of actualizing the existing store of meaning in its transcendence of the everyday world."

63 See in its bearing on our question the excellent summing up by J.-C. Goyon, "Dramatische Texte," *LÄ* 1 (1975) 1140–44, esp. 1141: "L'ensemble livret du dialogue et didascalies constitue donc le plan-directeur d'une action représentée. Pour cette raison, les D.T. présentent souvent une incohérence apparente et semblent incomplets. Il convient cependant de garder présent à l'esprit qu'il s'agit là seulement du 'squelette' du drame, où seuls sont mentionnés les éléments essentiels sur lesquels devait se concentrer l'attention du metteur-en-scène, à peine de voir toute la réalisation entachée de nullité."

64 I have to thank Oliver Taplin for the opportunity to discuss the drama thesis as we walked along the Thames in Oxford in April 1984.

65 On "The Beginnings of the Drama: Tragedy," see A. Lesky, *A History of Greek Literature*, trans. J. Willis and C. de Heer (1966), here 223–33 (lit. on 232–33) [*Geschichte der griechischen Literatur* (3d ed., 1971) 260–70 (lit. on 269–70)]. Lesky formulates his own view as follows: "Both myth and tragedy were profoundly influenced by the effect which hero-cults had in making tales of the heroes the normal subject of tragedy. In this way the myth, after its epic and choral-lyric phase, entered on its tragic phase in which poets made it the vehicle of ethical and religious problems" (227–28; he refers to B. Snell, *The Discovery of the Mind: The Greek Origins of European Thought* [1960] 90 ["Mythos und Wirklichkeit in der griechischen Tragödie," in *Entdeckung des Geistes* (3d ed., 1955) 138]). On the role of the chorus in the development of the drama, Lesky maintains: "Thus we come to a view which can lay every claim to internal probability: in the course of its development the choral ode came to

more than a remnant. But the literary form, structure, style, and above all language of these poetic works can be clearly observed from what is available to us. We know an adequate amount about authors and addressees, and about the function of the drama in its social context. Early accounts, vase paintings, and archaeological findings allow us to reconstruct the performance practice with a large degree of conviction.

2. Another reason is that, when we come to the date of composition, DtIsa and the classic period of Greek drama may not have lain so far apart. To cite a few dates: in 539 B.C.E. Babylon was conquered by Cyrus, king of Persia (559–530 B.C.E.). For the Israelites who had been deported and were living in exile, this meant the possibility of a return and, with Persian permission, the rebuilding of the temple in Jerusalem. This reconstruction was completed, and the temple consecrated, in 515 B.C.E. The building of Jerusalem's walls under the governorship of Nehemiah is dated 445 B.C.E. With their completion Jerusalem was newly constituted as a city.

In Greece the earliest tragedy we know anything about was written by Thespis. According to the *Marmor Parium*[66] it was performed during the 61st Olympiad (536/535–533/532 B.C.E.) at the great Dionysian festival.

The war against Persia lasted from 492 to 479 B.C.E. In 490 the battle of Marathon was fought, and in 480 the battle of Salamis. Aeschylus's drama the *Persians* was already performed in 472—only eight years after the Persians had been defeated at the battle of Salamis. It was contemporaries who provided the first audience for the tragedy. The Aeschylus text is of special interest for the present commentary because it also grapples with Persian rule. Here too, even from a Greek viewpoint, Cyrus is an ideal ruler.[67] The hubris of his successors is presented critically. But at the same time, with his warn-ing against the military adventure of an expedition to Sicily, Aeschylus was probably concerned about political decisions made by his own people. The *Persians* is a reminder of the past, but it is also a comment on a topical theme.

A comparison of the structure of the Attic plays is the first relevant point for the interpretation of Isaiah 40–55 as drama. Formally, this structure comprises the framework, with prologue and epilogue, and the division into separate acts and scenes (this being our own terminology, developed in the course of a long tradition since antiquity). The structure is evident in the text itself, above all in the choric songs. These separate the major units of the *epeisodioi* from one another. According to Aristotle, "an *epeisodion* is that part of the tragedy in its full extent which is played out between the complete choric songs."[68] The choric songs separating the *epeisodioi* served initially a practical purpose. There was no curtain in the Attic theatre, so the choric songs made a change of roles and costumes possible. But they also performed the function of interpreting the action for the audience, setting it in a wider context. In addition, they span the time elapsing between the different parts of the action.

Another important structural element, however, is the entry and exit of the dramatis personae. O. Taplin has worked this out convincingly.[69] One must remember that the texts originally included no stage directions. What was happening, and who was speaking, had to be deduced from the text. The place and time of the action are a further element in the structure. Here again the texts themselves include signals. Detailed points of comparison are considered below in the commentary.

Not only Attic tragedy, but Attic comedy also deserves attention as a dramatic genre.[70] In spite of the differ-

---

include themes presupposing more and more knowledge on the part of the audience. It was an obvious step to prepare the hearers for what was coming by means of a prologue. Similarly a sequence of choral odes dealing with the various phases of a mythical narrative could be made possible by the simple device of bringing on a speaker between odes. The next step was to have the narrator and the chorus-leader speaking to each other" (*History*, 231).

66   The *Marmor Parium* is a marble stele with a chronological inscription listing political, religious, and literary events; it was composed presumably in the middle of the 3d century B.C.E.; see the *Oxford Classical Dictionary* (3d ed. 1996) 927.

67   See below on 46:16-22; cf. Aeschylus *Persians* 768–72.

68   See Aristotle *Poetics* 1452 B 20-21. I follow here K. Aichele, "Das Epeisodion," in W. Jens, ed., *Die Bauformen der griechischen Tragödie* (1971) 47–83, esp. 48.

69   O. Taplin, *The Stage-Craft of Aeschylus: The Dramatic Use of Exits and Entrances in Greek Tragedy* (1977).

70   See A. Lesky, *A History of Greek Literature* (1966), here "Comedy," pp. 233–40, with lit. [*Geschichte der*

ences between the two, comedy shares a number of characteristics with tragedy, for example, the part played by the chorus. In comedy the link with the Dionysian cult is more clearly maintained. Festival and procession are important elements. Comedy is concerned preeminently with everyday life. The audience is directly addressed. The battle of words is an invitation to participation. References to the political situation, both open and covert, can be detected. Here ambiguous language is employed as a useful technique. The audience is supposed to laugh—at the obscenities too.

In antiquity, the fifth century is the age of Old Comedy. For us its climax means Aristophanes. He was born c. 445 B.C.E.[71] and his last datable work was *Pluto*, performed in 388 B.C.E. He died during the 80s of the fourth century.

Attic comedy is of interest for DtIsa because it offers a point of comparison for the artisan scenes and the "idol production,"[72] for the caricature of a procession in 46:1-7, and for the description of Jerusalem's drunkenness in 51:17-23.

d. The *Exagoge* of Ezekiel the Tragedian[73]

At the end of these reflections about liturgical drama as genre, yet another text must be mentioned, a text that is clearly a drama, has a Jewish author,[74] and was written in Greek, probably in Egypt, in Alexandria. It is the play about Moses written by the tragedian Ezekiel.[75] Its title is the *Exagoge* (the "bringing out"), and its subject is the exodus of the Israelites from Egypt. It is one of the ironies of literary history that Ezekiel's *Exagoge* should be one of the very few dramas (apart from comedies) to survive from the Hellenistic period.

Eusebius of Caesarea (c. 260/265–339/340 C.E.) gives excerpts from the text in book 9 of his *Praeparatio Evangelica*, in the framework of extensive extracts from the work of Alexander Polyhistor of Miletus (1st century B.C.E.). Clement of Alexandria (c. 200 C.E.) also mentions Ezekiel the Tragedian in his *Stromata* (1.23).

The date of the *Exagoge* is disputed, estimates ranging from the third to the first century B.C.E. K. Kuiper's suggestion seems worth consideration.[76] He associates the play with speculation about the appearance of the Phoenix during the reign of Ptolemy III Euergetes (246–222 B.C.E.), linking it further with Tacitus's note in *Ann.* 6.28. H. Jacobson thinks that the text could perhaps be assigned to the second half of the second century B.C.E.[77]

The *Exagoge* takes up the biblical text as we find it in the book of Exodus, but with additional elements from the Midrash. Formally speaking, the drama has five acts.[78] Three actors are envisaged. Whether there was a chorus is disputed; at all events we have no evidence of one. The play is clearly addressed to Jews and Greeks. Both the form of the text and its detail permit

griechischen Literatur, "Anfänge des Dramas: Komödie" (1971) 270–78, with lit.].

71 On the basis of the OT, Nehemiah's governorship is assumed to have lasted from 445 to 433 B.C.E.; see A. Tångberg, "Nehemia/Nehemiabuch," *TRE* 24 (1994) 244–45 (with lit.).

72 Isa 40:18-20; 41:6-7; 44:9-20; 46:5-8.

73 At the time when I was beginning to develop my drama thesis, R. Bartelmus drew my attention to this text.

74 See Clement of Alexandria *Stromata* 1.23 (155.1): ὁ Ἐξεκίηλος ὁ τῶν Ἰουδαϊκῶν τραγῳδιῶν ποιητής.

75 Eusebius, *Werke,* vol. 8: *Praeparatio Evangelica,* ed. Karl Mras (1954), GCS 43/1, 524–27 (5.1–67) and 529–38 (5.68–269); *Tragicorum Graecorum Fragmenta,* vol. 1 (ed. B. Snell, 1971) 288–301; H. Jacobson, *The Exagoge of Ezekiel* (1983) (text, translation and commentary with lit.); E. Vogt, *Tragiker Ezechiel,* JSHRZ 4: *Poetische Schriften* (1983) (with introduction, esp. on the question of "reading" and "acting," and lit.); "Ezekiel the Tragedian," new translation and introduction by R. G. Robertson in

J. H. Charlesworth, ed., *OTP* 2:803–21; *Ezekiel the Tragedian* in C. R. Holladay, ed., *Fragments from Hellenistic Jewish Authors,* vol. 2: *Poets.* SBLTT 30, Pseudepigrapha Series 12 (1989).

76 K. Kuiper, "De Ezechiele Poeta Judaeo," *Mnemosyne* 28 (1900) 237–80. See H. Jacobson, *The Exagoge of Ezekiel* (1983) 7, 11–12.

77 Jacobson, *Exagoge,* 10–11.

78 See Jacobson's arrangement (ibid., 29): "It is, however, generally believed that the play did consist of five acts nor does this strain the evidence: (1) Moses' monologue and his meeting with the daughters of Raguel; (2) Moses' dream and its interpretation by Raguel; (3) the burning bush and God's appearance to Moses; (4) the messenger speech recounting the crossing of the Red Sea; (5) the scouting report on the oasis at Elim and the Phoenix."

us to suppose that the play was modeled on Greek tragedy.[79]

A comparison between the *Exagoge* and DtIsa seems obvious. The title, the "bringing out," would fit Isaiah 40–55 as well. In my view, the decisive question is whether there was already a tradition of Passover/Mazzot plays at an early period.[80]

2. Conclusions Regarding Their Bearing on Deutero-Isaiah's Work

Compared with Attic drama, DtIsa seems more archaic. The liturgical drama is itself worship. Heaven and earth are joined. Tragic and comic elements are not separated. The sublime and the everyday take place simultaneously—a characteristic of biblical tradition.[81] At the same time, the action in DtIsa has a dynamic of its own. Compared with Egyptian texts, DtIsa departs more radically from ritual and its explication (the explanation of the cultic vessels, for example, or sacrifical ceremonies). The action is always announced by a speaker. Procession, dance and music fill up the time.

The brevity of the speech sections in DtIsa is strikingly different from the Attic texts. Only what is most important is stated—the *logia,* so to speak. We can observe no more than the very beginnings of dialogue. The number of the chief performers is small, especially the number of those with speaking parts. Two to three actors have to suffice. I see this as one reason why, for example, Jacob/Israel (from Isaiah 41 onward) and Zion/Jerusalem (from Isaiah 48 onward) do not appear simultaneously. The sole exception is 51:12-16. But there neither Zion/Jerusalem nor Jacob/Israel is called by name. They are a nameless pair. Nor do they themselves speak. This means that they could also be played by other people, not just by the main actors. Cyrus and Babylon do not meet either. All three groups of texts, Egyptian, Attic, and biblical, show the important part played by the chorus, although the emphasis varies in the different groups.

Finally, the comparison undertaken in the present commentary suggests the conclusion that Isaiah 40–55 was initially a "festival scroll" for the master of the ceremony. It is a kind of script—what modern authors writing about the Egyptian texts call a libretto or aide-mémoire (see above). It is only in performance that a drama, a living word, comes into being from the text. This is not at variance with the fact that the "festival scroll" as we now have it was performed,[82] and probably also written, with considerable artistry.[83]

For an understanding of DtIsa's work it is important to grasp that it was conceived in literary terms, but that as a liturgical drama it became through its performance literature for a (largely) nonliterary public. Whether other biblical writings should also be understood as "dramatic"—either because they were themselves parts of plays or because they provided a basis for a dramatization—is a question that still requires examination.[84] Similarly uncertain in the present state of research are: possible relationships with dramatic literature in Mesopotamia, influences in liturgies and processions, dramatization of epics, and the significance of the motif of the "two cities" in competition with each other (such as Jerusalem/Babylon).

---

79 See ibid., 23–28: "The *Exagoge* and Fifth-century Tragedy"; and E. Vogt, "Das Mosesdrama des Ezechiel und die attische Tragödie," in A. Bierl, P. von Möllendorff, and E. Vogt, eds., *Orchestra–Drama Mythos Bühne. FS H. Flashar* (1994) 151–60.

80 On the problem of the theater in Jewish tradition see Jacobson, *Exagoge,* 18–20.

81 See E. Auerbach, *Mimesis: The Representation of Reality in Western Literature* (1957) 1–20, "Odysseus' Scar." [*Mimesis. Dargestellte Wirklichkeit in der Abendländischen Literatur* (1946; 3d ed. 1964), esp. 1–26].

82 Cf. the so-called imperative hymns (see F. Crüsemann, *Studien zur Formgeschichte von Hymnus und Danklied in Israel* [1969]), which after all are initially directions for the performance before they become an art form of their own (see below on 42:10-13; 44:23).

83 The possibility that DtIsa's work was intended to be "read," not acted, cannot be excluded. This could be indicated by the beauty of the language, the dense interaction of word and action, and the content of the message. But the same might be said of the other supreme dramas in the literature of the world (see above for lit. on the *Exagoge* of Ezekiel the Tragedian).

84 Closest are parts of Trito-Isaiah; Isaiah 24–27; 34–35; also deserving of examination under this aspect are texts from the Psalms and, e.g., the prophetic texts of Micah and Joel; for Micah see Helmut Utzschneider, "Michas Reise in die Zeit. Ein Werkstattbericht," in W. Sommer, ed., *Zeitenwende–Zeitenende* (Theologische Akzente 2; 1997) 11–40.

It is striking that the Joseph story, the book of Job and texts from the book of Daniel have been drama-

E. The Structure of Isaiah 40–55[85]

1. Structural Characteristics and Basic Scenes

The exegesis shows that DtIsa's work is divided into six acts (1–6), framed by a prologue and an epilogue. The structure is clearly signaled by the hymns at the end of the respective acts. It is only at the end of Act VI that a hymn is missing, perhaps because of the immediate transition to the epilogue.

The survey also shows that in every unit there is at least one event where a group is moving along in an organized, often ceremonial fashion. This can take the form of a procession (Isa 52:11-12) or a parody of one (46:1-2). These movements are an essential component of the dramatic action.

The survey of the structure, finally, provides an explanation for the seemingly erratic distribution of the Servant of God texts. As the plan shows, the four texts are distributed among Act I (42:1-9), Act IV (48:16—49:12), Act V (50:2—51:16) and Act VI (52:13—53:12). No single act contains more than one of these texts.

The division of the acts into individual scenes follows a triadic pattern that is maintained with astonishing strictness.[86] This can be seen from the table of contents. The scheme is carried through right down to the smallest units. The length of a unit is not decisive. A single verse can introduce an extensive action. But the triadic pattern is even then maintained.[87] Various allocations are possible, especially in the case of the smallest units. A reason can sometimes be found for exceptions to the rule. For example, Act III, with the "homage paid by the foreign peoples to Cyrus" (45:14-17) and the "homage of the whole world paid to Yahweh" (45:20-24), contains two processions with heavy requirements for players and properties. Both preparation and performance would

have taken considerable time. This could account for the lack of a part C in Act III.

My own impression is that the Servant of God texts have a special position. They do not fall within the numbering of the structural elements. Act 6, which includes the most extensive of the servant texts, could be an exception in this respect. This would mean that 52:13—53:12 could serve as part B of this act.

DtIsa's liturgical drama uses a set with only a few basic scenes. These would require very little to make them identifiable in a performance. But they could also be elaborated further, according to circumstance and the means available. The scenes can take place on earth, but can be set in the heavenly sphere as well; the basic pattern remains. "Smallest units" belonging to the most varied genres can find a place within these basic scenes, for example, the disputation sayings, salvation oracles, and eschatological hymns of praise that have been worked out and discussed in the literature on DtIsa. Let us now look at each of these scenes in turn.

a. The Throne Scene

The throne scene belongs to the presentation of sovereignty. As illustrations from various areas of antiquity show, it has a common, traditional iconography. At the same time this iconography can be adapted to particular circumstances. The ruler sits on his or her throne. This can be either ostentatiously simple or magnificent. The insignia of the sovereign are the robes, crown and scepter. Special features in the interior architecture of the palace, a dais or a tent, give the throne prominence. The royal household, with its various functionaries, supports the ruler and increases his or her standing.

---

tized again and again in the course of literary history. Is this due, at least in part, to their dramatic structure? (Cf. the lists in the *Encyclopaedia Judaica* in the articles on Joseph, Job and Daniel, in the sections: "In the Arts. . . .") See also Christine Schenk's study, "Die Rezeption der Josephsnovelle (Gen 37–50) in den Patriarchaden 'Joseph und Zulaika' (1753) und 'Jakob und Joseph' (1754) von Johann Jakob Bodmer" (M.A. thesis, Munich, 1994).

85   For this section, see the table of contents and the plan of the structure. Details may be found in the exegesis of the texts referred to.

86   Indicated in the table of contents through the divi-

sion into A, B, C, and 1, 2, 3; cf. also the divisions in the translation as printed.

87   See already Muilenburg's observation about "triads" in his "Isaiah, Introduction, Chs. 40–66," *IB,* vol. 5 (1956) 390–91. The question about the origin of the triad pattern and its significance still requires investigation.

The functions of the throne scene as a sociomorpheme for declarations of sovereignty can generally be translated into action in the following ways:

1. through acclamation

    The court, the ruler's subjects, the peoples of the earth pay homage to the ruler. Here the hymn in its various forms has its place.

2. through the verbal exercise of rule

    The ruler consults with counselors; the ruler issues decrees. It is to these that I would assign salvation oracles/assurances of salvation, for example.

    The ruler enacts laws and administers justice, either personally or through someone he or she appoints.

3. through the appointment of representatives

    The sovereign decides who is to be chosen and legitimates that person. The ruler tells the appointed person what function to perform, and assigns special tasks.

The throne scene with the presence of God is of great importance for DtIsa. It is closely associated with the concept "Yahweh as king." It is with the help of this scene that the sovereignty of God is declared and presented. A high level of abstraction is thereby achieved, even through the scenes themselves take concrete form.

It is a heavenly throne scene that is assumed at the very beginning of DtIsa, in Isaiah 40. The decree goes forth: "Comfort, comfort my people . . ." (40:1-2). A speaker is appointed (vv. 6-8). The hymn is sung (vv. 12-17). In the same framework God then directly appoints Jacob/Israel (41:8-13; 43:1-7) and the Servant of God (42:1-9).

The throne scene in 44:24—45:25 is of fundamental importance, because it describes the relationship between the divine order and the earthly, political order, represented by the figure of Cyrus. Cyrus too is directly appointed by God (45:1-8, 9-13).

Another throne scene in heaven is 49:14—50:1. Here Yahweh is judge and ruler. In 51:4-8 the throne scene is linked with a mime that depicts the ruler's righteousness and justice. In 52:14-15 the divine judge's speech opens the proceedings.

The transition to an earthly throne scene is made when the foreign peoples pay homage to Cyrus (45:14-17).

In the parody in 47:1-7, Babylon is dethroned. In a corresponding mirror scene in 52:1-6 we are shown Zion/Jerusalem's investiture and enthronement.

A special problem for the throne scene was how to represent the divine presence. Could this take the form of an audition without a theophany? Was it presented symbolically? Did an authorized spokesman represent the Deity?

b. Lawcourt Scenes

Scenes in a court of law are frequent in DtIsa.[88] This has to do with the way lawcourts were constituted in Israel. The court sat publicly, "in the gate." Everyone could imagine it, for everyone would have experienced such a legal proceeding. A freeman would actually have taken part in legal proceedings as witness, plaintiff or defendant. The aim of a court procedure was first and foremost to get a settlement, *shalom*. Everyday disputes, and an action such as the one brought against the prophet Jeremiah (Jer 26:7-19), followed a similar pattern. The facts were established in the witnesses' speeches and counterspeeches. This promoted a "culture of dispute." Plato's dialogues are developed from "the banquet," the *symposium*. In Israel, dialogue grew out of legal proceedings. It is in dialogue that "the truth" develops. In DtIsa we can see how, in a process of abstraction, the so-called disputation sayings (or discussion sayings) could develop out of a speech made before a court of law.[89] In the case of the genre "lawcourt scenes" too, we find in DtIsa

---

88 Isa 41:1-5a; 41:21-29; 43:8-15; 43:22-28; 44:6-8; 47:8-15; 48:1-11; 49:14-16; 52:13—53:12. For the judicial system see H. J. Boecker, *Law and the Administration of Justice in the Old Testament and Ancient East* (1980), esp. 27–52; H. Niehr, *Rechtsprechung in Israel*, SBS 130 (1987); R. R. Wilson, "Israel's Judicial System in the Preexilic Period," *JQR* 74 (1983) 229–48; E. Otto, "Zivile Funktionen des Stadttores in Palästina und Mesopotamien," in M. Weippert et al., eds., *Meilenstein. FS H. Donner,* ÄAT 30 (1995) 188–97.

89 Begrich (*Studien zu Deuterojesaja*, BWANT 4/25 [1938; reprint 1963] 48–53) counts the following as "disputation sayings": 40:12-17; 40:18-20+25-26; 40:21-24; 40:27-31; 44:24-28; 45:9-13; 45:18-25; 46:5-11; 48:1-11; 48:12-15; 50:1-3. He was thereby proceeding from the "smallest units." For the

examples on the heavenly level[90] corresponding to the earthly one.[91] Yahweh and the gods, or "the peoples"[92] (but Israel too),[93] are shown locked in legal dispute. To this the disputation sayings correspond on earth. "Services to be rendered" (e.g., the divine predictions)[94] and contracts (e.g., the marriage contract between Yahweh and Zion/Jerusalem)[95] form the substance of the action. An action in civil law can be transferred to the relationship between God and a human being. As a sociomorpheme it becomes a way of making a theological statement or putting forward a theological interpretation.

c. Battle Scenes

Compared with the Egyptian dramatic texts, the battle scenes in DtIsa are strikingly restricted. Here all that is meant to be noted is that Yahweh goes forth to battle (Isa 42:13). How far we ought to imagine the battle as taking place behind the scenes is a point to be considered later in the exegesis of the individual passages.

Isa 43:14-16 is a reminiscence of the way the Egyptian army marched out at the Exodus. This may have been dramatically presented, but not necessarily so ("Do not remember the earlier [happenings]," v. 18). Isa 51:9-11 ("Was it not you who cut Rahab to pieces, pierced the dragon through," v. 9) can be compared with the description of the triumph of Horus in Edfu.[96] According to Isa 52:10, "Yahweh has bared his holy arm in the eyes of all peoples." But a battle is not described.

d. Scenes with Artisans (and Those in Other Professions)[97]

These scenes introduce an element of comedy into the seriousness of the drama. They show what was familiar to everyone. The audience probably included people with specialist skills. As in the old TV quiz show "What's My Line?" the fun depends on the accurate representation of different types. The significance of the scenes should not be underestimated, any more than we underestimate the importance of the comic scenes in Aristophanes or Shakespeare's clowns. They are an integral component of the play as a whole. It emerges from the exegesis of the passages in question that the theology in the artisan scenes is the same as that in the rest of the drama. God and the gods: that is DtIsa's theme throughout. Here it is related directly to the audience and their own experience.

e. Marriage[98]

Here too general experience is the point of departure. The women know how a tent is erected (see under 54:2). But the proper order of the ceremonies is also familiar (see 54:4-10). Marriage is the quintessential festival. There are examples enough of its dramatic presentation in literature. The connection with the cult is clear, and not just in antiquity (see below on 54:11-14a and 54:14b-17). Isaiah 54 shows how in this form of marriage ceremony, profound religious problems could be communicated to an audience.

f. Movements, Processions, *Pompa*

As has already been said, at least one organized movement has to be assumed in every act. In the ancient world—and not only there—the procession in its various forms is public, both a means of presentation and an opportunity for participation. The community's identity

---

discussion in research see D. Michel, "Deuterojesaja," *TRE* 8 (1981) 510–30, esp. 512.

90 See esp. 52:13—53:12.

91 Cf., e.g., the summoning of the court in 43:22; 49:14; on the speech before the court see 44:7.

92 Isa 41:1-51 (islands and nations in the underworld); 41:21-29 (gods); 43:8-15 (peoples and nations); 44:6-8 (gods).

93 See 42:18-25; 43:22-28.

94 See under 41:21-29; 48:1-11; 48:12-15.

95 See 49:14; 50:1; 54:4-10.

96 See H. W. Fairman, *The Triumph of Horus: An Ancient Egyptian Sacred Drama* (1974), esp. 27–33; text, 79–83 and 101–4.

97 The following texts may be assigned to this group:
40:18-20 caster or foundryman, gold- or silversmith
41:5b-7 specialist for metalwork, gold- or silversmith
44:9-20 specialist in iron/metalwork, v. 12
specialist in woodwork, v. 13
shepherd, v. 14a; farmer, v.14b
46:5-8 merchant, gold- or silversmith.

98 For the frequent and varied use of the *topos* "marriage" in the biblical texts cf. Genesis 24; Isa 62:1-5; Jer 7:34; 33:11; Ezek 16:8-14; Hos 2:18-25; Psalm 45; Tobit 6–8; Matt 22:1-14; 25:1-13; Luke 14:7-11; John 2:1-12; Rev 19:6-10; 21:9-11. In spite of all historically necessary differentiation, we may assume that the addressees in each given case would have been familiar with the more or less complete *topos* "marriage," both as a concept and in practice. Thus deviations from the traditional pattern would have been perceived as particular signals. On "marriage" and its presentation in drama, cf. in the genre of comedy, Menander (c. 342–292 B.C.E.) *Aspis* (The

can thus be presented in visual form. In DtIsa processions play an important role. A movement can have a positive character, such as the entry of the chorus in 40:12-17 (prologue) or the exit in 55:13 (epilogue). The entry with "the vessels of the Lord" (52:11-12 in Act VI) is a procession; and so, in contrast, is the train of prisoners captured from foreign peoples, who pass in front of Cyrus (45:14-17 in Act III), and also the homage paid by "the peoples" to Yahweh (45:22-24 in Act III). Here DtIsa has taken up elements of the *pompa*, the procession associated with the cult of the ruler (see also 52:11-12 with literature on *pompa*). Another contrasting pair is the train of the poor and wretched who look for water (41:17 in Act I)—they are going to be raised up—and the line of the (Egyptian) army that marches out to its destruction (43:16-17 in Act II). In both these cases, the transition between the procession and the actual play itself is fluid: The scenes could be presented in various ways.

The movement with the idols is a negative example ("Bel has collapsed, Nebo bends down"; see 46:1-4 in Act IV with literature on different types of *pompa*), and so is the procession of the merchants or traders in honor of their gods (46:5-8; see there also literature on the *pompa diaboli* in the Christian tradition). The survey shows the distribution of movements and processions throughout the different acts, and the shift from positive to negative examples. In this way too a dramatic tension is generated. The homecoming of the exiles must surely have been a colorful spectacle (49:22-23 in Act V; cf. 49:7-12).

These processions offered an opportunity for many people to participate, as actors or audience. How elaborate they were would have depended on the circumstances; the mere announcement of a procession may have been enough. As in the case of other elements in the liturgical drama, the mode of performance can have been adapted to the particular local and temporal circumstances. Thus processions may have been merely announced, so that the audience could imagine them. But the procession is a constitutive element of the liturgical drama and is essential to its understanding.

In terms of the performance practice, the processions could be an indication that the individual acts were performed on different days. If so many people took part, time would be needed for preparation. We must remember the part played by the costumes, when foreign peoples, kings, princes and idolaters appeared. Mardi Gras in its diverse modern variants offers an illustration. When at the end, in 55:12, the people exit and "the trees of the field" are supposed to clap their hands, the greenery must first of all have had to be procured.

g. Hymns—Music, Mime, and Dance

Hymns[99] are used to divide one act from another.[100] They are announced in particular detail. But hymnal elements can be found within individual acts too.[101] The hymn and the acclamation that corresponds to it are connected with the cult of the ruler. This may also be said of Yahweh as "king." Hymns presuppose performance by a chorus, with musical accompaniment. There are hints of this in the text,[102] but unfortunately no more than that. I would suppose that the overall impression made by a performance of DtIsa's work was rather akin to that of an oratorio. Mime and dance also played a part.[103] But here too, although there are hints in the text and some parallels in antiquity, we are by and large dependent on supposition.[104]

h. The Servant of God Texts

The special position of the Servant of God texts has been an unceasing subject of discussion in research ever since B. Duhm isolated these texts in his commentary

Shield) and *Dyskolos* (The Peevish Fellow) LCL 132, I (1979).

99 Of fundamental importance is F. Crüsemann, *Studien zur Formgeschichte von Hymnus und Danklied in Israel* (1969). A helpful contribution is A. Richter's "Literaturübersicht. Hauptlinien der Deuterojesaja-Forschung von 1964–1979, 4. Hymnische Redeformen," in C. Westermann, *Sprache und Struktur der Prophetie Deuterojesajas* (1981) 99–102; see also J. W. Kleinig, *The Lord's Song: The Basis, Function and Significance of Choral Music in Chronicles* (1993), with lit.

100 Act I: 42:10-13; Act II: 44:21-23; Act III: 45:25; Act

IV: 49:13; Act V: 52:9.

101 See among other passages:
40:12-17 entry of the chorus with a hymn
40:21-31 hymnal dialogue
45:5-8 self-presentation of the Deity
48:20-22 song of thanksgiving
54:1 call for jubilation; cf. 51:3.

102 See under 40:12-17 and 52:7-10. The rhythmical structure of many of the texts is also an indication of the hymnal character.

103 See under 40:15-17; 40:30-31; 41:15-16a; 45:1-8; 48:7-13, 20-22; 51:4-8. For music see also under 40:12-17; 49:13; 52:7-10.

(1st ed. 1892), terming them "Ebed-Jahwe-Lieder" ("servant of Yahweh songs"). According to the question raised, stress is laid either on the differences between these texts and their context in DtIsa or on the common ground they share with the rest of the work. The following summary presupposes the history of research on these texts as well as the exegesis put forward later in the present volume.[105]

1) Demarcation and Distribution

The survey of the structure of Isaiah 40–55 as a dramatic text makes possible an explanation of the irregular distribution of the servant texts. Act I contains one Servant text, Acts IV, V and VI (the last act) one in each case. The scenic repertoire is in accord with that of the whole work. Thus both the installation of the Servant in the first of the texts (42:1-9) and the (heavenly) lawcourt scene in the fourth (52:13–53:12) presuppose a throne scene. The difference is in the characters and the content.

2) The Servant Texts as "Biography"

As we shall see in the commentary, the demarcation of the texts is disputed, and with good reason. We shall start from the texts that are traditionally seen as central, about which scholars largely agree. The texts can be described as elements of an ideal biography.[106]

Servant Text I: Isa 42:1-9
The biography begins with the installation. God himself appoints his Servant, thus directly legitimating him. God's people and the foreign nations are the servant's sphere of responsibility. He has judicial functions. He sees to it that the rule of law is maintained. The proper hearing of cases and the liberation of prisoners are cited as specific examples.

Servant Text II: Isa 49:1-6 (as part of 48:16—49:12)
The Servant himself talks about the charge he has been given. He carries out his function through the power of the word, not through the sword. What he says is a word legitimated by God. In this respect he belongs to the prophetic tradition. This can also be discerned from a first announcement of suffering (v. 4). The Servant has a function to perform for the "islands" and "nations," as well as for Jacob/Israel.

Servant Text III: Isa 50:4-11 (as part of 50:2—51:16)
The text is autobiographical in style. What the Servant does is "to hear" and "to speak." But it is above all the Servant's sufferings that are reported. Closely related texts are, in the Psalter, the prayers of complaint uttered by the person who, though innocent, has been accused (cf., e.g., Psalms 5; 7; 17; 26; 27; 69), and the story of the prophet Jeremiah's sufferings.[107] The motif of trust, as a confession of faith, also belongs to the biography.

Servant Text IV: Isa 52:13—53:12
This text describes the Servant's exaltation and his rehabilitation in a heavenly court of law. His life is recollected and, contrary to all appearances, is interpreted in his favor.

---

104 See also C. Wilcke, "Hymne," *RLA* 4 (1972–75) 539–44; J. Assmann, "Hymnus," *LÄ* 3 (1980) 103–10; for the Attic drama see A. W. Pickard-Cambridge, *The Dramatic Festivals of Athens* (2d ed. 1968) "V. The Chorus, A. The Character, Functions, and Movements of the Chorus," 232–46; "B. Dancing in Drama," 246–57; "C. Music in Drama," 257–62"; T. B. L. Webster, *The Greek Chorus* (1970); J. Rode, "Das Chorlied," in W. Jens, *Die Bauformen der griechischen Tragödie* (1971) 85–115.

105 See the comprehensive bibliography on the servant of God in DtIsa (up to 1985) in H. Haag, *Der Gottesknecht bei Deuterojesaja* (EdF 233; 2d ed. 1993). See also D. Michel, "Deuterojesaja," *TRE* 8 (1981) 510–30; and the bibliography on Isaiah 53 by W. Hüllstrung and G. Feine in B. Janowski and P. Stuhlmacher, eds., *Der leidende Gottesknecht. Jesaja 53 und seine Wirkungsgeschichte* (1996) 251–71.

106 See K. Baltzer, "Zur formgeschichtlichen Bestimmung der Texte vom Gottesknecht im Deuterojesaja-Buch," in *Probleme biblischer Theologie. FS G. von Rad* (1971) 27–43; idem, *Die Biographie der Propheten* (1975) 171–77.

107 Beginning with Jeremiah 26, see my *Biographie der Propheten* (1975) 126–28. Of special interest are the so-called Confessions of Jeremiah: Jer 11:18—12:6; 15:10-21; 17:14-18; 18:18-23; 20:7-18. See the commentary on Isa 50:4.

The biography traced in the above texts binds together the Servant's words and his acts. It is an account rendered to God and human beings of the way he has carried out his commission. He is the righteous yet suffering person. He becomes the prototype with whom the individual or group can identify. These wisdom components are accentuated by the Servant's anonymity.

3) The Servant Texts as "Memorial" of Moses

Who was the Servant of God? This is the question that has continually been asked. The identification with Moses that is assumed in the present commentary is not new. A text in the Babylonian Talmud tractate *Soṭa* shows that Jewish tradition was familiar with the identification of the Servant of God with Moses.[108] In modern times it was most emphatically maintained by E. Sellin, although he later moved away from the identification.[109] A fundamental point underlying the argument of the following section is that it is strange that Moses should not be mentioned at all in a work whose theme is preeminently the exodus. I believe that the texts contain a whole series of signals that are intended to point to Moses. It is a veiled revelation. The most important instrument of identification are the pointers to Scripture, more specifically to the Mosaic Torah, the Pentateuch. A few examples may serve as illustrations, but more detail may be found in the commentary.

Servant Text I: Isa 42:1-9
The Servant's installation begins with a hymnal predication of God. This picks up Genesis 1–2, the beginning of the Torah. The catchwords from Genesis 1 are clearly evident: "create, heaven, firmament, earth, bring forth." Exodus 3 (esp. vv. 13-15) records the appointment of Moses. The heart of the text is the revelation of the divine name. Isa 42:8 takes this up: "I am Yahweh, that is

my name" (אֲנִי יהוה הוּא שְׁמִי). In addition, the charge to "bring out" (יצא), which occurs three times in Exod 3:10, 11, 12, is also given in thrice-varied form in Isa 42:1, 3, 7.

Servant Text II: Isa 48:16—49:12
Here the traditional boundaries drawn around the text should be extended. The "sending" of the Servant in 48:16 is the beginning (cf. Exod 3:10, 13, 14, 15). In Isa 48:17 the Servant himself opens with a divine speech: "I am Yahweh your God." Along with the phrases "a way that you can go" and "my commandments," this becomes a reminder of the proclamation of the Decalogue on Sinai through Moses. In turn, the use of "exodus"—this time from Babylon (v. 20)—and "water for him from the rocks" (v. 21) provide a new interpretation of the wanderings in the wilderness. If it was already the servant Moses to whom Yahweh said "You are my servant, Israel" (49:3), then this status does not obtain only from the time of the Davidic dynasty (cf. 1 Chr 16:13). Israel's legitimation through Moses is older than that, and that is the important point.

Servant Text III: Isa 50:2—51:16
According to this text the Servant is both teacher and taught (לִמּוּד, v. 4). This is the way Deuteronomy describes Moses (cf. Deut 1:5; 4:1, 5, 14; 5:31; 6:1).

Servant Text IV: 52:13—53:12
As the exegesis of the passage will demonstrate, the fourth Servant of God text is an interpretation of Deuteronomy 34, with Moses' rise, death and burial. The Servant's grave "among criminals and beside a rich man" can be understood as a contemporary interpretation, referring to the death of Moses in Moab, on Mount

---

108 There it is said in a divine speech addressed to Moses, with a quotation from Isa 53:12 (see also below on that text): "R[abbi] Simlai expounded . . . '*Because he poured out his soul unto death*'—because he surrendered himself to die, as it is said, *And if not, blot me, I pray thee* etc. [Exod 32:32]. '*And was numbered with the transgressors*'—because he was numbered with them who were condemned to die in the wilderness. '*Yet he bare the sins of many*'—because he secured atonement for the making of the Golden Calf. '*And made intercession for the transgressors*'—because he begged for mercy on behalf of the sinners in Israel that they should turn in penitence,

and the word *pegiʿah* ['*intercession*'] means nothing else than prayer, as it is said, *Therefore pray not thou for this people, neither lift up cry nor prayer for them, neither make intercession to Me* [Jer 7:16]," *b. Soṭa* 14a, quotation following the edition of I. Epstein, *The Babylonian Talmud*, vol. 20 (1932) 73–74, 55–56. See also *Sipre Deuteronomy* 355 on Deut 33:21/Isa 53:12, R. Hammer, trans. and ed., *Sifre: A Tannaitic Commentary on the Book of Deuteronomy* (YJS 24, 1986) 372–73. I am grateful to G. Stroumsa for drawing my attention to these texts.

109 E. Sellin, *Mose und seine Bedeutung für die israelitisch-jüdische Religionsgeschichte* (1922); see also, idem,

Nebo, opposite Baal-peor, before the entry into the promised land.

This survey shows that the four servant texts are a reflection on four stages in the life of Moses, the Servant of God, two of them taken from the book of Exodus (the installation at the burning bush, the revelation of the commandments on Sinai), two of them references to Deuteronomy (Moses the teacher, Moses' death). In its binding together of these traditions too, DtIsa's work is a unifying document.

The elimination of Moses' name is explained in 48:19. It was the consequence of Israel's disobedience—its failure to keep the commandments: "His name would not have been wiped out nor destroyed before me." This is probably an interpretation of Exod 32:32, the story of the golden calf (see below on the text). In DtIsa's work as a whole, *all* names eventually disappear, from Jacob/Israel to Cyrus, right down to Zion/Jerusalem. It is Yahweh's name alone that stands (see Isa 55:13 and below in the commentary on the text).

4) The Appearance of the Servant of God, Moses
If we look more closely, we discover that the Servant texts are more intimately bound into their context than is often assumed. This again has to do with the dramatic structure of Isaiah 40–55. The texts are already announced in the prologue (40:14).[110] It may be useful to go through the texts once more from the angle of the drama's action.

Servant Text I: Isa 42:1-9
The Servant of God appears. Yahweh himself presents him: "Look there: my servant whom I uphold." We therefore have to imagine the Servant as being present, although he himself does not speak. The content of the scene—perhaps also the emblems used (clothes, etc.)—

tells the audience that the Moses who had once departed is now present.

Servant Text II: Isa 48:16—49:12
Here, over against what is generally considered in research to be the core text (49:1-6), a broader text must be considered (see the commentary). The announcement of the Servant is followed by his appearance (48:16): "*But now*: the Lord Yahweh has sent me, and his spirit . . ." "Sending" is an identifying catchword taken from Exod 3:13ff. (see the commentary under Isa 48:26). The sending through Yahweh's spirit is what is happening *now*, in the framework of the liturgical drama. The following speeches remind the audience of Moses' function and his fate,[111] and in their bearing on past and future they are simultaneously prophetic speech. The Servant may perhaps only disappear again at the end of the act, with the hymn in 49:13.

Servant Text III: 50:2—51:16
The appearance of the Servant is emphatically marked: "Why did I come in and no human being is there? Why did I call and no one answers?" (50:2). Yahweh's hand itself has snatched him from the underworld. The speeches he makes after his appearance are again both a reminiscence of Moses and, at the same time, prophecy. After 51:15, with the confessional formula "Yahweh Sabaoth is his name," the Servant disappears again into the underworld, just as "Everyman" (אדם) did in 47:4 (see the commentary).

Servant Text IV: 52:13—53:12
The text is a self-contained dramatic action. Yahweh himself identifies the servant in his rising up and exaltation: "See, my servant shall be 'beatified'" (52:13). In the

---

"Die Lösung des deuterojesajanischen Gottes-knechtsrätsels," *ZAW* 55 (1937) 177–217. See also the review of research in O. Eissfeldt, *The Old Testament: An Introduction* (1965) 330–32, 340–41 [*Einleitung in das Alte Testament* (1964) 446, 448–52].

110 See the commentary under 40:13-14; 53:11; and K. Baltzer, "Jes 40,13-14–ein Schlüssel zur Einheit Deutero-Jesajas?" in *FS V. Hamp* (1987) 7–10.

111 The question remains: How did the audience come to know the traditions about Moses? The possible answers include (1) The role of narrative, oral tradition (which does not have to exclude basic written versions); (2) the reading of texts (such as we know

from the Pentateuch) in the context of worship; (3) and finally, as in the present case, a dramatic presentation. All these possibilities are open to discussion. A similiar problem exists in the case of Attic drama. How did the audience come to be familiar with the plot? Was there a "normal form," such as the versions known to us in "told to the children" editions?

heavenly judgment of the dead, the life of the servant Moses is interpreted. The purpose and goal are his exaltation.

The four Servant texts thus show themselves to be an integral part of the drama as we have it. It seems probable that they had their own earlier history in tradition. Every era also has its own picture of Moses. In the framework of the drama, the texts fulfill an important function in lament and in remembrance of the dead. The interpretation of the Servant texts will bring out this connection with the lament for the dead. In the Egyptian dramatic texts, the cultic ceremonies for the king's deceased predecessor form part of the performance.[112] In Attic drama, a constitutive element is the lament for the dead, the *threnos*.[113] A comparison with DtIsa's text exposes the shared characteristics and the differences.

F. Liturgical Drama and Festival

The following section rests on observations drawn from the text of DtIsa, although the interpretation depends to some extent on supposition. I hope that this may at least spark off a fruitful discussion. A more precise comparison in the context of ethnology and the history of religion is really required. The catchword "liturgical" is intended to make clear that the drama is still part of the act of worship. The "speaker" is appointed in Isa 40:6-8. In its formulations, the language follows the liturgical tradition passed down to us in the Psalter, while the use of direct divine speech belongs to prophetic tradition. Liturgy and drama are alike in linking past, present, and future. In DtIsa this takes place *sub specie Dei*. The purpose is the praise of God. That is why hymns conclude the different acts. The acclamation draws in the chorus, or the people.

A religio-historical comparison gives credence to the link among cult, drama, and festival. Where DtIsa is concerned, J. Eaton[114] has tried programmatically to provide the proof, carrying further the studies made by S. Mowinckel and I. Engnell on the feast celebrating Yahweh's accession to the throne. Eaton sees a close connection with the Davidic monarchy. On the basis of his study of the Psalms, he links the festal drama with the liturgy for the preexilic autumn festival.[115] His study is stimulating, even if one does not share his premises. Skepticism about "a pattern of divine kingship" in the ancient Near East has, if anything, increased. That the occasion for DtIsa's work was a cyclical renewal of Yahweh's kingship in the accession festival seems to me questionable. In 52:7, "As king reigns/rules your God," the point is that Jerusalem is again becoming the royal city; a renewal of Yahweh's kingship is not the theme (see below on the text of 52:7). "As king reigns" Yahweh in Jerusalem, and no other king.

If a consideration starts from the great feasts of the festal calendar, I believe that Passover/Mazzot, the main spring festival, comes into prominence as the occasion for the work's performance, rather than the autumn festival. In Passover/Mazzot the link with the exodus is obvious, as Exodus 12 shows.[116] It is generally assumed—irrespective of the view taken of the earlier history—that in the exilic-postexilic era the two festivals were combined. In DtIsa, however, the elements originally belonging to the Mazzot festival are noticeably more pronounced.[117] There the feast is a pilgrimage festival,[118] in which the participants go up to Jerusalem (see under 40:31; 49:7-12; 55:1-5). The food is bread, not meat (see under 55:1-2). There is no mention of an animal sacrifice, where blood is shed (see under 43:22-28; 52:5bβ). In Isa 53:7, 10, the killing of an animal serves only as a comparison with the sacrifice of the Servant. If this is a Passover, it is one without a Passover lamb. In the Persian period, the Persian aversion to blood offerings could have played a part.[119]

There are some small indications of the date of the feast. Isa 40:6-8 uses as a simile the drying up of the vegetation under the hot desert wind in the transition from spring to summer. The close in 55:10: "As the rain comes down . . ." probably points to the "late rain" in

---

112 See above on the Egyptian dramatic texts.

113 See F. R. Adrados, *Festival, Comedy and Tragedy: The Greek Origins of Theatre* (1975) 82–85 and 438–39.

114 J. H. Eaton, *Festal Drama in Deutero-Isaiah* (1979).

115 See ibid., chap. 2, 8–37 and 115.

116 See B. S. Childs, *The Book of Exodus* (1974) 178–214 (with lit.) on Exod 12:1-13, 16. Also J. B. Segal, *The Hebrew Passover from the Earliest Times to A.D. 70*,

LOS 12 (1963); R. Schmidt, *Exodus und Passah. Ihr Zusammenhang im Alten Testament*, OBO 7 (2d ed. 1982).

117 See E. Otto, *Das Mazzotfest in Gilgal*, BWANT 107 (1975), esp. 175–91.

118 Cf. Exod 23:15; 34:18.

119 See Herodotus (c. 490–425/420 B.C.E.) 1.131–32 (LCL, 1975, pp. 170–73); G. Widengren, *Die*

spring that "gives bread to the eater" (v. 10). The snow fits the spring better too. Cypresses and myrtles burst into leaf (55:13). Finally, in spring there is milk in plenty—but not in the autumn (see below on 55:1 and on the text).

A special problem is the question of the duration of the liturgical drama's performance. On the one hand, it is possible that it was played right through on a single day. In Athens the performances of classical dramas lasted from sunrise to sunset. For DtIsa a relevant point is the degree to which the times implied correspond to the actual situation, or are supposed to be imagined (e.g., 40:26: "Lift up your eyes and see: who has created these," with reference to the stars). Either is possible. Similarly, the processions could have been actually carried out, following the libretto, or could merely have been announced; this would also have had an influence on the duration of the performance.

An additional factor in judging length of performance is the relationship between the duration of the feast and the duration of the liturgical drama. A Passover play could begin in the evening and be continued on the following day.

The Mazzot festival, on the other hand, lasts seven days, or a week, not just a few days. Originally it probably led an independent existence as the festival of the barley harvest, but was later combined with the Passover (see Lev 23:4-8). The reference back to the exodus tradition links the two festivals,[120] and this same tradition is the basis for DtIsa. This is of interest in its bearing on the duration of the drama's performance as well as the number of acts—six, plus prologue and epilogue: perhaps one act of the drama was celebrated per day, the prologue possibly on the evening prior to the festival. A comparison with the *Exagoge* of Ezekiel the Tragedian

(see above) also raises the question of the tradition of the Passover/Mazzot feast.[121] There too the Feast of Passover is extended to seven days.

The reflections presented here are of interest in connection with the military colony in Elephantine/Syene in Egypt during the Persian period. "The land of Sinim" is mentioned in 49:12 (see below on the text). The Aramaic papyrus Cowley 21[122] records a letter written by a certain Hananiah to the community in Elephantine about the feast of the 14th–21st Nisan. The editors term the text a "Passover letter" and date it 419 B.C.E. But the word "Passover" does not occur, perhaps because of the papyrus's state of preservation. What is said suggests Mazzot, however. Would it have been possible to slaughter a Passover lamb in Elephantine, in the area dominated by the ram god Chnum? Is that also a reason why only food and incense offerings were permitted for the newly built temple in Elephantine?[123]

G. Where Was Deutero-Isaiah's Work Composed and Where Performed?

The place of composition has traditionally been assumed to be Babylon. B. Duhm is an exception: in his commentary he suggests Lebanon, probably on the grounds of 40:16. But if the place was Babylon, it is surprising that so little is said about Babylon's concrete situation, and that there is so little local color in the text. DtIsa's references to Babylon could be drawn simply from the Psalms and the Babylon sayings in Isaiah or Jeremiah. This does not exclude the possibility of close contact between the *gōlâ* in Babylon and Jerusalem (cf., e.g., Ez 8:1; 11:14-21; chap. 12; 14:21-23; 16:1-2; 22:2, 23-31; 24:1-2; 33:21-22; Jer 29:1-9).

The Babylonian gods Bel and Nebo (46:1) were known elsewhere as well (e.g., in Elephantine; see below on

---

Religionen Irans (1965) 28–35, 66; W. Hinz, *Darius und die Perser. Eine Kulturgeschichte der Achämeniden,* vol. 2 (1979), "Verpönung von Schlachtopfern," 197–202. See also in the *gāthās* of Zoroaster: *Yasna* 29:1-2; 32:8, 12, 14; 44:20; 48:10; text and German translation: H. Humbach, *Die Gathas des Zarathustra,* vol. 1 (1959). See also Heidemarie Koch, *Die religiösen Verhältnisse der Dareioszeit. Untersuchungen anhand der Elamitischen Persepolistäfelchen,* Göttinger Orientforschungen III. Series Iranica 4 (1977) 131–53, esp. 145, 176–78.

120 Cf. Exodus 12, esp. 12:29-34, 37-39; 23:14-17; 34:18-24; also Deut 16:1-8.

121 See Jacobson, *The Exagoge of Ezekiel* (1983) 124–25.

122 See B. Porten, *Jews of Elephantine and Arameans of Syene* (1980) 78–79.

123 See Papyrus Cowley 21; Porten, *Jews of Elephantine,* 99–100.

46:1-2 and also Papyrus Amherst 63). The Chaldean astronomy/astrology (see 47:8-15) was well known in the ancient world (we need only think of the "three wise men" from the east in Matt 2:1-12), so that familarity with their practices was not restricted to Babylon.

Moreover, the query about the place of performance and the query about the place where the author composed his work are two separate questions that must be distinguished from one another. I myself believe that Jerusalem is most probably the place where DtIsa's work was composed. One of DtIsa's themes is the restitution of Zion/Jerusalem. The walls are part of this restitution. Yahweh writes them into his hands (49:16), and the "mural crown" (see under 54:11-12) represents the new city. According to chap. 55 Jerusalem is the goal of pilgrimage.

A minor geographical detail could be of interest for the locality question: in 49:12 the directions or points of the compass are named, the already mentioned "land of Sinim" probably standing for the south. Seen from Babylon, Syene/Elephantine in Egypt does not lie to the south—this is rather the case if the standpoint is Jerusalem. The author seems to be familiar with Jerusalem's geographical position and incorporates it into his text.

If we wish to think of a performance in Jerusalem, the forecourt of the temple would be a possible venue. What speaks against this is DtIsa's reserve toward the temple and its priesthood: he does not mention them at all (44:28 is the exception). A situation on the southeast slope of Jerusalem would be a possibility.[124] Here no extensive theatrical sets would be required for the audience. "Go out from there! You should not touch anything unclean. . . . Purify yourselves, you who carry the vessels of Yahweh!" (52:11). These directions could have

a double meaning. They link the exodus from Babylon with the exit from the temple. The information could also have a point in the context of local geography, if the temple and the approach to it were on a single line (i.e., north; see below on the text). This would be so both in the case of the temple forecourt and in the case of a position on Jerusalem's southeastern slope.

When in 52:7-11 the watchmen announce Yahweh's return and his entry as king into Jerusalem, his royal city, the appearance probably comes from the east,[125] with the sunrise. That is the direction of the mountains on which the messengers appear; for Jerusalem this would mean the Mount of Olives.

Other local phenomena may be water from the rocks (48:21; 49:10), water on which Babylon travels through the underworld, a pool where, following the Egyptian model, Rahab can be symbolically slain,[126] and a cave as access to the underworld.

But the liturgical drama is not bound to this particular local situation. It would be sufficient if there were a tent, to hide the presence of the Deity and to serve as a place where Zion-Jerusalem could be adorned for the feast ("Make the cords of your tent long, . . ." 54:2). It is conceivable that other theatrical props were used to indicate place and time.

I think it possible that the play was not written in Babylon but was performed for the *gōlâ* there. For the work is also "publicity" for Jerusalem as a place of pilgrimage. This publicity could have had its place not only in Babylon but in other places in the Diaspora as well. It is Israelites and sympathizers to whom DtIsa addresses his work. "The islands and their inhabitants . . . the desert and its towns" are to join in raising a new song (42:10-13). That includes Greeks and Arabs. As far as the OT is concerned, it is worth considering whether DtIsa's

---

124 The situation of the Dionysius theater in Athens on the slope of the Acropolis would be comparable. On the importance of the points of the compass in the Attic theater see K. Joerden, "Zur Bedeutung des Außer- und Hinterszenischen," in W. Jens, ed., *Die Bauformen der griechischen Tragödie* (1971), "Exkurs II: Rechts und links; Die Bedeutung der Parodoi" (409): "For the awareness of the audience, above all the Athenian audience, who on the slope of the Acropolis were looking roughly south, the west (i.e., the right side) was always what was close at hand, embodied by the city in its varying character as farmland, port and city area, whereas the east

(the left) was always the road coming from far-off places."

125 Cf. Ezek 43:1-4.

126 On "sacred lakes" in the Egyptian cult, see B. Gessler-Löhr, "See," *LÄ* 5 (1984) 791–804, esp. 796 on Edfu.

text would still have been preserved if it had to be assigned to a single place only.[127] Its inclusion in the canon speaks in favor of wider recognition.

H. "Deutero-Isaiah" as Author

Our investigation of the literary form has shown how homogeneously Isaiah 40–55 is conceived and shaped. The various individual genres dovetail into the liturgical drama as an entirety. This is a highly developed literary work to which a highly developed theology corresponds. We should like to know who the author of this theological work of art was. But that is no doubt a modern question, and one that presupposes a different understanding of individual artistic achievement within a society. The names of the poets of Attic drama are known to us. In Athens, even vases are signed with the names of the artists who made them, as we can see from the exhibits in various museums at the present day. It is surely intentional when, in contrast, the original text of

Isa 55:13 closes by saying that only Yahweh's name will not be blotted out. We can encounter Deutero-Isaiah only in his work.

It is conceivable that this work was an individual achievement. But studies of the works of Shakespeare or Rembrandt have shown how closely these works of art, too, required for their production a group into which they were integrated.

One continual problem for me is the immense knowledge of Scripture that these texts demonstrate. They presuppose a library. Completeness cannot be shown, but important parts of the Pentateuch are known,[128] as well as Isaiah, Jeremiah, and Ezekiel.[129] It is striking, for example, that a number of sayings about Babylon are taken over.[130] Were there anthologies or concordances? The texts presuppose a tradition of scriptural interpretation, and at the same time an authoritative decision in favor of a particular, topical interpretation such as belongs to prophecy.[131]

---

127 Where Attic drama is concerned, we know of guilds for traveling players from the beginning of the 3rd century B.C.E. From the time of Alexander, we have evidence of new performances at festivals. See A. Pickard-Cambridge, *The Dramatic Festivals of Athens* (1968) 279–305.

128 Cf., e.g., for creation: Isa 40:26; 42:5; 44:9-11. For patriarchs and matriarchs: 51:1-3; 43:22-28; 44:1-5. For Exodus: 41:14-20; 43:16-21; 48:16-22; 51:9-11; 53:4-6. For Deuteronomy: 50:4-11; 51:1-3, 12-16; 52:13; 53:9. See K. Baltzer; "Schriftauslegung bei Deuterojesaja? Jes. 43,22-28 als Beispiel," in M. Görg, ed., *Die Väter Israels. FS J. Scharbert* (1989) 11–16; idem, "Jes. 52:13: Die 'Erhöhung' des 'Gottesknechtes'," in L. Bormann, K. Del Tredici, and A. Standhartinger, eds., *Religious Propaganda and Missionary Competition in the New Testament World: FS D. Georgi* (1994) 45–56. See also B. J. van der Merwe, *Pentateuchtradisies in de Prediking van Deuterojesaja* (1955); M. Fishbane, *Biblical Interpretation in Ancient Israel* (1985) (lit.!) and the review by B. Childs, *JBL* 106 (1987) 511–13; G. Vanoni, "Anspielungen und Zitate innerhalb der hebräischen Bibel. Am Beispiel von Dtn 4,29; Dtn 30,3 und Jes 29,13-14," in W. Gross, ed., *Jeremia und die "deuteronomistische Bewegung,"* BBB 98 (1995) 383–95 (with lit.).

129 For prophetic texts cf., e.g., Isaiah: see below on 51:11; 52:4; Jeremiah: see below on 41:8-13, 17-20; 48:20; 50:4-11; cf. Jer 26:18 and Mic 3:12; Ezekiel: see below on 41:1-5a. See also D. Baltzer, *Ezechiel und Deuterojesaja*, BZAW 121 (1971); H. Utz-

schneider, *Künder oder Schreiber? Eine These zum Problem der "Schriftprophetie" auf Grund von Maleachi 1,6–2,9*, BEAT 19 (1989).

130 See 46:1-4 and 47:1-7 in their relation to "the oracle/burden concerning Babylon" (Isa 13:1), Isaiah 13, 14, 21, and Jeremiah 50–51.

131 For the possibility of using the literary tradition by way of a "signal-word" system (*Leitwort-System*) see H. Utzschneider, *Gottes langer Atem: Die Exodus-erzählung (Ex 1–14) in ästhetischer und historischer Sicht* (SBS 166; Stuttgart: Katholisches Bibelwerk, 1996). His observations on Exodus 1–14 are comparable with those I have made in DtIsa. See also for the relation between Psalms 3–7 and 2 Samuel 15–19 B. Janowski, "JHWH der Richter—ein rettender Gott. Psalm 7 und das Motiv des Gottesgerichts," in *JBTh* 9: *Sünde und Gericht* (1994) 53–85; E. Zenger, "Was wird anders bei kanonischer Psalmenauslegung," in F. V. Reiterer, ed., *Ein Gott—eine Offenbarung. Beiträge zur biblischen Exegese, Theologie und Spiritualität: FS N. Füglister* (1991) 397–413; M. Millard, *Die Komposition des Psalters: Ein formgeschichtlicher Ansatz* (FAT 9; 1994) 127–32.

The wordplays, both those dependent on the ear and those dependent on the eye, are of a high standard.[132] Stylistic devices are richly diversified, for example, the play on series of vowels.[133]

All these factors speak in favor of a group with which DtIsa was closely associated.[134]

II. Historical Questions

A. The Period: The Rise and Fall of the Great Empires

DtIsa sets his work in the context of world history.[135] There is a reminiscence of Assyria (52:4). Babylon's downfall is announced (47:1-15). Cyrus brings about this downfall (48:14), and with it the era of Persian rule begins. "Islands" and "nations" are addressed by the Servant (49:1); his justice is "a light for peoples" (cf. 51:4-5). "The islands" (42:10), I believe, are the Greek world, while "peoples and nations" are the nations of the territories from Egypt to Persia. Egypt, Kush, and the Sabeans are mentioned among the foreign peoples (45:14); in the east Kedar, and Sela/Petra in east Jordan (42:11). The wide span of the geographical horizon that we find in 49:12 is in line with this. There, in naming the different directions or points of the compass, DtIsa lets "the land of Sinim" (today's Syene) stand for the extreme south. In antiquity, this was the place that under the name of

Jeb/Elephantine marked the frontier between Egypt and the Sudan, on the first cataract of the Nile.

DtIsa's perception of history reaches back to creation, the beginning of the world, and stretches forward to the world of his own day, taking in Noah/the flood, the patriarchs and matriarchs, the sojourn in Egypt, the exodus, the wanderings in the wilderness, the occupation of the promised land, David, and the exile. His picture therefore corresponds to Israel's historical creed in its most extensive form.[136] What historical experiences does DtIsa's view of history presuppose?

Among the important shifts that took place in world history in the sixth and fifth centuries B.C.E. were the emergence and growth of the great Middle Eastern empires of Babylonia and Persia, building on that of neo-Assyria of the preceding centuries.[137] Even for contemporaries, the relatively rapid succession of these empires must have been impressive; this is evident, not least, from the account in Daniel 7. Unfortunately we still know far too little about the underlying processes, and further research in this field is very much to be desired.[138]

1. The Neo-Assyrian Empire (911–612 B.C.E.)

What was new about the Assyrian rule was probably the deliberate formation of a major empire. The Assyrian Empire consisted of a central state with a number of

---

132 For "play on words" see, e.g., 40:22; 41:14-16; 49:24-26; 52:1-6; 54:14b-17. For possible "plays of the scribes" see below on 51:3; 51:10a; 52:4.

133 For play on series of vowels see below 40:12-17, 21-24, 30-31; 42:14, 18-25; 43:16-21, 22-28; 50:2-3; 51:9-11; 53:1; 54:7-8.

134 In considering the work, R. Albertz talks consistently about the "Deutero-Isaiah group" (*A History of Israelite Religion in the Old Testament Period* [1994] 2:414–26 [*Religionsgeschichte Israels in alttestamentlicher Zeit* (1992) 2:431–46]).

135 For this second part of the introduction, attention should be explicitly drawn to the various accounts of the history of Israel, as well as to studies of the individual ancient oriental epochs. Here it is only possible to mention the aspects that I believe are important for further discussion about the historical presuppositions of DtIsa's work.

136 Cf. the summaries Deut 26:1-11; Ezra 9; Nehemiah 9; and the historical works that are expanded forms of the same exposition: the Priestly writing, the Deuteronomistic history and the Chronicler's history. We may probably presuppose that these were

the background for DtIsa, perhaps in part even contemporary.

137 Of earlier works that have received too little attention I should like to mention here F. M. Heichelheim, *Wirtschaftsgeschichte des Altertums*, vols. 1 and 2 (1938).

138 See *Anfänge politischen Denkens in der Antike. Die nahöstlichen Kulturen und die Griechen*, Schriften des Historischen Kollegs, Kolloquien 24, ed. K. Raaflaub and E. Müller-Luckner (1993). Also requiring clarification is the terminology used in each case: "empire" or "state"? And in the case of ethnic groups, "people" or "nation" (or "foreign peoples/nations," as the case may be)? Different research traditions use different designations for the various epochs (e.g., "late Babylonian" or "Neo-Babylonian"). These also require discussion.

139 See on this P. Machinist, "Assyrians on Assyria in the First Millennium B.C.," in ibid. 77–104; and W. Röllig, "Politisches Handeln assyrischer Könige," ibid., 105–13. Talking about the area of the Assyrian Empire with its open frontiers, Röllig writes: "Consequently the strong kings tried to

provinces and vassals. These were acquired through conquest,[139] the result being the annihilation of a centuries-old structure. In the vassal system, the usual practice had been to force the local leaders of subjugated countries to pay tribute. When the supreme power changed, internal conditions altered very little. The province system enables the great empires to exercise firm control from the central administration. Now a dependent administration was built up in the provinces. It was for the benefit of this that, among other things, the upper classes were deported and settled in a different province. The system of deportations was further developed after some earlier, preliminary examples (e.g., in the period of Ur III and in the Middle Assyrian Empire). The replacement of the ruling classes led to a kind of merry-go-round. It was a system based on mutual dependence and mutual hate. It was in the course of just such a policy that in 722/721[140] Samaria was conquered and the Northern Kingdom of Israel brought to an end.

The inscriptions, but above all the military campaigns, show the sheer power and violence involved. The military achievements and the remarkable building activity are undeniable, and these are stressed in research. Assyria had impressive rulers. The question is only what this rule looked like from below, from the standpoint of the people affected (cf. Nah 3:1).

2. The Neo-Babylonian Empire (626–539 B.C.E.)

For a brief period the Neo-Babylonian Empire meant a continuation of the ancient Babylonian culture. Starting from Babylon as center, a whole series of countries were conquered, among them the states that had succeeded to the Assyrian Empire. As far as can be seen, the aim was to link the Persian Gulf with the Mediterranean. Tribute paid by the subjugated countries made the enterprise

profitable for the kings. This tribute was still paid in kind. In spite of the personal achievement of the rulers, especially Nabopolassar (625/624–604 B.C.E.) and Nebuchadnezzar II (604–562 B.C.E.), under Babylonian rule a whole series of problems remained unresolved. The relationship between monarchy and capital was full of tension, as were the relations between the urban and rural populations. The last Babylonian king, Nabonidus (556/555–539 B.C.E.), abandoned the capital for a time because of the conflict with the Marduk priesthood there. Nabonidus cultivated the cult of the moon god. By setting up his residence in the oasis Teiman, he sought ties with the Arab tribes. For Israel, Neo-Babylonian rule meant the destruction of the state of Judah and its capital Jerusalem. Under Nebuchadnezzar, the upper class was deported. Here no new foreign upper class was installed, and in this respect Judah differed from Samaria, which had fallen to the Assyrians in 722/721 B.C.E. The people who had been deported lived in places assigned to them by the Babylonians. This was the period of the exile. It is generally considered to have lasted from 598/597 B.C.E., the siege of Jerusalem and the first deportation (or sometimes from 587/586 B.C.E., the destruction of Jerusalem), until the return of the exiles, from 538 B.C.E. onward. The "seventy years" of exile go back to the prophecy of Jeremiah,[141] even if a precise application of this period of time remains problematical.

3. The Persian Empire (539–333 B.C.E.)

The Persian Empire followed directly on these earlier empires. The continuity is not in doubt. In spite of that, the differences and new developments in the Persian Empire must not go unnoticed. The empire's very duration—it lasted for about two hundred years—meant that it exerted an immense influence on the ancient world.[142]

---

secure the frontiers—and in doing so departed further and further from the center. Expansion and imperialism was therefore not a concept in itself, but was the result of the securing of the frontiers" (112). For the early development of the Assyrian provincial system, see, e.g., P. Machinist, *Assur* 3/2 (1982) 1–37 (for provinces). For a different view see M. Liverani, *State Archives of Assyria Bulletin* II/2 (1988) 81–98, esp. 90 n. 36.

140 One reason for the uncertainty in the dating systems is that it is not clear whether on a change of rule the years in which one rule ended and another began were counted once or twice. The way the

years of a joint reign were counted poses a special problem. In the case of Israel/Judah, the circumstance that in the postexilic period the beginning of the New Year was changed from the autumn to the spring may play an additional role. For the discussion see J. C. Vanderkam, "Calendars," *ABD* 1 (1992) 810–20, esp. 817 (3. The Year); and M. Cogan, "Chronology," *ABD* 1 (1992) 1002–11 (with lit.).

141 Cf. Jer 25:11; 29:10; see also Dan 9:2-3.

142 For the history of the Persian era see R. N. Frye, *The History of Ancient Iran*, HAW III/7 (1984); *The*

a. Conquests

The Persian kingdom begins with the rebellion of Cyrus II (559–530/529 B.C.E.) against the supremacy of the Medes. The Median capital Ecbatana was conquered in 550 B.C.E. The capture of Sardis, the capital of Lydia, in 547/546 was then decisive, this victory being achieved by Cyrus in an unexpected winter campaign. Croesus, the king of Lydia (c. 561–545 B.C.E.), was taken prisoner. The capture of Babylon in 539 marks the beginning of the Persian Empire.

b. Monetary System

More important for the development of the Persian Empire than the proverbial gold of Croesus was the adoption of the monetary system that had been set up by the Lydians. After some preliminary stages, the Lydians introduced traffic in gold and silver coins, stamped and of differing denominations. The coins made a direct transfer possible, both commercially and in terms of political power. Gold coins were a political instrument. Silver served foreign trade and was used to pay mercenaries. Copper made it possible to give change in the marketplace. The Persians permitted coins to be minted independently in different parts of the empire and their cities, and encouraged the exchange. It was probably in 502/501 B.C.E. that Darius I (521–485 B.C.E.) initiated the gold daric, named after him and stamped with his image.[143] With the gold standard the Persians also at once became "monetarists," and this had important consequences. They hoarded the gold that they acquired from the satraps and dependent countries, depositing it in the famous treasure-houses of their palaces. This made things difficult for countries such as Judah that had no mineral resources of their own. In these countries olives, oil, and wine as cash crops had to bring in the equivalent value. The currency problem will concern us again in DtIsa: "and will give you [Cyrus] treasures of darkness and hidden stores" (Isa 45:3). With Persian gold Alexander then financed his campaigns.

c. Administration[144]

The Persian Empire was a centralized, feudal society.[145] The emperor at the head united in his person the most important functions of rule over the whole empire. He led the army in war. As the supreme judge, he provided for law and justice. The edicts (*dāta*) he issued had the status of imperial law. He also headed the religious structure, responsible only to the imperial god Ahura Mazda, with himself, conversely, representing the deity.

The closer circle of rule was made up of the six families of "relatives" and "friends." A graduated system of personal loyalties supported the imperial power, or endangered it through rivalries. A network of satraps surrounded the Persian homeland, ruled by persons in the confidence of the emperor, some of them drawn from the local dynasties. The link with the outposts of the empire was secured by regular reports to the court, by the exchange of "gifts" on the occasion of festivals, and not least by a well-developed secret service.

The emperor was the only one to claim the title of "Lord" (*ahura*). Below him, on the different feudal levels, his dependents were called *manā bandaka*. It was a relationship of mutual obligation. Greek interpretation ren-

Cambridge History of Judaism, ed. W. D. Davies and L. Finkelstein (1984), vol. 1: *Introduction; The Persian Period* (with lit.); *The Cambridge History of Iran*, vol. 2: *The Median and Achaemenian Periods*, ed. I. Gershevitch (1985); M. A. Dandamaev, *A Political History of the Achaemenid Empire* (Eng. trans. 1989); J. L. Berquist, *Judaism in Persia's Shadow: A Social and Historical Approach* (1995); P. Briant, *Histoire de l'Empire Perse. De Cyrus à Alexandre* (1996).

143 I am grateful to Leo Mildenberg, Zurich, for useful information. See also his article "Über das Münzwesen im Reich der Achämeniden," *AMI* 26 (1993) 55–79 (pls. 6–13). On the coin findings in the Persian Empire see M. Thompson, O. Mørkholm, and C. Kray, *An Inventory of Greek Coin Hoards* (1973) and *Coin Hoards* I–VII, Royal Numismatic Society London (1975–85); J. Elayi and H. G. Elayi, "Trésors de monnaies phéniciennes et circulation monétaire (V^e–IVe siècles avant J.C.)," *Transeuphratène* Suppl. 1 (1993) 322ff.

144 See among other publications M. A. Dandamaev and V. G. Lukonin, *The Culture and Social Institutions of Ancient Iran* (1984); C. Tuplin, "The Administration of the Achaemenid Empire," in I. Carradice, ed., *Coinage and Administration in the Athenian and Persian Empires* (1987) 109–66.

145 See now also P. Frei and K. Koch, *Reichsidee und Reichsorganisation im Perserreich* (2d ed. 1996). The fundamental theses they develop require further discussion, especially if the proximity to DtIsa in both time and substance is greater than has hitherto been assumed (see among other publications the contributions to the discussion in *ZAR* 1 [1995]).

dered the concepts by *despotēs* (lord) and *doulos* (slave, servant).

In view of all this, it is conceivable that DtIsa's theme "God as Lord,"[146] "the servant" and "the servants" should also be seen against the background of Persian imperial ideology. It is a dispute about who the real Lord is, and whom the "servants" serve.[147]

d. The Political Position of the Ethnic Groups

The political position of the ethnic groups in the Persian system of rule was new. The reliefs in Persepolis show the throne of the emperor carried by the different peoples.[148] The Persians were concerned to win the assent of the subject nations. They drew on local dignitaries to administer their empire and to serve at the Persian court.[149] The picture the Persians give of themselves stresses their political and religious tolerance. In spite of that, however, it cannot have been pleasant to come into conflict with them. At the same time, Persian rule must have come as a relief to the east, especially in view of the empires that had preceded it. Merchants were soon traveling the roads that the Persians laid out for military purposes—and ideas traveled as well.

One problem we face is the picture of the Persians that has come down to us through the Greeks. According to Athenian propaganda the Persians were barbarians. But there was much more exchange between Greeks and Persians than this would suggest. Philip II of Macedonia, Alexander's father, built his palace on the Persian pattern. Greek architects and sculptors were at work in Persepolis and Pasargade, the royal Persian residences. We also have to remember the conflict arising from the collision of interests between Greek trade (e.g.,

settlements in Egypt) and the formation of the Persian Empire, with its consequences. The encouragement of the ethnic groups gave the different peoples more independence and responsibility. In this way they acquired a stronger identity, although the demarcation between them was thereby promoted as well. The danger of misuse was inherent in the instrumentalization of the ethnic groups, internally and externally. In the association of states that made up the empire, collaboration with Persian rule was an obvious subject of mutual reproach among the subject peoples. The problem of the relation between particularity and universality had continually to be solved afresh—as we can see from DtIsa.

e. The Importance of the Towns

The development of the towns (which, after Alexander, was then to put so enduring a stamp on the history of the Hellenistic period) already began in the Persian period. The refounding of Jerusalem is an example (see below under Isaiah 54). In the course of this development, differing political structures came into being. The city monarchies, originally dynastically founded, were replaced by the *tyrannis*, or absolute power, of an individual.[150] Other towns were governed by oligarchies of nobles and bourgeoisie. Athens is an example of development into a "democracy."

Through crafts and trade the towns became wealthy.[151] Greek became the language of commerce. The Athenian owl adorns silver coins as far off as Gaza and Egypt. What is known as Imperial Aramaic,[152] one of the official Persian languages, offered extensive

---

146 Cf. אדני יהוה, Isa 40:10; 48:16; 49:14, 22; 50:4, 5, 7, 9; 51:22; 52:4.

147 In Daniel 3 the conflict between earthly and divine sovereignty is clear.

148 See here now K. Koch, "Weltordnung und Reichsidee im alten Iran und ihre Auswirkungen auf die Provinz Jehud," in P. Frei and K. Koch, *Reichsidee und Reichsorganisation* (2d ed. 1996) 133–337, esp. "3. Der göttliche Schutz über Thron und Völker auf den Reliefs in Persepolis," 159–84; and "4. Das Völkergestell auf den Grabdenkmälern," 184–97. The reliefs are reproduced in G. Walser, *Die Völkerschaften auf den Reliefs von Persepolis*, Teheraner Forschungen 2 (1966).

149 OT examples are Nehemiah (cf. Nehemiah 1) and Daniel and his friends (Daniel 1–6). For conflicts

with the Persian rule see also Daniel; on the level of policy see A. Kuhrt, "The Cyrus Cylinder and Achaemenid Imperial Policy," *JSOT* 25 (1983) 83–97.

150 See V. Fadinger's paper, "Griechische Tyrannis und Alter Orient," in *Anfänge politischen Denkens in der Antike*, ed. K. Raaflaub and E. Müller-Luckner (1993) 263–316, and the following discussion (394–413) with my own contribution (412).

151 M. W. Stolper, *Entrepreneurs and Empire: The Murašu Archive, the Murašu Firm, and Persian Rule in Babylonia*, Nederlands Historisch-Archäologisch Instituut te Istanbul 54 (1985).

152 For a general introduction cf. S. Segert, *Altaramäische Grammatik mit Bibliographie, Chrestomathie*

opportunities for communication, even for people whose native language was Hebrew.

B. The Date of Deutero-Isaiah

The date of Deutero-Isaiah is hardly a matter of dispute among scholars. The *terminus a quo* is undoubtedly given by the mention of Cyrus in chaps. 44–45. But the *terminus ad quem* is not so certain. It is generally assumed that the work was written after the taking of Sardis in 547/546 B.C.E.[153] and before the capture of Babylon in 539 B.C.E. The reasons are that the capture of Babylon is not explicitly reported in DtIsa and—contrary to the biblical Babylon oracles—historically speaking took place peacefully. Cyrus's entry into the city was in fact welcomed in Babylon.

It is possible to assign the date of DtIsa to the end of the sixth century, with the beginning of Persian rule. But I believe that there are good reasons for assuming a later date—to be more specific, sometime between 450 and 400 B.C.E., the presupposition being a number of general considerations and the exegesis of individual passages.

DtIsa's theme is not the renewal of the dynasty and kingdom of David. We find no messianic expectations of the kind expressed during the exile (see Ezek 34:23-24; 37:24-25) and afterward (e.g., Hag 2:20-23; Zech [I] 4:1-14).[154] The transfer of imperial power (*translatio imperii*) to Cyrus, the Persian king, is fully accepted. The person who calls Cyrus "anointed" (45:1) is not still expecting a representative of the Davidic dynasty (see also the commentary on 40:6-8 and 54:3-4).

The rebuilding of the temple is not a theme that engages DtIsa's interest. It certainly took place on the orders of Cyrus (44:28), but DtIsa says no more about it than that, in contrast to the prophet Haggai, and probably Zechariah too. The new legitimation of the priesthood plays no part, as it does in the rehabilitation of the high priest Joshua in Zechariah 3, for example. On the other hand, DtIsa's critical attitude toward sacrifice is clear (see under Isa 43:22-28; 52:5). With the end of the exile, these were important themes. What is new for DtIsa is the close bond between the renewal of Jacob/Israel and the renewal of Zion/Jerusalem. The building of the walls makes Jerusalem a city. The point at issue is not just the return of the *gōlâ*, it is also the pilgrimage to Jerusalem (chap. 55).

In considering the probable date of the work, I am particularly struck by the parallels between DtIsa and the measures taken by Nehemiah, according to the book that goes under his name. These parallels include:

- the building of the walls (Isa 49:16, 17-19; 54:11-14a; cf. Neh 2:11–4:17; 6:15-16)
- the association of the cities of Judah with Jerusalem (Isa 40:9-11; 44:26; cf. Neh 3; 11)
- the liberation of people enslaved because of debt (Isa 42:22; 44:5; 46:10; 49:8-9, 24-26; 51:10-11; 51:13-14; cf. Neh 5)
- the link among the *gōlâ* (the group of the exiles), those who had remained in the country and the Diaspora (see Isa 49:12, 22-23; 51:1-3, 9-11 and the commentary; cf. the biography of Nehemiah).

There is a difference, inasmuch as DtIsa stresses so strongly the indissolubility of the "marriage" between Yahweh and Zion/Jerusalem. Could this indicate that DtIsa was against the dissolution of marriage in general? Texts from Elephantine dating from this period show the problems raised by divorce, especially in connection with property and inheritance. I would guess that this fact played a part in the so-called mixed marriages, in which the partners came from different ethnic communities. For Judah, and for Jerusalem's identity as a city, this was of particular importance. Nehemiah, however, thinks that mixed marriages can be dissolved, even if he does not take as rigorous a view as Ezra (Isa 49:14-15; 50:1; 54:6-7; cf. Ezra 9:1-4; 10:1-17; Neh 13:23-27). In connection with the theme of mixed marriages, it is also interesting to compare what is said about the Servant of God in Isa 50:6 and about Moses in Num 12:1-9 with Neh 13:25 (see below on the text of Isa 50:6).

---

und Glossar (1975) 31–56, esp. 39–46; for further literature cf. U. Weber and J. Wiesehöfer, *Das Reich der Achaimeniden. Eine Bibliographie,* AMI (sup. vol. 15) (Teheran) (1996) 81–82.

153 Isa 41:3, 25 could be a reference to Cyrus's unexpectedly swift winter campaign.

154 See K. Baltzer, "Das Ende des Staates Juda und die Messias-Frage," in R. Rendtorff and K. Koch, eds.,

Studien zur Theologie der alttestamentlichen Überlieferung. FS G. von Rad (1961) 33–43.

155 See under Isa 49:7 and 17; cf. Neh 2:19-20; 3:33–4:5; 6; see also under Isa 52:1 and 54:14b-17.

I think DtIsa may possibly contain references to the concrete political situation of Nehemiah's conflict with his opponents, Sanballat, the governor of Samaria, Tobiah the Ammonite and Geshem the Arab.[155]

Above all, however, the book of Nehemiah, like DtIsa, presupposes the concept of the Servant of God:

1. Moses is the servant of God (מֹשֶׁה עַבְדְּךָ, Neh 1:7-8). He is this as lawgiver and prophet. He is not a miracle worker. It is God alone who works wonders.
2. Nehemiah is the servant of God (עַבְדְּךָ, Neh 1:6, 11). He acts under the authority of Moses.
3. The Israelites are servants of God (עֲבָדֶיךָ בְּנֵי יִשְׂרָאֵל, Neh 1:6; see also vv. 10 and 11). They are his servants both individually and as a collective (Neh 1:10).[156]

Historically, this servant concept is bound up with the upheaval of the time. The "servant" and the "servants" constitute the new, or renewed, "Israel." What is being renewed is the early premonarchic period as utopia. It means the dissolution of the dynastic structure. Nehemiah and DtIsa are linked through their rejection of the Davidic monarchy and its polity. The appeal to Moses and the law makes possible isonomy, or equality before the law and with it the first beginnings of democratization. This picture fits together very well with the development of the cities in the Persian period before Alexander.

The date of Nehemiah is disputed.[157] This partly has to do with the difficulty of determining whether the king mentioned in Neh 2:1 is Artaxerxes I (465/464–425/424 B.C.E.) or the later Artaxerxes II (404–359). I myself think that the earlier date is more probable. The beginning of Nehemiah's activity could then be dated to 445/444, the twentieth year of Artaxerxes I's reign, and 433 would mark the end of his governorship twelve years later (Neh 5:14; 13:6). We should possibly assume that Nehemiah was active during a second period.[158]

The development of the scientific world picture that DtIsa presupposes also fits the period from about the middle of the fifth century B.C.E. until its end. The heavens are marked out, the mountains weighted (see under 40:12). Yahweh is enthroned over "the circle of the earth" (40:22). The heaven is "like gauze," not a firmament or solid dome, as the Priestly writing still assumed (40:22; cf. Gen 1:6-8; see also Isa 51:6). When Isa 40:26 says: "Lift up your eyes on high and see: who has created these? He brings out their host by number—he calls them all by name," that means that the stars too are created. It is not the stars that determine destinies (cf. 47:13 on Babylonian science). The order of the world is also God-given.

One final historical comment has a bearing on the date: Cyrus certainly already claimed sovereignty over Egypt, but that sovereignty was only implemented by Cambyses (529–522 B.C.E.). It resulted in a number of revolts in Egypt, with Greek support (e.g., in 460 B.C.E.). DtIsa gives the impression that Persian rule over Egypt is still the presupposition (see under 45:14-17). This rule ended initially about 405 B.C.E. According to DtIsa, Egypt was given to the Persians "as ransom" (43:3). This meant, conversely, that the Persians could not demand "ransom" again from Israel/Judah. The ever-increasing tribute that the Persians demanded until their downfall embittered the peoples of their empire. In Egypt the attitude to the Persians was ambivalent.[159] There is evidence of a Cyrus renaissance in the latter half of the Achaemenid period in Greece. He became the prototype of the ideal ruler. In his campaign against the Persians, for example, Alexander visited Cyrus's tomb first of all

---

156 See K. Baltzer, "Moses Servant of God and the Servants: Text and Tradition in the Prayer of Nehemiah (Neh 1:5-11)," in B. A. Pearson et al., eds., *The Future of Early Christianity: FS H. Koester* (1991) 121–30.

157 See A. H. J. Gunneweg, *Nehemia* (1987) 39–47 on Neh 1:1-4; idem, *Geschichte Israels bis Bar Kochba* (5th ed. 1972) 142–45.

158 See here now Koch, "Weltordnung und Reichsidee im alten Iran und ihre Auswirkungen auf die Provinz Jehud," in Frei and Koch, *Reichsidee und Reichsorganisation* (2d ed. 1996) 133–337, esp. 296–300.

159 See D. Valbelle, *Les Neuf Arcs. L'égyptien et les étrangers de la préhistoire à la conquête d'Alexandrie* (1990) 262–71. But nevertheless Darius I could later be depicted as an ideal lawgiver. See "V. Bericht über eine Sammlung ägyptischer Gesetze unter Darius (c, 6–16)," in W. Spiegelberg, ed., *Die sogenannte demotische Chronik des Pap. 215 der Bibliothèque Nationale zu Paris* (1914) 30–32; see also P. Kapolny, "Demotische Chronik," *LÄ* 1 (1975) 1056–60. The text is dated at the end of the 3d century B.C.E. See also Diodorus of Sicily 1.94–95, esp. 95.4-5 (LCL, 1968).

(Strabo *Geography* 15.3.7 C730; Arrian *Anabasis* 6.29.4-11). But Cyrus's renown also implied criticism of his successors on the Persian throne. Could it be that the naming of Cyrus in DtIsa, coming long after Cyrus's actual reign, belongs within the context of a critical movement of this kind, directed against the Persians? DtIsa stresses that the true king who rules over the world is Yahweh alone.

C. The Political and Social Situation

DtIsa's work conveys a more or less clear picture of the political and social situation in the world by which he was directly surrounded, even through we have to allow for the poetic form and language.

Zion/Jerusalem –Jacob/Israel

Jerusalem is an independent city within the Persian Empire. The intermediate political authorities and functionaries are viewed quite critically. According to 52:15, kings shut their mouths in the presence of the Servant of God. Kings and princesses act as servants (49:23). This can be a disparagement of rule by the nobility—even Israel's own (cf. 49:7). "Governors" ("those appointed," סְגָנִים, 41:25) are already treated "like clay" by Cyrus. "Dignitaries" (רוֹזְנִים) and "judges of the land" (שֹׁפְטֵי אָרֶץ) are "a nothingness" according to 40:23. The people have their own "rulers" (מֹשְׁלָו), but these are criticized, especially in connection with sacrifice (52:5).

Through its appeal to Cyrus, the city is laying claim to its political freedom. An edict of Yahweh (44:24-28) confirms that Cyrus has ordered the city and temple to be rebuilt, at Yahweh's commission.

According to 52:1, Zion/Jerusalem is עִיר הַקֹּדֶשׁ. This can be rendered "city of the sanctuary." But I have the impression that in DtIsa this ancient formula is understood programmatically as "the Holy City." There is no mention of the temple (except in 44:28), nor of priests.[160] Zion/Jerusalem is the city into which Yahweh enters as king (52:7)—i.e., it is "the city of God." This gives it a function as the goal of pilgrimage (see under 55:1-5; cf. 2:1-5).[161] Pilgrimage also means that gifts are brought by the wealthy and that the poor are fed (55:1). Loyal though the city was, one must ask whether its

status as "Holy City" did not call in question the rendering of military service (40:2) and the payment of tribute (see 43:3; 45:3; 52:3; cf. Ezra 4:13).

The city's independence becomes symbolically clear when Yahweh himself confers upon it the "mural crown" (54:11-12). Politically, Jerusalem is closely associated with the cities of Judah. The texts 40:9-11 and 44:26 show this precisely. This means that Jerusalem is claiming legitimate succession to the Davidic rule. At the same time a changed understanding of the relationship between "the city" and "the cities of Judah" can be detected. Jerusalem is the "mother" (51:17-23); according to 54:13-14 she has "sons/descendants." They help in the rebuilding. In my view, Jerusalem is thus elevated into a metropolis, over against the country towns. The relationship is meant to be characterized by peace and justice (54:13).

DtIsa's program is to link city, country, and Diaspora. The people belonging to these different sectors constitute the new Israel as the people of God (cf. 40:1-2). At the same time the texts show the tensions with which this program was confronted. If we look at the situation as a whole, we can reconstruct the picture of a differentiated society. The texts about the production of idols are especially interesting in their bearing on the professions and on social status. In the urban sector there are the merchants and traders ("those who pour gold out of the purse and weigh out silver in the scales," 46:6) and the artisans or craftspeople. There are experts for metal and woodwork (40:19-20; 44:12-13). The metalworkers are divided into blacksmiths and gold- and silversmiths (40:19; 41:5b-7; 54:16). They are probably organized in cooperatives (see under 41:6; 44:11, "all its comrades," כָּל־חֲבֵרָיו).

In the city there are intellectuals, "poets/prophets" like DtIsa himself (see under 52:5). The country population consists of shepherds and farmers (44:14-20). Their status is raised by the reactivation of tribal traditions. Jacob/Israel and Zion/Jerusalem are given equal space and equal attention in DtIsa's account. In both, the political and religious aspects play a part. In both city and countryside there are rich and poor (49:24-26). Economically, as we have noted, debt slavery is a danger for the

---

160 But see under 52:11-12.
161 For illustration see also Tob 1:3-9.
162 Cf. G. von Rad, *Old Testament Theology*, vol. 2 (trans. D. M. G. Stalker; 1965) 239 [*Theologie des Alten Testaments*, vol. 2 (1960; 7th ed. 1980) 249]: "The three election traditions (of the Exodus, of David, and of Zion) which are constitutive for the whole of

community as a whole (49:24; 51:13-14; cf. 44:5). How liberation/redemption is to be made possible is therefore one of DtIsa's fundamental themes ("Comfort, comfort my people," 40:1). The purpose of his message is the liberty of the liberated as the people of God.

III. Deutero-Isaiah's Theology

A. A Theology in Development

Deutero-Isaiah's theology is a theology of crisis and of hope. It reflects the collapse of the political existence of the kingdom of David and his dynasty. It preserves the experience of the exile. It makes Israel's religious traditions as they are preserved in the Scriptures fruitful for the grasp of present reality. The liberation from the burden of the past that God has made possible and the forgiveness of guilt make it possible to venture an outline for the future: "Comfort, comfort my people! . . . speak to the heart of Jerusalem" (Isa 40:1-2).

If we want to take in and apprehend DtIsa's theology today we must be aware that he is building on the abundant riches of Israel's traditions.[162] Knowledge of these is presupposed. Otherwise the brief references and hints would not suffice, even for the comprehension of the people he is addressing. What is new about DtIsa's theology is rather the way he selects, combines, and applies the traditions. The continuity of experience of God in past, present, and future rests on the continuity of God's word. As in prophecy in general, God's word proves itself efficacious in promise, fulfillment, and renewed promise. It is a "living word"; that is the way it is programmatically developed in Isa 40:8 and 55:11. The astonishing thing in DtIsa is that God's word is already at his disposal as a *written* word. As noted above and the exegesis of individual passages shows again and again, we have to reckon with written sources. We may assume that the Pentateuch and the prophetic writings are known to a great extent. Closeness to the Psalms is evident. DtIsa's work contains much learning, much that is the work of "a scribe." But in his work interpretation means application to the contemporary situation. Present experience is tested against the divine word that has been transmitted, and it can be communicated in

those terms. The sting and pungency of the topical application sets DtIsa in the succession of prophecy. Scripture and its message are not just something for the learned; they are there for God's people as a whole.

One element in prophecy is its concern for public proclamation. For this the drama is particularly well suited as a genre.[163] The content can be familiar, as it is in other dramas in the ancient world. The important thing is the way the familiar content is focused for contemporary understanding. The beauty of the language, the rich world of the images, the memorability of what is said—these things are all at the service of communication. In this sense the form and genre of DtIsa's work are themselves part of his theology.

In talking about DtIsa's theology we must be continually aware that our theology today is dominated by concepts and conceptual systems that have been developed in the course of our own theological and philosophical history. DtIsa works with "concrete abstractions." Many terms and concepts are still linked with primary experiences, and are consequently graphic, colorful and "tellable." The "way" is experienced in the going of it; "sowing, growing, reaping" make development clear. "Carrying, seeking, finding" are everyday activities, but they can also be an expression of abstract ideas.

Sociomorphemes play an important part in DtIsa's theological language. It is usual to talk about anthropomorphemes when human ways of behaving are ascribed to God (e.g., God repents).[164] God is imagined in human guise. But expressing the relationship to God with the help of relationships between human beings seems to me more important. The relations between master and servant or husband and wife would be sociomorphemes of this kind. Thus religious experience can be communicated with the help of the experience of everyday life. Here a highly differentiated yet consistent "language" (in the sense of a language system) is possible.

"Master-servant" is an example of the way DtIsa uses this sociomorpheme. Master-servant designates God's relationship to Jacob/Israel; and here the people as a whole, as well as every individual belonging to it, are addressed as "servant." The relationship is a mutual one. Demands are made on the servant or slave. But his

---

prophecy are all, we find, taken up by Deutero-Isaiah and used by him in striking poems."

163   See part I section D above: "Isaiah 40–55 as Liturgical Drama."

164   See J. Jeremias, *Die Reue Gottes: Aspekte alttestamentlicher Gottesvorstellung* (1975).

existence is constituted through the assurance of protection and provision. DtIsa can then term the historical experience of the exile as, for example, the selling of an unfaithful slave (42:24-25), the slave's repurchase (43:1-7; 50:1), and his liberation (manumission) or redemption (43:3; 44:1-5, 6, 21-23; 48:20: "Yahweh has redeemed [גָּאַל] his servant Jacob"; 51:10).

On a higher level of general applicability and abstraction, the Servant of God is the servant of his Lord. He is the one who, out of an immediate relationship to God, proclaims his Lord's will, represents God's people, and is given a task on behalf of "the peoples."

In spite of the different levels—though these correspond to one another—the sociomorpheme remains the same, so that the "language" is still consistent.

The sociomorpheme husband-wife is used by DtIsa for Yahweh's relationship to Zion/Jerusalem. It too reflects everyday experience. It can be differentiated into the choice of a bride and the marriage (54:1-17), the rights and duties in the relation of husband and wife, separation (49:14-21), or divorce (50:1). "Redemption" then means the wife's reinstatement: the lord restores her to her previous status. With this Jerusalem's destiny is now expressed (52:9, גָּאַל).

By linking the sociomorpheme master-servant with the sociomorpheme husband-wife, DtIsa initiates a process of abstraction. This can be grasped by way of the term "redeem" (גָּאַל), which runs right through DtIsa's work (17 times). In its conceptual context, it acquires the meaning "liberate, redeem, reinstate in the previous condition." For DtIsa it is an essential element in what he has to say about God: "Yahweh is your redeemer" (cf. 41:14; 44:24; 48:17; 49:26; 54:5, 8).

This example shows the "theology-in-its-becoming" that we can discern in DtIsa. He does not presuppose any abstract system in the modern sense, but he is nevertheless able to develop theological concepts that can arrive at a high degree of general validity.

B. Deutero-Isaiah's Declarations about God: The "Kingship" of God

In what he has to say about God too—theology in the true sense—DtIsa takes up the traditions that had been handed down to him. The concept of Yahweh as king is essential. Isa 40:1 begins: "Comfort, comfort my people!—says your God. Speak to the heart of Jerusalem."

This assurance presupposes that Yahweh is once more his people's God and king. Zion/Jerusalem is again his royal city. This is in line with the hymnic utterances in 52:7-10: "As king reigns your God. . . . Yes, Yahweh has comforted his people, he has redeemed Jerusalem."

With the acknowledgment of Yahweh as king, DtIsa stands in the succession of the first Isaiah, the eighth-century prophet. His theological program may be seen as comprehended in the installation account in Isa 6:3: "Holy, holy, holy is Yahweh Sabaoth, the whole earth is full of his glory"; and 6:5: "My eyes have seen the King, Yahweh Sabaoth."

This is the first datable designation of Yahweh as king, and it may be put at c. 740 B.C.E. But the concept is much older than that. Yahweh's kingship too can first of all be described as a sociomorpheme. A king has a palace. He sits on a throne. He is surrounded by a royal household. He rules over land and people. As a theological concept, the sociomorpheme "the kingship of Yahweh" permits the integration of extremely different subsidiary concepts—rule over the world, for example; or the exercise of sovereignty in Israel by way of word, covenant, and law; or Jerusalem/Zion as royal city. The concept of Yahweh's kingship therefore has an extremely high level of abstraction. It permits all-embracing statements, but it can also be partially applied, as when Yahweh is called Jacob's king, for example (41:21). DtIsa's work permits such a reconstruction from the whole to the parts, and vice versa. It thereby emerges that his "language system" is consistent.

But DtIsa does not stand still at levels of reflection such as this. In the liturgical drama the experience of divine sovereignty becomes utterable and communicable. The hymns are an important instrument here. The hymn is the genre through which both earthly and divine sovereignty are publicly presented. In the Psalter there are already hymns addressed both to the earthly sovereign and to Yahweh as king. The nature and program of rule are formulated in the listing of honorifics, predicates, and acts. The acclamation ("Yes, indeed, . . ." כִּי) sets the seal on the acknowledgment of sovereignty. In DtIsa the confession of God's sovereignty is given in the hymn, especially at the prominent points marking the end of the individual acts of the liturgical drama. The predominant theme is God's sovereignty over the whole world (42:10-12):

10 Sing to Yahweh a new song,
his praise from the ends of the earth!
<Let> the sea <roar> and all that fills it,
the islands and their inhabitants!

11 <Let> the desert and its towns <rejoice>,
the farmsteads that Kedar inhabits!
Let the inhabitants of the rock shout for joy,
let them shout from the tops of the mountains!

12 Let them give Yahweh glory
and make his praise known among the islands!

Other *topoi* comprehended in the concept of Yahweh's kingship are the redemption/liberation of Jacob/Israel (44:23), Yahweh's righteousness (45:25), his comfort for his people, and his compassion on the wretched (oppressed; 49:13).

In this complex, the acknowledgment of the divine sovereignty always also implies the possibility of criticism of earthly rule (see, e.g., 40:22-24; cf. under 52:5):[165] "He gives dignitaries over to nothingness—judges of the land he has made as nothing" (40:23). Earthly righteousness is measured against the righteousness of God (45:24-25; 46:12-13). We may perhaps be permitted to doubt whether Israel's kings and rulers were particularly enthusiastic if the people proclaimed "Yahweh is king" all too loudly!

As examples in the Psalter show, hymns forge the link between creation and God's acts in history. DtIsa picks up this approach programmatically (see esp. 40:22-24, 26, 28-31). The rule of God extends over the whole world, in both time and space.

C. The One and Only God

In the Psalms, and there again particularly in those that may be classified as hymns, Yahweh is presented as king over the gods.[166] In terms of the history of religion, this means taking up a predicate that, in the countries surrounding Israel, is used to designate the highest god.

That presupposes a pantheon, at least in the Canaanite area.[167] In the OT these polytheistic premises have been addressed and absorbed in different ways. In the heavenly throne scene in Isaiah 6, for instance, the seraphs are now merely ministering beings.

DtIsa has the proclamation: "As king reigns/rules your God." This proclamation is addressed to Zion/Jerusalem in 52:7. He explicitly uses the title "king" for Yahweh[168] in 41:21; 43:15; 44:6. Of these instances, 41:21 belongs within the context of the fictitious legal battle with the gods (v. 23: "so that we know that you are gods"), the outcome being:

See, you are (less) than nothingness,
and what you do is (less) than naught.
An abomination, whoever chooses you (v. 24).

According to 43:15, Yahweh is Israel's king because he is its creator. He makes possible the exodus from Egypt as well as the new "exodus" (43:16-21). Finally, in 44:6 Yahweh's uniqueness is proclaimed in solemn form:

Thus says Yahweh, Israel's king,
and its redeemer, Yahweh Sabaoth:
I am the first and I am the last,
and besides me there are no gods.

If we trace a line of development in Israel's faith, it may be seen to start from the commandment: "You shall have no other gods besides me."[169] This presupposes the existence of other gods, but rejects their worship where Israel is concerned. The prophet Jeremiah maintains that the other gods "do not help."[170] In DtIsa, however, the very existence of the gods is denied (41:21-29). This is therefore a development from monolatrism—the worship of only one God—to monotheism (see 44:6-8). In DtIsa this development into the confession of faith "Yahweh alone" can still be seen in its polytheistic context. The experience of exile in a foreign country plays a part. It is the experience of the historical turn of events

---

165 On this subject see R. Ishikawa, "Der Hymnus im Alten Testament und seine kritische Funktion" (diss., Munich, 1996).

166 See Psalm 95, esp. v. 3; 96, esp. v. 4; 97, esp. vv. 7-9.

167 Cf. still Psalm 82, esp. vv. 1 and 6; and W. H. Schmidt, *Königtum Gottes in Ugarit und Israel* (2d ed. 1966) 66ff., 80ff.

168 For a summary survey of earlier research see H.-J. Kraus, *Psalms 1–59* (1988), excursus 4 on Yahweh predicates [*Psalmen I* (5th ed. 1978), Exkurs 4, "Die Bezeichnungen Jahwes," 197–201]; also J. A. Soggin, "מֶלֶךְ *melek* King," *TLOT* 2:672–80 [*THAT*

1:908–20], and H. Ringgren, K. Seybold, and H.-J. Fabry, "מֶלֶךְ *melek* . . . ," *TDOT* 8:346–75, esp. 365–67 [*ThWAT* 4:926–57, esp. 947–52] (both articles with lit.).

169 Exod 20:3-6; Deut 5:7-10.

170 Jer 2:28; 10:5; 11:12.

and of conferred salvation, liberation/redemption. DtIsa is able to discuss Yahweh's uniqueness theoretically too. The consequences of the concept begin to emerge.[171]

The acknowledgment of the one God makes the distinction between imperial god (or goddess), city god (or goddess), and house god (or goddess) impossible. A religious segmentation is thus excluded. In Israel's surrounding world, each political unit is represented by its own deity; but now these units are no longer separate spheres of reality.

In the Persian Empire it seemed possible to assent to the existence of a supreme God. Ezra, for example, bears the official title "the scribe of the God of heaven" (Ezra 7:12), which he can accept, even according to Israelite interpretation.

For DtIsa, belief in the one God also makes a dualist position impossible.[172] The end of the address to Cyrus in 45:1-8 makes the point in emphatic terms:

> I am Yahweh and there is no other,
> who forms light and creates darkness,
> who makes peace/salvation and creates disaster (רע) (45:7).

From the viewpoint of the surrounding world, it would have seemed perfectly possible for Zion/ Jerusalem to be elevated to city goddess on its refounding. DtIsa takes considerable trouble to make clear that in the drama Zion/Jerusalem is *only a representation* of the city.[173] Faith in "the God of the fathers" as the patriarchs and matriarchs experienced him is completely integrated, even though the attribute itself does not appear. In DtIsa this becomes clear in a new way. Because individuals as well as the people as a whole are continually addressed, the need for a personal tutelary and house deity besides Yahweh is eliminated.[174] But with this the division between public and private religion also ceases to be applicable.

The centering on Yahweh brings about a change in the belief in God. The beginnings of this can be seen in DtIsa in an important sector: the one God means among other things that it is no longer possible to define the gender of the Deity in exclusive terms, or to make any gender-specific differentiation. DtIsa can venture to compare what Yahweh does with the shout of the warrior who goes forth to battle (42:13) and with the cry of the woman in labor (42:14).

DtIsa's stress on Yahweh's "mercy" and "compassion" has always attracted attention.[175] It is worth noting that in Hebrew the word for "have compassion" (רחם *rḥm*) can carry an overtone of the word for "womb" (רֶחֶם *reḥem*).[176] Compassion (רַחֲמִים *raḥᵃmîm*) is demanded of Babylon, the "daughter of the Chaldeans" and "mistress of kingdoms" (47:5-6). In contrast Yahweh shows his "wife"—Zion/Jerusalem is meant—"great compassion" (רַחֲמִים גְּדֹלִים *raḥᵃmîm gᵉdolîm*) according to 54:7. Yahweh is thereby displaying an attribute that is supposed to belong especially to women. But it is remarkable that the following text, 54:11-14 (particularly v. 14) then pursues the dispute about worship of the goddess Anat.[177] In the Ugaritic text Anat bears the cognomen *rḥm* "girl"[178] and *rḥmy*[179] "the merciful one." In DtIsa the experience of being the object of compassion, or of compassion itself, can be integrated into the acknowledgment of the one God.

---

171 As an approach to the problem of monotheism, see now F. Stolz, *Einführung in den biblischen Monotheismus* (1996), with extensive bibliography; also W. H. Schmidt, "Monotheismus," *TRE* 23 (1994) 233–62, esp. "II. Altes Testament," 237–48. See also *Monotheismus im Alten Israel und seiner Umwelt*, ed. O. Keel (1980), and *Gott, der Einzige. Zur Entstehung des Monotheismus in Israel*, ed. E. Haag (1985).

172 This is rightly observed by R. Albertz, *A History of Israelite Religion in the Old Testament Period* (1994) 2:418 [*Religionsgeschichte Israels* (1992) 2:435]. I differ from him as to the date and the question of the confrontation with Persian religion.

173 See in the commentary under 49:14-21; 51:17-23; 52:1-3; chap. 54, esp. vv. 11-14; and K. Baltzer, "Stadt-Tyche oder Zion-Jerusalem?" in *Alttestamentlicher Glaube und Biblische Theologie. FS H. D.*

Preuss (1992) 114–19; idem, "The Polemic against the Gods and Its Relevance for Second Isaiah's Conception of the New Jerusalem," in T. C. Eskenazi and K. H. Richards, eds., *Second Temple Studies* (1994) 52–59.

174 Cf. still Jer 7:18; 44:15-19, according to which the women bake cakes for the queen of heaven.

175 Isa 49:10, 13, 15; 54:8, 10; 55:7.

176 See H. J. Stoebe, "רחם *rḥm* pi. to have mercy," *TLOT* 3:1225–30 [*THAT* 2:761–68]; *HALOT* 3:1216–17; רֶחֶם, 1217–18 [*HALAT* 1134–35, 1136]. Cf. for DtIsa 46:3; 49:15.

177 See in the commentary under this text.

178 See *HALOT* 3:1218 on *רַחֲמָה [*HALAT* 1136], with reference to *KTU* 1.6 II 27.

179 Ibid., no. 2, with reference to *KTU* 1.23, 13, 16, 28, with further lit.

The phrase "Yahweh alone" lends the foundational declaration of the First Commandment new contemporary force. As in the Decalogue, the underlying reason for this confession of faith—election and God's acts of salvation—must always be remembered simultaneously.

The polemic against idols and the making of them has to be understood in the context of the prohibition of images (the Second Commandment). The theme is formulated programmatically in the prologue: "And with whom will you liken God, and with what will you compare him as likeness (דְּמוּת)?" (40:18). The polemic shows that it was by no means a matter of course to acknowledge the one God, who does not reveal himself in images, is not present in them and cannot be worshiped through them. As the exegesis of the individual passages shows, the theological approach in these texts is no different from that of the rest of DtIsa's work. Even the down-to-earth parody has to do with acknowledgment of the one God. Here again we are presented, as if in a mirror, with pictures of the different social sectors: the piety of home and clan practiced by the country people, the peasants and shepherds who make idols for themselves (44:14-20), and the urban population represented by craftsmen (40:18-20; 44:9-13) and merchants or traders (46:5-8). These are probably organized in cooperatives (44:11) and guilds. The address to people of different social statuses is comparable with the preaching of John the Baptist in Luke 3:1-20 and examples from church history. We see the same thing, for example, in medieval preaching and visual representations. The groups are presented with their special problems and temptations.

In Israel's surrounding world, particular deities were responsible for each of these sectors; Hermes/Mercury was the god of tradesmen, for example, while Herakles/Hercules was associated with shepherds and hunters. If it is Yahweh alone who is experienced and worshiped in all these different spheres of life, then the people belonging to them move very much closer to each other, and many forms of communication are possible. Individuals from different social spheres truly become one people. In the counterpicture, the manufacture of idols, the goal of the unity of all groups before Yahweh becomes clear.

Public, "state" religion is parodied in the procession of the Babylonian imperial gods Bel and Nebo (Isa 46:1). The real dispute with the theory and practice of the imperial cult is pursued in the throne scene with Cyrus (44:24—45:25). Cyrus is legitimated by Yahweh as "my shepherd" (44:8) and as Yahweh's "anointed one" (45:1). It is specifically said that Cyrus himself does not "know" Yahweh (45:4b-5).

For the peoples subjugated by the Persians, Yahweh is a "hidden god" (45:15a). But its own fate allows Israel to testify that "the God of Israel is one who helps" (45:15b).

Yahweh is no longer the "imperial God" of the kingdom of David, nor is he the "imperial God" of the Persian Empire. In the rise and fall of empires he remains the same God. His "empire" is the whole world: that is his kingdom.

1. "The Holy One of Israel"

The use of the epithet "the Holy One" for Yahweh in DtIsa shows that in this cultic sector too there was serious theological reflection.[180] What is developing is a radical rethinking of the concept of holiness. Yahweh is Israel's "Holy One."[181] This holiness is not a threat to his people. It is from "Israel's Holy One" that salvation for Israel proceeds (43:14-15): "I am Yahweh, your holy one, Israel's creator, your king" (43:15; cf. 45:11; 49:7 bis). As "Israel's Holy One" he is the God of the whole world (54:5). It is he too "who teaches you how to help, who lets you enter upon a way you can go" (48:17). In that particular context, this is a declaration made through the servant of God, probably casting back to the Decalogue tradition (see below on the text). Holiness is no longer restricted to the temple and priestly ministrations. To put it in epigrammatic terms: Jerusalem changes from being "the city of the sanctuary" (עִיר הַקֹּדֶשׁ)[182] to being "the Holy City." According to Isaiah 55, it is the place of pilgrimage, festival and a shared feast. This makes Jerusalem the royal city of the king who rules over the whole world.[183]

---

180 Isa 40:25. Lit.: H.-P. Müller, "קדשׁ, qdš holy," *TLOT* 3:1103–18 [*THAT* 2:589–609].

181 קְדוֹשׁ יִשְׂרָאֵל, see 41:14, 16, 20; 43:3; 47:4; 48:17; 54:5; 55:5.

182 Isa 48:2; 52:1.

183 On the importance of the royal city in the Persian period see P. Marinković, "Stadt ohne Mauern" (Th.D. diss., Munich, 1996), with lit.

2. Deutero-Isaiah's Attitude toward Sacrifice

In the ancient world, sacrifice was an important part of religious life. Its roots reach so far back into the *prehistory* of humanity[184] that the OT, for example, seldom provides a reason for sacrifice, but merely continually reinterprets it. Sacrifice too has its function on the different social levels, from individuals within the smallest social units to the overriding organizations of monarchy and temple. In prophecy, sacrifice was repeatedly called into question, from Amos onward (Amos 5:21-27). The essential difference between the outlook on the world prompting the sacrificial cult and the outlook of prophecy is the explanation of a discrepancy between act and consequence, and the reaction to it: Why does disaster happen? How can it be averted? Sacrifice is supposed to put an end to the unexplained discrepancy between act and destiny. Sacrifice is expected to eliminate or avert guilt. Prophecy is at one with the tradition of wisdom and law in seeing human destiny as the consequence of human acts. This is true in the life of the community and in individual life too. DtIsa belongs to the prophetic tradition. He sharply rejects sacrifice. With the help of a scriptural proof he substantiates his conviction that sacrifice serves only human beings, not God.[185] In 52:5 he criticizes the practice of daily sacrifice.[186] In one passage only does DtIsa use the concept of sacrifice in a positive sense, and that is when he is talking about the self-giving of the Servant of God "to wipe out debt/as an offering for sin" (אָשָׁם 53:10).

Experience may have played a part in forming DtIsa's attitude toward sacrifice. After the temple had been destroyed by the Babylonians, sacrifice was no longer possible in the country, officially at least (yet see Jer 41:5). This was especially the case since the sacrificial cult had come to be centered on Jerusalem, in the wake of Josiah's reforms. In Babylonian exile no sacrifice was possible—at least we hear of none. When the temple in Jerusalem was restored, sacrifice was resumed, as we can see from Haggai and Zechariah. But there may have been dissenting voices as well. Why should sacrifice be introduced once more, when people had gotten along without it for several generations, and had found their religious identity in a new way with different religious practices (prayer, sabbath and feasts)? We may assume that after the temple had been restored, DtIsa's public denial of privileges bought by sacrifice gave rise to conflict.

D. The One God and the One World

"In the beginning God created the heavens and the earth": that is the way the account of creation begins in Gen 1:1. The Priestly writing's version ends in 2:1-4a. The conclusion of the whole is given in Gen 2:1: "Thus the heavens and the earth were finished (וַיְכֻלּוּ), and all the host of them." DtIsa belongs within this tradition, but he addressed it and comes to terms with it afresh, as he does with the science of his time. We are too little aware of what an achievement it meant to talk about the one, whole world at all. Our modes of perceiving and grasping space and time are different. The attempt to understand the possibilities and limitations of the different world pictures and concepts is still a fascinating task. The following comments can be no more than an attempt.[187]

The important part played by the theme of "creation" in DtIsa has always been recognized.[188] DtIsa does not develop any theological system in the modern sense, however. He applies "theology" to the situation of the people he is addressing, and it is from this that we have to reconstruct his concept.

---

184 W. Burkert, *Homo Necans: The Anthropology of Ancient Greek Sacrificial Ritual and Myth* (1983) [*Homo Necans. Interpretation altgriechischer Opferriten und Mythen* (1972)].

185 Isa 43:22-28. On this text see K. Baltzer, "Schriftauslegung bei Deuterojesaja? Jes 43,22-28 als Beispiel," in *Die Väter Israels. FS J. Scharbert* (1989) 11–16.

186 This is obscured for us by the translation. See the commentary on the text.

187 I learned a great deal in the seminar titled "Was wusste die Antike von Welt, Raum und Zeit?" ("What was known in antiquity about world, space, and time?"), which I held in Munich in the winter semester 1993/94 jointly with Kai Brodersen und Manfred Krebernik; I would like to express my thanks to both of them here.

188 See G. von Rad, "The Theological Problem of the Old Testament Doctrine of Creation," in *The Problem of the Hexateuch and Other Essays* (trans. E. W. T. Dicken; New York: McGraw-Hill, 1966) 131–43 ["Das theologische Problem des alttestamentlichen Schöpfungsglaubens," (1936) in *Gesammelte Studien* I (ThBü 8; 1965) 136–47]; R. Rendtorff, "Die theologische Stellung des Schöpfungsglaubens bei Deuterojesaja," *ZThK* 51

We must remember that the fifth century B.C.E. was still the era of the Greek natural philosophers. These came from the most widely diverse cities of the eastern Mediterranean, and it was the exchange of questions, observations, and ideas that made the development of philosophy possible before Socrates, Plato, and Aristotle.

1. God as Lord over Space and Time
a. Space

When we are considering the ideas about space, it would be useful to gather together all the geographical information we find in DtIsa, and to inquire about its function.[189] "Countries" and "islands" comprise the whole inhabited world.[190] Yahweh "is enthroned above the circle of the earth, and its inhabitants are like grasshoppers" (40:22a). But nevertheless it was as a dwelling place that the earth was created (45:18).

Isa 49:12 offers a kind of compass: "far away . . . north . . . west . . . the land of Sinim." "The land of Sinim" stands for the south, as we have seen. It corresponds to Syene, today's Aswan, on the border between Egypt and the Sudan. At that time there was a Jewish military colony there, in Elephantine. "Yahweh's people, his afflicted ones" (49:13) are to come from all these different points of the compass. The most important group of exiles lived in Babylon, but there were "dispersed" Israelites in Egypt too, as well as in other countries, especially people who had been sold there as slaves. That it was possible to discuss questions of belief by way of letters and visits is evident from biblical testimonies (Jer 29:1-23, 24-32; Ezek 24:25-26; 33:21-22) and from archaeological findings (e.g., at Elephantine).[191]

The experience of a faith spanning space and the different countries was a reality, and is acknowledged in the hymn in 49:13.

Where "the heavens" are concerned, the contact between Babylonian and Egyptian astronomy in the Persian period led to an enormous expansion of astronomical knowledge. Greek mathematics, acquired above all through navigation, made it possible to work out the zodiac. From our point of view, it should be noted that this also meant a further development of astrology.[192] These presuppositions are necessary for an understanding of Isa 40:12, for example: "Who marked out the heavens with the span of his hand"—Yahweh determines destinies; compare 40:26, which says that Yahweh brings out the hosts of the stars. In my view, "their host" (צְבָאָם ṣebāʾām) is also an interpretation of Sabaoth (צְבָאוֹת ṣebāʾôt) as a divine predicate. Yahweh commands the stars as well.[193] There are no counterpowers. Here the temptation of a dualistic worldview is averted. In the same context 40:26 says of the stars: "He calls them all by name." The stars then cease to be anonymous powers; but Cyrus, the political ruler, is called by name in the

---

(1954) 3–13; M. Weinfeld, "God the Creator in Gen I and in the Prophecy of Second Isaiah," *Tarbiz* 37/2 (1968) 105–32; E. Otto, "Schöpfung als Kategorie der Vermittlung von Gott und Welt in Biblischer Theologie," in H. G. Geyer, et al., eds., *"Wenn nicht jetzt, wann dann?" FS H.-J. Kraus* (1983) 53–68; and J. Vermeylen, "Le motif de la création dans le Deutéro-Isaïe," in *La création dans l'Orient ancien* (LD 127; 1987) 183–240.

189 On the problem, cf. K. Brodersen, *Terra Cognita, Studien zur römischen Raumerfassung*, in *Spudasmata, Studien zur Klassischen Philologie und ihren Grenzgebieten* (1995) 59.

190 "The countries" probably means the land from Egypt to Persia, while "the islands" are the Greek part of the Mediterranean.

191 From the archive of the communal leader Jedanjah eight letters and a memorandum are extant, dating from the end of the 5th century B.C.E. They show that there were contacts between Elephantine and Jerusalem, but also with Samaria. Important is the letter instructing the recipient "to keep the (Passover? and) Feast of Unleavened Bread" (Cowley, *Aramaic Papyri*, no. 21; Porten, A 4.1), as well as the letters regarding the restoration of the temple in Elephantine (Cowley, nos. 30–33; Porten, A 4.7-10). See the texts in B. Porten and A. Yardeni, *Textbook of the Aramaic Documents from Ancient Egypt*, 1: *Letters* (1986).

192 See below on 40:12, 22, 25-26 and esp. 47:13: "You have labored with the multitude of your counselors . . . those who <divide up> the heavens, who observe the stars, who announce month for month <what> is going to befall you." See B. L. van der Waerden, *Die Astronomie der Griechen* (1988) (with lit.).

193 The LXX (quite appropriately) renders צְבָאוֹת by παντοκράτωρ.

same way (41:25; 45:3, 4); and, as servant, Jacob/Israel is called by name too (43:1). This calling by name places all three sectors under the same divine sovereignty; conversely, the Deity too is called on by name, Yahweh Sabaoth (47:4; 48:2; 51:15; 52:6). The whole world is no longer alien; it becomes familiar through its naming. It has a nameable, calculable order.

In his ideas about "the heavens" DtIsa corrects the view taken by the Priestly writing, incorporating new knowledge. The heavens are "stretched out" (נטה),[194] whereas the earth is "trodden fast" (רקע; cf. 44:25; 42:5). For Gen 1:6-8 heaven is a firmament or solid dome (רקיע). In DtIsa it can be compared with a garment (50:3). The heaven passes away like smoke (51:6). Ideas of this kind come close to the ancient doctrine of the four elements: fire, water, air, and earth.[195]

I suspect that when Yahweh is said to reign over "the circle of the earth" (40:22), or when he speaks from its uppermost height (ראש), DtIsa is presupposing that the heavens consist of different spheres. The Servant of God will be "carried up and be very high" according to 52:13. There he sees "light" (53:11). It is the light of the divine presence, but this is distinguished from the light of the sun.[196]

DtIsa knows about the underworld. It is the land of silence (41:1). There the rulers of primordial days can be found (41:1-4a). Babylon enters the underworld with its terrors (47:5-15). But the underworld is no longer a sphere beyond the sovereignty of God. Out of that underworld the Servant of God can appear (48:16b; 50:2). He can rise up to the heavenly judgment for his rehabilitation (52:13). And "Everyman" too can enter into the darkness without fear, provided that he knows the password: "Our redeemer, Yahweh Sabaoth is his name, the Holy One of Israel" (see under 47:3-5). The texts should be seen as part of the dispute with the gods and the contemporary cults of the underworld.

b. Time

When he is talking about time, DtIsa has a long list of terms at his disposal. The relation between past, present, and future can be made the subject of reflection. God's time, from eternity to eternity,[197] embraces earthly time. The fundamental point is Yahweh's proclamation (44:6):

> Thus says Yahweh, Israel's king and its redeemer,
> Yahweh Sabaoth:
> I am the first and I am the last,
> and besides me there are no gods.

To this the declaration in 48:12-13 corresponds:

> I am the One, I am the first, I am also the last.
> My hand also laid the foundations of the earth,
> and my right hand spread out the heavens.

In both texts, what is said about God's time is linked with statements about sovereignty. The beginning of time is constituted by creation. But the remarkable thing

---

194 On "heaven/the heavens" cf. 40:12, 22; 47:13; 55:8; see R. Bartelmus, "שָׁמַיִם šāmajim," ThWAT 8:204–39 (cf. נטה, 40:22; 42:5; 44:24; 45:12; 51:13; cj. 51:16; 54:2).

195 This doctrine is generally associated with Empedocles of Akragas. He lived c. 495–435 B.C.E. He could therefore, according to our assumption, have been a contemporary of Deutero-Isaiah. He is assigned to the so-called pre-Socratic philosophers. The places they came from show a distribution not restricted to Greece but spread over the whole of the Levant. This is an indication of the possibilities of communication open at that time.

Empedocles wrote about "the nature of Being" (περὶ φύσεως τῶν ὄντων) in epic form. In doing so he combined metaphysical, cosmological, and anthropological aspects. His concern was the question about the immutable basic elements of matter (he called them "roots," ῥιζώματα) and the moving forces, love and strife (φιλότης and νεῖκος); see G. S. Kirk, J. E. Raven, and M. Schofield, *The Presocratic Philosophers: A Critical History with a Selection of Texts* (2d ed. 1983).

Of special interest for us are the texts cited there: no. 342, frg. 2, Sextus *adv. math.* 7.123 (*Defense of the Senses*); and no. 345, frg. 111, Diogenes Laertius 8.59 (*The Power of Knowledge*). For DtIsa see below on Isa 40:25-31 under the key words "time," "space," and "force/power/strength" (כֹּחַ; see further 40:9, 26, 29, 31; 41:1; 44:12 [bis]; 49:4; 50:2). For water (מַיִם) see 40:12; 41:17, 18 (bis); 43:2, 16, 20; 44:3, 4, 12; 48:1, 21 (bis); 49:10; 50:2; 51:10; 54:9 (bis) and further below on 55:10-11. For wind/spirit (רוּחַ) see 40:7, 13; 41:16, 29; 42:1, 5; 44:3; 48:16; 54:6; see also K. Koch, "Wind und Zeit als Konstituenten des Kosmos in phönikischer Mythologie und spätalttestamentlichen Texten," in M. Dietrich and O. Loretz, eds., *Mesopotamica–Ugaritica–Biblica. FS K. Bergerhof* (AOAT 232; 1993). See also the concordance for "fire" (אֵשׁ, אוּר) and "earth" (עָפָר, אֶרֶץ, אֲדָמָה) in DtIsa.

196 Cf. Qoh 1:9: "There is nothing new under the sun," i.e., as far as the sphere of the sun; but above the

40

is that DtIsa does not restrict the incomparable divine act of creation—expressed in Gen 1:1 by the verb ברא—to creation-in-the-beginning.[198] Talking about new happenings and hidden events, he says: "They have been created (נִבְרְאוּ) now and not previously or yesterday" (48:7). Yahweh is the creator of heaven and earth (40:28; 42:5; 45:18). He created humankind (45:12), including Jacob/Israel (43:1, 15). But God also creates what is new (54:16). Here creation becomes part of history even more consistently than it does in the Pentateuch.

DtIsa shows how past salvation and disaster exert an influence right down to the present. Guilt is not forgotten; it is forgiven.

DtIsa uses all the potentialities of the theater in order to make past, present and future simultaneous in the time of the drama,[199] so that they can be experienced in the context of the fiction. He knows too that traditions and remembrance can paralyze. So he dares to declare (43:18-19):

> Do not remember the earlier [happenings],
> and do not consider the things of old!
> See, I am making something new!

Yet the context is, of all things, the exodus and the miracle at the Reed Sea (43:16-17)![200] The remembrance of the great acts of the past can cause the wonder of God's activity in the present to be overlooked. In this sense the past is not simply finished and done with. It has to be grappled with publicly if an understanding of it is to be arrived at; and here the festival offers an opportunity through the performance of the "liturgical drama."

One way of grasping time in the overriding sense is prophecy. It mediates and interprets God's word. The events announced are fulfilled, and in this fulfillment they become the means of new promises and fulfilments (44:26):

> Who confirms the word of his servant
> and will fulfill the counsel of his messengers.

In this respect prophecy is a contrast to pagan prediction (44:25). In DtIsa—as the exegesis shows—prophecy is, practically speaking, scriptural prophecy: it records what was once proclaimed, and what has been fulfilled.[201] I think it possible that the appearance of Cyrus has been interpreted also on the basis of scriptural prophecy (2 Chr 36:22; Ezra 1:1). Thus the promise has been fulfilled. Hope for the new constitution of Zion/Jerusalem follows the temporal line of renewed promise. The experience of time, the apprehension of time, and the interpretation of time are ways of approaching this text's understanding of history. This understanding provides temporal orientation in world-time as a whole, from creation, as the beginning, until its end. Individual elements of the history experienced can be linked together, as they are in 51:1-3, for example, where Abraham and Sarah are brought in together with Zion/Jerusalem, "to comfort."

Through faith in the continuity of God in all the different times, both community and individuals can acquire their identity. This is not a modern understanding of history. For instance, the universally accepted scale of years is missing as a yardstick ("the year . . . B.C.E./C.E."), and it is this scale that allows events to be defined as successive or simultaneous.[202] Associations of traditions and concepts such as we find in the texts of

---

sun, where God is, there is surely something "new" (cf. 3:16; 4:1, 3, 7, 15 and other passages)!

197 Isa 40:28: "An everlasting God is Yahweh, Creator of the ends of the earth" (אֱלֹהֵי עוֹלָם יהוה בּוֹרֵא קְצוֹת הָאָרֶץ).

198 DtIsa uses ברא 16 times!

199 The relative Hebrew time system increases the difficulty of translating into our own language system (see R. Bartelmus, *HYH: Bedeutung und Funktion eines hebräischen "Allerweltswortes"—zugleich ein Beitrag zur Frage des hebräischen Tempus-Systems* [1982]).

200 Perhaps it is not by chance, as well, that DtIsa should play down remembrance of the military defeat of the Egyptians at the Reed Sea: "who lets chariot and horse go forth, army and mighty men together—there they lie, can no longer get up"

(43:17). There is probably also criticism of the Song of Miriam in 41:16 as well (see below on that text). This would fit in with DtIsa's tendency, observable elsewhere too, to oppose warlike solutions (see, on the other hand, the description of the event at the Reed Sea in Josephus *Antiquities* 2.16 [349]). In their glorification of the past, "remembrance days" are often dangerous!

201 Cf. 44:7-8, 26; 45:21; 46:9; 48:3, 5, 6, 8, 14.

202 An initial approach to such a scale is the list of *toledot* in the Priestly writing. This is a way of grasping time from creation onward; see T. Krüger, *Geschichtskonzepte im Ezechielbuch* (1989).

antiquity can be more real, or at least can have a greater effect, than the reality of facts. Historical experiences can be grappled with if they are told afresh.

For DtIsa, the unity of the world in space and time is a recognition conferred by faith. Its foundation lies in the activity of the one God: "I am Yahweh who makes all things" (44:24; cf. 45:8). DtIsa discloses the tensions in which this confession of faith is permanently embedded. It is by no means a matter of course. His interest in the whole can be perceived, purely in terms of language, through the frequency with which he uses the term "wholeness" (כֹּל) in the sense of "all, everything, wholly, everyone" in its different forms (58 times). DtIsa does not (or does not yet?) use the absolute term, with the definite article: "the whole" (הַכֹּל), as does Qoh 11:5 (but cf. Jer 10:16; 51:19). We may think of the comparable development of the concept τὸ πᾶν, τὰ πάντα in Greek philosophy.[203]

E. The One Torah—the Law of the Servant of God

The word *tōrâ*—instruction, law—is used only five times in DtIsa.[204] This fact easily masks the key function that the Torah has for DtIsa. It is through the Torah that the sovereignty of the one God over the whole world is efficacious and discernible. It is the Torah of Moses, the Servant of God. The identification of the nameless Servant of God with Moses shows clearly how important the remembrance of Moses, his words and acts, is for DtIsa and his time. The Moses tradition is taken up, but at the same time it is understood in a new way. Conflicts are gathered up and resolved in the unity of Moses' Torah. Thus the first two Servant texts are linked with the Moses of Sinai (his installation, and the receiving of the law) and the third and fourth with the Moses of Deuteronomy (Moses the teacher and his death, down to his rehabilitation by his Lord). The unity of these two different Moses traditions is in dispute. We need only think of the two versions of the Decalogue, or the ten-

sions between the Book of the Covenant in Exodus and the laws of Deuteronomy, with their interpretation. These are not just modern exegetical problems.

In the first Servant text (42:1-9) *tōrâ* can be understood as instruction, and this is the way it is often translated. According to this interpretation, the Torah points the direction that the acts of human beings should take. These are not individual precepts. But I believe that the declaration "his [i.e., the Servant of God's] Torah" is deliberately taking up the formula "Torah of Moses."[205] As law, it is what von Rad calls "the whole of the revelation of the will of Jahweh to Israel,"[206] mediated through Moses. But according to DtIsa, "the law" understood in this way is now also addressed to the islands, as representing the foreign peoples; its importance for salvation is universal. Consequently, after his installation the Servant (Moses) is "a covenant to the people and light to the nations" (42:6). Covenant (בְּרִית) and law (תּוֹרָה) belong together.

The lawcourt scene in 42:18-25 mentions the Torah twice:

21   Yahweh is pleased for the sake of his righteousness
       to make the law great and glorious.

24   But they did not want to walk in his ways
       and did not listen to his precepts/his law.

The truth of the law also proves itself especially in the catastrophe resulting from its nonobservance. Blessing and curse are bound up with the law. It is one's relationship to the law that determines salvation and disaster. In the time of need that contrasts with the salvation promised, the recognition grows: "Is it not Yahweh against whom we have sinned?" (42:24). This confession of guilt is made at a decisive turning point in the liturgical drama as a whole. This corresponds to the prophetic call to repentance, and also to the structure of Christian worship, with the confession of sins (cf. Exodus 34; Ezra

---

203 See, e.g., Empedocles, frg. 13 "And nothing in the universe is either empty or overfull" (οὐδέ τι τοῦ παντὸς κενεὸν). Text following Hermann Diels, *Die Fragmente der Vorsokratiker*, vol. 1, ed. W. Kranz (6th ed. 1951) 314; and Plato *Timaeus* 28 C, 30 B (LCL, 1975). See also B. Reicke, *TDNT* 5:892–96 [*ThWNT* 5:890–95]; B. L. van der Waerden, *Die Astronomie der Griechen* (1988).

204 Isa 42:4, 21, 24; 51:4, 7. See now esp. I. Fischer, *Tora*

für Israel–Tora für die Völker (1995).

205 1 Kgs 2:3; 2 Kgs 23:25; Mal 3:22; Dan 9:13; Exod 3:2; 7:6; 2 Chr 23:18; 30:16; cf. Josh 8:31; 23:6; 2 Kgs 14:6; Neh 8:8.

206 See G. von Rad, *Old Testament Theology*, vol. 1 (1962) 219–31, esp. 222 [*Theologie des Alten Testaments*, vol. 1 (1960; 7th ed. 1980) 218–33] on Deuteronomy, esp. 221.

9; Nehemiah 9; Daniel 9).[207] It is the acknowledgment of righteousness as world order, and this acknowledgment also means a recognition of the sovereignty of God.

Righteousness and help are also bound up with the Torah, according to 51:4-8. It is a hope given to all nations and human beings. It spans the generations (v. 8) and reaches even beyond the end of the world (v. 6). The formulation in 51:4 is particularly remarkable: "Yes, law goes out from/beside me!" (כִּי תוֹרָה מֵאִתִּי תֵצֵא). This establishes that the Torah/law is immediate to God. The origin of the law is "beside" Yahweh. I suspect that a dispute underlies this pronouncement. According to Prov 8:22-30, Wisdom (חָכְמָה) is "beside" (אֵצֶל) Yahweh even before creation (v.30). Curiously enough, the word "wisdom" (חָכְמָה) is used only once in DtIsa, and then in a negative connotation: Babylon's wisdom (47:10). The noun "wise man" (חָכָם) is also used in a negative sense (40:20; 44:25). It could well be that here "law" (תוֹרָה) and "wisdom" (חָכְמָה) represent two competing *Weltanschauungen*, or bodies of opinion.

In the same context, 51:4-8, v. 7 talks about the "people with my Torah/law in their hearts."[208] The context shows that the people who are addressed here are those who are living in difficult conditions, subjected to the "reviling" and "mocking" of the world around (v. 7). In my view, the promise of the text is addressed to "sympathizers" who are restricted in their public acknowledgment of the Torah/law. In spite of that, God accepts them as people who "know salvation [or justice]."

Is DtIsa's theology universalist or particularist? This question is frequently discussed;[209] but as it stands, it is too narrowly formulated. His theology embraces the world and the nations. It starts from the special experience of Jacob/Israel. But the frontiers are traced out anew once the "people with my Torah/law in their hearts" are considered to belong to God's people.

"His Torah/law" (42:4)—that is, Moses' Torah—does not just mean individual legalistic regulations, or perhaps Deuteronomy. As far as I can see, in DtIsa the phrase "his Torah" already embraces the whole of the Pentateuch. This thesis would certainly have to be investigated in more detail; but the exegesis of individual passages shows again and again that what we are being given is an interpretation of pentateuchal traditions, and texts already existing in written form.[210] The cardinal points are, on the one hand, the account of creation given by the Priestly writer and the Yahwist in Genesis 1-2 and, on the other, the death of Moses, the Servant of God, in Deuteronomy 34. If we ask how Moses is able to tell about creation, Isa 51:12-16 could provide the answer. The first point is: "And I put my words in your mouth" (51:16). That could be said about a prophet too. That is why Moses was also able to describe his own end. But Yahweh goes on to say to the Servant (51:16):

> and in the shadow of my hand I have hidden you,
> to <stretch out> the heavens
> and to lay the foundations of the earth.

This may perhaps presuppose the preexistence of the Servant of God, an existence "hidden in the shadow of my hand." To say to Zion, "you are my people," is the function of the Servant of God now, in the present, after his appearance. This task goes beyond the framework of the Pentateuch—unless it is a reception of the message of Deuteronomy about God's chosen place.

If we list DtIsa's themes, we find that they are the essential traditions of the Pentateuch as the Torah of Moses. DtIsa can assume that these will be familiar to the people he is addressing. But at the same time the experience of the exilic period is passed on as well. Creation is acknowledged as something experienced in the present too. Yahweh is the first and the last. There are no other gods. The mythological traditions of Israel's surrounding world are disputed. There is a mention of Yahweh's oath given in his covenant with Noah (54:9). For even according to Genesis, this promise was given to the whole world. The promise is taken up again

---

207 See K. Baltzer, *The Covenant Formulary* (1971), chap. 3, "The Covenant Formulary at the Renewal of the Covenant," 39–62, esp. 50 [*Das Bundesformular* (2d ed. 1964) 48–70].

208 This formulation is probably taking up Jer 31:31-34, esp. v. 33.

209 See J. Hausmann, *Israels Rest* (1987) 246–53; and P. Marinković, "Stadt ohne Mauern" (Th.D. diss., Munich 1996), esp. "Universalismus und Partiku-

larismus als theologische Konzepte in exilisch-nachexilischer Zeit," 71–88; see further P. A. H. de Boer, *Second Isaiah's Message* (OTS 11; 1956) 90; D. E. Hollenberg, "Nationalism and 'the Nations' in Isaiah XL–LV," *VT* 19 (1969) 23–36; and H. Leene, "Universalism or Nationalism? Isaiah XLV 9-13 and its context," *Bijdr* 35 (1974) 324ff. and 329ff.

210 See esp. under Isa 52:13–53:12.

with the patriarchs and matriarchs, Abraham, Sarah, and Jacob.[211] This also means a casting back to the era before Israel became a state. There are still, ever and again, "father's houses," as the smallest units in which people both live and work.

As far as the themes of the exodus and the wanderings in the wilderness are concerned, for DtIsa too the fundamental experience is liberation. An exodus from Egypt was necessary at that earlier time, and a new exodus of the exiled people is necessary now. The example of liberation also shows that "remembrance" is not confined to the Torah as a lofty abstraction; it is translated into the practical necessity of liberation from debt slavery.[212] Lands that have been laid waste are to be passed on as an inheritance (49:8). But above all the settlement of the land is experienced in a new way as a pilgrimage (54:17b; 55:1-3a; see also under 40:31). The fundamental elements of the "historical creed" are thus evident. This "prehistory" provides the foundation for the relationship to God. Correspondingly the individual commandments follow from that relationship.

Here we can discern the structure of the covenant,[213] and here Torah and covenant (בְּרִית) cannot be separated. The link between the two is anchored in the figure of Moses, the Servant of God. This also makes it possible to resolve the tension between the covenant on Sinai and the covenant in the land of Moab according to Deuteronomy. DtIsa's work is a document of unity. The one Torah as the "declaration of Yahweh's will" is meant for the present.

Moses is the mediator of the covenant between Yahweh and his people. In the name of his God and at his God's commission Moses is the lawgiver. What has to be decided afresh in DtIsa is whether the Servant has a function for Israel alone. The answer given in 49:6 is unequivocal: "It is too little that you should belong to me as Servant, to raise up [restore?] the tribes of Israel." The Servant is destined to be a "light" of "nations" (42:6).

Looking back, we can perceive once more that the first Servant text (42:1-9) provides the program for the whole of DtIsa's message. The text declares three times, with different nuances, that the Servant has a charge to see that justice, or the decree of justice (מִשְׁפָּט), prevails (42:1, 3, 4). His Torah/law is valid for the islands too (42:4). The God Yahweh is the creator of heaven and earth (42:5). He is the selfsame God who gives life to the whole of humanity. Under this universal aspect it is understandable that the Servant of God should be destined to be "a covenant to the people and a light to the nations" (42:6). The foundation is God's "righteousness/faithfulness to the community." What is being paraphrased here is the sovereignty of God. In the form of kingship (Greek βασιλεία τοῦ θεοῦ), the one God, the one world, and the one Torah are experienced and acknowledged, and in this experience and this creed the OT and the NT are linked.[214]

For DtIsa the world under the aspect that we call nature and under the aspect of the social and political order that we call history are a *single* world. This recognition and this acknowledgment are perpetuated throughout Jewish and Christian tradition. The same conviction is expressed by Philo of Alexandria, for example (c. 40 C.E.), when he links φύσις (*physis*) and νόμος (*nomos*) and talks about "natural law," νόμος φύσεως.[215] The present generation is the first in humanity's history to have *seen* the earth as a whole, as a blue star, on a photograph taken from the Apollo space shuttle. Today too Deutero-Isaiah's theology is a challenge to inquire about the one God and the one world.

---

211 Abraham in 41:8; 51:2: Sarah in 51:2; Jacob, e.g., in 43:22; 44:1-2, 5; 45:4, 19; 49:26.

212 See K. Baltzer, "Liberation from Debt Slavery After the Exile in Second Isaiah and Nehemiah," in *Ancient Israelite Religion: FS F. M. Cross* (1987) 474–84.

213 See K. Baltzer, *The Covenant Formulary* (1971) [*Das Bundesformular* (2d ed. 1964)].

214 See the literature on the individual servant texts in the commentary, and now B. Janowski and P. Stuhlmacher, eds., *Der leidende Gottesknecht. Jesaja 53 und seine Wirkungsgeschichte* (1996), with extensive bibliography.

215 See H. Koester, "ΝΟΜΟΣ ΦΥΣΕΩΣ. The Concept of Natural Law in Greek Thought," in *Religions in Antiquity: FS E. Goodenough* (1968) 521–41.

Deutero-Isaiah

With the prologue in chap. 40, Deutero-Isaiah begins his work. Here the book's most important *themes* are announced: God's sovereignty over the whole world, the election and redemption of Jacob/Israel, the renewal of Zion/Jerusalem, the dispute with the foreign gods and their images, the revealing of the divine word. These are the old familiar themes that were treated again and again in the prophecy that followed the exile.[1] But here tension is built up: what fresh development are these themes now going to be given?

An infinite *space* is traversed in these verses, from the remoteness of the heavens where God is, over the wide spaces of the desert through which God comes, announced from the "high mountain," to the scene of events—the place where the hymn is heard, but where there are also craftsmen who are fashioning images of idols.

The *time* stretches from creation, by way of the present, in which Jacob/Israel laments and receives assurance, to the future following the return to Zion/Jerusalem. The point of intersection is what is proclaimed, and what happens, here and now.

The structure of the chapter and the division between the smallest units can be seen in various ways and justified accordingly, as the commentaries show. Many agree that vv. 1-11 form a kind of prologue.[2] To use this description for the text is to draw on a category originally belonging to the Attic theater. There the first explanatory speech that introduces the dramatic action is called the "prologue." According to Aristotle's definition in his *Poetics*, the prologue is "that whole part of the tragedy that precedes the entry of the chorus."[3] Both views—one substantial, one formal—have continued to exert an influence down to the present day. It is therefore not by chance that earlier authors have already noticed the dramatic or scenic character of the text.[4] I should like to expand this approach somewhat, so that it serves an understanding of the whole.

In order to separate the different units, we may ask about the speakers or the persons taking part in the action.[5] Anticipating results drawn from the individual analysis, we can establish the following:

A. 1. vv. 1-2 The (first) speaker is surely God himself ("says your God," v. 1).

A. 2. vv. 3-5 The (second) speaker is God's vizier ("Yahweh's mouth has spoken," v. 5).

A. 3. vv. 6-8 The (third) speaker is not identified but is evidently a heavenly being. He in his turn charges a (fourth) speaker: "Call . . . !" This speaker answers: "What shall I call?" (v. 6).

B. 1. vv. 9-11 The (fourth) speaker charges Zion/Jerusalem, the messenger of joy: "Say to the cities of Judah . . ." (v. 9).

B. 2. vv. 12-17 The chorus enters with a hymn.

B. 3. vv. 18-20 The fashioners of idols enter.

C. 1. vv. 21-24 The (fourth) speaker and chorus antiphonally.

C. 2. vv. 25-26 When "the Holy One speaks" (v. 25) it is again God himself (first speaker). It could also be a citation by the (fourth) speaker. What follows is again: the (fourth) speaker and chorus antiphonally.

C. 3. vv. 27-31 The (fourth) speaker asks Jacob/Israel directly: "Why do you say . . ." (v. 27). Conclusion by the chorus.

The structure is strikingly regular. The text consists of 3 x 3 units, equal in extent as far as the number of the verses goes. Only the choral passage in the middle (B.2, vv. 12-17) is longer. The scene of the first three units (A) is the heavenly sphere; the scene of the second three is earth (B). In the third part (C) the earthly and the heavenly spheres are linked.

---

1   Cf. for example the themes in Ezekiel. See D. Baltzer, *Ezechiel und Deuterojesaja* (1971).

2   Thus already Delitzsch, 139 [412]: "The first part, vv. 1-11, can be viewed as a prologue to all 27 speeches. Here the theme of the prophetic promise and the inevitability of its fulfillment are addressed" [trans. altered]. Cf. among others Muilenburg, 422; Westermann, 32–33 [31]; McKenzie, 16; Elliger, 34: "Prologkapitel"; Beuken, 15, 29–30.

3   *Poetics* 1452b17–27 (quote: 19–20): ἔστιν δὲ πρόλογος μὲν μέρος ὅλον τραγῳδίας τὸ πρὸ χοροῦ παρόδου. For the discussion see H. W. Schmidt, "Die Struktur des Eingangs" in W. Jens, *Die Bauformen der griechischen Tragödie* (1971) 1–46.

4   Muilenburg, 422–23; H. D. Preuss, *Deuterojesaja* (1976) 35, 41; Beuken, 15, 29–30; R. J. Clifford, *Fair Spoken and Persuading* (1984) 76; esp. J. H. Eaton, *Festal Drama in Deutero-Isaiah* (1979) 38ff.

5   Of fundamental importance here is F. M. Cross, "The Council of Yahweh in Second Isaiah," *JNES* 12 (1953) 274–77; also his *Canaanite Myth and Hebrew Epic* (1973) 187–88; further L. Krinetzki, "Zur Stilistik von Jes 40:1-8," *BZ* n.s. (1972) 57–58; O. Loretz, "Die Sprecher der Götterversammlung in Jes 40:1-8," *UF* 6 (1974) 489–91.

The assumption that there is a deliberate play on the number three here may be viewed with skepticism. But—as will be shown—"three" does in fact play a part on different levels, right down to the finest structure of the text.[6]

This is an indication of the text's conscious artistry,[7] its highly wrought composition, and the skill of its author. This is truly poetry, and that must be taken into account in the exegesis of the chapter as a single unit. The number three is a symbol of completeness or perfection; it is consequently appropriate for the divine presence. Formally speaking it underlines the solemn character of this text.

The function of chap. 40 as the entry into chaps. 40–55 as a whole can be perceived—even apart from the content—from the dramatis personae who are here presented: First, the "God of Israel" (the divine Presence). Then, in the "heavenly sphere" (A.1.-3, vv. 1-6), there are *three speakers*. It may be that here in the prologue they are represented only by voices. The *fourth speaker* is called, and is the one who calls. Perhaps "the one who calls" is his title. Here the full range of the verb קרא *qr'* should be taken into account: "call, call up, invite, proclaim, read, recite publicly." After his call and installation (vv. 6-8), the fourth speaker has an important function. He leads the ritual of the festival, he interprets the event, and he is authorized to say, "Thus says the LORD. . . ." As spokesman, he is one of the essential person in the "drama." Whether the different functions may have been indicated by some special emblem, head-dress, or perhaps a mask is in each individual case a possibility to be considered. The *chorus* is also necessary. It represents different groups of people as events progress. Here and in the "drama" as a whole, the fashioners of idols serve as comic relief. It is important for the dramatic unity and for the unity of theme that the personifications of both Zion/Jerusalem (v. 9) *and* Jacob/Israel (v. 27) are mentioned. This makes it impossible to separate chaps. 40–48 from 49–55, as various commentators have proposed.[8] Cyrus and "the Servant of God" are not yet mentioned here. But a closer glance shows that there is in fact a covert reference to them in vv. 13 and 14.[9] Only "Babylon" is not mentioned.

If we think in terms of a scenic performance, then—differentiating between persons who speak as part of the "drama" and others who only act—three "characters" are required, apart from the chorus and the artisans: a spokesman, the messenger of joy Zion/Jerusalem, and Jacob/Israel. The separate parts of this "prelude" follow closely on one another in rapidly shifting form. This increases the tension leading up to Act I, which opens with a court scene, beginning "Silence! (come) to me . . ." ("Listen to me in silence!" 41:1).

If the individual elements are so much part of the whole we can no longer expect to find preserved the original individual genres. These have been fused into the wider unity.

---

6   See Krinetzki, "Zur Stilistik," 54–69, esp. 58–60, with reference to Isaiah 6; Elliger, 42–43; but already earlier, L. Köhler, *Deuterojesaja (Jes 40–55) stilkritisch untersucht* (1923) 92; Muilenburg, 423; North, 72. Cf., e.g., 3 times כִּי in 40:2; 3 times הִנֵּה in vv. 9 and 10; 3 times participles in vv. 22 and 23; 3 times אַף in v. 24.

7   See here also K. K. Sacon, "Isaiah 40:1-11: A Rhetorical-Critical Study," in *Rhetorical Criticism. FS J. Muilenburg* (1974) 99–116; Y. Gitay, *Prophecy and Persuasion* (1981) 63–79.

8   See R. P. Merendino, *Der Erste und der Letzte* (1981).

9   See below on this passage; also K. Baltzer, "Jes 40:13-14—ein Schlüssel zur Einheit Deutero-Jesajas?" in *FS V. Hamp, BN* 37 (1987) 7–10.

40 Prelude in Heaven

1   Comfort, comfort my people!
says your God.

2   Speak to the heart of Jerusalem
    and call to her:
        Truly,[a] fulfilled is[b] her time of service.
        Truly, paid off is her indebtedness.
        Truly, she has received from Yahweh's
            hand
            double for all her sins.

3   Voice of one who calls:
        In the desert prepare the way of Yahweh!
        Make in the desert plains a straight high-
            way for our God!

4   Every valley shall rise up,
    and every mountain and hill shall sink
        down.
    And the crooked shall become straight,
    and the rounded heights valley plains.

5   And Yahweh's glory shall unveil itself,
    and all flesh together shall see it.
        Truly, the mouth of Yahweh has spoken.

6   Voice of one who speaks: Call!
    <Then I said>:[a]   What shall I call?
        All flesh is grass,
        and *all* its goodliness[b] like the flower of
            the field.

7   The grass is withered,
    the flower faded,
        for Yahweh's wind/spirit has blown upon
            it.
        Truly, the people are grass.

8   The grass is withered,
    the flower faded,
        but the word of our God
            will endure forever.

2[a]   For כִּי with an affirmative meaning see W. Schneider, *Grammatik des biblischen Hebräisch* (7th ed. 1990) § 53.3.1c.

2[b]   Thus MT (מָלְאָה). The pointing מִלְּאָה ("she has fulfilled") is also possible. 1QIsa[a] offers מלא. See below on this passage.

6[a]   The pointing in MT (וְאָמַר) presents difficulty if the verbal form as *wĕqaṭal* is taken seriously. LXX (καὶ εἶπα; cf. Vg) suggests the vocalization as *wayyiqṭol* (וָאֹמַר) 1QIsa[a] offers ואומרה. See below on this passage.

6[b]   Or "grace" (חסד): see below, and on 55:3b.

A. 1. 40:1-2
First Speaker, A Divine Speech:

"Comfort, comfort my people!" (40:1)

■ **1** "Comfort, comfort *my* people! says *your* God." This sentence sums up everything that DtIsa has to proclaim. It means a real turn of events—a new beginning and yet, at the same time, continuity. God's fundamental decision in favor of his people has been made: that is the note that irradiates all else. In it we can also hear an echo of the ancient formula in which the relationship between God and Israel is described in pregnant brevity: "I will be your God and you shall be my people." This is "the covenant formula,"[10] the definition that has to be newly developed in each situation, to meet the specific meaning and consequences of the "covenant" between Yahweh and his people. Its function in the "covenant formulary" (as genre)[11] is therefore to act as the "fundamental declaration." In this formulary, the historical introduction gives the presuppositions for the relationship with God, while the commandments then name the consequences, down to blessing and curse, that follow

---

10   R. Smend, *Die Bundesformel* (1963).

11   K. Baltzer, *The Covenant Formulary* (1971) [*Das Bundesformular* (2d ed. 1964)]. For the "fundamental declaration" or "statement of substance" see, e.g., pp. 12, 21, 37, 126; cf. Exod 6:7; Lev 26:12; Deut 27:9; 29:12 (29:13); Jer 7:23; 11:4; 13:11; 24:7;

conduct that either conforms to the covenant or contravenes it. It is in this context that the present time can in each given case be defined as a time of salvation or disaster.

By naming his son "Not-My-People" (לֹא עַמִּי, Hos 1:9; cf. 2:1-3 [1:10—2:1]), Hosea had announced the suspension of the relationship between God and his people. Jeremiah assumes that this relationship cannot be intact if the divine commandments are not kept; as he demonstrates, there is no "peace" (שָׁלוֹם) with either God or neighbor. The downfall of Jerusalem and Judah is the result of human acts. In the words that the text puts into the mouth of the commander of Nebuchadnezzar's bodyguard: "Yahweh your God pronounced this evil against this place; and now Yahweh has done as he said. For you have sinned against Yahweh (כִּי־חֲטָאתֶם לַיהוה) and did not obey his voice" (Jer 40:2-3). This approach toward interpreting personal acts and destiny in the context of the covenant relationship between God and people had become a basic element in Israel's self-understanding, enabling it to grapple and come to terms with the breakdown of its national and religious existence.

Ezekiel lets us see how hard this mourning process was—the process that German calls *Trauerarbeit*, "the work of grief."[12] For him, the whole of the history preceding the covenant—its "historical introduction"—can be seen as a history of disaster (Ezekiel 20). But at the same time he also sees the danger for people who take seriously their own responsibility for what has happened to them, in the sense of the proverb: "The fathers have eaten sour grapes, and the children's teeth are set on edge" (18:2).[13] He holds up to these people the opposite conviction: Yahweh is on the side of life (v. 23). Both Jeremiah and Ezekiel show in their individual ways hope for a new covenant; the same may be said of their tradition. It will then once again be true that "I will be their God, and they shall be my people" (Jer 31:33).[14] Theologically, this means the development of a

catastrophe theory based on experience.

DtIsa begins with an answer to the same questions: How can God's acts of judgment be accepted? How can one cling to one's identity even in guilt? How are collective and individual experiences to be linked? DtIsa's approach is in the prophetic tradition: the relationship between God and his people—"my people, your God"— has been constituted afresh from God's side. This gives a hope that makes life possible. The covenant with Noah ("covenant of my peace," בְּרִית שְׁלוֹמִי, 54:10) and the covenant with David (בְּרִית עוֹלָם; cf. 55:3) are given contemporary force. But, as we shall often see in DtIsa, the utterances have to be understood on several different levels, without our being able to (and without our having to) come down on the side of *a single* meaning, in the sense of an either-or. This can immediately be shown from the term "people" (עַם): Israel is "Yahweh's people" (עַם יהוה), or will become so, on the basis of its history; that is the train of thought followed in the more legal and constitutional category of the "covenant" between Yahweh and Israel. The presupposition is the concept of Yahweh's kingship. But עַם also has a nuance that puts it rather in the family context. It then means the people to whom one is related, one's "kin." This is probably the older meaning, so that "people" in the sense of "nation" would be an extension of the term for "family" or "clan." According to N. Lohfink,[15] עַם יהוה can be interpreted as "Yahweh's kin" or "Yahweh's relatives." His specific deduction from this is as follows: "When Yahweh heard the cry of distress of a group of his worshipers and resolved to rescue them, it was because he viewed this necessitous group of people as his own kin." We should be cautious about transferring modern terms like "family" to the concept; for the members of a "house" (בַּיִת or בֵּית אָב) are not merely linked with one another biologically and genealogically. The house (בַּיִת) is a community for living, an economic unit and a legal entity.

If we relate this to DtIsa, it emerges that the "family" meaning of עַם also fits the context very well. For

---

30:22; 31:33; 32:38; Ezek 1:20; 14:11; 36:28; 37:23, 27; Zech 8:8.

12 For Ezekiel's understanding of history see T. Krüger, *Geschichtskonzepte im Ezechielbuch* (1989).

13 K. Baltzer, F. Merkel, and D. Georgi, "Ezechiel 18,1-4.21-24.30-32," *GPM* 18 (1963/64) 233–38.

14 See Jer 31:31-34; 32:36-44 (esp. 38); Ezekiel 36 (esp. 26ff.); 37:15-27 (esp. 23, 26, 27).

15 N. Lohfink, "Beobachtungen zur Geschichte des Ausdrucks עַם יהוה," in *Probleme biblischer Theologie: FS G. von Rad* (1971) 275–305.

"redeem" (גאל), one of the most important key words in the whole work, is originally a term in family law.[16] This would mean that from the very outset we have here a sociomorpheme capable of seeing the *topos* "redeem" in a social as well as a theological context.

The term נחם may belong to the same context. In the *Piel* it is rendered by "comfort" (in the *Niphal* by "regret"); according to *HALOT* both forms have the same origin, "relieving one's feelings." Consequently the root has also been associated with "heaving a sigh of relief" or "taking a deep breath." Comfort is what human beings need when they are suffering or in some distress. Consequently personal attention—comfort through words—is included. But "comfort" is not restricted to verbal consolation in the OT. It also includes action. The whole range of the term can be seen in DtIsa too. We hear about "comfort" or the lack of it in suffering and death (51:9; 54:11 *Pual*); the revival of the land is "comfort" (51:3); "comfort" is set parallel to "will have compassion on his afflicted" (וְעֲנִיָּו יְרַחֵם, 49:13). The correspondence to "redeem" (גאל) in 52:9 is important. On the basis of these last two passages especially, H. J. Stoebe arrives at the conclusion that "the nuance of support is always involved in *nḥm* pi[el]."[17] In 51:12-14 "comfort" (v. 12) clearly takes concrete form in the liberation from captivity.

DtIsa uses נחם only for "comforting" through Yahweh. God is the one who comforts, who relieves, who liberates. But this does not mean that people ought not also to comfort, relieve, and liberate; and how much more if they themselves have been comforted, relieved, and liberated. This connection between the way God acts and what human beings do will become clear in the course of DtIsa's text. But we are already given a hint in this verse; we can ask who is being addressed—who is it that is supposed to comfort? If God is speaking, in the heavenly sphere, then it is "the heavenly ones" who first of all hear the announcement of salvation and the accompanying charge. These heavenly beings can then be called messengers or heralds. B. Duhm answers the question of the addressee by saying: "Not the priests, as the LXX believes; it is *everyone who is able to comfort*."[18] The bounds of the circle are intentionally drawn as widely as this. In the framework of the dramatic context, every listener also hears the commission. It is the prelude to the whole.

We should therefore also note the text's caution about saying directly: "Thus says Yahweh. . . ." Up to now there is no one who has been authorized to speak in Yahweh's name. So whether with "your God" listeners are hearing God himself or someone authorized in the heavenly sphere remains open. The preformative conjugation יֹאמַר is curious too. Ought it to be rendered: "He will say (in the future)"? Or does it mean: "He says (from now on)"?

■ **2** After the people for whom the message of salvation is intended have been described in the most comprehensive terms as "[God's] people," Jerusalem is now specially addressed. The city is personified—otherwise it would be impossible to "speak to her heart."[19] Yet it is neverthless the real city, to which the exiles are to return and whose walls are to be rebuilt—which, in fact, is going to be a "city" once more. It is not the exiles themselves who are meant here, in my view, and it is a mistake to relate the following pronouncements to them initially. Verse 2 is constructed in the feminine throughout because it is the city of Jerusalem that is being addressed.[20]

The proclamation to Jerusalem has three aspects: 1. The ending of her "time of service."[21] Here two renderings are possible: "she has fulfilled . . ." or "it has been fulfilled." In the first translation Jerusalem's role is more active, in the second more passive. צבא can be used for the work performed by a dependent, for example, compulsory labor (Job 7:1; 10:17; 14:14). This is also the way the word is generally interpreted here. But in the vast majoriy of cases it refers to military service. This meaning also applies to a whole series of other

---

16 See J. J. Stamm, "*Berît ʿam* bei Deuterojesaja," in ibid., 510–24.

17 H. J. Stoebe, "נחם *nḥm* pi. to comfort," *TLOT* 2:736 [*THAT* 2:62].

18 See B. Duhm, *Das Buch Jesaja,* on this passage.

19 For "speaking to the heart" as a phrase meaning the language of love, cf. Gen 34:3; Judg 19:3; Hos 2:16 (14); also Gen 50:21; 2 Chr 30:22.

20 As distinct from Jacob/Israel in v. 27.

21 See A. S. van der Woude, "צבא *ṣābāʾ* army," *TLOT* 2:1039–46 [*THAT* 2:498–507].

Semitic languages. In Egyptian the word *ḏabiʾn*, "army," is a loanword. I would not exclude the military overtone of the term here.[22] It would be entirely appropriate and comprehensible if we remember here that "Jerusalem" continually had imposed on her the obligation to participate in the military campaigns of the great powers.[23] We know that there was a Jewish military colony in Egypt.[24] As the Elephantine papyri show, there was close contact with Jerusalem from the Persian period onward, from the conquest of Egypt by Cambyses (525) until the end of Persian rule. For a city, the conscription of a troop of young men was a burden, and a sign of its dependence. A certain irony is implicit in Isa 40:2, when "the city "(fem.) performs military service. But the service for foreign masters is to be ended.

2. The abolition of the whole complex of indebtedness. Jerusalem is told in this announcement that her indebtedness will be forgiven. According to R. Knierim, commenting on the word עָוֹן, "Given the basic meaning, a translation 'bend' (deed and consequence)-'being crooked/crookedness' (fate, punishment)-'twisting/being twisted' or 'perversion/perversity/being perverted' seems most consistent."[25] This would then be a vividly comprehensible way of showing how Jerusalem was bowed down under the burden of its indebtedness. But now this has been discharged (נִרְצָה).[26] The form probably derives from a root רצה II,[27] which in the *Qal* means "pay, discharge." The *Niphal* form[28] here also leaves open whether Jerusalem itself has paid, or whether its debt has been settled by someone else. At all events the "perversity"[29] is now at an end.

3. Establishment of the city's status. What does it mean to say that Jerusalem has received "double" (כִּפְלַיִם) for all its transgressions? Since the language of the text is otherwise extremely precise, it is improbable that this expression is merely rhetorical hyperbole. A legal interpretation of the expression is possible. G. von Rad, following a suggestion of M. Tsevat, proposed that כִּפְלַיִם ("double") should be seen as parallel to שְׁנַיִם ("twofold" in the sense of equivalence or tit for tat) and should be rendered "correspondence, equivalent."[30] In the law of obligations, a claim is met "correspondingly" (quid pro quo); debt and payment are equal in value.

Other authors think that the "double" aspect should be given more force. For example, appealing to Jer 16:18, Elliger paraphrases: "The full amount—that is, twice her debt, first the debt itself and second the usual legal compensation."[31] In any event, the point is made that the debt has been settled.

A. Phillips introduced a new viewpoint into the discussion.[32] He assumes that the "doubling" refers to the length of time involved: the destruction of Jerusalem and the exile last longer than a single generation, so that the next, "innocent" generation is also involved in the consequences. If we reckon with about thirty years for a generation, we would arrive at sixty years here, which is not far from the seventy years of the exile according to Jeremiah's prophecy. Or, if the phrase is supposed to be interpreted in a temporal sense, ought Jeremiah's figure to be doubled, so as to arrive roughly at the time of the city's rebuilding?

22　P. R. Ackroyd (*Israel under Babylon and Persia* [1970] 108) translates: "Her warfare is ended (v. 2), perhaps better than the RSV margin 'time of service', the period of military service or of compulsory labour."

23　See, e.g., J. Elayi, "Les cités phéniciennes et l'émpire Assyrien à l'époque d'Assurbanipal," *RA* 77 (1983) 45–58.

24　Isa 49:12 mentions the return from the land of Sinim. This was probably identical with Syene, on the first cataract of the Nile, on the southern border of Egypt. Cf. Ezek 29:10; 30:6. See also below under 49:12. See also E. J. Bickerman, *From Ezra to the Last of the Maccabees* (1962) 34–35.

25　R. Knierim, "עָוֹן *ʿāwōn* perversity," *TLOT* 2:864 [*THAT* 2:245].

26　M. Buber (*Bücher der Kündung* [7th ed., 1978]) translates: "dass abgegnadet ist ihre Schuld." Is he basing

this translation on נרצה I?

27　See *HALOT* s.v.; also Elliger on this passage, 14–15.

28　G. Gerlemann, "רצה *rṣh* to be pleased with," *TLOT* 3:1260 [*THAT* 2:811]) thinks that רצה II means: "to let something come to one, to (have to) accept something as one's portion. . . . Even the ni[phal] in Isa 40:2 may be understood in terms of the basic meaning: guilt has been accepted by Jerusalem, i.e., the punishment due it has been acknowledged, and this is a fact judged to be a sign of remorse and penitence."

29　R. Knierim, "עָוֹן *ʿāwōn* perversity," *TLOT* 2:864 [*THAT* 2:245].

30　G. von Rad, "כִּפְלַיִם in Jes 40,2 = Äquivalent?" *ZAW* 79 (1967) 80–82.

31　Elliger on this passage.

32　A. Phillips, "'Double for All Her Sins,'" *ZAW* 94 (1982) 130–32.

I should like to propose a third possible interpretation here. It does not necessarily exclude the legal and temporal interpretation, but would take more account of the context in DtIsa. The passage 47:8-9 is important here. There the subject is the antitype to Jerusalem as city; Babylon says about itself (v. 8): "I shall not sit as a widow or be childless." But the divine saying to Babylon (v. 9) is: "These two things (שְׁתֵּי אֵלֶּה) shall come to you in a moment, in one day; the loss of children and widowhood shall come upon you like 'twins' (cj. תְּאֹמִים[33])." Childlessness and widowhood are the double fate that Jerusalem itself has experienced (54:1, 4). It has received "at Yahweh's hand the cup of his wrath" (51:17). There too (vv. 18, 20), the loss of sons is mentioned. 51:19 goes on: "These two things (שְׁתַּיִם הֵנָּה) have befallen you." As a woman, Jerusalem has in Yahweh lost her husband. The lost sons are the inhabitants of the city. But if the city is a "mother city," as in Greek (μητρόπολις), then her "children" are also the smaller cities that are subordinate to her. So in the immediate context it is no more than logical that Zion/Jerusalem's message should be sent to the cities of Judah (40:9). Yahweh is again Lord (אֲדֹנָי, v. 10). Jerusalem's "widowhood" and "childlessness" are now at an end.

This means that what is under discussion at the beginning of DtIsa's work is the restoration of Jerusalem. It is moving to see that here there is no casting back to a glorious past; it is indebtedness that is remembered. The new beginning rests on the forgiveness of debt—of guilt. It is a gift of God.

The first two verses give a comprehensive reason for the new beginning promised to the people of God. The good news is sent "orbi et urbi," one might say, adapting the papal blessing sent out from Rome.

A. 2. 40:3-5
Second Speaker:

". . . prepare the way of Yahweh!" (40:3)

■ 3 "Voice of one who calls": by rendering in this way the accents given for the construct compound by the

MT,[34] the indefinite nature of the situation is retained. This is a stage direction. What follows is still proclaimed in the heavenly sphere. We may perhaps suppose that these words are spoken from behind the scenes. It is clear that what is said is no longer uttered directly by God himself: the highway is designed for "our God" (v. 3). The one who calls is probably one of the heavenly beings. At the end (v. 5) he is identified as "the mouth of Yahweh." That is the highest rank that can be conferred. In Egypt, "the mouth of the king" is the pharaoh's vizier. In Israel the prophet can be "the mouth of Yahweh."[35] But the mouth is warranted to express the ruler's will completely, even in this mediated form. It remains his "word." The content of the message corresponds to a royal edict commanding the building of a road. It begins with the commission to build (v. 3), and defines the how (v. 4) and the why of its construction (v. 5). The radically new turn of events announced in vv. 1-2 is now to be given concrete form: the building, maintenance, and securing of the supraregional trunk road is a task for the ruler. These roads are the very quintessence of rule— indeed they are the first essentials for empire building, providing the infrastructure for military operations as well as for trade and communications. Rulers extol their own building activities in inscriptions, in the ancient world no less than in modern times. "The king's highway" (דֶּרֶךְ הַמֶּלֶךְ) is termed a "banked up track" (מְסִלָּה) in Num 20:17, 19. There it runs through Edom, and during the exodus from Egypt Moses wishes to take the people along it when they leave Kadesh. For Isaiah, the "prepared road" (מְסִלָּה) is associated with the new exodus.[36] He expects that such a connection between Egypt and Assyria will bring about peaceful times (19:23). In DtIsa it is the king, Yahweh himself, who issues the commission for the construction of his imperial highway. This, then, is also the first evocation of the renewed exodus tradition.

---

33   MT has כִּתְמָם, "to a full extent." The LXX reading ἐξαίφνης corresponds to פִּתְאֹם, "suddenly." The conjectural reading תְּאֹמִים, "twins," then "both together," was already proposed by A. Krochmal and F. Buhl; see Marti on this passage. It would intensify the "two" in v. 9a.

34   The consonantal text would also permit the translation: "a voice calls" or "a voice that calls."

35   See Jer 1:9; 15:19; cf. Aaron as the mouth of Moses in Exod 4:16.

36   Isa 11:16: "So there shall be a highway (מְסִלָּה) for the remnant of his people that Assyria has left, as

■ **4** This road is a wonderful road: that is evident, because mountains are leveled and valleys are filled up. The terminology of the royal inscriptions can be equally exuberant.[37] The preceding "every/all" (כֹּל; valleys and hills) is typical of DtIsa. No type of country is excluded if even the desert is no hindrance to God's coming—and to the return of the exiled people. The question "who will be the builder?" is not answered here.[38] According to 43:19 it is Yahweh himself who "makes a path through the desert."[39] Just as at creation, it is the word that sets events in motion.

In interpretations of the passage, scholars have continually discussed whether these utterances are to be taken literally. Is this about the building of a real road connecting Babylon and Jerusalem, or are the statements meant to be understood metaphorically? I believe that these two possibilities are not necessarily mutually exclusive, if we take into account the function of the prologue as a summing up of the action of the whole drama.

Of course, this has to do with the call for a real return of the *gōlâ*, and that it may be made possible with divine help. Of course the way is a genuine hindrance—if its difficulties and perils do not actually provide a pretext for not returning. But the choice of words allows the text to become transparent for more than the geographical facts. The desert can be the place of hostile powers (cf. Lev 16:10). גַּיְא, the word used for "valley" here, almost without exception means "the valley of death, darkness, putrefaction."[40] It is a word for a place that is anti-God. The "mountain" can be a symbol for political power, as it is in Jeremiah's saying against Babylon (Jer 51:24-26).[41] שָׁפֵל means "to be low, sink down"; the low foothills of the Judean mountains, for example, are called Shephelah (שְׁפֵלָה). But in most passages the expression is used for a socially humble position,[42] especially in the *Hiphil* form of the verb, which has the sense of "degrade, humiliate."[43] This would mean that v. 4a would already be a foretaste of what is directly expressed in 40:22-23, and of what the rest of DtIsa's text expounds: that earthly power is transitory.[44]

The statement that "the crooked shall be made straight" is also curious. Elliger, for example, renders v. 4bα as: "And what was rough ground will become level terrain." He points to "the word עָקֹב, 'nodule' or 'corm' (like the form of the heel), which is only found elsewhere, in a transferred sense, in Jer 17:9 . . . of course as an image for mountainous, hilly country."[45] But this is not as unequivocally plain as he suggests. As Elliger also points out, LXX, Targum, and Vulgate understand the sentence as: "(Everything) crooked will become straight."[46] A road can be straightened. But here too a double meaning would seem to be suggested. In Mic 3:9 "the heads of the house of Jacob and the rulers of the house of Israel" are reproached for abhorring justice

---

there was for Israel when it came up from the land of Egypt" (see also 12:1ff.).

37 Cf. the inscription of Nebuchadnezzar II, published by F. H. Weissbach, *Die Inschriften Nebukadnezars II. im Wâdī Brîssā und am Nahr el-Kelb* (1906; reprint 1978). Translations: *AOT*[2] 365–66, and *ANET* 307: "What no former king had done (I achieved): I cut through steep mountains, I split rocks, opened passages and (thus) I constructed a straight road for the (transport of the) cedars. I made the Arahtu flo[at] (down)." Later German trans. by R. Borger (*TUAT* 1/4 [1984]) 405:33–44, with lit.). Cf. also Herodotus's description of the royal highway (ἡ ὁδὸς ἡ βασιλική) from "Sardis to Susa" in the Persian period (5.52–54).

38 Duhm writes here: "according to other passages (41:18ff., etc.) the desert is transformed under Yahweh's footprints—here, however, through the activity of beings close to him. But only an invisible being can require these invisible ones to act." According to König, *Historisch-Kritisches Lehrgebäude* (349), the charge is given to the "hermits" who live in the desert.

39 Cf. 41:18; 42:15; 49:11.

40 See Deut 34:6; 2 Kgs 2:16; Zech 14:4; Ps 23:4; cf. esp. Ezek 6:3; also Ezek 31:12; 32:5; 35:8; 36:4.

41 Cf. Zech 4:7: "What are you, O great mountain? Before Zerubbabel you shall become a plain (לְמִישֹׁר)"; Dan 2:34, 35.

42 See *HALAT* 4:1506; Isa 2:9, 17; 5:15; Prov 16:19.

43 Ibid.; 1 Sam 2:7; 2 Sam 22:28; Ps 18:28 (27); Isa 13:11; 25:11; Ezek 21:31 (26); Pss 75:8 (7); 147:6; Prov 29:23.

44 Cf. Isa 2:12-16 and Mary's Magnificat in Luke 1:46-55.

45 Elliger on this passage.

46 καὶ ἔσται πάντα τὰ σκολιὰ εἰς εὐθεῖαν (Aquila: το περικαμπες εις ευθυτητα, 86, Chrysostom; see J. Ziegler, *Isaias* [*Septuaginta;* 2d ed. 1967]). In content, a comparison with the beginning of Hesiod's *Erga* is interesting. It is said there of Zeus that he "puts the crooked straight": ῥεῖα δέ τ᾽ ἰθύνει σκολιὸν (*Erga* 1.6). A. Lesky (*Geschichte der griechischen Literatur* [3d ed. 1971] 123) writes here: "Whereas the theogony was basically an *aristeia* or panegyric on Zeus, the *Erga* begins with a little hymn to the

and for making everything that was straight (הַיְשָׁרָה) crooked. Here we have the usual word for "crooked paths" (עקשׁ).[47]

The curious choice of words in DtIsa could again be connected with the character of the prologue, in which there is a play on what is to follow—in this case a play on the name Jacob (יַעֲקֹב) by way of the word "crooked" (הֶעָקֹב heʿāqob). In Isa 43:22-28 and 44:1-5 we probably have a Jacob midrash, which is picking up Gen 25:19—35:29. In Gen 25:25-26 the name "Jacob" is explained as meaning "heel" (עָקֵב), while in 27:36 its meaning is said to be "outwitter" (עָקַב). According to DtIsa, Jacob is no longer the cheat (cf. Hos 12:4-7; 14:9 <8>). He is given the name "Jeshurun" (יְשֻׁרוּן, 44:2). But this name includes the element "to be straight, just" (ישׁר); or, to paraphrase it in the words of our present text, 40:4, "the crooked shall become straight/upright."[48] The ethical understanding of the motif "prepare Yahweh's way," developed in later interpretation from Trito-Isaiah (Isa 57:14-21; cf. 62:10-12) by way of Malachi (3:1) down to the NT (Mark 1:2-3 and par.), would then already be implicit in DtIsa's poetry.[49]

Like vv. 1-2, vv. 3-5 are also words heard in the heavenly sphere first of all. All those who hear them are supposed to obey the charge: "Prepare Yahweh's way!" In the framework of the genre's construction, vv. 3-5 correspond to the *ethopoeia* of the drama.[50] The prologue does not merely develop the action; here the ethical exposition is given too, whether it be through the presentation of a conflict or the statement of the purpose.

According to the text, the royal highway will be prepared for Yahweh and his glory (כָּבוֹד).[51] But where Yahweh will come from, and where he is going, is initially left open. The construction of roads can have a military purpose, if the ruler uses them for going out to battle.[52]

■ **5** The appearance of Yahweh's majesty for "all flesh" could therefore be interpreted as a coming for war and

---

supreme God. To say that he has the power to cast down and to exalt is to introduce no new feature into his picture; but when it is said that he puts the crooked straight, this names two sustaining concepts of archaic legal language. One of the fundamental motifs is mentioned when the poet begs Zeus to establish the order of law."

47 See *HALOT* s.v.: *Niphal*, Prov 28:18: "follow crooked ways"; *Piel*, Isa 59:8; Prov 10:9: "choose perverse ways"; Hos 12:8 <7> (cj.) "defraud." As the adjective "perverse, wrong," Deut 32:5; 2 Sam 22:27; Pss 18:27 <26>; 101:4; Prov 8:8; 11:20; 17:20; 19:1; 22:5; 28:6; cf. Isa 59:13; Ps 73:8. DtIsa uses the root עקשׁ in 42:16. Marti's proposal that this passage too should be emended in the same direction actually does away with the real point of the text. For the same theme cf. also Qoh 1:5.

48 Unfortunately v. 4bβ eludes a precise interpretation. רְכָסִים is a hapax legomenon. According to *HALOT*, בִּקְעָה is the "valley-plain wide U-shaped valley with gentle sides." If the valley is well watered (41:18), its fertility is secured, and it is suitable for people to pass through.

49 Here an interpretation such as Fohrer's is justifiable: "In the desert and steppe of their hearts they should put aside all hindrances, their despair as well as their obstinacy, because of the forgiveness they have been promised (vv. 1-2)." See already Delitzsch on this passage. Duhm takes a contrary view: "An allegorical interpretation of our passage surely requires no detailed refutation." North writes here: "The description is primarily of physical hindrances, but it goes without saying that moral hindrances, as well as physical, must give way to Yahweh."

50 Cf. H. W. Schmidt, "Die Struktur des Eingangs," in W. Jens, ed., *Die Bauformen der griechischen Tragödie* (1971) 1–46, esp. 23–27, 31–32, 40–41.

51 Verses 3-5 offer an excellent example of the close relation between poetical form and theological content in DtIsa. Köhler (5) already noted the rhythm: 2+2 (v. 3aβ), 2+2 (v. 3b), 2+3? (v. 4a), 3+3 (v. 4b), 3+3 (v. 5abα). With some minor deviations from Köhler, R. P. Merendino (*Der Erste und der Letzte*) concludes rightly (41): "Through the gradual increase of stresses from v. 3 to v. 5, the whole text undoubtedly acquires more movement and intensity. This reaches its climax in v. 5—certainly intentionally, since v. 5 contains the text's decisive declaration." The connection between a triple rhythm and the divine epiphany is characteristic of DtIsa's work, as we shall frequently see. On the following passage see C. Westermann, "כבד *kbd* to be heavy," *TLOT* 2:590–602, with lit., esp. 598–600 [*THAT* 1:794–812, esp. 806ff.].

52 Here Young cites a provision in one of Esarhaddon's vassal treaties: "You shall indeed place a fair path at his feet," following D. J. Wiseman, *The Vassal Treaties of Esarhaddon* (1958) 54.

judgment.[53] That would correspond to Isa 66:15-17, 18-19, for example (cf. Zech 14:3). War or peace, a coming for doom or for salvation, is the question according to v. 5 too. It is only the context in vv. 9-11 that makes clear that this has to do with Yahweh's return to Zion/Jerusalem together with his people. Here the text is close to the Priestly writing's account of the wanderings through the desert (cf. Exod 16:7, 10; Num 14:10; 16:19; 17:7 <16:42>; 20:6). In that account Yahweh's glory has a protective function. The return of Yahweh's majesty is also reminiscent of the description in Ezekiel of the entry of the כָּבוֹד into city and temple (43:2ff.). In this way God's presence is once again closely linked with the Holy City.[54] Since "all flesh" sees Yahweh's glory, which is associated with the return of the exiles, the whole of humanity witnesses to his saving activity in history. Here, by way of the phrase "all flesh," the distance between God and human beings is especially emphasized.[55] בָּשָׂר is a key word that simultaneously establishes the link with the directly following part-unit in vv. 6-8. With the word "together" (יַחְדָּו) an idea important for DtIsa is formulated for the first time: the idea of the unity of all humanity before the one God.[56]

A. 3. 40:6-8
Third Speaker, Appointment of the Fourth Speaker as Herald ("Caller")

"All flesh is grass . . . , but the word of our God . . . forever" (40:8)

Verses 6-8 also begin once more in the heavenly sphere: "Voice of one who speaks." The speaker is not identi-

fied. The only thing that is clear is that this speaker has moved closer: he no longer needs to call (קרא); he can now speak (אמר). But what he says is just as much a command as what is enjoined in vv. 1-2 and 3-5. The imperative is now singular, differing from the imperatives in vv. 1-2 and 3-5. An "I" answers—a speaker, that is, who is different from the previous ones. He asks: "What shall I call?" But who is this "I"? The difficulty seems at first to be a textual one. The existing MT has "וְאָמַר" (i.e., the 3rd person masc. sing. perfect of אמר) "and he (or: one) said." But the Qumran Isaiah scroll (1QIsaª) reads ואומרה (i.e., the 1st person sing.).[57] This corresponds to the already known readings of LXX (καὶ εἶπα) and Vulgate (et dixi) "and I said." Most modern scholars have adopted this rendering. But the MT nevertheless offers the more difficult reading, and hence probably the original one. I do not myself think, however, that the deviation in the readings makes a substantial difference. It makes no difference to the fact that in this verse a speaker uses the direct first-person form for the first time.

Form criticism suggests a comparison between vv. 6-8 and installation accounts, especially the installation of prophets. The basic elements of these can be reconstructed as a throne scene, the installation in office and function, a statement of the tasks required, and finally encouragement to the person installed.[58] In the present text, the installation is reduced to an extremely succinct form. The throne scene has no pictorial elements but is entirely confined to the audition. Nevertheless, there is no doubt that the commission, even if it is mediated, comes from the divine sphere. The speaker is installed

53 See Jörg Jeremias, *Theophanie* (2d ed. 1976) 147: "If it is correct that in the descriptions of theophanies Yahweh originally drew near to battle, the reason why theophany descriptions penetrated into the prophetic proclamation of judgment and salvation would also be readily explicable; for the majority of such proclamations announce Yahweh's coming against his enemies in Israel, or against Israel's opponents"; see also 179, with reference to Lipiński's theory about the connection between the description of the theophany and Yahweh's war; see E. Lipiński, *La Royauté de Jahwé dans la Poésie et le Culte de l'Ancien Israël* (1965) 151ff. See also F. M. Cross, *Canaanite Myth and Hebrew Epic* (1973) 91–111; and P. D. Miller, *The Divine Warrior in Early Israel* (1975). On the same motif in apocalyptic literature see E. Brandenburger, *Das Recht des Weltenrichters: Untersuchung zu Mt. 25,31-46* (1980),

esp. 53, with reference to *1 Enoch* 1:3-9; 62:1-16; 90:13ff.; *As. Mos.* 10; 2 Esdras 11–12, 13; *Sib. Or.* 3:63ff.; 4:170ff.

54 Elliger believes here that "DtIsa's concept of Yahweh's כבוד is congruent with that in Isa 6:3, where the כבוד is the majesty of 'King Yahweh' (Isa 6:5), of which the whole earth is full." It is certainly true that the associated concept in Isaiah 40 is the kingship of Yahweh.

55 See N. P. Bratsiotis, "בָּשָׂר *bāśār*," *TDOT* 2:317–32, esp. 330 [*ThWAT* 1:850–67, esp. 861].

56 Cf. P. E. Bonnard, *Le Second Isaïe, Son disciple et leurs éditeurs. Isaïe 40–66* (1972) 89 n. 2.

57 Or is this a fem. sing. participle, showing that the speaker referred to is female?

58 See K. Baltzer, *Die Biographie der Propheten* (1975).

to act as "caller" (קרא). Resistance is expressed (vv. 6b-7), and encouragement given (v. 8). To this extent I would agree with the suggestion made, for example, by Habel,[59] that the text should be understood along the lines of a prophetic installation account. But unlike the prophets, "the one who calls" remains anonymous here. Nor is the whole range of prophetic functions detectible, at least in these verses.[60] Here again it can, in my view, be helpful to assume that DtIsa's work has a dramatic form. In his time, for an actor to "act" a role was not yet a matter of course. Nonetheless, it was still possible for a human being to represent the Deity as "speaker." In this respect the text is still archaic, close to cultic drama, although it has already moved away from that in its reflective character.[61]

■ 6 If we now assume that in vv. 6-8 the speaker who represents Yahweh in what follows is installed, his authorization here at the beginning as "caller" (קרא)[62] suffices; that describes his function sufficiently. In what follows he will have to utter the ancient, hallowed formula: "Thus says Yahweh" (כֹּה אָמַר יְהוה); he will have to speak in direct divine speech, and will have to announce and interpret the sacred events.

There is therefore good reason for the speaker to use the first person here.[63] It may thus well be that the reading "Then I said: What shall I call?" also has its point. But we cannot exclude the possibility that "and one said . . ." is one of the rare stage directions in the text. At all events, here a speaker appears on the scene for the first time in the text; everything earlier could have been presented from behind the scenes, being restricted to audi-

tion. In this way the transition to "earthly" events is clearly marked.

■ 7 The objection to the divine commission rests on the transitory nature of everything human (vv. 6b-7). The swift withering of the vegetation through the hot, dry, desert wind of early summer is turned into a metaphor.[64] Wisdom sayings are often found at an important point in installation accounts. But the proverb quoted here is already modified: it is not the strong wind that causes things to perish; it is "Yahweh's spirit" (רוּחַ יהוה). This is the threatening thing, not nature as such in its transience. Here Westermann's observation is appropriate; he points out that elements of the lament have been taken up, such as we find, in Psalms 39, 49, and 90, and in the book of Job.[65] Verses 6b-7 could be paraphrased with the words of Ps 90:5-7: "We are consumed by your anger." In the face of this, what is there still to preach?

In Attic tragedy too, lament has an important function in the framework of the prologue. It sounds the keynote, thrusting forward to the solution or to the catastrophe. In DtIsa it opens up the furthest horizon of human existence. The voice has just said that Yahweh's glory will be seen by "all flesh together" (v. 5); but now the very same key word evokes the transience of "all flesh."[66] It applies to the individual who is speaking here, as it applies to humanity in general (cf. 42:5).

"Truly, the people are grass!" is a phrase responding to the situation. Textually, the sentence could be a gloss, and has been presumed to be such ever since the eighteenth century, with Koppe. The sentence is missing in the LXX. That it is a later gloss would seem to be con-

59   N. Habel, "The Form and Significance of the Call Narratives," *ZAW* 77 (1965) 297–323.

60   In this respect there is at least a marked difference compared with the installation of the Servant of God in Isa 42:1-9.

61   A tradition where comparable circumstances can still be detected is that of the veil over the face of Moses in Exod 34:29-35 (see the commentaries on that passage).

62   *HALOT* under this heading gives for the Semitic languages (except Ethiopic): "call, recite, read." C. J. Labuschagne ("קרא, *qrʾ*, to call," *TLOT* 3:1158–64 [*THAT* 2:666–74]) maintains: "Strictly speaking, *qrʾ* has no synonyms, . . . because terms that could potentially be considered all have specialized meanings" (1159 [667]). "Closely related to the nuance 'to call to' is that of proclamation, declaration, and announcement" (1160 [668]).

63   But "the speaker" does not have to be identical with the author of the work!

64   For the comparison with grass: Pss 37:2; 90:4-6; 103:15; 129:6; see also Isa 28:1; Job 14:1-3. For the meteorology see M. Noth, *The Old Testament World* (1966) 28–33 [*Die Welt des Alten Testaments* (2d ed. 1953) 26–27].

65   Westermann, 41–42 [37].

66   The translation of חֶסֶד in this passage is difficult; see H. J. Stoebe, "חֶסֶד *ḥesed* kindness," *TLOT* 2:449–64 [*THAT* 1:600–621], with lit. specifically on Isa 40:6; also idem, "Zu Jesaja 40,6," *WuD* 2 (1950) 122–28; further L. J. Kuyper, "The Meaning of חסדו Isa. XL 6," *VT* 13 (1963) 489–92. If one starts from "the flower of the field," one arrives at "charm, beauty." The justification is usage in postbiblical Hebrew. Elliger (23–24), with others, has preferred the translation "force, strength," because this can be

firmed by 1QIsa[a], where it has been interpolated between the lines and in the margin. But the vocabulary is DtIsa's own; it does indeed sound like a lament. In this respect the sentence is comparable with another "interjection" in 42:24: "Is it not Yahweh against whom we have sinned?" Both passages are prose, neither being subject to the meter of the context. In this respect the cry in 40:7 is a "communal lament." The people—the people addressed in 40:1—have understood: they know what their true situation is.[67]

If the people are "grass," we may ask whether there is not a covert political allusion to rulers in the "flower" (צִיץ) that "fades." There would then be a correspondence between DtIsa's prologue and his epilogue. According to 55:3, the "enduring mercies of David" (חַסְדֵי דָוִד הַנֶּאֱמָנִים) now apply to the people as a whole.[68]

■ **8** This verse is the reversal of v. 7a both in its form and its content. First of all the preceding sentence "the grass is withered, the flower faded" is echoed word for word. But the conclusion is the exact opposite: in place of transience we find the endurance of the divine Word.[69] This is probably not a continuation of the spokesman's own speech; it is the answer to his lament. Again, however, the encouragement is not for him alone; it is addressed to "all flesh" and—if we allow the interjection in v. 7 to stand—specifically to "the people."

The "interjection" could also mark a change of speaker. This is perhaps indicated by the plural "our God." Up to now a plural has been used only in the heavenly sphere. It is from there that the fully authorized assurance comes, an assurance that runs counter to everything that can be seen on earth. Verse 8 would then mark the conclusion of the heavenly scene.

First the heavenly beings affirm the power and reliability of the divine Word. The "Word of our God" is a *topos* of fundamental importance for DtIsa. The assertion should not be confined to the immediate context. Its important position in the prologue[70] finds its correspondence in the epilogue, in 55:10-11, where the assertion is taken up once more. The two passages interpret one another mutually, bringing out one of the fundamental thrusts of DtIsa's theology.

The Word is creative. It is efficacious "like the rain" (55:10). It is the word of his servants that Yahweh himself puts into force (44:26). The validity of the pronouncements of judgment and of the promise of salvation depends on this. The reliability of the announcement of events is in dispute where the gods and their worshipers are concerned. What is "earlier" and what "later" comes together in the "Word" (cf. 41:42). The second exodus from Babylon corresponds to the first exodus from Egypt. The Word is also efficacious in the interpretation of tradition. Yahweh's Word manifests itself in each given case in a specific message, as it does

---

applied to both the image and the thing imaged. As evidence he adduces among other things the parallel with עֹז, "strength," in Pss 59:10 (9), 17–18 (16–17); 62:12-13 (11-12); Exod 15:13; also Ps 143:12; Jonah 2:8-9; further the Targum's interpretive translation (תקפהון). But I am not sure whether what is meant in v. 6 is not stronger than the original image. It is not a strong wind that causes decay; it is the wind of Yahweh. The normal use of the term in the context of a community relationship would then suffice, the sense being the "grace, goodness, solidarity" that would make the relationship the best possible. In 55:3 DtIsa does use the term parallel to בְּרִית, "covenant" (see below, and also under 54:8, 10). See still N. Glueck, *Das Wort ḥesed im alttestamentlichen Sprachgebrauche als menschliche und göttliche gemeinschaftgemässe Verhaltungsweise* (2d ed. 1962). [ET, A. Gottschalk, ed. E. L. Epstein, *Ḥesed in the Bible* (1967)].

67 I would not, therefore, go along with Elliger's surmise (26): "Even if one takes העם to mean humanity as a whole, the statement sounds like a complaint, whether one interprets this as the sigh of a 'reader'

conscious of failure (as Budde does) or as the confession of someone 'who was deeply moved' (Westermann). It has hence failed to grasp the tenor of the messenger's speech." Marti and Duhm also understand this as "a sigh" in their interpretations of the passage.

68 For צִיץ as "the frontlet on the high priest's headdress" (an artificial flower made of gold), see Exod 28:36; 39:30; Lev 8:9; Sir 40:4. See *HALOT* s.v. (with lit.).

69 For the phrase "establish the word" (קוּם דָּבָר) cf. 1 Kgs 2:4; 6:12; 8:20; as the opposite, Josh 21:45; *Hiphil*: Ps 119:38; Prov 19:21; Neh 9:8.

70 It is noticeable that in the last sentence of v. 8 דָּבָר, "word," is given a stressed position before the predicate.

here in chap. 40, with the "comforting" announcement of a return and a new beginning.

In vv. 6-8 DtIsa is not proclaiming a wisdom saying about the transitoriness of all earthly things. That can generally be preached in simpler terms. It is not natural transience that is the most important problem; it is extinction, perishing, through "indebtedness"—"guilt" (40:2). Over against this DtIsa testifies to the unlimited, enduring efficacy of the divine Word.[71]

"The wind of Yahweh" (v. 7), which can destroy, or "the Word of our God" (v. 8), which vitalizes and builds up—that is the alternative which the text presents. It is the most comprehensive theological perspective of DtIsa's work, already put forward here in the framework of the prologue.

---

71   עוֹלָם has not yet the metaphysical quality of "eternity" here; see E. Jenni, "Das Wort ʿōlām im AT," *ZAW* 64 (1952) 197–248; idem, *ZAW* 65 (1953) 1–35, 199–221; now summarized in "עוֹלָם ʿôlām eternity," *TLOT* 2:852–62 [*THAT* 2:228–43].

40

Entry

9
Get up on a high mountain,
messenger (of joy) Zion!
Lift up your voice with strength,
messenger (of joy) Jerusalem!
Lift (it) up! Fear not!
Say to the cities of Judah:
  See, your God!

10
  See, my Lord Yahweh will come <with
    strength>[a]
and his arm rules for him.
See, his reward is with him,
and his recompense is before him.

11
Like a shepherd does he pasture his flock.
He gathers lambs with his arm
and carries (them) in his bosom.
He leads those that are with young.

12
Who has measured (the) waters[a] in the hollow
    of his hand,
and marked out [determined] the heavens with
    the span of his hand,
and holds the dust of the earth in a measure,
and weighs mountains with scales
and the hills in a balance?

13
Who has directed Yahweh's spirit,
and his counselor—he will let him know it?

14
Whom has he consulted and to whom has he
    given knowledge
and instructed him about the way of law and
    justice
and taught him knowledge,[a]
and will let him know a way of understanding?

15
See, peoples are like a drop in a bucket,
and count as a grain of dust (on) the scales!
See, islands weigh as much as powder,

16
and Lebanon does not suffice for a fire,
nor are its wild beasts enough for a burnt
    offering!

17
All peoples are like nothingness before him,
less than nothingness[a] and emptiness are they
accounted by him.

18
And with whom will you liken God,
and with what will you compare him as
    likeness?

19
  Has not[a] a craftsman cast the statue,
  and a goldsmith overlays it with gold
  and fashions silver chains?

20
  When anyone sets up[a] an image
  does he not choose wood that does not rot,
  seek out a wise expert
  to set up a statue that is not unsteady?

10a 1QIsa^a (בחוזק) suggests that the pointing should be בְּחֹזֶק instead of MT בְּחָזָק. See below on this passage.

12a Instead of מים 1QIsa^a reads מ י ים ("water of the sea"; cf. B. Couroyer, "Isaïe, XL,12," *RB* 73 [1966] 186–96). The emendation ימים ("seas") has frequently been proposed. But the assonance מים ושמים in MT is surely intentional (cf. also במאזנים at the end of the verse: see Muilenburg, 435, on this passage).

14a וילמדהו דעת is missing in LXX. This could be a gloss (but if so an early one; cf. 1QIsa^a). See R. N. Whybray, *The Heavenly Counsellor in Is 40,13-14* (SOTSMS 1; 1971) 10 n. 1, and R. F. Melugin, "Deutero-Isaiah and Form Criticism," *VT* 21 (1971) 326–37.

17a Compared with וכאפס (1QIsa^a; cf. S, Vg), מאפס (MT) offers the more difficult reading (*lectio difficilior*) and hence the more probable one.

19a Contrary to MT, the ה in הפסל (v. 19) and המסכן (v. 20) ought probably to be understood not as an article but as an interrogative particle (see below on this passage). Otherwise we should have to translate (v. 19): "The statue was cast by a craftsman" (and in v. 20): "Anyone who sets up an image chooses wood."

20a For the interpretation of הַמְסֻכָּן תְּרוּמָה, see below.

B. 1. 40:9-11
Sending Forth of the Messenger Zion/Jerusalem: The Triumphal Procession of the Shepherd

"See, my Lord Yahweh will come . . ." (40:10)

The content of these verses is the message about "the shepherd's triumphal procession." We may expect a carefully crafted construction, even if details (e.g., the meter) cannot be determined with any certainty.[72] The three smallest units correspond to the divisions of the verse. The recurrent "threes" in the rhythm and structure of the poetry can be seen in the details too, for example: Zion—Jerusalem—cities of Judah (v. 9), or the triple "See" (הִנֵּה) in vv. 9c-10. The assonances are striking and correspond to the "call," for example: הַר . . . הָרִימִי . . . הָרִימִי (har . . . hārîmî . . . hārîmî) (v. 9), or עַל . . . עֲלִי . . . עָלוֹת (ʿal . . . ʿălî . . . ʿālōt) (vv. 9, 11)[73]— just as when we want to be heard a long way away we might call "yoo-hoo!"

In the structure of the prologue, the installation of the "caller" (vv. 6-8) is now followed by the sending out of the (female) messenger, as the first action to take place in the earthly sphere. The text is linked with vv. 1-2 through the personification of Jerusalem. It is also a continuation of vv. 3-5: the royal highway for the triumph has been prepared. In this way the individual sections of the prologue are closely interwoven.

As for genre, the text can be compared with the instruction to a messenger.[74] The messenger, the addressees, and the message to be passed on are all named. The verb בשׂר in itself says nothing about the content of the message that is to be conveyed.[75] It can be either good or bad. The verbal participle stresses the messenger's activity as conveying a message, as distinct from the fixed role of messenger (מַלְאָךְ). Zion/Jerusalem is acting as one who passes on a piece of news. But this does not exhaust her function, since according to 40:2 Jerusalem has performed military service. The feminine personification of the city runs right through DtIsa.[76] It is in this light that we have to solve the difficulty of the grammatical relationship. There are two possible ways of translating the genitive: (1) as objective genitive:[77] "You, who bring a message *for* Zion/Jerusalem"; or (2) as appositional or epexegetical genitive:[78] "Zion/Jerusalem *as* bringer of a message." In favor of the second possibility is that the addressees of the message are explicitly named in what follows, as "the cities of Judah." The feminine forms of the verbs would also fit in here. They are in the singular, so that Zion/Jerusalem has to be seen as a (female) messenger.[79]

The double term "Zion/Jerusalem" corresponds to the formula "Jacob/Israel" in DtIsa, and in both cases we may ask about the nuances implicit in the two terms.

---

72 See Elliger, 32–33; Beuken, 26.

73 Can one already here detect an echo of the *aliyah*, the going up to Jerusalem? L. Boadt ("Intentional Alliteration in Second Isaiah," *CBQ* 45 [1983] 353–61) draws attention to the alliteration *ʿălî-lāk* and the assonance with *qôlēk* (358). These observations are further indications that the text is a precise literary composition, but one designed to be spoken and heard.

74 See Begrich, *Studien zu Deuterojesaja* (1938, reprint 1963) 58–59, with reference to 1 Sam 31:9; 2 Sam 1:20; 18:19ff. and the scene in 2 Sam 18:19-21.

75 Cf. in DtIsa 41:27; 52:7; for TritoIsa, 61:1. For the proclamation of the divine sovereignty, see Ps 96:2. In Ps 68:12 (11) female messengers are also mentioned; see also *Odes of Solomon* 33. In my view the term is neutral. It becomes "joyful tidings" through its content. Thus the LXX's translation with εὐαγγελίζομαι is an interpretation. The NT can link on to the hope for the coming of the Lord when it talks about εὐαγγέλιον ("joyful message"). (See also the Targum's rendering of Isa 40:9: "The

royal rule of God has revealed itself.") For the discussion see O. Schilling, "בשׂר, *bśr*," *TDOT* 2:313–16 [*ThWAT* 1:845–49]; G. Friedrich, "εὐαγγελίζομαι," *TDNT* 2:707–10 [*ThWNT* 2:705–7]; M. Burrows, "The Origin of the Term 'Gospel,'" *JBL* 44 (1925) 21–33; D. J. McCarthy, "Vox *bśr* praeparat vocem 'evangelium,'" *VD* 42 (1964) 26–33; R. Fisher, "The Herald of Good News in Second Isaiah," in *Rhetorical Criticism. FS J. Muilenburg* (1974) 117–32; H. Koester, *Ancient Christian Gospels* (1990).

76 Cf. 49:14; 51:17; 52:1-2; chap. 54.

77 Of the commentaries see Grotius, Duhm, Marti, Sellin, and Fohrer on this passage.

78 See among others Volz, Begrich, and Westermann on this passage.

79 In favor of the first possibility, however, is that in the case of a genitive of apposition in the vocative we should really expect the definite article before the first noun: המבשׂרת. In the case of an objective genitive, i.e., a genuine construct, the first noun is codetermined by the proper name. In poetical

Zion is topographically the name of Jerusalem's eastern hill. It is the place that David conquered. The name then acquires a preeminently religious connotation as the place of Yahweh's presence, which is associated with the temple. Yahweh has chosen Zion. That is his dwelling place and the place of his throne. These are the traditions associated with "Zion," as we find them in the Psalms especially. Although the two names also become largely congruent with one another ("Zion" standing for the whole of Jerusalem and "Jerusalem" for the city chosen by Yahweh), the name "Jerusalem" nevertheless stresses the political stature of the city more emphatically. It is the more comprehensive term. When the two terms appear together in compound form, fused into a single personification, this no doubt embraces the city as a whole, as a religious and political entity, and brings out the unity of the two aspects.[80]

When the addressees are described as "cities of Judah," this shows that we have to presuppose quite precise constitutional and legal concepts. It is neither the tribe of Judah nor the country of Judah that is named. Jerusalem and the cities of Judah are set in a new relationship to one another. Historically speaking, the country towns had not been as depopulated as Jerusalem, the city of the court and the administration, the temple and the priesthood. This was bound to create problems when Jerusalem was newly constituted. It is not entirely a matter of course that Jerusalem's "city God" should be the "God of the cities of Judah" too. Were there not other city gods and goddesses as well?[81] The concept of Jerusalem as metropolis already begins

to take shape in this text, at least in outline; it is one of DtIsa's basic themes.

This is the background against which the content of the message is to be heard: "Your God . . . Yahweh" (vv. 9-10). It is from the center in Zion/Jerusalem that the message is sent out.

■ **10** In the divine predications we hear the echo of the perceptions hallowed from time immemorial. In 40:1 the phrase "your God" corresponds to "my people," the heart of the covenant assurance. If it is true that "the Lord is Yahweh," then his people are "Yahweh's servant," or they are "Yahweh's bondsmen, his servants"— the fundamental assertion of election. But when Zion/Jerusalem proclaims this here, then Yahweh is again simultaneously Lord of the chosen city; he is Lord (אֲדֹנָי), not "Baal."[82]

What is announced is Yahweh's return to Zion ("He will come").[83] This is the way a king enters his capital city; this is the way a procession of the gods is described in the civilizations surrounding Israel. The parade belongs to the return of the victorious general. Phrases in the text point to this, for example, "with strength/power"[84] (חֹזֶק)[85] and "his arm," as a way of describing his strength. The victor brings booty and prisoners with him. If we compare Ps 68:19-20 <18-19>, the people who go before him would be prisoners. This terminology belongs to the notion of Yahweh as "divine warrior."

But the terms "reward" or "wages" (שָׂכָר) and "recompense" (פְּעֻלָּה) are already an indication of the profound

---

texts, however, the determination can also be omitted.

80   One may ask whether a double city emblem corresponds to this construction, comparable with the double crown of the pharaohs, which symbolized the union of Upper and Lower Egypt. Cf. also the combination of mural crown and polos in the representations of city goddesses, for example.

81   Cf. Jer 11:13: "For your gods have become as many as your towns, O Judah."

82   Cf. Hos 2:17-18 (15-16).

83   See F. Schnutenhaus, "Das Kommen und Erscheinen Gottes im AT," *ZAW* 76 (1964) 1–21; J. Jeremias, *Theophanie* (2d ed. 1976).

84   Or: "Through a strong man/as a strong one" (see *HALOT* s.v.), to whom the following suffixes and statements would then also refer?

85   The punctuation presents a textual problem. The

plene form of 1QIsa[a] and the early translations (LXX, S) presuppose בְּחֹזֶק, "with power/strength" (as do most commentaries). The series of vowels with a succession of *ô* sounds could also speak in favor of the change. But L. G. Rignell argues ("A Study of Isaiah cc. 40–55," *LUÅ* [1956] 14) that this is already a reference to the exodus: "He reveals himself as the mighty God, who has brought the people out of Egypt." For the "outstretched arm" he points to Exod 6:6, and to the "strong hand" of Exod 13:3, 9. See also P. A. H. de Boer, *Second-Isaiah's Message*, OTS 11 (1956) 41, 69–70. De Boer believes that the Masoretic punctuation preserves a separate tradition. N. L. Tidwell ("My Servant Jacob, Is XLII 1," in *Studies on Prophecy* [1974] 15–27) even sees the form of the MT, with his use of a formula found also in Ezek 20:33-34, as an expression of DtIsa's own poetic achievement.

change the image has undergone; for they do not mean the spoils of war—they are the reward of labor.[86] The people in the procession are not slaves; they are those who have been saved.[87] For a person familiar with the biblical tradition—and this may be presupposed with DtIsa and those he is addressing—the very wording makes this clear; for this is the way that Jacob with his herds returned from Haran into the promised land.[88] Here we find the term "wages" mentioned (שָׂכָר, Gen 29:15; 30:32-33). In Gen 33:14 we find, finally: "I will lead on slowly, according to the pace of the herds that are before me and according to the pace of the children."[89] This is the way Israel came out of Egypt, led by Yahweh with "a mighty hand" and "an outstretched arm."[90] The God of Israel is king, as well as shepherd.[91] But DtIsa's picture is dominated by the peaceful return.[92] There can hardly be anything less military as comparison for a triumphal procession than the movement of flocks. It is above all the trouble and solicitous

care for those who are his that are extolled as predicates of DtIsa's God.[93] Sovereignty and help for the weak are not mutually exclusive. Here we are not far from Jesus' entry into Jerusalem.

The function of the prologue as summary again becomes plain, both from its content and from its form. Here what is going to happen in the future and what is already underway are announced.[94] The consequence is tension: how can this hope be fulfilled? The imperatives act as dramatic elements: "Get up on a high mountain!" This is already happening. The three demonstrative "See"s (הִנֵּה)[95] are designed to evoke a visual impression. Above all, however, the messenger scene is an essential dramatic element. It expounds salvation as coming through Yahweh's return to his city.

It is illuminating to compare this with Attic drama. The best known example is the messenger's report at the beginning of Aeschylus's *Persians*.[96] There the description of the disaster—the downfall of the Persian

---

86   For a different view see Begrich, *Studien zu Deuterojesaja* (1938, reprint 1963) 59 n. 222, contrary to Volz and pointing to Ezek 29:18-20. See also Jer 31:15-16.

87   See here the interpretation in TritoIsa, 62:11-12.

88   See also V. Maag, "Der Hirte Israels (Eine Skizze von Wesen und Bedeutung der Väterreligion)," in *Kultur, Kulturkontakt und Religion: Gesammelte Studien* (1980) 111–44.

89   Gen 33:13 has וְהַבָּקָר עָלוֹת עָלָי, "I have nursing animals"; cf. Isa 40:11 (and 9); Gen 33:14, וַאֲנִי אֶתְנָהֲלָה לְאִטִּי; cf. Isa 40:11b.

90   Deut 4:34; 5:15; 7:19; 11:2; 26:8; 1 Kgs 8:42; Jer 21:5; Ezek 20:33; Ps 136:12. Lit.: V. Hamp, "Das Hirtenmotiv im AT," in *FS Kardinal Faulhaber* (1949) 7–20; J. G. S. S. Thomson, "The Shepherd-Ruler Concept in the OT and Its Application in the NT," *SJT* 8 (1955) 406–18.

91   In this DtIsa corresponds to Psalm 23. נהל in v. 11 is the "solicitous accompaniment"; see *HALOT*. The verb is probably connected with the word for drinking place (נַהֲלֹל, Isa 7:19); see Isa 49:10; 51:18; and Ps 23:2; cf. Exod 15:13; Ps 31:4 <3>; for the shepherd image cf. Jeremiah 31; Ezekiel 34; Luke 15:3-7; John 10:1-18.

92   See W. Zimmerli, "Der Neue Exodus in der Verkündigung der beiden grossen Exilspropheten," in *Gottes Offenbarung: Gesammelte Aufsätze* (1963) 192–204.

93   The parallel should be noted between v. 10 "his arm rules (משל) for him," and v. 11, "with his arm" he gathers (קבץ) "lambs." For God's "rule" as a con-

trast to earthly rule, cf. 49:7; 52:5; for "gather" as a catchword for return and a new beginning cf. 43:5; 49:18; 54:7; see Beuken on this passage.

94   Again the connection with the framework in chaps. 54 and 55 is evident. Cf. also chap. 52. Westermann (44 [39]) writes: "These verses of the prologue (9-11) are the basis of the 'eschatological psalm of praise' peculiar to Deutero-Isaiah and found throughout his preaching. Here the call to praise is always substantiated by a verb in the perfect tense: God has already acted." He refers readers to his own book *Praise and Lament in the Psalms* (1981) 142–45 [*Lob und Klage in den Psalmen* (5th ed. 1977) 108–10].

95   On הִנֵּה see the lexicons; also C. J. Labuschagne, "The Particles הֵן and הִנֵּה," in *Syntax and Meaning: Studies in Hebrew Syntax and Biblical Exegesis, OTS* 15 (1973) 1–14. O. Taplin (*Stagecraft of Aeschylus* [1977] 150–51) makes an interesting comment on "the whole matter of deictic pronouns and physical presence in Greek drama": "It has sometimes been implied that for ὅδε to be used the person referred to has actually to be present in sight of the audience or at least to be imagined as within sight of the speaker. But, while this is usually the case, there are literally dozens of places in Greek tragedy and comedy where the deictic pronoun is used to refer to someone who is definitely not in view. In such cases the person is rather, 'vividly present to the speaker's thought'" (with a quotation from Lloyd-Jones, *CR* n.s. 15 [1965] 242).

96   Aeschylus *Persians* 243–527. See Taplin, *Stagecraft,*

army—is the starting point for the whole. The gods have ranged themselves against the Persians. The question why the catastrophe happened is developed in the drama. But elsewhere too the messenger (ἄγγελος) is an important figure in Attic drama.[97]

In DtIsa there is a difference, however. Here too, certainly, we have a messenger scene (the messenger being female), but the messenger's own speech is not given in the text. There can be a number of reasons for this. The messenger may have carried out the command at once, repeating the commission given to her "from the high mountain." In this case there would be no need to spell it out in the text.[98] Or "get up on a high mountain" perhaps announces Zion/Jerusalem's exit from the stage, so that she can carry out the commission in the meantime. In the second part of the prologue (v. 27), Jacob/Israel is addressed, and so is perhaps already personified here, like Jerusalem in v. 2. We may remember that classical theater had to get along with only a few actors, at least if they had speaking parts;[99] so it might perhaps be that the person speaking for "Zion/Jerusalem" had to go off in order to come on again as speaker for "Jacob/Israel."

In comparing Attic drama with the existing text of DtIsa, it is particularly interesting that in the Greek form there should also be a close link between messenger and chorus. The messenger gives an account of what is past or future. The chorus expresses the reaction of "the people." The following text, 40:12-17, can be seen under this aspect.

B. 2. 40:12-17
Entry of the Chorus with a Hymn

"Who . . . ?" [if not Yahweh alone is the Creator] (40:12-14)
"All peoples are like nothingness before him . . ." (40:17)

From v. 12 on, the theme is the incomparability of Yahweh as Creator and Lord of the world. But this theme is presented under a number of different aspects and in different ways, existing traditions thereby being taken up and related to the new situation. It is useful initially to look at each of the smaller units of text separately.

Like other commentators, I see vv. 12-17 as a first unit. This can be justified on formal grounds. Both vv. 12 and 13 are introduced with a question ("Who?" מִי). Verse 15 follows with a double conclusion issuing from these questions: ("See!" הֵן). Verse 17 adds a generalizing summary: "All peoples—before him they are as a nothingness." In v. 18 again new questions are then asked ("with whom?" אֶל מִי; and "what?" וּמַה), these being followed by a description of the fashioning of idols.

The essential factor in determining the division is a definition of the text's genre. Following the investigations of L. Köhler, J. Begrich and H. E. von Waldow, the prevailing opinion came to be that these are disputation sayings, like vv. 12-31 as a whole.[100] In favor of this was thought to be the series of questions, as well as the con-

---

80-91, the section headed "enter advance messenger: a) ἄγγελος and dramatic function"; 81 n. 2 gives lit. on "messengers." Taplin distinguishes the "aftermath" messenger, who is a frequent figure in Euripides (83). On the messenger in Aeschylus's *Persians* he writes: "The next most common structural function for an *angelos* is that of the herald or advance messenger; and this one in *Pers* is a variant of this type. . . . The events recounted in the vivid narrative speeches occurred in the past before the play began."(83) "The entry which the Herald in *Pers* foreruns does not materialize halfway through the play, but at the opening of the last act; and it does not precede the crucial catastrophe, it is—or rather it stands for—the catastrophe itself" (84). The same problem about sequence and levels of time can be found in DtIsa too.

97 Cf. in Aeschylus's prologues the lookout's report in *Seven against Thebes* and the watchman's account of the fire sign in *Agamemnon*.

98 See Taplin, *Stagecraft of Aeschylus* (1977) 16: "The text was only a convenient abstract of the real work"; see also p. 25.

99 E. Simon, *Das Antike Theater* (1972) 11 (*The Ancient Theatre* [1982]): "In the archaic period there was only a single actor, who 'answered' the chorus or 'gave a report' (ὑποκριτής). The original significance of the chorus can already be seen from this description, which is entirely related to him. Aeschylus diminished the preeminence of the chorus and introduced the second actor, Sophocles the third."

100 See R. F. Melugin, *The Structure of Deutero-Isaiah* (1968) 27–32; A. Schoors, *I Am God Your Saviour* (1973) 245–95 (a good review of the discussion). Schoors puts 40:12-31 among "The Disputations" (§3), though adding: "But 12-17 may also be a hymn" (250–51).

cern to win the assent of the listeners, and the wisdom terminology. The overriding argumentative structure of the larger unit to which these observations draw attention must still, in my view, be taken into account.

Hymnic elements, however, have continually been observed in vv. 12-31,[101] some commentators even going so far as to describe individual sections directly as a hymn (thus H. Gressmann, for example, with reference to vv. 12-26).[102] Westermann concludes: "The passage taken altogether is modelled on the structure found in descriptive praise." He also recognizes the link with the disputation (see his comment on this passage). Here he sees vv. 12-17 as a separate "section" or "part" of the greater whole.[103]

Of essential importance for understanding vv. 12-17 is, in my view, the question about the function of this section in its context. In form and content it can be described as a "hymn." But the hymn as genre includes the acclamation of the ruler: his power and his deeds are extolled, and his sovereignty is thereby acknowledged. Now the section vv. 12-17 was preceded in v. 10 by the proclamation "The Lord is Yahweh," with the anticipatory description of the "triumphal procession." The hymn in vv. 12-17 responds appropriately. At the same time, as I hope to show, it contains the "program" for everything that follows.

The unit vv. 12-17 has an extremely strict poetic structure. It consists of three "strophes" (I: v. 12; II: vv. 13-14; III: vv. 15-17).[104] The assonances in the text are striking:[105]

- Strophe I has the sound sequence *a-im* 4 times, slightly varied by way of a short or long *a* or, respectively, *yim* (3 times) or *im*.
- Strophe II has the sound *u* 5 times, in the sequence *ennû - ēhû - ēhû - ēhû - ennû*.
- In Strophe III the dominant tone coloring is *ē*. Twice *hēn - hēn* (v. 15) is followed by *ʾēn - ʾēn* (plus כְּאַיִן in v. 17?), giving an echo effect.

There are consonantal assonances too, for example, in I: וְשָׁקַל - וְכָל *wešāqal–wekol* (v. 12) and in III: כַּדַּק - וּכְשַׁחַק *kaddaq–ûkešaḥaq* (v. 15). Probably with better pronunciation even more assonances would emerge.

These observations lead to the question about the mode of rendition of this hymn. The rich linguistic modulation could indicate either speech or *Sprechgesang*, a mode of utterance between song and speech. The text may possibly also contain indications of musical performance, at least in strophe I. This would be the case if in the hymn "water, heavens, earth, mountains, hills" signaled the different height of the tone in each case. This could give the five tones of a pentatonic scale.

But in the case of the metric indications too we may suspect a double significance: as meter and as instructions for musical performance at the same time. Clap-

---

101 See among others H. Gressmann, "Die literarische Analyse Deuterojesajas," *ZAW* 34 (1914) 293–94; H. Gunkel and J. Begrich, *Einleitung in die Psalmen* (1933) 33; Muilenburg, 434ff.; C. Westermann, *Praise and Lament in the Psalms* (1981) 127 n. 81 [*Lob und Klage in den Psalmen* (5th ed. 1977) 95 n. 81].

102 Gressmann, *ZAW* 34 (1914) 293.

103 A "question" (which one would rather assign to wisdom) and "drama" do not have to be mutually exclusive. See Taplin, *Stagecraft of Aeschylus* (1977) 67, on Aristophanes' *Frogs* 971ff.: "Euripides boasts that he taught people to ask questions—πῶς τοῦτ' ἔχει; ποῦ μοι τοδὶ τίς τοῦτ' ἔλαβὲ. Observations of dramatic methods may underlie Aristophanes' joke here." The content of this passage from the *Frogs* is also interesting in comparison with DtIsa:

> I taught them all these knowing ways
> By chopping logic in my plays,
> And making all my speakers try
> To reason out the How and Why.
> So now the people trace the springs,
> The sources and the roots of things,

And manage all their households too
Far better than they used to do,
Scanning and searching What's amiss?
And, Why was that? And, How is this?
(971–80; trans. B. B. Rogers)

104 Elliger (42) talks about "a strophic structure of considerable artistry": "Each of the three verses consists of five half-lines, the first two and the last two of which are always more closely related, whereas the middle one inclines sometimes more to the one, sometimes more to the other. Each half-line has three stresses; only the last line (17) is rather a double line with four stresses in each half. Each strophe is a variation on a theme, drawing on different forms of *parallelismus membrorum*." Even though one may differ about the verse form, Elliger is correct in noting the high artistry of the text, an artistry evident not least in the different uses of chiasmus.

105 See here also Y. Gitay, *Prophecy and Persuasion* (1981), esp. 88–94.

ping with cupped palms or with the flat of the hand gives different tone colorings. Moreover the hands indicate the rhythm.

שָׁלִישׁ in v. 12 is a measure of capacity (cf. Ps. 80:6 [5])—perhaps, according to the word's literal meaning, "a third" of a seah; this would amount to 4.4 litres. At the same time it is the name of a musical instrument on which according to 1 Sam 18:6 the women play when they are "singing and dancing" in homage to Saul as king and to David. It has been conjectured that what is meant is a lute (because of the three strings), a triangle (because of the form), or a sistrum (because of the three transverse metal wires). Gressmann's interpretation that it was a small drum would link the different meanings together: it is a measure such as is used in a household; and if one stretches a membrane over it, it becomes a drum, a rhythm instrument. It is somewhat larger and hence deeper in tone (and fuller) than the tambourine (תֹף; cf. also 1 Sam 18:6). If the scale-pans of a large balance or of double scales are made of metal (as they still are today), they make good percussion and rhythm instruments. An indication of the kind of performance, finally, could be the dual at the close of strophe I ("double balance," בְּמֹאזְנַיִם $b^emôz^enayîm$), perhaps even the grammatical duals "water" (מַיִם $mayîm$[106]) and "heaven(s)" (שָׁמַיִם $šāmayîm$) as well. The hieroglyph for dual: \\, $ii = y$, is musically probably the repeat sign. As iy or iyy it kept this meaning right down to Gregorian chant.[107]

Strophe II is, musically speaking, much more measured and even, compared with the restlessness of strophe I. The five $û$ sounds see to this. These are missing entirely in strophe I, while in strophe III they are to be found only in the last line (וְתֹהוּ נֶחְשְׁבוּ־לֹו). One might ask whether the $û$ sounds also perhaps represent an instrument. Strophe III is much more strongly aligned toward visual impressions. It is not by chance that it begins with a double deictic "See!" (הֵן). Bucket and scales are objects of everyday use.

The hymn is very regularly built up. Unevennesses in the structure can therefore either be particular, emphatic signals, or they can indicate later alterations,

even glosses. This may possibly be of help in solving certain textual and literary problems.

In v. 14 the phrase "and [he] taught him knowledge" is missing in the LXX. It could be a doublet of the preceding "and instructed him." But 1QIsa[a], for example, testifies to the phrase. If it is deleted, strophe II has the characteristic u only 4 times instead of 5 times. If, with this in mind, one looks back at strophe I, one is struck by the clause: "And he holds the dust of the earth in a third of a measure (seah)." It is the only clause without the im sound. Some scholars have even suggested that it is prose. Without this sentence we should again have a four-cola structure.

In strophe III, v. 16 is textually suspect. But in the sequence "peoples—islands—Lebanon" the last of the three has its place as a geographical and political instance. Verse 16b is a different matter: "Its wild beasts are not enough for a burnt offering." One reason for objecting to it is that wild animals could not normally be used in sacrifice. But it would provide one more object in the series. If the two statements about "the peoples" are seen as a double assertion,[108] together with "islands" and "Lebanon" they would add up to four elements. Then "wild beasts" would make a fifth, if "all peoples" is taken as a final refrain.

My question is whether the hymn, as far as its form goes, was not originally designed for $3 \times 4 = 12$ elements (which would make an arrangement for a double chorus easier), but was then expanded to 3×5. This would explain the amplifications, which fit perfectly well into the logical progression of the whole and do not essentially alter the meaning. The expansion could be connected with the performance practice, and with the attempt to arrive at a special emphasis in each case. But further considerations of content are required for a decision.

40:12-17 is the first hymn in DtIsa's work. It therefore occupies a particularly prominent place in the whole. A comparison with Attic drama may help toward a better understanding of its function.

In his *Poetics* (1452b22) Aristotle writes: "In the choric song, the *parodos* is the first utterance of the whole

---

106 The sound sequence suggests that the change from "water" (מַיִם) to מִי יָם, "waters of the sea" (the reading in 1QIsa[a]), is not to be recommended. See Muilenburg, IB 5, on the passage; also B. Couroyer,

"Isaïe, XL, 12," *RB* 73 (1966) 186–96.
107 H. Hickman, *Musikgeschichte in Bildern*, II/1 (1961) 84.
108 The possibility that in these two statements a paral-

66

chorus." The term πάροδος has frequently also been understood as the song that the choir sings on its first entry. The *parados* took a number of different forms, astrophic and antistrophic, more or less mimetic.

Important elements in the choral song at the beginning are the description of the presuppositions for the drama, the development of the general principles required for an understanding of it (gnomic), and their application. Talking about Aeschylus's *Persians*, J. Rode sums the matter up succinctly by saying: "In fact the *parodos* contains the whole tragedy in a nutshell."[109]

Where Attic drama is concerned, the allocation of the individual verses and sections to persons and chorus has largely been made clear to us through the work of the scholiasts, scholars themselves still living in the ancient world. But the assumption that the hymn in Isa 40:12-17 was rendered by a chorus is an assumption that still has to be tested.

Having considered the apportioning of the voices, the sound and the rhythm of the text, we shall now turn to the content, considering particularly those aspects that suggest a comparison with the *parodos*.

■ **12, Strophe I** Two answers are possible in response to the question, "Who has measured (the) waters in the hollow of his hand?" The first response might be: "Yahweh!"; the second: "No human being!" In favor of the first answer are biblical traditions such as Job 28:12-28 (esp. 24ff.) or Job 38; in favor of the second, texts such as Prov 30:1-4, the beginning of the book of Sirach, and others. But these answers do not have to be mutually exclusive, if the point that is being made is the distinction between Creator and created being. This brings out all the more clearly the common ground this text shares with Greek tragedy, as well as the differences.

The *parados* in Aeschylus's *Agamemnon* includes the invocation of the deity too. And the famous hymn to Zeus (160-83) also begins with a question: "Zeus, whoever he is . . ." (ὅστις ποτ᾽ ἐστίν . . .). This, at all events, is not unusual. The theme is then that the future is uncertain. Through suffering the human being arrives at expe-

rience. The *parados* of Sophocles' *Antigone* (332–375) describes the grandeur of the human being; the limitation is death. Keeping "the divine laws that have been laid down" makes the survival of the city possible, as the further course of the drama shows.

In both these cases, however, in spite of the general statement in the *parados,* we can see that there is a specific reference. Where could this reference be found in DtIsa? 40:12 has always been compared with the divine praise of Marduk: "who measures the waters of the sea" (*mādidi mē tamtim*). We find this in a prayer for the Babylonian New Year Festival (although the texts themselves date only from the Seleucid period): "Who [. . .]s heaven, heaps up the earth. Who measures the waters of the sea, cultivates the fields" (*ANET* 332, ll. 240-41). In another prayer belonging to the same context, Bel-Marduk is invoked (*ANET* 309). After naming a series of stars, the text goes on: "The star Sirius, who measures the waters of the sea. My Lord, my Lord, be calm!" (ibid., 333). These texts show that the question "Who?" could receive different answers in the civilizations surrounding Israel, since water, the heavens, the earth, the mountains, and the hills could be assigned to entirely different deities. Cults of this kind probably also continued to be a temptation for Israel. The answer to the question "Who?" would then be here: "Yahweh alone!"[110] This, however, already gives us the perspective of DtIsa's book. According to our presuppositions, it is conceivable that question and answer are communicated for the first time through the chorus (who, as we shall see, may have been women).

Elements of dispute no doubt underlie the series of termini: "measure, mark out, hold, weigh." From the beginnings of the natural sciences down to the present day, these have been the means by which to apprehend and grasp the world of nature. It must be remembered that the fifth century B.C.E. brought an enormous expansion in the practical and theoretical knowledge of "nature" (or "the world"). Opportunities for exchanging

lel term to "peoples" (גּוֹיִם), namely "nations" (אֻמִּים), has been omitted is worth consideration; cf. Ps 117:1. In Isa 41:1 אֻמִּים is parallel to "islands" (אִיִּים).

109 J. Rode, "Das Chorlied," in W. Jens, ed., *Die Bauformen der griechischen Tragödie* (1971) 96.

110 See Delitzsch on this passage: "The questions . . . are designed to awaken awareness of the fact that

Yahweh and no one but he has given these components of the cosmos their quantitative measure, their particular form and their proper place in the universal whole" [147, trans. altered].

information in the Persian Empire and in the area of Greek colonization contributed greatly to this expansion. In terms of the history of philosophy, this is the age of Greek "natural philosophy," but it was not confined to Greece. For DtIsa, natural phenomena could not possess any divine quality. The unity of the world is given through creation. The greatness and sovereignty of his God is for DtIsa so all-embracing that the mighty work of creation *can* only be expressed in terms of the smallest human measures. He would certainly never have accepted the pronouncement made by Protagoras (481–411 B.C.E.) that the human being is the measure of all things (πάντων χρημάτων μέτρον ἄνθρωπος).

■ **13-14, Strophe II**[111] Both Luther and the 1611 English Bible (KJV) translated this text along similar lines: "Who hath directed the Spirit of the Lord, or being his counsellor hath taught him? With whom took he counsel, and who instructed him, and taught him in the path of judgment, and taught him knowledge, and shewed to him the way of understanding?"[112] This translation reflects a long interpretive tradition that has endured down to the present day. The text could also have been heard in this way, or very similarly, by DtIsa's own contemporaries, as a general glorification of Yahweh.

But a closer examination shows that the text is more closely linked with its specific context than this. The double question: "Who? . . . Whom?" is supposed to call attention and heighten expectation of what is to come. The answer to the question "Who?" could be here, as in v. 12: "No one"—at least no human being; or it could be: "Yahweh." In the second case it would be a tautological statement: "Yahweh has directed Yahweh's spirit." But if we take the same answer that we assumed above for v. 12, "Yahweh *alone*," then the decision in the dispute about the foreign gods becomes clearer.

Strophes I and II are linked together not only by the question "Who?" but also by the key word "direct" or "determine" (תכן). In view of the precision and economy of the hymn's formulation, this is a signal that has to be noted. The root תכן is probably connected with the Akk. *taqānu*, "to be put right." Whether it is related to the Hebrew כון, "to be firm," is a matter of dispute (see *HALOT* 2:464–65). The range of meaning is in the *Qal* "test," in the *Niphal* "to be tested," while in the *Piel* it means "to fix" in both the literal and the metaphorical sense, to the point of "determine or direct." The aspect of order could link the different nuances with one another.

Where the text we are considering is concerned, we may ask what the "determining" of the heavens (in the sense of "measuring" them) has to do with the "directing" of Yahweh's spirit. In both cases it is a matter of "determining" or "directing" destinies. The measuring out of the heavens is necessary if one wishes to calculate the position of the stars. According to Isa 47:13, Babylon has at its disposal the "dividers of the heavens" (הֹבְרֵי הַשָּׁמַיִם) as well as the "watchers of the stars, who predict from month to month what will befall you." Knowledge of the heavens is the necessary precondition for astrology. At that time this was a serious science, comparable with today's economic and political forecasts. People inquired about the rules and laws that govern the world. Israel's faith maintains that it is not the stars which decide destiny; it is Yahweh. The dispute with astronomy/astrology then immediately becomes the theme once more in 40:26.[113]

Yahweh determines, and his spirit becomes efficacious. Verse 13 shows God's freedom and self-determination in his works. If human beings wish to make or fashion something, they need Yahweh's spirit (רוּחַ יהוה,

111 On the following passage see K. Baltzer, "Jes 40:13-14—ein Schlüssel zur Einheit Deuterojesajas?" in *FS V. Hamp, BN* 37 (1987) 7–10.

112 For Luther's translation see M. Luther, *Biblia, Das ist: Die gantze Heilige Schrifft deudsch. auffs neu zugericht . . .* (Wittenberg: Hans Lufft, 1545).

113 The discovery of the zodiac is put at c. 450 B.C.E.—or to be more precise one would have to say: the "standardization" of the zodiac by the Greeks. It brought with it an enormous expansion of the possibilities open to astronomy and astrology. It meant a survey of the whole of the heavens, whereas until then most observations of the stars had been oriented

toward the horizon. This was the case in Babylon, for example. See "Astrologie," *LAW* (1965) 354–57; "Astronomie," ibid., 357–65; "Sternbilder und Sternsagen," ibid., 2912–21; H. Gundel and R. Böker, "Zodiakos," in PW, 2/19 (1972) 462–709.

Exod 31:3). They need it in order to be able to rule (Num 27:18; Deut 34:9; Judg 3:10). It would be a contradiction in terms if Yahweh were to need a different "spirit" (רוח) when he creates from when he directs. The selfsame spirit of Yahweh is efficacious in prophecy too.

But what decision is specifically meant? In order to be able to answer this we must first of all once again be clear about the double structure of vv. 13-14.[114] The first question "Who . . . ?" in v. 13 is completed by: "He will let him perceive/know" (יוֹדִיעֶנּוּ); the second question "Whom . . . ?" in v. 14 is also completed by: "He will let him perceive/know" (יוֹדִיעֶנּוּ).

Now, "perceive/know" (ידע) is of course a very common word, but Elliger, for example, has noticed that "in DtIsa ידע Hiphil occurs only in 40:13 and 14, as well as in 47:13." The two first passages are in the text we are considering; the third passage is related to this text because it has to do with Babylon's astrology. There Babylon's "advisers" are the ones who "let it be known (מוֹדִיעִם) what will happen to you." To "let it be known" in the sense of a prediction is one of DtIsa's most important themes. If one sees the connection here, it is a help in deciding how vv. 13 and 14 ought to be understood.

With regard to the first question, the statement that Yahweh has no "counselor"[115] can perhaps have its place in a polemic against notions connected with the primordial role of Wisdom according to Prov 8:22-31. But the revelations here refer to the future, at least as time is seen within the drama.

After what we have said it would seem possible to revert to Rignell's proposal,[116] even if Elliger decidedly rejects it: "Rignell has a highly singular view. He sees here the same covert reference to Cyrus that is to be found in 46:11, and consequently translates: 'and (who) makes known to him (= Yahweh) the man of his coun-

sel?'" I would make only one small change to Rignell: He (Yahweh) will "make known the man of his counsel"— that is, as in 46:11 Cyrus is the man of the divine resolve (אִישׁ עֲצָתוֹ), for whom Yahweh has decided, in order to implement his plans.[117] Then I can again agree with Elliger: "The Persian king is the executive organ whom Yahweh inspires with his will, and who acts even without knowing the innermost significance of events (45:4-5)."[118] The position in v. 13 can be compared with the beginning of the book of Ezra (1:1-4; cf. 2 Chr 36:22-23; Ezra 6:3-5): "In the first year of Cyrus king of Persia, in order that the word of the Lord by the mouth of Jeremiah might be accomplished, the Lord awakened the spirit (רוּחַ) of Cyrus king of Persia."

With regard to the second question in v. 14, according to the end of the verse, this question has to do with the revelation of "a way of insight." The inquiry is initially a question about a person: "Whom?" But there is a certain tension, because at the beginning and the close of v. 14 the root "to realize or understand" (בין) is used, which relates not to a person but to the content of the understanding given to him.

We found it useful in response to the first question to follow up a possible general interpretation by a search for a concrete answer (even if this answer was again veiled, in the context of the dramatic situation); so it would seem useful to try to do the same in the case of the second question too. One could then paraphrase this question and say: "For whom has Yahweh decided according to his resolve, so that he may give him insight." The rest of DtIsa's text expounds that it is just this which may be said of *the Servant of Yahweh.*" His election is the free decision of his "Lord."[119] Yahweh himself equips him with insight.[120] Understood in this way, the two following suffixes ("instructed/taught *him*")

---

114 The stylistic device "before/after" is the same in both cases. In each case what will be revealed later is stated beforehand.

115 On the possible translations and their difficulties see the commentaries; also R. N. Whybray, *The Heavenly Counsellor in Isaiah 40 13-14* (1971). We may assume that DtIsa, in chap. 40 especially, presupposes the idea of the heavenly council. We are indebted to Whybray for developing this idea in detail, but in my view the present text is actually precisely directed against the tradition of "heavenly counselors"; see also M. Dahood, "The Breakup of Two Composite Phrases in Isaiah 40:13," *Bib* 54

(1973) 537–38.

116 In L. G. Rignell, *A Study of Isaiah cc. 40–55,* LUÅ (1956) 15–16; see also Bonnard on this passage.

117 There may be other wordplays here too. 1QIsaᵃ like *Ketib* has עצתו; LXX in accordance with *Qere* presupposes the 1st person suffix (עֲצָתוֹ).

118 Elliger, 51.

119 Cf. 42:1: "my chosen one, in whom my soul delights."

120 Cf. 42:1.

would refer to the "Servant," for who can teach Yahweh?

The comparison with the Servant of God texts shows the correspondence: Thus we read in 40:14: "and [he] instructed him about the way of law and justice (בְּאֹרַח מִשְׁפָּט)." In the first of the Servant of God texts, it is said of the installation of the servant, 42:1: "I have put my Spirit upon him. (A decree of) justice will he bring forth to the peoples (יוֹצִיא מִשְׁפָּט לַגּוֹיִם)"; 42:3; "In truth will he bring forth (the decree of) justice (יוֹצִיא מִשְׁפָּט)"; 42:4: "till he has established law and justice (יָשִׂים מִשְׁפָּט) in the land (or: on earth, בָּאָרֶץ)"; cf. also 49:4; 50:8; 53:8. These texts are talking about judicial decisions, and at the same time "crises" in the Servant's life.

According to 40:14, "And [he has] taught him *knowledge* (וַיְלַמְּדֵהוּ דַעַת)." The third Servant of God text says (50:4): "The Lord God has given me the tongue of 'those who are taught,' that I may know how (לָשׁוֹן לִמּוּדִים לָדַעַת) to sustain with a word him that is weary. Morning by morning he wakens my ear to hear as 'those who are taught' (לִשְׁמֹעַ כַּלִּמּוּדִים)"; 40:14: "he will let him know a way of understanding/insight" (יוֹדִיעֶנּוּ דֶּרֶךְ תְּבוּנוֹת). The fourth and last Servant of God text, 52:15, offers a comparison: "Truly, what they had not been told they will have seen, and what they have never heard they will have understood/received insight" (הִתְבּוֹנָנוּ)." The very first hymn, in 40:13-14, thus already announces what is going to be expounded in what follows. The tension is engendered—"Who?"—and the lines of the interpretation indicated. This is not least a pointer to the unity of DtIsa's work. We shall therefore have to note even the finer points. In the context of the dramatic pre-sentation, the call and instruction of the "Servant" are in 40:14 already in the past; from this aspect the "way of insight" is still in the future. In the final Servant of God text the "Servant" is dead; he is rehabilitated in the heavenly judgment. From this, "insight" follows.

"Right" is not the same thing as "knowledge," which makes the consoling of the assailed possible (50:4). Both belong to the task of "Yahweh's Servant"; both are the theme of DtIsa's book. Consequently "and [he has] taught him knowledge" in v. 14 is by no means to be deleted, as textual considerations would initially seem to suggest. In the whole context of this verse we can see the LXX and their variants struggling with the terminology of their own time. Is "gnosis" in its Greek clothing the same thing that is proclaimed here as "knowledge"?

"Insights" proceeding from Yahweh's justice and knowledge are the enduring message of this verse.[121] Like the question, the answer is equivocal: "A way of insight *he* will let him perceive"—this "he" is a human being whom Yahweh in his resolve has chosen (v. 13b); and at the same time "he" is Yahweh himself, who permits the chosen one to perceive (vv. 13b and 14).

■ **15-17, Strophe III** The third strophe can be conceived as being more strongly mimetic.[122] Attention has already been drawn to the double "see" (הֵן).[123] In the progress of the drama, the third part of the chorus would enter at this point. "Water, dust, powder,[124] firewood"—all these are things carried in receptacles of one kind or another, and can be poured out. Afterward all that remains, clearly, is "a drop in the bucket" (v. 15).[125] If one pronounces the sequence כְּמַר . . . וּכְשַׁחַק . . . כַּדַּק (*kᵉmar . . .*

---

121 K. Elliger ("Der Begriff 'Geschichte' bei Deuterojesaja," in *Kleine Schriften zum Alten Testament* [1966] 199–210) thought that the concepts (as he translated them) "the path of justice" (אֹרַח מִשְׁפָּט) and "the way of insight" (דֶּרֶךְ תְּבוּנוֹת) could be rendered in modern terminology through the word "history." In my view, however, it is rather "the Servant's biography" in his words and deeds that leads to "insight."

122 In this respect there may be a difference from Attic drama here.

123 Cf. 40:9-10 (see above); cf. also D. Vetter's comment, *TLOT* 1:379 [*THAT* 1:505]: "hinnēh, (hēn, hē') can still be recognized as a component of a primitive command, presenting the substance of the command." Cf. C. J. Labuschagne, "The Particles הֵן and הִנֵּה," *OTS* 18 (1973) 1–14.

124 דַּק must derive from דקק, "to crush" (e.g., in a mortar), "grind finely" (in a mill). This can be grain (Isa 28:28), metal (Exod 32:20; Deut 9:21), ashes (2 Kgs 23:6), or incense (Exod 30:36).

125 Cf. Num 24:7; according to *HALOT* 1:222 it means: a "bucket of leather, the mouth of which is kept open by crossed sticks" (with reference to G. Dalman, *Arbeit und Sitte in Palästina*, 5 [1937; 9th ed. 1964] 189). We are indebted to D. W. Thomas for his detailed investigation, "'A Drop of a Bucket'? Some Observations on the Hebrew Text of Isaiah 40:15," in *In Memoriam P. Kahle* (1968) 214–21; but in my view he is not correct in his conclusion. The concern of the text in the series is the variation on the same idea.

ûkᵉšaḥaq . . . kaddaq)—and perhaps עוֹלָה . . . בָּעֵר (*bāᶜer . . . ᶜôlāh*) in addition—accentuated sound elements can be detected. But at the same time the double "See" (הֵן) is also a signal drawing attention to the content, and to the conclusion to be drawn from the first two strophes. The utterances about the uniqueness of God in "creation and preservation" point toward the question about the importance of the "peoples."

The problem about the world of people and nations continually occupied the minds of Israel, as the people of God. The "ocean of the peoples" was the frightening threat to the foundations of its existence. "Why do the peoples/nations rage?" (Pss 2:1; 65:8-9 [7-8]). It was the tormenting question for Israel in its political annihilation and its banishment. Had not the others been victorious? Were they not always stronger in their oppressive superiority? Was Israel not only one of many, even among the peoples deported by Babylon—and by no means "the people of election"? Linked with this was the hidden unspoken question: Were the hostile gods not greater?

The present hymn is addressed in concrete terms to the deep anxiety that "the peoples are too strong." This is true even in the Persian Empire, made up as it was of many different peoples. אִיִּים are the islands and coasts of the Mediterranean,[126] and, at this period, above all the Greek area too. "Lebanon" includes the Phoenician coast. This mention stands out in the hymn because it seems to be the only specific reference. Duhm concluded from this that DtIsa was living in Lebanon. He no doubt sensed that at this point the text could conceal some contemporary reference. But unfortunately references of this kind generally elude us. Without the scholiasts we should understand references in Aristophanes, for example, even less than we do.

Apart from being a mighty mountain range, "Lebanon" is associated with its wealth of forests. Wood, especially cedarwood, was needed for the rebuilding of Jerusalem. The agreement in Nehemiah 10 shows that lack of firewood was a problem for the restoration of the temple cult. Because of the various military conquests and the economic distress, wood was a raw material that had become scarce in the country. In Ezekiel 31 Pharaoh is compared with the cedars of Lebanon. "Lebanon" and its cedars can also be used in a transferred sense, as a symbol for power and greatness.[127] The way the name is used in Ezekiel 31 also suggests the question whether it could not also be a pseudonym, perhaps for Egypt. Lebanon is famous for its riches of wood and game. This argument runs *a minore ad maius:* "if not even . . . then how much less. . . ."

The statement about the game (חַיָּתוֹ) does not fit into the regular structure of this verse. But perhaps this is actually a way of emphasizing the statement particularly: if even the beasts of Lebanon are not sufficient for a burnt offering, how much less the (legitimate) offerings. Wild animals are not permitted as sacrifice, according to the OT. But a polemic against (blood) sacrifice can also be read into this assertion; for it is striking that in DtIsa there is hardly any mention of the temple, let alone of sacrifice, even though he is concerned with the reconstitution of Jerusalem. Criticism of sacrifice is taken up in 43:22-28 too.

The final refrain in v. 17 draws the appropriate conclusion from what has just been said: "All peoples are as a nothingness before him [Yahweh]." The declaration that they are "like a drop in a bucket" was already a drastic analogy, and here too the idea is taken to its extreme: "all peoples!" This relativizes all power, not only the power of rulers. This is a matter of faith, no longer something that can be demonstrated. Fear is confronted by experience of the reality of God's power. The reality that apparently means power—the peoples—is denied, and denied three times: it is "not present" (כְּאַיִן), "at an end" (מֵאֶפֶס),[128] "empty, void" (תֹהוּ). The last instance is

---

126 Young's comment (48) is of interest for the localization of DtIsa: "The second part of the Book of Isaiah often uses this word to designate those districts that are far from Palestine (41:1, 5; 42:4, 10; 49:1; 60:9; 66:19). It is an appropriate word for one who is residing in Palestine, but its appropriateness would be greatly weakened if the author were in Mesopotamia." See already Duhm, 295: "Sea-lands . . . perhaps because he lived at the sea."

127 Cf. 2 Kgs 14:9; Isa 2:12-13; 10:34; 35:2; Zech 11:1-2; Ps 92:13 (12).

128 It is possible to follow 1QIsaᵃ and Syriac, reading כְּ, "as nothing," but מִן as partitive would also make sense: "as part of nothing," "less than nothing"; see Young here. Duhm translates: "out of nothingness, without core and essence."

an allusion to a key word in Genesis 1.[129] The possibility that there is an echo here of the utterances in the creation account in the Priestly writing cannot be excluded: "Heaven . . . the earth without form and void . . . over the waters . . . the Spirit of God."

That is the beginning of the sovereign rule of God that the hymn extols. Peoples and kingdoms come and go—that is the experience which is then passed on again in Daniel 7. The verb at the close of the hymn is a genuine perfect, as an act that reaches right down to the present; "this is how he considers them: as a nothingness!" Belief in God's rule over the whole world from creation onward is the theological presupposition for DtIsa's work.

The first hymn therefore puts forward the *theological exposition*. This corresponds to the "mythos" in classical drama. The second function of the hymn is the *exposition of the persons* who play a part in the drama. Here, for the OT, Yahweh is the truly active one. But the characters involved in the historical events, Cyrus and the servant of God, are introduced in veiled form. Finally, the hymn also contains an *exposition of the text's ethic:* to trust the power of God in the face of all temptations to the contrary, and to walk "the way of insight" (v. 14).[130]

It is the theme "world—time—history" that is so resolutely addressed in this way. It is the mystery of the *deus revelatus et absconditus* (cf. Rom 11:34; 1 Cor 2:16). "Hymn" and "wisdom" are here closely linked with one another in form, function and content. This is the "inward exposition" of DtIsa's work.[131]

B. 3. 40:18-20
Appearance of the Idol Manufacturers

"And with whom will you liken God . . . ?" (40:18)

The solemn seriousness of the hymn is followed in vv. 18-20 by an entr'acte in which the same theme—Yahweh's incomparability—is presented on a different level. Many people, not least the commentators, have stumbled over the text, and have urged that it should be moved[132] or even expunged altogether.[133] But it is just as carefully thought out in its craftsmanship and theology as is its context; the only difference is that here the text is meant to raise a laugh. In this respect DtIsa's work is fundamentally different from Attic drama, in which tragedy and comedy are two quite separate genres. The brevity of the text indicates that, like the other smaller units in chap. 40, it should be seen as a "preview" or "trailer," and must therefore be considered in the context of the whole. The text also has ethopoetic functions: the senselessness of idol worship is demonstrated by way of the "idol production." That this was a real problem, in spite of all the parody, is evident not least from the fact that in v. 18—for the first time in chap. 40—the listeners or spectators are directly addressed: "With whom will *you* [plural] liken God?"

The series of alliterations and chiastic correspondences continues. Thus in v. 18 the first half-verse begins with the preposition אֶל ("with") and concludes with אֵל ("God"); in v. 19 צֹרֵף ("the one who works as a smith") occurs twice. But once again we have to be on the lookout for a double significance, as when לוֹ, "him," and לֹא, "not," alternate twice.

The *architecture* of the text can easily be reconstructed. The double question at the beginning: "With whom . . . ?" and "What . . . ?" corresponds to the double "image" (v. 19) and "stele" (v. 20). The ה in these two terms is probably the interrogative pronoun, not the article.[134] In the case of "image/stele" (פֶּסֶל), the article would be unusual in a poetic text; and it has always been noted that in "image/stele" (v. 20, הַמְסֻכָּן) the *dagesh* required for the article is missing. Again we have a striking sequence of sounds in what are then four questions in all: *mi-ma-ha-ha.*

---

129 DtIsa uses it 7 times in all: 40:17, 23; 41:29; 44:9; 45:18, 19; 49:4.

130 Duhm sums up something of this point (293): "The person who has properly grasped Yahweh's incomparable majesty and his preeminence in power and insight can no longer doubt, despair, or be overwise, nor can he commit the foolishness of the Gentiles."

131 Cf. P. A. H. de Boer, *Aischylos: Die Perser* (1972) 23, on the "*parados* of the chorus" (vv. 1-150): "It thus becomes clear that here in this choric song Aeschylus is puting together in a kaleidoscopic manner all the motifs that sustain the work and are important for an interpretation of the action; but that he completely avoids pressing them into service for an interpretation. It is accordingly not sufficient to see only the words of the leader of the chorus as

The second pair of questions contains implicit answers to the first two questions. But they are no less rhetorical, and are supposed to provoke the people addressed into giving the answer: "no, by no means!" Except for "no" (לֹא), these are the same negations with which the preceding hymn closed in v. 17.

■ **18** In v. 18 the theological point of departure is the assertion about God. Here the name "El" (אֵל) is used for God, a term found in almost all Semitic languages. In the Ugaritic pantheon, for example, El is the head of the gods. In the OT the term can have an archaic flavor, as it has, for example, in the Balaam oracles in Numbers 23–24. According to Elliger, when it is used without an article it is "comparable with our word 'God.' The name differs from the name Yahweh in that it already implies the claim that this is the only God—more even: that the one so named is alone truly God."[135] But it is striking that DtIsa uses the term "El" for God—although incidentally only in chaps. 40–46—particularly in passages where the point at issue is the dispute with foreign gods (i.e., in 43:10; 44:10, 15, 17; 45:20-22; 46:6-9). According to 45:14-15, the Gentiles too can acknowledge "God," even if he is a "hidden God"; and in spite of all the agressiveness of the polemic against idols—and for the ancient world this must have led to the reproach of wicked impiety—this suggests that the aim here is to win a consensus. There is an element of "enlightenment" in this approach: in the reverence for "God" there can be agreement, especially if images are rejected. Were there "heathens" too among the listeners or spectators?

In the progress of the argument that runs from v. 18 to v. 20 there is a still further aspect in El as the name for God. W. H. Schmidt has drawn attention to this strand of tradition: "The OT repeatedly juxtaposes ʾel 'God' and humans. 'God is not a human, that he should lie' (Num 23:19) paraphrases God's trustworthy faithfulness to his word. The prophet Hosea (11:9) justifies his interpretation of holiness as forgiving love instead of punishing wrath with the antithesis, 'I am God and not a human'"[136] (cf. also Isa 31:3; Ezek 28:2-9; Job 9:2; 35:4). Our present text is also dealing with the relationship between Creator and created being. God has created the human being—all human beings; the human being does not create God. That is the criticism of *homo faber*.

But what is the "image, likeness"(דְּמוּת) of God?[137] Elliger may well be right when he says: "דמות *never* means an image of God." But if we remember Genesis 1 (and this reminiscence would seem indicated after the allusions in the preceding hymn, vv. 12-17) then the human being is created to be "like" (כְּ, Gen 1:26) or "in (בְּ) the image of God" (Gen 5:1; cf. 5:3). Any other "image," such as those usually "set up in rows" (ערך) in the sanctuaries of the ancient world, infringes on the prohibition of images as it is formulated in the Decalogue.

■ **19-20** These fundamental assertions show us how to interpret what happens next.[138] We can best imagine them on the lips of the "speaker," who then also had to announce the entry of the other dramatis personae.

The first object to be shown is a פֶּסֶל. According to *HALOT*, this can be "a divine image carved from wood or sculpted from stone, but later cast in metal" (3:949). In our present text it was the last of these, for the following asyndetic relative clause explains that it was cast (נָסַךְ, perfect!). If we assume that what we have before us is a dramatic presentation, the first of the workmen would now come on. He is a skilled caster or foundryman. Schiller describes the foundryman in his poem "Die Glocke": "Von der Stirne heiss, rinnen muss der Schweiss, soll das Werk den Meister loben" ("The sweat must run if the work is to do honor to the master's skill"). Since casting involved working with charcoal, it was a sooty affair, and a founder was easily recognizable from his appearance.

---

an exposition, although they do certainly offer a sufficient exposition for the external action; the choric song must also be drawn in. It represents the 'inner exposition' of the work, so to speak."

132 Thus Duhm, who inserted it after 41:7; also Marti; H. E. von Waldow, "Anlass und Hintergrund der Verkündigung des Deuterojesaja" (diss., Bonn, 1953); Westermann.

133 See Volz on this passage.

134 Thus in v. 19a LXX, Vg; see Elliger.

135 Elliger, 72.

136 W. H. Schmidt, "אֵל ʾēl God," *TLOT* 1:107–12, esp. 112 [*THAT* 1:142–49, esp. 149].

137 See C. Westermann, *Genesis 1–11* 146 [202], and Excursus, 147–55 [203–14].

138 Cf. 44:9-11.

The second artisan is the gold- or silversmith. He works with metal too, but for the gold overlay of the statue[139] (see the suffixes) cleanliness is required (for gold is too costly to be wasted), and a very small hammer is used. There could be no greater contrast to the first workman in appearance and demeanor. The goldsmith's work is still going on; the verb is in the imperfect, as a general statement. רקע means the beating of metal into thin sheets. This is a laborious process, as anyone knows who has seen it in the Middle East. But the term is again reminiscent of Genesis 1, for it is the same root that is used there for the "firmament (רָקִיעַ) between the waters" that "God called heaven." God brings it into being by "speaking." Here again the contrast between the divine and the human activity becomes manifest.

The third kind of work to be mentioned is the manufacture of silver chains (רְתֻקוֹת).[140] The difficulty is to know whether another person is employed here, or whether the same smith is working with both gold and silver. There is a problem similar to the one we encountered in the preceding hymn: a 2×2=4 division is expanded to five elements. The form attributed to the final verb depends on the interpretation.

According to the text as we have it, it is at least possible that there is another smith who is manufacturing chains of silver wire. For this he has to weld the individual links together. צרף, meaning "fuse," is therefore appropriate. This too is a laborious activity, and the craftsman is actually engaged in it now (hence the participle). Then the chains can also be welded onto the figure, like the sheets of gold. But what have the chains to do with the statue of the god? Of course they could be a decoration. But perhaps the catchword "chains" has greater importance than that.

Karl Meuli has shown that there was a wide tradition of "chained gods."[141] There is evidence for this in mythology and cult, in the visual arts and in written texts. Different though the themes and their contexts are (and it is impossible to enter into that in any detail here), there is no doubt that there are stories about images of gods "that did not stay in their proper place but went elsewhere." Consequently the statues were tied to their place with cords and chains, and fastened to the pedestal or the floor—even if these are in part secondary interpretations. Famous examples are representations with chains and cords of Artemis (Cybele) as the city goddess of Ephesus, a type of representation that was widespread in Syria and Asia Minor. According to Plato's *Meno* (97 D and E), Socrates taught: "If one nevertheless values knowledge much more highly than right opinion, then this is very like the statues of Daedalus; for these too, if they are not tied down, play truant and run away; but when they are fastened they remain." As late as the fourth century C.E., on the founding of Constantinople, Constantine the Great had a statue of Tyche with chains set up, so that Tyche (= happiness) might remain in his new capital.[142]

It may therefore well be that the mention of "chains" is much more closely linked with the context than the notion of mere decoration would suggest.[143] The statue of the god is firmly established—but this means that it cannot move either;[144] that is the irony of it, an irony that DtIsa takes up again later, in his further polemic against idols.

According to v. 19 it is possible to assume that this is a single cultic object on which two or three craftsmen are working. So we may suppose that v. 20 is talking about only one object too. But here the object is made of wood, not metal. At the end of the verse it too is called

---

139 For examples of this technique see *ANEP* nos. 481, 483, 484, 497; *AOB* no. 347, and other examples in Elliger, 76.

140 Hapax legomenon; cf. 1 Kgs 6:21 and the root רתק in Nah 3:10.

141 K. Meuli, "Die gefesselten Götter," in *Gesammelte Schriften*, vol. 2 (1975) 1035–81. See also R. Merkelbach, "Gefesselte Götter," *Antaios* 12 (1971) 549–65; K. Baltzer, "Stadt-Tyche oder Zion-Jerusalem?" in *Alttestamentlicher Glaube und Biblische Theologie. FS H. D. Preuss* (1992) 114–19 (subsequently published in revised form as "The Polemic against the Gods and Its Relevance for Second

Isaiah's Conception of the New Jerusalem," in T. C. Eskenazi and K. H. Richards, eds., *Second Temple Studies*, vol. 2: *Temple and Community in the Persian Period* [1994] 52–59).

142 Greek and German text in Meuli, *Gesammelte Schriften*, 2:1081.

143 The fastening with "nails" (בְּמַסְמְרִים) in 41:7 would then indeed have to be seen as a parallel statement of the same phenomenon. See S. Smith, *Isaiah Chapters XL–LV* (1944) 171; and Schoors, *I Am God Your Saviour* (1973) 253. The correspondence to 40:19 and 20 ("that is not unsteady"; cf. 41:7) would also be clearer.

the image of a god (פֶּסֶל), but the beginning in v. 20a offers apparently insurmountable obstacles, even in the translation. P. Trudinger has carefully compiled the solutions that have been proposed. I myself should like to assent for the most part to T. N. D. Mettinger's conclusions for v. 20.

For him, too, the starting point is that v. 19aα and v. 20aα are parallel, and that both are concerned with a *single* object; further, that an emendation should initially be avoided, and that the text should first be taken seriously as it stands. Taking up a suggestion of J. Gray, Mettinger links מְסֻכָּן with the root *skn* (found in Ugaritic and elsewhere), meaning "to make a statue or image," as *Pual* participle: "something that is given form, the image." תְּרוּמָה could be the more or less voluntary contribution for the cult. In this way Mettinger arrives at the translation: "Maybe an image which is a sacred contribution." It was quite usual for an image of a god to be given to a temple as a votive offering; and if the text is interpreted in this way it would make sense.

My own feeling, however, is that the difficulty of the text is built in from the outset—that the ambiguity is intentional and is the reason for the unusual choice of words and forms. The early listeners could probably hear in these the whole gamut of possible interpretations that have been adopted down to the era of modern research. Which of these interpretations DtIsa was really appealing to can unfortunately no longer be established.

The same may also be said about the link with מִסְכֵּן, "to be in need, poor" (cf. Qoh 4:13; 9:15; also Deut 8:9). Thus Westermann translates: "wer zu arm ist für ein solche Stiftung" (in the ET: "who is too poor for such a work of art"). But who is "poor" here?[145]

In his monograph on the roots *skn* and *sgn*, E. Lipiński describes *skn* as meaning, among other things, "to run the danger of . . . ," particularly in unconsidered behavior.[146] He mentions the connection with the noun *sōkēn*, "governor," as the functionary of a ruler. By way of the meaning "substitute" (representative), in Sumerian it already acquired the meaning of a stele or statue in the sanctuary.[147] This semantic field is of course of the greatest interest for our text. It is only somewhat disappointing when at the end of his investigation Lipiński himself refers explicitly to this text and maintains, as possible meaning for Isa 40:20: "VII. *MSKN*, 'dalbergie, ébène,'" a kind of ebonylike wood. He derives this from Akkadian, and on the basis of the present context.[148] This is a possible interpretation, but surely the shallowest and most simplistic.

Who is it that chooses "a wood" or "a tree" that does not decay? Here it is not as simple as it was in v. 19, where it was possible to identify the craftsmen. But if one takes this section as a trailer or preview, then the rest of DtIsa's text has something to tell us. In 44:14 someone is described who chooses from among "the trees of the forest." The trees named are cedars, durmast oaks (RSV: holm trees), and oaks—kinds of wood, in fact, that do not easily rot. The type of person concerned is described as a real rough diamond, a Hercules who uses any amount of wood for roasting his meat and for warmth (44:16). The shepherd or hunter is probably meant.

There is an explanation for a second "character" too. The person who can seek out a "wise expert" is the merchant or trader. In 46:5-8 it is just this person who is described. But since, as we have seen, v. 20 is concerned with a single object, the shepherd or hunter and the merchant surely have something to do with one another. Then here, just as in v. 19, it is the contrast that is being brought out: if the "rough diamond" (or Hercules) is

---

144 Cf. also Psalm 115, esp. v. 7.

145 Cf. Westermann, 47 [56], as already Delitzsch, 2:146 [417]; see also Bonnard, 93: "Celui qui est démuni pour son ex voto" ["He is without means for his gift"].

146 E. Lipiński, "*skn* et *sgn* dans le sémitique occidental du nord," *UF* 5 (1973) 181–207.

147 Ibid., 200: "The term *skn* normally designated the functionary who represented the king in the exercise of his powers. He was therefore in some sense his substitute. Following the extension of the word's semantic value, it came to be used for the stele or statue which represented the author of the inscrip-

tion in the temple, and was supposed to carry out religious duties toward the deity. This object was thus the substitute or surrogate for the believer, who was often the king or a member of the royal family."

148 Ibid., 206. Jerome already declared that this was a kind of wood. Proposals have been the palm (Zimmern), the elm (Cheyne), and the mulberry (Smith).

"the" wise expert, he will no doubt see to it somewhat forcefully that the פֶּסֶל, the image of the god, is no longer shaky, unstable. But then it really will be firm (cf. 46:5-7)! We can imagine that at this point there was any amount of slapstick.

But again the rext has an astonishing depth. Behind all the jokes—some of them grotesque enough—we should not overlook that essential key words of faith are named in this "distancing" manner (*Verfremdungseffekt*): "choose" (בחר) and "seek" (שׁבקשׁ)—that is otherwise what is said about Yahweh.[149] The human being is supposed to "establish" his heart. "It will not be unstable." But if one reads לֹא יָמוֹת, that is, with ת instead of ט (hardly distinguishable when spoken), then, with slight changes in the vocalization (יָמוּת), the phrase reads: "He will not die!"

For the listeners of DtIsa's own day, it was probably also clear which gods were being alluded to in this entr'acte. Here people would be able to guess from the trades involved who was laughing at whom. The gold- and silversmiths have an interest in the city deity, since she encouraged the trade in devotional bric-à-brac (cf. Acts 19:28: "Great is Artemis of the Ephesians!"). In Greek terminology, this would point to Tyche, in combination with a female deity,[150] for the "chains" pointed us in the same direction (v. 19). The god of the merchants—and thieves—is, again in Greek terms, Hermes. Hermes is also the god who leads the dead into the underworld. (Are we supposed to hear: "it will not be shaky" or "he will not die"?) The "stele" as "Herma" would be just as clear, since a quadrangular pillar with a head would be sufficient.

If DtIsa's theme is the refounding of the city of Jerusalem, a beginning of this kind, affecting as it does the very foundations of the city's "religion," its fortunes and its commerce, is daring—and very much to the point.[151]

---

149 See J. C. Kim, "Das Verhältnis Jahwes zu den anderen Göttern in Deuterojesaja" (1962) 20–21.

150 On the tradition of the "Dea Syria" see M. Hörig, *Dea Syria: Studien zur religiösen Tradition der Fruchtbarkeitsgötter in Vorderasien* (1979).

151 The comparison with Attic drama may also make the position of the entr'acte with "the manufacture of idols" in chap. 40 comprehensible, if it is precisely there that the worship of idols in the *parados* is reflected. See J. Rode, "Das Chorlied," in W. Jens, ed., *Die Bauformen der griechischen Tragödie* (1971) 93, on the *parados* in Aeschylus's *Seven against Thebes* (78-149): "Prayers to Ares and the whole company of the gods (vv. 104-15) lead over to the third section (vv. 116-49), which depicts the whole procession of the chorus in front of the statues of the gods: Zeus, Pallas and Poseidon, Ares and Aphrodite, Apollo and Artemis are appealed to one after the other, and supplicatory gifts are offered. . . . When in the *Theoroi* the chorus supplies the statues with masks, this is the comic version of the rogatory procession in the *Seven*." Fragment Theoroi des Aischylos 17,4-17, Mette; see here K. Reinhardt, "Vorschläge zum neuen Aischylos," *Hermes* 85 (1957) 1–17. On the role played by images of the gods, see also O. Taplin, *Greek Tragedy in Action* (1978) 84 and 93, esp. on Euripides' *Hippolytos* (pp. 58–87). See also here the definition of "Hermes" in Webster's *New Twentieth-Century Dictionary* (2d ed. 1980): "In ancient Greece, a herma, a statue composed of a head, usually that of the god Hermes, placed on a quadrangular pillar, the height of which corresponds to the stature of the human body. Such statues were placed at the corners of streets, on high roads as sign posts with distances inscribed upon them, and on the boundaries of lands and states."

40 Speaker and Chorus Antiphonally: Hymnal Dialogue

21 Do you not know?
Do you not hear?
Has it not been told you from the beginning?
Have you not understood the foundations of
the earth?

22 He is enthroned above the circle of the
earth,
—and its inhabitants are like grasshoppers.
He spreads out (the) heaven like gauze,
—and he stretched it out like a tent to
dwell in.

23 He gives dignitaries over to nothingness,
—judges of the land he has made as
nothing.

24 Hardly are they planted,
hardly are they sown,
hardly has their shoot taken root in the
earth—
—(already) he blew on them
and they withered.
And the tempest will carry them away like
chaff.

25 And with whom will you compare me, that I
should be like him?
—says a Holy One.

26 Lift up your eyes on high
and see: who has created these?
He brings out their host by number,
—all of them he calls by name.
Of those <great> in power
and those mighty in strength[a]
not one is missing.

27 Why do you say, Jacob,
and speak, Israel:
My way is hidden from Yahweh,
and my rights are passed over in the face
of my God?

28 Do you not know?
Have you not heard?
An everlasting God is Yahweh,
Creator of the ends of the earth.
He will not grow weary
and will not become faint.
His insight is unsearchable.

29 He gives strength to the weary,
and to him who has no power he will
give increased strength.

30 But young men will be weary and grow
faint,
and picked men will stumble and fall.

31 But those who hope for Yahweh renew
(their) strength:
They let great wings grow like eagles,
they run and do not grow faint,
they walk and do not become weary.

26[a] Thus if the punctuation is corrected from מֵרֹב (MT) to מֶרֶב. It would also be possible to leave the consonantal text as it is and to read וְאַמִּיץ instead of וְאֹמֶץ (cf. 1QIsa[a] and the different versions): "Of the richness of power and <force> of strength."

C. 1. 40:21-24
The Creator of the World Is Also Lord over the Powerful

"He is enthroned above the circle of the earth . . ." (40:22)

Isa 40:21-24 is the first of three uniformly constructed, fairly short units. Questions are followed in each case by a hymnic section. It is possible to assign the questions to a speaker (or cantor) and the hymnic sections to the chorus. The self-contained hymn as we find it in vv. 12-17 now becomes a hymnic dialogue.[152] But the plural of the forms of address also draw in the listeners or spectators at the same time.

Again the text has a strict, carefully crafted construction.[153] The assonances are striking, with marked vowel sequences. The questions in v. 21 are introduced four times in succession by the interrogative particle ה, with the shortest of the *a* sounds, *ḥateph pataḥ*. This is followed by the confessional-like response with the triple article ה, with a short *a* sound, *pataḥ*. This gives a series of seven elements. In the four-times negated question v. 21 has four long *o* sounds (הֲלוֹא): "*hălô*" can easily be called out in every language. Verse 24 offers אַף בַּל three times. The quadruple אֶרֶץ ("land, earth"), once in each verse, however it is pronounced, with its *segol* offers sufficient *e* sounds. Finally, we should note the alternating sequence between a triple יָם in vv. 22-23a and a quadruple ו in vv. 23b-24; a similar alternation in the hymn in vv. 12-17 appeared to correspond to different groups within the chorus, high and deep voices.

There are wordplays,[154] for example in v. 22, where the root יָשַׁב, "sit, dwell," is used three times. Yet at the same time this is not really a "play," since it is in this very way that the essential utterances of the text are stressed. God as he sits "enthroned" (הַיֹּשֵׁב) is contrasted with the "inhabitants" of the earth (יֹשְׁבֶיהָ). The heavens are like a tent "to dwell in" (לָשֶׁבֶת). Frequent instances of chiasmus are mutually explanatory: "perceive/know (תֵּדְעוּ)—understand (הֲבִינֹתֶם)," "hear (תִּשְׁמָעוּ)—announce/tell (הֻגַּד)" in v. 21, for example.

■ **21** The temporal structure of the verse should probably be noted very precisely. The text can be translated: "Do you not know . . . do you not hear . . . ?"—that is, from now on, permanently. But gramatically two initial imperfects are set over against two following perfects. This stresses the direction toward future and past—the one is not yet complete, while the other already is. But in the concrete situation, as this is brought into the proem of the drama, the future rendering of the Hebrew imperfects has its place. This is especially so if one follows W. Schrottroff, who advocates the following meaning for ידע: "primarily the sensory awareness of objects and circumstances in one's environment attained through involvement with them and through the information of others."[155] The organs of perception are eyes and ears. The rhetorical question: "Will you not perceive and hear?" provokes the reaction: "Yes, we will!" This makes it even clearer that the other two questions, with their perfect tenses, are directed to tradition. Its content *has already* been made known—and understood.

A minor textual difficulty could be a pointer to the history of the tradition here. Although there is no textual evidence, and although the ancient translations are also unanimous, commentaries and *BHS* propose changing מוֹסְדוֹת ("foundations") into מִיֻּסַּדַת (Elliger: "since the earth was founded"), parallel to מֵראֹשׁ ("from the beginning"). But the question is, which kind of parallelism is the original? This is connected with another question, whether it is so much a matter of course that מֵראֹשׁ should be understood in a temporal sense.

If we assume a chiasmus in vv. 21 and 22, then the "foundations of the earth" (v. 21) and "the circle of the earth" (v. 22) correspond. They are at all events "below," while "above" is "(the) heaven" (v. 22). But the corresponding element to "heaven" in v. 21 would be ראֹשׁ, in the sense of "head, summit, topmost part." This would then mean: the world from its furthest height to its greatest depths witnesses to its Creator and Lord; as

---

152 Cf. O. Taplin, *Stagecraft of Aeschylus* (1977) 473 on πάροδος: "The first song is often not purely choral but takes the form of a lyric dialogue."

153 See Y. Gitay, *Prophecy and Persuasion,* (1981) 92–94, 97. Cf. North, A. Schoors (*I Am God Your Saviour* [1973]), and Beuken on this passage.

154 See here R. J. Clifford, *Fair Spoken and Persuading* (1984).

155 W. Schottroff, "ידע, *ydᶜ*, to perceive, know," *TLOT* 2:511 [*THAT* 1:686].

Ps 19:2, 5 [1, 4] says: "The heavens tell the glory of God, and the firmament proclaims (מַגִּיד) the works of his hands . . . and their words to the ends of the earth."[156] The world picture of these two texts is entirely comparable.

■ **22** What the "circle of the earth" (חוּג הָאָרֶץ) means in the present text, v. 22, is not entirely clear. According to Seybold this is "the notion of two horizon circles."[157] He believes that "this notion of two concentric circular coastlines, that of the earth disk and that of the heavenly mountain islands, is directly evident in Babylonian cosmology, as reflected, for example, in the Sippar world map (6th-5th century B.C.E., with earlier prototypes)."[158] If one thinks in term of a "horizon," then an "enthronement" at the zenith would be conceivable.[159] But I think it possible that here we already have a more developed form of astronomical assumptions. The "circle of the earth" could be the earth's equator. Job 22:14 and Sir 43:12 (cf. 24:5) talk about "the circle of heaven" (חוּג שָׁמַיִם). These too are hymnic, cosmological declarations. The two could fit together, for the celestial equator is simply the projection of the earth's equator into the heavenly sphere.[160] This is then of interest if it is assumed that both (seemingly) turn on a single axis that points to the north, to the polar star.[161] At the spring and autumn equinoxes the sun rises at the point of intersection between the earthly and the celestial equator with the "ecliptic."[162]

"The one who is enthroned above the circle of the earth" then has his place above the stationary pole around which the whole world turns. He is in fact in "the north" (41:25). From there he rules his world and awakens the spirit of Cyrus (41:25). From there he leads out the stars according to their number (46:26). He is close to human beings,[163] even though at this distance they seem as small "as grasshoppers." In the word used here for a kind of grasshopper (חֲגָבִים h^agābîm), just as in חָגַג hāghāg, '[form a procession, jump], dance, celebrate,' and חַג hagh, 'procession, (round) dance, festival,'" K. Seybold believes that there is again a connection with חוּג (hûgh) with the semantic element of "circular movement."[164]

The interpretations suggested here could also fit in with an initially spatial interpretation of "beginning" (רֹאשׁ) in v. 21. The text shows an astonishing achievement in the way it grasps, as an abstraction, the unity of experienceable reality. The spatial interpretation of רֹאשׁ, as the beginning of a certain stretch or distance, is developed, through a process of abstraction, into the temporal understanding of the beginning of a stretch of time. The most familiar example is the absolute use in Gen 1:1: "In the beginning God created the heavens and the earth." How close Isaiah 40 is to Genesis 1 can be seen again and again from the key words used in the text.

If we follow up the terms רֹאשׁ and רֵאשִׁית in DtIsa, we can see how here the category of time is discovered in its reference to the world as a whole. The presupposition is belief in the all-embracing sovereignty of God. In our modern categories we distinguish between nature and history. Here in this text it is *the unity* of the world that is emphatically adhered to. The one world corresponds to

---

156 Ps 19:5 (4) talks about a "tent" for the sun.

157 "חוּג chûgh," *TDOT* 4:244–47, esp. 247 [*ThWAT* 2:780–84, esp. 783].

158 Ibid., 247 [783], with reference to O. Keel, *The Symbolism of the Biblical World* (1978) 21, pl. 8 [*Die Welt der altorientalischen Bildsymbolik und das Alte Testament* (1972) 17, pl. 8, also 15–60, 13–48]: "Conceptions of the Cosmos."

159 Cf. Exod 24:9-11.

160 Probably on the same projected level (according to this cosmology) is the use of חוּג in Prov 8:27-28 and Job 26:10 (as a verb). Beneath this "circle" lies the "primordial flood" (חוּג עַל־פְּנֵי תְהוֹם, Prov 8:27; cf. 1QM 10:13; Sir 24:5) with its waters.

161 Here too the cosmology presupposed probably accords with Job 22:12-14. G. Fohrer (*Das Buch Hiob* [1963]) renders v. 12: "Is God not as high as the heavens? And see the uppermost star, how high it

is." For "head of the stars" (רֹאשׁ כּוֹכָבִים) he draws attention to G. Hölscher (*Das Buch Hiob* [2d ed. 1952] 55): "What is meant is the top of the astral heaven, i.e., the heavenly pole (Greek πόλος, really 'axis,' and then the end of the axis on which the wheel turns; cf. Euripides, *Orest.* 1685: ἄστρων πόλος)." Both Fohrer and Hölscher emend v. 12. But in association with v. 14, "the circle of heaven," both Job and DtIsa are concerned about the question of the remoteness and the nearness of God. This question is discussed in the context of the dispute with the world picture newly developed in the Persian era.

162 Cf. Job 26:10; Ps 19:7 (6); Sir 43:7, 12.

163 Cf. Isa 41:17-20.

164 K. Seybold, "חוּג chûgh" *TDOT* 4:244–45 [*ThWAT* 2:781].

the one God. God establishes its spatial and temporal continuum.

■ **23-24** The contrast is all the greater in vv. 23 and 24 when, with the greatest rigor, the discontinuity of earthly rule to divine rule is presented. This is in glaring contradiction to the claim to permanence made by the mighty, and their need for legitimation. These assertions are developed out of the third hymnic predication. It is impossible to miss the alliteration in "who spreads out" (הַנּוֹטֶה *haggôteh*) and "who gives" (הַנּוֹתֵן *hannôtēn*). For God, the one is as light a thing as the other. The very breadth and scope of the assertions shows that it is on the final element of this hymnic section that the main emphasis lies. Behind this is long experience. The lords of this world come and go. Their true Lord remains! The OT is full of bitter experiences with the powerful. Here is an opportunity to describe the decision makers as "nothingness" (כַּתֹּהוּ). Here again Gen 1:2 is not far away—or Daniel 7 either. Mary's hymn of praise in Luke 1:46-55 once more takes up these ideas about the relative nature of earthly power.

DtIsa shows the sovereignty of his God, who is the Creator of the world and the Lord over all political powers. That which claims dominance on earth becomes for him a nothingness. The rise of great powers and the splendor of their rulers do not impress him. He sees in them only the presumption that makes them arrogate to themselves a power that is not theirs to claim, for they must one day all vanish once more. The whole confusing ebb and flow of events is for him relative, and becomes clear to him, because he knows that behind it all is the concerted will of his God.

This makes the programmatic character of Isaiah 40 clear. What is acknowledged here in hymnic form is going to be developed in the rest of the text.

C. 2. 40:25-26
Acknowledgment of Yahweh, Who Guarantees the Order of the Stars (and Hence Destinies)

"He brings out the host [of the stars] by number . . ." (40:26)

In this small unit a double question is asked: "With whom (אֶל־מִי) will you compare me . . . ?" (v. 25) and "Who (מִי) has created . . . ?" (v. 26). The hymnic section in v. 26 gives the answer. The alternation between speaker and chorus is once again clear. Verses 25-26 are

the central section of the three units that make up vv. 21-31. Brief though it is, it is no less important than the other sections. Verses 21-24 contain three predications: "who is enthroned," "who spreads out," "who gives"; then in vv. 27-31 the name Yahweh follows, three times. Here, at the center of the unit, is a single predicate: "who brings out." In the hymn this predicate is developed in connection with the stars, but it could at the same time be the motto of the whole: the one who led the people out of Egypt is the very one who leads them out of exile.

The text is bound into its context in a number of different ways. The question: "With whom will you compare me?" was already asked in v. 18, in the introduction to the "idol manufacture" passage. It is later repeated word for word in 46:5, again as the introduction to a section about "the manufacture of idols" (vv. 5-8). In 40:26 God's creative activity is contrasted with the human being as *homo faber*, the one who creates his own work. This link with the context shows yet again the meticulous care that has gone into the text.

■ **25** This verse is *not* a direct divine speech; it is a quotation. The future "he will speak" (יֹאמַר) can be understood as a continuous form: from now on it is he who is speaking, and continues to do so. That would mean that a rendering in the present tense would be possible: "he says." But in the context of the drama it is quite clear that 46:5 is really a divine speech. Here in 40:25, in the framework of the proem, we have only the announcement.

This also provides an explanation for another anomaly in the text. It has often been noted that (in Marti's words): "קָדוֹשׁ without the article and without a dependent noun . . . as a proper name and in the sense of אֵל (v. 18) . . . is otherwise found only in Hab 3:3 and Job 6:10." It is then generally translated "*the* Holy One." Elliger interprets the expression as follows: "Yahweh is [the] Holy One per se; that is, he is the one who is set apart from all others without any exception, set apart even from those beings who may claim the predicate 'holy' for themselves." It is no doubt true that an absolute interpretation of this kind is possible. But in the context of DtIsa the expression should be heard in a more concrete sense. It is the question of who "God" (אֵל) is (40:18), and it is similarly the question of who is a "Holy One." If one translates the phrase exactly as it stands ("a Holy One will say . . ."), the result is the tense question: "which Holy One?" The answer is given again and again in everything that follows: "the Holy One of Israel." So we must agree with Elliger when he says: "It is not by chance that here, on this single occasion, over against thirteen other instances in 40–55, the addition יִשְׂרָאֵל [Israel] is left out." The section solves the puzzle set in the proem. Attention is heightened. Here too we may ask ourselves how far we ought to reckon with Gentile listeners.

The term "Holy One" again contains the whole message. "Holy One" as a name for Yahweh has a long history. קָדוֹשׁ was an important concept in the interpretation of the relationship betwen Yahweh and his people.[165] In Isaiah 6 Yahweh's holiness is proclaimed at a prominent point in the installation of the prophet. If this God binds himself to Israel, he is establishing a relationship that has as its goal a "holy people" (עַם קָדוֹשׁ), even if this goal becomes evident only in a remnant of the people.[166] The originally negative character of the "remnant" idea at the end of Isaiah 6 is given a positive turn. DtIsa takes up the term "the Holy One of Israel." The concept originally stresses God's tremendous "distance." But astonishingly enough he links it *with the idea of redemption* (41:14; 43:3; 45:18ff.; 47:4).

■ **26** The command: "Lift up your eyes on high and see: who has created these?" brings out the situation of the drama particularly clearly. It is noticeable that neither here nor elsewhere does DtIsa use the term "stars." We may compare Genesis 1 here, where the creation account avoids the words for "sun" and "moon," using instead the word "lighting appliances" (מְאוֹרֹת, Gen 1:14-16)! The names for sun and moon might have been misunderstood as meaning the names of gods. The stars are mentioned in Gen 1:6, however. "These" (אֵלֶּה) in Isa 40:26 is to be understood in a deictic, or demonstrative, sense, especially since the word is used in conjunction with "eyes" and "seeing." Again, a comparison with Attic drama is a help in the interpretation. There too there are no external stage directions, so the situation is indicated in the text itself. At the beginning of the drama, even the time of day when the events are taking place (and the time of day of the performance) is evident.[167]

Scholars discuss how far Attic drama too was realistic in its presentation, and how far it drew purely on the imagination. Taplin's investigations have convinced me that there was probably a considerable degree of realism in situational directions of the kind we are considering.

The two other calls to "lift up your eyes" in DtIsa do not speak in favor of an imaginary situation either. In 49:18 Zion, personified as a woman, is told to look round her. If one notes the perfect tenses, "her children" have been gathered together (v. 21: "Who has borne me these? . . . where were they?"). In 51:6 the gaze at heaven and earth is realistic, for the comparisons "like smoke" or "like a garment" only come afterward. Creation is acknowledged in the things that can really be seen.[168] It can be perceived and experienced in faith. The term בָּרָא, which is used for the divine creative activity, again suggests a relation to the account in Genesis 1.

The speaker's question and the chorus's answer are mutually explanatory. Even if here the terminology does not explicitly cast back to tradition, as it does in vv. 21 and 28, one can easily see how traditional phraseology and concepts have been taken over from the hymns; a comparison with Ps 147:4-5, for example (together with the context), makes this plain: "He numbers the stars, he calls them all by their names" (both phrases are expressions of sovereignty). Hymns of this kind were familiar to the listeners; they were their hymnbook, as it were.

The commentaries are unanimous in pointing out the extent to which words taken from the military sector are used here. This is of course connected with the fact that the stars are described as a "host" or army (צָבָא ṣābāʾ). One positively waits for the name Yahweh Sabaoth (יהוה צְבָאוֹת). But this is the very point at which it does not come. According to 42:13, Yahweh is like a hero and a warrior who goes forth to war against his enemies. But in the present text the warlike image is immediately corrected: "Not one of them is missing." The last saying takes up 40:11 again ("like a shepherd his flock . . ."). The one who leads out the stars is also "the good shepherd," and not any other God. If that can be said even about the stars, how much more is it true for

---

165 See M. Noth, *Das System der zwölf Stämme Israels* (1930, reprint 1966) 61ff.

166 G. von Rad, "Das Gottesvolk im Deuteronomium," in *Gesammelte Studien,* vol. 2 (1973) 83.

167 See H. W. Schmidt, "Die Struktur des Eingangs," in

W. Jens, ed., *Die Bauformen der griechischen Tragödie* (1971) 38–39.

168 For בָּרָא as technical term cf. the Priestly writing in Genesis.

every human being! The catchword "power/strength" already anticipates the following unit, vv. 27-28.

The beautiful picture of the stars and the flocks should not keep us from noticing what the text is actually saying, however. What is at issue here is a dispute with contemporary science and politics, for it was the general conviction that the stars determine the fates of human beings. To use the word "astrology" for this phenomenon could be to trivialize it. The savants of the time—"the people who knew"—believed that they were on the track of general laws. Knowledge meant power, and power made sure that it was supported by knowledge. Babylon was the classic country of astronomy/astrology. But it was not confined to Babylon. It was an international science.

"The one who brings/leads out" gives the stars their order and their laws. In the context of creative activity (ברא), "leading out" can mean the act of creation itself, so that the participle would have to be rendered by the perfect tense: "who has brought/led out." "Call by name" is imperfect (in the Hebrew sense), being related to permanence and future. "The Holy One" knows their number and their names, that is, he has power even over the stars, although human beings believe that in the face of the stars they are helpless.

C. 3. 40:27-31
God's Sovereignty over Time, Space, and Force Makes Hope Possible

"But those who hope for Yahweh renew (their) strength . . ." (40:31)

Verses 27-31 are the third and last unit in the complex 40:21-31. It completes the proem. Once again the unit consists of three parts:

1. vv. 27-28aα   2 x 2 = 4 questions
2. vv. 28aβ-29   3 hymnic assertions as response
3. vv. 30-31   mimetic conclusion.

Here too we may assume that the questions in (1) were asked by the speaker, whereas (2) and (3) belonged to the chorus.

In what went before, in vv. 21 and 25, the plural questions showed that there is a direct appeal to the audience; in v. 27 the addressee is singular. This fits with the content, for here an individual participant in the action is presented for the first time. The speaker calls this person "Jacob/Israel." No one else was present, apart from the speaker and the chorus, when Zion/Jerusalem received her commission in v. 9 above to go up on a high mountain and to speak to the cities of Judah. The commentators have therefore rightly noticed that it is from this point onward that Jacob/Israel is mentioned, and then (with small variations) seventeen times in DtIsa—up to chap. 49—and after that never again.[169] In 49:14 Zion is mentioned again for the first time since 41:27, and from that point on it is Zion/Jerusalem (with similar variations) who is once more the active person. The problem of the distribution of the names can therefore by no means be solved by the methods of literary or redaction criticism. In the proem both the female and the male representative are presented: together they are the whole people. In the form of Jacob/Israel the people are coactors in what follows.

The double name is a problem in the case of Jacob/Israel too. It may perhaps be a way of showing the plurality and the unity. We shall see in the further course of the text that the variation in the names can also go with particular emphases—for example, Jacob = the liar, Israel = the chosen one. How far double emblems may have corresponded to the double names is something we cannot answer.[170]

■ **27** The text begins with the question "Why?" A. Jepsen maintains here: "The human 'why' to God is generally (46 times) introduced by *lāmmâ;* that is to say, it is the reproachful question with which the community or an individual comes before God. This reproach is initially always evoked, no doubt, through a contradiction between the divine promise and election on the one hand, and what God does on the other."[171] A "why?" of this kind has its place especially in communal laments.[172]

Here the complaint is explicitly cited, and we may ask whether it is not Jacob/Israel himself that is speaking.[173] In spite of its few words, the complaint is a comprehensive one. נִסְתְּרָה can be translated as 1st person fem. sing. perfect *Niphal:* "My way has been hidden"; in that case the following imperfect would have to be rendered as

---

169 Isa 40:27; 41:8, 14a; 42:24; 43:1, 22, 28; 44:1, 5, 21a, 23; 45:4; 46:3; 48:1,12; 49:5, 6.
170 Cf. in Egypt the pharaoh's double crown, represent-

ing Upper and Lower Egypt, or the hieroglyph used to express the unity of the kingdom.
171 A. Jepsen, "Warum? Eine lexikalische und theologi-

subsequent: "My right will pass by." In the complaint, past and future are linked. Another possibility is to define נִסְתְּרָה as the *Niphal* participle. Then the following imperfect is making a general statement and a particular "time" is not fixed. The complaint is talking about situations of distress that continually recur. The "way" is the fate that Yahweh does not see, and מִשְׁפָּטִי is here probably the legitimate claim based on election and promise.

The complaint is set aside in the testimony of tradition. ידע has again the whole semantic scope of "experience, perceive, know." What can be heard in what follows is nothing new, but it has again and again to be tested afresh.

■ **28-29** In the hymn, the chorus confesses its faith and interprets events. It is once again a summary proclamation of the theology that is developed—or, better, presents itself—in what follows. At the same time this is also the pronouncement of the consequences for the life of the community and the individual. The message is not abstractly elevated, but it is related to the specific situation and distress.

In v. 27 the complaint named the name of Yahweh, as name of the one God who has turned away, even if he is "my God"; and in the same way the hymn proclaims the name of Yahweh first of all (v. 28). Three predications are linked with this name: "God," "Creator," "giver." In the preceding text (vv. 25-26) the article was not used for אֵל ("God") or קָדוֹשׁ ("Holy One"); and here the article is again not used. This is the invitation to the listener then to join in and assent: "Yahweh is *the.* . . ."

Three categorical assertions are bound up with the predications: The first is related to the time: "God from everlasting." Here it should be noted that עוֹלָם is initially time that is unlimited, and unlimited in both directions, past and future (as comes out clearly in the formula "from everlasting to everlasting").

The second is related to space: "Creator of the ends of the earth." What "the earth" is, is defined in light of its furthest frontiers. That was important at a time when experience and knowledge of the world was expanding, as it could do in the Persian period.

The third category mentioned is, astonishingly enough, "a giver of power/strength (כֹּחַ)." This catchword was already mentioned in the preceding verse, v. 26. There it was related to the "strength" of the Creator in the order and movement of the heavenly bodies. The same divine power/strength is especially efficacious in the weakest of all, "the weary" (v. 29); it gives new life to "those who put their hope in Yahweh" (according to v. 31). It is the third mention of the catchword "power/strength" (כֹּחַ) in this context.

The elaborately wrought interweaving from v. 26 onward of the other words as well shows that the interrelations in the passage are intentional. The twin words "weary" (יָעֵף) and "faint" (יָגֵעַ) in vv. 28-31 are varied three times, sometimes chiastically ("Yahweh will not . . . young men will . . . those who hope for Yahweh will no longer"). According to v. 26 Yahweh is rich in power, and according to v. 29 he gives power to the powerless. Here we can see how the small units of the text are closely linked by way of common catchwords and concepts.

In this regular if complicated structure, it is all the more noticeable when a single statement cannot immediately be fitted into the pattern. This is so in the case of the final sentence in v. 28: "His insight is unsearchable." Here, in my view, lies a key to the whole, an answer to the questions. One might paraphrase by saying: "There is no way of exploring his [God's] insight." To "search out" or "explore" (חֵקֶר) occurs only here in DtIsa. It is a term belonging to the wisdom tradition that we find in the corresponding OT texts. The way the word is used in the book of Job is worth noting for the interpretation of the present text (Job 5:9; 9:10; 11:7; 36:26). For Job's question corresponds very well to the complaint in Isa 40:27.

The exploration of time and space and force—a deliberate use of these categories is what science is about. The natural philosophy that was just beginning at this period, and with which we are familiar from Greek tradition, is not very far away in either time or space. In his work DtIsa shows an astonishing degree of abstraction.

---

sche Studie," in *Das ferne und das nahe Wort. FS L. Rost* (1967) 106–13, esp. 108, 113.

172 Pss 44:24, 25 (23, 24); 74:1, 11; 79:10; 80:13 (12); 115:2; Lam 5:20; also Isa 63:17; Jer 14:8, 9; Joel 2:17.

173 The *i* sounds in this statement of lament are striking.

At the same time he lets the chorus say: "His [God's] insight is unsearchable." It is in the tension between this assertion and the complaint in v. 27, "My way is hidden from Yahweh . . . ," that the inner exposition of DtIsa's work is to be found. It is the crisis of faith that is here being developed in dialogue. People experience this tension; how are they to deal with it?[174]

■ **30-31** The close of the chorus anticipates one answer: the hope for Yahweh will never be disappointed (cf. Rom 5:5). Here in v. 31 the name of Yahweh is mentioned for the third time in vv. 27-31. Yahweh is the one who can give new strength. That is vividly demonstrated in the contrast between the "stumbling and falling" of the people who are considered to be strong, and the "running" of the weary.

The structure of the verse is extremely strict. Two assertions about "young men" and "picked men" are contrasted with four statements about "those who hope for Yahweh." The "wearying" is described in v. 30 in relatively extensive terms; the close in v. 31b, with its series of verbs, seems staccato in comparison. In these verses the sounds again play an important part. If we note the sequence of vowels in the final syllables, separated according to the units of speech, we find the sequence: *û - îm - û - îm - û - û - û - îm - û - û - û - û*. These are the same vowels we noticed in the first hymn, in 40:12-17. I suspect that they also have to do with the pitch of the notes. If the earlier hymn marked the entry of the chorus, the hymn at the end of the proem would mark its departure.[175] The verbs of movement in vv. 30-31 lend support to a view of this kind. The section must be

imagined mimetically, as a dance, and the rhythm of the language would accord with this.

The section contains a whole series of words that occur only here in DtIsa;[176] נַעַר really means "the status of someone with few rights, a subordinate and dependent person."[177] A man is נַעַר as long as he is single. נַעַר is the quintessence of youth and hence also of youthful strength. בָּחוּר is really "the chosen one." "Elite" would be an accurate rendering, for the term is used in just this sense in the military sector.[178] It is precisely the people whose power and endurance is extolled who will become weak. Human strength is limited.

"Wings . . . like eagles . . . run and not faint"—when we hear that we think first of mythological figures.[179] Fabulous mixed beings are common in the pictorial art of the ancient world.[180] They can have the wings of griffins and the bodies of lions. But in our present text it is human beings to whom these features are specially applied.

There are difficulties in both the translation and the interpretation of v. 31aβ, however. The verbal form יַעֲלוּ can be both *Qal* ("they will mount up, go up") and *Hiphil* ("they will bring up, lead up"). But in the context this is probably once again an intentional ambiguity, not an alternative. The causative meaning of the *Hiphil* fits the "wings," and Delitzsch already translated: "They lift up their wings." If a huge bird raises its wings it can fly away immediately. The comparison has to do with the point in time. *As soon as* those who "hope for Yahweh" receive new strength, they begin to move. In German, to "let one's wings droop" ("die Flügel hängen lassen") is an

---

174 See here F. J. Arnecke, "Krisen und Krisenbewältigung bei Deuterojesaja und 4. Esra" (1979).

175 It may be that in vv. 30-31 three chorus groups can be detected, these corresponding to the three parts of the hymn in vv. 12-17. In 40:15-17 the third group could be recognized from the sharp sound כְּמַר . . . וּכְשַׁחַק . . . כַּדַּק. The closest correspondence here in v. 30 would be כָּשׁוֹל יִכָּשֵׁלוּ, i.e., the group of young men and chosen warriors. They march and stumble! The groups I (v. 12) and II (vv. 13-14) join together in v. 31. But "they walk and do not become weary" corresponds rather to group II in vv. 13-14, which represented insight, knowledge, and perception—i.e., these were the old, in contrast to the women's voices in v. 12; here in v. 31 these higher voices would represent the mounting flight of the eagle.

176 See the list in Elliger's notes on this passage.

177 See H.-P. Stähli, *Knabe, Jüngling, Knecht: Untersuchungen zum Begriff* נער *im Alten Testament* (1978) 275; on the text: 94, 97-98.

178 See Bonnard 103 n. 3: "An elite groups is really the translation of בחורים, from the root בחר, select, choose." He refers to Judg 20:15-16; 1 Sam 24:3; 1 Kgs 12:21; Jer 48:15. "In Israel one ought hardly to speak of 'selected men' in the modern sense of the word, since the first gymnasium did not appear until later on: 1 Macc 1:14" (ibid.). But perhaps the sporting aspect is not after all so remote.

179 As polemic this again suggests Hermes, the tireless messenger of the gods. He is winged, and one of the beasts who accompanies him is the eagle.

180 Cf. *AOB* nos. 374–403; *ANEP* 212–23, nos. 644–706.

expression for discouragement and inactivity. Here it is just the opposite that is meant. The figure of speech shows a good observation of nature. In what follows DtIsa is decribing the turn of events that put an end to the exile. To that extent the *Hiphil* translation has its place. But in this theme the *Qal* is equally appropriate: "They will mount up." In Jewish tradition, the root עלה in the form "Aliyah" is still a technical term for going up to Jerusalem. This double meaning can be grasped visually at the close of the proem. "An eagle dance" is quite conceivable in modern ballet too. The return of the exiles is symbolically anticipated.

Another difficulty is the answer to the question as to what kind of bird is meant. *HALOT* gives for נֶשֶׁר: "eagle" and "vulture" (2:731). Both are powerful birds, and one can very well talk about their "great wings." The problem would only be the zoological nomenclature. But when KB, referring to Isa 40:31 and Ps 103:5, interprets: "renews itself," the implicit assumption is that here we have a motif from the phoenix myth; for the phoenix can renew itself and its plumage. This assumption would mean that Isa 40:30 should be translated as יַעֲלוּ *Hiphil*, "grow great wings." This mythological explanation might be considered somewhat farfetched if it were not that the phoenix is also mentioned in the *Exagoge* ("The Leading Out"), a play written by the Jewish tragic dramatist Ezekiel, fragments of which have come down to us from the first century B.C.E.[181] Only in Isa 40:31 this motif is not actually developed. Human beings run and walk with new strength. This last utterance in the verse particularly—"walk and not be weary"—can very well be once more an anticipatory announcement of the return to Zion/Jerusalem.

The hymnic praise of Yahweh's power in vv. 28-29 is hence followed in vv. 30-31 by the "application."

Yahweh's supremacy over all the dimensions of time, space and force are compared with two possible modes of human existence: (1) The life of young men and warriors. The expectation of political and military success is bound up with men like these; yet they are bound to become "weary and faint." (2) The life open to the weak and powerless. Because they hold fast to Yahweh, or better, because he holds fast to them, they receive the power that he alone can give, and that is his own.[182] This is the possibility open to those who "hope for Yahweh."

"Hope" (קוה) is connected with the word for "a stretched string" (קָו). It means "to be tense, firm, strong," then also "hope, wait for." With the exception of Gen 49:18, it hardly ever occurs in the historical books of the OT. In Isa 59:2; Jer 13:16; Job 3:9 and 30:26 it means the waiting for the light. It is found frequently in the individual laments (see Pss 25:3-21; 27:14; 69:21 [20]; Jer 14:22). In Ps 69:7 (6), the prayer of an impeached but innocent person, it means the waiting for the verdict, the outcome of the divine judgment. It means renouncing the wish to act for oneself, and instead waiting for what Yahweh will do, and for his just decision, which is salvation (cf. Pss 37:34; 40:2 [1]; Prov 20:22; Isa 25:9; 26:8, finally in DtIsa 49:23).

In the text, "those who wait" are contrasted with young men and chosen warriors. This alternative has a long tradition. In a certain sense it is reminiscent of the antithesis between those who trust in "horses and riders" and "those who look to the Holy One of Israel" (Isa 31:1; cf. Psalm 33). "Those who wait" have nothing in their hand, neither material possessions (אוֹן, Hos 12:9; Job 20:10) nor bodily strength (Ezek 12:4); it is they who are out of breath (יָעֵף, Jer 2:24). Everything they have— even if it is only their "strength"—they have to be given. Israel is called to be "people who wait" like this. They

---

181   The phoenix appears to Moses and the Israelites at the exodus from Egypt in Elim, at the twelve springs of water; cf. Exod 15:27 and Num 33:9. Moreover in Ezekiel the Tragedian we can also read: (254) "But further we saw another strange beast, wondrous such as no one had ever seen. For it was almost double the size of an eagle . . . , (265). It seemed to be the king of all the birds, as one could perceive; for all the birds together hastened timidly behind him, while he himself moved ahead like a proud bull, strutting on with rushing, swift steps." Translation following the German trans. of E. Vogt, *Tragiker Ezechiel* (1983), with reference to M. L. Walla, *Der*

Vogel Phönix in der antiken Literatur und der Dichtung des Laktanz (1969); R. van den Brock, *The Myth of the Phoenix According to Classical and Early Christian Traditions* (1972).

182   Cf. v. 26; in Ps 29:3-4 power/strength (כֹּחַ) can be synonymous with glory (כָּבוֹד).

really are "powerless and weary." David sang that Saul and Jonathan, the gallant warriors, "were swifter than eagles." It is this that is now promised to Israel, in a new way. Yahweh himself has "great wings," according to Ezek 17:3; that is, he is long-suffering. This meets all the objections of the people who say: "We shall not survive the journey home, we have not the strength for a new beginning."

Act I: 41:1–42:13

"The earlier happenings—see, they have come about!
But new ones I declare—before they spring up I let (you)
hear of them" (42:9)

A. 1. 41:1-5a
Court Scene in the Underworld, with
the Announcement of Cyrus

41

"Silence, (come) to me islands . . . nations" (41:1)

1   Silence, (come) to me islands!
    And nations shall renew strength.ᵃ
    Let them approach, then let them speak.
    Let us draw near together for the dispute!

2   Who has aroused (him) from the rising (of
        the sun)?
        Salvation meets his foot,
        he delivers up nations before him
        and <makes kings go down>.ᵃ
        His sword grinds to dust,
        his bow to chaff that is blown away.
3   He pursues them, passes on victoriously,
        does not touch the path with his feet.ᵃ

4   Who has done (this) and brought it about?
        One who calls the generations from
                the beginning—
        I am Yahweh, the first,
        and with the last I am he.

5a Islands have seen (it). <They were afraid>.ᵃ
    The ends of the earth (will) tremble.

1a The difficult יַחֲלִיפוּ כֹחַ (cf. 40:31) is often corrected in order
    to establish a parallelism to v. 1aα (cf. *BHK, BHS,* and the
    commentaries). But in the framework of the scene presup-
    posed here the reading makes perfectly good sense (see below
    on this passage).

2a Read with 1QIsaᵃ and Θ' יוֹרִיד (or יֵרְד, respectively) instead of
    יַרְדְּ.

3a On the text of v. 3b cf. D. R. Ap-Thomas, "Two Notes on
    Isaiah," in *Essays in Honour of G. W. Thatcher* (1967) 45–55.
    1QIsaᵃ offers יבינו instead of יבוא.

5a Read וַיִּרְאוּ instead of וַיִּירָאוּ; cf. LXX, S, Vg.

The text of 41:1-5a can be viewed as a separate unit. The
beginning talks about the "islands" and "nations" (v. 1a),
and at the end we again hear about the "islands" and
"the ends of the earth" (v. 5a). The section is one of the
"court scenes." At the beginning we can initially discern
no indications of the situation. The text plunges in
immediately with a direct divine speech. This continues
up to v. 4. Verse 5 describes the reaction of those concerned. We might have expected a similar note at the
very beginning, saying that those addressed have come.
Various emendations to v. 1 are designed to remedy this
deficiency.

The section begins with a summons to a legal judgment (v. 1). Two questions are then asked: "Who has
aroused (him) . . . ?" (v. 2a) and "Who has done (this)?"

(v. 4a). These questions are reminiscent of the series of
questions: "Who . . . ? Whom . . . ?" (מִי) in the previous
chapter. The answer is given in v. 4, in hymnic predications: it is Yahweh himself who has acted. The text of vv.
1-5 is therefore relatively self-contained, but is also linked
with its context.

Formally, the text contains elements of the legal dispute. But according to today's view, civil proceedings are
meant rather than criminal ones. A claim made by one
party against another is to be settled by the court: "Who
has done what?" (see v. 4a). It is not certain whether the
islands and nations are being accused. According to v. 1
they are commanded to "speak" and, "together" (יַחְדָּו)
with Yahweh, are told to approach the court.[1] At the end
judgment is not given against them, but the islands

1   In this respect the text differs from Deut 25:1:
    there it is a legal dispute between different parties
    (. . . רִיב בֵּין).

"see." That is, they are witnesses to an event rather than one of the parties in the proceedings. This suggests that this is really a dispute between Yahweh and another party, who is not explicitly named in the text: Yahweh asserts his claim against the claim of other gods, although these gods do not appear directly here. But why the terror at the end? Of decisive importance for the interpretation of the text is the answer to the question: Where is the whole event taking place? Hence, what kind of court is this? The exegesis of chap. 40 showed that we cannot expect stage directions external to the text, but that indications of place and time are nevertheless found in the text itself.

The divine speech begins without any introduction, but the very first word offers one indication of place: "Silence, (come) to me . . . !" The action is therefore happening at a place where there is silence. This catchword itself places the scene: it is the underworld, as a comparison with Ps 115:17, for example, shows:

The dead do not praise Yahweh
Nor do any that go down into silence (דּוּמָה).[2]

Verses 2 and 4 see Yahweh's activity as already complete, as far as the legal proceedings are concerned, but the imperfects in vv. 2 and 3 must be understood in an iterative sense—the action is still continuing. But perhaps the temporal point of reference also changes: at the moment of the "awakening" the action was still in the future. But from the observer's standpoint, in terms of dramatic time, the nations have already been delivered up and the kings "made to go down"; they are like dust. From this too we could deduce that the scene takes place in the underworld. This is the court where the dead are judged. Yahweh himself is the judge, and calls the islands and nations to witness to their fate.

With this premise a whole series of details and difficulties in the text become comprehensible. As has already been said, at the beginning of the text v. 1 requires no emendation. "And nations will renew their strength"—so that, as the dead, they can still perceive something and can appear before the court as witnesses. It is Yahweh who confers this strength. Here we should note the context: in chap. 40 "strength" (כֹּחַ) is mentioned three times. It is the divine "power/strength" that

moves the heavenly bodies in their order (40:26); it is the same "strength" that is given to the "weary" (v. 28); and it is this strength, finally—with the same verb—that renews those who hope for Yahweh. This "strength" can even give new life to the dead. It is efficacious on all three levels: in the heavenly world, the earthly world, and the underworld. The whole world is governed by it. Even the dead obey the command.

What the text has to say about the underworld seems initially alien to the OT. But as an illustration of the situation that is being imagined here we may remember the Tyre texts in Ezek 26:1—28:19. There, 26:19-21 describes Tyre's descent to Hades.[3] Verse 20 reads: "Then I shall make you go down to the people of old with those who go down to the pit and will make you dwell, like the ancient ruins in the land, in the depths with those who have gone down to the pit, so that you will not rise again in the land of the living."[4] The technical term here is ירד *Hiphil*, "bring down, make [someone] go down." But this then solves a further textual difficulty in Isa 41:2. The variant in 1QIsa[a] (יוריד) fits in perfectly: "(He) brings the kings down" or "(he) makes them go down."

Finally, if we consider the fall of Tyre according to Ezekiel, the fear and trembling also have their place. For example, Ezek 26:15-16 reads: "Thus has the Lord Yahweh said to Tyre: 'Will not the islands shake at the sound of your fall? . . . and all the princes of the sea shall tremble and be appalled at you.'" In Ezekiel the motif of the "descent to Hades" is moreover related to Egypt and Pharaoh (Ezek 31:10-18; 32:17-32). In Isaiah 14 it is the king of Babylon who with a great tumult descends to the underworld, so that the rulers who are already gathered there start up in alarm to greet the newcomer and to bewail him.[5] DtIsa could evidently draw on traditions of this kind; he had no need to go into detail in order to be understood. But his interpretation is his own: the islands and nations are not greeting someone who has descended into Hades; they are witnessing the reason for their own fall.

The name of Cyrus is not yet mentioned here; DtIsa still avoids using it, just as he does in 41:25-29. Cyrus is named for the first time only in 44:28. This builds up

2   Cf. also Pss 31:18 (17); 51:16 (cj.); 94:17. Cf. Isa 47:5
      at Babylon's entry into the underworld (דּוּמָה).
3   See W. Zimmerli, *Ezekiel* 2 (1983) 38–39 [*Ezechiel*
      (1969) 621].
4   Trans. following Zimmerli, ibid., 31–32 [607].
5   See here O. Kaiser and E. Lohse, *Death and Life*
      (1981) 53–54 [*Tod und Leben* (1977) 47–48].

the tension in the composition as a whole. But because it is an exacting text, we may infer that if the islands and nations represent the Greek-speaking countries along the Mediterranean coasts of Asia Minor, then they are mentioned as being the first countries that Cyrus subdued (c. 545 B.C.E.). It was the winter war against Croesus of Lydia for the conquest of Sardis that first brought Cyrus renown. Now those who were vanquished witness to the cause of their defeat. Behind the text we can glimpse Cyrus. The text poses the question about the fulfillment of messianic hope, thus sounding one of DtIsa's main themes.

In v. 4 Yahweh himself is acknowledged as the real cause of political events. Although the one whom he "awakened" deposes kings, his power is merely relative compared with the power of Yahweh himself. Even the sovereignty of a Cyrus is limited.

The proclamation of Cyrus in these verses is up to this point quite consistent. It has to be seen in the context of DtIsa's critical engagement with OT traditions. We can see here fundamental approaches of prophecy to questions about rule.

If we look back, however, we are struck by the fact that at certain points it is not at all clear whether the text is talking about a real person, or whether mythical elements are being used as a way of proclaiming Cyrus's importance. Such mythical elements might be "the rising (of the sun)," that is, from the east, at the beginning, and at the end the remark that "he does not touch the path with his feet." But these could also be quite factual references to Cyrus's origins, and a pointer to the "rider." The two possibilities are not mutually exclusive.

■ **4** The central theophany utterance in this first scene is in v. 4. If we think in terms of a dramatic presentation, this would have been a severe cause of offense. Again and again, Jewish tradition strictly forbade the representation of God. But instances in the visual arts (e.g., the frescoes in Dura-Europus) show that a symbolic representation was possible. The exodus tradition shows that the presence of God could be perceived through the accompanying cloud and the pillar of fire. "The tent of meeting" was associated with the appearance of the "cloud," which was visible to the "people" too.[6]

DtIsa battles for the incomparability of God, out of theological conviction. But at the same time he makes theological statements visually apprehensible in drama, mediating them to the people he is addressing in the form of action. In v. 4 three hymnic declarations are made about Yahweh:

1. He is the one who calls.
2. He is the first.
3. He is with the last.

Here the climax is the self-introductory formula "I am Yahweh!" The third element in the formula is then again modified: "I am he." The use of the formula shows that here a dispute is taking place. The stress lies on the I: "*I* am he"—I, not some other god.

The present context suggests an interpretation of these declarations in terms of time. Yahweh's claim to recognition as Lord of the world rests on creation. Through his sovereign word, the generations have come into being from the beginning. If he is also with the last, that which is formulated as a confession of God's creation is established as valid for the present too. It is also true for those still to be born. God is not only at the beginning of the world, and its "prime mover." We shall see that the attempt to make statements about creation fruitful for the present is one of DtIsa's main concerns. This sentence is therefore not merely a gloss. The recognition that God is the same for those born later too means promise and assurance for all times.

How is the general concept of God's sovereignty related to concrete historical experience? It is this that is argumentatively developed in the form of a lawsuit. To put the matter the other way round: the concept of the sovereignty of God makes possible an understanding of past experience in the light of faith.

DtIsa introduces the sociomorpheme "trial, judicial hearing" in order to elucidate the fundamental conditions of the relationship between God and human beings. But the exegesis must still take account of the fact that here DtIsa has chosen a special form of legal proceedings. His choice must surely have been determined by some particular problem.

If we once more draw on the "descent to Hades" in Ezekiel 26 for a comparison, we should notice the time

---

6 See E. Jenni, "עָנָן *ʿānān* cloud," *TLOT* 2:937–39 [*THAT* 2:351–53].

factor there too: in the underworld, Tyre encounters "the people of old" (עַם עוֹלָם), "all that has been laid waste since olden times" (כָּחֳרָבוֹת מֵעוֹלָם, v. 20). Correspondingly, Egypt encounters those who have fallen by the sword: Assyria, Elam, Meshech-Tubal, Edom, the princes of the north. Here are lying "the heroes who fell 'in the days of old'" (Ezek 32:27).[7] "The one who calls the generations from the beginning" could also refer to Yahweh's sovereignty over the land of the dead.[8] He has called past generations, that is, he has determined their death. He—he and none other—will be with the last as well. Yahweh is the first, supreme, sole Lord, for the dead too—no other god, not even Osiris, or whatever his name may be.

The text would in this case belong in an eminent degree to the dispute about the other gods. For a long time the world of death was for Israel "far from Yahweh." It was possible to talk about death with a tremendous, cold matter-of-factness. But from the exilic period onward Israel was forced to come to terms in a new way with the cults of the dead encountered in the civilizations surrounding it. If, as chap. 40 maintains, space, time and eternity are part of creation, then the realm of death could no longer be excluded from Yahweh's sovereignty either. The "I am Yahweh" applies there too, and DtIsa passes on this discovery of faith. It is in line with utterances in the Psalms:

If I ascend to heaven, you are there.
If I make my bed in Sheol, you are there.
If I take the wings of the morning . . .
(Ps 139:8-9).[9]

---

7   See Zimmerli, *Ezekiel* 2 (1983) 168 [*Ezechiel* (1969) 778] on this passage. In line with LXX ἀπ᾽ αἰῶνος he proposes: "מֵעוֹלָם נֹפְלִים could also be translated: 'Those who lie there from of old.'" He asks whether this is a play on the נְפִלִים in Gen 6:4.

8   Cf. Isa 44:23: תַּחְתִּיּוֹת אָרֶץ. In the hymn this land too is included in Yahweh's sovereignty.

9   On the change of view in the history of OT tradition about Yahweh's relation to the realm of the dead, see Kaiser and Lohse, *Death and Life* (1981) 54ff., 68ff. [*Tod und Leben* (1977) 48ff., 68ff.].

41

". . . and says to his brother: be strong!" (41:6)

A. 2.   41:5b-7
The Smiths at Work
Idol Production and Commentary

5b   They drew near and approached—
6   one man will help his neighbor/comrade
        and says to his brother: Be strong!—
7   and the smith stood by/encouraged
            the goldsmith,
    the one who smooths with the hammer,
            he who strikes the mallet—
        by saying of the welding/bond, "It is good!"—
    and he fastened it with pegs, it will not
            shake/totter.

■ **5** The islands "see." That is not simply an observation about an optic impression. In the *parallelismus membrorum* it is said that the ends of the earth "quake." This is a sign of fathomless terror. They have experienced a theophany, the theophany of Yahweh as the God who has power over the whole world from its greatest heights to its extremest depths. This power is felt to the ends of the earth. It unleashes earthquakes.

In this way the departure of the "islands" could also be presented in theatrically effective terms. But at the same time this "finale" is intimately connected with the beginning of the next little scene. This emerges from the text through the very fact that it is not certain whether the last half-sentence of v. 5 belongs to what has gone before, or reaches forward to what comes afterward. But the sequence of events has been quite correctly preserved. "They approached . . ."—*who* is not yet clear. But the place—and perhaps the semi-darkness—of the underworld remains. It is the metalworkers who come, as we shall immediately discover. But anyone who is at all familiar with ancient mythology knows who is at work in the underworld: It is Hephaistos, or Vulcan, or whatever name he goes by, with his fellows. The earthquake has been a fitting introduction. Here we again have a comic episode, side by side with the serious court scene. But its content should be taken no less seriously.

The substance is the same as that of vv. 1-4, though transposed to a different level—the dispute with the "gods"; perhaps we may conclude even more precisely: the dispute with the gods of the "islands."

■ **6, 7** The manufacture of idols. Most scholars agree that vv. 6 and 7 constitute a separate unit. We might ask what the manufacture of idols has to do with the preceding court scene.[10] Duhm (probably following a proposal of Paul de Lagarde) has therefore added vv. 6 and 7 onto 40:19, because that also talks about the manufacture of idols.[11] Elliger thinks that the passage is a further "strophe belonging to the same poem" that has strayed into the wrong place.[12] Most modern exegetes follow Duhm, but his proposal has also met with opposition.[13] Muilenburg, for example, points to the intimate connection of the verse with its present context,[14] and Preuss reminds us of the "frequency of the link between these motifs," the "dispute or quarrel among the gods (ריב) and the mocking of [their] idols."[15]

I should like to assent to these observations while modifying the explanation. The verses originally formed a separate unit, belonging to a wider complex. What is being described is the manufacture of an idol; and in the present section the theme is the cooperation of the craftsmen: "A man (אישׁ) will help his neighbor/comrade" (v. 6).[16] The description of the process, with two

---

10   Thus Marti, 279.
11   Duhm, 270.
12   Elliger, 115–16, 128.
13   Volz, 14; North; J. C. Kim, "Das Verhältnis Jahwes zu den anderen Göttern in Deuterojesaja" (1962) 12, 16.
14   Muilenburg, 452.
15   H. D. Preuss, *Verspottung fremder Religionen im Alten*

Testament (1971) 202–3 on this passage; he bases his view on Judg 6:32; 1 Sam 5:1-5; 1 Kgs 18:19-40; 2 Kgs 1:1-8; Ps 82:1-7; and Jer 2:1ff.; further Exodus 1–12; Deuteronomy 32; 2 Kings 18–19.
16   Elliger (128 n. 1) points out that otherwise in DtIsa עזר is always used of Yahweh (41:6, 10, 13, 14; 44:2; 49:8; 50:7, 9).

verbs in the narrative form, can follow: "he stood by/encouraged (וַיְחַזֵּק)"—the craftsmen are meant—and "fastened 'it' (וַיְחַזְּקֵהוּ) with pegs." Here in the light of the suffix we would also be permitted to assume an idol (פֶּסֶל) as the object to be fastened.

In v. 7 as in 40:19, the first craftsman to be mentioned is the חָרָשׁ. He is the expert in the widest sense for metalwork (1 Sam 13:19; Isa 54:16; Hos 13:2), woodwork (2 Sam 5:11; 2 Kgs 12:12; 22:6; Isa 44:13; Jer 10:3), and stonework (Exod 28:11; 2 Sam 5:11). If we assume that there is a close connection between this verse and Isa 40:18-20, then here too the passage is talking about metal casting.

צֹרֵף is the craftsman who works with welding techniques especially. Here it is above all a question of the purifying of precious metals (2 Sam 22:31; Zech 13:9; Pss 12:7 [6]; 17:3; 18:31 [30]; 26:2; 66:10; 105:19; 119:40; Prov 30:5; Dan 11:35). The substantive is then generally rendered "silversmith" or "goldsmith" (Judg 17:4; Jer 10:9, 14; 51:17; Neh 3:8, 32). Isa 40:19 and 46:6 also show that the craftsman is dealing with precious metals.

It is not clear whether the same artisans are involved in the following two activities. I think it probable that a further example of cooperation is being given, perhaps here also between rough and precision work. פַּטִּישׁ is a heavy hammer (cf. Jer 23:29; 50:23). פַּעַם is frequently translated "anvil," but it may be a small hammer or mallet.[17]

If the sense is reconstructed in this way, then the passage does not have to be a lampoon; it is really a technical description. The impression only changes with the passages in direct speech.

■ **6b** "And says to his brother: 'Be strong!'" The word "brother" (אָח) stresses even more clearly than "neighbor" or "comrade" (רֵעַ) the relationship, or at least the

bond, among the people.[18] In plain words, the brother is being called upon to take part in idol worship; it is not merely that an artisan is being exhorted to work. The verb "to be strong or firm" (חזק) is introduced yet again, in a different sense from the way it is used in the technical process described in v. 7b. According to Duhm, "חזק is a cry with which workers fire one another on: Go to it! cf. Zech. 8:9."[19] But in Zechariah it is God's own call to rebuild the temple!

In the immediately succeeeding text, Isa 41:9, it is Yahweh who "seizes" (הֶחֱזַקְתִּיךָ) Israel, his servant, and 41:13 talks similarly about "your God, who seizes your right hand" (מַחֲזִיק יְמִינֶךָ). חזק ("to be or make strong or firm") is therefore a catchword that links the text with its context. But this is not merely a superficial link by way of the same catchword; in the context the point at issue is the question about Yahweh's power or the power of the gods, or of their peoples in each case.[20]

■ **7** Verse 7bα can be literally translated: "who says to the 'bond': that is good"; this is the second direct-speech section. The meaning of דֶּבֶק is not clear. In the OT the word occurs only here and in 1 Kgs 22:34 and 2 Chr 18:33, although there it is in the plural. In both these passages the word must refer to part of the armor. Bonnet supposes that what is meant are the armor's "'pendants' = scales"; others think it is the "belt" or "suspending straps."[21] S. Smith, following a suggestion of W. E. Barnes, has also related the "armor" interpretation in these passages to the text of Isa 41:6-7, thus arriving at a unified pattern.[22] But the parallelism to other texts about idols is closer still. Other commentators think of the technical process of fusing the nucleus

---

17　Targum 452 has קוּרְנָסָא, "mallet, hammer"; see also Muilenburg, who refers to A. D. Haldar, *The Notion of the Desert in Sumero-Accadian and West-Semitic Religions* (1950) 37. Since פעם really means "foot," Elliger (129) presumes in the light of the form that this is a term for "hammer"; see also *HALOT* s.v.

18　J. Kühlewein ("רֵעַ *rēaʿ* companion," *TLOT* 3:1245 [*THAT* 2:789]) writes about this passage: "Even in the meaning 'neighbour,' *rēaʿ* often stands in conjunction with an indication of relationship such as *ʾāḥ*, which can also be employed in an expanded usage for nonrelatives (cf. Deut 15:2; Isa 41:6; Jer 23:35; 31:34; 34:17)." All the other passages cited

refer to relationships within the people of Israel! Are the "smiths" "brothers," as descendants of Cain?

19　See Duhm on this passage.

20　See the previous comments on 41:1 ("renew strength") and what is said below on 41:10; Muilenburg on this passage; Preuss, *Verspottung fremder Religionen im Alten Testament* (1971) 202.

21　See *HALOT* 1:209 [*HALAT* 1:201]; H. Bonnet, *Die Waffen der Völker des Alten Orients* (1926) 213–14; H. Weippert, "Panzer," *BRL*² (1977) 248.

22　S. Smith (*Isaiah Chapters XL–LV: Literary Criticism*

of the statue to its precious-metal overlay, and translate: "soldering."[23]

A frequent *topos* in polemic against idols is that the idols "fall" or "topple over"; so we are then immediately told that they are pinned or pegged, so as to make them firm. Perhaps the passage in direct speech is an anticipatory interpretation, which is less interested in the technical process.

דֶּבֶק is an abstract formation; it can be translated "bond." A comparison of the different texts where the verb דבק occurs shows that it is used to designate the bond with other human beings,[24] but above all the bond with Yahweh.[25] The difficulty would then lie in the ambiguity of what is being said here: the technician thinks that the "welding/bond" is good, although it is known to be an idolatrous "bond," or a bond with "idols," instead of with Yahweh. To be attached to these foreign gods is certainly "not good." The craftsman says of his work "he [or: that] is good" (טוֹב הוּא), which is just what God says of his creation. But the work of the person who makes idols is not good at all. In the context of Isaiah 41 the "he" is contrasted with the "I am he" (אֲנִי הוּא) of v. 4 (see above).

"It will not shake/totter" (לֹא יִמּוֹט). This remark concludes the polemic against the idols. But grammatically the lack of a connecting link is not easily explained. Duhm has struck out the sentence altogether.[26] It can be understood as an implicit relative clause. But it also seems possible that it is the continuation of the commenting direct-speech section. The translation "it will not shake" is deduced from the context here, following 40:20.[27] This is not wrong, technically speaking. But we should rather expect "collapse" once more.[28] It is noticeable that here the verb is not נפל ("fall") but מוט.[29] In the *Qal* it means "totter." But the verb has a characteristic breadth of meaning. It is used for earthquakes among other things, especially if God causes them (Pss 46:3 [2]; 7 [6]; 60:4 [2]; Isa 24:19) and for the "slipping of the foot" (Deut 32:35; Pss 38:17 [16]; 55:23 [22]; 66:9; 94:18; 123:3). The finding in the *Niphal* corresponds to this (Pss 46:6 [5]; 82:5: "The foundations of the earth"; 93:1; 96:10; 104:5; and of human beings: 10:6; 13:5; 15:5; 16:8; 21:8 [7]; 30:7 [6]; 62:3; 112:5; Prov 10:30; 12:3). The two meanings are linked in Ps 125:1: "Those who trust in Yahweh are like Mount Zion, which does not move." The relation to Zion and to the "God is king" tradition in Psalms 46 and 96 is noticeable.[30] DtIsa is evidently familiar with this use of the verb, as we can see from 54:10:

> The mountains may depart and the hills totter (תְּמוּטֶנָה),
> But the proofs of my grace shall not depart from you,
> and the covenant of my peace shall not totter (תָמוּט).

---

and History [1944] 159) translates: "saying of the armour-joint: it is good."

23   Thus, among others, North, Fohrer, Westermann, McKenzie. Elliger (104, 130) understands it intransitively as "adhere"; cf. 1 Sam 5:3-4, which describes the overturned statue of the god Dagon.

24   Gen 2:24; 34:3; 2 Sam 20:2; 1 Kgs 11:2; Ruth 1:14; 2:23.

25   Deut 10:20; 11:22; 13:5 (4); 30:20; Josh 22:5; 23:8; 2 Kgs 18:6; see also Ps 119:31; for a negative sense, see the adherence to "Jeroboam's sins" in 2 Kgs 3:3.

26   Duhm, 220: "לֹא יִמּוֹט, which should at least have a ו in front of it, is probably an interpolation, since it disturbs the meter and is a repetition of 40:20, where it fits the context better." The ו ("and") now appears in 1QIsa[b]. But it has probably been introduced to smooth out the difficulty. See also Marti on this passage: "לֹא ימוט, which, closely conjoined without a ו, would refer to the subject of יחזקהו, has been added as an explanatory gloss, following 40:20."

27   If the reference is to an ichthyphallic idol—as, e.g.,

in the case of the Egyptian god of the underworld, Min—the irony is all the more cutting (cf. also the hermae).

28   Preuss, *Verspottung fremder Religionen im Alten Testament* (1971) 119 on Amos 3:9ff.; 4:4ff.; 5:5-6; 8:14: "The false worshipers of Yahweh, however, who think that they can make of Yahweh just some random god, will suffer the fate with which idols are often threatened, or which is described polemically as their typical characteristic: they will fall (נפל) and will not be able to get up again (קום)"; cf. 1 Sam 5:1-5 and in the parallel, Babylon—the image of her gods: Isa 21:9, 10; see also Ps 82:7.

29   There is also a difference in the choice of words compared with Jer 10:4. DtIsa takes an independent line in his interpretation.

30   Cf. also Hab 2:5ff., 19.

So when the comment says that the idols "do not shake/totter," this seeming firmness is an illusion. The idols will certainly fall when the whole world trembles.[31] In the context of Isaiah 41, there is also a contrast between Cyrus's rapid movements and the immovability of the idols (cf. 46:7).

This makes plain that the comment in the direct-speech passages is intended to achieve a parodistic effect. At the same time, it is these sections especially that establish the link with both the immediate and the wider context of DtIsa's book. This lends the text its significance in its present position.

---

31 Frey (47) brings out the wordplay very well in his interpretation: "The stem 'to be firm' . . . shows the attitude of the idol worshipers as a search for support and stability. But in the general lack of stability no one can receive support from anyone else. Everyone has in fact to support the other. One person urges the other one on, saying 'be firm!' and through a firm bearing compensates for what is lacking in inward stability and support. And since they cannot receive support from one another, they feel particularly strong because they need support from another world. . . . Religion is having a heyday. The manufacture of idols is in full swing."

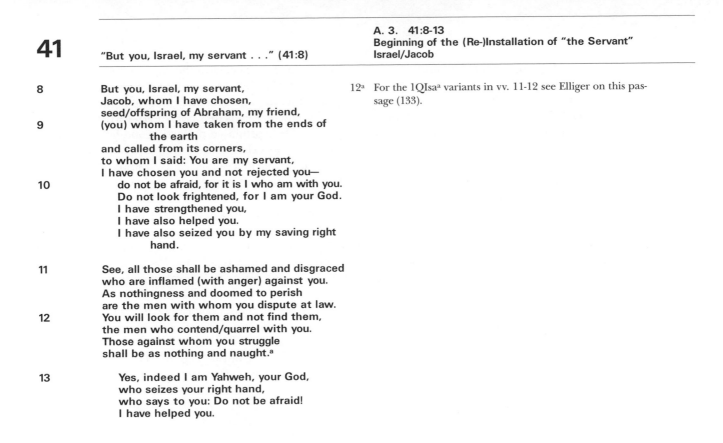

8   But you, Israel, my servant,
Jacob, whom I have chosen,
seed/offspring of Abraham, my friend,

9   (you) whom I have taken from the ends of
the earth
and called from its corners,
to whom I said: You are my servant,
I have chosen you and not rejected you—

10   do not be afraid, for it is I who am with you.
Do not look frightened, for I am your God.
I have strengthened you,
I have also helped you.
I have also seized you by my saving right
hand.

11   See, all those shall be ashamed and disgraced
who are inflamed (with anger) against you.
As nothingness and doomed to perish
are the men with whom you dispute at law.

12   You will look for them and not find them,
the men who contend/quarrel with you.
Those against whom you struggle
shall be as nothing and naught.[a]

13   Yes, indeed I am Yahweh, your God,
who seizes your right hand,
who says to you: Do not be afraid!
I have helped you.

12[a]   For the 1QIsa[a] variants in vv. 11-12 see Elliger on this passage (133).

The text is well preserved. Textual changes are generally connected with differing interpretations. 1QIsa[a] has considerable gaps in the text of vv. 11 and 12. Fohrer thinks that this shorter text is the original.[32] For a contrary view see Elliger, and especially his reference to the full text in 1QIsa[b].[33] The omission of v. 13bγ in the LXX is probably also merely an oversight.

The divisions in the section 41:8-13 and the definition of the genre are the subject of dispute.[34] This affects the interpretation of the text to some extent. Opinions differ as to whether the individual units are short or more extensive. Delitzsch divides the pericope into vv. 8-10, 11-13, 14-16, 17-20, and he is followed by Muilenburg and North, among others. Duhm and Marti put vv. 8-10 and 11-16 together. More recent commentators generally see vv. 8-13 as a single unit, and vv. 14-16 and 17-20 as other units (thus Mowinckel, Westermann, Melugin, Schoors, and Spykerboer).[35]

Westermann blazed a new trail here when he defined vv. 8-13 as an "oracle of salvation." In so doing he was taking up Begrich's theory[36] about the "priestly oracle of salvation" as a response to the complaint of the individual, which he thought to be the genre providing the background for DtIsa's proclamation. Von Waldow had developed these theses further by showing firm "formal components" and by assuming that there are quite close

32   See G. Fohrer, "Zum Text von Jesaja 41,8-13," *VT* 5 (1955) 239–49, reprinted in his *Studien zur alttestamentlichen Prophetie 1949–1965* (1967) 182–89.

33   See Elliger on this passage.

34   See also the arrangement in Fohrer, "Zum Text von Jesaja 41,8-13," in *Studien*, 182 (see above, n. 32). Cf. J. Ziegler, "Die Vorlage der Isaias-Septuaginta (LXX) und die erste Isaias-Rolle von Qumran (1QIsa[a]),"

JBL 78 (1959) 34–59.

35   See also the survey in L. Boadt, "Isaiah 41:8-13: Notes on Poetic Structure and Style," *CBQ* 35 (1973) 22 n. 10.

36   J. Begrich, "Das priesterliche Heilsorakel," *ZAW* n.s. 11 (1934) 81–92, reprinted in his *Gesammelte Studien zum Alten Testament* (1964) 217–31.

links between DtIsa and the situation of worship.[37] Westermann finds a special group of salvation sayings in DtIsa that he calls "assurances of salvation."[38] They are characterized by the call "Do not be afraid" (41:8-13, 14-16; 43:1-4, 5-7; 44:1-5; 54:4-6). Taking 41:8-13 as an example,[39] he develops an "identical structure":

> Address (with expansions)
> Assurance of salvation: Do not be afraid!
> Reason, Justification
> (a) nominal (I am with you, I am your God)
> (b) verbal (I strengthen you, I help you [perfect])
> Consequence (future) for the one imploring help, and directed against his enemies (purpose)

The sections shaped by this formulary "are no longer cultic texts, however; they are free apostrophes addressed to the congregation."

R. P. Merendino has criticized Westermann's approach because the association with a "complaint" situation cannot be proved.[40] As for genre, he himself proposes "a promise of salvation or victory, freely given by Yahweh without any previous request, in the style of the divine assurance that belongs to the tradition of the Yahweh war."[41]

Some of Westermann's and Merendino's observations are undoubtedly complementary. Merendino does not dispute either that the "assurance of salvation" is a special form of "the 'oracle' genre in general."[42] But in my view the present text allows us to discover more than that about the "occasion"[43] of the "salvation oracle."

Verses 8-13 as *Installation*. If we begin by analyzing vv. 8-13, it emerges that the text obviously consists of a single scene. At least two "persons" are present, a master

and a servant. The content of the happening can first of all be described as follows: a servant is given his master's assurance that he is his servant (vv. 8a, 9b: "you are my servant"). The servant is in—or gets into—difficulties (vv. 11 and 12). He is promised protection and help (vv. 10 and 13). Now, it is clear that this is not just any "master" or lord, for he introduces himself as "Yahweh, your God" (v. 13). So we must again presuppose that the place of the action is this Lord's heavenly (or earthly) palace. It is also unambiguously clear in this text who the servant is. It is "Israel/Jacob" (v. 8). Since the text goes on in the singular form of address, the servant is initially a single individual. The name "Israel" and his description as "Abraham's seed/offspring" give the figure its special significance: he is the personification of God's people. But if the name of the servant can be given here, he will hardly be the same servant as the one who remains unnamed in 42:1-9.

What is the nature of the "action"? The visual elements have been pushed completely into the background, but in spite of that, important information can be deduced from v. 10 especially. The servant "is afraid" (v. 10aα). That is understandable, since this is a direct encounter with God; the servant's experience is no different from the experience of Moses (Exod 3:6) or of one of the prophets on their installation.[44] That "places" the Lord's self-introduction here. This is the God of the servant Israel/Jacob and none other ("It is *I* who am with you").[45] The verb in the *parallelismus membrorum*, אַל־תִּשְׁתָּע (v. 10aβ), also probably embraces the "fearing" element. The Masoretic punctuation suggests that it

37 H.-E. von Waldow, "Anlass und Hintergrund der Verkündigung des Deuterojesaja" (1953) 11–28, esp. 27.

38 C. Westermann, "Das Heilswort bei Deuterojesaja," *EvTh* 24 (1964) 355–73; also his "Sprache und Struktur der Prophetie Deuterojesajas," in *Forschung am Alten Testament*, vol. 1 (1964) 117–20; and his commentary on this passage.

39 Westermann, "Sprache und Struktur," 118.

40 R. P. Merendino, "Literarkritisches, Gattungs-kritisches und Exegetisches zu Jes 41,8-16," *Bib* 53 (1972) 1–42. See also his commentary *Der Erste und der Letzte: Eine Untersuchung von Jes 40–48,* 135–77.

41 Merendino, "Literarkritisches, Gattungskritisches," 28.

42 Ibid., 32.

43 Ibid.: "Decisive for a determination of the genre, however, is a decision about the place (temple, mili-

tary camp, court) . . . the method (the drawing of lots, divine omen in the context of a sacrifice, dream, vision . . .) and the precise occasion on which the oracle is conferred in any given case." (See also his commentary, 167.)

44 Thus Isa 6:5; Ezek 2:1. This contrasts with the "Do not be afraid" of v. 13, being here "an entry formula for the theophany"; see Elliger, who points to L. Köhler, "Die Offenbarungsformel 'Fürchte dich nicht' im AT," *SThZ* 36 (1919) 33–39.

45 For the emphatic position of the "I" (אֲנִי) see Elliger on this passage; also H. D. Preuss, "Ich will mit dir sein," *ZAW* 80 (1968) 139–73.

should be understood as *Hitpael* of שעה, "look," which in light of the situation led to the interpretation "looking frightened." Several authors assume that the word is derived from a root שתע, meaning "fear," that can be found in Phoenician and Ugaritic.[46] In the present text, however, ירא, "fear," is also to some extent a deduction based on the *parallelismus membrorum*. The verb then occurs again almost immediately in 41:23, where it is associated with a divine appearance that is judged to be negative. The reaction that must be meant could be described as *stupor*, a word that can cover fear, awe, astonishment, and paralysis.[47]

Verse 10aβ also stresses that the one whom the servant has experienced (or fears) in the theophany is his God ("I am your God"). In the context of the dispute with the "gods" in DtIsa, this statement then acquires new weight.

The double command, formulated by way of אל with the jussive, is followed by three verbal elements in the perfect tense. They describe an action that begins in the present and persists from then on. It is first said that the servant is "strengthened." אמץ can in general mean "to be strong, sturdy." According to van der Woude, the term "occurs only with a personal subj[ect] (God, human)."[48] But the use in the encouragement formula is characteristic: "Be firm and strong." It is found several times in connection with installations.[49] Of special interest for the present text is the context in the "royal oracle" in Ps 89:20-38 (19-37);[50] cf. vv. 20-21 (19-20):

> I have exalted one chosen from among the people.
> I have found David my servant (עַבְדִּי),
> with the oil of my holiness I have anointed him,
> my hand shall continually hold him fast,
> [and] my arm surely strengthen him (תְּאַמְּצֶנּוּ).
> No enemy shall fall upon him.

In Psalm 80, which takes up a series of earlier traditions,

v. 18 (17) reads: "Let your hand be over the man at your right hand" parallel to: "over the person (בֶּן־אָדָם) whom you have strengthened (אִמַּצְתָּ) for yourself." In these texts there is a comparable semantic field, so that a reference to "installation" in the declaration in v. 10 of the present DtIsa text would seem possible.

The servant is lent the strength that is to accompany him from now on.[51] The promise of help (עזר) is so general that a specific understanding of what is meant here cannot initially be discerned. In the context of DtIsa's book, "help" comes to be a connecting catchword.[52] All the more precise is the formulation: "I have also seized you by my saving right hand" (cf. v. 9). This can be understood in a transferred sense as a further declaration about Yahweh's help. But in the civilizations surrounding the OT, "to take by the hand" was a technical term for the deity's installation of a king. It is understandable that in light of its understanding of God the OT should have been shy about any such direct presentation and declaration. In the installation of Isaiah, it is only the seraphs who act (Isa 6:6-7). But in Jeremiah's installation it was at least possible to say that Yahweh put out his hand and touched his lips[53] (Jer 1:9). And this gesture and the words of installation are closely connected.

In the framework of the scene in Isa 41:8-13, however, the gesture of taking by the hand also has its exact place. The "lord" himself installs the servant.[54] So it is not by chance that the other instance of תמך in DtIsa should be

---

46 See *HALOT* s.v., with lit.

47 Cf. the Greek translations: for 41:10, LXX μὴ πλανῶ, α′ ἐπικλίνου, σ′ ἀπατηθῇς, ϑ′ παρειου; 41:23, ϑαυμασόμεϑα. For the substance, see Ezekiel's reaction at his installation (Ezek 1:28; 2:2), and Paul's according to Acts 9:3-4. See Jörg Jeremias, *Theophanie* (2d ed., 1976) 1, 18, 20ff., 90, 160.

48 A. S. van der Woude, "אמץ ʾmṣ to be strong," *TLOT* 1:158 [*THAT* 1:210].

49 For Joshua, Deut 3:28 *Piel*; 31:7 *Qal* (cf. v. 6); Josh 1:6 *Qal*; Solomon, 1 Chr 22:13; 28:20 *Qal*.

50 See also H.-J. Kraus, *Psalms 60–150* (1989) 207–10

on Psalm 89 [*Psalmen* 2 (5th ed. 1978) 621–24].

51 See also 1 Cor 16:13.

52 See in contrast Isa 41:6, where the reference is to human activity (always otherwise as a divine act in DtIsa: 41:13, 14; 44:2; 49:8; 50:7, 9).

53 Or should the *Hiphil* be translated: "and he let my mouth touch"?

54 Fohrer (37–38) has seen this particularly well: "Since the expression means originally 'to install in an office' . . . it is also simultaneously to be seen in relation to Israel's description as *servant*—that is, as

found at the beginning of the first Servant of God text (Isa 42:1), which again has to do with the installation of a "servant."[55]

God's right hand is more precisely defined through צִדְקִי (*sidqî*) ("my righteousness, my salvation"), that is, Yahweh has seized Israel/Jacob, his servant, by his "saving right hand." This is the only passage in the whole OT where this combination is found.[56] It is peculiar to the context in the book of DtIsa, for which צֶדֶק *ṣedeq* is a key concept. In chap. 41 it establishes a parallel between Cyrus—צֶדֶק calls or "follows his foot" (v. 2)—and the servant, whom the right hand צִדְקִי grasps. In both cases "righteousness, salvation" issues from the same source. What concerns the servant is as real as that which concerns Cyrus. If the text is seen in context in this way, it is clear that this closer definition already yields the level of interpretation in which this servant is Israel.

If v. 10 is the core or essence of an installation, we may ask what other elements also belong to the installation. The *speech of encouragement* is one of them. It can contain a brief or more extensive assurance, given by the designator to the one designated.[57] It has to do with the promise of authority and help in the difficulties of administering the office to which he has been appointed. With these presuppositions, vv. 11-13 can be understood as a speech of encouragement. Verses 11-12 list the possible trials to which the servant will be exposed.

Verse 13 gives the reason why these trials will be surmounted.

If the servant has enemies, these are "men" (vv. 11, 12, אֲנָשִׁים). That suggests that here an individual is confronted by many people. One has the impression that there is a buildup from "be angry,"[58] "to burn with anger," by way of "legal dispute" (רִיב) to "downright conflict"[59] and "strife." It is a pattern of the way things go among human beings, and in this sense it could equally well be found in a wisdom context.[60] The terms point to the personal sphere rather than to a war.[61] The motif of a threat by "enemies" can also be found in the prayers of complaint of the individual in the Psalter.[62] The catchword "legal dispute" permits an even more precise reference to the "prayers of those accused but innocent."[63] The description in vv. 11-12 of the servant's difficulties would allow us to infer a complaint, while the assurances would suggest a prayer for help. But we must take into account the special situation of the present context, which has to do with the "servant" and his installation.

This being said, the terminology and the complex of ideas suggest a comparison between this passage and the so-called confessions of Jeremiah. The confessions presuppose that Jeremiah is involved in a legal dispute.[64]

---

one specially authorized by God." Why Elliger on this passage immediately withdraws from his observation that a gesture is meant is not clear to me: "But his answer is not merely a gesture but in a deeper sense a response through action."

55 In 42:1 it is constructed with בְּ. See below on that passage.

56 See Merendino, "Literarkritisches, Gattungskritisches und Exegetisches zu Jes 41,8-16," *Bib* 53 (1972) 9.

57 See K. Baltzer, *Die Biographie der Propheten* (1975) under "Ermutigungsrede" ("speech of encouragement"): Gideon (Judg 6:16), 33; Moses (Exod 3:12), 41; (Exod 4:11 and 12), 42; Jeremiah (Jer 1:8), 117; (Jer 1:17-19), 121–22; Ezekiel (Ezek 2:3—3:11), 131.

58 *Niphal* participle of חרה, "to become or be hot," "to become angry." Cf. 45:24; cj. 45:16. *Hiphil* Job 19:11; Sir 51:19. *Hitpael* Ps 37:1, 7-8; Sir 11:9. Both G. Driver and North read the *Qal* participle from נהר, "breathe angrily"; see *BHS*.

59 מַצּוֹת from נצה; see Exod 2:13: "When he went out the next day, he saw two Hebrew men fighting; and

he said to the one who was in the wrong, 'Why do you strike your fellow?'" Cf. Deut 25:11; 2 Sam 14:6.

60 Cf. Juvenal *Satire* 15.33–58:
First insults and curses
sound the trumpet for battle,
stirring their hearts with fury,
then with answering shout
fierce battle is joined
but, in default of weapons, a battle of fists
(*The Satires of Juvenal*, trans. C. Plumb, London: Panther, 1968).

61 Duhm (278 on this passage) makes a correct observation when he writes: "Israel is thought of as a private person whom ill-disposed neighbors attack, compelling him to go to law."

62 H. Gunkel and J. Begrich, *Einleitung in die Psalmen* (1933) 196. For an example cf. Psalm 22.

63 H. Schmidt, *Das Gebet des Angeklagten im AT* (1928). For an example cf. Psalms 7 and 35.

64 Jer 11:20: "Yahweh of hosts judges righteously . . . to you I have put forward my case (רִיבִי)" (cf. 15:18;

The point at issue is his conduct of his office.[65] He is innocent and can therefore claim the help of his Lord.[66] His opponents[67] are threatened with a curse.[68] In the end the prophet is endorsed. Closest to the present text in these confessions is Jer 15:19-20,[69] where Jeremiah is once more confirmed in his office. He is exhorted to stand firm, even in the face of hostility. The section closes with encouraging promises. The reference back in this text to Jeremiah's installation as it is described in Jeremiah 1 is striking.

With these presuppositions, Isa 41:9b-13 can be interpreted as a text in the tradition of prophecy.[70] It begins with the confirmation of the "servant" *as* servant. At the beginning, in v. 9, he is called "my servant." At the end of v. 10 it is obvious that "Yahweh, your God" is imagined as speaking. The title "servant of Yahweh" (עֶבֶד יהוה) is not yet actually pronounced here, but it is already implicit. The direct address by God as Lord is decisive for the rank of the person named, as it is in the other installation accounts in the OT.[71]

In this way the perfect tenses in vv. 9 and 10 ("I have chosen you . . . not despised . . . strengthened . . . helped . . . seized by my saving right hand") acquire their meaning as references to the past. As far as the present is concerned, and from now on, the same reason for assurance is once more given in v. 13: "who seizes your right hand" and "who says to you: Do not be afraid!" But here it is

not some numinous terror that is meant; it is fear of quite specific human enemies (vv. 11 and 12). They are going to be destroyed. The text of vv. 9b-13 puts into words the experience that as God's servant a prophet can count on the help of his or her Lord. The conclusion in v. 13: "I have helped you" is therefore a good summing up. It also already prepares the transition to v. 14.

The text can therefore be understood in the prophetic tradition as a scene in which the human "servant" is installed by the divine "Lord." But the very first sentence in v. 8 already lifts the interpretation to a new level: "But you Israel (are) my servant." Here, placed emphatically at the beginning, we have the name "Israel," instead of the sequence Jacob/Israel, which is otherwise usual in DtIsa.[72] By way of v. 8, the "servant" is interpreted as a collective.

The problem of a collective or individual interpretation is therefore already posed in the very first passage in DtIsa's book where Israel is called "servant." Statements about the "servant" can be related to Israel and vice versa. But one must also be aware that in the dramatic performance "Israel" could still simultaneously be imagined and presented as an individual person.

■ **8-9a** These verses begin by addressing Israel as "servant." This address contains the assurance of the election that has already taken place, thus corresponding to

---

18:19; cj. 20:12); 15:10: "A man of strife and contention to the whole land."

65 Jer 11:21: "You shall not prophesy in the name of Yahweh"; 15:11, 15; 17:15-16; 18:20; 20:10.

66 Jer 15:11, 15ff.; 17:14-16.

67 Jer 11:21: "The men of Anathoth"; 20:10:"All my close friends" (כֹּל אֱנוֹשׁ שְׁלֹמִי).

68 Jer 11:22-23; 17:18; 18:21, 23.

69 Jer 15:19-21:
    Therefore thus says Yahweh:
      If you repent, I will let you stand before me again.
      If you let what is noble and not what is mean go
        out of your mouth,
      you shall serve me as my mouth.
    Then they will turn to you and you will not turn to
        them.
    And I will make you for this people a bronze, an
        insurmountable wall.
      Though they fight against you
      They will not prevail over you,
    for I am at your side
      to help you

and to save you—saying of Yahweh—
and will save you out of the hand of the wicked
and will deliver you from the fist of the violent.
    (trans. following W. Rudolph, *Jeremia* [1968]).

70 Comparable in function among the Servant texts are Isa 49:4, 5; 50:5b-9.

71 See K. Baltzer, *Die Biographie der Propheten* (1975) 219, under the catchword "unmediated relation to God."

72 Isa 40:27; 41:14; 42:24; 43:1, 22, 28; 44:1, 5, 21, 23; 45:4; 46:3; 48:1, 12; 49:5, 6; see Merendino, "Literarkritisches, Gattungskritisches und Exegetisches zu Jes 41,8-16," *Bib* 53 (1972) 4–5; L. Boadt, "Isaiah 41:8-13: Notes on Poetic Structure and Style," *CBQ* 35 (1973) 27, with reference to S. Gevirtz, *Patterns in the Early Poetry of Israel* (1963) 53.

the prophetic *vocation oracle*. The reason is given in an explicit reference to the tradition of the patriarchs. In Jacob, Israel is already present. For Genesis, Jacob is the bearer of blessing.[73] To him the promises given to Abraham are transferred.[74] But Ps 105:6 explicitly calls Jacob "the chosen one" (בְּחִיר),[75] and parallel to this is the description of Abraham as "servant" (עַבְדּוֹ; cf. v. 42). The psalm is especially interesting because it links the early traditions with the present in a similar way to the passage we are considering.[76] Yahweh is Lord over the whole world; he keeps his covenant and remains faithful. "His people" are "his chosen ones."[77] To them the land is promised. It is possible that the election tradition had long been associated with Jacob, in the context of faith in "the God of the fathers."[78] Pronouncements about the choosing of the king (especially David and his dynasty)[79] and the election of Jerusalem and Zion[80] are frequent in the OT; any mention of the divine election of priests is more rare.[81] It is noticeable that DtIsa looks back to the era before the formation of the nation, an era not affected by the collapse of national and cultic existence through the exile. He relates election to Israel as a people, as Deuteronomy and the literature dependent

on it had also done in its different way.[82] Election stresses the unique nature of Israel's existence, its commitment, and the special protection under which it stands. In DtIsa election is mediated neither through the institution of the monarchy nor through the sanctuary. One cannot expect this if, as in the present text, Israel itself is addressed as servant and is confirmed in its function.

Descent from Abraham, finally, also belongs to Israel's legitimation as servant. Only a few passages in the prophetic books mention Abraham,[83] so the reference here strikes a particular note. A ruler asserts his legitimation through an appeal to his dynasty; but Israel claims this legitimation as "Abraham's seed/offspring." The "many" appeal to the "one." They are the fulfillment of the promise given to the patriarchs.

It is not quite certain how אֹהֲבִי should be translated. It can be literally rendered: "who loves me (Yahweh)"[84] or "whom I (Yahweh) love."[85] Either seems possible. I myself believe that the second translation, with Yahweh as subject, is the more probable. In the text אֹהֲבִי, "my friend," stands in apposition to "*my* servant." The installation in the first Servant of God text (42:1) is comparable.[86] There too the commitment is from Yahweh's

---

73   Gen 27:1-29; 30:27, 30; 32:27-28 (26-27); 33:11; 48:8-9.

74   Gen 28:13-14; cf. 12:2-3.

75   See here *BHS* and the commentaries.

76   See K. Koch, "Zur Geschichte der Erwählungsvorstellung in Israel," *ZAW* 67 (1955) [1956] 205–26, esp. 206–7 and 219ff.

77   Ps 105:42 For he remembered his holy word
             to Abraham his servant,
   v. 43 and he brought out his people with joy,
             with rejoicing his chosen ones (בְּחִירָיו).
   v. 44 He gave them the lands of the nations.
   Cf. H.-J. Kraus, *Psalms 60–150* (1989) 305ff. [*Psalmen* 2 (5th ed. 1978) 716ff.].

78   A. Alt, "The God of the Fathers," in *Essays on OT History and Religion* (1967) 59ff. ["Der Gott der Väter," in *Kleine Schriften* 1 (1968) 64ff.].

79   1 Kgs 8:16; 11:34; 2 Sam 16:18; Pss 78:67ff.; 89:4 (3), 20-21 (19-20); cf. 132:10ff.

80   Pss 132:13; 78:68. In the form of the place "which Yahweh (your) God has chosen," see Deut 12:5, 11; 14:23ff.; 16:2, 6-7, 11, 15-16; 17:8, 10; 18:6; 26:2; and frequently.

81   Deut 18:5; 21:5; Pss 65:5 (4); 105:26.

82   Deut 7:6-8; 10:12ff.; 1 Kgs 3:8. Cf. H. Wildberger, "בחר *bḥr* to choose," *TLOT* 1:209–26; on the present text, 219–20 [*THAT* 1:275–300; on the present text: 290]; G. E. Mendenhall, *IDB* 2:76–82; H. Seebass,

"בָּחַר *bāchar*," *TDOT* 2:73–87 [*ThWAT* 1:592–608]; G. E. Wright, *The Old Testament Against Its Environment* (1950) 46–54; H. H. Rowley, *The Biblical Doctrine of Election* (1950); T. C. Vriezen, *Die Erwählung Israels nach dem Alten Testament* (1953); K. Koch, "Zur Geschichte der Erwählungsvorstellung in Israel," *ZAW* 67 (1956) 205–26.

83   Apart from 51:2, where Abraham is called "your father" (in contrast to 63:16), only Ezek 33:24. Isa 29:22, Jer 33:26 and Mic 7:20 are considered to be "secondary" (see Elliger on this passage). It is noticeable that Jer 33:23-26 resembles DtIsa in its semantic field, but that in its hope for rulers from the two families of Jacob and David it arrives at a different political decision.

84   Thus Westermann.

85   Elliger (138) points out that in 48:14 and 43:4 Yahweh is also the subject of אהב, and further that the LXX translates: ὃν ἠγάπησα; Aquila: ἀγαπητοῦ μου, and in comparison 2 Chr 20:7, τῷ ἠγαπημένῳ σου.

86   "Look there: my servant whose hand I take, my chosen one (in whom) my soul delights (רָצְתָה נַפְשִׁי בְּחִירִי)." Cf. Sir 46:13 on Samuel as prophet: Ἠγαπημένος ὑπὸ κυρίου αὐτοῦ (רצוי || אהוב) according to *HALOT* 3:1281 [*HALAT* 4:1195] on רצה). See also 1 Chr 28:4.

side first of all. What is meant, then, is the love that Abraham experienced, so that he could be called "friend."[87]

Abraham is called[88] "from the furthest ends of the earth."[89] This, of course, is viewed from the traditional perspective of Jerusalem, for which—if we follow the account in Genesis—Ur and Haran are far-off countries. K. Koch assumes that there is a connection with a "concept of creation" and links this with the notion of "unknown remoteness and what is uncanny and void."[90]

But anyone who can call someone else to his service even in a far-off place is also exerting sovereignty there. Consequently there is a cross-reference here to 41:5, where "the ends of the earth" tremble at the acts of God. The call of the prophet Isaiah occurs in the holy place in the land. Jeremiah does not leave the land voluntarily. That is why Ezekiel's installation at the river Chebar, in the far-off, impure country, is so surprising—no less surprising than Paul's call outside Damascus.

As far as content goes, what is stated here can be interpreted as pointing to Abraham. All this has already been said about him. But syntactically the declarations can be directly related to "Israel." Israel now receives its call in the alien land, no less than before. Wherever it may find itself, it is not cut off from the rule of its God. That is why the assurance that Israel can—once again—view itself as "servant" is "a salvation oracle." It implies the promise of protection from the side of its Lord, as well as its own obligation to serve him.

■ **9b** Verse 9b looks initially like a repetition of v. 8a. But here the assurance of election is linked with the abjura-

tion of rejection. We know from a whole series of texts that the question whether the collapse of national existence and the exile were to be interpreted as rejection by Yahweh was the subject of discussion in Israel. Opinions apparently differed.[91] The book of Lamentations closes with the question (5:22): "Have you utterly rejected us?" (מָאֹס מְאַסְתָּנוּ).[92] But Leviticus 26, the end of the Holiness Code, justifies the exile on the grounds of the people's transgressions, and goes on: "Yet even then, when they are in the land of their enemies, I have not rejected them (מאס), or abhorred them (געל), so as to destroy them utterly by breaking my covenant with them; for I Yahweh am their God; I will remember on their behalf the covenant with their forefathers."[93] This passage too holds on to the reminder of, and retrospective bond with, the covenant with the patriarchs (v. 42) and the exodus generation (v. 44).

The proclamation in the DtIsa text that Israel is "not rejected" means that a decision has been made: the relationship with God has not in principle been ended. But in the light of this presupposition Israel had to address and come to terms with the exile in a different way. It is here that the statement about "redemption" has its place (see the comment on 41:14), as well as in the conceptual complex of the relationship between "lord" and "servant."[94]

We may therefore say that three complementary levels of interpretation can be discovered in the text of 41:8-13:

---

87 This corresponds to the understanding of the Koran, Sura 4:125; see Young, 82, n. 17: "'And who is better in respect to religion than he who has submitted himself (lit., his face) to Allah, while he is doing good and he follows the faith (lit., word) of Abraham the Upright, and God took Abraham as a friend (ḥalîl).' Actually, the word means *he who loves me,* the suffix being objective." Cf. 2 Chr 20:7; Jas 2:23.

88 חזק Hiphil is probably "to take the hand," corresponding to 42:6; 51:18 (cf. 41:13; 45:1). The parallel to chap. 42, esp. v. 6, sugggests that in the chiastic formulation חזק Hiphil–קרא has here also to do with call and installation.

89 אָצִיל is a hapax legomenon. The *parallelismus membrorum* suggests that it means "furthest parts" (see *HALOT* s.v.).

90 Koch, "Zur Geschichte der Erwählungsvorstellung in Israel," *ZAW* 67 (1955) 219–20.

91 See also Jer 33:23-26 for the contrasting of בחר and מאס.

92 Cf. Ps 89:39-40; 2 Kgs 17:20.

93 Following K. Elliger, *Leviticus* (1966); cf. Jer 14:19-22. There the catchwords "reject" (מאס), "abhor" (געל), "remember the covenant" (זכר ברית) also occur; see further Jer 31:37.

94 See K. Baltzer, "Liberation from Debt Slavery," in *Ancient Israelite Religion: FS F. M. Cross* (1987) 478–84; idem, "Moses Servant of God and the Servants," in *The Future of Early Christianity: FS H. Koester* (1991) 121–30.

1. "Lord—servant," in their everyday sense;
2. "Yahweh the Lord—his servant," in the sense of the prophetic tradition in particular;
3. "Yahweh the Lord—Israel as his servant," in the sense of this DtIsa text.

Common to all three levels is the act of installation. The lord-servant relationship becomes the sociomorpheme with whose help Israel's particular situation in relation to its God can be presented and reflected.

Complicated though the evolution and structure of the text are, in its final version it has nevertheless acquired a strikingly unified form. Various scholars have noted that the section has rhythmical characteristics.[95] In this relatively short section, eighteen words end with the second person masculine suffix. In the present MT at least, the *kā* (ךָ) echoes throughout; it may even have already been the earlier pronounciation.[96] It contrasts with the fourfold *î* (יִ) of the first person masculine singular suffix ("*my* servant"; twice "*my* friend"; "*I*"). But this is not merely a superficial literary device. The correspondence between the "you" of the servant and the "I" of God is the real theme of the passage. What applied "earlier" in his election (cf. Gen 28:13) now applies "anew" to the servant Israel/Jacob. This is confirmed in the heavenly sphere. In this section, which is so intimately interwoven with the content and theology of the whole book, the hand of the author whom we call Deutero-Isaiah can be traced with particular clarity.

---

95 See here J. Muilenburg, "A Study in Hebrew Rhetoric: Repetition and Style," *Congress Volume: Copenhagen 1953* (VTSup l; 1953) 97–111; further L. Boadt, "Isaiah 41:8-13: Notes on Poetic Structure and Style," *CBQ* 35 (1973) 26–34, esp. 33–34. "The investigation of the structure of Isa 41:8-13 has revealed a prolific use of poetical devices: chiasm, parallelism, word repetition, inclusions, metrical changes, reversal of fixed pairs, alliteration, asso-nance, and end-rhyme. . . . The evidence indicates that a high degree of craftsmanship is involved" (34).

96 See D. N. Freedman and F. M. Cross, *Early Hebrew Orthography* (1952) 65–67.

41 "Do not be afraid, you worm Jacob, people of Israel!" (41:14)

B. 1. 41:14-16
Double Divine Oracle:
Jacob/Israel as "Worm" and "Threshing Sledge"

14 Do not be afraid, you worm Jacob, people[a]
    of Israel!
  I have helped you—saying of Yahweh—
  and your redeemer is the Holy One of Israel.

15 See, I have appointed you to be a threshing
        sledge,
  new, with many teeth.
  You shall thresh mountains and crush them,
  and you shall make hills like chaff.
16 You shall winnow them, and a wind will
        raise them up,
  and a storm will scatter them.

  But you shall rejoice over Yahweh,
  in the Holy One of Israel you shall glory.

14[a] See the comment below.

■ **14-16** These verses join immediately onto vv. 8-13. It is the same scene; Yahweh is speaking to Israel. The same catchwords occur too: "Do not be afraid" (vv. 10, 14); "I have helped you" (vv. 10, 14).[97] In the framework of the installation, this section ends with an oracle. Oracles are frequent in installations. One instance is the installation of Jeremiah, in which a special commission is formulated in two "parables," the branch of the almond tree and the boiling pot, each of them containing a wordplay.[98] In the present text there are also two metaphors in which word and image coincide: Jacob/Israel as "worm" (v. 14) and the "threshing sledge" (vv. 15-16). In both cases it is quite probable that we can no longer fully understand the connection and the possible allusions. The same is true today in the case of political caricatures, even if they are only a few years old. So the interpretation can be no more than an attempt.

■ **14** In the OT the word "worm" (תּוֹלַעַת) is associated with a feeling of revulsion. Worms feed on the dead (Isa 14:11; 66:24; see also Exod 16:30).[99] If a human being is called a worm, this is an expression of contempt (Ps 22:7)[100] or disdain (Job 25:6). So does Jacob himself feel that he is a "worm," or is this the way he is regarded? We can also ask if this is the opinion of the world around, or if it is resentment against the *gōlâ* in exile on the part of the people who had remained in the land. "Creeping things" are cultically impure,[101] and it is the most extreme contrast possible when Yahweh, "the Holy One of Israel," addresses this "worm Jacob" and promises him his help.

97 It is striking that in this section the MT treats Yahweh as feminine. But this may be connected with the feminine "worm" (תּוֹלַעַת).

98 שׁקד, "branch of an almond tree" and "be awake" (Jer 1:11); נפח, from "the heating of the pot" and "disaster" (Jer 1:13-14); see also Amos 8:1-3: קַיִץ, "harvest" and "end." The connection with the oracle tradition requires investigation here.

99 The תּוֹלַעַת שָׁנִי, the scale insect (*lecanium illicis*) from which carmine is extracted, forms a special group. תּוֹלֵעָה is then the color red (often in Exod 25:4; 26:1, 31, 36; and frequently elsewhere), or red fabric (see also Isa 1:18). It shows that the writer is not necessarily thinking of "worm" or "maggot" but rather of vermin (see also Deut 28:39).

100 Ps 22:7-9 (6-8) (trans. H.-J. Kraus, *Psalms 1-59* (1988) [*Psalmen* 1 (5th ed. 1978)]):

7 (6) But I am a worm (תּוֹלַעַת) and not a man,
    the ridicule of men, despised by the people.
8 (7) All who see me scoff at me,
    screw up their mouth, shake their head.
9 (8) "He put it in the hands" of Yahweh
    (גֹּל אֶל־יהוה, or should the reading be
    גַּאֲלוֹ? see *BHK*), let him free him,
    let him rescue him,
    for he is obviously well disposed to him.

101 Lev 11:10, 23; cf. Acts 10:11ff.

The next two words, מְתֵי יִשְׂרָאֵל,[102] can be translated: "people of Israel." This phrase often has the connotation of "a small number of people" (מְתֵי מִסְפָּר, Gen 34:30 and frequently; Deut 26:5, מְתֵי מְעָט; "remnant," Deut 28:62). There is therefore nothing in the wording to prevent us from interpreting the phrase "worm Jacob" here as meaning: (these are) "the few people of Israel." This is especially true if with Gen 34:30, Ps 105:12 = 1 Chr 16:19 and above all Deut 26:5 the reference to the Jacob tradition is clear, and with Deut 4:27 (cf. 28:62) the reference to the exile. 1QIsa[a] already has מיתי, probably a plural participle from מות, that is, "the dying." The translation in Aquila and Theodotion and the Vulgate's "qui mortui estis in Israel" correspond to this. Ever since Ewald, the word has generally been emended to רִמַּת, which is also a kind of creeping thing, mentioned in Isa 14:11 and Job 25:6 parallel to תּוֹלֵעָה. But this emendation introduces no new emphasis and is hence superfluous. It would be much more important to decide the question whether, comparable with oracles, the meaning of the term תּוֹלֵעָה, "scarlet-grain coccid > scarlet cloth" (see *HALAT* 4:1568), could also play a part in the interpretation.

The help given to the despised people is justified in v. 14 on the grounds that "the Holy One of Israel" is "your redeemer" (גֹּאֲלֵךְ). Here the legal term גאל is introduced for the first time. In his lexicon, Köhler interprets the word as follows: "To lay claim to a person, a thing > claim back from an other's authority, redeem . . . buy back."[103] It is one of DtIsa's key terms,[104] and belongs to the conceptional context of "lord and servant" and "serve" (עבד).[105] The slave who has been sold by his master because of some misdemeanor will be bought back and readmitted to the relationship of protection and service. That is "redemption." It is both promise and requirement. Verse 14 is therefore also a summing up of what has been said in vv. 8-13. Israel can depend on help. The transference to the community as a whole of what were originally individual categories makes it possible to use such highly personal concepts, derived from family law. Before God the community is not an "it"; it is a "you."

But what is the relation of the metaphorical "worm, maggot" to the image of the threshing sledge? In order to understand this, we have to take account of the different levels of time. The installation of Jacob/Israel as servant took place in the primeval era, the era of the patriarchs—that is why the reference to Abraham in v. 8 is important. From the standpoint of this early era, everything that is thereby promised is in the future. In the situation of the drama, the audience is taken back to the beginnings, and becomes contemporary with the inception of Jacob/Israel's history. In Jacob the collective is already present. The listeners know and can witness to the fact that the promise to Jacob/Israel has been fulfilled. Yahweh has chosen and has led along marvelous ways, even though Jacob/Israel was "a worm."

■ **15-16** With the word "See," a new section begins. Jacob/Israel is no longer a "worm"; he is now a "threshing sledge."[106] If we note the connection with oracles, it will be clear that שׂים has to be translated by "destine" or "appoint,"[107] not by "make into." At the installation the task is laid down and the history determined.[108] But how ought we to understand the tense of שַׂמְתִּיךְ? In the "installation" of Jacob/Israel it is a kind of *perfectum propheticum*: "I appoint you to be a threshing sledge." It is directed toward the future, although for the listeners it is in the past. Consequently it is also correct if we hear the divine speech in the perfect tense: "I have appointed you to be a threshing sledge." In this case the pronouncement would be a summing up of Jacob/Israel's history.

But I am not certain that vv. 15-16 as a whole should be heard in a positive sense. It could well be that one oracle ("worm") is positive, and the other ("threshing sledge") negative.[109] This becomes understandable once we assume that here too there is a reference to traditions such as the Hosea tradition. In Hos 10:9-17[110] peaceful agricultural activity (v. 11: "Ephraim [was] a trained

---

102 For detailed textual criticism see A. Schoors, *I Am God Your Saviour* (1973) 59–61.

103 KB (1st ed. 1953) 162, drawing esp. on J. J. Stamm, *Erlösen und Vergeben im AT* (1940) 27ff.

104 Isa 43:14; 44:6, 24; 47:4; 48:17; 49:7, 26; 54:5, 8.

105 See K. Baltzer, "Liberation from Debt Slavery," in *Ancient Israelite Religion: FS F. M. Cross* (1987). 477–84.

106 This term is otherwise found in the OT only when Araunah gives the "threshing sledges" to David when the latter buys the threshing floor at Jerusalem. Cf. 2 Sam 24:22; 1 Chr 21:23.

107 See Exod 9:5; Job 34:23; cf. Ps 104:9; Prov 8:29.

108 At his installation Jeremiah's fate is announced in images and wordplay (Jer 1:18).

109 Isaiah also receives an unfavorable oracle at his

heifer that loved to thresh . . . Judah must plough, Jacob harrow"; v. 12: "Sow according to the law of the covenant and you will reap in accordance with faithfulness to the covenant") is contrasted with false trust in "'your chariots', in the multitude of your warriors." According to Hosea, this will bring about Israel's downfall.

There can be no doubt that Israel and its kings "threshed" other peoples.[111] But nevertheless, among the "crimes against humanity" listed in the sayings against the foreign nations, Amos also names "threshing with threshing sledges of iron" (1:3). Hosea declares (9:1): "Do not rejoice, O Israel! Do not exult as other nations do!" Here "rejoice" (גיל) is used as it is in our present text (v. 16). H. W. Wolff describes the special character of this term (*Hosea*, 153): "The 'rejoicing' is expressed by noisy applause and enthusiastic commotion (cf. Judg 16:23; 2 Sam 6:12) . . . [it] is expressed by shrill, unrestrained screams. . . . It is evident from [Hos] 10:5b that the screams are a special part of the bull cult. Thus it is not surprising that גיל, as it is first used by Hosea, is found neither in the Pentateuch, nor in the Deuteronomistic History, and that the prophets Amos, Micah, Jeremiah . . . and Ezekiel strictly avoid the word;[112] Isaiah uses it once (9:2)." Perhaps DtIsa also thinks that this form of victorious song is inappropriate for the praise of Yahweh.[113] It is a "rejoicing for idols!" This is not the way to praise "the Holy One of Israel." On the contrary, it is actually "self-praise," as the text points out (הלל *Hitpael*).[114]

The "installation" of Jacob/Israel (4:8-16)—personified as "servant"—would then, according to this analysis, encapsulate a recapitulation of Israel's history. The primeval era is presented as a time when the weak, the despised, the little flock were marvelously guided. This

is of course also said as hope and model for the present. The time in which Israel could "thresh"—the time of the kings—must be viewed critically. It ends in "false jubilation."

These presuppositions make the dramatic switch from v. 16 to v. 17 comprehensible: "The poor and needy seek water and there is none." For this has been preceded by the catastrophe. But that raises the question of how the servant Jacob/Israel can be restored to his relationship with his Lord. It is from this tension that the next scenes live, up to 43:1ff., the renewed installation of Jacob/Israel. The wheel comes full circle in 44:21. There the chorus raises the proper jubilation (44:23).

The text contains a few hints about the mode of performance. With the beginning of the image in 41:14, the text shifts from the suffix of the second person masculine singular to the second person feminine singular. This makes clear that with v. 13 the address to the servant as the personification of Jacob/Israel is at an end. If a feminine personification now follows, this could be connected with the feminine gender of the image "worm"; but the feminine is still used for "threshing sledge" as well. One possible explanation, it seems to me, is that here a female chorus enters or, to be more exact, that the "images" are mimetically presented in dance. The repeated "see" (הִנֵּה) at the beginning of v. 15 speaks in favor of this: here is something that can be shown and something that can be seen. The activities—threshing, grinding, making like chaff, winnowing—easily lend themselves to a presentation in visual terms. The rhythm in vv. 15-16a is $3 \times 3 + 3$. A comparison with Greek shows that a triadic strophe division is typical of dithyrambs and triumphal songs. In the dithyramb a chorus of women dances for Dionysos, with the shrill cries that were also a feature of the paean. The גיל of

---

installation: Isa 6:9-11. It is the biblical problem about "the hardening of the heart" (cf. Exod 4:21; 7:13; 10:20; 14:17; 1 Sam 6:6; and frequently). Cf. J. Jeremias, *Hosea* (1983), on Hos 11:7-11.

110 On the text see H. W. Wolff, *Hosea* (1974), esp. 185–86 [*Hosea* (3d ed. 1976), esp. 197].

111 See Judg 8:7, 12; Hab 3:12; Mic 4:13; cf. Mic 4:14 (5:1).

112 One ought probably to add: in distinction from the tradition of the Psalms. DtIsa otherwise uses the expression only in 49:13, where the earth is told to "sing for joy." But there it is a question of the peaceful return to the home country.

113 It is therefore understandable that LXX, or the text on which LXX is based, should have changed the reading here (see also Elliger on this passage).

114 Elliger sees this correctly, but then declares: "The *Hitpael* is not reflexive."

v. 16 would again be explicable against this background: "rejoicing over Yahweh" or "unrestrained screams"? Acoustically too, it is conceivable that the "false jubilation over victory" could have been presented by way of the chorus.[115]

But after the orgiastic dance, the transition from v. 16 to v. 17 is then also convincing. After the collapse, "the poor and needy seek water, but there is none. Their tongue is parched with thirst." This too could undoubtedly be mimetically presented, if indeed the textual complex does not actually extend directly as far as, and including, v. 20.

---

115 For the whole passage cf. Exod 15:21-27; 32:17ff.

41

"The needy and the poor seek water . . ." (41:17)

B. 2. 41:17-20
**Double Scene: Description of the Misery on Earth—
Resolve in Heaven for Salvation**

17   The needy and the poor seek water, but
           there is none.
    Their tongue is parched with thirst.
    I, Yahweh, will hear them,
    (I) the God of Israel will not forsake them.

18   I will open rivers on bare heights
    and wells in the midst of the valley plains.
    I will turn a steppe into a marshy pool
    and parched land into springs of water.

19   I will put cedars in the steppe,
    acacias, myrtles, and "oil trees."
    I will set cypresses in the desert,
    "plane trees"(?) and "box trees"(?) together[a]

20   so that they may see and know
    and heed and perceive together
    that the hand of Yahweh has done this,
    and the Holy One of Israel has created it.

19[a] On the various tree species see below.

The section 41:17-20 can easily be seen as a single unit;[116] the only disputed point is the degree to which it is independent of its context. Scholars agree that the genre to which the text belongs is the "salvation oracle." Begrich justifies this allocation,[117] but already sees difficulties too.[118] Von Waldow agrees, but only with some qualification.[119] Westermann has modified the genre definition by talking about a "proclamation of salvation relating to the future,"[120] instead of a salvation oracle. Elliger's criticism is more basic,[121] but his own definition of the genre is vague: he calls it a "prophetic promise."[122]

I want to start from one of Elliger's observations, however. He notes that "the needy are never actually addressed."[123] But according to the text they are present! The complex can be viewed as a kind of double scene. On the earthly level, human beings are wandering about in search of water. On the heavenly level we have a divine monologue.[124] The dramatic tension arises from the fact that, from the human viewpoint, the two levels

---

116 See also the scribe's arrangement of the text in 1QIsa[a] and [b].

117 J. Begrich, *Studien zu Deuterojesaja* (1938, reprint 1963) 15: "The following common features show that the text is a salvation oracle: in all such texts Yahweh speaks in the first person; in all of them the person seeking help is addressed in the second person; the structure clearly betrays that the text originated in the situation to which the salvation oracle belongs; and, finally, the details of the material treated often have to do with the related genres of the individual and the communal lament."

118 On the address in the second person: "Exceptions are 41:17-20 and 42:14-17, two salvation oracles for the people. But this is not a counterargument." He refers to H. Gunkel and J. Begrich, *Einleitung in die Psalmen* (1933) § 4, 14, pp. 137–38.

119 H.-E. von Waldow, "Anlass und Hintergrund der Verkündigung des Deuterojesaja" (1953) 91: "The sections Isa 41:17-19 and 42:14-16 will also belong to the same theme 'general assurances of salvation.' But here it is not easy to decide. Concrete events do not seem to be meant."

120 C. Westermann, "Sprache und Struktur der Prophetie Deuterojesajas," in *Forschung am Alten Testament* 1:120–22; also his commentary on this passage.

121 Elliger concludes (159): "But the characteristic form elements are missing."

122 Ibid., 159, 160.

123 Ibid., 159.

124 See here W. A. M. Beuken, "Mišpāṭ. The First Servant Song and Its Context," *VT* 22 (1972) 21, esp. n. 3 with lit. For Beuken, one result of the exegesis of vv. 17-20 is: "We shall come to see that this very portrayal of God as making his salvific decisions without any consultation whatsoever of men, forms a basic supposition of the first Ebed Song" (23).

do not communicate. The chorus (which presumably represents "the needy and poor") remains dumb; "their tongue is parched with thirst" (v. 17a). For this very reason they are unable to complain. Here there is no mediator between the earthly and the heavenly world.[125] Here there is no proclamation to human beings. What we have instead is an exposition, still in the heavenly sphere, of what God is going to do (vv. 18-19). It is only God's acts that will convince people when they are in distress (v. 20). Details show how carefully crafted the section is, and make its content more comprehensible.

■ **17a** This verse offers a description of the distress.[126] The syntax of the sentence can be understood in the following way. Verse 17aα is a nominative clause with a predicative participle, which stresses the enduring character of the action. Verse 17aβ emphasizes the urgency by using the perfect tense of the verb: their tongues are already parched.

The people are described as "the needy and the poor" (הָעֲנִיִּים וְהָאֶבְיוֹנִים).[127] This double formula is not found anywhere else in DtIsa, but it is by no means rare in other texts.[128] It describes men and women who are low in the social scale,[129] without any influence, and whose rights are restricted.[130] They suffer under the powerful. Because they can no longer help themselves, they are dependent on special protection. This is an obligation laid on the community.

Because God is a just ruler, he takes up the cause of the underprivileged. In the Psalter especially, God's help for "the poor and needy" is frequently acknowledged in intercession and thanksgiving.[131] God is on the side of the people without any rights. If one wishes to differentiate between the two terms here, עָנִי points more to being "bowed down or oppressed,"[132] אֶבְיוֹן to "neediness."[133] So when DtIsa uses these terms for the people,[134] their semantic scope already indicates that what he is talking about is not merely that they have no water. But this already raises the question about the link with the tradition to which the text belongs.

The *topos* "the people have no water to drink" plays an important part in the exodus tradition. We need only think of the places where the people rested in the desert: Marah (Exod 15:22-26), Massah, and Meribah (Exod 17:1-7; Num 20:1-13).[135] We must expect the *topos* to have a significant place in DtIsa's announcement of the new exodus too. But we must first examine the present text in order to see whether it is linked with another tradition complex as well.

One possibility is to see it against the background of the drought described in Jeremiah 14–15. There we are told about a service of intercession held because the rains had failed. Jer 14:2-9 quotes an extensive communal prayer of complaint. It describes the distress suffered by the different classes and groups in town and country,

125 Elliger writes (159): "The prophet is addressed; that is his secret experience; hence the people are referred to in the third person, but the prophet passes on to them what he has heard." But the aspect Elliger is referring to requires further explanation. In drama too the author and the audience "know" more than the actors. For the scene, see also the presentation of people seeking help from the vizier in N. de Garis Davies, *The Tomb of Rekh-mi-Re at Thebes* (1943, reprint 1973) 68–69 and pl. 72.

126 One really has to hear the verse in Hebrew. I would therefore agree with C. Stuhlmueller (*Creative Redemption in Deutero-Isaiah* [1970] 70–71 n. 229): "BH suggests changes in TM *metri causa*, but the alliteration and assonance are too exquisite to be tampered with: the four opening words ending in *îm* (the long seeking), and the quick reversal *maim wā'ain*; then the rasping, dry sound of seven successive *ā* vowels." See also North, 101.

127 For the lit. see J. J. Stamm's account, "Ein Vierteljahrhundert Psalmenforschung," *ThR* n.s. 23 (1955) 55–60; also the excursus in Kraus, *Psalms*

1–59 (1988) 93–94 [*Psalmen* 1 (5th ed. 1978) 82–83]. Further E. Gerstenberger, "אבה *'bh* to want," *TLOT* 1:17–18 [*THAT* 1:23–25], and R. Martin-Achard, "ענה *'nh* II to be destitute," *TLOT* 2:933–94 [*THAT* 2:344–46; G. J. Botterweck, "אֶבְיוֹן *'ebhyôn*," *TDOT* 1:27–41 [*ThWAT* 1:28–43].

128 Pss 35:10; 37:14; 40:18 (17); 70:6 (5); 74:21; 86:1; 109:16, 22; Deut 24:14; Jer 22:16; Ezek 16:49; 18:12; 22:29; Job 24:14; Prov 31:9.

129 Lev 19:10; Ezek 22:29; Isa 58:7; Ps 74:21.

130 Isa 10:2; Zech 7:10; Job 24:9.

131 Pss 9:19 (18); 10:2, 8-10; 18:28 (27); 35:10; 74:19; Job 36:6.

132 R. Martin-Achard, "ענה *'nh* II to be destitute," *TLOT* 2:933 [*THAT* 2:344].

133 E. Gerstenberger, "אבה *'bh* to want," *TLOT* 1:17 [*THAT* 1:23]; Botterweck, "אֶבְיוֹן *'ebhyôn*," *TDOT* 1:27–41 [*ThWAT* 1:37–39].

134 See also the parallels in 49:13; cf. 14:32.

135 Cf. Pss 78:15-16; 114.

down to the animals. Reasons are given why God should intervene. But in the name of his God, the prophet Jeremiah has to proclaim judgment because of Israel's sins. The covenant is not intact (v. 21). The false gods cannot give rain (v. 22). The curse will continue until the captivity (15:2) and the annihilation (15:9). Here, in the context of the drought, the prophet Jeremiah proclaims collapse and exile. The DtIsa text would then, against the background of Jeremiah 14–15, be a retraction of earlier prophecy, a lifting of the curse.[136]

Another Jeremiah text, Jeremiah 2, is interesting as well, because there the protection given in the period of the exodus is set over against the present time of apostasy. Israel was holy (קֹדֶשׁ) for Yahweh, and that lent it protection (cf. v. 3 with Isa 41:20). In a list of attributes comparable with Isa 41:18-19, the desert is described as a dry land.[137] But in the cultivated lands Israel has exchanged Yahweh for gods who are no gods at all (vv. 8-11): "For a twofold evil did my people: they forsook me, the well of living water, in order to build cisterns, cracked cisterns that do not hold the water" (v. 13; translation following Rudolph). The theme "water—drought" is also given different variations.[138] Here we see how in

DtIsa the exodus theme is interwoven with others.

The description of the distress reaches a climax if we also hear an echo of Isa 5:8-24, and 10:1-4 here. In Isa 5:13 the upper class is named because of its economic practices:

> Therefore my people must go into exile,
>   since it has no insight,
> and its nobles are "robbed of strength" by hunger,
>   and its populace is dried up completely by thirst
>   (translation from H. Wildberger, *Isaiah*).

Isa 41:17 would then be an illustration of how "the common people" (הָמוֹן) are faring, the people who in the text are called "the needy and poor." Finally, a reference suggests itself, as Elliger thinks, to the "certain, unique event of the trek home."[139] The passage describes the fear of dying of thirst on the long march.

■ **17b** The decision to help: the earthly distress is not hidden from Yahweh. He learns directly how desperate the situation is, and he reacts. That is surely the sense of ענה.[140] The fate of the "needy and poor" is not a matter of indifference to him. The promise not "to forsake" (עזב) them belongs here too. In the tradition of the covenant, and related to Israel, the verb means the falling away, or defection, from Yahweh and the breach

---

136 See also McKenzie, 32, with reference to Isa 34:8-15.
137 Jer 2:6-7:
>   "Where is Yahweh, who brought us up out of the
>   land of Egypt,
>   who led us in the desert, in the land of the
>   steppes
>   and gorges, in dry and gloomy country,
>   in the land through which no one passes?"
>   It was I who brought you into the fruitful garden
>   land."
(trans. following W. Rudolph, *Jeremia* [1968]; see the comment in B. J. van der Merwe, *Pentateuchtradisies in de Prediking van Deuterojesaja* [1955] 54–55.)
138 See also vv. 18; 31; 3:3.
139 Elliger, 169. See Dillmann, 374; also the list in C. Stuhlmueller, *Creative Redemption in Deutero-Isaiah* (1970) 272. That the text is not simply and solely a matter of the facts is also suggested by the following interpretations (to take some examples). An allegorical interpretation is attempted by E. Hessler, "Die Struktur der Bilder bei Deuterojesaja," *EvTh* 25 (1965) 360: "The action is undoubtedly directed towards 'tree planting.' We are familiar with this motif in reversed form as 'tree felling' in Isa 2:10ff.; 10:16ff.; 3:3ff. . . . In that case 'the planting of trees' would conversely be the building up of the people [with reference to Isa 60:21; 61:3 and 5:7]. . . . Even

on gentile soil, therefore, Israel will be established as Yahweh's plantation, after Yahweh himself has already opened up the water of life in the country." Cf. C. C. Torrey's spiritual interpretation, *The Second Isaiah* (1928) 317: "Spiritual blessings are here pictured in the usual and (for an oriental) most forcible way, by the figure of desert land turned into an oasis. The 'thirst' is the same which is spoken of in 55:1. See 35:6f.; 43:19ff.; 44:3 (where מים is interpreted by רוחי); 49:10." Stuhlmueller (*Redemption,* 72) talks about "combining the symbolic with the real." For a critical interpretation see J. H. Eaton, *Festal Drama in Deutero-Isaiah* (1979) 46–47.
140 See C. J. Labuschagne, "ענה *ʿnh* to answer," *TLOT* 2:927 [*THAT* 2:335–36]: "Proceeding from the assumption that *ʿnh* meant originally 'to turn around,' particularly either turning the countenance in order to display attention or turning the eyes in order to observe a person or a thing, one can deduce on semasiological grounds a basic meaning 'to react, respond.'" There may be a wordplay on הָעֲנִיִּים in v. 17a and אֶעֱנֵם in v. 17b. The sound of אֲנִי יהוה, "I (Yahweh)," suggests that v. 17bα should perhaps be included.

of the covenant.[141] If Yahweh then "forsakes" his people,[142] this means that they are cut off from salvation and life. That is true for the people as a whole, and for the individual. That is why the word has its place in the complaint.[143]

In the heavenly sphere God's decision for commitment has already been made,[144] but on earth it still has to be enacted. The decisive point is the assurance of God's presence for his people. That means hope. It is the fundamental reversal of the presuppositions that were evident in Jeremiah 14, for example.[145] DtIsa therefore belongs to the prophetic tradition in that he claims the authority to decipher the mystery of God's intentions for the future, and to testify to the turn of events that has taken place.

■ **18-19** These verses are closely knit with v. 17. The sovereign "I, Yahweh" (v. 17b) is followed by six pronouncements in the first person imperfect: "I will . . ." or "I shall. . . ." These sound like a government declaration. All the activity is God's. But in what colors is the future painted? Is the text related to the trek home, or is it referring to the restoration of the home country? Or does it embrace both?

It is worth defining more precisely the elements with which the writer is working. It is noticeable how many different terms occur in these two verses, even if some of them are difficult to define lexically. These terms can be divided into three groups:

1. Different kinds of water (the catchword was already used in 41:17a)
2. Different kinds of dry land
3. Different kinds of trees.[146]

The lists are comparable with the onomastica found in the wisdom traditions of Egypt especially. They are part of encyclopedic science. For example, they list natural phenomena in a certain order.[147] Von Rad showed the influence of these onomastica on the OT.[148] In Psalm 148 a list of this kind provides the foundation for the praise of Yahweh. Verse 9 calls on "mountains and all hills, fruit trees and all cedars (וְכָל־אֲרָזִים)" to praise him. It is noticeable that, compared with the psalm, in this DtIsa text the fruit trees are missing, whereas the cedar (אֶרֶז) is named first of all.

As a comparable text, the Priestly writing's creation account in Genesis 1 is interesting. It too is based on an onomasticon and begins with heaven and earth, proceeding to human beings. In the list for the third day, water, land, and plants are mentioned side by side, and there are again beginnings of a specification (vv. 9-13). In the book of *Jubilees,* the corresponding text expands this further, taking up other lists of a similar kind.[149] *Jubilees* distinguishes among different kinds of water, as well as among fruit trees, "groves" and the garden of Eden. If with these presuppositions in mind we come to the present DtIsa text, we shall not look first for direct geographical information about the stretch of country

141 See H. P. Stähli, "עזב ʿzb to abandon," *TLOT* 2:866–68 [*THAT* 2:249–52, esp. 251]. Cf. Deut 29:24 (25); 31:16-17; Josh 24:16, 20; Judg 2:12-14; 10:6, 10, 13; 1 Sam 8:8; 12:10; 1 Kgs 9:9; 11:33; Isa 65:11; Jer 22:9; Pss 89:31 (30); 119:53, 87; Ezra 8:22; 9:10.

142 Deut 31:17; Josh 24:20; Judg 6:13; 2 Chr 12:5; 15:2; 24:20.

143 Ps 22:2 (1); see also vv. 25, 27ff.

144 See also Deut 31:7-8.

145 Jer 14:9 was a false demand on the part of the people: "And you, Yahweh, are in the midst of us, and we are called by your name; do not forsake us"; v. 12: "Although they fast, I do not hear their cry."

146 See the list in Elliger, 158.

147 See A. H. Gardiner, *Ancient Egyptian Onomastica,* vols. 1 and 2 (1947). The onomasticon of Amenope is entitled: "The teaching . . . for learning all things that exist: what Ptah created, . . . heaven with its affairs, earth and what is in it." He lists under nos. 18–48(?) different kinds of water, under nos. 49–62 different kinds of land (Gardiner, pp. 4*–13*).

148 See G. von Rad, "Job XXXVIII and Ancient Egyptian Wisdom," in *The Problem of the Hexateuch* (1966) 281–91 ["Hiob XXXVIII und die altägyptische Weisheit," in *Wisdom in Israel: FS H. H. Rowley* (VTSup 3; 1955) 293–301; reprinted in *Gesammelte Studien zum Alten Testament* 1 (1973) 262–71].

149 *Jub.* 2:4-7: "(7) And on this day he created for them all *seas* according to their places and all *rivers* and the places for the *waters on the mountains* and *on the earth* and all the *dew* of the earth, and *seed* that is sowed, with all its crops, and *everything that is eaten,* and *the trees that bring fruit* and the *trees of the forest* and in Eden the *Garden of Eden* for their pleasure, and all plants according to their kind. And these four works he performed on the third day" (trans. following K. Berger, JSHRZ 2/3). See also *1 Enoch* 28–32; 2 Esdr 6:42.

150 Elliger, 166: "On the other hand the riddle is at once solved if one assumes that the steppe is the concrete situation of the return home." For a contrary view see H.-E. von Waldow, "Anlass und

between Mesopotamia and Judah.[150] The trees do not necessarily permit the conclusion that the writer came from Lebanon.[151] He was describing the world on the basis of what he knew, and with the help of testimonies about creation. This is also shown in v. 20 by the word ברא, which is used for the act of divine creation.[152] Since these are pronouncements about the future, this is a *new* creation. It is the utopia of a parkland with water and shade or, to adopt the originally Persian term, a "paradise."[153]

■ **20** Of decisive importance for the reception of traditions such as these in the context is the announcement of the fundamental change.[154] In this framework, the journey home from the exile is conceivable too. The change announced sets in motion a process of perception,[155] the goal of which is shared understanding[156] of God's power in creation and preservation. This gives this text its wide scope. The Lord of the whole world identifies himself with the fate of little, unimportant people and those without rights. He is able to overcome the adversities and to bring about the turn of events. Out of this contrast, the scene thrusts inescapably toward the question: "How can this happen?"

Here an ideal landscape is depicted, and this makes the similarity to other ancient utopias clear. Very close to it is the description of the temple of Zeus Triphylius given by the Greek philosopher Euhemerus (c. 300 B.C.E.). This probably goes back to Egyptian sources and has been passed down by Diodorus of Sicily (5.42-44). The trees have been selected according to their "pleasing aspect." Euhemerus mentions cypresses and plane trees first of all. The columnlike cypress and the spreading plane tree (from Gk. πλατύς, "broad")[157] form an antithetical pair. If we then turn back to Isa 41:19, בְּרוֹשׁ can perhaps be assumed to be the "cypress," which is what the LXX (κυπάρισσος) also understood it to be. But in form, the juniper (*Juniperus phoenicea*) is not as

---

Hintergrund der Verkündigung des Deuterojesaja" (1953) 217 n. 1: "In reading Isa 41:18-19, it will hardly be correct to think of the return through the desert (thus Duhm und Volz on this passage). If this was really what the writer was thinking of, Yahweh would have done better to create roads instead of swamps, and more fruit trees instead of wood and flowering plants" (etc.).

151 See Duhm, 280: "DtIsa must surely have lived in a place where he was able to see these trees, i.e., certainly not in Babylon, but more probably in Lebanon."

152 Cf. Gen 1:1.

153 See *HALOT* 3:963 [*HALAT* 3:907] under the heading פַּרְדֵּס: "Avestan *pairidaēza* rampart; a domain of the King in the Achaemenid period. . . . Late Bab. *pardēsu* . . . a marvellous garden . . . parkland Song 4:13; Qoh 2:5. . . . forest . . . Neh 2:8; . . . on [פַּרְדֵּס] in general see [*BHH* 3:]1386f." παράδεισος is used by Xenophon as a term for the royal Persian gardens (*Anabasis* 1.4.10). The LXX translates גַּן in Gen 2:8 by παράδεισος. It should at all events be noted that in DtIsa the "arboreum" belongs to the open country, and is not enclosed.

154 See Ezekiel 47, esp. vv. 7 and 12; other comparisons are Genesis 2; Ezekiel 31; Isa 60:13; Deut 8:7; Rev 22:3. Muilenburg, 459: "The transformation of nature is a central feature of Second Isaiah's eschatology (42:18-21; 48:21; 49:9-11; 55:13)."

155 The starting point here is seeing, not hearing, as so often elsewhere in the OT. Perception leads to knowledge (ידע). This is stored up in the heart (שׂים, "set, lay"). The word should probably be expanded by לִבּוֹ, "his heart," with a preposition. Cf. 41:22; 47:7; *HALOT* 2:513-15 [*HALAT* 488-89]; it should be noted that the preceding vv. 18 and 19 talk twice about Yahweh's "setting" or "putting." The result is "insight" in the literal sense, but it can also be rendered "clarity" (for שׂכל see M. Sæbø, "שׂכל *śkl* hi. to have insight," *TLOT* 3:126-72 [*THAT* 2:824-28]). Personal involvement and reflection are linked. As background I would assume wisdom anthropology, rather than a breakdown into formal categories, "recalling the paraenetic expansiveness of Deuteronomy" (thus W. Zimmerli, "Knowledge of God according to the Book of Ezekiel," in *I Am Yahweh* [1982] 54 [*Erkenntnis Gottes nach dem Buch Ezechiel*, AThANT 27 (1954) 31; reprinted in *Gottes Offenbarung, Gesammelte Aufsätze* (1963) 70]). Cf. also Prov 1:1-7; Dan 9:25.

156 See יַחְדָּו, "together"; in this way the same word used at the end of v. 19 is taken up again. Is it only those named in v. 17 that are meant, or the whole of Israel, or—following 40:5—"all flesh together" (יַחְדָּו)?

157 Curiosity suggests the question whether "plane trees" is not already an interpretation. Could the "broad" tree next to the cypress not be the pine? As a child, I learned to distinguish "closed umbrellas" (cypresses) from "open umbrellas" (pine trees).

111

different as most commentators assume. Köhler's proposal to translate the second tree, תִּדְהָר, by "plane tree" then seems in comparison not quite so impossible.[158]

Of the second pair of tree species, the myrtle is mentioned in both texts. It is valued because of its sweet-smelling oil. The ancient world was already familiar with the myrtle wreath (הֲדַס, *Myrtus communis*; Pindar 1.3.88), and in Germany it is still used in the bridal wreath.[159]

In view of all this, it will be permissible to wonder whether the "oil tree" (וְעֵץ שָׁמֶן) in the parallelism can also be explained. In Euhemerus it is the laurel. That too is a scented tree. According to Hippocrates, oil (ἔλαιον) is extracted from it, according to Theophrasus, chrism, the oil used for anointing (χρῖσμα).

But why has DtIsa used a description here and not a name? In the Greek world, the laurel (ἡ δάφνη) is definitely associated with Apollo. His temple can be called "δαφνηφορεῖον" (Athenaeus 10.424f). Among the people of Syracuse Apollo was known as "the one crowned with laurels" (δαφνίτης). The laurel belongs to the "grove." People adorned themselves and were adorned with laurel wreaths and branches. It played a part in a particular kind of round dance. So when the name of the tree is not mentioned here, the omission could have to do with DtIsa's polemic against idols.

We may assume that the first pair, cedars and acacias, is also chosen because they are an antithetical pair. The cedar has dense foliage, while the true acacia is feathery.

DtIsa resembles Euhemerus not only in his description of the trees but also in his account of the wealth of water in the region. But the differences should be noticed too. DtIsa talks about neither birds nor animals, neither human beings nor a temple. It is—still—the divine vision of a landscape. But it is aligned toward a real future.

This becomes clear when we arrive at Isa 51:3: there desert and steppe are part of Zion. The city lies in ruins. But it will once again become an Eden (cf. Gen 2:8-10; 4:16), and Yahweh's garden (cf. Gen 13:10). It is the city that lies in paradisal surroundings, not just the temple or the palace. This new city will be filled with people

rejoicing and singing. We are of course also intended to think of the Ezekiel traditions: according to Ezek 47:1-12 the spring that streams out from the temple brings water to the dry places, so that trees can grow. Ezek 36:29-38 establishes the link between new fertility and the process of perception.

Right at the end of the DtIsa text, the same theme is taken up once more, in 55:12-13. There too the subject is an ideal landscape. The cypresses and myrtles represent it. Here the exodus and the Zion traditions are finally interwoven. Conversely, 55:12-13 now also gives a hint of the way other passages were performed. If "mountains" (הֶהָרִים, masc. plur.) and "hills" (הַגְּבָעוֹת, fem. plur.) break into jubilation and all the trees of the fields clap their hands, this is also a clear stage direction for a chorus, with mimetic elements. In contrast, 41:18 has twice the feminine plural וֹת-, "rivers and wells," and twice מַיִם, "water" (masc. plur.) at the end. The observation that the trees come in pairs (3 x 2) also suggests that this may have been a scenic representation. The expansion to the number 7 (the box tree) requires a separate explanation (see below). Greek vase paintings especially show that trees could be made identifiable through twigs or wreaths, and waters through emblems. The subject of 55:12-13 is the joy of the new exodus of those who are led out—but here in peace!—in contrast to the threat to the people at the first exodus from Egypt. All the jubilation is for Yahweh's glory.

If from this point we come back once more to the three units 41:15-16, 17, and 18-20, their profile becomes even more distinct. For one of the questions that arose was whether the second oracle ("threshing sledge") given to Jacob/Israel at his installation as servant should really be understood in a positive sense. Against this background, the answer is again: No! In what follows I hope to show that here it is a question of real conflicts and arguments in the tradition.

I should like to start by assuming that the three sections of text are a midrashlike exposition of Exod 15:15-20. This may sound surprising, but the similarities are striking. The Exodus text has to do with the passage

---

158 See L. Kähler, *Deuterojesaja* (1923) 13; also *Zürcher Bibel* (1931). C. Westermann adds, "The translation is only conjectural" (*Isaiah 40–66*) [1969] 78. But see KB (1st ed. 1953) 1019: "unknown species of tree on Lebanon . . . not elm-tree." Cf. *HALOT* under this heading. According to *HALAT* the derivation of תְּאַשּׁוּר is uncertain or unknown (see also lit.). The word is missing in the LXX, but S, Vg and Tg render it in the sense of "box tree."

159 הֲדַסָּה means "bride, just married, epithet of Ishtar"; cf. Esth 2:7 (*HALOT* 1:239 [*HALAT* 1:229]).

through the Reed Sea. It is preceded by Moses' hymn of praise, and followed by the note: "Then the prophet Miriam, Aaron's sister, took a tambourine in her hand; and all the women went out after her with tambourines and with dancing. And Miriam sang to them (vv. 20-21)." Isa 41:15-16 is also talking about a "triumphal song." Neither Miriam's name nor the names of Aaron and Moses are mentioned in DtIsa. But the feminine suffixes in vv. 14 and 15 (which are otherwise hardly explicable; see above) could conceal a small pointer to Miriam. I would guess that in v. 16 the "you" is also feminine, if—without changing the consonants—one reads "you" (את) followed by an interrogative pronoun (ה). In the Exodus text it is clear that in Miriam's paean of praise it is solely Yahweh's act that is extolled; but, as we shall see, DtIsa has some reservations with regard to this song.

In the Exodus text, Miriam's song and the dances are followed by the Marah story: "They went three days in the wilderness and found no water. . . . They could not drink the water of Marah because it was bitter" (vv. 22-23). Isa 41:17 would correspond to this: "The needy and the poor seek water, but there is none. . . ." Unlike the Exodus text, there is no mention of the complaint and of Moses' cry for help (צעק). Yahweh hears directly, without any appeal.

In Exod 15:27 we hear of the next stopping place, Elim, "where there were twelve springs of water and seventy palm trees; and they camped there by the water." Isa 41:18-19, with its marvelous landscape, would correspond to this.

One would only like to know more about the interpretation of these texts in DtIsa's own time. But perhaps some conclusions can all the same be drawn from later texts, especially if they are closely linked with DtIsa's own themes.

Philo is the most important example. In *De Vita Mosis* he twice treats the theme "songs following the miracle at the Red Sea." In *Vit. Mos.* 1 the people respond to the unexpected, bloodless victory with songs of thanksgiving to God (εὐχαριστικοὺς ὕμνους εἰς τὸν θεὸν), Moses and his sister leading the chorus of men and women respectively (1.180; LCL, pp. 368–69). We can see that there are problems here if we compare the second version in *Vit. Mos.* 2.256-57. There, in ever new phraseology, Philo stresses that the chorus of men and women sing in concord (συμφωνίαν) and harmony (ἁρμονίαις), and finally: "for the voices of men are bass and the women's

treble, and when they are blended in due proportion, the resulting melody is of fullest and sweetest harmony." But for this Moses needs the full force of his persuasive power. There were therefore evidently discussions about the performance of Miriam's song particularly, as we already conjectured on the basis of Isa 41:16.

Josephus shows that it was not merely a question of the form taken by the women's song. In *Ant.* 2.16.4 (346), he certainly lets Moses express his thanksgiving in the classical form of hexameters. But, above all, he has the Egyptian weapons collected at the sea, so that when the Hebrews march on to Sinai they are armed. According to Josephus, therefore, Moses is also a general (στρατηγός *stratēgos*, e.g., *Ant.* 3.1.3 [12])! There could be no more radical difference between this and DtIsa. But the alternative "through Yahweh alone" or "with the help of one's own weapons" must surely have been discussed in DtIsa's own time as well. His own position is unambiguous, when at the close in 42:13 he lets Yahweh "go forth like a hero."

Speaking of Marah, Philo stresses the people's forgetfulness of God's past goodness when they were in distress (*Vit. Mos.* 1.181-87). He links his account with general anthropological reflections about the thirst and the marvelous, yet natural, succor.

But Philo introduces Elim as "well watered and well furnished with trees" (εὔυδρόν τε καὶ εὔδενδρον, *Vit. Mos.* 1.188-90). This would be an apt description of the landscape in DtIsa too. Philo interprets the twelve wells and the seventy palm trees as meaning the twelve tribes and the seventy rulers over the tribes: "while the heads of the whole nation (γενάρχαι δὲ τοῦ σύμπαντος ἔθνους) are seventy, who may properly be compared to the palm, the noblest of trees (ἀρίστῳ *aristō*), excellent (κάλλιστον) both in its appearance and in the fruit which it bears." He sees this as a clear indication of "national blessings" (ἀγαθῶν τῶν ἐθνικῶν *agathon tōn ethnikōn*). But these may be the very reasons why DtIsa does not mention the number twelve in talking about the wells ("It is too light a thing that you . . . should [again] raise up the tribes of Jacob," says 49:6, talking about the Servant of Yahweh), and the seventy palms have been replaced by seven species of trees. DtIsa does not show even the beginnings of an oligarchical constitution for God's people.

Josephus's description of Elim is absolutely negative. It is a place that looks fine from a distance, but at closer quarters it proves to be anything but (*Ant.* 3.9-11). Josephus had no opinion at all of utopia!

The account in the *Exagoge* of the tragic playwright Ezekiel is all the more interesting. He links the deliverance at the "Red Sea" (206) directly with Elim (243-69). In his commentary, H. Jacobson postulates that Marah was left out because "Ezekiel constantly avoids those episodes which place the Jews in a bad light."[160] The sojourn in Elim is described in detail instead.

Ezekiel's drama probably actually ended with Elim. According to Jacobson, "It will be taken as a sign of divine favor that their first camping place turns out to be a virtual Utopia. Ezekiel may even have intended it as a foreshadowing of the entry into Palestine."[161] In the scout's description, the "ideal landscape" element again emerges.[162] So here too it has its place in the exodus. The description of the phoenix in the *Exagoge*'s account

of Elim is strange. It could be connected with speculations about time.[163] An association between the Greek word for palm tree (φοίνιξ *phoinix*) and the bird's name (φοίνιξ *phoinix*) cannot be ruled out, even if in the *Exagoge* this is not explicit. The association could go further: the palm tree (φοίνιξ *phoinix*) is a symbol for Phoenicia.[164] So Elim could be a foreshadowing of the occupation of the promised land.

There are no palm trees in DtIsa, either here or anywhere else.[165] Could this be connected with the fact that his goal is not "Phoenicia," the *country* of the palm, but Zion/Jerusalem? Nevertheless, an anticipatory vision of what is to come—hope for future glory—is no less evident in this text of DtIsa. The desert poses a threat to life; and if even that desert is already transformed into a peaceful oasis, then the return home from exile is also conceivable.

---

160 H. Jacobson, *The Exagoge of Ezekiel* (1983) 156.
161 Ibid.
162 "Good Moses, see what a place we have found in this fresh, wooded valley. There it is as you also surely see. There a light now shines for us in the night, as a sign, like a pillar of fire. There we found a shady meadow and running water; (there was there) a deep thicket, twelve springs poured from a single rock, but there were many mighty palm trees (there), full of fruit, ten times seven, and young grass was growing there, surrounded by water, grazing for the cattle" (243–53; trans. following E. Vogt, *Tragiker Ezechiel*, JSHRZ 4).

163 Jacobson, *The Exagoge of Ezekiel* (1983) 157–64. See also Vogt, JSHRZ 4:132 n. 255, with lit.
164 Cf. even later the palm trees on the Roman coins commemorating the fall of Jerusalem (so-called *Judaea capta* coins).
165 For the possibility that he was familiar with the myth of the phoenix, see above on Isa 40:31.

B. 3. 41:21-29
Court Scene in the Heavenly Sphere:
Yahweh (and the Gods)—
Judgment over the Announcement of Cyrus

41

"Come forward and set forth your case!" (41:21)

21   Come forward and set forth your case! says
       Yahweh.
    Put forward your proofs! says Jacob's king.

22   Let them <come forward>[a] and tell us
    what is going to happen.
    The former (things)—what were they?
    Tell us, so that we may take note (of it)
    and know their outcome.
    Or the coming (things)—let us hear (them).

23   Tell us what will happen hereafter
    so that we know that you are gods.
    Yes, do something, good or evil,
    so that we are astonished and <see>[a] (it)
       together.

24   See, you are (less) than nothingness,
     and what you do is (less) than naught.
     An abomination, whoever chooses you!

25   I have awakened (one) from the north,
    and he came from the rising of the sun,
    <and I called him by his name>.[a]
    <And he trampled> governors <down>[b] like
       clay
    and as a potter treads loam.

26   Who declared (that) from the beginning, so
       that we knew (it),
    and beforehand, so that we can say: that is
       right?
    No one at all declares it,
    no one at all lets us hear,
    no one at all hears you speak.
27   First to Zion—see, see them![a]—
    and to Jerusalem I will give a messenger.

28   And I look there[a]—but there is no one,
    and among these there—but there is no
       counselor
    whom I could ask, and they give an answer.
29   See, they are all evil,[a]
     futile are their deeds,
     wind and emptiness their images.

22a   Instead of MT יַגִּישׁוּ ("they shall bring forward") the LXX reading (cf. Tg, Vg) יִגְּשׁוּ is probably correct.

23a   Thus with *Qere* (וְנִרְאֶה; *Ketib:* וְנִרָא, "and may be afraid").

25a   Read with 1QIsaᵃ ואקרא בשמו instead of MT יקרא בשמי; cf. below on this passage.

25b   Instead of MT ויבא, read וַיָּבָס.

27a   Thus with MT הנה הנם; others correct to הגדתי, "First <I have declared> (it) to Zion"; cf. below and the extensive discussion in Elliger on this passage (174–75).

28a   Or <"Then I looked there"> (וָאֵרֶא; cf. Vg, S, Tg)?

29a   See below.

Most recent commentaries agree as to where this unit begins and ends, and its definition as a legal procedure.[166] The scene and its content show a striking similarity to 41:1-4.[167] But in spite of the resemblances, the differences must be noted too.

The text is obviously structured in two artistically

---

166   North; McKenzie; Westermann; Schoors, *I Am God Your Saviour* (1973); H. E. Spykerboer, *Structure and Composition of Deutero-Isaiah* (1976); Elliger.

167   For the judicial speeches see lit. on 41:1-5.

wrought halves, vv. 21-24 and vv. 25-29. There is a whole series of correspondences—the beginning of vv. 22 and 26, for example, and the close of vv. 24 and 29. Schoors notes the word parallels in the two halves,[168] and Young the verbal links even within vv. 21-24.[169] These are indications of the exacting literary technique used in the shaping of the text.[170] As a catchword נגד *Hiphil* ("bring forward, tell, proclaim") in all its various nuances binds the unit into a whole (vv. 22a, b; 23; 26a, b; 27a?). But to say this is already to touch on the heart of the text itself, which has to do with the authoritative announcement of the future.

The catchword "trial" (רִיבְכֶם, "your case") in v. 21 makes clear that this is a legal action.[171] But the structure shows this too. Two sets of evidence are brought, one by each of the two parties. The first part of the dispute (vv. 21-24) has to do with the foreign gods and their prophecies; the second part (vv. 25-29) with Yahweh and *his* prophecy. The confrontation generates a violent contrast. Each body of evidence is followed by a judgment (vv. 24 and 29), introduced by "see" (הֵן). As in 41:1-5, the object of the proceedings is the legal settlement of a claim—the claim to be God. And divinity can be experienced in the congruity between word and deed, promise and fulfillment.

In the introduction, Yahweh is introduced with the title "king" (מֶלֶךְ, v. 21).[172] Because of the context, this leads on to the phrase "*Jacob's king*," an expression that occurs nowhere else in the OT, and that proclaims God's relationship of sovereignty and protection toward his people.[173] But in the framework of the scene, the title "king" is preeminently a mark of rank. In the history of religion, when the title "king" is given to the supreme god this points first of all to his rule over the other gods.[174] The description "court scene" makes it easy to overlook the fact that the present text is picking up age-old motifs about the assembly of the gods.[175] This means that the pointer to Psalm 82 is important, even if the psalm is talking about a different kind of trial. As king, Yahweh is also judge. That is evident even from the external framework. According to v. 21 he summons, pronounces judgment and, according to v. 28, declares the proceedings to be ended. "Gods" are explicitly named as one party to the action (v. 23). But the plural is used on Yahweh's side too. There is no doubt that this is supposed to be the description of a scene in heaven.

---

168 Schoors, *I Am God Your Saviour* (1973) 214: "Their literary unity is clearly marked by a striking word parallelism. To be sure, there is a certain caesura after vs. 24, but we see in the first part a sequence *yaggîdû* (vs. 22a)—*wᵉnēdᵉʿâ* (vs. 22c)—*hēn . . . mēʾayin* (vs. 24)—*ʾepes* (vs. 24 emended), which is to be found exactly in the second one: *mî-higgîd* (vs. 26)—*wᵉnēdāʾâ* (vs. 26)—*hēn ʾayin* (vs. 29)—*ʾepes* (vs. 29). We have, beyond any doubt, two parts forming one unit."

169 Young (95): "The challenge is expressed in four closely knit verses. Verses 21 and 22 are tied together by the presence in both of the words *haggishu (draw near)* and *yaggishu (let them draw near)*. Verses 22 and 23 are connected by the presence in each of the word *haggidu (make known)*, which is found in the middle of 22 and at the beginning of 23. Again 23 and 24 are formally connected by the presence of *ʾattem (ye)* in the middle of the verse 23 and at the beginning of 24 (hen *ʾattem*). There is probably also a formal connection between verses 21 and 24 in that in both of them the plural suffix *kem (your)* is found."

170 For the reconstruction of a metrical structure, see the chart in Elliger, 180.

171 עֲצֻמוֹת in the sense of "proofs" is probably legal language, although it is a hapax legomenon. It is

derived from עצם I, "to be mighty, strong," i.e., "strong words"; see *HALOT* 2:870 [*HALAT* 3:823]. Cf. also LXX βουλαί. On the other hand Spykerboer (*Structure and Composition of Deutero-Isaiah* [1976]) views it as an abstract in the fem. plur., derived from the adjective עָצוּם: "It really means 'strong things' and the phrase . . . could thus be (like כֹּחַ כֹּחַ יַחֲלִיפוּ in 41:1) a sarcastic call to the gods to show their strength" (73). The verbs קרב ("bring forward"), נגש ("approach"), נגד *Hiphil* ("declare") also make sense in the context of legal proceedings.

172 In view of the content of the following text, one may ask whether here the term for God (אֵל or אֱלֹהִים) was not originally used too; cf. 40:18; 43:12; 45:22; 45:5, 14, 18; 46:9. This could also be indicated by the LXX's reading, κύριος ὁ θεός, and was already Duhm's view; for a contrary opinion see Torrey on the passage.

173 Cf. 43:15; 44:6.

174 See the summing up in Kraus, *Psalms 1–59* (1988) 81–89 [*Psalmen 1* (5th ed. 1978) 197–205 (excursus on Psalm 24)]; F. M. Cross, *Canaanite Myth and Hebrew Epic* (1973), esp. 79–111.

175 See F. M. Cross, "The Council of Yahweh in Second Isaiah," *JNES* 12 (1953) 274–77.

The place of the action is the "palace" of the king, the "highest god," and it is to him that the other gods have to come. If we go along with the sociomorpheme in the correspondence to earthly kingship, then this is probably even more precisely the palace gate, where judgments are pronounced.[176]

So from the outward form of the text down to its grammatical details, what is depicted here is a dispute between the gods, in which the head of the gods arbitrates. The fascination of this DtIsa text too is that a monotheistic theology is developed with the help of polytheistic traditions. The myth that has been handed down becomes the linguistic matrix for communicating the new experience of reality. In the trial described, the ineffectiveness of the gods is proved, and hence their nonexistence. Verse 28 declares laconically: "I look there, but there is no one (no man)." The gods have left without a word. This heaven is empty.

When an established form is put to so radically alien a use, it will be permissible to ask whether there is not an element of parody here—whether this sentence in v. 28 is not intended to raise a laugh. This is always difficult for us to decide in the case of an ancient text, as the discussion about Aristophanes, for example, shows. In his case, it is only the scholiasts' indications that allow us to recall to life what the audience laughed at. Here the possibility is at least worth considering. It makes the subject of the text no less serious.

Different levels of understanding are the reason for a number of tensions in the text, but these must be examined individually in the course of the exegesis.

■ **22-24** In the first presentation of evidence, the initial question is the general one of whether the gods can "tell what is going to happen" (v. 22).[177] In the situation of the exile, and no less in the later period, this must have

been an entirely practical problem. Babylon and the Chaldeans are proverbial for their prophecies. The excavations in Mesopotamia give us even today a picture of oracle techniques and the interpretation of the stars. Astronomy and astrology were not yet distinguished from one another. They were the sciences of the time. They demonstrated the power of the gods and their priests. Even today, predictions and the handling of them confer considerable power.

The story in Daniel 2 gives us a good idea of the nature of the dispute in DtIsa. If we assume that it dates from the Persian period, the basic substance of the text is not very far removed in time from the DtIsa text. The situation of life under foreign hegemony and the need to preserve the faith are common to both texts. In the literary technique used to build up the scene they are quite comparable. The king who in the book of Daniel demands an interpretation of the future is "Nebuchadnezzar." He calls "the diviners, the soothsayers, the sorcerers and the Chaldeans" (v. 2), but they are unable to solve the task of "telling the dream and its interpretation." It is only Daniel who can do so, because God reveals the mysteries to him. The narrative character of the text easily obscures the fact that in Daniel too the subject is a dispute about the interpretation of the future in the field of tension between political power and faith. It is in the interpolated *logia* that the theoretical concern of the text comes out especially clearly.[178]

But the relationship to "heathen" interpretations of the future is already a problem for the Joseph story in Genesis. There the question is answered in the sense of

---

176 This is not a "throne accession" scene. An ascent to the throne would take place *in* the palace.

177 נגד *Hiphil* has a double reference here. In the OT it can be used on the one hand for declarations before a court of law (see Lev 14:35; Prov 12:17; cf. 1 Sam 27:11; Jer 20:10); on the other hand it takes on the meaning of "disclose," for example, in the context of dream interpretations (see Gen 41:24-25), or in the case of a riddle (Judg 14:12ff.; 1 Kgs 10:3), or as interpretation of the future (Qoh 6:12 [7:1]; 10:14; see C. Westermann, "נגד *ngd* to communicate," *TLOT* 2:715; also 716–17 [*THAT*

2:34; also 36]). Both levels play a part in the present text; see below.

178 Dan 2:10ff. (trans. following O. Plöger, *Daniel* [1965]):

10 "There is no one on earth who could perform what the king demands!

11 For the king's commandment is hard, and there is surely no one else who could perform it for the king, apart from the gods, whose dwelling is not among human beings. . ."

prophecy, by way of Joseph's endowment with the Spirit.[179]

These comparable texts give us an impression of the social situation in which the problem of interpreting the future arises. Joseph and Daniel are examples of intellectuals holding high government positions, and their opponents belong to the same social group.[180] So it will have been all the more difficult for them to preserve their identity in their faith in the "God of the fathers." We should like to know more: where was the common ground and what were the differences compared with the interpretation of the future practiced in the surrounding world? Certain mantic techniques were rejected.[181] According to the story of Joseph, and also Daniel 2, the interpretation of dreams is possible if the interpreter is divinely authorized.

The dispute in the present DtIsa text has to do with prognostication too. The precise meaning of the passage is disputed. It depends especially on the interpretation of the terminology in v. 22: רִאשֹׁנוֹת ("earlier events/circumstances") and אַחֲרִיֹתָן ("later events/circumstances").[182] There are two possible views. The first assumes that v. 22a is talking about the future in general. The conclusion would then be (to adopt Delitzsch's classic formulation): "The antithetical terms here both lie on the line of the future—what is immediately future, and what will continue to be future."[183] This certainly

avoids the problem presented by the text: that something that happened in the past is to be "noticed" for the future. The second view maintains that רֹאשׁ in its different forms as a determination of time otherwise always means "earlier events" in the sense of what is past; so here too these are prophecies made in the past. In contrast to this, אַחֲרִית is the "future."

It seems to me important for an understanding of the text that what is at issue here is not simply a question about prophecies as such; the point is their interpretation. Here we must briefly consider the linguistic and conceptual background of the text. "Earlier events" can certainly be known, but it is more important to know what they mean. That is implicit in the question in v. 22: "What were they? (They should explain!)"[184] When Ezekiel's wife dies and, at the divine command, the prophet fails to observe the mourning customs, the people ask: "Will you not tell us what these things are?" (Ezek 24:19).[185] The facts of the symbolic action are known but the interpretation is lacking. This shows that Westermann is correct[186] when he notes that נגד *Hiphil* in the sense of "interpret" can be used parallel to פתר in the Joseph story[187] and פשר in the book of Daniel[188]—the two groups of texts that we have already drawn on as a comparison for our present text.[189]

---

19 But when the mystery was revealed to Daniel in a vision of the night, Daniel praised the God of heaven:

20 "His name, the (name) of God, be praised for ever and ever, for wisdom and strength are his!

21 He changes times and seasons, removes kings and installs kings, gives wisdom to the wise and insight to those of understanding,

22 Discloses the depths and what is hidden, knows what is in the darkness, whereas light dwells with him.

23 You, God of my fathers, I bless and praise, for you have given wisdom and strength. . . .

27 Wise men, soothsayers, interpreters of signs, astrologers cannot tell the mystery that the king demands.

28 But there is a God in heaven who reveals mysteries, and he has let King Nebuchadnezzar know what will happen at the end of days. . . ."

47 "Truly your God is the God of gods, the lord of kings and revealer of mysteries."

179 See Gen 41:38: "Can we find anyone else like this—one in whom is the spirit of God?"

180 See also Ezra and Nehemiah, who were in the Persian administration.

181 See even earlier 1 Samuel 28: v. 9 compared with v. 15!

182 Cf. Isa 41:22; 42:9; 43:9, 18-19; 46:9; 48:3, 6. See A. Bentzen, "On the ideas of 'the old' and 'the new' in Deutero-Isaiah," *StTh* 1 (1948) 183–87; C. R. North, "The Former Things and the New Things in Deutero-Isaiah," in *Studies in Old Testament Prophecy. FS T. H. Robinson* (1950) 111–26; A. Schoors, "Les choses antérieures et les choses nouvelles dans les oracles Deutéro-Isaïens," *EThL* 40 (1964) 19–47 (with further lit.).

183 Delitzsch, 2:168 (trans. altered) [435].

184 V. 22bα: מַה הֵנָּה הַגִּידוּ.

185 V. 19bα: . . . הֲלֹא־תַגִּיד לָנוּ מָה־אֵלֶּה.

186 C. Westermann, "נגד *ngd* to communicate," *TLOT* 2:715 [*THAT* 2:34].

187 Cf. Gen 41:24 with Isa 40:8, 16, 22; 41:8, 12-13, 15. For the substantive "interpretation" see Gen 40:5, 8, 12, 18; 41:11.

188 As a verb, Dan 5:12, 16; as a substantive, 2:7; 4:15-16; 5:8,12; plural 2:4-7, 9, 16, 24-26, 30, 36, 45; 4:3-

The end of the book of Daniel (12:1-13), finally, is important. The book again sums up what has been said in the preceding chapters. Then two heavenly persons appear, one of whom tells Daniel that "it would be for a time, times, and half (a time)" (v. 7). Daniel goes on: "I heard but could not understand; so I said: 'My lord, what is "the future' of these things . . . ?'[190] He (the messenger) said: 'Go your way, Daniel, for the words are to remain secret and sealed until the time of the end.'" Only "the discerning" (מַשְׂכִּלִים, v. 10)[191] understand. The heavenly representative is not telling Daniel anything new. He is quoting what has already been said in Dan 7:25. Daniel "knows." But the application is still not clear to him. It is only the future which will make that clear—for "the discerning." In the book of Daniel, past history is interpreted with the help of prophetic words so that it may be made plain for present and future. The premise is the belief that God guides history, and that his word retains its validity. The conclusion drawn from this basic assumption is that history can be understood through an interpretation of Scripture, and that prediction is possible.[192] This takes place under authority, through divine revelation.

This particular hermeneutical approach in the book of Daniel corresponds in many respects to what we find actually practiced in the book of DtIsa. In the present text it is reduced to the most succinct formula. With these presuppositions, v. 22 can be paraphrased more or less as follows: "The gods should interpret relevant events of the past, as they have been handed down, in such a way as to show their permanent validity. This interpretation should be noted,[193] so that whenever in the future events occur that have to be understood as a fulfillment of prophecy, it will be possible to discern the agreement between prophecy and fulfillment (and hence the truth of the prophecy), as well as, finally, the authority for the revelation and its interpretation." The interest in both the "earlier" and the "coming" time is directed toward the future. Consequently in this interpretation it is also quite logical when the introductory sentence in v. 22a demands that "what is going to happen" should be "told."[194]

In the alternative ("or . . . ," v. 22) that is put before the gods, the subject is initially the events that are going to "come" or "be"—the announcement of the future. It is "pure prophecy," so to speak, without recourse to tradition. The conclusion that is the presupposition for an understanding of the passage is: that which the gods are denied the power to do, Israel's God can really perform.

The demand in v. 23b, "do something good or evil," can be understood in the sense of "doing *something*"; this is the way in which antithetical pairs of this kind are often used. I myself think it more probably refers to the practice of oracles, in which the main question put to the gods was whether their attitude was favorable or unfavorable.[195] The "astonishment" can certainly be ironical. But in connection with the problem of prophecy and fulfillment, I believe that the reading "so that we may see it together" is more probably a demand for testimony.

It is noticeable that on Yahweh's side too a plural is several times used in the text.[196] This originally has its

---

4, 6, 15-16, 21; 5:7-8, 12, 15-17, 26; 7:16.

189   In the interpretive literature from Qumran an explanatory הוא ("that is . . ." or "means . . .") alternates with various forms of פשר; see, e.g., the *pesher* on Habakkuk 1QpHab 2:5; 3:2, 4, 13; 4:1, 5, 14; 5:3, 6; 9:7; 10:3 and frequently. This *pesher* is precisely the kind of literature that, taking the prophetic word spoken in the past, interprets it for the present, while also looking forward to the future.

190   מָה אַחֲרִית אֵלֶּה, v. 8. LXX has here: τίς ἡ λύσις τοῦ λόγου τούτου, καὶ τίνος αἱ παραβολαὶ αὗται; Theodotion: τί τὰ ἔσχατα τούτων;

191   See Isa 41:20.

192   See, e.g., Daniel 9, esp. vv. 2, 22ff., 25. O. Plöger (*Daniel* [1965]) writes about v. 24: "'Vision' could be a reminiscence of Daniel's vision in chap. 8, and 'prophet' could be a reminder of Jeremiah's saying,

so that the prophetic word of the 70s and Daniel's vision in chap. 8 could be shown to agree when the final state of things is brought about" (140).

193   וְנָשִׂימָה לִבֵּנוּ; cf. Dan 7:28; Luke 2:19, 51.

194   A reversal of the order in v. 22 such as is generally suggested (cf. *BHS* and most commentaries) is not merely unnecessary; it does not improve "the meaning and parallelism" either, as Marti believes. It actually destroys the sequence of the three hermeneutical steps: (1) interpretation of the past; (2) documentation; (3) testing on the basis of events.

195   Cf. also Jer 10:5; Zeph 1:12.

196   V. 22, "tell us; we take note . . . know"; v. 23, "we know; we are astonished and see"; v. 26 "we knew . . . we can say."

point in the case of arbitration between two parties. But in the present context Yahweh has become one of the parties himself and confronts the gods. The solution that Yahweh is accompanied by subordinate heavenly beings, and that these are the reason for the "we," is not explicitly supported by the text either. The remaining possibility is that the listeners are being included, or—to take up the catchword in v. 21—Jacob, as the community whose "king" is Yahweh. In this case we should here have a development comparable with the link in Daniel between the heavenly and the earthly community as "saints of the Most High" (Daniel 7).

In the liturgical drama, the inclusion of the listeners is an essential element. They become contemporaneous with past and future. The polemical harshness, especially at the end in v. 24, permits the assumption that this was a sharp challenge to the group who are being addressed here. According to E. Gerstenberger, "the word *tôʿēbâ* indicated originally that which was deemed dangerous on the basis of group norms and hence that which aroused anxiety and repulsion."[197] "To choose abomination" is the opposite of "choosing Yahweh." What is rejected here is a false way of prediction.[198]

The text of vv. 22-24 shows the capacity for theoretical reflection. The different possibilities are worked through in an almost scholastic way, to the point of denying the existence of the gods themselves. For DtIsa's addressees, the solution means: if this is already true in the heavenly sphere, how much more on earth! In a situation of difficulty and oppression, the judgment in v. 24 that the gods "are a nothingness" is an assertion of faith.

■ **25-29** The second set of proofs in vv. 25-29 is in many ways the mirror image of the first. It begins with what Yahweh has done (v. 25). This is followed by an examination of the predicted events. If divine action and what has been proclaimed correspond, history becomes comprehensible. In the context of DtIsa's book, this culminates in the practical experience of the coming of a person called by God, who is victorious at God's commission and on his behalf. Cyrus's name is still not yet mentioned, although Yahweh already knows him[199]—another element that heightens the drama. It is more important for Zion/Jerusalem to know that the turning point is impending.

Now, we may ask: is the text referring to salvation oracles in general, or is it thinking of specific prophecies?[200] Among the oracles against foreign nations, there are sayings against Babylon, for example, in Isa 13:1—14:23 and Jeremiah 50–51. But the relationship of these texts to one another and to DtIsa would require further clarification. An interpretive tradition in the OT connected with the name of Cyrus can definitely be established. It is found in the introduction to the book of Ezra:

> In the first year of Cyrus (כּוֹרֶשׁ), king of Persia, in order that the word of Yahweh by the mouth of Jeremiah might be accomplished, Yahweh stirred up the spirit (הֵעִיר יהוה אֶת־רוּחַ) of Cyrus, king of Persia, so that he sent the call (וַיַּעֲבֶר קוֹל) throughout all his kingdom, and also through a written edict (בְּמִכְתָּב)" (Ezra 1:1).

This is followed by the charge to build the temple and to return home. In Ezra 1 the prophecy given through

---

197 E. Gerstenberger, "תעב *tʿb* to abhor," *TLOT* 3:1428–31, quotation 1431 [*THAT* 2:1051–55, quotation 1054.

198 In Isa 44:19 the idol itself is an "abomination." In the circle round DtIsa, this is the way Ezekiel describes foreign cultic practices (Ezek 16:47, 50; 22:11). Ezekiel uses the term particularly frequently (43 times). In the Chronicler's history, it is also applied to cultic practices such as the cult in the Valley of Hinnom (2 Chr 28:3) and the worship of the heavenly host (2 Chr 33:2-5); cf. 2 Chr 34:33; 36:8, 14. The mingling with foreign peoples is mentioned in Ezra (Ezra 9:1, 11, 14). Mal 2:11 refers specifically to marriage with foreigners. The LXX renders the term with βδέλυγμα, in Ezekiel with ἀνομία. See P. Humbert, "Le substantif *toʿēbā* et le verbe *tʿb* dans l'Ancien Testament," *ZAW* 72 (1960) 217–37.

199 The text has יִקְרָא בִשְׁמִי, "he will call on my name." It is the more difficult reading. The formula means "to invoke, worship a deity"; cf. Gen 4:26; 12:8; Isa 12:4. DtIsa otherwise avoids any direct declaration that Cyrus worships Yahweh. It seems to me more probable that a change has been made here, and that the original reading was וָאֶקְרָא בִשְׁמוֹ "I have called him by his name." That [is also the version in 1QIsaᵃ; see Elliger on this passage.

200 McKenzie, 35: "It is impossible to find in the OT the passages he may have had in mind. He had available, as we have said, history and prophecy; and the prophetic collections include oracles of deliverance and salvation."

Jeremiah is explicitly linked with the prophecy's fulfillment through Cyrus.[201] In Daniel 9 the prophecy of the seventy years is called "the word of Yahweh to the prophet Jeremiah" (v. 2), which has now been fulfilled. What is meant here is probably a text such as Jer 24:12-13 or 29:10-11.[202] In Dan 9:24-27 the seventy years are interpreted yet again. According to v. 25a, there is a first period of seven year-weeks (amounting to 49 years) from "the time that the word went out"—that is, from Jeremiah's prophecy about the rebuilding of Jerusalem—"until the coming of an anointed *nāgîd* (מָשִׁיחַ נָגִיד)." The title actually belongs to Israel's early traditions. It was applied to the person "designated" by Yahweh and was then associated with the monarchy.

If this is linked with DtIsa, then in 45:1 Cyrus is called Yahweh's "anointed one"—an exciting designation. The present text, Isaiah 41, plays several times with the word "announce" (נגד *Hiphil*). The verb is used twice in connection with the veiled announcement of Cyrus in v. 26. One can either translate: "Who has proclaimed from the beginning (or from earlier)" or "Who has designated." It would therefore seem possible to apply the title "anointed, designated one" in Dan 9:25 to Cyrus,[203] and to relate to the Persian era the interpretation of the period of time announced in Jeremiah's saying. In Dan 10:1 Cyrus is expressly named. The terminology with which Daniel 9 describes the reception and interpretation of the tradition is also striking, in light of the language used in DtIsa.[204]

It emerges that there are points in common in the semantic field, in concepts, and in political position among the texts of DtIsa, Ezra 1, and Daniel 9. These can be explained as a recourse to shared traditions, if not actually as literary dependencies. The temporal relationship requires further clarification, but the texts will not be far apart in time. For the interpretation of the present DtIsa text, it is sufficient initially to presuppose that Jeremiah's prophecy was actually applied to Cyrus.

■ **25a** In referring to Cyrus, the text, like Ezra 1:1, talks about "awakening" (עור *Hiphil*).[205] It is difficult to reconcile the two directions "from the north" and "from the rising" (of the sun). They can be explained either as the two directions from which Cyrus actually did come to Babylon,[206] or they can be combined as an expression for northeast.[207] I myself think it is more probable that "north" describes the place where Yahweh is, from whence he calls,[208] whereas Cyrus comes from the "rising (of the sun)." Both would then be initially mythological declarations that were then applied to real circumstances. In the structure of DtIsa's book, it would be clear that here Yahweh had not yet returned home to Zion.

The image of the potter who treads the clay to make it soft and pliable fits well into the context of Cyrus's call.[209] It is understandable that H. L. Ginsberg should feel that the object "governors" (סְגָנִים) ought to be emended to "peoples" (גּוֹיִם),[210] for one does indeed expect a *wider* reference. But the text is probably unimpeachable. The title is an Akkadian loanword (*šakun*, *šakin*).[211] It could refer to the Babylonian governors whom Cyrus is to conquer,[212] for Jeremiah too had already threatened that they would be annihilated

---

201 Cf. also 1 Esdras!

202 Cf. also Jer 27:21-22.

203 Plöger (*Daniel* [1965]) thinks that this "probably refers to the high priest Joshua rather than to the Persian king Cyrus" (141, on 9:9-27).

204 Cf. Dan 9:2, 11, 15, 21-23.

205 Also Isa 41:2; 45:13. Westermann's excursus on v. 25a (88–90 [73–75]) shows the link with the tradition of "the holy war."

206 Thus Muilenburg.

207 Thus North.

208 Cf. Ezekiel's installation in Ezek 1:4 and W. Zimmerli, *Ezekiel* 1 (1979) 120 [*Ezechiel* (1969) 52]; Isa 14:13 in the song of triumph over the king of Babylon. Ps 48:3 (2) shows the connection between "the mountain of God in the north" and Zion; see Kraus, *Psalms 1–59* (1988) 462–63 [*Psalmen* 1 (5th

ed. 1978) 342–43, excursus on Psalm 46].

209 On the images used in the framework of installations, see K. Baltzer, *Die Biographie der Propheten* (1975) 118–19. For visual presentation, Young refers to *ANEP* nos. 309, 314, 330, and 345.

210 H. L. Ginsberg, "Some Emendations in Isaiah," *JBL* 69 (1950) 51–60: "The text originally had ויבסגום, i.e. ויבס גוים 'and he has trampled nations'" (59); he refers to 41:2; 45:1; 63:6.

211 See *HALOT* s.v.

212 See Duhm; for a different view, see Dillmann on this passage.

(according to 51:57; cf. vv. 23-28).[213] In the later period סְגָנִים are the leaders of the Jewish community, with whom Ezra has adverse experiences (9:2) and Nehemiah mainly good ones (Neh 5:7, unfavorable; 2:16?; 4:8 [4], 13 [19]; 5:17; 7:5; 12:40; 13:11). With such ambiguity, does not the threat of intervention by the Persian power still hold?

■ **26-27** These verses return to the subject of prediction. According to v. 26a, the conclusion from the evidence of prophecy ought to be that the witnesses declare: צַדִּיק. Köhler proposes that this should be translated in the objective sense: "That is correct."[214] But the question at the beginning "Who has . . ." makes it probable that the point is also the justification of the person who has predicted the future correctly.[215]

Verse 27 presents a textual difficulty.[216] It could be translated: "First to Zion—see, see them!—and to Jerusalem *I will give*[217] a messenger (masc.)." The verb at the end is in the imperfect, so we may assume that the text is now talking about the future. According to the context of the book, however, the (female) messengers were already appointed and equipped for their task in 40:9-11. But probably that is a scene that takes place in heaven. On earth nothing has as yet been seen and heard. It is only in 51:17-18; 52:1-2, 7-8 that we are told for the first time that the task has actually been carried out. The scene described in 41:21-29 also takes place in heaven. So MT's "see, see them" could be an interjection, referring to these very messengers, who have already been appointed and are present. The only difficult point is the gender of the "messengers," for in 40:9-10 they are feminine, while in 41:27 and in 52:7 the masculine gender is used.

Commentators have proposed the most widely differing emendations. The insertion of a הִגַּדְתִּי ("I have proclaimed") would seem the most probable, in view of the different uses of נגד *Hiphil* in this section. But this necessarily assumes a change of tense. Begrich has grasped the scenic character of the text very well when, talking

about vv. 27-28, he writes: "The facts have therefore now been established and the hearing could go forward to the judgment. But this does not happen because the other party has silently left the place of jurisdiction, under the impression of their defeat."[218] One might add: although they had just been present; for this is clear from the indication "and among these there" (v. 28).

■ **29** At the end of a text we are once more in danger of missing a point if אָוֶן, "evil/power of evil," is replaced by אַיִן, "nothingness."[219] In the consonantal Hebrew text the words are very similar, only ו and י are exchanged. But again, familiarity with Scripture is presupposed. The well-versed reader knows that Hosea, for example, replaces the word אֵל ("God") in the name of the sanctuary Beth-El ("house of God") by אָוֶן ("iniquity").[220] Here DtIsa's proof that the other gods are no gods at all culminates in the assertion that they are "iniquity." Thus in v. 29 the repetition is associated with the rejection of images. So that is the conclusion of this "court scene" also.

In this text, a historical, political event is seen in the framework of the dispute about the gods and their power. The extent to which the possibility or assertion of prediction plays a part here is rightly recognized. In this text especially, Yahweh is explicitly called king (v. 21), and we can see how political power can be relativized with the help of the concept of the kingship of God. A number of commentators find the emotional solemnity of this text distasteful. But it should be noted that when Yahweh is called "king" here, it is as *Jacob*'s king." His kingship is linked with the Israel of the patriarchs' era. In the rise to universalism its historical perspective is not lost—nor indeed (if we think of the OT figure of Jacob) its human dimension either.

If we notice the text's hermeneutical approach in vv. 21-29, its place in the context also becomes clearer. In 41:8-9 the installation of Israel/Jacob begins. Verse 14 gives him a favorable oracle on his way, and vv. 15-16 an unfavorable one. But in content, vv. 15-20 are an inter-

---

213 Cf. also Ezek 23:6, 12, esp v. 23.
214 L. Köhler, *Deuterojesaja* (1923) 114.
215 Cf. 43:9, 26.
216 For the suggested emendations, see Elliger, 174–75.
217 Most commentaries translate in the perfect: "I have given," though without giving any reason. McKenzie takes the future tense; Torrey, Young and Bonnard the present.

218 Begrich, *Studien zu Deuterojesaja* (1938, reprint 1963) 46.
219 Thus already 1QIsaᵃ.
220 Hos 4:15; 5:8; 10:5; cf. Josh 7:2; 18:12; 1 Sam 13:5; 14:23.

pretation of Exodus 15. The listeners were quite well able to grasp this. The "saying" was fulfilled in the first exodus from Egypt. It is at the same time a summing up of Israel's history. It is still valid, as hope. The one who now speaks is the same God, *Jacob*'s king from the beginning. But he is also *king*. Israel/Jacob then no longer needs an earthly king. With that the listeners could agree, and were intended to do so. At the same time vv. 21-29 establish the link with what follows. The proclamation of Cyrus's coming shows the king of the world ("and he came from the rising of the sun, and I called him," v. 25) as the ruler who determines destinies. The dramatic tension is accentuated when, instead of the Cyrus who is expected in 42:1-9, another "servant" now appears first.

1 Look there: my servant whom I uphold,
my chosen one, (in whom) my soul delights.
I have put my spirit upon him.
(A decree of) justice will he bring forth to
the peoples.

2 He will not cry and will not lift up his voice
nor let it be heard in the street.

3 A bruised reed he will not break,
and a smoldering wick he will not extinguish.
In truth/faithfulness will he bring forth (the
decree of) justice.

4 He will not be quenched and will not <be
crushed>[a]
until he has established justice in the land.
And the islands wait for his instruction/his
law.

5 Thus says the God Yahweh,
who creates the heaven and stretches it out,
who spreads out the earth and what
proceeds from it,
who gives breath to the people on it
and spirit to those who walk on it:

6 I, Yahweh, have called you in righteousness.
And I <took>[a] your hand
and <formed>[a] you and <made>[a] you
to be a covenant to the people and light to
the nations,

7 to open blind eyes
and to lead prisoners out of the prison,
out of the dungeon those who sit in
darkness.

8 I am Yahweh, that is my name,
and I give my glory to no one else
and my praise (not) to idols.

9 The earlier happenings—see they have come
about!
But new ones I now declare—
before they spring up I let you hear of them.

4[a] Read יָרוּץ instead of יָרוּץ, "he will (not) run." See below on this passage.

6[a] As in Sr, Vg (cf. LXX, Tg), the three verbs should probably be pointed as *wayyiqtol* forms (וַ instead of וְ). Otherwise they would have to be translated by the future or the present tense.

"See" (הֵן) introduces a new scene. Ever since Duhm, the text has been called the first Servant of God song, although there have been differing views about the extent of the text, with differing reasoning. The exegesis must take account of the text's special character *and* its place in the context. It is preceded by a court scene in the heavenly sphere (41:21-29)—a lawsuit between God and the "gods." The subject of the dispute is the ability to predict. Isa 41:25-27 deals specifically with the announcement of Cyrus, although his name is not yet mentioned. At the end, in v. 28, heaven is empty. The conclusion is that the gods are futile. This is balanced by the hymn in vv. 10ff., which extols Yahweh as Lord over the whole world.

Verses 1-9 describe a presentation or installation.[221] God himself installs his "servant." A comparison with other texts shows that in genre this is closely related to the "installation accounts," of prophets especially. The twofold division of the text may be connected with the requirements of the genre: vv. 1-4 comprise the presentation and calling of the servant. Its "place" (according to the form) should be the council of the heavenly house-

---

221 See K. Baltzer, "Zur formgeschichtlichen Bestimmung der Texte vom Gottesknecht im Deuterojesaja Buch," in *Probleme biblischer Theologie.* *FS G. von Rad* (1971) 27–43, esp. 30ff. Beuken (106) with other commentators defines 42:1-4 as an "'installation speech' (presentation saying)."

hold. But what is possible in Job 1:6-12 ("and Yahweh said to Satan: 'Have you not set your heart on my servant [עַבְדִּי] Job?'" v. 8), and what can still be detected in Isaiah 6, at Isaiah's installation ("I heard the voice of the Lord [אֲדֹנָי], saying: 'Whom shall I send and who will go for us?'" v. 8) is expressly excluded in this DtIsa text by the immediately preceding verse, 41:28: "but there is no counselor. . . ." The whole emphasis lies on Yahweh's own resolve. In DtIsa only title and functions are named. Verses 5-7 bring the actual installation, with the direct address to the Servant. This address is mediated through a spokesman. It delineates the Servant's sphere of competence, both for the people (עָם) and for the foreign nations (גּוֹיִם). According to v. 7, the special instructions he receives are: "to open blind eyes and to lead prisoners out of prison." A series of catchwords points to the servant's function in the sphere of justice and its administration.

But if this is an installation it will be permissible to ask: "Who is the Servant?" This question has indeed been asked continually. The one appointed is never named. This is not entirely unusual. In Jer 1:11 Jeremiah is addressed by name, but Isaiah and Ezekiel are not, at their actual installation. But in both cases it is obvious from the context who the person appointed is.

One of the earliest interpretations of the text, the LXX, interpolates the name "Israel" after "my servant"[222] in v. 1, and "Jacob" after "my chosen one." But that would mean that this is a doublet of the installation of Israel/Jacob as servant in 41:8-16. If there are two installation accounts, it would seem obvious to assume that two different servants are being appointed. But if Jacob/Israel (in 41:15) is the first servant, who is the second? The question can be posed in this form if one assumes that in DtIsa we have a continuous, uninterrupted action.

Isaiah 41:8 also suggests a sequence: Israel/Jacob is "the seed/descendant of Abraham, my friend." Who comes then? I would think it likely that the name expected is Moses. The reasons for omitting his name are, I believe, theological ones. This postulate must be justified in more detail in the immediate context. For the moment it must suffice to say the following: It is striking that in a work whose theme is the exodus, and in which the first exodus from Egypt is skillfully linked with the new exodus from Babylon, Moses should not appear at all, although other names are mentioned, from Noah (54:9), by way of Abraham (41:8; 51:2), Sarah (51:2), and Jacob/Israel, down to David (55:3). Here we should allow for the fact that there was a tradition that Moses' name should not be named. We find this from Hosea ("a prophet," Hos 12:14 [13]) and Psalm 78, down to the Wisdom of Solomon.

DtIsa himself probably gives one of the reasons for the elimination of Moses' name: it is Jacob/Israel's fault, because it did not obey Yahweh's commandments. In the context of the second Servant of God text in 49:1ff., 48:18-19 reads: "O that you had paid attention to my commandments! . . . His name would not be cut off and not destroyed before me." This, in my view, is an interpretation of Exod 32:31-32,[223] where, because of the golden calf, Moses prays: "Alas, this people has sinned a great sin; they have made for themselves a god of gold. But now, if you will only forgive their sin (all will be well); if not, blot me out of the book that you have written!"[224]

The sequence from Israel to Moses is also found in the praise of the patriarchs in Sir 44:23-45:1 (Hebr.). The text is interesting because here, as in DtIsa, there is a play on the term "lead out."[225] In Ezekiel's *Exagoge* (as far as it is known to us) Moses begins his prologue:

---

222 It is remarkable that here and in 41:9 the LXX should render עבד by παῖς (Aquila and Symmachus have ὁ δουλός μου). The different semantic fields of עבד and παῖς should be noted in this connection. This plays a part in the reception in the NT; cf. Matt 12:18-21. See also W. Zimmerli, "παῖς ϑεοῦ," *TDNT* 5:656-77 [*ThWNT* 5:653-76].

223 In the Samaritan tradition the same text is cited as reason for the omission of the name of Moses in the Decalogue. See M. Gaster, *The Asatir: The Samaritan Book of the "Secrets of Moses"* (1927) pitron 11.19; trans. 283. See also *b. Soṭa* 14a on Isa 53:12.

224 For criticism of the interpreters of this passage, see B. S. Childs, *Exodus* (1974) 578.

225 [ויוֹצ]א ממנו איש מוצא חן בעיני כל חי; καὶ ἐξήγαγεν ἐξ αὐτοῦ ἄνδρα ἐλέους. . . . On the text see F. Vattioni,

"When *Jacob* left the land of Canaan" (1) and then proceeds immediately to his marvelous deliverance (14).[226]

Reasons can therefore be given for relating the installation of Jacob/Israel (41:8-16) closely to the installation of "Moses" (42:1-9). These are two "servants of God" who have to be differentiated.[227] The historical perspective becomes clear when the installation of Cyrus is desribed in 45:1-7.

There is something mysterious about the not naming of the one whom Yahweh installs.[228] The name is "hidden" with God—*in petto*, so to speak. This intensifies the dramatic tension. But this tension only works for listeners or readers if they have been "initiated," if what they know allows them to make a more or less appropriate guess. This could explain the covert allusions and ambiguities of the text. But it also makes it difficult for any exegesis to arrive at a secure result: the game is still going on, as it were.[229]

In the modern period, E. Sellin most forcefully maintained the interpretation that the Servant is Moses.[230] He met with little concurrence, at least among OT scholars.[231] But his observations are worth consideration even today, especially in connection with the Servant of God texts. In what follows I shall try to interpret the text of vv. 1-9 in the light of the supposition that Moses is the Servant of God.

The word "servant" (עֶבֶד) can cover a number of very different functions. The title presupposes the relationship between master and servant. The servant is obliged to serve, the master to give the requisite care and protection. In this relationship the social rank can vary considerably. It is determined above all by the position of the master on whom the servant is dependent. In the context, in 41:21, Yahweh is called "Jacob's king" (מֶלֶךְ יַעֲקֹב). The servant who is called and appointed by Yahweh himself therefore enjoys a high rank.

Although *everyone* in Israel is certainly in duty bound "to serve God (as servant) (עבד)," the title "Servant of Yahweh" is used in a special way for *Moses*; there is evidence for this throughout the whole OT.[232]

When the OT talks about individuals being chosen by God, this probably refers initially to the kings. It is God's free resolve that distinguishes, legitimates and binds the one chosen. So it is astonishing when, in contrast to the ideology of kingship, *Israel* is called "servant" in 41:8 and is described as "chosen" (also 45:4). In the present text

---

Ecclesiastico: Testo ebraico con apparato critico e versioni greca, latina e siriaca (1968).

226 In his commentary on *The Exagoge of Ezekiel* (1983), Jacobson offers the following explanation as to why, before an audience living in Egypt, a close link should have been made between Jacob and Moses, while Joseph and his period were excluded: "What [the reason] was can, I think, be discovered in the anti-Semitic elements preserved in Manetho (*apud* Jos. *Contra Apionem* 1.75-90, 103, 224, 228). There was evidently an Egyptian tradition that identified the Jews with the hated Hyksos" (73). Did similar considerations play a part for DtIsa too? Did the name "Moses" sound too Egyptian—above all in the Persian period, in which Egypt was notoriously restive, with a number of revolts against Persian rule? On the Egyptian form of the name "Moses" see J. W. Griffiths, "The Egyptian Derivation of the Name Moses," *JNES* 12 (1953) 225ff.; S. Herrmann, "Mose," in *Gesammelte Studien zur Geschichte und Theologie des Alten Testaments* (1986) 47–75, esp. 49.

227 See also H.-J. Hermisson, "Israel und der Gottesknecht bei Deuterojesaja," *ZThK* 79 (1982) 1–24.

228 On the problem of the anonymity, see also W. M. W. Roth, "The Anonymity of the Suffering Servant," *JBL* 83 (1964) 171–79.

229 Here we require a more precise knowledge of the interpretation in midrash, among the church fathers, and above all, as we shall see, in pictorial tradition. It may perhaps be useful to stress that it is not the historical Moses who is in question here, but the picture of Moses cherished in the postexilic period. Here too there are hardly any precise studies. I am also thinking at this point of the way biblical texts were illustrated in Bavaria in the baroque period. Theological programs are implicit in these too, and their influence is apparent even today.

230 E. Sellin, *Mose und seine Bedeutung für die israelitisch-jüdische Religionsgeschichte* (1922) 77–113, chap. 4: "Die Mosetradition bei Deuterojesaja." This is true even if Sellin himself wavered! As identification of the Servant he proposed: (1) Zerubbabel (in *Serubbabel; Ein Beitrag zur Geschichte der messianischen Erwartung und der Entstehung des Judentums* [1898]); (2) Joiachin (in *Der Knecht Gottes bei Deuterojesaja* [1901]); (3) Deutero-Isaiah himself (in *Geschichte des israelitisch-jüdischen Volkes* [vol. 2; 1932]) 66–79.

231 His theories play an important part in Freud's book *Moses and Monotheism* (1939). Cf. S. Freud, *Complete Works*, vol. 23.

232 See here Exod 14:31; Num 12:7-8; Deut 34:5; Josh 1:2, 7; 18:7; 1 Kgs 8:53, 56; Isa 63:11; Mal 3:22 (4:4); Ps 105:26; Dan 9:11; Bar 2:28; Wis 10:16; also Heb

as well, the two declarations are linked with one another. Ps 106:23 stresses that Moses is Yahweh's chosen one, and in that passage this is the precondition that makes it possible for Moses to intercede with Yahweh on behalf of his people in the catastrophe of the golden calf. It could well be that the catchword in Ps 106:23[233] is already a reference to the tradition: "Moses who turns away destruction"—the tradition that then plays an important part in the Servant of God texts.

"In whom my soul delights/I delight": it is personal affection that is more strongly emphasized here. DtIsa dares to talk about Yahweh's "I," his "soul" (נֶפֶשׁ). Delight is elsewhere the Deity's response to sacrifice (Lev 1:3; 7:18). Here it is the response to a person instead.[234] The three predications are closely related to one another and outline the servant's position. Tonally, because of the suffix of the first person singular "my," they all end in an *i* sound, and this is carried through in the second half of the verse as well.

In the framework of an installation, the gift of God's spirit (רוּחַ) can be understood as an equipping for office and function. In Israel's early period, the charismatic leaders, as saviors and judges, were endowed with the spirit in just this way (Judg 3:10; 6:34; 11:29; 1 Sam 11:6). It was probably because of this that the kings also claimed the gift of the spirit in association with their anointing (see 1 Sam 16:13-14; cf. Isa 11:2). It is striking that the formulation we find in the present text, "to put spirit on someone" (נתן על) is otherwise found only in Num 11:25, 29, where it has to do with the "spirit" of Moses, which is transferred to the seventy elders by Yahweh himself. It is then interpreted as the spirit of

prophecy, which Moses actually hopes will be given to the whole people (v. 29).

If the underlying traditions are also taken into account, the two declarations in v. 1b are closely related to one another.[235] The formulation "decree of justice . . . cause it to go out, bring forth (מִשְׁפָּט . . . . יוֹצִיא)" is found only in this text (vv. 1 and 3) and is hardly translatable as it stands. The formula has to be unpacked before its tension can be understood. The term מִשְׁפָּט is used three times in this text as well as the term יצא; both terms in shifting significance. "To go out" (יצא) is among other things a technical term for going forth to war.[236] In the *Hiphil* it is then much the most frequent term for the bringing out of Egypt.[237] Here it should be noted that Exodus 14 describes Israel's passage through the Reed Sea in language taken from the tradition of the "holy war." Yahweh is the one who alone acts to deliver his people. But it is Moses, after he has received his installation at the burning bush (Exodus 3), who is charged: "You shall bring out (וְהוֹצֵא) from Egypt my people, the Israelites" (v. 10). Against this background, the text might be paraphrased: in this installation (the *new*) Moses is given the gift of the spirit, not in order to bring out a more or less peaceful body of volunteers, but so as to bring forth "a decree of justice." From this "the gentile peoples" (לַגּוֹיִם) will profit too.[238] In the wider context of DtIsa's book, a new leader is not required for the new exodus if Yahweh himself enters with them "as a shepherd pastures his flock" (40:11).

"To go out" and "to bring out/bring forth" in their various combinations are important catchwords in

---

3:5; Rev 15:3. See also K. Baltzer, "Moses Servant of God and the Servants: Text and Tradition in the Prayer of Nehemiah (Neh 1:5-11)," in *The Future of Early Christianity: FS H. Koester* (1991) 121–30.

233   Cf. Sir 45:4; *1 Enoch* 45:3-4; 55:4; Luke 9:35.

234   Cf. at Jesus' baptism, Mark 1:11; Matt 3:17; Luke 3:22; at the transfiguration, Mark 9:7; Matt 17:5; Luke 9:35.

235   See Beuken on this passage.

236   Important for the present text at this point is the programmatic declaration to Othniel in Judg 3:10: "And the spirit of Yahweh came upon him, and he judged Israel and he went out to war (לַמִּלְחָמָה וַיֵּצֵא)." Cf. also 1 Sam 11:6-7; further Gen 14:8; Num 1:3, 20-21; Deut 20:1; 23:10 (9); 1 Sam 8:20; 18:30; 2 Sam 18:2-4; Amos 5:3; see E. Jenni, "יצא *yṣ'* to go

out," *TLOT* 2:561–66, esp. 562–63 [*THAT* 1:755–61, esp. 757]. On Yahweh's "going out" see Judg 4:14; 2 Sam 5:24; see also J. Jeremias, *Theophanie* (2d ed. 1976) 10.

237   According to Jenni, "יצא *yṣ'* to go out," *TLOT* 2:565 [*THAT* 1:760, 76 times; he refers to the table in P. Humbert, "Dieu fait sortir," *ThZ* 18 (1962) 357–61 and 433–36, as well as to J. Wijngaards, "הוֹצִיא and העלה, a Twofold Approach to the Exodus," *VT* 15 (1965) 91–102, esp 92.

238   Exod 3:21-22 was a stumbling block even for early interpretation.

DtIsa.[239] The same may be said about מִשְׁפָּט (which according to *HALOT* means "decision, judgement . . . dispute, case . . . legal claim . . . law," 2:651–52); it is one of DtIsa's key concepts. W. A. M. Beuken and J. Jeremias have shown how, through these catchwords, a network of relationships is built up between this text and the other texts of the book. By way of this network, the history of God's activity for his people is proclaimed, its goal being a new righteousness. G. Liedke describes שׁפט as "an action that restores the disturbed order of a (legal) community. . . . [This should] be understood not only as a one-time act but also as a continuous activity, as a constant preservation of the *šālôm*."[240] This comes about when a judge pronounces a judgment, deciding about guilt or innocence. Because, in the OT, law developed out of individual decisions (case law), the substantive מִשְׁפָּט becomes the term for legal tenets.

■ **1** If according to the text of v. 1 מִשְׁפָּט goes out to the peoples, this initially means a greater degree of abstraction. Law, an order of law, is to be established. This is in line with the basic task for which the Servant is sent: he has the world of the nations in view, not just Israel.[241] The suffering of God's people is connected with the disrupted order of the community of law among the peoples. But God is not prepared to put up with this state of affairs. Here the Servant has a task that is as fundamentally important as the exodus from Egypt.

■ **2-4** In spite of this wide perspective, vv. 2-4 still do not forget that an order of law is built up on small, everyday, legally relevant decisions. Law is indivisible. Its life-furthering power can be seen especially in the people who no longer know how to help themselves. As is often the case, the installation includes practical instructions, these being found in the acts that the Servant is said to be going to perform.

■ **3** For v. 3 I would follow Begrich's view that מִשְׁפָּט is the "judgment," or more precisely the "legal decision." In association with לֶאֱמֶת, it would then be a matter of "the correctness and unimpeachability of the judgment," so that, with Begrich, one may render v. 3: "He will make the judgment known as truth."[242]

A judgment can have favorable or unfavorable consequences for the person concerned. The judge's task is first of all to clarify something that is in dispute. The community lives from the quality of this clarification. In a criminal case, acquittal or punishment is the consequence of the decision—the accused is guilty or not guilty. But how is a just judgment achieved? If we look back from the conclusion of v. 3, we must expect that in an installation, qualifications will be conferred that the person who has to pass judgment—a judge—needs to have. In the OT, a passage that is comparable in genre is the "mirror for judges" in 1 Sam 12:3, with which, at the end of his work, Samuel begs for formal approval of what he has done.

In v. 2 three negative examples are given first of all. These are for a judge three unacceptable ways of speaking. They are acutely observed.[243] A good judge does not "shout." In ancient German law *zetern* meant the cry for help that obliged everyone who heard it to go to the assistance of the person concerned. In this sense Cain's blood "cries out (צעק) from the ground" and Yahweh intervenes on his behalf (Gen 4:10). But later the same word became the quintessence of a high, complaining cry.

A good judge has no need to raise his voice. He has sufficient authority without that. The worst thing that can be said of a judge is that his voice can be heard in the street, outside the place of judgment, because he is shouting so loudly.[244] This unfavorable picture allows the

---

239 Elliger, 207 n. 1.
240 See G. Liedke, "שׁפט *špṭ* to judge," *TLOT* 3:1392–99, esp. 1393–94 [*THAT* 2:999–1009, esp. 1001–2]; also idem, *Gestalt und Bezeichnung alttestamentlicher Rechtssätze: Eine formgeschichtlich-terminologische Studie* (1971).
241 Cf. Isa 2:1-5.
242 Note the close connection between v. 3b (יוֹצִיא מִשְׁפָּט לֶאֱמֶת) and v. 1bβ (מִשְׁפָּט לַגּוֹיִם יוֹצִיא)!
243 The topic of the "shouting judge" appears throughout the history of exegesis, e.g., Abraham Ibn Ezra (1089–1164) s.v.: "He shall not cry, as the judge is used to do"; David Kimchi (c. 1160–1235): "The

judge addresses the accused in a loud and harsh tone, in order to impress him with the sense of his authority." See M. Friedländer, *The Commentary of Ibn Ezra on Isaiah*, vol. 1 (1873; reprint 1965) 187 and n. 1; and Hugo Grotius (1583–1645), *Annotationes*, s.v.
244 For the issue of the "shouting judge" see also Aristophanes (c. 445–385 B.C.E.), *The Wasps* (422 B.C.E.), esp. 619–31. In the comedy the judge Philocleon compares himself to Zeus. Aristophanes lets him say:

positive one to be deduced without any difficulty. The Servant will speak quietly and comprehensibly.[245] The ability to speak appropriately in public is one of the goals of wisdom training. So this same *topos* can also be found in the biographies of prominent Egyptian officials, from the Middle Kingdom down to the late period. It is here that I should most readily look for comparable pronouncements.[246]

This is also true of the second group of functions assigned to the Servant in v. 3. I would not myself assume, like Begrich, that the breaking of the reed and the extinguishing of the lamp are legal customs. These are probably initially simply metaphors for "being weak."[247] In the biographies, to intercede with the court on behalf of the weak is considered praiseworthy.[248] But above all, there is the group of petitioners who are mentioned in the text and depicted in pictures in the tombs of high-up Egyptian officials. The person who holds an office is judged by his treatment of people who are living on the fringes of society. If the Servant is thus presented as a model judge, what does this have to do with Moses? Here a comparison with the late texts (e.g., Ezekiel's *Exagoge* or Philo's *Vita Mosis*) can help us to grasp the point more clearly. The premise is Moses'

biography as it is described in Exodus 2. After his birth and his early years at Pharaoh's court, the first thing the adult Moses does is to kill an Egyptian who had struck "a Hebrew, one of his kinsfolk" (v. 11). What Moses has done becomes known, and when he tries to intervene in a dispute between two Hebrews, he is reproached with wanting "to be a ruler and judge over us" (שַׂר וְשֹׁפֵט עָלֵינוּ). This episode reflects both national pride and skepticism. But at the same time, here Moses is definitely described as "judge" for the first time. Even though Exod 18:13 then also shows him as a patient judge who is not weary of exercising justice for the people from morning to night, his first act nevertheless remained a scandal for those who came later. It can be passed over in silence or explained in different ways. Acts 7:24 is a biblical example that also shows that the case was the subject of discussion.

Again the solution given in Ezekiel's *Exagoge* is especially interesting. As H. Jacobson shows convincingly in his commentary, this drama was meant for a non-Jewish public too. National tones are excluded, and the two who are quarreling belong to the same people (συγγενεῖς, *Exagoge* 49). Moses intervenes by saying: "Why

ἆρ᾽ οὐ μεγάλην ἀρχὴν ἄρχω	"Is this not a fine dominion of mine?
καὶ τοῦ Διὸς οὐδὲν ἐλάττω,	Is it less than the empire of Zeus?
ὅστις ἀκούω ταῦθ᾽ ἅπερ ὁ Ζεύς;	Why the very same phrases, so grand and divine,
ἢν γοῦν ἡμεῖς θορυβήσωμεν,	For me, as for Him, are in use.
πᾶς τίς φησιν τῶν παριόντων,	For when we are raging loud and high
"οἷον βροντᾷ τὸ δικαστήριον,	In stormy, tumultuous din,
ὦ Ζεῦ βασιλεῦ."	*O Lord! O Zeus!* say the passers-by, *How thunders the court within!*"

(According to B. B. Rogers, LCL 178, I, 468–69)

245 There may be a joking reference here that permitted the spectators to identify the Servant as Moses. In the second element of the series in v. 2, "voice" is left out, whereas in the third element "his voice" is placed in a prominent position at the end. What is the point of mentioning "his voice"? Everyone who was familiar with Moses' installation as described in

Exod 2:23—7:7 knew about his speech difficulties (Exod 4:10-12; 6:12, 30). But now the Servant who has been announced can speak in a wholly appropriate way. He has made a virtue of necessity, he does not shout. The political dimension of the joke is that in Exodus the solution is that Aaron takes Moses' place as spokesman. But here this is no longer necessary, and there is no such mention in DtIsa (cf. also Philo *Vit. Mos.* 1.83–84, which shows a similar trend, unlike Sirach for example).

246 See Baltzer, *Die Biographie der Propheten* (1975) 41–43, 136–46; E. Otto, *Inschriften der ägyptischen Spätzeit* (1954).

247 For the proverbial use of "the broken reed" cf. 2 Kgs 18:21; Isa 36:6. Young suspects that there may be a wordplay here on "oppress." See also Torrey, 325–26. Cf. Deut 28:33; Isa 58:6.

248 The verb "ill treat" (רצץ) is used in Samuel's "mirror for judges," 1 Sam 12:3, 4; cf. Amos 4:1; Hos 5:11.

do you strike someone weaker than yourself?" ($\tau\acute{\iota}$ $\tau\acute{\upsilon}\pi\tau\epsilon\iota\varsigma$ $\mathring{\alpha}\sigma\vartheta\epsilon\nu\acute{\epsilon}\sigma\tau\epsilon\rho\sigma\nu$ $\sigma\acute{\epsilon}\vartheta\epsilon\nu$, 50). That Isa 42:3 was understood as a requirement to the Servant to strengthen the weak is evident from its early interpretation.[249] Seen from the *Exagoge*'s standpoint, this could have been a new definition of Moses' judicial function.

Another Moses biography shows *why* it was important to depict him as judge, however, and it is probably not by chance that this biography comes from the same milieu. Philo's *Vita Mosis* is structured: Moses as judge ($\kappa\rho\iota\tau\acute{\eta}\varsigma$) and Moses as lawgiver ($\nu\sigma\mu\sigma\vartheta\acute{\epsilon}\tau\eta\varsigma$). Only the good judge is suited to be a lawgiver—that is Philo's thesis.

■ **4** Whereas the theme of vv. 2-3 is the Servant's conduct of his office, v. 4 touches on his personal fate. The chiastic use of the two verbs "break" (רצץ)[250] and "quench" (כהה) already shows that the two things cannot be separated. The Servant shares the fate of the people for whom he intercedes. The office in which the Servant has been installed is a difficult one, but he is given the assurance that in the end he will not fail.

Those who are familiar with the life of Moses can read the verse as a prophecy of his death, once more given in the form of a veiled revelation. The first concealed hint is "he will not be quenched" (לֹא יִכְהֶה). In Deuteronomy 34, the last chapter of the Pentateuch, we are told (vv. 5, 7): "Then Moses, the servant of Yahweh, died there. . . . And Moses was a hundred and twenty years old when he died, his sight was not quenched (לֹא כָהֲתָה) and his vigor had not abated."[251]

If we assume that there is a connection here, then אֶרֶץ in v. 4 is the *land* about which Deut 34:1 says: "And Yahweh showed him the whole land." Moses had then already finished his bequest to his people. Deut 32:44-47 reads like an exposition of what might be meant by "living rightly" (מִשְׁפָּט). There Moses says: "Take to heart

(שִׂימוּ לְבַבְכֶם) all these words." How close this text is to DtIsa has occasionally been noticed, and not without good reason.[252] For in DtIsa this is the clearest exposition of what 40:14 announced about the Servant.

The last statement in the verse is closely bound up with the preceding one. In the parallelism, the horizon extends further: אֶרֶץ (*'ereṣ*) is the land of Israel, not the world, but "islands, coastlands" (אִיִּים *'îyîm*) leads into a wider vista. תוֹרָה (*tôrah*) can be the Servant's "instruction," his "decision." That would mean that the Servant gives individual directives, and hence acts as "judge." But if the name of Moses is added here too, the sentence takes on a different profile. "The law of Moses" (מֹשֶׁה תּוֹרַת) becomes a technical term.[253] We must remember in this connection that this is the law God gave to Moses (see Neh 10:30). The "law of Moses" (תּוֹרָה) stands ultimately for the Pentateuch.

If the text is read in this way, it becomes clear that it contains "signals" that point far into the postexilic period. DtIsa thereby shows a freedom that cannot have won him unquestioned assent. He does not talk about himself but points to another. He is true to his tradition, interpreting Scripture and at the same time opening up a vista into the future: "The islands will. . . ." When "the law" goes out, Moses—to talk in Philo's categories—is not merely "judge"; he is also "lawgiver." But if, even in the Persian period, "the islands" were already associated with Greek culture, then we may ask even more pointedly: Is Moses greater than Solon?

■ **5-9** The Masoretic tradition made a heavy caesura after v. 4 (פ for *petucha*). It has been followed by a whole series of commentaries. There is certainly a break here; a new divine speech begins. This is no longer direct, but is mediated by someone who has been empowered to utter the formula: "Thus says Yahweh." The sequence of

---

249 See Elliger for textual criticism of v. 3: "The subgroup *cI* of the Catenen group has for $\tau\grave{\eta}\nu$ $\kappa\acute{\alpha}\lambda\alpha\mu\sigma\nu$ the interesting explanation $\tau\grave{\eta}\nu$ $\tau\hat{\omega}\nu$ 'Ioυδαίων $\mathring{\alpha}\sigma\vartheta\acute{\epsilon}\text{-}$ $\nu\alpha\iota\alpha\nu$. T [Targum] has a similar explanation: 'the humble, who are like a broken reed' and correspondingly $\alpha\beta$ 'the poor who are like a quenched wick.'"

250 Generally, following MT, יָרֹוץ (*Qal*) is emended to יֵרֹוץ (*Niphal*): "it will be broken" (see *BHS*). But Elliger thinks here: "It is possible that רצץ *Qal* (on û see Ges-K §67q) was also used intransitively (thus Levy, North) or that a cognate form רוץ had this meaning." The sound in the chiasm רָצֹוּץ (v. 3) could speak in favor of such a possibility (cf. also LXX).

251 It should be pointed out here that in Deut 34:8 a note on the lament for Moses immediately follows. This is important for a definition of the genre of the Servant texts and for the comparison with the *threnos* in drama.

252 See G. von Rad, *Deuteronomy* (1966) 201 [*Das fünfte Buch Mose* (2d ed. 1968) 143–44]. Also G. E. Wright, "The Lawsuit of God: A Form-critical Study of Deuteronomy 32," in *Israel's Prophetic Heritage: FS J. Muilenburg* (1962) 26ff.

253 Josh 8:31; 23:6; 1 Kgs 2:3; 2 Kgs 14:6; 23:25; Mal

speakers is similar to that in 40:1-11: It begins with God speaking in the heavenly sphere (which could be presented as a pure audition but is also conceivable as being heard from behind the scenes), and this is followed by a spokesman who represents the Deity. But the speech still belongs to the installation account that begins in v. 1. As the series of second person suffixes shows, the Servant is now directly addressed. As far as the genre is concerned, the distinction between vocation oracle (vv. 1-4) and act of installation (vv. 5-9) is not unusual. It will also quickly appear that there are inward connections between the two sections. The pivot is the Torah (of Moses). For what appears here as a hymnic predication of God is an exceedingly concise interpretive "reception" of Genesis 1 and 2—that is, the beginning of the Torah. One may have doubts as to whether v. 4 refers to the end of the Torah, Moses' death, but the verbal concurrences in vv. 5ff. are clearer. The two *topoi,* creation and the death of Moses, play a part in the later discussion: How can Moses know the beginning of the world, and how can he describe his own death? Here the answer would be: these things have already been revealed to him by God himself at his installation. His Torah by no means merely comprises legal precepts.

■ **5** This is the sole instance in the OT where God is termed "the God Yahweh" (הָאֵל יהוה; but cf. Ps 85:9). The appellation is an acknowledgment of Yahweh's uniqueness. It is the first of the three namings of the divine name Yahweh in vv. 5-9. The echo of the age-old formula of prophetic revelation: "Thus says Yahweh" is obvious. DtIsa uses "El" as name for God especially when, as here, he is touching on the relationship to the gentile peoples (see, e.g., 45:14-15). Behind the link between "the God" and "Yahweh" is the hermeneutical decision to put together the names used for God in Genesis 1 and 2. It is the same God who has created both the world and human beings. The cardinal catchwords in Genesis 1 can be recognized: "create" (ברא, v. 1), "heavens" (שָׁמַיִם, v. 1), "firmament" (רְקִיעַ, v. 6),

"earth" (אֶרֶץ, v. 1), "bring forth" (יצא, v. 12). But they are newly interpreted.

The most interesting change is that the heaven is "stretched out" (נטה), whereas the earth is "firm" (רקע). I see this as a correction of Genesis 1, made because of the presuppositions of a modified worldview. "Heaven" is no longer something fixed; it is like a tent, "like a web" or piece of gauze that can be "spread out." "What comes out/proceeds from it" (צֶאֱצָאִים) is a more abstract statement[254] than "the earth brings forth" in Gen 1:24. It is a phrase in which DtIsa can also include "descendants" (Isa 44:3; 48:19). It is amusing that it enriches "go out" (יצא), the key word of the present text, by a further variant.

"Breath" (נְשָׁמָה) is the key word at the creation of the human being according to Gen 2:7. "Breath" is given not only to "Adam," the human being (הָאָדָם) as an individual; it is given to "the people on it" (לְעָם עָלֶיהָ), that is, on the earth. This can hardly mean a single people, although it must certainly have been a provocation when DtIsa relates the term "people" (עַ) inclusively to the whole of humanity. In the parallelism רוּחַ is then the "breath, spirit." If it is given to those who walk on the earth, this relativizes the frontiers of the peoples as ethnic units.[255] The hymnic predications are therefore precisely tailored to the context. The creation of humanity is the reason for the sending of the Servant, and the reason too for the universality of his Torah—its validity for all human beings. Here the whole dynamic of the statements about creation becomes evident.

■ **6** In the act of installation the Servant's call is again summed up in a brief formula: "I will give you for a covenant to the people, to be a light to the nations." This formula is so central, and yet so difficult to grasp in its precise significance![256] Its two halves stand parallel to one another. Thus the grammatical explanation of the two constructs must accord with this.

If one assumes that "light to (of) the nations" is an objective genitive, in the sense of "in order to bring light

---

3:22 (4:4); Dan 9:11, 13; Ezra 3:2; 7:6; Neh 8:1; 2 Chr 23:18; 30:16.

254 For further examples of the expression (according to *HALOT* 3:993 tantum plur.) see Isa 22:24; 34:1; 61:9; 65:23; Job 5:25; 21:8; 27:14; 31:8; Sir 47:20.

255 After Yahweh has put (נתן) his spirit (רוּחַ) upon the Servant in v. 1, he now puts it upon all human beings. Perhaps the reception and further develop-

ment in Num 11:24—30:31 can be detected here.

256 See here Muilenburg.

to the nations," the corresponding interpretation of "covenant to (of) the people" would be "the one who brings the covenant to the people."[257] In this way an attempt can also be made to arrive at an understanding in light of the previous presuppositions for interpreting 42:1-9.

Beuken has pinned the problem down to the grammatical point: are עַם (*ʾam* "people") and גּוֹיִם (*gôyim* "[Gentile] peoples") in synonymous or in antithetical parallelism?[258] That is, does עַם *ʾam* mean Israel, or is it meant to be understood collectively as the whole of humanity? But this makes clear that this is the same problem as the one encountered in the hymnic utterance in v. 5. In both cases the word used is עַם *ʾam*. "Peoples" (גּוֹיִם *gôyim*) would then correspond to "those who walk on the earth." But in v. 5 עַם *ʾam* can hardly refer to Israel alone; the collective interpretation seems more probable, although this could of course be different in v. 6.

But we started from the assumption that this whole complex continually circles around the interpretation of Scripture or, to be more precise, the interpretation of the "Torah of Moses." Could that be the case here too, and could the tensions in the text be explained in that light?

Here Sellin already offered a clue that is worth following up. He believed that Gen 12:2 is the closest parallel. Talking about Abraham, this verse reads: "And he will be a blessing (בְּרָכָה)." But perhaps, in the Abrahamite tradition, the substance of Genesis 17 is more important still: 17:2 has the key phrase "And I will give (וְאֶתְּנָה) my

covenant," while v. 4 goes on: "See, my covenant (בְּרִיתִי) is with you, and you shall become the father (לְאָב) of a throng of nations (גּוֹיִם)."

In Isa 42:5 the statement about the "breath" was related to עַם, as the whole of humanity, instead of to Adam. Could it not be that here the covenant[259] is also related to עַם as humanity instead of to Abraham? "Throng (הֲמוֹן) of peoples" would be replaced by "light (אוֹר) to the nations." Such a suggestion can hardly be proved, but it could be in line with the train of thought in the text.[260]

If we compare Ezekiel's *Exagoge*, it becomes strikingly evident that this too is full of midrashlike traditions.[261] Perhaps the question whether עַם *ʾam* relates to Israel or collectively to humanity as a whole is not an alternative. Jacobson thinks it possible that the text of the *Exagoge* was heard differently according to the presuppositions of its listeners.[262]

That the Servant is also sent to the foreign peoples is not in dispute; the question is whether they are included in the one people (עַם, *ʾam* sing.!) for whom the covenant is valid.

■ **7** The possibility of several interpretations is also latent in the practical instructions given to the Servant (v. 7). The reference of the statements can be divided if we assume a chiasmus: the "Gentiles" (the peoples) are blind and their eyes will be opened; Israel is in prison and will be freed. But cannot Israel be blind too? This is the way the Targum understands it: "To open the eyes of the house of Israel who are as it were blind to the law." Is this meant in a mental or spiritual sense, or more

---

257 See already J. Fischer, *Isaias 40–55 und die Perikopen vom Gottesknecht* (1916) 86–87: "The *ʾor goyim* is the touchstone for the correctness of the interpretation of the *berit ʿam*. . . . *Berit ʿam* and *ʾor goyim* are the Ebed's professional titles; on the one hand the Ebed has received from God the assignment to mediate the covenant with Israel, to restore the covenant relationship; on the other hand he has been given the task of illuminating the gentile world—of passing on the light to them."

258 Beuken on this passage; see also J. Kugel, *The Idea of Biblical Poetry; Parallelism and Its History* (1981).

259 For the "new covenant" cf. Jer 31:31-34; Ezek 16:60ff.; 37:26.

260 M. S. Smith puts forward a suggestion that is interesting because it also assumes both the reception of tradition and different levels of meaning; see his "*Bĕrît ʿam/Bĕrît ʿôlām:* A New Proposal for the Crux

of Isa 42:6," *JBL* 100 (1981) 241–43: "The obvious phonetic resemblance between *bĕrît ʿôlām* and *bĕrît ʿam* suggests that Second Isaiah is playing on the memory of the Davidic covenant theology [cf. Isa 55:1-5 and 2 Sam 23:1-7]. . . . The slogan of the old dynasty is *bĕrît ʿôlām*, while that of the new is *bĕrît ʿam*." The connection with 2 Samuel 7 (the Nathan prophecy) should also be noted, especially the dispute in vv. 24 and 25.

261 Jacobson, *The Exagoge of Ezekiel* (1983) 20–21.

262 Ibid., with reference to *Exagoge* 42–58 (in correspondence to Exod 2:13-14): "Here then we are witness to a phenomenon that occurs a number of times in the *Exagoge*. Ezekiel constructs his narrative in such a fashion that it can be taken in one way by the Jews in the audience, in another by the non-Jews" (80).

practically? Is the Servant to heal the physically blind? Or is it a matter of blindness of heart?

It is certainly deliberate when the key word "lead out" (לְהוֹצִיא) is used a third time in the text here. It is again a reminder of the exodus from Egypt. But at the beginning of the Decalogue, for instance, there is a mention of the "house of bondage" (מִבֵּית עֲבָדִים). "House of imprisonment" (מִבֵּית כֶּלֶא), like "stronghold, dungeon" (מַסְגֵּר), sounds much more like imprisonment in the factual sense. Liberation from prison where someone is imprisoned for debt is one of DtIsa's themes.[263] The infinitives can also be related to Yahweh, as the active subject. He is the one who really liberates. The Servant delivers on his instructions and in his name. But are these merely directives to the Servant or are they also requirements to the listeners, if they wish to follow the Servant's example?

These questions have received different answers in the history of the passage's interpretation, down to the NT itself. No doubt this ambiguity is intended; the answers depend on who hears the questions and feels addressed.

■ **8** The conclusion is the utmost intensification of the whole text. It contains the full proclamation of theophany, which is fundamental for the OT and its tradition. Here the revelation of the divine name is renewed. After the "preliminary signal" in v. 6: "I am Yahweh," the beginning of v. 8 brings the full formula: "I am Yahweh, that is my name." The echo—indeed the reception—of Exodus 3 is unmistakable. This is one of the most highly wrought creations of the author of the book of DtIsa. For it is a call that literally "re-collects," and identifies

with, an earlier call. Who does not know the scene with the burning bush, which has its center in the revelation of the divine name![264] Now, in the installation of the Servant, everything that has already been said becomes once more transparent, and discloses the installation of Moses. The center of the message is the confession of the one God and the rejection of cultic images (פְּסִילִים).[265] Verse 8 could also be the summing up in a single sentence of the "Torah of Moses."

It may well be that the new formula הָאֵל יהוה in v. 5 takes up and makes unambiguous the continual shift between אֱלֹהִים and יהוה in Exodus 3. הָאֵל יהוה is the description and name of the *one* God, who calls his Servant.[266]

■ **9** Seen as a unit, the text ends in v. 9 with a turn to the listeners: "I let you hear (them—new happenings)." This verse once more makes the hermeneutical problem of the text clear. As the commentaries show, the temporal structure of the text presents difficulty. Here the ancient versions of the text already waver, as do the commentaries: what should be understood as perfect, and what as imperfect?[267] But this is not merely a textual problem; it is a problem about the actual substance of the text. Even its original hearers probably found it difficult to grasp the interlacing of past, present, and future in the tenses.

Here the comparison with drama and the theater suggests itself generally, in a profounder sense. One fundamental element in theater is fiction. With its help, conflicts in the experience of reality, above all in the world of accepted rules and values, can be addressed

---

263   See K. Baltzer, "Liberation from Debt Slavery After the Exile in Second Isaiah and Nehemiah," in *Ancient Israelite Religion: FS F. M. Cross* (1987) 474–84.

264   This is avoided in the corresponding scene in the *Exagoge* (90–119).

265   On פֶּסֶל see C. Dohmen, *Das Bilderverbot: Seine Entstehung und seine Entwicklung im AT* (1985, 2d ed. 1987), and the lit. there cited.

266   Beuken has described very well the importance of the name יהוה for the text (120): "*hā᾽ēl yhwh* in v. 5 is also polemical in tone (otherwise found only in Ps 85:9 (8). The definite article makes clear that YHWH alone can call himself God: 'thus says "*the true God*" YHWH' . . . the Holy Name—which does not occur again in this passage or afterward—thus forming a stylistic link binding the beginning of v. 5b to v. 6 and v. 8." See also Childs, *Exodus* (1974)

46–89: "The Call of Moses" (Exod 3:1-4, 17), with lit. on the divine name (60–61) and on the history of interpretation.

267   Cf. Elliger (239): "The imperfect takes up the participial predicate of the nominative clause in the preceding line of the previous verse. It is not, therefore, as Fohrer believes, a future tense, consoling the postexilic community with the promise of something ahead; it is a present tense, or to be more precise an example of 'the general present, i.e., statements applicable for all time' (Ges-Bergst II §7a). Yahweh draws the conclusion from what he has already said."

and worked through. At its best, fiction can actually make it possible to arrive at a common understanding of reality.

One method in fiction is the more or less pronounced abolition of normal categories of time and space. In this text the time dimension plays a prominent part.[268] To recapitulate this in broad terms: for the spectators—and for us too, when we read the text—the present is initially the Servant's installation. We ourselves witness it. The future is everything that is announced with the phrase "lead out" or "bring forth"; the past is everything else. On the "Moses" level, his installation at the burning bush is present, this being signaled by the quotation from Exodus 3 among other things. The past is then everything from creation onward, down to Moses, while the future is the leading out (from Egypt), the death of Moses, and everything else.

These two levels are explicitly linked with one another in the final saying addressed to the listeners. Then "earlier happenings" (הָרִאשֹׁנוֹת) means that which has taken place from the beginning of creation, to use the phrase in Gen 1:1 (בְּרֵאשִׁית). What was laid upon Moses, the first exodus, has already come about. The prophecy of his death has also come true. To that extent Scripture has been fulfilled. As far as the future is concerned— "new happenings" (חֲדָשֹׁות)—these are what the listeners have just heard and are still going to hear. What is meant here is the new exodus, a new fulfillment of Scripture. The historical experience with Yahweh makes new, genuine hope for "his people" possible. His way and his justice are not hidden (Isa 40:27). The "present presence" of the Servant does not permit a historicizing smoothing out of the past, in the sense of "at the time when Moses was alive. . . ." The interpreted Scripture is the present Word. This too makes plain that the "Torah of Moses" is

more than legal provisions. What is new, and yet also based on creation and the promise to the patriarchs, is the proclamation that the Torah can apply to the gentile peoples too.

Verse 5 makes the time question even more complicated: "Thus has the God Yahweh spoken." This is a citation of the solemn opening formula of prophetic utterance. If we take the tense to be a perfect, then we must doubtless understand the dependent participles as past as well, and take them to refer to creation in the beginning. But the Word of God is proclaimed *now*; and this means a simultaneous assertion of God's present activity in creation—its preservation down to the human beings living on earth now.

The problem about faith in God in its bearing on being and time—the problem thought about in this text— does not seem unusual if its scriptural basis is Exodus 3.[269] There Yahweh's name is paraphrased: "I will show myself as the one I shall show myself to be" (אֶהְיֶה אֲשֶׁר אֶהְיֶה, v. 14). If the "islands" are to hear and understand the Torah of Moses, there is bound to be a clash here with the Greek interpretation "I am the one who is" (LXX: Ἐγώ εἰμι ὁ ὤν).

Another problem has been noticed by commentators who relate vv. 5-9, or the whole text, to Cyrus.[270] For this, reasons can undoubtedly be adduced. Elliger, for example (231), mentions the connection with the Cyrus song in 41:21-29 and (228) the installation terminology. "For Cyrus, the political effectivity that is the sole subject of v. 7 is a matter of course" (236). "Yahweh has taken Cyrus into his service to bring light into the present darkness" (ibid.).

The composition is correctly observed, but it is explicitly only in 45:1-7 that Cyrus's installation takes place. If it were already the subject here, it would be merely a

---

268 See the discussion in the early versions, MT, LXX, 1QIsa, Tg, S, and the commentaries: Elliger on this passage; Beuken, 122–23; H. Haag, "Bund für das Volk und Licht für die Heiden (Jes 42:6)," *Didaskalia* 7 (1977) 4 n. 3; and O. Kaiser, *Der königliche Knecht* (1959) 33.

269 Cf. Luke 20:37. For the understanding of time, see R. Bartelmus, *HYH: Bedeutung und Funktion eines hebräischen "Allerweltswortes"—zugleich ein Beitrag zur Frage des hebräischen Tempussystems* (1982), esp. 232: "And this again means for our question that the phrase אהיה אשר אהיה can syntactically be clearly described as a combination of a classifying and an

'existential' statement, with the temporal relation 'future,' the initial clause being given an indeterminate aspect through the combination with the paronomastic relative clause. The sentence can then, however, be clearly translated and simply means: 'I will be whoever I will be.'"

270 Bonnard's heading is: "(42,1-4 + 5-9) A. The Servant Cyrus" (123).

doublet. Cannot the Servant be "politically effective"? We need only think of Moses. Cyrus's important role in DtIsa is undisputed. He is even ascribed the predicate that really belonged to the Davidic kings: "anointed one" (מָשִׁיחַ). But "light" = savior for the world—that is something else again! It is precisely at this point that, in my view, the tension of the text arises. Cyrus is expected, but it is the Servant who comes. We shall have to return to this when we consider the question about the dramatic shaping of the material. It could perhaps be that the text is criticizing the people who expect everything from "Cyrus" and who, for example, do not ask what can already be done even without him. (Here "Cyrus" is merely the emblem of Persian rule, its symbolic representative.) When prisoners are kept in prison because of their debts, only "Moses" and his commandments[271] are required for them to be set free.[272] That is in itself political enough. God's covenant with his people, and with humanity too, is a matter for Moses, not for Cyrus. There even his power comes up against its limits. Yahweh is "Jacob's king" (41:2)—that is the way the preceding scene begins, with its announcement of Cyrus in 41:25-26. The recognition of Persian rule is not without a certain reservation.

■ **1-9** Finally, we have to address the question: How is 42:1-9 to be understood if it is part of a drama? How, even, was it performed?[273] The exegesis has shown that the text is probably a quite particular scene, but that it is at the same time part of the whole, to a much greater degree than is often assumed. In the progress of the action too it has its particular, unique place.

The installation is one of the fundamental elements of the OT's scenic repertoire. We find comparable descriptions in the tomb biographies of prominent Egyptian officials, showing their installation by the pharaoh; and these give us an impression of the way the installation could be pictorially presented.[274] The relation there between inscription and painting also indicates the relationship between word and act. At the same time, the comparison can initially offer no more than indications, as illustration. But DtIsa's text has no doubt biographical elements, especially those appropriate to the "ideal" biography. The subject is the installation of a single individual, the Servant.

The clearest element in the action is the taking of the hand (v. 6).[275] This has its place in the installation. It is the way in which a ruler bridges the distance between him- or herself and the one the ruler appoints. It is a gesture of closeness and strengthening. A representation of this kind (though certainly later) is the typical scene "Moses at the burning bush," depicted above the Torah shrine in Dura-Europos; its characteristic features are preserved with only few changes even in Christian illustrations.[276] Remembering the close relationship between vase painting and drama in the Greek world (substantial evidence for wall painting unfortunately dates only from the Roman period), one can see from this genre indications of what may have been the performance practice. The hand of God is shown reaching out of the cloud, while Moses is portrayed with an adoring gesture. The shoes he has taken off are enough to indicate the place. The Deity himself has no need to appear; only the voice is heard.

---

271 A NT example is the story of Dives and Lazarus (Luke 16:19-31).

272 See K. Baltzer, "Liberation from Debt Slavery After the Exile in Second Isaiah and Nehemiah," in *Ancient Israelite Religion: FS F. M. Cross* (1987) 474–84. Cf. Deut 5:15; 15:12-18; Jer 34:8-22 on laws about slavery and release from debt.

273 For the tonal structure of this and the following text, with their alliteration and assonance, see Y. Gitay, *Prophecy and Persuasion* (1981) 129–32, under "D. Style."

274 See Baltzer, *Die Biographie der Propheten* (1975).

275 For v. 1 cf. Duhm (311): "Behold my Servant! Here Yahweh is speaking . . . Yahweh is, as it were, pointing to him as to an outstanding and long-awaited personality; cf. John 1:29, 30." Beuken (109): "God

takes the Servant by the hand and thus leads him in. The imperfect shows accurately that this gesture is continued while God is speaking." See also O. Keel, *The Symbolism of the Biblical World* (1978) 258–59 and pl. 347 [*Die Welt der altorientalischen Bildsymbolik und das Alte Testament* (1972) 238 and pl. 347]; as well as S. M. Paul, "Deutero-Isaiah and Cuneiform Royal Inscriptions," in *Essays in Memory of E. A. Speiser* (1968) 182.

276 See E. R. Goodenough, *Jewish Symbols in the Greco-Roman Period*, vol. 11 (1964), color pl. V, West Wall, and pl. 325.

But the main problem about the text's dramatic realization is that in the situation it assumes Moses is already dead, and everyone in the audience knows this. This is a further aspect of the complicated relationship between the Servant and Moses. But how can the simultaneity of past and present event be represented, if this is so important for the understanding of the text itself?

The most probable solution, as I see it, is that the Servant appears as Moses. We shall see presently how cautiously DtIsa handles this possibility. Any confusion with necromancy had to be avoided. Saul attempted to conjure up Samuel with the help of the witch of Endor, in order to learn his fate (1 Samuel 28), and ever since then, at latest, this form of divination had been taboo.[277] In that light, Isa 42:1b can be read in a new way: "I have put my spirit upon him." On the "inward" side of the text, this has to do with the equipping of the Servant for his office.[278] Elliger says about 44:3: "In 44:3 Yahweh's 'spirit' is clearly the vital force." Could the same be true of 42:1? Moses is not a spirit, but Yahweh has once again given him vital force. The appearance is not without the Lord's will or contrary to it. A comparable statement is repeated before the second Servant of God text in 48:16: "The Lord Yahweh has sent me and his spirit." Here *the Servant himself* is speaking.[279] Yet the appearance is not without the will of *the Lord* Yahweh. Neither the Servant nor human beings can bring about the epiphany. In any event there is no mention at all of rites or accompanying phenomena.

The decisions that DtIsa has made here become plain if one compares the different solutions found in the framework of the ancient theater. The best-known example of the appearance of a dead person in Attic drama is the spirit of Darius in Aeschylus's *Persians* (681–842). The Persian queen Atossa is awaiting her son Xerxes. Instead, the spirit of her dead husband Darius appears. Lament and sacrifice have brought him up from his grave. In his speech Darius tells of the catastrophe suffered by the Persian army at the hands of the Greeks. He interprets these events as the result of his son's hubris. An essential part of his speech is the glance back to his predecessors, among them Cyrus (768-72).[280] A more detailed comparison would be interesting. Here we must confine ourselves to the question of function. The appearance is not part of the action, and yet it provides the general perspective for the understanding that the poet intends. In the dead man's speech the ethos of the drama is formulated. The same might be said about the Servant of God texts. They are the focus of the whole.

For a pictorial presentation, the so-called Basel crater is instructive;[281] on this, a chorus dances and a dead person is seen on his own tomb.[282] The correspondence between the chorus and the person who appears is clear, since they are both depicted through series of letters as speaking or singing, as the case may be. The sequence of vowels (*OIOOA*) and the gestures show that the chorus is engaged in a lament.

---

277 But see K. van der Toorn, "Echoes of Judaean Necromancy in Isaiah 28,7-22," *ZAW* 100 (1988) 199–217.

278 See A. N. Michelini's comment in her *Tradition and Dramatic Form in the Persians of Aeschylus* (1982): "The ambiguous position of drama between the real theater and the illusory stage world makes it entirely possible for a word or statement to have one meaning for the stage character and another for the audience" (128 n. 2, with reference to lit.).

279 For more detail, see below on the text.

280 He says about Cyrus: "Third, after him, Cyrus, blest in his fortune [εὐδαίμων ἀνήρ], came to the throne and stablished peace for all his people. The Lydians and Phrygians he won to his rule, and the whole of Ionia he subdued by force; for the gods hated him not, since he was right-minded [θεὸς γὰρ οὐκ ἤχθηρεν, ὡς εὔφρων ἔφυ]" (trans. H. W. Smyth [LCL]).

281 I am indebted to Margot Schmidt of the Museum of

Antiquities in Basel for the elucidation of this dancer crater. Perhaps the interpretations—tragic chorus with the eidolon of a dead person and dithyramb with the figure of Dionysos Eleutheros—are not necessarily mutually exclusive, at least in a sphere where the dead person becomes a god, as in Egypt. Vera Slehoferova generously placed at my disposal her manuscript on this colonnette crater (BS 415, Corpus vasorum Basel 3) even before its publication. Now see there also for a precise description, with lit.

282 O. Taplin kindly made clear to me that this is a tomb and not an altar. It was his book that first drew my attention to this representation; see Taplin, *Greek Tragedy in Action* (1978) plate 3 and note.

In drama, there is a whole series of literary examples of spirits appearing.[283] With regard to the performance practice, I should at least like to suggest that the Servant who appears in Isaiah 42 might be identifiable in another way still. The series of *i* vowels in v. 1 has already been mentioned. In vv. 2-4 (לֹא *loʾ*) follows seven times. For the listener who heard here an echo of the Decalogue, with its series of commandments "You shall not . . ." (לֹא *loʾ*), an association with Moses would suggest itself. If the text is spoken, and not just thought of as written, the first (and in content somewhat strange) "he will not shout" (לֹא יִצְעָק *loʾ yiṣʿāq*) can also be heard as "not Isaac" (לֹא יִצְחָק *loʾ yiṣḥāq*). The second statement too, "he will not lift up" (לֹא יִשָּׂא *loʾ yiśśaʾ*), in the text curiously without the object "his voice,"[284] can be confused with "not Jesse" (לֹא יִשַׁי *loʾ yišay*). The one who appears must not be confused with Isaac, the father of Jacob, or with Jesse, the father of David. As we have seen, the substance of the passage in itself excludes confusion with Cyrus. If with all this in mind we look again at the third element in the series, "and he will not hear" (וְלֹא־יִשְׁמִיעַ *wᵉoʾ yišmîʿa*), the association with a name is not so clear. But שָׁמַע (*šmʿ* "hear") and the first element in the name Samuel (שְׁמוּאֵל *šᵉmûʾēl*) are not so far apart in sound. Perhaps the poet deliberately leaves it at that, with only this slight echo. It is too dangerous to pronounce the name of Samuel because of its use in magic (right down to the wolf's glen in Weber's *Freischütz*). But it is at least clear that it is not Samuel who has risen up. That is important for the listeners and spectators.

These things can be seen as mere sophisticated intricacies, but their connection with genre and function is worth consideration. The two examples given, the one from Attic drama (Aeschylus's *Persians*) and the other the pictorial representation on the Basel crater, show the connection with the lament or, to be more precise, with the lament for the dead. In DtIsa this only becomes clear if the four Servant of God texts are kept together. But the content of even the first text makes it obvious that this has to do with the dead Moses, who is being remembered here—who even, if our assumption is correct, actually "appears" in the framework of the liturgical drama. It is the Moses of the burning bush, the Moses to whom, according to Exodus 3, the divine name is manifested at his installation.

But an indication of his fate is already given in the first Servant of God text (42:4), in the pronouncement "He will not be quenched and will not be crushed." That is a reason for lament and for hope. The lament (ϑρῆνος *threnos*) was probably from the very beginning a fundamental element in Attic drama. In Egypt the remembrance of the dead was an intrinsic part of festivals. Remembrance and lamentation have their firm place in DtIsa's work also.

Isa 42:1-9 closes without the Servant's having spoken. The tense expectation of the second Servant of God text in 49:1-6 is thereby intensified. Instead of further lamentation the chorus now sings a "new song" (42:10). Dramaturgically, this gives the Servant the opportunity to go off. The hymn is a completion, and at the same time an announcement of the theme of what follows.

---

283 See R. M. Hickman, *Ghostly Etiquette on the Classical Stage* (1938).
284 See Delitzsch on this passage.

42

"Sing to Yahweh a new song . . ." (42:10)

42:10-13
Hymn
Going Forth of Yahweh (Exit)

10	Sing to Yahweh a new song his praise from the end of the earth. <Let> the sea <roar>[a] and all that fills it. the islands and their inhabitants.	
11	<Let> the desert and its towns <rejoice>,[a] the farmsteads that Kedar inhabits. Let the inhabitants of the rock shout for joy, let them shout from the tops of the mountains.	
12	Let them give Yahweh the glory and make his praise known among the islands.	
13	Yahweh goes forth like a hero, like a warrior he awakens zeal. He raises the war cry, the shout of battle, over his enemies he shows himself as hero.	

10a Read instead of יוֹרְדֵי הַיָּם ("who sail the sea"): יִרְעֲמוּ; see below on this passage.

11a For נשא in the sense of נשא קול cf. 42:2. Perhaps it should here be corrected to יָשִׂישׂ (cf. LXX: εὐφράνϑητι); see below.

Where the section begins and where it ends is disputed in the relevant literature.[285] It can be established first of all that both in the preceding section (42:1-9) and in the one following (42:14-17), we have a direct divine speech in the first person; whereas in vv. 10-13 Yahweh is talked about in the third person. Unlike their context, vv. 10-13 are hymnic in character; at least they have a meter of their own. As far as the content goes, v. 14 is a new beginning, and there could be no greater contrast to the immediately preceding verse. In v. 13 Yahweh is presented as warrior, while in v. 14 he appears in the image of a woman in childbirth. On the other hand the link with the foregoing section is a close one.[286] Yahweh's proclamation of "the new thing" (in v. 9) evokes as response the call for a "new song" (v. 10).[287] The new happenings (חֲדָשׁוֹת) are therefore not a prophecy of some far-off future. But the expectation of "the new thing" was already the theme of the wider context, and explicitly so in 41:21-29. Moreover the theme is certainly already stated with the beginning in 40:1-2.

An essential element in the dramatic buildup is the chorus, which can be used to signal the end of an act, a further indication being the exit of the main personages.[288] Both are found here, on the one hand in the call for the hymn, on the other in the declaration in v. 13 that Yahweh "is going forth" (יצא). The function of vv. 10-13 would then be to mark the end of Act I. This should be borne in mind in the interpretation.

Both form and content make clear that vv. 10-13 are a hymn.[289] The beginning, "Sing to Yahweh a new song," is in line with the hymns in the Psalter (e.g., Psalms 96, 98, and 149).[290] It is an announcement that probably had its place in worship. We may assume that the call for a hymn came from a precentor. The choir or the congregation responds with the actual hymn. Of course individual elements in the hymn could be developed

---

285 See the survey in Spykerboer, *The Structure and Composition of Deutero-Isaiah* (1976) 93; also Elliger, 243–44. A careful justification of the independence of vv. 10-13 is given by J. Morgenstern, "Isaiah 42:10-13," in *To Do and to Teach: FS C. L. Pyatt* (1953) 27–38.

286 See Gitay, *Prophecy and Persuasion* (1981) 122–23, 128.

287 Spykerboer, *The Structure and Composition of Deutero-Isaiah* (1976) 94.

288 For Greek theater see Taplin, *The Stagecraft of Aeschylus* (1977), esp. §5: "Action and Formal Structure," 49ff.: "As I see it, then, the formal struc-

ture of Greek tragedy is founded on a basic pattern: enter actor(s)—actors' dialogue—exeunt actor(s)/choral strophic song/enter new actor(s)—actors' dialogue . . . and so on: Beneath the many complexities of the construction of the plays there lies, I suggest, this simple form" (55).

289 Thus already H. Gressmann, "Die literarische Analyse Deuterojesajas," *ZAW* 34 (1914) 254–97; Begrich, *Studien zu Deuterojesaja* (1938, reprint 1963) 54. C. Westermann ("Sprache und Struktur der Prophetie Deuterojesajas," in *Forschung am Alten Testament* 1 [1964]) assigns the text to the "eschatological hymns of praise" (157).

independently, so that the invitation to the hymn turns into a poetic form of its own.[291] Conversely, the answer of the choir or the congregation might consist only of a refrain, in response to the cantor. We should not assume that there was any rigid pattern here. The hymn especially has always set free spontaneous emotions. We should remember here that for the whole of the ancient world the hymn's functions were not primarily aesthetic. This was the form given to recognition of the ruler, whether this be a person or a god. Outside Israel, in the cult of the ruling prince, god and sovereign could be united. It is therefore not by chance that the psalms cited have as their theme the praise of Yahweh as king (see Pss 96:10; 98:6; 149:2).

■ **10-12** The invitation to the hymn is given in vv. 10-12, with a number of different verbs. The series includes minor textual difficulties. In v. 10 the MT (יוֹרְדֵי הַיָּם) can be translated: "who sail the sea,"[292] which would mean that a further group of human beings is mentioned. But Lowth already proposed emending this to יִרְעַם, "let (the sea) roar, thunder."[293] In v. 11 יִשְׂאוּ could be an elliptical expression for "to raise the voice (קוֹל)" (cf. 42:2). But because of LXX εὐφράνθητι, it is generally deduced that the original reading was יָשִׂישׂ "let it (or them) rejoice."[294] The character of the sequence is hardly altered through corrections of this kind; it describes a loud, joyful call.

With regard to those who are exhorted to magnify Yahweh, one has the impression that an order is being followed that we can simply no longer reconstruct with any certainty. It begins with the "end of the earth," and it is noticeable that here only the singular is used, and not the phrase "from one end of the earth to the other." In other passages "the end" can mean the north. Does the hymn mean the north here? "Sea" and "islands"

follow. For DtIsa the sea (יָם) is the great ocean of the world.[295] In 49:12 the sea is also the west (as a compass point) in a list of the countries from which the exiles return. In that passage it also occurs in the context of a concluding hymn. The commentaries stress that "islands" (אִיִּים) can include coastlands, for example, the coasts of Asia Minor and Syria. Verse 11 names the people who live in the desert (מִדְבָּר). Kedar is mentioned. In the OT this name is used for the bedouin who live in the east, in the Arabian area, with their flocks.[296] The name may be connected with their dark skins.[297] "Rock" (סֶלַע) can also be a name. If so, it probably refers to the city of Petra, in the mountains southeast of the Dead Sea. Of course we cannot exclude the possibility that the hymn is simply talking about rocks and mountains in a quite general sense. But in what follows we shall have to ask whether there is not also a reference here to a particular political situation.

Elliger and others assume that what we have here is "a deliberate threefold division of the world, which is addressed as a whole," a division into "coastlands, steppe and mountains" as "the three zones of the earth in which human beings live."[298] This is a possible interpretation, which is in line with the concern of hymns for all-embracing praise: the whole world participates in the joy of God's people. But it is also worth considering whether there is not a closer connection with v. 13. For it is in v. 13 that the new happening which provides the reason for jubilation is named for the first time: it is Yahweh's going forth to battle. But then the point of departure—the furthermost regions of the earth, by way of coastlands, steppe, and mountains—could also indicate the direction of Yahweh's coming.[299] It is at all events clear that as yet he is not coming from Jerusalem.[300] But he is going forth to the place where the

---

290   Compare also Pss 33:3; 144:9; Jdt 16:15; Rev 14:3.

291   To that extent F. Crüsemann's definition of this as an "imperative hymn" is correct; see his *Studien zur Formgeschichte von Hymnus und Danklied in Israel* (1969). On 42:10-13 see 69–70.

292   See already Naegelsbach on this passage, with reference to Ps 107:23: ירד as "go down," because optically the horizon seems high above the sea (cf. Luke 5:4).

293   With reference to Pss 96:11 and 98:7.

294   Or יָשׂוּשׂ; see Elliger here. 1QIsa^a has ישׂא.

295   See here Elliger and 40:12; 42:10; 43:16; 48:18; 50:2; 51:10, 15.

296   Cf. Isa 21:16; Ezek 27:21; Jer 25:23-24; 49:28-29; Gen 25:13. See W. Zimmerli, *Ezekiel* 2 (1983) 68 [*Ezechiel* (1969) 655–56]; H. P. Rüger, "Das Tyrusorakel Ez. 27" (1961) 92–96.

297   Cf. Cant 1:5. Or is it the land of Hauran, which is "dark" because of its basalt rocks? For "Kedar" see also E. A. Knauf, *Ismael, Untersuchungen zur Geschichte Palästinas und Nordarabiens im 1. Jtsd v. Chr.* (1985), esp. 96–108, 109 n. 596.

298   Elliger on this passage.

299   For directions of this kind, indicating from whence the divine appearance is coming, see also Deut

battle is going to be fought; and he is accompanied by the acclamation of all countries. A chorus representing the different groups of human beings would then also have a dramatic function.

But where does the battle take place? Before this question can be answered in its reference to v. 13, the preceding context should once more be noted—the "earlier happenings," as v. 9 puts it. The hymn is a general, comprehensive praise of Yahweh. But nevertheless some of the things said can be understood in a quite concrete sense: Selaᶜ-Petra as a city, Kedar as the term for an Arabian tribe, perhaps also the towns in "a particular desert," as *HALOT* paraphrases מִדְבָּר. But what region is meant?

Curiously enough the Servant of God text to which the hymn is a response gives some indications here. This applies first to the comprehension level: Moses is installed at the burning bush. We may remember the beginning of Exod 3:1: "Moses was a shepherd, keeping the flock of his father-in-law Jethro, the priest of Midian. . . ." Tradition already testified that Moses found refuge from Pharaoh among the Midianites. There he married a Cushite (and therefore dark-skinned) woman (Num 12:1). The geographical information in the hymn can quite well be reconciled with "Midian." What Midian's actual limits were—how much of northern Arabia it covered—is a matter of dispute; but it is clear

that it included the southern part of east Jordan. Thus it is no contradiction when Philo makes Moses escape into neighboring "Arabia" (*Vit. Mos.* 1.47). This country and its inhabitants rejoice, and begin to sing a "new song."

Thus on the comprehension level of the Servant's installation—referring to the comprehension of DtIsa and his audience—the statements take on a political emphasis; for the Persians claimed *Arabāya* as part of their empire, and it is as such that it appears in lists of countries and peoples.[301] At the same time it was evidently difficult to incorporate, and Arabia kept a relative degree of freedom.[302]

The "Arabs" are also recognizable in paintings and reliefs. They bring incense as a gift for the Persian kings.[303] The "Servant's Torah" can and will be proclaimed in Arabia too, as well as in the "islands." These countries also belong to the Persian Empire.[304] If Yahweh's "light" rises upon them, this is a reason for rejoicing (cf. vv. 4, 9, 10).

But perhaps the text has a more topical background still. In Ezekiel 27, the lament over Tyre, we find in the parallelism in v. 21: "Arabia and all the princes of Kedar, they were the buyers at your side. For lambs and rams and goats. . . ."[305] According to Ps 120:5-7, Kedar is by

---

33:2; Judg 5:4-5; Hab 3:3; (Hos 5:8-9); Ezek 1:4, with the comments of Jörg Jeremias, *Theophanie: Zur Geschichte einer alttestamentlichen Gattung* (2d ed. 1976) 6ff., 8; "Excursus: Die Ausgangsorte Jahwes," 115–17.

300 It is noticeable that the borders of a settlement are named, down to "the desert and its towns" (v. 11), but not the cultivated lands and their townships.

301 See P. Calmeyer, *Die "Statistische Landcharte" des Perserreiches* (1982) 1:109–87, esp. 124–25; and 2:141–222.

302 "A comparison of the satrapies under Cyrus as given by Xenophon [*Cyrop.* 8.6.7-8] and under Darius reveals a number of differences: Arabia under Darius no longer forms either the whole or part of a satrapy; if Cyrus actually appointed a satrap of Arabia, his successors found it expedient to withdraw him; they were content with maintaining a good understanding with Arabs, which was essential for the safety of their communication with Egypt, without persisting in the attempt to subject them to more direct Persian government" (J. B.

Bury, S. A. Cook, and F. E. Adcock, *The Persian Empire and the West* [1964] 195). For the geographical and historical discussion, see E. A. Knauf, *Midian: Untersuchungen zur Geschichte Palästinas und Nordarabiens im 1. Jahrtausend v. Chr.* (1989) 988.

303 See, e.g., G. Walser, *Die Völkerschaften auf den Reliefs von Persepolis: Historische Studie über die sogenannten Tributzüge an der Apadanatreppe* (1966) 97–98; pls. 27 and 76.

304 Cf. the Behistun inscription of Darius; col. 1: "Said Darius the King: These are the lands which came to me. I became their king by the will of Ahuramazda: Persia, Elam, Babylonia, Assyria, *Arabia*, Egypt, *those by the sea*, Sardis, Ionia, Media . . . a total of twenty-three lands" (trans. R. N. Frye, *The History of Ancient Iran* [1983], appendix 2, 363, italics added. Cf. also the wider context. Unfortunately this section of the text has not been preserved in the Aramaic translation of the Behistun inscription found in Elephantine, Egypt. But the translation shows that the text was known even in the Jewish Diaspora.

305 See W. Zimmerli, *Ezekiel* 2 (1983) 68 [*Ezechiel* (1969)

no means a peaceful country. In Nehemiah's time, Geshem the Arab, like Sanballat the Horonite and Tobiah the Ammonite, was among the opponents of Nehemiah who formed a league to prevent the rebuilding of Jerusalem as a city.[306] This would be the first of the possible references to this situation in DtIsa. If "the inhabitants of the desert," Kedar and *Sela*ᶜ-Petra "give Yahweh the glory" (v. 12), this also means the end of "Geshem's" enmity—reason enough for "a new song."

■ **13** As climax and conclusion, Yahweh's going forth is described in hymnic form. The verse is built up with complete regularity. This becomes especially evident if we follow D. N. Freedman's suggestion.[307]

יצא also has the special meaning "to go forth to battle and war."[308] It was used from early times as an element of a theophany when Yahweh goes forth to the "holy war."[309] According to Exod 15:3, Israel already extolled Yahweh as a warrior (אִישׁ מִלְחָמָה) at the Reed Sea.[310] In the "holy war" Yahweh himself fights, and is simultaneously the leader of the heavenly and the earthly army. At the sound of the war cry (תְּרוּעָה), the fear of God—the terror induced by the appearance of the God himself—falls upon the enemy.[311] Here it is Yahweh himself who sounds the battle cry.

Even in earliest times, the struggle takes place on two levels, according to the Song of Deborah. On earth it is the kings who fight (Judg 5:19), in the heavenly sphere it is the stars (Judg 5:20). This parallelism between earthly and heavenly events continues to be an element in "the day of Yahweh." The seer in Daniel 10 and 11 still experiences the battles that are going on in the heavenly

sphere as a way of understanding earthly events. So if in the context of DtIsa's book Yahweh goes forth to battle, this will hardly be any battle other than the one that Cyrus wages in the earthly sphere to bring about the downfall of Babylon.[312]

In considering the connection with the first Servant of God text, we should again note that the element of Yahweh's "going forth to war" also has its place in the Moses tradition and its interpretation. Thus the Egyptian plagues are interpreted as Yahweh's battle against Pharaoh. According to Isa 51:9, Yahweh slays "Rahab." That must be understood in the framework of the mythology of the primordial dragon; but Rahab is also a code word for Egypt. And Israel's deliverance at the Reed Sea is portrayed as Yahweh's "holy war" against the pharaoh and his military power. Only in DtIsa neither Moses nor the Servant goes forth to battle! There may be several reasons why the battle itself is not described in DtIsa. It is characteristic of later accounts of the "holy war" to be less interested in the battle than in the victory and peace achieved.[313] Isa 40:9ff. does indeed describe proleptically Yahweh's return from battle. But another reason might be that in the Greek theater actual battle scenes are also rare. In Aeschylus's *Persians*, the battle is described retrospectively through the reports of messengers and participants. In the structure of DtIsa's book, the battle takes place after Yahweh has gone forth as warrior; the going forth to battle and

---

655–56) on this passage. Cf. also Isa 60:7; further Gen 25:13; 1 Chr 1:29; Isa 21:16; Jer 25:23-24; 49:28.

306 Neh 2:19; 4:1-2; 6:1-2. See F. M. Cross, "Aspects of Samaritan and Jewish History in Late Persian and Hellenistic Times," *HTR* 59 (1966) 201–11, esp. 202.

307 Cited by McKenzie, 42, note a on the text "Let the sea and its fullness thunder": "Reading as in Pss xcvi 11, xcviii 7; Heb. 'those who go down to the sea.' The corruption may have arisen from a haplography that has left us parts of two different lines."

308 Deut 20:1; 23:10; Judg 20:28; 1 Sam 8:20; 18:30— 2 Sam 11:1; 18:2; Amos 5:3; 1 Chr 20:1; 1QM 1:13; 2:8; 3:1, 7.

309 Judg 4:14; 5:4; 2 Sam 5:24; 2 Chr 14:15; Isa 26:21; Mic 1:3; Hab 3:13; Zech 14:3; Ps 68:8 (7).

310 Cf. also Isa 28:21; 31:4; 59:16-17; Zech 9:13-14.

311 See G. von Rad, *Holy War* (1991) 48–49 [*Der Heilige Krieg im alten Israel* (1951; 5th ed. 1969) 11]. For the war cry see Josh 6:5; Judg 7:20; 1 Sam 17:20, 52; 2 Chr 20:21-22; cf. 1QM 2:15; 7:13; 8:10, 15; 9:1; 17:11; 18:2.

312 Thus the close of the act in 42:13 corresponds to the beginning in 41:1-4; cf. Spykerboer, *The Structure and Composition of Deutero-Isaiah* (1976) 96.

313 See the theory about the "holy war" according to 2 Chronicles 20, esp. v. 24.

the close of the first act therefore coincide. They are linked in the dramatic hymn, which celebrates Yahweh's power and glory (כָּבוֹד, v. 12).[314] We find the warlike

aspect in the picture of God alien, or at least strange; yet it does raise the question of the way in which God's sovereignty is actually realized.

---

314 J. Morgenstern ("Isaiah 42:10-13," in *To Do and to Teach: FS C. L. Pyatt* [1953] 36, 37) has perceived the special status of this hymn very well. He writes, however, that it is only a "fragment of a longer poem." "But we may at least be grateful for this small fragment of what must once have been a psalm of literary beauty and of religious fervor." But perhaps the whole text has after all been preserved? Its expansion through responses and repetitions (e.g., v. 12) can certainly have required some time. On Greek theater, Taplin writes in *The Stagecraft of Aeschylus* (1977) 49 n 2: "The playwright did not compose special choral songs, but simply put χοροῦ in script and left the matter in the hands of χοροδιδάσκαλος (in the fifth century the playwright himself; but things changed)."

Act II: 42:14–44:23

"Yes, Yahweh has redeemed/liberated Jacob and in/through Israel will he glorify himself" (44:23)

A. 1. 42:14-17
Monologue in the Heavenly Sphere with Yahweh's
Declaration of His Will for Salvation
The Inescapability of Salvation, Comparable with a Birth
The Way Is Made Possible
Exit of the Idol Worshipers

42 "These are the things that I do and do not
cease to do" (42:16)

14 I have been silent for a long time,
have been dumb and have restrained myself.
[Now] like women in labor I will cry out,
I will groan and gasp (for breath) at once.

15a For the textual problems see below.

15 I will dry out mountains and hills
and I will let all their verdure wither.
And I will turn rivers into <islands>ᵃ.
and will let swamps dry up.

16 And I will lead the blind on a road they do
not know,
on paths they do not know will I guide them.
I will turn the darkness into light before them
and rough ground into a level place.
These are the things that I do and do not
cease to do.

17 They withdraw behind.
They are ignominiously put to shame
who trust in a statue,
who say to a cast image:
"You are our gods!"

Verses 14-17 are a monologue spoken in the heavenly sphere. It is conceivable that it was spoken from behind the scenes. Yahweh alone is speaking, and we participate in his innermost thoughts. The subject is annihilation and deliverance, which will come about in what follows.

The grammatical structure is striking. A first person singular in the perfect tense in v. 14aα is followed by a series of imperfects, as many as ten of them in the first person singular, two of them imperfect consecutives. The series is concluded in v. 16bγδ by two perfects in the first person singular.

In the interpretation it will therefore be permissible to assume that here there is a consecutive progression. The meter may also be the same throughout.[1] Only v. 17 is clearly set apart from the rest, but the verse does not belong to the following section and can also be interpreted as part of the preceding divine speech. But in the passage as a whole there is then a tension between the external unity and the thematic divergences. What do the cries of a woman in labor (v. 14) have to do with the withering of nature (v. 15) and the guiding of the blind (v. 16), and finally with idol worship (v. 17)?

1   Elliger (256) thinks "that at least in vv. 14-16 the
original form is not a mixed meter but is throughout a five-stress unit in both its forms."

■ **14** The mention of Yahweh's "cries" in v. 14 was for many interpreters a reason for assuming that the verse is closely connected with v. 13. A catchword link by way of "cry out" is possible. But in v. 14 we are presented with a completely different scene. Yahweh's behavior is compared with a woman in childbirth—that is quite clear because of the particle "like" (כְּ). What is not so certain is the factor linking the two points of comparison. It could be the "crying out."[2] But I myself believe that on the metaphorical level a single, unified process is being described: at the end of a pregnancy there is a birth. It is the inescapability and logic of this birth that provides the link between the two halves of the comparison.

The three verbs in v. 14a describe the pregnant woman's passivity. First she is "silent for a long time"[3]—that is, for nine months. After the perfect of חשׁה the process begins with the imperfect of חרשׁ, "to be deaf, dumb." A first act of will is going on.[4] The next step is "the restraining of oneself," because the labor pains are beginning. It is now that we learn for the first time how to interpret the process: "like a woman in labor." Immediately there comes the shift from passive to active behavior on the part of the pregnant woman. This is also described with three verbs, as a process: "cry out, groan, gasp for breath"[5] and that "all at once" (יַחַד)—it would be impossible to describe labor pains better in literary terms.[6] In view of the taboo with which religions frequently surround the birth process, the description in this passage is highly outspoken. It is also worth noting that here what God does can very well be compared with a woman's behavior.[7]

The comparison, then, rests on the inescapability and logical nature of birth. In v. 14 the levels of image and fact are closely linked. One ought probably to say, even, that it is our understanding of what an image is that divides the two levels from one another. The ancient author was interested in the actual *unity* of the processes.

Factually, the observations made by Westermann, for example, are correct: v. 14a contains linguistic elements belonging to the "lament."[8] The reproach that God does nothing and is silent is an element in both the communal[9] and the individual[10] lament. The questions whether God intervenes and when, can be presupposed in the text. The implicit answers are: "Yes" and "soon"! Thus this is a "proclamation of salvation"[11];more, it is actually the beginning of salvation's realization. The apparent quiet ("for a long time," מֵעוֹלָם, v. 14a) is interpreted as preparation of the coming one. The waiting for God finds an end when he acts, to bring about disaster (v. 15) and salvation (v. 16).

■ **15** In the light of the text's structure one must be clear that the series of imperfects immediately continues. In v. 16 too we learn for the first time the resolves that Yahweh has made for himself in the monologue. The subject is his coming into the world with the signs of elemental divine power. When Yahweh appears all the vegetation droops and withers, and even the rivers dry up. Underlying v. 15 is the tradition of the "theophany account," which Jörg Jeremias has worked out.[12] In the description of the circumstances accompanying the divine appearance, we must especially expect that

---

2   This is the explicit view of, e.g., A. Schoors, *I Am God Your Saviour* (1973) 91: "The woman in travail is only a term of comparison to picture Yahwe's loud crying. In short, there is no metaphor but a simile."

3   For the meaning of חשׁה, "to remain quiet," cf. in the *Qal* Isa 62:1 (parallel to שׁקט, "keep quiet, behave peaceably"); 64:11 (12); Pss 28:1; 107:29; *Hiphil* Judg 18:9; 1 Kgs 22:3; 2 Kgs 7:9; Neh 8:11; cf. Isa 57:11. In Qoh 3:7; 2 Kgs 2:3, 5 and Ps 39:3 (2) the translation "to be silent" would seem rather to be suggested; see already Naegelsbach (484): "חשׁה . . . is rather 'to be quiet', whereas חֶרֶשׁ according to the basic meaning *incidere, insculpere* would initially mean deaf and dumb . . . and only after that 'silence.'"

4   For the progression see R. Bartelmus, *HYH* (1982) 67–73. For a contrary view cf., e.g., Marti on this

passage: "The imperfects אַחֲרִישׁ אֶתְאַפָּק are subordinate to the main verb הֶחֱשֵׁיתִי and through it are moved into the sphere of the past: For a long time I have been silent, keeping still, restraining myself." This construction destroys the subtlety of the text.

5   It is interesting that the LXX probably links the comparison with "to control oneself": ἐκαρτέρησα ὡς ἡ τίκτουσα.

6   Especially if one notes the onomatopoeic character of the verbs. Verse 14 is one of the passages that was certainly designed to be heard, not read.

7   Cf. 46:3-4; cf. 66:13.

8   Westermann, 105–6 [87–88].

9   Pss 83:2 (1); 109:1; cf. Isa 62:1; 64:11 (12); Hab 1:13.

10   Pss 28:1-2; 35:22; 39:13 (12).

11   Thus Westermann on this passage.

12   Jörg Jeremias, *Theophanie* (2d ed. 1976) 151: "Theophany descriptions were given a stressed posi-

ancient Near Eastern mythological traditions have been taken up and modified.

In the text as we have it, it is possible to identify a limited semantic field that can be found in a series of other OT texts as well. Closest to it is Nah 1:2a, 3b-6,[13] as well as Hab 3:3-15 and Psalm 114. Sea and rivers, mountains and hills are mentioned. We are told in various different ways that they will dry up. Then there is a transition to statements that are reminiscent of earthquakes or battle. In each case the natural elements are built into the context of Yahweh's appearance.[14]

DtIsa himself already refers in 40:7 to "Yahweh's wind" (רוּחַ יהוה), which makes the vegetation dry up. In the Yahweh edict in chap. 44 the depths (צוּלָה) and the rivers are mentioned, and in 50:2-3 the sea and the rivers.[15] The mythological background is still detectable in the personal address to the elements (44:27) and in the "reproach" (50:2). The language is a reminder of the dying of nature in the vegetation cycle.

If we come back to 42:15 in the light of these presuppositions, it is noticeable that here the rivers are mentioned but not the sea (יָם). The islands (לָאִיִּים) are referred to instead. There are then two possibilities. Either the text is corrupt[16] or it has been adapted to the context. The purpose of Yahweh's coming is, after all, to make the trek back possible (the journey mentioned at the beginning of v. 16). But then, if it was the road from Babylon to Jerusalem that was in the author's mind,[17] it would be odd to mention the sea. It makes more sense if one imagines that if the water level drops, it leaves "islands" by way of which the the rivers can be crossed. All the same, the sentence remains artificial.[18] In the already mentioned Psalm 114 (v. 8), the "reedy pools" (אֲגַם־מָיִם) are seen as a welcome source of water.[19] But if they dry out, as they do here, they are certainly more easily crossed. The demonstration of Yahweh's power is not an end in itself. Its goal is and remains the bringing

---

tion at the beginning of the triumphal songs that Israel sang at the end of Yahweh wars and that celebrated Israel's victories as triumphs. They consist of two elements, the first being Yahweh's coming, the second the uprising of nature."

13   Following Jeremias's translation, ibid., 31–32 (shortened):

2a A zealous and an avenging God is Yahweh . . .

4   He rebukes the sea and dries it up,
    and lets all the rivers run dry.
    Bashan and Carmel languish
    and Lebanon's bloom withers.

5   Mountains quake before him
    and the hills rock to and fro.
    The earth lies desolate before him,
    the mainland and those who dwell there.

Amos 1:2 is also important for the background in the history of the tradition:

    Yahweh roars from Zion,
    from Jerusalem he lifts up his voice.
    the shepherds' pastures wither
    and the top of Carmel dries up.

14   In this light it is understandable that different interpretations should already be possible in the biblical tradition itself. Natural and political events are described in the same language. Consequently Fohrer, for example (56), can suspect that "the mountains and hills, rivers and pools are concealed terms for the Babylonian Empire, which God must put an end to in battle, so that the new world era can dawn."

15   Jeremias (*Theophanie* [2d ed. 1976] 93) draws atten-

tion in this connection to the title of Baal's opponent: *zbl . ym . tpṭ . nhr*, "Prince Sea, Judge River." The iconography used in depicting Jesus' baptism in the Jordan by John the Baptist is also interesting: a man and a woman are often visible in the water. These are explained as originally representing the river god and the goddess of the sea.

16   The emendation of לָאִיִּים ("islands") to לְצִיָּה ("arid landscape, waterless region") has been proposed, e.g., by Oort (cf. Isa 41:18; 49:8 cj.; 53:2); or the plur. לְצִיּוֹת has been suggested, by a series of more modern commentators; or the plural formation לְצִיִּים, e.g., already by R. Lowth. Did the sentence once run: "I will make water and sea become desolate" (וְהִשְׁאֵיתִי נְהָרוֹת וְיָם, or וְיָם אַשֶּׁאָה נְהָרוֹת) using שאה Hiphil? In *Qal* the word means "lie desolate" (Isa 6:11), in *Niphal*, "be desolate," Isa 6:11; in *Hiphil* Isa 37:26; 2 Kgs 19:25, "make desolate"; cf. Nah 1:4, 5. Does the peculiar *qameṣ* under ל derive from an original יָם? (cf. שֵׁאת, "devastation," Lam 3:47).

17   Isa 50:2 talks generally about Yahweh's power. In 51:10 it is an element in the remembrance of the exodus.

18   The change from the series of first person imperfects to perfect consecutive could speak in favor of an intervention here (see below).

19   Cf. Isa 35:7; 41:18; Ps 107:35; in contrast cf. Exod 7:19; 8:1 (5); Isa 14:23.

home of the exiles. That is the purpose of the final resolve in v. 16 about the safety of "the road."

■ **16** The key word "blind" is used for the first time in the Servant of God text in 42:7, where it is connected with deliverance from prison and from the "darkness" of the dungeon. The prisoners would have become "blind" because they had been in darkness for so long.[20] In the text that directly follows, blindness is mentioned five times (42:18, 19 a, bα, β; 43:8). The present text is related entirely to its context.[21] The earlier v. 7 makes plain that it is real blindness that is meant, blindness that makes guidance along the road necessary: light in the darkness as liberation from imprisonment.[22] But the following text, 42:18ff., shows that it is also the blindness that culpably (v. 14) fails to observe Yahweh's acts and word (vv. 20, 24, 25).[23] Both aspects come together in Yahweh's resolve: solicitude for the blind, which leads to their liberation, and accusation against the blindness of his people.

It is possible that the expressions "lead,"[24] "the road they do not know,"[25] the darkness,[26] which is lit up before them by Yahweh,[27] are reminiscences of the language used in the account of the first exodus from Egypt. It is now a question of bringing the people home from exile. The person who thinks: "We don't know the way" is put right. Again the text expresses itself in extreme terms: even the blind will be led, darkness will be light. It is a testimony to God's forbearing patience.

Verse 16βγ is the summing up of Yahweh's declaration of will. What is going to happen in the future is now stated, the perfect tense being used as an expression of certainty.[28] In the dramatic structure, from this point the arc reaches over to the close of the act. What Yahweh resolved in his monologue at the beginning is endorsed by the hymn at the end in 44:23: "Rejoice, you heavens: yes, Yahweh has acted (כִּי עָשָׂה). . . . Yes, Yahweh has redeemed/liberated Jacob and in/through Israel will he glorify himself (יִתְפָּאָר)." Here further themes sounded at the beginning are taken up once more, with "the depths of the earth" and "the mountains" and their vegetation, which are to acknowledge Yahweh in the hymn.

■ **17** It is in this context, in my view, that v. 17 ought now to be seen—the rejection of idol worshipers. In both grammatical structure and theme, the verse clearly differs from what has gone before. It is therefore understandable that it can be viewed as a later addition.[29] But in the composition it has its place, for it announces what are to be essential scenes in this act: the description of the manufacture of idols in 44:9-20. This is in fact the most extensive piece of polemic against idols in DtIsa. In this respect too the monologue in 42:14-17 is both prediction and summing up.

Other than in the preceding declaration of will, here there is no need for Yahweh to do anything more. The idol worshipers themselves experience the consequence of what they do in the form of their ignominy.[30] The gods are human products, whatever technology may be used to produce them;[31] so there is no reliance on them. DtIsa does not lose sight of the overriding theological orientation. "God and the gods" is for him not an abstract theme. It is a daily experienced confrontation. Otherwise he would not bring it up again and again, like

---

20 Cf. Isa 49:9; 51:14.

21 It is noticeable that here once again the series of first person imperfects is interrupted by a perfect consecutive. This could suggest that the original text was regular in form, and has been revised to fit the context.

22 Cf. 49:9. The Targum establishes the unity by explaining in 42:7 as well: "The eyes of the house of Israel, which are as if blind for the law" (see Elliger on this passage).

23 Also important in the context is 44:18, because it shows the introductory character of the monologue. It is true that there the term "blind" (עִוֵּר) is missing, but in the framework of the polemic agaist idols it is said that "their eyes are sealed (טַח) so that they cannot see."

24 הלך Hiphil; cf. Deut 8:15; Jer 2:6; Pss 106:9; 136:16; see also Isa 48:21 (following A. Schoors, *I Am God*

Your Saviour [1973] on this passage).

25 Cf. Exod 33:12-17.

26 Jer 2:6.

27 Exod 13:21-22; Deut 1:33; Neh 9:12, 19.

28 See Bartelmus, *HYH* (1982) 51ff.

29 See Elliger, 267.

30 On שׁוֹשׁ, בּוֹשׁ, בֹּשֶׁת see M. Klopfenstein, *Scham und Schande nach dem AT* (1972). In Jeremiah בֹּשֶׁת is a code word for Baal (see Jer 3:21-25; 11:13; cf. 2:26-28).

31 For details and on the terminology see below on 44:9-20.

a constant refrain. The reproach by no means applies only to "the Gentiles"; it can very well be directed to Israelites too, just as the preceding section enters into Israelite arguments about whether, when, and how God intervenes. When life is shared with foreigners in a foreign land, the cult of idols is a particular temptation, as the book of Daniel was again to show later.[32] But the formulation in the text is so broad that it includes every kind of idol cult.

As regards the dramatic structure, v. 16 announces the procession of the blind ("lead . . . on the road," וְהוֹלַכְתִּי . . . בְּדֶרֶךְ), while v. 17 announces the exit of the idol worshipers ("they withdraw behind" נָסֹגוּ אָחוֹר).[33]

---

32   For the problem one may point to Exod 32:4 (thus Young on this passage) and to Hosea.

33   According to Elliger on this passage, the phrase means "literally 'to retreat backward,' i.e., 'to withdraw, to make off'; it is a favorite expression in the Psalter (Pss 35:4 [3]; 40:15 [14]; 44:19 [18]; 70:3 [2]; 129:5; further 2 Sam 1:22; Jer 38:22; 46:5)." As a stage direction, cf. Isa 44:25: "turn round, [go off] to the back" (מֵשִׁיב . . . אָחוֹר).

A. 2.   42:18-25
The "Blind Servant" and the "Deaf Messenger"
as a Contradiction in Terms
Knowledge on the Basis of Experience
"Who has surrendered Jacob to a plunderer
and Israel to robbers?" (42:24)

42

"Is it not Yahweh against whom we have
sinned?" (42:24)

18	You deaf, listen, and you blind, look up and see!
19	Who is blind if not my servant, and (who is) deaf like my messenger whom I send? Who is blind like měšullām,[a] and (who is) blind like Yahweh's servant?
20	You[a] have seen much but do not regard (it). With open ears he yet does not hear.
21	Yahweh is pleased for the sake of his righteousness to make the law great and glorious.

22	But that is a robbed and plundered people.
	<trapped in holes>[a] are they all,
	and in prisons are they hidden.
	They have become spoil, and there is no
	    deliverer,
	(have become) prey and there is no one who
	    says: "Give back!"

23	Who among you heeds this? Let him attend and listen for later!
24	Who has surrendered Jacob to a plunderer[a] and Israel to robbers? "Is it not Yahweh, against whom we have sinned?" But they did not want to walk in his ways and did not listen to his precepts/his law.

25	Then he poured out the embers of his anger
	    on them
	and the violence of war.
	And they scorched him from all sides, but
	    he did not regard (it),
	and they burned him, but he did not take (it)
	    to heart.

19a On the various interpretive possibilities, see
below on this passage.

20a Thus the *Ketib* (רָאִיתָ = ראית). The *Qere* reading is
an infinitive (רָאוֹת = רָאֹת).

22a The infinitive הָפֵחַ can stand for a finite verb.
Otherwise it would have to be emended to הֻפַּח
or הֻפְּחוּ (cf. Tg). Instead of MT בַּחוּרִים, "young
men," the reading in the parallelism should
more probably be בְּחֹורִים, "in holes" (cf. LXX).

24a In the parallelism the *Ketib* לִמְשֹׁוסֶה, "to a plunderer," is more probable than the *Qere* לִמְשַׁ[ו]סָּה,
"to plundering."

This section presents a number of difficulties, as commentators agree. The variants in the transmitted text
already show that attempts have been made to iron out
the cruxes, and the same may be said of the early translations. Modern commentators generally try to arrive at
a consistent sense by way of emendations and by assuming secondary additions.[34] In principle, however, an
effort should be made to preserve the text as it stands as
far as possible. Some of the problems can be solved if
here too we start from the following premises. DtIsa is
taking up traditions, to the point of working up already
existing literary material. This leads to tensions, because
the literary and conceptual adaptation to the particular
context is not always smooth. One reason for this can be

---

34   See the list in Elliger (278) and Schoors, *I Am God
Your Saviour* (1973) 202.

the respect for tradition that wishes to leave traditional material as unaltered as possible. But we also have the impression that DtIsa loves to oscillate between different interpretations. A further presupposition is that here too the text has a dramatic structure. In spite of the difficulties, however, the actual content of the section is clear enough.

Verses 18-25 constitute a transitional section between vv. 14-17 (the monologue with Yahweh's resolve) and 43:1-7 (God's address to Jacob/Israel, with the announcement of salvation). The link with the previous text is forged through the catchword "blind" in vv. 16 and 18-19. The section is linked with what follows through the connecting "but now" (וְעַתָּה) in 43:1. But there is a link with the still wider context as well: v. 23 demands that the proclamation should be noticed "for later." What this "later" can refer to becomes evident in the next unit but one, 43:8-15; for there the blind and the deaf are to be God's witnesses to the nations. That is why they must listen now. The introduction in 43:8 is picking up 42:18: "Bring forward the blind people—it has eyes; and the deaf people—it has ears." The question is how Israel can become a witness for its God, even though it has shown itself to be blind and deaf. So the section of text we are considering here is only relatively self-contained. In literary character, the section can most readily be assigned to the trial scenes.[35]

It is clear that a group of listeners is being addressed. In v. 18 this group is challenged with "listen . . . look . . . !" and in v. 23 similarly: "Who among you will heed this!" From v. 24 onward this "crowd" or group is included in the "we sinned." Finally, v. 22 points to "that people" (וְהוּא עַם). In the drama "the crowd" could be the listeners or the chorus—perhaps even both at once.

It is harder to answer the question about who the speakers are in each given case, and to decide where the different sections of the speech begin and end. In v. 18, at least, a divine speech begins. Yahweh talks about "my servant . . . my messenger" (v. 19). I would assume that

this speech includes the whole *indictment* down to v. 20.[36] Verses 21-22 do not continue the divine speech. Yahweh is now spoken about in the third person. A speaker gives *a description of the distress* and turns to the crowd (vv. 21-23). The heart of the last speech section (vv. 24-25) is the *contrite confession of sin*: "we sinned" (v. 24ba). It is possible that this is formulated by the same speaker, who is now associating himself with the many in the "we." His speech, with the description of the distress, goes on immediately: "but they did not walk . . ." and continues through v. 25. But it is more probable that vv. 24-25 were spoken by the crowd, or by the chorus as representing them; we may compare the "interjection" used in drama.[37]

■ **18-20** The assertion that the people addressed are "blind and deaf" (see v. 18) is an unheard-of provocation. Who welcomes a reproach of this kind! But DtIsa carries the metaphor to the point of absurdity when he calls the people "a blind servant" and "a deaf messenger." To begin the scene like this is to be sure of the listeners' attention. A blind servant is useless, a deaf messenger ineligible. Everyone must realize that from his or her own experience. That is reason enough for agreeing with the judgment. The assertions presuppose the technique of figurative speech employed by the prophets.[38] Its instrument is wordplay. But this does not exclude a precise terminology and concept.[39]

The conclusion that is put forward here means: if Israel was the "servant" of its Lord and God, then it showed itself to be blind and deaf, and must take the consequences.[40] This can also mean implicitly that Yahweh is exonerated from the reproach of insensibility to Israel's suffering. That is what Westermann assumes when (pointing to 40:27) he assigns the text to the trial speeches or, more precisely, to the appeal to the judge.[41]

■ **19** In v. 19 the link is forged between an individual and a collective interpretation of the "Servant." The

---

35 With Westermann; Schoors, *I Am God Your Saviour* (1973) 202; cf., e.g., 43:22-28.

36 See the exegesis of this passage.

37 See below on this passage.

38 Cf., e.g., the prophet Nathan's parable, 2 Sam 12:1-15, esp. vv. 7, 10 and 13, as well as Isaiah's Song of the Vineyard, Isaiah 5.

39 L. Köhler (*Deuterojesaja . . . stilkritisch untersucht*

[1923] 113) thinks that v. 18 is picking up the "two-witness testimony" before a court of law.

40 Cf. the interpretation in the Targum: "You evildoers, who are like the deaf, have you no ears? Listen! And you guilty ones, who are like the blind, have you no eyes? Understand and see!"

41 Westermann on this passage; Schoors, *I Am God Your Saviour* (1973) 202.

double understanding can be detected even in the textual variants. The MT here has the singular "my servant." The LXX interprets this—correctly according to the facts—with the plural "my 'servants'" (οἱ παῖδές μου). But this does not necessarily presuppose a different original reading.

The second half of v. 19 is disputed, and is often even viewed as a complete interpolation.[42] I myself want to propose a different solution. The two halves of the verse, 19a and 19b, are certainly almost parallel—but only "almost." The first half (a) fits the context better. Israel is termed "servant" and "messenger." Could v. 19b be an added quotation, which DtIsa varies in v. 19a? If this is a quotation, that would explain the phrase "Servant of Yahweh" (עֶבֶד יהוה) in Yahweh's own speech. It is otherwise conspicuously avoided in DtIsa. The meaning of *mĕšullām* (כִּמְשֻׁלָּם), which many commentators consider inexplicable,[43] could be connected with this. In a quotation, a word that does not completely fit the context would not be unusual. If we therefore start initially from the immediate context of this word, we expect that in the *parallelismus membrorum* "Yahweh's servant" will be balanced by another singular, also signify-

ing a title or, to be more precise, a compound title. A title that could be one of the word's components is "ruler" (מֹשֵׁל, *Qal participle* of משׁל II).[44]

As has long been recognized, the LXX version, οἱ κυριεύοντες αὐτῶν ("who rule over them"), suggests such a derivation. Retroverted into Hebrew, the reading could then be כְּמֹשְׁלֵיהֶם.[45] One must bear in mind, however, that in the LXX the verse is plural throughout: "my servants."[46] But the reading could also have been singular originally. The second part of the word would then still require explanation, however: ־ָם *([mĕšull]ām)* or, in the retroversion into Hebrew, ־ֵיהֶם. Could this not conceal an original עַם ("people") or הָעָם ("the people," with the definite article)? Then only one letter, ע, would have dropped out in the consonantal state: כמשל [ע]ם for the singular, כמשלי [ע]ם for the plural.

On the basis of these reflections, and preserving the consonantal text as far as possible, I would emend to מֹשֵׁל הָעָם or מֹשֵׁל עַם, and render the title: "(the) ruler of the people."[47] The catchword "people" (עַם) will be taken up again almost immediately in v. 22,[48] while "rulers" (מֹשְׁלִים) are also mentioned in DtIsa in 49:7 and 52:5, also in unfavorable terms. A "blind ruler" is impos-

---

42 Already Duhm's view, and almost unanimously so seen by modern commentators too; see here Fohrer; Westermann; Schoors, *I Am God Your Saviour* (1973) 202; and Elliger.

43 *mĕšullām* can be a proper name, e.g., 2 Kgs 21:19; 22:3; Neh 8:4; 10:8; 12:3. According to M. Noth (*Die israelitischen Personennamen im Rahmen der Gemeinsemitischen Namensgebung* [1928; reprint 1966] 174; cf. 258) it means that the Deity has "replaced" a dead child (*Piel* of שׁלם). J. L. Palache (*The Ebed-Jahweh Enigma in Pseudo-Isaiah* [1934] 30–42) identifies it with the name of a son of Zerubbabel, mentioned in 1 Chr 3:19; but in spite of this theory a name at this point in v. 19b hardly makes sense. An appellative meaning may therefore be assumed. (For a survey of the various attempts at an interpretation, see Elliger on the passage, and Schoors, *I Am God Your Saviour* [1973] 203–4.) The explanations can be divided according to whether they assume a derivation from the root שׁלם. If this derivation is correct, a *Pual* participle could then be translated: "one who is or will be compensated." This can then be understood in a whole range of meanings, from "the day laborer" (P. A. H. de Boer, *Second Isaiah's Message* [1956] 11) to "the one who finds revenge" (Fohrer). The old interpretation "the perfect one" (supported by Torrey [*Second Isaiah*

(1928)] among modern commentators) also belongs here (see Symmachus: ὁ τέλειος; cf. also Heb 5:9). Other commentators proceed from the *Hiphil* meaning: "to make peace with" (see Josh 10:1, 4; 11:19; 2 Sam 10:19), perhaps as a *Hophal* participle (cf. Job 5:23). This gives the rendering "the covenanted one" (Kissane, Muilenburg) or "he who has been granted my covenant of peace" (North); cf. also Isa 54:10. The translation "the one whom I send, my envoy" requires emendation to the root שׁלח (see the proposal in *BHK, BHS*).

44 Elliger has developed a derivation from משׁל I, "to utter a saying," and מֹשְׁלִים as "one who talks big." But this does not seem to me to fit the context.

45 Thus already Duhm, 292.

46 οἱ παῖδές μου . . . οἱ κυριεύοντες αὐτῶν . . . οἱ δοῦλοι τοῦ θεοῦ.

47 For משׁל see J. A. Soggin, "משׁל *mšl* to rule," *TLOT* 2:689–91 [*THAT* 1:930–33]. Cf. K. Baltzer, *Die Biographie der Propheten* (1975) 26–27 on 2 Sam 23:1-7; p. 35 on Judg 8:23; pp. 73 and 151 on the problem of avoiding established titles in titular use. Cf. Gen 45:8, 26; Josh 12:2, 5; 2 Sam 23:3; 1 Kgs 5:1 (4:21); Isa 16:1; Jer 22:30; 51:46; Mic 5:1 (2); Hab 1:14; Pss 22:29 (28); 59:14 (13); 66:7; 89:10 (9); Prov 23:1; 28:15; 29:12, 21; Qoh 9:17; 1 Chr 29:12; 2 Chr 7:18; 9:26; 20:6. The word is generally linked by way

sible;[49] here the expression is certainly used in a transferred sense, rather like the way it is used in the saying about "the blind leading the blind" in the NT.[50] That would mean that DtIsa is picking up a saying about a "servant of Yahweh" and a "ruler of the people" who were proverbially incapable, and is applying the saying to Israel as a whole.

■ **20** After the pointed question "Who?" which can only be answered by "Israel, Yahweh's servant," v. 20 appears to be a summing up of the accusation. The text of the verse is not quite clear. The person and gender of the verbal forms change continually. The text may be corrupt. Or it is intact and the difficulties must once again be put down to the style.[51] But behind the textual problem there is a difficulty of content too. In v. 18 a number of people are addressed; v. 19 then talks about them in the terminology "servant" in the singular form. In light of the context, for v. 20 to be addressed to a singular "you" would thus be comprehensible and would make sense. I would therefore read v. 20aα as: "you [sing.] have seen," רָאִיתָ (cf. 1QIsaᵃ).[52] There is no need to be disturbed by the fact that v. 20bβ then goes on in the third person: "he does not hear";[53] that would correspond to the shift from the second to the third person in vv. 18-19.

The commands to "keep" (שמר) and to "hear" (שמע) are among the fundamental requirements of the OT.

"Keep, preserve" almost becomes a technical term for religious conduct. The object can be God's commandments (e.g., Gen 26:5; Deut 4:2; cf. Psalm 119; Prov 4:4), justice (Hos 12:7 [6]; Isa 56:1), or the covenant (Gen 17:9-10). What is striking about the present text is that it is *what happens* which is especially to be preserved, this probably meaning Yahweh's acts. But in the "covenant" two things are united:[54] Yahweh's activity constitutes the relationship with him—the keeping of the commandments is the result. "Hearing" or "listening to" can also be used in the semantic field that includes the terms "commandments," "law" and "covenant."[55] In relation to God it often means "obeying."[56] Conversely, "not to listen" is a threat to the relationship with God.

People do not necessarily translate what they know into action: that trial to faith finds expression in this verse. But the failure is due to guilt, not fate.

■ **21** A key statement for the interpretation of the section is the declaration in v. 21 that Yahweh has made the law great and glorious because of his faithfulness to the community. A speaker begins this declaration after Yahweh's accusation has been heard (vv. 18-20). Some scholars suspect that the sentence reflects a later understanding of the law, and it is hence frequently deleted as secondary. But it seems to me so firmly bound up with the logic of the argumentation in the context that omission is

---

of a בְּ, e.g., מוֹשֵׁל בְּיִשְׂרָאֵל (Mic 5:1 [2]; 2 Chr 7:18), but it does occur without a preposition, e.g., מֹשֵׁל עַמִּים (Ps 105:20 for Pharaoh). For the plural cf. הַמּוֹשְׁלִים בָּעָם, 2 Chr 23:20, and מֹשְׁלֵי הָעָם, Isa 28:14. Elliger also points to the Syriac translation: "Who is blind like the ruler" מנו עוירא איך שליטא.

48 The Lucianic recension of the LXX has an ὁ λαός in front of παῖδες.

49 This infringes on his physical wholeness. The blinding of Zedekiah puts an end to his rule (2 Kgs 25:7); Eli's blindness (1 Samuel 3) perhaps calls his legitimation in question. See, even in modern times, the discussion about the blindness of the last king of Hanover when his country was annexed by Prussia under Bismarck.

50 Matt 15:14; Luke 6:39; cf. Rom 2:19.

51 E. Z. Rodriguez ("Filologia y critica textual en Is. 40–55," *Burg.* 11 [1970] 101) talks about "el estilo vehemente retorico del contexto."

52 Here too LXX has the second person plural.

53 On the basis of various manuscripts, Elliger pleads that this was originally an impersonal formulation

throughout. He renders the passage: "Sees so much, yet notices nothing; has open ears, and yet hears nothing." It is, however, at least worth considering whether v. 20b might not already belong to what follows. The divine speech would then end in v. 20a, and what the speaker says would begin with v. 20b. It would be the beginning of "the description of distress."

54 See also the formula about keeping "the ways of God" (Gen 18:19; 2 Sam 22:22; Ps 18:22 [21]; Job 23:11; and frequently).

55 Gen 26:5; 1 Kgs 11:38; 2 Kgs 18:12; Isa 30:9; see H.-J. Kraus, "Hören und Sehen in der althebräischen Tradition," *StGen* (1966) 115–23; reprinted in *Biblisch-theologische Aufsätze* (1972) 84–101.

56 E.g., in the phrase "listening to his voice." H. Schult (שמע *šmᶜ* to hear," *TLOT* 3:1375–80 [*THAT* 2:974–82]) draws attention to the following point (1379 [981]): "According to contextual evidence the apparently general demand to hear Yahweh's word often masks the demand for exclusive worship of Yahweh (e.g., Deut 11:13, cf. 16:27f.; 30:16 LXX;

impossible. Here "Torah" is not the individual precept; it is Yahweh's declaration of will[57] as a whole, the will that he has revealed and put into force. Indeed we already find this interpretation in Hosea.[58] "Joy in the Torah" does not necessarily begin only with the so-called Torah psalms (1; 19; 119), even though there too it is particularly related to the individual. In Deuteronomy and the literature associated with it, the regulations of the law, being Yahweh's will, are linked with blessing and curse. The covenant between Yahweh and his people is the overarching factor. Both Jeremiah and Ezekiel interpret Israel's fate with the help of these categories. This approach must be presupposed for DtIsa too (see above on 40:1).

In the present text, the Torah is bound up with God's faithfulness to the community.[59] The judgment in v. 20 is: "not kept and not obeyed"; so the situation of the people is a result of what it has done. With this conclusion the text also belongs completely within the prophetic tradition.

■ 22-23 Verse 22 describes the present distress. Israel is a robbed and imprisoned people. We may again ask how far traditional phraseology is being used to describe the situation of the exile, and how far the language is prompted by topical issues.

Westermann has found general acceptance with his assumption that here we have terminology and motifs belonging to the complaint.[60] This conclusion was a step forward compared with the alternative approach, which asked whether this account was an accurate picture of the exilic situation.[61] Particular exception had been taken to the declaration that the exiles were living in "prisons," a statement that contrasts with the picture that can be deduced from the book of Ezekiel, for instance, which suggests that the exiles lived rather in conditions of compulsory settlement, with limited freedom of movement. Probably the circumstances of the text itself are complicated, since here the intricate play between individual and collective declarations is continued. We have accounts telling us that individuals as well as the kings were really prisoners.[62] Here this is extended to "all" (כֻּלָּם)—a forcible way of expressing what Elliger calls the "loss of liberty." I would also ask: what better way could there be of depicting exile scenically than through "prisoners"?[63] We can here surely perceive the concept, expressed in poetic language, that because

---

Judg 2:17, 20; 3:4; 2 Kgs 21:8f.; 22:13 [cf. v 17]; Jer 9:12-13; cf. also Ps 81:9f. [8-9], 12 [11], 14[13])." This could be true of the context in DtIsa as well.

57   On חפץ see G. Gerlemann, "חפץ ḥpṣ to be pleased" *TLOT* 2:466-67, esp. 467 [*THAT* 1:623-26, 625]: "ḥpṣ is distinguished from ʾhb primarily by means of the fact that 'to be pleased' expresses a particular class distinction between subj[ect] and obj[ect]—it deals mostly with affection on the part of the superior (cf. 1 Sam 18:22)."

58   See Hos 4:6; 8:1, 12; H.W. Wolff, *Hosea* (2d ed. 1965) 138 [*Hosea* (3d ed. 1976) 176-77]; cf. Isa 8:16; Zech 7:12; Jer 31:33.

59   Cf. also v. 24, where Yahweh's ways and the Torah are parallel to one another.

60   For the whole see C. Westermann, "The Structure and History of the Lament in the Old Testament," in *Praise and Lament in the Psalms* (1981) 165–213, esp. 178–81 ["Struktur und Geschichte der Klage im Alten Testament," in *Forschung am Alten Testament* 1:266–305, esp. 277–79]; also his commentary on the present passage, where he points out that all the statements in v. 22 are in the third person, i.e., are elements in the lament that have been transposed into description. He comments that as soon as they are once more transferred into the first person it becomes obvious that they are utterances belonging to a popular lament. Cf. Schoors, *I Am God Your Saviour* (1973) 206 with reference to Pss 7:3 (2); 71:11; Job 5:4; 10:7 for מַצִּיל אֵין; cf. Pss 44:11 (10); 89:42 (41); further 141:9.

61   Still of contemporary importance in the discussion are Delitzsch's opinion, 2:188 [449]: "An allegorizing, embroidered picture of the homelessness and servitude of exile" [trans. altered], and Marti's (293): "It cannot be deduced from the passage that DtIsa did not know the true conditions in which the individual exiles lived"; also Duhm (293): "Even if we view this as extreme hyperbole, it is proof that DtIsa did not live in Babylon." It has also been repeatedly maintained that this is an image about the robbing of a caravan during the journey through the desert; thus Volz, Muilenburg, and Young. Cf. also Abraham's intervention on Lot's behalf in Genesis 14, and as a counterpart to the crime of Joseph's brothers (Genesis 37).

62   2 Kgs 25:7: "They . . . put out the eyes of Zedekiah; they bound him in fetters and took him to Babylon" (cf. 2 Chr 36:6); 2 Kgs 25:27: "King Evil-merodach of Babylon . . . released King Jehoiachin of Judah from the dungeon (מִבֵּית כֶּלֶא)."

63   "That" (הוּא) people, so emphasized at the beginning of v. 22, can again be an indication that "the people" are conceived of as being present.

they did not obey Yahweh, their God, and keep his covenant, he was not "in their midst." So the people had no one who could save them, or who could claim back the people who had been taken prisoner. The same applies in the civil-law categories of the relationship between master and servant. At the same time, this is doubtless where the topical reference to DtIsa's own time begins. That is particularly true if the text is associated with the postexilic period and the country's restoration. The experience of the Babylonian exile is applied to the misery of the people who have been enslaved because of their debts.[64] The description of the distress is part of the complaint; but it can also be the first step toward ending the affliction. So here the explicit demand to the listeners in v. 23 has its proper place.

■ **24-25** In many respects these verses are parallel to vv. 21-23. Expressions used in v. 22 are taken up once more. The argument is if anything even harsher and more bitter. It is not just that God has passively done nothing to save his people; he has actually himself delivered up Jacob/Israel (v. 24). In his anger he has played an active part (v. 25). The reason is Israel's sin; this is seen with equal clarity. It is exegetically absurd to dispute DtIsa's authorship of individual sayings, or parts of verses, on the grounds that they are "Deuteronomistic." He is very well able to think in the tradition of the covenant. Language and total concept coincide. He takes up the parenetic application too,[65] objectively establishing the fact of guilt. "We have sinned" (חָטָאנוּ): that is the central declaration.[66] It is first formulated as a question, but it requires the assent of the listeners all the more just because of that. The confession makes the way free for a new start, which then begins in 43:1ff. with the assurance of redemption and reinstallation.

But the word order, with its emphatic anterior position, also deserves note: "Is it not *Yahweh* . . . ?" The commentator generally explain the question as a rhetorical one,[67] but perhaps it really was a question requiring a decision. We know from Jer 44:15ff. that there was undoubtedly a discussion as to whether the catastrophe was not due to the discontinuance of sacrifice to "the queen of heaven." Verse 24 would then belong entirely to the dispute about "idols" in DtIsa.

Verse 25 describes the threat in the colors of the "holy war" that had turned against Israel in "the day of Yahweh," as Amos had already predicted.[68] "Burned earth" means utter catastrophe, and raises the question: "What now?"

■ **18-25** If, finally, vv. 18-25 are once more considered under the aspect of dramatic structure, then the monologue that opens Act 2 (42:14-17) is followed in v. 18 by the announcement of the entry of Jacob/Israel, an announcement made by Yahweh himself. There is something "to see" (לִרְאוֹת). Since in the text individual declarations ("Yahweh's servant") alternate with collective ones, it is possible that Jacob/Israel was represented by a single person. That would also be true for the scene that follows in 43:1-7, the reinstallation of "the servant Jacob/Israel."

When from v. 22 onward the speaker points to "that people" (הוּא עָם), one should think rather of the crowd represented by the chorus. Here the correspondence between chorus and listeners or spectators is especially close. The beginning of v. 18 is therefore a skillful one: "You deaf hear, you blind look, so that you may see." The miserable procession of "the robbed and plundered people" could of course be presented without difficulty. The procession of prisoners is a widespread motif in visual art.[69] These people were joined by the fettered occupants of the prisons.

---

64   Cf. Neh 5:1-13; see K. Baltzer, "Liberation from Debt Slavery After the Exile in Second Isaiah and Nehemiah," in *Ancient Israelite Religion: FS F. M. Cross* (1987) 477–84, esp. 480.

65   "They did not want to walk in his ways, did not listen to his precepts/law. . . . They did not perceive them/it . . . but he did not take (them/it) to heart."

66   For a recognition of guilt like this cf. Nehemiah 9; Ezra 9; Daniel 9; see K. Baltzer, *The Covenant Formulary* (1971) chap. 3, "The Covenant Formulary at the Renewal of the Covenant," 39–62 (*Das Bundesformular* [2d ed. 1964] 48–70). The following

reasons are put forward for supposing v. 24bβγ to be a later addition: (1) The passage is prose (Westermann); (2) the order of words is an Aramaism (Marti, Duhm); (3) זוּ as relative pronoun is unusual (see Schoors, *I Am God Your Saviour* [1973] 206–7).

67   Thus Marti, Duhm; see also Westermann here.

68   See Amos 5:18-20; cf. Joel 2:1-11.

69   AOB[2] nos. 128, 133, 141 (the conquest of Lachish by Sennacherib; relief from Nineveh, London, British Museum); see *ANEP:* Mari, no. 305; Egypt, 1, 7, 49, 50, 57, 323, 325, 326, 347; Assyria, 10, 167,

The text is apparently again working with sound sequences. The question "who?" (מִי *mî*) is asked 2 × 2 times (vv. 19, 23); what Jacob/Israel has neglected to do is asserted 3 × 2 times with "not" (לֹא *lōʾ*): "not regarded, . . . not listened to" (v. 20), "they did not want to walk . . . they did not listen" (v. 24), "he did not regard it . . . he did not take it to heart" (v. 25).

Form and content correspond. What is generally valid leads to a conclusion about the specific situation. It is a list of mistakes and transgressions. One need then only notice the accumulation of *ô* sounds from v. 23 onward to comprehend the "complaint" character of the text. If from this point one again looks at v. 24bα, it emerges that the text as a whole builds up to an extreme tension that finds release in the cry: "Is not Yahweh the one . . . ?" The commentators are right in pointing out that the sentence is probably prose, and that the זוּ *zû* as relative pronoun can be an aramaism. But this is a good way of characterizing the people who are acting as chorus. Verse 43:21 then corresponds when, in his compassion, Yahweh talks about "the people there" (עַם זוּ *ʿam zû*). These are the only two occurrences of זוּ in the whole of DtIsa.

In view of the associated sounds, the sentence appears much more firmly embedded in its context than is often assumed. It begins with v. 22: "But that [people], it is a robbed people (עַם־בָּזוּז *ʿam bāzûz*)." In the following passage, v. 25a has "the violence (וֶעֱזוּז) of war." The sequence of vowels in v. 24bα (if we leave the name Yahweh aside) fits the fear and lament: *ǎ ô û ā ā û ô*. If the sentence is the cry of the people, it was probably not merely spoken once; it would have been repeated. For it is in a few words the radical confession of sin to which 43:1 responds: "But now (וְעַתָּה), thus says Yahweh."

Here DtIsa witnesses to the laborious process by which Israel addressed and worked through its grief over the calamity. The catastrophe of the collapse was certainly open to different interpretations. The cause could be seen in adverse circumstances, in the superiority of the enemy and their gods. The downfall of Jerusalem meant the end of national existence and—with the destruction of the temple—the end of Israel's religious center too. It is hardly possible to overestimate the total character of the disaster. It affected society in all its aspects.

Prophecy had made it possible to accept that in the catastrophe Israel had encountered not something alien but its own God. As far as we can see, the foundations for this idea were laid in the book of Jeremiah especially. Central to the viewpoint is the concept of "the covenant," which was a focus for Israel's faith. The tenaciously held conviction that the destiny of human beings is the consequence of what they do was the corollary. This text offers a good example of the way experience can be formulated with the help of concepts such as "covenant-law," or "master-servant," or their combination. Here the experience of faith becomes communicable.

One more small observation can be made about the mode of theological argumentation in this text. Its harsh stringency could hardly be outdone, but in v. 24—one of the key points, as we have seen—DtIsa does not relinquish his solidarity with the people to whom he is speaking. Here, quite unexpectedly, stands a "we": "Is not Yahweh the one against whom *we* sinned?" Is it still necessary to defend DtIsa against the charge of a false understanding of the law? For we must not and cannot isolate this passage from its context. Only Yahweh himself can restore the relationship with the divine: DtIsa has already made this plain with his very first saying, "Comfort, comfort my people." The present passage asks first about the reason for the distress. Salvation can then be proclaimed in what follows: "Fear not. . . ."

357, 358, 365, 373. See also O. Keel, *The Symbolism of the Biblical World* (1978) 323–24 [*Die Welt der altorientalischen Bildsymbolik und das Alte Testament* (2d ed. 1977) 280–81].

A. 3.   43:1-7
Renewed Installation of Jacob/Israel, with the Assurance
of Protection
The "Redemption" of Jacob/Israel
The Gathering of Jacob/Israel from the Whole World

43

"For I, Yahweh, am your God, the Holy One
of Israel, your savior" (43:3)

1	But now—thus says Yahweh,
	your creator, Jacob, and the one who
	    formed you, Israel:
	
	Do not be afraid, for I have redeemed you,
	I have called you by name,ᵃ it is to me you
	    belong.

2	When you go through water I am with you,
	and (when you go) through rivers, they will
	    not sweep you away.
	When you walk through fire you shall not be
	    burned,
	and a flame shall not scorch you.

3	For I, Yahweh, am your God, the Holy One of Israel, your savior. I have given Egypt as a ransom for you, Cush and Sheba in exchange for you.
4	Because you are precious in my sight, greatly valued, and (because) I love you, I give \<islands\>ᵃ in exchange for you and nations for your life.
5	Do not be afraid, for I am with you. From the rising (of the sun) I will bring your offspring, and from (its) setting I will gather you,
6	saying to the north, "Give (them) up!" and to the south, "Do not withhold (them)! Bring my sons here from far away and my daughters from the end of the earth,
7	everyone who is called by my name, and whom I have created for my glory, whom I have formed and made!"

1a   For קְרָאתִי בְשִׁמְךָ cf. הַקּוֹרֵא בְשֵׁם in 45:3; קָרָאתִי בְשֵׁם, Exod
31:2; קָרָא יהוה בְשֵׁם, Exod 35:30. An emendation to בִשְׁמִי/
קְרָאתִיךָ בְשִׁמְךָ, "I have called you by your/my name" (*BHS;* cf.
v. 7), is not necessary.

4a   Thus with a correction from אָדָם, "human being(s)" to אִיִּים;
see below.

■ **1-7** The text is self-contained.[70] Ever since Begrich's investigation,[71] it has been termed a "salvation oracle." The introductory "But now" (וְעַתָּה, v. 1) links the section with what has gone before. It is a kind of summing up: this is now a new hour, a new situation.[72] In the present context this is preceded by a description of the distress and, at the same time, by a confession of sin (42:24). In the prayer of complaint too the acknowledgment of guilt is the precondition for the assurance of salvation. The unequivocal assurance of salvation is the *cantus firmus*

---

70   R. F. Melugin ("The Structure of Deutero-Isaiah" [1968] 173–81) offers a convincing discussion of the unity of vv. 1-7, assuming an internal subdivision into vv. 1-3a, 3b-4 and 5-7. The threefold division— the promise of protection (vv. 1-2), the redemption (vv. 3-4), and then the gathering (vv. 5-6)—is clear. What still seems to me uncertain is whether v. 3a is the close of the promise of protection or the beginning of the announcement of redemption. The ter-minology of v. 1a corresponds closely with that of v. 7.

71   Begrich, *Studien zu Deuterojesaja* (1938; reprint 1963) 12.

72   Cf. 44:1; 49:5. "And now" (וְעַתָּה) can mark "the turn from the complaint that has been brought to a responding oracle": thus H. E. von Waldow, *Denn ich erlöse dich: Eine Auslegung von Jes 43* (1960) 15; see also Schoors, *I Am God Your Saviour* (1971) 68.

for the text. It is uttered throughout as God's own speech, delivered under his authority.[73]

God's word is mediated through a "spokesman" (cf. 40:6-8). The formula "thus says Yahweh" is his legitimation as messenger in the prophetic tradition. This probably also offers an indication of the performance practice. The "spokesman" is a prophetic figure. As a "persona" in the sense of the ancient theater, his function is to utter the divine speeches. His outward appearance may also have shown what his role was, if it was in accordance with what a prophet was supposed to look like at that time.[74]

It is noticeable that in this Act II, the formula "thus says Yahweh" occurs five times (43:1, 14, 16; 44:2, 6). It is possible that all five speeches that begin with this introductory formula were spoken by the same "persona." But it is also conceivable that they were divided among as many as five speakers, according to circumstances. This would presuppose a further differentiation of the tasks of proclamation, in which the messengers could have had varying ranks and importance.[75]

The unambiguous character of what is said easily obscures the fact that the text is the result of a highly complicated process of theological reflection; but though intricate, the steps can still easily be traced. The passage takes up and passes on experiences of faith. It has often been observed that in this text utterances

applied to individuals are linked with others that are directed to Israel as a whole.[76] But this corresponds precisely to what we already discovered about the statements describing Jacob/Israel as Servant.[77] Thus it is advisable here too to follow the interpretive approach chosen there, so as to understand the structure of the text more fully. That the term "servant" (עבד) is missing here is not an obstacle, since it will presently emerge that the semantic field to which the word belongs is undoubtedly represented.

■ **1-3a** If the address to Jacob/Israel in v. 1 is excluded for the time being, the verses can again be understood as having an individual reference. The address is in the second person singular throughout. An assertion of ownership is put forward ("you belong to me," v. 1), and the promise of protection given (vv. 2-3). But if God himself is speaking directly to a human being ("Do not be afraid!"), then—if we ask about the presuppositions of a text of this kind—the number of possible genres can easily be narrowed down. Here again, in my view, elements[78] in the installation accounts of prophets[79] are again comparable. This may be demonstrated from the installation of Jeremiah.

1. The vocation oracle in Jer 1:5 declares expressly that Jeremiah has been chosen and created by God. It is a salvation saying that is directly related to the prophetic office. Creation is the justification for the right of own-

---

But this is not the only possible use of the formula. The initial concern is to affirm the "beginning of the present" in each case. It therefore also has a characteristic place, for example, in historical surveys such as Josh 24:14, at the end of the retrospective review of the redemptive history, and in Neh 9:32, at the end of the history of disaster. The description of wretchedness in Isa 42:18-25 is not far removed from the prayer of lament. In this way the link with the context can remain, without its being necessary first to construct a prayer of lament to precede the present oracle of salvation.

73 The messenger formula "Thus says Yahweh . . ." is characteristic of OT prophecy. The prophet represents Yahweh to his people. He can therefore be termed Yahweh's "mouth" (פֶּה, Jer 15:19; cf. Isa 30:2; 51:16; 59:21; Jer 1:9, 10; 5:14) or "voice" (קוֹל). That is this messenger's rank. As an aid to understanding I have therefore drawn on the institution of the vizier in Egypt (Baltzer, *Die Biographie der Propheten* [1975] esp. 153–56), his judicial functions being a particularly important point of comparison. For the

present text, this means that the closest parallel is not the *priestly* salvation oracle. Thus I would agree with the criticism of R. Kilian, "Ps 22 und das priesterliche Heilsorakel," *BZ* n.s. 12 (1968) 172–85; and R. P. Merendino, "Literarkritisches, Gattungskritisches und Exegetisches zu Jes 41,8-16," *Bib* 53 (1972) 1–42. If the structure and content correspond to those of a salvation oracle (see Schoors, *I Am God Your Saviour* [1973] 32ff., "§1. Definition of the Genre"), one could more readily talk here about a *prophetic* salvation oracle.

74 For the NT cf. Mark 1:6.

75 Cf. below on 52:7-10; 54:4, 5, 6, 7-8, 9-10.

76 See Westermann, 116 [95].

77 See esp. 41:8-13.

78 Cf. above on 42:1-7.

79 See Baltzer, *Die Biographie der Propheten* (1975) 113ff.

ership. Against this background, the reference to creation in Isa 43:1 would not seem to be fortuitous.

2. An essential element in the installation is the "word of encouragement."[80] In Jer 1:8 this runs: "Do not be afraid of them, for I am with you to deliver you." This agrees with the present text right down to the wording. The fear is not a numinous fear. It is the fear of enemies. This becomes clear through the repetition of the word of encouragement in Jer 1:19 and the way it is taken up again in the framework of Jeremiah's so-called confessions.

3. Words of encouragement often include extremely vivid comparisons.[81] That does not mean that the dangers are any less concrete. Yahweh makes of Jeremiah "a fortified city, an iron pillar, and a bronze wall, against the whole land." This is a way of promising him that "they will fight against you; but they shall not prevail against you, for I am with you, says Yahweh, to deliver you" (Jer 1:19). Yahweh himself protects the one who enters his service. He confers immunity on that one. In the present text, danger is described through the elements of water and fire.[82] Even in these extremes Yahweh stands guard. As for genre, this should be interpreted as an "image" saying,[83] in the framework of the installation.

It is interesting that the legends in the book of Daniel describe deliverance from fire and flame quite literally. The story of "the three men in the burning fiery furnace" (Daniel 3) reads positively like an illustration of the promise in Isa 43:2. Daniel's friends are explicitly called "servants of the Most High God" (Dan 3:26; cf. vv. 16-18, 28). The protection that is originally given to the prophets in particular is in the book of Daniel granted to the devout individual too.[84]

In the context of the book of DtIsa, the main concern is to testify to the hope for deliverance in every conceivable peril. But the link with the context is not given merely by way of a superficial association with the catchword "water"; because Israel as a whole is a "servant,"[85] it succeeds to everything that was once promised to the special "servants," the prophets, at their installation, and to which they testified with their lives. The calling by name is a declaration of possession. It is a legal act that comprises at one and the same time a claim to mastery or control and the assurance of protection.[86]

Jacob/Israel is protected in this very way. Isa 40:26 acknowledged that God "calls by name" the countless host of the stars. Everyone is unique in just this sense. The name means more than that God is interested in people personally. To give a name is also to give a charge and an authorization. Thus Cyrus is called to his task through the naming of his name (44:28; 45:1). He is trusted, and God cannot and will not simply do without him in his plans. But this is true not only of the great ones of history, nor does it apply only to prophets. It is true for every single individual among God's people. Jacob/Israel has dared to make the test as to whether it is true that it is not the people's own diligence and competence that can make a name for them; it is God alone who gives them their name, and lets them be his people, even if the historical continuity cannot be discerned by human eyes.

---

80 Ibid., 121.

81 Cf. Ezek 2:6; 3:8.

82 See Pss 21:10 (9); 32:6; 66:12; 69:3 (2), 15-16 (14-15); 78:13; 88:17-18 (16-17); 124:4-5; 144:5-7. For Ps 66:12, H.-J. Kraus (*Psalms 60–150* [1989] 38 [*Psalmen* 2 (5th ed. 1978) 459]) points to "an old mythical motif (H. Gunkel, "Das Märchen im AT," *Religionsgeschichtl. Volksbücher* [1921] 65f. [*Folklore in the Old Testament* (1987) 80–81]) or to uses of the ordeal (H. Schmidt)." See also H. Otten, "Das Hethiterreich," in H. Schmökel, ed., *Kulturgeschichte des Alten Orients* (1961) 395–96; cf. H. Ringgren, "Gottesurteil, Ordal," *BHH* 1:600; H. H. Cohn,"Ordeal," *EncJud* 12:1448–50. Cf. Luke 10:19; Rom 8:38-39. North (119) sees a close connection with the preceding 42:25: "The assurance that flames will *not* now scorch is intended as a contrast with the flames that *did* scorch."

83 For the "going through" (עבר) water it is worth considering whether this is not also a play on the Jacob tradition of Gen 32:23-33 (22-32).

84 In the application to Israel there may also be a reference to the rescue at the Reed Sea. D. N. Freedman has therefore proposed the reading: "*beô yam*, 'through the sea,' instead of 'through waters'" (in McKenzie, 49). For a contrary view see C. Stuhlmueller, *Creative Redemption in Deutero-Isaiah* (1970) 13 n. 397: "The combination of water and fire is reminiscent of a more general overwhelming danger." Cf. also the rescue of Jonah from the sea in comparison with the utterances of the psalm in Jonah 2, esp. vv. 4-7 (3-6).

85 Cf. Jacob/Israel in v. 1.

86 Amos 9:12; 2 Chr 7:14; Isa 63:19; Deut 28:10; Jer 14:9; Isa 62:2; Zeph 3:12.

If we start from the assumption that vv. 1-3a have to be understood in the context of prophetic installation accounts, then one catchword attracts attention because it does not immediately seem to fit the context: "for I have redeemed you" (כִּי גְאַלְתִּיךָ, v. 1). At an installation someone is taken into service. But only someone who was already in a master's service can be redeemed. So what we have here can only be a *re*installation.[87] It is only in the light of the overriding understanding in DtIsa of what it means for Israel to be a servant that the word "redeem" emerges in its full meaning in this text. According to L. Köhler,[88] גאל is "a term of family law." It means "to lay claim to a person, to something > to demand him, to redeem." We can reconstruct a sociomorpheme of "redemption" that looks roughly as follows: a master has a slave who serves him; since the master is no longer satisfied with this slave because of some culpable failure, he sells him; the slave thereby becomes entirely a "commodity," also losing any such rights as he still possesses; he finds that with his new master conditions are considerably worse; remorsefully he turns to his old master again; this master is prepared to buy the slave back—to redeem or ransom him.

A number of OT texts show that this sociomorpheme drawn from the sphere of private and labor law had already been used as a way of describing the relationship between Yahweh and Israel. In the book of Judges, the sociomorpheme is part of the overriding framework. With the help of the semantic field it can easily be discerned, especially through the key word "sell."[89] The pattern can already be detected in Judges 2:

(v. 11) The Israelites did what was evil in the sight of Yahweh and served (וַיַּעַבְדוּ) the Baals. . . . (v. 12) . . . and they provoked Yahweh to anger. . . . (v. 14) Then the anger of Yahweh was kindled against Israel, and

he gave them into the hand of . . . and he sold them (וַיִּמְכְּרֵם); . . . (v. 15) . . . and they were hard pressed. . . . (v. 18) And he delivered them (וְהוֹשִׁיעָם) from the hand . . . for Yahweh was moved to pity by their groanings because of those who persecuted and oppressed them.

The same pattern is behind 1 Sam 12:8-15.[90] Within the semantic field, individual terms can be exchanged. This probably reflects the particular interest of the author concerned. In the book of Judges, the "redemption" (in the sense of גאל) is described in the words "help, save" (ישע), in 1 Samuel 12 with "draw out, rescue" (נצל). Exod 6:6 puts "deliver from slavery" and "redeem" parallel to one another.[91] For DtIsa "redeem" (גאל) is the dominant term, as the very frequency and distribution of the instances show.[92]

The transference to Israel of this sociomorpheme, whose original habitat was the sphere of private law, was therefore not new; DtIsa was taking over an already existing usage. We may assume that his addressees too were familiar with this tradition. When the key word "I have redeemed you" appears in vv. 1-3, it acts as both a reminder and a signal. For the question is: can Israel still be a "servant" after all that has happened? The answer here is: "Yes—a servant who has been bought back!" The problem of "redemption" is one of the central issues in this text, and this was precisely perceived by the version in the Qumran Isaiah scroll (if indeed this does not actually offer the original reading). There vv. 1-3a end: "Yahweh . . . who redeems (גואלך) you," instead of "who helps/saves you."

87 Cf. Jer 15:19-20.
88 *HALOT* 1:169 [*HALAT* 1:162] under this heading, drawing on J. J. Stamm, *Erlösen und Vergeben im AT* (1940) 27–45: see also Stamm, "גאל *gˀl* to redeem," *TLOT* 1:288–96 [*THAT* 1:383–94, esp. §4f, 293–94 [390–92]; H. Ringgren, "גאל, *gāˀal*" *TDOT* 2:350–55 [*ThWAT* 1:884–90]; A. R. Johnson, *The Primary Meaning of gˀl* (1953) 67; A. Jepsen, "Die Begriffe des 'Erlösens' im AT," in *FS R. Hermann* (1957) 153–63; N. H. Snaith, "The Hebrew Root gˀl," *ALUOS* 3 (1961–62) 60–67; F. Holmgren, "The Concept of Yahweh as Goˀel in Second Isaiah" (1963); C. Westermann, *Sprache und Struktur der Prophetie Deuterojesajas* (1964) 157–60; Stuhlmueller, *Creative Redemption in Deutero-Isaiah* (1970) 99–131; Baltzer, "Liberation from Debt Slavery After the Exile in Second Isaiah and Nehemiah," in *Ancient Israelite Religion: FS F. M. Cross* (1987) 477–84, esp. 479–80.
89 See Judg 2:14; 3:8; 4:2; 10:7. Cf. Ps 44:13 (12) as an indictment of Yahweh within the song of lament: "You sold your people for nothing, and had little profit from the price."
90 See "sell" (מכר), v. 9; "serve the baals" (עבד), v. 10.
91 Exod 6:6: וְהִצַּלְתִּי אֶתְכֶם מֵעֲבֹדָתָם וְגָאַלְתִּי אֶתְכֶם; cf. Exod 15:13.

In this part of DtIsa, up through Act IV (49:13), "redemption" (גאל)[93] is an indicator for the sociomorpheme "master-servant" as a description of the relationship with God. The use of redemption (גאל) in the sociomorpheme "man-woman" for Yahweh's relationship to Zion/Jerusalem from Act V onward (49:19ff.) must be distinguished from this.[94]

When God "redeems" human beings, he begins something new by so doing. All previous history, with its diverse vicissitudes, is finished and done with. There is no longer any outside power of disposal. To be ruled by forces outside one's own control (*Fremdbestimmung*) is a familiar aspect of modern experience too. Redemption" is the gift of freedom.

■ **3b-7** The second part of this section is in many respects parallel to the first.[95] Some of the correspondences are almost word for word.[96] But the differences should be noticed too. At least in vv. 5, 6, and 7 those addressed are, in sense, plural. This is especially notable in v. 7, where the corresponding v. 1 of the first part is in the singular. The impression given is that the second part (vv. 3b-7) is an exposition, or interpretation, of the first part (vv. 1-3a), or, to be more exact, it is an application to the specific situation. "Redemption" is understood as return from exile.

■ **3b-4** Within the pattern of this sociomorpheme as we have developed it, the argument can be carried forward in quite precise terms. If someone or something is "redeemed," compensation must be offered. The compensation normally takes the form of money or goods.[97] In the present case it is countries or their inhabitants who are given in exchange for the exiles.[98] It is, so to speak, merely a step-by-step barter (תַּחְתֶּיךָ, v. 3; cf. v. 4: bis).[99] The parallel text in 45:13 and 14 will make plain that this is neither a price paid for the thing purchased nor a gift. It is a quite particular "redemption" such as one could not expect. What it *means* bursts the bounds of the traditional linguistic *form* in which it is expressed.

The comparison with chap. 45 supports the supposition that 43:3b already contains a specific topical allusion, for vv. 13 and 14 of this later chapter are declarations about Cyrus. This would point to a political constellation in which Cyrus had subdued Egypt, Cush and Sheba (i.e., the parts of Africa and southern Arabia known to Israel).[100] How far this was historical fact, or was claimed as such, cannot be said with any degree of certainty.[101] DtIsa announces the claim as actually fulfilled.

---

92   Isa 41:14; 43:1, 14; 44:6, 22-24; 47:4; 48:17, 20; 49:7, 26; 51:10; 54:5, 8.

93   See 49:7.

94   Cf. 49:26; (51:10); 52:3, 9; 54:5 and 8. Stuhlmueller has noted the difference; see his *Creative Redemption in Deutero-Isaiah* (1970) 115ff.

95   See Westermann on this passage, with a somewhat different demarcation.

96   In order to make this clear, the parallel passages may again be cited here: 43:1-2 (I) and 43:5, 7 (II)—partly in literal translation:

   I   vv. 1-2   Do not be afraid . . . you are mine . . . I am with you.
   II   v. 5   Do not be afraid, for I am with you.
   I   v. 1   I have called you by your name.
   II   v. 7   everyone who is called by my name.
   I   v. 1   your creator . . . the one who formed you.
   II   v. 7   Whom I have created . . . whom I have formed.

97   E.g., כֹּפֶר, Gen 32:21(20); Num 35:31; Ps 49:8(7); Job 33:24; cf. also on פדה; פְּדְיוֹךָ.

98   By contrast, in a similar context Isa 11:11-12 talks explicitly about "buying" (לִקְנוֹת): "On that day the Lord will extend his hand yet a second time to recover the remnant that is left of his people, from Assyria, from Egypt, from Pathros, from Ethiopia, from Elam, from Shinar, from Hamath, and from the coastlands of the sea. And he will raise a signal for the nations and will assemble the outcasts of Israel, and gather the dispersed of Judah from the four corners of the earth." With reference to individuals, cf. Prov 11:8; 21:18.

99   אָדָם is difficult to explain. In the parallelism to "nations" (אֻמִּים) one would expect something like "islands" (אִיִּים), following 41:1; 49:1 (thus Graetz, Klostermann, Torrey). Other commentators emend to (among other things) אֲדָמוֹת, "countries" (Duhm, Marti, Cheyne, North, Westermann, Fohrer; for a contrary view cf. Volz). Did a later period relate this to "Edom"? The consonants would make this possible.

100 Cf. Gen 10:6-7.

101 For the dating see below. For criticism see Duhm and Cheyne on this passage; also Muilenburg (483) on 43:4.

Verse 4b is similar in content to v. 3b, differing only in being once more formulated in quite general terms.[102] In both cases it may be assumed that the "you" (sing.) addressed is not an individual person. This has to do with *Israel's* redemption. The reason for the "buying out," redemption or liberation is given: it is simply God's love.[103] The phrase "and I love you" (וַאֲנִי אֲהַבְתִּיךָ) can still have a legal overtone in the sense of a bond of loyalty, but at the same time it undoubtedly expresses God's whole personal bond with his people, which rests on his free election.

■ **5-6** Whereas vv. 3 and 4 could initially still be restricted to the liberation of the men and women in Babylonian exile, in vv. 5 and 6 the horizon widens out: those who have been scattered will come from all directions, from the very ends of the earth.[104] It is only this that is really the turning point of the exile,[105] and with it the beginning of the era of salvation. Here the text follows the trend of the whole book toward as wide and general an application as possible. At this stage in the interpretation, too, the concept of the "*servant*

Israel/Jacob" is abandoned. The word now used is "seed." This can still refer to Israel/Jacob as progenitor. The new community will correspond to the beginning. "My sons . . . my daughters" (v. 6): the relationship to God is thus directly described in family categories. The declaration implies that God is not merely the "lord" or "master" of a "servant"; he is also the "father" of "sons *and* daughters."[106] So the whole of God's people is now embraced.

■ **7** This verse forms the conclusion and also the climax and most extreme intensification of the passage. "All who are called by Yahweh's name" means all the men and women who belong to him. The fact of creation justifies the right of ownership. The formulations in v. 1 are taken up once more. But now they are related to individuals, so that "creation" is not just something that happened at the beginning of the world.[107] The close of the passage says emphatically: "I have made them."[108] It is understandable that this could be the start of an interpretation that no longer accepted the restriction to the descendants of Jacob/Israel.[109]

---

102 See also above on 42:10-12.

103 Here the traditions of Hosea, Deuteronomy and Jeremiah have been taken up. On אהב see W. L. Moran, "The Ancient Near Eastern Background of the Love of God in Deuteronomy," *CBQ* 25 (1963) 77–87; N. Lohfink, *Das Hauptgebot: Eine Untersuchung literarischer Einleitungsfragen zu Dtn 5–11* (1963) 73–74, 78, 80 chart IV, 303–4; E. Jenni, "אהב *ʾhb* to love," *TLOT* 1:45–54, esp. 51–53 [*THAT* 1:60–73, esp. 69–71; T. C. Vriezen, "Bubers Auslegung des Liebesgebots, Lev 19,18b," *ThZ* 22 (1966) 4–7.

104 The points of the compass are addressed as if they were persons (with feminine forms). But they are no longer deities. They have been demythologized, as it were. And yet they obey commands! At the same time a dramatic element is again conceivable here: in other scenes in DtIsa the representatives of foreign countries are present; here, similarly, it is the points of the compass.

105 Cf. Jer 40:12; K. Baltzer, "Das Ende des Staates Juda und die Messias-Frage," in *Studien zur Theologie der alttestamentlichen Überlieferung: FS G. von Rad* (1961) 35; also Acts 2:5ff.; John 11:51-52; Luke 13:29.

106 At this point Muilenburg points to Exod 4:22-23; Hos 11:1; Isa 1:2; further Jer 3:4, 19; 31:9; Hos 1:10; Isa 63:16; 64:8 (9); Mal 1:6. Also important in this connection, however, is Paul's argument that liberation from the "slavery" of the law through Christ

means liberation for a relationship as a child to God (Rom 8:12-18; Gal 4:1-7, and frequently).

107 See B. J. van der Merwe, *Pentateuchtradisies in de Prediking van Deuterojesaja* (1955) 1–38, esp. 38, and 172–75. P's term for creating (ברא) and the word used by J (יצר) are combined here.

108 None of the three verbs can be dispensed with here (for another view see Duhm, Marti, and Cheyne on this passage), for in this act, 43:1 onward (cf. vv. 15, 21; 44:2, 21, 24), these catchwords establish the link with the making of idols (44:9ff.). Here Torrey draws attention to the conclusion of a poetic unit, with its triple elements. For the nuances of the terms see Delitzsch, 2:39 [452]: "The three synonyms bring out the power, the liberty and the riches of grace with which Jehovah called Israel into existence, to glorify himself in it, and that he might be glorified by it. They form a climax, for בָּרָא signifies to produce as a new thing; יצר to shape what has been produced before, and עשׂה to make it perfect or complete—i.e., *creavi, formavi, perfeci*" [trans. altered]. Stuhlmueller (*Creative Redemption in Deutero-Isaiah* [1970]) interprets as follows (115): "*brʾ* emphasizes that only Yahweh, no other kinsman, can perform a redemptive act as glorious as this one . . . *yṣr* enunciates the tender and careful way in which Yahweh forms the new life of his child Israel."

109 Cf. Fohrer's interpretation, 61.

B. 1. 43:8-15
Court Scene with the Dramatis Personae:
Yahweh Himself, Israel as a People, the "Peoples"
and "Nations"
Yahweh's Ability to Act

43

"You are my witnesses . . . and my servant whom I have chosen" (43:10)

8   Lead out[a] a blind people—and yet there are
            eyes;
     and deaf—and yet it has ears!

9   All the peoples have gathered together,
     and nations are to assemble.
     Who among them can declare this
     and tell us of earlier (events)?
     Let them bring their witnesses, so that they
            may receive justice,
     and hear and say: "It is true/It is right."
10   You are my witnesses—saying of Yahweh—
     and my servant whom I have chosen
     so that you may know and believe me
     and understand that I am he:
     before me no god was formed,
     and after me there will be none.

11   I, I am Yahweh,
     and besides me there is no helper.
12   I have made known and have let be helped
            and have let be heard,
     and no stranger among you,
     And you are my witnesses—saying of
            Yahweh—but I am God.
13   From henceforth also I am the one,
     and no one can deliver from my hand.
     I act—and who can avert it?

14   Thus says Yahweh, your redeemer, the Holy
            the Holy One of Israel:
     For your sakes I have sent (him) to Babylon,
     and will break down all bars.[a]
     And the Chaldeans: their jubilation will
            become <lamentation>.[b]
15   I am Yahweh, your Holy One,
     Israel's creator, your king.

8a   Following 1QIsa[a] read הוֹצִיא instead of MT הוֹצִיא; cf. below on
     this passage.
14a Cf. below on this passage.
14b Read בָּאֳנִיּוֹת instead of בָּאֳנִיּוֹת, "on ships"; see below.

Verse 8 clearly marks the beginning of this section of text.[110] Where the section ends is not quite so clear. Most commentators assume that it closes with v. 13. Verses 14-15 could be a separate unit or could also belong to the following text. But it would be very short for a separate unit. Because of their content, I would rather add the verses onto vv. 8-13. They give concrete

form to the future that has previously been announced in general terms. In the passage as a whole, vv. 16-21 then pursue the ideas in vv. 8-15. We may thus assume that vv. 8-15 is a unit with a (relatively) consistent sense.

The basic elements of the text show that its genre is again a trial scene. The dramatis personae are:[111]

---

110 For a different view see J. D. Smart, *History and
     Theology in Second Isaiah* (1967) 98; also Bonnard on
     this passage, 140–41.

111 See Muilenburg here (486): "Present again are the
     three major dramatis personae of the poems: God,
     the nations, and Israel. A strophe is devoted to

Yahweh himself; Israel as a people (עַם), also termed "my witnesses" (עֵדַי, vv. 10, 12) and "my servant" (עַבְדִּי, v. 10); and in addition the "peoples" (הַגּוֹיִם) or "nations" (לְאֻמִּים, v. 9).

If we assume that Yahweh is talking as God (אֵל), in direct speech (v. 12), the *scene of the action* must be the heavenly sphere. That the peoples are represented by their gods would fit in with this. But here we run up against one of the difficulties about the text, for the reality of the foreign gods is precisely the point under dispute. Thus the content modifies the form. The same applies to "Israel." It could be represented by a "servant of Yahweh." Moses, like the prophets, has access to the heavenly sphere where no mortal person can otherwise be. But for DtIsa, Israel as "the servant" is understood in a collective sense, and this change of stance makes itself felt right down to the grammar of the text.[112]

Elements in the *action* are "Israel's" entry (v. 8)[113] and the assembly of the peoples (v. 9). Yahweh speaks, turning to the different groups and thus to the auditorium as well. The text is therefore also a divine speech. But it again includes the elements: question ("Who among them . . . ?" v. 9) and answer ("It is true!" v. 9).

If we presuppose that the overriding genre of the book of DtIsa has to be defined as drama, the scenic elements fit perfectly. It is striking that the scenic character of the present text was recognized long ago but was then brushed aside. Duhm talked about "an imaginative play on judicial proceedings."[114] Begrich[115] described the passage as "an almost scenically composed description of a trial. . . . The characteristic thing about the text is that it lets the trial be seen through the eyes of the witnesses who appear." To term the text "a trial *speech*"[116] robs it of its character as an account of action; for in the speech the action is described and interpreted, as is often the case in the drama of the ancient world. The number of speaking parts is limited, compared with the number of the people taking part in the action.

On the first interpretive level, it is clear that the text contains elements of a lawsuit. For otherwise listeners and spectators would not understand what is going on at all. This is the way—or similar to the way—a court is held in the town's gateway, or in the prince's judgment hall. Köhler has shown this especially well.[117] Elements include the summons to appear (v. 8), the calling of witnesses (vv. 9, 10, 12), and the decision or judgment (vv. 11-13). Public oration and counteroration as a way of clarifying the facts of a case are part of Mediterranean culture. Consequently, the transition from judicial procedure to disputation and vice versa is a fluid one.[118]

On a second level, the text presupposes the tradition about "the dispute between the gods." In the heavenly sphere too, courts of justice are held and disputes settled. This presupposes the polytheistic worldview that

---

112 See the comment on v. 10.

113 הוֹצִיא, following the MT, is *Hiphil* perfect: "He has brought out." 1QIsaᵃ has the more probable reading הוֹצִיאוּ, "Lead out . . ." (cf. Vulgate, LXX). Duhm and others already proposed reading הוֹצִיא (infinitive absolute), though then in an imperative sense. The infinitive "to lead out" makes sense if v. 8 is initially a stage direction indicating what is happening (vv. 8-9aβ), and if the speech only begins again in v. 9aγ with "Which of them. . . ."

114 Duhm, 297; see also 296: "the lively imagination of the author, who has already several times depicted legal proceedings of this kind."

115 Begrich, *Studien zu Deuterojesaja* (1938, reprint 1963) 47; see also 27. Schoors (*I Am God Your Saviour* [1973] 223) renders Begrich by saying: "to him it is a quasi-scenic description of a lawsuit." H. E. von Waldow, "Anlass und Hintergrund der Verkündigung des Deuterojesaja" (1953) 46: "The legal issue in the judicial speeches is either Yahweh's faithfulness . . . or his exclusive claim . . .

each, with God the speaker throughout (vss. 9c-13)."

recognition of him is imposed upon the doubters in dramatic form."

116 See, e.g., Westermann here; Schoors, *I Am God Your Saviour* (1973) 223: "is a trial speech"; R. P. Merendino, *Der Erste und der Letzte: Eine Untersuchung von Jes 40–48* (1981) 324: "It is generally accepted that 43:8-13 is a trial speech," with an excursus on "Deutero-Isaiah's trial speeches," 225ff.

117 L. Köhler, *Deuterojesaja (Jes 40–55) stilkritisch untersucht* (1923), 110–20, esp. 113–14.

118 See von Waldow, "Anlass und Hintergrund der Verkündigung des Deuterojesaja" (1953) 46: "This inner relationship between trial speeches and disputation sayings makes it permissible, in what follows, to treat the two genres no longer separately but together."

was a matter of course for the countries belonging to the OT world. In the OT itself this worldview can still be detected behind a text such as Psalm 82, which begins: "God (Yahweh)[119] stands in the divine assembly (בַּעֲדַת־אֵל), in the midst of the gods he holds court." This DtIsa text is part of the confrontation with these traditions, and its tensions can be explained in that light, as the detailed exegesis will show.

In the trial described, the object of dispute is the ability to act and to proclaim the future as well as the past (v. 9; cf. v. 12). A claim of this kind is to be endorsed or confuted before the court. The claimant is Yahweh as "God" (וַאֲנִי אֵל v. 12).

Up to this point the basic pattern of the scene agrees with the trial scenes hitherto. This makes it all the more important to inquire about the nuances. Here we have to look for the "dramatic progression" that seems to us to be lacking, because of the apparent poverty of action, compared with our modern Western understanding of drama.

■ 8 The very first sentence in v. 8 is a powerful signal that makes the spectators or listeners prick up their ears: the people are "blind" and "deaf." Now, this is doubtless a catchword linked with the beginning of this Act II. Isa 42:18-25 (cf. 42:16) made abundantly clear the sense in which the blindness and deafness of Israel[120] as servant are meant to be understood: as Israel's culpable failure to keep the law (42:20, 21). The catchwords have undergone variations in the present text. Duhm has aptly described the circumstances, and the wordplay: "'The blind people, and eyes exist' does not mean: the people that is blind and yet has eyes."[121] A blind or deaf witness is a contradiction in terms. But here the important thing is that in spite of its blindness and deafness, Israel was in a position to see and hear what happened—it had the

necessary organs. This means that it can testify to the connection between prediction and its God's fulfillment of that prediction. It is an important concern of this text to state that Israel is a "witness."[122] It has meanwhile been reinstalled as "servant," the decision to redeem it has been taken. But it still does not "see" again, and its sins are still the subject of dispute (43:22-28; 44:9-20), until the point comes when conversion is demanded of it (44:22). The "witnesses" too are supposed to arrive at knowledge and insight through the trial (see v. 10).

The special thing about this trial is that here the people (עַם) and the (foreign) peoples (כָּל־הַגּוֹיִם) confront one another as witnesses. In the first trial (41:1-5), the islands are mentioned (vv. 1, 15); in the second (41:21-29), the gods (v. 23).[123] According to the symmetry of the present text, Yahweh, with his people as witness, ought really to be balanced on the other side (in v. 9) by the peoples, with their gods: "Who among *them* can declare this?" The announcement of the future is really a matter for the gods. The people can *be* witnesses of the fact, but they cannot *appear* as witnesses in court. But DtIsa avoids even the *word* "gods" in this text. That is no more than consistent in a text that pleads so unconditionally for the singularity, the uniqueness of Yahweh. "God or the gods"—this was an alternative that was still possible in Josh 24:15-16; Yahweh or Baal was a decision that Elijah had demanded of the people on Carmel.[124] Here there is now only Yahweh, and Yahweh alone. The "dispute between the gods" therefore turns into the dispute between "the witnesses." Israel must enter into this dispute on the earthly level. That is what the listeners can experience.

■ 9 What is the "this" that "is to be declared"? The question is not easily answered.[125] "This" (זֹאת) is a feminine demonstrative pronoun "that almost always points to

---

119 "God" (אלהים) is here generally emended to "Yahweh" (יהוה); see the commentaries on this passage. Cf. also comments on 1 Kgs 22:19ff.; Isa 6:3; Job 1 and 2; Ps 103:19ff. For the lawcourt see Dan 7:9ff.

120 On "seeing" and "not seeing," "knowing and "not knowing" in ancient drama, cf. D. Seale, *Vision and Stagecraft in Sophocles* (1982).

121 Duhm on this passage.

122 "You are my witnesses," vv. 10, 12; see also 44:8.

123 That in 41:1 as in 43:9 the nations (לְאֻמִּים) are mentioned, and that the trial described here presupposes "the gods" (43:9), does not affect the different

emphasis. The distinction for Israel between "people" (עַם) on the one hand and "peoples" (גּוֹיִם) and "islands" (אִיִּים) on the other is already present in 40:1 and 15. It corresponds to the postexilic development of the terminology. See E. Schwarz, *Identität durch Abgrenzung* (1982); A. R. Hulst, "גּוֹי/עַם ʿam/gôy, people," *TLOT* 2:896–919 [*THAT* 2:290–325] (with lit.).

124 1 Kgs 18:21ff., 37, 39.

125 See the summing up in Schoors, *I Am God Your Saviour* (1973) 224–25.

some present (new) . . . person or thing."[126] There is general agreement that it refers to something quite close,[127] in either the immediately preceding[128] or the immediately succeeding[129] sense. Here "this" probably refers to the announcement of saving events, including the restoration of Israel.

But perhaps we can come closer than this to the precise meaning of the text. Elliger has approached v. 9 from the meaning of the verb "make known" (נגד Hiphil). He notices that of twenty-one instances in DtIsa "human beings [are] the subject in only three cases. . . . In sixteen instances the subject is the gods or Yahweh." He concludes from this that for DtIsa the verb also means "the prediction of the course of history as proof of God." Elliger sees a difficulty in the following: "The object זאת 'this,' which turns up so abruptly and without any closer definition, can in itself certainly only mean the present, a present event, especially in its surely antithetical parallelism to ראשנות, 'earlier [events].'" In addition, the verb here is in the imperfect (יַגִּיד), so that it has to be rendered at least by the present, if not even by the future tense. In 41:22 we assumed that נגד Hiphil, "interpret," is used in the sense of the interpretation of Scripture. If we approach the present passage with the same understanding, then in the immediate context "interpretation of Scripture" is being demonstrated in temporal terms too—in 43:16-21 as the history of salvation, in vv. 22-28 as the history of iniquity. What is "interpreted" is the meaning of "my servant whom I have chosen" (43:10; cf. 44:1, 2). Past, present and future are thus once again intimately linked, because it is the selfsame God who acts. "The gods" or their representatives do not understand an interpretation of this kind.

Elliger thinks that "Who among them . . . ?" (v. 9aγ) might possibly indicate "that at this moment he [the speaker] points to their group [the group of the opposing party]." If one accepts this as a possible interpretation, one can then go on to ask whether "this" (זאת) might also be some specific object, perhaps a scriptural scroll. "Scriptures" can be "interpreted" for the present day; they record "the earlier (events, ראשנות)," which "we can be told of" if we read them. In exactly the same way the opposing party can "hear," and then say: "That is right!" (lit.: "it is truth," אֱמֶת).[130] The dramatic situation makes it possible to conceive of a solution to the problem of what "this" (זאת) means that takes the context into account. Verse 9 makes clear that in the contest of ideas[131] foreigners too can come to the conclusion that God's Word is dependable.[132] How much more ought that to be true for Israel itself!

■ **10** In vv. 10ff. reasons are given and expounded for the function of God's people as witness: "You are my witnesses" (vv. 10 and 12). Both times this statement is followed by the formula: "saying of Yahweh" (נְאֻם־יהוה).

---

126 Thus already GKB §136: (p. 436); on the present text: "In Isa 43:9 זאת is used in the sense of our neutral 'such.'"

127 J. Morgenstern, "The Message of Deutero-Isaiah in Its Sequential Unfolding," *HUCA* 30 (1959) 1–102: "זאת has the force of a pronominal suffix. Its antecedent must be some momentous event very soon to happen" (66).

128 Muilenburg on this passage: "Who can foretell the imminent redemption described in vss. 1-7," with reference to 41:2a; 42:23a; 48:14b.

129 North, 122: "This זאת must refer to something specific, most likely the conquest of Cyrus."

130 The resemblance to Daniel is again striking. Unfortunately the text of Dan 10:21—11:2 is corrupt (see the commentaries). Dan 10:21 talks about a "book of truth": "I will tell you what is written in the book of truth" (אַגִּיד לְךָ אֶת־הָרָשׁוּם בִּכְתָב אֱמֶת); see also 11:2a: "Truth (אֱמֶת) will I announce to you." A historical survey then follows in 11:1-12, 13 in the form of a disclosure of the future. It is puzzling why the LXX should have associated this historical note

with Cyrus's first year. For "the book of truth," cf. "the heavenly tablets and what is written thereon" in *1 Enoch* 81:1.

131 McKenzie, 53: "The challenge as in the preceding confrontation is to match prophecy with prophecy. Yahweh presents Israel as his evidence . . . Israel alone among the nations has a true history and an interpretation of the meaning of history; Israel alone is conscious of its destiny and of the path which it must follow to attain its destiny."

132 On אמת see H. Wildberger, "אמן ʾmn, firm, secure," *TLOT* 1:151–57 [*THAT* 1:201–9]: "ʾemet in a profane usage means not only subj[ect]-oriented 'dependability, uprightness,' but also obj[ect]-oriented 'something dependable, truth.' (155 [207])." He takes Isa 43:9 as an example of the juridical arena, where objective truth, not merely subjective truthfulness, is definitely in view. Witnesses before the court can declare the statement of a litigant ʾemet 'it is true,' i.e., the relevant statement agrees with reality" (153 [203]). But in view of the context in Isa 43:9, the use of אֱמֶת in the book of Daniel is not as

Duhm is irritated by the use of the formula here, and in his irritation has made a correct point.[133] In DtIsa's time this was already an age-old formula.[134] I myself believe that here it introduces a divine saying in quoted form.[135] This becomes clear if the content of the two statements is seen together: "my servant whom I have chosen" (v. 10)—"I am God" (אל, v. 12). A quotation can often be detected because it does not completely fit the context. Many commentaries would like to change the singular "my servant" into the plural "my servants."[136] But this would actually wreck DtIsa's theological approach: the *one* servant has become *many* witnesses.[137] Who is the "chosen[138] servant" here? According to the (re)installation in 41:8-13 it is Israel/Jacob, "the seed of Abraham, my friend"; in the passage soon to follow (44:1, 2) he is actually named.[139] So we may ask whether there is not a play on the Jacob tradition in the present text too, or, to be more precise, a reference to Jacob's encounter with God at Bethel (Genesis 28).[140] Its subject is the revelation that Yahweh is the God of the patriarchs, the election of Jacob and his descendants, and the promise of a return to the land of the fathers.

God's speech is citing an ancient divine saying, and that a quotation should be used is in line with the hermeneutical approach developed in the preceding verse, v. 9. The word is valid now, in that present-day Israel becomes a witness. Because it is chosen, the peo-ple can know and acknowledge Yahweh. The verbs "know" (ידע), "believe" (אמן *Hiphil*) and "understand" (בין) name the criteria for Yahweh's witnesses. All these concepts have to do with knowing; that is their common ground. The content of what is known is described immediately afterward. At the same time it becomes clear that this is not merely a question of knowing in the intellectual sense. An attitude and a kind of behavior are implied too. Experience and knowledge are not separate from one another.

The word "witness" defines afresh the function of Israel/Jacob, beyond the confines of this text. Israel/Jacob is to witness to Yahweh and his activity before the peoples. That is the task. The basis of a people's existence can certainly be defined in very different ways. It can be oriented toward the concept of domination, for example. The relationship to the other nations could be differently defined too. Witness means neither subjugation nor conversion. Sovereignty over the world belongs to God alone. The nations themselves must be able to say—in the final words of v. 9—that what is said of this God "is true/is right" (אמת).

The whole text takes a special turn because one might really expect[141] that here the peoples already "perceive . . . believe . . . understand. . . ." Instead the requirements are directed to "the witnesses" themselves first of

---

unique as Wildberger and others assume. Dan 8:26 is explained as follows: "can only mean that the vision is true because one can depend upon it, certain that the fulfillment will not fail" (156 [208]); but this could apply to the present text too.

133 Duhm, 297, on this passage: "One is therefore surprised by this unusual expression . . . and cannot understand why in the middle of his speech Yahweh should stress so simple a statement as that the Israelites are Yahweh's witnesses and servants through the phrase 'murmur of Yahweh.'"

134 See D. Vetter, "נְאֻם *neʾum* utterance," *TLOT* 2:692–94 [*THAT* 2:1–3]; also his *Seherspruch und Segensschilderung* (1974); W. F. Albright, "The Oracles of Balaam," *JBL* 63 (1944) 207–33.

135 According to Vetter, "נְאֻם *neʾum* utterance," *TLOT* 2:694 [*THAT* 2:3], the formula is used, for example "in Jer[emiah] 35x concluding a speech of Yahweh, 31x in introductions, 42x between elements of a parallelism."

136 E.g., Duhm (297): "In the second stichos of v. 10a the reading must be עֲבָדַי, for it is the Israelites who

are the subject here, not the hero of the Servant songs."

137 Schoors (*I Am God Your Saviour* [1973] 226) has noted this correctly.

138 For the use of "choose" (בחר) in DtIsa see R. Lack, *La symbolique du livre d'Isaïe: Essai sur l'image littéraire comme élément de structuration* (1973) 99: "If we examine the successive instances of *bḥr*, we arrive at the following result: the artisan chooses the material for his images (40:20)—idolatry is a choice (41:24). Conversely, Yahweh chooses Jacob (41:8, 9)—Israel is chosen to be a witness (43:10)." See further on 42:8–44:23.

139 See also 49:7.

140 Verse 13 is particularly important: "I am Yahweh, the God of (אֲנִי יהוה אֱלֹהֵי) Abraham your father and the God of Isaac; the land on which you lie I will give to you and to your offspring." See further vv. 15, 17, and 19: "He called that place Beth-El" (וַיִּקְרָא אֶת־שֵׁם־הַמָּקוֹם הַהוּא בֵּית־אֵל), v. 21).

141 For that reason many commentators change the second person plural into the third person plural.

all. For DtIsa too these are the initial addressees, not those far off. The quality of the witness is important for God's Word.

In vv. 10-13, "that I am he" (כִּי אֲנִי הוּא, v. 10bα) introduces Yahweh's speech defending his own position, according to the tenor of the context. Logic would require Israel itself as witness to say: "it is true," "it is right" (אֱמֶת; cf. v. 9). The section contains hymnic elements. Traditional phrases are taken up. But in spite of that, the passage is more firmly incorporated in the context than one immediately notices. Verses 10-12 especially talk about the past, telling who Yahweh is and what he has done; v. 13 has to do with the future. It declares what is going to happen: "I will act" (v. 13). But the claim to let "earlier things" be heard and to proclaim what is future is the very point at issue, according to v. 9.

The divine speech begins afresh in v. 13 with a self-introduction: "From henceforth also I am he" or "I am the one" (אֲנִי הוּא). The formulation is a curious one.

Does "the one" (הוּא) mean the one who is already known?[142]

"Before me no god was formed and after me there will be none." That is the monotheistic formulation in succinct form.[143] The Yahweh religion has always insisted on the sole worship of its God. That is also the core of the First Commandment in the Decalogue. There were other gods for other peoples—about that there was no question. At this stage, therefore, the word "monolatry" should be used for the worship of the one God. The ineffectualness of the foreign gods is already one of Jeremiah's themes. Now the actual existence of other gods is denied, from the very outset.

Theogonies, which tell how the gods came into being, played an important part in the worldview of peoples in the countries surrounding Israel.[144] These theogonies made it possible to bind together different religious traditions. Political changes—for example in the position of the most important state gods—could be expressed by

---

Thus again Duhm on this passage, as a possibility. See Schoors, *I Am God Your Saviour* (1973) 226, in dispute with Zimmerli, "Knowledge of God according to the Book of Ezekiel," in *I Am Yahweh* (1982) 54–55 ["Erkenntnis Gottes nach dem Buche Ezechiel," in *Gottes Offenbarung; Gesammelte Aufsätze zum Alten Testament* (1963) 70].

142 Or is a "God" (אֵל) avoided here because it could collide with the continuation "no God" (אֵל)? Verse 12 has the sequence "I am God" (אֲנִי אֵל) with the continuation in v. 13: "I am that one" (אֲנִי הוּא).

143 F. M. Cross, *Canaanite Myth and Hebrew Epic* (1973); E. Haag, ed., *Gott, der Einzige* (1985); O. Keel, ed., *Monotheismus im Alten Israel und seiner Umwelt* (1980); K. Koch, "Šaddaj: Zum Verhältnis zwischen israelitischer Monolatrie und nordwest-semitischem Polytheismus," *VT* 26 (1976) 299–332; B. Lang, ed., *Der einzige Gott: Die Geburt des biblischen Monotheismus* (1981); M. C. Lind, "Monotheism, Power, and Justice: A Study in Isaiah 40–55," *CBQ* 46 (1984) 432–46; H. Wildberger, "Der Monotheismus Deuterojesajas," in his *Jahwe und sein Volk: Gesammelte Aufsätze zum AT* (1979) 249–73.

144 For *Egypt*, see the texts in *ANET* 1–7; e.g., from the Bremner-Rhind Papyrus (British Museum 10188) XXVI: "After I had come into being as the sole God, there were three gods beside me. I came into being in this land whereas Shu and Tefnut rejoiced in Min, in which they were. . . . Then Shu and Tefnut brought forth Osiris, Horus Khenti-en-irti, Seth, Isis, and Nephthys from the body, one of them after another; and they brought forth there

multitudes in this land."

For *Babylon*, see the creation epic *Enuma eliš*, *ANET* 60ff.; *AOT* 108ff. It begins with the genesis of the gods. The most important of them is Marduk, the god of Babylon. In the Assyrian period, Marduk was sometimes replaced in Assyria by the god Assur.

For the *Hittites*, see the myth about "the kingdom in heaven," *ANET* 120–21. H. G. Güterbock and H. Otten have pointed to the link with Hurrite theogonies on the one hand and with Greek theogonies (following Hesiod) on the other: H. Otten, *Mythen vom Gotte Kumarbi* (1950); H. G. Güterbock, *The Song of Ullikummi* (1952); also his "Hittite Mythology," in S. N. Kramer, ed., *Mythologies of the Ancient World* (1961) 155–72.

For *Phoenicia,* the texts found in Ugarit/Ras Shamra are especially informative. See *ANET* 129ff. The god El has the title "Father" (ʾab). He and his consort Ashera are the parents of the gods, who can be called the sons of El (bn il) or "the seventy children of Ashera." See M. H. Pope, *El in the Ugaritic Texts* (1955); F. M. Cross, *Cannanite Myth and Hebrew Epic* (1973) 13–75, esp. 44–48, 70. For Phoenicia, the tradition of Sanchuniathon should be noted. This was passed down by Philo of Byblos in his Phoenician history (φοινικικά) and is extant in Eusebius *Praeparatio Evangelica.* Text: K. Mras, *Eusebius Werke,* 8/1 (1954). Lit.: O. Eissfeldt, *Ras Schamra und Sanchunjaton* (1939); also his *Sanchunjaton von Beirut und Ilumilka von Ugarit* (1952).

The connections between the different theogo-

way of the sequence in the genealogies. Systematizing elements developed into approaches toward a natural philosophy. The best-known ancient theogony is Hesiod's (c. 700 B.C.E.).[145] There, after the proem, the poet, summoned by the muses, sings of the things to come and the things of the past.[146] In the genealogical arrangement Ouranos, Kronos, and Zeus succeed one another. The goal and purpose is to glorify the Olympic Zeus and his world order.

This example (Hesiod's theogony) brings out all the more distinctly the decisions that lie behind the present DtIsa text. The procreation about which the myth tells is no longer acceptable. The gods are not created, let alone born. This means that in DtIsa the distinction between God and the world has now been finally completed: the world, in all its phenomena, has become creation. To say that Kronos precedes Zeus is also to hear the echo of the Greek word for "time" ($\chi\rho\acute{o}\nu o\varsigma$). But neither before Yahweh nor after him is there any (other) God (אֵל, v. 10). Thus Yahweh is not subject to time either.[147] This is a decision of far-reaching consequence for the concept of the world. As far as the function of the theogonies is concerned, the different pantheons of different ethnic

groups can then no longer be integrated by way of genealogical relationships.

The identification of Yahweh with El picks up, consciously or unconsciously, a long chain of tradition, the traces of which can be seen preeminently in hymnic poetry.[148] But that the identification should be made at this particular point, in the dispute with the nations (גּוֹיִם, v. 9), is surely not fortuitous.

■ **11** This verse begins with the full revelation formula: "I, I am Yahweh." This certainly signals a dramatic climax.[149] The self-introductory formula might have continued: "and besides me there is no God." But there is no need to say that again here. Instead the utterance stresses that Yahweh is a "helper" or, as others translate the word, "a savior." This is a catchword that has also already been used in this context.

■ **12** What v. 11 declares to be permanently valid (the permanence being expressed through the participle, a "helping" one), v. 12 establishes as having actually taken place: "I have helped." This sums up in a single word the history of salvation for Israel.[150] Taking up the point under dispute in v. 9, v. 12 declares: "I have made known

---

nies are striking, but still await a precise clarification through interdisciplinary research.

145   Herodotus describes it as follows (2.53): "The Greeks received the names of their gods afterwards from the Pelasgians. But how each of the gods was born or whether they had all been from everlasting, and what manner of form they have, they knew not, in a manner of speaking, until yesterday or the day before. For I deem that Hesiod and Homer were four hundred years earlier than me, and no more; and these are they that made for the Greeks a genealogy of the gods, and gave them their surnames, and divided the offices and arts among them, and described their forms" (trans. J. Enoch Powell, LCL, 1949).

For the Hesiod text see H. G. Evelyn-White, *Hesiod* (LCL, 1936); W. Marg, *Hesiod: Sämtliche Gedichte* (1970); Hesiod, *Theogony*, ed. M. L. West (1966); on Hesiod see M. P. Nilsson, *Geschichte der griechischen Religion*, 1 (1941) 587–92 (on the Orphic theogony, 647–51); Albin Lesky, *Geschichte der griechischen Literatur* (3d ed. 1971) 113–30 (with lit.).

146   *Theogony* 38–39 (LCL, pp. 80–81): "Come thou, let us begin with the Muses (Τύνη, Μουσάων ἀρχώμεϑα) who gladden the great spirit of their father Zeus (ταὶ Διὶ πατρὶ) in Olympus with their songs, telling of things that are and that shall be and that

were aforetime (τά τ᾽ ἐόντα τά τ᾽ ἐσσόμενα πρό τ᾽ ἐόντα) with consenting voice."

147   It seems possible that in the (lit.) "he will not be" (לֹא יְהְיֶה, v. 10) with the following "I, I am Yahweh" there is a wordplay similar to that in Exod 3:14; see J. Morgenstern, "The Message of Deutero-Isaiah in Its Sequential Unfolding," *HUCA* 30 (1959) 72; Bartelmus, *HYH*, 226–35.

148   See here Cross, *Canaanite Myth and Hebrew Epic* (1973): "ʾEl and the God of the Fathers," 13–43; "Yahweh and ʾEl," 44–75, with lit.

149   W. Zimmerli has worked out the special character of this formula in "I Am Yahweh," in *I Am Yahweh* (1982) 1–28 ["Ich bin Jahwe," in *Gottes Offenbarung. Gesammelte Aufsätze* (1963) 11-40].

150   Why *BHK* should have suggested that the word be eliminated as a dittography is for me a puzzle. The alliteration lends solemnity to the statement, just like the double "I" at the beginning of the same verse.

. . . and have let it be heard." God's acts and proclamation belong together.

The final statement of this section is curious (literally): "And there (is) not a stranger (זָר) among you." Various possible interpretations have been proposed.[151] A complement has been supplied: "a strange *God*."[152] That could refer to the "foreign gods" that have been discarded,[153] or to Yahweh, who is not a "strange God." Some commentators interpret "strange" as "unknown": Yahweh is (or will be) no longer "unknown." Relating the declaration to human beings, Elliger paraphrases: "and there is none among you to whom it (that which I have proclaimed) would be strange."[154] But if the meaning of the root means "diverge from, turn away, be far from," as Snijders maintains,[155] then it is worth considering whether what we have here is not a motif from the prayers of complaint.[156] If Yahweh is "a stranger," then he is not in Israel's midst; he has forsaken Israel. But this complaint is now no longer necessary. Yahweh is present.

■ **13** The verse turns to the future. The form of the verbs (preformative conjugation) makes this clear: "I act and who will avert it?" In my view this also explains the beginning of the verse (literally): "*Seen from the (present) day*, I am the one." It is not the beginning of time in general that is the theme;[157] it is the present time.[158] What is still in the future is described as what God is going to do. The criterion given is that it is irresistible, and that

only God determines its direction. This is saying the same as what we mean with our abstract concept "future." The term is still lacking, but the idea itself can very well be expressed.[159]

■ **14-15** The close of the divine speech in v. 13 is still formulated in quite general terms. But we have already seen several times that an elevated level of reflection allows conclusions to be drawn about the actual situation. This is achieved here by way of the composition. It is true that the saying is introduced as being God's own word; but it is no longer part of the divine speech. It is conveyed through a messenger. Nevertheless the connections with the context are close.

The phrase "your redeemer" in v. 14 has been prepared for through the catchword "redeem" (גָּאַל) in 43:1-7, as has also the title "the Holy One of Israel" (cf. 43:3) and "Israel's creator" (cf. 43:1). It is noticeable, however, that vv. 14-15 then thrice use the plural form of address: "your redeemer . . . your Holy One . . . your king," which often points to an interpretation related to every individual. What applies to Israel as a whole is true for individuals too. It is promised to everyone, in pastoral solicitude. Taking up the catchword in v. 14, Elliger has therefore rightly headed his exegesis of this passage (43:14-15): "for your sakes."[160]

---

151 See the discussion in Elliger here.

152 In correspondence to אֵל נֵכָר (Mal 2:11), thus, e.g., Marti, Torrey, North with reference to texts such as Deut 32:12; Jer 2:25; 3:13; 5:19; Pss 44:20-21 (19-20); 81:10 (9).

153 In this case it would be parallel to the close of the previous v. 11: "there is no helper beside me"; on אֵין זָר in the sense of "none other" see 1 Kgs 3:18; cf. Job 19:27, with the commentaries.

154 Elliger, 327.

155 L. A. Snijders, "The Meaning of זָר in the OT," *OTS* 10 (1954) 1–21.

156 The lament in Jer 14:7-9 might be cited, for example. It is interesting because certain terms used there also play a part in DtIsa: (v. 8) "You are the hope of Israel and its savior (מוֹשִׁיעוֹ) in time of trouble. Why have you become like a stranger (גֵּר) in the land and like a traveler, who only remains overnight? (v. 9) Why do you behave like one who has failed, and like a hero who cannot help (לְהוֹשִׁיעַ)? For you, O Yahweh, are in the midst of us (בְּקִרְבֵּנוּ) and we are called by your name. Do not

forsake us." But the beginning, "When our sins testify against us, help us, . . ." turns this lament into a parody, for through its sins Israel has lost its right to invoke God as its helper. Consequently the prophet Jeremiah has to announce that the complaint has been rejected.

157 Thus the LXX interprets by ἀπ᾽ ἀρχῆς; see also Tg, S and Vg. There is no need to emend MT to מֵעוֹלָם; see Elliger's analysis here; Begrich, *Studien zu Deuterojesaja* (1938, reprint 1963) 41: "from today on, i.e., the day when judgment was pronounced"; von Waldow, *Anlass und Hintergrund der Verkündigung des Deuterojesaja* (1953) 71: "i.e., from the day when I ascended the throne and from the day of this trial."

158 In contrast to מִיּוֹם, 48:7 talks about "before the (present) day."

159 The same may be said about the concept "history" in DtIsa.

160 Elliger on this passage.

Unfortunately the text has been corrupted in the process of transmission, but its essentials can still be reconstructed. The name Babylon is explicitly mentioned here for the first time, paving the way for 46:1–47:15.[161] Who is sent to Babylon is not stated. But a comparison with the other texts that make direct political statements show that for this "X" we should again read Cyrus. The perfect tense is probably accurately used, for according to 41:1-5a, 25-26 the mission has already taken place: "I *have sent* (him)" (v. 14).

According to the MT, the rest of the statement runs literally: "I will bring down refugees, them all."[162] But the vocalization probably should be slightly altered, so as to read "bars" (בְּרִיחִים)[163] instead of "refugees" (בְּרִיחִם). The verse is then saying that the "bars"—all the bars—will be broken down. That is the specific and practical hope. What it means as far as Cyrus is concerned is explained in 45:1-2, in varied phraseology. This latter passage talks explicitly about the bursting open of "iron bars," and the opening of gates and doors. But there it is also clear that the passage is referring to future events.

The third and last statement is clearly talking about the Chaldeans, who are also named for the first time. But what does MT's reading ("their jubilation [is] on ships") mean?[164] Here too it is possible, without altering the consonantal text, to read "into lamentation" (בַּאֲנִיּוֹת)[165] instead of "on ships" (בָּאֳנִיּוֹת).[166] What could

conceivably have dropped out at the end would be a verb, such as "I (or they) will change" (their jubilation into lamentation), unless this is a simple main clause: "their jubilation will become lamentation."[167] This would refer to the far-off future, after the defeat. The perspective is the switch over from the enthusiasm of a great power into despair. But perhaps the different readings and interpretive possibilities are also intentional.

Looked at from the aspect of the dramatic buildup, vv. 14-15 can be seen as a description of the happenings that form the background to the text. Their function is comparable to the function of the messenger reports in Greek drama. They tell what cannot be seen on the stage itself, yet provides the driving power for events. Thus within the dispute about fundamental theological problems, a brief topical reference is slotted in: Cyrus—the still anonymous anointed one—is already on the move.

It would be worthwhile pursuing the Yahweh predicates and their relation to one another. Here we may simply note the description of Yahweh as "your king." The royal title for the deity originally had to do with his kingship over the gods. This was the title enjoyed by the highest god in the pantheon. But in the present context the *nonexistence* of the gods has just been attested. So

---

161 "Babylon" occurs otherwise in 47:1; 48:14, 20. Torrey explains the mention of Babylon and the Chaldeans here as a later interpolation. This does away with the specific historical aspect at which the text is aiming. The same may be said of J. D. Smart's comment in his *History and Theology in Second Isaiah* (1967) 105: the text concerns "the eschatological event that the prophet anticipated in which not only Babylon but all the nations would have their power broken, and exiles would be gathered in, not only from Babylon but from the four corners of the earth." Smart also denies that there is a reference to Cyrus here. But the trend toward an "eschatologization" belongs to later interpretation; it is not true of the original text.

162 The MT is unequivocally endorsed by LXX: πάντας φεύγοντας; S ˀrwqˁ.

163 The Vulgate is doubtless already making this suggestion when it translates *vectes* ("bolts") *universos*. For the various solutions proposed see Köhler, *Deuterojesaja . . . stilkritisch untersucht* (1923) 20; T. J. Meek, "Some Passages Bearing on the Date of

Second Isaiah," *HUCA* 23 (1950/51) 175–77; M. Dahood, "The Linguistic Position of Ugaritic in the Light of Recent Discoveries," *BETL* 12–13 (1959) 275–76; P. Humbert, "A propos du 'serpent' (*bšn*) du mythe de Môt et Alein," *AfO* 11 (1936/37) 235–37; A. Ravenna, "Isaia 43,14," *RevB* 12 (1964) 293–96; Elliger and Volz on this passage.

164 On LXX see I. L. Seeligman, *The Septuagint Version of Isaiah* (1948) 10.

165 See the survey in Elliger (332). The suggestion was probably made first by Ewald. But we must also reckon with the possibility that, as frequently in DtIsa, the double reading is intentional.

166 Supporters of the reading "on ships" refer to Herodotus 1.194 for the ships of the Babylonians.

167 See Ps 30:12 (11); Amos 8:10: "I will turn (וְהָפַכְתִּי) your feasts into mourning and all your songs into lamentation." For the construction הפך with an accusative and בְּ see Ps 41:4 (3). Closest to the text in content—comfort for Jerusalem and disaster for the cities of the oppressor—is 1 Bar 4:34: καὶ τὸ ἀγαυρίαμα αὐτῆς [A add. ἔσται] εἰς πένθος. Here

Yahweh's kingship is related to his rule over Israel. One can then also go on to ask: if Yahweh is so emphatically called "your king," is an earthly king still expected? Finally, the use is not arbitrary. A king can "send," and he can "break down bars." The concept of Yahweh's kingship is not restricted to this text. It is one of the sustaining pillars for DtIsa, as it is for his addressees. The catchword "king of Israel" is taken up again almost at once, in 44:6.

---

too a nominative clause in the Hebrew is doubtless presupposed. ἀγαυρίαμα corresponds to תְּהִלָּה in the Hebrew text of Isa 62:7.

43

**"The people whom I have formed for myself,
they will tell of my glory" (43:21)**

16   **Thus has Yahweh spoken,
he who makes a way in the sea,
and a path in the mighty waters,**

17   **who lets chariot and horse go forth,
army and mighty men together—
there they lie, can no longer get up,
are extinguished, quenched like a wick:**

18   **Do not remember the earlier (happenings)
and do not consider the things of old!**

19   **See, I am making something new.
Now it is springing up—do you not notice it?**

    **Yes, I am making a way in the desert,
in the wilderness, streams.**

20   **The beasts of the field will honor me,
jackals and ostrich hens (owls?),
because I have brought water into the desert,
streams into the wilderness,
to give drink to my chosen people.**

21   **The people there whom I have formed for myself,
they will tell of my glory.**

Verses 16-21 can be marked off as a relatively independent text unit. It has an introductory formula of its own, and the following verses, 22-28, begin a new theme. The genre to which the text should be assigned is disputed.[168] It is generally viewed as a salvation oracle, though the emphases of the different commentaries vary.[169] But in what way is salvation proclaimed here?[170]

The "messenger formula" in v. 16 offers the starting point for the interpretation: "Thus says Yahweh" (כֹּה אָמַר יהוה). The same formula introduced the previous information about what is happening in and around Babylon (v. 14). It meant above all: Cyrus is on the move! The insider can know this. That is exciting enough. But vv. 16-17 increase the tension even more. A new report is given in similar form.[171] It is true that this formula frequently introduces the messenger's speech, especially in prophecy. In the dramatic buildup too the messenger would have an important function,[172] describing the

---

168 See the discussion in Melugin, "The Structure of Deutero-Isaiah" (1968) 181–85.

169 See Begrich, *Studien zu Deuterojesaja* (1938, reprint 1963) 6, 14; Merendino, *Der Erste und der Letzte: Eine Untersuchung von Jes 40–48* (1981) 343–44; von Waldow, "Anlass und Hintergrund der Verkündigung des Deuterojesaja" (1953) 240–41; C. Westermann, "Sprache und Struktur der Prophetie Deuterojesajas," in *Forschung am Alten Testament* 1 (1964) 120; Westermann, 126–27 (104); Schoors, *I Am God Your Saviour* (1973) 93–97.

170 See Schoors's questions, *I Am God Your Saviour* (1973) 93.

171 In both cases, the whole messenger speech is given in Yahweh's name. Consequently I cannot follow Elliger's division "between the introduction of the messenger saying, in which it is the prophet who is speaking, and the Yahweh speech proper" (Elliger on this passage; see also 351).

172 On the part played by the messenger in Greek drama, see W. Jens, ed., *Die Bauformen der griechischen Tragödie* (1971) 66, 122, 135–40, and 176–79. As an example see O. Taplin's comments in *The Stagecraft of Aeschylus* (1977) 80–85, 167–68: "The next most common structural function for an *angelos* is that of the herald or advance messenger; and

events that are taking place in the background.[173] The battle—marvelous happenings—the announcement of new events and actors: all these things can be communicated by the messenger.[174] And all this may be said of this text. The messenger's[175] rank is clear: he is Yahweh's messenger. So what he reports is authentic.

■ **16-17** Yahweh is shown to be one who performs marvels: that is why the participles with the article have their place here. The events cannot be separated from the God who is acknowledged as a person: "He makes a way in the sea . . . he lets chariots and horses go forth." But every child who has ever heard the Passover story[176] knows what this is talking about, and knows too what happens. Except Egypt and the pharaoh are not mentioned by name here. Nor are listeners supposed to think of the past. They are intended to think of the present, and there can then be no doubt that the army whose downfall is described is the army of the Babylonians.

The whole passage is artistically shaped, and there can be no doubt that many of the finer points escape us. We lack, for example, the sound of the words. The waters are עַזִּים (ʿazzîm), "powerful,"[177] "horse" is סוּס (sûs), "the

mighty one" is עִזּוּז (ʿizzûz).[178] One can almost hear the army coming up. But even if this is the sinister enemy army, it is Yahweh who lets it go forth—it is he who permits it.[179] But the battle is at an end before it has even begun. Two verbs in the imperfect tell what happens: the enemy will lie there and will not get up again.[180] Then the tense changes to the perfect (again twice!): the action is at an end. The army has been extinguished like the wick of a candle or a flaming torch. In this way the listener participates directly in what has happened.[181]

The presupposition for the text is quite clearly the exodus tradition. It takes up the mode of argument and the concept of the "holy war" or the "Yahweh war."[182] Yahweh alone is the one who fights for Israel. The people itself can do nothing, nor does it need to do anything. In the words of Isa 7:9: "If you do not stand firm in faith, you shall not stand at all."

In the structure of DtIsa's book as a whole the "battle" account has an important function, even if the struggle takes place "offstage"—or perhaps for that very reason. If we assume that at the end of Act I (42:13) Yahweh goes forth to battle,[183] then this battle has raged meanwhile; but now the victory has been won. We are told that

---

this one in *Pers* [the *Persians* of Aeschylus] is a variant of this type. He usually leads up towards the arrival of a central character, and hence towards the catastrophe. . . . Also, the events reported by most advance messengers arise out of the course of the play, and are supposed to have been happening simultaneously with the earlier scenes" (83).

173 See K. Joerden, "Zur Bedeutung des Ausser- und Hinterszenischen," in Jens, ed., *Die Bauformen der griechischen Tragödie* (1971) 369–407.

174 See among other things the charts for Greek drama, ibid., 403.

175 Comparable here is the *Exagoge* of Ezekiel, in which the passage of the Israelites through the sea and the downfall of the Egyptians are described from the Egyptian standpoint by a messenger, in the form of a battle report (193–242).

176 The link between Passover and Exodus is probably an old one; see Exodus 14–15. Cf. in the historical summaries: Deut 26:8; Josh 24:6-7; Pss 78:13; 106:7-12; Neh 9:9-11. In the prophetic texts: Isa 11:15-16. Ps 72:17-21 also comes very close. On the whole subject see van der Merwe, *Pentateuchtradisies in de Prediking van Deuterojesaja* (1955) 176–88.

177 The same word is also used in connection with the passage through the sea in Neh 9:11. In Exod 14:21 it is used to describe the "strong east wind" that

makes the water retreat; for עזז meaning "to be strong, powerful, defiant" see *HALOT* 2:808–9 [*HALAT* 3:764–65].

178 Delitzsch (2:196) translates here: "The army with the hero (heroes) at its head" [trans. altered], referring to Ps 24:8. Schoors (*I Am God Your Saviour* [1973] 93 n. 2) presumes that "commander of the army" is meant; cf. Dan 10:20.

179 Cf. Gog's departure according to Ezek 38:4; the wider context in Ezekiel is also worth noting. For "leading out" as a technical term, see also Isa 40:26.

180 Cf. among the Zion psalms Pss 48:5-7 (4-6); 76:5-7 (4-6); and 2 Kings 19, esp. vv. 32-37.

181 The dramatic character has been noted by Delitzsch (2:196 [455]: "We are transported at once into the very midst of the scenes of destruction"); and North (125): "The hearers are either transported into the past, or the past brought into their present, for them to see what is happening." Was the extinguishing of the lamp an image or something that the spectators could see? Is פִּשְׁתָּה here the flaxen wick, or a torch made of rolled linen and saturated with pitch?

182 G. von Rad, *Holy War* (1991) [*Der Heilige Krieg im alten Israel* (5th ed. 1969)]; R. Smend, *Yahweh War and Tribal Confederation* (1970) [*Jahwekrieg und Stämmebund* (1966)]; F. Stolz, *Jahwes und Israels*

here.[184] Consequently, in the following act (44:24-28; 45:13), Cyrus can already be given the commission to rebuild Jerusalem. True, the gates still have to be opened for him (45:1-3), but then Babylon's gods and the men who are their bearers will be taken away into captivity (46:1-2). Victory has already been won, even before Babylon has fallen. It is striking that this picture is not very far removed from what can be reconstructed about the capture of Babylon from other historical texts—that it was more or less peaceful. But in his theological tradition DtIsa holds fast to two convictions: First, the deliverance was not due to Israel's own strength. This awareness is implicit in the acknowledgment of the deliverance at the Reed Sea. He adheres just as firmly to the second conviction, that it was not the military strength of Cyrus and the new imperial power that brought deliverance. The deliverance comes from Yahweh.[185] The actual course of the struggle is not described. It is only the outcome—the deliverance—that is important.

■ **18-19a** That DtIsa should so turn against "former things" has continually caused astonishment,[186] for hardly any other prophetic writing appeals so strongly to tradition. How can we explain this contradiction? One important factor seems to me to be that DtIsa works with interlocking arguments. One conclusion leads to a counterargument, which is then confuted, so that the next conclusion follows. In this process, new aspects can lead to the repeal of a previous conclusion. But that conclusion does not thereby lose its value on the earlier levels of the argument. DtIsa does not develop any "system" of

theological declarations that are generally applicable irrespective of their context. His emphasis varies in the different argumentative complexes and in the dispute with varying counterpositions, to the point when his individual statements are (apparently?) mutually contradictory.

What was announced in the past has actually come to pass: this is stressed several times. Yahweh has thus been proved reliable. But it is possible to go along with tradition in acknowledging that the exodus was an act of deliverance without believing that God can save now as well. When this skeptic hears God's word about "the way" and "the water in the desert," he thinks only of the past. But for DtIsa faith does not have to do only with the past. It is focused on the present, which means the "*now*" (v. 19a), and on the future.

Like the past, the future is seen in personal categories: "Look upon me as one who makes something new" (thus literally v. 19a). The participial style is consistently preserved, because it belongs intrinsically to what is being said. The continuum is not some abstract concept, such as "time" or "history." It is conceivable and experienceable in faith in the one *God*. The future has already begun. "It is springing up *now*" (v. 19a).[187]

Everyone knows from experience that once a plant "springs up" it goes on growing; and God's activity goes forward in just the same relentless way.[188] One must only perceive the "springing up." The single concept is therefore an image that corresponds both to the image of the cries of battle and to the image of the cries of the

---

Kriege (1972); F. M. Cross, *Canaanite Myth and Hebrew Epic* (1973).

183   2 Chronicles 20 illustrates the theory of the "holy war" here, esp. vv. 15, 17, and 20-24.

184   There is therefore no contradiction between Isa 42:9: "before they spring up I let you hear of them," and v. 19: "now it is springing up" (contrary to Muilenburg and Elliger on this passage). The difference is the point of time in the progress of the drama.

185   The sectors therefore cannot be separated, as Torrey tries to do on literary grounds: "The prophet is not dealing with such passing trifles as the campaigns of a king, or changes of the political horizon; he has before his eyes something immensely more important, the spiritual awakening and salvation of his people" (*Second Isaiah* [1928] 340).

186   For the discussion, see A. Schoors, "Les choses antérieures et les choses nouvelles dans les oracles Deutéro-Isaïens," *EThL* 40 (1964) 19–47, esp. 23–25; also his *I Am God Your Saviour* (1973) 94–95; further Elliger, 352–53.

187   Duhm writes here: "lively rhetoric, which is intended to make readers feel the closeness of the miracle." Young on this passage points to the connection with 42:9: "This verse probably represents a step in advance, in that here the new thing is already incipient. The word *now* seems to suggest that even as the Lord speaks, this new thing is coming into being." This is in fact a good description of a cultic drama.

188   For the discussion, see R. Lack, *La symbolique du livre d'Isaïe* (1973) 94–95.

woman in labor in Isa 42:13-14. At all events the process is irreversible.

■ **19b-21** The divine promise at the close of v. 19 is decisive. It is formulated in the continuous tense (Hebrew imperfect): "Yes, I am making a way in the desert." This gathers up the whole of chap. 40. The reasoning is directed against the opinion that "there is no path in the desert."

In the promise in v. 19 the second train of thought is intimately linked with the first. It differs in content inasmuch as it now promises "in the wilderness streams."[189] This is an answer to the person who believes that "paths in the desert" are certainly possible, but who then says: "There is no water, we shall die of thirst." Formally, the structure of the second train of thought is the mirror image of the first. It begins with the promise and then reverts to tradition. We see this recourse to tradition when v. 20 picks up a motif belonging to the extensive complex about the marvelous transformation of the desert into a paradise.[190] "The jackal and the ostrich" are the timid inhabitants of the desert,[191] whom human beings hardly ever catch sight of. Even they will honor Yahweh. Nature is completely incorporated into Yahweh's future activity on behalf of the homecomers.

Strikingly enough, v. 20b again employs the perfect tense: "I *have put* water in the desert."[192] We also find again the not very common phrase "streams in the wilderness" (בִּישִׁימוֹן),"[193] as in v. 19. The saying is introduced in Hebrew by כִּי, "because" or "for," which often signals the beginning of a quotation. For the reasons already mentioned, I would assume that here too this is a reference to tradition. After the mention of the exodus and Reed Sea in vv. 16 and 17, this would be a reminder of the wanderings in the wilderness. The conclusion would be the same. At that time "my chosen people" (v. 20) were given water to drink, and they will again be given water now. Then "that people there (עַם־זוּ)[194] whom I have formed for myself" (v. 21) will also tell of the wonderful acts of its God. Present experience becomes part of the confession of faith.

The detailed exegesis of this text shows DtIsa's hermeneutical approach particularly clearly. This is not limited to the terms "what was earlier" (רִאשֹׁנוֹת), "what was of old" (קַדְמֹנִיּוֹת) and "what is new" (חֲדָשָׁה), and to their interpretation. Nor is some random "earlier time" meant; it is the time named in the text. "Path" and "water" are expected in the future, in a quite practical sense. Elliger is probably right when he says (355): "Only the hostile power of the Egyptians (v. 17)[195] finds no correspondence in v. 19." The struggle is now past. We

---

189 The reading in 1QIsaᵃ, which gives "paths" (נתיבות) instead of "streams" (נְהָרוֹת), could be a harmonization, but in view of the artistic chiasmus in the passage it is not necessary. See also the analysis in Schoors, *I Am God Your Saviour* (1973) 95. For water in the desert see Exod 15:22-26; 17:1-7; Ps 78:15-16; Neh 9:15. In distinction from other texts, "water" is a positive term in DtIsa here.

190 Cf. Isa 41:17-20; 55:10, 12; Ps 65:13 (12); further Isa 11:6-9; Joel 1:20; Ps 42:2 (1).

191 The identity of the animals named is not quite certain. They are also mentioned together in Isa 34:13; Mic 1:8; Job 30:29. For תַּן, plur. תַּנִּים see *HALOT* s.v., with lit. For בְּנוֹת יַעֲנָה see also *HALOT*. יַעֲנָה is listed among unclean animals (Lev 11:16; Deut 14:15). Whether the term refers to a kind of owl, not to the ostrich, is the subject of discussion. Perhaps North's rendering "These desert howlers" is correct (see North on this passage, with lit.). The howling of jackals and the cry of owls can be heard. They are not precisely melodious, and yet they serve the glory of God (v. 20). But v. 23 goes on to say that

Israel has not "glorified" Yahweh—that is the dreadful thing! See Muilenburg here: "The pervasive emphasis upon singing belongs to the same complex of thought." Elliger on this passage (with lit.) sums up: "But whether ostriches or owls, whether jackals or wolves, the beasts of the steppe will 'glorify' Yahweh."

192 1QIsaᵃ has the imperfect, but MT is the more difficult reading and is therefore more likely to be correct; for v. 20b is not just a simple repetition of v. 19b. See here Merendino, *Der Erste und der Letzte: Eine Untersuchung von Jes 40–48* (1981) 334. He asks: "Is it appropriate to describe this new thing with phraseology reminiscent of the old exodus event?" But this is precisely what DtIsa is doing!

193 Deut 32:10; Pss 68:8 (7); 78:40; 106:14; 107:4. Does the word contain an echo of the root "shudder" (שׁמם)?

194 This is Delitzsch's rendering here. זוּ as the demonstrative pronoun makes sense if it points to the "people" sitting there (cf. 42:24). They are *now* "the chosen people."

174

might therefore paraphrase: "From now on, when they hear the words: 'there is a way . . .' (v. 16) they should no longer think of the first exodus but of the second.[196] Only the wanderings in the wilderness and the entry into the promised land are still to come for the people whom I have formed for myself."

This text is a model for the function of biblical tradi-

tion. The experience of the past helps toward an understanding of things in the present. The continuity of God's faithfulness makes hope for the future possible. This is in itself an exposition of tradition. But there are no superficial quotations. What we are offered is a further transmission of the testimony that this is "the fulfillment of the Scriptures."

---

195   The naming of Egypt is perhaps intentionally avoided here in the context of the going forth to war of the army. In the Persian period Egypt was notoriously restive. There could also be a topical allusion for DtIsa's own time.

196   The Gospel of Mark is taking up this approach when it links the first exodus (Mark 1:2; cf. Exod 23:20) and the second exodus (Mark 1:3; cf. Isa 40:3) with Jesus' baptism in the Jordan. If we follow the thinking of the present text, we might say that this was the beginning of the third exodus. See also Mark 1:15. The coming of Jesus is described with the categories of the first and second exodus.

43

"Yet it is not me on whom you called, Jacob!
Have you really concerned yourself about me,
Israel?" (43:22)

22 Yet it is not me on whom you called, Jacob!
Have you really concerned yourself about
me, Israel?[a]

23 You have not brought me sheep and goats
for your burnt offerings,
and have not honored me with[a] your
sacrifices.
I have not made you serve with meal offering,
and have not wearied you (with a plea) for
incense.

24 You have not bought me spicy cane for silver,
and have not let me slurp the fat of your
sacrifices.
You have only made me serve with your
transgressions/sins,
you have given me trouble with your
iniquities.

25 I, I am he who blots out your crimes for my
own sake,
and I will no longer remember your
transgressions/sins.

26 Remind me! Let us go to law with one
another!
Set forth your case, so that you may be
proved right!

27 Your father, the earlier one, did wrong/sinned,
and your spokesmen have broken with me.

28 Then I profaned the princes of a sanctuary
and delivered[a] Jacob to anathema,
and Israel to reviling.

22a See below on this passage.

23a One would expect the preposition בְּ here, and it is in fact the
reading in 1QIsa[a] (ובזבחיכה; cf. S).

28a Contrary to MT (וְאֲחַלֵּל) the reading here should probably be
וָאֲחַלֵּ֣ל (cf. LXX).

■ **22-28** The text is a relatively independent unit, clearly distinguished from its context in both form and content. It is preceded by two communications in the form of "messenger sayings" that tell of the saving events which are afoot (vv. 14, 15, and 16-21). The conclusion was the promise that the people (עַם) as Yahweh's chosen people (עַמִּי בְחִירִי) will once more tell of his glorious acts, will recognize him as God and Lord. All the more marked is the contrast when vv. 22-24 begin with a series of negative pronouncements or a list of sins.

The unit begins with the mention by name of Jacob/ Israel (v. 22) and it ends in the same way (v. 28). The following passage explicitly confirms that Jacob/Israel is a chosen servant (בְחַרְתִּי בוֹ, 44:1). The very structure makes clear that it is not Israel's merits that have

brought about the turn of events. The whole text takes the form of a divine speech, but it is not a monologue. Jacob/Israel is addressed, v. 26 being a challenge to action and to dialogue. The verse is an indication that here too we have to imagine a trial: "Let us go to law together" (נִשָׁפְטָה יָחַד), the text says explicitly. This also defines the opposing parties. On the one hand is Yahweh himself, on the other, this time, Jacob/Israel. So here, after Yahweh has turned to the islands in 41:1-5, to the gods in 41:21-29 and to the nations in 43:8-15, he now again turns to his people. The passage is thus comparable to the beginning of this act in 42:18-25. But the unique character of the proceedings should be noted. The trial is not simply a repetition, for it presupposes that the accused is really Yahweh.

There is a large measure of agreement about the genre to which the text belongs.[197] Begrich already assigned the text to the "appeals of the accused," in the wider category of "judgment speeches." Even more precisely, he thought he could discover "an alteration to the basic form" in which "the person under attack . . . defends himself against a claim leveled against him."[198] Here Begrich goes into the first part in particular detail. But according to Westermann the close should be taken into account too. According to that, this is a genuine indictment of Yahweh for having pronounced the "anathema."[199]

The text is comparable to a judicial hearing, but if it is viewed in the light of the genre in general, the special character of this particular trial comes out more strongly.[200]

■ **22** The text, and with it the action, begins with an assertion and a question. This already allows the subject of the dispute to be deduced: "It is not me upon whom you have called, Jacob!" The word "me" (אֹתִי, v. 22) is put in the emphatic antecedent position. When Yahweh says this, it means that other gods have indeed been invoked.

The assertion therefore belongs to the dispute about the foreign gods.

The כִּי in v. 22b is emended in most commentaries (as already in the LXX) to וְלֹא, "and not."[201] But MT has the more difficult reading (*lectio difficilior*) and is confirmed by 1QIsaᵃ. It is therefore worth considering whether here כִּי does not begin an interrogative sentence, which might be rendered: "Is it really the case that you have concerned yourself about me, Israel?"[202] A negation (which the sense demands) does not have to be expressly formulated.[203] What is emphasized this time is the "taking pains," the "bothering about." It is this which is also developed in what follows. One may also ask whether the antithesis to "about me, for me" (בִּי) should not be "for you." But that can only be decided in the light of the interpretation as a whole.

■ **23-24** These verses first of all give a list of sacrificial offerings. It is not always easy for us to say exactly what is meant in each case.[204] עֹלָה is the burnt offering ("what rises up in smoke"). The whole animal is sacrificed, but the animal's skin is left for the priest (Lev 7:8; 2 Chr 29:34). זֶבַח really means only "the slaughtering." Parts of

---

197 Von Waldow, "Anlass und Hintergrund der Verkündigung des Deuterojesaja" (1953) 40–41. "In the present trial speech Yahweh opens the proceedings by declaring that this legal relationship, which allegedly rests on performance and reward, does not exist at all in this form, and even if the people have rendered services, these cannot have been meant for him." Cf. idem, *Denn ich erlöse dich: Eine Auslegung von Jes 43* (1960) 74. H. J. Boecker, *Redeformen des Rechtslebens im Alten Testament* (2d ed. 1970) 54–55; Schoors, *I Am God Your Saviour* (1973) 189–97.

198 Begrich, *Studien zu Deuterojesaja* (1938, reprint 1963) 31, on the text: "The premise of the text is that Israel declares that, because it has rendered particular services, Yahweh is obliged to help it." But Begrich goes on: "Without the understandably indignant question in response to the reproach of a misdemeanor, he begins at once with a defense addressed to the party who is making the claim"; here it is noticeable that he does not discuss the possibility that the clause introduced by כִּי implies the question that we should expect from the genre ("Is it the case that . . . ?"). Without giving a reason he changes this, following LXX, into וְלֹא (see Begrich, 32 n. 91).

199 C. Westermann, "Sprache und Struktur der

Prophetie Deuterojesajas," in *Forschung am Alten Testament* 1:142: "The whole is therefore not a real trial speech but rather a pre-trial disputation"; also Westermann, 130–31 [107].

200 On the text see K. Baltzer, "Schriftauslegung bei Deuterojesaja?–Jes 43,22-28 als Beispiel," in *Die Väter Israels. FS J. Scharbert* (1989) 11–16.

201 See the list in Elliger here.

202 For the meaning of the question in the framework of the genre, see n. 97 above with Begrich, *Studien zu Deuterojesaja* (1938, reprint 1963) 31.

203 That the series of 1 + 6 negations (לֹא) is retained can also be a reason in view of the artificial character of the text.

204 For lit. see G. B. Gray, *Sacrifice in the OT: Its Theory and Practice* (1925, reprint 1971); H. Ringgren, *Israelite Religion* (1966) [*Israelitische Religion* (1963)]; R. Rendtorff, *Studien zur Geschichte des Opfers im Alten Israel* (1967); R. Hentschke, "Opfer II im AT," *RGG*³ 4:1641–47 (with lit.).

the animal, such as the blood and the fat,[205] are offered as sacrifice. This is essentially the cultic meal of a community.[206] מִנְחָה is "a gift, present . . . as an expression of respect, thanksgiving, homage, friendship, dependence."[207] As sacrifice, it means the meal offering, for which vegetable gifts especially were brought.[208] "Incense" (לְבֹנָה)[209] and "spicy cane" (קָנֶה)[210] are costly components of a sacrifice, and could also be used as luxuries.[211]

Up to this point the text can be read as an exposition on the basis of the Torah about sacrifices given on Sinai, after the exodus from Egypt. The outcome is negative. The sacrifices have apparently not been made in accordance with Yahweh's ideas. But what is the reason for the criticism? Various possibilities have been canvassed for their bearing on the interpretation of vv. 22-24.[212]

1. The text means the rejection of the preexilic cult.
2. The text means the rejection of the sacrificial cult in exile.
3. The text means the rejection of sacrifice in general.

In all three variants, the distinction between the external observance of the cult and inward conviction plays a part in the argument, whether this distinction is positive or negative.[213]

It is clear that the text belongs to a long tradition of dispute about the sacrificial cult in the Bible.[214] It begins with the matter-of-course acceptance of it, taken over from primeval times. Sacrifice is interpreted in the OT, but the reasons for it are not actually given. The sacrificial cult ended in 70 C.E. with the destruction of the temple in Jerusalem. Both the Jewish and the Christian community addressed and came to terms with this event in different ways, in the light of tradition and the new interpretation of tradition. The question is: to what point in the development does the present text belong? In the OT the relationship to God is not constituted through sacrifice. For prophecy, the fundamental question is whether the relationship to God is intact—whether there is "peace" (שָׁלוֹם). If the relationship to God exists not only for the individual but also for Israel as God's people, that relationship cannot be separated from the relationship with one's neighbor. When Amos criticizes sacrifice (Amos 5:21-27), he does so because it was assumed in his time that the cult had a point, even without "justice and righteousness" in social dealings

---

205 See the ordinance in Leviticus 3.

206 See Gen 31:54; Exod 18:12; 1 Kgs 8:62.

207 *HALOT* 2:601 [*HALAT* 2:258–69]. See Gen 32:14 (13), 19 (18), 21-22 (20-21); 33:10; 1 Sam 10:27; 2 Kgs 16:15; 20:12; 2 Chr 9:24; 17:11; 26:8.

208 R. Hentschke, "Opfer II im AT," *RGG*³ 4:1645: "It consists of flour or some baked product to which salt, usually also oil and incense, were added. Only when it was offered as a sin offering were the last two ingredients omitted (Lev 5:11-13)." So when incense is mentioned in the present text, the מִנְחָה is not being understood as a sin offering.

209 Resin from the *Boswellia Carteri* and *Frereana*, produced especially in Ḥadhramaut and Somalia. According to Jer 6:20 it is imported from "Sheba"; cf. Isa 60:6. See *HALOT* 2:518 [*HALAT* 2:493].

210 Really קָנֶה טוֹב, "sweet-smelling cane"; cf. Jer 6:20; Ezek 27:19; Cant 4:14; see Akk. *qanū ṭābu*, "Parker's Cymbopogon" according to I. Löw *Die Flora der Juden* 1:692–93, or "Parker's Citronella grass" according to J. W. Bews, *The World's Grasses* (1929) 48.

211 Cf. Exod 30:7-9, 34-38; see M. Löhr, *Das Räucheropfer im AT* (1927).

212 See the commentaries and the survey in T. Booij, "Negation in Isaiah 43,22-24," *ZAW* 94 (1982) 390–400, esp. 392.

213 Young (160): "There was no true bringing of the sheep of burnt offering to the Lord. 'What you brought,' we may paraphrase, 'was a sham offering and not the real thing.'" Von Waldow, "Anlass und Hintergrund der Verkündigung des Deuterojesaja" (1953) 79: "With a life of faith that has become mere formalism, and with the sacrificial practice that has been petrified into an *opus operatum*, the covenant could not be preserved. Living obedience was missing." Schoors, *I Am God Your Saviour* (1973): "The reproach only concerns the formalistic cult without righteousness" (191); "The overestimation of cult is not wanted by God" (192). Elliger (374): "[DtIsa] makes Yahweh contest the honesty and inner sincerity of 'tribute' of this kind."

214 H. W. Hertzberg, "Die prophetische Kritik am Kult," *ThLZ* 75 (1950) 219–26, reprinted in *Beiträge zur Traditionsgeschichte und Theologie des AT* (1962) 81–90; R. Hentschke, *Die Stellung der vorexilischen Propheten zum Kultus* (1957); J. P. Hyatt, *The Prophetic Criticism of Israelite Worship* (1963); E. Würthwein, "Kultpolemik oder Kultbescheid?" in *Tradition und Situation: Studien zur alttestamentlichen Prophetie: FS A. Weiser* (1963) 115–31; M. Sekine, "Das Problem der Kultpolemik bei den Propheten," *EvTh* 28 (1968) 605–9.

(vv. 22-23). Hosea is more radical still in his judgment, because he was convinced that Israel had ceased to be Yahweh's people (see Hos 1:8-9). The breakdown of the "institutional world" of the Northern Kingdom also meant the downfall of the cult at the national sanctuary in Bethel (see Hos 6:4-11; 7:1ff.).[215] Isaiah (Isa 1:10-17) rejected the attempt to restore the relationship with God through sacrifice.[216]

The overall impression is that the prophets did not reject the sacrificial cult completely, but that for them dealings with one's fellow men and women are the premise for the relationship to God. Ezekiel was a prophet, yet he planned a new order for the temple in Jerusalem, to take effect after the exile, when God's presence would again be linked with Zion and "the land" (Ezek 20:40-41; 40:1—47:12). DtIsa could be interpreted as belonging to the same framework. But I suspect that the text also contains a hint of new developments;[217] and I should therefore like to ask once more what the real issue is, if we take as our point of departure the accusation in vv. 22-24.

If we examine the verbs in vv. 22-24, it emerges that they all have to do mainly with "concerning oneself" (יגע, 3 times) and "serving" (עבד, 2 times). What a master can demand of his servant in the way of behavior is specified. "Honoring" is one of the elements (v. 23). But honor has not been offered. The servant has not "con-

cerned himself" or "served." This places the text in the field of the "master-servant" sociomorpheme in DtIsa. But up to this point the level of the image is equivocal; for when the master says that the servant "has made me serve . . . and has given me trouble," this goes against all economic logic—this is the world turned upside down. The point of dispute would then be the reversal of the relationship between master and servant. That can be described precisely as "a breach of community" (פשע, v. 25).[218] Here too, as elsewhere in the prophetic tradition, misbehavior in the cult is the outcome of faulty social behavior, not its cause.

But the text may contain a further level of meaning too,[219] emerging from an interpretation of the Jacob story. In its own way this emphasizes that the concern is not on behalf of Yahweh but has been undertaken for Jacob's own sake (v. 22).

The sacrifice that Jacob brings is for himself. He has the profit. If Jacob is Israel, then Israel is also bringing its sacrifice for its own sake. This can imply a criticism of sacrifice such as is clearly detectible in polemical form, in the Jewish context, in Bel and the Dragon, one of the additions to the book of Daniel. This text is extant only in Greek in the LXX and in Theodotion, or in their translations. It tells how Daniel convinces the king of Babylon (in Theodotion it is Cyrus) that the offerings in the temple of the god Bel are consumed by the priests

215 See H. Utzschneider, *Hosea, Prophet vor dem Ende* (1980); H.W. Wolff, *Hosea* (1974) 80–81, 100, 120 [*Hosea* (3d ed. 1976) 100, 127, 153].

216 See H. Wildberger, *Isaiah 1–12* (1991) 40, on Isa 1:10-17, with lit. [*Jesaja* (2d ed. 1980) 38]: "When Isaiah utters a sharp No! here, he unmasks a conception of sacrifice as magic, showing it to be nothing more than a dangerous illusion. But sacrifice and festivals are not in any way rejected out of hand."

217 It is also worth considering how far the dispute about "blood " sacrifice in the Persian period plays a part. Cf., e.g., the text in Cowley, no. 33, ll.8–12 from Elephantine; text edition: B. Porten, *Jews of Elephantine and Arameans of Syene; Aramaic Texts with Translation* (1980) 100, as well as Isa 66:3.

218 See R. Knierim, "פשע *pešaᶜ* crime," *TLOT* 2:1033–37 [*THAT* 2:488–95]. "Whoever commits *pešaᶜ* does not merely rebel or protest against Yahweh but breaks with him, takes away what is his, robs, embezzles, misappropriates it. Although it always implies a conscious behavior, the term per se does not describe

the attitude but the criminal act (1036 [493]). Delitzsch, 2:199–200 [457]: "Israel's sins weigh heavily on him, like a burden on a slave. . . . But the active power of the divine love is greater than the weight of the divine wrath" [transl. altered].

219 For the following passage see Baltzer, "Schriftauslegung bei Deuterojesaja?—Jes 43,22-28 als Beispiel," in *Die Väter Israels: FS J. Scharbert* (1989) 12–13. For multiple levels of meaning in a text see the interpretation of the vineyard song in Isaiah 5 in K. Baltzer, D. Georgi and F. Merkel, "Jes 5:1-7," *GPM* 18 (1964) 391–95; H. Utzschneider, *Künder oder Schreiber? Eine These zum Problem der "Schriftprophetie" auf Grund von Maleachi 1,6–2,9* (1989). On the problem of interpretation within the OT, see M. Fishbane, *Biblical Interpretation in Ancient Israel* (1985) (esp. the lit.) and B. S. Childs's review in *JBL* 106 (1987) 511–13.

and their families. The background is the dispute with the heathen gods and their idols.[220] This was the temptation of the Diaspora. As far as the matter itself is concerned, DtIsa is no less definite. He condemns the cult if it is an end in itself. A criticism of sacrifice that takes as a starting point its utility for the sacrificers is a delicate matter politically speaking, and not only in the ancient world. It inevitably lays itself open to the charge of impiety. Thus in DtIsa form and content coincide: the text demands men and women who know this, and that applies especially when DtIsa confesses his faith in "the living God."

To assume that Jacob traditions[221] lie behind the text is not wholly unreasonable. The name Jacob/Israel is mentioned at the beginning (v. 22) and at the end (v. 28), and is probably presupposed in v. 27 in the reference to "your father . . . the earlier one." "Take pains" (יגע, vv. 22, 23, 24) and "serve" (עבד, vv. 23 and 24) are used chiastically. "Not" (לא *loʾ*) follows 1 + 6 times in the series. Finally, the suffixes of the first and second person masculine singular, "me" (י-) "you" (ך-), alternate throughout, and hence also the sounds *î* and *kā*.[222] These are signals one should also take into account in the interpretation.

If one starts tentatively from the fact that the text talks about "father 'Jacob,' your earlier/your first one" (הָרִאשׁוֹן אָבִיךָ, v. 27), then the catchwords "serve" (עבד) and "take pains" (יגע) take on a new meaning. The concordance already shows that these catchwords in the Jacob story occur together only in Gen 31:41, 42, in Jacob's speech to Laban: "This (means) for me (זֶה־לִּי): these twenty

years have I served you in your house (עֲבַדְתִּיךָ), fourteen years for your two daughters and six years for your flock. . . . God has seen my affliction and the labor of my hands (יְגִיעַ כַּפַּי)." For whom has Jacob labored and whom has he served? According to this text, the answer is not Yahweh, at least! What Jacob was concerned about was (his) own wage (אֶת־מַשְׂכֻּרְתִּי), and the one he served was Laban.[223] But it is only through the help of "the God of his fathers" that Jacob can keep what belongs to him on his return.

Verse 23aα, "You have not brought me sheep and goats/a young animal" (לֹא־הֵבֵיאתָ לִּי שֵׂה): the listener may of course remember that, on his mother's advice, Jacob brought two kids from his flock (Gen 27:9-10) as a way of extorting Esau's blessing from his father by trickery.[224] The skins served the deception. The animals were certainly not designed for burnt offerings. But in the Jacob story the term "sheep and goats/young animal" (שֵׂה) occurs only in Gen 30:32, where Jacob's share of the flock is separated from Laban's: "I will go through all your flock today, removing from it every speckled and spotted young animal (כָּל־שֶׂה) [and every black lamb (וְכָל־שֶׂה־חוּם)][225] . . . and it shall be my wage (שְׂכָרִי)." In this case too the point is to increase Jacob's possessions. That already provides the link with the next statement in DtIsa.

Verse 23aβ, "you have not honored me (לֹא כִבַּדְתָּנִי)": Gen 31:1 talks about Jacob's "honor" (כָּבוֹד). According

220 See the discussion at the beginning of the text Bel and the Dragon (following Theodotion) 4-6: "But Daniel worshipped his own God. And the king said unto him, Why dost thou not worship Bel? But he said, Because I may not do honour to idols made with hands, but to the living God, who hath created the heaven and the earth, and hath sovereignty over all flesh Then the king said to him, Thinkest thou not that Bel is a living god? Or seest thou not how much he eateth and drinketh every day?" (trans. following RV as printed in R. H. Charles, ed., *Apocrypha and Pseudepigrapha of the Old Testament* [Oxford: Clarendon, 1913, reprint 1963] 1:659).

221 For the reception of the patriarchal traditions in DtIsa see already van der Merwe, *Pentateuchtradisies in de Prediking van Deuterojesaja* (1955), esp. § 33, p. 130. On Jacob cf. pp. 132–33. Deut 32:1-44, esp. v. 7, seems to me important in this connection, for

there after the reminder of former days the demand is made: "Ask your father!" The context makes clear—particularly in the LXX version—that it is Jacob whom the text then goes on to talk about. That it is Jacob who is meant is the view of most modern exegetes. Earlier interpretation related "your father . . . the earlier/first" to Adam (thus already Kimchi; cf. also 2 Esdr 7:11; Rom 5:12-14) or Abraham (thus Jerome and Rashi).

222 According to the MT 13 and 11 times, respectively.

223 Gen 29:15, 18, 20, 27 (bis), 30; 30:26 (bis), 29; 31:6, 41; in relation to Esau: 32:5 (4), 19 (18), 21 (20); 33:5, 14.

224 According to v. 10, Rebekah says: "Take [the savory food] to your father to eat (וְהָבֵאתָ לְאָבִיךָ וְאָכָל), so that he may bless you"; cf. vv. 4, 7, 12, 18.

225 See C. Westermann, *Genesis 12–36* (1985) on this passage [*Genesis* (2d ed. 1989)].

to the context, the Hebrew term here means "possessions, wealth."[226] Laban's sons complain: "He has gained all this wealth (כָּבוֹד) from what belonged to our father." Against the background of this Genesis text, the irony in DtIsa becomes clear if one translates: "As far as your sacrifices go, you have not made me rich [instead of 'honored' for כִּבַּדְתָּנִי]"—which has to be complemented by the words: "but only yourself!"

Verse 23bα, literally, "I have not made you serve with meal offerings (בְּמִנְחָה)": The term מִנְחָה is used five times in the Jacob story.[227] But there it is not the meal offering that is meant but the "present" for Jacob's brother Esau. So here too it is correct to say: not for Yahweh!

Verse 23bβ, "I have not wearied you with incense (בַּלְּבוֹנָה)": Here the connection with the Genesis text may be indicated by way of a play on the Hebrew word. The word "incense" means "what is white"[228] (probably because of the color of the resin). According to Gen 30:37, Jacob increases his flocks through a trick: "Then Jacob took fresh rods of storax (לִבְנֶה) . . . and peeled white streaks in them (פְּצָלוֹת לְבָנוֹת), exposing the white (הַלָּבָן) of the rods." The storax is called לִבְנֶה because of its white fronds.[229] Here too "white" is something that is to Jacob's advantage.

Verse 24aα, "You have not bought me spicy cane (קָנֶה) for silver": In this case DtIsa is playing on the words "buy" (קנה) and "cane" (קָנֶה). One of the words formed from the root "acquire, buy" (קנה) is the substantive "property, possessions" (קִנְיָן). When Jacob returns home, we are told (Gen 31:17-18): "So Jacob arose, and set his children and his wives on camels; and he drove away all his livestock (אֶת־כָּל־מִקְנֵהוּ), the livestock that belonged to him (מִקְנֵה קִנְיָנוֹ), which he had acquired in Paddan-aram . . . to go to his father Isaac in the land of Canaan." Through his labor, Jacob had acquired his own personal property. The statement therefore fits better under the heading "Jacob's acquisitions" than in the list of sacrifices. It has always been noted that "spicy cane" does not appear in these lists.[230]

Finally, one may ask why it is said of Jacob: "you have not let me slurp the fat of your sacrifices" (זְבָחֶיךָ, v. 24aβ). Again a Genesis text can have been taken up quite literally. After the contract with Laban has been completed the text reads (Gen 31:54): "and Jacob offered a sacrifice (וַיִּזְבַּח יַעֲקֹב זֶבַח) on the hilltop and called his kinsfolk (וַיִּקְרָא לְאֶחָיו) to eat the meal, and they ate the meal and tarried all night on the hilltop." The meal is for Jacob and his family! For the exilic and postexilic period, a sacrifice (זֶבַח) on the "hilltop" must surely have been suspect. Could it seriously be "for Yahweh"?

If we thus read the series of "nots" (לֹא) against the background of the Jacob texts in Genesis, their individual declarations seem like "findings." It was quite true that Jacob "was concerned" for himself and did not "serve" Yahweh. The alternative is obvious, as the very suffixes and their sounds show: "for me" or "for you."

If the text can be read as an interpretation of Genesis 30–32, we may go on to ask whether the introduction in v. 22 does not also have a particular function in this connection. Verse 22a can simply be translated: "You have not called me, Jacob" (וְלֹא־אֹתִי קָרָאתָ יַעֲקֹב). It is then usually understood to mean "calling upon Yahweh." But this does not eliminate the tensions in the text. After all, an invocation in prayer could be made in exile too. Does the cry not reach the one to whom it is addressed? Are other gods meant? These are possible explanations.[231] But the key text in the Jacob story in Genesis makes a strikingly similar statement. Esau says about Jacob (Gen 27:36): "Is it so that he is called Jacob, that he has gone behind my back (וַיַּעְקְבֵנִי הֲכִי קָרָא שְׁמוֹ יַעֲקֹב) these two times?" It is Jacob who is called a "cheat," not Yahweh. In this light the antithesis and the emphasis are understandable: "But it is not me that you have called 'Jacob.'"

This could be a signal for anyone who had even the slightest remembrance of the Jacob story, a reminder that later we hear about "Jacob, the cheat."[232] The person who is well versed in Scripture knows that הֲכִי (hªkî)

---

226 Cf. Isa 10:3; 66:12; C. Westermann, "כבד kbd to be heavy," *TLOT* 2:590–602 [*THAT* 1:794–812]; C. Dohmen and P. Stenmans, "כבד kābēd," *TDOT* 7:13–22 [*ThWAT* 4:13–23]; M. Weinfeld, כָּבוֹד kābôd," ibid., 22–38 [23–40].

227 Gen 32:14 (13), 19 (18), 21 (20), 22 (21); 33:10.

228 See *HALOT* 2:518 [*HALAT* 2:493]: "Frankincense, the white and at the fracture yellow resin of

Boswellia Carteri and *Frereana* from Ḥaḍramaut and Somaliland . . . the best kind is white" (with references).

229 Cf. *HALOT* 2:578 [*HALAT* 2:492]; according to other authorities the white or silver poplar.

230 See McKenzie, 59.

231 Cf. also Gen 33:20.

232 This explains why in the following salvation oracle

as a question,[233] meaning "is it the case that . . . ?" occurs here, in Gen 27:36, as a question put by Esau, as well as in 29:15, where Laban says to Jacob: "Is it not so that you are my brother (הֲכִי אָחִי), should you serve me (וַעֲבַדְתַּנִי) for nothing ? Tell me, what should your wage be (מַה־מַּשְׂכֻּרְתֶּךָ)?" That is precisely the theme of Genesis 30–32 and of Isa 43:23-24. Could the sentence in v. 22 that begins with כִּי not be an introductory question in DtIsa too? "Is it the case that you have taken pains about me . . . ?" The answer is then No!—as it is in the whole series of questions. The text takes a critical view of Jacob's gainful employment. At least it is not a fulfillment of religious duties. The interpretation of the Jacob tradition would then be not far removed from Hos 12:1-15 (11:12–12:14), esp. v. 13 (12):[234] "Israel served (וַיַּעֲבֹד) for a wife, and for a wife he tended (שָׁמָר) sheep."

In texts of this kind, scriptural interpretation does not mean simply preserving a text for its own sake; it serves an understanding of present-day problems. In order to comprehend it we are dependent on reconstructions that may be more or less certain. In the context of DtIsa it is a question of Israel's reconstitution after the exile. According to the Genesis texts, Jacob wanders from Laban to Esau, until he again settles in the land of his fathers. Laban stands for Mesopotamia, Esau for the road back to Canaan.[235] Does this means that "Jacob" is typical of the homecomers from exile? According to the texts he is "rich." The DtIsa text is critical: "you have made me serve" הֶעֱבַדְתַּנִי (the verb form can also be rendered: "You have simply given me work," v. 24). Is this addressed to wealthy homecomers, a reminder of their duty as regards their "service for Yahweh"? We are familiar with this problem from the book of Nehemiah, for example.[236]

The approach thus developed would mean that what we have here is an extremely highly wrought, artistic text. It can be understood on different levels. On one level the methods of scriptural interpretation are employed. This is a cryptic communication. The basis is a standardized text whose overall meaning is presupposed. Word-for-word quotations are used to identify the context. Since knowledge of the text is presupposed, the writer can play with individual formulations, often giving them a new, topical meaning in the process. Irony and wit are not excluded.

On the one hand the complicated nature of the interpretive process speaks in favor of a written composition, oriented toward the texts. On the other hand the use of aural elements suggests that this was meant for an auditorium. And some of these listeners, at least, were expected to be well versed in the texts.

■ 25 If both levels of meaning—the question of sacrifice and the question of Jacob's transgressions—have to do with "not serving God," we should expect the verdict: guilty! No defense is possible on these counts. There are no extenuating circumstances. Not to serve God is a breach of community (פֶּשַׁע)"; these are transgressions/ sins (חַטָּאוֹת).[237] So the promise that the Lord will blot out the guilt is all the more surprising. A solemn declaration is made in the style of the revelatory speech: "I, I am he/the one. . . ." Other masters do not do this. To cancel a debt without compensation makes economic nonsense.[238] So the result of the trial is in the end in favor of the party who actually loses the case.

■ 26 But since the lawsuit originally involved an indictment of Yahweh, claiming that he had not fulfilled his obligations to his people, the proceedings conclude with a declaration of the legality of Yahweh's acts. Here we

---

in Isa 44:1-5 "the servant Jacob" is called "*Jeshurun*" (יְשֻׁרוּן).

233 See GKC §150e (p. 474); *HALOT* 2:470 [*HALAT* 2:449].

234 Cf. H. W. Wolff, *Hosea* (1974) on this passage [*Hosea* (3d ed. 1976)]; also J. Jeremias, *Der Prophet Hosea* (1983); H. Utzschneider, *Hosea: Prophet vor dem Ende* (1980) 201–2.

235 Cf. Gen 33:18.

236 Cf. Baltzer, "Liberation from Debt Slavery After the Exile in Second Isaiah and Nehemiah," in *Ancient Israelite Religion: FS F. M. Cross* (1987) 477–84.

237 See R. Knierim, *Die Hauptbegriffe der Sünde im AT*

(1965); idem, "פֶּשַׁע *pešaʾ* crime," *TLOT* 2:1033–37 [*THAT* 2:488–95]; idem, "חטא *ḥṭʾ* to miss," *TLOT* 1:406–11, esp. 410 [*THAT* 1:541–49, esp. 547]; von Waldow, "Anlass und Hintergrund der Verkündigung des Deuterojesaja" (1953) 80–81.

238 מחה is "blot out." Closest are passages in which what has been written is "blotted out": Exod 32:32; Num 5:23 (see F. Crüsemann, "Kritik an Amos im deuteronomistischen Geschichtswerk: Erwägungen zu 2. Könige 14,27," in *Probleme biblischer Theologie. FS G. von Rad* [1971] 61 n. 25). Names can be blotted out: Deut 9:14; 29:19 (20); 2 Kgs 14:27; Ps 9:6 (5). So can the remembrance of human beings:

have the germ of a theology of history that interprets Israel's past not as a history of salvation but as one of disaster and guilt.[239]

■ **27-28** The transgression of the "forefather Jacob" was proved in vv. 22-24. But that is only the beginning. The breach of community (פֶּשַׁע) continues. The meaning of מְלִיצֶיךָ is uncertain. It is a *Hiphil* participle from the root לִיץ. According to H. N. Richardson, "the verb 'talk freely or big' and the noun 'babbler' seem to satisfy the sense of the context best." That would be conceivable as a description of the country's leaders.[240] It is noticeable how imprecisely DtIsa uses institutional terms. This does not necessarily mean that he had no precise notion about them. But perhaps he avoids pinning himself down for political reasons.

The same may be said about the phrase שָׂרֵי קֹדֶשׁ, "the princes of a sanctuary" (v. 28).[241] The coordination of the two terms may perhaps suggest that this is a refer-ence to the worldly and the spiritual heads (the kings and the priests).[242]

The harsh verdict is that Jacob/Israel's downfall is due to the action of those who rule over it.[243] Act and destiny belong together. It is not that a somber fate has simply overtaken Jacob/Israel. Yahweh, its God, has brought about this fate himself. These final sentences belong entirely to the prophetic tradition. In misfortune[244] it is God himself who is encountered, and nothing else.

Essential for understanding the salvation that God brings about is the recognition that the background of this salvation is human sin. The past remains part of the present and the future. The identity of God's people is still preserved. But the past is not painted in rosy colors. It is addressed for what it is, and worked through. This experience is passed on. Hope for the future is based on the impossible possibility of God's goodness. The "trial" in this text makes that clear.

Exod 17:14; Deut 25:19. For the "wiping out of sins" cf. Isa 44:22; Ps 51:3, 11. The verb possibly again indicates an action that can be seen, such as the wiping clean of a tablet recording the debts of a customer in the bazaar. We can speak of something being "chalked up" against a person, either as the record of a debt or in a transferred sense.

239   Cf. Ezekiel 20; Nehemiah 9; Daniel 9.

240   Richardson, "Some Notes on לִיץ and Its Derivatives," *VT* 5 (1955) 179. LXX renders it οἱ ἄρχοντες αὐτῶν (or ὑμῶν). Syriac by שׁליטניך, "your ruler." Aquila and Symmachus translate οἱ ἑρμενεῖς σου. The Vulgate's "interpretes tui" corresponds to this. Elliger's supposition (385): "that in מליצים there is a deliberate derogatory wordplay—perhaps even with the undertone 'braggard,'" has something to be said for it in view of the style of the context. Cf. Hos 7:16; 10:4, 7.

241   This is the way the leaders of the twenty-four divisions of priests in the temple are designated in 1 Chr 24:5 too. The more usual term is שָׂרֵי הַכֹּהֲנִים. But DtIsa evidently deliberately avoids using the term "priest" (כֹּהֵן) in general. In this context in DtIsa, however, this expression too may not be a particularly friendly one, perhaps being used in the sense of "princes of holiness" = cult officials. It is they of all people who are "profaned." North translates here: "'and I profaned . . . the holy princes' . . .

'profane' must be in the sense opposite to 'sacred'— so 'de-sacrated,' somewhat as the fruit of the vine after being 'holy' (i.e., given to the sanctuary Lev 19:23-25) in the fourth year was thereafter 'profaned,' i.e., put to everyday or secular use (cf. Deut 20:6; 28:30; Jer 31:5)."

242   Cf. also Neh 9:32, 34; 10:1-29 (9:38—10:28); further Zech 3:1-7.

243   The MT suggests that both verbs should be translated by the future tense, as if the curse is still ahead. But with only a minor change it can be pointed as וָ—imperfect consecutive. Both the patriarch and the leaders have sinned, so Yahweh imposed disaster. The present day is reached only with the following "but now" (וְעַתָּה, 44:1); cf. Neh 9:32, 36.

244   For "curse" (חרם) see Schoors, *I Am God Your Saviour* (1973) 196, with references to Num 21:2-3; Josh 6:21; 1 Samuel 15; Jer 25:9; see further Exod 22:19 (20); Lev 27:29; Deut 13:13-19 (12-18); Isa 34:2; 2 Chr 20:23; C. Brekelmans, "חֵרֶם ḥērem ban," *TLOT* 2:474–77 [*THAT* 1:635–39]; N. Lohfink, "חָרַם ḥāram," *TDOT* 5:180–99 [*ThWAT* 3:192–213]. According to Lev 27:28 and Mic 4:13, what has been consecrated to Yahweh through the curse is excluded from "redemption" (גאל). For "blasphemous words" cf. Ps 44:14-17 (13-16); Jer 51:7; Ezek 5:15; Zeph 2:8.

C. 1. 44:1-5
Court Scene:
The Liberation (from Slavery) of the Servant Jacob/Israel
The Restoration of God's People

44

"Do not be afraid, my servant (is) Jacob,
and Jeshurun, I have chosen him!" (44:2)

1   But now hear, Jacob my servant,
and Israel whom I have chosen!

2   Thus says Yahweh, the one who made you
and formed you—from the womb he helps
       you.[a]
Do not be afraid! My servant (is) Jacob,
and Jeshurun, I have chosen him!

3   Yes, I will pour water onto thirsty (land)
and floods onto dry land.
I will pour my Spirit upon your descendants
and my blessing on your offspring.

4   And they shall spring up <as>[a] between
       grass (?),
like poplars beside ditches.

5   The one there will say: "I belong to Yahweh,"
and the one there will <be called>[a] after
       Jacob,
and the one there will write <on>[b] his hand:
       "Yahweh's (property),"
and with the name of Israel he will <be
       honored>.[c]

2a   Or, following the MT: "and he who has formed you from the womb—he helps you (or: he will help you)."

4a   MT בְּבֵין חָצִיר ("in the space between grass"?) should probably be corrected to כְּבֵין חָצִיר, following a number of manuscripts (cf. LXX, Tg).

5a   Thus with a correction of the vocalization from יִקְרָא ("he will call/name") to יִקָּרֵא (cf. σ´: κληθήσεται).

5b   Thus with a correction from יָדוֹ ("his hand [will write]") to בְּיָדוֹ; (cf. LXX^B, α´, ϑ´: (τῇ) χειρὶ αὐτοῦ (see also L, Vg).

5c   Thus if the active יְכַנֶּה is corrected to יְכֻנֶּה (cf. S, Tg, Vg).

The section can be seen as a unit with a distinct content of its own.[245] It begins with the naming of Jacob/Israel in v. 1 and closes similarly in v. 5. In the composition as a whole, it is linked with the preceding section, 43:22-28. The remembrance of guilt is linked with a new promise of salvation. The text begins afresh with "But now" (וְעַתָּה, v. 1). The sequence can be compared with 43:1-7 and 43:14, 16. The following unit begins again with the formula: "Thus says Yahweh" (v. 6).

There is a wide measure of agreement that in genre the text may be defined as a "salvation oracle" or "salvation saying."[246] But how is salvation proclaimed here, and in what sense? Taking the context into account, R. P. Merendino assigns the text to "the genre 'announcements of salvation,' . . . but in a special sense: here

Yahweh as sovereign judge pronounces his judicial pardon."[247] To say this brings out that this is initially an event; Yahweh speaks through his messenger: "Thus says Yahweh . . . ," and Jacob/Israel is addressed (vv. 1-2). This directness is by no means a matter of course. It indicates the importance of the event. Just as a king is represented by his vizier, so "Yahweh, king of Israel," is represented in the legal proceedings that follow by his authorized spokesman.

■ **1-2** The twice-used designation "my servant" serves as a hint, permitting the deduction that we can again expect the sociomorpheme "master-servant." What happens here is the legal implementation of a redemption (גְּאֻלָּה). It speaks in favor of this interpretation that Jacob/Israel should be the first to be told the circum-

---

245   For the interpretation see E. Kutsch, "Ich will meinen Geist ausgiessen auf deine Kinder," in *Das Wort, das weiter wirkt. FS K. Frör* (1970) 122–33.

246   See Begrich, *Studien zu Deuterojesaja* (1938, reprint 1963) 14; C. Westermann, "Sprache und Struktur der Prophetie Deuterojesajas," in *Forschung am Alten Testament* 1 (1964) 117–18; see also idem, "Das Heilswort bei Deuterojesajas," *EvTh* 24 (1964)

355–73; Schoors, *I Am God Your Saviour* (1973) 78–79; Elliger, 368.

247   Merendino, *Der Erste und der Letzte: Eine Untersuchung von Jes 40–48* (1981) 371.

stances. He is once again a servant, because Yahweh has chosen him. Then there follows the "official" declaration, so to speak: "Thus says Yahweh . . ." (v. 1). The "redeemer" justifies his claim in two ways: (1) he "has made" Jacob/Israel, so he has a right to him; he is his own property; (2) "from the womb"—that applies to slaves born in the household. The master of the house has a claim on them. For his part, the "master" is in duty bound to provide protection and help (עזר). This he promises to do. Consequently the "servant" has no need to be afraid.[248]

Legally, the redemption of a slave means reinstallation, or restoration to his earlier status. That is why Yahweh declares—reversing v. 1—"my servant (is) Jacob," at the same time giving him a new name, *Jeshurun*, "I have chosen him." The declaration is not directed preeminently to the servant himself; it is addressed to the witnesses, so that they know what the master intends. The difficulty of the text is again due to the fact that we have the content of the speech, but not a description of what is happening. We may assume, however, that "the redemption" (גאל) is accompanied by some action or other.

In this case a comparison with "redemption" procedures otherwise described in the OT makes it possible for us to acquire an idea of what is occurring here, at least in broad outline. In the following two cases it is a matter of settling questions of ownership, in the widest sense. The prophet Jeremiah "redeems" a field during the siege of Jerusalem. His uncle's son sums up the nature of the legal act in a single sentence: "Buy my field that is at Anathoth in the land of Benjamin, for the right of possession by inheritance and the 'redemption' (הַגְּאֻלָּה) is yours" (32:8). But in what detail the act is described, with the drawing up of the double document, the weighing up of the price—all of it in the presence of witnesses!

According to the book of Ruth (chap. 4), Boaz employs the practice of "redemption" (אֶגְאָלָה, v. 4; cf. vv.

1, 3, 4, 6, 7; הַגְּאֻלָּה, 8) and acquires a field. For this he enters into the levirate marriage that is bound up with the inheritance. The completion of the legal act is described precisely. It even goes so far as to explain the ancient custom of handing over a shoe, when it was a matter of "redeeming and exchanging, to confirm a transaction" (v. 7). This is really the narration of a scene. But that means that we have first to reconstruct what was a matter of course for the ancient listener and reader, even if he or she was not actually a spectator.

As far as the text is concerned, this means that Yahweh took advantage of the opportunity to buy back, or redeem. That explains the jubilation in vv. 3-5. Verse 6 goes on appropriately: "Thus says Yahweh, Israel's king and its *redeemer* (וְגֹאֲלוֹ)." But this text too can be understood on several different levels. We have tried to show that an interpretation of the Jacob story underlies the preceding text, 43:22-28. It is possible to suppose that this interpretation goes further, and that it can help to explain certain curious features of the present text too.

The naming of the name—Jacob's own name, instead of the name of God—was the element that triggered off the charge in 43:22. In 44:1 and 4, Yahweh himself now names the name of Jacob. The theme is explicitly taken up again in v. 5. But the most striking feature is Jacob's new name: "*Jeshurun*" (יְשֻׁרוּן)[249]—new, inasmuch as he has never been called this up to now in DtIsa's book. A comparison with Deut 32:15; 33:5, 26; Sir 37:25 (Hebr. MSS. D and B) shows that the name is not DtIsa's own independent formation. Its interpretation is disputed. L. Wächter follows earlier commentators in concluding that it is "a honorific and a pet name." "The root is *yšr*, so the best translation would be 'the upright one' or 'the dependable one.'" Irrespective of whether this is the original or the correct meaning, it is difficult in the case of biblical etymologies especially to distinguish between a primary and a secondary usage; but the context in DtIsa must at all events be noted. Here this passage is preceded by the unfavorable description of Jacob in

248 Cf. 41:10, 13-14; 43:1-2, 5.
249 See here W. Bacher, "יְשֻׁרוּן," *ZAW* 5 (1885) 161–63; L. Wächter, "Israel und Jeschurun," in *Schalom. FS A. Jepsen* (1971) 58–64; G. Wallis, "Jeschurun," *BHH* 2:858; M. J. Mulder, "יְשֻׁרוּן *yᵉšurûn*," *TDOT* 6:472–77, esp. 476–77 [*ThWAT* 3:1070–75, esp. 1074–75]; G. Liedke, "ישׁר, *yšr*, to be straight, right," *TLOT* 2:588–90 [*THAT* 1:791]; H. Ringgren, L. Alonso-Schökel, and W. Mayer, "יָשַׁר *yāšar*," *TDOT* 6:463–72, esp. 469 and 471 [*ThWAT* 3:1059–70], esp. 1066 and 1069].

43:22-28. The text is evidently taking up Jacob traditions. In Gen 27:36 and Hos 12:3-4 (2-3) these are linked with the interpretation of his name as "Jacob the deceiver." So when Jacob is now reinstalled in his position and rights as servant (because he has been redeemed), he is "the righteous, the upright one" (יְשֻׁר). We find the wordplay again almost immediately, I believe, when the pronouncements about Jacob as an individual are related to the community (v. 5). Here the "name of Jacob" (בְּשֵׁם יַעֲקֹב) and the "name of Israel" (בְשֵׁם יִשְׂרָאֵל) are parallel designations. For Jacob and Israel to be identified is nothing new. But this may mean that for us the special point is lost. In v. 5 we should pronounce יְשָׁר־אֵל, i.e. yāšar ʾēl,[250] and translate: "righteous, upright is God." That is the confession of faith of those who call themselves afresh after Jacob/Israel. The parallelism in the roots "to be crooked" (עקב) and "to be straight" (ישר) is found in DtIsa at the very beginning, in the prologue in 40:4: "The crooked will become straight" (הֶעָקֹב לְמִישׁוֹר). I believe it possible that this is already an allusion to 44:1-5—a preliminary statement at the very beginning of the text's still hidden program, so to speak.

These are perhaps not unexceptionable philological derivations.[251] They are developed from the sounds, and therefore have their proper place in the spoken word of the drama. But they are not simply wordplays, without a proper understanding of the meaning. What happens to Jacob as servant—that he is newly declared "righteous" because God is righteous—applies also to the community of God's people.

■ **3, 4-5** Blessing is promised in words rich in imagery

reminiscent of the hymn. The blessing consists first of all in the fertility of the land. Rain falls after the dry season. Water means life. Green grass, trees—in the parched land of the Middle East there is hardly anything that arouses more wonder. We find similar utterances in the descriptions of paradisal conditions. We are reminded that "dew from heaven" is also promised in the blessing given to Jacob.[252] Here there is new blessing after the "anathema" (חֵרֶם, 43:28). But v. 3b gives this declaration of blessing a new dimension.[253] Now the outpouring of water becomes an image for the outpouring and efficacy of the Spirit. Like rain on the seed (זֶרַע, v. 3), the Spirit of God works on "the seed of human beings," letting it "spring up" (צמח, v. 4).[254]

The comparison embraces the plant's whole development, with the irresistible beginning of growth after the rain.[255] The Spirit gives life. But what is the significance of the comparison? Attention has been drawn—rightly, I believe—to the closeness between this passage and Ezek 37:1-4, the vision of the "raising of dead Israel."[256] There the Spirit brings the "dry bones" to life again. The subject is the revivification of the people and the return to the land. I believe that in this DtIsa text too the initial point is the restoration of God's people. Its fate is represented in the fate of Jacob and his descendants. They have experienced the curse; they will partake of the blessing. Is the Spirit of God the life-giving Spirit or the Spirit of prophecy? This does not have to be an alternative. If Jacob is a "servant," his descendants are

---

250 For the exchange of the sibilants (שׂ und שׁ) see G. E. Mendenhall, "Puppy and Lettuce in Northwest-Semitic Covenant Making," *BASOR* 133 (1954) 29 n. 14, with reference to G. A. Danell, *Studies in the Name Israel* (1946); cf. Judg 12:6.

251 But see Wächter, "Israel und Jeschurun" in *Schalom. FS A. Jepsen* (1971) 59–60.

252 See Gen 27:28; conversely, v. 39. Cf. Deut 32:10-14 (9-13); Zech 8:12.

253 The uncertainty whether כ should be read twice in v. 4 could be another indication of the change into a comparison. On the theme "blessing" see J. Scharbert, "ברך, brk" *TDOT* 2:279–308, esp. 298–99 [*ThWAT* 1:808–41, esp. 831].

254 Kutsch ("Ich will meinen Geist ausgiessen auf deine Kinder," in *Das Wort, das weiter wirkt. FS K. Frör* [1970] 130) sees here a special word addressed to the young: "DtIsa promises . . . that the younger

generation, which has already departed from the faith of their fathers or is in the process of doing so, through the efficacy of Yahweh's spirit will return to Yahweh and hence to his people, and will again acquire vitality through his blessing."

255 See S. Amsler, "צמח ṣmḥ to sprout," *TLOT* 3:1085–87 [*THAT* 2:563–66]; H. Schlier, "ἀνατολή," *TDNT* 1:352–53 [*ThWNT* 1:354–55]; cf. Hos 8:7; Gen 2:5; Pss 65:11(10); 104:14. For DtIsa see 42:9; 43:19; 45:8.

256 See Kutsch, "Ich will meinen Geist ausgiessen auf deine Kinder," in *Das Wort, das weiter wirkt. FS K. Frör* (1970) 124–25; R. Bartelmus, "Ez. 37,1-14, die Verbform wᵉqatal und die Anfänge der Auferstehungshoffnung," *ZAW* 97 (1985) 366–89.

"servants" too, and the gift of the Spirit is given to them as it was to the prophet.[257]

Verse 5 joins onto the declaration that Jacob is "my Servant." A servant (עֶבֶד) is the property of his master. To say "for Yahweh" or "belonging to Yahweh" (לַיהוה) is comparable to the formula that we find, for example, in the inscriptions on pitcher handles, which mark the contents as being for the king (לַמֶּלֶךְ)—as royal property. Whether slaves had any special mark in Israel is a matter of dispute.[258] But to give a name is also a declaration of ownership.

When people call themselves "Jacob/Israel" or "belonging to Yahweh," this can be understood in different ways. It can be the sign of adherence to an ethnic community, or to a religious community, or to both. Here it depends on the period when it is used, and on the sound that the descriptions carry. When Jonah is compelled to identify himself, he declares "I am a Hebrew (עִבְרִי) and fear Yahweh" (Jonah 1:9). That is what distinguishes him from the "foreigners." But it probably already has an old-fashioned sound. "Belonging to Judah" (יְהוּדִי) was an ethnic or political description, the emphasis varying before and after the exile.[259] But as far as we can see, "Jacob/Israel" was not a political entity at this time; it was rather a program. The person who used this name for himself was making a confession of faith.[260]

Did the chorus act this out in the drama? "This one . . . this one . . . this one" (זֶה) is said three times (v. 5), like a stage direction. It could be that three or four different groups were thereby named. "Foreigners" could be "Yahweh's property" too, and Israel as an honorific[261] was not confined to the *ethnos*. But the claim to be Yahweh's property had practical consequences too. We must remember that in the ancient world when a slave was freed (*manumissio* was the Latin term) the slave's name was registered in the sanctuary. This meant that the previous owner had given up all rights, and that the former slave was free of his or her obligations. Jeremiah 34 shows how manumission could be misused for the purpose of psychological warfare. Yahweh himself watches to see that the commandment to set the slaves free is kept (see v. 14; cf. Exod 21:2; Deut 15:12). The consequence of the broken promise is the destruction of the city of Jerusalem and the cities of Judah (Jer 34:22). Neh 5:1-13 shows quite clearly that the problem remained acute. Thus at this point listeners probably pricked up their ears. This vision of the future was something that concerned them personally.

The text initially envisages only the restoration of "Jacob," in hope for a new beginning that would bring blessing and the return from exile; but the amazing thing is that this hope should have been fulfilled in a measure that was undreamed of. The gift of the Spirit is also the miracle of Pentecost, in which the people of God grew beyond the bounds of Jacob/Israel. The group of those who confess Yahweh is an open group: that is already implicit in this text. The interpretation that non-Israelites can belong to it as well is no more than consistent. This text too can be read in a series of steps. It is a testimony to an extended process of perception and interpretation.

257 Cf. Zech 14:21.

258 According to Lev 19:28 tattooing is forbidden; but see the piercing of the lobes of the ear according to Deut 15:12-18. Identifying marks are mentioned in Ezek 9:4; Rev 7:3; 13:16; Gal 6:17-18. Cf. also Gen 4:15. For the tattooing of slaves at Elephantine see P. Grelot, *Documents araméens d'Egypte* (1972) no. 41. For signs bound on the hand cf. Exod 13:16; Deut 6:8; 11:18; Prov 7:3.

259 *HALOT* 2:394 [*HALAT* 2:377]; see below; H.-J. Zobel, "יְהוּדָה *y°hûdâ*," *TDOT* 5:482-99 [*ThWAT* 3:512-33] (lit.).

260 Cf. Isa 7:10-17 and the name Immanuel.

261 See *HALOT* 2:483 [*HALAT* 2:460 s.v. כנה with reference to Isa 45:4; Job 32:21-22; Sir 36:12 (Hebr.), 17 (LXX); 44:23; 45:2 (margin); 47:6. On manumission of slaves, see W. L. Westermann, *Sklaverei*, PW Suppl. 6 (1935) cols. 894-1068, esp. 933ff. On registration of slaves' names, see, for example, the inscriptions from Delphi, nos. 1684ff., in *Sammlung der griechischen Dialekt-Inschriften von I. Becktel*, ed. H. Collitz, 4 vols. (Göttingen, 1884-1915).

"Thus says Yahweh, Israel's king, and its
redeemer, Yahweh Sabaoth . . ." (44:6)

6   Thus says Yahweh, Israel's king,
    and its redeemer, Yahweh Sabaoth:

    I am the first and I am the last,
    and besides me there are no gods.

7   But who is like me? <Let him come forward
        and>ᵃ call
    and declare it and expound it to me!
    <Who has proclaimed from of old future
        (events)>ᵇ
    or can tell (us)ᶜ what is going to come?

8   Do not be frightened and do not panic!
    Have I not told you from of old and declared
        (it)?
    And you are my witnesses:
    Is there any God besides me?
    No, there is no other rock. I know of none.

7a Expand, following LXX (στήτω καί): וְ יַעֲמֹד.

7b Thus with a conjectural emendation to מִי הִשְׁמִיעַ מֵעוֹלָם אוֹתִיּוֹת
(cf. *BHS*). MT (מַשְׁמִעִי עַם־עוֹלָם וְאֹתִיּוֹת . . .) would have to be
translated more or less as follows: "Since I have installed an
eternal people, they are told the future (events) and what is
going to come."

7c Thus with a conjectural emendation לָנוּ for לָמוֹ ("to them").

If, in closing, we survey the wider complex 43:8—44:5,
we see that it began with a trial scene in which the
peoples are gathered together before Yahweh (43:8-13;
see v. 9: "all peoples" [כָּל־הַגּוֹיִם] . . . and nations"
[לְאֻמִּים]). Yahweh's people is presented as a "blind witness." Action is announced in two brief messages. In vv.
14-15 it is the fall of Babylon, in vv. 16-21 the downfall
of the Babylonian army. 43:22-28 and 44:1-5 are linked.
A direct accusation is made against Jacob/Israel. After
he has been pardoned, he is "redeemed." If we take 44:1-
5 as a starting point, we may ask whether the course of
events is not similar to that in 41:8-16; 42:1-9; and 43:1-7.
Where is the dramatic progression? The exegesis has
shown that here the Jacob aspect is in the foreground.
This time it is the people, as the collective "Jacob my
Servant," which is taken back into its election (43:10;
44:1, 2). 44:6-8 is a link passage. The titles ascribed to
Yahweh pick up the preceding themes once more.

■ **6** Yahweh is Israel's king. Two things are bound up
with this assertion. When the royal title is given to the
deity, it means first of all that he is "king over the gods."

A god proves his kingship by acting as judge over the
gods. But because the gods do not exist (אֵין אֱלֹהִים, 44:6),
only the peoples stand before Yahweh. The denial of a
theogony is endorsed once more (44:6; cf. 43:10-11). But
if Yahweh himself is Israel's king,[262] then this can also
mean that no human king for Israel can be expected. It
is Cyrus, the foreign ruler, who is sent to Babylon (43:15)
to bring about the liberation. It is Yahweh himself who
wages the real battle (43:16-21). It is he, as Yahweh
Sabaoth (v. 6).[263] In the trial described in this scene too,
Yahweh is probably represented by a spokesman, as the
introductory formula "thus says Yahweh" shows.

■ **7** "The gods" are once more asked to make a statement, but the result is the same as it was at the beginning of the trial in 43:8-13.[264] The other party in the
dispute does not come forward; it simply fails to appear.
But nevertheless there is one essential difference in this
symmetrical structure. Yahweh's own summing up establishes: "I am the first and the last, and besides me there
are no gods" (v. 6).

---

262 Cf. 41:21-22; 43:15; Zeph 3:15.

263 1QIsaᵃ stresses the solemn character of the proclamation by inserting in the text "is his name" (שְׁמוֹ).
Here for the first time in DtIsa; also 45:13; 47:4;
48:2; 51:15; 54:5; but in substance cf. also 40:27. See
also North on this passage, A. S. van der Woude,
"צָבָא *ṣābāʾ* army," *TLOT* 2:1039–46 [*THAT*
2:498–507].

264 The text of v. 7c is unequivocally attested (see

1QIsaᵃ, LXX, Tg). But the meaning of "from my
establishing of an eternal people and things to
come" remains obscure. An emendation to
מִי ישמיע מעולם אתיות, "Who has proclaimed from
days of old future events" (thus the proposal in
Schoors, *I Am God Your Saviour* [1973] 230), seems
possible. מֵעוֹלָם, "since oldest times" (lit.: "since
always"), can be referring to all the traditions that

■ **8** The intention of v. 8 is a final explicit affirmation of what was stated in v. 6.[265] At the beginning of this trial it was said (43:8) that the people (עַם) was "blind" and "deaf";[266] but we hear no more about that now. For Jacob/Israel has heard and seen what Yahweh is doing. It is Yahweh's "redeemed servant." That is the reason why there is again a turn to "the chorus," or to the spectators and listeners as the case may be: "You are my witnesses" (44:8). Human beings can witness to the acts of God, but what they do cannot be a substitute for what God does. This is a critical question addressed to the compulsions of false missionary ambition. The credibility of the testimony stems from the experience that one's own "blindness" and "deafness" have been healed. To be able to see and hear freely is the fundamental presupposition for life with one another.

"Rock" in v. 8 is a divine epithet.[267] In 48:21 it is an allusion to the exodus tradition (the rock from which Yahweh makes water flow), while in 51:1 it is a reference to the tradition of the patriarchs. It is thus a theologoumenon that is presupposed and interpreted in different senses. In view of the special character of the text as a summing up of what has gone before, Deuteronomy 32 again deserves particular attention here, because that text was bound up especially closely with the Jacob tradition. In the Deuteronomy passage, "rock" is the outstanding predicate for God. It is used explicitly six times (vv. 4, 15, 18, 30, 31, 37). "Jeshurun" has rejected its God, according to Deut 32:5, and its "rock" has therefore sold it (v. 30). This is the sociomorpheme "servant/lord." The passage ends, in words slightly different from those in Isa 44:8: "There is no other God besides me" (Deut 32:4). In the light of the theme, the catchword "rock" provides a good transition to vv. 9-20, the dispute about idols.

Isa 44:6-8 and 21-23 correspond, forming a kind of framework for this section. Thus v. 6 begins with "Yahweh, Israel's king and its redeemer," while v. 23 ends: "Yes, Yahweh has redeemed/liberated Jacob, and in/through Israel will he glorify himself" (cf. v. 22). A further series of catchwords can be found in the formula about "forming" (יצר). These are not merely verbal links; they also signal a link in substance. In the "redemption" Yahweh justifies his right to his servant with the claim that he had "formed you" (v. 2). Verse 10 asks: "Who has formed (מִי יָצַר) a god," and the end (v. 21) says once more: "I have formed you" (יְצַרְתִּיךָ). The character of vv. 6-8 as a link passage is thus clear.

DtIsa takes up—creation, the patriarchs, or the exodus.

265 Verses 6-8 are assigned to the genre "trial speech" by Begrich, von Waldow, Fohrer, Muilenburg, Westermann, Elliger and Schoors. I would agree, with the proviso that I do not see the text as an independent unit. Consequently in the framework of the legal proceedings the final saying can be a salvation oracle for Israel. In v. 8a 1QIsaᵃ has תיראו, probably rightly.

266 Here the text takes up catchwords from the beginning of Act II (42:16, 18).

267 For the divine predicate "rock" (צוּר) see *HALOT* 3:1017 [*HALAT* 3:953 (with lit.); A. S. van der Woude, "צוּר *ṣûr*," *TLOT* 2:1067–71 [*THAT* 2:538–43, esp. 542-43]. A connection with the traditions of the Jerusalem cult is generally assumed in the literature. See C. J. Labuschagne, *The Incomparability of Yahweh in the OT* (1966), esp.

70–72, 114–17 (on Deuteronomy 32); L. Delekat, *Asylie und Schutzorakel am Zionsheiligtum* (1967) 379–80 and 209 on Deut 32:37; D. Eichhorn, *Gott als Fels, Burg und Zuflucht: Eine Untersuchung zum Gebet des Mittlers in den Psalmen* (1972) 30–91, esp. 76 and the summing up 89–91; H. Wildberger, *Isaiah 1–12* (1991) 359 [*Jesaja* [1972] 338] on Isa 8:14-15; H.-J. Kraus, *Psalms 1–59* (1988) 404 [*Psalmen 1* [5th ed. 1978] 287–88]; G. H. Davies, "Psalm 95," *ZAW* 85 (1973) 183–95, esp. 189–90. The divine predicate "rock" (צוּר) is a "motif of trust" (Begrich); see esp. Deut 32:4, 15, 18, 30, 31, 37; further Pss 18:3 (2); 47 (46); 62:3 (2); 89:27 (26); 95:1; in DtIsa also 48:21; 51:1. The Jacob tradition and its connection with Deuteronomy 32, as we saw, already played a role in Isa 43:22ff. (see above). Cf. also Wolff, *Hosea* (1974) [*Hosea* (3d ed. 1976)] on Hos 12:5.

9   The makers of images, they all are nothing,
and their darlings do not help,
and their witnesses <. . .>[a] do not see
and do not perceive, so that they may be
shamed.

10   Who has fashioned a god and cast an image
that is of no use?

11   See, all its comrades will be ashamed,
and <its>[a] fashioners too, they (are
descended from) a human being.
Let them assemble all of them! Let them all
come forward!
Let them be terrified! Let them all be
ashamed!—Together!

12   A specialist for iron—he cuts off/hammers (?),
and works with charcoal,
and forms it with hammers,
and forges it with his strong arm.
He also becomes hungry and (has) no (more)
strength.
He has drunk no water and has become tired.

13   A specialist for wood—he has stretched a
measuring line.
He traces it out with a stylus,
fashions it with carving tools,
with the rounding tool he makes his contours,
<so as to make it>[a] like the (ideal) image of
a man,
like a splendid example of a human being—
to dwell in a house.

(Herdsman)

14   (A man has come)[a] to fell cedars
and he took a durmast oak and an oak tree
and he made himself strong under the trees
of the wood.

(Farmer)

A man has planted a laurel,
and the rain makes it big,

15   and it can serve someone for a fire.
Then he took part of them and warmed
himself:
in part he kindles (it) and bakes bread,
in part he makes (of it) a god <and bows
down (before it) in worship>.[a]
He has made an image and thrown himself
down in front of it.

(Herdsman)

16   His (one) half he took to burn in the fire,
in part he eats meat,
he roasts the meat so as to eat his fill.
In part he warms himself too and says,
"Ah! now I am warm! I have seen firelight!"

17   And the remainder he has made into a god,
into its image.
He throws himself down before it <and
worships it>[a]

9a   MT הֵמָּה with its *puncta extraordinaria* is missing in some manuscripts and should probably be omitted.

11a   וְחָרָשָׁיו should probably be read instead of וְחָרָשִׁים.

13a   The *wayyiqtol* form וַיַּעֲשֵׂהוּ is difficult to understand in the context. The pointing should probably rather be וְיַעֲשֵׂהוּ (*weyiqtol* in
the final or purpose sense).

14a   A finite verb—בָּא, for example—should be thought of as preceding לִכְרָת (see below on this passage). A correction to כָּרַת,
"one man has felled (cedars for himself)," would also be possible; cf. LXX, Vg.

15a   Read וְיִשְׁתַּחֲוֶה in place of וַיִּשְׁתָּחוּ.

17a   Read וְיִשְׁתַּחֲוֶה in place of וַיִּשְׁתָּחוּ.

and prays to it and says:
"Save me, for you are my god!"

(Speaker)

18   They have not perceived and do not understand
that their eyes are sealed so that they cannot
see,
their hearts (are sealed) so that they cannot
understand.

(Herdsman)

19   And he does not take it to heart,
and has not the perception and not the
insight to say:
"His half I have burnt in the fire."

(Farmer)

"And on the embers of part of it I have baked
bread."

(Herdsman)

"I roast meat and eat."

(Farmer)

"And the remainder I turn into an abomination/
a horror."

(Herdsman)

"Do I throw myself down in front of a block
of wood?"

(Farmer and Herdsman?/Speaker?)

20   He grazes on ashes. A deluded heart has led
him astray.
But he will not save his life,
and will not say: "Is it not a lie (which is) in
my right hand?!"

The very first words in v. 9 (יֹצְרֵי־פֶסֶל) encapsulate the problem posed in the following unit: What should we think about the production of idols? Seen in its wider context, the reasoning here moves a step further. The existence of other gods was initially called into question; what is in doubt here is whether it is possible to "fashion a god" (v. 10). The manufacture of an image is apparently attributed to the foreign cult as a matter of course. Belief in Yahweh is irreconcilable with idols.[268] Here the starting point is and remains the prohibition of images as this is summed up for us in the Decalogue.[269] It is one of the central elements constituting Israel's unique character as the people of God, and an essential mark differentiating its people from the world around. Here the

268 See Exod 20:4; Deut 5:8; Exod 20:23; 34:17; Deuteronomy 4; 27:15; Daniel 3. This corresponds to the Islamic faith; cf. what is said in the Qurʾan 19:42; 21:66; 25:55; 26:72; 29:17; 37:86, 95.

269 See P. Welten, "Bilder II, AT," *TRE* 6 (1980) 517–21 (with lit.); W. Zimmerli, "Das zweite Gebot" (1950), in *Gottes Offenbarung: Gesammelte Aufsätze zum Alten Testament* (1963) 234–48; K. H. Bernhardt, *Gott und Bild* (1956); G. von Rad, *Old Testament Theology* 1 (1962, reprint 1975) 212–19 [*Theologie des Alten Testaments* 2 (1957; 8th ed. 1982–84) 211–18]; C. R. North, "The Essence of Idolatry," in *Von Ugarit nach Qumran. FS O. Eissfeldt* (1958) 151–60; J. Gutmann,

"The 'Second Commandment' and the Image in Judaism," in *No Graven Images: Studies in Art and the Hebrew Bible* (1971) 3–14; R. P. Carroll, "The Aniconic God and the Cult of Images," *StTh* 31 (1977) 51–64; T. N. D. Mettinger, "The Veto on Images and the Aniconic God in Ancient Israel," in *Religious Symbols and Their Functions* (1979) 15–29; F.-L. Hossfeld, *Der Dekalog: Seine späten Fassungen, die originale Komposition und seine Vorstufen* (1982) 268–73; F. Crüsemann, *Bewahrung der Freiheit: Das Thema des Dekalogs in sozialgeschichtlicher Perspektive* (1983) 47–50; C. Dohmen, *Das Bilderverbot: Seine Entstehung und seine Entwicklung im AT* (2d ed.

fundamental point is the understanding of reality. What is the relationship between reality and image? In what way is the divine present in the world? Where is the borderline between human and divine activity? These are questions that we might ask too. The author of our text has a long period of dispute behind him. But it becomes clear in the polemic that even for him and his time the problem is by no means finished and done with.

Whether vv. 9-20 are "genuine" has long been a subject of dispute among scholars.[270] Duhm's view is already typical: "The section shatters the connection between vv. 6-8 and vv. 21-26 and no more belongs to DtIsa than Jer 10:1-16 belongs to Jeremiah.[271] Even the language displays peculiarities, and the difference in rhythm and style is more striking still; above all, it is impossible to see the grandiloquent DtIsa engaging in this finicking painting."[272] It is literary criteria for the most part that induce critics to detach the text from its context. A particular view of the author and his theology also plays its

part. But on the literary level some arguments suggest that the passage is intimately connected with the rest of the book. Above all, the same vocabulary is used here.[273] This is true both of the sustaining terms and the individual particles.[274] The terms are brought together into concepts that are comparable to what has gone before. Catchwords provide a link with the immediate context,[275] and this is an indication that the argument is connected too.[276]

There is no question that the text has a particular content of its own. But it has points in common with other texts in DtIsa that have to do with "idols" and their manufacture. These texts pick up traditions about "the mocking of foreign religions," as H. D. Preuss especially has shown.[277] The particular content conditions the particular poetic form. Significantly enough, *BHS* now also sets the text as poetry, not as prose.[278] Another point common to these texts, as Westermann has acutely observed, is that they "cause a break in the context."[279]

1987); J. M. Kennedy, "The Social Background of Early Israel's Rejection of Cultic Images: A Proposal," *BTB* 17 (1987) 138–44; O. Keel and C. Uehlinger, *Gods, Goddesses, and Images of God in Ancient Israel* (1998) [*Göttinnen, Götter und Gottessymbole: Neue Erkenntnisse zur Religionsgeschichte Kanaans und Israels aufgrund bislang unerschlossener ikonographischer Quellen* (1992)].

270 Merendino (*Der Erste und der Letzte: Eine Untersuchung von Jes 40–48* [1981] 385 n. 208) names the following as rejecting the "genuineness" of the passage (including himself): Cheyne, Duhm, Marti, Köhler, Elliger, Fohrer, North, and Westermann. According to him the following assume that the author is DtIsa himself: Guillet, Bonnard, Lack, McKenzie, Rignell, Steinmann and Ziegler. North, however, is inclined to waver (139), and the same may be said of Schoors (279). Muilenburg and Preuss also plead for Deutero-Isaian authorship. See also J. Kim, "Das Verhältnis Jahwes zu den anderen Göttern in Deuterojesaja" (1962) 64–65; and Spykerboer, *The Structure and Composition of Deutero-Isaiah* (1976) 118–19.

271 See this argument again in North, 139–40.

272 Duhm, 305.

273 See the list in H. D. Preuss, *Verspottung fremder Religionen im AT* (1971) 209–10, with reference to vv. 9-11. He lists: אֵל, בוש, עֵד, הוֹעִיל, תֹהוּ, פֶסֶל, יֵצֶר, נָסַך, חרשׁ, יַחַד, עָמַד; see also Spykerboer, *The Structure and Composition of Deutero-Isaiah* (1976) 119ff.; Elliger, 415–16.

274 Spykerboer, *The Structure and Composition of Deutero-*

Isaiah: 120, on "they all" (כֻּלָם); 121, on "nothing" (לְבִלְתִּי, בַּל); and 122, on "see" (הֵן).

275 "Form" (יצר) in 44:9, 10, 12, as in the context 44:2, 21, 24; "witness" (עד) in 44:8 in the context of v. 9. Cf. 43:8-13.

276 See Westermann, 146 (119): "his declaration that Yahweh is the one God; hence the catchword with which 44:9-20 makes the link is 'no god beside me' (44:8b)." Westermann disputes DtIsaian authorship, however, arguing: "This taunt song differs from all the rest of Deutero-Isaiah in that it says nothing about Yahweh and his dealings with Israel" (146 [119]). We shall return to this point in the discussion about the genre of the text.

277 This is the title that Preuss gives his book (*Verspottung fremder Religionen im AT* [1971]); see also J. Guillet, "La polémique contre les idoles et le Serviteur de Yahvé," *Bib* 40 (1959) 428–34; W. M. W. Roth, "For Life, He Appeals to Death (Wis. 13:18): A Study of OT Idol Parodies," *CBQ* 37 (1975) 21–47. For further texts see 2 Kgs 19:15-19; Isa 37:14-20; Jer 10:2-16; Hos 8:4-7; Hab 2:18-20; Psalms 115 and 135; Baruch 6 (Letter of Jeremiah); Wisdom 13–15; on the last of these texts and its connection with Isa 44:9-20, see D. Georgi, *Weisheit Salomos* (1980).

278 See here the editor of the book of Isaiah in *BHS*, D. W. Thomas, "Isaiah XLIV, 9-20: A Translation and Commentary " in *FS A. Dupont-Sommer* (1971) 319.

279 Westermann, 146–47 [119].

But this too does not necesarily sugggest that they should be excised, since throughout the book DtIsa works with contrasts. A literary explanation for the tensions in the text itself becomes problematical, however, once this becomes material only for the construction of different versions.[280] In what follows the attempt will therefore be made to arrive at an understanding of what the passage is saying through a determination of the genre to which it belongs, as far as possible preserving the text as it stands. The special character of this passage, vv. 9-20, must emerge from its detailed exegesis.

The text has been defined as a "taunt song."[281] Other descriptions—trial speech[282] or sermon[283]—take into account only a single aspect in each case. The elements in the presentation of the action, the characters as "types," as well as—in the formal sphere—the straightforward sequence of individual verses and the use of fixed formula could all speak in favor of an epic genre. But in the epic we should expect a clearer description of the circumstances, for example,[284] so that in their imaginations *listeners* are able to *see* what is happening. In this particular respect the text is relatively sparing. Action is certainly interpreted. I would therefore once more assume that this is a scene belonging to a drama.

The dramatic character of the text has long been recognized, for example by D. W. Thomas, who takes up observations made by C. C. Torrey.[285] This dramatic character determines both the content and the form. The scene takes place entirely in the earthly sphere. The most important scenes of the action are the workshop and the home. A speaker introduces the event, explaining what is going on in each case and interpreting it. This is one of the occasions where we have an explicit stage direction: "Let them assemble, all of them, let them come forward" (v. 11). The actors have at least a few words to say: "Ah, now I am warm, I have seen firelight (אוּר, *ʾûr*)" (v. 16);[286] and: "Save me, for you are my god!" (v. 17). Perhaps they speak again at the end of the passage (vv. 19 and 20). In each case the actors come forward in pairs. In the first part (vv. 12-13) they are craftsmen, specialists in metal- and woodwork, and thus artists too. In the second, longer and more detailed section (vv. 14-20) they are the "bread-eater" (v. 15) and the "meat-eater" (v. 16)—that is, they initially represent "the common people."

In this part (vv. 14-20), where "the people" are shown as actors, we again find aramaisms,[287] and a seemingly inconsistent use of tenses.[288] This is one more indication of DtIsa's skill in the use of language, not an indication that the passage is not genuine (i.e., is the work of another hand). Here too it would be worthwhile comparing the language of comedy—the comedies of Aristophanes, for example.

---

280   Thus, e.g., Merendino (*Der Erste und der Letzte: Eine Untersuchung von Jes 40–48* [1981] 386) distinguishes between an "author (who is thinking) more about the makers of the idols and less about the process of manufacture of the idols itself" (to which author he attributes 44:9-13, 18b, 20a, 20bβ) and an "interpolator" in 44:14-18a, 19; cf. Fohrer, 75–77 on this passage.

281   See Elliger, 420–21.

282   See H. Gressmann, "Die literarische Analyse Deuterojesajas," *ZAW* 34 (1914) 278.

283   P. R. Ackroyd, *Israel under Babylon and Persia* (1970) 118–19: "We must assume that this sermon is adressed to members of the Jewish community who are tempted by the rich religious life of their environment."

284   See E. Auerbach, *Mimesis: The Representation of Reality in Western Literature* (1953), esp. 1–19: "Odysseus' Scar" [*Mimesis: Dargestellte Wirklichkeit in der Abendländischen Literatur* (3d ed. 1964), esp. 5–27: "Die Narbe des Odysseus"].

285   Torrey, *The Second Isaiah* (1928) 329: "The verses under consideration provide a fine example of the poet's dramatic power. In them is presented to our gaze in the most vivid way a scene of craftsmen at their work." Muilenburg, 510: "He has observed the idol makers at their work, and has stood there, watching the process step by step"; and 515 on v. 20: "and his people have witnessed the same scene."

286   Cf. 53:11: "Because of the anguish of his soul he shall see <light, אוֹר, *ʾôr*)> <and> be satisfied." Compared with 53:11, 44:16 is a parody of the beatific vision (Lat. *fruitio dei*).

287   Cf. above on 42:24. "Kindle" (השׂיק, v. 15) and "throw himself down" (סגד, vv. 15, 17, 19) are cited. See S. M. Wagner, *Die lexikalischen und grammatikalischen Aramaismen im alttestamentlichen Hebräisch* (1966), esp. nos. 202 (p. 87) and 195 (p. 85); see here Elliger, 416, 423; also his comment: "The language is consciously that of everyday speech" (427).

288   Elliger, 416: "Another reason (why this is not genuine) is the confusion of the tenses, with the

■ **9-11** Verse 9 introduces the dramatis personae who play a part in what follows: "sculptors of statues or figures" (יֹצְרֵי־פֶסֶל).[289] That can refer particularly to the artists described in vv. 12-13, who manufacture images for the cult; but in a wider sense the idols of the ordinary people are included (vv. 14-20).[290] The choice of words at once brings out the contrast here between "form, shape, create" (יצר) and "emptiness and nothingness" (תֹהוּ *tohû*). The word תֹהוּ is used for wasteland, in contrast to the land that is cultivated. It is also "devastation."[291] The manufacturers of idols want to give something form, but the result is in fact "formless," "nothingness." They wish to be creative, and destroy even themselves.

At this point we are surely meant to hear the antithesis to creation when God is the creator. That is the conclusion that 44:21 then draws: "I have fashioned/formed you" (יְצַרְתִּךָ). The earth was not created as a wasteland (45:18). A connection with what is said about creation in Gen 1:1-2 suggests itself. But it is not necessarily a single tradition only that is taken up here, for v. 10 varies v. 9: "Who has fashioned a god (מִי־יָצַר אֵל)?" To this v. 11 contrasts the skilled craftsman as a human being (מֵאָדָם *mēʾādām*). Here we should rather compare Gen 2:7-8.

The text works with shifts in the meaning of the words. "Their darlings" (חֲמוּדֵיהֶם, v. 9), the objects of their desire, refers initially to the idols. Dan 11:27, to

take one example, suggests that the object of the "desire" (חמד) is really the Deity–in Dan 11:27 Tammuz-Adonis, as "the darling of women." But since for DtIsa there are no other gods, all that is actually left are idols. The text is addressing the manufacturers of images, and *their* concern is not devoid of an additional commercial interest: that is where their "desire" lies.

DtIsa varies individual termini. The gods cannot "help" (יעל): this has been the theme of polemic for a long time; we find it in Jeremiah, for example. "Do not help–do not see–do not know": according to DtIsa this applies both to the gods and to their images. It is the very opposite of what is acknowledged of Yahweh.[292] According to 48:17, Yahweh is the one "who teaches (Israel) what helps (it)." The verb is used again here in v. 10. Of course here too the word can be rendered "help," but the meaning is more probably "to have the benefit of, to profit from."[293]

"To be ashamed" (בּוֹשׁ) is actually used three times in these verses. According to M. A. Klopfenstein, "the word group *bôš* in all its forms . . . has to do with the ambivalence between the subjective 'to be ashamed of oneself' and the objective 'to be put to shame.'"[294] "In content *bôš* etc. often describes the failure of particular expectations, either social or practical."[295] As examples of the latter, Klopfenstein points to the disappointment of merchants (Job 6:20)[296] and farmers (Joel 1:10-12, 17).[297] If

---

unregulated and promiscuous use of perfect, imperfect and imperfect consecutive, which can otherwise be evidenced especially in later Hebrew poetry."

289 See on פֶסֶל, פֶּסֶל, *HALOT* 3:949 [*HALAT* 3:894]; C. Dohmen, *ThWAT* 6:688–97: "It means a three-dimensional representation" (692); on DtIsa see 696–97.

290 Also in 44:11. Spykerboer (*The Structure and Composition of Deutero-Isaiah* [1976] 120) renders it by "the whole sorry lot of them." For DtIsa's concern for comprehensive formulation, cf. כלם, "all," in 40:26; 41:29; 42:22; 43:14; 45:16; 49:18 (bis); 50:9.

291 Cf. in DtIsa 40:17, 23; 41:29; 45:18, 19; 49:4; see *HALAT* 4:1556–57; C. Westermann, *Genesis 1–11* (1984) 103–4 on Gen. 1:2 [*Genesis 1* (1974) 142]; Spykerboer (*The Structure and Composition of Deutero-Isaiah* [1976] 34–35) has drawn particular attention to the connection between the term תֹהוּ, as well as the parallel terms "nothingness, vain" (אֶפֶס אַיִן), and the statements about Yahweh's incomparability and uniqueness.

292 See H. D. Preuss, *Verspottung fremder Religionen im AT* (1971) 215: "Thus mockery of the idols is the reverse side of the hymn to Yahweh."

293 D. W. Thomas ("Isaiah XLIV, 9-20: A Translation and Commentary," in *FS A. Dupont-Sommer* [1971] 320) translates (יעל) "to be of no profit whatever." See also Bonnard, 159 n. 3, "to profit"; J. Steinmann (*Le livre de la consolation d'Israël et les prophètes du retour de l'éxil* [1960] 129) explains: "DtIsa's thesis is that the Babylonian sculptors are acting out of self-interest."

294 M. A. Klopfenstein, *Scham und Schande nach dem AT* (1972) 49. Cf. F. Stolz, "בּוֹשׁ *bôš* to be ashamed," *TLOT* 1:204–7 [*THAT* 1:269–72]; H. Seebass, "בּוֹשׁ *bôš*" *TDOT* 2:50–60 [*ThWAT* 1:568–80].

295 Klopfenstein, *Scham und Schande nach dem AT*, 89.

296 Ibid., 44.

297 Ibid., 46–47. Klopfenstein assumes that here too there is "a play on the objective and the personal subject: where the products 'are shamed,' the farmer is 'shamed' also."

one wishes to differentiate between the emphases in our present text, then v. 11a refers to the commercial "disappointment" of the producers of idols, whereas v. 11b points to the subjective "being ashamed," parallel to "tremble, be afraid" (פחד).[298] Here it is a matter of life and death for every individual, because each of them has entered into dealings with "nothingness."[299]

An old difficulty is how to render חֲבֵרָיו.[300] Does the suffix refer to the idols, so that the word has to be translated: "his [the idol's] comrades," in the sense of "*worshipers*," or does it refer to the *producers* of an idol, its comrades in this sense? As the commentaries show, one can adduce good reasons for both views. I myself believe that there is no real alternative here, and that the ambiguity is intentional.

"Comrades" (חֲבֵרִים) are members of a "cooperative" (חֶבֶר). The verb חבר II means "to bind oneself or unite." In the world to which the OT belongs, the term could be used for professional associations, especially associations formed for economic purposes. These purposes could be the management and cultivation of the land, or commercial undertakings;[301] but there were also associations of artisans.

The term is not very frequently used in the OT itself, but where it does occur the background is evidently the same in each case.[302] Fishermen and tradesmen form guilds (see Job 40:30 [41:6]; cf. Luke 5:10). Fellow herdsmen are called חֲבֵרִים (Cant 1:7;

8:13). Jehoshaphat, king of Judah, and Ahaziah, king of Israel, formed a commercial association to build ships for the trade with Tarshish—an undertaking that came to grief (2 Chr 20:35-37). According to Isa 1:23 even thieves can be "comrades"; and Hos 6:9 criticizes the college (חֶבֶר) of priests for having become a band of robbers.[303]

Mutual obligation was part of this. Qoh 4:9-10 formulates the matter in classic terms: "Two are better than one, because they have a good reward for their toil; for if one 'falls,' his comrade (חֲבֵרוֹ) will help him up." A community of this kind enjoyed the special protection of the gods. This was probably connected with the sworn commitment assumed when a person entered into an association of this kind.

A good example is the association of Syrian merchants on the island of Delos. They jointly owned a trading post, and jointly pursued the cult of "Poseidon."[304] Occupation and religion were therefore closely linked. "Guild" or "corporation" are terms we still use that have come down to us from the world of medieval commerce. Others, such as "cooperative" or "trade union," are more recent. The terms must of course be differentiated, but the link between a professional organization and a particular ideology can be observed again and again.

With these presuppositions, we must assume that, in the exilic situation especially, conflicts inevitably arose for the Jewish community through the side-by-side existence in professional life of different religions and

---

298 For פחד, "to shake with fear," cf. Deut 28:66; Isa 12:.2; 19:17; 33:14; Jer 33:9; 36:16, 24; Pss 27:1; 78:53; 119:161; Prov 3:24; Job 23:15. The verb stands for "the terror of the Godhead" in Sir 7:29. For the substantive see 1 Sam 11:7; Isa 2:10, 19, 21; Ps 36:2 (1); 2 Chr 14:13 (14); 17:10; 19:7; 20:29. It is a paniclike fear. See also H. P. Stähli, "פחד *phd* to shake," *TLOT* 2:979–81 [*THAT* 2:411–13]; H.-P. Müller, "פָּחַד *pāḥad*," *ThWAT* 6:552–62.

299 This is clear from the psalms of lament. See F. Stolz, *TLOT* "בוש *bôš*," 1:206 [*THAT* 1:271–72]: "The supplicant, then, lays claim to God's help and protection from destruction; because the enemy cannot expect this aid, he/she is abandoned to annihilation" (with reference to Pss 22:6; 25:2-3, 20; 31:2 [1], 18 [17]; 69:7 [6]; 71:1). It is hence consistent when Isa 44:20 says that "those who worship idols will not save their lives." See also 45:17, 24; 49:23; 54:4. Further H. Seebass, "בוש *bôš*," *TDOT* 2:50–60 [*ThWAT* 1:568–80].

300 Thus the Syriac translation renders it "their craftsmen"; Targum: "their worshipers" (see Elliger, 409).

301 See the account of Wen-Amon (I, 7–II, 1); *ANET* 25–29; K. Galling et al., *Textbuch zur Geschichte Israels* (1950) 36–43. Also W. Helck, "Wenamun," *LÄ* 6 (1986) 1215–17.

302 See H. Cazelles, "חֶבֶר *chābar*," *TDOT* 4:193–97 [*ThWAT* 2:721–26]. Referring to Isa 44:11, Cazelles writes: "The prophet plays on the ambiguity of *ḥbr* and *ḥrš* ('workman'/'magician'; cf. Isa. 3:3)" (195 [723]). M. Noth (*Die Ursprünge des alten Israel im Lichte neuer Quellen* [1961] 35) renders חבר as "association" ("Verband"). See also *HALOT* 1:288 [*HALAT* 1:276] s.v. חֶבֶר I: "association . . . corporation; . . . Akk. *bīt ḫubūri* storehouse, community house; Eg. *ḫubūr* commercial association."

303 Cf. also 47:9.

304 See H. Koester, *Introduction to the New Testament* (1982) 1:65–67, esp. 66 [*Einführung in das NT* (1980) 65-67, esp. 66].

ethnic communities. Where the "scribal" level is concerned—that is, the class of prominent officials—the Daniel legends in Daniel 1–6 offer a good picture. The artisans mentioned in vv. 12 and 13 of the present DtIsa text are also specialized technicians of some standing.[305] To be a blacksmith in particular required special knowledge and skills. The text attacks the manufacture of idols in general. But I myself wonder whether this text is directed against heathen artisans only, or whether there were not Jewish technician artists too. The conflict arises especially where art for religious purposes is concerned, from statues of the gods down to devotional bric-a-brac. Was it possible to participate in the manufacture of these things even if one no longer believed in the gods?[306] "Comrades" of the idols and comrades belonging to the same guild are on this level identical. The full sting of the polemic becomes clear if it is a dispute with questionable belief as well as with a questionable business.[307]

The conclusion (הֵן) that (guild) comrades are also put to shame if they manufacture a god is added parallel to a statement about the craftsmen. "Artisans are only human beings": this is the sense of Elliger's translation.

This is certainly correct, and also meets the sense in the present context, with its antithesis between God and human beings. But Duhm (who had an acute sense for such nuances, even if one often cannot accept his conclusions) already stumbled over the flat triteness of the statement, and "the puzzling מִן (of)." We should expect a plural, "human beings."[308] I should like to suggest tentatively that here too there may be a reference to the Genesis traditions. If the phrase is rendered: "metalworkers—they are descendants of Adam," the text requires no emendation. The first time that "ore smelters and blacksmiths" are mentioned in the OT is in Gen 4:22.[309] The Genesis text as we have it is corrupt; so the mention of Tubal-cain as the father of the smiths is missing. But the catchword כָּל־חֹרֵשׁ[310] ("everyone who works with ore and iron") can clearly be detected. In DtIsa the genealogy[311] would then be traced back not to Cain but straight to Adam. If the metalworkers are descended from Adam, they are not divine: that would then be the argument.

■ **12-13** After the general introduction in vv. 9-11, a pair of artisans is introduced in vv. 12 and 13:[312] the "specialist"[313] for ironwork[314] (חָרַשׁ בַּרְזֶל) and the "specialist" for

---

305 Cf. 2 Kgs 24:14.

306 In this connection the attention drawn by commentators to 1 Cor 10:20 (κοινωνοὶ τῶν δαιμονίων) is interesting. The comparison is not merely a matter of terminology, however, but of Paul's whole argument in vv. 14-22, which deals with a similar problem. Verse 19 asks explicitly about the significance of the idol (ὅτι εἴδωλόν τί ἐστιν); see the commentaries on this passage.

307 In the NT, Acts 19:23-40 offers a good illustration of this tradition:
"²³ There arose about that time no little agitation concerning the 'Way.' ²⁴ For a silversmith by the name of Demetrius, who manufactured silver Artemis temples, brought no little business to the craftsmen. ²⁵ He gathered them together, and the workers of like trade, and said: 'Men, you know that our prosperity comes from this business, ²⁶ and you see and hear that not only at Ephesus but in almost the whole (province of) Asia this Paul has persuasively turned away many people by saying that there are no gods who are made with hands. ²⁷ But not only does this our branch of business threaten to fall into disrepute, but also the temple of the great goddess Artemis may be accounted for nothing, and she may in the future be deprived of her majesty,

which all Asia and the entire world revere.'
²⁸ When they heard this they became angry and cried: 'Great is Artemis of the Ephesians!'
²⁹ And the town was thrown into confusion" (trans. in E. Haenchen, *The Acts of the Apostles* (1965) 570 [*Die Apostelgeschichte* (12th ed. 1959) 547]).

308 Cf. the list of proposed emendations in D. W. Thomas, "Isaiah XLIV, 9-20: A Translation and Commentary," in *FS A. Dupont-Sommer* (1971) 323.

309 See Westermann, *Genesis 1–11* (1984) 332–34, with lit. [*Genesis 1* (1974) 450–53].

310 Unlike Westermann, ibid., I suspect that an original לטשׁ, "hammer, sharpen," has been explained through the more common חרשׁ, "to work metal"; see also *HALOT* s.v.

311 For מִן in the sense of descent and affiliation, cf. the use in the lists in Chronicles (1 Chronicles 9; 2 Chronicles 17 and 29).

312 We may compare the beginning of Aeschylus's drama *Prometheus Bound*. Two workmen called "Power and Strength" (Κράτος Βία τε) bring on the bound Prometheus and hammer him to the mountain on the seashore of Scythia, under the supervision of the god Hephaistos.

313 For "artisan" (חָרָשׁ) see *HALOT* 1:357, 358 [*HALAT* 1:343, 344]; and V. Hamp, "חָרַשׁ *ḥāraš* I," *TDOT*

woodwork (חָרַשׁ עֵצִים). The structure is the same in both cases. The name of the occupation is followed by three sentences describing what is done, to which a brief commentary is then added. The process is described in expert terms, from the rough work to the finer processing.[315] It is only difficult for us to understand because we do not know some of the technical terms.

The descriptions of these occupational activities belong to the tradition of wisdom texts.[316] They are also a part of encyclopedic knowledge.[317] Even today, quiz shows in which occupations have to be guessed ("What's My Line?") live from the pleasure viewers get from them. The description of the occupation does not have to be seen as derogatory, even though we may suppose that there is some exaggeration in what is said. We must remember that in the world that surrounded Israel, descriptions of idols and the making of them had an entirely positive character. Some of these descriptions are couched in hymnic form. The satire in the text is derived from the interpretation in each case.

■ **12** What does the metalworker do? The first word, מַעֲצָד, presents difficulties. As it is pointed in MT, it means a "cutting tool," perhaps an axe or a sickle.[318] But then the verb required by the sense is missing, and something would have to be added—for example, "make" or "manufacture" (עשׂה). But the passage is concerned with the making of an idol, not a tool. We should expect the preparation of the raw material, parallel to the work performed by the woodworker (v. 13).[319] The pointing as a Piel participle מְעַצֵּד, which was already proposed by

---

5:220–23 [*ThWAT* 3:234–38]. H.-P. Müller ("Magisch-mantische Weisheit und die Gestalt Daniels," *UF* 1 [1969] 79–94) derives the noun from the root חרשׁ III, "to practice magic." He thinks that this "points to a way of thinking that considers that manual and technical activity is useless without accompanying magic" (80).

314 See *HALOT* 1:155–56 [*HALAT* 1:148–49] s.v. with lit.

315 Elliger on this passage.

316 Artisan scenes are a *topos* in Egyptian tomb representations. They give a good impression of various kinds of craft activity. Archeological finds of tools and other things confirm the precision of the presentation. For the present DtIsa text the pictures of workers in wood and metal in the tomb of the vizier Rekh-mi-Re, for example, are of interest; see N. de G. Davies, *The Tomb of Rekh-mi-Re at Thebes* (1943, reprint 1973) pls. LII, LIII, LV, text: 50–54; see also *ANEP* nos. 122–24 (pp. 37, 264) and no. 133 (pp. 40, 265). Literary descriptions of professional activity can be found in a number of different contexts. An Egyptian example is "The Instruction of Kheti." It is thought to date from the Middle Kingdom, but may possibly be older. It is extant in a number of copies of varying date, including a series of ostraca. It is a wisdom text that also includes satiric elements. Various trades are described, always from the standpoint of a "scribe." Life in the "bureaucracy" is the way of life that is superior to all others—or so the young scribes learn in the course of copying the text at school. The difference of status is not the problem in the biblical text. Both technician and simple farmer are in similar danger of idolizing their work (cf. also Sir 38:24-34, esp. v. 28). At the beginning of "The Instruction of Kheti" metal- and woodworkers are presented: "I have never seen a sculptor on an errand nor a goldsmith when he was sent out. (But) I have seen the metalworker at his work at the mouth of his furnace. His fingers were somewhat like crocodiles; he stank more than fish roes. . . . Every craftsman that wields the adze, he is wearier than a hoeman. His field is the wood, and his *job* is the metal. At night, though he is released, he does more . . . than his arms can (really) do. At night *he has to strike a light*" (*ANET* 432–34), See also (German) trans. in W. Helck, *Die Lehre des Dwȝ-Ḫtjj*, part 1, *Kleine Ägyptische Texte* (1970); also H. Brunner, *LÄ* 3:977–78 with lit.; H. Brunner, *Die Lehre des Cheti, Sohn des Duauf* (1944) 22, translation of 4,7–5,3; 28–30.

317 In the OT cf., e.g., Job 28:1-12, the description of the mine; Psalm 104 describes the activity of the worker on the land.

318 *HALOT* 2:615 [*HALAT* 2:581–82] renders it: "bent pruning knife, agricultural implement, blacksmith's tool," probably also in view of Jer 10:3. Duhm says here. "And why should the sharpening of the tool also be mentioned, especially since in what follows it is only the hammers of the metalworkers that play a part? Nor does מעצד, the axe, fit this craftsman, since the axe is used for felling trees (Jer 10:3)."

319 Elliger correctly supposes here that "the expert in iron cuts out the prototype."

R. Lowth in 1839, therefore deserves reconsideration.[320] The blacksmith is a man "who cuts off iron" from the pig iron, in order to shape it. But perhaps the direct working of a piece of iron ore as it comes from the smelting is meant. It has to be hammered to make it smooth. The connection between hammering and cutting can be explained by the technical problem of how to make a cutting edge out of iron. This can be done by grinding, but also by hammering, as in the case of a sickle, reaping hook or scythe.[321]

If we assume that the word means "to hammer in order to make something smooth or sharp,"[322] this would be the first thing a metalworker did in working the wrought iron. For this the iron would have to be heated in the fire.

The further precision work consists of beating into shape with the help of various hammers.[323] If this is presented in a practical demonstration, it is certainly a noisy affair.

The point of the commentary in v. 12bγ-c is the ironical contrast between "his strong arm" (בִּזְרוֹעַ כֹּחוֹ) and "no strength" (וְאֵין כֹּחַ). Even the mighty smith is dependent on food and drink. That makes him a human being.

The attentive listener of course knows that otherwise in DtIsa "arm" always means "Yahweh's arm."[324]

■ 13 What does the woodworker do? The first thing is to measure and make a drawing.[325] Work with various tools follows. What is precisely meant we have not hitherto been able to determine. If Egyptian descriptions of woodworking are taken as illustration, then two kinds of tool especially were used, a small pickaxe and various sizes of a carving tool or chisel. This fits in with the archeological finds. The final process has again to do with "form" (תֹּאַר). According to Isa 52:14 and 53:2, this includes the element of "harmonious appearance, beauty."[326] The tool used is generally called a "compass," although the meaning is actually obscure.

מְחוּגָה is connected with the root חוג, "to revolve round, to draw a circle." This can refer to the fact that the tool is round, that it can be used to make circular movements, or that with its help something round can be made. The Egyptian artisan scene may once more offer a useful illustration. There in the "wood department" workers are seen using a piece of sandstone to finish the wood. Sandstone is a practical natural product used for polishing.[327] So the tool has the same function as our

---

320 See D. W. Thomas, "Isaiah XLIV, 9-20: A Translation and Commentary," in *FS A. Dupont-Sommer* (1971) 324.

321 Cf. the root לטש, which also covers "hammer" and "sharpen." In Gen 4:22 it is also parallel to חרש: "Tubal-cain, a hammerer (לֹטֵשׁ), 'father' of all experts (כָּל־חֹרֵשׁ) for bronze and iron." See Westermann, *Genesis 1–11* (1984) 332 [*Genesis 1* (1974) 451] on this passage: "either in the general sense of 'hammer' or the specific sense of 'sharpen,'" with reference to J. Gabriel, "Die Kainitengenealogie," *Bib* 40 (1959) 409–27, esp. 411; cf. 1 Sam 13:20; Ps 7:13 (12); 52:4 (2); Sir 31/34:26. On the problems about the working of iron in the ancient world, see R. J. Forbes, *Studies in Ancient Technology* 8 (2d ed. 1971) 54–104: "The Evolution of the Smith, His Social and Sacred Status," 87 on the present text; vol. 9 (2d ed. 1972) 187–288.

322 The LXX translation "it sharpens" (ὤξυνε τέκτων σίδηρον) does not therefore require us to assume any other Hebrew text. The process is only obscure here when the LXX talks about the "two-edged carpenter's axe" (σκεπάρνῳ εἰργάσατο αὐτὸ) and about "boring with the drill." The Syriac links the two actions: "He smooths it with the carpenter's axe."

323 The description for pl. LV in N. de G. Davies, *The Tomb of Rekh-mi-Re at Thebes* (1943) 52, illustrates

the point: "Smiths beating out the metal: The first operation is to beat out the rings into thin plates. This is done by a maul of hard stone on an anvil of the same material (both blue) mounted on a wooden block. A disk of flat metal is seen as the result." And on "soldering": "The body of the vessels could be beaten into shape, but other parts called for soldering, hence the blowpipe, the furnace and the tongs." In this case the material is doubtless precious metal.

324 Isa 40:10, 11; 48:14; 51:5, 9; 52:10; 53:1; see Elliger here.

325 This is the only instance of שֶׂרֶד in the OT. *HALOT* 3:1354 [*HALAT* 4:1262] concludes that it less likely means ochre (Fe_2O_3); rather, following others, e.g., D. W. Thomas, who connect it with Arabic *sarada*, "engrave," it is therefore usually translated "stylus."

326 D. W. Thomas, "Isaiah XLIV. 9-20: A Translation and Commentary," in *FS A. Dupont-Sommer* (1971) 327: "The idol has not only the form of a man, but it possesses also the splendour of a man!"

327 Cf. the description in N. de G. Davies, *The Tomb of Rekh-mi-Re at Thebes* (1943) 51: "In the latter scene (plate LII) the chair legs, provided with tenons which hold them to the frame, are receiving their final form under a little slip of sandstone. The three men who are shaping a papyrus column of wood (Plate LIII, row 2) are smoothing it with semi-

files[328] and emery paper. Today one would use a polisher with sandpaper, on a drill. It is a matter of the final precision work. So when E. Jenni renders תאר as "drawing the contours" this is probably quite appropriate. In the *Piel* form it would mean smoothing the curves "as a final process."[329]

Up to this point the text is once more a simple description of the work. It is only the commentary in v. 13b that gives the interpretation and brings out the real point. After so much trouble one would expect that the result for the artisan would be: "He has made it into a god" (thus lit. v. 17; cf. v. 10). Instead what emerges is (to follow Elliger's translation): "And he makes it like the image of a man, like a splendid example of a human being, so that it remains in the house." The contrast here too is between God and human being. The image of the man is still no more than human work. The human being lives in a house, not in heaven. I would rather suppose that "to dwell in a house" (לְשֶׁבֶת בָּיִת) refers to "a human being" (אָדָם ʾādām). That is his nature, like eating and drinking (v. 12).[330] But there may be a deliberate ambiguity here: the figure is set up in the "house" (בָּיִת), which can be both a private house and the temple. Here too the practical contrast between God–idol–human being is the ironical point of the text. This is deliberate comedy, intended to raise a laugh. But I believe that the text had a further dimension for people familiar with tradition.

The term "image" (תַּבְנִית) is not found in many texts, but the texts in which it does occur are significant. According to Exod 25:9 and 40, Moses receives from Yahweh the "prototype" (תַּבְנִית) of the tabernacle and its furnishings, the design according to which it is to be built. This might be viewed as the heavenly blueprint that has to be realized in the earthly sphere. In the Platonic sense it might be seen as the Idea of the tabernacle. Its character as model or blueprint also comes out in the directives David gives to Solomon in 1 Chr 28:11-12 and 18-19 for the building of the temple and its furnishing.[331] In Deut 4:16-18 the term is used in connection with "the evidence of tradition" for rejecting the worship of Yahweh in images of any created things.[332] According to Ezek 8:10, the prohibition of images in the temple in Jerusalem had been infringed.[333] The word and the thing meant may already occur in Hosea.[334]

Who is "the prototype of a man"? Anyone who knows the biblical creation traditions would reply: Adam. A prayer taken from the Qumran War Scroll (1QM 10.8ff., 14)[335] reads: "O God of Israel, who is like you in heaven or on earth? Who accomplishes deeds and mighty works like yours? . . . (You are the Creator [הבורא] of) the earth . . . of the beasts and birds and of 'the primordial image

---

circular pieces of sandstone (white). The disk between the men is probably the base."

328   The Vulgate version is therefore interesting: "The woodworker has worked with the file" ("*faber lignarius lima operatus est*"). Then the Vulgate has again: "He rounds it on the lathe" ("*et in circino tornavit*"); see Elliger, 441.

329   E. Jenni, *Das hebräische Piʿel* (1968) 214; *HALAT* 4:1545 under this heading; cf. also *HALAT* 4:1545–46 s.v. תאר.

330   Cf. Jer 36:22; Job 15:28; see also Gen 4:20 and 25:27 on the tent.

331   Cf. also 2 Kgs 6:10 for an altar.

332   See G. von Rad, *Deuteronomy* (1966) 47 and 49–50 [*Deuteronomium* (1964) 33 and 36]; v. 16: "lest you act corruptly by making a graven image for yourselves, in the form of any figure, the likeness of male or female, the likeness of any animal"

(פֶּסֶל תְּמוּנַת כָּל־סָמֶל תַּבְנִית זָכָר אוֹ נְקֵבָה . . .). Cf. also Ps 106:20.

333   In this text "all kinds of creeping things and loathsome animals" (תַּבְנִית) can be an interpretive addition based on Deut 4:16-17. See W. Zimmerli, *Ezekiel 1* (1979) [*Ezechiel* (1969)] on this passage.

334   Hos 13:2: "They make for themselves a molten image from their silver (according to the type) (כְּתַבְנִית with LXX) of the idols. All of it is the work of craftsmen." See H. W. Wolff, *Hosea* (1974) on this passage [*Hosea* (3d ed. 1976)]. On the text of Hosea 13 see also H. Utzschneider, *Hosea: Prophet vor dem Ende* (1980) 102–4, 119–25.

335   D. W. Thomas ("Isaiah XLIV, 9-20: A Translation and Commentary," in *FS A. Dupont-Sommer* [1971] 326) draws attention to this passage (with reference to A. Dupont-Sommer, *The Essene Writings from*

of the human being' (תבנית אדם)."[336] Or should this final phrase be translated: "the primordial image of Adam"?[337] Of course the Qumran text is much later than DtIsa, and we know relatively little about speculations over creation, especially the creation of human beings and their beginnings.[338] But if we look back to Isa 44:13 from a text such as 1QM, the parallelism between "prototype of a man" and "splendor of a human being" (תִּפְאֶרֶת אָדָם) is striking. Could the phrase here also be rendered: "the splendor of Adam"?[339] The theological argument underlying the text would then be: even Adam in all his ideal beauty was created by God.[340] That means that he is not a god—and how much more is this true of figures representing a human being "like" (כְּ) Adam. The text would therefore indicate on an elevated theoretical level which problems about archetype and image in the cult and in art could be discussed.[341]

■ **14-20** First of all I want to make some observations about the difficulties in the text. Its relation to its immediate context is not clear. Grammatically, to begin with an infinitive ("in order to fell . . . ," v. 14a) is unusual.[342] About the content Elliger writes: "The strange thing . . . is that the master procures the material only after he has already finished the image."[343] Singular and plural alternate apparently without rhyme or reason. To quote Elliger once more: "The attempt has occasionally been made to salvage the unity of the whole by excising v. 18.

. . . It is true that this gets rid of the troublesome plural in an account that is in the singular from v. 12 onward, but the content remains confused."[344] In the progress of the action the felling of the trees is mentioned before the plants.[345] Some things are said twice or even three times,[346] for example the "bowing down in reverence" (vv. 15, 17), "throwing oneself down" (vv. 15, 17, 19). Most attempts to find a solution have had recourse to literary interventions in the text. Some sections are viewed as "glosses"[347] or "additions."[348] I should like to take up some of the observations that have been made, while myself attempting a different explanation.

There is a "double movement" here, as Elliger has rightly noticed.[349] In each case an action is described, and a comment then given. The fundamental principle behind the buildup of the text is thus no different from that in vv. 12-13. But are the "actors" the same? Delitzsch observed about v. 14: "The subject is *not* the carpenter of the preceding verse, v. 13; it is just someone or other."[350] The two "movements" are distinguished through the fact that in the one case baking bread is mentioned (v. 15) and in the other roasting meat (v. 16).

Bread and meat as basic nourishment traditionally characterize different ways of life and occupational groups. According to Gen 4:2, Abel is a herdsman (רֹעֵה צֹאן) and Cain a farmer (עֹבֵד אֲדָמָה). Cain sacrifices "from the fruits of the earth" (v. 3), Abel "from the firstfruits

Qumran [1962] 185). See G. Vermes, *The Complete Dead Sea Scrolls in English* (1997).

336 Translation following E. Lohse, *Die Texte aus Qumran* (1964) 202ff.

337 Dupont-Sommer translates: "The shape of Adam."

338 See also R. Kittel, "εἰκων," *TDNT* 2:381–97 [*ThWNT* 2:378–96]; W. Staerk, *Soter: Die biblische Erlösererwartung*, part 1 (1933); E. Brandenburger, *Adam und Christus* (1962).

339 It would thus be the same problem as in 44:11; see above on that passage. See also McKenzie, 68: "In vs. 13 the prophet seems deliberately to reverse the process of Gen I, 26-27; God made man in his image and likeness, and now deluded man makes God in his image."

340 According to 46:13 Israel is lent Yahweh's splendor (תִּפְאַרְתִּי).

341 For the further development in the Hellenistic period see Wisdom 13–15, esp. 13:13, "he forms it in the likeness of a human being (εἰκόνι ἀνϑρώπου)."

342 See Duhm here.

343 Elliger on this passage.

344 Elliger, 417.

345 D. W. Thomas, "Isaiah XLIV, 9-20: A Translation and Commentary," in *FS A. Dupont-Sommer* (1971) 326: "The mention of cutting down before planting is strangely premature." Delitzsch, 2:210 [465]: "The description is genealogical, and therefore moves retrogressively, from the felling to the planting."

346 Torrey, *Second Isaiah* (1978), on this passage.

347 For vv. 15b-16a Schoors refers to Condamin and Loisy, but rejects the proposal where v. 18 is concerned.

348 Elliger, 420, referring to vv. 19-20. He sees v. 14 as the beginning of a quotation (419).

349 Elliger, 418.

350 Delitzsch on this passage.

351 The hunter would be possible too. But I think that "herdsman" is more probable (see below on v. 20). It is probably impossible to draw a firm line between hunter and herdsman.

of his flocks" (v. 4). The pair Jacob and Esau in Genesis 25 is comparable. Here Esau is "a skillful hunter, a man of the field" (v. 27). He brings his father game. Jacob, in contrast, is "an orderly man who stayed by the tents." He gives Esau not only the famous "mess of pottage" (lentil stew), but bread too (v. 34). So the catchwords "bread" (Isa 44:15) and "meat" (Isa 44:16) in this DtIsa text could also be a way of describing different people. Probably the first is a farmer, the other a herdsman.[351]

These are the two basic occupations that make up "the people." Whereas the technicians and artists in vv. 12 and 13 must be assigned to the privileged classes, farmer and herdsman represent the simple folk. The bread-eater and the meat-eater also come forward as a pair. This would explain the change from singular to plural: it depends on whether they are addressed separately or together. The detailed exegesis will have to show whether what is said can be assigned to the two different roles.

■ **14a** The beginning with an infinitive construction is unusual and therefore attracts attention. "In order to fell" would have to be completed either by: "one man is there," or by taking up the stage direction in v. 11: "one

man has come forward."[352] The man who appears here is a rough type. He walks in the woods and takes on the big trees.[353] He shows that he is strong.[354] It is worth considering how far in the figure of this rough diamond the text is also attacking the Hercules cult.[355] This had taken on a growing importance in the fifth century B.C.E. As a hero, Hercules was a folk figure, but the Hercules myth plays an important part in literature too.[356] Hercules is famous for his mighty deeds and his prodigious appetite. He is the prototype of the strong man. It is not enough for him to fell one cedar—it has to be several. There is a touch of the grotesque here. This is the way the "meat-eating" herdsman is introduced.

■ **14b** Here the bread-eating farmer is presented. He has planted his tree.[357] That is the civilization of the cultivated lands. Then he has to wait patiently for the rain to make it grow. A reminiscence of the Garden of Eden in Genesis 2–3 (see esp. Gen 2:8)[358] suggests itself. Again, it does not seem to me fortuitous that for the third time in this text "human being–Adam" is mentioned. He is the bread-eater, not the meat-eater! In v. 14a and b the two prototypes are introduced with three statements in each

---

352 Cf. Delitzsch's translation: "He sets out to fell cedars, and takes . . ." (2:209 [trans. altered]).

353 The precise identification of the trees named still presents difficulties. אֶרֶז is generally translated "cedar" (*Cedrus libani Barrel*), see I. Löw, *Die Flora der Juden* (1924–34) 3:17–26; according to L. Köhler, "Hebräische Vokabeln II," *ZAW* 55 (1937) 163ff., it is *Abies cilicia* "or another tall conifer." At all events it is a tree coming from Lebanon (Judg 9:15; Isa 2:13; 14:8; Ps 29:5 [4]; 104:16). תִּרְזָה could be a hardwood tree, in view of Arab. *taraza*. אַלּוֹן is originally "any tree of considerable stature" according to J. J. Hess, "Beduinisches zum Alten und Neuen Testament," *ZAW* 35 (1915) 214–15; according to *HALOT* 1:54 [*HALAT* 1:52] here the word then means "oak." Because of the parallels, two different kinds of oak are generally assumed.

354 The formulation וַיֹּאמֶץ־לוֹ is strange. According to J. Schreiner ("אָמַץ *'āmats*," *TDOT* 1:323–27 [*ThWAT* 1:348–52]) "Strength, when it is designated by the root אמץ, is almost always viewed as a quality of a person" (324 [349]). He cites the present text, Isa 44:14, as an exception. But perhaps it is not an exception at all. There is an echo of the "strengthening" or "encouragement" formula "be strong and bold" (חזק ואמץ) as God's promise: Deut 31:6, 7, 23; Josh 1: 6, 7, 9, 18; 10:25; Ps 27:14; 1 Chr 22:13. In

the negative sense it means "to make the heart strong " in the sense of hardness of heart (see Deut 15:7; 2 Chr 36:13). Schreiner comes to the conclusion: "Seen as a whole, the theological content of אָמַץ is an avowed or concealed praise of God, who alone is strong" (327 [352]); cf. Job 9:4, 19; 17:9; 36:19 and in DtIsa 40:26; 41:10. See also A. S. van der Woude, "אמץ *'ms* to be strong," *TLOT* 1:157–59 [*THAT* 1:209–11].

355 A. Dihle, "Herakles," *RGG*³ 3:227–28; H. Sichtermann, *LAW* (1965) 1258–62.

356 See A. Lesky, *History of Greek Literature* (1966) [*Geschichte der griechischen Literatur* (3d ed. 1971)] s.v. "Herakles." As examples may be named Sophocles' *Trachiniae* (before 425 B.C.E.) and *Philoctetes* (409), Euripides' *Heracles* (between 421 and 415), and Aristophanes' *Frogs* (405).

357 I therefore consider the reading "cedar" (אֶרֶז) to be improbable. It would be a doublet of v. 14a. The cedar is above all a tree found in forests. *HALAT* defines אֹרֶן as "laurel," *Laurus nobilis* L., citing I. Löw, *Die Flora der Juden* (1924–34) 2:119–23. See also the earlier sources cited by Delitzsch and Elliger for this passage.

358 LXX has κύριος, probably reading אדן, "which the Lord planted." This makes the echo of Genesis 2

case. In the same way as in vv. 12 and 13, here we have initially only descriptions of what actually takes place.

■ **15** This verse gives the farmer's comment.[359] The antithesis is to be found in the contrast between the double use of the wood: in part (אַף) for utilitarian purposes, in part (אַף) for a god (אֵל). But the contrast between what the human being does and can do, and what God does, is again implicit. The close of v. 15 declares coolly: when the human being thinks that he has made a god, all he has done is to manufacture the image of a god (פֶּסֶל).

■ **16-17** These verses give the comment on the herdsman. It is parallel to the preceding one, with obvious differences. "His half" (חֶצְיוֹ) is the part he takes for his own personal use. Since it is taken from the forest, this part is certainly not small, nor is the fire. In order to bake the farmer's bread, the hot embers of the charcoal suffice (v. 19). The meat-eater eats his fill. This was surely presented both audibly and visibly.[360] The farmer is silent in what he does. The herdsman makes primitive noises—we need only count the gutturals and *r* sounds in what he says in v. 16. The idol is made out of what is left over (v. 17); there are no artistic ambitions here. The theology of the herdsman's prayer becomes disturbing if one

follows the proceeding: what the human being himself has made cannot save him.[361]

■ **18-20** Verse 18 begins with declarations in the plural. The two examples of wrong behavior are subjected to a summary evaluation that we might compare with "the moral of the tale" told by a balladmonger in the days of broadsheets. It is part of the burlesque character of this text—and part too of the author's dramatic achievement—that in vv. 19 and 20 the two typical figures are again allowed to speak for themselves. They do so alternately, in a kind of duet, and in so doing pass judgment on themselves.

But the comedy should not make us overlook the theoretical claims of the text. Even in the vocabulary the abstract terms are noticeable: knowledge (דַּעַת),[362] insight (תְּבוּנָה, v. 19),[363] abomination (תּוֹעֵבָה, v. 19)[364] and lie (שֶׁקֶר, v. 20),[365] terms in which the basic theological

---

even more marked. In the case of "the rain makes it big" also, one may ask how far the reader is supposed to have in mind that it is God who causes it to rain (cf. Gen 2:5 and Isa 55:10).

359   For an attempt at a reconstruction of the text of vv. 15-16 see A. Gelston, "Some Notes on Second Isaiah," *VT* 21 (1971) 517–22.

360   1QIsaᵃ has instead of רָאִיתִי, "I have seen," נֶגֶד, hence: "I am warm *in front of* the fire."

361   Is the assonance intentional: v. 14, אַלּוֹן ("oak"); v. 17, לְאֵל ("to God"), לוֹ ("to him"), וַיִּתְפַּלֵּל אֵלָיו ("he prays to him"), הַצִּילֵנִי ("save me"), אֵלִי ("my God")?

362   On דעת see W. Schottroff's account in "ידע *ydᶜ* to perceive, know," *TLOT* 2:512 [*THAT* 1:687]: "The knowledge that results from realization, experience, and perception and that one can learn and transmit." The term is put parallel to "understanding" (תְּבוּנָה) also in Prov 2:6, 10-11; 17:27; 24:3-4; cf. Exod 31:3; 35:31; 1 Kgs 7:14. In Prov 3:19-20 both terms are divine attributes.

363   H. H. Schmid ("בין *bîn* to understand," *TLOT* 1:230 [*THAT* 1:306]) distinguishes between "*bînâ* 'insight, understanding' and *tᵉbûnâ* 'insight, facility.'" For the present text, the way the term is used in Chronicles as "to be able to do something well professionally" is illuminating (1 Chr 15:22; 25:7; 27:32; 2 Chr 34:12; cf. Dan 1:4, 17; 8:23). For the link with wis-

dom traditions see H. H. Schmid, *Wesen und Geschichte der Weisheit* (1966).

364   See E. Gerstenberger, "תעב *tᶜb* pi. to abhor," *TLOT* 3:1428-31 [*THAT* 2:1051-55]. "That which is excluded by the set of one's own nature, that which seems dangerous or sinister" (1429 [1053]). Hence: "Certain things are incompatible with Yahweh's nature and are rejected by him" (1430 [1053]). Of special interest for the present text is the Ezekiel tradition found in Ezek 8:9-13 and 5:9, 11; 7:3, 4, 9; 16:6, 22. Lit.: P. Humbert, "L'étymologie du substantif *toᶜēbā*," in *Verbannung und Heimkehr. FS W. Rudolph* (1961) 157–60; idem, "Le substantif *toᶜēbā* et le verbe *tᶜb* dans l'Ancien Testament," *ZAW* 72 (1960) 217–37.

365   See M. A. Klopfenstein, "שקר *šqr* to deceive," *TLOT* 3:1399–1405 [*THAT* 2:1010–19]: "The primary 'Sitz im Leben' is thus to be sought in the law of contract, and the original meaning should be paraphrased as 'breach of a relationship of faithfulness and trust, contractually regulated or otherwise presupposed as a matter of course'" (1012). It means "the aggressive deceit, breach of faith, or perfidy that is designed to harm one's neighbors. . . . In most cases . . . a mode of action or behavior" (1400 [1011]). The Jeremiah tradition in Jer 3:23;

position can be detected. There are catchwords and repetitions taken over from what has gone before. Certain formulations are modified. "Save me, for you are my god" (v. 17) becomes "he will not save his life" (or "his soul," נַפְשׁוֹ, v. 20).[366] The herdsman/hunter has certainly "seen fire" (v. 16, רָאִיתִי אוּר *rāʾîtî ʾûr*), but fire turns into ashes, and these cannot "pasture" the herdsman either (v. 20, רֹעֶה אֵפֶר *roʿeh ʾēpher*). "See" (ראה) can also have the semantic range "to see with an emotional reaction."[367] This can be positive (e.g., "view with joy," 1 Sam 6:19; Qoh 2:1) or negative ("rejoice over the downfall of the enemy," Obad 12; Ps 22:18 [17]; 37:34; 54:9 [7]; 112:8). The experience of fire, however, is unambiguously negative in DtIsa. Isa 47:14 says about Babylon: "They will not be able to save their life from the power of the flame. No coal for warming oneself is this, no fire (אוּר *ʾûr*) to sit before" (cf. also 50:11). Both passages are talking about the fire of the underworld.

But in a much deeper sense the one who is strong in himself loses (v. 14). If one traces the arc forward to 53:11, the Servant of Yahweh is promised that "out of the anguish of his soul he shall see [light] ([אוֹר] יִרְאֶה *yirʾeh ʾûr*);[368] he will become satisfied through his knowledge." That is the true *fruitio dei*.

The present text as a whole puts forward a progressive argument in which one thing is listed after another, point for point. The negation "not" (לֹא) occurs seven times. From the behavior described in such negative terms it is not hard to discover what is positively required.

Two proverbial sayings are probably implicit, and interpreted, in the section. They betray themselves because they are not completely integrated into their context. The first is in v. 18bα. What does (literally) "their eyes are sealed from seeing" mean? The verb

derives from a subsidiary form, טחח, of the verb טוח as *Qal* perfect. In the present context it is then generally corrected to the plural טַחוּ. The verb is used for the plastering of a house with clay (Lev 14:42, 43-48), or when it is whitewashed (Ezek 13:10, 12, 14-15). In a transferred sense it is used for false prophecy, according to Ezek 22:28; and this would offer a possible comparison for the present text. In 1 Chr 29:4 it means the overlay with precious metal. All in all the lexical result remains unsatisfactory.[369] I think it is just possible that here the word refers to the farmer's weather lore, which tells him when rain is coming (cf. 44:14).[370] In Job 38:22-38 we find a description of meteorological phenomena and their meaning in the divine order. Verses 36-38 read (following Fohrer's translation):

36 Who has put wisdom in the ibis (בַּטֻּחוֹת חָכְמָה)
    or given understanding to the cock? (לַשֶּׂכְוִי בִינָה)
37 Who can in wisdom number the clouds,
    and the water pitchers of heaven—who tilts them,
38 when the dust of the earth becomes a single casting
    and the clods of earth stick to one another?

The text is disputed. According to Fohrer, "the weather prophets of the animal world are named, the ibis and the cock, . . . because God has given them the ability to announce the coming thunderstorm in good time."[371] In the present DtIsa text too, it is a question of "insight"; but instead of being wise like an ibis, "their eyes are sealed."[372] Thus this could be an intentional distortion, instead of טֻחוֹת *ṭuḥôt*, מֵרְאוֹת[טַח[*ṭaḥ[mēr]ôt*. The text could then be paraphrased: people who live in the country are certainly weather-wise, knowing the rules

---

10:14; 13:25; 16:19-20 and 51:17 is important. See also idem, *Die Lüge nach dem AT: Ihr Begriff, ihre Bedeutung und ihre Beurteilung* (1964).

366 Here again, the sequence of sounds may well not be fortuitous: v. 16, "he roasts meat" (יִצְלֶה צָלִי); v. 17, "save me my God" (הַצִּילֵנִי כִּי אֵלִי); v. 19, "I roast meat"(ר)(אָצְלֶה בָשָׂר); v. 20, "he will not save his life" (וְלֹא־יַצִּיל אֶת־נַפְשׁוֹ). These are all texts that have to do with the herdsman/hunter. For the content see 44:9-11 above on בּוֹשׁ, "to be ashamed."

367 See *HALOT* 3:1158–59 [*HALAT* 3/4:1080–81], s.v. ר, with a reference to *TLOT* 3:1178 [*THAT* 2:694].

368 For the text and its textual problems, see below

under that passage. 1QIsaᵃ has here יראה אור. Cf. LXX.

369 See *HALOT* 2:374 [*HALAT* 2:358] s.v. טחח.

370 See above on "knowledge" (דֵעַת) and "professional skill" (תְּבוּנָה) in the wisdom tradition.

371 G. Fohrer, *Das Buch Hiob* (1963) 508 on this passage.

372 Even the lexicons consider that there may be a connection in Hebrew between טֻחוֹת and the roots תוח, טחח or טחה. טֻחוֹת occurs in another difficult passage in the OT, in Ps 51:8 (6). There too it has to do with knowledge. Because of the parallelism, NRSV renders it "in the inward being." But it was probably

determining the weather;[373] but if they worship their gods, they do not yet have the true knowledge that is necessary for life.

A second proverb can be found in v. 20. Here too it is difficult to understand what is meant. After what has gone before, it seems perfectly appropriate that there should be talk of "pasturing." What is described is what would be a senseless occupation for a herdsman, so to speak: "pasturing ashes."[374] Ash, especially wood ash, cannot be held together. It flies away at the slightest breath. So the two "proverbs" would then also refer to the farmers and the herdsmen.

The dramatic structure is also detectable at the end. Verse 19 can be split up and distributed to different voices and persons.[375] The introductory comment continues to be given by the speaker. "His half" (חֶצְיוֹ) in v. 16 was twice a catchword for the herdsman; now he takes it up himself: "His half I have burnt in the fire." "Part" (אַף) the farmer says twice (v. 15). Now it is again a question of baking bread. "I roast *meat* and eat," says the herdsman. If the antiphony is continued, then "abomination" (תּוֹעֵבָה) belongs to the farmer, the "block of wood" (בּוּל עֵץ) to the herdsman.

Under this aspect the language of the very last half-sentence has a twisted logic. It contains a double negative with לֹא ("not"), in one case linked with the interrogative particle. We should probably also hear the sentence spoken with changing emphasis. Who is speaking? If it is "the speaker," this is simply a statement of fact. If spoken by one or both actors, "Is it not a lie (שֶׁקֶר) in my right hand" is a confession of faith.[376] According to the Psalter, Yahweh leads the human being "by his right hand." In Jeremiah, for example, "lie" is code for the gods. The "lies" are the idols. This would be made drastically clear if the actors exited with a "block of wood." The ambiguity is hence preserved to the very end. The text is therefore highly demanding. It displays the same literary techniques and the same concepts as the rest of the work.[377] Perhaps we even come particularly close to its author in these everyday scenes.[378] The detail is lovingly observed. Irony and seriousness are inextricably linked.[379] The incomparable nature of their God is made clear to human beings on the level of their own experience. Only God must be worshiped, not the product of human labor.[380] This perception of faith makes further life possible (v. 20).

originally the name of the Egyptian god Thoth (*ḏḥwty*), whose bird and symbol are the ibis. Whether and how far the god Thoth and his ideology play a part for the text can only be a matter for speculation. The correspondence with the god's name Thoth could be a further reason for the ridicule (cf. the change from *Baʿal* [בעל] into *Bošet* [בֹּשֶׁת], Hos 9:10; Jer 3:24; 11:13, and also in names, 2 Sam 2:8; 11:21; 21:8).

373 The argument in Matt 16:1-4 and Luke 12:54-56 would be comparable. Jesus' listeners can read the signs of the weather but not the signs of the time. See also G. von Rad, *Wisdom in Israel* (1972): "The Doctrine of the Proper Time," 138–43 [*Weisheit in Israel* (1970): "Die Lehre von der rechten Zeit," 182–88].

374 There is a comparable expression in German about "trying to keep a sack full of fleas"; see also on Hos 12:2, where there is probably an intentional ambiguity as well.

375 Muilenburg on v. 19: "The following lines are the words of the idol maker."

376 See North, 142: "The climax of irony comes when the accuser puts the indictment into the mouth of the idol-worshipper, as if he would perforce acknowledge the 'truth of it,' if only he had any sense."

377 See the summing up by R. Lack in *La symbolique du livre d'Isaïe* (1973) 98–99: "The pattern of the 'formation' of Israel evokes in this section the complementary pattern of the formation of idols and the 'nonformation' of Yahweh. . . . In reality, 44:9-20 is again picking up the theme of 'anti-creation.'"

378 In this respect the text is comparable with the artisan (clown) scenes in Shakespeare. I received essential stimulus for the understanding of the text developed here from a performance of *Hamlet*.

379 Torrey's judgment on this passage is still valid (*Second Isaiah* [1928] 345): "This poem is fully up to the standard of those which surround it. The description of the making of the idol, in particular, is very spirited and picturesque. If it were to be turned into prose (!), and interpreted without the least appreciation of the writer's sense of humor, it would indeed be a tiresome composition and worthy of the scorn which has been dealt out to it in some of the most recent commentaries."

380 In conclusion Muilenburg (515) sums up as follows: "The tragedy of false religion is that its devotees become incapable of facing reality . . . (I John 5:20-21)."

21   Remember these things, Jacob,
and Israel, for you are my servant.

I have formed you, you are a servant for me,
Israel, you will not be forgotten by me.

22   I have wiped away your transgressions like a
cloud,
and like clouds your sins.
Return to me, for I have redeemed/liberated
you.

23   Rejoice, you heavens: yes, Yahweh has acted!
Cry aloud, you depths of the earth!
Break out in jubilation, you mountains,
you forest and every tree in it!
Yes, Yahweh has redeemed/liberated Jacob,
and in/through Israel will he glorify himself.

The text has a triple function. It underlines yet again what is presented in vv. 9-20. It takes up vv. 6-8, thus forming the framework for vv. 9-20.[381] But above all it constitutes the close of the whole second act, from 42:14 onward.[382] We should therefore not expect new ideas; this is rather a summing up of what has already been said. The sense to be given to the concepts must be deduced from what has gone before.[383] The creation, election and redemption of Jacob/Israel: these provide the theme. The statements now aim directly at the behavior of those addressed.

■ **21** The author is concerned that they should "remember these things" (זְכָר־אֵלֶּה).[384] According to the Aristotelian definition, the function of Greek drama was to awaken "pity and fear." Here the appeal is to remembrance, which also means knowledge. The misunderstanding that "the making of idols" can be viewed merely as a heathen affair is resisted. The exegesis has made plain that difficulties encountered by the community in the temptations of the surrounding gentile world also underly the text.[385]

The reason (כִּי) given is also connected with what has gone immediately before. What is true, living "creativity"? In contrast to the way human beings "form" things, God is the one who has "formed" (יְצַרְתִּיךָ) his servant. Consequently God has a claim to him.[386] The subject is Jacob/Israel as a whole, but we must imagine the immediate effect on every individual listener, who is reached through the second person singular formulation, and the emphasized singular "you" (bis). "You will not be forgotten by me"[387] is a consolation directed toward the events to come.

■ **22** What was said at the beginning of this act is again endorsed: Jacob/Israel has accepted its fate as being the result of its sin (42:24-25). God has freed it and declared it once more to be his servant and property (43:1-7; 44:1-5). This makes repentance and a new beginning possible.

---

381   See Delitzsch on v. 23: "This exulting finale is undoubtedly a boundary-stone marking the end of the fifth speech" [trans. alt.]" (2:214 [469]). For Delitzsch the fifth speech begins in 44:6.

382   See Marti: "The song indicates the end of the section about Israel, Yahweh's servant, and his secure future." Marti (305) puts the beginning of the section at 42:1. See also the division in Elliger, 450.

383   Commentators who view the text as an independent unit and do not accept the thesis of a total composition must come to different conclusions at this point.

384   On זכר see W. Schottroff, *Gedenken im alten Orient*

und im Alten Testament (2d ed. 1967); also his article "זכר *zkr* to remember," *TLOT* 1:381–88 [*THAT* 1:507–18]; H. Eising, "זכר *zākhār*," *TDOT* 4:64–81 [*ThWAT* 2:571–93].

385   Contrary to Elliger's verdict, I would therefore still maintain that "these" (אֵלֶּה) relates to what has gone before; see also Spykerboer, *The Structure and Composition of Deutero-Isaiah* (1976) 127. Schoors and Fohrer plead that it is related to what follows.

386   Cf. 49:5.

387   The form תִּנָּשֵׁנִי *Niphal* with suffix as dative object is difficult and occurs nowhere else. A number of different emendations have been proposed: תִּנְשֵׁנִי from

It is impossible to declare the gospel in terser or clearer terms. Yahweh rules over natural phenomena: that is the conviction of faith in the wisdom tradition.[388] In the same way he can set aside human crimes and their consequences.[389] Human beings and "nature" belong to a single world. I would be cautious about viewing the text merely as pictorial, a *Bildwort*. For believers these are realities.[390] The return to Yahweh[391] is already an announcement of the return to Zion too.

■ **23** This verse brings us to the close of the larger unit 42:14—44:23.[392] In terms of dramatic structure, the verse corresponds to the final chorus, the chorus concluding the second act. At the same time it forges the link with what is going to follow. The section is assigned to the hymns.[393] F. Crüsemann has described the special form of the "imperative hymn":[394] "In this type of hymn the participants in the cult, or individual groups of these participants, are called with plural imperatives to praise Yahweh. This exhortation is obeyed, the true hymn itself then being raised. The sentence introduced with a deictic—not a justifying!—כִּי, in which Yahweh's saving act is extolled, must be seen as this [i.e., the hymn itself]."[395] This description is in full accord with the present text,

about which Crüsemann has made some excellent observations.[396] This כִּי also has an emphatic meaning, in the sense of "yes!" I would have some reservation only about Crüsemann's conclusion: "These are therefore not real hymns, sung by chorus and congregation, but here the hymnic form serves the assurance of salvation."[397]

The imperatives are a call to action: "Rejoice . . . cry aloud . . . break out in jubilation!" Musically speaking, v. 23 is then not itself a hymn; it is the announcement of the hymn. The section is intended for the precentor. It contains the most important information to be passed on to those taking part, the chorus and the musicians. I would assume that the announcements about the content are also directions for the performance.[398] The particular degrees or intervals and their sequence are laid down. The hymn begins "high" (heavens), then "low" (earth). The "depths of the earth" (תַּחְתִּיּוֹת) probably announces a specially deep register. A middle register follows, with mountains and forests. The degrees or intervals are initially directives for the instruments. They also correspond roughly to the particular registers of the singers, men and women. The way the hymn is to be sung is also stated. רנן is a kind of high-pitched song with

נטש, "give up, cast away," e.g., Deut 32:15 and Jer 15:6; thus Klostermann, Cheyne, Marti, Morgenstern; *HALAT;* תִּנָּשֵׁנִי from נשא II, "deceive"; thus Muilenburg, North, Bonnard (also 1QIsaᵃ?). A pointing תִּנָּשֵׁנִי as *Qal* from נשא corresponding to נשה, "forget," would also be possible for 1QIsaᵃ. Duhm, Haller, Kissane, and Elliger assume a misreading: instead of the original הָ, a suffix נִי. Torrey believes that this is possibly an intentional double reading, in the sense of "you shall not be forgotten" and "you shall not forget me." I myself, however, would in poetry be prepared to accept the unusual form. See also Delitzsch on the passage. For its content cf. 40:22; 48:14-15 and the argument in Spykerboer, *The Structure and Composition of Deutero-Isaiah* (1976) 127.

388   See also Job 38:22-38.

389   In Hos 13:1-3 the makers of idols are threatened with disappearing "like the morning mist." The text here says the very opposite. Cf. Jer 31:27-38 and Psalm 130. See here Delitzsch: "The point of comparison is not the dark, heavy multitude of sins, but the facility and rapidity with which they are expunged" (2:213 [468]). Elliger (447) stresses "the thoroughness with which they disappear," pointing to Job 7:9; 30:15; Hos 6:4. See R. Knierim, "פֶּשַׁע pešaʿ crime," *TLOT* 2:1033-37 [*THAT* 2:488-95];

and idem, "חטא *ḥṭʾ* to miss," *TLOT* 1:406-11 [*THAT* 1:541-49]. See also K. Koch, "חטא *chāṭāʾ*," *TDOT* 4:309-19 [*ThWAT* 2:857-70]; H. Ringgren and H. Seebass, "פשע *pāšaʿ*," *ThWAT* 6:791-810. For the content of the verse cf. 43:25.

390   Muilenburg, 509: "It is not so much his people's captivity that occupies God's concern, but their sin."

391   See H. W. Wolff, "Das Thema 'Umkehr' in der alttestamentlichen Prophetie" (1951), in his *Gesammelte Studien zum AT* (2d ed. 1973) 130-55; Jörg Jeremias, "Zur Eschatologie des Hoseabuches," in *Die Botschaft und die Boten. FS H. W. Wolff* (1981) 217-33; J. A. Soggin, "שוב *šûb* to return," *TLOT* 3:1312-17 [*THAT* 2:884-91].

392   See also Westermann; further Spykerboer, *The Structure and Composition of Deutero-Isaiah* (1976) on this passage.

393   Thus among others Gressmann, Begrich, Hessler, and Elliger; see the survey of the research in F. Crüsemann, *Studien zur Formgeschichte von Hymnus und Danklied in Israel* (1969) 45-46. For the text and its function, see F. Matheus, *Singet dem Herrn ein neues Lied: Die Hymnen Deuterojesajas* (1990) 67-77.

394   Crüsemann, *Studien,* 19-82.

395   Ibid., 80.

396   Ibid., 47-48.

397   Ibid., 80.

long, sustained notes.[399] רוע *Hiphil* are the deep men's voices, which correspond to the war cry.[400] They are incidentally mentioned here for the last time in DtIsa. According to 44:27 "the depths" dry up. From then on things take an upward turn. Hence the higher notes predominate. פָּצְחוּ . . . רִנָּה is sung in the middle register but is probably also a special way of singing, "breaking out into jubilation."[401]

Finally the text of the hymn is given. It is the brief sentence: "Yes, Yahweh has acted." It may have been sung in varying antiphony between high and deep voices. The second text is: "Yes, Yahweh has redeemed/liberated Jacob, he will glorify himself in/through Israel." As a double declaration, it would have been distributed between the "mountains" and the "forest and all the trees in it."

If we assume that this was a scenic performance, then various forms of antiphony are conceivable: between precentor and chorus; between different choruses; or between chorus and listeners. The brief cries of acclamation: "Yes, Yahweh has acted," and "Yes, Yahweh has redeemed/liberated Jacob," suggest in my view that the listeners were included.[402] This gives us the most impor-

tant directives for the performance. The length of the individual variations would be ad lib.

In the present text there seems to be a discrepancy between the length of the whole unit 42:14—44:23 and the extent of its close, with v. 23. But these instructions for the hymn allow us to suppose that there were repeats.[403] The fundamental themes, which can be varied, are announced in the text. Yahweh is acclaimed in the way that earthly rulers are also acclaimed. In the hymn the power and greatness of sovereignty is proclaimed—but also the way in which it is exercised. God's sovereignty is "liberating," "redemptive."

For the content of the hymn, this means that the whole world, described by its extremes, heaven and earth, is to join in the jubilation. A special point is that "the forest and every tree in it" are to participate. The word "forest" (יַעַר) otherwise occurs in DtIsa only in 44:14. Here we must assume that the intention is to forge a link with the preceding scene. For there the most important trees in the forest were named.[404] But now they need no longer fear that their wood will be misused for idols.[405] Here again the text is intended to raise a smile.

---

398 The "figures" in the theory and practice of baroque music are perhaps comparable. The musical "figure" "anabasis/ascensus/rise" is described by A. Kircher (1650): "Anabasis or Ascensio (rise) is a musical period through which we express something outstanding or something that is in the process of rising, or something sublime, as for example: Ascendens Christus in altum [Christ ascending on high]." See D. Bartel, *Handbuch der musikalischen Figurenlehre* (1985) 84–85; "Catabasis": 115–16. The use of "figures" as a way of interpreting a text can be seen particularly well in Heinrich Schütz (1585–1672); see, e.g., the "octave progression" in *Psalmen Davids*, Gesamt Ausgabe III, 157: "*Der Himmel und Erde gemacht hat*"; *kleine Geistliche Konzerte II, Nr. XIV "im Himmel und auf Erden. . . ."* See also the comments by H. H. Eggebrecht, *Heinrich Schütz, Musicus poeticus* (2d ed. 1984), esp. 97–99.

399 רנן, "rejoice," in Isa 42:11; 49:13; 52:8, 9; 54:1; as substantive: 43:14; 48:20; 49:13; 51:11; 55:12. It is the shrill crying or high-pitched singing of women especially (see Isa 12:6; 54:1; Zeph 3:14; Zech 2:14 (2:10); Prov 8:3; Lam 2:18). It can express either joy or grief. According to the text it is "the heavens" that are to rejoice.

400 רוע *Hiphil* means "crying." Since it is also a tech-

nical term for the war cry (see Josh 6:10 and frequently; 1 Sam 17:52; Hos 5:8; Joel 2:1; 2 Chr 13:15—thus also Isa 42:13!), it corresponds to the pitch of men's voices. The term "depths (תַּחְתִּיוֹת) of the earth" is appropriate.

401 See also H. Seidel, *Musik in Altisrael: Untersuchungen zur Musikgeschichte und Musikpraxis Altisraels anhand biblischer und außerbiblischer Texte* (1989), with lit.

402 Again, consequently, Crüsemann's observation in *Studien zur Formgeschichte von Hymnus und Danklied in Israel* (1969) 48 is important: "Instead of שיר, הלל *Piel*, זמר *Piel*, and so on, the text has here אִיל, רנן, פצח and so on. Whatever these words may derive from, they at all events do not mean an articulate speaking or singing, which would be in line with the meaning of the verbs otherwise typically used in this genre." Anyone who has ever heard the rhythmical shouting of a crowd in the East will not forget it!

403 Crüsemann (ibid.) draws a comparison with the Song of Miriam in Exodus 15, and this does indeed suggest itself.

404 "The trees of the fields" rejoice for the first time only in 55:12. According to this text, a newly cultivated countryside has come into being, with cypresses and myrtles, a paradise (*paradeisos*—garden).

405 Cf. Isa 14:8: "The cypresses exult over you, the cedars of Lebanon, saying, 'Since you were laid low,

One subtlety in the text is that the two first verbs of the acclamations are in the perfect:[406] "Yahweh *has* acted (עָשָׂה)" and "Yahweh *has* redeemed (גָּאַל)." This is in line with the dramatic structure, and this, in DtIsa's opinion, is what has already taken place. The last verb is in the imperfect: "He will glorify himself" (יִתְפָּאָר).[407] This is still to come. One can hesitate about how to translate it.

Does it establish what is going to happen, or is it, as part of the acclamation, a wish that Yahweh will glorify himself? In either case the final saying points to coming events with the implicit question: How will Yahweh show his glory in and through Israel? How can this come about?[408]

---

no one comes to cut us down.'" This is a section from the song of triumph over the fall of the king of Babylon.

406 See Crüsemann, *Studien zur Formgeschichte von Hymnus und Danklied in Israel* (1969) 47; Elliger, 452, on this passage.

407 The word also contains an element of "adornment, beauty, splendor." See North's comments here (143): "The nouns *pᵉʾēr* and *tipʾeret* suggest that the action of the verb was accompanied by the wearing of finery, particularly on the head. A *pᵉʾēr* was some kind of festive garland or head-dress." He points to Isa 62:3: "The promise is that Israel is to be 'a crown of beauty in the hand of Yahweh' and there

is much in Isa xl–lxvi to suggest that the redeemed Israel is his proudest achievement." In the present context it is interesting that 44:13 talked about "a splendid example of a human being" (אָדָם תִּפְאָרֶת) that the artist is going to produce. Conversely, here Yahweh "glorifies" himself. For Zion's crown see below on 54:11-14. Marti (305) translates: "He entwines himself with Israel into a wreath of glory." In the text the appointment of Cyrus follows here. In 46:13 it stands before the deposition of Babylon.

408 It is therefore understandable that, following the arrangement of the text in the manuscript, 1QIsaᵃ should have assigned the verse to the following section.

Act III: 44:24–45:25

A Throne Scene

"Who says to Cyrus: 'My shepherd!'
and 'All that I wish he will fulfill . . .'" (44:28)

"Only in Yahweh [is there] . . . righteousness and strength"
(45:24)

44

"I am Yahweh, who makes all things" (44:24)
"Who says to Jerusalem: 'she shall be
inhabited!'" (44:26)

A. 1. 44:24-28
Theophany and Yahweh Edict

24   Thus says Yahweh, your redeemer,
who formed you from your mother's womb:

I am Yahweh, who makes everything,
who alone stretches out the heavens,
who treads fast the earth—who is beside me?

25   who breaks the signs of functionaries,
and makes fools of oracle priests;
who pushes the wise back,
and makes their knowledge foolish;

26   who confirms the word of his servant,
and will fulfill the counsel of his messengers;

who says to Jerusalem: "She shall be
    inhabited,"
and to the cities of Judah: "They shall be
    built,"
and "I will rebuild their ruins";

27   who says to the depths: "Run dry!"
and "Your rivers I will dry up";

28   who says to Cyrus: "My shepherd!"
and "All that I wish he will fulfill,
saying to Jerusalem: 'She shall be built,
and the foundations of the temple shall be
    laid.'"

■ **44:24–45:25** In 44:24—45:25 Yahweh's rule over the whole world is presented in a throne scene. The themes of the individual smaller literary units are subordinated to the fundamental idea of God's sovereignty. The beginning of this compositional unit is clearly marked through the close of the preceding description of the manufacture of idols, and the hymn in 44:23. At the end the "Hallelujah" is announced in 45:25. In the following chapter, chap. 46, something new begins: the procession of the heathen gods. Most commentaries assume that the units are shorter than this analysis postulates,[1] but then have difficulty in explaining their cohesion and sequence. But among earlier commentators Delitzsch, for example, pleaded for more extensive units. For him,

---

1   See the survey in Elliger, 456.

44:24-45 is "the sixth discourse of the first third."[2] Among more recent commentators, Spykerboer takes this division (with the subsidiary sections 44:24—45:7, 45:8 and 45:9-25).[3] The genres assigned to the different sections vary, being determin by the divisions of the text; they must therefore be considered at the appropriate points.

It is noticeable that certain motifs run right through this whole scene. The first of these is the formula: "I am Yahweh" (44:24; 45:3; 5, 6, 7, 8, 18, 19, 21). The very distribution shows a certain rhythm. The "self-introductory formula" signals the presence of the one who thus introduces himself. In whatever form it occurs, it is the epiphany of the deity. The formula "Thus says Yahweh" is also frequently reiterated (44:24; 45:1, 11, 14, 18). This formula is found in each case at the beginning of subsidiary units. It corresponds to the five-times repeated messenger formula in 42:14—44:23, the second act.[4] It is again possible that either a single messenger authoritatively proclaims: "Thus says Yahweh . . . ," or that the message is distributed among five speakers. 45:13 ends: "Says Yahweh Sabaoth." 45:24 confirms at the end: "he has told me." The word of God goes out to the world. Various addressees are named, and there is hardly a sector that is not addressed. The word of God is the theme of the whole unit. This is once more stated at the end, in 45:23: "From my mouth has gone forth righteousness

(צְדָקָה), a word (דָּבָר), and it will not return." This, both in wording and in substance, carries the arc back to the beginning in 40:8 (cf. 40:5), and forward to the end in 55:11. This too is an indication of the central position of the unit 44:24—45:25. God's sovereignty is exercised through the word uttered by the Lord of the whole world.

If we assume that the whole structure of DtIsa's book is dramatic, the unit can in my view be defined as a third act. This is interesting, because a comparison with Attic drama shows that there too special emphasis is laid on the third "epeisodion."[5] It is one of the climaxes of the drama, whether it be the zenith or the nadir of events. In what K. Aichele calls "the architectural plan of the drama," it is at this point that the "reversal" in the action[6] often takes place—the appearance of the helper or savior,[7] and the interpretation of the future.[8]

However one explains the relationship and tradition of such "dramatic plans," the comparison with the biblical text brings out the important position given to Cyrus's appearance.[9] In his person, the turn of events becomes evident. The several announcements preceding his appearance have built up the tension.[10] Now his name is explicitly mentioned for the first time, and mentioned twice (44:28 and 45:1). In this way he is visibly introduced as a "character."

The theme of this compositional unit is Cyrus's legiti-

2   Delitzsch, 2:214 [469; trans. altered].

3   H. E. Spykerboer, *The Structure and Composition of Deutero-Isaiah* (1976) 129–30.

4   See 43:1, 4, 16; 44:2, 6.

5   See K. Aichele, "Das Epeisodion," in W. Jens, ed., *Die Bauformen der griechischen Tragödie* (1971) 48–83, esp. 67–68, 71, 75, 79ff.: "In all Aeschylus's tragedies, the second dramatic thrust and the real main act of the drama takes place in the third epeisodion. In all the dramas, the new act begins immediately at the start of the third epeisodion" (67). As examples he names *The Persians, Seven against Thebes, Supplices, Choephori, Agamemnon, Eumenides,* and *Prometheus.* In this comparison the varying length of the dramas must be taken into consideration. To give the number of acts in Attic drama as five is undoubtedly a schematization. For me, the important point about the comparison is the function of the third epeisodion, and the rough distribution of the climaxes in the total structure. If we assume that there are six acts in DtIsa, then in light of the whole, and according to the division of

the chapters, the third act lies at the end of the first half.

6   For Euripides see ibid., 75, 79.

7   For Aeschylus: "In *Agamemnon* the long-heralded hero now comes on for the first time" (ibid., 67). For Sophocles see *Oedipus Coloneus* (71). For Euripides: "The deliverer or helper of the side that is hard pressed either comes on the second part of the second epeisodion (Heracles, Orestes) or at the beginning of the third (Alcestis, Medea), or in the course of it (Hippolytus, Andromache, Hecabe). The reversal of action in the *Bacchae* (palace wonder, the freeing of Dionysus) takes place at the beginning of the third epeisodion" (75).

8   North (143) heads 44:24-28 "The Curtain Rises for Cyrus."

9   For Aeschylus: "In *The Persians* Darius interprets the catastrophe and offers vistas of the future" (Aichele, "Das Epeisodion," 67); see also the appearance of Io in *Prometheus.*

10   Isa 41:1-4, 21-26; see also above on 42:5-9.

mation and his commission to rebuild Zion/Jerusalem and the cities of Judah, and to free the prisoners. But the outstanding importance of Cyrus should not lead us to overlook that each individual scene of this act also has its particular importance for the progress and meaning of the whole, especially in respect to the future. This must be shown in the detailed exegesis.

■ **44:24-28** The genre of the first section, 44:24-28, has been very varyingly defined in research.[11] The most important suggestions were already made at the beginning of the scholarly discussion. Gressmann[12] treats the text as a hymn,[13] dividing it into a "prophetic introduction" (v. 24a) and "the self-predication of the Deity" (vv. 24b-26a), which serves as an introduction to "the body of the oracle itself, the promise for Jerusalem" (vv. 26b-28).[14] According to Gressmann, the special mark of the hymn is "the participial style" that runs throughout. Begrich assigns the hymn to the disputation speeches, because of its use of literary forms.[15] A double chain of evidence (first, Yahweh's acts, vv. 24-26; second, Yahweh's words, vv. 27-28) proceeds in each case "quite deliberately from the indisputable assertion . . . to what is disputed."[16] Begrich here also draws on texts from chap. 45. He assumes "that in his argumentation the prophet is taking up hymnic material."[17] The attempt has since been made to combine these two positions.[18] A new factor in the discussion is that, starting from the

self-introductory formula (Zimmerli), scholars have drawn for comparison on the ancient oriental hymns in which the deity (or the king) extols him- or herself.[19] These self-acclamatory hymns have the function of "legitimating the ruler."[20] This can be the heavenly ruler, in disputes with a hierarchy of gods, or it can be an earthly sovereign whose "divine authorization is demonstrated."[21]

These observations about the form can be drawn from the history of research. A few preliminary considerations about the style should be added. The text is shaped with extreme artistry. Elsewhere too DtIsa works with the stylistic devices of *parallelismus membrorum*, chiasm, and various types of correspondence. But here everything is intensified, form and content hardly being separable from one another. One striking feature is the continual triple beat. In vv. 24b-28 each of the three new statements begins with three participles. The stylization goes so far that in vv. 25-28 three participles begin with מֵ *mē* and the following three with הָ *hā*. In v. 24 there is a sequence of three words ending with *yod*: "I" (אָנֹכִי *ʾānokî*), "alone" (לְבַדִּי *lᵉbadî*), and "who is beside me" (מֵאִתִּי *mēʾitî*).[22] But this triple pattern also runs through the whole succeeding text.[23] This is a further indication of the unity of the composition, from 44:24 through 45:25. But we may then ask whether the "threeness" is not already present in the first statement, v. 24a: Yahweh

---

11   See the survey in R. F. Melugin, "The Structure of Deutero-Isaiah" (1968) 55–56; C. Stuhlmueller, *Creative Redemption in Deutero-Isaiah* (1970) 196–97; Spykerboer, *The Structure and Composition of Deutero-Isaiah* (1976) 130–31; and the discussion in Elliger, 456–65.

12   H. Gressmann, "Die literarische Analyse Deuterojesajas," *ZAW* 34 (1914) 254–97. On the text see also M. Weippert, "Erwägungen zu Jes 44,24-28," *DBAT* 21 (1985) 121–32.

13   Gressmann, *ZAW* 34 (1914) 283ff.

14   Ibid., 289–90.

15   J. Begrich, *Studien zu Deuterojesaja* (1938, reprint 1963) 50–53.

16   Ibid., 51.

17   Ibid., 52.

18   See, e.g., E. Jenni, *Die politischen Voraussagen der Propheten* (1956) 100–101: "A disputation saying with a hymnic touch"; Fohrer: "A mixture of hymn . . . and discussion saying."

19   C. Westermann, "Sprache und Struktur der Prophetie Deuterojesajas," in *Forschung am Alten*

Testament 1 (1964) 92–170, esp. 145ff.; H. M. Dion, "Le genre littéraire de l'Hymne," *RB* 74 (1967) 215–34. H. P. Müller, "Altes und Neues zum Buch Hiob," *EvTh* 37 (1977) 284–304, esp. 295–96 with lit.

20   C. Wilcke, "Hymns," *RLA* 4 (1972–75) 541–42.

21   Example: "Ištar of Arbela, Hymn with Oracle," in M. Weippert, "'Heiliger Krieg' in Israel und Assyrien," *ZAW* 84 (1972) 473–74; Inanna in: *ANET* 578–79; *SAHG* 67, 115.

22   See also Elliger, 467, on v. 24bγ אָנֹכִי: "Because in addition the metrical stress twice falls on this resounding 'I,' the formula becomes a half-stichos with three stresses, in which the measured, solemn progress of the speech is clearly audible."

23   For example, in 44:24–45:25 "I am Yahweh" is pronounced 9 times (3 × 3): in 44:24 אֲנִי יהוה; אָנֹכִי יהוה in 45:3, 5, 6, 7, 8, 18, 19, 21.

speaks as redeemer and creator. We shall also have to note the correspondences in the text. For example, "who makes everything (כֹּל)" in v. 24 is taken up again in v. 28: "and everything (וְכָל־) that pleases me/all that I wish he will fulfill (יַשְׁלִם)." This last is again announced in v. 26: "The counsel of his messengers he will fulfill (יַשְׁלִים)."

In this way the text takes on a ceremonial, solemn character. In spite of the literary subtleties, it ought really to be read aloud and listened to. These observations are also indications of the scenic character of the text. It is here that its unity as genre is to be found.[24] But in my view the text is also closely structured within itself, and this has not hitherto received sufficient attention.

■ **24** Since the text begins directly with the divine speech, we again initially lack information about the more immediate circumstances. But this is the declaration of a theophany.[25] The speaker is one who has the authority to use the age-old prophetic formula: "Thus says Yahweh." He passes on directly what has been revealed in an epiphany. This is again indicated by the "self-introductory formula."[26] Since the subject of the utterance is the exercise of divine sovereignty, the "throne scene" suggests itself. This must be assumed in the case of other DtIsa texts too. The special point here, compared with a text such as 42:1-4, for example, is that the listeners are directly included. What happens does not take place in heavenly remoteness. Heavenly and earthly spheres are related to each other to a degree hardly found elsewhere. It is an epiphany. Of course it would be possible to represent Jacob/Israel through the Servant in the heavenly sphere. But in what follows earthly persons such as Cyrus (45:1), prisoners (45:14), and people from all over the world (45:20, 22) appear too. So the direct address: "*your* redeemer, who has formed *you* from the womb" establishes contact with everyone who is listening, and again with tremendous dramatic intensity. At the same time, a certain distance remains. Cyrus does not encounter Yahweh directly, but only in the messenger's word.

The catchword "redeem, liberate" (גאל) links up with what has gone before.[27] Yahweh as ruler of the world is none other than "your redeemer." In the ancient world the accession of a ruler was often the occasion for a remission of debts; this was a way of showing that a new era had begun.[28] The "government program" in the text mentions the gracious acts of God to his people first of all. But this already states the theme of the following passage in quite concrete terms: if God "has redeemed you," how much more should you "redeem" or free debtors! That God's sovereignty rests on his act of creation is again maintained through the corresponding formulation: "who has formed you from the womb."[29] Creation is not merely something belonging to the primordial era. It takes place in the present too, and justifies both gift and claim.

Verse 24b draws in the universal horizon of creation: awareness of the unity of the world corresponds to belief in the one God. "Who makes all things (עֹשֶׂה־כֹל)"– not even the definite article (which one would expect in Hebrew) is used here. It is impossible to think of anything more comprehensive than this. It is hard for us modern people to conceive how difficult it was for the ancient Near East, and the ancient world in general, to arrive at concepts like "everything" or "nothing." It was possible to list the works of creation as the Priestly writing does, and at the end talk about "all the work that God had done" (Gen 2:3). But here in DtIsa the abstract formulation comes at the beginning. In its inclusiveness it also draws in all the activity that is mentioned in what follows. DtIsa is on the way to a formulation of the concept "all." But this is intimately connected with his theological approach, which starts from the unity and uniqueness of God. Our division between nature and history seems artificial in comparison, because for DtIsa there is only a single reality.

The way in which statements about the world are developed out of the tradition of the hymn can still be

---

24   Elliger (465) has recognized something of this: "The question about the genre can therefore surely be answered unequivocally: the Yahweh speech is structured in the form of a royal edict. The divine ruler proclaims his will to the heavenly assembly."

25   Jörg Jeremias, *Theophanie* (2d ed. 1976); J. Muilenburg, "The Speech of Theophany," *HDSB* 28 (1963–64) 35–47.

26   See W. Zimmerli, "I Am Yahweh," in *I Am Yahweh* (1982) 1–28 ["Ich bin Jahwe," in *Gottes Offenbarung: Gesammelte Aufsätze* (1963) 11–40].

27   Cf. 41:14; 43:1, 14; 44:6, 22, 23, 24.

28   For the release from debt, see K. Baltzer, "Liberation from Debt Slavery After the Exile in Second Isaiah and Nehemiah," in *Ancient Israelite Religion: FS F. M. Cross* (1987) 474–84.

perceived. "Spreading out the heavens" and "treading fast the earth" are ancient mythologems. They belong within the group of traditional divine predications.[30] But one can perceive in this passage that they are not used at random. Basing his work on other studies, N. C. Habel has worked out the presuppositions of the formula "who spreads out the heavens" in DtIsa.[31] He sees a specific tabernacle tradition in both the Deuteronomistic tradition (2 Sam 6:2, 17) and in the Priestly writing (Exod 37:1-9; 40:20-21). In the psalms these statements are bound up especially with the theophany (Pss 104:2-5; 144:5-7; 18:9-13 [8-12]; cf. Job 26).[32] They must be distinguished from general declarations about creation. The heavenly and the earthly "tent" correspond (Exod 25:9, 40; 40:16-38; cf. also Wis 9:8-10; Heb 8:5; 9:11).[33] We already assumed for different reasons that the scene in Isa 44:24a represents an epiphany. This assumption is endorsed by v. 24b. The hymnic declarations are at the same time descriptive elements in the scene. The tent over the throne *is* the heavens. That is evident right down to the star-studded canopy of Christian art; there too the stars belong to the iconography of epiphany and sovereignty.[34] In the drama the

"speaker," as Yahweh's representative, probably had his place in the tent.

Verse 24b can be defined on the basis of its form and content as a "self-predication hymn."[35] It provides the legitimation for Yahweh's acts, which are described in what follows. This is necessary because what happens here is a cause of dispute.[36]

■ **25** There is almost complete consensus that vv. 25-26a belong to the genre "hymn." Many assume that in vv. 24-28 we have an almost unbroken series of participles. But the grammatical structure is probably more complicated than that. Participles alone do not make a hymn. Further, it is noticeable that the three participles are not determined (as might be expected in Hebrew) and that they are followed by three sentences in the imperfect, in which the verbs are in the third person. This suggests that the intention is to express action that is going on now: "He is in the process of . . . and. . . ." W. A. M. Beuken is one of the few to have seen the difficulties.[37] He distinguishes v. 24b as "God's word" from vv. 25-28 as "the prophet's word."[38] In any event, we may assume that a speaker is describing what is happening, in the same way as in the preceding unit, 44:9-20, for example.

---

29   Cf. 43:2; 49:5.

30   Cf. F. M. Cross, *Canaanite Myth and Hebrew Epic* (1973); J. J. M. Roberts, *The Earliest Semitic Pantheon* (1972); M. Dijkstra, *Gods Voorstelling: Predikatieve expressie van zelfopenbaring in oudoosterse teksten en Deutero-Jesaja* (1980).

31   N. C. Habel, "He Who Stretches out the Heavens," *CBQ* 34 (1972) 417–30. Cf. 40:22; 42:5; 45:12; 48:13; 51:13, 16.

32   See also R. J. Clifford, "The Tent of El and the Israelite Tent of Meeting," *CBQ* 33 (1971) 221–27.

33   Habel ("He Who Stretches out the Heavens," *CBQ* 34 [1972] 427 n. 20) also makes what I think is an important point when he compares the symbolic action in Jer 43:8ff., on the grounds that it shows the connection between the representation of the earthly ruler (Nebuchadnezzar) and the representation of divine sovereignty. "The association with sky in Job 26 suggests that the idea of Jer 43 is that of a shining canopy overhead. Be that as it may, the throne of the king is set up on foundation stones and then some kind of tent is pitched over it."

34   See here, e.g., F. Gerke, *Spätantike und frühes Christentum* (1967) 141–44, for the significance of the curtains. On "spreading out the earth" (הָאָרֶץ רֹקַע) see T. M. Ludwig, "The Traditions of the Establishing of the Earth in Deutero-Isaiah," *JBL* 92

(1973) 345–57, esp. 347ff. רקע is used for the embossing of a metal bowl by the goldsmith—hence the translation "spread out." See *HALOT* 3:1291–92 [*HALAT* 4:1204–5]; cf. also Gen 1:6-8.

35   מֵאִתִּי, "from with me," in the sense of "through me myself," "on my own initiative," has the support of good manuscripts as well as the *Qere*. Yet from the point of view of the sense there is something to be said in favor of the proposal מִי אִתִּי, "who is with me" (thus the *Ketib*, 1QIsa[a]; LXX, Aquila, Vg). Jerome uses both readings (see B. Kedar-Kopfstein, "Divergent Hebrew Readings in Jerome's Isaiah," *Textus* 4 [1964] 176–210, esp. 184).

36   Cf. Exod 34:6-7; Ps 81:7-8 (6-7).

37   Beuken, 228–29: "The three participles . . . should be understood as predicative nouns, not as appositions: 'He annihilates . . . He causes to withdraw . . . He fulfills'" (229). On page 322 n. 2 he refers for support to König, *Lehrgebäude* II 2, §§409b; 411e, h; 413k.

38   Beuken, 229. R. P. Merendino (*Der Erste und der Letzte: Eine Untersuchung von Jes 40–48* [1981] 410) observes rightly: "If one follows Crüsemann's critical observations about the genre (cf. Crüsemann, *Studien zur Formgeschichte von Hymnus und Danklied* [in Israel (1969)] 91–95, 152–54), vv. 25-28a do not display the characteristics proper to hymnic partici-

The form-critical reflections are in accordance with the grammatical ones. In a throne scene the description of the ruler is often followed by statements about his royal household.[39] What happens in the present text is the choosing of the proper counselors. That is one of the most important tasks for the one who exercises sovereignty. The details of the text also become clearer if we compare it with its counterpart, the throne scene with the "daughter of the Chaldeans," Babylon, in 47:1-15 (esp. vv. 13-15).

First of all the subject is the group of those who divine the future.[40] At all periods, prediction is part of the exercise of rule, extrapolation into the future and manipulation of the future here being closely connected. In the ancient world, divination was already a science involving large numbers of people, as well as considerable skill and resources.[41] The more developed the political structures, the more there were differentiated professional groups concerned with the future and its interpretation. For us, at this distance in time, the terms and distinctions are often no longer fully comprehensible.

בַּדִּים are initially (if it is permissible to link the word with Akk. *baddum*) "functionaries" generally.[42] According to Hos 11:6 they have to do with plans. According to Jer 50:36 they belong to the "executive officers" in Babylon. Since in the reversal they "show

themselves to be fools," wisdom is apparently expected of them. That fits the context in the present text. קֶסֶם is the inquiry put to the oracle, in the OT especially through the drawing of lots.[43] So if their "signs are broken" that could mean their insignia or tools. Ezek 21:26-27 (21-22) gives a vivid account of the arrow oracle of the king of Babylon. Arrows could be broken. But lots could also be drawn with sticks. When the soothsayers' instruments are destroyed, their techniques are destroyed too. In this way the people who are really responsible for making things clear are themselves "confused."

There is also irony in the verb הלל. The root הלל I (like Akk. *ellu*) means "to be or to become bright." It is used about the light of the stars (Isa 13:10; Job 29:3; 31:26); in Job 31:26 there is an association with forbidden practices.[44] הלל III is explained on the basis of הלל I as meaning "to be moonstruck," and then "to be confused, mad" (*Qal*) or to make so (*Poel* Ps 102:9 [8]; Job 12:17; Qoh 7:7; cj. 2 Sam 22:4 par. and Ps 18:4 [3]). In the DtIsa text it stands in the latter form, and "madness" of this kind can of course also be acted.[45] The literary character of the text suggests that the contrast with הלל II, "praise, extol," is probably intentional. The praise of Yahweh, the Hallelujah, would actually have its appropriate place in the throne scene. In their "frenzied" condi-

---

ples." But he then still goes on to talk about the hymn, and describes the text as "a kind of response" (410).

39 Cf., e.g., Isa 6:1-3; 1 Kgs 22:18-22; Dan 7:9-10.

40 On the following see esp. H.-P. Müller, "Magisch-mantische Weisheit und die Gestalt Daniels," *UF* 1 (1969) 79–94. He perceives rightly that: "Isa 44:25-26 therefore reflects the rivalry of the 'prophets' on both sides, in accordance with DtIsa's theme of the competitive struggle of the gods" (82). Only the text is closer to those in which the "rivalry of the divining sages . . . can be presented in narrative form." Müller refers to Genesis 41 E [i.e., the Elohist version]; Exod 7:11; Daniel (1) 2; 4-5.

41 For an introduction see J. P. Vernant et al., *Divination et rationalité* (1974); F. H. Cryer, *Divination in Ancient Israel and Its Near Eastern Environment* (1994).

42 See A. Finet and J. Bottéro, *Répertoire analytique: Archive royal de Mari XV* (1954) 192. The often proposed change to בָּרִים, corresponding to an Akkadian term for a group of oracle priests, is

unnecessary. The alteration also destroys the antithesis between "I (Yahweh) alone" (לְבַדִּי, v. 24) and "functionaries" (בַּדִּים, v. 25). It is probable that in Heb. בַּדִּים, there is also an echo of בַּד from בדא, "empty talk, untruthful speech" (cf. Isa 16:6; Jer 48:30; Job 11:3). *HALOT* (1:109 s.v. בַּד [*HALAT* 1:105] renders it "oracle priest."

43 Num 22:7; 23:23; Deut 18:10; 1 Sam 15:23; 2 Kgs 17:17; Jer 14:14; Ezek 13:6, 23; 21:26-27; Prov 16:10. According to *HALOT* 3:1115–16 [*HALAT* 3:1042] the noun means "prediction, survey of future events." It is the term used for consulting an arrow oracle in particular (Ezek 21:26-27 [21-22]). Cf. also Num 22:7.

44 See G. Fohrer, *Das Buch Hiob* (1963) 438 on this passage.

45 See 1 Sam 21:14, where it is said about David: "So he changed his behavior before them; he pretended to be mad (הלל III *Hitpoel*) in their hands, beat on the doors of the gate and let his spittle run down

tion these "counselors" have to disappear. The second half-verse says this explicitly about "the wise."

"Who pushes the wise back" (מֵשִׁיב חֲכָמִים אָחוֹר) can also be understood literally: "He turns to the back [of the stage]," and would then, as a stage direction, have its proper place in the scenic structure.[46] Since there are as yet no stage directions in the modern sense, what happens is announced in the text. So the exit demonstrates what is meant with additional clarity.

Again the irony of the text is perceptible. The MT preserves the joke by writing יְשַׂכֵּל, which is ambiguous. 1QIsaᵃ spoils it through its reading סכל, which means "to allow to be foolish" (סכל *Piel*). According to the sense of the whole passage, this סכל is what is meant; the text's שׂכל is a variant form.[47] The effect is here again "to behave foolishly" (סכל *Niphal*), which already implies the interpretation.[48] But what one really expects of the wise (חֲכָמִים) is that with their knowledge (דַּעְתָּם) they "understand,[49] have insight,[50] make wise,[51] have success[52] and thus act discerningly, devoutly";[53] this indicates the semantic range of שׂכל I.[54] "To be foolish" (סכל) or "understand" (שׂכל)—the difference is only a single *s* sound, comparable with the famous "shibboleth."[55] This is once more an indication that the text is conceived for speaking and listening.

According to DtIsa, the decision is that between false and true wisdom. All forms of magic are rejected, under the premise of v. 24, that Yahweh "makes everything," not any human being. Consequently the oracle priests and "the foolish wise" are not required in Yahweh's council. Those who exercise power through knowledge, the technicians of prediction, lose the power they have acquired for themselves.

In Israel the proclamation of the future is bound to the revealed word of God. God's will remains the same in past, present and future. That is DtIsa's great theme. After the false prophets have disappeared, his servant and his messengers remain. They form the "royal household" of God, and he is present among them.

■ **26a** If we again ask first of all about the persons involved, we come up against a textual problem; but behind this is actually a problem of interpretation.[56] Is the text talking about "his servant" (sing.) or "his servants" (plur.)? The Masoretic textual tradition clearly has the singular. 1QIsaᵃ and 1QIsaᵇ (though unpointed) probably agree—at all events there is no plural *yod*. Only the LXXᴬ and Targum have a plural, but this provides a sufficient reason for many commentators to follow this view. But the present text has the more difficult reading and deserves to be given preference. The text shares the difficulty of all statements about "servant" (עבד) in DtIsa: their complexity. The context would initially suggest that the servant should be viewed as the representation of Jacob/Israel. This is also in accordance with 45:4. An identification of the servant with Jeremiah would be interesting, for Cyrus's legitimation is traced back to his prophecy.[57] Thus it would be true that the word of his servant comes into force through that which follows. Under the general aspect of prophecy, the plural "his servants" (meaning prophets) would also be conceivable.

But if one starts from the specific framework of the throne scene, then it is plain that "his servant" is a single figure, the one who—whatever title and name he may have—heads the royal household and is responsible for forging the link between ruler and people, people and

---

his beard." See H. J. Stoebe, *Das erste Buch Samuelis* (1973) on this passage. Also see Jer 25:16 on drunkenness, as well as 50:38 and 51:7; Jer 46:9 and Nah 2:5 (4) on "driving as if mad" with chariots.

46   On אחר in DtIsa in the spatial sense, cf. 42:17; 50:5.

47   Elliger (454) thinks here that "the שׂ in MT is simply an abnormal spelling."

48   Cf. 1 Sam 13:13; 2 Sam 24:10; 1 Chr 21:8; 2 Chr 16:9.

49   Cf. Deut 32:29; Pss 64:10 (9); 106:7; Dan 9:13, 25; Neh 8:13.

50   Cf. Isa 41:20; Dan 1:17; 11:33, 35; 12:3, 10; Neh 9:20.

51   Ps 32:8; Dan 9:22.

52   Deut 29:8 (9); Josh 1:8; 1 Sam 18:5, 15; 1 Kgs 2:3;

2 Kgs 18:7; Isa 52:13; Jer 10:21; 20:11; 23:5; 50:9; Prov 17:8.

53   Isa 52:13; Ps 101:2.

54   According to *HALOT* s.v.

55   According to Judg 12:6 as well it was a matter of the varying pronunciation of *s*: v. 6 "They made (an Ephraimite) say Shibboleth (שִׁבֹּלֶת, 'torrent of water'), but he said Siboleth (סִבֹּלֶת), for he could not pronounce it right. Then they seized him and killed him at the fords of the Jordan."

56   See the survey of the research in Elliger, 454; on this passage, 470.

57   See 2 Chr 36:22-23; Ezra 1:1-4; Dan 9:2.

ruler. He is the first, after the ruler. In terms of political structures, it would seem to me appropriate to describe him as the king's vizier. His word corresponds to the ruler's will, he is the "mouthpiece" or "voice." Insofar as this is a heavenly scene and figure, the prophecy of all time can find its unity there.[58] The way in which prophecy is represented on earth in any specific case must be distinguished from this. In this text "his servant" and "his messengers" are clearly on the side of the heavenly One. The messengers support the servant. They are part of the heavenly council. The very term shows that their task is to send, to communicate, and to counsel. If 44:24—45:25 is surveyed as a whole, then these functions really are exercised in this scene, as must be shown in detail.

■ **26b-28** After the royal household has been constituted, the sovereign's activity begins with an edict. The comparison with royal edicts in the countries of the OT world suggests itself. Grammatically, a direct connection with the self-proclamation in v. 24b is effected. The determined Hebrew participles (English: "who speaks . . .") refer to "I am Yahweh."[59] His word is command; in it, he himself acts (first person of the verbs). The link in content is the fact that his edict applies to his whole sphere of sovereignty (cf. "everything," כָּל, v. 24).

The first charge has to do with Jerusalem and the cities of Judah. What is most remote for the exiles has to happen first of all. How long will the restoration take? That could be the anxious underlying question. On the other hand Jerusalem is the center of all hope. Jerusalem is "the city of God" (Pss 46:5 [4];[60] 48:2 [1]).

That the king builds his capital is one of the sovereignty themes.[61] Building ordinances played a part in the king's accession to the throne especially.

The theme of the outward and inward rebuilding of Jerusalem and the cities of Judah was already heard right at the beginning of DtIsa's book (40:2, 9). Here the same theme is similarly addressed as a whole. From 49:14 through chap. 54 DtIsa especially expounds the reinstallation of Zion/Jerusalem to its former status and condition. Jerusalem is once more to become a metropolis (49:21; 54:1-3).[62] The first and most important thing is that Jerusalem will be populated. The people come first, and then the buildings—a good rule for the establishment of every community.

But another special note in the DtIsa context deserves attention. In the OT the *Hophal* of ישׁב, "to sit down, dwell," is otherwise found only in Isa 5:8. Wildberger writes about this Isaiah text:[63] "Owning land was not only a question of the economic condition in which an Israelite found himself, but it also identified his position as a citizen within the community. Whoever had to give up land and property became a simple day laborer or slave and thereby lost his ability to influence public affairs."[64] "The *hophʿal* הוּשַׁב means to be resident in the country, equipped with all public rights and duties. . . . The greed for possession on the part of the rich therefore comes down to depriving their fellow countrymen of their rights. . . ." Wildberger has grasped an important point. I do not share Elliger's skepticism, for the relationship to Isaiah 5 does not depend only on a single verb.[65] Both the context and the conceptional link must

58 See K. Baltzer, *Die Biographie der Propheten* (1975) 110–12, 126, 130, 168.

59 Melugin ("The Structure of Deutero-Isaiah" [1968] 57) has perceived very well the special character of the determined participles: "Normally the hymn uses participial style for past events or for all attributive statements which are essentially timeless . . . vv. 26b-28, in my opinion are the conclusions of the disputation; Yahweh has argued from the known in order to convince doubters of that which is not yet generally agreed upon."

60 See H.-J. Kraus, *Psalms 1–59* (1988) 458ff. on Psalm 46, esp. 462–63 on the glorifying of the city of God [*Psalmen* 1 (5th ed. 1978), esp. excursus 5, "Die Verherrlichung der Gottesstadt"].

61 1 Kgs 9:10-28; 16:23-28; Dan 4:27.

62 Textual operations that eliminate "the cities of Judah" are unnecessary from the standpoint of the content. Jerusalem will again become the "mother city" (μητρόπολις), which has "daughter cities."

63 H. Wildberger, *Isaiah 1–12* (1991) 197–98 [*Jesaja 1–12* (2d ed. 1980) 183].

64 He refers to L. Köhler, "Die hebräische Rechtsgemeinde," in *Der hebräische Mensch* (1953) 147 ["Justice in the Gate," in *Hebrew Man* (1956) 130].

65 In Ezek 35:9 the *Hophal* is conjugated from ישׁב, "to be inhabited" (see KB s.v.). The subject there is the judgment on "Mount Seir," i.e., Edom. In antithesis to the present text of 44:26 the Ezekiel text threatens (v. 4): "I will make your towns ruined towns (חָרְבָּה) and a desolation (שְׁמָמָה)." In the context, the seizure of land is given as a reason for the annihilation (vv. 10, 12; 36:2). The land is legally "the inher-

be noted. The point is Yahweh's gift of the land, in which everyone has a share. The instrument of redemption (גְּאֻלָּה) makes the restoration of solidarity in Israel possible—the adjustment of interests among "brothers," as equals. Basically, this is all formulated in Leviticus 25. But this approach, which is founded on faith, is continually endangered. Ps 69:34-37 (33-36) is no less a program:

> 34   For Yahweh listens to the poor
> and does not despise those of his who are in prison.
> 35   Him heaven and earth must glorify,
> the seas and all that moves in them!
> 36   For "Yahweh" helps Zion,
> will build the cities of Judah.
> They take dwelling and possession there,
> 37   The children of his servants will inherit it,
> and they who love his name will dwell there.
> (Translation following H.-J. Kraus)

The closeness to the DtIsa text is striking, however one defines the precise relationship between the two. The psalm again makes clear that what the text is talking about is the restoration of the rights of free people. Redemption, liberation from debt (גְּאֻלָּה, Lev 25:24) is one of DtIsa's fundamental themes. What follows is an exposition of what it means to say about Jerusalem (and the cities of Judah): "It will be inhabited." That is already the case in 45:18-19, where the reason for the restoration goes back to the creation of the earth: "He did not create it as an empty wasteland (תֹהוּ); he formed it to be inhabited."

Yahweh himself will raise up the "rubble." The word חָרְבָּה is generally found in connection with destroyed cities. It refers to the ruins of houses. But a text such as Ezek 36:35 makes us suspect that in connection with cities it may have had a more particular meaning. In Ezekiel "ruined towns" (הֶחֳרָבוֹת) are contrasted with "fortified towns" (בְּצוּרוֹת). The best illustration is found in

the book of Nehemiah. Nehemiah complains that "the place of my ancestors' graves lies waste (חֲרֵבָה) and its gates have been destroyed by fire" (2:3, 17). What follows is an account of the building of the walls with divine help (2:18; 4:3, 8, 14; esp. 6:16).

Where the present DtIsa text is concerned, this would mean, according to Elliger: "Yahweh personally intervenes on behalf of Jerusalem's rebuilding." But this is apparently necessary because the resistance is so great. It is only when Jerusalem has walls once more that it again has city rights and can enforce them. Under this aspect, what v. 28 says about Jerusalem is not simply a doublet that should be eliminated. To put it in somewhat oversimplified terms: "building" when it means the building of houses is something different from the building of walls. When a city has walls again, this also means the reversal of many prophetic judgment sayings, which cried out that sheep and goats would graze in the place, or that wild animals would slink through the alleys. That is no longer possible once walls and gates protect the city. In DtIsa the theme of the city walls goes further still when, according to 54:11-12, Zion/Jerusalem is crowned with "a mural crown."[66]

The content of the first commission in the divine edict is the charge to populate, build, and protect. It should be noted that the cities of Judah are also mentioned here. It is not only the capital city that is important. The second commission is given to the deep (צוּלָה)[67] and her rivers. The depths too are addressed in personified form.[68] Otherwise they are demythologized. The charge has its practical purpose in the context. DtIsa several times touches on the fear that the rivers could prevent the return (cf. 42:15; 43:2, 16). This would mean that preparations for the return are also part of the theme here. But this section of text is a good

---

itance of the house of Israel" (נַחֲלָה, 35:15). The whole complex of Ezekiel 35–36 is of the greatest interest for DtIsa. See also W. Zimmerli, *Ezekiel* 2 (1983) on the text [*Ezechiel* (1969)], and D. Baltzer, *Ezechiel und Deuterojesaja* (1971).

66   See below on that passage and K. Baltzer, "Stadt-Tyche oder Zion/Jerusalem," in *Alttestamentlicher Glaube und Biblische Theologie: FS H. D. Preuss* (1992) 114–19. English version: "The Polemic against the Gods and Its Relevance for Second Isaiah's Conception of the New Jerusalem," in *Second Temple Studies* (1994) 52–59.

67   "The deep" is fem. here: she possesses "rivers" (see

the suffix of the second person fem. sing.). One would not be surprised if "she" were to appear as personification.

68   This is the only occasion on which the word for the "deep" (צוּלָה) occurs in this form in the OT. It derives from צלל II, "to sink down" (see *HALOT*), which also occurs only once, in Exod 15:10, in the context of the miracle at the Reed Sea: "You let your wind (רוּחַ) blow, and the sea covered them, and they sank down like lead in mighty waters." For מְצוּלָה cf. Exod 15:5; Jonah 2:4 (3); Mic 7:19; Zech 1:8; 10:11; Pss 68:23 (22); 69:3 (2), 16 (15); 88:7 (6); 107:24; Job 4:23; Neh 9:11.

example of the many-layered character of DtIsa's work. In the throne scene as genre, the control over the depths has its place, since the depths are the quintessence of the forces of chaos.[69] The ruler creates the order that makes life in the fullest sense possible, and at his accession above all.

"The depths and their rivers" reflect a mythological geography of the kind found in the Ugaritic texts, for example.[70] El has his seat "at the source of the two rivers, amid the springs of the two depths." These notions have been taken up in the Psalms, and associated with Jerusalem especially.[71] Of special interest for the present text is the struggle between Baal and Yamm in the Ugaritic tradition. As an illustration, O. Kaiser[72] has drawn on the text ʿnt III:33-44, for example,[73] showing that there is probably a connection between the myth and Egyptian traditions (Astarte papyrus,[74] Book of the Dead 108.14-43[75]), as well as with the Typhon myth according to Apollodorus.[76] The background to the myth are the storms that blow up from the sea at the beginning of winter and beat against the coasts from Egypt to Syria.[77] The subduing of the sea as a deity or monster is common to the traditions. In Ugarit this subjugation is the result of Baal's struggle; in Egypt it comes about at Seth's command.[78] The latter view is undoubtedly closer to Isa 44:27. Depths and rivers are banished through Yahweh's word.

For many commentators, the mention of the depths and rivers at this point seems curiously erratic.[79] What has this to do with Cyrus and the rebuilding of Jerusalem? But it could be that this very element is part of the basic fabric of the text. If the development of

44:24 is hypothetically traced (the description of the enthronement of a god, perhaps even the supreme god, who rules over the world—an assembly of the gods, with varying groups, the god's "servant" and his messengers— his sway over the powers of sea and rivers) then this reconstruction corresponds quite strikingly to the picture that can be put together from the texts on which Kaiser draws.

I myself suspect that in writing his work DtIsa was able to find support in traditional forms. The question of already existing dramatic accounts again becomes acute here. DtIsa has taken up the pattern underlying the action entirely along his own lines and has transformed it. He is simply doing what the Christian mystery plays, and even carnival customs, did with the pagan traditions connected with the nature festivals and the seasonal feasts. We can easily imagine that a dragon was one of the stage props here. For his conceptions DtIsa was able to draw on existing traditions such as we find in the Psalms.

Elsewhere too DtIsa shows his familiarity with "the waters of the great primeval flood" (מֵי תְהוֹם רַבָּה, 51:10). In this passage the victory over Rahab and the dragon is equated with the passage through the sea (see also Exod 15:10; Jer 23:7-8). In Isa 54:9 he talks about "the waters of Noah," the primeval flood; for his own day this means the renewed assurance of the covenant of peace given by "Yahweh the merciful one." DtIsa can draw on the biblical tradition in all its breadth, in order to make his testimony for his own day clear. In so doing he is not bound to any particular terminology.[80] "The depths" can in general mean the sovereignty over the world to its

---

69 Cf. Daniel 7.

70 See M. H. Pope, *El in the Ugaritic Texts* (1955) 61–81; F. M. Cross, *Canaanite Myth and Hebrew Epic* (1973); R. J. Clifford, *The Cosmic Mountain in Canaan and the OT* (1972); W. H. Schmidt, *Königtum Gottes in Ugarit und Israel: Zur Herkunft der Königsprädikationen Jahwes* (2d ed. 1966).

71 Ps 29:2ff.: "Yahweh's voice is over the waters"; v. 10: "Yahweh sits enthroned over the flood (לַמַּבּוּל); Yahweh sits enthroned as king forever." Cf. Pss 46:3ff. (2ff.) and 96:11.

72 O. Kaiser, *Die mythische Bedeutung des Meeres in Ägypten, Ugarit und Israel* (1962); see also Jörg Jeremias, *Theophanie* (2d ed. 1976) 90–97, 182–93.

73 Kaiser, *Die mythische Bedeutung*, 74–75.

74 Ibid., 81–91, 150.

75 See ibid., 87.

76 Ibid., 75, 86–88.

77 See ibid., 91.

78 Ibid., 89.

79 Westermann (155 [126]) refers to M. Haller, *Deuterojesaja* (1925): "The idea [image] of the drying up of the deep which now comes in strikes a foreign note." He sees a connection with the "descriptive praise" of God.

80 Cf. Jonah 2:3-4 (2-3), which talks about both Sheol (מִבֶּטֶן שְׁאוֹל), and the deep in the midst of the sea (מְצוּלָה), as well as about the river (נָהָר); cf. also the Ugaritic text ʿnt III:33-44 (C. Gordon, *UL*, 9–11); see Kaiser, *Die mythische Bedeutung des Meeres in Ägypten, Ugarit und Israel* (1962) 69–77, 149.

farthest bounds. But in this passage the phrase can also have been heard in a much more precise sense.[81] In the context of the first instruction to Jerusalem (v. 26), we pointed to the text of Isaiah 5, because that also has to do with slavery for debt. Isaiah announces that the consequence will be that "Sheol opens its jaws wide, opens its mouth beyond measure, so that her [Jerusalem's] glory and her multitude may go down." In Isaiah the destruction of social solidarity brings chaos, as a threat to existence itself. In DtIsa the threat is ended through the divine word. He goes on to expound in 45:18-19 what he means by this.

The third charge mentions Cyrus by name for the first time.[82] He too receives a specific commission.[83] At the same time he is given the title "my shepherd." We have evidence that the ruler was described as shepherd from earliest times, both in Egypt and in Mesopotamia.[84] A king should lead his people, care for them and protect them like a shepherd. The iconography of the shepherd carrying a sheep is also widespread.

Israel knew that Yahweh is a shepherd for his people (Psalms 23; 68:8 [7]; 74:1; 77:21; 78:52-53; 79:13; 95:7; 100:3; 121:4). DtIsa takes up the idea in 40:11. Texts in Jeremiah, Ezekiel and Zechariah show that there were expectations that in the future there would be "good shepherds"—expectations fed not least by the disappointing experiences the people had had with their kings.[85] Of these shepherds the restoration of Israel in the postexilic period was expected. The link between the shepherd concept and the Davidic dynasty is clear. So it must have been all the more shocking when the foreign ruler was described as Yahweh's shepherd.[86] But the idea also implies that the authority of the person bearing the title is a derived authority. If Yahweh himself is the shepherd of his people, "his shepherd" must conform to his edicts and is responsible to him. The first sentence in v. 24 already made clear who *the shepherd's* Lord is too. The textual variant "who says to Jerusalem" (הָאֹמֵר) instead of "in order to say to Jerusalem" (וְלֵאמֹר) shows that there was a factual problem here: who gives the commision to build Jerusalem and the Temple?[87] That Yahweh does so directly would seem to be the easier reading. The series of participles would simply be prolonged.

But the complicated form of the text as it stands brings out something important. Attention has continually been drawn to the Cyrus edict, and we shall go into

---

81   The Targum already suggests the expectation of a pointed historical reference when it renders the passage: "Who says to Babylon it shall be dried up and I will dry out its rivers." Commentators refer frequently to the account of the capture of Babylon by Cyrus in Herodotus (1.189). See also A. Schoors, *I Am God Your Saviour* (1973) 272 on this passage.

82   On the name of Cyrus II (559-529), king of Persia, Heb. כֹּרֶשׁ, Gk. Κῦρος, Old Pers. Kūruš (*Handbuch des Altpersischen* [1964] 130), see W. Eilers, "Kyros," *Beiträge zur Namenforschung* 15 (1964) 180-236, esp. 194 (lit.). In the OT Cyrus's name is mentioned in Isa 44:28; 45:1; Ezra 1:1-2, 7-8; 3:7; 4:3, 5; 2 Chr 36:22-23; Dan 1:21; 10:1. On the problems connected with the mention of Cyrus, see also R. G. Kratz, *Kyros im Deuterojesaja-Buch* (1991) 72-92.

83   There is no reason at all to eliminate v. 28b. Fohrer (81) writes: "This section of the verse should be moved from v. 28, where it is superfluous, to this point (v. 26), where something of the kind is required." Cf. Westermann 152 [124]: "The text is deranged in v. 28b; the first part of 26b is repeated in 28b. The simplest solution is to take the second part of 28b along with 26b."

84   Joachim Jeremias, "ποιμήν," *TDNT* 6:485-502 [*ThWNT* 6:484-501] (further lit.). See also J. A. Soggin, "רעה r‹h to tend," *TLOT* 3:1248 [*THAT*

2:794]; V. Hamp, "Das Hirtenmotiv im AT," in *FS Faulhaber* (1949) 7-20; J. G. Botterweck, "Hirte und Herde im AT und im alten Orient," in *FS Frings* (1960) 339-52; D. Müller, "Der gute Hirte. Ein Beitrag zur Geschichte ägyptischer Bildreden," *ZÄS* 86 (1961) 126-44; M. J. Seux, *Épithètes royales akkadiennes et sumériennes* (1967) 244-50, esp. 441-46; 2 Sam 5:2; Jer 3:15; 23:1ff.; Ezek 34:23; Mic 5:5 (6).

85   Negatively, Jer 2:8; 10:21; 12:10; 23:1-2; 25:34-38; 50:6; Ezek 34:1-10. Positively, Jer 3:15; 23:3-6; Ezek 34:23-24.

86   In my view, to point רע as רֵעַ in the sense of "friend, counselor" weakens the sense (this is Marti's proposal but see already 1QIsaᵃ). David is called "shepherd" in 2 Sam 5:2: "Yahweh said to you: It is you who shall be the shepherd of my people Israel." The mention in Ezekiel corresponds to this (34:23): "I will set up over them a shepherd, my servant David." Cf. 1 Kgs 22:17; Jer 23:4; Mic 5:4 (5).

87   I assume with Schoors, *I Am God Your Saviour* (1973) 267 on this passage, that הֵיכָל, "palace, temple," is here treated as fem.

this presently. For our present DtIsa text, what the original edict looked like is not so important. The real point is: in what transmitted form did DtIsa know it? If we compare 2 Chr 36:23 and Ezra 1:2-4, we see that the essential point there is the building of the temple. The permission given to the exiles to return is bound up with that. The version in Ezra 6:1-6 also has to do solely with the temple.[88] What Cyrus orders according to Isa 44:28b is that Jerusalem should be built and the foundations of the temple laid. But v. 26 went much further when it talked about the founding of the city. The text therefore differentiates very precisely, making clear that the refounding of the city is Yahweh's direct command, while this is only indirectly true of the command to lay the foundations of the temple. That Cyrus gave the commission for the sanctuary is probably also correct historically speaking.

According to OT tradition, the Cyrus edict is more a kind of "protective charter" for the sanctuary. These protective promises and legitimations can be found right down to modern times in inscriptions and plaques on buildings. A promise given by Cyrus could thus have been generally known in the Persian period. Here in DtIsa the refounding of the temple is put down solely to Yahwh's own resolve: "Everything that pleases me/that I wish he will fulfill."

One of the striking facts in DtIsa is that, although there is so much talk about Zion/Jerusalem, temple and cult play a minor role. His mention of the founding of the Temple here is the only time it is mentioned at all. In this respect he differs fundamentally from Ezekiel, Haggai, or Zechariah, for example, or even Ezra. In comparison with them, DtIsa's position here too is more like that of Nehemiah: the temple is mentioned, but that is not where his heart is. The temple is doubtless the place of God's presence in his city, but this presence does not depend on the sacrificial cult.

If Cyrus can be described in a single sentence as shepherd and founder of the temple, this does not look as if a new David was expected. To found the temple is the right of kings, and this right is indirectly exercised by Cyrus. But perhaps this position is not so far removed from that of Chronicles, where David is described as the founder of the temple, while at the end Cyrus orders the rebuilding with prophetic legitimation. This shows that it was possible both theologically and politically to distinguish between the expectation of a messiah-king and the hope for Zion. This will become clearer still in what follows (45:1).

These few verses, 24-28, therefore sound the essential themes of DtIsa's book from chap. 40 to chap. 55.[89] They are woven together with the greatest artistry. A turn of events in heaven and on earth has begun to show itself.

---

88 Cf. also Josephus *Ant.* 11.1.2.
89 Muilenburg, 516: "All the major elements of the prophecy are present in the introduction: redemption, creation, history, monotheism, prophecy, sovereignty and purpose."

45

"Thus says Yahweh to his anointed one, to Cyrus" (45:1)

A. 2. 45:1-8
Installation of Cyrus

1 Thus says Yahweh to his anointed one,[a]
   to Cyrus, whom I have taken by his right hand,
   to subdue peoples before him—
   and I will ungird the hips of kings,
   to open doors before him—
   and gates will not be closed:

2 I myself will go before you
   and will level "city walls" (?).
   I will break bronze doors,
   and I will destroy iron bars,
3 and will give you treasures of darkness
   and hidden stores,
   so that you may know that I am Yahweh.—

   Who calls you by your name, the God of Israel,
4 for the sake of my servant Jacob,
   and Israel my chosen one.
   So I called you by your name.
   I will give you a title of honor, although you have not known/do not know me.

5 *I am Yahweh,* and there is no other.
   Besides me there are no gods.
   I gird you although you have not known/do not know me,
6 so that they may know in the east and in the west[a]
   that besides me there is no other.

   I am Yahweh, and there is no other,
7 who forms light and creates darkness,
   who makes peace/salvation and creates disaster.

   I am Yahweh who does all this.[a]
8 Drop, heavens, from above!
   And let clouds trickle down salvation.
   Let the earth open itself, so that help may <ripen>,[a]
   and let righteousness spring up with it.
   I Yahweh have created it/him.

1[a] See below on this passage.
6[a] Literally: "in the region of the rising of the sun and the region of (its?) setting"; cf. below.
7[a] According to *HALOT* (1:52 [*HALAT* 1:50]) אֵלֶּה ("these, this") can be related (1) to what has been said previously; and (2) to what then follows. In view of the triple "I am Yahweh" I would relate the statement to what follows (contrary to the Masoretes).
8[a] The sing. וְיֵפֶר (cf. LXX[Mss], Vg) should probably be read instead of the plur. וְיִפְרוּ." 1QIsa[a] has ויפרח, "so that . . . springs up/blossoms."

After the communication of the divine edict, which concerns the whole world, an installation follows, in the framework of the throne scene. In this scene Cyrus's legitimation is made plain.[90] The text continues the skillfully crafted structure and the interlaced statements of 44:24-28. "I am Yahweh" is uttered three times (45:5, 6, 7). The sovereign's will is proclaimed, and the reasons for his intentions given in three declarations:

---

90 M. Haller, "Die Kyroslieder Deuterojesajas," in *Eucharistērion I: Studien zur Religion und Literatur des Alten und Neuen Testaments. FS H. Gunkel* (1923) 261–77; E. Jenni, "Die Rolle des Kyros bei Deuterojesaja," *ThZ* 10 (1954) 241–56; idem, *Die politischen Voraussagen der Propheten* (1956) 100–103; N. E. Simon, "König Cyrus und die Typologie," *Judaica* 11 (1955) 83–89; G. Reinwald, *Cyrus im zweiten Teil des Buches Isaias* (1956); further lit.: see P. Auvray, "Cyrus, instrument du Dieu unique," *BVC* 50 (1963) 17–23; and Kratz, *Kyros im Deuterojesaja-Buch* (1991), esp. 19–35.

1. (vv. 2-3) I myself will go before you . . . so that (לְמַעַן) you know . . ."
2. (v. 4) "For the sake of (לְמַעַן) my servant . . . I will give you a name of honor . . ."
3. (vv. 5-6a) I gird you . . . so that (לְמַעַן) they may know . . ."

It is not a rigidly consistent series; the sequence is varied. "Although you have not known me" links vv. 4 and 5; "and there is no other" links vv. 5 and 6.

The triple repetition of the vowel sequence ă - a - ē in 45:2 can hardly be fortuitous: "I will level" (אֲיַשֵּׁר), "I will break" (אֲשַׁבֵּר), "I will destroy" (אֲגַדֵּעַ). The final phrase in 45:7, "who does all this," again takes up 44:24, the beginning of the throne scene. The style has the dignity appropriate to the action. The stylistically elevated elements are in accord with the content. Yahweh is the ruler, not Cyrus. This already indicates the tension that then makes itself clearly felt in 45:9-13: has Cyrus not been assigned too high a rank?

That the text is not a unified whole has continually been felt to be a difficulty in determining the *genre* of this section. Begrich assumed it to be a "salvation oracle." This designation can then be modified. From a literary standpoint, the passage can be divided into two salvation oracles, as Fohrer proposed, vv. 1-3 and 4-7. A closer definition would be "royal oracle," this being the suggestion of von Waldow and Weippert,[91] for example. Westermann assumes that "its original place was the king's enthronement."[92]

If we assume that a scene is being played, the connection between what is done ("take his hand") and what is said becomes comprehensible. Cyrus is directly addressed in vv. 2-5;[93] the third person masculine suffixes already make this clear. In 45:1 the suffix is second person masculine; Cyrus is presented to an auditorium,[94] which then again appears as plural in v. 6 ("so that they may know . . .").

■ **1-4** What we have here is not just a random salvation saying. It is connected with the special function that Cyrus is supposed to exercise. But we are still left with the question: What is this person being installed *as*? If the answer is put in negative terms, it can be said that the royal title is not used, nor is there any mention of a throne. The text says "whom I have taken by his right hand" (v. 1), not "sit down at my right hand!"[95] The functions are initially warlike, as they already were in 41:2-3 and 41:25: "I will . . . ungird kings" (45:1) and "I will gird you" (v. 5). To take someone's hand is certainly a gesture, but it is a gesture signaling a purpose. If one takes someone's hand, one can guide and lead that person. This is the way Yahweh led Israel out of Egypt, according to Jer 31:32.[96] In a transferred sense, it means the promise of guidance and protection.

Cyrus's sovereignty is legitimated in three ways: peoples will be subjugated (לְרַד־לְפָנָיו),[97] kings disarmed, and cities and palaces thrown open. The same thing is again

---

91 M. H. E. Weippert, "De herkomst van het heilsorakel voor Israel bij Deutero-Jesaja," *NedThT* 36 (1982) 1–11, esp. 9–11.

92 Westermann, "Sprache und Struktur der Prophetie Deuterojesajas," in *Forschung am Alten Testament* 1 (1964) 150.

93 LXX inserts in v. 1 κύριος ὁ θεός, and Duhm suggests adopting this reading by following יהוה with a הָאֵל, "the god." This proposal is worth consideration. DtIsa uses אֵל or אֱלֹהִים as the term for God particularly in contexts that have to do with foreign nations; see 45:15; cf. Jonah 1:6; 3:5, 8-9.

94 See here Merendino, *Der Erste und der Letzte: Eine Untersuchung von Jes 40–48* (1981) 417: "The deictic character of the אשר at the beginning (v. 1)–'This one there . . . I have'–speaks in favor of this being an identification proceeding" (with reference to 1 Sam 9:17; 10:24; 16:12). See also the installation in the monarchy in the framework of the assembly of the gods, R. J. Clifford, "The Tent of El and the Israelite Tent of Meeting," *CBQ* 33 (1971) 221–27.

95 Ps 110:1.

96 See also Exod 23:20ff. For the installation cf. Isa 42:6.

97 The form לְרַד is unusual. It is generally considered to derive from רדד, "drive back, subject"; thus Torrey (*Second Isaiah* [1928]), who refers to Ps 144:2. One would expect לְרֹד. Further instances of the verb in this sense are uncertain (see *HALOT* 3:1189–90 [*HALAT* 4:1110]). One might consider whether originally a form of ירד, "to go down," should be assumed. It can be used in the sense of "fetch down," e.g., Edom from its mountains, to compel it to leave its dwelling places (Jer 49:16; Obad 3–4). In a transferred sense in the *Hiphil* it can mean "bring down" as a humiliation (Jer 49:16; Hos 7:12; Amos 9:2). But ירד is frequently used for the descent to the underworld, for the death of individuals and peoples (cf. Isa 14:4-21, with the fall of the universal ruler [vv. 11, 15], who according to vv. 22-23 is identified with Babylon). In Ezek 32:17-32 it is Egypt's descent into the underworld (vv. 18, 24-25; cf. 31:15-18). In Ezek 26:19-21 Tyre or its princes are threatened with the same fate (28:1-16).

specifically confirmed in v. 2 through the announcement that cities will be taken.[98]

But even if the world of myth can still be detected, in the present text this is transmuted into a historical account of Cyrus's deeds. For "the depths and their rivers" have already been subjugated by the divine word, according to 44:27. Torrey has rightly observed that Cyrus's name has been inserted here.[99] But it is not merely a matter of the interpolation of the name in this passage, for that could easily be expunged. The conflicts and problems of the Persian era are much too deeply woven into the whole present book of DtIsa for a simple elimination of the name to make any essential difference. That is why Cyrus is now the subject.

Attention has continually been drawn to the relation between this text and the so-called Cyrus edict.[100]

Marduk's choosing of Cyrus and the renewal of sanctuaries and cult have been compared with the DtIsa passage. These statements are not specific to this Babylonian Cyrus text. They belong to a long tradition in Mesopotamia of royal inscriptions on buildings. It is unlikely that the DtIsa text derives directly from these. But the Cyrus cylinder indicates the religious policy of the Achaemenids very well,[101] and shows the expectations that were linked with Cyrus in Babylon. The point of comparison is that Cyrus sees himself as legitimated by a foreign, Babylonian god, Marduk, and that he reverences the god accordingly.[102]

It was not least through his (relative) tolerance that Cyrus II became a model for people living later. For the Greeks, and for the Athenians above all, the Persians after their invasion were "the barbarians." This picture was passed on to us in the West by way of a classical education, and still exerts an influence down to the present day.[103] But even for the Greeks,

---

Isa 41:2 must be understood in the sense of "go down," especially if the reading in 1QIsaᵃ יורד Hiphil is adopted (see above on this passage; cf. also Num 16:30; Ps 55:16 [15]). There the subject is the "islands and nations" that are already in the underworld. See G. Mayer, "ירד yārad," TDOT 6:315–22, esp. 319–21 [ThWAT 3:894–901, esp. 898–900] on the descent into Hades. But it is also possible that DtIsa is already correcting the traditional mythological language about the *nations* who go down to the underworld, since he talks about "subduing" here.

98   A. Hoffmann explains convincingly that הַדוּרִים in v. 2 means a ring of walls; see his "Jahwe schleift Ringmauern—Jes 45:2aβ," in *FS J. Ziegler* (1972) 2:187–95.

99   Torrey (*Second Isaiah* [1928] 41) on what he considers to be "The 'Cyrus' Interpolations in 45:1 and 44:28": "The conclusion, supported by such evidence, internal and external, ought to be no longer in doubt; the word is *an explanatory addition to the text*, by a later hand." My own opinion, however, is that this "later hand" is DtIsa's own. See also Smart on this passage.

100 For the text of the Cyrus cylinder, see A. L. Oppenheim, *ANET* 315–16; K. Galling, *TGI*² 82–84; *TUAT* 1:407–10 (with lit.).
     (11) . . . All countries together he [Marduk] inspected, he examined (them). (12) He sought for a just ruler after his own heart, he took him by his hand: he called Cyrus, the king of Anshan, he pronounced his name to exercise rule over the whole universe. (13) He put

Gutium and the whole of Ummanmanda under his feet. The black-headed people whom he allowed his hands to subdue (14) he kept in law and justice. Marduk, the great Lord, who cares for his people, looked kindly on his good deeds and his righteous heart. (15) He commanded him to go to his city Babylon and let him take the path to Babylon. He went at his side like a friend and comrade. (16) His extensive troups, the number of whom was as immeasurable as the waters of a river, marched armed with weapons at his side. (17) He let him enter his city Babylon without struggle and battle. . . . (27) Me, Cyrus, the king, who worships him, and Cambyses, the son of my body, as well as all my troops, (28) he graciously blessed. In prosperity we [walk] joyfully before him. . . . (32) I brought the gods who were living there [in the aforementioned countries and cities] back to their own place and let them occupy an eternal dwelling. I gathered all the people and took them back to the places where they lived" (translation following *TUAT*).

101 On the problems see A. Kuhrt, "The Cyrus Cylinder and Achaemenid Imperial Policy," *JSOT* 25 (1983) 83–97.

102 Westermann ("Sprache und Struktur der Prophetie Deuterojesajas," in *Forschung am Alten Testament* 1 [1964] 148) sees this correctly.

103 For the historical discussion see H. Bengtson, *Griechische Geschichte* (1977) 130–31; R. N. Frye, *The History of Ancient Iran* (1983); A. R. Burn, "Persia

Cyrus was a good ruler. In his drama the *Persians* (472 B.C.E.) Aeschylus makes the spirit of Darius say of Cyrus:[104]

> Since our Lord Zeus first ordained this high estate that one ruler should bear sway over all Asia with its flocks and wield the sceptre of its government . . . third, after him, Cyrus, blest in his fortune, came to the throne and stablished peace for all his people. The Lydians and Phrygians he won to his rule, and the whole of Ionia he subdued by force; for the gods hated him not, since he was right-minded.[105]

Herodotus (c. 484–430 B.C.E.) cites the saying of the Persians:

> In the reigns of Cyrus and Cambyses after him there was no fixed tribute, but payment was made in gifts. It is by reason of this fixing of tribute[106] and other like ordinances, that the Persians called Darius the huckster, Cambyses the master, and Cyrus the father;[107] for Darius made petty profit out of everything, Cambyses was harsh and arrogant, Cyrus was merciful and ever wrought for their well-being.[108]

The function of the positive Cyrus picture as a criticism of the present day is perceptible in Xenophon's *Cyropaedia* 8.8 (Xenophon lived c. 430–354 B.C.E.):[109]

> 1. That Cyrus's empire was the greatest and most glorious of all kingdoms in Asia—of that it may be its own witness.[110] For it was bounded on the east by the Indian Ocean, on the north by the Black Sea, on the west by Cyprus and Egypt, and on the south by Ethiopia. And although it was of such magnitude, it was governed by the single will (γνώμη) of Cyrus; and he honored his subjects and cared for them as if they were his own children; and they, on their part, reverenced Cyrus as a father.[111] 2. Still, as soon as Cyrus was dead, his children at once fell into dissension, states and nations began to revolt, and everything began to deteriorate."[112]

> 27. For I maintain that I have proved that the Persians of the present day and those living in the dependencies are less reverent toward the gods, less dutiful to their relatives, less upright in their dealings with all men, and less brave in war than they were of old.

Finally we may remember that Alexander the Great claimed to be Cyrus's successor. This was one of the reasons why he visited Cyrus's tomb and had it restored.[113]

If we draw for comparison upon the Babylonian and the Greek reception of the Cyrus tradition, we can see that DtIsa offers a further variant, with both similarities and differences. The favorable presentation of Cyrus is clearly a common denominator, and so is the character of his rule, which embraced many peoples and kingdoms. According to 45:4 Yahweh gives Cyrus a title of honor (אֲכַנְּךָ). Verse 1 is now interpreted as the subjugation of peoples and the "ungirding" of kings.

The dispute is already implicit in the first word of the divine speech in v. 1: "Thus says Yahweh to his anointed one (לִמְשִׁיחוֹ), to Cyrus." This already sounds the keynote.[114] For Israel this designation must initially have been a tremendous provocation, for it was on this concept that the whole monarchical tradition depended.[115]

and the Greeks," in I. Gershevitch, ed., *The Cambridge History of Iran*, vol. 2: *The Median and Achaemenian Periods* (1985) 292–391.

104 Aeschylus *Persians* 308–9.

105 θεὸς γὰρ οὐκ ἤχθηρεν, ὡς εὔφρων ἔφυ.

106 κατεστηκὸς οὐδὲν φόρου πέρι, ἀλλὰ δῶρα ἀγίνεον· διὰ δὲ ταύτην τὴν ἐπίταξιν του φόρου. . . .

107 Δαρεῖος μὲν ἦν κάπηλος, Καμβύσης δὲ δεσπότης, Κῦρος δὲ πατήρ.

108 Trans. A. D. Godley, *Herodotus* 3.88–89 (LCL 2:116–17 [1921; rev. 1938, reprint 1971]).

109 Trans. W. Miller, Xenophon *Cyropaedia* 8.8.1–2, 27 (LCL 2:438–41, 452–53 [1914]). See also Herodotus's presentation of Cyrus as a contrast to Xerxes.

110 Ὅτι μὲν δὴ καλλίστη καὶ μεγίστη τῶν ἐν τῇ Ἀσίᾳ ἡ Κύρου βασιλεία ἐγένετο αὐτὴ ἑαυτῇ μαρτυρεῖ.

111 καὶ ἐκεῖνός τε τοὺς ὑφ᾽ ἑαυτῷ ὥσπερ ἑαυτοῦ παῖδας ἐτίμα τε καὶ ἐθεράπευεν, οἵ τε ἀρχόμενοι Κῦρον ὡς πατέρα ἐσέβοντο.

112 πάντα δ᾽ ἐπὶ τὸ χεῖρον ἐτρέπετο.

113 Texts: Strabo *Geography* 15.3.7 (730); Arrian *Anabasis* 6.29.4–11. See S. Lauffer, *Alexander der Große* (lit. updated by K. Brodersen; 3d ed. 1993).

114 Young thinks here (195): "The form *mashiaḥ* (anointed) is stronger than the passive participle, *mashuaḥ*. It denotes in the first place the fact that an anointing has taken place." This could suggest that the account is describing the anointing of Cyrus. Cf. the anointing of David in the synagogue at Dura-Europos: E. Goodenough, *Jewish Symbols*, vol. 11: *Symbolism in the Dura Synagogue* (1964), pl. VII West Wall. On the anointing see E. Kutsch, *Salbung als Rechtsakt im AT und im Alten Orient* (1963).

115 See K. Seybold, "משׁח *māšaḥ*," *ThWAT* 5:46–59; M.

"David" was the prototype of the anointed one.[116] Of course prophets[117] and priests[118] can also be said to be anointed in the OT. But in a scene that is so unequivocally linked with statements about sovereignty, and in which the argument is pursued in quite precise political or constitutional terms ("Jerusalem," "the cities of Judah"), we can assume that for listeners the declaration of the anointing established the link with the Davidic dynasty and its claim. To put it somewhat drastically: Cyrus is the new David! The dignity of the "anointed one" is transferred to a foreign ruler.[119] According to 44:24-28, this ruler was Cyrus as founder of the temple; here it is Cyrus as sovereign.

The conflict becomes clear if we compare the positions of the Deuteronomistic history on the one hand and the prophet Jeremiah and the Chronicler on the other.[120] There was a messianic-royal expectation that hoped for the restoration of the Davidic dynasty and of Israel/Judah's existence as a state. The Nathan prophecy in 2 Samuel 7 remained in force, even when in a later generation Jehoiachin, the last legitimate king, was in exile. From this, a position that proceeds from the premise of divine sovereignty over the whole world must be distinguished. This second position was maintained above all in prophecy. It was able to address and come to terms with the collapse of national existence through the downfall of Jerusalem and the exile, and could therefore see even foreign rulers as legitimate. The reference to Jeremiah at the close of the Chronicler's history is an example.

The foundation for this theology was laid when Isaiah felt able to call the Assyrians the instrument of his God (Isa 10:5), and when Jeremiah terms Nebuchadnezzar "my servant" (Jer 43:10; also 25:9; 27:6). Belief in Yahweh as creator and king of the world makes it possible to relativize earthly sovereignty. This corresponds to DtIsa's position too, and puts him in line with prophetic tradition. Anyone who can call Cyrus "the anointed one" will hardly expect a new Davidic king.

A comparison with the Greek texts leads us to suspect that in DtIsa there may also be latent criticism of the present situation in the ideal figure Cyrus-David. This is especially possible if we assume a date for DtIsa in the Nehemiah period. Appeal was made to Cyrus to uphold the rights already conceded. Cyrus's legitimation through Yahweh is not affected. But present-day practice was measured against him.

It is moving to see in DtIsa the way in which tradition draws to a point in a historical figure like Cyrus. One may ask theologically how identification with the Persian ruler could be possible without any restriction, as it apparently was. The following texts show that this was already a problem in DtIsa's own time. But in the reception of DtIsa the question of the relationship between divine and earthly sovereignty was continually thought about afresh, with Cyrus as an example. For faith in this God, rule over the world was never again unquestioned.

According to the present text, 45:2 can be viewed as a description of the capture of Babylon. This is especially probable if one accepts the explanation of הֲדוּרִים as "ring of walls."[121] The parallelism between Jerusalem, whose walls are to be rebuilt, and Babylon, whose walls

---

Noth, "Office and Vocation in the Old Testament," in *The Laws in the Pentateuch and Other Studies* (1966) 229–49 ["Amt und Berufung im Alten Testament (1958)," in *Gesammelte Studien zum Alten Testament* (3d ed. 1966) 309–33]; E. Kutsch, *Salbung;* T. N. D. Mettinger, *King and Messiah: The Civil and Sacral Legitimation of the Israelite Kings* (1976), esp. 185–232.

116 Cf. 1 Sam 12:3; 16:1-13, esp. v. 6; 24:6-7, 10; 26:9, 11, 16, 23; 2 Sam 1:14; 2:4; 5:3; 19:22; also Pss 2:2; 18:51 (50); 20:7 (6); 28:8; 84:10; 89:39 (38); Lam 4:20. The anointing secures the king's inviolability and dignity.

117 See 1 Kgs 19:16; cf. Isa 61:1 (?).

118 See Exod 29:7; 30:30; Lev 4:3, 5, 16; 6:15 (22); 8:12; cf. Zech 4:14; also Dan 9:25; 1 Chr 29:22 for the postexilic high priests.

119 This is also in contradiction to Deut 17:15.

120 See K. Baltzer, "Das Ende des Staates Juda und die Messias-Frage," in *Studien zur Theologie der alttestamentlichen Überlieferungen. FS G. von Rad* (1961) 33–43.

121 In accordance with the Masoretic pointing. The connection with Akk. *dûru,* meaning a particular kind of wall, has recently become clear; see A. Hoffmann, "Jahwe schleift Ringmauern—Jes 45:2aβ," in *FS J. Ziegler* (1972) 187–96; C. H. Southwood, "The Problematic *hᵃdûrîm* of Isaiah XLV 2," *VT* 25 (1975) 801–2.

are razed to the ground (v. 2), would then be even clearer. We know that Babylon was captured by Cyrus, and the sources show that it probably fell without a struggle.[122]

The mention in the text of the "treasures and stores" (v. 3) that Cyrus will receive is strange. In the framework of the installation, this is a "privilege" for the one installed. The Persians were well known in the ancient world for their purposeful accumulation of treasure.[123] They built up a good administration that extended over their whole empire. The books of Daniel, Ezra, and Nehemiah give an impression of it from the Jewish perspective. For the subjugated countries, Persian practice was a positive change from the policy of the Assyrian conquerers.

By introducing coined money for the payment of taxes the Persians achieved a more effective income and a link between decentralized and centralized elements in government. If too little capital flowed back into the different parts of the empire, however, and the ability to pay taxes was unduly strained, tensions inevitably arose.

It is against this background that we can also hear the promise to Cyrus that he has received "treasures and stores." That meant that his claim had been met. This is all the more the case because in the same scene, in 45:13 and 45:14, the question of costs comes up again. The biblical text knows, and states austerely as a matter of simple fact, that Cyrus did not know Yahweh (vv. 4 and 5).[124] But Yahweh's uniqueness will become evident to the whole world.

■ 5-8 Verses 6-7 contain three statements in which at this point Yahweh's all-embracing sovereignty is acknowledged. In each case they are paired antitheses that embrace and declare the "all" (כָל־אֵלֶּה).[125] "From the rising of the sun (the east) until its setting (the west)"[126] means the whole world. Yahweh is not the God of a single country, and cannot be identified with a single people. His lordship is therefore not nationally limited. "Light and darkness"—the antithesis explicitly declares that both are created. The creation account in the Priestly writing in Genesis 1 is not far off, and there is also an echo of the hymnic declarations in the Psalms. The comparison between Psalm 104 and Akhenaton's "Hymn to the Sun" makes one difference clear. The sun as god rules only over the day. In the darkness the forces of chaos arise. But according to Psalm 104 God cares even for the sustenance of the lions. Here the darkness is part of his creation, and hence of his sovereignty.

If we look forward from these two double declarations to the third, it is probable that it too establishes an "everything." Peace (שָׁלוֹם) is a condition in which interests and claims are brought into a balanced relationship to one another. Consequently the rendering "salvation"

122 Cf. from the Cyrus cylinder 17: "He [Marduk] let him enter his city Babylon without struggle and battle." Cf. Herodotus *History* 1.191. The date is probably October 29, 539 B.C.E. (see Frye, *The History of Ancient Iran* [1983] 94).

123 Herodotus *History* 1.178–83; Xenophon *Cyropaedia* 5.2.8; 7.2.11; see also Jer 50:37; 51:13; Hab 2:6-8. The victory over Croesus of Lydia and the conquest of Sardis in the winter of 547/546, with the seizure of Croesus's proverbial treasure, made Cyrus famous and was not the least of the factors that made his later campaigns possible (see Herodotus *History* 1.69–93; D. Schlumberger, "L'argent grec dans l'empire achémenide," *MDAFA* 14 [1953] 55–57).

124 But see Josephus *Ant.* 11.1.2–3: "Cyrus knew these things since he had read the book of his prophecy which Isaiah had left behind two hundred and ten years earlier."

125 G. Lambert, "Lier et délier: L'expression de la totalité par l'opposition de deux contraires," *VivPen* 3 (1943/44) 91–103; P. P. Boccaccio, "I termini contrari come espressioni della totalità in Ebraico," *Bib* 33 (1952) 173–90.

126 Delitzsch: "The *ah* from וּמִעֲרָבָה is is not a feminine ending (LXX, Targ., Jer.), but a feminine suffix with *He raphato pro mappic* (Kimchi); cf. 23:17, 18; 34:17 . . . שֶׁמֶשׁ here, as in Gen 15:17, Nah 3:17; Mal 3:20 and always in Arabic, is feminine, for the west is everywhere called מַעֲרָב (Arab. *magrib*)" (2:220 [altered; 473]). North (148): מערבה Lit. 'its place of setting,' though there is no need to insert *mappîq* in the *hē*: cf. GK 91e." See H. Ringgren, "זרח *zārach*; מִזְרָח *mizrāch*," *TDOT* 4:141–43 [*ThWAT* 2:661–62]; H. Niehr, "עֶרֶב *ᶜereb* . . . מַעֲרָב *maᶜᵃrāb*," *ThWAT* 6:359–66.

is appropriate. This is especially the case in a legally ordered relationship, for example in the framework of a covenant (בְּרִית). In this context "evil" (רָע)[127] is the supervention of the curse that follows a breach of the covenant.

In the countries surrounding ancient Israel and Judah, it was the gods responsible for oaths who pursued people who broke covenants. Since for DtIsa no other gods exist, Yahweh himself is responsible for "evil." Evil can hence in no way be ascribed to the creation of any other metaphysical being.[128] Salvation and disaster are set over against each other. The responsibility of human beings for salvation and disaster as a consequence of what they do is adhered to. In the context of DtIsa, this third double declaration is certainly a further step, an intensification. Nothing that happens is outside Yahweh's will and sovereignty.[129]

These formulations mean a clear rejection of every kind of dualism. If the starting point is the belief in creation that DtIsa proclaims, this is no more than consistent. It has many times been pointed out that the dualisms light-darkness and correspondingly good-evil are characteristic of Persian religion.[130] Right down to the gnosticism of all ages, dualism remains a temptation, because it seems so convincing. Israel endured the acceptance even of disaster at the hand of its God. By doing so it held fast to the assurance that no power can

be stronger than God, and that whatever happened it could never be wrested from his hand.

Again, the declarations in this verse can be heard in different ways. For Israel they mean: Yahweh can end the curse and its consequences, even Jerusalem's destruction and the exile; and he has in fact done so. For those listening this was reality: "they have perceived it" is the sense in which the tense in v. 6a can be altered. If it is taken in the narrower context of Cyrus's installation, commissioning, and prerogative, the sentence can also, I believe, be heard as: "'Peace' (שָׁלוֹם) is there for Cyrus, but in abolishing 'peace' Yahweh can also create 'evil.'"[131] DtIsa is not unreservedly on the side of the great power. It is salvation and disaster, blessing and curse—which Israel has faced from the very beginning through its relationship to God, a decision that the spectators face too.

This text is the passage in which Cyrus is actually named. Twice earlier he has been announced (41:21-29; 42:5-9) and twice named; in this act he remains present (44:24—45:17), and then follow only two other mentions without the name (46:9-11; 48:12-15). Because of the way he is introduced in 41:2, one has the impression that he moves through the whole section.

The link of v. 8 with vv. 1-7 is clear. Again the text repeats: "I am Yahweh." In vv. 5 and 6 this was twice linked with "there is no other," in v. 7 with "who does *all*

---

127 1QIsa[a] reads instead of "peace" (שלום) "good" (טוב), thus making the proximity to blessing and curse even clearer.

128 If we presuppose a scenic presentation, it is worth considering whether the three pairs did not also come on as personifications. They can at all events be imagined iconographically. Cf. the sun and moon in representations of the crucifixion and throne scenes in Christian iconography. See also, e.g., the rising quadriga of Sol and Luna's chariot and horses, which are driving into the sea, on the Arch of Constantine in Rome: F. Gerke, *Spätantike und frühes Christentum* (1967), plate appendix no. 4 and 2.

129 For the dogmatic discussion about this text, see Young, 200: "The Bible teaches that there is a *decretum absolutum,* that God has foreordained whatsoever comes to pass. Likewise, the Bible also teaches the responsibility of the creature. . . . There is a third position, namely to accept both aspects even though one cannot harmonize nor reconcile them" (with reference to Ps 33:11; Isa 14:24; 46:9, 10; Dan

4:35; Acts 2:23; Rom 11:33-36; Eph 1:4; 3:9, 11; 2 Tim 1:9; 1 Pet 1:20; Rev 17:17). Other commentators mention Gen 1:9; Jer 33:25; Amos 5:8. See also H. Haag, "'Ich mache Heil und erschaffe Unheil' (Jes 45,7)," in *FS J. Ziegler* (1972) 179–85. Beuken makes an important comment (238): "The sayings that God creates darkness and woe do not just mean . . . that he produces them, but above all that he holds sway over them." He points out that the terms used in DtIsa characterize cosmic and historical phenomena (cf. for "light" 42:6, 16; 49:6; 51:4; for "darkness" 42:7; for "peace" 41:3; 48:8, 22; 52:7; 53:5; 54:10, 13; 55:12; for "evil" 41:23; 47:10).

130 E.g., by Fohrer.

131 Fohrer (84) on this passage : "It is not a question of Persian or Israelite policy, but of God's. . . . Since God has not called him [Cyrus] because of his glorious deeds, but since the deeds follow only on the call, the glory is not the king's but God's."

this." Now we are told in v. 8: "I have created it." The purpose is to extol Yahweh's uniqueness; in a further intensification, v. 8 proclaims the divine lordship. In its very essence this lordship means salvation, help, and righteousness. But there is a tension in these declarations that becomes clear only against the background of the tradition history of this unit.[132] In the exegesis of the throne scene from 44:24 onward, it proved useful to inquire first of all about the earlier forms of the text.

In v. 8 the mythological complex of ideas is easily detectable, as is the link with the cycle of the seasons. Here we may leave aside for the moment the terms "salvation," "help," and "righteousness." The rain makes the earth fruitful; this is declared to be an engendering and a giving birth. Grammatically, "heavens" and "clouds" are masculine, so the corresponding verbs also take the masculine form.[133] The earth is feminine, so what it does also takes the feminine form. The verbs have a sexual connotation that can be heard more or less unequivocally. Since the text has to do with the sexual realm, the early versions already had difficulties with it. The rain corresponds to the dripping of the semen (רעף). The earth opens itself (פתח)[134] to conceive. What follows

requires familiarity with the ancient understanding of procreation and birth. We should now expect declarations about the growth of the embryo. There was already a rough knowledge of this, as Job 10:10-12 shows. But according to the present MT, it is the male procreative force that effects "the bringing of fruit" (פרה).[135] Consequently the verb is again masculine plural and continues to be so until the time of birth. Then the woman comes into her own: she lets the child grow or "spring up" (צמח) by nourishing it. The same sequence is somewhat clearer in 55:10: the rain (masc.) descends, drenches the earth, "and lets it give birth" (וְהוֹלִידָהּ). This last phrase takes the place of "they bring fruit" (וְיִפְרוּ), which is so disputed in 45:8. In 55:10 we again have a mention of "growing, springing up" (וְהִצְמִיחָהּ). There too it is the rain that causes this to happen. But the reference may be intended as a comparison with the universal efficacy of the "word" (דבר, v. 11), a comparison that runs throughout.

Fertility in nature and human fertility belong together, resulting from the same vital force. One can infer this from many biblical texts. It is Yahweh who confers this vital force. But there is a decisive conflict here.[136] Other

---

132 The commentators are very uncertain in their definition of the genre of v. 8. According to Duhm it is "a little lyrical eruption like 42:10ff. and 44:23ff.," Marti calls it a "lyric intermezzo," and Muilenburg takes a similar view. According to Westermann it is "a short hymn" as a "distinctive ending" to the Cyrus oracle; cf. North. In contrast, Crüsemann (*Studien zur Formgeschichte von Hymnus und Danklied in Israel* [1969] 45 n. 2) rightly objects that there is no invitation to praise. See also Beuken; Merendino (*Der Erste und der Letzte: Eine Untersuchung von Jes 40–48* [1981]) calls it an "implementation saying," but thinks the verse is secondary (424), as Fohrer did earlier.

133 Job 36:27-29 partly uses the same verbs, but is clearly more interested in the scientific description of the process. On the other hand, in Ps 72:6 the king is compared with rain. See H.-J. Kraus on that passage in *Psalms 60–150* (1989) 78 [*Psalmen* (5th ed. 1978) 658–59], with parallels "from ancient Near Eastern kingship."

134 With reference to the possible sexual interpretation, M. H. Goshen-Gottstein ("Theory and Practice of Textual Criticism," *Textus* 3 [1963] 155 n. 93) draws attention to the Midrash (*Gen. Rab.* § XIII):
"תפתח ארץ"—כנקבה זו שהיא פותחת לזכר;
"ויפרו ישע"—שהן פרין ורבין

135 For the reading ויפרח in 1QIsaᵃ in place of MT's

reading, see P. A. H. de Boer, *Second Isaiah's Message* (1956) 71–72. One has the impression that the Qumran Isaiah scroll is already eliminating the offensive features of the text! For example, instead of "The earth opens" (תִּפְתַּח־אֶרֶץ) it has "he speaks to the earth" (האמר לארץ). According to K. Elliger, "Dubletten im Bibeltext," in: *A Light unto My Path. FS J. M. Myers* (1974) 131–40, esp. 135–37, the copy used for the LXX text had the original: "let it ripen" (וְיִפַּר). Even this is an easier reading, however. In contrast, Naegelsbach (527 on this passage) already observed correctly: "The already mentioned heaven and earth are the subject of יפח. The heaven is thought of as a masculine and fertilizing potency, the earth as a feminine potency that conceives and brings forth."

136 In this dispute the text belongs to the theological tradition of prophecy, especially Hosea's; cf. Hos 2:20-25.

137 See *CTA* 3 II = V AB-B = ˤnt II, cited in W. Beyerlin, *Near Eastern Religious Texts Relating to the Old Testament* (1978) 193; cf. 195 [*Religionsgeschichtliches Textbuch zum Alten Testament* (1975) 215; cf. 218]: After the struggle the goddess Anat washes "the blood of soldiers from her hands" (l. 34). "She draws water and washes herself—dew of the heaven, fat of the earth, a shower of rain from the rider on the clouds [term for Baal], the dew of heaven which

gods claim this same sovereignty over nature—in the OT world Baal, the weather god, especially. So it is not by chance that texts close to 45:8 are found among the mythical Ugaritic texts from Ras Shamra.[137] But we must expect that there was a whole variety of traditions, of which undoubtedly only a fraction have come down to us. Individual motifs are combined in different ways and newly interpreted. Deut 28:12 acknowledges: "Yahweh will open for you his rich storehouse, the heavens, to give rain to your land in its season, in order that he may bless all the work of your hands." It is Yahweh who does this, and no other god.

The special thing about the present text (v. 8) is that it does not stop at the orders of nature, their restoration and preservation. Reality is not just nature, engendering, and fertility. Reality is justice in social behavior too, justice in relation to God and one's neighbor. The terms "salvation," "help," "righteousness," or "justice" are artistically interpolated into the mythological texts that we may suppose provided the background. According to its form, "salvation" (צֶדֶק) is masculine, "righteousness" (צְדָקָה), from the same Hebrew root, is feminine. The "shoot" that comes from them and is called "help" (יֶשַׁע) is again masculine.

Is it still possible to trace mythological elements in the three concepts? If the context were different, one could conceive of a male deity, a female deity, and a child or youthful deity—a kind of triad. But in this context it is belief in Yahweh as creator that is acknowledged, over against speculations of this kind (v. 7b: "I am Yahweh who does all this"). Yahweh sets the process going through his proclamation. The concepts therefore become personifications[138] of his will. They are now sent out into the world.

A survey of the wider context of DtIsa's book gives us a strange picture that supports these reflections. Salvation (צֶדֶק) occurs in DtIsa nine times, four instances before 45:8 and five after. But the four instances before 45:8 are significant. Twice salvation is found in conjunction with the installation of the "servant" (41:10; 42:6), in both cases linked with "Yahweh's hand." In 41:2 salvation (צֶדֶק) confronts Cyrus,[139] and this is the passage where he is mentioned for the first time. It would seem reasonable to suppose that here "salvation" (masc.) should be imagined in personified form. These three passages are connected by the fact that the encounters are not public—not yet! Only 42:21 cannot, as far as I can see, be fitted in here. All the other mentions occur after 45:8. As a substantive יֶשַׁע, "help," is found only here and in 51:5,[140] which states that "help" has gone forth. In the case of righteousness (צְדָקָה)[141] the analysis gives a clear result: all further nine instances occur after 45:8 (45:23, 24; 46:12, 13; 48:18; 51:6, 8; 54:14, 17). Concept and personification can hardly be

---

137 the clouds pour down, which is given by the stars" (ll. 38–41); *CTA* 3 III/IV = V AB-C/D = ʿnt III IV: "And say to the virgin Anat, present this message to Yabamat Limim: 'Message of the mighty Baal, a word from the one who is exalted among the heroes! Come to me from the land of battle! Bring love into the earth, pour peace into the heart of the earth, much love into the depths of the fields!'" Cf. also *1 Enoch* 11:1-2, which is preceded by a description of judgment. "In those days I will open the heavenly storerooms of blessing, in order to let them descend upon the earth, on the work and the labor of the children of men, and then salvation and justice all the days of the world, and men and women of all human generations, shall couple with one another" (trans. following G. Beer in E. Kautzsch, *Die Apokryphen und Pseudepigraphen des Alten Testaments* (1900, reprint 1921) 243. *T. Jud.* 24:2 reads according to the Armenian version: "And the heavens shall open and the blessings of the holy Father shall stream down, and he will pour out the Spirit of truth upon us." Cf. also *Jub.* 36:27–28; *Ps. Sol.* 17.

138 The development in the Greek world is comparable. See here L. Petersen, *Zur Geschichte der Personifikation in griechischer Dichtung und bildender Kunst* (1939).

139 Muilenburg's comment on the passage (525) is also of interest for the iconography that we must assume here; he points to 41:21, "where the meaning is 'victory'; here the meaning is the divine activity which brings about the triumph of righteousness."

140 The nine instances of "help" (יְשׁוּעָה, fem.) also occur after 45:8.

141 In the present text it is not entirely clear who "lets spring up." Like other commentators, de Boer (*Second Isaiah's Message* [1956] 49 on this passage) thinks that "the subject of the next verb תצמיח is again the earth, the subject of תפתח." This certainly makes sense. But could not "righteousness" "make spring up" too? Is the object contained in יַחַד: "community, totality, then together" (cf. 40:5)? Perhaps the difficulty is again connected with the history and development of the text. We should expect a parallel term for "earth" (אֶרֶץ), e.g., "field" (שָׂדֶה) cf.

separated. The concern is to depict their efficacy in the context of the divine commission.

In terms of dramatic structure, in v. 8 we experience the sending forth of salvation, help, righteousness.[142] To put it metaphorically, what comes from heaven is not just rain; it is the water of life, which benefits the whole world. In this linguistic form it is obvious that righteousness from heaven and righteousness on earth correspond; this is the way in which "help" materializes.[143]

It is not quite clear what the final declaration about creation refers to, with its third person masculine suffix. Is it what is said in v. 8 as a whole: "I Yahweh have created *it*,[144] but especially the help (יֶשַׁע masc.)"? This would once more make clear that powers and forces do not have a life of their own. Or is the suffix related to Cyrus, who was the subject of what was said earlier, and who is mentioned again in 45:13?[145] Finally, "who created it/him" (in Hebrew indistinguishable) could anticipate the twice-mentioned "its maker" (יֹצְרוֹ), which refers to Israel, in vv. 9 and 11.

But perhaps v. 8 is really a link section, intended to make clear the dimensions of God's whole activity? In this case the interpretation need not be an alternative. Creation as new creation links what has gone before with what follows.[146] In the time of the drama itself, it is the turn from the past to the future. What is to come is prepared: the new foundation of the city Zion/Jerusalem and the return of all Israel as a manifestation of God's sovereignty. The turn of events does not take place in a mythical era, however; it has its historical dimension, which is here declared through the name of Cyrus.

It was hence a consistent interpretation that showed a grasp of much of the tradition history behind the text when Jerome interpreted the text christologically: "Rorate caeli desuper, et nubes pluant *iustum* [the just one]; aperiatur terra, et germinet *salvatorem* [the savior]. Et iustitia oriatur simul: Ego dominus creavi eum." This turned into the Advent cry of the church: "Rorate coeli desuper et nubes pluant iustum," which can still be heard in the Christmas hymns: "He shall come down like showers/upon the fruitful earth"; or the German, "O Heiland, reiss die Himmel auf."[147]

With v. 8, the first part of Cyrus's installation in the throne scene is complete. Looking back, one may ask whether v. 6 does not already introduce a kind of entr'acte? This would be the case if, along with salvation, help, and righteousness in v. 8, we ought also to imagine the other concepts from v. 6 onward as personified figures in a performance. For a singular picture emerges. Beginning with east (sunrise)—west (sunset), and going on to light-darkness, and peace-evil, vv. 6-7 give us three contrasting pairs. Verse 8 adds: heavens, clouds, earth, as well as the already mentioned salvation, help, righteousness. All in all there are twelve terms, nine of which are masculine and three probably feminine: west (according to MT: מַעֲרָבָה), earth (אֶרֶץ), and righteousness (צְדָקָה). Did they come on as a kind of ballet? The terms would have been recognizable in each case by way of their

---

Gen 2:5; Isa 55:12), or perhaps "ground" (אֲדָמָה; cf. Isa 28:24). Then "lets spring up" makes sense and the double parallels "heavens-clouds" and "earth-field" are preserved. But as it is, the interpolated "righteousness" heightens the—probably intentional—tension. The change is the signal. In 55:10 it is "the word" that lets it (the earth) spring up. That is just as unusual, if one presupposes that it is the earth that permits the springing up (cf. Genesis 1)!

142 For the combination of the terms, cf. 46:13; 51:1-6; also Ps 85:9-14 (8-13); see also Schoors, *I Am God Your Saviour* (1973) 285.

143 See E. Hessler, "Die Struktur der Bilder bei Deuterojesaja," *EvTh* 25 (1965) 364–67 on this passage.

144 Thus McKenzie's translation (76); Young (202 n. 16), with reference to Amos 1:3: "The m. suffix refers to the general proposition previously stated."

145 That is the view taken by the LXX. See also Ibn Ezra: "I, the Lord . . . have created righteousness for Cyrus; he will establish rightousness in the world."

146 See here Spykerboer, *The Structure and Composition of Deutero-Isaiah* (1976) 134–36. He points out that "the verb 'to create' (ברא) connects v. 8 with v. 7, where it appears twice. It is found again in v. 12 and twice in v. 18, altogether 6 times in ch. 45 (16 times in the whole book)" (134). See also R. Lack, *La symbolique du livre d'Isaïe* (1973) on this passage.

147 See F. Ruffenach, "Rorate, caeli, desuper et nubes pluant iustum (Is. 45,8)," *VD* 12 (1932) 353–56; M. Adinolfi, "De Mariologicis Lyrani Postillis in Prophetas' Medii Aevi Exegeseos Lumine Perpensis," *SBFLA* 9 (1958/59) 199–250, esp. 225–30.

emblems. The "perceiving, recognizing" (יֵדְעוּ) in v. 6 would then have to be taken much more literally, and also the pointer to "all these" (כָל־אֵלֶּה) at the end of v. 7. The contrasting pairs are summoned. "From above" (מִמַּעַל)[148] and "together" (יַחַד) in v. 8 would then also be implicit stage directions. Dance is one of the fundamental elements in ancient drama. It would then also have its place here.[149]

---

148 It is interesting that in his interpretation Ibn Ezra (ed. M. Friedländer [1873, reprint 1965] 207; see also n. 97) assumes personifications as angels: "Drop down. This is a command to the angels that they shall drop righteousness, and cause salvation and truth to succeed."

149 See also below on 51:4-6.

"Woe to the one who quarrels with his maker" (45:9)

A. 3. 45:9-13
Consultation and Resolve in the Heavenly Sphere:
The Legitimation and Commission of Cyrus

9   Woe to the one who quarrels with his maker—
a clay vessel among clay vessels, earthenware!
Does clay say to its maker: "What are you
     making?"
and: "It is your work, it has no hands!"?[a]

10   Woe to the one who says to a father: "What
     are you begetting?"
and to a woman: "With what are you in labor?"

11   Thus says Yaweh,
the Holy One of Israel and its maker:
<Will you question me about future (events)?>[a]
Will you command me about my sons and the
     work of my hands?

12   *I* have made the earth,
and I have created humankind upon it!

My hands have stretched out the heavens,
and I have commanded all their host!

13   *I* have roused him in righteousness
and I will make all his paths straight.
He will build my city
and send my deported people (home)—
not for a price and not for a gift (as bribe),
says Yahweh Sabaoth.

9a   Perhaps instead of וּפָעָלְךָ אֵין־יָדַיִם לוֹ, the reading should be
וּפָעֳלוֹ . . . לְךָ, "and (to) its fashioner: 'Have you no hands?'"
(cf. LXX, S; *BHS*).

11a   Thus with a correction to הָאֹתִיּוֹת תִּשְׁאָלוּנִי from MT:
הָאֹתִיּוֹת שְׁאָלוּנִי, "ask me about future (events)!" It would also be
possible to emend to הָאֹתִי תִּשְׁאָלוּנִי or הַאַתֶּם and thus to link up
with עַל־בָּנַי: "*You* want to ask me . . ." or "you want to ask *me*
about my sons? And you want to give me orders about the
work of my hands?" (cf. *HALAT* 4:1277; see below on this passage).

With these verses[150] we participate in a deliberation that
takes place in the heavenly sphere. What was said at the
beginning of the throne scene is now elaborated: that
Yahweh "carries out the counsel of his messengers"
(44:26). The decision in v. 13 again confirms Cyrus's
legitimation and commission (cf. 44:26-28). This presupposes that the interpretation of Cyrus as "the anointed
one" (45:1) has been resisted and queried, and that this
opposition is to be countered here.

The text is a scrupulously constructed literary composition. The triple beat is continued.[151] The verses are
closely interwoven by means of catchwords and thematic
links.[152] The most important terms for the Creator's
activity are used in characteristic variation.[153]

Begrich already assigned the unit to the "disputation
speeches." But the genre can be more precisely defined
than that. It is modeled on the ruler's consultation with
his counselors. According to 2 Samuel 7, King David
consults the prophet Nathan about his resolve to build
the temple. The prophet gives his consent: "Go, all that
you have in mind, do it (לֵךְ עֲשֵׂה), for Yahweh is with you"
(v. 3). But he is then corrected by Yahweh himself. 2 Sam

---

150   On the text see esp. H. Leene's careful study
"Universalism or Nationalism? Isaiah XLV 9–13 and
Its Context," *BTFT* 35 (1974) 309–34, although I
cannot share his overall conclusion: "This unit is
not directed to Israelites who considered the message of Second Isaiah to be too 'universalistic,' but
to non-Israelites, who found it too 'nationalistic'"
(309). Also Schoors, *I Am God Your Saviour* (1973)
261–67; J. L. Koole, "Zu Jes 45:9ff," in *FS M. A. Beek*
(1974) 170–75; B. D. Naidoff, "The two-fold structure of Isaiah xlv 9–13," *VT* 31 (1981) 180–85.

151   "His maker" (יֹצְרוֹ, v. 9, bis; v. 11); "I" (אָנֹכִי, v. 12; אֲנִי,
v. 12; אָנֹכִי, v. 13); "my sons" (בָּנַי v. 11); "my city"
(עִירִי, v. 13); "my prisoners" (גָּלוּתִי, v. 13).

152   Earth (אֲדָמָה, v. 9)—"I have made the earth and
humankind upon it" (עָשִׂיתִי אֶרֶץ וְאָדָם עָלֶיהָ); "hands"
(v. 9, יָדָיִם; אֵין־יָדַיִם; v. 11, פֹּעַל יָדִי; v. 12, יָדַי); "my sons"
(בָּנַי, v. 11); "he will build my city" (הוּא־יִבְנֶה עִירִי,
v. 13); see also the list in Leene, "Universalism or
Nationalism? Isaiah XLV 9–13 and Its Context,"
BTFT 35 (1974) 317.

153   "Form, make" (יצר, vv. 9, 11); "do, make" (עשׂה, vv.
9, 12); "effect" (פעל, vv. 9, 11); "create" (ברא, v. 11);
see also "command" (צוה, vv. 11 and 12) "stretch
out the heavens" (אֲנִי יָדַי נָטוּ שָׁמַיִם, v. 12). See E.
Hessler, "Gott der Schöpfer: Ein Beitrag zur

16:15—17:14 describes a controversial consultation between Hushai, "David's friend" (רֵעֶה, 16:16), and Ahithophel about the way Absalom, the claimant to the throne, should proceed. The example of King Rehoboam in 1 Kgs 12:3-16 shows quite clearly how an opinion was arrived at. Israel's "popular assembly" (כָּל־קְהַל יִשְׂרָאֵל) makes a request. The king consults the council of elders (vv. 6-7) and the council of young men (vv. 8-11), and then conveys his decision to the people (vv. 13-14). We find an example of the royal council in heaven[154] in 1 Kgs 22:19-22 (and correspondingly in 2 Chr 18:18-21). In the vision, the prophet Micaiah ben Imlah sees Yahweh on his throne, surrounded by the heavenly host. In the deliberations, questions are put and answers given: "One said one thing and another said another."[155] Yahweh himself decides, and what he has let the prophet proclaim comes to pass. We may also, finally, compare the beginning of the book of Job (1:6-12; 2:1-7).

If from this background we come to the present text, some of the singularities and difficulties can be more readily understood. In vv. 11-13 Yahweh himself is speaking; that is clear. But who is the speaker in vv. 9 and 10? It is Yahweh's "counselors"! This fits in with observations made in the commentaries that here prophetic and wisdom elements are present. There are two double verdicts, each of them introduced by "woe!" (הוֹי, vv. 9 and

10). The number of verdicts allows us to conclude that there were four counselors. This could also be an indication of the performance practice.

"Woe" cries are one of the "basic forms of prophetic speech."[156] Westermann presumes that they developed out of curse oracles. "Woe" (הוֹי) announces doom to evildoers, a doom that in the final analysis can end in death. The link between the "woe" and a following participial construction[157] describing the misconduct is strange. Such constructions are connected especially with some typical group behavior.[158] For these reasons E. Gerstenberger and H. W. Wolff assume that there was a link with the wisdom tradition. As the announcement of a critical verdict, "Woe" (הוֹי) occurs only here in DtIsa.[159] Thus it may be called a prophetic oracle. Here a certain kind of behavior is thought about on the basis of examples; this is a method found in wisdom literature too.

■ **9** The first example is taken from the potter's world,[160] as is shown by the catchwords "fired clay/clay vessel" (חֶרֶשׂ)[161] and "clay" (חֹמֶר). But it should be noted that the verse contains *two* verdicts; these are not completely identical but are designed to make different aspects clear. Consequently v. 9a begins with the clay product, v. 9b follows with clay as raw material. Nowadays we would probably proceed in the reverse order.

It is immediately signaled that this is not a matter of

Komposition und Theologie Deuterojesajas" (1960) 109ff.; Leene, "Universalism or Nationalism? Isaiah XLV 9–13 and Its Context," *BTFT* 35 (1974) 312–13.

154 See F. M. Cross, "The Council of Yahweh in Second Isaiah," *JNES* 12 (1953) 274–78; Zimmerli, *Ezekiel* 1 (1979) 98–99 [*Ezechiel* (1969) 19–20]; R. N. Whybray, *The Heavenly Counsellor in Isaiah 40, 13–14: A Study of the Sources of the Theology of Deutero-Isaiah* (1971), esp. 49–53. Whybray does not consider the present text 45:9-13, however.

155 See MT and the commentaries on this passage.

156 Lit.: C. Westermann, *Basic Forms of Prophetic Speech* (1967; reprint 1991) 190–98 [*Grundformen prophetischer Rede* (1960) 137–42]; E. Gerstenberger, "Woe-Oracles of the Prophets," *JBL* 81 (1962) 249–63; H. W. Wolff, *Amos the Prophet: The Man and His Background* (1973) 17–34 [*Amos' geistige Heimat* (1964) 12–23]; G. Wanke, "אוֹי und הוֹי," *ZAW* 78 (1966) 215–18.

157 Cf. Isa 5:18, 20; 33:1; Amos 6:1; Hab 2:6, 19.

158 G. Wanke, "אוֹי und הוֹי," *ZAW* 78 (1966) 218: "The

phrases הוֹי + participle lack the sharp personal reference; human emotions do not play an essential part in them. In the הוֹי-sayings, the criticism of personal behavior rather presupposes deliberation and reflection." E. Gerstenberger, "Woe-Oracles of the Prophets" *JBL* 81 (1962) 252: "The normal prophetic woe-form contains general and timeless indictments of historically unspecified evildoers."

159 As a consequence this passage has been ascribed to a hand other than DtIsa's; thus Elliger, Westermann; see also 55:1: there הוֹי is an "inviting summons"; see Wanke, *ZAW* 78 (1966) 117.

160 For the "potter" comparison cf. Isa 29:16; Jer 18:1-11; 19:1-13; Job 4:19; 33:6; Sir 33:13; Rom 9:20-24.

161 For this translation cf. *HALOT* 1:357 [*HALAT* 1:343], on the basis of J. L. Kelso, *The Ceramic Vocabulary of the Old Testament* (1948). According to Kelso's definition in *IDB* 3:849, "pottery" is "the technical term for any kind of fired ware." See also Leene, "Universalism or Nationalism? Isaiah XLV 9–13 and its Context," *BTFT* 35 (1974) 310.

technical or professional information, however; it is really an abstraction on the basis of this occupational background. It is nonsense for the product to attempt to fight a case (רִיב) against the one who has produced it.[162] Common sense tells us that the two are simply not on the same level. The reason then explicitly given in v. 9aβ is more closely bound up with the context than is generally appreciated. The human being is a "clay vessel[163] among (or: together with)[164] earthenware vessels."[165] This gives the play on the words "earth" (אֲדָמָה ʾᵃdāmāh, v. 9) and "human being" (אָדָם ʾādām, v. 12) its point. But the statement is in fact simply an echo of the tradition of Genesis 2–3. According to this view, it is nonsense for human beings to quarrel with the one who has made them. This is the opposite position to that of a Job,[166] but accords with the view of Job's friends. The verdict's conclusion makes plain that the maker (יֹצְרוֹ, v. 9a) is the potter, and at the same time Yahweh is the creator.[167]

The second verdict begins as a question, thus underlining the discussion character of the text. It is equally nonsensical for the clay to call the potter to account for his plans—"what are you making" or "what will you make?"[168] (imperfect tense in Hebrew). The material has no right of consultation in the potting process. The potter decides on the form. That makes sense to everyone. The reason given is again drawn from creation theology. The clay too is created, for "[it is] your work (וּפָעָלְךָ)."[169]

The second person masculine singular suffix has always caused difficulty[170] and has hence often been emended. But in the framework of the consultation in the heavenly household the direct address to Yahweh has its point. The underlying conviction is the unity of creation. What can be said of clay can be said of human beings too. This is the only way in which the comparison makes sense. A further declaration follows, also as a nominative clause.

The intended parallelism to v. 11—"work of my hands" (פֹּעַל יָדִי)—also makes the curious "it has no hands" comprehensible.[171] Like "his work" it refers to the clay. This is therefore the subject throughout. The clay as raw material cannot form itself. It needs the hands of the potter. It is in this way that Yahweh forms human beings for the task given to them. In the way he does it he is free.

■ 10 The second contribution is initially more difficult to understand, if one looks for the point of comparison. Again it is a double verdict, here with a comparison drawn from the sphere of begetting and giving birth. We may exclude an interpretation in the sense of Jer 20:14-18, which calls the prophet's own birth in question. It is not the individual's father who is the subject, let alone his mother.[172] The context leads one to expect a generally applicable statement describing behavior that is really nonsensical.

---

162 Beuken (242) refers to Isa 10:15; 29:16 and the sayings of Ahikar: "Why should wood strive with fire, flesh with a knife, a man with [a king]?" (*ANET* 429). This comparison again makes the link with the wisdom tradition plain.

163 Cf. Prov 26:23; Jer 19:1 "burnt clay" (חֶרֶשׂ) as an abbreviation for "a vessel of . . ." (כְּלִי חֶרֶשׂ); see *HALOT* 1:357 [*HALAT* 1:343] with lit. But probably an indication of the material is enough, so that a possible rendering would also be: "A product of clay among clay products."

164 For את as meaning "together with, among others," cf. *HALOT* 1:101 [*HALAT* 1:97–98].

165 The text is not corrupt and requires no emendation. For a textual discussion see G. R. Driver, "Linguistic and Textual Problems: Isaiah XL–LXVI," *JTS* 36 (1935) 396–406, esp. 399. Driver observes rightly: "The jingling play on two similar but distinct groups is characteristic of this author." Cf. C. F. Whitley, "Textual Notes on Deutero-Isaiah," *VT* 11 (1961) 458; A. F. Johns, "A Note on Isaiah 45:9," *AUSS* 1 (1963) 62–64; G. R. Driver,

"Isaianic Problems," in *FS W. Eilers* (1967) 43–57. For the LXX version see I. L. Seeligmann, *The Septuagint Version of Isaiah* (1948) 22–23. Ibn Ezra (207) already wrote about this passage: "*The potsherd. The man who is like a potsherd of earthern ware.*"

166 See Job 9 and 10, esp. 10:8.

167 Thus already the Targum.

168 On this question cf. 2 Sam 16:10; Job 9:12; Dan 4:32.

169 See J. Vollmer, "פעל *pᶜl* to make do," *TLOT* 2:1014–18 [*THAT* 2:461–66]; K.-J. Illmann, "פָּעַל *pāʿal*," *ThWAT* 6:697–703.

170 For the attempts at a solution see Leene, "Universalism or Nationalism? Isaiah XLV 9–13 and Its Context," *BTFT* 35 (1974) 311–12. 1QIsaᵃ: "No one has hands for your work" (ופועלכם אין אדם ידים לו); cf. 1QH 18:11-13.

171 RSV's translation: "Your work has no handles" presupposes יְדוֹת instead of יָדִים in the text; see North, 153 on this passage, with reference to GKC § 87o.

172 "The wife of your father" is the stepmother (cf. Lev

234

The question in the first verdict is not why a father begets, but "what" (מַה) he begets. Moreover we should once more note the Hebrew imperfect, used in the future sense.[173] The question thus corresponds exactly to the question put to the potter in v. 9. A father does not know whether he is going to beget a son or a daughter,[174] who the child is,[175] or what it will be like.[176] The same is true of a woman. When she is in labor she does not know what kind of child she is going to bring into the world. The comparison with labor pains may also involve other aspects too. The birth pangs are an image for fears, incalculability, and in DtIsa (e.g., in 42:14) for an irreversible, inexorable process.[177] So here too, when birth is used as a comparison the "time" aspect could also play a part.

But these verdicts about both the "father" and the "woman" must again be understood against the background of the context. God is the true father. He alone knows what kind of child is engendered and born. He also determines the birth. Everyday experience makes God's sovereignty over human beings clear. Anyone who calls it in question puts him- or herself outside the coherent warp and woof of this life; he becomes subject to the "woe!" (הוֹי).[178] Both double verdicts arrive at the same conclusion and intensify one another: the human being can neither question nor determine what God does.[179] This already touches on what is said in Yahweh's verdict in vv. 11-13.

■ **11** The solemn titles stress God's remoteness ("the Holy One" קָדוֹשׁ) and yet his closeness for Israel in his very sovereignty ("its maker", יֹצְרוֹ).[180] The verse has given rise to a whole series of textual emendations.[181] The present MT expresses the command: "Ask me about future (events)!" (imperative). But in the parallelism the verb is: "you will command me" (תְּצַוֻּנִי).[182] Since this can hardly apply to Yahweh, it has been assumed that the second verb is meant ironically. But the quintessence of the verdicts in vv. 9 and 10 was that the human being

---

18:8, 11); see Leene, "Universalism or Nationalism? Isaiah XLV 9–13 and Its Context," *BTFT* 35 (1974) 313 on this passage. This applies also to Muilenburg's interpretation, 527: "It is gross impiety for the child to rebel against his birth and the subsequent nurture which belongs to his parents (cf. Mal 1:6)."

173 Young (204) rightly adheres firmly to this point.

174 יֹלד is frequently used with indications of gender: Gen 5:3-4; Exod 21:4; Deut 28:41; Jer 16:2; 29:6; Ezek 18:10, 14; Job 1:2; Qoh 6:3.

175 The name is generally given only after the child has been born. God alone knows a human being from his mother's womb. On יֹלד with certain names see, e.g., Gen 5:21, 32; 11:10, 12, 26; 25:19; Ruth 4:22.

176 Prov 17:21; 23:24.

177 See G. Bertram, "ὠδίν, ὠδίνω," *TDNT* 9:667–74, esp. 668–69 [*ThWNT* 9:668–75, esp. 670–71]; J. Scharbert, *Der Schmerz im Alten Testament* (1955), esp. 25. On חיל, "to be in labor," see *HALOT* 1:310 [*HALAT* 1:298].

178 See Gerstenberger, "Woe-Oracles of the Prophets," *JBL* 81 (1962) 258 n. 33 on this passage: "If these two woes belong together, then they seek to express the inviolability and inscrutability of the natural, cosmic order, a theme which is so fundamental to the wisdom literature that the whole books of Job and Ecclesiastes are founded on it. Prov 30:3-4 takes a similar attitude." Isa 64:7 (8) seems like an exposition of the same tradition: "Yet, O Yahweh, you are our Father; we are the clay, and you are our potter; and we are all the work of your hand" (see also the

rest of the passage). Cf. also 63:16; Mal 2:10. The context and the dispute with the El-traditions should also be remembered here. For El's title *ab adm* see M. H. Pope, *El in the Ugaritic Texts* (1955) 47, with reference to I Krt 37, 43, 136, 151, 278.

179 For the other tradition of representing the nature of human existence in its lowliness before God's greatness, see E. Brandenburger, *Fleisch und Geist: Paulus und die dualistische Weisheit* (1968), esp. 86–87 on 1QH 15:8-25; 103 on 1QH 18:3-30.

180 Cf. Isa 43:1, 21; 44:2, 21, 24.

181 See again the discussion of the attempts at a solution in Leene, "Universalism or Nationalism? Isaiah XLV 9–13 and Its Context," *BTFT* 35 (1974) 315; Beuken, 243–44 on this passage; also P. Wernberg-Møller, "Studies in the Defective Spellings in the Isaiah-Scroll of St Mark's Monastery," *JSS* 3 (1958) 244–64, esp. 263–64; M. Bogaert, "Les suffixes verbaux non accusatifs dans le sémitique nord-occidental et particulièrement en hébreu," *Bib* 45 (1964) 238. 1QIsaᵃ and ᵇ combine the phrases differently: "Thus says Yahweh, the Holy One of Israel, who forms the future (Isaᵇ: האתיות)—or: the signs (Isaᵃ: האותות): 'Ask me about my sons.'" The LXX takes the same view: "ὁ ποιήσας τὰ ἐπερχόμενα. Ἐρωτήσατέ με περὶ."

182 On the basis of 1 Chr 22:12, Delitzsch (2:233[476]) understands צוה in this passage as meaning "to commend something to the care of someone" and translates: "Thus says Yahweh, Israel's Holy One and its maker: About the future ask me, let my sons and

cannot question (in the sense of requiring a justification), let alone command.[183]

Here we must come back once more to the definition of the scene as a heavenly deliberation. In 1 Kings 22 too, after the verdicts and proposal of the counselors, Yahweh puts a question once more, before he announces his decision.[184] If we read the ה in הָאֹתִיּוֹת not as an article—*the* future (events)" (הַ)—but as interrogative particle (הֲ), it can be the introduction to a double question. It would then correspond to the question in v. 9b: "Does . . . perhaps say . . . ?" (lit. "Will . . . say . . . ?" הֲיֹאמַר) and continue the deliberation.[185] The only change required in the consonantal text is then a change from the imperative to "you will command" (תְּצַוֻּנִי), corresponding to a future tense; this is effected simply through the addition of a ת: "Do you wish to ask me (תִּשְׁאָלוּנִי) . . . ,[186] do you wish to command me . . . ?" The implicit answer is exactly the same as in the previous verdicts: No! The questions are initially directed to the "counselors" who are present, and hence of course to the listeners too. It is the future that is in question; this was already evident in the future-tense declarations in vv. 9 and 10. This is stressed by the emphatic anteposition given to "future (events)" (אֹתִיּוֹת).[187] Only Yahweh has control over "his sons"[188] and "the work of his hands."[189]

■ **12** Yahweh once more gives a fundamental declaration of what he has done. Here the self-predications again have their proper place and function. The universal order is expounded in comprehensive phraseology. This is the earthly sphere where humanity (אָדָם) has its place. It is not initially the individual who is created. In this respect we are struck by the closeness to Genesis 1. Here the creation traditions of P and J have been absorbed. The heavens are the place of the "host" (צְבָאָם) whom Yahweh commands.[190] We may ask whether the "time" aspect has not been taken up again here, for it is not the stars themselves that determine destinies, time, and the hour. It remains in general astonishing that for DtIsa a "heavenly deliberation" should take on the forms and intellectual patterns of wisdom. For him, the validity of these statements is not confined to Israel. Yahweh is God for the whole world.

The presupposition underlying the logic of the whole text is the unity of reality as creation. The text gives us an insight into the way in which at this period common experience was argumentatively employed for the mastery of practical political problems. This is an interpretation of wisdom traditions that embraces the whole of reality and makes it communicable; it is not yet the

---

the work of my hands be commended to my charge" (trans. altered).

183 See G. Liedke, "צוה ṣwh pi. to command," *TLOT* 2:1062–65 [*THAT* 2:530–36].

184 Verse 21 (22): "and Yahweh asked him, 'With what' (בַּמֶּה)?"

185 The transference into the interrogative form is again based on the emendation in *BHS:* "Do you ask *me* (הַאֹתִי תִשְׁאָלוּנִי) about my sons?" See also A. B. Ehrlich, *Randglossen zur hebräischen Bibel* 4 (1912) 166; G. R. Driver, "Studies in the Vocabulary of the Old Testament," *JTS* 34 (1933) 39; P. W. Skehan, "Some Textual Problems in Isaiah," *CBQ* 22 (1960) 54–55; Schoors, *I Am God Your Saviour* (1973) 264.

186 Thus already Marti, 311, on the basis of "Secker and others." Duhm takes a contrary view: "One cannot see why one should not ask what Yahweh has resolved." An objection of this kind probably led early on to a change in the text such as the rendering in the MT. This view is certainly in line with biblical testimony, but does not fit the logic of the present text. One reason is probably the varying weight given to שאל—whether it is merely a "questioning" or rather a "demanding an explanation" in the sense of "calling to account."

187 Cf. 41:23; 44:7.

188 The LXX has here: "Ask me about my sons and about my daughters" (περὶ τῶν υἱῶν μου καὶ περὶ τῶν θυγατέρων μου). It could be that a translator added a mention of daughters, especially since the previous verse talks about "father" and "wife." But perhaps an early reading has been preserved. The Hebrew corresponding to this would be: עַל־בְּנֵי וְעַל־בְּנוֹתַי . Here there is a striking echo of El's title "Creator of the created," *bny bnwt.* Is this chance, or is it intentional? In a text so heavily weighted with statements about creation, which works with word-plays, and in the framework of the throne scene, the question is at least permissible. See also H. Ringgren, "אָב ʾābh," *TDOT* 1:1–19, esp. 16–17 [*ThWAT* 1:1–19, esp. 16–17]. For the title see Pope, *El in the Ugaritic Texts* (1955) 47; W. H. Schmidt, *Königtum Gottes in Ugarit und Israel: Zur Herkunft der Königsprädikation Jahwes* (2d ed. 1966) 49; with reference to *UT* 49, III, 5, 11 (*CML* 112a); 51, II, 11; III, 32 (*CML* 92–94) 2 Aqht I, 25 (*CML* 48b).

189 Cf. Isa 44:24; 45:2, 5–7, 8.

190 Cf. 40:26.

interpretation of law—unless indeed Genesis 1–2 is to be understood as the beginning of the Torah.

■ **13** The transition from the general legitimation of divine authority to the decision arrived at in the consultation is clearly marked by the change to the future tense in v. 13aβ. Cyrus is not named, but he is the subject. It is this crystallization toward which the text draws.[191] His, Cyrus's, rousing[192] is part of the total order.[193] Yahweh sees to it that he observes this order and the thereby given limitations of his power (אֲשֶׁר). Through the rebuilding of the city[194] and the liberation of the prisoners the Yahweh edict in 44:24-28 is once more endorsed, although in the present passage liberation is given the greater emphasis. But this has an important function in providing a link with the following complex.

Part of the resolve is the decision that no purchase price and no bribe[195] are to be paid. Many commentators stumble over these concluding words, and maintain that v. 13bγ is the work of another hand.[196]

There is no doubt that in this scene the problem that lay heavy on the listeners is under discussion: Why was a Persian of all people needed to bring about salvation? The answer is: God is free in his resolves and in what he does. The reconstruction of the situation underlying a text is always a question of greater or lesser probability. But if we look at the series in v. 13: "righteousness" (צֶדֶק), "makes his paths straight" (יֹשֶׁר) and the word "gift" in the severe sense of "bribe" (שֹׁחַד), then we may ask whether a further problem is not the integrity of the Persian administration. Was everything that Cyrus did correct? In the present text the point is initially that the prisoners do not have to pay for their liberation. That does not have to be a contradiction of the fact that Cyrus receives compensation.[197] But the next scene deals with this point.

---

191 McKenzie (79) writes about the text: "That an Israelite prophet should view the conquest of Cyrus purely as directed to the restoration of Israel may seem an intolerably narrow view of history. But it is a fact that the restoration of a Jewish community in Palestine has had a more lasting effect than anything else accomplished by Cyrus, who has been given in history the title of the Great."

192 Cf. 42:2, 25, 2 Chr 36:22 = Ezra 1:1.

193 H. H. Schmid, *Gerechtigkeit als Weltordnung: Hintergrund und Geschichte des alttestamentlichen Gerechtigkeitsbegriffs* (1968) 133: "צדק in Deutero-Isaiah accordingly means Yahweh's order, which—in accordance with the order of creation—will establish itself in the time of salvation that is at hand. The distinction between צדק as a term for the order

itself and צדקה as the acts that accord with that order is gradually becoming blurred." See C. F. Whitley, "Deutero-Isaiah's Interpretation of *ṣedeq*," *VT* 22 (1972) 473; Schoors (*I Am God Your Saviour* [1973] 265) thinks: "In connection with Cyrus, *ṣedeq* designates the victories of this king inasmuch as they have been given by Yahwe and thus represent a salvific reality."

194 Jerusalem is "my city," no longer "the city of David"! Cf. 46:13.

195 Cf. Isa 1:23; 5:23; 33:15; Mic 3:11; Ps 26:10; Prov 6:35; Job 15:34; and from the judicial texts Exod 23:8; Deut 10:17; 16:19; 27:25; also 1 Sam 8:3.

196 Duhm, 309; Marti, 311.

197 Cf. 43:3-4; 52:3; see also Duhm on this passage.

45

"The God of Israel is one who helps!" (45:15)

B. 1.   45:14-17
Homage of the Foreign Peoples before Cyrus
(Procession)

14   Thus says Yahweh:
The produce of Egypt and the profit of Kush
and the Sabaeans, men of tall stature,
pass in front of you and belong to you.

They go behind you. In fetters they pass by.
And they throw themselves down in front of
      you, they cry to you:

"Yes, a god is with you!
and besides him there is no other!
There are no gods!

15   Truly, you are a hidden God!"

The God of Israel is one who helps!

16   They are all put to shame and have also been
      confounded.
They have gone in shame, the experts for
      images.

17   Israel has been helped by Yahweh,
a help for most distant times.
You will not be put to shame and will not be
      confounded
to all eternity.

This text has been subject to dispute from earliest times. It is questionable whether it constitutes a genuine unit at all.[198] Its genre is difficult to define.[199] Above all, the content presents us with a number of stumbling blocks. To whom is the text addressed? Is it Israel or Cyrus? Is this a piece of triumphalist theology and inappropriate bragging? In a situation like this every explanation will have its weak points. Nevertheless an attempt must be made.

It is once more noticeable that the text is consciously shaped. There are intertwinings[200] and repetitions designed to stress points of particular concern.[201] It is closely connected with its immediate context, as H. Leene especially has shown.[202] The text begins in v. 14 with "Thus says Yahweh. . . ." If Yahweh is thus presented as speaking—at least through a representative—this indicates that we are still within the framework of the throne scene, in which the divine sovereignty is presented in various ways. The section is preceded in vv. 9-13 by the *topos* "consultation." I should like provisionally to give the present text vv. 14-17 the title: "Tribute from Foreign Countries," one aspect of "Homage of Foreign Peoples."

G. Walser begins his study about the peoples depicted on the Persepolis reliefs with the sentence: "In the East, the portrayal of subjugated and tribute-bringing peoples is one of the earliest representations of royal power."[203] An early example is the so-called standard from the royal burial place in Ur, which dates from the first half of the third millennium B.C.E.[204] Of particular interest for the OT is the so-called black

---

198 Westermann, 169 [337]: "We must reckon with the possibility that the verses are a combination of fragments which could only have been preserved as fragment." But see the careful discussion in Spykerboer, *The Structure and Composition of Deutero-Isaiah* (1976) 136–41, esp. 138.

199 Begrich (*Studien zu Deuterojesaja* [1938, reprint 1963] 14, 22–23) assigns it to the "salvation oracles, or assurance oracles answering a plea." For a contrary view see Schoors, *I Am God Your Saviour* (1973) 151.

200 Egypt (מִצְרַיִם *miṣrayim*, v. 14), "idols" (צִרִים *ṣirîm*,

v. 17), "they walk in fetters" (הלך בְּ, v. 14), "they walk in shame" (הלך בְּ, v. 16).

201 God (אֵל . . . . אֱלֹהִים . . . אֵל, vv. 14-15); ישׁע, 3 times, vv. 15, 17; כלם 3 times, vv. 16, 17; אַךְ *ʾak* (v. 14); אָכֵן *ʾākēn* (v. 15). Close in v. 17, 3 times ע (עַד־עוֹלְמֵי עַד).

202 Leene, "Universalism or Nationalism? Isaiah XLV 9–13 and Its Context," *BTFT* 35 (1974) 324ff. and 329ff.

203 G. Walser, *Die Völkerschaften auf den Reliefs von Persepolis: Historische Studien über den sogenannten Tributzug an der Apadanatreppe* (1966) 11.

204 *ANEP* nos. 303–4 (pp. 97, 284).

obelisk of Shalmanesar III of Assyria (858–824), because it shows tribute being brought by King Jehu of Israel.[205] In their link between text and visual presentation, examples from Egypt offer a good illustration for the scene in DtIsa, with "the tribute from foreign countries."

Rule over foreign countries is one element in the Egyptian conception of the state. Pharaoh's victory over the foreign nations is at the same time a victory over chaos and the establishment of order. This is confirmed by the tribute. Here even the earliest representations show a striking attempt at precise characterization of the foreigners and their countries. An established iconography develops in the way they are portrayed.

The picture cycle of the tribute scene is well preserved in the tomb of Rekh-mi-Re. Here the annotation explains: "*Rekh-mi-Rēʿ* receiving the tribute of the southern land along with the tribute of Punt, the tribute of Retenu-land and the tribute of Keftin-land, together with the captives of the various lands, brought away for the glory of His Majesty, the King of Egypt, *Men-kheper-Rēʿ*, who lives for ever."[206]

Of special interest for the DtIsa text (see 45:14) is the presentation of the Nubians, because the biblical Kush (כוש) probably corresponds to the Egyptian "South-land" as far as Ethiopia. The annotation here runs: "The arrival in peace of the chiefs of the southern land, (namely) the *Inutiu-sety* and *Khenty-ḥen-nūfer*, with respectful obeisance and prostration, bearing their tribute . . . (to) the King of Both Egypts, *Men-kheper-Rēʿ*—may he live forever—in the hope that there would be given to them the breath of life."

The pictures show precisely the most widely varying products, plants and animals, minerals and artifacts that are being brought in a long procession by representatives of the different countries. For Nubia, N. de Garis Davies draws up a list: "The pile of offer-

ings includes the regular products of the land—ostrich feathers and eggs, logs of ebony, gold in bars and rings, three baskets filled with '*ḏʿm*' gold, a green monkey on its special stool, six jars of '*sty*' ointment (?), five 'leopard' skins, six 'tusks,' a basket of red '*ḥmꜣgt*' stone, and one of green '*šsmt*' stone."[207]

Distinguished from these are the groups of slaves—men, women and children from the subjugated countries.[208] They are truly prisoners, led by soldiers.

Bringing forward the children of the chiefs of the southern lands, together with the children of the northern lands, brought away as the pick of the booty of His Majesty, King of Both Egypts, *Men-kheper-Reʿ*—may life be given him—from all lands, to fill the workshops and to be serfs of the estate of his father *Amūn*, lord of the thrones of Egypt; even as all lands had been given him (the king), grasped together in his fist and their chiefs flung [down] under his sandals. It was the seigneur, etc. [*Rekh-mi-Rēʿ*] who received the booty of the various lands, brought away from the victories of His Majesty.

The Persian kings took up the ancient Near Eastern tradition of visual presentation of a throne scene with a procession of subjugated peoples bringing tribute. But the tradition is significantly modified because of a different ideology of rule.[209] The peoples of the empire carry the Persian throne. Representatives of the nations are bringing their offerings voluntarily, on some peaceful occasion.[210] This program is artistically presented in impressive form in the architecture and pictorial ornamentation of Persepolis. On the eastern staircase of the great *apadana* we see the procession of twenty-three delegations in different national costume, who are depicted bearing the different products of their countries, the whole empire being summed up in the different ethnic groups.[211] It is a celebration, preserved in stone,

---

205 *AOB* pls. 54–55, nos. 121–24; *ANEP* nos. 351–55 (pp. 120–22, 290–91).

206 N. de Garis Davies, *The Tomb of Rekh-mi-Re at Thebes* (1944, reprint 1973) 17.

207 Ibid., 26. The pictures explain the "strange defilement of the acquisition" (Marti) and help us to imagine "the people of Kush." "The text presents difficulties, both formally and in content: the double יַעֲבֹרוּ is awkward, and it is then incomprehensible why the text should talk about the 'acquisition' and the 'profit of the trade' as 'going' (or 'passing to' or 'passing over to') so that these belong to the Israelites instead of Cyrus (cf. 43:3, 4), and that the Sabeans should offer themselves in chains to Israel" (Marti on this passage).

208 See the captions to the pictures in Davies, *Tomb*, 29.

209 See G. Walser, *Die Völkerschaften auf den Reliefs von Persepolis: Historische Studien über den sogenannten Tributzug an der Apadanatreppe* (1966) 26; K. Koch, "Weltordnung und Reichsidee im alten Iran," in P. Frei and K. Koch, *Reichsorganisation im Perserreich* (1984).

210 The Behistun relief still gives a a negative view of the different peoples. But it shows Darius I and the so-called kings of lies (actually the leaders of local revolts) tied to each other by a rope.

211 See P. Calmeyer, "Die 'statistische Landcharte' des Perserreiches" 1 (1982) 105–88; 2 (1983) 141–222.

of Persia's royal rule in the framework of the world of the nations and the whole universal order.

For our question about the description of the foreign peoples in DtIsa, the base of a statue found in Susa is of particular interest.[212] There the representatives of the nations are also presented in supporting attitudes. Probably this statue dates from the period of Darius I (522–486 B.C.E.), when extensions were made to his palace in Elam. Twenty-four nations are depicted and represented through explanatory texts, the names in each case being surrounded by a wall cartouche. Remarkably enough, the statue was probably made in Egypt. But the potentates of the foreign nations are not prisoners, as they are in Egypt. They are "carrying" the king with upraised hands. This example shows the exchange of ideas and pictorial representations in the Persian period, and indicates quite specific solutions in the acceptance and rejection of different traditions.

In Isa 45:14-17 we see in its essentials the iconography of the traditional scene: the listing of countries and peoples, and the homage to the ruler. But here the foreigners are prisoners (v. 14); they are bringing in their train the produce of their countries as tribute. We may of course ask which picture is closer to reality—voluntary gifts or enforced tribute? That would also depend on the perspective, whether the matter is seen from above, or from the angle of the people affected; and here differences of degree can undoubtedly be acknowledged.

But this makes it all the more imperative to ask: to whom is the tribute and homage being paid in this scene? The MT has pointed the suffixes in v. 14 as feminine throughout. Since there is no feminine to be found in the text itself, the antecedent has first to be discovered. "My city" (i.e., Zion/Jerusalem) and "my prisoners" (גָּלוּתִי) in v. 13 are possibilities. Both have been proposed. But this double proposal is itself difficult, if the point of reference is intended to be only one of the two. If we assume that it is only Zion/Jerusalem, then we are struck by the fact that in v. 13 the city is not addressed as a person, as it so often is in DtIsa. Here it is

the real city that is to be rebuilt. Muilenburg's proposal that in this passage "Israel" should be assumed to be feminine is improbable.[213]

I should therefore like to take up the early proposal already made by Ibn Ezra that the original addressee was Cyrus.[214] This would require no change in the consonantal text; only the vocalization of the suffixes would have to be changed to masculine. I would like to add to the early arguments that in the whole act from 44:24 onward Cyrus is one of the main characters. His legitimation and commissioning are the essential theme. This also applies to the "consultation" in vv. 9-13. But there too he is not again mentioned by name. Nor would this be necessary in the case of a scenic performance or a tableaulike presentation, because the dramatis personae could be seen, until they went off. The scene expounds what Cyrus's installation means. In DtIsa announcement and exposition frequently correspond.

What takes place here was announced for the first time in 43:3: Egypt, Cush, and Sheba as ransom for Israel's release. Thus it is only a seeming contradiction of 45:13. The difference is that Israel does not have to pay for its liberation itself. The term "bribe" (שֹׁחַד) is used only in 45:13. A bribe is not what one offers a ruler such as Cyrus. Israel's God offers compensation (תַּחַת), pays a price (כֹּפֶר, 43:3). From the point of view of those liberated, who have no hope of ever being able to find the means to buy their liberty, the liberation is "free of charge." The logic of the text is consistent in itself, even if we find it hard to accept. But the problem makes a curiously modern impression. How many countries, and not only in the past, take money in return for setting people free! This is the way the text can also be heard: as an admonition to the Persian administration. You have received enough compensation—now set the prisoners free!

It is an element in the iconography of the presentation that the ruler receives tribute. But Yahweh does not take the spoils, and Israel even less so.[215] Cyrus obvi-

212 See G. Walser, *Die Völkerschaften auf den Reliefs von Persepolis: Historische Studien über den sogenannten Tributzug an der Apadanatreppe* (1966) 36–38; P. Calmeyer, "Landcharte" 1:109–24, esp. 109–10, 117, 124; M. Roaf, "The Subject Peoples on the Base of the Statue of Darius," *Cahiers de la délégation archéologique française en Iran* 4 (1974) 73–160; K. Koch, "Weltordnung und Reichsidee im alten Iran,"

in P. Frei and K. Koch, eds., *Reichsorganisation im Perserreich* (1984) 113 n. 45.

213 Muilenburg (529) on this passage: "The use of the feminine suffixes supports the view that Israel is meant (cf. 18:7; 23:18; 60:5ff.)."

214 Skinner (70) on this passage also quotes from the early interpreters Jerome and Hugo Grotius.

215 In this respect the position in Isaiah 60 differs. See

ously has the profit. In a deeper sense it becomes clear that even Cyrus with all his power is not an "autonomous" ruler. Even his political actions are subject to God's consent.

Through its different verbs, the text allows us to see the to-and-fro of the procession.[216] It is certainly an opportunity to offer something to the eye and the imagination. It is comparable with the earlier scenes with the artisans. Compared with the relatively high degree of abstraction in the speeches in the throne scene, here there is action. But that does not mean that this individual scene is less thought through theologically. It is reminiscent of the medieval nativity plays, with their portrayal of the Three Wise Men, with their pomp. One can just see them "following behind (Cyrus)." In הלך אחרי there is also an echo of "follow," in the sense of discipleship, just as Israel "followed strange gods." "In fetters" corresponds to "in shame" (v. 16). The climax is the homage to Cyrus. But for Israel's ears it is also a climax of error, if not of blasphemy, for both the verbs used are pre-eminently technical terms for the worship of God, to which the earthly ruler simply cannot lay claim.[217] This homage is a terrible misunderstanding that can come about only through force ("in fetters"). It will end only in 45:23, when Yahweh affirms: "To me every knee shall bow."

■ **14-15a** The prisoners' lament is hence a moving one. The word אֵל (*ʾēl*), which is twice used for God in vv. 14 and 15a, shows that it is the foreigners who are speaking here. They recognize ("Yes truly!" אַךְ, v. 14) that a god is with Cyrus. In their fate they experience divine power. This was a widespread view, and means subjection to the aggressor. Remembering the introduction of the text ("throw oneself down/fall down and worship," v. 14), we may even ask whether Cyrus too can be invoked as "god" (אֱלֹהִים), in the sense: "there is no mighty one except him." For this is then Babylon's error according to 47:8, 10—to think that it is unique. In the more immediate context the lines are again a prelude to 45:22.

The third declaration of the foreign peoples is then already on the right track when, with "you" (אַתָּה), it turns to "the hidden God." "You" is clearly not Cyrus, since in the present scene he is visible, not "hidden." This in itself corrects the possible misunderstanding of "Elohim."[218] A detail shows how the author can build up and resolve tension.

Westermann, 169 (138): "It is a feature that does not suit Deutero-Isaiah: the ambassadors of the nations come *with their treasures* and appear all together, as in a procession, to pay homage."

216   Duhm rightly comments here: "What a remarkable confusion!"

217   שׁחה, traditionally *Hitpael* means "to bow deeply, to incline oneself." It is "the highest performance of homage . . . frequently expressing cultic homage" (KB 959; see also *HALOT* 1:296 [*HALAT* 1:283–84] חוה II as *eštaf*, and שׁחה *HALAT* 4:1351–52 with lit.). The *proskynesis* or prostration can be made before a ruler or other powerful figure (see Gen 42:6; 43:26, 28; but cf. 37:10; 50:18; 1 Sam 2:36; 24:9; 28:14; 2 Sam 9:8; 14:33; 15:5; 28:8 and elsewhere). It also stands for the prostration before God (Gen 24:26; Ps 95:6). Isa 49:23 talks about the "falling down" of kings and princes. פלל *Hitpael* occurs 79 times in the OT. Its basic meaning is "to make intercession," from which it then acquires the general meaning "pray." According to H.-P. Stähli, "פלל *pll* hitp. to pray," *TLOT* 2:991–94 [*THAT* 2:427–32]: "The contexts of most passages, however, suggest that *pll* hitp. designates an intercessory and/or complaint form of prayer, whether the prayer of an individual (1 Sam 1:10, 12, 26f.; 2 Kgs 19:15, 20 and par.; 20:2 and par.; Jonah 2:2 [1:17]; 4:2; Pss 5:3 [2]; 32:6;

2 Chr 32:24; 33:13), or a prayer of the people in general (1 Kgs 8:33, 35, 44 and par.; Isa 16:12; cf. Dan 9:4), brought before God in view of a crisis" (993 [430]). Stähli establishes (992 [429]): "Prayer is directed, explicitly or implicitly, to God (otherwise only in Isa 16:12; 44:17; 45:20, where prayer is addressed to a foreign deity, an idol, and Isa 45:14, where Israel is the obj[ect]" (he refers to Duhm and Westermann). If this is so, 45:14 would be the only exception (thus already Delitzsch on this passage). This is for me a further reason for thinking it improbable that here Zion or Israel was originally the object of the veneration. In the immediate context, in 44:17 and 45:20, פלל is the term for the false cult (see also 46:6 for שׁחה). Daniel 3 should be compared for the whole complex. See also E. Gerstenberger, "פלל *pll*," *ThWAT* 6:606–17.

218   It is of course also possible to interpret אֱלֹהִים as a plural, "gods": "and there are no gods besides him."

The statement about the hiddenness of God is a key to an understanding of the text.[219] It is noticeable that in the OT this is mainly an element of complaint.[220] It can be found in both individual[221] and communal[222] laments. God has turned away. Instead of grace, human beings experience disfavor; instead of salvation, disaster. God's will can therefore no longer be discerned. It is called in question. If the prisoners from foreign countries have experienced "God" (אֵל), then it is only as the one "who keeps himself hidden" (סתר *Hitpael*). That is the reason for their lament.

With this in mind, we can hear vv. 14-15 in a new way. As assurance and emphasis, both אַךְ *ʾak* and אָכֵן *ʾākēn* mean "indeed, truly";[223] but the sound of the words is hardly distinguishable from the differently written אָח *ʾaḥ*, the onomatopoeic interjection of pain.[224] Here a chorus of prisoners is lamenting, in contrast to the closing chorus in 45:24. There the "yes, truly" (אַךְ) sounds very different. For people who worship only power—even in their own downfall—Yahweh remains a hidden God.[225]

■ **15b-17** If the understanding of vv. 14-15a is developed in this way, v. 15b remains incomprehensible. How should the foreign peoples know that the God of Israel helps? After all, in terms of the dramatic structure they have only just arrived. They have not yet encountered Israel at all. But this has nothing to do with some arcane knowledge or other. The foreign nations cannot utter this sentence, nor do they have to do so—at least not yet, we may again say. The assertion belongs on Israel's lips. The division of the verse should be corrected. As it is at present, it bears out the view of the exegetes who see the homage as given to Israel, not to Cyrus. But how could the declaration that the God of Israel helps be spoken by people in fetters?

The decisive contribution to an interpretation of this verse was made by Beuken, when he observed that this psalmlike, thanksgiving section is a *tōdâ*. In the Psalms, lament is frequently followed by thanksgiving. People who have been liberated from their distress testify to their deliverance before the congregation. It is the motif of the ex-voto, which has belonged in the sanctuary from time immemorial. At the beginning of the *tōdâ* the naming of God has its appropriate place, and so has the declaration that he is one who helps. Thus the change in the division of the verse enables the thrice-repeated root "help" (ישׁע) to be retained.

If the genre is defined as a *tōdâ*, the didactic character also becomes comprehensible. Positive and negative behavior[226] are contrasted. The correlation is help and downfall, like blessing and curse. What has been learned from the experience of faith is passed on. As in every *tōdâ*, what is said applies beyond the particular case in point, and is valid for everyone who hears it.[227]

219 For the whole see L. Perlitt, "Die Verborgenheit Gottes," in *Probleme biblischer Theologie. FS G. von Rad* (1971) 367–82.

220 See M. Dijkstra, "Zur Deutung von Jesaja 45,15ff.," *ZAW* 89 (1977) 215–22, esp. 218; for examples from nonbiblical texts see Perlitt, "Die Verborgenheit Gottes," 367–68.

221 Cf. Pss 10:1, 11; 13:2; 27:9; 30:8 (7); 55:2 (1); 69:18 (17); 88:15 (14); 89:47 (46); 102:3 (2); 143:7; Lam 3:56.

222 Ps 44:25 (24).

223 N. H. Snaith ("The Meaning of the Hebrew אַךְ," *VT* 14 [1964] 221–25) believes that in אַךְ "there is an idea of contrariness, exception, restriction and even contradiction" (225). He paraphrases 45:14: "Contrary to what we have previously believed, El is in thee, and there is none apart from God" (223).

224 Cf. Ezek 6:11; 18:10; 21:20; as הָאָח, Ezek 25:3; 26:2; 36:2; see LXX and the commentaries on this passage.

225 See M. Dijkstra, "Zur Deutung von Jesaja 45,15ff.," *ZAW* 89 (1977) 219: "Isa 45:15 is in its compressed form a 'lament,' inasmuch as it embraces the element of complaint—you are a God who hides himself—and the motif of the hearing of a prayer—you are Israel's God, the Deliverer." Cf. J.-G. Heintz, "De l'absence de la statue divine au 'Dieu qui se cache' (Esaïe, 45/15). Aux origines d'un thème biblique," *RHPhR* 59 (1979) 427–37. Also see G. Wehmeier, "סתר *str* hi. to hide," *TLOT* 2:813–19 [*THAT* 2:173–81]; and S. Wagner, "סתר *sātar*," *ThWAT* 5:967–77.

226 The manufacture of idols is again negative. צָרִים is unusual. It may perhaps be due merely to a word-play with מִצְרַיִם (see Bonnard, 176–77 under this heading). There is probably an echo of יצר, "form, make," as well. The Targum explains it as צלמין מציירין, "artistic representations," as does Delitzsch, following a reading in Codex Reuchlin. Torrey (*Second Isaiah* [1928]) on this passage believed: "The use of צרים, 'pangs,' in place of צורות, 'images,' is a characteristic bit of massoretic humor" (cf. 41:21; 48:5).

227 On v. 17 see Merendino, *Der Erste und der Letzte:*

But then the question can be pursued a step further: Who is speaking here, and to whom?[228] Verse 17a says: "Israel has been helped by Yahweh." That is a collective testimony. It does not have to be uttered simply by a single individual. I believe that the people who make this confession of faith can be defined even more precisely. In the verse that immediately precedes this part-scene (45:13), Yahweh talks about "my city and . . . my deported people" ("my *gālût*"; וְגָלוּתִי, i.e., the group of the exiled/deported people). The verse again shows itself to be a link passage. Now in vv. 14-15a and vv. 15b-17 two groups of "prisoners" stand over against each other: the ones who have now been put in fetters, and the ones who have been set free. "Yahweh's prisoners" testify that Israel's God can save, for ever and ever. They pass on their own experience: that people who make idols will be put to shame. They themselves have been forced to experience this. The deliverance is not merely a fact belonging to the past. It is fundamental for present and future, forever—to all eternity.[229] This help is not limited in time. A subtle theology of history here also explains the enslavement of nations who have given themselves up to idolatry. In this passage Israel does not exclude itself from this danger. For the text, the fate of the imprisoned foreign peoples (represented by the three African countries) is by no means a matter of indifference. The existence of these people means that there is no reason for triumph. Israel testifies to its hope—to the prisoners too. In doing so Israel here already fulfills its function as "witness," the function in which, according

to the second act (42:14—44:23), it has once more been installed.[230]

If the content of vv. 14-15a and vv. 15b-17 is examined, the programmatic character of these verses becomes clear. F. Delitzsch already talked about "an antiphonal response by the congregation to their (the heathen's) confession of faith."[231] Lament and thanksgiving, chorus and counterchorus alternate. As so often elsewhere in the drama of the ancient world, one of the chorus's functions is to show how the action is meant to be interpreted. Thus these verses are already a preparation for the end of the throne scene in vv. 21-25. At the same time these are themes that are taken up again in the remaining acts of the drama. First (v. 13) came the question whether Israel has to pay for the liberation and will continue to be indebted to Cyrus. The answer at the close of this section is also implicitly unequivocal: "No." Israel has been helped by Yahweh. That is an everlasting help (v. 17).

At the close of this section we may ask whether historical reminiscences are not also involved in the text. Why does the procession of prisoners consist particularly of peoples belonging to Egypt? Cyrus claimed sovereignty over Egypt too, as the tutelary deity with an Egyptian crown in the entry hall of his throne chamber in Parsargadae shows.[232] It was only his successor Cambyses II (529–522 B.C.E.) who actually conquered Egypt (between 525 and 522), declaring himself "king of Egypt, king of the country."[233] Persian lordship over Egypt lasted until about 405 B.C.E., the beginning of the 28th

---

Eine Untersuchung von Jes 40–48 (1981) 440: "The second person plural form of address shows that these saying too have their *Sitz im Leben* in the assembled congregation."

228   For the various proposals, see the survey in Beuken, 248.

229   The frequency of the indications of time should be noted. See E. Jenni, "Das Wort ʿōlām im AT" (diss. 1953); printed in *ZAW* 64 (1953) 197–248, and *ZAW* 65 (1953) 1–35; summary now in "עוֹלָם ʿôlām eternity," *TLOT* 2:852–62, esp. 859–60 [*THAT* 2:228–43, esp. 239]; further H.-D. Preuss, "עוֹלָם ʿôlām," *ThWAT* 5:1144–59.

230   Cf. esp. 42:18-25; 43:10, 12; 44:8.

231   Delitzsch, 2:226 [477] on this passage.

232   See M. Mallowan, "Cyrus the Great (558–529 B.C.)," in *The Cambridge History of Iran* 2 (1985) 392–402 (with lit.); cf. also Xenophon *Cyropaedia*

1.1.4; 8.6.20.

233   See E. Bresciani, "The Persian Occupation of Egypt," in *The Cambridge History of Iran* 2 (1985) 502–28; K. M. T. Atkinson, "The Legitimacy of Cambyses and Darius as Kings of Egypt," *JAOS* 76 (1956) 167–77 (with references to texts); O. Kaiser, "Der geknickte Rohrstab. Zum geschichtlichen Hintergrund der Überlieferung und Weiterbildung der prophetischen Ägyptensprüche im 5. Jahrhundert"; also his "Zwischen den Fronten. Palästina in der Auseinandersetzung zwischen Perserreich und Ägypten in der ersten Hälfte des 4. Jahrhunderts," both now in O. Kaiser, *Von der Gegenwartsbedeutung des Alten Testaments, Gesammelte Studien* (1984) 181–88 and 189–98.

Egyptian Dynasty. There was a series of revolts against Persian domination, the best known being led by Inaros, son of Psamtik, a Lybian. It began about 460 B.C.E. and was supported by the Athenians, who took a fleet up the Nile as far as Memphis. The revolt was put down by Megabyzus, the Persian satrap of Syria. Inaros was brought to Persia with other leaders and was put to death there in 454.[234] Upper Egypt and the "Jewish" military colony in Elephantine remained on the side of the Persians.[235] In view of these historical facts it is interesting that the legitimacy of Persian rule over Egypt should be acknowledged in the DtIsa text.

---

234 Herodotus 3.12; Thucydides 1.104–10.

235 This is clear from the fact that the Aramaic papyri from Elephantine are dated according to the years of Artaxerxes I's reign (465/464–425). See A. E. Cowley, *Aramaic Papyri of the Fifth Century B.C.* (1923; reprint 1967) nos. 8 and 9 from the 6th year, no. 10 from the 9th year and no. 11 from the 10th year.

18 Yes, thus says Yahweh,
who has created the heavens—
he is the God

who has formed the earth and made it—
he founded it,

he did not create it as a wasteland,
he formed it to dwell in:

19 "I am Yahweh and there is no other.
I have not spoken in hiddenness,
in the place of the land of darkness.

I have not said to Jacob's descendants:
'Seek me in the wasteland <for nothing>!'

I am Yahweh who speaks righteousness,
who proclaims what is right."

The commentators are at one in viewing vv. 18-25 as a unit, vv. 18-19 perhaps forming a subsection within it. They therefore also observe the *parashah* division, which begins a new section with v. 18. The content suggests this division. The theme of Yahweh's uniqueness is carried though to the end of the chapter.[236] This declaration is constitutive for the whole throne scene.[237] To that extent there is a connection throughout. But it seems to me that the link with vv. 14-17 is relatively close, and that it permits a better understanding of the special statement made in vv. 18-19.

The verses form the conclusion of the individual scene, which was originally concerned with the bringing of tribute as a manifestation of rule. It is only in v. 20 that a new action is announced: "Gather together . . . !"

In v. 18 a connection with what has gone before is established through the signal "yes indeed!" (כִּי).[238] The catchword "hide" (סתר) is a clear link: v. 15, "a hidden God"; v. 19, "I have not spoken in hiddenness." Consequently the double "he" (הוא, v. 18) in the sense of "he, that one" as a statement of identification can also point back to the God about whom the lament asked in vv. 14-15a: "*he* is the God!" (with the definite article). In the framework of the throne scene Yahweh confirms the word of his witness in vv. 15b-17. The original *topos* "tribute of the foreign countries" changes, and is now the proclamation of God's gift in his creation. It is noticeable that in v. 18 the act of creation is described with four different verbs ("create," ברא, bis; "form," יצר, bis; "make," עשׂה; "found," כנן), whereas in v. 19 the divine Word is announced with three verbs ("speak," דבר, bis; "say," אמר; "proclaim," נגד *Hiphil*).

Verses 18-19 contain at heart Yahweh's reiterated self-introduction. He is "*the* God," who reveals himself as "I am Yahweh" (vv. 18 and 19). A series of participles[239] expresses the importance of Yahweh's commitment to the world. The declarations correspond to titles known from the hymnic tradition. "Heaven and earth" means the whole world that Yahweh has created and over which *this* God therefore rules.[240] These titular declarations are not chosen at random, however. They are in their function, although not the contents, comparable with the

---

236 Verse 18: "I am Yahweh and there is no other"; cf. vv. 19, 21, 22.

237 Cf. 45:3, 5, 6, 8, and the recapitulation and further development of the theme of Yahweh's uniqueness in 46:8.

238 Marti has noted this: "You will never be put to shame, *for* Yahweh's word is true." See also Muilenburg and Spykerboer, *The Structure and Composition of Deutero-Isaiah* (1976), on this passage; also M. Dijkstra, "Zur Deutung von Jesaja 45,15ff.," *ZAW* 89 (1977) 220.

239 On the meaning of the participle see R. Bartelmus, *HYH: Bedeutung und Funktion eines hebräischen "Allerweltswortes"–zugleich ein Beitrag zur Frage des hebräischen Tempussystems* (1982) 49–51.

240 Cf. the Greek κόσμος, "cosmos." For the comparison with Egyptian throne names, see A. Alt, "Jesaja 8,23–9,6 . . . ," *Kleine Schriften* (Munich, 1953) 206–25, esp. p. 219; S. Morenz, "Ägyptische und davidische Königstitulaten," *ZÄS* 79 (1954) 73–74.

throne names of the pharaohs in Egypt, which also signify a particular program. It is noticeable that the earth is characterized as creation in three ways.[241] This shows the direction in which the whole is moving.

■ **18** Yahweh's actual declaration begins only in v. 18b, with the finite verbs. The conviction that the world was created as dwelling place is the theological application of belief in creation. This belief is subjected to doubt by the experience of destruction, either through natural forces (when during earthquakes the ground ceases to be firm, or when floods lay the country waste) or, and above all, when the land is devastated by war. But the chaos is not God's will, and not the purpose of creation. The catchword "barren, waste" (*tohû*, תֹהוּ), in any event, is reminiscent of Gen 1:2.[242] DtIsa draws hope from the promise of his God that even the ravaged land of Israel can be restored. Thus v. 18 could anticipate the theme that is then especially expounded in chap. 49.[243] But in its immediate context, Yahweh's resolve that the world should be created not as a wasteland but as a dwelling place has probably a more practical and direct reference, if it refers to the lament of the prisoners.

תֹהוּ is the term for "desert, waste place, nothingness."[244] There is also an echo of "the frightening desert waste that brings destruction."[245] "Especially in proclamations of judgment, it means a desert or devastation that is threatened."[246] Isa 24:10 is important for our pres-

ent text because this is the word used there for the city that has been laid waste and is deserted. More common are compounds of שמם, "to lie waste."[247] In the return to the era of salvation in 54:3, DtIsa talks about "the desolate towns" that will be inhabited once more. It is not God's will that human beings should be led into imprisonment in fetters (v. 14), or sold into slavery, not even if they are Egyptians and Africans. If cities and countries are "laid waste" and lose their populations, this is the result of human acts. The cause is seen to be idolatry. This is true for all nations, Israel included.[248] It is an explanation that is put forward as a divine oracle by which to interpret the presentation of the prisoners.

■ **19** The second declaration in v. 19 is also difficult for us to understand. It will be permissible to assume that here too, in correspondence to v. 18, general statements are linked with a practical reference. What is "the place of the land of darkness"?[249] Is the land dark because Yahweh has withdrawn his light from it?[250] Or is it the land of death, in contrast to "the land of the living"?[251] There are reasons for supposing that the underworld is meant.[252] Isa 5:8ff. could again speak in favor of this, for there, after the devastation (v. 9), the throng of human beings disappears into Sheol (v. 14).[253]

If we assume that there is a close connection between vv. 18 and 19 on the one hand and vv. 14-17 on the other, Ezekiel's seven oracles against Pharaoh and Egypt

---

241 On *he* has founded it" (lit. "it is he who founds it") see E. Gerstenberger, "כון *kûn* ni. to stand firm," *TLOT* 2:602–6 [*THAT* 1:812–17]; K. Koch, "כון *kûn*," *TDOT* 7:89–101 [*ThWAT* 4:95–107, esp. 104].

242 Muilenburg (531) on this passage: "God did not leave the earth empty and unoccupied; he created it for the purpose of making it a home for men." See also Young on the passage. Duhm takes a different view here.

243 Cf. esp. 49:8, 19, 20.

244 See *HALAT* under this heading.

245 C. Westermann, *Genesis 1–11* (1984) 102 on Gen 1:2 [*Genesis 1* (1974) 142] (with reference to Deut 32:10; Job 6:18; 12:24 = Ps 107:40).

246 Ibid., 103 [142], on the basis of Isa 24:10; 34:11; 40:23; Jer 4:23.

247 See F. Stolz, "שמם *šmm* to lie deserted," *TLOT* 3:1373 [*THAT* 2:972]: In the *Qal* "when the objective aspect dominates, the verb can best be rendered 'to lie devastated.' Subj[ect]s are usually the earth, the fields, etc. (Gen 47:19; Ezek 12:19, etc.; likewise *šāmēm* 'devastated' in Jer 12:11; Lam 5:18;

Dan 9:17 of the sanctuary. . . . One should perhaps understand the [Niphal] as more pass[ive] than the qal, i.e., 'to be abandoned' (of streets and cities: Lev 26:22; Isa 33:8; Jer 33:10; of the land: Jer 12:11; Zech 7:14; of buildings and altars: Ezek 6:4; Joel 1:17; Zeph 3:6)."

248 Cf. Isa 5:8-14, 17, esp. v. 9; Jer 34:8-27, esp. v. 22.

249 In Hebrew the definite article in the construct is missing in חֹשֶׁךְ "darkness, gloominess." So the translation could also be "place of *a* land of darkness." But it is probably a particular darkness that is being announced. Delitzsch writes on this passage (2:227–28 [479]): "According to Ps. cxxxix.15, the interior of the earth, and according to Job x.21, Hades, in contrast to the heathen cave-oracles and spirit-voices which seemed to rise up from the interior of the earth, which were evoked by the necromancers (see ch. lxv.4; viii.19; xxix.4)" [trans. altered].

250 See Amos 8:9; Ezek 32:8; cf. also Isa 9:1 (2), 18 (19).

251 Cf. Isa 53:8; 38:11; Jer 11:19; Ezek 26:20; Pss 27:13; 52:7 (5); 116:9; 142:6 (5); Job 28:13.

in Ezek 29:1—32:32 are of especial interest, for there we find a series of elements that are comparable with the present DtIsa text. These very similarities also bring out the differences. According to Ezek 29:17-21, Nebuchadnezzar, the king of Babylon, is given Egypt as compensation. The judgment is the result of Egypt's pomp (הָמוֹן) "in which there is concentrated everything that is vain and immoderate, everything boastful from the political or the religious point of view."[254] In a lament over the pharaoh the text reads:

> 32:8 All the bright lights in the sky I shall darken on your account, and I shall set darkness over your land, says [the Lord] Yahweh (אֲדֹנָי יהוה).
> 9 And I shall trouble the hearts of many nations when I lead ‹your hosts of captives› among the nations, to lands which you (formerly) did not know. . .
> 15 When I make [the land of] Egypt into a wilderness and the land ‹lies waste›, stripped of all that fills it—when I smite all who dwell in it, then they will know that I am Yahweh.[255]

Above all, however, the passage describes in detail how Egypt with its pomp descends to the underworld, into the realm of the dead.[256] The DtIsa text is much terser, and lacks any kind of mythological exposition. There can be nothing more here than a mere allusion to the Ezekiel tradition. The text is more interested in the counterpart—the deliverance. The prisoners themselves lament. What are they told?

Perhaps it can take us a little further if we ask how the declaration in v. 19 would sound if it were put in positive terms: "Yahweh has spoken in a place, he has said to the seed of Jacob (there) seek me!" For Israel, "the place" (מָקוֹם) is especially Zion and the temple in Jerusalem.

"To seek God,"[257] particularly in the form of "seeking God's face," is a paraphrase for participation in the cult. In that context "cult" can also mean the inquiry of an oracle and invocation in lament. All this was for Israel again bound up with Zion and the temple. In his revelation Yahweh had bound himself to Zion; that was the place where he could be invoked. But here we must remember the context in DtIsa: it is the Creator of the heavens and the earth who is speaking here. So at the same time he is not spatially bound.

But what is the counterpart to the "seeking of God" that is described here? The supposition that Osiris[258] is meant no longer seems to me impossible, remembering the context and the complaint of the Egyptians. The irony is that the search for Osiris in the underworld really does lead to the underworld, to downfall. In the text no name is mentioned, in contrast to 46:1-2, where Bel and Nebo are named. Unlike the foreign gods, Yahweh brings about "salvation." That is the testimony here for Israel, and for the foreign nations too.

The purpose in both verses, 18 and 19, is Yahweh's proclamation: "I am Yahweh." The revelation of the name is intended for the foreign peoples. For Israel the name is familiar. Nevertheless Israel also hears the definition of Yahweh as the Only One (v. 18)[259] and the one who establishes "justice, righteousness" (צֶדֶק) through his word.[260] Yahweh's sovereignty is manifested when men and women live in accordance with that word, not through the presentation of tribute.

252 See W. A. M. Beuken, "The Confession of God's Exclusivity by All Mankind," *Bijdr* 35 (1974) 335–56, esp. 343 n. 28; and Beuken, 324 n. 71, with reference to N. J. Tromp, *Primitive Conceptions of Death and the Nether World in the Old Testament* (1969) 96ff.

253 See above on 44:27.

254 Zimmerli, *Ezekiel* 2 (1983) 135 on 30:1-19 [*Ezechiel* (1969) 739].

255 Translation following ibid.

256 See 31:16, אֶרֶץ תַּחְתִּית . . . בוֹר . . . שְׁאוֹלָה; 32:17-32.

257 See C. Westermann, "Die Begriffe für Fragen und Suchen im AT," in *Forschung am Alten Testament* 2 (1974) 162–90, esp. 165; Bonnard on this passage;

S. Wagner, "בָּקַשׁ *biqqeš*," *TDOT* 2:229–41, esp. 238 [*ThWAT* 1:754–69; 765 on 45:19].

258 See Duhm here.

259 For the grammatical construction of v. 18, see Beuken, "The Confession of God's Exclusivity by All Mankind," *Bijdr* 35 (1974) 336–56.

260 C. F. Whitley, "Deutero-Isaiah's Interpretation of *ṣedeq*," *VT* 22 (1972) 469–75. He translates here (473): "I Yahweh uttereth a divine decision (*ṣedeq*), I declareth *what is destined* (*mêšārîm*)." See also F. Crüsemann, "Jahwes Gerechtigkeit im Alten Testament," *EvTh* 36 (1976) 427–56. Cf. Prov 1:3; 2:9; 12:17; also Isa 33:15; Pss 9:9 (8); 58:2; 99:4.

45

"Turn to me and let (me) help (you),
all the ends of the earth!" (45:22)

B. 3.   45:20-24
Homage of the Whole World before Yahweh
(Procession)

20   Assemble yourselves and come in,
draw near together,
those who have escaped from the nations!

They have not perceived (it),
those who carry the wood of their idols
and pray to a god who does not help.

21   Declare and present your case!
Let them consult together!
Who told this from long ago,
and proclaimed it of old?
Was it not I, Yahweh?
And there are no gods besides me.
Besides me there is no just and helping
God.

22   Turn to me and let (me) help (you),
all the ends of the earth!
For I am God and there is none besides.

23   I have sworn by myself,
from my mouth righteousness has gone
forth,
a word that will not return.
Yes, to me every knee shall bow,
every tongue shall swear!

24   "Only in Yahweh, he has told me, <is there>
proof of righteousness and strength."

To him all who were incensed against him
<shall>ᵃ come in and be ashamed.

24ᵃ   Following numerous manuscripts (1QIsaᵃ, LXX, S, Vg), one
should read the plur. יָבֹאוּ here instead of the sing. יָבֹא.

■ **20-22** A new scene begins with v. 20.²⁶¹ This is signaled by three verbs of movement ("assemble . . . come in . . . draw near").²⁶² It is still part of the throne scene, for Yahweh himself is the speaker who gives the instructions (v. 21). There are elements that are also found in the trial scenes: "assemble . . . proclaim . . . put forward the case . . . consult."²⁶³ But at the end there is not a judgment; instead there are two questions: "Who . . . ? Is it not I . . . ?" This does not look like the end of a trial scene.

It is important for the interpretation to decide who is meant by "those who have escaped from the nations" (פְּלִיטֵי הַגּוֹיִם).²⁶⁴ The group can be seen in positive terms. In that case it is Israelites who have survived from the

261   It is therefore possible that Cyrus with his prisoners has already gone off; see v. 14: "they go behind you in fetters."

262   Instead of "together" (יַחְדָּו) 1QIsaᵃ has "and comes" (ואתיו), as another verb.

263   For the interpretation as a "court speech" see Muilenburg, Westermann, Melugin, Stuhlmueller, Schoors; for the view that it is a "dispute" see Begrich, von Waldow, Fohrer. The section is generally defined as comprising 45:18-25, however.

264   This means understanding the construction as a partitive genitive. See E. Ruprecht, "פלט *plṭ* pi. to save," *TLOT* 2:986 [*THAT* 2:420–27]: "*pālîṭ/pālêṭ* is

an 'escapee,' almost without exception one who escaped the sword in war, who barely survived the defeat in war by flight (. . . Jer 44:28; Ezek 6:8; Jer 51:50)" (988 [424]). "An 'escapee' is occasionally the messenger who reports devastating defeat (Gen 14:13; Ezek 24:26f.; 33:21f.)" (989 [424]). See also G. F. Hasel, "פלט *pālaṭ*," *ThWAT* 6:589–606.

nations, or "Gentiles who have been preserved."[265] As far as I can see, however, the group is clearly characterized in unfavorable terms, whether they be "Israelites" or "Gentiles."[266] According to v. 20b they are people "who carry the wood of their figure ['their idol' is meant] and pray to a god who does not help."[267] Here the remnant notion is still used entirely in its original sense; those who have escaped are the ones who announce the downfall of their peoples and countries.[268] The idols and their worship are the visible reason for the catastrophe.

With these presuppositions the link with the context becomes clearer. This part of the scene is parallel to 45:14-19. As is often the case, the presentation is in parallel form.

Again it is a question of "foreign peoples" (גּוֹיִם). "They pray to a god" (מִתְפַּלְלִים אֶל־אֵל, 45:20)[269] corresponds to v. 14: "They cry to you (in prayer)." "There are no (other) gods besides me" (v. 21) takes up from v. 14: "Besides him there is no other! There are no gods!" The goal is again to testify to Yahweh's help (vv. 20 and 21; cf. 15 and 17). If the one group carries the products of its country and is in chains, the others carry the emblems of their gods.

The scene also serves as preparation for the following act in chap. 46. That is why the scene here can be so brief. The catchword "carry" (v. 20: נשׂא) is taken up again and expounded in 46:1-4. There the idols are Bel and Nebo. This suggests that in 45:20 the "nations" (גּוֹיִם) means the peoples who have been vanquished by Cyrus in the east.[270] This part of the scene therefore belongs to

the theme "sovereignty over the foreign nations." The different countries are portrayed in stylized form and those who appear here could be the pair Africa and Asia.[271]

But what does DtIsa do with the elements that are already at his disposal? Here the text's concern is not Cyrus's triumph but the question: what is going to happen to the conquered peoples? The reasons for the catastrophe are pointed out to them: they themselves are responsible. They could have been aware of the fate that threatened them. They should "discuss" this (v. 21: "let them consult together").[272] They have experienced the "righteous God" (אֵל־צַדִּיק). He can become the "helping" (מוֹשִׁיעַ) Yahweh for them too (v. 21). To put it somewhat too succinctly, this is theology for the nations in the tradition of Deuteronomy. The text is astonished that people who have escaped the catastrophe should still be dragging idols with them. With this the writer turns to his own people as well—they are the listeners. They were, and are, "survivors" too.

The unit vv. 20-24 forms the finale of the throne scene. What is presented is the homage of the whole world, or to be more exact, it is the anticipation of this homage. The beginning of the final part-scene is marked by the announcement of a new entrance: "Turn to me (פְּנוּ־אֵלַי) . . . all the ends of the earth." They are not prisoners any more, and they turn no longer to Cyrus, but directly to the Lord of the whole world.

The ends of the earth (אַפְסֵי־אָרֶץ),[273] in the spatial sense first of all, means the all-embracing sphere of God's sovereignty. They could then be portrayed

---

265 Delitzsch on this passage.
266 Bonnard particularly has made this point here.
267 Westermann explains the sentence as "a marginal gloss."
268 This means understanding the grammatical construction as a partitive genitive: "those *of the nations* who have escaped," not as a separative genitive: "those *out of the nations* who have escaped."
269 The onomatopoeia with *l* should be noted. Their speech is slurred as they pray!
270 Ibn Ezra on this passage: "Ye, that are escaped. . . . The Babylonians are addressed."
271 Cf. again the representation in the tomb of Rekh-mi-Re and the caption: "The arrival in peace of the chiefs of Retenu and all the lands of Further Asia in deferential obeisance, their tribute on their backs, in the hope that there would be given to them the breath of life because of loyalty to his Majesty; for

they have seen his very great victories—yea his terribleness has dominated their hearts" (Davies, *The Tomb of Rekh-mi-Re* [1943, reprint 1973] 27). Here too "those who escaped" are shown and described.
272 With reference to the situation of the drama, Beuken observes acutely in "The Confession of God's Exclusivity by all Mankind," *Bijdr* 35 (1974) 347: "It is a climax, for now God is successfully pleading in front of his main adversaries what he has so far been contending about them before Israel. . . . The switch from the second to the third person is not surprising if we interpret it as an aside to Israel."
273 For this phrase see 52:10; also Deut 33:17; 1 Sam 2:10; Jer 16:19; Mic 5:3 (4); Zech 9:10; Pss 2:8; 22:27; 59:14 (13); 67:8 (7); 72:8; 98:3; Prov 30:4; Sir 36:33; cf. Matt 12:42; Mark 1:45; 13:27; Luke 11:31; Acts 1:8; 17:30; 21:28; 1 Cor 4:17; Rev 20:8.

emblematically, for example as the four points of the compass.[274] The whole horizon of the world is also comprehended in the fourfold "all" (כֹּל): "all the ends of the earth" (v. 22), "every knee . . . every tongue" (v. 23), "all who were incensed against him" (v. 24). This last "all" in particular is important: even God's opponents are included.

■ **22-24** These verses do not turn initially to Israel especially. The description of God is again "El" (אֵל), as it is elsewhere too in the case of the foreign nations. This is the God who calls, the only God for everyone. The action is at heart a double oath ceremony. Yahweh's oath (נִשְׁבַּעְתִּי)[275] corresponds to the oath of human beings (תִּשָּׁבַע) (v. 23). Here elements of the covenant tradition are taken up in astonishing abstraction. Yahweh's oath is uttered in the perfect tense: "I have sworn." His righteousness holds good in both salvation and disaster. His word has already been realized in creation, and in the fulfillment of the future that has been announced,[276] a link thus being forged with 40:6-8 and 55:10-11.

The "bending of every knee" could well be understood as an element in the action. It is part of the divine speech, but corresponds to what would be a stage direction in the modern theater. To bend the knee is an act of homage to the ruler.[277] The oath of "Everyman" (v. 24) is directed to the future. It expressly names salvation and disaster, blessing and curse. The proofs of righteousness (צְדָקוֹת)[278] can be experienced, and so can the downfall of those who are against Yahweh. Sovereignty has two creative aspects: grace and what makes life possible on the one hand, and the judicial and punitive aspect on the other. The structure of the eschatological divine judgment on humanity is here fully developed.[279] It is closely connected with the theophany, and with the response of the human being to it.[280]

Attention should be drawn to one detail here. The first person singular is used in v. 24, apparently without any transition: "He has said to me" (לִי אָמַר). In view of the textual evidence, neither deletion nor a conjectural emendation would seem justified.[281] The text continually works with correspondences. Immediately before, in v. 23, "to me" (לִי) refers to Yahweh. In v. 24 it is at all events a human being who speaks the "to me" (לִי). It is thus made clear for the listener too that the previous divine speech has ended. Yahweh is now talked about in the third person. But who can the speaker be? Right at the beginning, in 40:6, an equally unexpected first person asked: "What shall I cry?" There the question is part of the "spokesman's" installation. He is accredited in his prophetic function. I would assume that in 45:24, at the end of this act, the "speaker" steps out of his role again. It is as a human being that he now utters the confession of faith in Yahweh: "Truly, with Yahweh. . . ." He speaks first what everyone is then supposed to echo. To be the spokesman for men and women is as much a prophetic task as it is to be the spokesman of God.[282]

Thus vv. 22-24 are entirely universal. The "ends of the earth" should allow themselves to be saved (v. 22)[283]— that is the message of this theophany. Here the frontier between heaven and earth is permeable. Earthly circumstances are presented in the form of heavenly events.

---

274 See Rev 20:8.

275 Cf. Gen 22:16; Exod 32:13; Deut 32:40; Amos 4:2; 6:8; Jer 22:5; Heb 6:13-18; N. Lohfink, *Die Landverheissung als Eid. Eine Studie zu Gen 15* (1967). See also *HALAT* 4:1298–1301 under the heading שבע (with lit.); C. A. Keller, "שׁבע *šbᶜ* ni. to swear," *TLOT* 3:1292–97 [*THAT* 2:855–63].

276 For the construction see Marti (314) on this passage: "The main subject is דָּבָר, hence יָצָא is masculine: Gone forth from my mouth as truth is a word that shall not be rescinded, will not be withdrawn before it has been fulfilled." But in my view "righteousness, justice" (צְדָקָה) and "word" (דָּבָר) are parallel and interchangeable.

277 Cf. also 1 Kgs 19:18.

278 Cf. Judg 5:11; 1 Sam 12:7; Mic 6:5; Pss 71:19; 103:6; 1QS 1:21-22.

279 See here E. Brandenburger, *Das Recht des*

Weltenrichters: Untersuchung zu Matthäus 25, 31–46 (1980) 25, with reference to Ps 37:22.

280 See Bonnard's summing up of the passage (179): "It is in Yahweh alone that power and 'justice' can be found, that is to say fidelity—translated into action—to the plan of salvation, according to which he wishes at once to judge, justify, pardon and restore."

281 Torrey (*Second Isaiah* [1928]) has proposed reading here instead of "he has said to me" (לִי אָמַר) "one will say" (*Niphal*, יֵאָמֵר). This could accord with 1QIsaᵃ, provided that one does not point as לִי יֹאמַר, "he will say to me." Other commentators, appealing to LXX (λέγων) and Syriac wnʾmrwn, change to "as follows," as the beginning of the sentence.

282 Cf. the double charge given to Moses in Exod 18:19-20; Jer 15:19; 18:20.

283 This is the third use of the root "help, save" (ישׁע) in the context; cf. vv. 20, 21, 22.

25   **"Through Yahweh all the descendants of Israel
       shall be righteous and triumph" (45:25)**

But then what is the function of Israel's "seed" ("all descendants")?[284] Verse 25 gives the answer. Once more an "all" (כָּל) is uttered. In the four preceding instances of "all, every" (כָּל־) in vv. 22-24, Israel is part of the nations. Now the subject is Israel's unity, and its task. Israel's unity is also an eschatological wonder, like the gathering of the nations. It is experienced, presented, and at the same time hoped for in the future.[285] The whole book shows that Yahweh "makes righteous."[286] This is explicitly stated in the framework of the throne scene, in 45:8. But here the new catchword is: "They shall praise" (יִתְהַלְלוּ yithalelû), that is, "the whole of Israel's seed" is to raise the "Hallelujah."[287]

In the framework of the dramatic structure, it is noticeable that a hymnic conclusion by the chorus such as we find as in 44:23, for example, is missing. But the hymn is implicit. The "hallel" does not have to be explicitly "performed." It is enough if the precentor announces it, as in the psalms. The congregation responds with the cry "hallelujah!" In this way it identifies itself with the aknowledgment of v. 24. The hymn is "the people's acclamation of the ruler." Here it is the recognition of God as Lord of the whole world.

The throne scene thus reaches a moving conclusion, which presents the way in which the divine sovereignty in all its aspects is implemented. It is universal and yet at the same time related to the individual fate. It is realized in faith in the one who is above all earthly rule, and yet it is eminently political. It acts with strength, and yet has compassion on prisoners and those who suffer. Humanity is a unity for God, and is yet divided into different peoples, each with its special destiny. Not all human beings can be "Israel's seed," but all can acknowledge Yahweh when they hear the testimony that Israel now already speaks.[288] It is impossible to miss the conviction that runs through the whole scene that the God of Israel is a saving, helping, liberating God.

I believe that historically speaking this text already

---

284 Beuken (255) on this passage observes that there is a functional tension between the use of the names Jacob and Israel in DtIsa. He therefore thinks (pointing to Delitzsch, Westermann, and Bonnard) that "seed of Israel" is not the same as "seed of Jacob" in v. 19: "What is meant here is not the historical Israel, defined as nation, but the Israel to which 'outsiders' can also come, under the influence of God's Spirit." There may perhaps be a wordplay here. Verse 19 has to do with Yahweh's hiddenness. According to Gen 32:23-33 Jacob became Israel at the Jabbok. He saw God face to face and his life was preserved (v. 31). Is there an echo in v. 25 of "seed of Israel" as "seed of the man who saw God"?

285 See F. Crüsemann, "Jahwes Gerechtigkeit im Alten Testament," *EvTh* 36 (1976) 444–46, on this passage: "The connection with the 'judgment' genre, which is otherwise wholly alien to the mention of Yahweh's ṣĕdāqâ, permits us for the first time to talk about anything in the direction of justification: through Yahweh's salvific act (termed ṣĕdāqâ) both Yahweh *and* Israel receive justice."

286 See Beuken, 258: "DtIsa's picture of the future is entirely eschatological, but we do well to understand the term qualitatively, not quantitatively. He is not talking about something that is far away, and hence abstract, but about events here and now."

287 North interestingly enough paraphrases the verse, in view of the dramatic character of the text: "Shall be victorious . . . and glory. 'Paeans of victory' might serve, but the 'paean' was essentially Greek. The natural way for Hebrews to 'triumph and glory (*hithallel*) in Yahweh' would be to sing 'Hallelujah' psalms such as Psalms 104–106, 111–113, 115–117, 135, 146–150. These psalms are full of the 'praiseworthy' deeds of Yahweh." For the hallelujah see, e.g., Ps 106:48: "Blessed be Yahweh, the God of Israel, from everlasting to everlasting. And let all the people say, 'Amen.' Hallelujah!"; and 1 Chr 16:36; 2 Chr 5:13-14. It shows how close DtIsa is to liturgical celebration. See also the end of the *Odes of Solomon;* Tob 13:18; 3 Macc 7:13; Rev 19:1, 3, 4, 6. For lit.: C. Westermann, "הלל *hll* pi. to praise," *TLOT* 1:371–76 [*THAT* 1:493–502]. H. Ringgren, "הלל *hll* II," *TDOT* 3:404–10 [*ThWAT* 2:433–41].

288 By saying this I should like to take up and correct Leene's conclusion in "Universalism or Nationalism? Isaiah XLV 9–13 and Its Context," *BBTFT* 35 (1974) 334: "I hardly consider the terms 'universalism' and 'nationalism' appropriate to the adequate description of the theology of Isa. xlv. Second Isaiah expects the universal acknowledgement of Yahweh as the only God. . . . Every 'goy' may know: I am not

embodies the beginnings of a "missionary" theology. In interpreting the text we should note that it argues out of a situation not of triumph but of trial.[289] Is it true that the word of God holds good? Will it be efficacious in earthly history? Thus Rom 14:7-12 and Phil 2:9-11 are applied interpretations of the text by Paul.

---

an exchange-medium in Yahweh's plan, but a potential Israelite." For the discussion see also P. A. H. de Boer, *Second Isaiah's Message* (1956) 90; D. E. Hollenberg, "Nationalism and 'the Nations' in Isaiah XL–LV," *VT* 19 (1969) 32.

289 Spykerboer rightly draws attention to this; see *The Structure and Composition of Deutero-Isaiah* (1976) 143.

Act IV: 46:1–49:13

"Yes! Yahweh has comforted his people and has compassion on his afflicted [opressed] ones" (49:13)

In 46:1—47:15 Babylon's "deposition" is described. It begins with the parody of a procession (46:1-4).[1] The name "Babylon" is not yet mentioned. Hitherto also, it has only been used in connection with the announcement of Cyrus in 43:14. There it is prophesied that the "Chaldean's" jubilation will be transformed into lamentation. This is what is now happening. With the naming of the Babylonian gods Bel and Nebo (46:1) we are given a first indication of what is to come.

A second scene is 46:5-8. It too contains elements of the procession (v. 7: "lift onto their shoulders . . . drag . . ."). It is traders and their activities that are parodied here. It is to them that Babylon owes its proverbial wealth. Verses 9-13 are a direct divine speech with an announcement of the turn of events.

In a further scene (chap. 47), in an evident intensification, the personified "Babylon"[2] herself appears. "The mistress of kingdoms" (v. 5) is degraded to a slave. She goes off, together with her counselors (47:13): "Everyone staggers to their own side" (v. 15).

That is in brief the substance of the first part of this act, where "Babylon" is at the center. The text is full of action, and certainly offers an opportunity for a colorful spectacle. But for all that, one should not overlook the deliberate skill of the literary shaping. This act too lives from its words. As I hope to show in the detailed exegesis, the individual sections are again elaborately linked through pointers to what is to come and to what has gone before, by way of ambiguous catchwords. In spite of the burlesque, this is a document belonging to a dispute. We can see this from the intermediate argumentative sections, which are introduced by "Listen . . ." (46:3), "remember . . ." (v. 9), "listen . . ." (v. 12). Even when parodied, the foreign cult is still a question addressed to Israel's own faith.

A 1. 46:1-4
Parody of a Procession (*Pompa*) and "Burden" on Babylon

46

"Bel is broken down, Nebo bends down" (46:1)

1   Bel is broken down, Nebo bends down.
Their images are packed onto beasts and
    cattle,
loaded onto them as a burden for the
    exhausted.

2   They are bent down, they are all broken
    down.
They were not able to save a burden,
and they themselves went into captivity.

3   Listen to me, house of Jacob,
and the whole remnant of the house of Israel,
who have been borne from birth,
who were carried from the womb—

---

1   The dramatic character of the text from v. 1 onward is stressed by Y. Gitay, *Prophecy and Persuasion* (1981) 201, 205; R. J. Clifford, *Fair Spoken and Persuading* (1984) 130.

2   In what follows the *personified* Babylon is always set between quotation marks, in distinction from the *city* of Babylon, as a political entity.

253

4
    and even until your old age it is I,
    and until you turn gray I will drag you along.
    I have done it and I will carry
    and I will drag and save.

The text is clearly divided into two halves. In vv. 1-2 an action is described; in vv. 3 and 4 it is interpreted. In structure, and probably in genre too, this is comparable with the narrative visions and their interpretation in the book of Daniel. The action serves as an oracle. This partly explains the difficult choice of words in the text, a difficulty intensified by the auditory effect that the writer intends. In this passage particularly, it is again obvious that the text is not written merely to be read; it should be heard.

The essential catchword is "burden" (מַשָּׂא *maśśāʾ*). It is found explicitly twice in vv. 1 and 2. In addition we twice have the root נשׂא ("bear") in vv. 1 and 3. In sound, *maśśāʾ* is striking for its double sharp *s*. We need only imagine what it sounded like when it was cried out by a big crowd! Until the final "I will . . . save" there is no section of text without a more or less sharp *s* sound. One only needs to underline them. In vv. 3 and 4 the shift among the different degrees of sharpness in the *s* sound is fascinating. But this may also have to do with the content. The hiss is a gesture of repulsion and defense. According to Jer 50:13, "Everyone who passes by Babylon shall be appalled and hiss (יִשֹּׁם וְיִשְׁרֹק) because of

all her wounds."[3] On the other hand Yahweh can "whistle" in order to call up the forces of destruction (Isa 5:26; 7:18). In Zech 10:8 "whistling" is used in a positive sense, for the gathering together of the exiles for their return. In its interaction of listening and performance, the dramatic action here is still close to the cult.

The term "burden" (מַשָּׂא) also shows that form and content cannot be divided in this text. Derived from the root נשׂא, "carry, lift," the word means especially the "load" that has to be carried. But it can also be a technical term for the prophetic oracle. Jer 23:33-40 is already a play on this ambiguity.[4] In the text the "load for pack animals" is initially the primary meaning. The animals can no longer carry their burden, the idols. It is useless to flee with these valuables. The end is "captivity" (v. 2).

At the same time the text can also be viewed as a prophetic oracle—as "burden" (מַשָּׂא) in this sense—about the downfall of Babylon,[5] or more precisely as the fulfillment of this oracle, for the downfall is now taking place. This leads to the question whether DtIsa would have been able to draw upon prophetic oracles about Babylon of this kind.[6]

---

3   Translation following W. Rudolph, *Jeremia* (1947; 3d ed. 1968) 300. Jer 51:37 also talks about "horror and whistling" (שַׁמָּה וּשְׁרֵקָה) in connection with the destruction of Babylon. See also *HALAT* 4:1527–28 under שׁרק; R. Lasch, "Pfeifen und Dämonenglaube," *ARW* 18 (1915) 589–92.

4   For the wordplay on "burden" in Num 4:27, 32, 49, see M. Gertner, "The Masorah and the Levites," *VT* 10 (1960) 241–84, esp. 252 n. 1.

5   On the connection between procession and omen/oracle in Babylon, see H. D. Preuss, *Verspottung fremder Religionen im Alten Testament* (1971) 222, with reference to A. L. Oppenheim, "Zur keilschriftlichen Omenliteratur," *Or* 5 (1936) 221–22; also Beuken, 326 n. 27, with reference to R. Borger, "Gott Marduk und Gott Šulgi als Propheten. Zwei prophetische Texte," *BiOr* 28 (1971) 16–17, 21–22. For Egypt see J. Assmann, "Das ägyptische Prozessionsfest," in J. Assmann and T. Sundermeier, eds., *Das Fest und das Heilige: Religiöse Kontrapunkte zur Alltagswelt* (1991) 105–22, esp. 108 on oracle.

6   The present interpretation is based on the assumption that collections of Babylon sayings were available to DtIsa. In the OT such sayings can be found in the framework of sayings regarding the foreign nations, especially in Isaiah 13–14 and 21, and in Jeremiah 50–51. They raise a whole series of problems, both literary and tradition-historical. The connection with the omen/oracle literature of the ancient world requires a much more detailed investigation than it has as yet received. It is not easy to elucidate how far interpretations after the event are present and how far, conversely, historical events contradict the prophecies. I should like explicitly to draw attention here to S. Erlandsson's study *The Burden of Babylon: A Study of Isaiah 13:2—14:23* (1970), with lit.; see also J. H. Hayes, "The Usage of Oracles Against Foreign Nations in Ancient Israel," *JBL* 87 (1968) 81–92. As nonbiblical examples Hayes gives two oracles against Babylon from Mari: *Archives royales de Mari XIII: Textes divers*, ed. G. Dossin (1964), text nos. 23 and 114, with reference to A. Malamat, "Prophetic Revelations in New

For this there are examples in connection with the book of Isaiah. Isa 13:1 begins: "The oracle ('burden') concerning Babylon that Isaiah son of Amoz saw" (מַשָּׂא בָּבֶל אֲשֶׁר חָזָה). One may doubt Isaianic authorship and yet agree with Wildberger: "Thus the possibility is still worth mentioning that the author of Isaiah 13 may have written at a time before the Persian leader Cyrus seized control of the empire of the Medes and that the destruction of Babylon at the hand of the Medes may indeed have been anticipated."[7] According to Wildberger, this would mean dating the text before 539 B.C.E. Isa 13:1 is the beginning of a collection of oracles that describe the downfall of Babylon in various ways. What is worth noting for the present DtIsa text is that "the burden" (מַשָּׂא) can be seen, and is therefore part of a visionary action. The reference back to what was proclaimed earlier—in 46:10 in this case—becomes comprehensible through such texts. Whether details in DtIsa also derive from prophecies of this kind can hardly be established.

Isaiah 21 is of interest, since it is also a "burden" (מַשָּׂא, v. 1) about the fall of Babylon. According to vv. 6-7, a watchman is to be posted to await a "caravan of pack animals"[8]—horses, donkeys, and camels. The caravan comes and the message is announced:[9] "Fallen, fallen is Babylon, and all the images of her gods lie shattered on the ground" (v. 9). For the person who was familiar with an oracle of this kind, the train of pack animals would already be an indication of Babylon's fall, which is otherwise not explicitly mentioned.

But the irony surely goes further. What is expounded here is the parody of a solemn procession (Latin *pompa*).[10] This was one of the most important public religious and political occasions in the whole of the ancient world. In a ceremonial procession, the gods, their images and symbols, as well as vessels used in cult and sacrifice, were carried around.[11] The *pompa* was an essential element in festivals. There the particular society presented itself in the identity and power it assumed for itself.[12]

In his commentary, Delitzsch already detected a connection between the DtIsa text and the *pompa*. The carrying of images of the city and state gods, as well as other precious objects, and finally the inclusion of animals of all kinds (לַחַיָּה וְלַבְּהֵמָה) were all part of a procession of this kind. But what was otherwise an occasion for the greatest admiration is here profoundly called in question as a glorification of human power directed against God.

■ **1-2** To come down to details: in v. 1 Bel and Nebo are named as Babylonian deities. "Bel" is really only the designation for "lord" (Akk. *bēlu*), comparable to the OT "Baal." It then became one of the names for Marduk, the chief god of the Babylonian kingdom. His temple in the

---

Documents from Mari and the Bible," *Volume du Congrès: Genève 1965* (1966) 206–27.

7 H. Wildberger, *Isaiah 13–27* (1997) 18 [*Jesaja* (2d ed. 1980) 511].

8 See *HALAT* s.v. רָכַב on this passage.

9 On the various possible interpretations of "the trek of chariots, riders and animals" already in an earlier text, Isa 21:1-10, see O. Kaiser, *Isaiah 13–39* (1974) on this passage [*Der Prophet Jesaja: Kapitel 13–39* (1973)]. Kaiser suspects an intentional ambiguity. As oracle this would correspond to the DtIsa text.

10 See F. Bömer, PW 21/2 (1952) 1878–1994 under the heading *Pompa 1* "pompa (πομπή) Prozessionen und Umzüge"; W. Burkert, *Greek Religion* (1985) 99–101 [*Griechische Religion der archaischen und klassischen Epoche* (1977) 163–66].

11 Best known are the phallephoric processions of the Dionysos cult. But a whole series of other objects "are carried" too. Burkert (*Greek Religion*, 99 [*Griechische Religion,* 164]) says here: "There were all kinds of appurtenances to be carried and corresponding roles with fixed titles such as basket

bearer, water bearer, fire bearer, bowl bearer, and bough bearer. In the Demeter and Dionysos cult covered containers whose contents are known only to the initiate are carried around in connection with the Mysteries—the round wickerwork basket with a lid, *kiste,* and the veiled winnowing fan, *liknon* and consequently there are *kistephoroi* [carrying chests] and *liknophoroi* [fan-shaped baskets]." Cf. PW 21/2, 1890–92, 1903–4. A good illustration is the panathenaean frieze in the Parthenon.

12 As an example of a *pompa* that was carried out but that was only the result of a long development, see the list of *pompa* in Daphne near Antioch (PW 21/2, 1955, no. 197). The *pompa* was organized by Antiochus IV Epiphanes c. 167 B.C.E. 2 Macc 6:7 reports a *pompa* of the same ruler in Jerusalem (PW 21/2, 1941, no. 125). Cf. also no. 196 on the *pompa* in Alexandria put on by Ptolemy II Philadelphus and Berenice c. 270 B.C.E. (PW 21/2, 1954–55) and the comments by E. E. Rice, *The Grand Procession of Ptolemy Philadelphus* (1983).

capital city Babylon was Esagila, with the famous temple tower Etemenanki. "Nebo" (Akk. *nabû*) was the god of the town of Borsippa, which was not far from Babylon. He was the god of science and was responsible for determining destinies, among other things. In the Babylonian pantheon he was reckoned to be Marduk's son. He was later identified with Hermes-Mercury.[13] In the text of the clay Cyrus cylinder found in Babylon, Bel and Nebo are named as Cyrus's tutelary gods.[14] In the OT the name of the god "Nebo" occurs only in the present text. It is probably included in the name Nebuchadrezzar, Heb. נְבוּכַדְרֶאצַּר (Akk. *Nabū-kudurri–uṣur*, "may Nabu protect the border"), Nebuchadrezzar being the Babylonian king who conquered Jerusalem.[15] The last Babylonian king, Nabonidus, also had a name incorporating the element Nabu. More important is the picture of Bel that OT tradition built up. The earliest OT instances are probably in Jer 50:2 and 51:44, that is, again in prophetic oracles about Babylon that are also similar in content to the present DtIsa text. In the additions to the book of Daniel that have come down to us in Greek, Bel has become the quintessence of Babylonian deity, and the object of polemic against idols.[16] Verse 1 here too is polemic; and polemic is generally an indication that a nerve has been touched. Bel "is broken down."[17] The verb כרע means first of all the kneeling in homage or prayer.[18] The people kneeled as the procession passed by.

Because of the context of the sentence, כרע is rendered "he is bent." Both in the oracle to Judah (Gen 49:9) and in the blessing of Balaam (Num 24:9), the word is used for the "crouching" of the lion. It is the quintessence of power. The verb can be used in a positive sense for kneeling in prayer and homage.[19] It has this sense in the immediately preceding text, Isa 45:23. To Yahweh "every knee shall bow" (תִּכְרַע כָּל־בֶּרֶךְ).

If one takes account of this context, an ironical note can at all events be detected. "Bel bows down." The variant in Isa 10:4 is then strange, where a possible reading could be: "The one who does not bow down among the prisoners will fall under the slain." Or—a reading closer to the present text of 46:1—"Belthi collapses, Osiris is broken and they fall among the slain."[20]

But now it is the "Bel" who collapses. We would like to know more exactly what the emblems for the gods Bel and Nebo were. The text may be thinking of statues. Marduk is represented by a mythical beast, half serpent and half griffin.

The text immediately adds here that it is certainly not the gods themselves who are being carried; "these are their images, (lit.) their fabrications." The suffix can be related either to the gods—they are only pictorial representations—or to the worshipers who have made the images (cf. 48:5). At all events I would relate the comment to Bel and Nebo, not to the pack animals.

עָצָב is the "fabrication, image of a god (used derogatorily)."[21] In this sense the Babylon oracle in Jer 50:2 is a close parallel: "Babylon is taken, Bel is put to shame, Merodach is shattered. Her images (עֲצַבֶּיהָ) are put to shame, her idols are shattered." On the other hand in the Babylon oracle in Isaiah 14 עצב II is used in the sense of "complaint, hardship," in the same series as "agitation," "excitement" (רֹגֶז), and "hard servitude"

---

13   The LXX tradition has Δαγων (*dagōn*)! I. L. Seeligmann (*The Septuagint Version of Isaiah* [1948] 77) points to Philo of Byblos: "Hellenistic conceptions occurring also in Philo Byblius may have served as source of origin." It would seem to me possible that in the LXX the text is linked with 1 Samuel 5, the story about the capture of the ark by the Philistines, and the setting up of their god Dagon in the sanctuary, with the consequent shattering of their idol. See also the illustration of the text in the synagogue at Dura-Europos.

14   The two deities are also mentioned on the clay Cyrus cylinder: "Cyrus . . . whose dynasty is loved by Bel and Nabu" (l. 22; see also l. 35); *AOT* 368ff.; *TUAT* 1:407–10, esp. 409; *ANET* 315–16. For the mention in the Aramaic texts from Elephantine (Egypt) see B. Porten, *Archives from Elephantine: The*

Life of an Ancient Jewish Military Colony (1968): "Aramean Deities," 164–173.

15   See also Nebushazban, Jer 39:13 (Akk. *Nabū-šēzibanni*, "Nabu save me"); see *HALAT*.

16   Cf. also the *Ep. Jer.* 40 and the context.

17   A change in the pointing such as *BHS* proposes is not required. Bel's "breakdown" has begun when the speaker begins; the "bending down" (participle) of Nebo still continues.

18   1 Kgs 8:54; 19:18; Pss 22:30 (29); 72:9.

19   Pss 22:30 (29); 72:9; 95:6; Ezra 9:5; 2 Chr 7:3; 29:29; and elsewhere.

20   Following the emendation proposed by P. de Lagarde; see *BHS* and the commentaries on this passage, esp. H. Wildberger, *Isaiah 1–12* (1991) 193–94 [*Jesaja* (2d ed. 1980) 179–80].

21   *HALOT*, s.v.

(הָעֲבֹדָה הַקָּשָׁה). Yahweh will "give rest" from them. In Isa 46:1 עֹצֶב stands in connection with a series of "burdens." One asks who the bearer is here.

"Collapse" and "bend" are chiastically emphasized. Even the pack animals break down under the load, until with the end of v. 2 the whole nightmare vanishes: they "go into captivity." This also announces the exit from the stage.[22] It is curious that "their soul" (וְנַפְשָׁם) is explicitly mentioned. This is usually understood as an intensification meaning *they themselves.* But perhaps "soul" is really meant (cf. 44:20; 47:14). What does the suffix in "their soul" (וְנַפְשָׁם) refer to? Could it be the citizens of Babylon, their supporters, just as the suffix on עֲצַבֵּיהֶם, "*their* images/fabrications" refers to the supporters of "the gods"? For they go along with this procession, as "chorus." The "soul" would be comparable with the "breath of our nostrils" (רוּחַ אַפֵּינוּ) in Lam 4:20 as the title of the imprisoned king, describing his vital importance[23] for the inhabitants of Jerusalem. People expect of "Babylon" what only Yahweh can actually give: life (cf. Gen 2:7; Ps 104:29).

After the taunt song about Babylon has been raised in Isa 14:3-23 (וְנָשָׂאתָ הַמָּשָׁל הַזֶּה, v. 4), Babylon disappears into the underworld (שְׁאוֹל, v. 9). Is "captivity" in the present DtIsa text thinking only of prisoners of war, or does it also mean being carried away without there being any return? Is this a "burden" (מַשָּׂא) for a "weary person" (עֲיֵפָה)[24]—that is, Babylon—whose name is not yet mentioned?

■ **3-4** These verses directly continue the play on the double sense of "burden" (מַשָּׂא) as prophecy and load.

Here the prophetic oracle is a new interpretation of the Babylon oracle. It is in some sense a third level of meaning. First, Babylon's triumphal procession and its gods turned into a lamentable caravan; but out of this now comes the promise of salvation for Jacob/Israel.

The technique of interpreting oracles is handled with complete mastery. The most important words are taken up again and acquire a new meaning. Instead of "(kneeling before) Bel" we now have "listen to *me*" (אֵלַי ʾēlay), where it will surely be permissible to hear the echo of אֵלִי ʾēlî, "my God." The person who has not grasped this immediately hears once again "Isra*el.*" Then follows the assurance "I am the one," as catchword from the revelatory utterance, in all five times "I" (אֲנִי).[25] The conclusion is "I will save" in the sense of "and I will bring to a safe place," instead of v. 2: "they were not able to save a burden" in the sense of "they were not able to bring it to a safe place." The sound changes too: instead of "they [their soul] went (off)," הָלְכָה with a triple *ā* sound (as in the lament?) as the final word in v. 2, a triple short *a* (וַאֲמַלֵּט) is used in v. 4. In chiastic alternation "your burdens are laid upon them" (v. 1) becomes "borne from birth and carried from the womb" (v. 3).[26] In "womb" (רֶחֶם) one can hear the ancient acknowledgment of the God who is "compassionate" (רַחוּם).[27] "To carry a child" is what a mother does especially. Here it is a divine predicate. But then the text talks about the carrying of the old. That is not a task for the woman.

It emerges yet again how problematical it is to transfer our notions of gender to God. The important thing is the "carrying."[28] That runs across the whole semantic

22   See also Beuken here on *mlṭ*, "save": "like *plṭ* in 45:20 [*mlṭ*, 'save'] is a verb of movement; cf. v. 4; 49:24-25; Jer 50:2, 8; 51:6, 44-45" He refers to E. Ruprecht, "פלט *plṭ* pi. to save," *TLOT* 2:986–90, esp. 988 [*THAT* 2:420–27, esp. 423].

23   4:20: "Yahweh's anointed, the breath of our life, is
taken captive in their pits—
the one of whom we thought, under his protection
we shall live among the nations."
See H. J. Kraus, *Klagelieder* (1968) on this passage.

24   H. D. Preuss (*Verspottung fremder Religionen im Alten Testament* [1971] 223) suspects "that in v. 1 there may even (cf. Isa 14:4bff.) be an echo of elements belonging to the lament for the dead."

25   For DtIsa's number symbolism the number 5 is somewhat unusual. But a further "I" is implicit in "and *I* will save." This would mean that the 6 = 2 × 3

would again be reached in the divine speech.

26   See Duhm's interpretation (351): "If the idols are the precious load of their worshipers, so conversely Yahweh's worshipers are the burden of their God—a pertinent reversal! And the consequence accords with this: where the human being carries God, the result is downfall; here, where God carries human beings, they are saved."

27   Exod 34:6; Deut 4:31; Pss 78:38; 86:15; Joel 2:13; Jonah 4:2; Neh 9:17, 31.

28   Cf. also Num 11:12; Deut 1:31; 32:11. J. Rabinowitz ("A Note on Isa 46:4," *JBL* 73 [1954] 237) assumes that "carrying" in 46:4 can have a specific legal meaning. It is the duty of a freed slave to look after his master in his old age. Rabinowitz draws this conclusion from the terminology of an Aramaic papyrus dated 427 B.C.E., published by E. G. Kraeling, *The Brooklyn Museum Aramaic Papyri*

range, from the tender carrying of the baby, by way of "carry" (נשא) as catchword in vv. 1-2, down to the dragging (סבל) of burdens.

The statements apply initially to Jacob/Israel as a collective. But the text also appeals to the individual, and its emotional content must also be noted. It is characteristic of DtIsa to describe in personal categories something that applies to all Israel. First of all, one can really say of an individual that he is "carried" from the womb until he is old. God gives life its continuity. It is not the human being who "drags" him- or herself through to the end. It is Yahweh who "drags" the human being.[29] But what applies to the individual is also true for all Israel. Again the argument is quite precise. That which was true in the past ("I have done it") will be true in the future too (cf. the futures in v. 4). In contrast to the gods "who are unable to save a burden" or load (v. 2), v. 4 says: "I will carry and I will . . . save." That is the real climax of the text in the interpretive part.

"Until you are gray" (עַד־שֵׂיבָה ‘ad-śêbāh) again metamorphoses a catchword from vv. 1-2, replacing "in captivity" (בַּשְּׁבִי baššᵉbî). 47:1 sounds like an echo: "sit down in the dust" (שְׁבִי šᵉbî, twice addressed to Babylon).

According to v. 3 "the whole remnant of the house of Israel" is told to listen. We may ask whether some special group is meant by this. One proposal among others is that it is those who remained in the country who are the target, as distinct from the Babylonian gōlâ. I have the impression that it is again initially a matter of a scriptural proof. Investigations have continually shown that the term "remnant" is an ambivalent one.[30] The "remnant" of a people actually served originally as a witness to its complete downfall in judgment and war. It was a long time before the remnant idea could be interpreted positively, as a sign of the compassion of Israel's God.[31] It was probably only in the postexilic period that it became a sustaining theologoumenon with which to acknowledge new salvation after the catastrophe.[32] Jer 50:20-22 is important for the present DtIsa text because it belongs within the framework of the collection of oracles about Babylon. "In those days and at that time, saying of Yahweh, the iniquity of Israel shall be sought, and there shall be none; and the sins of Judah, and none shall be found; for I will pardon them those whom I have spared." According to W. Rudolph,[33] "those whom I have spared" (אֲשֶׁר אַשְׁאִיר) is a play on the usual שְׁאֵרִית—the "remnant." It therefore seems possible, because of the Babylon context, that it is the Babylonian gōlâ who are initially meant.[34] But in view of the tradition history of the "remnant" concept, the decisive point is the unequivocal character of the promise of salvation in the present text.[35]

(1953) no. 5, p. 180; see also J. C. Greenfield, "Adi balṭu—Care for the Elderly and Its Rewards," *AfO* Beiheft 19 (1982) 309–16, esp. 313.

29   In the following section (v. 7) the catchword "drag" (סבל) is again used for idols.

30   See H. Wildberger, "שאר šʾr to remain," *TLOT* 3:1284–92 [*THAT* 2:844–55] (with lit.), as well as J. Hausmann, *Israels Rest: Studien zum Selbstverständnis der nachexilischen Gemeinde* (1987).

31   See 1 Kgs 19:10ff.; Amos 5:15.

32   See Isa 10:20-22; Zeph 3:12ff.

33   W. Rudolph, *Jeremia* (1947; 3d ed. 1968) on this passage.

34   But the problem that Knight raises (*Deutero-Isaiah*, 147) is worth noting: "The conversation overheard in this verse is almost certainly apocryphal. No displaced persons, aliens, foreigners would dare make sarcastic remarks such as these as they elbowed their way on the sidewalk when the procession of gods was going by."

35   Cf. also 49:21-22.

5   To whom could you liken me and make me
        equal
     and compare me, as if we were alike?

6   Those who pour gold out of the purse
     and weigh out silver in the scales,
     they hire a goldsmith that he may make it
        into a god,
     they bow down, even throw themselves
        down,

7   lift it on to their shoulders and carry it,
     so that they may put it in its place, so that
        it may stand—
     it will not move from its place—
     yes, one cries to it, but it does not answer,
     it will not save anyone from his distress.

8   Think of this and <be ashamed>!ª
     Take it to heart, you apostates!

8a   Thus with a correction of the incomprehensible וְהִתְאֹשָׁשׁוּ ("acknowledge your guilt"?) to וְהִתְבֹּשָׁשׁוּ (cf. Gen 2:25); but see below on the text.

The parody of a procession continues. The next group follows. The catchwords "carry, lift" (נשׂא) and "drag" (סבל) are maintained (v. 6). But the text is much more serious than the preceding one, the burlesque elements being almost entirely lacking. The personal disquiet and concern is greater, as will become clear from the content. The structure is clear. The action in vv. 6-7 is framed by two introductory questions in v. 5 and a first application in v. 8.

The very sounds intensify the sinister impression. When the text talks about "making a god" (v. 6), five verbs end with *û* (v. 6) and the following three verbs with *ûhû* (v. 7). "It will stand" in v. 7 gives *ô* seven times in all, three of the instances being *lô* ("not," לֹא). Verse 7 closes: "he/it will not (לֹא) help him/save him." This, then, is once more a text designed to be heard.

■ **5** The introductory questions about the incomparability of God establish a link with the proem in 40:18 and 25. This underlines the importance of these questions. For in 40:19 the "goldsmith" (צֹרֵף) already made an appearance. And we already asssumed that the person who can afford "a wise expert" means the merchant.

■ **6-7** The "purse" (כִּיס *kîs*) as an appurtenance or emblem is the sign of the merchant or trader.[36] Who else can "pour out gold" (זוּל *zul*)? Perhaps there is also an echo of (זלל *zalal*), "to be immoderate, irresponsible."[37] In the texts that polemicize against idols in DtIsa we were already struck by the list of classes or social groups, lastly—in 44:9-20—the artisans (v. 12, "specialist for iron/metalwork"; v. 13, "specialist for wood") as well as the shepherd (v. 14a) and the farmer (v. 14b). For an urban community, whether it be Babylon or Jerusalem, the merchant is an important figure.

A noticeable feature of the text is that v. 6 immediately uses the plural. The people do everything together; it is only in his or her distress that an individual cries out (v. 7b). My guess is that the merchants are presented as a guild who are performing their public and religious duties. If this is so, we may assume that the deity who is represented is also the god of the merchants, whether his name be Nebo, Hermes, or Mercury. If the figure typifies Hermes/Mercury, the irony in v. 7 is particularly apt, for he is the god who actually hurries from land to land, with his winged shoes or cap. But here (literally) he "will stand still, he will not move from his place."

36   In German even today *Kies* is a slang word for money. It was originally thieves' cant, and such language is frequently a source for the most widely varying linguistic traditions. See *HALOT* 2:472 [*HALAT* 2:450]: "Akk. *kīsu*, bag used by Babylonian merchants for their weights," with reference to H. Zimmern, *Akkadische Fremdwörter* (2d ed. 1917) 20; W. G. Lambert, *Babylonian Wisdom Literature* (1960) 319–20; Y. Yadin, *The Finds from the Bar Kokhba Period in the Cave of Letters* (1963) 160–61; *AHw* 487b. Cf. also Deut 25:13; Mic 6:9-11; Prov 1:13-14.

37   Cf. Deut 21:20; Prov 23:20-21; 28:7; Lam 1:11; Sir 18:33. See Duhm (324) on this passage: "The money for the idol is thrown away."

The text is full of action, the series of imperfects announcing what is happening in each given case. The procedure in which the idol is worshiped is precisely described in a long series of imperfects (from v. 6aβ): "then they will. . . ." In style the piece can very well be compared with the instructions for a ritual.[38] According to Westermann,[39] "A description is given of the three most important acts [of such worship]: the obeisance or proskynesis, the procession, and the prayer." Just as in the texts about the making of the idol, we can assume that the description of the ritual was in no way a source of offense for Israel's surrounding world. Even the carrying of the god or its image is not in itself derogatory. The polemical stings probably lie initially in small modifications.

The gold or silversmith is not commissioned to make an image;[40] he makes "for him [the commissioner of the work] a god." But that is precisely the point from which the argument in DtIsa often starts: a god cannot be "made." If the carrying is described by the word "drag it away" (סבל, v. 7), this has a flavor of "burden, forced labor."[41] But this is precisely the term that establishes the unity with what has gone before (v. 4) and that is used in 53:4 to desribe what the Servant of God does in his suffering.[42]

That a cultic image should be set up in its place is a matter of course. This is generally accompanied by particular rituals. The irony emerges only through the clause "it [the cultic image]—or: he [the god]—will not move from its/his place" (v. 7). But the same verb (מוש muš) is used again in DtIsa, this time in a positive sense, in 54:10: "Even if mountains depart (move) from their place . . . my steadfast love (חַסְדִּי) will not depart from you."

Finally, the catchword "save, help" (ישׁע Hiphil) in v. 7

associates the text with one of DtIsa's themes. In the dispute about the gods a fundamental question is: Who can really help in distress? It is only the confession of the experienced and hoped-for help of its God that makes the worship of other gods and their images an absurdity for Israel. The conclusion in the text is that a god of this kind is no help in distress (v. 7); how can it be, when it is the product of human hands?[43]

■ **8** The line of argument seems convincing and the application in v. 8 takes this up explicitly: "Think of this. . . ." Two further imperatives follow. They require a particular kind of behavior, but what is really meant at first remains unclear. The derivation of the second verb is disputed, and we do not know why the text suddenly talks about "sinners, apostates."

In order to understand the real point of dispute, a comparison with a text from the apocryphal Epistle of Jeremiah can, I believe, be helpful. Here we shall for the moment exclude the question about the literary and historical context.

A copy of a letter which Jeremiah sent to the prisoners who were to be taken to Babylon as exiles by the king of the Babylonians, to give them the message that God had commanded him. (1) Because of the sins that you have committed before God, you will be taken away to Babylon as exiles by Nebuchadnezzar, king of the Babylonians. (2) When you have come to Babylon, you will have to remain there for many years, for a long time, up to seven generations; after that I will bring you away from there in peace. (3) Now in Babylon you will see gods made of silver and gold and wood, which people carry on their shoulders, and which cause the heathen to fear. (4) So beware lest you become like the foreigners or lest fear for these gods possesses you, (5) when you see the multitude

38   For an example see K. F. Müller, "Das assyrische Ritual I," MVÄG 41 (1937) 14ff.

39   Westermann, 183 [148].

40   Cf. the ritual for the New Year Festival in Babylon: F. Thureau-Dangin, *Rituels accadiens* (1921) 127–54; *AOT* 297; *ANET* 331–32.

41   Gen 49:15; cf. 1 Kgs 11:28; Ps 81:7 (6); Neh 4:11 (17); Isa 9:3 (4); 10:27; 14:25.

42   Cf. Lam 5:7.

43   In Egypt an oracle could be given by an idol carried by priests. This was used by the kings, e.g., in determining the successor to the throne. See G. Roeder, *Kulte, Orakel und Naturverehrung im Alten Ägypten*

(1960) 22; on Thutmoses III, 195–200, 202; on Sheshonk, 223–25; 228–30. Private persons had the same opportunity. A stele of the priest Pa-ser is interesting. The top part of the stele shows him standing with raised hands before the boat that is carried by priests with the image of the god, in order to ask for a decision in a matter connected with a piece of land. The petition is rejected with the phrase: "The god stood still." If it is accepted, the phrase was: "[It then happened that] the god nodded his head vigorously in the presence of the priests." Text published by G. Legrain, *ASAE* 16

(which goes) before and behind them worshiping them. But say in your hearts, "It is you, O Lord, whom we must worship." (6) For my angel is with you, and seeks your souls.[44]

The text offers an interpretation of history that is not far from DtIsa's. The Babylonian exile is the consequence of sin. We may assume that there is a reference to Jeremiah 10, especially to v. 5, which mentions the carrying of gods (נְשׂוֹא יִנָּשֵׂא). But "carrying on the shoulders" is still closer to the DtIsa text, and so is the connection with a procession: "When you see the crowd before and behind them (the gods made of silver, gold and wood). . . ." The decisive thing, however, is the mental reservation that is enjoined: "Say in your conscience (τῇ διανοίᾳ): 'It is you, O Lord, whom we must worship'" (Ep Jer 5). For this an angel is at hand to help, who "seeks your souls (ψυχὰς)" (Ep Jer 6). In my view this is the precise opposite to the position taken by the DtIsa text. There the demand is: "Turn away!" In practical terms that would mean: neither take part in the spectacle, nor look on. The "pure heart" is not possible. "Sinners, apostates at heart" are addressed.

Here a difficult decision has to be made about the rendering of עַל־כָּתֵף (lift, carry) , "on the shoulders" and "to the heart" (lit. "on the heart," עַל־לֵב). I think it is possible that the second application contains a further

intensification. The verb וְהִתְאֹשָׁשׁוּ cannot be understood as it stands.[45] But if the double š sound (שׁ) is replaced by a double r (ר), we have the root אָרַר. In the *Piel* it means "to bring about a curse" (cf. Num 5:18, 19, 24, 27). A *Hitpael* would mean "to lay a curse on oneself." But that would be the equivalent of a renunciation, with a conditional self-curse: "If I continue to do this, may I be cursed."

The change from ר to שׁ can already have been made in the text itself. In the preceding text we also noticed the frequency of *s* sounds. There it was a question of "repelling demons." A conditional self-curse is no less dangerous. But the demand would then correspond to the requirement later made of those brought for Christian baptism: to renounce the devil and his *pompa*![46]

With so strict an attitude as the one DtIsa maintains, how would it still have been possible to live as a merchant in the Babylonian *gōlâ*? Could a merchant hold aloof from public and religious occasions? Could he trade without cooperating with the "guilds"? It is the old and ever new question: how far can one "go along" with things? That is the question here. For DtIsa there was only one possibility: "Go out from Babylon!"

(1916) 161–70; *ANET* 448. See Roeder, *Kulte,* 238–41, pl. 17.

44 Ep Jer heading and vv. 1-6; trans. following A. H. J. Gunneweg in JSHRZ 3/2 (1975) 187; see also the rest of the text.

45 For the attempts at an explanation see Muilenburg, 541: "is a *hapax legomenon* which some derive from the noun אִישׁ, 'man' (cf. KJV, **show yourselves men**), but with little support. The LXX reads στενάξατε, 'groan'; the Vulg., *confundamini* (cf. Hebrew התבוששו), which is accepted by Lagarde and others. Torrey takes it as an Aramaic loan word meaning 'to found,' hence 'put yourselves on a secure foundation' (cf. Arabic *assasa*, 'to be well grounded'; cf. the Palestinian Syriac of Matt. 7:25) or 'be assured.'

This is the best solution. The RSV follows the Syriac in rendering **consider** (*hithbônānû*)." See also Bonnard on the passage; A. Schoors, *I Am God Your Saviour* (1973) 274; Beuken, 263 on the passage.

46 On the rejection of the *pompa diaboli* by Christians, see the baptismal formula: ἀποτάσσομαι τῷ Σατανᾷ καὶ τῇ πομπῇ αὐτοῦ in *Constitut. apost.* 7.41.2 as well as: "renuntio diabolo et pompae et angelis eius" in Tertullian *De corona* 3.2 (*Tertulliani Opera* part II [1954] 1037–65); cf. J. Köhne, "Die Schrift Tertullians 'Über die Schauspiele' in kultur- und religionsgeschichtlicher Beleuchtung" (diss., 1929); H. Jürgens, *Pompa Diaboli: Die lateinischen Kirchenväter und das antike Theater* (1972).

"Remember the former things since earliest time" (46:9)

A. 3.   46:9-13
Yahweh's Plan

9   Remember the former things since earliest
          time:
     Yes! I am God,
     and there is no other deity,
     and nothing is as I am!

10   Who from the beginning declares the end,
     and from primordial time things that have
          not (yet) happened,
     who says: "My plan will be fulfilled!"
     and "I will carry out all my purposes!"
11   who from the rising (of the sun) calls the
          bird of prey,
     from a far-off land the man of his purpose—
     yes, I have spoken, I will also bring it about,
     I have formed (it), I will also do (it).

12   Listen to me, you who are mighty of
          heart/courage,[a]
     who are far from righteousness/salvation:
13   I have brought my righteousness/salvation
          near, it is not far off,
     and my help will not tarry.
     And I will give help in Zion,[a]
     give Israel my glory.

12a Instead of אַבִּירֵי לֵב, LXX (οἱ ἀπολωλεκότες) probably read
     אֹבְדֵי לֵב, "whose courage [is failing]"; see below on the text.
13a Cf. below on this passage.

■ 9 The procession with the idols has gone off, and it is not likely that anyone "turned back" from it (cf. v. 8). The elements in the action will be intensified with the appearance of "Babylon" in 47:1. Between the two episodes is a divine speech with hymnic self-predications (vv. 9-11) and a further critical appeal: "listen to me" (v. 12). The initial "remember"[47] acts as a catchword linking the passage with what has gone before (v. 8). But there it had a negative overtone: in a time of disaster the people will remember that gods made by human beings cannot help them. Now it is a positive remembrance of "earlier things that have happened[48] from time immemorial/the earlier events since earliest times." This can refer to creation or to history. But the little signal "Yes!" (כִּי) makes clear that God is in any case the origin of events. The unalterable declaration that God is incomparable is cited. The resemblance to the First Commandment is clear. This is a revelatory speech: "I am. . . ."

The special subtlety of the text is that in the double divine statement it begins with the name "El" for God. This is the term that DtIsa often uses when he is talking about the whole world, including the "Gentiles"—and in this particular case, when the subject is Babylon and Cyrus. The God of the whole world is Israel's God too.

The name Yahweh is not used here (cf. 45:6), but the divine name "Elohim" (אֱלֹהִים) does occur in the parallelism. It then echoes throughout this whole text—literally so, for v. 9 has the e sound (as in Heb. ʾĕlōhîm) three times, v. 10 seven times and v. 11 also seven times. This would hardly be by chance. The first declaration sounds the keynote. In content, the assertions of incomparability are certainly directed at Babylon's claim: "I and none else" (אֶפֶס, 47:8 and 10). The ancient confessional formulas are highly topical, or better: their consequences must be discovered afresh. It is a widespread modern

47   See W. Schottroff, "זכר zkr remember," TLOT
     1:381–88 [THAT 1:507–18].
48   See H. P. Müller's translation in "ראֹשׁ rōš head,"

TLOT 3:1190 [THAT 2:710], with lit. A. Schoors,
"Les choses antérieures et les choses nouvelles dans
les oracles Deutéro-Isaïens," EThL 40 (1964) 32–34.

misunderstanding that hymns make only general declarations; they are allegedly merely poems without any binding force.[49] But the hymnic declarations in the text allow us to perceive precise reflection. They have to do with the relationship between divine proclamation and divine action; that is, they have to do with the mode of God's rule. The three hymnic verbal participles stand parallel to three statements about God's activity (עשׂה). This makes it clear: God has acted and he acts still!

■ **10-11** The declarations develop what the Being of God means ("who declares . . . ," v. 10; "who says . . . ," v. 10; "who calls . . . ," v. 11). These are the modes of revelation. They are always directed to human beings. The human being is permitted to know what is from the beginning. God's plan does not remain secret. In these declarations the most extreme past and future are linked in a unique way. The world is a unity in time and space— the greatest unity that can be thought. But the recognition does not remain a purely general one. It is bound up with concrete political events in the calling of Cyrus.

The argument could run as follows: one can accept that the creation was announced beforehand (v. 10); that is the case in Genesis 1 too. That God has a plan and decides according to his good pleasure[50] is continually called in question on the basis of experience, but for all that, it is the essential substance of prophetic proclamation and tradition. The rule of God is not something arbitrary. According to the testimony of this text, God binds himself to his word as it has been revealed through "the law and the prophets." His "plan" belongs here too (cf. Isa 44:28; 48:14; 55:11). But once again, what about

Cyrus? The catchword "counsel" (עֵצָה) is taken up once more.[51]

Does God need a "man of counsel"[52] such as every ruler has, with his often problematical advice? The answer is no! Here too, the "man of his counsel" is clearly the person who is called on the basis of the divine resolve.

Cyrus's name is not mentioned any more. After his appearance in Act III (44:24—45:25) he gradually disappears. More important than this particular person is his place in God's "plan." Consequently he is here described in his function as "bird of prey" (עַיִט ʿayyîṭ). It is difficult for us to grasp exactly what is meant by this. The word עַיִט is used for a number of different birds of prey. They have been identified as eagles,[53] vultures or falcons.[54] But initially the name derives not from the bird's predatory character but from its cry: the verb עיט means "screech." But I do not think we should start from the zoological question, which bird? For the text contains a throng of set formulations. It should be noted that it is "the (bird) from the rising." On the basis of the anonymous Cyrus text in 41:25 we can say more precisely: "from the rising of the sun" (cf. also 41:2). If one assumes a Near Eastern tradition here, the bird could be the legendary Anzu bird, which is associated with the sun and the ruler. In Egyptian traditions there is the special kind of Horus falcon who, as *Harachte*, is linked with the rising sun, and with whom the pharaoh is identified. This is not out of the question if we remember that the tutelary deity represented in Cyrus's palace in Pasargadae has the inscription: "I (am) Cyrus the king

---

Schoors sums up his conclusion: "In all the texts relative to the question, the word designates events predicted and not the predictions themselves" (Schoors, *I Am God Your Saviour* [1973] 276).

49 See R. Ishikawa, "Der Hymnus im Alten Testament und seine kritische Funktion" (diss., Munich, 1996).

50 One must agree with A. Hurvitz, "The History of a Legal Formula, *kōl ʾašer-ḥāpēṣ ʿāśāh* (Psalms cxv 3; cxxxv 6)," *VT* 32 (1982) 257–67, when he maintains that the formula "do according to his good pleasure" has a legal aspect. It has its place in agreements made under civil law. In the political sphere, depending on the nature of its structure, the ruler's will can be law. Power can be arbitrary, or it can be bound to law and justice. This plays a part in the application of the sociomorpheme "monarchical rule" to the relationship to God.

51 See 40:13; 44:26.

52 "My man of counsel" should be read, following the *Qere;* cf. LXX.

53 Because of the sound, older commentators saw a connection between עַיִט and Gk. ἀετός, "eagle"; they pointed to the golden eagle, which was Cyrus's standard according to Xenophon *Cyrop.* 7.1.4; *Anab.* 1.10.12.

54 The point of comparison is the swiftness of Cyrus's rise or the unexpected capture of King Croesus's capital city Sardis in the winter campaign of 545 B.C.E. See North, 166: "'Falcon', with its 'stooping' flight would suit Cyrus well."

an Achaemenian" and wears an Egyptian crown.[55] We must also remember that according to Isa 43:3 and 45:14 Egypt, Cush, and Sheba are assigned to Cyrus. There is evidence that the Horus title was ascribed to Cambyses in Egypt.

The Persians therefore certainly laid claim to foreign symbols of power too. For more or less peaceable countries to be depicted in the form of birds of prey of various kinds has been common practice down to the present day. In the ancient world the symbol stressed the worldwide, divine power of the ruler. But if one reverts to the beginning of the argumentation in v. 9, with its thesis: "there is no other deity (אֱלֹהִים *ʾelohîm*)," then even Cyrus as ruler is not divine. He too is called—but called he is! That is his legitimation.

If the text thus forms a single unit in content, we may go on to ask whether the theme "fulfillment of earlier prophecies" does not run throughout as well. In v. 10 this was generally assumed to be the case with "creation" and "history."[56] But where does the specific announcement of Cyrus belong here? The biblical references to "birds of prey" shed little light where prophecies are concerned. More interesting is the detail "from a far-off land" (מֵאֶרֶץ מֶרְחָק), for this particular form occurs only in Isa 13:5, the oracle about Babylon. There vv. 1-4 describe the summoning and gathering of an army by Yahweh. Then we are told in v. 5: "They come (בָּאִים) from a far-off land." The LXX uses the singular for Yahweh and his army at this point: "He comes. . . ." Had this prophecy about Babylon and the Day of Yahweh been interpreted as referring to Cyrus?

Now, it is true that 48:15 says in reference to Babylon, again taking up a Cyrus text: "I have let *him* come/ brought *him* in" (Cyrus; masc. suffix). That would also fit in well with the prophecy according to Isaiah 13. But here in 46:11 we have a feminine suffix: "I [fem.] will bring in." The close of the verse corresponds to this: "I [fem.] will do." To what do these two suffixes refer? Possibly there is here a further "scriptural proof" that is picking up the prophecies of disaster to Babylon. According to Jer 51:59-64, Jeremiah writes "in a scroll all the disasters that would come on Babylon." This is intended to be understood literally. Jeremiah asks a certain Seraiah "when you come to Babylon" to read it aloud there (v. 61). Then, in a symbolic act, he is to weigh down the scroll with a stone and throw it into the Euphrates: "Thus shall Babylon sink, to rise no more, because of the disasters that I am bringing on her." So there was already an oracle about Babylon, ascribed to Jeremiah, the heart of which are the catchwords "come in, bring in" (בוא) and "evil, disaster" (רָעָה). "Evil, disaster" (רָעָה, fem.!) is what is brought into Babylon.

DtIsa can say of disaster too that it is "made" by Yahweh; this was already explicitly declared in 45:7, where "weal and woe" are linked with "create" (בָּרָא). But these two Cyrus texts are so similar in content and choice of words that they can explain one another. The fall of Babylon, as it will then immediately be depicted in chap. 47, really is then an event that was announced "earlier"!

■ **12-13** The announcement of Babylon's immediately impending fall means salvation for Israel. It is easy to

55   See the illustration in Gershevitch, *The Cambridge History of Iran,* vol. 2 (1985) pl. 6a; cf. pls. 8, 25 and 26b. The seal in pl. 48b shows joss stands and winged wild goats in Persian court style linked with the Egyptian "eye of Horus" and a falcon. The seal dates from the period between the 5th and the 4th centuries B.C.E. It is now in the British Museum in London.

56   See H.-P. Müller, "ראשׁ *rōʾš* head," *TLOT* 3:1190 [*THAT* 2:710]: "*rēʾšît* in Isa 46:10 concerns the beginning of time per se. . . . Gen 1:1 and Sir 15:14 also used the word in this abs. sense" (with lit.). On אחרית see E. Jenni, "אחר *ʾḥr* after," *TLOT* 1:83–88, esp. 87 [*THAT* 1:110–18, esp. 115]: "Process and end are contained in the meanings 'outcome, end (of a thing).'" He points here to Isa 41:22; 46:10; 47:7; Amos 8:10; Prov 14:12=16:25; 14:13 text emended; 20:21; 25:8; Qoh 7:8; 10:13; Lam 1:9.

With respect to DtIsa's complicated time-situation interpretation (which is also connected with the dramatic structure), one can agree with Jenni that, seen from the beginning, everything later "comes afterward" (see 86 [115] § 4a) down to the present in any given case. Seen from the point of view of the present, everything future again comes afterward. It is all the more surprising that v. 13 should establish that help for Zion does not "come afterward" (לֹא תְאַחֵר). This gives rise to the difficulty in translating the following verb, "and I have given help in Zion" or "I will give help in Zion," this depending on whether the w' is understood in a copulative or a consecutive sense.

57   ἀπολωλεκότες corresponds to Heb. אֹבְדֵי; see also Westermann here. Schoors, (*I Am God Your Saviour* [1973] 150–54) follows Westermann in defining vv. 12-13 as a "proclamation of salvation." He

imagine the national rejoicing that news of this kind would have caused. So the continuation of the text in 46:12 is all the more astonishing—so astonishing indeed that the LXX already changed the wording in order to make it a clear oracle of salvation: "Who are strong in heart" becomes "whose courage is failing."[57] Many commentaries have followed the LXX here, down to the present day. But if we note the context and the choice of words, it emerges that the text is critical and does *not* permit cheap rejoicing, since it begins: "Listen to *me*."[58] This critical note was sounded first in 46:8: "Rebels, apostates, take it to the heart." Here in v. 12 it is also a question of the "heart," surely in the sense of "innermost ideas, attitude of mind." This therefore sounds the theme that is then further developed after the judgment over Babylon in chap. 48—the critical dispute with a contemporary Jacob/Israel. The slogan "And we were victorious in spite of it all" is impossible here. Salvation and disaster come from God alone.

The negative note is already indicated in the description "the stouthearted, the stubborn of heart" (אַבִּירֵי לֵב).[59] In the only other passage where this compound occurs in the OT, Ps 76:6 (5), it refers to the proud warriors who have come forward against the God of Israel and Zion, and who are destroyed in the judgment. It means the power and strength characteristic of great animals, especially the bull. So when the attribute is applied to human beings it can stand for the mighty as such (Isa 10:13; Job 24:22; 34:20; Lam 1:15). The saying about Egypt and the reference to Apis in Jer 4:15 suggest that the connection with the bull's potency still plays a part.[60] That was why the ancient description of God as "the Mighty One of Jacob" was suspect. The Masoretes tried to establish a differentiation between "bull" and "Mighty One" by way of a different pointing (אביר with or without *dagesh* in the second radical, respectively). The five instances are in Gen 49:24; Isa 49:26; 60:16; Ps 132:2, 5; also Isa 1:24: "Mighty One of Israel." In this series, Isa 49:26 also gives an indication of why "mighty" has a negative sense in the present text. The attribute "mighty" in this sense can be applied only to "the Mighty One of Jacob," the God who helps and redeems.

If we remember the critical position taken by v. 12a, we may assume that v. 12b too is meant in a negative sense. The acts of these people are "far from righteousness."[61] But they do not escape "the righteousness of God." They must take responsibility and will be called to account. There is a play both on the term "righteousness"[62] and

---

assigns vv. 5-11 to the "disputations" (273–78). He adheres to the Hebrew text "stubborn of heart," observing rightly: "In a proclamation of salvation, it sounds somewhat strange" (278). But when he then paraphrases v. 12b: "You who think you are far from salvation" (154), this parallelism between vv. 12a and 12b actually moves in the opposite direction.

58   R. Lack (*La symbolique du livre d'Isaïe* [1973] 103) accords with the facts when he contrasts the "denigration of the makers of idols" and "the call to reflection." He points especially to the parallels between 44:23 and 46:13. See also H. C. Spykerboer, *The Structure and Composition of Deutero-Isaiah* (1976) 151–52.

59   See *HALAT* under this heading; also A. S. Kapelrud, "אַבִּיר, ʾābhîr" *TDOT* 1:42–44 [*ThWAT* 1:43–46].

60   The LXX has ὁ Ἄπις (according to LXX numbering, 26:15).

61   A. Schoors (*I Am God Your Saviour* [1973] 151) takes a contrary view: "Thus righteousness is certainly not a moral quality which the hearers lack (subjective righteousness)." But v. 12 is related to human

beings, and the suffix that could point to the divine righteousness is missing. The suffixes and final vowels again alternate very skillfully in vv. 12 and 13: *â* ("righteousness")—*î* ("my righteousness")—*î* ("my help")—*â* ("help")—*î* ("my glory"). In the case of the second "help" the relation to God is unequivocal because of the "I have given."

62   Torrey (*Second Isaiah* [1928] 241, 367) has clearly seen this when he renders צדקה first by "righteousness," then by "triumph." "Wherever the saving order, which is what is meant by צדק, is damaged, then Yahweh must step in; then, the punishment of the wicked person would also be part of Yahweh's acting in a righteous way. If that would not take place, then the holy God would not be preserving his holiness" (H. Wildberger, *Isaiah 1–12* [1991] 206–7 on Isa 5:16 [*Jesaja* (1972) 192]) (as a correction to the opinion of K. Koch, G. von Rad and F. Horst). Cf. also E. Brandenburger, "Gericht Gottes III. Neues Testament," *TRE* 12 (1984) 469–83; also his "Pistis und Soteria. Zum Verstehenshorizont von 'Glaube' im Urchristentum," *ZThK* 85 (1988)

on the term "far off."[63] The "far-off" God is neither an excuse nor a way of escape. He reaches human beings both near and far. "Righteousness," both as "judgment" and as "help," characterizes God's activity. Whereas 46:7 establishes that the gods and their images do not help, the commentary on this pseudo-procession ends with the assurance of help for Zion.

After 40:9 and 41:7, this is the first mention of Zion prior to the Zion texts from 49:14 onward. Before the description of Babylon's downfall, "Zion" is mentioned once more; everything is directed toward nothing less than its renewal. That this announcement seems to be made almost in passing should not be allowed to diminish its importance.[64] It is an indication of the closely woven fabric of DtIsa's text, which cannot simply be cut up into separate pieces. The glory of this God appears in his help for human beings, who are summed up in "Zion" and "Israel" as unity.[65] This makes it possible for human beings to have the assurance of faith in an alien environment.

165–98; idem, "Gerichtskonzeptionen im Urchristentum und ihre Voraussetzungen," *SNTU* 16 (1991) 5–54.

63 The root "far" (רחק) occurs three times in the text. God calls from a "far-off land" (v. 11), human beings are "far from righteousness/salvation" (v. 12), "my righteousness/salvation will be far off" (v. 13). When the text announces God's sovereignty over the whole world, space and time are fused in the term "far."

64 See Spykerboer, *The Structure and Composition of Deutero-Isaiah* (1976) 152 on this passage.

65 The proper translation of the end of v. 13 is disputed. It can be a separate nominative clause, "my righteousness (is) for Israel"; or is "my glory for Israel" a further object for "give"? Schoors (*I Am God Your Saviour* [1973] 153) points to the parallelism with 44:23 and renders the sentence: "I give salvation in Zion and so I show my glory in Israel." But why do the two possibilities have to be mutually exclusive? DtIsa loves to give a many-layered force to his utterances.

47   "Step down and sit in (the) dust . . ." (47:1)

B. 1. 47:1-7
**Deposition of Babylon and Descent to the Underworld
("Babylon's Descent into Hell")**

The account of Babylon's deposition and end is full of dramatic tension. "Babylon" appears and disappears again. As the verbs already show, the cohesion is given through the continuous action. The chapter can be subdivided into 2 x 3 sections: (1) vv. 1-7: 1-3a, 3b-4, 5-7; (2) vv. 8-15: 8-9, 10-12, 13-15.

An exegesis of the chapter is fraught with a number of difficulties. Attempts have been made to solve the problems through the methods of literary criticism, most radically by disputing DtIsa's authorship of the entire chapter, or by leaving merely a severely mutilated text. But since the text is of such an exacting literary quality, and since it is very closely bound up with its context, a solution along these lines is improbable.

Recent attempts to assign the text to a particular genre have resulted in definitions such as "taunt song" (Begrich), "oracle to the nations" (Westermann; cf. Bonnard) or "judgment oracle and threat" (Merendino). These definitions are always based on certain aspects of the text. But what they exclude are the elements of the *action*. Consequently Beuken's pointer to "rites of self-deprecation," and aspects of lament and mourning, is of particular interest. The text, fifteen verses in all, actually has the second person feminine suffix "ךְ-" as many as thirty times, with different conjunctive vowels, especially *ṣērē* (ךְ ֵ -; cf. v. 10). The direct address to Babylon could be expected in this text, but the note of lamentation is brought out acoustically at the same time: אֵיךְ *ʾêk* or אֵיכָה *ʾêkah*.[66] The tone is certainly not triumphant.

If we view the text as a scene, or a succession of short scenes, in the framework of the liturgical drama, I believe the different elements of the text can be convincingly fitted together. We must once again note particularly that in this text—as in other ancient dramas—we have hardly any stage directions. The action has to be deduced entirely from signals in the text itself.

A further premise for understanding the text in the context of DtIsa's book is the correspondence between Babylon's deposition here and Zion's installation in chap. 51. Babylon's "divestiture" corresponds to Zion's "investiture" in 51:1-2. More details might be added.

A further dramatic feature is the contrast between the two cities, who are represented by two women. This is an age-old motif, taken up in different ways, right down to the representation of church and synagogue in Christian art. Literary criticism, in the widest sense of the term, talks about "mirror scenes," which explain each other mutually.[67] The subject of the scene(s) in chap. 47 is certainly the deposition and condemnation of Babylon. But this does not sufficiently bring out its special character. As I hope to show in the detailed exegesis, a whole series of statements in the text are open to different levels of interpretation. If we put the observations together, they give us an indication of the most important place of the action: it is the underworld. We might therefore in anticipation even head the scene: "Babylon's descent into hell."

The motif of the descent into hell is not unusual in the OT.[68] It is explicitly applied to Babylon in the present context in Isa 14:1-23.[69] We shall see that DtIsa has probably taken over individual elements from this text too. In the way it takes up and reworks traditional oracles to Babylon, our present text, chap. 47, would then fit precisely into the context of chap. 46.

We may assume that some of the scenes in DtIsa take place in the underworld. The exegesis of chap. 41 already indicated this. Here DtIsa was able to draw on existing OT utterances about the underworld.[70] The OT's severe reserve toward every cult of the dead or speculations about the underworld is well known. This

---

66   אֵיכָה *ʾêkah* is "the standing opening word of the lament for the dead": *HALOT* s.v., with reference to H. Jahnow, *Das hebräische Leichenlied im Rahmen der Völkerdichtung* (1923) 136; cf. Isa 1:21; Lam 1:1; 2:1; 4:1, 2. אֵיךְ *ʾêk* is the shorter form with the same meaning; cf. Isa 14:4, 12; Jer 50:23; 51:41; see W. Zimmerli, *Ezekiel* 2 (1983) [*Ezechiel* 2 (1969)] on Ezek 26:17, whereby the texts Isa 14:4, 12; Jer 50:23; and 51:41 are sayings about Babylon, while the subject of Ezek 27:27 is the downfall of Tyre. See below.

67   See O. Taplin, *Greek Tragedy in Action* (1978) 122–39.

68   Cf. Ezek 26:1-21; esp. vv. 19-21 (on Tyre); 28:1-10; esp. v. 8 (on the princes of Tyre); 31:1-18; esp. vv. 14, 15-18 (on Pharaoh); 32:17-32; esp. vv. 18-19 (on Egypt); and W. Zimmerli, *Ezekiel* 2 (1983) [*Ezechiel* 2 (1969)] on these texts.

69   See O. Kaiser, *Isaiah 13–39* (1974) [*Der Prophet Jesaja, Kapitel 13–39* (1973)] on this passage; S. Erlandsson, *The Burden of Babylon: A Study of Isaiah 13:2—14:23* (1970).

70   See G. Gerlemann, "שְׁאוֹל *šeʾôl* realm of the dead" *TLOT* 3:1279–82 [*THAT* 2:837–41] (with lit.); B. Kedar, "Netherworld," *EncJud* 12 (1971) 996–98

reserve was based on Israel's faith in what Zimmerli calls "God's bias in favor of life." Nevertheless, the poets always felt able to say more here than the dogmaticians. But perhaps behind DtIsa we can also see first traces of the discovery that God's sovereignty knows no frontiers but reaches even to "the depths of the earth."

It is difficult to decide how far DtIsa was working with a combination of different traditions about the underworld. The period of Persian rule was a time of intensive interchange between east and west. In the present state of research it is impossible to offer more than scattered hints here. Egypt is the classic land for knowledge about the underworld.[71] In Mesopotamia the descent to the underworld was an element in the Inanna-Ishtar myth. In the Gilgamesh epic too the underworld is a world without light, "a house of dust."[72] Phoenicia had its own traditions of which the Ugaritic texts give us a small glimpse. Greek literature has something to say about "Hades."[73] There too "dark/darkness" is a primary characteristic of the underworld (Homer *Il.* 8.368: Ἅδης; *Od.* 11.37: Ἐρέβευς; 12.81: Ἔρεβος).[74] Book 11 of the *Odyssey*, "Nekyia," gives a detailed account of the underworld.

(lit.); N. J. Tromp, *Primitive Conceptions of Death and the Nether World in the Old Testament* (1969); L. I. J. Stadelmann, *The Hebrew Conception of the World: A Philological and Literary Study* (1970) 165–76.

71 See H. Kees, *Totenglauben und Jenseitsvorstellungen der Alten Ägypter* (1926); H. Bonnet, "Jenseitsgericht, Jenseitsglaube," *RÄRG* (1952) 334–55; E. Hornung, "Jenseitsführer"; C. Seeber, "Jenseitsgericht"; and U. Rössler-Köhler, "Jenseitsvorstellungen"; all in *LÄ* 3 (1980) 252–67.

72 See Gilgamesh Epic, Tablet VII, col. iv, 33–54, esp. 36 and 40; *ANET* 87; A. Heidel, *The Gilgamesh Epic and Old Testament Parallels* (2d ed. 1949).

73 O. Gigon and K. Schubert, "Hades," *LAW* (1965) 1180; D. Wachsmuth, "Unterwelt," in *KP* 5 (1975) 1053–56.

74 See, e.g., Homer, *The Iliad*, vol. 1 (LCL; 1924, reprint 1971) 364; Homer, *The Odyssey*, vol. 1 (LCL; 1919, reprint 1976) 388 and 438.

1   Step down and sit in[a] (the) dust,[b]
     virgin [of?] Babylon's daughter!
     Sit down on the ground without a throne,
     daughter of the Chaldeans!
     No, you will no longer (be able to) let
                yourself be called[c]
     "tender" and "precious/spoiled"!

2   Take a hand mill and grind flour!
     Raise your veil!
     Lift the hem of your skirt!
     bare your legs!
     cross/wade through rivers!

3   Your nakedness will be exposed,[a]
     and your shame become visible.[b]

     Revenge I take
     <and will not allow myself compassion>.[c]

     A man/a human being:[d]
4   Our Redeemer?—
     Yahweh Sabaoth is his name,
     the Holy One of Israel.

5   Sit down in silence
     and enter into the darkness,
     daughter of the Chaldeans!
     No, you will no longer (be able to) let
                yourself be called[a]
     "mistress of kingdoms."

6   I was angry with my people,
     I have profaned my heritage,
     and I have given them into your hand.
     You showed them no mercy.
     (Even) on the old you made your yoke
                exceedingly heavy.

7   And you thought: I shall be forever,
     an everlasting mistress!
     You did not take that to heart,
     did not think of its outcome/end.

1[a]   Or "on the dust"?
1[b]   Or "in (the) rubble"? Cf. 1 Kgs 20:10; 2 Kgs 23:12; Ps 102:15
        (14); Neh 4:4 (10); pile of ashes: Neh 3:34 (4:2).
1[c]   Lit.: "You will not continue (that) one calls you."
3[a]   Short form = jussive.
3[b]   Long form = indicative.
3[c]   Proposed emendations: cj. to *Niphal* אֶכָּנֵעַ (thus *HALOT* 3:910
        [*HALAT* 3:861]), "and will allow myself to be implored by no
        one"? Or to יַפְגִּעַ (thus *BHS*; cf. σ´ ἀντιστήσεται [similarly
        Vg]), "and no one will oppose (me)/will intervene"? But for
        the translation see below on the text.
3[d]   = stage direction; see the interpretation below; cf. εἶπεν in
        LXX (L, Syh, E, A); see BHS.
5[a]   See v. 1 above.

■ 1 "Step down!" Who can give a command such as this to Babylon? The beginning already makes clear that this is a direct divine speech. "Babylon" is the ruler. But instead of sitting on the throne she has to sit on the ground. "Babylon" is the representative of the power of the Babylonian Empire. This is an announcement of its end. Power, even the greatest power, can pass away.

The figurative way of talking about Babylon as a woman is more complicated than would at first appear, however.[75] The theme of the reevaluation of all values is sounded and played through on several levels. This shows an author's poetic skill; but it also leads to tensions in the text.

75   Comparable in this respect is the song of the vine-
      yard in Isaiah 5; see K. Baltzer, D. Georgi, and F.
      Merkel, "Jesaja 5,1-7," *GPM* 18 (1963/64) 391-95.

Babylon is a "daughter" (בַּת). As such she shares in the luxury of the house. She can be called "tender and precious/spoiled."

■ **2-3a** The daughter is a free woman. Now she is going to become unfree instead. She has to perform a slave's work. She is no longer the mistress but is told what to do: "Take a hand mill and grind flour!"[76] She also loses the signs of her high rank, which meant going veiled and wearing long skirts. These things merely hinder the work. For that it is better to go bare-legged, with the dress kilted up, especially if one has to wade through water. Mesopotamia is an alluvial country, where a good deal of work has to be done in water. "By the waters of Babylon we sat down . . .": we know this from Ps 137:1.

But probably the catchword "cross rivers" belongs to another pictorial level too, when "Babylon" is told to lift her skirts. "Babylon" is a "virgin" (בְּתוּלָה, v. 1).[77] She will be so no longer: "your nakedness will be exposed" (v. 3a). The sexual connotation of the verb "expose" (גלה, v. 2), which has already been used twice, is now plain.[78] It is a particularly drastic reinforcement of the motif of the revolution in values.

Some commentators see "Babylon" as the rich, spoiled people who are then carried off into captivity. The reference to the crossing of the rivers (v. 2) is thought to point to this.[79] Babylon is experiencing what Israel experienced with the exile. "To expose" (גלה) in the sense of "to take into exile" is a technical term. But curiously enough DtIsa never uses it in this sense, except in the phrase "my [i.e., God's] deported people/exiles" in 45:13, and even there it is connected with a particular feature, the lifting of the garment.[80] Thus the text can be directly experienced and understood on this level of action. Its message is the reversal of values: the mistress becomes the slave. But individual terms have to be understood in a more precise sense than is immediately evident. They seem like quotations from other conceptional contexts.

Babylon is "the virgin Babylon's daughter." This description has a long prehistory.[81] The personification of cities as women was connected with the development of city goddesses. The city goddess was associated with the tutelary god of the city or kingdom, the two being wife and husband. That is why capital cities particularly were entitled "virgin" and "daughter." For the OT a deification of the city was impossible, but the traditional sociomorpheme can still be detected. In order to preserve the legal character of the description, A. Fitzgerald paraphrases v. 1: "virgin daughter Babylon! . . . daughter/capital of the Chaldeans."[82] The epithets "tender" and "precious" can be viewed ironically, as "programmatic throne names predicting that the bearer of them will have good fortune."[83] We should like to know with what emblems "Babylon" was identified as the representation of the city.

The terms bring out the political dimension of Babylon's deposition. But in the negative "Babylon" we can hear overtones of Zion/Jerusalem and its functions too. Up to this point vv. 1-3 can be consistently explained as "Babylon's deposition." But this does not yet make the connection with the rest of the chapter clear, the first question being: Why does the deposition precede the judgment? This becomes comprehensible only if we become aware of the second level of the text, which depicts the descent to the underworld.

The terms used are ambiguous. One after another, they are allusions to the underworld, only the term "realm of the dead" (שְׁאוֹל šeʾōl) evidently being avoided.[84] This second interpretive level begins with the first word: "Step down" (רְדִי from ירד). The word is used

---

76   Exod 11:5.
77   See J. Bergman, H. Ringgren, and M. Tsevat, "בְּתוּלָה bᵉtûlāh," *TDOT* 2:338–43 [*ThWAT* 1:872–77].
78   Cf. Lev 18:6-19; 20:11; Deut 23:1 (22:30); 27:20.
79   Duhm, 327; but see also Dillmann's criticism.
80   Cf. Isa 20:2-4.
81   A. Fitzgerald, "The Mythological Background for the Presentation of Jerusalem as Queen and False Worship as Adultery in the OT," *CBQ* 34 (1972) 403–16; idem, "*BTWLT* and *BT* as Titles for Capital Cities," *CBQ* 37 (1975) 167–83.
82   Fitzgerald, "*BTWLT* and *BT*," 171.
83   "Programmatische en geluk voorspellende troon-namen" (Beuken's description, 269); he refers to Deut 28:54, 56 and the connection with utterances of blessing and curse: "ᶜng Isa 55:2; Jer 6:2; Mic 1:16; 2:9; Ps 37:11; rkk Lev 26:36; Isa 1:6; Jer 51:46."
84   But see 47:11 below on "disaster" (שׁוֹאָה).

in different constructions for the descent to the realm of the underworld and death.[85] In this context both "dust" (עָפָר)[86] and "earth" (אֶרֶץ)[87] are frequent terms. When v. 1 says (lit.), "there is no throne," a particular point is being made. According to the account of Babylon's "descent to Hades" in 14:1-22, former rulers certainly have thrones in the underworld (v. 9), but it is just this that Babylon is denied. It must descend to the deepest "pit" (v. 15). Even in a detail like this, there is surely a link between DtIsa and the tradition of the Babylon oracle.

When "Babylon" is told to cross rivers (v. 2), this can be explained, as we have seen, on the level of "a slave must work" as well as in the light of Babylon's geographical position. Only it is never said that Babylon now has to go into exile in a reversal of Israel's fate, and in the process must "cross rivers." But the belief that "rivers" belong to the underworld was familiar to the OT too,[88] even if it does not itself name them as precisely as does Greek mythology, with the rivers of Hades, Acheron, Kohytos, Pyriphlegeton, and Styx.[89]

If we assume that motifs from different traditions about the underworld may have been combined, the "stripping" of "Babylon" may be compared with Inanna-Ishtar's entry into the realm of the dead.[90]

If we understand the text as part of a drama, the scenic presentation of Babylon's deposition can easily be imagined. Some of the text's caustic points then emerge even more strongly.

The place of the action is first the palace. "Babylon" appears as female ruler, on her throne. If we assume that the setting was similar to that of a Greek theater, only the central door would have to be opened. This also makes a surprise effect possible: the splendor becomes visible. But even a royal tent would suffice (cf. 54:2). A ruler has her household. So we may assume that the "counselors" mentioned in v. 13 appear here too, as the chorus so to speak. At the command in v. 1, "Babylon" descends from her throne.

The "dust" can actually be seen too. "The virgin Babylon" first sits down *on* (עַל) the ground. The spectators know that this is only the beginning. The ruler who has descended from her throne in all her robes is forced to "grind." We may be sure she finds it a struggle. If this was the ancient method of grinding, she would have to kneel down and rub the upper millstone forward and back with both hands. Onomatopoeia brings out the grating sound produced: each of the four words contains a ḥ. In a gesture of humiliation, "Babylon" kneels in front of the empty throne on which she has just been sitting.

The word צַמָּה is variously interpreted: as a veil (over the face) or as "plaits of hair" that must now be loosened. As a parallel to "Jerusalem's coronation" in 54:11-14, we would expect some headdress or other. This may have been the *polos*, or cylindrical headdress, with veil, but it may also have had to do with the way the hair was worn.[91]

The rest of the divesting—to the point when "Babylon" has to "cross, wade through rivers"—can well be imagined, especially if the crossing was accompanied by splashing water. The audience gets its money's worth! But then, in v. 3a, the text suddenly switches to the future: "Your nakedness will be exposed . . . your shame will become visible." But this is not actually shown. Drastic though DtIsa can be, here—especially since this is a divine speech—the utmost limit has been reached. But, as we shall see, in this way difficulties in the dramatic composition of the text are also cleverly covered up.

85   See G. Wehmeier, "עלה ʿlh to go up," *TLOT* 2:892 [*THAT* 2:284]: "In contrast, *yrd* is a technical term for the descent of the dead into the underworld" (with text references). For Sheol cf. Gen 37:35; Num 16:30, 33; Ezek 31:15-17; Ps 55:16 (15); Job 7:9; Qoh 3:21; Jonah 2:7 (6); Ps 44:26 (25); see also G. Mayer, "ירד *yārad*," *TDOT* 6:315-22 [*ThWAT* 3:898-900] (with text references).

86   ירד with עָפָר Ps 22:30 (29); see N. H. Ridderbos, "עָפָר als Staub des Totenortes," *OTS* 5 (1948) 174-78, with reference to Job 19:25; 41:25 (24); 21:26; 17:16; 40:13 (8); Pss 22:30 (29); 30:10 (9); Dan 12:2; cf. also Isa 26:5, 19; further G. Wanke, "עָפָר *ʿāpār* dust" *TLOT* 2:939-41, esp. 941 [*THAT* 2:353-56,

esp. 355].

87   See 1 Sam 28:13; Jonah 2:7 (6); Ps 44:26 (25); Job 10:21-22; Qoh 3:21; Exod 15:12; Isa 14:12; 29:4, L. I. J. Stadelmann, *The Hebrew Conception of the World: A Philological and Literary Study* (1970) 167-77.

88   Cf. Ps 24:2; Ezek 31:15.

89   See G. Wentzel, "Acheron," PW 1/1:217-19; see above on Isaiah 41.

90   See "Descent of Ishtar to the Nether World," *ANET* 106-9, esp. ll. 36-63.

91   See also E. Kerrn-Lillesø, "Stirnband und Diadem," *LÄ* 6 (1986) 45-49.

I assume that 47:1-7 is a double scene. The first part takes place in the upper world, the second in the underworld. This would require a rapid change of scene, but it also intensifies the tension.

With the close of v. 2, "cross . . . ," the actress (or actor?) is simultaneously given a sign to go off; עבר also means literally "to go away, take one's departure." Everything now happens behind the scenes.

■ **3b** The divine speaker is still talking in v. 3a, but certainly not in v. 4. Verse 3b could be part of the divine speech, but I think that this is improbable. So who else could the speaker be?

The word "revenge" (נָקָם) does not otherwise occur in DtIsa.[92] The modern interpretation of the term is loaded, because nowadays vengeance or revenge has a strongly emotional connotation. Vengeance takes place outside the confines of law, and goes beyond the law. The avenger puts himself and what he does in the law's place. But in the OT the whole purpose of נָקָם ("revenge/requital") is to restore the order of law. It belongs to the wider complex of the concept "peace" (שָׁלוֹם), as a balanced and equitable order for the world. Yet DtIsa does not otherwise argue directly with a principle of "revenge." In the following passage what interests him is precisely a more distinct proof of Babylon's guilt. Babylon is also directly indicted because of the fault committed and the guilt incurred.

The compound "to take revenge" (לקח נקם) is also unusual.[93] H. H. Schmid[94] adduces this instance as a "unique instance" as related to God and observes that in the whole of the OT "Relatively infrequently God is the sub[ject] of the verb [take] (something over 50x)."[95]

The second statement is strange too: "I will not allow myself compassion." It stands in immediate tension to v. 4, which talks about "redemption" through Yahweh.

This initially leaves aside the last word of the verse, "a man, a human being" (אָדָם ʾādām), which is also difficult to fit in grammatically. But who could be speaking here, if it is not Yahweh? I should like to suggest that v. 3b should be understood as a saying of Sheol: "Revenge I take—I will not allow myself compassion."[96] For the action makes clear that we are at the exact transition point between the upper and the lower world. According to the OT's understanding too, the underworld is entered through "gates."[97] In more strongly personified form, it has a "throat" with which it swallows up people.[98] According to Prov 30:15-16, Sheol never says: "It is enough!"

■ **4** But the situation at the entrance to the underworld could now explain v. 4 too, and first of all the strange "a man/a human being" (אָדָם ʾādām) that stands, lost, at the end of v. 3. It is one of the rare direct stage directions in the text. It is required in order to rule out any misunderstandings. The speaker who otherwise explains what is going on is not available, because in the wake of the rapid change of scene he has to change his position. The person who comes on to bridge the interim and draw the attention of the audience to himself (since there is no curtain) is "a human being."

He says something before he has even been asked, thereby signaling his haste: "Our Redeemer?" This must be understood as a question in response to another question that is really required here: "Who is your Redeemer?" But he knows the right password at the "gateway"; he knows the name:[99] "Yahweh Sabaoth is his name, the Holy One of Israel." With these words he can pass without fear.

This is one of DtIsa's enchanting miniatures. There is a lighthearted touch here. Everyone can understand the

---

92 See G. Sauer, "נקם nqm to avenge," *TLOT* 2:767–69 [*THAT* 2:106–9].

93 It otherwise occurs only in Jer 20:20, and there it refers to human beings.

94 H. H. Schmid, "לקח lqḥ to take," *TLOT* 2:648–51 [*THAT* 2:875–79].

95 Ibid., 650, 651 [878].

96 See also the appearance of the spirit of Darius in Aeschylus's *Persians* 688–93. Cf. H. W. Smyth, *Aeschylus* 1:164–65: "Not easy is the path from out the tomb; for this cause above all—that the gods beneath the earth are readier to seize than to release."

97 Isa 38:10; Wis 16:13; Matt 16:18.

98 Isa 5:14; Hab 2:5; Prov 1:12; Sir 51:6.

99 Especially close to this motif are the Egyptian traditions, e.g., the *Amduat* and the Book of the Gates; see E. Hornung, *Ägyptische Unterweltsbücher* (1972) 128. See also Ps 24:7-10.

100 See *HALOT* s.v. A. Baumann, "דמה II dāmāh II," *TDOT* 3:260–65 [*ThWAT* 2:277–83]; see also H. D. Preuss, "דמה dāmāh," *TDOT* 3:250–60 [*ThWAT* 2:266–77]; also Tromp, *Primitive Conceptions of Death and the Nether World in the Old Testament* (1969) 76–77 on "*Dûmâ* (Fortress-Silence)" with reference to Ezek 27:32b; in addition Pss 94:17; 115:17.

situation, even children have no need to be afraid, even if what follows is somewhat "hellish." At the same time the scene is completely serious, for the password contains the whole message of hope in a single phrase. It is not just a chance association if at this point we think of Dante's *Divine Comedy*, where over the entrance to hell stand the words: "Abandon hope, all ye who enter here" ("Qui si convien lasciare agni sospetto," canto III, 14). Here the gate itself is also speaking: "Through me. . . ."

■ **5-7** With v. 5 we are in the underworld. It is again a divine speech and the context makes clear that "Babylon" is being addressed. The text gives clear signals about the place of the action. "Silence" is characteristic of the underworld. But whereas in 41:1 it was possible to doubt whether this particular "silence" was meant, here the choice of words is more decisive. As an adverb, דּוּמָם means "silently." But the form also corresponds to the substantive "quietness, silence." The connection among the roots דמה II, "be silent"; דום, "be silent" and דמם, "to be motionless, rigid," has not been completely clarified.[100] In the semantic field of these roots we can continually see connections with judgment and death,[101] even to the world of the dead, with the corresponding taboos and alterations that are used to disguise the context. Thus in Ps 51:16 (14) מִדָּמִים should probably be emended to the same word as in the present text, "land of silence." In Pss 94:17 and 115:17 דּוּמָם is the name for the underworld.[102] "Darkness" (חֹשֶׁךְ) is its characteristic mark.[103] Job 17:13 talks about "darkness" in parallelism to Sheol. According to 18:18 "darkness" is the opposite of life in the world. It is into darkness such as this that "Babylon" has to go.

If this makes clear the background of what actually happens in the text, we may then at once add a question about the performance practice. The indication "darkness" could point to the time of day of the performance, but this is not necessarily the case. Greek vase paintings showing mythological scenes make it evident that two torches were sufficient to characterize Hades as a place

of darkness.[104] The following action could therefore be played on a normal stage.

Verse 5 immediately gives two stage directions: "Sit down . . . go in/enter." We should actually expect the reverse order. If someone has to sit down in order to arrive at a particular goal, some conveyance is required. It is by no means impossible that it is just this that is meant. In the underworld one cannot simply wander around. In Egyptian representations, for example, the dead person is taken part of the way in a small sailing boat.[105] The command to sit down corresponds to the later command in v. 12 to "stand up/come forward" (עִמְדִי־נָא).

It is noticeable that in the underworld "Babylon" is no longer called by her name. She is a "daughter of the Chaldeans" (v. 5), which can also be rendered as "Chaldean woman"—one among many, an anonymous person. She also loses her title "mistress of kingdoms."

In vv. 6-7 the indictment against "Babylon" is brought forward. That means that "the Holy One of Israel" is judge in the underworld too. Even the "mistress" does not escape. It is an indication of the limits that DtIsa's theology dares to explore. Here belief in the *one* God is consistently carried through: it is also *one* world, in which the realm of the dead is included. Here heaven and hell as a dualism is ultimately no longer possible. God's sovereignty is unlimited.

This means that the disaster which comes upon his people can also come from God's hand. It is not the power of Babylon that has won the victory: "I gave them into your hand." The age-old formula from the "holy war" is here taken up once more. But—and this is typical of prophetic tradition since Amos—the identity between God and people is not a matter of course. Yahweh can be against his people.

On the other hand God's sovereignty over the whole world and over the nations means that every people has to render an account of its actions and behavior. "Compassion" with the losers is rare in power struggles,

---

101 See Isa 6:5; Jer 8:14; 25:37; 47:5; 49:26; 50:30; 51:6; Hos 10:7, 15; Obad 5; Zeph 1:11.

102 LXX renders it by ᾅδης ("Hades").

103 See Tromp, *Primitive Conceptions of Death and the Nether World in the Old Testament* (1969) 142–43, with reference to Job 18:18; 17:13; 15:22; 19:8; Pss 107; 35:6; 88:7 (6), 13 (12); D. Wachsmuth, "Unterwelt," *KP* 5 (1975) 1053–56.

104 See, e.g., A. W. Pickard-Cambridge, *The Theatre of Dionysus in Athens* (1946): volute crater from Canosa, scenes in Hades [in Antikensammlung Munich, SH 3297] (fig. 24); volute crater from Ruvo, scene in Hades (fig. 27) (95); fragments of volute crater from Ruvo, Fenicia (fig. 29) (98).

105 Cf. also Charon's bark in Greek mythology. As god of the underworld, Hades has a chariot.

especially if one party believes that it has right on its side. But the text does not stop short at wholesale abuse of the powerful. The oppression of old people is expressly mentioned. The commandment to honor the old is not specifically meant for Israel alone. Nothing more is demanded of "Babylon" than what is generally humane. To lay a heavy yoke on the old is simply unacceptable behavior. In taking as the standard what is generally valid, DtIsa is adopting the same practice as the prophets in their oracles to the nations (cf. e.g., Amos 1:3–2:3).

At the heart of the indictment is "Babylon's" claim to be divine. The assertion that she is eternal is part of this. With this claim, power absolves itself of the need to give a reason for its legitimation. The predicate "eter-nal" belongs to God alone. "Babylon" should remember this, with heart and head. This also means that the problem of the limits of power does not end with "Babylon" but has to be continually raised afresh.

"Babylon" has not considered the consequences of her arrogance. אַחֲרִית is the "end" (just as רֵאשִׁית is the "beginning"). The word can be used for the end as downfall, or for the end of a period of history. "Babylon" had to take the consequences. At the same time the text announces the close of this double scene and establishes the link with what follows. "What comes afterward" (the literal rendering of אַחֲרִית) is impressively shown immediately afterward. So it is appropriate that v. 8 should begin by pinpointing the time: "But now. . . ."

8   But now, hear this, (you) libertine,
who dwells securely,
who thinks in your heart:
I and no one else!
I will not sit there as widow,
and will experience no barrenness.[a]

9   But these two things will come to you,
suddenly and on one and the same day:
barrenness and widowhood.

Utterly[a] have they come upon you,
in spite of the number of your sorceries,
in spite of the great power of your
          invocations.

10   You have trusted in your wickedness,
you have thought: no one sees me!
Your wisdom and your knowledge,
they have led you astray.
So you thought in your heart:
I and no other!

11   But wickedness/evil will come upon you—
you know no charm against it.
And affliction will fall upon you—
you cannot atone for it.
And disaster/ruin will suddenly come upon
          you—
you do not know (it <as yet>).[a]

12   Come forward with your invocations
and with the multitude of your enchantments,
with which you have labored since your
          youth!
Perhaps you can help,
perhaps you will frighten away—.

13   You have labored with the multitude of your
          counselors.
Let them come forward and save you,
those who <divide up> the heavens,[a]
who observe the stars,
who announce month for month
<what>[b] is going to befall you.

14   See, they have become like stubble,
fire has burnt them,
they cannot save their lives
from the violence of the flames—
(these are) no charcoal embers <with which
          to warm oneself>,[a]
(no) fire that one can sit before.[b]

15   Thus have they become for you, those with
          whom you have labored,
<your sorcerers>[a] since your youth.
Everyone of them staggers over to his own
          side,
There is no one who helps you/saves you.

8[a]   Or: "and come to know no barrenness."

9[a]   Lit.: "in accord with their perfection/completeness."

11[a]   Or: "you do not see it beforehand" or "you do not know it
(and therefore do not know how to deal with it)"?

13[a]   Following the *Qere,* read הֹבְרוּ instead of הָבְרוּ ("they have divided up"). 1QIsa[a] has הוברי ("who *put a spell* on the heavens").

13[b]   With a correction to אֲשֶׁר יָבֹא (cf. LXX, S, and Tg).

14[a]   MT has לַחְמָם, "their food." The translation follows 1QIsa[a]
לחומם; cf. *BHS.*

14[b]   Or "at which one could warm oneself . . . ," or "which one
could sit in front of. . . ."

15[a]   Thus with a correction from סֹחֲרַיִךְ ("your traders") to שֹׁחֲרַיִךְ;
see *HALOT* 2:750 [*HALAT* 3:708].

■ **8-12** This can again be interpreted as a double scene. "Babylon" continues her journey through the underworld, two stages being described. The first is covered by vv. 8-9. Initially, "Babylon" is again accused. As in v. 7, the central point is her claim to divinity. Here she bases the claim on her uniqueness. For those who pick up the reference to Zeph 2:15, this claim is therefore full of irony, since the reference shows that other capital cities before "Babylon" have also claimed to be unique. In Zephaniah it was Nineveh, the capital of Assyria, which plumed itself in the very same words. Everyone who is familiar with the Scriptures knows how this arrogance was brought low.[106] Babylon's claim, like that of Nineveh, is blasphemous; it testifies to the arrogance of power. According to DtIsa, uniqueness is a predicate that belongs to God alone.[107]

Instead of security "Babylon" will experience widowhood and barrenness. To be a widow meant to be without any material provision, and to have neither legal rights nor protection.[108] To be childless counted as shameful. It too was a threat to a woman's material security and protection. But to transfer these categories to the political level was not new.[109] We may therefore assume that the phraseology was immediately comprehensible. The point is Babylon's loss of power. Relationships to other peoples come to an end. The population is destroyed. In a continuation of the sociomorpheme "the city as mother," the loss of children can also mean the loss of "daughter" or satellite cities. In a polytheistic environment, "widowhood" means that a city's tutelary god has left the goddess representing the city. In DtIsa, as in the rest of the OT as well, this figurative language is still easily detectable. Here Ezekiel 16 and 23 are of particular interest for the present text,[110] for there Jerusalem is reproached with whoredom and the sacrifice of her children. According to 16:38 (cf. 23:45), she is subject to the law condemning adulteresses and murderesses. One may therefore ask whether "widowhood and barrenness" are meant as the punishments appropriate for this state of affairs. In Ezekiel "fury and jealousy" fall upon Jerusalem. In DtIsa it is "Babylon" who is impeached.

"Babylon" thought that she could escape "widowhood and barrennness" as the consequences of what she has done. To avert evil consequences is the purpose of magical practices. But it is useless. Disaster will catch up with "Babylon" unexpectedly, suddenly, once and for all, and totally. This will be visibly demonstrated, according to the text. We have to imagine that "barrenness and widowhood" were presented in personified form, like "Babylon" herself. They are announced in v. 9a: "They will come (in) to you" (future). It was possible to point to them: "These two . . ." At the end we read: "They have come upon you" (perfect tense). Something terrible has therefore happened in the meantime.

We should like to know more about the emblems used. How could barrenness and widowhood be recognized? We may assume that the widow wore mourning clothes. But with us too, it is not very long since it was possible to deduce the marital status of a village woman from her dress.[111]

For the text there is no doubt that Yahweh is the Lord of the underworld too. He gives the command "hear this . . ." (v. 8). But this acknowledgment is made—especially where the underworld is concerned—with the expedients of polytheistic tradition and in dispute with that tradition. "These two" in conjunction with the feminine plural suggests the myths associated with the goddesses of the underworld Demeter and Persephone-Kore (to adopt their Greek names).[112] Together they are termed

---

106 But anyone who knows the context knows also that in Zephaniah 3 a judgment speech directed against Jerusalem, the "soiled, defiled, violent city," follows.

107 See Isa 45:5, 14, 18, 21, 22; cf. Deut 4:35, 39; Joel 2:27.

108 See, e.g., Deut 10:18; 14:29; Pss 94:6; 146:9; Prov 15:25.

109 As an example of a political application, cf. the beginning of Lamentations (1:1ff.): "How forsaken lies the city that once was full of people! How *like* a widow. . . ."

110 T. Krüger has drawn my attention to these texts. Cf. W. Zimmerli, *Ezekiel* 1 (1979) [*Ezechiel* 1 (1969)] on these passages.

111 Could the assonance between "childlessness" (שְׁכוֹל *šobel*) and "long skirt" (שֹׁבֶל *šᵉkôl*, v. 2) be intentional? See O. Kern, "Demeter," PW 4/2:2734, l. 40: "Her black garment reaches down to her *toes*." Cf. Pausanias 8.5.8 and 8.42.

112 O. Kern, "Demeter," PW 4/2:2713–64; K.-H. Roloff, "Demeter," *LAW,* 708–10; M. P. Nilsson, *Griechische Feste von Religiöser Bedeutung. Mit Ausschluß der Attischen* (1906, reprint 1975), "Demeter" 311–54; idem, *Geschichte der griechischen Religion* vol. 2 (2d ed. 1961), "Die Mysterien der Demeter," 345–58; E. Simon, *Festivals of Attica: An Archaeological*

"the two deities" (τὼ θεώ).[113] They are linked through the fact that both belong to the underworld and because both have the gift of fertility, for grain especially. The element "mother" (μήτηρ) is clearly recognizable in the name Demeter; the daughter, Kore, is "the girl." If we hear the present text with Greek ears, then according to the myth—especially in its Eleusinian form—Demeter is "childless."[114] Her daughter Persephone is carried off by the god of the underworld, Hades-Pluto.[115] Demeter, the mother, goes through the whole world looking for her, in the guise of an old woman. Kore-Persephone becomes "a widow" because she abandons her husband in the underworld, at least for two-thirds of the year. This background could explain why there is a chiastic change of sequence in v. 9 compared with v. 8: first barrenness, then widowhood. An explanation of this kind presupposes that DtIsa's polemic against the gods may be more precisely targeted than is often assumed.

■ **10-12** The second half-scene leads to a further stage in the journey through the underworld. It begins with a double accusation (v. 10) and shows the consequences of the deed (vv. 11-12). For the spectators, v. 10a contains a double witticism. When "Babylon" is quoted as saying "No one sees me," that is of course true; for she is in the underworld. But at the same time it is the longstanding error of rulers to believe that their secret intrigues will never be seen. Yet they are noted and have consequences; otherwise "Babylon" would not now be in the underworld.

Faith has known, at least since the history of the patriarchs (Genesis 6), that Yahweh is a God who "sees."[116] He "saw" the misery of his people in Egypt (Exod 3:7), and he sees "the heart" (1 Sam 16:7). "Babylon" has overlooked this, for all her "wisdom and knowledge." In her "trust" (בטח), "Babylon" is the antitype to those who trust in God.[117] Her repeated assertion "I, and beside me there is no one at all" (lit.: "I and beside me no one is there," vv. 8a, 10b) shows that the point here is the fundamental decision whether the human being or God

is the criterion for everything. But this means that there can also be no one to whom "Babylon" has to render an account.

The specific point in the dispute is Babylonian science, which is paraphrased in v. 10 as "wisdom and knowledge" (חָכְמָתֵךְ וְדַעְתֵּךְ). For Babylon's power did not rest merely on its military and economic strength; it was due to its scientific and cultural achievements too. Because of archeological finds and newly discovered texts we know more about this than ever before. Then as now, science and religion could not be separated. It was this that made the dispute of such vital importance. Verse 11 says that the function of science is to avert disaster ("to charm away"—as countercharm—"to atone") and its ability to predict. Here theory and practice are closely linked. We may use the terms "magic, mantic and astrology,"[118] but the negative overtones that these words have for us must not make us forget that this was the science of the time.

It is interesting that formulations such as "affliction (הוָה)" or "disaster/ruin (שׁוֹאָה) will come upon you" contain polytheistic assertions that are no more than slightly veiled. It is easier to present gods or demons "falling upon you" or "coming (in)," until the point when they are "frightened away" (v. 12). But DtIsa is consistent. Here too the foreign gods are empty and futile, and "evil" is an abstraction of reality.

The section is linked with the polemic against idols in the rest of DtIsa's book by way of the catchword "your knowledge" (דַעְתֵּךְ, v. 10), which really means a "not-knowing" (לֹא תֵדְעִי, v. 11), of the future especially, as well as the inability to help by way of religious practices (here termed sorcery). Because of this link we should in this case too like to be able to identify the deities who are under dispute. For this three terms offer themselves, רָעָה ("wickedness/evil"), הוָה ("affliction") and שׁוֹאָה ("disaster/ruin"). The terms are difficult to define exactly. "Evil" (רָעָה) is too general. On the other hand "misfortune" (הוָה) in this sense is otherwise found in this form

---

Commentary (1983) 17–27; F. Bräuninger, "Persephone," PW 19/1:944–72; K.-H. Roloff, "Persephone," *LAW* 2260.

113 See Kern, "Demeter," PW 19/2:2753.

114 Cf. the chorus in Euripides' *Helena* 1301ff., where Demeter is equated with Rhea.

115 See Hesiod, *Theogony* 912–14; *Homeric Hymns* II.

116 Cf. רְאָנִי.

117 See E. Gerstenberger, "בטח *bṭḥ* to trust," *TLOT* 1:226–30 [*THAT* 1:300–305]. Cf. 2 Kings 18–19; Isa 30:12, 15; Jer 7:3-15; 17:5, 7.

118 See Fohrer, 109.

only in Ezek 7:26. It derives from a root הוה, but the root's meaning is disputed.[119] "Disaster/ruin" (שׁוֹאָה) is probably connected with the Hebrew word for the underworld, Sheol (שְׁאוֹל).[120] The use of the word שׁואה for disaster in the present text may therefore be seen as a signal, showing that the term Sheol is being avoided. The meaning is traced back to a root שׁאה. But here the demarcation lines are disputed. There is probably a connection with "wasteland, disaster."

The early hearers too were probably uncertain what exactly is meant here, and the uncertainty increased the sinister impression. The very words themselves have a sinister sound. One can probably say that this is a triad of terms, but that these are treated as female personifications. The triad belongs to the underworld. We cannot detect any connection with particular deities. But in the history of religion a triad formation, and the personification and deification of terms, is possible and can be found, for example, in Egyptian religion and in the Greek world.

The three statements introduced by "not" (לֹא) can be rather better differentiated. שׁחר belongs to the group "magic-sorcery,"[121] so it can be rendered "charm it away, put a spell on," since it is a question of defense. כפר is what a priest does when he averts misfortune from the community by way of ritual acts.[122] These might be expiatory rites, for example (which were often associated with blood), and certain forms of sacrifice. To "know" (ידע) what is coming, that is, what is going to happen in the future, is the function of the most varied forms of mantic. It therefore includes a wide range of practices used in the world that surrounded Israel. In Israel these practices were suspect, as the lists in Deut 18:10-11, Jer 27:9 and Dan 2:2 show. Among Israel's neighbors, particular deities were responsible for these practices in each given case. Babylon was famous for its sorcery.

Verse 12 adds two other terms for practices that from the OT's point of view were sinister: חבר was already used in Isa 44:11, in the description of the artisans'

cooperatives. The link by way of "oath" is probably the common element. Thus in the text it can acquire the meaning "charm or invocation." כשׁף has the clearest overtone of magic. It "corresponds to Akk. kašāpu, kuššupu, 'to bewitch, cast a spell on' (AHw 461; CAD K 284–85), with the nominative formations kišpu, 'magic, witchery' (AHw 491)."[123] But according to the text none of these practices can "help" (v. 12b); they are useless. That is the message of the text. It requires a certain degree of knowledge and the ability to go along with the argument.

But action is clearly involved in the text too. It begins in v. 11: "But wickedness/evil will come upon you . . . and (affliction) will fall upon you . . . and disaster/ruin will suddenly come upon you." In the Hebrew the feminine is carried through in both the verbs and the suffixes. 1QIsaᵃ's reading "it (she) will come in" (וּבָאָה) undoubtedly has its place in the series of feminines. Here it is difficult to translate the term by way of the neutral "it." It is possible that here too the concepts "wickedness/evil," "affliction," and "disaster/ruin" should be imagined as personified. According to the text, the action takes place on different levels, either because "Babylon" is first sitting down, or because the beings come from somewhere above. They come on one after another, as they are announced. A conclusion, as in the first half-scene in v. 9, is not mentioned.

"Babylon" is told to stand up (v. 12: "come forward"), whereas from v. 5 onward she must be imagined as sitting down. But even then she is not able to catch or frighten away the ominous beings that buzz round her like flies. This brings the first half-scene to an end. Perhaps the whole nightmare throng disappears behind the scenes. But it is conceivable that the whole scene was presented as a whirling dance. It is noteworthy that apart from "Babylon" five active persons appear on the stage in vv. 8-12, though without speaking parts.

■ **13-15** Events hasten toward their end. The brief double scene begins with renewed proceedings against

119 See S. Erlandsson, "הוה havvāh," TDOT 3:356–58 [ThWAT 2:379–81]. He paraphrases the meaning as follows (357 [380]): "The word havvah is usually connected with men who are unfaithful and rebellious against God, who are not willing to adapt themselves to the good ordinances of God, but pervert the right according to their evil desires."

120 Thus first L. Köhler, "Alttestamentliche

Wortforschung scheʾōl," ThZ 2 (1946) 71–74; idem, "Problems in the Study of the Language of the Old Testament," JSS 1 (1956) 9 and 19-20; G. Gerlemann, "שׁאול šeʾôl realm of the dead," TLOT 3:1279–82 [THAT 2:837–41].

121 See G. André, "כשׁף kāšap," TDOT 7:360–66, esp. 366 [ThWAT 4:375–81, esp. 380].

"Babylon" (v. 13) and closes with "Babylon's" annihilation (vv. 14-15). "Babylon" enters again. "You have labored . . ." establishes the link with what has gone before, which the audience has already seen.

"The counselors" are commanded to stand up (come forward). This may first be understood literally, as in v. 12. For they will have been sitting, especially if—as the ruler "Babylon's" retinue—they already entered in 47:1, and have been surrounding the throne. Another possibility is that they now enter as the chorus and thus "appear" before the court of law. They are required to make a prediction of future events, on the basis of the position of the stars.

Here Babylon's age-old knowledge of astronomy (which was also astrology) is apostrophized. I do not think it is out of the question that the "dividing of the heavens" with the observation of the stars refers to the discovery of the zodiac, which was made during this period.[124] Earlier Babylonian astronomy had been more closely related to the horizon, being based on observation of the rising and setting of stars and constellations. The division into months by way of the zodiac and its constitutive parts made a much more differentiated astronomy and astrology possible.[125] חֳדָשִׁים can refer both to months and to "new things."

The theme of prediction is taken up again here, at the end, because it is connected with one of DtIsa's main concerns, his acknowledgment of his God's ability to create and proclaim something new. At the same time, it is this final section that focuses most clearly on the concrete situation. Here too the dispute is about who knows the future (מוֹדִיעִם, v. 13; cf. ידע in v. 11) and who helps/saves (וְיוֹשִׁעֵךְ, v. 13; יַצִּילוּ, v. 14; מוֹשִׁיעֵךְ, v. 15). In this way prophecy competes with astrology.

One may very well ask today too about the data on which predictions are made. Today too the claim to be able to predict confers power. But if we have now ceased to admit the predictive value of astronomy, terming attempts of this kind "astrology," this criticism puts us in line with the tradition of DtIsa. Only we should be aware of what a venture this first step was, and that it was a step which DtIsa undertook on the premises of faith.

The story about Daniel and his friends in Daniel 2 provides a good illustration for this text and for the dispute with Babylonian science. The story tells of Nebuchadnezzar's dream about the four empires, which the friends have to interpret. The texts are probably not far removed in date. The same catchwords and methods of argument are found in both. Although the stress is different in some particular respects, common to both texts is the stress on the precedence of revelation compared with the techniques of divination, as well as the preeminence of God's sovereignty over against the lordship of the great earthly power.

What then happens in vv. 14 and 15 can only be understood in terms of action. The text does not in any way require emendation. "See" (הִנֵּה) is the renewed signal that there is in fact something to be seen. "Babylon" and her royal household disappear in "fire" and "flame." Anyone who knows anything at all about the underworld of "hell" knows too that at its end the fire of annihilation blazes.[126] Thus "Babylon" is finally overwhelmed by the disaster she has called down upon herself.

It seems probable that the performance was accompanied by pyrotechnic effects. A straw fire burns swiftly "like stubble." But so that we are sure to recognize the place where we and "Babylon" are standing, and understand the seriousness of the situation, the text declares explicitly: "These are no charcoal embers with which

122   See B. Lang, "כִּפֶּר kipper," *TDOT* 7:288–303 [*ThWAT* 4:303–18].

123   See G. André, "כָּשַׁף kāšap," *TDOT* 7:361 [*ThWAT* 4:376]; also B. Lang, "כִּפֶּר kipper," *TDOT* 7:290 [*ThWAT* 4:305]: "Babylonian incantation and ritual texts, especially from the first half of the first millennium, use the term *kuppuru* (D stem of *kapāru* [*AHw* 1:442–46] with the meaning 'purify cultically'; it refers to acts performed by an incantation priest."

124   See above on 40:12.

125   For Egypt, e.g., E. Brunner-Traut, "Mythos im

Alltag. Zum Loskalender im Alten Ägypten," *Antaios* 12 (1971) 332–47. She makes an interesting reference to Papyrus Chester Beatty I: "On this day the fight between Horus and Seth took place. The one smote the other. The two pressed against each other, changing themselves into two hippopotamuses at the gate of the gods of Babylon" (336 n. 21). It is the indication of a "bad day"!

126   From Egyptian sources cf. the 5th and 11th Hour of Amduat; also the 10th, 22nd, 41st, and 59th scene of the Book of the Gates; see Hornung, *Ägyptische Unterweltsbücher* (1972) 44.

one can warm oneself, not a fire to sit in front of" (v. 14). The experience of a devouring fire is conveyed although the modern inferno had not yet been invented, nor the laser technology that is so effective on the stage.

The sentence "everyone staggers over to his own side" signals that the actors go off and that this is the end of the scene. "There is no one to help you (מוֹשִׁיעֵךְ)" is the final word, which is an encouragement to reflection. The catchword "help" (הוֹעִיל) appears in three variations from v. 12 onward. The irony is that the wise men cannot even help themselves, let alone "Babylon." "Babylon" has no "helper." This is the exact opposite and counterpart to what is promised to "Zion/Jerusalem."

"For my sake, for my sake I will act . . . ,
and my glory I will not give to another" (48:11)

B. 3. 48:1-11
Judgment on Untrue Jacob/Israel

---

1 Hear this, O house of Jacob,
who are called by the name of Israel—
but they have come forth from the womb[a]
of Judah—
who swear by the name of Yahweh—
and they wish to remember the God of Israel
(but) not in steadfastness/truth and not with
righteousness.

2 Yes, they are called after the city of the
Holy One,[a]
and they lean on the God of Israel—
Yahweh Sabaoth is his name.

3 The earlier (happenings) I have already
proclaimed,
and they went out of my mouth,
and I caused them to be heard.[a]
Suddenly I acted, and they have come to pass.

4 Because I knew that you are hard,
and your neck is an iron sinew,
and your forehead (made of) bronze,

5 I proclaimed it to you before,
before it came about I let you hear (it),
so that you cannot say:
    My idol brought it about!
    or: my carved image or my cast image
        commanded it!

6 You have heard it—but see all this—
can you not declare it?
From the beginning I have let you know new
(happenings)
and hidden (circumstances) that you did not
know.

7 They have been created now and not
            previously
or yesterday, and you have not (yet) heard
            them,
so that you cannot say:
            See, I knew it.

8 You   neither heard
                nor knew
                nor was your ear <opened>[a]
        before;
for I knew: you will be utterly faithless/are
            utterly faithless,
and you are called a rogue from your
        mother's womb.

9 For my name's sake I will defer my anger,
and (for) my praise's (sake) I will restrain
        myself toward you,
so that I do not wipe you out.

10 See I have refined you, but not for silver,
I have tested[a] you in the furnace of misery.

11 For my sake, for my sake I will act,

1a Thus with a correction from MT (וּמִמֵּי, "and out of the water"
or "the waters") to וּמִמְּצֵי; cf. 1QIsaᵃ (see *BHS*).

2a A possible translation is also "city of the sanctuary" or "holy
city." See below on 52:1-2.

3a וְאַשְׁמִיעֵם is a more probable reading than וָאַשְׁמִיעֵם (see *BHS*).

8a Thus with a correction from פִּתְּחָה, "she has opened," to פִּתַּחְתָּ;
cf. 1QIsaᵃ, Tg; Cairo Genizah, S, Vg seem to presuppose a
Pual (פֻּתְּחָה, "she" or "it [your ear; fem.] has been opened");
but there is no supporting evidence for this (see *BHS*).

10a The variant בחנתיכה in 1QIsaᵃ confirms that here בחר is used
in the sense of "test"; see here *HALAT*. See also below on the
text.

for how <I am profaned>,^a
and my glory I will not give to any other.

11a MT (יֵחָל, "he is/will be profaned") is incomprehensible in the context. LXX adds τὸ ἐμὸν ὄνομα (= שְׁמִי). The most probable solution would seem to be to read the first person sing. (אֵ[ו]חָל) together with 1QIsa^a (איחל; cf. S, Vg).

Many commentators agree in pronouncing chap. 48 to be "difficult."[127] But in my view the difficulty has to do with the specific character of this text, which artistically weaves together a number of different elements and levels of meaning. On the one hand it winds up the theme of "Babylon"; on the other, after Zion has been named in 46:13, here the phrase "city of the Holy One" (v. 2) prepares the theme "Zion/Jerusalem" (from 49:14 in Acts V and VI). Jacob/Israel is mentioned (v. 12), and there is a reference to Cyrus, but above all the "servant" is announced once more. All in all, the text is a summing up of what has gone before.[128]

The text works with proofs from tradition, indeed scriptural proofs, in the sense of prophecy and fulfillment. Here again, indications are found in the catchwords "earlier things" (רִאשֹׁנוֹת, v. 3) and "new things" (חֲדָשׁוֹת, v. 6). It is not easy to pinpoint the references in individual cases, but the attempt should be made.

The most regrettable thing, however, is that we can no longer understand the topical references that we must suppose the text contains. Here we lack explanations from ancient times, of the kind that have been passed down by the scholiasts for Aristophanes' comedies, for example. On the dramatic level, it is important to note as closely as possible who is speaking in each case.

If we take first, as indications of the structural divisions, the imperatives "hear" (שׁמע), the following more or less extensive units emerge:

48:1-11   "Hear this, O house of Jacob . . ."
48:12-15 "Listen to me, O Jacob . . ."
48:16-22 "Draw near to me and listen to this . . ."
49:1   "Listen to me, you islands . . ."

"Hear, listen to" in fact proves to be an important catchword in the text, for the root שׁמע is used twelve times in all, in different forms (including 49:1).

In the context of the major unit that begins with chap. 46, an element of action is followed in each case by a parenetic application in the form of a divine speech. After the "procession of the idols" in 46:1-2, the "house of Jacob" is also addressed, associated there with "all the remnant of the house of Israel." The manufacture and procession of the idols in 46:5-7 is linked in vv. 8-12 with a comment that is initially clearly critical: "Rogue . . ." (פֹּושְׁעִם v. 8). The term covers "to do evil/injustice, to be/to become an apostate." This connection should also be noted in the third divine speech in the present text. The action is not an end in itself. The purpose of Babylon's downfall is not to triumph over her; it is a challenge requiring listeners to question their own history and conduct.[129]

■ **1-3** The place of the action is doubtless still the underworld. At all events there is nothing in the passage to suggest the contrary. This may explain why here the past history of the "house of Jacob" can be addressed; and in this connection the perfects in vv. 1 and 2 should be noted. The actual divine speech begins only in v. 3.

On the level of the action, vv. 1-2 are an announcement. The speaker comes forward like a herald: "Yahweh Sabaoth is his name." This, then, is a new part-scene.

In structure the text must be assigned to the scenes that take place in a court of law. The point is again the claim of true prophecy. The special nuance is derived from the "summons" of one of the parties in vv. 1-2.

127 For a survey of the research see Schoors, *I Am God Your Saviour* (1973) 283–92; Beuken, 277–79 with nn. 1–7 (327); Spykerboer, *The Structure and Composition of Deutero-Isaiah* (1976) 156–62, 230–31.

128 See Naegelsbach 517 [552]: "This chapter reproduces the chief ingredients of the foregoing discourses from chap. xl on. By this brief recapitulation, it aims a mighty effect on the spirits of the hearers by means of a total impression. A glorious redemption, analogous to that wrought by Moses, is presented to the view of the people of the Exile,

from whose blessings, of course, the wicked are excluded."

129 Cf. here H. Leene, "Juda en de heilige stad in Jesaja 48:1-2: Verkenningen in een stroomgebied," in M. Boertien, ed., *Proeven van oudtestamentisch onderzoek ter gelegenheid van het afscheid van Prof. Dr. M. A. Beek* (1974) 80–92.

This party is described with the catchwords "house of Jacob," "Judah," "called after the city of the Holy One," that is, Yahweh's. It is therefore a group that appears, not the "servant" Jacob/Israel alone.

In this text particularly it is a question whether the address "house of Jacob" should be understood in a positive sense from the outset, or whether criticism of the past does not already begin at this point. The Jacob tradition is ambivalent. "Jacob" is the vehicle of blessing, but he is also "the liar."

Apart from the Genesis story, this tradition can already be seen in Hos 12:1-7 (11:12—12:6):

> 3(2)   Yahweh has a lawsuit with Judah <Israel>,[130]
> to call Jacob to account according to his ways;
> according to his deeds he will requite him.
> 4(3)   In the womb he tricked his brother,
> in his "wealth" he strove against God.[131]

According to Hosea, Jacob's guilt begins already in the womb. In view of this it is striking that Isa 48:8 should run: "For I knew: you will be utterly faithless/are utterly faithless, and you are called a rogue from your mother's womb." The doxology in Hos 12:6 (5), "And Yahweh is the God of hosts, Yahweh is his name (זִכְרוֹ),"[132] with its context, can also be compared with the divine predication here in vv. 1-2.

Jeremiah also alludes to this negative tradition about Jacob (Jer 9:3 [4]):

> Beware of your neighbors,
> and put no trust in your brother,
> for one brother deceives the other (כִּי־כָל־אָח עָקוֹב יַעְקֹב).

Here as in Gen 27:35-36 there is a wordplay on "Jacob" and "deceive" (יַעְקֹב ya'aqōb, from עקב).[133] The remarkable thing is that according to the compositional text of the book as it stands, the prophet Jeremiah begins his proclamation of judgment: "Hear the word of Yahweh, O house of Jacob, and all the families of the house of Israel" (Jer 2:4, cf. 5:20-25). This is preceded by the charge to proclaim to Jerusalem (Jer 2:2). This leads to the question whether, quite apart from points of detail, there is not a general connection between our present DtIsa text and the Jeremiah tradition, especially Jeremiah 1–6.

Here we must start from our previous conclusion that when DtIsa speaks about "former things" he is referring to specific scriptural testimonies. His account of the downfall of Babylon had as its presupposition the sayings about Babylon in the books of Isaiah and Jeremiah. Could there not be something similar behind the present declaration of judgment? If this is the case, the remarkable link between the house of Jacob, Judah, and the city of Jerusalem would be noteworthy. I should like at least to put forward this possibility for discussion, in the hope that it might help us to understand some of the difficulties in the text.

Jeremiah is not mentioned in DtIsa any more than are other prophets, not even in connection with Cyrus, as 2 Chr 36:22 and Ezra 1:1 at least do. But a hint could perhaps be given in v. 3a to the "well-versed" listeners who are several times apostrophized in the text. According to this, the earlier "happenings" (הָרִאשֹׁנֹת) have been revealed in a triple step: they were proclaimed, they proceeded out of the mouth (of Yahweh), and they were brought to the ears of the people—only after that did Yahweh act (עשׂה). "The mouth (פֶּה) of Yahweh" can be used generally in a transferred sense for the word of God.[134] It is found in this sense too in the prophetic tradition. There "voice" (קוֹל) can be used in a similar sense.[135] But at the installation of Jeremiah the phrase is an emphatic one: "See, I am putting my words in your mouth." In Jer 15:19 Jeremiah is explicitly called Yahweh's "mouth." He can exercise his prophetic func-

---

130 H. W. Wolff (*Hosea* [1974] 206 [*Hosea* (2d ed. 1965) 267]) thinks that "Israel" was the original reading: the Hebrew text "Judah" "probably originates from the book's Judaic redaction (cf. 4:15; 5:5; 6:11)." But for DtIsa it is precisely the link between "Jacob" and "Judah" that is of interest. I would therefore propose retaining the reading "Judah," contrary to Wolff's view. It seems possible that DtIsa already presupposes the "Judaic redaction" of Hosea.

131 Trans. following Wolff, ibid., 206 [266]; see also 185 [239–40] on Hos 10:11.

132 See Wolff, ibid., 205–7, 213–16 [266, 276–77] on this passage.

133 W. L. Holladay (*Jeremiah: Chapters 1–25* [1986] 298) translates here: "for every brother acts like a Jacob."

134 See F. García López, "פֶּה *pæh*," *ThWAT* 6:522–38, esp. 529–33.

135 I would suppose that in a number of passages קוֹל stands for the function of a prophet, similar to פֶּה. "Listen to the voice (קוֹל) of Yahweh" would accordingly also mean "listen to the prophet." Cf. B. Kedar-Kopfstein, "קוֹל *qôl*," *ThWAT* 6:1237–52, esp. 1251.

tion again when he allows what is "precious" to proceed (יצא) from himself, not what is "common." Jer 9:10-15 (11-16) prophesies the downfall of Jerusalem and the cities of Judah. The text asks the question: Who is a wise man? It goes on: "Let him understand it and let the one to whom the mouth of Yahweh has spoken declare it"[136]—explain, that is, why the land has been destroyed. I believe that here too "mouth" is a term for the prophet Jeremiah.

That for later generations Jeremiah was "the mouth of Yahweh" in a very particular way is shown, finally, by 2 Chr 36:12, which says about Zedekiah: "He did not humble himself before the prophet Jeremiah, before the mouth of Yahweh" (מִלִּפְנֵי יִרְמְיָהוּ הַנָּבִיא מִפִּי יהוה). "The mouth of Yahweh" would then stand for "Jeremiah."[137] But the links between the present DtIsa text and texts from the book of Jeremiah go further even than that.

Verse 1 talks about "swearing by the name of Yahweh"; this theme is treated in three places in the book of Jeremiah. In Jer 4:2 the right way of swearing is named as a precondition for conversion. Here the agreements reach as far as the actual wording.[138] In Jeremiah the declaration is part of a threatening oracle that according to Jer 4:1 is addressed to "Israel." In v. 3 "the man of Judah" and "the <inhabitants> of Jerusalem" are named (cf. v. 4). According to the context the point is to announce "the enemy from the north": (v. 5) "Declare (נגד) in Judah, and let it be heard (שמע) in Jerusalem, and say. . . ." But this is what Isa 48:3, 5 says with the very same verbs, "declare" (נגד *Hiphil*) and "allow to be heard" (שמע *Hiphil*): Yahweh announced the disaster to Judah and Jerusalem beforehand. If we compare the texts, we can be more precise and say: Yahweh announced the disaster through *Jeremiah*. If we remember Jer 4:6, "for I am bringing in disaster (רָעָה אָנֹכִי מֵבִיא) from the north and a great destruction," then "they have come in" (וַתָּבֹאנָה, v. 3), instead of the more abstract

"they have arrived," also acquires a more precise meaning. This would mean that DtIsa is not concerned about prediction in general; he is referring specifically to the announcement through Jeremiah of the downfall of Judah and Jerusalem.

Jer 5:2-6 (cf. v. 7-9) talks a second time about swearing, also in a threatening oracle addressed to Jerusalem: "They swear falsely."[139] There the statement is linked with the theme that in order to prevent themselves from repenting, the people "make their faces harder than rock." The final catastrophe is still to come.

According to Jeremiah 44 this catastrophe has now taken place. Yahweh has "brought on" the disaster to "Jerusalem and all the cities of Judah" (v. 2; cf. vv. 6, 22-23). Jeremiah is in Egypt, together with a remnant of the population. Now matters are reversed: according to v. 26b, Yahweh says: "See, I have sworn by my great name, says Yahweh, that it shall not be, nor shall my name be named on the lips of any man of Judah who says 'as Yahweh lives—in all the land of Egypt.'" The disaster is to continue. The reason is worship of "the queen of heaven."

One can get the impression that Isaiah 48 is entering into complexes like this. The theme "oath" or "swearing" is linked with the question about "steadfastness/truth and righteousness." The oath is an instrument in the relationships between people, in social behavior. The community is disrupted when someone misuses God's name in an oath.[140] The text criticizes the discrepancy between the acknowledgment of God and the acts committed. History is interpreted as a consequence of what Jerusalem and Judah have done. To disobey the commandments of God leads to misfortune. In this approach Jeremiah and DtIsa are at one. This is a question of the fundamental relationship to God in the sense of the confession of faith: that is made clear by the additional clause "and they wish to remember (יַזְכִּירוּ)[141] the

---

136 On the difficulties of translating the text, see Holladay, *Jeremiah: Chapters 1–25* (1986) 307.

137 Comparable would be the iconography in baroque churches, for example in Bavaria, where a flaming heart indicates Augustine, a beehive Ambrose, as doctors of the church.

138 Jer 4:2
        בְּמִשְׁפָּט וּבִצְדָקָה   בֶּאֱמֶת   וְנִשְׁבַּעְתָּ חַי יהוה
Isa 48:1
    הַנִּשְׁבָּעִים בְּשֵׁם יהוה . . . לֹא בֶאֱמֶת וְלֹא בִצְדָקָה

139 Cf. also Jer 7:9 with its context; also Hos 4:2; Lev 5:24 (6:3); 19:12; Zech 5:4; Mal 3:5.

140 See K. Baltzer, "Namenglaube II. Im AT," *RGG*³ 4:1302–4.

141 On the connection between זכר and the worship of the congregation, see Westermann, 196–97 [160]. Cf. H. Eising, "זָכַר *zākar*," *TDOT* 4:64–82 [*ThWAT* 2:571–93]; W. Schottroff, "זכר *zkr* to remember," *TLOT* 1:381–88 [*THAT* 1:507–18].

God of Israel" in the context of "swearing" (48:1). This is not merely something in the past. It still has topical relevance. It is the sole formulation in the context that is definitely in the imperfect.

■ **4-7** The "hardness" of "the house of Jacob" is given in v. 4 as the reason for the disaster that was announced earlier and has now taken place. It has often been claimed that this verse is by another hand, since it is allegedly "Deuteronomistic" and contains a series of terms found only here in DtIsa. But there is a reason for this, if in this passage DtIsa is pursuing a kind of scriptural proof. If we compare the passages already put forward in the past by Duhm, Deut 31:27, for example, comes from the testament of Moses before his death: "For I know well . . . how stiff-necked you are."[142] Three Jeremiah texts are relevant: Jer 7:26, along with vv. 25 and 27, establishes the line running from "the fathers" at the exodus from Egypt, by way of "all my servants the prophets," down to Jeremiah himself.[143] Jer 17:20 shows that 17:23 is directed to "the kings of Judah and all Judah and all the inhabitants of Jerusalem." Jer 19:15 is the announcement and justification of disaster, after the inspection of the Tophet of Jerusalem, the place of child sacrifices and foreign cults, "because they have stiffened their necks, refusing to hear my words."

DtIsa does not simply take over a sentence word for word, and yet he does not change its substance; that is his literary achievement. He splits up the formula "hard as to their necks." The strange "sinew" (גִּיד *gîd*) has no doubt something to do with the wordplay on "proclaim" (הִגִּיד *higgîd*) in vv. 3 and 5. But as everyone who is familiar with Gen 32:33 (32) knows, this is the term for the hip nerve, on which Jacob was struck.

According to Jer 6:28 the prophet Jeremiah called Yahweh's people "bronze and iron," and we should take the continuation of this text into account when considering v. 10. Perhaps there is an echo of other traditional sayings too—Prov 29:1, for example, for the sudden downfall, and Ezek 3:7 for the "hard forehead."[144]

The word that announces and interprets is part of the divine act. That is a prophetic tradition, which DtIsa clearly acknowledges here. It excludes two misunderstandings: first, that what human beings experience is not Yahweh's doing (v. 5: "so that you cannot say . . ."); and second, that discernment depends on human knowledge, not on revelation (v. 7: "so that you could not say . . ."). The "foreign gods" could be rivals to Yahweh's words and works. Consistently enough, these gods are no longer named in the text. Verse 5 talks only about "images." But as we know from DtIsa's polemic, they can neither act nor speak. In this approach too DtIsa belongs to the tradition of Jeremiah (cf. Jeremiah 10).

The aim of the argument is to make the experience of God's reliability in crisis (in this case the downfall of Jerusalem and, with the exile, the end of Judah's existence as a state) the reason for deducing the reliability of God's word in the present. The radical nature of the new salvation can only be understood as a new creation (v. 9, בְרָא). The mediation between this discontinuity of disaster and salvation on the one hand, and the continuity of history on the other, is possible only by way of a theological understanding of God. To believe in the continuity presupposes a community that accepts the past, including its guilt and the disaster that has been experienced. This means that in the present text too emendations should be viewed with suspicion.

■ **8-11** Many commentators view vv. 8-11, or part of them, as a later addition, and this is of course a possibility. The vocabulary has suggested to some commentators the influence of Trito-Isaiah. But it may also be pointed out that the style and argument hardly differs from that of the context. Verse 8b pronounces the verdict "guilty." Verses 9-11 state what the consequences of this verdict really ought to be.

■ **8** This verse continues the statement of the evidence in the court proceedings that, we may assume, are the setting here. A triple series with "not either" (גַּם לֹא): "neither . . . nor . . . nor . . ." establishes tersely that over a prolonged period there has been neither hearing nor knowledge.

Verses 6-7 changed the form of address between the collective singular "you" to a differentiating plural. This collective is evidently responsible for the proclamation.[145] From v. 8 the singular is once more used, probably again in a collective sense.

---

142 Cf. also Exod 32:9.
143 Cf. also Neh 9:16-17, 29.
144 Cf. Jer 5:3.

145 But there may possibly also be a connection with the "Chaldeans" in 47:13 and 48:14.

"Because I knew . . ." introduces a proof from tradition, in correspondence to v. 4. The reproach of "faithlessness" (בגד)[146] in relationship to God is in line with the understanding that we already find in Hosea, which sees the sociomorpheme of marriage as linked with the idea of the "covenant."[147] But again Jeremiah is particularly illuminating.[148] In this case, we can actually point to a chapter in which the theme is dominant: Jeremiah 3. It may be summed up in the words of Jer 3:20: "But as a woman is faithless to (בגד מן) her beloved, so you have been faithless to me (בגד בי), O house of Israel, says Yahweh." But in this chapter the faithlessness applies especially to Judah (see vv. 7, 8, 10, 11). It consists of serving foreign gods ("committing adultery with stone and tree," v. 9) and "not obeying Yahweh's voice" (v. 13).

If we assume that there is a connection here, then the reproach "rogue from the womb"[149] can refer to the descendants of the adulterously ended "marriage," the annulled relationship to God.[150] In view of DtIsa's pleasure in complex levels of meaning, we cannot exclude the possibility that there is a reminiscence of Jacob's beginnings here. But it is noticeable that in the context of Jeremiah 3 the recreant Israel is told to repent (v. 12), is assured that Yahweh's wrath will not last forever (v. 12; cf. Isa 48:9), that she should admit her guilt toward Yahweh (פְּשָׁעַתְּ, v. 13), and that finally the "faithless children" will be brought to Zion (v. 14). These are all elements in the Jeremiah text that can be compared with the approach taken by the present text in DtIsa. What is promised in Jeremiah is announced here as immediately impending.

■ **10** Again a comparison with Jeremiah 6 can help to solve difficulties in the present text. The catchwords "refine" (צרף), "silver" (כֶּסֶף) and "(small) furnace" (כּוּר) in the text lead us to expect that the subject is the extraction of silver. But then why does the text run "not for silver"? Instead of "test" (בחן),[151] which we should expect as a parallel to "refine" (צרף), we have בחר, which can mean "test" but is generally used in the sense of "choose"; and the furnace is "a furnace of misery." From the earliest versions down to modern commentators, textual changes or emendations have been proposed. But changes would destroy the subtlety of the text. As it stands, it is certainly not consistent. Nor does it have to be, if the consistency lies outside this text itself, in the text on which it is commenting.

The process of extracting pure silver lies behind a number of biblical texts.[152] The most detailed description and application is to be found in Jer 6:29-30. Jeremiah is appointed tester (בָּחוֹן) of the people. "Bronze and iron are they" (v. 28)[153] may also belong to the metallurgical process. We are indebted to W. L. Holladay for his clear description of the process that is the background of the Jeremiah text.[154] He shows how precisely the text describes a smelting process that has gone wrong, with its result: "In vain the refiner has refined" (לַשָּׁוְא צָרַף צָרוֹף)[155] and—in the interpretation—"They are called rejected silver" (כֶּסֶף נִמְאָס).

The catchwords are again recognizable. But DtIsa alters the sense. Instead of "null and void" (לַשָּׁוְא) he says: "not for silver." But this is his theme otherwise too (52:3): "You have been sold for nothing, and you will not

---

146 See S. Erlandsson, "בָּגַד bāghadh," *TDOT* 1:470–73 [*ThWAT* 1:507–11]; M. A. Klopfenstein, "בגד bgd to act faithlessly," *TLOT* 1:198–200 [*THAT* 1:261–64].

147 See for בגד Hos 5:7; 6:7; Mal 2:10-16.

148 It is curious that the paronomastic construction found in v. 8 is used especially in the book of Isaiah (Isa 21:2; 24:16; 33:1), but that there the meaning is so different in that context the translation has to be "rob" (see S. Erlandsson, "בגד bāghadh," *TDOT* 1:470–73 [*ThWAT* 1:507–11] on this passage).

149 On פשע (Isa 48:8) see R. Knierim, *Die Hauptbegriffe für Sünde im Alten Testament* (1965) 113ff.

150 Cf. Jer 3:11ff.; v. 14 "faithless children," with Hos 5:5-7, "they are unfaithful (בגד) toward Yahweh and beget alien children (בָּנִים זָרִים, v. 7)"; as well as Mal 2:10ff.: "Why are we faithless to one another (בגד)." Consequently according to v. 15 they are no longer "God's offspring" (זֶרַע אֱלֹהִים).

151 Cf. Jer 9:6 (7); Zech 13:9; Pss 17:3; 26:2; 66:10. The very change in the formula as it might be expected is a marked signal that arouses attention.

152 Cf. Isa 1:22 and 25; Zech 13:9; Ps 66:10; Dan 11:35.

153 See above on 48:4.

154 Holladay, *Jeremiah*, 1 (1986) 230–32 on 6:29a: "Excursus: The Cupellation of Silver"; further R. J. Forbes, *Metallurgy in Antiquity* (1950); also his *Studies in Ancient Technology* 8 (1964).

155 See here Holladay, *Jeremiah*, 1 (1986).

be redeemed for silver (וְלֹא בְכֶסֶף)" (cf. 45:13 in the saying to Cyrus, and 55:1).

We can make the change clear to ourselves through the double meaning of the English phrase "for nothing." "For nothing" in the sense of "in vain" becomes "for nothing" meaning "costing nothing." The "testing" of the people that Jeremiah undertakes at his Lord's charge, with an unfortunately devastating result, becomes—a new—election. And the "misery" is now at an end.

The image of "the furnace of wretchedness" too (v. 10) clearly has tradition behind it.[156] The sojourn in Egypt is often called a "furnace."[157] The catchword "wretchedness" is also often used for the period in Egypt. What is special in DtIsa is the combination of the two terms. But DtIsa himself does not mention Egypt here, thus arriving at a process of abstraction. The special acknowledgment of the exodus from Egypt has passed down an experience that has general validity. It offers the approach that makes it possible to surmount crisis. Guilt can be expressed without its involving the deprivation of all hope. Guilt is not repressed. God's "praise" (v. 9) and "glory" (v. 11) are preserved. Even in disaster "election" still stands. Hope remains in the Babylonian exile, or wherever men and women are driven, in whatever "misery" they may land.

Since the text of vv. 1-11 takes the form of court proceedings, we should expect that the statement of the evidence and the verdict "guilty" (v. 8) would be followed by an announcement of the consequences of this judgment—the punishment. But it is just this which is missing in the present text. We may ask ourselves, why? The answer is briefly given by Yahweh through the triple "for the sake of . . ." (לְמַעַן): "for my name's sake" (v. 9), and "for my sake, yes for my sake" (v. 11). In spite of all the trenchancy of the "reproach," this is the presupposition for everything that follows.

---

156 Deut 4:20; 1 Kgs 8:51; see esp. once more the book of Jeremiah, Jer 11:4. Duhm already remarked in connection with the present DtIsa passage: "The glossator may mainly have had Jer 6:29 at the back of his mind."

157 Gen 41:52; Exod 3:7, 17 (מֵעֳנִי מִצְרַיִם); 4:31; Deut 16:3; 26:7; Neh 9:9. For Jacob cf. Gen 31:42 and 36.

48 "I am the One, I am the first, I am also the last" (48:12)

C. 48:12-15
Yahweh's Proclamation
The Homage of "the Chaldeans"

12 Listen to me, O Jacob,
and Israel, whom I have called!
I am the One, I am the first,
I am also the last.

13 My hand also laid the foundations of the
earth
and my right hand spread out the heaven.
When I summon them, they stand there
together.

14 Assemble all of you and listen!
Who among them has declared those
(events)?

"Yahweh loved him—
he will perform his will to Babylon and his
arm."a
(The Chaldeans)

15 I, I have spoken, and I have called him.
I have made him come/brought him in, and
his way will prosper.

14a Some commentators have proposed replacing וּזְרֹעוֹ, "and his arm," by וְזֶרַע (or וּבְזֶרַע): "<and (other) descendants> of the Chaldeans" (cf. LXX σπέρμα; see *BHS*).

If we again take the summons to listen (vv. 12, 14, 16) as a signal indicating a division in the text, then vv. 12-15 consist of two brief units, vv. 12-13 and vv. 14-15. There is an intimate connection with the more extensive unit that follows in vv. 16-22.

Verse 14b has a position of its own. In my view this is an entr'acte on the part of "the Chaldeans." Otherwise we may assume that the speaker is always the Deity, directly or indirectly. A number of stage directions go together with "listening": "come forward together, stand up, stand there" (עמד, v. 13), "assemble" (קבץ, v. 14) and "draw near, approach, come forward" (קרב v. 16). As regards the type of scene, we should imagine this as a royal audience. It is divided up into three subscenes, these corresponding to the units mentioned. As we shall see, different persons are at the center of interest in each case; they are either addressed or represent the audience or spectators. Yahweh is once more presented as ruler, and the special aspects of his sovereign activity should be noted in each case.

Over and above the individual units, there is an overriding "I" (אֲנִי) that appears seven times between v. 12b and v. 16a. This, therefore, is a revelatory speech, in which theological approach and tonal form correspond. If the scene is viewed in the context of the drama, one should remember that at the beginning of this fourth

act, in 46:4, there was also a fivefold "I" sequence. It too begins with "It is I," "I am the one" (אֲנִי הוּא). Now the act is moving toward its end and—with "the appearance of the Servant" (in chap. 48 from v. 16)—toward one of its climaxes.

■ **12-13** The address "Jacob and Israel" establishes the link with what has gone before. There is first of all the connection with 48:1-11, but there is also a reference back to 46:3 in the same act. The situation has not changed. As will presently emerge from v. 14, the underworld is probably still presupposed as the place of the action. An essential change compared with 48:1 is the combination "Jacob *and* Israel." The claim to be "Israel" is no longer called in question. That is indeed the step forward compared with vv. 1-11: the proceedings against Jacob, with the false claim to be Israel ("not in steadfastness/truth and not in righteousness," v. 1) have now been closed. The punishment that is really due has been set aside for Yahweh's sake (and for his "name" [cf. LXX] and his "glory," v. 11). What takes place now is intended as a new beginning (cf. v. 6).

Part of this new beginning is that "Jacob and Israel" are addressed as one who has been "called." The singular is striking. It corresponds to the installation of the Servant Israel/Jacob in 41:8 (cf. 41:14) as well as to the "redemption" of Jacob/Israel in 43:1 and 44:1 (cf. also

48:20 + 49:3). The chiasmus in the altered sequence Jacob/Israel is certainly not fortuitous. I have the impression that "Jacob" stresses the worldly existence, "Israel" the spiritual qualification. The participial construction "my called one" (מְקֹרָאִי) stands for the enduring quality of the call: it applies in the past, in the present and in the future.

The text begins with the singular "my called one" (מְקֹרָאִי, *Pual* participle with suffix). This is in line with the interpretation of "the Servant Jacob/Israel" as an individual. At the end of this brief unit we hear (in v. 13) about a plural subject whom Yahweh "summons" or "calls" (קֹרֵא אֲנִי). The two forms of "call" (קרא)[158] correspond in their participial construction, with the sole difference that in the one case the *Pual* is used and in the other the *Qal*. Here too we have to assume that there is a switch to a "collective" interpretation, as in the case of "the Servant Jacob/Israel." It is the "house of Jacob" of 48:1 that can now once more be addressed as "called," in both senses of the word.

This is the deeper reason for a difficulty that is probably connected with the performance practice in this fourth act. We might expect the "Servant Jacob/Israel" to appear once more. Apart from the divine speaker he is the most important person in the first two acts. After "Babylon's" exit in 47:15, a second actor was perhaps initially not available. But this actor is imperatively required for the immediately following entry of "the Servant of God" (Moses) from 48:16. Consequently here the section of the chorus already representing the house of Jacob now comes into play. It does not itself speak, but "standing up" and "assembling" are actions that could be mimed.

Apart from the "I" sequence, Yahweh's great self-predication in vv. 12 and 13 deserves special attention. In spite of its solemn generality, it is nonetheless quite precisely embedded in this particular context. That becomes clear if we view it for itself and then draw on its parallels elsewhere in DtIsa.

There are five divine declarations. Three nominative sentences with "I" (אֲנִי) are followed by two verbal clauses. The declarations can also be divided into contrasting pairs. Then the first statement: "I am the One"

is followed by the antitheses: first-last, earth-heaven. The different declarations are artistically intertwined and also have different vowel sequences.

"I am the One" (אֲנִי הוּא, *ʾanî hûʾ*), means the one who is already known. There is a play on the divine name Yahweh, perhaps in its abbreviated form יְהוּ *yahû*. It is in a sense a revelation of the name without the name itself being named here. The divine identity is declared as applying in the past ("I am the First," רִאשׁוֹן) and in the future ("and I am the Last," אַחֲרוֹן). This was a problem in the preceding texts: is God always the same, for example even in the misfortunes of his people? Even if one accepts his revelation in the past, is it still possible to hope for a future (cf. 40:21-24)?

The catchwords "first" (רִאשׁוֹן) and "last" (אַחֲרוֹן) are used in 41:4 for the first time. Common to the two texts is the assumption that the scene takes place in the underworld. In the first text at least the temporal components are linked with the spatial ones. In the underworld the generations of the past are all simultaneously present; yet it is a separate space—a space separated from the upper world and from heaven. Consequently when we come to the text of 48:12-13 we may ask whether here too Jacob/Israel includes past generations. The rule of the God who is speaking here embraces both time and space. The second mention of the paired "first"-"last" occurs in 44:6, where it is also a divine self-predication—there an element in the dispute with other gods. The subject is the announcement of Cyrus (vv. 7-8). The latter would correspond to 48:14. But it is especially interesting that in 44:6 Yahweh is explicitly called "king of Israel." The third and last occurrence of the formula is here in 48:12. Here too we may assume that this is a throne scene.

God's sovereignty over the world is justified through the two wider predications, which have to do with creation. Here too the categories of time and space are closely connected.

The foundation of the earth and the spreading out of the heavens[159] took place at the beginning (cf. the perfect tenses of the verbs). But at the same time these phrases circumscribe the space of the divine sovereignty. In this particular context that means that the founda-

---

158 The word קרא is used a third time almost immediately afterward (v. 15) for Cyrus, in the sense of "call" or "appoint." This shows the importance of

"call" (קרא) in the present text.

159 The word chosen at this point is strange. For the "spreading out of the heaven" DtIsa uses נטה six

tional "pillars" of the earth are included in the sphere of Yahweh's power—that is, the underworld too.[160] For the Yahweh religion this was by no means a matter of course. Does Sheol not cut off human beings from Yahweh? In a period and environment in which the gods of the dead were taking on increased importance, this was probably a matter of considerable dispute. These divine predications are intended as a response to assailed faith.

If we look back, we can see that the titular predications can be compared with the throne names used in the royal ritual. There is evidence for this in the OT, but it goes back ultimately to Egyptian models.[161] That there are five predications in the existing passage is not the least important feature speaking in favor of this, in view of the five predications found in the Egyptian texts. But the DtIsa text emphasizes that Yahweh is the real "king" of the whole world.

There is a difficulty about v. 13b and the transition to v. 14 because it is not quite clear who is being addressed in each case. Is it Jacob/Israel, the nations, or their gods? As the textual criticism shows, the use of the suffixes is also uncertain. Various emendations have been proposed.

In my view we have to start from the stage directions contained in the text:

1. "When I summon them, they stand there together!" (v. 13)
2. "Assemble, all of you!" (v. 14)
3. "Draw near to me!" (v. 16)

This is a clear sequence. It does not presuppose that the persons differ. It fits into the framework of a royal audience. If we presume that this was a scenic performance, the commands are an implicit stage direction for the chorus. If "all" assemble, there are certainly choreo-

graphical elements too. But in content the scene is more important than is immediately perceptible. We may ask why so solemn a form of address is required simply in order that the smallest unit should end: "When I summon them, they stand there together" (יַעַמְדוּ יַחְדָּו). But it becomes comprehensible if we take the context and situation into account. "Stand" (עמד) presupposes "getting up." Here it also means the "getting up" of those who are resting in the world below. "Jacob and Israel" (v. 12) are only "together" (v. 13) and "all" (v. 14) if past generations are included. Now something really "new" begins (cf. v. 6), which all are to witness. With these presuppositions the text can be compared with the "raising of dead Israel" in the valley of dry bones in Ezekiel (Ezek 37:1-14).[162] The essential passage is Ezek 37:10-11:

> So I prophesied as he commanded me,
> and the breath (הָרוּחַ) came into them, and they lived,
> and stood upon their feet (וַיַּעַמְדוּ עַל־רַגְלֵיהֶם),
> an exceeding great host.
> Then he said to me: "Son of man/human being (בֶּן־אָדָם),
> these bones are the whole house of Israel (כָּל־בֵּית יִשְׂרָאֵל)."[163]

■ **14-15** After the whole of "Jacob and Israel" have gathered together in this way, they become the first witnesses of a fulfilled prophecy. The question is: who does "you all" comprise? Is the whole auditorium addressed too? Although the name is no longer mentioned, it is clear that this has to do with Cyrus. He too has been called (קְרָאתִיו, v. 15) by Yahweh. In this sense he corresponds to "Jacob and Israel" (מְקֹרָאִי, v. 12). This is the tremendous arc that DtIsa can span because of his conviction about the activity of his God in history. With this position, DtIsa cannot have expected unanimous assent; about that there can be no question. Did it not cast doubt on the exclusivity of Israel's call?

Brief statements once more recapitulate what was previously said about Cyrus's call and installation. Here in

times (40:22; 42:5; 44:24; 45:12; 51:13; cj. 51:16; 54:2). Only here is שׂפח *Piel* used. This verb, again, occurs only here in the OT. According to *HALOT* the verb is related to Akk. *ṭepū*. The connection with "clap the hands" is striking. Is the present text associated with a gesture?

160 Cf. Pss 18:16 (15); 95:4; Isa 24:18; Jer 31:37; Jonah 2:7 (6); Mic 6:2.

161 See G. von Rad, "The Royal Ritual in Judah," in *The Problem of the Hexateuch and Other Essays* (1966) 222–31 ["Das judäische Königsritual," (1947) in *Gesammelte Studien zum Alten Testament* (4th ed. 1971) 205–13]; H. Bonnet, "Krönung," *RÄRG*

395–400; M.-T. Derchain-Urtel, "Thronbesteigung," *LÄ* 6 (1986) 529–32; Wildberger, *Isaiah 1–12* (1991) [*Jesaja 1–12* (2d ed. 1980)] on Isa 9:5-6.

162 See W. Zimmerli, *Ezekiel* 2 (1983) 253–66 [*Ezechiel* 2 (1969) 885–902] with lit.; R. Bartelmus, "Ez 37,1-14. Die Verbform *wᵉqatal* und die Anfänge der Auferstehungshoffnung," *ZAW* 97 (1985) 366–89.

163 On v. 11 see esp. R. Bartelmus, "Textkritik, Literarkritik und Syntax. Anmerkungen zur neueren Diskussion um Ez 37,11," *BN* 25 (1984) 55–64.

v. 15, in a divine speech, his legitimation and his success are explained in three ways: "I have called him, I have made him come,[164] and his way will prosper."

The important point in the text, however, is again the prophetic proof. This is of interest because it bears on the validity of the divine word in the future too. Here Israel is engaged in a dispute with the prediction practice of its environment. This problem is the subject of v. 14.

The verse is considered difficult, but the difficulty disappears once we assume that DtIsa, serious though his purpose is, works with surprise effects and in this case with an almost macabre wit. If we note the directions given to the speakers, the instructions ("Listen . . .") and the question "Who . . . has declared?" in v. 14a are still part of the divine speech. The same is true of the beginning of v. 15: "I, I have spoken."

What does not fit in is the second half of v. 14: "Yahweh loved him" (אֲהֵבוֹ). The text has been unequivocally transmitted, but three interventions have been proposed, these generally being based on the interpretation of LXX and 1QIsaᵃ:

1. To expunge the name of Yahweh. But this does not eliminate the difficulty of the change of speaker.
2. To change the suffixes and punctuation from "he loved *him*" to "*my* beloved, *my* friend" (אֹהֲבִי, see *HALAT* under this heading) and from "*his* will" to "*my* will."
3. To change "his arm" (וּזְרֹעוֹ) completely to "seed (וְזֶרַע) of the Chaldeans."

But the difficulty about the change of speaker was felt in the original DtIsa text too. Consequently we have here one of the very rare stage directions, similar to the one we already noted in 47:3. There it was "a human being" (אָדָם) who was supposed to speak the sentence that follows in 47:4. Here the direction "Chaldeans" (כַּשְׂדִּים) is put at the end, or has perhaps strayed there in the course of the copying. As the verdict of "the Chaldeans," the sentence is quite comprehensible as it stands.

The Chaldeans are the people of Babylon, but the name is already used in the OT as a designation for "sages, astrologers" (cf. Dan 2:2, 4). In this act they have already appeared as the attendants of Babylon, the "daughter of the Chaldeans" (47:1). In 47:13 they are presented in their function as foretellers of the future. Together with Babylon, they disappeared into the fire of the underworld (47:14-15).

If with these presuppositions we again read the present text of v. 14, it becomes clear that it is Yahweh himself who asks: "Who among them has declared those (events)?" The "them" (בָּהֶם) refers to the other gods, who are no longer named here because they are nonexistent. "Those" are the events connected with Cyrus, which are named in what follows. The answer to the question "who?" which is by no means purely rhetorical, is "Yahweh." That is, he is the only God, and no other has "proclaimed," "declared" it. The answer probably came swiftly, since it simply takes the form of the name, not of a complete sentence, such as: "It is Yahweh" (יהוה הוא).

The content of the pronouncement is cited. The sequence of the suffixes is quite correct: "loved him . . . his will . . . his arm." Here it is noticeable that three words with the *o* sound of the third person masculine suffix ("his . . .") alternate at the end with two words "he will do it" (יַעֲשֶׂה) and "to Babylon" (בְּבָבֶל). Purely acoustically, we are reminded of "wailing and gnashing of teeth."[165] The irony of the text is that the "Chaldeans" probably do not appear again. Their cries out of the fire are heard from behind the scenes. There is nothing to be seen—hence the command at the beginning of the verse: "Listen!" Whether they like it or not, the Chaldeans have to recognize the truth of prophecy. Do they repent of their error?

As always in DtIsa, the jesting conceals the completely serious point. This is the last reference to Cyrus, and he does not appear here either. The phrase used to describe him, "Yahweh loved him," will surely have been a cause of offense to some listeners, if we remember that in 41:8 Abraham is addressed with the title "my beloved, my friend" (אֹהֲבִי). But the two other statements have to do with the relationship to the Persians and their rule,

---

164 If the translation were to assume בוא *Hiphil.* "I have brought him in," and if the phrase "to Babylon" is added, there could be a specific historical reference. The verb is in the perfect tense. This would indicate that the fall of Babylon is already presupposed.

165 Cf. Matt 8:12; 13:42, 50; 22:13; 24:51; 25:30; Luke 13:28.

and here the implication is: "They cannot do what pleases them" ("*his* will," חֶפְצוֹ), and: "they are not almighty" ("*his* arm," זְרֹעוֹ). Cyrus makes this clear. This can sometimes be said more explicitly in a "distanced" form such as this.

With the three final *o* sounds of the third person masculine suffix (twice "I have . . . him," "his way") the sequence of v. 14 is carried forward into v. 15. The sense sounds more positive, but vv. 14 and 15 belong together, politically and theologically.

The idea that foreigners also confess Yahweh—indeed, that they are ahead of Israel in their acknowledgment—is a motif used in other texts too. But here it introduces a theme that is developed in what follows.

48

"The Lord Yahweh has sent me and his spirit"
(48:16)

48:16
Appearance of the Servant of God

16a Draw near to me, hear this!
Not *from the beginning/from the summit*
        \<have I spoken\>,
I have spoken in hiddenness.
Since the time it came to be I was there.

16b *But now:*
The Lord Yahweh has sent me, and his spirit!

According to vv. 12-15 Jacob/Israel has gathered together and is now in v. 16 commanded to "draw near to me." What follows is therefore part of the throne scene. The difficulty of the text is in v. 16, the authenticity of which has, with varying reasoning, been wholly or partially disputed.[166] Schoors and Spykerboer give good reasons, however, for doubting that the problem can be solved by the methods of literary criticism. They see that the connection with the context is closer than is often assumed; and with this one must agree. If we once more start from the question: who is speaking? then in v. 16a the speaker is Yahweh. The end of the speech is marked in Hebrew by אֲנִי, "I," the last in the series of "I"s that begins in v. 12. Some commentators doubt whether the "But now" in v. 16b belongs here too, or whether it should be assigned to what follows. At all events, it is clear that from this point on someone else is speaking. He is identified through the first words. Since he talks about "the Lord Yahweh" (אֲדֹנָי יהוה), he is "the servant" (עֶבֶד). We may ask, which servant? The text's answer is a veiled revelation.

The person who comes forward here says: "The Lord Yahweh has sent me" (שְׁלָחַנִי). This is to echo a keyword in the account of Moses' call at the burning bush. The text is a carefully crafted reflection of Exodus 3, especially 3:13-15. There it is Moses who asks about the name: "See, if I come to the Israelites (אֶל־בְּנֵי יִשְׂרָאֵל) and say to them, 'The God of your fathers has sent me (שְׁלָחַנִי) to you' and they say to me 'What is his name?'

what shall I say to them?" According to the DtIsa text too the whole of Israel is gathered together. Here Yahweh's name is not in question. The Servant actually pronounces Yahweh's name three times in vv. 16-17. But the name of Moses has been expunged, as will presently emerge from v. 19.

Further pointers in vv. 16-22 to the revelation on Sinai and to the exodus will have to be considered in the course of the exegesis. First, however, an attempt must be made to reconstruct the action accompanying the text; and here again we have to assume that this is a liturgical drama. This allows us to compare it with other forms of drama, especially in the ancient world. Both similarities and differences should be noted.

The Servant comes forward unexpectedly. He is quite suddenly there. Nothing is said about his coming, in the way that, for example, the people who are present in the throne scene "come forward": "Draw near to me" (v. 16). The Servant himself speaks here, in contrast to 42:1. If he is supposed to be Moses, then there is a time problem in the drama: what does Moses have to do with the Persian period? Where is the present supposed to begin, and what is past and future? Drama can abolish the frontiers of space and time, and it can do this by letting persons belonging to the past appear in the framework of the action.

---

166 See Schoors, *I Am God Your Saviour* (1973) 281: "The commentaries are divided over the question of whether vs. 16 belongs to the same unit. . . . The meaning of vs. 16b is not very clear either. . . . Virtually no one accepts the authenticity of vs. 16c, although it is very well attested in textual tradition" (see also Schoors on the discussion in the research, with lit.).

A famous example that is also particularly suggestive here is the appearance of Darius's ghost (Gk. εἴδωλον) in Aeschylus's *Persians* (ll. 681–842). The chorus prepares for the appearance through an invocatory song that conjures up his spirit (ll. 623–68), and through libations offered by Queen Atossa, Darius's widow.[167] The dead king rises from his burial mound. He can be recognized by his clothing.

The essential point of the scene is Atossa's account of the defeat of the Persian army under Xerxes. Darius interprets the catastrophe: guilt and destiny are inextricably linked.[168] The real cause is the ruler's hubris. Darius looks back to the series of five (in the transmitted text seven) rulers who preceded him. His judgment on them is favorable, with one exception, Mardus.[169] On this basis Darius gives counsel and prophesies the future.[170] For Aeschylus's first listeners, victory over the Persians would have been much closer, and the resulting joy more immediate. But at the same time the poet's warning about hubris could not be overlooked or disregarded, particularly in this passage, which is central to the drama.

The dramatic function of the speeches in the *Persians* is comparable with their function in DtIsa. A great man belonging to the past appears, and offers listeners an interpretation of history from which they can and should learn. The Servant's first speech already includes the same basic elements:

1. Lament over the present time (vv. 18-19). The reason for the wretched state of affairs is the guilt of the past: "If only you had obeyed my commandments . . ." (v. 18).

2. Practical instructions for future action (v. 20): "Go out of Babylon."

3. The glance back to the story of the exodus, with its encouraging message (v. 21). The decision is between "your peace" (שְׁלוֹמֶךָ, v. 18) and the ending of peace: "There is no peace/salvation (אֵין שָׁלוֹם), Yahweh has said, for the wicked" (v. 22).

An essential difference between this passage and the appearance of Darius is that here there are no invocatory elements.[171] In the whole scene from v. 12 onward it is Yahweh himself who determines who comes where and when. The Servant's speech after his appearance is actually a divine speech: "Thus says Yahweh . . ." (v. 17).

One phrase in v. 16 still requires explanation, for though brief it is important for the interpretation. When the Servant identifies himself on the basis of Exodus 3 by saying "The Lord Yahweh has sent me," the phrase "and his spirit" (וְרוּחוֹ) is an addition, compared with the Exodus passage. At all events, there is no mention of "Yahweh's spirit" in Exodus 3. But in the present scene the spirit as vital force is initially required so that the Servant Moses can appear. The motif is hence compara-

---

167 Aeschylus *Persians* 620–22 (trans. H. W. Smyth; LCL 145 [1922, reprint 1973] 160–61):
"But come, my friends, do ye chant solemn songs as I make these libations to the dead, and summon forth the divine spirit of Darius (τόν τε δαίμονα Δαρεῖον ἀνακαλεῖσθε [ἀνακαλεῖσθαι M]) while I convey, in honour of the nether gods, these offerings for the earth to quaff."

168 Ibid., 739–49 (selected verses) (172–75):
Darius:
739 "Alas! Swift indeed has come the fulfilment of the oracles, and 'tis my son upon whom Zeus hath caused their issue to descend. . . ."
744 "A son of mine it was who, in his ignorance (οὐ κατειδὼς), brought these things to pass through youthful recklessness. . . . "
749 "Mortal though he was, he thought in his folly that he would gain the mastery over all the gods, aye even over Poseidon" (θνητὸς ὢν θεῶν τε πάντων ᾤετ᾽ οὐκ εὐβουλίᾳ).

169 The judgment about Cyrus is particularly interesting, especially since it is the judgment of a Greek. It is not far removed from that of DtIsa; ibid., 768–72 (pp. 174–75):

τρίτος δ᾽ ἀπ᾽ αὐτοῦ Κῦρος, εὐδαίμων ἀνήρ,	Third, after him, Cyrus, blest in his fortune,
ἄρξας ἔθηκε πᾶσιν εἰρήνην φίλοις·	came to the throne and established peace for all his people.
Λυδῶν δὲ λαὸν και Φρυγῶν ἐκτήσατο,	The Lydians and Phrygians he won to his rule,
Ἰωνίαν τε πᾶσαν ἤλασεν βίᾳ.	and the whole of Ionia he subdued by force;
θεὸς γὰρ οὐκ ἤχθηρεν, ὡς εὔφρων ἔφυ.	for the gods hated him not, since he was right minded.

170 See the question asked by the chorus (ibid., 787–89).

171 It may be asked whether the sequence of vowels in אֲנִי (vv. 12-16), which occurs seven times, was an indication to early listeners of a coming event. In the invoking of Darius, the chorus cries: ἠέ (651 and 656), οἶ (663 and 671), αἰαῖ αἰαῖ (673).

ble with the underworld scene in 41:1-5, where the "islands and nations" have first to be given "vital power" (כֹּחַ) so that they can come forward and speak. But the nature of the strength that Yahweh confers has been prepared for by three declarations in 40:26, 29, and 31.

The passage is preceded comparably by the divine utterances in 48:12-15 about "my hand" and "my right hand" (v. 13, with reference to creation), and about "his arm" (v. 14, with reference to the prophetic word). In the postexilic period all four theologoumena are important ways of describing God's activity, which is thus stated in its full scope. "Vital force" and "spirit" are seen as one and the same (cf. 42:5). Whereas the first Servant of God text, 42:1, said that Yahweh's "spirit" (רוּחַ) had been given to the Servant, here we have the corresponding statement that the Servant has been sent by Yahweh's "spirit." According to Num 11:16-17 and 24-30, Moses is the bearer of the divine spirit in a special way. This enables him to give of his spirit to the seventy elders and thus to authorize them. In this Numbers text the spirit is linked with prophecy (cf. vv. 26 and 29), although there it is the elders and the people who prophesy.

DtIsa is making a definite decision when he lets the Servant begin his speech with the prophetic formula "Thus says Yahweh" (כֹּה־אָמַר יהוה, v. 17). So that there can be no misunderstanding, the formula is repeated in 49:7 and 8. This thrice-repeated formula therefore also implies a decision in favor of a particular view of Moses' office and function, a view corresponding to Hosea's: "By a prophet Yahweh brought Israel up from Egypt, and by a prophet it was guarded" (Hos 12:14 [13]).[172] This tradition also matches the content of the following passage. Verses 21-22 make quite clear that it is the exodus that is being talked about. There is an exodus from Babylon too (v. 20), but in my own view the theme of the whole unit vv. 16-22 is Moses and the exodus from Egypt.

A first signal is already set in v. 16, in Yahweh's own speech: "Not from the beginning (מֵרֹאשׁ) <have I spoken>, I have spoken in hiddenness." The parallelism to "since the time . . ." (מֵעֵת) certainly suggests that רֹאשׁ should be interpreted in a temporal sense. But the spa-

tial interpretation "top, summit" is also possible, as an extension of the meaning "head," which was probably the primary sense of the word. If we look back from the end of the unit it becomes plain that the spatial meaning is also intended, although in a quite particular sense. For this, a comparison with Exodus 19 is required. This is the text describing Israel's arrival at Mount Sinai, after the exodus. The key word comes in v. 20: "And Yahweh descended upon Mount Sinai, to the top of the mountain (אֶל־רֹאשׁ הָהָר); and Yahweh summoned Moses to the top of the mountain (אֶל־רֹאשׁ הָהָר), and Moses went up." The text explains that the people (including the priests, vv. 23 and 24) are forbidden to approach the mountain. Moses is the mediator. The proclamation of the Ten Commandments follows in 20:1-17: "And God spoke all these words . . ." (v. 1). But if we add to this the framework of the story in Exod 20:18-22, there is a tension. Because they are so terrified by the theophany (vv. 18-19), the people implore Moses: "You speak to us, and we will listen; but God should not speak to us" (v. 19). As a result, according to v. 21: "The people stood at a distance, while Moses drew near to the darkness (הָעֲרָפֶל) of which it was said that God was there (אֲשֶׁר־שָׁם הָאֱלֹהִים)." In the light of this statement, v. 22 sounds like an explanation or a correction: "You have seen for yourselves that I spoke with you from heaven (מִן־הַשָּׁמַיִם דִּבַּרְתִּי)."

If we read Isa 48:16 once more against this background, it seems possible that the text is wrestling with the Sinai tradition.[173] The name of the mountain is not given. Yahweh has "not spoken in hiddenness from the top of the mountain!" The limitation to a particular earthly place is thus ended. Then it is not far to the statement in Exod 20:22 that Yahweh has spoken from heaven. If heaven is the space out of which Yahweh has spoken, then the "there" (שָׁם) in v. 16 corresponds to this in the spatial sense: "I am there," that is, in heaven. Here there may even be a wordplay on "there" (שָׁם šām) and "heaven" (שָׁמַיִם šāmayim). It is not clear to what the third person feminine suffix in "its" refers (הֱיוֹתָהּ). The divine predicates at the beginning of the unit in v. 13 talked about "earth" and "heaven." Earth is feminine. If this is the antecedent, the half-verse would also be talk-

---

172 Cf. Deut 18:15-16.

173 Cf. the same motif, God's address from Mount Horeb, in the introduction to the Decalogue in Deut 5:4-5.

ing about creation. "From the time of its being . . ."—
Gen 1:1-2 can be read in just this way: "And the earth
was (וְהָאָרֶץ הָיְתָה) without form and void." In this way creation and the revelation of the commandments are
closely connected. It is the abolition of time before God,
all times being immediate before him. "Top" (רֹאשׁ) is no
longer merely a mountain peak. It is the zenith of the
world, as we already assumed in 41:4: "the one who calls
the generations from the beginning and the topmost
point" (מֵרֹאשׁ). At all events it is Moses who proclaims the
divine word. But in DtIsa his name is not mentioned.

Finally, it is striking that v. 16 should begin with the
command to "Jacob and Israel" to "Draw near to me,"
whereas Exodus 19 stresses precisely the distance and
the borderline.

Accordingly even Isa 48:16 would seem to suggest that
this is again a topical interpretation of well-known texts.
As the text goes on, this assumption will be still more
clearly substantiated. As regards its content, the dere-
striction of the revelation on Sinai is the preparation for
the law's universal validity (cf. 49:1 and 6). The Creator
is the lawgiver.

48

"I am Yahweh your God,
who teaches you how to help,
who lets you enter upon a way that you can go"
(48:17)

17   Thus says Yahweh, your Redeemer, the Holy
         One of Israel:
     I am Yahweh your God,
     who teaches you how to help,
     who lets you enter upon a way that you can
         go.

18   If only you had listened to my
         commandments
     your peace/salvation would have been like
         the river
     and your righteousness like the waves of the
         sea.

19   Then your descendants would have been like
         the sand,
     and the offspring of your body like its
         grains.
     His name would not have been wiped out
         and not destroyed from before me.

■ **17** The Servant's speech is a prophetic divine utterance. The titles are closely linked with the context. "Your redeemer" is taken up again in v. 20: "Yahweh has redeemed his servant Jacob." Judgment and salvation are bound up with the name "the Holy One of Israel."[174] But when the Servant then says: "I am Yahweh, your God," the echo of the beginning of the Decalogue is unmistakable. Yahweh is once again the God of his people, and the covenant relationship has thus been restored.

Yahweh himself teaches Israel: this is acknowledged in the Psalms, but especially in Deuteronomy and Jeremiah. Thus the introduction to the Decalogue according to Deut 5:1 runs: "Hear, O Israel, the statutes and ordinances that I am proclaiming to you today; learn them (וּלְמַדְתֶּם) and observe them diligently."

In the text, what Yahweh teaches is more closely defined as that "which helps" (לְהוֹעִיל). Now, H. D. Preuss has surely rightly observed that it is only here in the prophetic tradition that this verb for "help" is used in a positive sense.[175] It is the converse of the usual "not being able to help," which is said of the gods in the polemic against them. Unlike these gods, Yahweh "helps." This statement therefore has to do with the fundamental definition of the relationship to God in the First Commandment. But now the "gods" are not so much as mentioned any more. The other commandments are summed up in the second declaration under the heading "way" (דֶּרֶךְ). The commandments are the "way" that Yahweh prepares. Here DtIsa is clearly taking up the theme of 40:3-5 again. "Way" means the possibility of a return, but it is at the same time a way of life that makes salvation possible.

Another method of structuring v. 17 is at least worth consideration. It assumes that DtIsa is taking over traditional formulations but is also modifying them. Here word-for-word quotations are often used only up to the point where they become recognizable. They are then expanded or abbreviated.

---

174   See Isa 41:14, 16, 20; 43:3, 14; 45:11; 49:7; 54:5; 55:5.

175   H. D. Preuss, "יעל *y⁽l*," *TDOT* 6:144–47 [*ThWAT* 3:709]; see also M. Sæbo, "יעל *y⁽l* hi. to be of use," *TLOT* 2:554–56 [*THAT* 1:746–48].

297

The formula for the prophetic oracles is of course: "Thus says Yahweh" (כֹּה־אָמַר יהוה). It could well be, however, that this is indeed the same formula, but that it has been expanded by "your redeemer" (גֹּאֲלֶךָ), since this is the most important message that the Servant now brings. In what has gone before, the key word "redeemer" was used for the last time in 47:3-4 as a question asked by the person who is hastening into the underworld: (Who is) "our redeemer?" The answer is, "Yahweh Sabaoth is his name, the Holy One of Israel" (47:4). He is now, according to v. 17, speaking through the mouth of his Servant: "Thus says Yahweh, your redeemer."[176] A further variant after 48:20 is the naming of the redeemer in 49:7: "thus says Yahweh, Israel's redeemer, its Holy One."

The beginning of the Decalogue runs "I am Yahweh, your God," but it is common knowledge that both in Exodus 20 and in Deut 5:6 the form used for "I" is אָנֹכִי, not אֲנִי. The beginning then has a particularly solemn force, but is somewhat "distanced." The brief אֲנִי then sounds a little flat. But it is nevertheless used in the long "I" (אֲנִי) series that begins in 48:12, where its position in the sentence varies. In vv. 12 and 15 it is placed at the beginning, in v. 16 at the end.

When the "I" is stressed, it means that this is a new message: "The Holy One of Israel am I!"[177] This would indicate that the real substance of the prophetic oracle was about to be given. It will emerge that the question about Yahweh's holiness is especially important for an understanding of the following verses, 21-22. Then the name of Yahweh follows along with the assurance "your God." The result would then look as follows:

Thus says Yahweh, your redeemer:
"The Holy One of Israel am I, Yahweh, your God,
who teaches you how to help,
who lets you enter upon a way that you can go."

The pregnancy of the Hebrew cannot be conveyed in translation. If we omit the introduction, the Hebrew sentence consists of precisely ten words. The remarkable thing is that according to Exod 34:28 Moses writes "on the tablets the words of the covenant, ten words." It is the covenant that has been renewed after the catastrophe of the golden calf. Is that why DtIsa also writes "ten words" here? If we remember the situation—Moses as the Servant is speaking and what he says is a continual play on the Sinai tradition—that could provide an explanation for this verse. I would not make this proposal if it were not that we continually find a play on words and numbers in DtIsa.

■ 18-19 The remembrance of the revelation of the commandments is the prelude to the lament. Grammatically, this interpretation presupposes that in לוּא ("If only you . . .") "the perfect [is] the expression of a wish that something might have happened in past time."[178] The following imperfect consecutive is in accord with this: it "is likewise used only in a hypothetical sense."[179] It would be equally possible to translate it by the future tense. The problem about the tenses in the text is that the Servant Moses who has now appeared interprets the past. Through his interpretation listeners are supposed to learn something for both the present and the future.[180] A number of commentators have also pointed to Psalm 81 as a parallel.[181] There too lament and wish are linked with each other, and there too the theological point of departure is the First Commandment and the requirement to walk in Yahweh's ways.

The individual commandments were called "my commandments" (מִצְוֹתָי). Now, we may ask: whose commandments are they? For it is Moses who is speaking. But for the text it is clear: they are and remain Yahweh's commandments. The introduction "Thus says Yahweh . . ." (v. 17) makes this clear. Moses is—merely—a prophet.

As W. Schottroff has observed,[182] it is noticeable that in the exilic and postexilic periods the verb "heed, pay attention to" (קשׁב Hiphil) "always occurs in negative

176 The Masoretic pointing endorses that the terms should be linked in this way.

177 In this case contrary to the division in the MT.

178 Thus the explanation in GKC § 151e (p. 477), with reference to Num 14:2 and Josh 7:7. GKC itself thinks that in Isa 48:18 and 63:19 the form should be considered "to express a wish that something expected in the future may already have happened" (ibid.).

179 GKC § 111x (p. 330). Here too GKC assumes a futurist sense for Isa 48:18: "if that were so = it would be so."

180 North (182) on this passage paraphrases the sense of the tense as follows: "The sense of the whole is: 'Would that you had' (but you did not), and yet you still may."

181 Westermann, 203 [165] on this passage.

statements describing Israel's disobedience." The only exceptions, in his view, are the occurrence in the "promise" in Isa 32:3 and in the "admonitions" in 42:23, as well as in the present text, 48:18.[183] But if the text is interpreted as a lament, in my view the link with the texts that Schottroff adduces in support of his view is closer (Jer 6:10, 19; Zech 1:4; 7:11; Neh 9:34; 2 Chr 33:10).

The salvation that has initially been forfeited is first of all described in four comparisons. These are arranged in two pairs: peace and righteousness, and in a double sense "descendants." That this is poetic language is also made clear by the sequence of sounds. The final syllables alternate (i–e–i–e), and the suffix "-kā" ("your," sing.) is used four times. This suffix also provides a link from v. 17 onward, where it is used four times.

In content, we have to assume that there are connections here with the promises, the promises to the patriarchs particularly,[184] for they received the promise of blessing and offspring. The greatness of the promise is at odds with the reality experienced.[185] According to the context, the reason for this discrepancy is the "breach with the relationship to God." This raises the question how there can be any hope that the promises will be still be fulfilled.

The end of the lament is the extirpation of the name. But whose name does "his name" (שְׁמוֹ) refer to? One solution is that it is the name of Jacob/Israel. The series of unfulfilled promises would then be prolonged. Like Beuken,[186] we might suppose that Yahweh acts as redeemer (גֹּאֵל, v. 17) in the positive sense, thus preventing the name from disappearing (we may think similarly of Boaz in the book of Ruth, 4:10).

The LXX is most unambiguous in its prolongation of the series including the suffixes. "Your name" (τὸ ὄνομά σου) would then correspond to שְׁמֶךָ. It is more difficult if we relate "his name" to "your seed" (זַרְעֶךָ, v. 19a),[187] for this is only one element in the series. Moreover, the name of Jacob/Israel is not blotted out.

I would like to propose a different solution, one based on the text as it stands. If there is any name that is consistently blotted out in DtIsa it is the name of Moses. This is all the more striking in this particular passage, which is talking about the commandments given by Yahweh (vv. 17-18) and the miracles performed during the wanderings in the wilderness (v. 21). The names of Abraham's "offspring," Jacob/Israel, Judah and David are certainly given at various points. Yet the name of Moses is missing, even when the subject is the exodus. It could perhaps be that a motif belonging to the interpretation of the exodus tradition plays a part here. In Exod 32:32, at the end of the story of the golden calf, Moses suggests that his own name should be blotted out:

31 So Moses returned to Yahweh and said:
    "Alas, this people has sinned a great sin;
    they have made for themselves a god (or: gods) of gold.
32 But now, if you will forgive (their) sin (it is well),
    but if not, blot me out of the book
    that you have written."

Here Moses' offer is not accepted. Immediately afterward he is given the charge: "Lead the people to the place about which I have spoken to you" (v. 34).[188]

A Samaritan commentary called "The Secrets of Moses"[189] suggests to me that it was because of this text, Exod 32:32, that Moses' name is omitted in DtIsa. The commentary passage runs:

"Now if thou wilt, forgive their sin, and if not, blot me out from thy book which thou hast written."

And if we should say that this was referring to the two tablets, we find that there was no mention of Moses to be found on the Tablets—(Woe unto those

---

182 W. Schottroff, "קשׁב qšb hi. to pay attention," *TLOT* 3:1171–74 [*THAT* 2:684–89].

183 Ibid., 1174 [689].

184 Especially to be mentioned here is Gen 13:16 and 22:17, the promises to Abraham; cf. also 2 Sam 17:11; Gen 32:13 (12); 1 Kgs 4:20; Hos 2:1 (1:10).

185 It is noticeable that here the promise of the land is missing.

186 Beuken on this passage.

187 With Skinner and Slotki; see Beuken on the passage.

188 The closeness of these texts to one another is also

of interest for the interpretation of Isaiah 53; see below on that text.

189 M. Gaster, *The Asatir: The Samaritan Book of the "Secrets of Moses" together with the Pitron or Samaritan Commentary and the Samaritan Story of the Death of Moses* (1927) 40, with the translation on p. 238: וְאָן אמרנו מדרשו . . . אן לא יש למשה על הלוחות זכרון בהם.

who forsake the Law of Moses for there is no salvation for them!)

The blotting out of Moses' name in DtIsa would have to be understood as a sign that the people had continued to sin, above all through the manufacture of idols. Moses has therefore become the Servant without a name.[190]

This final element in the lament is expressed in quite personal terms. Moses speaks about himself and for himself, as Yahweh's prophet.[191]

---

190 This does not exclude the possibility that there may be other reasons too—historical or tradition-historical—for the omission of Moses' name. For the "blotting out" of names in Egypt, see E. Brunner-Traut, "Namenstilgung und -verfolgung," *LÄ* 4 (1982) 338–41.

191 Cf. also the earlier explanation of Deuteronomy 34, that Moses prophesied his own death; see Philo *De Vit. Mos.* 2.291: "The divine spirit fell upon him and he prophesied with discernment while still alive the story of his own death."

20   Go out of Babylon!
       Flee from the Chaldeans!
       Declare (it) with a voice of joy,
       let this be heard,
       let it go out to the end of the world/earth,
       say: Yahweh has redeemed his servant Jacob!

21   And they were not thirsty.
       In the "deserts" he led them/let them wander.
       He let water flow for him from rocks,
       and he split open a rock
       and the water gushed out.

22   There is no peace/salvation, Yahweh has said,
         for the wicked!

■ **20** Among the listeners (whether chorus or audience), the lament evokes the question: "What can we do?"[192] So the lament over the forfeited blessing is followed by the proclamation of a new beginning. The reason is given in the appropriate terms in v. 20 (cf. v. 17): "Yahweh has redeemed his servant Jacob." This is still prophetic speech, now related to the future. The speaker has not changed: it is still Moses, in his appearance as Servant. Just as at the charge of his God he once gave the command for the exodus from Egypt, he now gives the command for the new exodus from Babylon.

Dramatically, this is a tremendously dense composition. Past, present, and future are seen as one, and are yet differentiated. There can be no doubt that a great deal of discussion about the exodus must lie behind v. 20. What is in question is also the content of the Passover pericope, which is freshly actualized every year at the Passover feast. Are the people to leave in haste, or is there no hurry about the new exodus? The decision here is: "Flee!"[193] Is the exodus to take place in secret or not? The answer is, it is to be public, "with a voice of joy . . . to the end of the earth." Event and announcement are described with the same word: "go out" (צֵאוּ) and "let it go out" (הוֹצִיאוּהָ).[194]

It is impossible to miss the fact that here again DtIsa is applying to his own time a prophecy from the book of Jeremiah. The beginning of v. 20 sounds like a quotation from Jer 50:8: "Flee from the midst of Babylon, and go out of the land of the Chaldeans!" DtIsa changes the quotation slightly. In Jer 50:8 the people have to flee from the city because it is going to be destroyed. It is clearly the country that is meant, not the people, "the Chaldeans." But perhaps DtIsa is again thinking of the Chaldeans as soothsayers, who ought to be shunned or "fled from"? But the whole quotation may possibly point to the wider context in the book of Jeremiah, with its account of Babylon's downfall, the lament "of the people of Israel and the people of Judah" (Jer 50:4), and finally the deliverance. Again, however, there is a notable difference compared with DtIsa: "Declare among the nations and proclaim . . . do not conceal it, say . . ." (Jer 50:2) refers to the news of Babylon's fall. In DtIsa the corresponding passage refers to the message that is to go out to the ends of the earth: the message of redemption:

192 Cf. the chorus as reply to Darius's historical survey in Aeschylus *Persians* 787–89: "What then, O King Darius? What is the goal toward which thou dost direct the issue of the speech? How, after this reverse, may we, the people of Persia, prosper best in time to come?" (πῶς ἂν ἐκ τούτων ἔτι πράσ- σοιμεν ὡς ἄριστα Περσικὸς λεώς;).

193 Cf. Exod 14:5.

194 See Beuken, 302–3: "The leave-taking does not take place without testimony being given, and the start of the journey is linked with rejoicing over God's deliverance."

He says explicitly: "Let *this* (זֹאת) be heard. . . ." The song to be raised is a song of thanksgiving, not a song of triumph.

■ **21** This verse is a reminiscence of the first exodus. For this Moses is competent. It is initially a continuation of the speech made in Yahweh's name. The remembrance is designed to give hope for the new exodus, and to disperse doubt. This, then, is a preparation for everything that is to follow.

"They were not thirsty" is parallelled by 55:1: "Everyone who thirsts, come to the waters!"[195] "They will not be thirsty" is the most important message. It can be heard in both the literal and the transferred sense.

We may also assume that the phrase (lit.): "walk in dry or waste places (בָּחֳרָבוֹת)" also has several different levels of meaning. The verb חרב means "dry out, become dry," in reference to water (cf. Gen 8:13).[196] The meaning "desert places" would therefore seem to be the obvious one.[197] But at the same time the root and its derivatives stand for "lay waste, make waste, reduce to rubble" (*Hiphil*), to the point of destruction in the ultimate degree: "to lie in rubble" (*Qal*). This can be said of the land (Isa 43:10), the city (Jer 26:9; Ezek 6:6; 12:20) or the sanctuary.

DtIsa uses the substantive for "place of ruins" (חָרְבָּה) in 44:26; 49:19; 51:3; and 52:9. It has been proposed that in the present text the *o* sound of the *qāmeṣ ḥāṭûp* should be changed into a long *ā* (*qāmeṣ*) (*HALOT* 1:350 [*HALAT* 1:3, 6]: "rd. variant חֳרָבוֹת [*ḥārābôt*] deserts"). But this may well rob the text of one of its points: the echo of the name Horeb (חֹרֵב *ḥōreb*), the name given to the mountain of the giving of the law, instead of Sinai, in Exod 3:1; 17:6 (associated in this passage with the miracle of the water from the rock!), 33:6, and throughout Deuteronomy. That is where Israel wandered in times past.

Water from the rock: this *topos* clearly belongs to the wanderings in the desert that followed the exodus from Egypt. In the Pentateuch there are two versions of this motif: Exod 17:1-7 and Num 20:1-13. According to the structure as we have it, before Sinai (or Horeb) the miracle takes place at Massah and Meribah (Exod 17:6-7), after Sinai at Kadesh at the "waters of contention" (Num 20:1, 13). The two versions have features in common

and also differences in the mode of the miracle and the role of Moses and the people. Other biblical texts show that the theme was a matter of controversy.

In using the catchword "rock" (צוּר) DtIsa follows the version in Exod 17:1-7 (v. 6), which corresponds to Pss 78:15, 20; 105:41; 114:8. Num 20:1-13 uses another word for "rock," סֶלַע (v. 8 twice; v. 10 twice; v. 11 once). Ps 78:16 has the same word and so has Neh 9:15.

In his choice of other catchwords DtIsa is closer to Psalm 78:

15 "He split the rocks open" (וַיְבַקַּע צוּרִים).
16 "He made 'what flows' (נֹזְלִים) come out of the rock."
20 "Water gushed out" (וַיָּזוּבוּ מַיִם).

I think, however, that DtIsa is also wrestling with the tradition of Numbers 20. The point at issue is the role of Moses and Aaron. Numbers 20 is clearly critical of them both. Moses makes a mistake in smiting the rock twice with his staff, instead of trusting in the power of the word. He is arrogant when he gathers the people together, calls them "mutineers" (הַמֹּרִים) and claims: "Can we perhaps let water flow for you out of this rock?" The emphasis here is on the "we." Taken to its logical conclusion, it would mean that Moses and Aaron want to be divine miracle makers for the people. But only Yahweh can perform the miracle. So "Yahweh's holiness" is at stake, and that is why Moses and Aaron are told: "You shall not bring this assembly (הַקָּהָל הַזֶּה) there into the land that I have given them" (vv. 12-13).

Under these presuppositions, DtIsa is making an important decision when he says: "He lets water from rocks flow *for him*" (לָמוֹ). In the whole verse Yahweh is the sole agent. The name of Moses is never mentioned.[198] But we saw that in v. 19 "his name" (שְׁמוֹ) is a pointer to Moses without this being stated, and similarly Moses is the subject of this verse too. What Yahweh has done, he has done for him. It is again a clear matter of rank—the difference between what God does and what the human being can do, even if he is the leader of the people or the congregation. Moses, the person who has appeared and who is speaking here, can testify to that.

One last point in this connection: the speech begins with the declaration that Yahweh is "the Holy One of

---

195 Cf. also Isa 41:17; 44:3; 50:2.
196 Cf. Isa 19:5-6; 44:27; Hos 13:15; Ps 106:9; Job 14:11.
197 On the substantive חָרְבָּה see *HALOT* 1:350 [*HALAT* 1:336]: "dry land" (in contrast to sea and river); see

Gen 7:22; Exod 14:21; Josh 3:17; 4:18; 2 Kgs 2:80; Ezek 30:12; Hag 2:6.
198 There is no mention of Aaron at all.

Israel" (v. 17). If it is Yahweh alone who performs wonders, his holiness is upheld.[199] The passage ends: "There is no peace/salvation (שָׁלוֹם), Yahweh has said, for the wicked (לָרְשָׁעִים)." The texts that have to do with the "water from the rock" are full of the "murmuring" of the people, their "tempting" of God, and remembrance of the sin of Jacob/Israel. This is developed most clearly in Psalm 78, especially in vv. 15-22. Even the leaders of the people are no exceptions, as Numbers 20 shows. Thus the declaration at the end of this passage has its proper place here. Moses testifies that this is true.[200] As in v. 19, there is an element of complaint in the comment too: he has not entered into the peace of the land.

This wider horizon does not diminish the joy over the people's undeserved preservation in their journey through the wilderness. Blessing and curse, salvation and disaster, life and death, are all elements in Moses' proclamation.

■ **22** This verse brings us provisionally to the end of the prophetic speech that began in v. 17. The listeners were "Jacob and Israel" who, v. 12 tells us, were gathered together. In 49:1-6 the Servant is still speaking, but the listeners have changed. Now they are the "islands and nations." This is not the beginning of a new act. One can at most talk about a new scene. The content is also comparable. The conclusion to the whole act follows only in 49:13, with the hymn.

In spite of this, the observation that there are hymnal elements in vv. 20-22 is quite correct—for example, the invitation: "Declare it with a voice of joy" or, if we turn to the form, the chiastic alternation: water-rock, rock-water in v. 21. This could be explained if the Servant's speech simultaneously announces the exit of the chorus Jacob/Israel. In the context of the drama, the instructions about movements should be taken literally, begin-

ning with "Go out" in v. 20. The drama acts out what is supposed to take place in reality.

Here the tone that the chorus is to take is also precisely given: בְּקוֹל רִנָּה. This can be translated "in an exulting voice." According to *HALOT,* רִנָּה is "a loud, resounding cry." It is the "cry of joy," but can also be the "cry of lament." The transition from the one to the other is not great, as 43:14 already showed. There Babylon's rejoicing changed into lament. Here it is the reverse. After vv. 18-19, with the new exit (vv. 20-21), lament turns into rejoicing.

This is not to be merely a "cry." The declaration "Yahweh has redeemed his servant Jacob" is articulated and, since this is an exit, we may presume that it was spoken in chorus: "Say . . . !" (אִמְרוּ). The conclusion is probably also spoken: "There is no peace/salvation for the wicked"—an echo of what Yahweh had said first.

Between vv. 20 and 22, however, five declarations are made (v. 21), each of which can be matched by some particular action. If we think back to the fivefold division in 40:12 and 15, the possibility of a mimed presentation is worth considering. We might think of a play with water.[201] If this is a dance, then it is not a "dance round the golden calf." The final note "water" (מַיִם) again suggests that this was a sign for a repeat. Here it is actually mentioned twice.[202]

The exit of Jacob/Israel as chorus brings to an end in some sense the unit that begins in 47:1. Jacob/Israel, or particular sections of the people, have continually been addressed, though the form of the address changes: first (in 46:3) "house of Jacob," then (48:1) "house of Jacob who are called by the name of Israel," and finally (48:12) "Jacob and Israel." Now the name "Jacob" disappears, and from 49:14 onward the name "Israel" too. Cyrus is not mentioned either in what follows, nor is there any

---

199 Cf. Ps 105:42.

200 We may assume that DtIsa's contemporaries knew much better than we who were meant by "the wicked" (רְשָׁעִים) referred to here. At the same time the formulation permits new topical references in any given case.

201 Cf. the description of different forms of libation, esp. in Egypt.

202 H. Hickmann (*Musikgeschichte in Bildern, Ägypten* [1961] 84) supposes that there could be a connection between repeat signs in Egypt and the neume used to indicate a repeat in plainsong: "The 'da

capo' or repeat sign is therefore indicated in ancient Egypt, as it is with us, by a sign made up of strokes and points, or by circular signs. The fact that the double stroke \\ also means the form indicating the dual, or ii = y in general, is reminiscent of the double accent of this form and of the sign iy or iyy used to indicate a repeat in plainsong notation."

further reference to him. From 49:14 onward "Zion" is at the center of events. These observations have led commentators to see 48:22 as a decisive caesura in DtIsa's book—sometimes to the point of calling into question DtIsa's authorship of everything that follows. But the continuity must be seen as well. The "Servant of God" texts link the different sections together, and there are correspondences in content. The (new) exodus has Jerusalem/Zion as its goal. 49:1-13 can be seen as a bridge passage pointing both forward and backward. This must be borne in mind in the exegesis of what follows.

49

"And he has said to me: You are my servant,
Israel . . ." (49:3)
"He said: . . . Thus I shall make you to be
a light of nations <a light to the nations> so that
my help reaches to the end of the earth" (49:6)

1   Listen to me, islands,
    and heed this, nations from far away!
    Yahweh called me from my mother's womb;
    from my mother's womb he thought of my
        name.

2   And he has made my mouth sharp as a sword
        <or: like a sharp sword?>—
    in the shadow of his hand he kept me safe.
    And he has made me into a sharpened
        arrow—
    in his quiver he hid me away.

3   And *he has said* to me:
    You are my servant, Israel:
    through you I will be glorified.

4   But *I said:*
    I have labored in vain,
    for nothing and nothing at all <?> have I
        spent my strength.
    Yet my rights <claim?> are <is> with Yahweh
    and my reward with my God.

5   But now *Yahweh has said*—
        he who formed me from the womb to
            be his servant,
        to bring Jacob back to him,
    and Israel <to him>[a] it will gather/will be
        gathered.
        but I will be/was[b] honored in his eyes,
        and my God has been my strength <my
            protection?>—

6   *he said:*
    It is too little that you should belong to me
        as servant,
    to raise up <restore?>[a] the tribes of Jacob
    and to bring back <those who have been
        preserved> of Israel.
    Thus I shall make you to be a "light of
        nations" <a light to the nations?>,
    so that my help reaches to the end of the
        earth.

5[a]   Thus with a correction from לֹא to לוֹ in accordance with the
Qere, which is supported by a number of manuscripts: 1QIsa[a],
LXX, α', E (cf. Tg). The *Ketib* can perhaps be understood in
the sense of: "so that Israel does not disappear (is not gathered <to the dead>)." Another possibility would be a further
correction from יֵאָסֵף to אֶאֱסֹף, following S (*'knš*; cf. A): "so
that I may gather Israel together with him (and be honored)."
Cf. below on this passage.

5[b]   According to L as ו + imperfect, according to S (Vg) pointed
as narrative form.

6[a]   Thus following the *Qere* (וּנְצוּרֵי instead of וּנְצִירֵי <aramaized
passive form?>).

With v. 1 a new scene begins. The "islands" and "the
nations from far away" are addressed and probably again
appear in the form of their representatives.[203] The
Servant is still the speaker. But here he does not begin
with the formula "Thus says Yahweh," which proved him

---

203 Cf. 41:1ff.

to be a prophet. There are no indications that the place where the action is taking place has changed.

The verses can be divided up as follows: The command to the foreign peoples to listen (v. 1a) is followed in vv. 1b-4 by a reflection about the past. This is shown by the perfect tenses of the verbs in v. 1b: "he has called me" and "he has thought of my name." From then on (v. 2) the narrative uses the *waw* consecutive: "*and* he has made my mouth," "*and* he has made me," in each case expanded through perfect forms, as far as "and he has said to me" (v. 3). The answer given in v. 4 is also in the perfect.

The second unit is introduced by: "But now (וְעַתָּה) Yahweh has said" (v. 5a). This already makes the time change clear. The text is now concerned with the present, and hence with a briefly formulated decision about both the Servant and "Israel."

Verse 5b begins with a renewed declaration by the Servant himself: "But I . . ." and a further citation of God's words: "he said . . ." (v. 6). Grammatically, this is again the narrative form. As regards the content, v. 6b again points to the future, with the new task given to the Servant. At the same time the mention of "the nations" establishes the connection with v. 1a.

The part played by the Servant differs in each of the units. It is notable that in each of them the name "Israel" is also mentioned (vv. 3, 5, 6). The fate of the Servant and the fate of Israel are connected. All in all the structure is built up with considerable artistry, right down to the details.[204] This makes it easy to overlook the cryptic character of the text. The divisions themselves bring out the importance of the verbs that have to do with speaking. Even though the Servant is the speaker throughout, in each case he cites what Yahweh has said, and what he himself has said or says. It is the approach to a dialogue, a "sham dialogue," so to speak. Here we may ask whether this was because the dialogue as dramatic form had not yet been fully developed, or whether there were theological reasons for avoiding a real dialogue between God and a human being at this point.[205] At all events the dialogue form should be noted in the interpretation of the text. It can help to explain some of its difficulties.

Ever since Duhm, the text has been traditionally termed the second "Servant of God song." I myself have interpreted the text as being part of an "ideal biography."[206] I would still maintain that it contains biographical elements, and that it has to do with the ministry and authority of the Servant, particularly toward the foreign peoples. But I have come to see more clearly how the text is bound up with its context. Here too the identification of the Servant with the appearance of Moses must prove its plausibility.

■ **1-4** By turning to the foreign nations the Servant asserts his Lord's claim that his sovereignty reaches to the ends of the earth. אִיִּים *ʾiyyîm* is the term for the Mediterranean islands and coastlands.[207] It means the Greek-speaking world particularly.[208] The content of the following text will make clear why "the islands and nations" are supposed to listen with such keen attention to the message about the new, changed role of Israel and the Servant. If, as W. Schottroff maintains in his reference to this passage, the command does not indicate the beginning of "a judicial assembly" but is the formula introducing a didactic discourse, this would stress the peaceful character of the scene.[209]

The Servant begins his speech by pointing to his legitimation: he has been called by Yahweh from his mother's womb. It is striking that "from my mother's womb" should be so much stressed in the text, twice here in the parallelism, and a third time in v. 5. There is no mention of the father. In a Greek environment, this could point to a hero who is of divine descent on the father's side. But the phrases "called by Yahweh" and "he thought of my name" speak against that here.[210]

If we read the text as referring to Moses, an observation of C. J. Labuschagne is worth noting: "Notably, *qrʾ* as the designation of an act that establishes contact with

---

204 See Beuken, 22–23. There is a striking frequency of *i* sounds in the text.

205 For the dialogue form cf. Philo's explanation in *Vit. Mos.* 2.187–91.

206 K. Baltzer, "Zur formgeschichtlichen Bestimmung der Texte vom Gottes-Knecht im Deuterojesaja-Buch," in *Probleme biblischer Theologie. FS G. von Rad* (1971), esp. 35–38; see also idem, *Die Biographie der*

Propheten (1975) 171–77, esp. 174.

207 See *HALOT* s.v. אִי.

208 Cf. the list in Aeschylus *Persians* 864–908; cf. also 185–90.

209 W. Schottroff, "קשׁב *qšb* hi. to pay attention," *TLOT* 3:1171–74, esp. 1173 [*THAT* 2:684–89, esp. 687] (with lit.).

210 Cf. Exod 33:17.

Yahweh . . . has Moses as the exclusive obj[ect] in the Pentateuch (Exod 3:4; 19:3, 20; 24:16; Lev 1:1)."[211] But the connection with Moses is closer still: the relationship to Moses' real mother becomes important when his growing up at the Egyptian court as the son of Pharaoh's daughter becomes suspect. Both the biblical tradition itself and later interpretations show that discussions about his descent existed.[212]

E. Sellin says about v. 2: "The very images picturing the mouth and the tongue of the Servant as a sharp weapon that could not at first be sufficiently used reminds us of the qualms of tradition because Moses was not a speaker, even through he had the support of the Almighty; cf. Exod 4:10-16."[213] But the connection goes deeper still, and the text indicates that contemporary issues are being touched on here.

The basis for this supposition can be found in v. 2, with its image of Yahweh as warrior. One feature of this image is the sharp sword on which he has already laid his hand, ready to draw. One can talk in Hebrew about the "mouth of the sword" that eats up the enemy. The arrows in the quiver are ready. They are sharpened (ברר II), that is, they are shining arrows. LXX (βέλος ἐκλεκτόν) derives the verb from ברר I, "choose, select." The sword is the weapon for close combat, bow and arrow can be used at a distance. The picture that emerges is identical with ancient Near Eastern presentations of the deity as warrior. Among biblical texts, the theophany description in Habakkuk 3 is of special interest. It shows the God who tramples down the foreign peoples (גּוֹיִם) in his wrath (v. 12) and sallies forth as help (לְיֵשַׁע) for his people (v. 13; cf. v. 8). It is noticeable that the two texts draw on a similar semantic field, although the interpretation differs.

Hab 3:4 is an example, even though this is a very difficult text. We can see that the text as we have it is talking about a splendor "like light" (כָּאוֹר). "Rays" (קַרְנַיִם)[214] go forth from the Deity's hand (מִיָּדוֹ). The final words are: "and there is the covering (חֶבְיוֹן) of his strength (עֻזּה)."

According to v. 11, sun and moon pass away "before the light of your arrows" (לְאוֹר חִצֶּיךָ). "Covering" (חֶבְיוֹן) is a hapax, but it is connected with the root "hide" (חבה), which is a key word for Isa 49:2. Yet the DtIsa text does not mention "splendor, light, rays," but talks instead about the Servant and his mouth. There is glorification here too, but according to v. 3 "through you—the servant Israel—I will be glorified (אֶתְפָּאָר)." It is only in v. 5 that we hear about "power, strength" (עֻזּי) for the first time, while "light" (לְאוֹר) and "help" (יְשׁוּעָתִי) are mentioned only in v. 6.

In Deut 32:39-43 the Song of Moses uses the same warlike language as Habakkuk 3. Arrow and sword rage. "No one can deliver from my hand" (וְאֵין מִיָּדִי מַצִּיל, v. 39). Instead, Isa 49:2 says that the Servant is kept safe "in the shadow of his hand" (בְּצֵל יָדוֹ).

The transformation of the sword into a simile ("*like* a sword") and the stress on the Servant's "mouth" are decisive for an understanding of DtIsa. But how do the Servant's "mouth" and the idea of the "holy war" go together? There is in fact a text in the Moses tradition that meets this specification, associating the two concepts, and that also fits in with the context in vv. 2-4. It is the slaughter of the Amalekites in Exod 17:8-16. This should be read, however, together with the summary in the Vulgate version of the book of Judith: "Think of Moses, the servant of the Lord, who smote the Amalekites, not with the sword but with holy prayer, who relied upon their power and might, upon their army, shield, chariot and riders" (Jdt 4:13); and also 5:16-17 generally: "And wherever they went without bow, arrow, shield or sword, God fought for them and was victorious. And no one could harm this people except when it departed from the commandments of the Lord its God."

Anyone familiar with the "labor" Moses endured in the battle with the Amalekites can understand the complaint here in v. 4, that it was all for nothing. Just as in the case of the later battles that followed the exodus, whether against Balak, the king of the Moabites, or

---

211 C. J. Labuschagne, "קרא *qrʾ* to call," *TLOT* 3:1163 [*THAT* 2:673].

212 See esp. the accounts in Philo *Vit. Mos.* 1.5–33 and Josephus *Ant.* 2.9.4-7.

213 E. Sellin, *Mose und seine Bedeutung für die Israelitisch-Jüdische Religionsgeschichte* (1922) 90.

214 Cf. Exod 34:29-30, 35.

against Sihon and Og, victory over the enemy was followed by apostasy and distress. From Moses' point of view, this labor is completely in vain (הֶבֶל, תֹּהוּ, רִיק) even if his rights (מִשְׁפָּט) and reward (פְּעֻלָּה) with God remain.[215]

We can again ask whether it is possible to reconstruct a situation in which as radical a position as this could have its place. Josephus's account of the battle with the Amalekites (*Ant.* 3.39–62) can be read as an antitype. Here Moses is the general pure and simple, who prepares his army with word and deed.[216] On "the raising of Moses' hand" Josephus expends no more than two sentences (53). It is a difference similar to the one we already noticed in the reception in Isa 41:15-16 of the Song of Miriam from Exod 15:20-21. There גיל, "cry ecstatically, shout for joy," is probably a quotation from the Song of Miriam. But in DtIsa גיל has an unfavorable sense. Thus Isa 41:15-16 is also an ambiguous oracle. A military solution is at least for DtIsa "in vain."

This, of course, is information that is of the greatest importance for the "islands and nations" (see v. 1). They no longer need to fear the "holy war." "Moses" himself has confirmed this. It is an essential alteration of tradition by way of a new interpretation. For the moment we must leave open the question about where to place this position, historically speaking.

The trend of the whole text vv. 1-4 now makes it easier to understand v. 3. The main difficulty of the exegesis is eliminated if we assume that here "the Servant Moses" is citing a divine oracle about "the Servant Israel." The formulation: "You are my servant, Israel," corresponds to 41:8: "And you, Israel, are my servant" (cf. 41:9b). This is Israel/Jacob, "Abraham's seed." In chap. 41 too we find this designation, after the speech to "the islands and nations" (41:1-5). In both cases the subject is election. Outside DtIsa the explicit description of "Israel" as servant is relatively rare, compared with the verbal statement that Israel "serves" (עבד) Yahweh. One passage where it is emphasized particularly is 1 Chr 16:13, which describes the people as "seed of Israel, his servant, sons of Jacob, his chosen one." According to the context, David calls on the Levites to "give thanks to the Lord" for the first time when the ark is brought to Jerusalem.

At this point the version in Psalm 105 has "seed of Abraham, his servant," instead of Israel. So the pronouncement "Israel, his servant," was evidently a matter for discussion. In this case the sentence: "He said *to me*: you are my servant, Israel," in v. 3 must be understood in a polemical sense: it was not just David who received this promise; the promise was already given to Moses. It is noticeable that in the context of the declarations about the future, 49:6 also immediately turns back to the tradition of the tribes. "Glorification" through the "servant Israel" has initially come to nothing, according to v. 3: "In vain. . . ."

If the text is examined under literary criteria it becomes plain that "Israel" is an integral part of the declaration; it cannot be eliminated, nor is it a later addition. The textual transmission is thoroughly well attested.[217]

■ **5-6** At first sight v. 5a seems to be a tiny unit, but commentators have doubted whether this sentence is a self-contained utterance at all, or whether it is not merely a preparation for what follows. But the "now" (וְעַתָּה) is a clear signal that this is a new beginning. The center is again a statement about "Israel." The name introduces the one sentence containing a main verb in this unit. We expect it to contain information about what Yahweh said to "his servant." But this is only the start of the textual and lexical difficulties presented by the text.

The sentence as the MT gives it runs: "And/But Israel, it will not be gathered," and in this form the sentence can certainly stand. We have only to explain "where" or "where to" Israel will be gathered (אסף), or *not* gathered, as the case may be. One possibility is to supplement "gather" with the phrase "to its fathers" or "relatives"; in this case the word means "dies." "A few passages use *'sp* in the context of burial (2 Sam 21:13 qal; Jer 8:2 ni.; 25:33 ni.; Ezek 29:5 ni. with *qbṣ* ni.; . . . cf. Sir 38:16)."[218] But the verb needs no further definition provided that the meaning is obvious from the context; for example, when it is said that Aaron "was gathered and died there" (יֵאָסֵף וַיָּמָת שָׁם, Num 20:26). But if in the present DtIsa text the action takes place in the underworld (as we have assumed under quite different presuppositions), then here too it would be superfluous to

---

215 See below on the interpretive reference to Nehemiah; cf. Neh 5:19; 13:14, 22, 31.

216 Josephus *Ant.* 3.52: "For himself, having thus animated the forces by his words and by all these active

preparations, he withdrew to the mountain, consigning the campaign to God and to Joshua" (LCL, 342–43).

217 See the commentaries here.

indicate a particular place for "gather." The meaning would be: Israel is *not* to disappear in the underworld like other peoples, for example, Babylon (47:1-14).

Again we may ask what this has to do with "Moses." A hint may be given by an obscure story that exercised later minds too: "the rebellion and downfall of the Korahites" in Numbers 16–17. Here Moses' authority was at stake (see 16:2, 29).[219] It was only through his intercession—and the intercession of Aaron too, at least according to Num 16:20—that "the whole congregation" (אֶת־כָּל־הָעֵדָה) was saved from annihilation. Only Korah and his followers "went down alive into Sheol; the earth closed over them, and they perished from the midst of the assembly" (הַקָּהָל, Num 16:33). Even if the verb "gather together" (אסף) is missing, Korah and his people were "snatched away" to the underworld, but *not* "Israel."

If from this point we return to the DtIsa text, the "bringing back" (שוב *Polel*) also has its point.[220] It is associated with the concept of Yahweh's covenant with his people.[221] His people's rebellion puts an end to the relationship to God, with all the consequences that this breach involves, to the point of complete annihilation. In this context "return" means the "return to the original relationship to Yahweh."[222] Its premise is that Yahweh is prepared for a "restoration of the original status."[223]

The era of the wanderings in the wilderness is full of Israel's rebellion against its God. "Murmuring" is a constant theme, down to the story of the golden calf. After Sinai things become even more critical, as can be seen from the already mentioned story about the Korahites, or the narratives about the spies.[224] Moses can avert the worst, especially through his intercession. Deut 30:1-10 and Neh 1:9, among other passages, show that he exhorts the people to repent in exemplary fashion.

Isa 49:5a brings out Moses' double function. He is Yahweh's "servant" (עֶבֶד לוֹ), his representative. At the same time, for the people he is the one who brings them back "to him" (אֵלָיו), that is, to Yahweh. Here again the name of Jacob is found in a context that stresses the existence of the people as pardoned sinners.

Looking back, one can also see that the version which the Masoretes already proposed as *Qere*, "And Israel, to him it will be gathered," also has its point (cf. 1QIsaᵃ and LXX, as well as textual note 5a above). Here לֹא is read as *lô*, "to him," instead of as *lôʾ*, "not." I would assume that this artistic "ambivalence"[225] reflects DtIsa's own intention. When read aloud, the two versions are indistinguishable. The first version, in the sense of "will not be snatched away/will not disappear," looks back to the time of distress. The second version gives hope—the hope that Israel too will be "gathered" anew. This version has therefore been taken into account in the translation, in view of the later texts in DtIsa.

In content, v. 3 and v. 5a correspond, inasmuch as in both verses the Servant of God makes a declaration about "Israel," supported by divine authority. Verse 3 refers to the past, Israel's beginnings: "And he said to me: 'You are my servant, Israel.'" Verse 5a refers to present and future: "But now Yahweh has said . . . 'Israel <to him> it will gather/will be gathered."

"To him" or "for him" leaves open whether this means Yahweh himself (cf. Num 11:16-17; Ps 50:5[226]), his pres-

218   See J. F. A. Sawyer, "קבץ *qbṣ* to assemble," *TLOT* 3:1100 [*THAT* 2:585].

219   Num 16:28: "And Moses said: this is how you shall know"—in the framework of the Persian policy toward different nationalities, as well as in relation to Egypt, this can also have been a point where there was a difference of opinion—"that Yahweh has sent me" (שְׁלָחָנִי).

220   See H. W. Wolff, "Das Thema 'Umkehr' in der alttestamentlichen Prophetie," *ZThK* 48 (1951) 129–48, reprinted in Wolff, *Gesammelte Studien zum Alten Testament* (2d ed. 1973) 130–50; G. Fohrer, "Umkehr und Erlösung beim Propheten Hosea," *ThZ* 11 (1955) 161–85, reprinted in *Studien zur alttestamentlichen Prophetie* (1967) 222–41; J. A. Soggin, "שוב *šûb* to return," *TLOT* 3:1312-17 [*THAT* 2:884–91].

221   W. L. Holladay, *The Root Šûbh in the Old Testament: With Particular Reference to Its Usages in Covenantal Contexts* (1958); M. L. Barré, "The Meaning of *lʾ ʾšybnw* in Amos 1:3–2:6," *JBL* 105 (1986) 611–31.

222   Wolff, "Das Thema 'Umkehr' in der alttestamentlichen Prophetie," *ZThK* 48 (1951) 129–45, reprinted in Wolff, *Gesammelte Studien zum Alten Testament* (2d ed. 1973) 130–50.

223   Ibid.

224   See A. Schart, *Mose und Israel im Konflikt. Eine redaktionsgeschichtliche Studie zu den Wüstenerzählungen* (1990).

225   This is well observed by Sawyer, "קבץ *qbṣ* to assemble," *TLOT* 3:1100 [*THAT* 2:585].

226   "Gather for me my faithful ones (אִסְפוּ־לִי חֲסִידָי), who made a covenant with me by sacrifice." The LXX has συναγάγετε αὐτῷ τοὺς ὁσίους αὐτοῦ. To

ence in Jerusalem (cf. Joel 1:14; Mic 4:6) or Moses and his Torah (cf. Deut 33:4-5; Neh 8:1). Different theological perspectives would be involved here in each case.

Verse 5b begins with a double statement reflecting the Servant's biography. Whereas vv. 1 and 5a talk about his legitimation through his birth, the subject now is the honor given to him by his Lord, which is in accord with the Servant's trust. The recollection of honors conferred and the listing of the different stages of the person's activity (including his advancement) are characteristic of Egyptian ideal biographies.[227] The present text is comparably structured. If the Servant is to be identified as Moses, it is hardly possible to determine with any certainty what specific "honors" the writer has in mind. It could be that Moses was permitted to approach God all by himself, and to talk to him face-to-face. The plea to be allowed to see "Yahweh's glory" (Exod 33:18)—a plea that is complied with, even if in modified form—belongs to this context (cf. Exodus 33–34). Moses' song in Exodus 15 begins: "My strength (עָזִּי) and my song is Yahweh, he has become my help, yes he is my God" (v. 2).[228]

Two stages in the Servant's activity are named, and these make immediately clear that there is progression from an easier task to a more difficult one. The meaning of the greater task, which points toward the future, can be judged when one knows how difficult even the first task was—"to raise up the tribes of Jacob." To put this into the mouth of Moses is to make an eminently political statement, for it takes up the prenational, premonarchical traditions of the tribal league.[229] If these traditions are already legitimated by Moses, why should the monarchy be restored? This shows how consistently DtIsa carries through his antidynastic line of argument. Moses observed the order of the tribes in the wander-

ings through the wilderness: that is the generally accepted picture.

The texts emphasize that this order already existed before the settlement of the promised land. Before his death Moses blesses the tribes (Deuteronomy 33, esp. v. 5). But since in the present context the recurring topic is Sinai/Horeb and the giving of the commandments (see esp. 48:17), one may ask whether DtIsa did not have a particular passage in mind. According to Exodus 24, when the covenant is concluded on Sinai, after Moses had written down Yahweh's words he "built an altar at the foot of the mountain, and set up twelve *maṣṣeboth* (מַצֵּבָה), corresponding to the twelve tribes of Israel" (v. 4). That Moses should have set up *maṣṣeboth*, steles or (cultic) pillars, must surely have been a cause of offense to a later era. Even the LXX already changed the word to the Greek equivalent for "stones," at least. Is the strange "raise up the tribes of Jacob" (לְהָקִים . . . אֶת־שִׁבְטֵי) a further interpretation designed to exonerate Moses?[230]

Verse 6 also contains a declaration about "Israel." If we follow the reading put forward in the Masorah, it is those who have been saved (נְצוּרֵי)[231] who will be brought back by the Servant. This can mean the people who were left over at the exodus, but it is also a transparent reference to the return of the exiles, which was DtIsa's contemporary situation. To have indicated any particular place would not have permitted this double meaning, and there is sufficient talk about Zion/Jerusalem in what follows.

The climax and conclusion of the Servant's address to the foreign peoples is the information that he himself is

---

this אֶסְפּוֹר־לוֹ would correspond, and hence—instead of a direct divine speech—the formulation in the third person singular, as in the present text Isa 49:5: "Israel <for him> it will gather/will be gathered." Ps 50:5 is close to Isa 49:5 and its context. Kraus calls the psalm a prophetic judgment liturgy. Here theophany and the Zion tradition are linked (50:1-3). See Kraus, *Psalms 1–59* (1987) [*Psalmen I* (5th ed. 1978) on Psalm 50.

227 See Baltzer, *Die Biographie der Propheten* (1975) 24, 136–49; E. Otto, *Die biographischen Inschriften der ägyptischen Spätzeit*, Probleme der Ägyptologie 2 (1954).

228 On the text see Jörg Jeremias, *Das Königtum Gottes in den Psalmen* (1987) 93–106 (with lit.).

229 See O. Kaiser, *Der königliche Knecht* (1959) 63.

230 On קוּם Hiphil see J. Gamberoni, "קוּם qûm," *ThWAT* 6:1252–74, esp. 1258: "In late texts the hiphil is largely used for the setting up and arrangement of cultic stones (Josh 4:9, 20; 24:26; Deut 27:2), heaps of stones (Josh 7:26; 8:29), *maṣṣeboth* (Deut 16:22; Lev 26:1 forbidden; uncontested: Gen 28:18 *śym* qal; 35:20 *nṣb* hiphil)."

231 As passive participle from the root נצר. For the meaning see G. Sauer, "נצר *nṣr* to guard," *TLOT* 2:762–63 [*THAT* 2:99–101]: "The meaning of *nṣr* in

to be a "light of nations" (לְאוֹר גּוֹיִם).[232] Both "light" and "help"—help, that is, for Israel—can mean disaster for the nations in the framework of the "holy war." But here the two things are closely associated with the person of the Servant.[233] "Light" (אוֹר) is the quintessence of justice and righteousness,[234] and means "deliverance, help, salvation" (יְשׁוּעָה) for the nations too. 51:4-6 will make even

clearer how this is connected with "precepts-law" (תּוֹרָה) and "justice" (מִשְׁפָּט). It is indeed nothing other than the Torah that has been given to Moses on Sinai, but that is now valid for the whole world.[235] This is the "greater" message. It is a message for the future.

OT Hebr[ew] is clearly 'established, to protect, guard, preserve'; it corresponds roughly to the meaning of *šmr*" (762 [100]).

232 See M. Sæbø, "אוֹר *ʾôr* light," *TLOT* 1:63–67 [*THAT* 1:83–90; S. Aalen, "אוֹר *ʾôr*," *TDOT* 1:147–67 [*ThWAT* 1:160–82].

233 See Aalen's observation, *TDOT* 1:164–65: "In the OT, men are not usually represented as participating in the divine light. Moses, whose skin shines (verb *qaran*) after his meeting with the Lord (Ex. 34:29f., 35), is an exception. It is not explicitly stated that this shining originated with God, but it is probably assumed (cf. *kabhodh* in 33:18)." The

link with Moses could explain the strangely personal mode of expression: "I have given you to be a light." See also Isa 42:6-7 in the first Servant text. The spiritualization of the "light" concept in later tradition is already heralded here. See also in the NT John 8:12 (9:5): "I am the light of the world."

234 See Aalen, ibid., 163.

235 For "to the ends of the earth" cf. Isa 48:20; also 40:28; 41:5, 9; 42:10; 43:6.

"He chose you" (49:7)

49:7-12
Divine Speech—A Threefold Revelation:

1. Lifting of the Threat (to the Servant)
2. The Servant as "Covenant for the People"
   for the Restoration of the Land and for the
   Liberation of Those Enslaved (Because of Debt)
3. Announcement of the Pilgrimage
The Return of Those Who Have Been Scattered
(Procession)

49

"See, these come from afar" (49:12)

7   Thus says Yahweh,
    Israel's redeemer, its Holy One,
       to one whose person <is despised>,ᵃ
       to one who <is abhorred by peoples>ᵇ
       to a servant of rulers:
    Kings will see it and stand up,
    princes, so that they prostrate themselves in
          reverence,
    for Yahweh's sake, who is dependable/faithful,
    the Holy One of Israel—and he chose you.

8   Thus says Yahweh:
    at an acceptable time [lit.: "at a time of
          favor"]
       I heard you,
    and on a favorable day [lit.: "on a day of
          salvation"]
       I helped you,
    so that I may form you and giveᵃ you a
          covenant for the people,
    to raise up <restore?> the land <the earth?>,
    to hand over devastated possessions as an
          inheritance,
9   to say to the prisoners: Go out!
    and to those in darkness: Come into the light!
    [lit., perhaps: "let yourselves be seen!" or
          something similar].

    Along the ways they shall feed,
    and along all the trails shall be their pasture.
10 They shall have no hunger and no thirst,
    and heat and sun will not strike them,
    for he who has compassion on them <their
          compassion?> will guide them
    and lead them to springs of water.
11 And I will make all hills <mountains?> a way
          <surmountable?>,
    and my highways shall lead high up.

12 See, these come from far away,
    and see, these from the north and west
          <from the sea>,
    and these from the land of Sinim.

7ᵃ   With a correction from לְבַזֹה to לִבְזוּי; cf. 1QIsaᵃ, α´, σ´, ϑ´, S,
     Tg. Cairo Genizah and LXX read לִבְזֹה, "to one whom every-
     one despises." On the text of v. 7 according to the Masoretic
     transmission, see below.
7ᵇ   With a correction from גּוֹי (Gentile) sing. to plur. and from
     לִמְתָעֵב to לִמְתֹעַב; see LXX; cf. Vg, Tg. See the comment below.
8ᵃ   It would also be possible (following a number of versions; see
     BHS), to point וָאֶצָּרְךָ and וָאֶתֶּנְךָ as narrative: "and I have
     formed you and given you. . . ." See below.

With the ancient introductory formula "Thus says Yahweh" (כֹּה־אָמַר יהוה), 48:17 is followed by two other prophecies (49:7, 8). Here too the triple number has its special significance.[236] The last element acquires special weight. The first oracle, in v. 7, echoes motifs belonging to the lament.[237] The second, in vv. 8-12, 13 is aimed at rejoicing and thanksgiving. The text offers some difficulties, especially in v. 7. Among other things, it raises the question: who is being addressed? In the text as we have it, the active form is used twice: "because of contempt," "because of one who abhors." Textual critics generally change these forms into the passive: the one despised, the one abhorred. To whom does the sequence from "someone" (נֶפֶשׁ) to "princes" (שָׂרִים) refer? What do "kings and princes" see? It could be that the difficulties are not due to the transmission of the text at all, and cannot therefore be eliminated by the methods of literary criticism. They may be connected with a characteristic that we have already observed several times in DtIsa: his tendency to play on different levels of meaning. It is on this assumption that we shall attempt to clarify the difficulties of the text.

On the first, immediately accessible level, it is the Servant who is being referred to. He is addressed in the masculine singular form—clearly so at the end of v. 7: "and he chose *you*" (suffix = ך)—and then immediately afterward four times in v. 8. Yahweh is certainly presented in the introductory formula as "Israel's redeemer and its Holy One (קְדוֹשׁ)," but it is as "the one who chooses" that he is "Israel's Holy One." From v. 8 on, it is clear that the Servant has tasks to perform on behalf of Israel, the "people."

If we see the Servant as the subject of the text, the change to the passive in v. 7 certainly has a point; and this is the rendering of the ancient translations and most commentators. The Servant is despised and abhorred, and by everyone.[238] That he of all people should be chosen by Yahweh is a reason for the mighty to be astonished. It signifies a fundamental reversal. In this sense the passage already points toward the final Servant of God text (Isa 52:13—53:12), particularly to 52:15.

On a second level, the text can be interpreted as referring to Moses as the Servant, even if the indications are less clear than they are otherwise from 48:16 onward. The speaker remains the same in v. 7. It is still "Moses," speaking as a prophet. He suffered under human hostility, and later tradition—drawing on Deuteronomy 34—believed that he also predicted his own death. But is this tradition sufficient to explain the "despised and abhorred"?

The declaration that Yahweh is faithful (נֶאֱמָן) to his election could be linked with the Moses tradition. Num 12:7 says of Moses that he is נֶאֱמָן. A. Jepsen says here: "One possibility is that *ne'eman* is to be understood as 'reliable'. . . . In this case, it is said of Moses: in contrast to Aaron and Miriam, he is faithful and loyal in my whole house."[239] But according to Jepsen it might perhaps be possible "that the participial forms here should be understood more like verbs: 'he is entrusted, he is authorized.' In this case, Nu. 12:7 would mean: 'He (alone) is entrusted with all my house.'" In spite of grammatical difficulties, "it is clear that [on the basis of 1 Sam 3:20—Ed.] a statement was made about Moses and Samuel which expressed a unique relationship to the deity, indeed, a special divine evaluation of these two men." If, as Jepsen maintains: "Yahweh is called *ne'eman*, 'faithful,' only in Isa. 49:7,"[240] this could be connected with DtIsa's general tendency to acknowledge statements about Moses and his acts as brought about by Yahweh.

---

236 One should not, therefore, expunge the formula for the prophetic saying in v. 8a, as Schoors suggests in *I Am God Your Saviour* (1973), 98, commenting on this passage.

237 Ibid., 99–100: "Also the recipient, Israel, is indicated in vs. 7b with expressions that clearly recall the lament to which the proclamation replies: 'deeply despised, abhorred by the nations' (Ps xxii 7; xliv 14-17; lxxix 4, 10, 22; lxxx 7; lxxxix 42, 51-52; cxv 2; cxxiii 3-4; Jer xxxi 19; Lam i 8, 11; iii 45; v 1)." He refers to H. Gunkel and J. Begrich, *Einleitung in die Psalmen* (1933) 126.

238 For נֶפֶשׁ as meaning "someone" see H. Seebass, "נֶפֶשׁ,

nepeš," *ThWAT* 5:531–55, esp. 536: "A technical use of the name can be found in P^G, P^S, H in legal texts and lists of persons, in which the gender-specific '*îš* ('*ādām* very seldom) is avoided, so as to make it all the clearer that any person at all is meant"; see also 550.

239 A. Jepsen, "אָמַן *'āman*," *TDOT* 1:292–323, esp. 296 [*ThWAT* 1:313–48, esp. 318].

240 Ibid., 295 [317], with reference to Deut 7:9.

If we read v. 8 as referring to Moses, the key word "covenant" (בְּרִית) can be linked with Sinai-Horeb. Moses allocated the land to Israel, at least according to Deuteronomy. At the same time, we should then rather expect the verbs to be in the past tense. The LXX already acted on this assumption: "I formed you" and "I made you." This would make the reference back to the installation of the Servant in 42:6 patent. The subject would then be "Moses'" authority, which is now once more endorsed. But we must nevertheless remember that the Masoretic reading is an unequivocal "and" (וְ) with the preformative conjugation of the verb—it supports a "future" interpretation.[241]

The description in vv. 9b-11 of the exodus as a wandering in the wilderness is clearly taking up traditions about the exodus from Egypt under Moses. Thus it is possible to interpret the text consistently on this level. Yet tensions remain that cannot be eliminated through a change of tense. Why, for example, are the "possessions devastated" (נְחָלוֹת שֹׁמֵמוֹת)? Why are the prisoners in the dark? Observations of this kind make us wonder whether here again the text should not be understood on a third level. Many more topical references might then perhaps be detected. But this requires a further excursus.

The introductory formula in vv. 7 and 8 designates the text as a divine oracle. It can be viewed as a double oracle. In content, the first saying (v. 7) is negative in trend, the second (vv. 8-12) positive. Double oracles of this kind can be found elsewhere in the ancient world too. As for genre, the oracle is ambiguous. The present text is working with the several meanings possible. For DtIsa, the oracle's realization in history, according to God's will, is clear.

As regards the dramatic structure, the second Servant of God text (from 48:16) is marked by the theme Sinai-Horeb. From there one can look back to the installation in 42:1-9 and forward to the settlement of the promised land. This would be on the "Moses" level. But Moses becomes a genuine prophet, prophesying the far-off future of his people. He points beyond himself to the new Moses. This new Moses already emerges in the picture presented by the previous text, 49:1-6, with which

DtIsa is probably also addressing his own time.

If the message of 49:1-6 to "the islands and nations" is again given a particular political focus, from the point of view of the outside addressees, we arrive at the following picture:

1. The Servant (Moses) was legitimated by virtue of his birth, even though this legitimation was kept hidden. The descent from his people is clear, because of his mother (vv. 1a, 5a).
2. He was not a soldier, or he failed in this role (vv. 1-4).
3. He was a mediator between God and his people. Through his authority he put the religious affairs of his people in order (v. 5a).
4. He reorganized "Israel" on the foundation of the tribal order. He himself had no royal ambitions.
5. His position in the world rests on the law that he brought (vv. 5b-6).

If this description of the Servant's (Moses') role is read against the background of the Persian era, it seems probable that it had topical relevance; and for this the following text is already important.

One element should be noted once more here. Descent on the mother's side acquires new importance in the Persian period. For the Persian administration, Moses is a "Judean/Jew" (יְהוּדִי). But then the whole context from 48:1 onward could be illuminating. For this passage has to do with descent from "Judah" (48:1), even though what was behind the conflict is not wholly clear. The Servant himself talks three times about Israel (49:3, 5, 6). For him the important thing is evidently this religious and political foundation or legitimation. With this picture in mind, we may ask, Who is it?

One can argue that various attributions are possible, and have indeed continually been put forward. It is possible to dispense with an attribution altogether, giving as one reason among others that we know too little about the Persian period that we may assume is the target. But I should like to mention a few hints that all point to a historical person, and that suggest that the person whom DtIsa has in mind and whom we are seeking is Nehemiah. The role description in 49:1-6 could fit him, and this identification would explain certain details in

---

241 See the discussion in Beuken, 38–39.
242 On לְ see GKC § 119u: The use of לְ "In loose connection with some verbal idea in the sense of *in reference to, with regard to* . . . so after a *verbum dicendi*."

243 M. Görg, "בָּזָה *bāzāh*," *TDOT* 2:63 [*ThWAT* 1:582–83].

the present text. If we follow it through, we come upon the following passages in v. 7. These passages also include the very points at which we run into difficulties of interpretation on the other levels.

■ **7** The text as the Masoretic tradition gives it can be translated as follows (in distinction from the ancient translations):

Thus says Yahweh . . .

because of contempt of someone	(לִבְזֹה נֶפֶשׁ[242])	[infinitive with accusative object]
because of a contemptuous "Gentile"	(לִמְתָעֵב גּוֹי)	[attributive phrase with the participle in a curious antecedent position]
because of a servant of rulers . . .	(לְעֶבֶד מֹשְׁלִים)	[construct state]

With this we can compare Neh 2:19. The Nehemiah passage has to do with the building of Jerusalem's walls under Nehemiah's direction.

And there heard of it	
Sanballat the Horonite	
and　Tobiah the servant of the	(הָעֶבֶד הָעַמֹּנִי)
Ammonites	
and　Geshem the Arab	(הָעַרְבִי)
They mocked us and they despised us.	(וַיַּלְעִגוּ לָנוּ וַיִּבְזוּ עָלֵינוּ)

In Neh 3:36-37 (4:4-5) the subject is also "contempt" (substantive בּוּזָה *bûzāh*). God is invoked so that he may put into force the link between act and destiny. The enemies named are to be given over "as plunder (לְבִזָּה *lᵉbizzah*) in a land of captivity." One can almost go on in DtIsa's words: "princes and kings" will of course see this reversal of fortune for the three evildoers, especially if it lands the miscreants in the underworld.

We may agree with Görg when he says: "Thus the contempt comes back upon the author of the *bazah* ['contempt']. . . . Consequently, he who carries out a *bazah* ['contempt'] against one chosen by Yahweh is himself condemned to insignificance."[243] Election is the pivot or heart of DtIsa's argument (about the person: "and he chose you," 49:7), just as it is in the book of Nehemiah ("I will bring them to the place that I have chosen," Neh

1:9). In Nehemiah this declaration is part of Nehemiah's prayer, in which Moses is termed "servant" (Neh 1:7, 8), and the people "servants" (vv. 10, 11), but where, above all, Nehemiah calls himself "Yahweh's servant" (v. 11). The link between the DtIsa and the Nehemiah texts therefore does not rest solely on verbal echoes. The passages are connected by their theological argument and by the situation: the rebuilding of Jerusalem.[244]

The phrase "because of a contemptuous 'Gentile'"[245] acquires its full pungency if it is linked with "Geshem the Arab" or the "Arabs, Ammonites and Ashdodites" in Neh 4:1 (7). The irony is that it is the foreigners themselves who are hostile toward other foreigners. According to Gerstenberger, "the word *tôᶜēbâ* indicated originally that which was deemed dangerous on the basis of group norms and hence that which aroused fear and disgust. Cultic usage may have led to legal and ethical usages; the word may also have been used simultaneously, however, in several areas of life to guard against that which was alien. . . . In the pi. it expresses emotional revulsion against that which is strange."[246] Here too, in the context of the link between act and destiny, the question is: who is endangered, the one who despises or the despised servant?

"Servant of rulers" is defined more closely through "servant of the Ammonites." But it is a description that people probably cast up at one another at a period when, under Persian sovereignty, ethnic and national identity were particularly stressed.

■ **8-12** The tenses in v. 8 (in Hebrew futures: "I will form you" and "I will give you") make sense if "Moses" is announcing the far-off future. Moses concluded the covenant for the people, and this will remain valid in the future too (cf. 42:6).

If we read this against the background of the book of Nehemiah as we have it, Nehemiah 8–10 provides an astonishing illustration. Chapter 10 is clearly talking about a renewed obligation assumed by the whole people "to walk in God's law, which was given by Moses, the servant of God (עֶבֶד־הָאֱלֹהִים)." In the existing text Nehemiah's role is disputed. As governor, he is the first

---

244　K. Baltzer, "Moses Servant of God and the Servants: Text and Tradition in the Prayer of Nehemiah (Neh 1:5-11)," in *The Future of Early Christianity. FS H. Koester* (1991) 121–30.

245　Here גּוֹי probably stands on the borderline between

"people" (meaning Gentile nations) and the later singular "an individual non-Jew."

246　E. Gerstenberger, "תעב *tᶜb* pi. to abhor," *TLOT* 3:1431 [*THAT* 2:1054–55].

to sign the document (10:2 [1]). But at the reading of the law in chap. 8 Ezra "the priest and scribe" (8:9) plays a decisive role. As a result, this whole complex in the book of Nehemiah has been viewed as secondary, and the event has been associated with Ezra. But in DtIsa there is never any explicit mention of priests at all. The temple is mentioned only indirectly, in Cyrus's edict, and the criticism of sacrifice is unambiguous. This could also suggest that this passage too in DtIsa is not without topical polemic. The "hearing" and the "help" (49:8) come about with the help of "Yahweh's Servant," not through Ezra, the priest! We could therefore reverse the whole argument and say: the link between the measures taken in Nehemiah 8–10 and Ezra is secondary, and expresses a different position.

One of the measures to be carried out according to vv. 8-9 is the new distribution of the "devastated possessions" and "the liberation of prisoners." On the one hand, if we look closely at the phraseology, it does not fit Moses—why are the inherited lands "devastated" (שְׁמֵמוֹת)?—nor are the exiles in Babylon "in chains" (אֲסוּרִים). On the other hand, if we compare Nehemiah's reforms in Neh 5:1-13, and especially the freeing of people enslaved for debt, the statements fit one another very well.[247]

Finally, we may assume that when the close of this whole section runs: "Yes, Yahweh has comforted (niḥam) his people" (כִּי נִחַם יהוה עַמּוֹ, v. 13) there is a direct play here on the name Nehemiah (נְחֶמְיָה). This verse also forms a link both with the beginning of 40:1 and with what follows (cf. 51:3; 52:9).

Even though it is impossible to arrive at complete certainty, the parallels between DtIsa and Nehemiah are so striking that they should be taken into account in interpreting the text and its dating. One detail in the text as we have it then deserves special attention from a historical point of view. Among the people who have returned from exile, 49:12 mentions "those from the land of Sinim" (מֵאֶרֶץ סִינִים). G. Lambert's exhaustive study[248] has led to general agreement that this is the name for Syene[249] (the name still found in its modern equivalent, Aswan). Better known in the ancient world was the island in the Nile whose Greek name is Elephantine, and which lies opposite Aswan, on the first cataract, at the southern frontier of the Egyptian kingdom. The island was called Elephantine because of the ivory trade that passed through it. The earlier, Egyptian name Yêb already derives from the word for elephant. In the Persian period (from 525 B.C.E.) a military garrison there included a unit of Jewish mercenaries.[250]

Aramaic papyri found on the island have shed some light on the history of this remote place. The Jews had their own temple there. In 411 B.C.E. this was destroyed by the priests of the Egyptian god Khnum. In letters of 410 and 407, the Jews in Elephantine appeal to the Persian governor of Judah, Bagoas, begging for his support for the rebuilding of their temple. Bagoas's assent led to tension between Samaria and Jerusalem, and also in Jerusalem itself, the question being whether the temple cult was permissible outside "the land" itself. Against this background, the mention of "these from the land of Sinim" would acquire an additional sting, for it would mean acknowledgment of Jerusalem's unique status. "They come" as liberated people even from there; we might amplify and say: even if they come as pilgrims. At all events, this is a date that one should take into account in considering the time at which DtIsa was writing.[251]

On the dramatic performance: If we look at the text of vv. 7, 8-12, 13 once more with a view to its "action," we can discover a number of hints that suggest a

247 See here K. Baltzer, "Liberation from Debt Slavery After the Exile in Second Isaiah and Nehemiah," in *Ancient Israelite Religion: FS F. M. Cross* (1987) 474–84.

248 G. Lambert, "Le livre d'Isaïe parle-t-il des Chinois?" *NRT* 85 (1953) 965–72.

249 The consonantal text in 1QIsaᵃ, סוניים, supports this explanation; see also I. L. Seeligman, *The Septuagint Version of Isaiah* (1948) 79.

250 See esp. K. Galling, *Bagoas und Esra. Studien zur Geschichte Israels im persischen Zeitalter* (1964) 149–84; A. Schalit, "Elephantine," *EncJud* 6:604-10; B. Porten, *Archives from Elephantine: The Life of an Ancient Jewish Military Colony* (1968).

251 As far as can be seen, the sequence in v. 12 follows the points of the compass. North and west (from the sea) are clear. Then Sinim/Elephantine would stand for the south. Problematical though statements about the points of the compass are in the ancient world, one can say that this indication of "south" is only valid for a limited geographical situation—not, for example, as seen from Babylon.

dramatic presentation. I think it possible that the "contempt" of v. 7 was mimed, for it is striking that a series of five persons or groups is again listed: "someone" (נֶפֶשׁ), a foreigner (גּוֹי), a servant of rulers (עֶבֶד מֹשְׁלִים), kings (מְלָכִים), princes (שָׂרִים). These people could have been made easily identifiable through emblems. It would have been specially effective if there was also a covert reference here to particular, more or less contemporary, people. Particular sounds may have accompanied "despise" (בזה),[252] and particular gestures "abhor" (תעב).

In the situation we are assuming for this act, the "seeing" refers first to the appearance of the three evildoers in the underworld.[253] An adoring prostration is made before Yahweh in acknowledgment of his power. The ambiguity of the wording would also allow the scene to act as an anticipation and preparation for the exaltation of the "despised and abhorred" Servant in 52:13—53:12.

In dramatic terms, this would be a "mirror scene" clearly designed to bring out the reversal of values.

Verse 9 onward describes the return of the people who have been liberated. The "springs of water" (מַבּוּעֵי מַיִם, v. 10) fit in with the wanderings in the wilderness. But they can also represent paradisal conditions, in distinction from the fire of the underworld into which Babylon disappears with its followers (cf. 47:14). There are verbs of movement. It is impossible to say with any certainty whether they were backed up by actions. But that this was the case from v. 12 is clear, for here again we have the deictic particles: "see these . . . see these. . . ." People come streaming in from all sides. It is a turbulent choral end to the whole act. This time the stage fills up instead of emptying. The emotional climax is made plain.

---

252 See M. Görg, "בָּזָה bāzāh," TDOT 2:61 [ThWAT 1:581]: "Of course, there is no proof that these words have any semantic relationship to West Semitic languages. And yet, one cannot exclude the possibility that a short onomatopoetic word imitat-ing the sound of loathing or indicating disapproving conduct may be the common term lying behind these roots in the two languages" [trans. slightly altered].

253 Again one is reminded of Dante's *Divine Comedy*!

49

"Yes! Yahweh has comforted his people, and has compassion on his afflicted (oppressed) ones" (49:13)

49:13
Hymn

13   Rejoice, O heavens,
and exult, O earth,
<and break out>ᵃ into jubilation, O hills
<mountains>!
Yes! Yahweh has comforted his people,
and has compassion on his afflicted
<oppressed> ones.

13a Following the *Qere* and numerous manuscripts: וּפִצְחוּ instead of יִפְצְחוּ, "they should break out (in jubilation)."

■ **13** This verse calls for a hymn. The pitch of the notes and their sequence is announced: high (heaven), low (earth), middle register (mountains). The marks of expression are also roughly detectable: "shout for joy, rejoice" (רנן), "cry" (גיל), "break into jubilation" (פצח רנה). The "-*ayim*" (the dual ending) in "heaven" (שָׁמַיִם) could again signal the repeat. One problem is the voice of the earth. It is usually assumed that the earth "exults." But 41:16 makes clear that for DtIsa גִּיל is by no means a positive term. We may therefore ask whether there is not a tension in the present text. Up to the close of this act, "earth" (אֶרֶץ) could mean the underworld. It is compelled to join in the rejoicing with its own (false) notes, whether it likes it or not. Yahweh, to whom the hymn is addressed, is Lord over the whole world from the heavens to the depths, just as the mountains reach from the underworld to the heights. The music is part of the message, not merely an embellishment at its end.

This can also be heard as a topical theological program. If *Yahweh* is the God of heaven, this means conflict with the Persian imperial ideology. The assertion that Yahweh is Lord over the underworld as well acquires a sharper edge in contrast to the polytheistic environment, above all the underworld cults associated with Osiris, Demeter, and others, which in this period were taking on increased importance. The revelation on Sinai-Horeb manifests Yahweh as the God of the moun-

tains—but so does his association with Zion/Jerusalem. The hymn is a confession of faith.

The marked caesura in the dramatic structure at this point is shown, finally, by the close of v. 13. "Yes!" (כִּי) can be used emphatically.²⁵⁴ It introduces a kind of refrain. It sums up everything that has gone before in an easily remembered way. It is an active recollection (memorial), and it is supposed to be engraved on the minds of the people who listen to it. The first exodus from Egypt, the revelation of the law on Mount Sinai-Horeb, and the exodus from Babylonian exile are all linked together in a confessional formula. That is liberation and compassion for the poor. This is lament and jubilation simultaneously, in remembrance (זִכָּרוֹן *zik-kārôn*) of the "Servant without a name," Moses. It is also a reminder of the "servant Nehemiah." His name too is held in remembrance in the song praising Yahweh for his liberation of his people; this is the enduring proclamation. Nehemiah and his reform belong to the past. But God continues to have compassion on his poor and wretched human beings.

---

254 See R. Ishikawa, "Der Hymnus im Alten Testament und seine kritische Funktion" (diss., Munich, 1996).

"Zion" is the goal of longing and hope.[1] Zion is the place where God is present and people can live together in justice and peace. The idea of Zion exerts an enduring influence throughout the times, binding and separating. DtIsa contributed essential elements to this tradition. He is not the initiator of this tradition in the OT; his concern is the *renewal* of Zion/Jerusalem. Nor is he the last in the Bible to make a contribution to that tradition—right down to the Revelation of John in the NT where, in the vision of the heavenly Jerusalem, the divine sovereignty is depicted as the city of the future.[2]

In DtIsa's work 49:14 signifies a new beginning. From this point on, "Zion/Jerusalem" is the main figure, no longer "Jacob/Israel" as was the case hitherto, and in chaps. 41–44 especially. In this way DtIsa links two concepts with differing traditions—the idea of God's people as Jacob/Israel, and the idea of God's city as Zion/Jerusalem. It seems probable that the two themes were fostered by different groups and that they had different addressees. But both themes are already programmatically stated in the prologue to chap. 40 (see 40:1 and 2; cf. 51:16).

Just as in the first part there were tensions in the theme "Jacob/Israel," there are now tensions between "Zion/Jerusalem" as personification and statements about the real city of Jerusalem and its inhabitants. This is one reason for some of the exegetical difficulties.

As personification of the city, "Zion/Jerusalem" is set over against the figure of "Babylon." The movement in the texts is almost mirrorlike. Whereas Act IV, from chap. 46 onward, shows the descent of "Babylon," now—up through 52:10—the rise of "Zion/Jerusalem" from the depths of its humiliation is presented. This then finds its crowning conclusion in 54:11-14. The artistry of DtIsa's composition shows itself once more in these broadly sweeping lines.

49:14—50:1
Throne Scene: Yahweh as Judge and Ruler (Proem)

In the structure as a whole up to chap. 55, this section serves as a kind of proem. In this sense we can compare it with chap. 40. Here the themes of what follows are already announced: the restoration of the walls (cf. 49:16); the creation of living space (49:19); and then the return of the exiles (49:22-23) and the liberation of the prisoners (49:24-26). Overriding everything is the promise that Yahweh has not forgotten (שׁכח, 49:14) "Zion."

In this unit too the action that follows is probably a kind of trailer or preview. There is a direct address to various characters. Thus by way of simple demonstratives (v. 21: 3 times "these," אֵלֶּה) "Zion" can indicate different groups of "children/descendants." "See" in vv. 22-23 introduces the procession of homecoming sons and daughters, this too corresponding to chap. 40. For the listeners, this preview builds up the tension.

The text is clearly structured within itself. In the first unit, 49:14-21, there are three different variations on the theme of "Zion." Three "wonders" are announced:

---

1   N. W. Porteous, "Jerusalem-Zion: The Growth of a Symbol," in *Verbannung und Heimkehr. FS W. Rudolph* (1961) 235–52; J. Jeremias, "Lade und Zion: Zur Entstehung der Zionstradition," in *Probleme biblischer Theologie. FS G. von Rad* (1971) 183–98; B. C. Ollenburger, *Zion, the City of the Great King: A Theological Symbol of the Jerusalem Cult* (1987).

2   See D. Georgi, "Die Visionen vom himmlischen Jerusalem in Apk. 21 und 22," in *Kirche. FS G. Bornkamm* (1980) 351–72; idem, "Who Is the True Prophet?" in *Christians among Jews and Gentiles. FS Krister Stendahl* (1986) 100–126; idem, "Auf dem Weg zu einer urbanen Theologie," public lectures delivered at the symposium on "Protestantismus als integrative Kraft in der multikulturellen Gesellschaft" (typewritten record, Frankfurt University, 1991).

1. Vv. 14-16: Zion is a woman who has not been forgotten (v. 14).
2. Vv. 17-19: Zion will again look "like the bride" (v. 18).
3. Vv. 20-21: Zion, the childless one (v. 20), will have children.

The second unit, 49:22—50:1, is divided up by a triple use of the formula that also introduces the prophetic oracle: "Thus says Yahweh" (כֹּה־אָמַר יהוה, 49:22, 25; 50:1). These sayings too are declarations about the future. The first two end with what W. Zimmerli calls the "recognition formula": "You will know . . . [or: they will know . . .] that I am Yahweh" (vv. 23, 26). According to Zimmerli, the "statement of recognition . . . originally belonged in the context of symbolic events."[3] The recognition formula demonstrates "an original inclination to any context in which decisions are made or ambiguous situations are clarified by means of symbolic events." The sign "manifests from the very start a certain alternative character." If we apply these findings of Zimmerli to the present text, it may be said to contain three "signs":

1. 49:22-23: The return of the exiles.
   This is a salvation oracle for Zion.
2. 49:24-26: The liberation of the enslaved.
   This is also a salvation oracle for Zion.
3. 50:1: The declaration of the guilt of Zion's "children/descendants."
   This is an oracle of doom.

The recognition formula is missing at the end of the third sign. This leaves the text open. It ends with the description of the distress that is the consequence of the "children's" sin. In what follows Yahweh's power is demonstrated (50:3) and the event of Jerusalem's downfall is reconstructed (see esp. 51:17-21). These things make it possible for repentance and the perception of Yahweh to develop.

Analyzed in this way, the structure of the text also allows us to discern the theological program that it presupposes. But we should nevertheless note that the text clearly involves action too. These action elements have often been used as clues for determining the genre. As a whole, the unit 49:14—50:1 presents a throne scene in which Yahweh acts as judge and ruler. The chief "characters" are Yahweh and Zion. Various groups of people appear. These are brief partial scenes in each given case. In the progress of the drama, the action announced takes up more time than the spoken sections. 49:22-23 again offers the opportunity for a procession.

---

3   W. Zimmerli, "Knowledge of God according to the Book of Ezekiel," in *I Am Yahweh* (1982) 29–98, esp. 77 [*Erkenntnis Gottes nach dem Buche Ezechiel. Eine theologische Studie* (1954), reprinted in his *Gottes Offenbarung. Gesammelte Aufsätze zum Alten Testament* (1963) 41–119, esp. 95].

14 But Zion said:
Yahweh has forsaken me,
and my Lord has forgotten me.

15 Does a woman forget her baby?
Does she not have compassion on the child
of her womb?
Even if these forget
I do not forget you.

16 See, I have engraved you on the palms of
my hands,
your walls are always present to me.

17 Your descendants/<builders>[a] have hastened,
your "destroyers" and your "desolaters"
begin to depart from you.

18 Lift up your eyes all around and see:
They have all gathered and come in to you!
As I live, saying of Yahweh:
Yes, you will put them on like an ornament,
you will bind them round like the bride.

19 Yes, your ruins and your waste places
and your devastated land—
yes, now it will be too confined for its
inhabitants,
but your "swallowers up" are far away.

20 The descendants of your childlessness
will yet say in your hearing:
The place is too narrow for me!
Make room for me, so that I can sit
down/dwell!

21 And you will think to your heart/to yourself:
Who has borne/begotten me these, when I
am childless and barren,
exiled and put away?
And who has brought these up?
When I alone was left—
<and>[a] these, where were they?

17a בניך can be pointed both as בָּנַיִךְ, "your descendants" (as in MT), and as בֹּנַיִךְ, "your builders" (as 1QIsaᵃ, α′, Vg; cf. LXX, ϑ′, Tg). The ambiguity is probably intentional.

21a וְאֵלֶּה should probably be read instead of אֵלֶּה, following numerous manuscripts (cf. LXX, Tg, Vg).

A. 1. 49:14-16
Zion's Appeal as a Forsaken Wife to the Judge

"*I* do not forget you!" (49:15)

In my view, we should assume that the framework of the action is again a kind of judicial scene. Difficulties of interpretation arise because DtIsa is working with different levels of meaning simultaneously. On the everyday level, the scene begins when a woman appeals to the judge because her husband has left her. She is therefore taking him to court. H. J. Boecker describes this by saying that it is the "transition from the prejudicial accusation to regular court proceedings."[4] The woman is in a predicament. "Forsaken" (עזב) probably means that she has *not* been divorced; she is merely separated.[5] This puts her in a wretched position between marriage and divorce. If she is divorced, she can at least demand back her dowry (*mōhar*) and can return to her own family home, or can remarry. In this situation she needs clarification by the court.

---

4   H. J. Boecker, *Redeformen des Rechtslebens im Alten Testament* (2d ed. 1970) 47.

5   See H.-P. Stähli, "עזב *ʿzb* to abandon," *TLOT* 2:867

[*THAT* 2:250]: "The expression (*ʾiššâ*) *ʿazūbā* 'abandoned wife' occurs 3x in imagery (Isa 54:6; 60:15 par. *śnʾ* 'to reject [a woman]'; 62:4; cf. 49:14). *ʿzb*

If it is true that "in regular court proceedings . . . a woman had no right to speak or express an opinion,"[6] the text is making a subtle point when it turns the "judge" into an advocate.[7] It is he who transforms her personal appeal into regular court proceedings. It is not "Zion" herself who is speaking in v. 14; this is a quotation by Yahweh himself.[8] His public advocacy on behalf of a woman builds up the initial tension. What is going to happen now? This question has particular force in a male-oriented society. The unexpected then happens: the "Lord" (אָדוֹן) acknowledges his wife, and at the end of the scene, in 50:1, the accused turns into the accuser, who explicitly denies that a divorce has taken place.

On the initial level of everyday experience, the text is consistent. A further level of interpretation emerges for anyone who is familiar with the tradition of the lament over the downfall of Zion/Jerusalem, if not actually with a text such as Lam 5:17-21:

Because of this our hearts were sick, because of these
    things our eyes are dim:
because of Mount Zion, which lies desolate, on which
    jackals/foxes play.
But you, Yahweh, are forever, your throne from gener-
    ation to generation.
Why will you forget us (שׁכח) for ever, and forsake us
    (עזב) time without end?
Bring us back to yourself.

The devastation of Zion (cf. Isa 49:19) raises the question of Yahweh's forgetfulness and abandonment. An acknowledgment of sin (Lam 5:7, 16) is part of the lament, as is the plea for restoration of the former status (v. 21).

On this theological level, it is then noticeable that in 49:14 and 15 the key word "forget" (שׁכח) is used four times. In the OT "forgetting" is an important term or concept that is used to describe the abrogation from the human side of the relationship to God.[9] It is used in this way in Deuteronomy particularly, and in the literature dependent on it. Conversely, the promise of salvation includes the assurance: "Yahweh your God is a merciful God (אֵל רַחוּם). He will not forsake you and will not destroy you and he will not forget (שׁכח) the covenant with your forefathers that he swore to them" (Deut 4:31). Against the background of this well-established theological language, the promise in the present text "I do not forget you" (v. 15) emerges in its full import. The significance is expressed through the action. The husband has not "forgotten" his wife, any more than Yahweh has forgotten Zion.

But then the text initiates a further process of abstraction. Contrary to all experience, the writer maintains that a mother is more likely to "forget" her child than Yahweh is to forget Zion. This makes the exceptional quality of Yahweh's commitment plain.

But again, the small literary unit ends in v. 16 with the announcement of a quite practical problem. The city of Jerusalem has to be protected by walls. Only walls lend her legal status as a city. The historical dispute about

---

here probably means a temporary abandonment, neglect and, paralleled with śn', a rejection and disregard of others, although the textual evidence is hardly sufficient to support the conclusion that it is a fixed legal term for divorce, as it may clearly be shown to be in Akk."

6   Boecker, *Redeformen des Rechtslebens im Alten Testament* (2d ed. 1970) 63.

7   See here in ibid., excursus 3: "Der Hilferuf הוֹשִׁיעָה als Formel des alttestamentlichen Zetergeschreis" ["The cry for help הוֹשִׁיעָה as formula for a hue and cry in the OT"], 61–66: "The so-called 'hue and cry' is often used by a person with few rights, who is unable to gain a proper hearing in the legal community and therefore has recourse to this cry for help. It is therefore not by chance that, as the instances in the OT show, the 'hue and cry' was raised especially by women" (63). For texts Boecker

cites 2 Kgs 8:1-6; 4:1; 6:26ff.; Judg 2:11-19; 3:9, 15. He comes to the conclusion: "The מוֹשִׁיעַ (môšia') was the helper in time of need to whom the hue and cry was directed" (65). But this is precisely the title which Yahweh claims for himself in the present text 49:26!

8   If we think in terms of a scenic performance, then the triple i of the final vowels, which are also linked with the a sounds, would signal the high pitch of the women's voices. That "Zion" then still does not speak herself can be connected with the fact that in the ancient world women's roles in drama were generally taken by men. Thus, in the delicate situation described at the beginning of the present text, the intention could have been to avoid raising an involuntary laugh at the words "My lord has forsaken me."

9   W. Schottroff, "שׁכח škḥ to forget," *TLOT* 3:1325

this emerges from the book of Nehemiah, for instance (esp. 2:11–7:3). If the walls are always "before" Yahweh, he cannot forget them.

Commentators have continually puzzled over what is meant by saying that Zion is etched into the two hands, or palms. Some exegetes have thought of a kind of tattooing, either of Jerusalem's name or of the plan of the city. The objection is that Lev 19:28, for example, explicitly forbids tattooing. Others have suggested phylacteries as a comparison. I should like to suggest as a possibility that it is the lines on the palm that are meant, lines in which people thought they could discern the plan of Jerusalem: the wrist could be the north, the one side being the Kidron Valley, the other the Hinnom Valley. In the middle is then the "central" valley, with various ramifications, and the sharp bend-back of the wall. At all events, in this way the southeast and southwest hills could be distinguished—a simple but topographically conceivable map,[10] and one that everyone held in his or her own hand, so to speak—not least Yahweh. In this way the Lord's reacceptance of Zion and the rebuilding of the city are already linked in the very first unit. Both are "wonders."

A. 2.   49:17-19
Zion as "the Bride"—the New Settlement

"Yes, now it will be too confined for its inhabitants . . ." (49:19)

There is a close connection between these verses and the preceding and succeeding passages.[11] The interweaving of statements about the city (ruins, devastations,

v. 19) with statements based on its personification as "Zion" ("like the bride") is clear.

Acoustically, the striking sequence of ךְ- (-ek) and ךְ- (-ayik) sounds at the end of words is prolonged (from 49:15 through 49:21). But now new characters enter the scene: "descendants/<builders>" and "destroyers-devastators" (v. 17). From v. 17 onward, we can also clearly detect more action. "Zion" is told to "lift up her eyes all around and see" (v. 18). Dramatically, these are implicit stage directions: "They have hastened . . . they begin to depart from you" (v. 17); "they have all gathered, they come in to you" (v. 18). The question is whether the action takes place behind the scenes or on the stage. In favor of the latter assumption is the continuation in v. 21, with its triple demonstratives: "these (there) . . . ," where there is evidently no need to name the groups directly.

A textual variant in v. 17 is interesting. According to *BHS*, the MT is pointed בָּנַיִךְ, "your sons," but the emendation בֹּנַיִךְ, "your builders," has been proposed on the basis of 1QIsa[a], Aquila and the Vulgate, as well as the renderings in LXX, Theodotion, and the Targum. This would fit the immediate context better (antithesis "builders"-"destroyers"), whereas MT's reading accords better with the wider context, which has to do with the "sons" or "descendants." I think that this double interpretation may possibly be intentional, especially since we have the same problem in 54:13. Everyone can hear what is said in his own way. The question is whether the "descendants/<builders>" here are simply and solely the returning inhabitants of Jerusalem, or whether the

---

[*THAT* 2:902]: "In the theological usage of the OT *škh* applies to people, esp. in reference to Yahweh, but also in reference to Yahweh's demonstrations of salvation and saving acts in history, to his *bᵉrît* and his commandments. 'Forgetting' refers in these contexts less to the human act of remembering than to practical behavior: active turning away and opposition."

10   For archeologically attested examples of maps, see the clay fragment showing the drawing of a town plan of Nippur (c. 1500 B.C.E.), *ANEP* 80, 278 (no. 260); see also P. Lampl, *Cities and Planning in the Ancient Near East* (1968) 12 and figs. 16–18 with further examples (fragment from Nuzi, c. 2500 B.C.E., and the fragment of a plan of Babylon dating from the 6th century B.C.E.). Ezek 4:1 should probably be understood in a similar sense; see C. Uehlinger,

"'Zeichne eine Stadt . . . und belagere sie!' Bild und Wort einer Zeichenhandlung Ezechiels gegen Jerusalem (Ez 4f.)," in M. Küchler and C. Uehlinger, eds, *Jerusalem: Texte–Bilder–Steine, zum 100. Geburtstag von H. und O. Keel-Leu* (1987) 111–200. On the topography of Jerusalem see the drawing in A. H. J. Gunneweg, *Nehemia* (1987) 182: excursus by Manfred Oeming on the topography and archeology of Jerusalem.

11   On the text of 49:18-21 see D. Baltzer, *Ezechiel und Deuterojesaja* (1971) 169–70.

towns of Judah (40:9) are meant as well. If these towns are the children or sons of the "mother city" Jerusalem, that implies a connection and dependency. A relationship of this kind would inevitably have involved conflict. We need only think of our metropolises today (our word "metropolis" is derived from the Greek for "mother city").

The image that follows in v. 18 permits a similar ambiguity. "Zion" puts on her bridal ornaments once more. עֲדִי means "ornaments" in general. According to Ezek 16:11, 13, this was the way Yahweh adorned Jerusalem, but she was then unfaithful. The topos was therefore familiar. According to *HALOT*, קְשֻׁרִים are "ribbons, breast-sashes (of women) Is 3:20; Jer 2:32; for Is 49:18 קשר pi." The present text uses a verbal form of the root קשר. The Masoretic pointing gives an imperfect *Piel* with suffix: "You will bind her round." The apparatus in *BHS* records that a fragment from the Cairo Genizah reads the form as *Qal*. An examination of the concordance shows that although the *Qal* form of the verb can certainly mean "bind on," the more general meaning is "to combine or associate" in the political sense, to the point of "hatching a plot." The related substantive קֶשֶׁר also means "association, conspiracy" (see *HALOT*). The way the image is introduced in v. 18 lends it marked emphasis: Yahweh himself swears by his own life! The question is whether there is not a topical reference as well, beyond the image level. Why "ornaments" and not "conspiracy"?

The verb קשר occurs twice in a text whose theme resembles the text we are considering. In Neh 3:38 (4:6) (*Niphal*) it means the closing of the ring of walls surrounding Jerusalem, and in Neh 4:2 (8) (*Qal*) a conspiracy against the building of the walls. If the DtIsa and Nehemiah texts are read in parallel, a number of other points must be noted. The decision to build the walls recorded in Nehemiah (2:20: "The God of heaven will give us success") is immediately followed first of all by the list of the "builders" (הַבּוֹנִים 3:37 [4:5]; cf. Isa 49:17). Among other things, this is a list of the towns and regions in Judah from which people have come to help in the rebuilding of Jerusalem's walls. Neh 3:5 remarks: "Next to them the Tekoites made repairs; but their nobles would not put their shoulders to the work of their Lord"; so we see that the help given was not entirely a matter of course. We may ask which towns are missing

from this list. What emerges is the picture of a relatively small area.

Thus when we read in DtIsa (49:17), "Your descendants/<builders> have hastened," this is an astonishing piece of information. In Nehemiah the grouping in the political conflict is clear. Neh 4:1 (7) gives the names: "Sanballat and Tobiah and the Arabs and the Ammonites and the Ashdodites." This means that Jerusalem, and the Judean towns loyal to it, were almost entirely surrounded. Neh 4:2 (8) goes on: "And all plotted together to come and fight against Jerusalem (וַיִּקְשְׁרוּ כֻלָּם יַחְדָּו לָבוֹא לְהִלָּחֶם) and to cause confusion in it." In DtIsa this is replaced by a peaceful coming: "Lift up your eyes round about (סָבִיב) and see: all have gathered together, they have come in to you! (כֻלָּם נִקְבְּצוּ בָאוּ לָךְ)" (v. 18). The enemies depart, the "descendants" or "builders" move in. There is no report of any struggle. This peaceful coming instead of warlike action transforms an element in the tradition of the holy war.

DtIsa names no names. But we may ask whether the text is not ridiculing the names of Nehemiah's opponents, as is the case in 49:7: "Your pullers down"/ "destroyers" (מְהָרְסַיִךְ, v. 17). Neh 3:35 (4:3) gives us Tobiah the Ammonite's bon mot: "That stone wall they are building—any fox (or jackal) going up on it would break it down!" For "break down" Tobiah actually uses the word פרץ, but it is possible that he had the reputation of being a "breaker down."

"Your desolaters" (מַחֲרִבַיִךְ, *maḥᵃribayik* v. 17): in its more precise meaning the root signifies "dry out, to be without water and plants," and then in the *Hiphil* "dry out, lay waste, make desert." Neh 4:1 (3:7) talks about the Arabs (הָעַרְבִים *hāʿarbîm*). But עֲרָבָה is nothing other than "the desert, a region without water." Neh 2:19 and 6:1 also give us the name of Nehemiah's Arab opponent. He was a man called Geshem (גֶּשֶׁם or גַּשְׁמוּ). Geshem means "rain." If someone called Geshem is numbered among the Arabs, with their proverbially arid lands (cf. Neh 2:19; 6:1), this is probably a veiled political joke on the name.

"Those who swallow you up" (מְבַלְּעָיִךְ, v. 19): in the *Qal* בלע means "swallow up, swallow down." L. Koehler (see *HALAT* here) notes the amusing turn of phrase in Job 7:19: "until I swallow my spittle," that is, in a very short time. In the *Piel* it is used for the "swallowing up" of land (2 Sam 20:19-20) and of people (Hab 1:13; Ps 35:25; Lam 2:16; Qoh 10:12), also several times in the sense of "destroy" (Isa 25:7-8; Ps 21:10 [9]).[12] Sanballat (סַנְבַלַּט) is the third in the group of Nehemiah's opponents, and as the governor of Samaria certainly the most important. In this function he is also known to us from the Elephantine papyri. His Akkadian name *Sin-uballit* means "(the moon god) Sin gives life." According to the Elephantine texts, his sons were called Delayah and Shelemyah. So Sanballat is not necessarily a foreigner, since he gives his children names that include the element Yahweh. The distortion of סַנְבַלַּט *sanballat* into מְבַלְּעָיִךְ *mᵉballᵉ'āyik* is considerable, but it shows who is meant. The leaders and their people are together summed up as "pullers down," "destroyers" and "swallowers up." If these topical explanations of DtIsa's text are correct, they would give it a much more precise historical reference. Like political jokes in general, references of this kind are comprehensible only for a brief period.

The statements about Zion's enemies are closely interwoven with the rest of the text. "Break in, destroy" (הרס) is picked up again in v. 19; chiastically, "destroyed land" becomes "lays waste" (חרב), "devastation, ruins." "Your waste places" (שֹׁמְמֹתַיִךְ) is added as a third element. When it refers to what were once dwelling places, it means "to be empty of people, become desolate," and it always carries the sense of something uncanny. It is the second endorsed statement in Yahweh's oath (introduced by כִּי). What is important about it is that the town with its ruins, the forsaken settlements and the land (אֶרֶץ) are mentioned together. This is the situation.

Then the third statement (with כִּי) follows, as an intensification: "too confined for its inhabitants." This initiates a new theme, after the building of the walls, and it

is immediately set forward in v. 20, until the arc that reaches forward to the final section in 54:2 is completed. The problem—to put it in negative terms—is the inadequate population of the restored city. Yahweh swears "now" (עַתָּה), but the implementation is still to come.

A. 3.   49:20-21
Zion as "Mother City"

"See, I alone was left . . ." (49:21)

With the close of v. 19, the rulers who are hostile to Zion and their people have gone off ("and are far away . . ."). Here too the text itself contains indications of the action. With v. 20, the "descendants/children of childlessness" are gathered together—so many of them that the place is crowded. It is a brief scene, comparable with the scenes with the artisans. The tone is rough throughout. Ibn Ezra already pointed to Gen 19:9 in his interpretation.[13] There "the men of Sodom, both young and old, all the people to the last man" (v. 4), gathered together in order to force an entry into Lot's house, crying "Get out!" (גֶּשׁ־הָלְאָה, v. 9). The present text is also extremely tersely formulated with the same verb: "Move up!" (גְּשָׁה־לִּי). אֵשֵׁבָה can mean both "I want to sit down" or "I want to live here," "to settle." This is not the way people talk in polite Jerusalem circles, but it is the language of the "descendants-builders" (v. 17), who have hurried to the scene. The chorus shouts so loudly that it rings in Zion's ears (בְאָזְנָיִךְ), which does not mean that the jostling is not quite friendly. Everyone eagerly participates. As Dieter Baltzer has acutely observed,[14] the quotation is closely bound up with its context. In Yahweh's speech in v. 19 he says, "Yes, now it will be too confined for its inhabitants (תֵּצְרִי מִיּוֹשֵׁב)." This corresponds to "it (is) narrow for me" (צַר־לִי) on the level of the people. Factually it means the same thing. "The place" (הַמָּקוֹם) talked about by the people is again ambiguous. It can be translated "the space, the place," but it is also the term for Jerusalem (1 Kgs 8:30; 2 Kgs 22:16; Jer 7:3; 19:3), the

---

12   We cannot exclude the possibility that there is also an echo of בלע II *Pual*, "be informed," in the sense of "calumny" (cf. Ps 55:10 [9] cj.), and בלע III *Niphal*, "be confused," *Piel* "confuse," *Pual* participle "confused" (מְבֻלָּעִים), *Hithpael* "appear confused." For בְּלִיַּעַל in connection with chaos, see B. Otzen, "בְּלִיַּעַל *bᵉlīya'al*," *TDOT* 2:131–36, esp. 134 [*ThWAT* 1:654–58, esp. 656].

13   Ibn Ezra, 227 on this passage.
14   D. Baltzer, *Ezechiel und Deuterojesaja* (1971) 169.

place that Yahweh has chosen (Deut 12:5; 14:23, 25; 1 Kgs 8:29),[15] the place of the sanctuary (cf. Isa 60:13; Ps 24:3; Ezra 9:8).

Since it has now become clear that the content of the text, the plan for the building of the walls in 49:16, and the implementation of their building in 49:17 can be compared with Nehemiah's measures as recorded in the book of Nehemiah, it will be permissible to ask whether v. 20 does not also have to do with the increase of Zion's population ("space to live in") in the same context. According to Neh 11:1-2, a synoecism took place on behalf of Jerusalem:[16] "Now the leaders of the people lived in Jerusalem, and the rest of the people cast lots to bring one out of ten men to settle in Jerusalem, the holy city,[17] whereas the other nine (were to remain) in the villages. And the people blessed all the men who decided voluntarily to settle in Jerusalem."[18] The reason for this measure was that the population was too small (cf. 7:4) to meet the economic and defense requirements of the restored city. The mutual loyalty of town and country was to be encouraged. The link with the countryside also secured the city's supplies. The briskly cheerful tone in the DtIsa passage suggests that the city population was not wholly enthusiastic about the newcomers.

When the present text has the people streaming in, so that there is not enough room for them, this is intended as an encouraging sign of hope and an inducement to other settlers. The proem to the two following acts (which have to do with the restoration of Zion) sounds the theme that is then taken up once more from chap. 54 onward. According to the Nehemiah text, the synoecism initially affected the inhabitants of the surrounding towns and country communities. That may be important for an understanding of the following verse, 49:21.

The key word "childlessness" (root שׁכל) links vv. 20 and 21. Through a miracle, the mother who has lost her children will have children once more: that is the image.[19] But image and fact are closely connected when Zion is depicted as the mother city. The question is only:

who are her "children" here?

The text distinguishes three groups, pointing to each of them with the word "these" (אֵלֶּה). In 49:12 three groups coming from all corners of the globe are addressed. In spite of that, this text too has a specific point of reference with Syene-Aswan, if we remember the Jewish military colony in Elephantine.

If we assume that one problem about the refounding of Jerusalem was the integration of different groups, the first point to be considered on the basis of the text of v. 21 and its context is, who could be meant by these groups?

The first group are the people who have been "brought forth" (ילד) for Zion. The text is curious, however, for the verb is masculine in form, so that the translation would have to be: "Who has 'begotten' for me these people here?" On the other hand, J. Schreiner observes: "Since, however, the causative hiphil was available for the meaning 'beget,' the qal with the meaning 'bear' is reserved for women."[20] Most translations and commentaries go along with this explanation in their interpretation of the present text too. But, as we have so often noticed in DtIsa, the double meaning "beget" and "bear" could be intentional. A passage from the letter sent from Jerusalem by the prophet Jeremiah to the people who had been carried off to Babylon is interesting in this connection: "Take wives and beget sons and daughters (וְהוֹלִידוּ) and take wives for your sons and give your daughters husbands so that they may bear (וְתֵלַדְנָה) sons and daughters, so that you multiply there and do not decrease" (Jer 29:6). Here the writer is working with the double meaning of the root ילד, even if in different stems. Jeremiah's letter is concerned with the gōlâ, a term used here as a technical term for those in exile in Babylon.[21] In the same context, Jer 29:10 announces the return from Babylon "after seventy years." In the present DtIsa text (v. 21), "Zion" is given the appellation "the exiled one" (גֹּלָה gōlāh) and she sees the "children" who have returned—that is, she sees the fulfillment of the

---

15 H. Koester, "τόπος," *TDNT* 8:187–208.

16 Following Gunneweg's translation in *Nehemia* (1987) 140.

17 לָשֶׁבֶת בִּירוּשָׁלַם עִיר הַקֹּדֶשׁ.

18 הַמִּתְנַדְּבִים לָשֶׁבֶת בִּירוּשָׁלָם.

19 See Bonnard, 226 on this passage: "our French language uses the word 'orphans' to designate children who no longer have any parents; it is short of vocab-

ulary to describe parents who no longer have any children."

20 J. Schreiner, "ילד yālad," *TDOT* 6:77 [*ThWAT* 3:634–35].

21 Verse 4: לְכָל־הַגּוֹלָה אֲשֶׁר־הִגְלֵיתִי מִירוּשָׁלַם בָּבֶלָה; cf. vv. 1 and 7. See H.-J. Zobel, "גֹּלָה gālāh," *TDOT* 2:476–88 [*ThWAT* 1:1018–31]: "The Heb. nouns *golah* and *galuth*, which the LXX usually translates

promise. The return is then actually implemented in vv. 22 and 23. It would seem obvious to see this group of "children" as the people who have returned home from exile in Babylon.[22]

The second group are those who "are made great/have been brought up" (גֻּדָּל).[23] The people meant by this group could be implicit in Zion's declaration: "I only was left (נִשְׁאַרְתִּי)." The declaration about the "remnant" (שאר) is an important theologoumenon that was intended to help the people to come to terms with the collapse of national existence and the exile, both in the negative sense (seeing them as judgment: "only a remnant remains") and in the positive one (as a sign of hope).[24] The concept has above all been developed in the book of Isaiah in its present form. Right at the beginning of the book (chap. 1) we are told: "Your country lies desolate (שְׁמָמָה), your cities are burned with fire . . . Daughter Zion is left (וְנוֹתְרָה) like a booth in a vineyard" (vv. 7-8). Here Isaiah, like other writers too, can use both שאר and יתר for "remnant."

According to this text, Jerusalem "is left," over against the country towns. But can we deduce from this that because of the downfall of the capital and the duration of the exile the situation had become reversed? The country towns have "become larger"! In the interpretation of 49:17-19 I tried to show on the basis of the building lists in the book of Nehemiah that it was the help of the people in the country towns especially that made the rebuilding of Jerusalem's walls possible. This group would accordingly have already been presented in the preceding text.

The third group designated are, "<and> these, where were they?" This is evidently a group not so readily identifiable politically as the gōlâ and those who have "grown up" in the land, but the group is nevertheless distinguished from the others ("these," אֵלֶּה). I should like to anticipate, and suggest that these are the people "enslaved for debt" who are mentioned in 49:24-26.

All three groups could certainly have been easily distinguished on their entrance by their appearance, clothing, and—as 49:20 showed—by their manner of speech. Socially they are totally different groups. To bring them together in spite of all the tensions was the task facing the rebuilders of Jerusalem; and it was a task that was both political and theological. Here too DtIsa's work emerges as a document of unification.

In favor of the thesis I have put forward, and as comparable model in its problems and solutions, I may point to Solon's new constitution for Athens as Aristotle describes it:

---

by *apoikesía*, 'emigration,' *metoikesía*, 'deportation,' or *aichmalōsía*, 'captivity,' mean 'exile' or 'those who are exiled, exiles,' and the same is true of the Biblical Aram. noun *galu*, 'exile.' They are derivatives of the root *glh* meaning 'to go into exile,' and are of as little help in determining the original meaning of this root as the occurences of *glh* in the other Semitic languages" (478 [1020]). "A brief word must also be said concerning the theological evaluation of the term *golah* in the Chronicler's work. The Chronicler also knows and uses the meaning 'exile,' 'exiles,' which was suggested above. But in Ezr. 9–10, he also connects *golah* with 'remnant,' and extends it to include the whole Jerusalem cult community in order to contrast it with the Samaritans" (487–88 [1031]); with reference to H. C. M. Vogt, *Studie zur nachexilischen Gemeinde in Esra-Nehemia* (1966) 158: "Those who belong to this cult community, repeatedly pardoned by God and established by God, are a part of 'those who returned home' and of 'the remnant.'"

22   The meaning of the cognomen "expelled" (סוּרָה)

can no longer be determined. It may be used in the sense of "displaced persons." According to S. Schwertner, "סור *sûr* to deviate," *TLOT* 2:796 [*THAT* 2:148]: "The many textual difficulties in MT in passages that use *sûr* are remarkable"; cf. among others Isa 17:1, in the saying about Damascus, "Cease to be a city" (?); see H. Wildberger on this passage, *Isaiah 1–12* (1991) [*Jesaja* 1–12 (2d ed. 1980)]; also Jer 2:21; 6:28; 17:13; Hos 4:18; 7:14). Are *gōlâ* and *sûrâ* subgroups of the people who were exiled or who emigrated?

23   See E. Jenni, "גָּדוֹל *gādôl* great," *TLOT* 1:304 [*THAT* 1:405]: "The pi. of *gdl* is mostly factitive 'to make great' (Gen 12:2; Num 6:5; Josh 3:7; 4:14; 1 Kgs 1:37, 47; Esth 3:1; 5:11; 10:2; 1 Chron 29:12, 25; 2 Chron 1:1)."

24   On שאר and שְׁאֵרִית see H. Wildberger, "שאר *š'r* to remain," *TLOT* 3:1284–92 [*THAT* 2:844–55] (with lit.), as well as J. Hausmann, *Israels Rest: Studien zum Selbstverständnis der nachexilischen Gemeinde* (1987).

And many sold away I did bring home
To god-built Athens, this one sold unjustly,
That other justly; others that had fled
From dire constraint of need, uttering no more
Their Attic tongue, so widely they had wandered,
And others suffering base slavery
Even here, trembling before their masters' humours,
I did set free.[25]

Problems today are not very different. It is only on the foundation of liberty that diverging traditions can be united.

---

25 Aristotle *Athenian Constitution* 12.4 (trans. H. Rackham; LCL, *Aristotle* XX; 1935, reprint 1971) 39; cf. also Plutarch *Solon* 15.5 (trans. B. Perrin; LCL, *Plutarch's Lives* I; 1914, reprint 1967) 445: "And of the citizens whose persons had been seized for debt, some he brought back from foreign lands, 'uttering no longer Attic speech, [s]o long and far their wretched wanderings; [a]nd some who here at home in shameful servitude were held' he says he set free." Cf. here also K. Baltzer, "Liberation from Debt Slavery After the Exile in Second Isaiah and Nehemiah," in *Ancient Israelite Religion. FS F. M. Cross* (1987) 482 and 484 n. 28.

22   Thus says the Lord Yahweh:
See, to peoples I will lift up my hand,
and to nations raise up my signal,
and they will bring your sons in their skirts,
and your daughters will be carried on
     shoulders.

23   And kings will have the care of you,
and princesses will be your wet nurses.
With their faces to the ground they will
     prostrate themselves before you,
and will lick the dust of your feet.

And you shall know that I am Yahweh;
those who hope for me will not be put to
     shame.

24   Can what a strong man has taken away[a] be
     taken from him?
And can the prisoner of a "righteous" man[b]
     escape?

25   Yes, thus says Yahweh:
Even the prisoner of a strong man can be
     taken away (from him)
and what a man of power has taken away[a]
     can escape.
And I myself will contend with the one who
     contends[b] with you,
and I myself will save your sons.

26   And I will let your oppressors eat their (own)
     flesh,
and they will become drunk with their (own)
     blood as with juice.

And all flesh shall know
that I am Yahweh, your savior
and your redeemer, the Mighty One of Jacob.

50:1   Thus says Yahweh:
Where is your mother's bill of divorce
with which I am supposed to have sent her
     away?
Or who is the one of my creditors
to whom I am supposed to have sold you?

See, because of your iniquities you were sold,
and because of your crimes/sins your
     mother was sent away.[a]

24a   Lit. "his booty," מַלְקוֹחַ. The noun derives from the same root
לקח as the verb (הֻ)יֻקַּח).

24b   1QIsaᵃ, S and Vg read עָרִיץ, "a man of violence, a tyrant." LXX
has ἀδίκως, "an unjust man." But MT clearly has the more difficult reading (*lectio difficilior*). With גִּבּוֹר (cf. 1 Chr 9:26) and
צַדִּיק, v. 24 is probably ironically echoing the self-descriptions
of particular persons or groups.

25a   See the comment on v. 24.

25b   Or should the plural be read ("with those who contend with
you") following a number of manuscripts and Vg (cf. S, Cairo
Genizah)?

50:1a   The root שלח is used twice in the text: the first time in the
legal sense of "release" (see *HALAT* 4:1402 on this passage,
on the *Piel*), the other time in the sense of "sent away" (see
HALAT 4:1403, on the *Pual*), probably in reference to the
exile.

B. 1.   49:22-23
The Return of the Exiles (Procession)

". . . those who hope for me will not be put to shame" (49:23)

The section 49:22—50:1 opens in vv. 22-23 with a salvation oracle. The homecoming of "sons and daughters" is
announced. The future form of the verbs suggests that
this is an event still to come. But at the same time the
opening "see" is striking, as well as the fact that what is
described is a continuous action: Yahweh's command—
the transport of the homecomers—then the *proskynesis* or
prostration. It is therefore worth considering whether

here too a kind of prologue is not being acted out (or could be acted out ad lib) in correspondence to what is said in the text. It is something like a "sign" for the event that in the drama begins with 52:11-12 (cf. 55:12-13) and is then expected to take place in reality. What is described is a kind of triumph, comparable to 40:9-11.

Babylon is not mentioned here. The text talks generally about the foreign peoples (גּוֹיִם *goyim*), and about peoples (עַמִּים) in general. Yahweh is Lord (אֲדֹנָי).[26] He has the right of command. A wave of his hand[27] and "his signal" (נֵס)[28] suffice. It is understood by the peoples too. The return home puts the world of the nations on the move. Thus this means more than the command to leave Babylon in 48:20.

As "sign," the text is an answer to the question that can be reconstructed from v. 23: "Will those who hope for Yahweh be put to shame?" The answer is no because Yahweh rules over the nations. Because of the bitter experience of severance from news about the home country—an experience shared by every diaspora—it is a welcome promise that Yahweh will give signals to the whole world.

One does not have the impression here that the return is taking place in the framework of warlike events. This is rather the picture of a great pilgrimage to Jerusalem. The foreign rulers, men and women both, come to pay homage.[29] They bring the homecomers with them, and see to it that they have every care.[30] That is a miracle, for this too would have been entirely contrary to everyday experience in the foreign land, where hope was often all that was left.[31]

But anyone who is carried by kings and princesses must through that very fact count as belonging to "the best society." The peaceful picture is intensified because it is the children who are carried home. Even this detail could indicate what could have been a problem, if the homecomers had been just the old people, who longed for their own country and who wanted to die and be buried in Jerusalem. But they are young people who still have the future before them, and who in the near future will have the task of reconstruction.

With regard to the performance: the group according to vv. 22-23 can easily be identified as one section of the chorus. Kings and princesses, especially foreign ones, are easily represented, as our own carnival processions today show. The children take part in the performance too. A procession of this kind, ending with the people falling on their faces in the *proskynesis*, must have been good fun.

B. 2.   49:24-26
The Ransoming from (Debt) Slavery

"Yahweh . . . , your savior and your redeemer" (49:26)

The text is closely bound up with its context. It is a brief scene that once more reveals DtIsa's supreme artistry. The situation is the same as it was at the beginning of the act, in 49:14: Zion is complaining to Yahweh. We probably have to *listen* to v. 24 in order to understand this fully. The verse has the *i* sound five times in a series of seven words in all. The first word is *hăyuqqaḥ*, and the half-line ends with *(mal)qôaḥ*. Here Zion is complaining

---

26 For discussion of the reading "my Lord" or "the Lord" see O. Eissfeldt, "אָדוֹן *'ādhōn*," *TDOT* 1:59–72, esp. 62–70 [*ThWAT* 1:62–78, esp. 67–75]. The reading "my Lord" would permit the text to be understood as a speech made by Zion (with reference to v. 14b). But in my view it is more probable that the three oracles are parallel to one another, stylized as an address by Yahweh.

27 See A. S. van der Woude, "יָד *yād* hand," *TLOT* 2:497–502 [*THAT* 1:667–74].

28 Cf. Isa 5:26; 11:10, 12; 13:2; 18:3; 30:17; 62:10. See here esp. A. Schoors, *I Am God Your Saviour* (1973) 109–10; Beuken, 63 on this passage.

29 For the practice of the *proskynesis*, see R. N. Frye, *The History of Ancient Iran* (1983) 142, esp. n. 7; M. A. Dandamaev and V. G. Lukonin, *The Culture and Social Institutions of Ancient Iran* (1989) 346 (414, 436) with reference to E. J. Bickerman,

"A propos d'un passage de Charès de Mytilène," *ParPass* 91 (1963) 241–55, esp. 252–53; and G. Widengren, "The Sacral Kingship of Iran," in *Sacral Kingship* (1959) 242–57. Cf. also the representation on the so-called black obelisk showing "Jehu, the son of Omri" [*sic*] falling at the feet of Shalmaneser III, *ANEP*, nos. 351, 355 (pp. 120, 122, and 290–91).

30 For kings as "nurses" cf. Num 11:12, in connection with Moses; also 2 Kgs 10:1; Esth 2:7.

31 See C. Westermann, "Das Hoffen im Alten Testament," in *Forschung am Alten Testament* (1964) 219–65.

even more than in 49:14, where there were only three *i* sounds. Here too one can ask whether Zion herself is speaking, or whether she is being quoted. But why does she continue to complain, even after she has been assured that her husband has not divorced her, and her children "are hastening" to her from far and near? For the glorious return from exile has just been announced in the immediately preceding verses (vv. 22-23). Some of the exiles are still missing, however: the third—and most difficult—group of "sons" and "children" (cf. 49:21).

Zion cries out her plea again, and Yahweh is invoked as savior and redeemer (v. 26: מוֹשִׁיעֵךְ וְגֹאֲלֵךְ).[32] The word "redeem" (גאל) is a first indication of the problem with which the text is concerned, the liberation of the people who have been enslaved because of debt.[33]

The procedure of invocation is described as if this is an inquiry put to an oracle. Zion asks, and receives a divine word. This probably drew on everyday experience too. A woman could visit a sanctuary or a prophet and ask for advice. The answer to the question "Can one . . . ?" could be either yes or no. In the present case, Zion is given a divine saying: "Even the prisoner of a strong man can be taken away (from him)" (v. 25a), which is then interpreted (vv. 25b-26a), in order finally to be proclaimed as a "sign" for humanity ("all flesh," v. 26b). Thus different levels of meaning are interwoven. This is also where the difficulties of the text lie. Once again, the text's point and esprit show themselves in the form of a textual problem.

"And can the prisoner of a 'righteous' man escape?" "Righteous man" (צַדִּיק) is the plain and unequivocal reading of the MT. It is undoubtedly the more difficult reading and according to the established rules of textual criticism is therefore probably the original version. 1QIsaᵃ has "man of power," עָרִיץ, parallel to v. 25, and this reading has been adopted by a whole series of translations, both ancient and modern.

But how can someone be "a righteous man" and still have prisoners? The text of Neh 5:1-13 is a good illustration. It describes how people in Jerusalem had to sell their children into slavery because they could no longer pay their debts (see esp. v. 5). Here Gunneweg writes in his commentary: "As a rule the complained-of giving of pledges, and even enslavement for debt, was legally incontestable, as the provisions in Exod 21:1-11; 22:25 (26); Lev 25:39 teach (for the practical application of these provisions cf. 2 Kgs 4:1). . . . Amos (2:6; 8:4, 6) and others like him had already protested against the misuse of such legally permitted possibilities."[34] In her complaint, Zion assumes that "the strong" have the law on their side, so that nothing can be done.[35] That is the reason why she appeals to Yahweh himself. In the divine answer "the righteous man" (צַדִּיק, *ṣadîq*) becomes "the man of power, the oppressor" (עָרִיץ, *ʿārîṣ*)—that is, the view taken of "righteousness" of this kind is plainly expressed. "Righteousness" is being viewed ironically, as the equivalent of violence. Luther's exposition of the commandment "Thou shalt not steal" in his Small Catechism: "nor acquire for oneself under the semblance of right," fits the case exactly. The words of Zion's complaint are taken up with this seemingly small change from "righteous man" to "man of power."

"Booty" (מַלְקוֹחַ) and "prisoners" (שְׁבִי) initially suggest warlike events. Consequently the text has been associated, more or less as a matter of course, with the exiling of the people. In Num 31:11-12, 26-27, 32, it is "the spoils of war" that are meant. But in the broadest sense the root לקח means "take, grasp, seize, take away." So the *Pual* as passive of the *Qal* can also mean "to be stolen" (e.g., in Judg 17:2). According to *HALAT*, שְׁבִי is

---

32 See here Boecker, *Redeformen des Rechtslebens im Alten Testament* (2d ed. 1970) 63–65.

33 See Baltzer, "Liberation from Debt Slavery After the Exile in Second Isaiah and Nehemiah," in *Ancient Israelite Religion. FS F. M. Cross* (1987), esp. 481.

34 Gunneweg, *Nehemia* (1987) 86 on this passage.

35 That may perhaps explain the phrase in Neh 5:5 that is so hard to translate: "Our hand is not our God." Gunneweg (ibid., 84, and note b on v. 5) translates in the sense of "We can do nothing about it." On "Can what a 'strong man' (מִגִּבּוֹר) has, be

taken away from him": The root גבר means "to be or become superior, strong" extending to: "be violent." The substantive גִּבּוֹר is used for the "warrior." From the time of the monarchy onward, the "warriors" were the members of the crack regiments. The term acquires the meaning "hero." It can be used in a transferred sense; cf. Ps 112:2; Isa 5:22; Ps 78:65. But above all, "strength" is also said to be an attribute of God. See Isa 9:5 (6); 10:21; Jer 20:11; 32:18; Zeph 3:17; Ps 24:8 cf. Deut 10:17; Neh 9:32. See J. Kühlewein, "גבר *gbr* to be superior," *TLOT* 1:299–302 [*THAT* 1:398–402].

"what is taken away as having been seized in war." But שְׁבוּת or שְׁבִית, especially in connection with the verb שׁוּב, becomes a technical term for "imprisonment for debt" or its termination.[36] The oscillation between a warlike and a judicial meaning is perhaps intentional: "the strong" wage war—even against their own people.

The answer given to Zion is a clear yes. This contravenes all human experience, according to which the strong are the victors. In approach it also corresponds once more to 49:15. In a second step, the answer leads to the implied question: How is this possible? The explanation is: because Yahweh himself conducts the case or trial. He does so, for example, by bringing an indictment. He can "save." "Lawsuit, action" (רִיב) fits the categories of a dispute in civil law better. It is a theme that DtIsa already touched on in 41:11, in connection with Jacob/Israel (cf. 42:22). It is developed further in the second part, in 51:12-16 and 54:14-15.

These sections form an artistically crafted oracle of salvation and disaster. R. P. Merendino has noted "the symmetrical structure of v. 25b." "The two half verses display the same sequence . . . , and every word or word formation begins with the letter *aleph*."[37] The result is six times א. The series is perhaps continued in v. 26. But the text is more complicated—in content too—than would at first appear.

The oracle of disaster (v. 26a) can include a curse such as the one in Deut 28:53-57 (cf. Lev 26:29). Jeremiah (19:9) and Ezekiel (5:10; 39:18-19) explicitly threaten that the people will eat human flesh, this being a sign of Jerusalem's most extreme necessity. Commentators frequently deny the authenticity of the sentence, because it does not fit in with the rest of DtIsa's theology. But perhaps here too he is interpreting prophetic tradition in an extreme form trimmed to his concrete situation. If the sentence is read against the background of a text like Neh 5:1-5, we find that there too the very same reproach is leveled against the "nobles and representatives"[38]—that they compel the lower classes and the impoverished to

give their children in pledge and to sell them into slavery. The reason, according to v. 2, is that "we must get grain, so that we may eat and stay alive." According to v. 5, the people affected argued, "Our flesh is the same as that of our kindred;[39] our children are the same as their children." Transferred to the DtIsa text, this would mean: what the impoverished citizens of Jerusalem and Judah are doing now—living from the money for the children they have given in pledge—will happen to the "oppressors"[40] too.

To "eat meat and drink wine" is really a sign of good living (see Isa 22:13; cf. Dan 10:3; Neh 5:18). The rich can afford this. But here DtIsa does not use the word for "wine" (יַיִן), as we should expect. According to 55:1, wine is poured out without payment at the final feast. But here the rare word עָסִיס is used instead.[41] It is generally translated as "sweet wine" or "grape juice." In the context the root עסס is more important for an understanding of the text. It means "tread down" (Mal 3:21). Thus what they are drinking is what has been "pressed out." This can also be a reference to the social situation. In our language too, "squeeze" can be used in the sense of pressure, or obtain by force; and "to squeeze dry" expresses ultimate extortion.

Finally "to be or become drunk" (שׁכר): with a minimal change of the verb's consonants—שׂ (*ś*) instead of שׁ (*š*)[42]—the word means: "They will have to hire themselves out." The verb is used in Hannah's hymn of praise in 1 Sam 2:5: "Those who were full have had to hire themselves out (נִשְׂכָּרוּ) for bread, those who were hungry cease 'to serve.'"[43] The relation between "the strong" (גִּבֹּרִים) and "those who have stumbled" (נִכְשָׁלִים, 1 Sam 2:4) is reversed.

This would give us a consistent interpretation of DtIsa's oracle of disaster in a particular social context. It would be a good example of the connection betweeen act and destiny. What "the strong" do will happen to them themselves. That DtIsa works with allusions as he does—allusions that those familiar with Scripture could

---

36 See *HALAT* s.v.

37 See R. P. Merendino, "Jes 49:14-26: Jahwes Bekenntnis zu Sion und die neue Heilszeit," *RB* 89 (1982) 321–69.

38 Thus v. 7; see Gunneweg's translation in *Nehemia* (1987) 84 and 87.

39 וְעַתָּה כִּבְשַׂר אַחֵינוּ בְּשָׂרֵנוּ.

40 For "oppress" (ינה) cf. Exod 22:20 (21) Lev 19:33;

25:14, 17; Deut 23:17 (16); Jer 22:3; Ezek 18:7, 12, 16; 22:7, 29; 45:8; 46:18.

41 Otherwise only in Joel 1:5; Amos 9:13; Cant 8:2 according to *HALOT*.

42 Cf. the famous "shibboleth" in Judg 12:6; there, however, it is the shift from שׁ (*š*) to ס (*s*).

43 Thus at least if one follows the reading in *BHK*

easily interpret—also speaks in favor of a tense political situation.

For his part DtIsa expounds this tradition and by so doing legitimates his message. Verse 26 ends: "Your redeemer (גֹּאֲלֵךְ) is the Mighty One of Jacob (אֲבִיר יַעֲקֹב)." By his time, this was certainly an old-fashioned title for God (cf. Gen 49:24; Isa 60:16; Ps 132:2, 5). It is strange that this particular title should crop up in the text here. But אָבִיר means "strong, mighty," originally probably "the bull." That Yahweh is "strong, mighty" is important in a context that talks about human beings who display their strength: compared with "mighty rulers," Yahweh is mightier still.

But it is noticeable that in the text—following the method of oracle interpretation—the title אֲבִיר ʾābîr, "strong man" (v. 26) is changed into אָרִיב ʾārîb, "I will fight a case" (v. 25). Only the two letters ב beth and ר reš are interchanged. This is the interpretive method used by the scribes. The interpretation can be paraphrased: by fighting the case, by saving, Yahweh is now "the strong one." But at the same time, in the mordancy of his social message, according to this text DtIsa was a faithful follower and exponent of prophetic tradition. Where his intervention on behalf of the weak of society is concerned, Amos, Hosea, and Jeremiah are not far off.

In comparing this passage with Neh 5:1-13, I should now like to go one step further. The resemblances to Isa 49:24-26 are not merely literary or a matter of tradition. We may also hazard that the historical circumstances were comparable too. The structure of Nehemiah 5 is similar. It starts with the lament of the people (v. 1): "Now there was a cry of lament (צַעֲקַת) of the people and their wives." In Isa 49:14 it is Zion who laments. The rest of the Nehemiah text deals with slavery as a consequence of debt. I have tried to show that the DtIsa text can also be understood in this light. It is then noticeable that where the DtIsa text promises that Yahweh will intervene in the legal action on behalf of Zion's "children" (אָנֹכִי אָרִיב, v. 25), the Nehemiah text runs (v. 7): "I entered into an action (וָאָרִיבָה) against the freemen (חֹרִים), the nobles and the governors, officials (סְגָנִים)." These are in fact the "strong." Nehemiah takes up the matter in the name of his God (v. 13) and gets the

assembly (כָּל־הַקָּהָל, v. 13) to pass a resolution about the remission of debts.

If from this point we look back at the proem in 49:14-21, the building of the walls, the settlement of the population and the remission of debts are three measures that we may deduce made Zion's new beginning possible. They are the very measures that Nehemiah is said to have implemented according to the book that bears his name. I therefore think that here too there may very well be a historical link with DtIsa.

In the dramatic structure, the proem acts as a kind of trailer or preview for what is to come. But it is not yet complete: the little scene in 50:1 is still to come.

B. 3.   50:1
The Establishment of Guilt

". . . because of your crimes/sins your mother was sent away" (50:1)

Salvation has been announced in two divine sayings (49:22, 24). Here the verdict "guilty" is once more pronounced, with the prophetic formula, "Thus says Yahweh." Previously the question discussed was whether help was possible, and if so how; now the question is again the reason for the disaster. DtIsa does not maintain any ideology of a new beginning bought at the price of the suppression and forgetfulness of guilt. This makes clear how undeserved the new turn of events is.

The connection with what has gone before is a close one. The scene is still the same as it has been since 49:14. Yahweh is presented as the judge who clarifies the facts of a case. Zion is no longer alone. Her children are there once more. Dramaturgically, this permits a kind of flashback to the beginning of the conflict between Yahweh and his people. The legal situation corresponds to 49:14, with the problem: is this a divorce or just a separation?[44] Apart from the difficulty that Yahweh plays the part of both judge and husband, the decision pronounced to Zion as wife is clear: her husband has not "forgotten" her—the two are not divorced. In 50:1, in my view, the same decision is passed on to the children: no bill of divorce exists.[45] It is conceivable that the children are claiming their mother's dowry on her behalf. But if

---

(חָדְלוּ עָבַד); cf. also *BHS* (חדלו עד?) and the commentaries.

44   See North (198): "separation, not divorce."

45   Cf. the bills of divorce from Elephantine: E. G. Kraeling, *The Brooklyn Museum Aramaic Papyri: New Documents of the Fifth Century B.C. from the Jewish*

the marriage still exists, they have no right to do so. The mother has been "sent away" because of the children's sins.[46] That would mean that the separation is only temporary, until the reason for it—the children's sins—has ceased to exist.

The second theme taken up from what has gone before is enslavement for debt. Now exile is viewed as the equivalent of being sold into slavery as a consequence of debt. Whether this was due to something for which the father was responsible or whether it was the fault of the children is disputed. This is clarified in a kind of trial, the presupposition being that if his debts have compelled the father to sell his children, then the father must have creditors. But the children cannot present them; they do not exist. The economic background is that in an emergency the children were given in pledge first of all. Only if the debtor still could not pay after a reasonable time was the "pledge" sold as a slave.

It is possible that children had a right to be redeemed if the father had the necessary financial resources. In the present text this case is explicitly excluded. The reason for the "sale," if one accepts R. Knierim's rendering of עָוֹן,[47] is the "wrongness" or "disorder" of the relationship between father and children. That is why they have been sold as slaves. But the children are responsible for this, not the father.

Neh 5:1-13 is the best illustration of the economic pro-

cedure "to give in pledge" (ערב, cj. vv. 2, 3) to the point of enslavement (עבד, v. 5). The argument that the father has not the necessary capital to redeem the sons and daughters also plays a part. "Our fields and our vineyards belong to others" (v. 5). The key word "hire out" (נשא) to the point of "profiteering"[48] can be found in Neh 5:7, 10-11, as in the present text Isa 50:1, "my creditors." Neh 5:1-13 is the same text on which we already drew for the preceding verses, 49:24-26. That would mean that the listeners were fully familiar with the legal background. It was everyday reality. The only question is whether a person was one of the "strong" ("just," v. 24) or one of the "weak." But if this is the situation—and it was in fact the situation before the exile—then have "Zion's children" any claim against their "father"?

The irony and tension of this text can hardly be exceeded. Separation or divorce in the case of the mother (Zion); the guilt of the father or of the children—the two cases are artistically and chiastically interwoven. In both of them the conclusion ("see," הֵן) is that the children are guilty in every respect. No contradiction follows. The question is: what happens now? This is the appropriate end of the proem. "You were sold" and "your mother was sent away" probably also indicate the exit of the chorus, which represented Zion and the children.[49]

Colony at Elephantine (1953); see no. 2, esp. ll. 7-9, and no. 7, esp. ll. 21-28, 30-40; B. Porten and A. Yardeni, eds., *Textbook of Aramaic Documents from Ancient Egypt: Newly copied, edited and translated into Hebrew and English,* vol. 2: *Contracts* (1989), see B 2.6; A. Cowley, ed., *Aramaic Papyri of the Fifth Century B.C.* (1923, reprint 1967) 15, esp. ll. 22–36. See here M. Fander, *Die Stellung der Frau im Markusevangelium. Unter besonderer Berücksichtigung kultur- und religionsgeschichtlicher Hintergründe* (1989) esp. 215–33 (with lit.).

46 It is striking that in the oracle of disaster that Micah pronounces over the cities of Judah (Mic 1:10-16) it is said that Lachish was "the quintessence of transgression" (רֵאשִׁית חַטָּאת) for the daughters of Zion, and that in Lachish are found "the sins of Israel"

(פִּשְׁעֵי יִשְׂרָאֵל, v. 13). Verse 14 goes on: "Therefore there will be a 'dowry' (שִׁלּוּחִים) to Moresheth-gath." The text is difficult; see the commentaries on this passage, esp. A. S. van der Woude, *Micha* (1976). Is the double "send" (שלח) in the present text connected with "dowry" (שִׁלּוּחִים) (cf. also 1 Kgs 9:16; Exod 18:2)? Cf. further M. Delcor and E. Jenni, "שלח *šlḥ* to send," *TLOT* 3:1330–34 [*THAT* 2:909–16].

47 See "עָוֹן *ʿāwōn* perversity," *TLOT* 2:862–66, esp. 864 [*THAT* 2:243–49, esp. 245]. Also *HALOT* s.v.

48 See *HALOT* here; cf. Deut 15:2; 24:10, 11; Jer 15:10; Isa 24:2; 1 Sam 22:2; 2 Kgs 4:1; as well as Exod 22:24 (25); Ps 109:11.

49 Cf. O. Taplin, *The Stagecraft of Aeschylus* (1977), with the investigation indicated by his subtitle: *The Dramatic Use of Exits and Entrances in Greek Tragedy.*

"The Lord Yahweh has given me the tongue
of the learned . . ." (50:4)

50:2-3
Appearance of the Servant of God

50

"Why did I come in and no human being is
there . . . ?" (50:2)

2   Why did I come in and no human being is
        there?
    Why did I call and no one answers?

    Is my hand really too short to deliver?[a]
    And have I no power to save?

    See, with my rebuke I can dry up the sea,
    I can make rivers into a desert—
    their fish will rot without water,
    <the hippopotamus/crocodile>[b] dies of
        thirst.

3   I clothe the heavens in darkness
    and make sackcloth their clothing.

2a   LXX (τοῦ ῥύσασθαι; cf. Tg, Vg) presupposes מפדות as the
infinitive of פדה with מן (מִפְּדוֹת, "to ransom," instead of
מִפְּדוּת).

2b   It has been suggested that after MT וְתָמֹת," "and die of thirst,"
בְּהֶמְתָּם, "their beasts," should be added (see *BHS*). Instead I
would propose the addition בְּהֵמוֹת, "hippopotamus/croco-
dile." In the context of sea and rivers, this would preserve the
parallelism to the fish. See below on the text.

Many commentators find themselves at a loss with the
beginning of v. 2: "Why did I come in and no human
being is there?"—if indeed they grapple with the difficulty of these sentences at all. Who is coming where? Why
is he alone? F. Delitzsch makes an interesting suggestion
when he links Yahweh's coming with the coming of
"Yahweh's Servant."[50] The relationship between Yahweh
and the Servant here and in the following text requires
closer clarification, however. It is one of the passages in
which I believe that to define the whole as a liturgical
drama can be helpful for an understanding of the text.
Here too there is a striking similarity to the mystery
plays.

Isa 50:1 concludes the proem to 49:14—52:10. After
the chorus and Zion have gone off, the stage is empty.
There really is "no human being there" any more when
the "Servant" comes in (בָּאתִי), that is, enters the stage.
He is now the main character, until Jerusalem "stands
up" (קוּמִי) in 51:17. To be more exact, Jerusalem, presented as a woman (as the feminine forms indicate), is
briefly addressed beforehand in 51:12: "Who are you?"
(מִי־אַתְּ). Between these two verses it is either the Servant

or Yahweh who is speaking. With the confession
"Yahweh Sabaoth is his name" the Servant of God disappears again to the place from whence he has come. The
Servant of God text III therefore extends from 50:2
through 51:16.

But where does the Servant come from? The comparison with 48:16 suggests that it will be permissible to
assume that in 50:1 we also have an appearance of the
Servant of God. The appearance in 48:16 is followed
only in 49:1-6 by the second Servant of God text (if we
apply the traditional division); but it is probably more
closely bound up with its context than is often assumed.
The same is true of our present passage too, only here
the third Servant of God text (traditionally 50:4-11)
begins already with v. 2.

In 48:16 too Yahweh's speech and the speech of the
Servant can hardly be separated from each other.
According to 50:2 the Servant must "come in." Yahweh
is still present, following the preceding scene. But, as the

50   Delitzsch on this passage: "For there is One who
     speaks, and who should it be except Yahweh's
     Servant, who elsewhere in these speeches too is

introduced with dramatic immediacy as speaking
himself? That is to say: in his Servant, Yahweh himself has come to his people. We know who this

Servant rightly says,[51] he is not a "man," a "human being" (אִישׁ) The spectators are of course "there." So the first two questions can be assigned to the Servant. According to these questions, he himself does not know how he has come to be where he is.

Yahweh himself at once gives the answer with a double question: "Is my arm really too short . . . or have I no strength?" The implied answer is: "Yahweh's hand reaches so far . . . and he has strength!" But where to, and what for? The translation "to ransom or free" (מִפְּדוֹת) and "to deliver" (לְהַצִּיל) is not wrong, but it is apt to obscure the point, if we are concerned about the consistency of the statements in these two verses.

C. R. North gives us a clue with his awareness of the violent tone of לְהַצִּיל; the sense is roughly "snatch away."[52] But who is being snatched from whom? A comparison can be of help at this point. On the appearance of Darius in Aeschylus's *Persians*, the text runs:

> But it is no easy journey out of those regions below.
> Not in any circumstances, and the gods
> below the earth are more skilled in seizing than
>   releasing.[53]

The present DtIsa text probably also has to do with the underworld, as we can see from the immediate continuation, with its parallelism of "sea" and "rivers." Here we should think above all the language of the Psalms.[54] Ps 93:3-4 describes the waters of the primordial flood, and in Jonah 2 Jonah sinks into the depths. According to Ezek 26:19-21, the primordial flood (תְּהוֹם) and "many waters" overwhelmed the city of Tyre before it "went down . . . to the land of the deep below, among those who have gone down to the pit."[55] But so that we notice in the present text that we have to do with the realm of the dead, the stinking fish are explicitly mentioned.[56] Once sea and rivers dry up, the way out of the underworld is open.

The text is again a dispute with the cults of the underworld and its gods. Yahweh's hand reaches into the underworld[57] and his "strength" (כֹּחַ) extends over the whole world.[58] That is why in hymnic fashion the text mentions the two extremes "sea" (for the depths), and "heavens" (for the heights). The possibility that there is an intentional reference to creation and the exodus cannot be excluded.[59] But I would see no alternative here; such deliberate ambivalences are characteristic of DtIsa's method.

Yahweh himself enables the Servant to appear. A comparison with the conjuring up of the dead in Aeschylus's *Persians*[60] again reveals both similarities and differences. There the invocation is preceded by sacrifices and above all by libations made by the Persian queen mother and

Servant of Yahweh is, in the historical fulfillment" (2:276 [514]) [trans. altered].

51 Beuken offers a fine translation:
"Why is no one now there, when I come?
[Why] does no one answer, when I call?"

52 North (200) on this passage: "*to set (you) at liberty.*] A mild translation of a vb. (*haṣṣîl, Hiph.*) which commonly expresses forcible capture, snatching away (Gen. 31:9; 1 Sam. 17:35; Amos 3:12). For *hiṣṣîl* || *pādāh* see not only here, but Jer. 15:21: 'I will snatch you from the hand of the wicked and rescue you from the grasp of the ruthless.'" For פדה "ransom, liberate" cf. also Ps 49:16 (15); Job 33:28; Sir 51:2 (Heb.).

53 Aeschylus, *Persians* 688–90.

54 N. J. Tromp, *Primitive Conceptions of Death and the Nether World in the OT* (1969) 59–66; D. M. Gunn, "Deutero-Isaiah and the Flood," *JBL* 94 (1975) 493–508, esp. 499–501. See also O. Kaiser, *Die mythische Bedeutung des Meeres in Ägypten, Ugarit und Israel* (3d ed. 1962).

55 See W. Zimmerli, *Ezekiel* 2 (1983) [*Ezechiel* 2 (1969)]

on this passage.

56 *BHS* suggests interpolating בְּהֶמְתָּם, "their beasts," in parallelism to "fish." Could the word בְּהֵמוֹת also have stood here? This was the name given to the hippopotamus (*Hippopotamus amphibius*). It would fit in better with "rivers." Job 40:23 says of the hippopotamus: "Even if the river is turbulent, it is not frightened; it is confident though Jordan rushes against its mouth." See G. Fohrer, *Hiob*, on this passage. I myself would only suggest that in view of the present DtIsa text "Jordan" should not be expunged. For the hippopotamus as an animal belonging to the deities of the underworld, see L. Störk, "Nilpferd," *LÄ* 4 (1982) 501–6. Other commentators assume that בְּהֵמוֹת, as "mighty beast," means the crocodile; see *HALOT* s.v.

57 Cf. Pss 18:17 (16); 139:7-10; 144:7.

58 Cf. Isa 40:26, 29, 31; 41:1 (see above on these passages).

59 Cf. also the first and ninth plagues in the exodus (Exod 7:14-25; 10:21-29).

60 See also R. M. Hickman, "Ghostly Etiquette on the

Darius's wife, Atossa.[61] The chorus laments and invokes the gods of the underworld and the spirits of the dead. In Isa 50:2 the Servant appears completely unexpectedly. The external accompaniments, thunder ("my upbraiding," v. 2) and smoke ("darkness," v. 3), come only later. Yahweh acts. He does not allow himself to be conjured up. But the degree to which DtIsa ventures into this dispute with his time becomes clear from small details. The ending "-ayim" in mayim ("waters," v. 2) and šāmayim ("heavens," v. 3) again suggests that in the hymnlike section vv. 2b-3 from "see" (הֵן) onward there were several repeats.[62]

K. van der Toorn has pursued traces of the calling up of the dead in the OT,[63] and has drawn attention to the resemblance between the sounds that spirits make and bird calls. Isa 29:4b is an example: "And your voice (will come) from the underworld (מֵאֶרֶץ mēʾereṣ) like a ghost, and out of the dust your speech will chirp (תְּצַפְצֵף tᵉṣaphṣēph)." Here ṣpp Pilpel is obviously meant to be onomatopoeic. According to Isa 38:14 (cf. Jer 8:7) it echoes the call of the swift (סִיס or סוּס, L. Apus apus)[64] or the bulbul (עָגוּר, Bulbul pycnonotus Reichenovi). In rereading the present text of Isa 50:2, or in listening to it, one is struck by the sequence: wᵉʾên . . . wᵉʾên . . . wᵉʾimʾên . . . hēn ... mēʾên, perhaps with a preceding or following i-sound. Is this an imitation of spirit/bird calls?[65] Should the sounds be interpreted by translating: "not . . . not . . . if not . . . see . . . of nothing," so that there is a series of negations? Or are these just incomprehensible sounds, like those uttered by the chorus in the Persians: ἠέ . . . ἠέ . . . οἳ . . . οἳ . . . αἰαῖ . . . αἰαῖ (652–73)?[66]

The theater of course offers possibilities for representing thunder (which is the way Yahweh's "upbraiding" [גְּעָרָה] is to be understood), while clouds of smoke could produce the darkness (קַדְרוּת); but apart from that, we are left only with a realization of how little we can probably appreciate the text's finer points. At all events, after this prelude the tension has been sufficiently prepared: the Servant can now begin his speech.

Classical Stage," ISCP 7 (1938), esp. 17–31; S. Eitrem, The Necromancy in the Persians of Aeschylus, SO 6 (1928) 1–16. The comparison with the 11th book of Homer's Odyssey is important ("Nekyia").

61   Aeschylus, Persians 597–680.
62   H. Hickmann, Musikgeschichte in Bildern, vol. II/1: Ägypten (1961) 84.
63   K. van der Toorn, "Echoes of Judaean Necromancy in Isaiah 28,7-22," ZAW 100 (1988) 199–217.
64   See HALOT; also L. Köhler, "Hebräische Vokabeln I," ZAW 54 (1936) 288–89. Others believe that סִיס is the swallow.
65   Cf. W. G. Lambert, "The Sultantepe Tablets IX: The Birdcall Text," AnSt 20 (1970) 111–17. In the texts, particular birds are assigned to particular gods, and their calls are interpreted. For example, the text KAR 124, recto, l. 3, says of the swallow: "The swallow is the bird of Zû / Baʿu [its cry is] 'Who crosses the sea' (Tiāmat)[. . .]."
66   Cf. the Basel crater; see M. Schmidt, "Dionysien," in Antike Kunst, 10.Jh. (1967) 70–81. "As they walk the young men sing a choric song. Single letters issue from their open mouths . . . the legible letters are the vowels I E (issuing from the mouth) in the case of the middle couple; perhaps the cry ἰή, familiar from dithyramb and paean" (71 with n. 4).

50

"Who among you fears Yahweh, listens
to the voice of his servant . . . ?
He trusts in the name of Yahweh" (50:10)

4   *The Lord*[a] *Yahweh* has given me the tongue
       of a disciple/scholar,
   so that I may know how <to answer>[b] the
       wearied with a word.
   He wakes me in the morning,
   in the morning he wakens my ear,
   so that I may hear like the disciples/the
       scholars.

5   *The Lord Yahweh* has opened my ear,
   and I was not intractable.
   I did not draw back.

6   I gave my back to those who smote me,
   and my cheeks to those who plucked out.[a]
   I did not hide[b] my face
   from insults and spitting.

7   *But the Lord* will help me <or: continually
       helps me>,
   therefore I have not been not put to shame,
   therefore I have made my face (hard) like flint.
   And I know that I shall not be put to shame.

8   The one who vindicates me is near.
   Who will contend with me?
   Let us stand up together!
   Who is my opponent in the case?[a]
   Let him come here to me!

9   *See, the Lord Yahweh* helps me.
   Who is it who could put me in the wrong?
   See, they all fall to pieces like a garment,
   the moth will eat them up.[a]

10   Who among you fears Yahweh,
   listens to the voice of his servant,[a]
   who has gone through darknesses
   and no light lights him?
   He trusts in the name of Yahweh
   and relies on his God.

11   *See,* you all fan fire,
   <kindle>[a] firebrands.
   Go into the embers[b] of your fire
   and into the firebrands (arrows) that you
          have kindled.
   You have this from my hand.
   You shall lie down in the place of torment.

4a   Or should אֲדֹנָי אֲדֹנָי, "*my* Lord," be read here and in this whole textual unit?

4b   Thus with a correction from לָעוּת ("to support"?) to לַעֲנֹת.

6a   Instead of לְמֹרְטִים, "the pluckers out," from מרט, "pull or pluck out" (e.g., hair, Ezra 9:3; Neh 13:25), 1QIsa[a] has למטלים. The root מטל has to do with "forge iron." It has been suggested that the word should be derived from טלל II, "injure" (see *HALOT*).

6b   1QIsa[a] הסירותי, "turned away."

8a   בַּעַל מִשְׁפָּטִי, "the master of my rights" or "my lawsuit, legal action."

9a   Or should the second person plural be read, with LXX: "*You* all fall to pieces like a garment, the moth will eat *you* up"?

10a   Or: "Let anyone among you who fears Yahweh listen." LXX (ἀκουσάτω; cf. S) presupposes יִשְׁמַע, "let him hear."

11a   Thus with a correction from מְאִירֵי ("prepares"?) to מְאַזְּרֵי (cf. S).

11b   LXX (τῷ φωτί; cf. S, Vg) reads בְּאוֹר, "into the light."

So that there can be no doubt at all as to who has appeared here, the first saying begins: "the *Lord,* Yahweh."[67] "The *Servant* of Yahweh" is the correspondence, even if this is not expressly said. "The Lord, Yahweh" is repeated three times in what follows (vv. 5, 7, 9), linking the smallest units of this text together.

Verses 4-11 cover the first of three speeches made by the Servant, who has now appeared. Two others follow in 51:1-3 and 51:9-11. The first speech serves to identify the Servant. In form, it is a piece of autobiography.[68] The piece is more closely connected with its immediate context and the book of DtIsa as a whole than I previously realized. Thus this text is already heralded in the prologue, in 40:14, by way of the key word "learn" (למד).[69] In defining the situation, we should note that here a human being is talking to the assembled listeners after his death. In spite of all the textual difficulties, the tripartite structure is obvious. First the Servant presents his task and his authority (v. 4).[70] Then he tells what has happened to him (vv. 5-8). Blessing and curse form the conclusion in vv. 9-11.

■ **4** What is said makes clear that the one who is introducing himself here is a "teacher." His function is to speak and to listen. He is himself a "disciple," "a scholar" (למוד),[71] and he passes on that which he has heard from his Lord and master. He is not just any teacher; he has a direct relationship to God himself. There is no higher rank. It is also important that he has been given a divine word not only once but "every morning." This indicates the continuity of his office.

Now the term "disciple, scholar" (למוד) is not common in the OT. In 54:13 the term is evidently picked up again. There Zion/Jerusalem's "children/descendants" are supposed to become once more "pupils taught by Yahweh." Isa 8:16 suggests that there was a teacher-pupil relationship in the framework of the prophetic institution,[72] and on the basis of what has already been said the Servant's position and function permit a comparison with the prophetic office. This impression becomes stronger still if vv. 5-11 are added, for these are statements that recall the installation of prophets—for example, the divine words heard by and spoken to Jeremiah (Jer 1:7, 9) and Ezekiel (Ezek 3:10). When the face of the prophet who is treated with such hostility is said to be as hard as flint (v. 7), this echoes the comparison found in Jer 1:18 and in Ezek 3:8-9.

Above all, however, in explaining the DtIsa text commentators have continually drawn on Jeremiah's confessions.[73] As genre, these confessions are the prayers of complaint of a person falsely accused. They are not merely concerned with Jeremiah's person; they have to do with his prophetic function. A comparison allows us to perceive the most important themes in the present text:

---

67 See here O. Eissfeldt, "אָדוֹן ʾāḏōn," TDOT 1:59–72, esp. 62, 70 [ThWAT 1:62–78, esp. 66, 76].

68 See K. Baltzer, "Zur formgeschichtlichen Bestimmung der Texte vom Gottesknecht im Deuterojesaja-Buch," in Probleme biblischer Theologie: FS G. von Rad (1971) 27–43.

69 "And he taught him knowledge" (וַיְלַמְּדֵהוּ דָעַת); see K. Baltzer, "Jes 40,13-14—ein Schlüssel zur Einheit Deutero-Jesajas?" BN 37 (1987) 7–10. Also E. Jenni, "למד lmd to learn," TLOT 2:646–48, esp. 648 [THAT 1:872–75, esp. 875]; A. S. Kapelrud, "לָמַד lāmad," TDOT 8:4–10 [ThWAT 4:576–82].

70 I think it possible that "he [Yahweh] wakes me in the morning" is one of the dramatic indications of time, comparable with 40:26, where the evening, or the night, is announced by way of a reference to the stars (see above on this text; cf. also 51:9, 17; 52:1, 7). It would mean that the appearance of the Servant takes place in the morning, when he "is woken." See B. Janowski, Rettungsgewissheit und Epiphanie des Heils. Das Motiv der Hilfe Gottes "am Morgen" im Alten Orient und im Alten Testament, vol. 1: Alter Orient (1989). J. Schreiner, "עור ʿwr," ThWAT 5:1184–90, esp. 1185. עור has the basic meaning "'excite,' in the sense of 'to become or to make active,' so that someone or something enters into activity and remains active. . . . It is generally

YHWH who makes someone (or something) act." The word is used in the sense of "wakening from sleep" in Hab 2:19; Zech 4:1; Pss 44:24 (23); 73:20; for the connection with death, the realm of the dead, cf. Isa 14:9 and Job 14:12. The transferred meaning of "awakening the ear" must be distinguished from this. There is not necessarily a dittography here, as many commentators assume.

71 Is the "tongue of a disciple" a correction of the "slow tongue" (וּכְבַד לָשׁוֹן) attributed to Moses in Exod 4:10? The contrast to the "tongue of a wicked man, a mocker" should also be noted, see B. Kedar-Kopfstein, "לָשׁוֹן lāšôn," TDOT 8:23–33 [ThWAT 4:595–605].

72 Cf. the relationship between Elijah und Elisha (2 Kgs 6:1-7), and between Jeremiah and Baruch.

73 Jer 11:18-23; 12:1-6; 15:10-21; 17:14-18; 18:18-23; 20:7-13, 14-18.

- personal vilification and threats (vv. 5-6):
  cf. Jer 11:19;   15:10;   17:15;   18:18;   20:10
- the invocation of Yahweh and expressions of trust (vv. 7-8):
  cf. Jer 11:20;   17:14;   20:11, 13
- the judicial clarification of the accusations (vv. 8 and 9):
  cf. Jer 11:19;   15:10-11; 17:15-16; 18:18-20; 20:10
- the deflecting of the threatened fate on to the enemy (v. 9):
  cf. Jer 11:21-23; 15:15;   17:18;   18:21-23; 20:12

In the postexilic period the picture of "the suffering prophet" was clearly molded by the biography of Jeremiah. He became the prototype. There is no doubt at all that DtIsa has taken up Jeremiah traditions. They were of decisive importance for addressing and working through the catastrophe of Jerusalem and Judah, and thus for an understanding of the exile. The one who appears in DtIsa in chap. 50 bears all the marks of a prophet. But is he Jeremiah or someone else?

It is improbable that the four Servant of God texts (which are already heralded in 40:14) are talking about different "servants." These are pieces of a single biography, segments that belong together, from the Servant's installation until his death and what may be considered his elevation. But if, as I believe, the nameless Servant of the first and second Servant of God texts is "Moses," this identification must prove itself in the third Servant of God text too. The biggest surprise is then to discover that a number of pointers suggest that what is presented here is not just some random portrait of Moses; this is the Moses of Deuteronomy. We find a first indication of this in what has already been said, since for Deuteronomy Moses is a prophet (נָבִיא), even if in an exceptional sense. The end of Deuteronomy states explicitly (34:5, 10):

And there Moses the servant of Yahweh (מֹשֶׁה עֶבֶד־יהוה) died in the land of Moab, at Yahweh's command (עַל־פִּי יהוה). . . . Never since has there arisen a prophet (נָבִיא) in Israel like Moses, whom Yahweh had made familiar face-to-face (יְדָעוֹ יהוה פָּנִים אֶל־פָּנִים) . . . (see also the rest of the passage).

Something of this "familiarity" (to take von Rad's translation)[74] also emerges from DtIsa 50:4: "Every morning he awakens my ear." But according to Deuteronomy Moses is not merely a prophet; he is a teacher too.[75] That points us to the beginning of Deuteronomy: 1:1, "These are the words (אֵלֶּה הַדְּבָרִים) that Moses spoke to all Israel beyond the Jordan." And the text goes on: 1:3, "Moses spoke to the Israelites just as Yahweh had commanded him to speak to them." According to 1:5 Moses then began "to expound this law" (בֵּאֵר אֶת־הַתּוֹרָה הַזֹּאת).[76]

Isa 50:4 might be called a good summing up of this beginning of Deuteronomy, and in that book the key word למד is used in various forms with striking frequency.[77] The detailed exposition begins in Deut 4:1:

1 So now Israel give heed to the statutes and ordinances that I [Moses] am teaching you (מְלַמֵּד) to observe, so that you may live and enter and inherit the land . . . that Yahweh, the God of your fathers, will give you. . . .

5 See, I have taught you (לִמַּדְתִּי) statutes and ordinances as Yahweh my God has charged me [Moses].

10 Assemble the people for me, so that I may let them hear my words, so that they may learn (יִלְמְדוּן) to fear me as long as they live in the land, and may teach them (יְלַמֵּדוּן) to their children.[78]

A special point that may be mentioned here is that for practice hymns can be marked למד *Piel*, as is the Song of Moses according to Deut 31:19, 22 (see Deuteronomy 32). We shall come back to this in connection with Isa 51:1-3.

According to Deuteronomy, God's people is a community for learning and teaching. Moses is not merely "the prophet." He is "the teacher" too. In DtIsa, correspondingly, Yahweh himself teaches Israel (48:17), Moses is both a learner and a teacher (50:4), and, finally, Zion's "children/descendants" are "taught by Yahweh" (54:13).

---

74   See G. von Rad, *Deuteronomy* (1979) [*Deuteronomium* (2d ed. 1968)] on this passage.

75   See P. D. Miller, Jr., "Moses My Servant: The Deuteronomic Portrait of Moses," *Int* 41 (1987) 245–55.

76   On the verb בָּאַר *Piel* see *HALOT*. It otherwise occurs only in Deut 27:8 and Hab 2:2.

77   See E. Jenni's list in "למד *lmd* to learn," *TLOT*

2:646–48 [*THAT* 1:872–75]: "Of the total of 94 instances of the root, 27 fall to Ps[alms], 17 to Deut[eronomy], 15 to Jer[emiah], 13 to Isa[iah] (other books 0-3x)" (646 [872]). See also A. S. Kapelrud, "למד *lāmad*," *TDOT* 8:5–7 [*ThWAT* 4:578–79].

The roots of synagogue and church reach far back. If as teacher Moses' ear is opened again and again, then he did not receive only the Ten Words on the tablets as at Sinai; he proclaimed the whole law, precepts and statutes, as well as their interpretation as this is found in Deuteronomy.

If we reread the continuation in Isa 50:5-8 with the assumption that this is "Moses," we have to ask what stories of suffering are being thought of here. The tales about the "murmuring" in the exodus tradition come to mind,[79] especially Massah Meribah and Baal-Peor. But it is not easy to find any very precise reference to the physical threat referred to in 50:5-6, or to a court action, as in 50:8. Similar problems will meet us in Isaiah 53. One possible explanation might be that there were Moses traditions that have not been preserved in the canonical writings.

I think it probable that one factor may be early interpretations of the existing texts. Here some work would have to be done on the beginning of the exegesis in the OT itself. The opening of Deuteronomy, which we have already cited, says of Moses (1:12), "How can I bear all by myself the weight (טָרְחֲכֶם) and the burden (מַשַּׂאֲכֶם) of you, and your strife (רִיבְכֶם)?" If we look back, we discover that "strife" (רִיב) is a catchword from the story of the murmuring in Exodus 17. The people demand: "Give us water to drink" (v. 2), and Moses replies, "Why do you quarrel with me (מַה־תְּרִיבוּן)? Why do you test (תְּנַסּוּן) Yahweh?" This provided the basis for the aetiology of Massah and Meribah (v. 7). There are three references to this story in Deuteronomy (6:16; 9:22; 33:8), but the name Meribah has been expunged, unless there is a covert reference to it in 1:12.[80] In DtIsa, finally, "strife" (רִיב) is interpreted as a legal dispute (50:8): "Who wishes to dispute with me (יָרִיב)? . . . Who is the opposite party?"—that is, the accuser. This opens the way for the transposition into a legal action according to the understanding of the day.

I should like to put forward for discussion a further

example of a possible dramatized, interpretive transposition of a scriptural narrative in the present DtIsa text. Verses 5-6 describe the Servant's meekness and humility: he does not retaliate. Numbers 12 tells how Miriam and Aaron criticize Moses, the grounds being his Cushite wife (v. 1) and the question of his authority: "Has Yahweh spoken only through Moses? Has he not spoken through us also?" (v. 2). The text then interposes that Moses was "a very humble man (עָנָו), more so than anyone else on the face of the earth" (v. 3).

Numbers 12 says that Yahweh talked to Moses "face-to-face (פֶּה אֶל־פֶּה), clearly, not in riddles" (v. 8). He is even permitted to see Yahweh's "form," "appearance" (v. 8), for he is "my servant Moses." These statements are related to the close of Deuteronomy (34:10), although with corrections, for at the end it is not in fact Yahweh's "appearance" that Moses sees, as is said in Num 12:8. But the close of Deuteronomy was the very text that came into question as background for Isa 50:4. If one rereads v. 4 in the light of Numbers 12, the statement "Yahweh has given me the tongue . . ." is ambiguous. It might mean "he gave *me*, and not Aaron." This could be a correction of Exod 4:10, according to which Moses was "slow of tongue," so that Aaron had to come to the rescue. According to Numbers 20, Aaron is already dead when Moses begins his farewell speech in Deuteronomy. Deut 9:20 says of Aaron only that Yahweh was "very angry" with him. Does this reflect a conflict between the institutions represented by Moses and by Aaron, respectively? In DtIsa Aaron is no longer mentioned.

■ **5-8** Verse 5 begins: ". . . has opened *my* ear." It has been suggested that this sentence should be deleted, as a repetition. But perhaps it is the appropriate introduction to v. 5, and lends the verse an additional aspect. We know no details about any invective directed against Moses. But if we again take Numbers 12 as the background, we see that there Miriam is treated "as one whose father has spat in her face (יָרֹק יָרַק): would she not <then> bear her shame (תִּכָּלֵם) for seven days?"

---

78   For the *Qal*: 5:1 (to introduce Deuteronomy's version of the Decalogue); 14:23; 17:19; 31:12, 13; *Piel*: 4:14; 5:31; 6:1; 11:19.

79   See A. Schart, *Mose und Israel im Konflikt: Eine redaktionsgeschichtliche Studie zu den Wüstenerzählungen* (1990).

80   Does "burden" (מַשַּׂאֲכֶם *maśśaʾakem*) stand for "quarrel, tempt" (מַסָּה *massāh*), in view of the similar

sound? Is it a correction of the obscure story about Massah and Meribah?

(v. 14). The question here is who spat at whom: the text of v. 14a is corrupt. According to the conclusion drawn from the analogy in the text, it looks more as if it were originally the daughter who spat in her father's face. She is shut out of the camp for seven days. Moses' punishment is therefore comparatively mild. In DtIsa it is the Servant of Yahweh who endures the "vilification, insults" (כְּלִימוֹת) and "spitting" (רֹק), according to 50:6. The problem of Miriam's leprosy—it is sent by Yahweh—and Moses' intervention on her behalf must be examined once more in connection with the fourth Servant of God text, 52:13–53:12. The whole text emerges as being a passage of extreme density and tension, especially if we admit reflections of this kind. It addresses the different levels of understanding about the authority of the Servant of Yahweh, Moses. This is discussed. According to the text, the Servant is a prophet and teacher in an exceptional sense. To the extent to which this is in question, he expects speedy clarification through a court action: "The one who makes me just is near" (v. 8). In the framework of the drama, this is also an announcement of what is going to follow in 52:13–53:12, where elements of the divine judgment are clearly detectable. We shall only have to consider whether contemporary problems are not also the subject of reflection here, under the same guise.

■ 9-11 I am still of the opinion that on the general biographical level the concluding verses are addressed to those who will come later. But if the Servant represents the Moses of Deuteronomy, then he is also the one who according to Deuteronomy 28 announces blessing and curse: "And if you will only obey the voice of Yahweh your God . . ." (v. 1), "But if you will not obey the voice of Yahweh your God . . ." (v. 15). Deuteronomy 30 interprets this as the choice between life and death: "See, I have set before you today life and the good, death and evil" (v. 15).

Particular statements in this DtIsa text can be understood as curses. In a similar way, the Song of Moses in Deuteronomy 32 talks about fire that burns to the depths of the underworld (v. 22), while in the same context Yahweh says: "I will heap disasters upon them, spend my arrows against them" (v. 23). But the terminology here suggests that these are probably all statements about the underworld. The positive aspect is that the "walking through dark places" is protected by Yahweh's name. In the negative one, striking phrases are "the embers of your fire" and "the place of torment"; it is here that the Servant's enemies are going to lie.[81] In the context, if the Servant has appeared from the underworld, these statements all dovetail. He has experienced Yahweh's protection. He knows what it is and can testify accordingly to those who fear Yahweh (v. 10). They have no need to fear others unless they are those who insult the Servant—whoever "you all" (כֻּלְּכֶם, v. 11) are.

But with these statements at the end of this biographical section, the Servant acquires another, additional role. He becomes the one who also knows the mysteries of the underworld. He has gone through darkness (v. 10) and finally decides about life and death (v. 11). Are there signs here that Moses is also a mystagogue? This is obviously the case later, in Philo.[82] But in Philo what traditions have coalesced?

At the end of this section one can ask why the invocation of "Moses" as he is presented in Deuteronomy should take place at precisely this point in DtIsa's work. There may have been already existing traditions about the different stages of Moses' life. The reason could also be dramaturgical. But it is also worth considering whether there were contemporary grounds as well.

---

81 Does this verse also contain a reference to the story about the rebellion and downfall of the Korah "gang" (Numbers 16)? There too it is a matter of Moses' authority, which is called in question. The text says about Korah and his people that after "each man [had taken] his censer and they [had] put fire in the censers and laid incense on them" (v. 18), Korah assembled the whole congregation against them (i.e., Moses and Aaron) at the entrance of the tent of meeting (v. 19). At Moses' plea (v. 28) the earth opens and they go down alive to the dead (vv. 30 and 33). The fire goes forth from Yahweh (v. 35) and destroys the rest. Numbers 16 therefore also has to do with the underworld, and with "something new" (v. 30)!

82 See E. R. Goodenough, *By Light, Light: The Mystic Gospel of Hellenistic Judaism* (1935, reprint 1969), esp. 199–234 "The Mystic Moses," with texts from Philo.

83 A small detail could indicate that Nehemiah is not simply being presented as a "new Moses." We are told that in his opposition to mixed marriages Nehemiah "beat" some of the Jews and "pulled out their hair" (מרט, Neh 13:25). This is just what the Servant does not do; he does not strike back, and does not pull out their beards (מרט, 50:6). In this

342

The preceding proem in the last section (49:1—50:1) reflected important social measures known to us from the book of Nehemiah, among them the liberation of people enslaved for debt.[83] Deuteronomy with its laws is characterized by intervention on behalf of the socially weak. It is to this context that the laws about the remission of debts (Deut 15:1-11) and the freeing of slaves (15:12-18) belong. Isa 50:4-11 could therefore be seen as a legacy of the dead Moses to "the wearied" (v. 4)[84] and all who hear his message afresh. The passages that follow then present two examples of prophetic interpretation in Moses' spirit (51:1-3 and 51:9-11).

---

respect he is humble like Moses (cf. Num 12:3). It is striking that in the Numbers passage too it is a question of a mixed marriage. Moses is accused among other things of having a Cushite wife (Num 12:1). Is the DtIsa passage an implicit criticism of Nehemiah's measures in the mixed-marriage question?

84 Cf. Isa 40:28-31.

51:1-3
Revelatory Speech by the Servant of God
The Link between the Patriarchs and
Matriarchs and the Zion Tradition
Turn to the "Yahweh Seekers"

51

"Look to Abraham, your father, and to Sarah . . ."
(51:2)

1
Listen to me,
you who pursue salvation <or: justice?>,
you who seek Yahweh!

Look to the rock (out of which) you were
hewn,
and to the hollow of the well/the cistern[a]
(out of which) you were dug/bored.[b]

2
Look to Abraham, your father,
and to Sarah, who (in labor) brought you
forth.[a]

Yes, as the only one <or: as a single person>
I called him,
so that I might bless him and make him
many.[b]

3
Yes, Yahweh has comforted Zion,
he has comforted all her ruins,
and made her desert like Eden
and her steppe like Yahweh's garden.
Rejoicing and gladness are found in her,
thanksgiving and the sound of song.

1[a]   For the translation and on the text see below.

1[b]   LXX has two active verb forms here: "(which) you have hewn"
and "(which) you have dug."

2[a]   On חִיל see *HALAT*. The form is an imperfect. It could be
rendered in an iterative sense: "has continually born you."

2[b]   Thus MT. The early translations read the text as narrative:
"and I have blessed and increased him." 1QIsa[a] has "make
fruitful" (ואפרהו) instead of "bless."

The commentaries are largely at one in seeing this as a
difficult text. There is a whole series of disputed questions:

Who is speaking?	Yahweh, the Servant, a speaker?
To whom?	To the exiles, the residents, foreigners?
When?	The tense structure of the text is not clear.
What about?	For example, is Yahweh the rock, or is it Abraham?

In my view, the difficulty is due to the fact that the text
itself is speculative. It contains a kind of "revelation
speech," and it has a wide horizon: remembrance of the
exodus tradition (evoked through the catchwords "rock"
and "spring")[85] reaches forward to the traditions about
the patriarchs and matriarchs (by way of the names of
Abraham and Sarah), and the text finally looks forward
to "Zion." The primeval period (Eden and Yahweh's

garden) is linked with the future. It is clear that in
"Zion" all these traditions find their goal (v. 3).

With regard to the question, who is speaking? the context deserves more attention than it generally receives;
for the text is preceded in 50:4-11 by one of the Servant
of God texts, and it is by no means certain that someone
different is speaking in 51:1-2. According to our previous
assumptions, "Listen to me" in 50:2 is pronounced by
the Servant of God "Moses," after his appearance. He
shows how tradition should be applied to the present.
He expounds his Torah. So he is still Moses the teacher.
Only the addressees are different. Thus this is a new
scene.

■ **1a** "Those who fear Yahweh" (50:10) and the evident
opponents, who exit after 50:11 ("Go in . . ."), are fol-

---

85   This applies only under the presupposition that in
the case of "hollow" no differentiation is made
between "well" (בְּאֵר *bᵉʾēr*) and "cistern" (בּוֹר *bôr*).
The forms of בּוֹר and בְּאֵר have influenced one
another mutually; see, e.g., Jer 6:7, which is obviously talking about a bubbling well, and בָּאֹר is to be
read as בּוֹר; see *HALOT* and GB[18]. A number of
commentators, including Duhm, North,

Muilenburg, and McKenzie among others, take בּוֹר
to be a explanatory gloss to the hapax legomenon
מַקֶּבֶת ("hollow").

lowed by "those who seek Yahweh" (51:1). In the *parallelismus membrorum* they are called רֹדְפֵי צֶדֶק, "those who pursue salvation." This can mean that they work for justice, peace, and the well-being of the community.[86] The law about "the judges and officials" (Deut 16:18-20) concludes (v. 20), "Justice (צֶדֶק) and only justice you shall pursue, so that you may remain alive and receive as your own the land that Yahweh your God will give you."[87] The phrase can be used in a transferred sense. But רדף is also a verb of movement, meaning "to pursue, hunt, follow someone."[88] If we assume that this was a dramatic performance, the verb could also be one of the implicit stage directions. The group that comes onto the stage "pursues," and with the utmost speed! We should again have to imagine "salvation, justice" (here in its masculine form, צֶדֶק) as personified. As we shall see, this is also a preparation for the following section, vv. 4-6.

We may assume that in this text the phrase "seek Yahweh" (בקשׁ יהוה *Piel*) has a similar double meaning. It can be used (there are about 30 instances) as a term for the "proper behavior before Yahweh, repentance and fear of God."[89] Deut 4:29 uses it in this sense for the exiles, parallel to דרשׁ: "If from there[90] you will seek (בִּקַּשְׁתֶּם) Yahweh your God, you will find him, if you search (תִדְרְשֶׁנּוּ) for him with all your heart and with all your soul." It is worth considering how far the participial form "seeker of Yahweh" has become the technical term for particular groups, whether as a way of distinguishing them within Israel itself, or to differentiate them from adherents of other religions.[91]

Indeed, G. Gerleman maintains that "*bqš* pi. is not used as a verb of motion, 'to search for a place.'"[92] But "seeking God" in the original cultic sense does in fact include seeking out (or visiting) the sanctuary. This is the way one betakes oneself to an audience with a king;

one "seeks" the king's face (Prov 29:26; cf. 1 Kgs 10:24; 2 Chr 9:23). In the same way one also "seeks" Yahweh's face (2 Sam 21:1; Pss 24:6; 27:8; 105:4; 1 Chr 16:11; 2 Chr 7:14; cf. Hos 5:6, 15; Exod 33:7). One "seeks" his presence. Specifically, for the present text, this can mean that a group of devout people—perhaps pilgrims—is being addressed under the name of "Yahweh seekers." They "are hastening" (רדף) to Zion. Their identity could perhaps have been shown through their behavior and clothing.

In the context, the beginning of this scene takes on a special importance. In the laws about the annual feasts laid down in Deut 16:16 we read: "Three times a year all your males shall appear before the face of Yahweh your God at the place that he will choose:[93] at the festival of unleavened bread, at the festival of weeks, and at the festival of booths." The special thing about the Deuteronomy version is that the Passover also turns into a pilgrimage festival, which has to be celebrated at the place of the sanctuary. It was originally a festival whose basic unit was "the house"—the association of families or clans (cf. Exod 12:1-13, 16). Moreover, in Deuteronomy the Passover becomes a sacrifice. A curious point is the relation to the Mazzot festival (the Feast of Unleavened Bread) expressed in this final note on the order of feasts. For here only Mazzot is mentioned, not the Passover. But if in the third Servant of God text in DtIsa (50:4-9) the Moses of Deuteronomy is speaking, it could be that DtIsa is supporting Deuteronomy's position: if Zion is the goal of pilgrimage, that is a reason for rebuilding the city.[94]

■ **1b-2a** If we assume that in this text the Servant Moses is first speaking to devout pilgrims, then the mention of "rock" and "well" (not "cisterns" in this case) suggests an association with the wanderings in the wilderness. Both

---

86   See K. Koch, "צדק *ṣdq* to be communally faithful, beneficial," *TLOT* 2:1046–62, esp. 1059–60 [צדק *ṣdq* gemeinschaftstreu/heilvoll sein," *THAT* 2:507–30, esp. 527].

87   In the Zurich translation; cf. Prov 21:21.

88   See *HALOT* s.v.

89   See G. Gerlemann, "בקשׁ *bqš* pi. to seek," *TLOT* 1:251–53, esp. 253 [*THAT* 1:333–36, esp. 335].

90   The specification "from there" (מִשָּׁם) shows that the sense of space is not completely lacking in this text either.

91   See S. Wagner, "בקשׁ *biqqeš*," *TDOT* 2:229–41, esp. 239 [*ThWAT* 1:754–69, esp. 766], with reference to

Zeph 1:6. For the participial use cf. Pss 40:17 (16); 69:7 (6); 70:5 (4); 105:3-4; 1 Chr 16:10-11; 2 Chr 11:16; Ezra 8:22.

92   Gerlemann, "בקשׁ *bqš* pi. to seek," *TLOT* 1:252 [*THAT* 1:334].

93   See *BHS* and commentaries on the text.

94   The problem of Passover—sacrifice—Mazzot requires further consideration; see below on 55:1-3.

rock and well gave water,[95] and there are traditions that both journeyed with the people in their wanderings.[96] But strangely enough there is at first no mention of water in the text. Yet water is surely the precondition if Zion's "desert" is or will be "like Eden, and her wilderness like the garden of Yahweh" (v. 3).

That stones should be hewn out of rock is understandable. It is harder to understand the metaphor that cisterns—no doubt made of stone too—are "dug/bored" (נקר Pual). But in Palestine's soft chalk the possibility that underground quarries could become cisterns cannot be excluded.

The text is more complicated than this, however, and that is probably connected with the type of scriptural proof that DtIsa is putting forward.[97] "Rock" is an image for God's protection and help.[98] It becomes a divine title.[99] Now, there is one text in which as nowhere else in the OT "rock" is used as a term for God himself. It is the so-called Song of Moses in Deut 32:4-43. Before his death, Moses proclaims this song to "the whole assembly of Israel" (31:10). It is his "teaching" ("my teaching," לקחי, 32:2). This text from Deuteronomy therefore once again fits precisely into the context at this point in DtIsa's work. The song begins: "The rock, his work is perfect" (Deut 32:4). One can refer to it simply by quoting the first word, "rock." This word is repeated five times in the song as a divine title (vv. 4, 15, 18, 30, 31). Once it stands for the rock out of which the people "sucked honey" (v. 13). Twice it is used for the foreign gods, over against Yahweh (vv. 31, 37). But Deut 32:18 can actually offer a key for an understanding of Isa 51:1-2:

The rock that begot you, 'you were unmindful of'[100]
(צוּר יְלָדְךָ תֶּשִׁי),

and forgot the God who in labor gave you birth
(וַתִּשְׁכַּח אֵל מְחֹלְלֶךָ).

According to the context (Deut 32:19: "Yahweh saw . . . his sons and daughters"), this is saying that the God of Israel is simultaneously father and mother—in whatever transferred sense this may be understood. The first word of this quotation ("rock") and the last phrase ("in labor bore you") are found in Isa 51:1-2 as well. Here too Yahweh is "the rock," but now *Abraham* is "your father" and *Sarah* has "in labor brought you forth" (תְּחוֹלֶלְכֶם)! Neither "begotten" nor "born": that is a correction which unequivocally excludes divine descent. "Jacob" (43:1)/"Israel" (43:15) is created (ברא) by God. In the dispute about heroes and "divine human beings," a clear limit is thereby drawn between the divine and the human sphere. This may have been the subject of discussion, especially now, in connection with the refounding of Zion/Jerusalem, in view of the foundation of Greek cities and Greek colonization in this period. Many Greek cities claimed heroes as founders and worshiped them in their cult.[101]

Against this background, at least some of the tensions in the text can be explained. From "the rock" stones are now hewn. They are needed for the rebuilding in the literal sense, and as "living stones," to use the language of 1 Pet 2:5-6.

מַקֶּבֶת בּוֹר, "hollow of the cistern," is strange. It has also been rendered "mouth of the cistern."[102] It has been hazarded that an echo of נְקֵבָה, "woman, womanly," is intended, by way of the root נקב, "pierce, bore through";[103] this would fit in with the "father-mother" *topos*. The "boring" or "digging" (נקר) could be a reminder of the "well song" in Num 21:16-18: "this is the

95 For "rock" see Exod 17:6; Deut 8:15; Pss 78:15, 20; 105:41; 114:8; cf. also 48:21. On "well" see esp. Num 21:16-18.

96 On "rock" see A. S. van der Woude, "צוּר ṣûr rock," *TLOT* 2:1067-71 [*THAT* 2:538-43] (with lit.); H.-J. Fabry, "צוּר ṣûr," *ThWAT* 6:973-83, esp. 982 on Deut 32:18 and Isa 51:1. On "cistern" (בּוֹר) see *HALOT* s.v.

97 K. Baltzer, "Schriftauslegung bei Deuterojesaja? Jes 43,22-28 als Beispiel," in *Die Väter Israels: FS J. Scharbert* (1989) 11-16.

98 See van der Woude, "צוּר ṣûr rock," *TLOT* 2:1070 [*THAT* 2:542], with reference to Pss 18:47 (46);

28:1; 31:3 (2); [31:4 (3)]; 62:3 (2), 8 (7); 71:3; 78:35; 94:22; 144:1; etc.; see also D. Eichhorn, *Gott als Fels, Berg und Zuflucht* (1972).

99 See 1 Sam 2:2; 2 Sam 22:32 par. Ps 18:32 (31); Hab 1:12.

100 See MT and the commentaries on this passage.

101 See R. Bartelmus, *Heroentum in Israel und seiner Umwelt* (1979).

102 See *HALOT*. Westermann translates by "Brunnenschacht" ("well shaft").

103 On the text of 51:1 see also N. A. van Uchelen, "Abraham als Felsen (Jes 51,1)," *ZAW* 80 (1968) 183-91, esp. 189. Cf. also Prov 5:15.

well that the princes sank," although there the verbs חפר and חקק are used for "dig." But the text has given rise to further speculation.[104]

The text aquires a new aspect if it is also read as an address to a group of pilgrims. Then the double "Look!" (הַבִּיטוּ) should no longer be understood in a merely mental or spiritual sense; there really is something to be seen. This is the way things are pointed out to pilgrims (and tourists). "Rock" and "caves" can be observed on Zion. One can tell their story, the *hieros logos* or sacred legend of their origin, and describe hopes for the future. A "rock" is pointed out to visitors to Jerusalem down to the present day. According to Ezekiel 47, a marvelous river issues from the temple. Rock and "cistern mouth" (if this is then the opening of a cistern from which water can be drawn) are not necessarily confined to their own actual place. Like other pilgrimage destinations, they can be copied; we need only think of the Calvaries and holy graves of Christian tradition. They are also conceivable as requisites in a play. More problematic, but suggested by the parallelism in the text, is the assumption that there were also pictures of Abraham and Sarah that could be "looked at."

■ **2b** To revert to the textual level, this section of the verse, and this section alone, is clearly a direct Yahweh speech. Here the first person is used, while v. 3 goes on to refer to Yahweh in the third person. No literary operations are required here. The Yahweh saying has its place and function in the context.

Three things are said about Abraham: "I called him so that I might bless him and make him many." The last two statements are reminiscent of the promises to the patriarchs, especially those given to Abraham in Genesis 12 and 17. But anyone who is familiar with the Bible knows that the promises to the patriarchs in their full form contain three assurances: descendants, blessing and land. The last of these is missing in our present passage. This is all the more striking because in Ezek 33:24 the same saying about Abraham as being "the only one"

is given as a reason why the many who have remained in the land ought to possess it.

The double promise of people and land is an ancient one. G. von Rad observes: "Deuteronomy, which appeals with extreme frequency to the promise to the patriarchs, understood this promise only as a promise of land (Deut 6:18, 23; 8:1, 7; 9:5, 28 and frequently)."[105] This is interesting, because in the context of our present text Deuteronomy plays so important a part. As regards the promise of the land, at all events, Deuteronomy is not followed here. In this text, the third element is Abraham's call, which indeed was also already formulated in 41:9 as a call from the furthest regions.

The echo of the promise to the patriarchs and the alterations to that promise acquire their significance in the present text if the divine word is addressed to the pilgrims. They are to come, but they are not to remain! They are called, in both senses of the word. For them it is perhaps a problem that they are merely single individuals (כִּי־אֶחָד). On the pilgrimage they experience community. The first thing that they receive is blessing; increase follows.

The text and the performance practice are again closely connected. "The seekers of Yahweh" (v. 1a), the pilgrims, are given a direct Yahweh word. The promise to Abraham has been fulfilled. But they are the children of Abraham and Sarah, so *this* promise is theirs afresh. With it they can also go back to the place where they live. The rapid switch from the Servant Moses' speech: "Listen to me . . ." to Yahweh's and back again makes it seem probable that at the performance there were two different speakers—unless only the masks were changed.

■ **3** Here Moses is again speaking as a prophet. He proclaims the redemption of Zion and reveals the divine resolve (וַיְשֶׂם), already made, that there will once more be an "Eden" such as is described in Gen 2:8, 10; 4:16, and a "garden of Yahweh" as in Gen 13:10.[106] The goal

---

104 See Philo *Som.* 2.269–71; E. R. Goodenough, *By Light, Light: The Mystic Gospel of Hellenistic Judaism* (1935, reprint 1969); also his *Jewish Symbols in the Greco-Roman Period* 10 (1964) 132–36.

105 G. von Rad, *Theologie des Alten Testaments* 1 (1957; 8th ed. 1982) 172 (this sentence has been omitted from the English translation); for the promise to Abraham see Deut 9:5; 34:4.

106 Cf. *Jub.* 11:18ff.; 13:6ff.

of the pilgrimage—Zion as "paradise"—exerted a lasting influence, putting its impress even on the architecture and iconography of Christian churches.

The joy of being on Zion finds expression in the songs. It could be that here the songs are merely referred to, but it is also possible that the text is indicating the point at which pilgrims' songs would be sung, songs such as we find in the Psalter, or perhaps the Song of Moses recorded in Deuteronomy, perhaps also "the well song" of Numbers 21.[107]

As the exegesis of the individual verses has shown, 51:1-3 is more consistent than is generally assumed. The program behind it is to link the tradition about the patriarchs with the Zion tradition. The connection is legitimated by "Moses." But the program is also the renewal of Zion as a center of pilgrimage. The counter position would be to acknowledge descent from Abraham and Sarah, but to have no desire for a return to Jerusalem. This is a position that one can imagine may well have existed among people in the Diaspora. These people had come to be at home in the foreign country, where they lived and worked as the prophet Jeremiah, for example, had recommended (Jeremiah 29). Why should they think of returning? But through the pilgrimage, those who have not returned are also numbered among Yahweh's people. Not to make *Jerusalem* the goal of pilgrimage then became the position held by the Samaritans, even though they claimed descent from Abraham and Sarah, and thus membership of the people of Israel.

Finally, we may perhaps deduce that descent from Abraham and Sarah, and with it membership in Jerusalem's cultic and civic community, was denied by the authorities in Jerusalem to those born in a foreign country. The disputes about the register of families in the books of Ezra and Nehemiah reflect these problems. This could have been the topical reference of the text.

When DtIsa maintains that the people and Zion belong together (cf. 51:16), this is one more indication that his work can be seen as a document concerned for the uniting of God's people.

---

107 One strange observation may be mentioned. If the Hebrew text is written with one word beneath the other, we have the impression that there is a play on the letters here. They concentrate on the sequence of consonants בר (*br*) and רב (*rb*). בר is contained in בור ("cistern") and in the name A*br*aham. רב means "much." בר and רב alternate. Is there a play on the name Abraham here, comparable with that in Gen 17:2-6? Gen 17:2, "I will multiply you" (אַרְבֶּה), is striking. Is this a kind of oracle interpretation, which is intended to lead from "Abraham" by way of "promises" and "dryness" in various forms to "joy"? These cryptic, acrosticlike links would have been accessible only to those who could read, however. They would presuppose that the original manuscripts were of a high quality. Of course we cannot exclude chance as explanation.

51:4-8
Divine Speech on the Law
(Throne Scene with Mime)
Turn to the "Sympathizers"

51 "Yes, law goes out from beside me" (51:4)
"People with my law in their hearts" (51:7)

4   Listen carefully to me, my people,
    and my nation—give heed to me!
    For law goes out from "beside me,"
    and my (judicial) decision as a light for
          peoples.

5   <In an instant>ᵃ I will bring my salvation <or:
              my justice?> near,
    my help has gone forth,
    and my arms will judge peoples <or: help
              peoples to justice>.
    Islands hope for me,
    and for my arm they wait.

6   Lift up your eyes to the heavens,
    and look down to the earth beneath!
    Though the heavens vanish in tatters of
          smoke
    and the earth passes away like a garment
    and its inhabitants die <like gnats>,ᵃ
    yet my help will endure forever,
    and my justice will not be broken.ᵇ

7   Listen to me,
    you who know salvation <or: justice?>,
    people with my law in their hearts!
    Do not fear human reviling,
    and do not be shattered by their mocking.

8   for "the moths will eat them up" like a
              garment,
    and "the clothes moths" will eat them up
              like wool.
    But my justice will remain to furthest time,
    and my help from generation to generation.

5ᵃ   For the separation of vv. 4 and 5 see below.
6ᵃ   If כְּמוֹ־כֵן is corrected to כְּמוֹכֵן, following 1QIsaᵇ, the transla-
     tion should perhaps be "like locusts"; see *BHS*.
6ᵇ   LXX: "cease" (ἐκλίπη); cf. Vg.

Verses 4-8 constitute a unit, linked by way of the catch-words (law, salvation, help, justice) and the common theme. The double demand: "Listen carefully to me" (v. 4) and "Listen to me" (v. 7), divides the unit into two sections. The unit as a whole should probably be understood primarily as a divine speech. The self-declarations ("my salvation/my justice . . . my arms") are so weighty that we can hardly suppose that Moses is the speaker, as he is in both the preceding and the succeeding texts. At the same time, the connection with these texts is close, for example in the reference to "my law" (תּוֹרָתִי, v. 7; cf. v. 4). Verse 5b corresponds almost word for word to the first Servant of God text in 42:4 (cf. also 49:1-6). The law, the Torah of Moses, is identical with the law of God. What is now said is a direct divine revelation. That lends the text particular weight. Its subject is knowledge of God, the world, and human existence. What is presented here is nothing less than a total worldview. For whom is this "teaching" meant? Apart from the content, which is bound to awaken the interest of the people addressed, the introductory formulas in vv. 4 and 7 give the first indication.

349

According to the text of v. 4, attention (קָשַׁב) is demanded of "my people" (עַמִּי), and "my nation" (לְאוּמִי) is told to listen. Even the ancient versions felt obliged to make a whole series of textual alterations to the text here.

Twelve Hebrew manuscripts and the Peshitta change both substantives into the plural ("peoples" and "nations"), so that they agree with the plural form of the verbs. That means that this is a universal proclamation, addressed directly to "the empires of the world." But it is possible, with Schoors, to argue in favor of a construction that follows the sense, not the grammatical rules. It is the individuals constituting people and nation who are being addressed. The striking series of first person singular suffixes ("my") in the whole text, including the effect of the *i* sound at the end of the Hebrew words, also speaks against a change to the plural.

Another solution, already suggested by LXX, leaves "my people" in the singular but changes "nation" into the plural "nations." Then "my people" is addressed to Israel, "the nations" meaning all the others. The stumbling block is that otherwise "nation" (לְאֹם) with the first person suffix never means Israel. The present text is undoubtedly the more difficult reading. To change it would also spoil the fine chiasm of the introduction in v. 4. But perhaps the stumbling block is intentional, in the sense that people belonging to different peoples and nations are *all* addressed as "my people" and "my nation." They are to belong to Yahweh. For the text goes on immediately afterward to talk positively about the "islands" too (אִיִּים), and in v. 7 "people" (עַם) is also singular.

The second summons to listeners in v. 7 can also help to identify the people addressed. They are those who "know salvation/justice" (יֹדְעֵי צֶדֶק). This takes up and modifies the identification sign already given in 51:1. Both have to do with salvation/justice. In 51:1 it was pilgrims who "pursue salvation/justice" (רֹדְפֵי צֶדֶק). Now it is others. They know salvation/justice—according to the

dramatic context in v. 5, they have been able to see salvation/justice (צֶדֶק). At the same time they are those who "know"—in the fullest sense of the term ידע. As in v. 1, the *parallelismus membrorum* gives a further clue to an identification of the group: they are people who "have my law in their hearts."[108] If they have it in their "inmost being" they have no need to show it outwardly. In the following passage the difficulties these people have with the world around them is also immediately mentioned. The conclusion could be that here a group of sympathizers from other "peoples and nations" are being addressed.[109] Like the pilgrims in the preceding passage (51:1-3), they come from "far off"—at least from the standpoint of Jerusalem. The kind of knowledge that is communicated to this group could also suggest that they are interested strangers.

■ **4-6** The whole text can be viewed under a number of different aspects. It is again a throne scene. Comparable are texts such as 1 Kgs 22:19-23; Isaiah 6 and the other prophetic installation accounts; Job 1:6-12; Daniel 7. Common to them all is the idea of God as king, surrounded by his royal household. It is a formalized scene with static elements (the order of precedence can be seen from the placing) and action too—consultations, and the coming and going of people with special briefs or assignments.

A scene of this kind serves to illustrate sovereignty. It is a kind of concrete abstraction—that is to say, a conceptual abstraction (such as sovereignty) is made describable and communicable through something concrete (such as a throne scene). Today the same function is fulfilled by group photographs of executive bodies—cabinets, political party leaders, or company directors. In the world of the ancient Near East, the delineation of hierarchies of the gods also had the function of making the order of world and society clear. In the development of cosmologies there is a connection between lists of the gods and encyclopedias. The apocalyptic texts still show that the transitions are fluid. In the gnostic systems hierarchical

---

108 For the plural see *HALOT*, s.v., under this heading, with reference to this passage.

109 On the subject of "non-Israelites as a part of God's people" and "Yahweh-worship by non-Israelites" see Peter Marinković, "'Geh in Frieden' (2 Kön 5,19). Sonderformen legitimer JHWHverehrung durch 'Heiden' in 'heidnischer' Mitwelt," in R. Feldmeier and U. Heckel, eds., *Die Heiden. Juden, Christen und*

das Problem des Fremden (1994) 3-21.

110 "Arm" (זְרוֹעַ) is generally feminine. The plural is hence often formed with the feminine ending וֹת (19 times). It is only in the present text and in four further instances that it is treated as a masculine. The singular "Yahweh's arm" is viewed as feminine in DtIsa in 52:10; 53:1 and hence probably in 51:9 too. The rare masculine plural form זְרֹעֵי could actually

order and development are linked. The problem is the connection between the divine and the human world, and the way the relationship should be evaluated. The degree of abstraction varies in each given case.

The present text belongs within this development, even though it is difficult to place it with any exactitude. The throne scene is still quite concrete. The Deity speaks directly, and those whom he commissions go out (חָצָא, v. 4; יָצָא, v. 5). But since one of DtIsa's fundamental principles is his rejection of the polytheistic world, those who go out cannot be gods. There is no genealogical order of descent and rank in relation to the one God. "Goings out" could, indeed, be understood in the Gnostic sense as emanations. But right at the beginning a remarkable subtlety in the text preserves both the nearness to God and the distance from him. The *Torah* goes out "from 'beside God'" (מֵאִתִּי, v. 4): that would be the literal rendering of the text. This closeness lends the Torah its status. But it is not identical with God.

In what follows, up through v. 6, seven terms end with the first person singular suffix, spoken by God: "my. . . ." Acoustically, the sequence is stressed through the *i* sound with which the terms end. Two terms belong together in each case. The first "Torah" is also included in the series, so that four pairs emerge, eight terms in all. There is an irregularity in the series in v. 5 (and hence a special signal) through the interpolation of "for me . . ." (a further 1st person masc. sing. suffix) between the statements about Yahweh's "arms." The following picture then emerges:

law (fem.)	(legal) decision (masc.)
salvation (masc.)	help (masc.)
arms (masc.)	arm (fem.)
<Yahweh's, to judge>	<Yahweh's, for hope>
help (fem.)	justice (fem.)

Against the background of ancient cosmologies, it is striking that, as is often the case there, the terms are paired. The change of gender should be noted: at the beginning feminine-masculine, then twice masculine. The third pair is not quite clear, but it should probably also be understood as masculine-feminine.[110] The final two terms, again, are both feminine. This would therefore give four feminine and four masculine terms in all, the alternation giving a somewhat artificial effect because in two instances a single term appears in both its masculine (v. 5: "salvation," צֶדֶק; "help," יֵשַׁע) and its feminine form (v. 6: "help," יְשׁוּעָה; "salvation, justice," צְדָקָה)—chiastically reversed in addition. In the genealogies, pairs of gods have their place; here only the different genders of the terms are left.

The number eight plays a role in Egyptian theogonies down to the Ogdoad in the gnostic texts. The text could hint at a change here, when "hope for me" (אֵלַי, preposition with 1st person sing. suffix) is inserted in the text between "arms" and "arm." The Deity is named again. Are there then nine elements in the series?

The Torah takes first place in the sequence, according to the text; whereas if one takes Prov 8:22–30 as an example, Wisdom (חָכְמָה) was beside Yahweh (אֶצְלוֹ, v. 30) even before the creation. The connection in the history of religion between this idea, the Egyptian *maat* tradition and Hellenistic *Sophia* speculation, down to Gnosticism, is well known. Here DtIsa puts the Torah at the beginning.[111]

"Torah" (תּוֹרָה) can be an individual precept of Yahweh. But its position in the series of terms in the text suggests that we have to assume a more comprehensive meaning here. H. W. Wolff shows that Hosea already understands Yahweh's Torah as "the entire disclosure of Yahweh's will, already fixed in writing."[112] A similar development may be presumed for Isaiah.

But as a unified complex of revelation for Israel, Torah is preeminently the distinguishing mark of

---

be intentional because of the ordered structure of the text. In the masculine and the feminine, the plural form can mean "the armies" (cf. Dan 11:31; 11:15, 22 and the context). The subject is therefore Yahweh's military power. See *HALOT*, s.v.; K. Albrecht, "Das Geschlecht der hebräischen Hauptwörter," *ZAW* 16 (1896) 41–121. H. L. Ginsberg, "The Arm of YHWH in Isaiah 51–63 and the text of Isa 53:10-11," *JBL* 77 (1958) 152–56; A. S. van der Woude, "זְרוֹעַ *zerôaʿ* arm," *TLOT* 1:392–94 [*THAT* 1:522–24]. F. J. Helfmeyer, "זְרוֹעַ

111   *zerôaʿ*," *TDOT* 4:131–40 [*ThWAT* 2:650–60].

111   John 1:1-5 probably continues this dispute: "In the beginning was the Word, and the Word was beside God" (Ἐν ἀρχῇ ἦν ὁ λόγος, καὶ ὁ λόγος ἦν πρὸς τὸν θεόν).

112   H. W. Wolff, *Hosea* (1974) 138 [*Hosea* (3d ed. 1976) 176–77]; see also idem, "'Wissen um Gott' bei Hosea als Urform von Theologie," in his *Gesammelte Studien zum Alten Testament* (1964) 192–205, esp. 194 and 197.

Deuteronomy. This comes out in the very terms themselves. That here in DtIsa there should be a link with Deuteronomy is not surprising, in a context where—starting with the third Servant of God text in 50:4-9—Moses is presented as "teacher," just as he is in Deuteronomy. But the present text offers a special emphasis compared with Deuteronomy, and probably an expansion as well, since it includes the cosmological aspect. Verse 6 makes this particularly evident. We must be clear from the very outset that our concepts of nature and history did not yet exist, and above all not the division between them. For DtIsa the world is a unity, and consequently the Torah can be the term for a unified world order. It embraces "the law" that is designed to govern the conduct of human beings, as well as "the law" for the rest of the created world of "the heavens . . . and the earth . . . and its inhabitants" (v. 6). Here again, we see the influence of the already mentioned link with Wisdom traditions in the interpretation of "Torah."

If we assume that the text can be assigned to the fifth century B.C.E., we may also assume that the Greek philosophy of nature provides the background for the dispute about the concept of law and world order. I do not believe that it is by chance that here vv. 4-5 again talk about "the islands." They represent the Greek world. It is impossible to differentiate the other terms precisely with any degree of certainty, but it is clear that they all revolve around the question of the justice of God's sovereignty.

Mišpāṭ (מִשְׁפָּט) is the judicial decision. It can be an individual legal pronouncement. But according to the present context something more general is to be expected. If we take the verb as a starting point, we can follow G. Liedke in saying: "In accord with perhaps the most common description, *špṭ* designates an action that restores the disturbed order of a (legal) community."[113] In v. 4, this community would be the community of peoples within the divine sovereignty. If everyone in this community is to be given his rights, "judging" is necessary. This term comprises both "giving judgment in someone's favor, helping someone to arrive at his or her rights," and "condemnation." This becomes clear in the example from Deuteronomy that Liedke cites, Deut 25:1: "If a dispute (*rîb*) is pending between two parties, they should go

to the *mišpāṭ*, who should pronounce justice (*špṭ*) for them: one should set the righteous in the right (*ṣdq* hi.) and declare the guilty party guilty (*ršʿ* hi.)."[114] So "*mišpaṭ* as verdict can signify deliverance or condemnation."[115]

For this term too, with its roots, the concordance alone shows that Deuteronomy offers a wealth of material in illustration. It is important to note that מִשְׁפָּט and the parallel terms in the text, "faithfulness to the community, salvation" (צֶדֶק צְדָקָה), differ from our modern abstractions because they involve the notion of an "efficacious sector or sphere." This too underlines their cosmological reference.

Yahweh's "arms" are his army,[116] and according to 40:26 are therefore the stars, which he leads out and knows by name. According to v. 5 Yahweh's "arms" "judge peoples," and in view of what has been said about שׁפט this can mean either salvation or doom for them. That depends on what they do, since act and destiny are linked. The parallelism "my arms . . . my arm" could also indicate an antithesis: judgment for the peoples—salvation for the islands. But this is not certain. Only the islands' "hope" for Yahweh is clearly positive.

The series of terms preceded by Yahweh's "my" (possessive ending in Hebrew) is clearly interrupted in v. 6a. This passage at first looks like an erratic block, but it is in fact closely connected with its context. In the previous text (vv. 1-3) v. 2b is comparable—a part-verse that was also important for the contemporary understanding of the text.

It is striking that "heaven" and "earth" are not included in the series of terms. In a world where cosmologies were viewed as genealogy, this would have seemed obvious, especially since it would be a further pair of antitheses: heaven (masc.)—earth (fem.). But unlike the concepts from "Torah" to "justice," heaven and earth are created and transient. If the heavens vanish "like smoke," then they are not a "firmament," as they are in Gen 1:8, for example. Smoke is formed through fire and air. This corresponds much better than "firmament" to beliefs about the elements at that period. That the earth "is used up, disintegrates" (בלה), or "grows old" like clothes (Josh 9:13; cf. also Josh 9:4-5; Neh 9:21) or an old woman (Gen 18:12) is hardly con-

---

113 G. Liedke, "שׁפט *špṭ* to judge," *TLOT* 3:1392–99, esp. 1393 [*THAT* 2:999–1009, esp. 1001].
114 Ibid., 1392 [1002].

115 Ibid., 1396 [1006].
116 See above for lit. on "arm," זְרוֹעַ.

ceivable either, according to the teaching about creation in Genesis 1 or 8:22. But perhaps this verse is a nutshell version of a dispute over doctrines about the world aeons—ideas that had been familiar in the Greek world ever since Hesiod (c. 700 B.C.E.).

If what has always been considered lasting—heaven and earth—are so no longer, this presupposes either new knowledge or the experience of catastrophe. At all events it arouses fear. Human beings die "like gnats"—if indeed this is the proper translation for the uncertain כְּמוֹ־כֵן. DtIsa counters this by saying that Yahweh's "help" is forever (לְעוֹלָם). This can be understood in different ways. It means either the expectation of "a new heaven and a new earth," after this heaven and earth have passed away, or "eternity" in the metaphysical sense. עוֹלָם (ʿôlām) is the Hebrew term used to render the Greek αἰών ("aeon"). The people who are addressed here are assured that God's promise is sure, in spite of all change.

Verses 4-6 are therefore an extremely dense text in which a whole worldview is developed.[117] An attempt to reconstruct the contemporary background leads us to suspect that here the text reflects an acute dispute, with the Greek world especially.

This comes out once more if one asks how the text could have been dramatically presented. The throne scene is not a problem. It is one of the main components in DtIsa's store of dramatic resources. It should only be noted that in the framework of the liturgical drama there is evidently—as yet—no difficulty about presenting God as speaking.

Another striking point is again the way the apparently abstract terms are linked with verbs of movement. Law and justice "go out" (יצא). Their place of departure is "from 'beside Yahweh,'" as we have already seen. "In an instant I will (bring near)" (אַרְגִּיעַ). As stage directions, the text is perfectly acceptable, only the verb has to be shifted to the following infinitive "to draw near," contrary to the verse division. "My help" again moves in the contrary direction (יצא). After all, the text says that "help" and "justice" do not move.

The concepts appear in pairs, half of them feminine, the other half masculine. They are probably individual figures. Only "the arms" (masc.) are given as a plural. These observations suggest that we again have to do with a dance in the framework of the throne scene. The terms could presumably be identified as personifications through their appearance, clothing, and emblems. Greek vase paintings give a good impression of the way this could be done. But even earlier, in Egypt, the deities represented could be recognized by their masks and head-dresses.[118]

The interpolation in v. 6a is explicitly introduced. The spectators are told to look up and look down.[119] As in 51:1-2, "Look" (הַבִּיטוּ) is evidently meant as a real seeing. The directive is also a friendly warning to the spectators, for if the heavens pass away "like smoke" we may suppose that there were pyrotechnical effects. Tearing lengths of material can also produce an explosive sound, as anyone who has shaken out a blanket too vigorously knows. In the face of so many terrors, it can well be imagined that the earth's inhabitants might die. Delitzsch's supposition that כְּמוֹ־כֵן (lit. "as . . . so") combined with a gesture means "as nothing" is very much to the point, if it was a gesture pointing to the scene in a dramatic performance.[120]

When "light" goes forth to the peoples, it is easiest to imagine that in the performance a torch was used. Like the fireworks, this perhaps suggests that this scene was played at dusk.

---

117 Thomas Krüger has drawn my attention to the fact that in the text here an "eschatology of world history" and an eschatology of "the end of the world" are being taken up and corrected. This is the case if we presuppose that the translations of v. 5, "judge" or "help peoples to justice," and v. 6, "Though . . . yet," are correct renderings.

118 "Yahweh's arm" as his (heavenly) army can be conceived of as angels. They can be indicated as warlike through sword and/or lance. Since according to 40:26 "the stars" are Yahweh's army, a star would also suffice as symbol. In the case of a nocturnal sit-uation (see v. 4 on "light"; v. 6 on "smoke") this could also have been a dance with lights.

119 This suggests that the audience were seated in at least a raised position. Otherwise "the earth" would not be "beneath" (מִתַּחַת).

120 Delitzsch (2:285 [520–21]): "As in 2 Sam 23:5, Num 13:33 [34], and Job 9:35, כ must be explained as nothing other than ita, sic [thus]; but in the classical languages these words are frequently given their meaning through the gesture with which they are pronounced (e.g., in Terence's Eunuch: Cape hoc flabellum et ventulum sic facito); and in the same way

The form and content of this text are intimately connected. What takes place here in dramatic form is the revelation of divine mysteries. The Greek correspondence is again the initiation into a mystery. But here it is probably not individual privileged *mystēs* who are being initiated; it is all the people who have participated in the dramatic event hitherto. They see the divine presence and hear the voice, they experience the heavenly world as a dance, and they are nerved and fortified against their fears. This is a public initiation, so to speak, in which the audience is both witness and participant.

■ **7-8** If we come to vv. 7-8 with these presuppositions, the function of these verses in the context becomes comprehensible. The seeing of the mystery is followed by the instruction of "the knowers." "Listen to me, you who know salvation." This is the way Wisdom can speak, or—in later Gnostic texts—the *Sophia*.

In the correspondence between the heavenly and the earthly sphere four concepts are picked up once more: salvation, law, justice, help. "Yahweh's arms" remain in the heavenly sphere. According to the rule that "like can only be known by like," the Torah is both in heaven and in the hearts of those who belong to God's people.

The fears are still there. They are experienced in the revilings and invective of other people. This suggests that the environment was hostile toward believers, a conclusion already suggested at the beginning of the exegesis of this passage. But the people who have thus been initiated must not be afraid. They will not "be broken" (חתת, v. 7), just as the righteousness of God will not be broken (חתת, v. 6) either—as they have seen. That is the vision's final word.

The enemies are transitory, even if they pose as strong. The use of אֱנוֹשׁ (*ʾenôš*) for "human being" makes this point. In the end they will be eaten up by עָשׁ (*ʾāš*)

and סָס (*sās*). The words are generally explained as names for different kinds of moths. But perhaps "the devourers" are two monsters who are paraded at the end of the scene.[121] Fear of the succession of aeons is countered by the promise of God's faithful help from generation to generation. The struggle to come to terms with frightening views of the universe, fed by knowledge and experience, is still a problem today. Faith in the righteousness of God is the hope even for those far off.

At the end of this unit (vv. 4-8) one may again ask: What has this to do with "Moses"? Having appeared as the Servant of God, "Moses" has spoken in the previous unit, 51:1-3, and will speak again in vv. 9-11. Since according to v. 4 the Torah, the law, "goes out from 'beside' <God>," it is clear that the Torah, "the law of Moses," is not Moses' own. It is heavenly in origin. Moses is only the mediator, the lawgiver in God's name.

One may also ask: What has this to do with Zion? Zion/Jerusalem is the theme of this whole act, from 49:14 onward. Zion is mentioned in 51:3, immediately before the present text, and v. 17 onward describes the resurgence of Jerusalem. Anyone familiar with Isa 2:1-5 knows that "out of Zion 'Torah', law, goes out, and Yahweh's word from Jerusalem" (v. 3b). Here again "Torah" is also instruction, the living word. But in Isaiah 2 the addressees are first "all the Gentiles" (כָּל־הַגּוֹיִם) and "many peoples" (v. 3): they come "at the end of days" (v. 2) as pilgrims, a model for the house of Jacob too, "to walk in the light of Yahweh" (v. 5).

This hope is now fulfilled for God's "people and nation" from all over the world (Isa 51:4). They see "light" (v. 4). This unit (vv. 4-8) is, I believe, particularly directed to "the sympathizers" or foreigners among the people who come to Zion/Jerusalem from afar.

---

we should think of כְּ as being spoken everywhere in the sense of *hujus* in the comic *hujus non facio* (Zumpt, §444); cf. 'Eat, drink and joke—the rest is not worth *that* much' on Sardanapalus's tomb in Strabo 14.5.9. Luther's *wie das* is meant in this sense according to his gloss; cf. Rückert: 'and their inhabitants, they die off in any case.' 'Like' is here the equivalent of 'as nothing'" [trans. altered].

121 The interpretation "moths" and "clothes moths" is suggested by the connection with "garment" and "wool." In this case the reference would be to transience. But the point of the comparison could also be that the devouring "twins" eat up garment and

wool like a shredding machine, a fate intended for the mockers. Do they belong to the underworld? Cf. also the monster in Bel 27, according to Theodotion; cf. the LXX version (translation following O. Plöger, "Zusätze zu Daniel" [1973] 63–86): "Then Daniel took pitch and fat and hair and mixed them and made flat cakes which he pushed into the dragon's jaws, and it ate them and burst. And he said: 'Look what you are worshiping!'"

51:9-11
Revelatory Speech by the Servant of God
The Link between the Exodus and Zion Traditions
Turn to Those "Freed/Ransomed" by Yahweh

51

"Awake as in primeval days . . ." (51:9)
". . . who made the depths of the sea a way
for those freed to cross over" (51:10)

9

Awake! Awake!
Put on/dress yourself with strength, arm of
Yahweh!
Awake as in primeval <primordial?> days,
the generations of oldest times!

Was it not you who cut[a] Rahab to pieces,
pierced the dragon through?

10

Was it not you who dried up the sea,
the water of the great flood?
Who made the depths of the sea a way
for those freed to cross over?

11

But the ransomed of Yahweh shall return
and come to Zion with rejoicing,
with lasting joy upon their heads.
Rejoicing and joy will arrive,
sorrow and sighing have flown away.

9[a] MT (הַמַּחְצֶבֶת) derives the verb from חצב *Hiphil*, see *HALOT* 1:342 [*HALAT* 1:329]. The weapon would then probably be the sword. According to 1QIsa[a] (המחצת) the verb would derive from מחץ, in the sense of "shatter"; see *HALOT* 2:571 [*HALAT* 2:541]. In this case the weapon would probably be a cudgel (cf. Job 26:12).

Verses 9-11 constitute a separate scene. Catchwords and themes link it, no doubt designedly, with the scene immediately before ("arm of Yahweh"; cf. v. 5) and with the one that follows ("liberation," cf. vv. 13-14). But this is no longer a divine speech, as are vv. 4-8 and again v. 12. But then who is speaking? It is "Moses," who has reappeared. He calls on Yahweh on behalf of the new exodus. A close examination suggests that here too the Moses of Deuteronomy is meant, for as J. J. Stamm pointed out: "As an innovation Deut[eronomy] applied the verb *pdh* [ransom, liberate] to the liberation from Egypt (7:8; 9:26; 13:6 [5]; 15:15; 21:8; 24:18)."[122] The present text has to do with the exodus and according to v. 11 with "the ransomed, liberated" (פְּדוּיֵי) people. Another striking point is the meaning of "Yahweh's arm" in Deuteronomy, in the formula "with a strong hand and an outstretched arm." According to van der Woude, "This usage . . . is limited to Deut[eronomy] (4:34; 5:15; 7:19; 11:2; 26:8) and the literature influ-

enced by Deut[eronomy] (Jer 32:21; Psa 136:12), and always refers to the divine act of redemption in the exodus [the bringing out] from Egypt."[123] Here, however, this Moses interprets Scripture afresh when, in the text, creation, the miracle at the Reed Sea and liberation are linked in a new way.

To whom is this teaching directed? To "the redeemed, the freed" (גְּאוּלִים, v. 10), who are now described more precisely as "Yahweh's ransomed ones" (פְּדוּיֵי יהוה). Legally, when a slave was redeemed in the ancient world, ownership was symbolically transferred to the deity. The names of redeemed slaves were therefore written on altars, for example. A ransom had to be paid for the manumission. But if "the ransomed of Yahweh," the former slaves, return to Zion (v. 10), this means that a third group of people from far afield is being addressed, following the pilgrims (51:1-3) and the sympathizers (vv. 4-8). The text attacks the problems of this group too in a fundamental theological disquisition.[124]

122 J. J. Stamm, "פדה *pdh* to redeem, liberate," *TLOT* 2:964–76; quotation on 975 [*THAT* 2:389–406; quotation on 405].

123 Van der Woude, "זְרוֹעַ *zᵉrôaᶜ* arm," *TLOT* 1:393 [*THAT* 1:524].

124 This is true even if v. 11 is supposed to be a quota-
tion from Isa 35:10. There the verse is the close of a paradisal scene. What follows in Isaiah 36 is the threat to Jerusalem through Sennacherib and the city's miraculous rescue. If we take this context into account, it would seem all the more appropriate that DtIsa should interpolate the verse into his text

■ 9a The text begins with a triple reveille: "Wake up!" (עוּרִי). According to the Masoretic notation, the stress in the first two of these calls is, unusually, on the second syllable, the third time on the first: "*urí, urí, úri.*" That has a somewhat military sound, if one thinks of the "Hurrah" cries with which the German and English armies attacked one another in the world wars (the Russian version was "*Ura!*"). But here it is not human beings who are fighting. "Yahweh's arm" is invoked. Nor is there any mention of the hand of Moses, which, according to Exod 14:16, 21, 26, and 27, he stretched out in order to bring about the miracle at the Reed Sea. This Moses, here in DtIsa, is not a miracle worker. But he can invoke Yahweh's help like a prophet. The connection with the popular lament has been correctly observed.[125] For slaves, this lament is particularly appropriate.

It is notable that "Yahweh's arm" is feminine, and that the feminine form of address is maintained throughout the text. "She," really "Yahweh's arm,"[126] is the representation of his power, which is substantiated through the acts of primeval (or primordial) days (v. 9a) and the expectation of events in the future (v. 11).

■ 9b-10 But what happens between the two, between past and future? The temporal structure of the text is important for its interpretation. On the one hand, as Seidl has observed, on the vocabulary level "only dynamic verbs are used, stative verbs are lacking altogether—an important observation, because it defines the whole unit as dynamic and determined by action."[127] On the other hand, the three nominal clauses that follow in vv. 9b-10 make a strangely static impression. The action becomes a title or form of address for "Yahweh's arm." God's sovereignty is recognized and praised in a series of participles, as in a hymn.[128] But before the text's temporal structure can be clarified further, what it is saying requires examination.

Rahab (רַהַב *rahab*), dragon (תַּנִּין *tannîn*), sea (יָם *yām*), and primordial flood (תְּהוֹם רַבָּה *tᵉhôm rabbā*) are names or descriptions that make clear that this is the stuff of myth. All these terms can be found in other biblical texts, for example, in Job 26:12-13, in the sequence: sea, Rahab, heaven, the fleeing serpent. Sea, dragons and Leviathan are mentioned in Ps 74:13-14, waters and the primordial flood in Ps 77:17 (16). Not least, the primordial flood has its importance at creation, according to Gen 1:2. The Psalms especially show that the conflict motif also belongs to these mythical traditions. Yahweh is victorious over the hostile powers that have taken form in these beings (see Ps 50:3; 74:13-14; 77:17-18 [16-17]; 89:10 [9]; etc.).

A whole series of investigations, some as early as the nineteenth century, have shown that the terminology and concepts here reflect an encounter with the surrounding world of the ancient Near East. A reconstruction of the myths has made it seem probable that there is a link with theogonies and the cult, even with the rhythms of the seasons themselves. Where precisely the individual myths should be localized, and what mutual influences can be assumed, are still matters of dispute. In the OT in general, as in this present text, slight references to these mythical traditions suffice; the wider context must have been familiar to the addressees. Otherwise they would not have been able to understand the text at all.

In this passage a tetrad of beings is built up. I have the impression that this gives a more or less complete picture of uncanny and threatening powers. For the OT, *Rahab* and *Tannin* are associated with Egypt. Ugaritic texts clearly show the connection between *Yam* as sea and the battle between the gods. How far the statements

---

at this point; for the restitution of Zion/Jerusalem is the subject. The verse is therefore by no means an erratic block. See Stamm, "פדה *pdh* to redeem, liberate," *TLOT* 2:974–75 [*THAT* 2:403–4], with reference to this text.

125 Westermann (240) on this passage.

126 See T. Seidl, "Jahwe der Krieger—Jahwe der Tröster. Kritik und Neuinterpretation der Schöpfungsvorstellungen in Jesaja 51:9-16," *BN* n.s. 21 (1983) 116–34: "It cannot be Yahweh as in the previous context (50:10—51:8): this is made clear by the vocative *zᵉrôaʿ YHWH*, which introduces the addressee of the speech, metonymically for Yahweh" (124). "This

addressee, as grammatical subject, links the sentences 9a-10, as can be verified by the consistently preserved feminine congruence" (125).

127 Ibid., 120–21.

128 T. Seidl (ibid., 121) goes along with W. Richter in describing the sentences as "identification utterances." "The direct form of address 'arm of Yahweh' (taken up pronominally) is identified with the titles that follow, which are in the definite form in Hebrew: 'Are you, arm of Yahweh, not identical with the one who cut Rahab to pieces, who pierced the dragon through, etc.?'"

about *Tehom* as the primordial flood have to do with the Babylonian Tiamat-Marduk myth is a matter of dispute.

In my view, Daniel 7 is an important point of comparison for Isa 51:9-11. There the divine sovereignty is presented in a throne scene (vv. 2-3): "I, Daniel, saw in my vision by night the four winds of heaven stirring up the great sea, and four great beasts came up out of the sea, different from one another."[129] In the book of Daniel, the beasts are four empires. According to v. 12, "their dominion was taken away, since the length of their lives was restricted to a certain time and hour." In the present text, the four monsters are also linked by their association with the waters of chaos. Unlike the beasts in Daniel, they do not surrender this form of existence.

The conflict motif is still easily recognizable in the text's terminology. *Rahab* is cut to pieces and *Tannin* is pierced through. The verbs therefore presuppose that "Yahweh's arm" is doubly armed, with both sword and lance.[130]

In v. 10, in the second pair, "drying out" through "rebuke" is conceivable, if one remembers 50:2 and Nah 1:4. But in the present text הַמַּחֲרֶבֶת *hammahᵃrebet* suggests an association with חֶרֶב *ḥereb*, "sword."[131] It is noticeable, however, that the word for sword is never actually used, even when the text talks about Rahab being "cut to pieces." This could be an example of DtIsa's repression of warlike elements. Indeed, the description could also be interpreted as a hunting scene.[132]

In biblical tradition, for chaos to be overcome at the beginning and for its limits to be established by Yahweh is part of creation and the preservation of the world. In the text the world order is expressed in mythical categories. But in addition these mythical images are now unequivocally linked through v. 10b with the miracle at the Reed Sea, at the exodus from Egypt. The "sea" image is therefore preserved throughout the text. The same association must be assumed in Isa 43:16 and 50:2, and is presupposed in Psalm 77 too.

A comparison with the different versions of the miracle at the Reed Sea in the Passover pericope in Exodus 14 suggests itself. In the version generally attributed to the Yahwist (J), "Yahweh drove the sea back by a strong east wind all night, and turned the sea into dry land" (v. 21). This offers a relatively natural explanation for the miracle. It includes elements from the holy war, for example, when the people "have to keep still" (v. 14) because Yahweh is fighting for them, and when the enemy panics (v. 24). It is also an endorsement of Moses, since at the end the text says: "So the people feared Yahweh and believed in Yahweh and in his servant Moses." In the second version, ascribed to the Elohist (E), the waters "form a wall for them on their right and on their left" (v. 22). Here the miraculous elements are more marked, in what Moses does too, as we have already seen (vv. 26-27).

Compared with the versions in Exodus 14, the mythical elements in the present DtIsa text are strongest of all. The event is given timeless validity. The legitimation reaches back to primordial times. At the same time, the context makes clear that it is Moses who again initiates the liberation. The conclusion is now that there is a way (דֶּרֶךְ, v. 10bβ) where "those who have been freed can cross" (לַעֲבֹר). This may also be a reference to the crossing of the Jordan and the entry into the promised land.[133] "Way" is meant to be understood literally, although at this period it also began to be used as the embodiment of a righteous life. There is a "way" even in the perilous deep. These few verses therefore sum up the whole tradition of salvation. It is an attribute of the divine sovereignty. Consequently the participial constructions are appropriate. What has been said is valid for all time.

■ **11** As Seidl maintains,[134] "primordial days" in v. 9 indicates "clear references to undefined events in the past"; but it should equally be noted that the turn to the future in v. 11 is intentional, as the very forms of the verbs show. The experience of foundational saving events is brought to bear on contemporary behavior in a quite

129 Thus the translation in the NRSV; cf. also Plöger, *Daniel*.

130 See the translation in textual note 9ᵃ above.

131 In the context of the passage through the Jordan the term is used for the drying out of the riverbed (Josh 3:17; 4:18).

132 Cf. in Egypt the mutual interchangeability of the hunt and war. Through both, the pharaoh establishes the order of the world.

133 The crossing of the Jordan under Joshua is depicted in Joshua 3–5 as a renewal of the Reed Sea miracle (thus explicitly Josh 4:21-24). On "way," דֶּרֶךְ, see Josh 3:4. Cf. also the renewal of the Passover and the Mazzot in Josh 5:10-12. With this renewal the manna simultaneously ceases.

134 T. Seidl, "Jahwe der Krieger—Jahwe der Tröster.

specific sense: "The ransomed of Yahweh" are to come to Zion. "Liberation" is the overarching horizon of the text. Liberation of the world from whatever threatens its existence, liberation from Egypt, and the liberation of people who have been enslaved: all these correspond.

It is difficult to decide how far the text also includes direct political references. *Rahab* is a name for Egypt in Ps 87:4; Isa 30:7 (cf. Ps 89:11 [10]; Job 9:13; 26:12). *Tannin* (cf. *BHS*) can stand for Pharaoh (Ezek 29:3; 32:2) and for Nebuchadnezzar (Jer 51:34)—both of them later favorite code names used for political communication in difficult times.

With this text too one can ask about the theory and practice of the performance. Here again the problem of time has a special relevance. If we do not confine ourselves to the formula about the unity of time and place as a theatrical rule, then events on the stage can very well bind together different times and present them as simultaneous. The cultic drama in particular regularly presents past as present.

The text is extremely dense in content, as must have been the action that we may assume accompanied it. It begins with a powerful acoustic effect: a call to wake up, uttered three times. One can again ask whether this is not also an indication of time, either fictitious or real. According to Genesis 1, the creation begins with the creation of light, the division of light from darkness. "At the morning watch Yahweh looked down upon the Egyptian army" (Exod 14:24)—and its downfall begins. As we have seen, both these traditions are linked in the present text. In the parallelism of a liturgical performance, one could imagine that this scene was played at first light. This would suggest that the act as a whole was performed at night. "Wake up!" would then waken the participants too. But a fictitious time would also be possible in the framework of the drama.

I already pointed out earlier in the exegesis that in vv.

9 and 10 verbs of action are used; but their grammatical and syntactical form is descriptive of a "state." All the verbs, however, are saying something about "Yahweh's arm" (fem. in Hebrew). Since the forms are feminine throughout, a female character is conceivable. The first act after the reveille is to put on "strength" (עֹז). That can be understood in a transferred sense, but the combination of strength and "putting on" is unusual. A piece of clothing can be put on. Soon afterward, in 52:1, Jerusalem is also supposed to put on "strength/power" (עֹז). There strength is parallel to "beautiful garments," but both are to be put on (לבשׁ). Is the "strength" (עֹז) that is to be put on here actually armor? This would fit the situation before a battle,[135] and would also be appropriate for "Jerusalem" as a representation of the walled city.[136] Once "strength" has been put on, then into battle! But there are no battle scenes in DtIsa. According to 42:13 Yahweh raises the war cry, and the battle itself can be imagined as taking place behind the scenes.[137] The same could be true of the present text, but it is also possible that the attributes applied to "Yahweh's arm" in this text merely herald the event while the type of presentation remains open.

Horus kills Seth in the form of a crocodile. Saint George slays the dragon, and in medieval pictures the dragon is still usually green, like a crocodile. So tenacious are traditions! A folk play about the slaying of the dragon that is still performed in Furth im Wald in Bavaria continues to celebrate the victory of good over evil. The dragon belongs to mythology as far afield as India and China, and continually plays a part in festival processions. According to the present text, as many as four different dragons are conquered by Yahweh's arm. A dramatic presentation is conceivable.

The return to Zion of the people who have been "ransomed" is explicitly described.[138] Verse 11 elaborates, depicting the return as a festive procession: "with lasting

---

Kritik und Neuinterpretation der Schöpfungsvorstellungen in Jesaja 51:9-16," *BN* n.s. 21 (1983) 123.

135 Cf. Ps 93:1; Isa 59:17; Eph 6:10-17. Apart from the donning of a suit of armor, a helmet and shield would also be conceivable. For the scene cf. also the vase paintings that show men arming for battle.

136 Cf. Isa 26:1; Cant 8:9-10.

137 The struggle is accompanied by the sound "*e, e.*" In vv. 9-10 the double segol is used five times, an indi-

cation that the text is designed to be heard. On the other hand, in v. 10a the written impression made by the Hebrew מִי יָם is striking. It can be read forward and backward, and could be an indication of the calligraphical form given to the original text. The water is optically divided, so to speak.

138 That this could also be a quotation from Isa 35:10 is no hindrance; see above on 51:9-11.

joy upon their heads." Again an abstract concept, joy, stands for something that can literally be carried on the head. Is it laurel wreaths? These can be preserved as a remembrance ("lasting," עוֹלָם). But flowers and other greenery could also be meant. Rejoicing and joy is the general mood—gratitude for the liberation that has been experienced, and that is relived in cultic drama and in reality. At the close, another stage direction can be detected in the text. Jubilation and joy "arrive," sorrow and sighing "flee away." We may assume that in a dramatic performance the concepts were again personified. With this the scene ends.

"... to plant the heavens and to lay the foundations of the earth and to say to Zion: You are my people!" (51:16)
"And I put my words in your mouth, and in the shadow of my hand I have hidden you ..." (51:16)

51:12-16
Antiphonal Speech by God and the Servant of God
The Link between Creation, Liberation and Salvation (for Zion/Jerusalem and Jacob/Israel)
Exit of the Servant of God

12   I myself, I myself am the one who comforts
          you [2d masc. plur.].
    Who are you [2d fem. sing.]?
    And you [2d fem. sing.] are afraid of human
          beings who will die,
    and of a human being who will become as
          grass?

13   And you [2d masc. sing.] forgot Yahweh
          who made you [2d masc. sing.],
    who stretched out the heavens
    and who laid the foundations of the earth,
    and you trembled continually all day long
    because of the fury of the oppressor,
    when he tried to destroy.
    And where (now) is the fury of the oppressor?
14   The one who is in chains shall speedily be
          freed.
    And he will not die in the pit,
    and he will not lack for bread.

15   But I am Yahweh, your God,
    who stirred up the sea, so that its waves
          roared.
    Yahweh Sabaoth is his name.

16   And I put my words in your mouth,
    and in the shadow of my hand I have
          hidden you,
    to plant[a] the heavens
    and to lay the foundations of the earth
    and to say to Zion: You are my people!

16[a] Probably "stretch out" (נטה) should be read here instead of "plant" (נטע); cf. v. 13 and the commentaries.

The text is a challenge, for, as C. North writes about these verses: "Compared with the rest of DI [Deutero-Isaiah] they are 'jumpy' and inconsequent."[139] He maintains (thinking not least about the relation of this text to the Servant Songs): "All things considered, li. 12-16 is the Achilles heel of the theory that DI 'wrote' and edited a book to which no subsequent additions were made."[140] Contrary to this view, I should like to put forward the following hypothesis: the rapid change in the persons addressed is connected with the dramatic structure of the text, and this text is an important element in the

presentation of the Servant of God, "Moses."

This is a transitional passage. It takes up what has gone before (e.g., picking up in v. 14 the theme of liberation from v. 11), while with v. 12, as we shall see, it points to what is to come: the rise of Zion/Jerusalem (v. 17 onward) and its "liberation" (52:2).

The repeated changes of speaker and addressees are a noticeable feature of the text. Yahweh's name is pronounced three times (once in v. 13, and twice in v. 15). Verse 13 names him in the third person, v. 15a is a first person declaration, and v. 15b is again third person.

139 North, 213–14.
140 North, 214.

Verse 12 begins with a plural form of address but everything else is in the singular. Masculine forms are generally used for the addressees, but in 51:12 we find the feminine. We shall try to discover the reason for this rapid alternation.

■ **12a** *God's address to all who listen.* The text begins in v. 12a with what is clearly a divine speech. This is a "self-introductory formula," beginning with the solemn-sounding double "I" in the longer form of the personal pronoun (אָנֹכִי). Here God himself is speaking in the form of the "participial predicate" otherwise characteristic of hymnic acclamations: "I myself, I myself am the one who comforts you." That implies: I and none other! As Seidl stresses, "comfort" as promise and help is contrasted with the warlike picture of the preceding text, vv. 9-11.[141] It thus again takes up the proclamation of 40:1 in succinct, emblematic form. In the more immediate context, the theme is taken up in 49:13; 51:3 (bis); and in 52:9. Since there is a close link between "comfort" (נחם) and "release" (גאל, פדה),[142] the divine speech also heralds in appropriate form what is said in the following verse. The message is addressed to all those present, and hence to the listeners too.

■ **12b** *God's address to "Zion/Jerusalem."* Since there is no interruption to the whole, not even by way of an "and," a "but" (וְ) or any other signal, we may assume that this is a continuation of the divine speech. It is addressed to a single (grammatically fem.) person. In the preceding vv. 9-11, "Yahweh's arm" is feminine, but this cannot be the addressee, since the text talks about "fearing." "Jerusalem" is a possibility, however, since in the following passage from v. 17 onward it appears as "poor" (עֲנִיָּה, fem., v. 21) and oppressed. We may assume more exactly that in v. 12b "Zion/Jerusalem" (the main character in the following scenes) comes on again, her exit, accompanied by her children, having been signaled in 50:1. The units 51:1-3, 4-8, 9-11 were certainly concerned in a different way with the theme of Zion, but not in the form of a personification.

It is possible that "Zion/Jerusalem" is not immediately recognizable here. "Who are you?" is the question asked on behalf of children watching a Punch and Judy show, when a new character comes on. Perhaps Zion/Jerusalem cannnot actually be seen the whole time by the spectators, for it is not until v. 17 that she is told: "Stand up, Jerusalem!" Through the catchwords "I myself am the one who comforts you" (cf. 40:1: "Comfort, comfort my people") and "You are afraid of . . . a human being who will become a grass?" (cf. 40:6: "All flesh is grass . . .") chap. 40 is called to mind. From that context we also know that Jerusalem is or was liable for military service or forced labor (צָבָא, 40:2). Isaiah 40 emerges once more as being a prologue, a summing up of the whole, for the following sections describe the raising up of Jerusalem. In the present text the argument is based on the transience of human beings, and especially rulers and their power.[143] Fear of other human beings is misplaced. God is not mortal: he "ruleth on high, almighty to save," as the hymn says.

■ **13-14** *The Servant of God's address to "Jacob/Israel."* The continuation is certainly not spoken by Yahweh, for the first two words in v. 13 make clear that Yahweh is being talked about in the third person, and that it is now no longer a female who is being addressed; it is a male in the singular. Who is the addressee? No name is mentioned, but the third saying, "who made you" (עֹשֶׂךָ), permits the identification. It is, in my view, "Jacob/Israel." The reinstallation of Jacob/Israel began in 43:1: "But now, thus says Yahweh, your creator, Jacob, and the one who formed you, Israel." The rather colorless "make" (עשה) in the present text covers the creating (ברא) and the forming (יצר) of 43:1. The name Jacob is never used after chap. 49 (vv. 5, 6, 26). Cyrus was a similar case: his name is not pronounced after 45:1, although he is talked about. He disappears, so to speak.

Even if this is the personification of Jacob/Israel, it is at the same time the nameless person enslaved for debt whose fear emerges from the text. A comparison with

---

141   Seidl, "Jahwe der Krieger—Jahwe der Tröster. Kritik und Neuinterpretation der Schöpfungsvorstellungen in Jesaja 51:9-16," *BN* n.s. 21 (1983) 129–31, esp. 130 on this passage.

142   See K. Baltzer, "Liberation from Debt Slavery After the Exile in Second Isaiah and Nehemiah," in *Ancient Israelite Religion: FS F. M. Cross* (1987) 477–84, esp. 477.

143   אֱנוֹשׁ *ʾenôs* has a collective meaning "human beings." In the late period it stresses the fragility and limitation of human existence. בֶּן־אָדָם *ben-ʾādām* is someone who belongs to the species human being (lit. "son of man"), i.e., is not divine. But there is also an echo of "descendant of Adam"; see C. Westermann, "אָדָם *ʾādām* person," *TLOT* 1:31–42 [*THAT* 1:41–57, esp. 43–45].

42:22-25 and 49:8-13 shows that the subject is not exile in general; it is institutionalized slavery for debt. This is a special form of slavery.[144] The free man can be forced to give himself in pledge because of debts, famine, or for other reasons. The creditor can try to compel the debtor's family to redeem him. He also retains the right to exploit the labor of the debtor, or to sell him into slavery. Laws such as the ones found in Exod 21:1-11, Leviticus 25, and Deut 15:12-18 show that attempts were made to regulate this practice legally, since its effect on the community was ultimately destructive. Jer 34:8-22 and above all Neh 5:1-13 reflect the theory and practice of liberation from slavery for debt.

In light of these presuppositions, the present text gives a consistent picture. The daily affliction suffered by the debtor is caused by the creditor. In chains, in prison, without sufficient food (see v. 14)—this in extreme cases was the debtor's situation.

But in a marvelous way his fortunes change. The speech indicates a whole series of actions illustrating both the affliction and the liberation. It is conceivable that these actions were dramatically performed. But who announces what is happening? Who is speaking, if it is not Yahweh? A number of observations can first be gathered together, as a help toward answering this question.

In this fifth act, from 50:4 onward, the Servant of God speaks. This is so in 50:4-11 and in 51:1-3. In contrast, 51:4-8 is presented as a divine speech. In 51:9-11 the Servant of God is again speaking; in 51:12 it is Yahweh himself. We must assume that the following vv. 15 and 16 are also a divine speech for the most part. If we look at the alternation of speakers in this whole context, it would seem obvious to assume that vv. 13 and 14 are spoken by the Servant. No other person is introduced.

Another aspect of the text suggests the same conclusion. According to the first Servant of God text, the Servant's task is to bring the people out of "the dungeon," "the house of captivity." Before the reinstallation of Jacob/Israel in 43:1-7, 42:22-23 describes the "robbed and plundered people," and there is again talk of prisons. In the context of the second Servant of God text, the Servant is given the commission (49:9): "to say to the prisoners: Go out! and to those in darkness: Come into

the light! [lit., perhaps: 'Let yourself be seen!' or something similar]." The description of distress in the present passage is comparable with these other texts. The Servant is therefore once more fulfilling the charge given him to proclaim "liberation." But if the Servant of Yahweh who also leads out of the dungeon (see יצא, "to lead out," in 42:7; 49:9) is "Moses," the present text acquires a further point. Finally, in interpreting the different units from 50:4 onward it proved helpful to see the Moses who has appeared as the Moses of Deuteronomy. In this case, however, we shall have to look at the laws in Deuteronomy about enslavement for debt (Deut 15:12-18) and the social legislation there (24:6-22), subjecting them to a careful comparison. In these laws the indebtedness of the poor is a recurring theme. In an emergency these people were forced to give in pledge objects of even such small value as a hand mill (v. 6) or a garment (v. 17). The ultimate object of value that could be offered as pledge was the debtors's own life and liberty (Deut 15:12-13). The line between this and abduction could evidently be a fine one, for the series of enactments also forbids Israelites to sell a "brother," or fellow Israelite, into slavery (24:7). The laws are several times justified by a reminder of the time in Egypt and Yahweh's liberation (15:15; 34:18, 22).

But the "oppressors" (הַמֵּצִיק) also acquire a profile in the present text, in light of 51:13. According to Deut 24:6-7, the kidnapper "acts violently" (עמר *Hitpael*). The day laborer must not be "oppressed" (עשׁק, Deut 24:14; cf. 28:29, 33, and Isa 52:4; 54:14). Even the comment: "You tremble continually all day long" (51:13) acquires a special point if the time unit for calculating pledges and wages is only a day (Deut 24:13, 15). It is also noteworthy that these laws are to apply to Israelites and foreigners alike. They are therefore just what the headings in some modern Bibles call them: "humanitarian precepts."

Through allusions of this kind, the text signals that "Moses," the Servant of God, is giving these commandments new, contemporary validity. In Deuteronomy they are promulgated in the context of Moses' farewell address, so they are at the same time his last will or bequest. That the same may be said about the present

144 See Baltzer, "Liberation from Debt Slavery After the Exile in Second Isaiah and Nehemiah," in *Ancient Israelite Religion: FS F. M. Cross* (1987) 477–84, with lit.

DtIsa text will be shown in what follows, in light of the exegesis of vv. 15 and 16.

If we appeal to this speech as "Moses'" bequest, we may also ask whether there is not a contemporary reference here as well. The implicit demand, several times repeated, is that the people who have been enslaved for debt must be redeemed or freed, if Jerusalem as city and Jacob/Israel as people are to rise again. This is clearly DtIsa's message at this prominent point.[145] But that is Nehemiah's program too (cf. Nehemiah 5; 1:5-11).[146] Prophetic tradition, particularly Jeremiah (cf. Jer 34:8-22), had already initiated the theme, in all its theological and political implications. Without liberation from the fear of "oppressors," there can be no future for the community. This is the enduring, implausible message: that according to God's will human beings should have no fear of other human beings.

■ **15a** *God speaks.* In v. 15 a divine speech clearly begins once more: "But I am Yahweh, your God." In this context the second person masculine singular suffix in "your God" (אֱלֹהֶיךָ) can refer to a number of different people: to the Servant of God (Moses), to the nameless prisoner (Jacob/Israel), and to whoever feels included, up to v. 16b—that is, up to "my people." It may be that all three are addressed. The following three divine predications are strange from a literary point of view, for—as the commentators have continually pointed out—this is a quotation from Jer 31:35, the passage promising the new covenant. And it looks as if that was the context to which it originally belonged. There the text is talking about laws for sun, moon, and stars. The roaring of the waves is then, as Beuken shows, a sign "of obedience and subservience."[147] The waves do what they are created for. They are under restraint, wild though they may seem. This is proclaimed by the Creator himself.

■ **15b** *The Servant of God's confession of faith.* In Jer 31:35 "the Lord Sabaoth is his name" is an affirmative summing up of the kind found elsewhere too. No special emphasis can be detected. But in a text like the present one in DtIsa, the change from direct address to the third person ("his name")—and hence the change of speaker too—is a clear signal. Who is now uttering the confession of faith: "Yahweh Sabaoth is his name"? In my view it is again the Servant of God. He is addressed immediately afterward, in v. 16, and he is authorized to speak. That all the people can, and should, echo this confession of faith—about that there can be no question. The only striking point is once again DtIsa's special predilection for the formulation "Yahweh Sabaoth" (6 times), a predicate never used by Trito-Isaiah or Ezekiel, for example.

The way DtIsa uses the acknowledgment "Yahweh Sabaoth is his name" in 47:4 is especially important.[148] In 47:1 the descent of the daughter "Babylon" into the underworld begins: "Step down and sit in (the) dust" (v. 1).[149] "Sit down in silence and enter into the darkness" (v. 5). For "Babylon" this is a "descent into hell" because she has to experience the consequences of her guilt (47:3). At this particular point in the drama DtIsa introduces "a human being." On his way into the underworld he behaves in a suitable way. He knows who his redeemer is. He knows the password: "Yahweh Sabaoth is his name, the Holy One of Israel."

I think it possible that this passage in chap. 47 corresponds to the present one. "Moses" utters the name of Yahweh Sabaoth in the same way as "Everyman." This would also be a sign that Moses, the Servant of God, is (again) entering the world of the dead. He has truly died, as he prophesied according to the end of the book of Deuteronomy.

In place of "Step down and sit in (the) dust"—the command to "Babylon"—another imperative immediately follows in 51:17: "Rouse yourself! . . . Stand up, Jerusalem!" There can be no clearer contrast between the two "cities." Out of the depths a new life begins.

■ **16** *God's address to the Servant of God.* "I put my words in your mouth." God can do this when he authorizes a human being and equips him as prophet. In Deut 18:18

---

145 Comparable in early Attic comedy would be the chorus's *parabasis*, in which the writer turns to the audience critically, with his own personal and political ideas; see, e.g., Aristophanes *Acharnians* 625–718; *Frogs* 674–737.

146 See Baltzer, "Liberation from Debt Slavery After the Exile in Second Isaiah and Nehemiah," in *Ancient Israelite Religion: FS F. M. Cross* (1987), esp.

481–82; and idem, "Moses Servant of God and the Servants: Text and Tradition in the Prayer of Nehemiah (Neh 1:5-11)," in *The Future of Early Christianity: FS H. Koester* (1991) 121–30.

147 Beuken on this passage.

148 Cf. 44:6; 45:13; 48:2; 54:5.

149 See above on this passage.

the prophetic office is derived from Moses in almost the same words: "I will raise up for them a prophet like you from among their own people and I will put [lit. 'give,' נתן] my words in his mouth." At the same time the text demonstrates Moses' unique position, the incomparability of which is established at the end of Deuteronomy, after Moses' death (Deut 34:10). "Never since has there arisen a prophet in Israel like Moses, whom Yahweh knew face to face."[150] It is precisely this unique position that the present text asserts. But it is remarkable that this comment should be among Deuteronomy's final words, and therefore belongs to the conclusion of Moses' Torah.

Some commentators are bothered because the sentence "In the shadow of my hand I have hidden you" appears almost word for word in 49:2, although the phrase "in the shadow of his [or my] hand" never occurs anywhere else.[151] But we should note that the statement is made by the Servant of God about himself in 49:2, and belongs to the second Servant of God text. When it is reiterated here as a divine utterance and promise, that establishes a link, making clear that here too it is the Servant of God who is being talked about.

The whole passage right to the end acquires its significance if Yahweh is presented as speaking to "Moses." That can be made clear through a paraphrase: That God put his words in Moses' mouth is familiar enough, where the laws are concerned; but here the statement applies to the whole of Moses' Torah. Yet how could Moses talk about the creation of heaven and earth when he was not there? DtIsa answers by saying that Moses was hidden and kept safe in the shadow of God's hand. This means that his preexistence was a conceivable idea. As a prophet, Moses is in this respect unique. With this utterance the text looks back to the beginning of things. But

Moses also looks forward, away from his own time into the future.

The ancient foundational declaration of the covenant was: "I will be your God and you shall be my people." This is clearly echoed at the beginning of v. 15 and at the close of v. 16. This is the way the declaration was revealed to Moses. But now Moses is authorized "to say to Zion: You are my people." Without the divine commission, Moses would not have been able to know about "Zion" any more than he could have known about the creation.

There is a tension in the final formulation of the text that we ourselves hardly notice: the tension between the ancient traditions that appeal to Jacob/Israel as a representation of the people of God, and the traditions about Zion/Jerusalem that, as is generally known, were linked with Israelite traditions as a whole only from the time of David onward. The partition of the Davidic kingdom again called in question, at least to some extent, the association of these different traditions.

The exile and the postexilic period had to take up these problems once more. At the reconstruction one of the main problems was the tension between town and country. DtIsa links the two strands of tradition. "Zion—God's people" is his program too. Could this have been presented in more dramatically enthralling terms than by first letting the nameless pair come forward: (Zion) as a woman in fear, (Jacob/Israel, the people) as a man in utmost necessity?

The "Moses" who has appeared, the nameless Servant of God, proclaims the liberation, the promise of God's new beginning. "Yahweh Sabaoth is his name": that is his final word. With it Moses disappears once more to the place from whence he came, the world of the dead, until in 52:13—53:12 his exaltation is presented.

---

150 Trans. as in NRSV; see also von Rad, *Deuteronomy* (1979) 209–10 [*Deuteronomium* (2d ed. 1968)] on this passage.

151 It could very well be a modification of the statement in Exod 33:22, however. Moses desires to see Yahweh's glory. That is not possible: "For no one shall see me and live" (v. 20). For his protection Moses is given the assurance: " I will cover you with my hand (וְשַׂכֹּתִי כַפִּי) until I have passed by" (v. 22). The hollow hand provides shadow and protection against the radiant light of glory (כְּבֹדִי, v. 22). Only after his death does the Servant of God–Moses enter into the glory of God (see below on 52:13–53:12).

C. 1. 51:17-23
Jerusalem's "Drunkenness"

51

"See, I have taken out of your hand the cup of staggering" (51:22)

17 Rouse yourself! Rouse yourself!
Stand up, Jerusalem!
you who have drunk from the hand of Yahweh
the cup of his wrath,
who have drunk and drained to the dregs
the bowl, the cup of staggering.

18 There was no one to guide her
among all the sons she had borne,
and there was no one to take her by the hand
among all the sons whom she had brought
up.

19 These two [or: both these things?] have
befallen you.
Who laments over you?
The devastation and the collapse and the
famine and the sword—
who <comforts>ª you?

20 Your sons fainted, they lay there,
at every street corner, like an antelope in a
net,
filled with Yahweh's wrath,
with the rebuke of your God.

21 Therefore hear this, you who are poor
and drunk, but not with wine!

22 Thus says your Lord Yahweh,
and your God, who fights the case for his
people:
See, I have taken out of your hand
the cup of staggering,
you will no longer have to drink
the bowl, the cup of my wrath.

23 But I will give it into the hand of those who
torment you,ª
who have said to you:
Bow down, so that we can walk on you!
So that you had to make your back like the
ground
and like a road for them to walk on.

19ª מִי יְנַחֲמֵךְ, "who comforts you?" should probably be read, with 1QIsaª and the early versions, rather than מִי אֲנַחֲמֵךְ, "how could I comfort you?"

23ª Here 1QIsaª adds וביד מעניך, "and into the hand of those who oppress you"; cf. LXX.

The text is the antitype to a Dionysian scene: "Drunk, but not with wine" (v. 21). Jerusalem experiences its most profound humiliation, and yet at the same time the turn of its fortunes. Let us first trace the argument of the text.

The section is again dominated by the idea of Jeru-salem as a woman. It is an extremely daring, even grotesque, picture. Normally, in Israel's surrounding world the city goddess is actually the personification of the city's virtues. She is frequently identified with Tyche, the goddess of fortune.[152] Tyche can be amalgamated with other goddesses, for example, Cybele, Astarte, Artemis[153] and Isis.[154] Tyche as city goddess bears as symbols the mural crown and the cornucopia, or horn of plenty. It is worth considering whether this iconographical presentation is the presupposition for an understanding of the present text.[155] In Isa 54:11-12 Zion is adorned by Yahweh with the mural crown.[156] The horn of plenty could be parodistically "defamiliarized," so as to become the model for the present text's "cup of staggering" (כּוֹס הַתַּרְעֵלָה). The curiously twisted form of the cornucopia and its frequent association with symbols for the gods could have suggested a transformation of this kind. Perhaps the "children" also belong to the iconography of Tyche as city goddess. They represent the city's wealth. That is why the goddess can carry the boy Pluto in her arms, or is shown with children beside her. In the present parody the children have to lead their drunken mother. Finally, it is conceivable that the antelope or gazelle,[157] which crops up so surprisingly in v. 20, originally—like other animals belonging to the goat family—typified a goddess as the mistress of animals.[158] Caprids are symbols of life and fertility. In the text, this motif too is perverted into its very opposite: the antelopes are imprisoned in the net. With this city iconography in mind, one can judge what it means when in this scene the city's personification appears as a drunken woman.

The image and the thing imaged go back to prophetic tradition.[159] Particularly in its present form[160] Jeremiah 25 can be read as an apt illustration of the point that is being made here. The fall of Jerusalem is not an inexplicable fate. It came about because God caused it, and in accordance with his will. What one sees is the loss of all rational political decision-making.[161] Whole nations can "be drunk." The image about the drinking of "the cup of staggering"[162] is a pictogram of its own, used to express calamity and its sequel. In Jeremiah 25, when the exile is announced, an explicit link is forged between the banishment and what Judah and Jerusalem have done (vv. 14-15): "So I will repay them according to their deeds and the work of their hands; for. . . ." The administration of the "cup of staggering" is therefore not simply an act through which God arbitrarily decides the fate of peoples.

■ **17-20** With these presuppositions, the present passage can be seen to be a retraction of the prophetic proclamation of doom.[163] It would seem possible for us still to reconstruct from it a prophetic oracle and its interpretation. The oracle would have begun with the announcement (v. 17): "You have drunk . . ." (שָׁתִית, bis) or "drink . . ." (שְׁתֵה). Then v. 19 follows with a wordplay: "There are two . . ." (שְׁתַּיִם or שְׁתֵּי). In the text as we have it, this phrase stands in curious isolation, for in fact four

152 For "Tyche" as city goddess see L. Ruhl, "Tyche," in W. H. Roscher, ed., *ALGM* (1916–24, reprint 1965) 1309–80; O. Waser, "Tyche in bildlicher Darstellung," ibid., 1357–80; G. Herzog-Hauser, "Tyche 1," PW 7/A2 (1948) 1643–89; M. P. Nilsson, *Geschichte der griechischen Religion* vol. 2 (3d ed. 1974) 200–218.

153 The description of Artemis as the city goddess of Ephesus (cf. Acts 19:21-40) is of special interest, since iconographical elements are present, e.g., mural crown, fetters and goatlike creatures, all of which indicate cultic connections.

154 See Herzog-Hauser, "Tyche 1," PW 7/A2 (1948) 1680–82.

155 See K. Baltzer, "The Polemic against the Gods and Its Relevance for Second Isaiah's Conception of the New Jerusalem," in *Second Temple Studies* (1994) 52–59.

156 See below on this passage.

157 See A. Terian, "The Hunting Imagery in Isaiah li 20a," *VT* 41 (1991) 462–71, esp. 470.

158 See O. Keel and C. Uehlinger, *Gods, Goddesses, and Images of God* (1998) index s.v. "Mistress of the Animals" [*Göttinnen, Götter und Gottessymbole* (1992), index s.v. "Herrin der Tiere, Capriden"].

159 Cf. Isa 28:1, 7; 29:9; Jer 13:12-14; 49:12; 51:7; Ezek 23:32-34; Nah 3:11-12; Hab 2:16; Ps 60:5 (3); Lam 4:21.

160 For the literary problems of the text see W. L. Holladay, *Jeremiah*, on this passage.

161 Isa 19:14; Ps 107:27: "stagger like a drunkard." "He was at his wits' end."

162 For the metaphorical meaning of "the cup of staggering" see H. A. Brongers, "Der Zornesbecher," *OTS* 15 (1969) 177–92, esp. 178–79.

163 Cf. v. 17, "stand up, Jerusalem," with Jer 25:27, for example: "Drink (שְׁתוּ), get drunk and vomit, fall and rise no more (וְלֹא תָקוּמוּ) before the sword that I am sending upon you."

plagues are initially mentioned. It is only in v. 20b that two threats follow: "the wrath of Yahweh and the rebuke of your God." From this "they [the sons] are full" (i.e., drunk).[164]

The text contains an interpretation. As Duhm already observed,[165] v. 18 is not smoothly welded into the context. But in DtIsa Zion/Jerusalem's "sons" undoubtedly have their place.[166] The text is criticizing the "sons" who have not helped their mother in her degradation.

Verses 19 and 20 describe the downfall of the city in traditional phraseology. "Famine and sword" are hardships included in curse lists. We can see DtIsa's tendency toward abstraction when he adds to this pair "devastation (הַשֹּׁד) and collapse (הַשֶּׁבֶר)." In Nah 3:7, to say that no one bemoans and comforts is a way of making Nineveh's downfall clear. What is striking in DtIsa at this point is that the future tense of the verbs "lament" and "comfort" is used. It is as if this utterance originally belonged to a prophecy of disaster, not to the description of the time of distress that is now past. In content, these are all declarations that also have a place in the popular lament.[167]

■ **21-23** These verses give the promise of salvation in the form of a divine saying. It is expressed in the same language as the description of distress that precedes it. There is a reversal of fortune once God takes away "the cup of staggering" from Jerusalem and gives it to Jerusalem's enemies. Jerusalem is no longer explicitly named; she is now "you who are poor" or "wretched" (עֲנִיָּה).[168] The image is thus already extrapolated when the drunkenness is explained as not being due to wine (v. 21).

The basis of the argument is the statement of faith: "Yahweh . . . your God . . . his people." If that is again true, then there is hope that Yahweh will "plead the cause of his people," in the sense of fighting a case (יָרִיב) on their behalf. The turn of events is due solely to God's resolve.

It has been made clear that Jerusalem was not guiltless of the fate meted out to her. Her downfall was not the arbitrary act of her God. In the same way her enemies are told why they have fallen victim to a similar destiny: their guilt is their brutal subjugation of those they had conquered. Even though in the ancient world brutality may have been normal practice in warfare, the text sees this as a transgression of the limits that are laid down for the mighty too. It had by now come to be a conceivable idea that God himself was still at work even in what the enemies of God's people did to them; and this means that a limit is laid down for these enemies also, in what they do. Here they are not judged according to the laws special to Israel; they are weighed in the balance and found wanting because of what was generally held to be the arrogance of the victor.[169]

The dramatic presentation begins right away in v. 17. Again, we have to assume that there was a spokesman who explained what was happening. (It is only in v. 22 that God begins to speak.) "Rouse yourself! Rouse yourself![170] Stand up!" This is the way one talks to a drunk, and there is already an element of parody about it. In what follows, everything that has happened is acted out once more. So that the spectators know who it is that is "staggering," she is named: this is Jerusalem. The name "Zion" is heard again only in 52:1. At the moment she is still the one who is humiliated. Perhaps there is a suggestion here that it is still night or early morning. It is only in 52:1 that Zion/Jerusalem is woken: "Awake, awake!" (עוּרִי). The triple reveille for "Yahweh's arm" was already sounded beforehand, in 51:9. "The heavenly ones" rise earlier!

---

164 "Being full" or "drunk" has its significance in connection with the saying about the "cup." Duhm thought it was "an appalling mixture of images for which the poet is not responsible" (360).

165 Duhm (359): "must have strayed into the text from the margin."

166 Cf. 54:13.

167 See Westermann, 244ff. [198]; A. Schoors, *I Am God Your Saviour* (1973) 129.

168 Cf. the comment on 54:11.

169 Cf. Isa 10:5-15, 24-27a; Jer 51:20-26, 34-40; Zech 1:15; 2:10-13 (6-9).

170 הִתְעוֹרְרִי. The verb "wake up," עור, is the same as in 51:9 and 52:1. But the form is a *Hitpolel* with a reflexive meaning (otherwise found only in Isa 64:6 [7]; Job 17:8). One cannot "wake" oneself, though one can "rouse oneself." Does the form הִתְעוֹרְרִי *hithʿôrᵉrî* (2x) also have onomatopoeic qualities when used in connection with הַתַּרְעֵלָה, "staggering, drunkenness"?

What was viewed favorably in the nightly revels of the Dionysian cults is given a bad mark here. The vase pictures illustrating the Greek wine festivals of the *oenotheria,* for example, show revelers being led home by young men. Naegelsbach[171] already noticed the frequent *lall* sounds in v. 18, which are perhaps intended to indicate indistinct speech.

The tense structure in vv. 17-20 is striking, with its combination of perfects and participles. If the verbs are to be interpreted as present perfects, then the action is still going on. The deictic "These" at the beginning of v. 19 suggests that there was something to see. Four sinister powers "fall upon" (קרא) "Jerusalem." Perhaps they were personified. Since "two" are mentioned, there may have been two pairs.[172] The attack may also have been presented in the form of a dance. The question: "Who laments over you?" could expect the answer: "no one." There is no one left on the stage who can lament. But the question could also have been designed to provoke the reaction of the audience and incite them to "lament."

The parallel question "Who <comforts> you?" means that the speaker himself is not in a position to do so. So the tension is built up in the direction of the utterances in vv. 21-22.

In v. 21 the speaker completely reverses the judgment passed on what has been seen. "Jerusalem" is a "poor woman," and her drunkenness is not due to wine. Verse 22 then introduces the divine speech in solemn form. The turning point is already indicated in an extraordinarily subtle but precise way before Yahweh himself

speaks, when he is announced as "your Lord" (אֲדֹנַיִךְ): the marriage tie with Jerusalem has been restored. Jerusalem has been accepted once more. "Jerusalem's" God is the very one who intervenes on behalf of his people and their rights. Here too the connection with the preceding text, 51:16, is maintained.

Again "the cup of staggering" is shown ("See . . . ," v. 22), before it is passed on to the tormentors (v. 23). The reproach leveled against them is their subjugation of "Jerusalem." As illustration, attention is frequently drawn to pictures in which kings tread on the backs of their subjugated enemies. There could conceivably be a military connotation if the phrase is rendered: "Like a road for them to walk on."[173] The only curious point is that Jerusalem herself is active, not just the tormentors. The sentence can also be translated: "You make your back like the land, as it is outside (חוּץ) for those who walk on it." If this is not just interpreted in a metaphorical sense, it could be describing the open, unwalled city. But the walls and the splendid form given to them are the theme of 54:11-14. There in v. 11, as here in 51:21, "the poor" and "the one who is not comforted" (cf. 51:19) are addressed. It may therefore be that catchwords for what is about to come are already given here in chap. 51. It is worth noting that there could hence also be references to the contemporary situation: the building of the walls under Nehemiah.[174]

---

171 Naegelsbach on this passage.
172 Again the sound of this sequence should be noted, above all the double *segol.*
173 The text may also have an obscene connotation. The tormentors say: "Bend down so that we can go over you." In its Aramaic *Pael*-form, עבר can mean "to cover, to mount"; cf. the *Piel* in Job 21:10.

According to *HALOT* (2:780 [*HALAT* 3:737]), it also has this meaning in "Jewish-Aramaic" in the *Pael* form. The city and her "soul" (נַפְשֵׁךְ) have been raped. Strikingly, obscenities also belonged to the Dionysian scene that the present text mirrors.
174 Cf. Nehemiah 1–6; 12:27-43.

"You were sold for nothing, and not for money will you be ransomed" (52:3)

C. 2. 52:1-6
Investiture and Enthronement of Zion/Jerusalem

---

1   Awake, awake!
Dress yourself with your strength, Zion!
Dress yourself in your state robes,
Jerusalem, you holy city!
Yes, an uncircumcised and an unclean person
shall enter you no more.

2   Shake off the dust from yourself!
Stand up, sit down, Jerusalem!
The chains round your neck have loosed
     themselves,[a]
(you) captive daughter Zion!

3   Yes, thus says Yahweh:
You were sold for nothing,
and not for money will you be ransomed.

4   Yes, thus says the Lord Yahweh:
My people first went down to Egypt,
to live there in the foreign land,
and Assyria has oppressed them without
     cause <for nothing>.

5   But now, what have I here?—saying of
     Yahweh.[a]
Truly, my people was taken away for nothing.
Its rulers <praise>—saying of Yahweh.
But continually, every day, my name is
     mocked.
[or: and where *tamid* (sacrifice) is concerned
     my name is mocked every day].

6   Therefore my people shall learn my name,
therefore,[a] on that day.
Yes, I am he who speaks! See: I!

2[a]   Thus following the *Ketib* (התפתחו). The *Qere* (which is followed by LXX, α', σ', ϑ', S and Vg) vocalizes as an imperative הִתְפַּתְּחִי, "free yourself <from the chains round your neck>." But we should then expect מִמּוֹסְרֵי rather than מוֹסְרֵי (see *BHS*).

5[a]   On the textual difficulties in v. 5, see the commentaries and the discussion below.

6[a]   Perhaps the second לָכֵן should be deleted, following 1QIsa[a], LXX, S, and Vg (see *BHS*); but see below on the text.

This scene shows the rise of Zion/Jerusalem out of deepest humiliation. Yahweh's entry into his royal city follows, with the choral ending in vv. 7-10. It is a "mirror scene,"[175] corresponding to Babylon's descent in chap. 47, so that the similarities and the differences in the fate of the two cities are brought out with particular clarity. Listeners are intended to learn from the cities as types of political and religious behavior. At the same time, as we shall see, there is a highly contemporary reference here. The subject is the restored city.

Our premise being that the text is a unified whole,[176] we shall try to understand the section on its different levels as an entirety. The literary operations frequently proposed in the commentaries are not required here.

In vv. 1-2 the "speaker" gives the directions and com-

ments on the action. But he is probably also speaking with prophetic authority ("thus says Yahweh," vv. 3 and 4; "saying of Yahweh," vv. 5 a and b). It is difficult to see this as a direct divine speech, since Yahweh's coming is announced in the following passage (v. 8, בְּשׁוּב יְהֹוָה צִיּוֹן).

Up to v. 9, Zion/Jerusalem is addressed, in an artistically contrived sequence: Zion—Jerusalem—Jerusalem—Zion—Zion—Zion—Jerusalem—Jerusalem. In the preceding scene of profoundest humiliation (51:17-23) the name of Zion was avoided. Now all Jerusalem is again "the holy city" (v. 1).[177]

Compared with 51:17, the "awake, awake" in v. 1 has again a positive sound. In the earlier passage Jerusalem was not asleep, but was just supposed to struggle to her feet in her drunken condition. The night is far

---

175   See here O. Taplin, *Greek Tragedy in Action* (1978) 122–39: "Mirror scenes."

176   Cf. the survey of the various possible divisions in

Beuken, 151 and 337 n. 1.

177   יְרוּשָׁלַם עִיר הַקֹּדֶשׁ could also be translated: "Jerusalem, city of the sanctuary." The grammatical

advanced, for in 51:9 "Yahweh's arm" (masc./fem.)[178] had to be woken three times. This implicit indication of time seems to me important for an understanding of vv. 7-10.

■ **1-2** To look first at the progress of the action: Zion/Jerusalem is told to dress herself (לבש). Seen as an investiture, this is also an act of state. Dress signals function and rank. An obvious example is the investiture of the high priest Joshua in Zech 3:1-7.[179] But now the whole personified city is given her "festal robe."

Here the abstract and the concrete are interchangeable. עז is "force, energy, power."[180] According to Isa 26:1, Jerusalem can be extolled in song as: "We have a strong city (עִיר עָז לָנוּ), help builds walls and bulwarks."[181]

But how can one "dress oneself" with strength (עֹז ʿoz)? I suspect that a breastplate is meant, as in 51:9. תִּפְאֶרֶת means "decoration, adornment, pomp."[182] In this case the word "robes" (בִּגְדֵי, plur.) clearly indicates that "glory" can be put on. As we can see especially from the statues of rulers down to Roman times, a surcoat could be put on over the armor. Veil (צַמָּה) and train (שֹׁבֶל) are signs of Babylon's noble status, according to 47:2.[183]

The clothes are also a program.[184] Jerusalem is pro-tected by her walls as if by armor. There is no mention of any weapons that could also be used for active fighting, such as a sword or spear.[185] If weapons of this kind are required, "Yahweh's arm" will fulfill their function (cf. 51:9-10), even if only as a deterrent (cf. 52:10). What the city desires is peace.

Jerusalem is to be a glorious city whose beauty can be a source of pride. But it must not be forgotten that "strength and glory" are divine attributes (cf. Pss 89:18 [17]; 96:6). That is why she is "the holy city."

Shaking off the dust is the next clearly visible gesture to be mentioned. Its special significance only becomes plain in the context of vv. 3-6. Babylon went down and sat down in the dust (47:1). So "stand up, get up" (קוּמִי) could, conversely, already have to do with the ascent to the throne, which was probably placed on a raised dais (cf. כִּסֵּא in 47:1). There "Jerusalem" is to take her place.

Up to this point the action is logical. The investiture and throne scenes in Attic drama and vase paintings provide a good illustration.

But according to the present text, Jerusalem/Zion is sitting on the throne with fetters around her neck—that is, chains or a rope. This is absurd and anything but

---

structure allows both possibilities. But according to GKC § 128k, p the closer definitions of the characteristic of a person or thing added to the construct state should be viewed as "merely formal genitives (*genit. explicativus* or *epixegeticus, genit. appositionis*). . . . Thus especially קֹדֶשׁ *holiness* very frequently serves as a periphrasis for the adjective קָדוֹשׁ, since קָדוֹשׁ is used almost exclusively in reference to persons" (according to GKC § 128p the use of צַדִּיק, צֶדֶק, and צְדָקָה is analogous; see, e.g., Lev 19:36). A series of examples of this use of קֹדֶשׁ is cited by GB under that heading (704), e.g., הַר הַקֹּדֶשׁ, "the holy mountain," Isa 27:13; Jer 31:23; Zech 8:3; Ps 87:1; Dan 9:20; אַדְמַת הַקֹּדֶשׁ, "the holy land," Zech 2:17 (13), as well as עִיר הַקֹּדֶשׁ, "the holy city," Isa 48:2; 52:1; Neh 11:1. It is noticeable that otherwise DtIsa never talks anywhere about the temple or the sanctuary (for 44:28 see above under that passage). His concern is always the unity of Zion/Jerusalem. It would therefore seem justifiable to render the phrase in 52:1 by "Jerusalem, the holy city" (thus also H. Ringgren in W. Kornfeld and H. Ringgren, "קדש *qdš*," *ThWAT* 6:1179–1204, esp. 1195). It is possible that there was a dispute precisely about this formula in its alternative meanings: "Jerusalem, city of the sanctuary" or "Jerusalem, the holy city." In each case the interpretation reflects different con-cepts about the relationship between city and sanctuary; cf. Zechariah 1–8 and esp. Zech 14:20-21, as well as Ps 46:5 (4); Neh 11:1, 18; Dan 9:24. For the rendering "holy city" see also Bonnard, 258 on this passage, and 203 on Isa 48:2; also *HALOT* 3:1077 [*HALAT* 3:1007]. A possible rendering as "the city of the Holy One" (i.e., God) cannot be excluded either.

178 See above on this passage.
179 Cf. also Jonathan's arming of David in 1 Sam 18:4.
180 See A. S. van der Woude, "עזז *ʿzz* to be strong," *TLOT* 2:868–72 [*THAT* 2:252–56].
181 See the commentaries on this passage; for עז in connection with fortifications cf. Judg 9:51; Amos 3:11; Jer 51:53; Pss 8:3 (2); 61:4 (3); Prov 10:15; 18:10, 11, 19.
182 See D. Vetter, "פאר *pʾr* pi. to glorify," *TLOT* 2:963–64 [*THAT* 2:387–89].
183 Cf. the list of the luxurious appointments for "the daughter of Zion" in Isa 3:16-24.
184 Cf. the descriptions of Athene; see D. Willers, "Athene," *LAW* 384–85 (with lit.).
185 The helmet is also missing. But see below on "mural crown" in 54:11-14.

logical,[186] and the audience of the time was probably not intended to see it as such either. The paradox that Jerusalem/Zion is an enthroned prisoner is probably the very point on which this text hinges, as I hope to show.

A first skillfully contrived signal is given in the text through the letter combination שׁב (*šb*). It is present in v. 2: "sit down" (שְׁבִי *šebî* from ישׁב, "sit"), and "prisoners" (שְׁבִיָּה *šebîyyāh* from שׁבה, "to take away as prisoner"), but also and above all in "return" (שׁוּב *šûb*) in the following v. 8: "They will see on Yahweh's return <to> Zion" (בְּשׁוּב יהוה צִיּוֹן). The same letter combination therefore occurs three times with three different verbs. This raises the question: how is Zion/Jerusalem's restoration related to the fact of her captivity (probably not as prisoner of war here,[187] but as a consequence of her debts) and to Yahweh's return to Zion? This would be to some degree the internal political problem of the text.

But this means that the text also intertwines with this a problem about relations with the outside world. Verse 1 already makes this plain: "yes, an uncircumcised and an unclean person shall no more enter you." This sentence is interposed into the action described, as an explanation of the phrase "holy city." In trying to solve the problem of the relation between internal affairs and the outside world according to the text, this sentence, I believe, must be taken as a starting point. What it says is unusual, in view of the openness toward foreigners that DtIsa shows elsewhere. "Circumcised" or "uncircumcised," "clean" and "unclean" are rather categories in priestly theology. A general interpretation is possible, but why is the plural not used ("uncircumcised and unclean persons") instead of the double singular? DtIsa himself likes to insert an "all" (כָּל־) when he is talking about groups; but he does not do so here. If people who are uncircumcised are not to be allowed in the city, some of the neighboring peoples would be permitted to enter, and others not.[188] It might be possible to exclude "unclean persons"[189] from the temple, but it would be difficult to exclude them from a whole city population, even if examples of such an exclusion can be found, as we can see from Mecca.

In this dilemma, E. J. Kissane is probably on the right track in his commentary when he writes about v. 1: "The new Sion will be free from foreign oppressors (cf. XXV.10; XXV.1; XXXII.18; XXXIII.18ff.). There is probably an allusion to the prophecy in Chapter XXXV concerning the 'holy way' to Sion over which the unclean shall not pass (XXXV.8)."[190]

Isa 35:8 says:

A <pure> highway shall be there,
<it> is called the Holy Way.
No unclean person shall walk on it,
<nor may a fool set foot upon the way>.[191]

But this is probably more than a mere "play on" Isa 35:8, for DtIsa has already taken up the promises to Zion in Isaiah 35 at two prominent points in the present act. In Isa 51:11 he cites the text of 35:10, and in 51:3 the whole ending of the same verse.

The immediate continuation of 35:10 in the book of Isaiah as we have it,[192] chaps. 36–37, is the account of how "Jerusalem was threatened by Sennacherib and

---

186 See Beuken (151) here: "It would be logical if Zion were first to loose her fetters (v. 2b) and then shake off the dust from herself, and take her place on a throne (v. 2a), in order finally to appear splendidly garbed (v. 1b)."

187 Thus *HALAT*, s.v.; cf. also *HALAT* on שׁוב II and שְׁבוּת, שְׁבִית.

188 F. Maas, "טָמֵא *ṭmʾ* to be unclean" *TLOT* 2:495–98 [*THAT* 1:664–67]; G. André, "טָמֵא *ṭmʾ*," *TDOT* 5:330–42, esp. 341–42 [*ThWAT* 3:352–66, esp. 364].

189 Cf. Jer 9:24-25 [25-26]; also on this passage W. Rudolph, *Jeremia* (3d ed. 1968), and W. L. Holladay, *Jeremiah* 1 (1986). Holladay points to the ancient texts cited in E. Schürer, *The History of the Jewish People* 1 (rev. ed. 1973) 537–38 [*Geschichte des jüdischen Volkes* 1 (1901) 675–76] and to J. M. Sasson,

"Circumcision in the Ancient Near East," *JBL* 85 (1966) 473–76; see also F. Dexinger, "Beschneidung," *TRE* 5:714–24.

190 Kissane, 167.

191 Thus the English translation of O. Kaiser, *Isaiah 13–39* (1974) [*Jesaja: Kapitel 13–39* (2d ed. 1976)]. The text is corrupt (see *BHS*); cf. the commentaries.

192 The problems of the composition of the book of Isaiah cannot be discussed here, but see Kaiser, *Isaiah 13–39*, on this passage; also C. Seitz, "Isaiah 1–66: Making Sense of the Whole," in C. Seitz, ed., *Reading and Preaching the Book of Isaiah* (1988) 105–26, and—esp. on Isaiah 36–39—idem, *Zion's Final Destiny: The Development of the Book of Isaiah* (1991); C. Hardmeier, *Prophetie im Streit vor dem Untergang Judas. Erzählkommunikative Studien zur Entstehungssituation der Jesaja- und Jeremiaerzählungen*

wondrously delivered":[193] "In the fourteenth year of King Hezekiah, King Sennacherib of Assyria came up against all the fortified cities of Judah and captured them. The king of Assyria sent the Rabshakeh from Lachish to King Hezekiah at Jerusalem, with a great army" (36:1-2).

Isa 37:33, finally, quotes as a saying of the prophet Isaiah: "Therefore thus says Yahweh concerning the king of Assyria: He shall not come into this city . . ." (לֹא יָבוֹא . . . אֶל־הָעִיר הַזֹּאת). This is not far removed from 52:1: "For an uncircumcised person will enter you no more" (כִּי לֹא יוֹסִיף יָבֹא־בָךְ עוֹד עָרֵל).

There can surely be no doubt that Sennacherib, the king of Assyria, was "an uncircumcised person." But Isaiah 36–37 as a whole complex is of particular interest for the present DtIsa text because of the brief comment in 52:4: "And Assyria has oppressed them [i.e., 'my people'] without cause (בְּאֶפֶס)." This could refer to the oppression of the Assyrians in general, an oppression that above all meant the end of the northern kingdom, Israel, in 722 B.C.E. and the downfall of Samaria. But in the present DtIsa context Zion/Jerusalem is the subject, and thus the threat to Jerusalem in 701 B.C.E. would seem to be the special reference. This is the situation that Isaiah 36–37 also reflects.

We can go further. Apart from Isaiah 36–37, there are two other versions of events during the siege of Jerusalem in Hezekiah's reign: 2 Kgs 18:13—19:37 and 2 Chr 32:1-23. The Deuteronomic version differs from that given by the Chronicler and the book of Isaiah in one essential point. 2 Kgs 18:13-16 reports the heavy tribute that Hezekiah had to pay Sennacherib. There is no mention of this in the other versions. They all agree in recounting that the Assyrians did not enter the city but withdrew in a miraculous fashion.

DtIsa's position agrees, provided that "for nothing" (בְּאֶפֶס) is understood as meaning "in vain." It is in contradiction to the Deuteronomic version if "for nothing" is interpreted to mean "not for money." But this is precisely the point under discussion, according to 52:3. I think it is most probable that DtIsa is following the Isaiah version, because he takes up Isaiah 35 too. That would mean that elements of Isaiah's theology about Yahweh's presence as protection for Jerusalem are revived at this point in DtIsa. Jeremiah had cast profoundest doubt on this theology. For him, appeal to the temple offered no security (Jer 7:1-15; cf. Jeremiah 26). DtIsa takes up Isaiah's tradition, but—as we see—Jeremiah's social criticism too. He is not concerned about the temple as such; his concern is the connection between "the holy city" (v. 1) and Yahweh's people (vv. 3-5: עַמִּי 3 times).

In DtIsa scriptural interpretation is always at the service of communication for his own day. The terminology "at the beginning, earlier" (בְּרִאשֹׁנָה, v. 4) and "but now" (וְעַתָּא) recurs in this text. In what follows we shall once more try to see this text too against the backdrop of the postexilic situation, and more precisely the Nehemiah era. The Isaianic prophecy about Assyria and the threat by the Rabshakeh and Sennacherib can be read afresh if one adds to 52:1 ("For an uncircumcised and an unclean person shall no more enter you") Neh 4:1-5 (7-11):

(v. 1 [7]) Now when Sanballat and Tobiah and the Arabs and the Ammonites and the Ashdodites heard that the repairing of the walls of Jerusalem was going forward . . .

(v. 2 [8]) they all plotted together to come in (לָבוֹא) and fight against Jerusalem . . .

(v. 5 [11]) And our oppressors said: "They will not know or see anything before we come in, into the midst of them (נָבוֹא אֶל־תּוֹכָם)."

According to v. 9 (15), the enemy's plan is foiled by God and by Nehemiah's measures. In retrospect, we may speculate as to whom can be meant in Isa 52:1 by "an uncircumcised person," and who the "unclean person" is. Since according to the note at the end of the book of Nehemiah (13:28-29), the family tie with "Sanballat the Horonite . . . defiled the priesthood" (גָּאַל II!), Sanballat would come into question as the one who was "unclean." In this case Tobiah the Ammonite would be the man who was "uncircumcised." And they were indeed unable to go ahead (לֹא יוֹסִיף, v. 1 [7]) with their plan to enter Jerusalem.

This may seem a bold reconstruction. But in the preceding fourth act too, we saw that there was presumably a topical political reference in 49:7, in the final scene

---

in II Reg 18–20 und Jer 37–40 (1990); cf. also O. H. Steck's redaction-history reconstructions, *Der Abschluß der Prophetie im Alten Testament. Ein Versuch zur Frage der Vorgeschichte des Kanons* (1991).

193 The heading in the Luther translation.

before the end. There it was probably the same people, Sanballat and Tobiah, who were the targets.

■ **3-5** Even if Zion/Jerusalem's outward safety is secured—since she has "put on "strength"—the "fetters" (מוֹסְרִים, v. 2) are still around her neck. Verses 3-5 explain what this means.

"Fetters" are mentioned three times in DtIsa, the form differing in each case: "But this is a people robbed and plundered, trapped in holes" (הָפֵחַ from פַּח, "snare, trap-net") (42:22); "to say to those in chains (לַאֲסוּרִים): come out!" (49:9); "Those in chains (צֹעֶה) will speedily be released" (51:14). In these cases the subject is probably enslavement because of debt.[194] We may assume that this is the background of the present text as well. Yahweh is "Lord" (v. 4a). That determines the status of "my people" (3 times) as "servants." Only the Lord can dispose over his servants, since they belong to him.

For this, "Egypt" is given as the first example: "My people went down into Egypt to live there as foreigners (לָגוּר שָׁם)" (52:4). As everyone knows, this was not the way things remained. Israel lost its status as "foreigner" (גֵּר) and was enslaved, until it was redeemed by its rightful Lord, Yahweh. In return for this redemption, compensation had neither to be given nor taken; this is in accord with Koehler's definition of חִנָּם ("for nothing").[195] It is the free "distributive" righteousness of God that is efficacious here.[196]

As I have said, the example of Assyria is applied to the city of Jerusalem, the two being initially linked through the aspect "for nothing." But in substance v. 5 is directly linked with the example of Egypt. The theme "my people" is pursued: "But now, what have I here. . . ." This, then, is not a matter of past problems. The point is the situation here and now.[197] According to the context, the *place* is clearly Zion/Jerusalem.[198] That means that "its

rulers" (מֹשְׁלָו) too will hardly be foreigners; it is its own ruling class that is meant. For here too "my name is mocked continually, every day" (v. 5b).

There is no reason to split up the unity of v. 5. But if its unity is preserved, the preliminary sentence "my people was taken (לֻקָּח) for nothing" also acquires a negative coloring. The enslavement brought the people no profit. לקח means "take, grasp, capture," so the meaning is very general. H. H. Schmid writes: "The verb acquires a more precise meaning 'to take forth, take away, take with one.'"[199] The substantive "booty" (מַלְקוֹחַ) also belongs here. In Gen 43:18; 2 Kgs 4:1; and Job 40:28 (41:4) the verb is used to mean "take as slave." In the *Pual* it stands in Judg 17:2 for theft. But above all the double use in 49:24 (with "booty," מַלְקוֹחַ) and v. 25 is striking. In 49:24-26, at the beginning of Act V, the text developed the theme of enslavement for debt, which is now summed up here, at the end, as a brief formula. The rulers have sold Yahweh's people "for nothing" (חִנָּם). It is the prophetic message as Amos formulated it, brought up to date: "They sell the righteous for silver, and the needy for a pair of sandals" (Amos 2:6; cf. 8:6).

Through injustice like this God's name is "mocked" (נֹאָץ), if the premise is the unity of God's people.[200] The confession of the one God has its social consequences. Through its ending, with its echo of the Amos saying, the verse is given a sinister, ironic turn. If we note the context we see that the example of Assyria is picked up again; for Isaiah 36–37 are full of the mockery of "the living God" (37:4) by the Rabshakeh and Sennacherib at the siege of Jerusalem, insults that almost seem like model examples of speeches deriding the God of Israel. But in the present text it is not the foreigners who blaspheme the name of Yahweh through what they do; it is his own people.

---

194 See Baltzer, "Liberation from Debt Slavery After the Exile," in *Ancient Israelite Religion: FS F. M. Cross*, esp. 480–81.

195 *HALOT* 1:334 [*HALAT* 1:321]; Koehler adds: "(cf. Lat. *gratiis > gratis*) Gen 29:15; Exod 21:2, 11; Num 11:5; Isa 52:3, 5; Jer 22:13; Job 1:9."

196 See K. Baltzer and T. Krüger, "Die Erfahrungen Hiobs. 'Konnektive' und 'distributive' Gerechtigkeit nach dem Hiob-Buch," in *Problems in Biblical Theology: FS R. Knierim* (1997) 27–37.

197 In my view the *Qere* וְעַתָּה מִי־לִי־פֹה can be rendered in this way. Perhaps it was a proverbial saying on the

lines of "*hic et nunc*." The *Ketib* means: "Whom have I here?"

198 Already Naegelsbach's view. Others assume that Babylon is meant, e.g., Delitzsch and Volz; see Beuken on this passage and North (220): "Presumably Babylon, not Egypt or Assyria." This is important for DtIsa's geographical identification in general.

199 H. H. Schmid, "לקח *lqḥ*, to take," *TLOT* 2:648–51, esp. 649 [*THAT* 1:875–79, esp. 876].

200 See S. H. Blank, "Studies in Deutero-Isaiah," *HUCA* 15 (1940) 1–46, esp. 1–8.

At three places we may suspect that the text is making an additional point. First, in v. 4: this is more of a scholarly joke, which DtIsa makes in order to show that this is within his capacity. [201]

36:2: וַיִּשְׁלַח מֶלֶךְ־אַשּׁוּר אֶת־רַב־שָׁקֵה

"The king of Assyria sent the Rabshakeh"

52:4: אַשּׁוּר בְּאֶפֶס עֲשָׁקוֹ

"And Assyria: for nothing has it oppressed"

It is a wordplay on the title *Rabshakeh*. In Akkadian it probably means "head of the cupbearers." In DtIsa רַב, "many," becomes אֶפֶס, "nothing,"[202] and שָׁקֵה is interpreted through עשׁק ("to act unjustly, oppress"[203]—i.e., "the nothing-oppressor"). That accords with Isaiah 36–37, but in the DtIsa context it does not let "the rulers" get off unscathed.

Second, in v. 5bα: "his ruler *yĕhêlîlû*" (מֹשְׁלוֹ יְהֵילִ֑ילוּ) is in my view deliberately ambiguous. Beuken has suggested a number of possibilities.[204] The verb can derive from the root ילל; in the *Hiphil* it means "howl, wail, lament." But according to Hos 7:14 the imperfect form ought to be יְיֵלִ֫ילוּ.

Then the various derivations of the root הלל come into question.[205] I would not exclude הלל I (contra *HALOT*). In the *Hiphil* it means "make shine" (Isa 13:10; Job 41:10 [9]), "shine" (Job 29:3; 31:26). That would please the rulers! But the form ought to be יָהֵלּוּ. הלל II *Piel* is "praise," especially "praise God," "raise the hallelujah." הלל III has a negative meaning throughout its range: in *Qal* "to be blind" (Pss 5:6 [5]; 73:3), in the *Poel* "to make a fool of, to make the object of mockery." This is the way DtIsa uses it in 44:25 (cf. Ps 102:9 [8]).

The undertones may be present, but the ambiguity is greatest when there is a deliberate "perversion" of הלל II, "praise, raise the hallelujah." The rulers praise themselves as do the godless their lusts, according to Ps 10:3.

But in the text the irony is surely given a further twist. מֹשְׁלוֹ are "the rulers," according to משׁל II. But the same participial form can also be derived from משׁל I:[206] "to make a saying, a parable: to act as rhapsodist (or reciter of poems)."[207]

According to Isa 28:14, the מֹשְׁלֵי הָעָם are "the (satirical) spokesmen, or balladmongers, of the people"—there too, probably, with similar ambiguity (cf. Num 21:27; Sir 44:4). Is DtIsa hitting out at his own writers' guild here? They give themselves airs and cannot even raise a decent "hallelujah"! Correctly speaking, the form should be יְהַלְלוּ from הלל *Piel*, if they "praise God," or *Hitpael* יִתְהַלְלוּ, if they "praise themselves."

It would be a further point if the verb were an artificial formation from הֵילֵל, the name for the morning star. It is true that the word occurs only once in the OT as הֵילֵל־בֶּן־שָׁחַר in Isa 14:12. In his commentary O. Kaiser translates it as "shining star, son of the dawn."[208] There is a connection with הלל I, "shine." But it stands at a very prominent point in the taunt song over the fall of Babylon, the lord of the world. In 14:4 and 5 there is also a wordplay on משׁל; the text of Isaiah 14 has therefore already been echoed once in the present verse. Moreover, this text conceals a number of mythical elements, centered on the paling of the morning star in the face of the rising sun. The LXX therefore uses ὁ ἑωσφόρος in 14:12, and the Vulgate *lucifer*.

In the present DtIsa text the dawn follows immediately—the dawn of the day on which Yahweh's royal rule over the whole world will be manifested.[209] To say that they are "morning star-ing"[210] (52:5bα) could be a malicious way of describing the veneration of Venus by

---

201 Cf. the *mene tekel* in Dan 5:1–6:1 (5:1-31), esp. 5:25-28.

202 See *HALOT*, s.v.; V. Hamp, "אֶפֶס *'ps*," *TDOT* 1:361–62 [*ThWAT* 1:389–91]: "*'ephes* is never used for 'end' in the temporal sense, thus in Isa. 52:4 it should not be translated 'in the end' (contra F. Zorell, *Lexicon Hebraicum* [1966] 74; *ZDMG* 70 [1916] 557)" (361 and n. 4 [389–90]); and "The privative meaning 'nothing' appears in Isa. 34:12; 40:17; 41:12, 29; 52:4" (362 [390]).

203 See *HALOT* on עשׁק, עֹשֶׁק, עֲשֻׁקָה.

204 Beuken (155) on this passage; see also North (218).

205 See *HALOT*, s.v.; C. Westermann, "הלל *hll* pi. to

praise," *TLOT* 1:371–76 [*THAT* 1:493–502]; H. Ringgren, "הלל *hll* I and II," *TDOT* 3:404–10 [*ThWAT* 2:433–41].

206 Thus already Ibn Ezra on this passage. For the wordplay with משׁל I and II the saying about Babylon in Isa 14:4 and 5 is interesting (see below).

207 See *HALOT*; S. Mowinckel, "Hat es ein israelitisches Nationalepos gegeben?" *ZAW* 53 (1935) 142.

208 Thus the English translation of O. Kaiser, *Isaiah 13–39* (1974) 28 [*Jesaja. Kapitel 13–39* (2d ed. 1976) 26].

209 See below on 52:7-10.

210 In Isa 14:12 Jerome read *hēlîl* instead of *hêlēl*. This

"rulers/poets"—but it would be in line with DtIsa's polemic against idols. For DtIsa it is a matter of the praise of Yahweh alone, through the raising of the hallelujah.

Third, in v. 5bβ: "But continually (וְתָמִיד wᵉtāmîd), every day, my name is mocked." Could this also be read: "And as for tamid (sacrifice), every day my name is mocked"? תָּמִיד "with a preceding term for a sacrifice" signifies the regular sacrifice in the temple[211] (see Num 28:1–29:39; Neh 10:34 [33]). Finally הַתָּמִיד, even when it stands alone, is the technical term for regular sacrifice (Num 28:3; Dan 8:11-14; 11:31; 12:11). DtIsa avoids the theme "temple, cult." His criticism of sacrifice is already obvious from 43:22-28.[212] Here v. 5 could imply a highly critical attitude toward the daily sacrifice: "it mocks my [Yahweh's] name."

Even if there can be different opinions about the details, the textual unit vv. 1-6 gives an impression of considerable harshness. That speaks in favor of the text's contemporary reference. The text's different strands are artistically interwoven; a catchword often suffices. This presupposes, initiates, and suggests a background of political pressure. In view of our basic historical assumption, we may in closing draw on a Nehemiah text as illustration: Nehemiah 5, which discusses the abolition of slavery for debt.[213]

Both texts might be headed by the same motto, Isa 52:3: "You were sold for nothing, and you will not be redeemed for silver." The heart of Nehemiah's reform is to be found in Neh 5:9-11. Its consequence for the creditors was: "We will restore it ['the debt'; נָשִׁיב] and demand nothing more (לֹא נְבַקֵּשׁ) from them" (v. 12). They swear an oath to this effect. The reason is twofold, according to v. 9: "Should you not walk in the fear of our God, in order to prevent the taunts (מֵחֶרְפַּת) of the Gentiles who are hostile to us?" The argument about the family relationship of people and congregation is clear (cf. vv. 1-2, 5, 8, 10, 13).

If from this point we come back to the action—the installation of Jerusalem—even small points can be explained. Zion/Jerusalem is explicitly told in v. 2: "shake off the dust from yourself" (הִתְנַעֲרִי). There could be a natural reason for this: she is getting up out of the dust. But why should the gesture be made only after the investiture? In Nehemiah, when he shakes the skirts of his garment it is a symbolic act: "So may God shake out everyone from house and from property who does not perform this promise" (נער, three times in 5:13!).

It seemed probable that "the fetters round your neck" (v. 2) in DtIsa refer to enslavement for debt. Again a textual variant is interesting. The Qere reading "Loose (הִתְפַּתְּחִי) the fetters of your neck" fits the progress of the action better. But if—by some miracle—a remission of debts is possible, then the Ketib reading would fit too: "The fetters have loosed themselves (הִתְפַּתְּחוּ)."

■ **6** This verse draws the conclusion from the whole passage. It is a double conclusion, corresponding to the different lines of argument in the text. The double לָכֵן in the sense of "Therefore . . . truly" must hence stand.[214]

On the one hand: if Yahweh's people know his name, they are legally the people he has freed (cf. 44:5).[215] On the other hand: if it is Yahweh who says, "Yes, I am he who speaks! See: I!" then it is no longer Babylon in its vanity (cf. 47:10)—but it is not Jerusalem either. Yahweh will prove himself to be the one he has proved himself to be, as already became plain at the revelation of the Name to Moses in Exodus 3.

would also justify the vowel sequence (וְהֵילִילוּ); see I. L. Seeligman, *The Septuagint Version of Isaiah* (1948) 100.

211 See *HALOT*, s.v.; cf. also עֹלָה תָמִיד (ʿōleh tāmîd Ps 74:23) on the desecration of the sanctuary in the context of a psalm of lament. See also on *tamid* A. Rothkoff, "Sacrifice: Second Temple Period," *EncJud* 14 (1971) 607–10 (lit.!); H. Seebass, "Opfer II. 4.5. tāmîd," *ThRE* 25 (1995) 263.

212 See K. Baltzer, "Schriftauslegung bei Deutero-

jesaja?—Jes 43,22-28 als Beispiel," in *Die Väter Israels. FS J. Scharbert* (1989) 11–16.

213 Baltzer, "Liberation from Debt Slavery After the Exile," in *Ancient Israelite Religion: FS F. M. Cross* (1987) 481–82.

214 See B. Jogeling, "*Lākēn* dans l'Ancien Testament," *OTS* 21 (1981) 190–200, summary on 200.

215 See above the lit. for Isa 44:5.

52

"How beautiful upon the mountains are the feet
of a messenger . . . one who says to Zion:
'As king reigns—your God'" (52:7)

7   How beautiful
       upon the mountains
       are the feet of a messenger,
       one who lets peace be heard,
       one who announces good,
       one who lets help be heard,
       one who says to Zion:
       "As king reigns—your God!"

8   The voice of your watchmen:
       They raise their voice,
       they rejoice together,
       for eye to eye they see
       Yahweh's return to Zion.

9   Be joyful, rejoice together,
       you ruins of Jerusalem!

       Yes! Yahweh has comforted his people,
       he has redeemed Jerusalem.

10   Yahweh has bared his holy arm
       in the sight of all peoples.
       And all the ends of the earth see
       the help of our God.

According to vv. 1-6 Zion/Jerusalem has again been accepted by its God. It is reinstalled in its original status. When chains are loosed and guilt among men and women is forgiven, "peace, good, and help" can be proclaimed, according to vv. 7-10. Then Yahweh can return to his city as king, and the jubilation fitting for a king can break forth. Verses 1-6 and 7-10 are thus closely connected.[216]

In the dramatic structure as a whole, vv. 7-10 form the conclusion to Act V. The unit embodies hymnic elements in both form and content. There is an invitation to shared "jubilation"[217] (רנן, vv. 8 and 9). Both the formula or watchword: "as king reigns your God" (v. 7) and the acknowledgment: "Yahweh has comforted his people, he has redeemed Jerusalem" (v. 9) have their place in the hymn. In this way the text is comparable with the hymnic conclusions to the previous acts: Act I, 42:10-12 (13); Act II, 44:23; Act III, 45:25; Act IV, 49:13. A striking feature of the present text is the number of acoustic terms. In each given case these terms are connected with what is happening.

216 On the text see A. S. van der Woude, "Hoe de Here naar Sion wederkeert. Traditio-historische overwegingen bij Jesaja 52:7-8," in *De Knecht. Studies rondom Deutero-Jesaja. FS J. L. Koole* (1978); P. D. Hanson, "Isaiah 52:7-10," *Int* 33 (1979) 389–94; R. F. Melugin, "Isaiah 52:7-10," *Int* 36 (1982) 176–81.

217 See R. Ficker, "רנן *rnn* to rejoice," *TLOT* 3:1240–43 [*THAT* 2:781–86]. Ficker establishes: "The majority of cases use *rnn* in the context of God's praise" (1241 [784]).

In what follows I shall try to reconstruct the action in this scene and shall attempt to elucidate its link with liturgical performance. I am well aware that here especially much more investigation is required.

The scene is split up into three parts, these also allowing us to perceive a certain progression in the action. This section is throughout an address by the speaker, who reports and comments on events and also gives directions. The actors or characters[218] and the place of the action vary.

Section	Scene of the Action	Characters
v. 7	"On the mountains"	Messenger
vv. 8-9	"Jerusalem"	Watchmen and "ruins of Jerusalem"
v. 10	"The ends of the earth"	Yahweh, the peoples

How do these parts fit together? Their unity can be thematically formulated: they all have to do with the manifestation of the divine sovereignty. But in the text this is presented in the form of action, which clearly moves purposefully in a certain direction. What can happen in such rapid succession on the mountains, in Jerusalem, and right to the ends of the earth? The external course of events corresponds to the sunrise. It is visible on the mountains first of all, then the sun's rays reach Jerusalem. Finally "the ends of the earth" see the sun. But the key word "sun" does not occur in the text; perhaps it has been deliberately avoided.

The comparison with Isaiah 60 is important. The Trito-Isaiah text shows correspondences with the motifs and probably also with the action of 52:7-10, though these things have undergone a characteristic change. 60:19-20 declares explicitly that Yahweh will be an "eternal light" (לְאוֹר עוֹלָם) for Zion, and will take the place of sun and moon (v. 20). The terminology in 60:1-3 is still drawn from the sunrise, however. We hear about the coming of light[219] (בָא אוֹרֵךְ) and about rising[220] (זרח, 3

times in vv. 1-3), these now being related to Yahweh. "Darkness covers the earth and darkness the peoples" (v. 2) too should now, in the context, be understood in a transferred sense. But even the command to Zion "stand up" (קוּמִי) is still detectable (v. 1; cf. 52:2). "Awake, awake" (עוּרִי) has become "shine" (אוֹרִי), by means of a slight modification. What is missing in chap. 52 is the vivid description of the triumphal procession for Zion as we find it in chap. 60.

It remains important for an understanding of DtIsa that in his text the sunrise should be interpreted by way of Yahweh's coming to Zion/Jerusalem. The prophet Ezekiel's criticism (Ezek 8:16-18)[221] shows that there was a problematical cult of the rising sun in the Jerusalem temple. The dispute had to do with the worship of the sun as god, whether in the form of the Babylonian Shamash or as the imperial Egyptian god Amon-Re.[222] The consequences of the sun cult for the interpretation of the world and society can be seen if Psalm 104 is compared with Akhenaton's great hymn.[223] Two aspects of this controversial tradition are important for an understanding of DtIsa: Yahweh's sovereignty extends over the whole of time, night as well as day;[224] and Yahweh is king for his people, so that neither the institution of monarchy nor the temple is required. He makes the "sun of righteousness "rise" (Mal 3:20 [4:2]).

In the context of DtIsa's text, what happens at night and what happens by day are interrelated events. "Yahweh's arm" (masc. or fem.) is active at night ("Awake!" 51:9, three times), and now all peoples "see it" (52:10) in the full light of day. Zion/Jerusalem arose while it was still night ("Awake!" 52:1, two times). Now it is told: "as king reigns your God" (v. 7). The catchword "day" ("on that day," בַּיּוֹם הַהוּא) is found in 52:6, and also signals the turn from night to daytime. We may

218 See also Hanson's division, "Isaiah 52:7-10," *Int* 33 (1979) 389: "A bi-polar pattern is discernible at each of the four stages of this expanding proclamation: Description of *dramatis personae*/reason for this response."

219 Job 25:3; 31:26; 37:11, 15, 21; Hab 3:4; cf. Judg 16:2; 19:26.

220 The rising of the sun: Gen 32:32 (31); Exod 22:2 (3); Judg 9:33; 2 Sam 23:4; 2 Kgs 3:22; Jonah 4:8; Nah 3:17; Mal 3:20 (4:2); Ps 104:22; Qoh 1:5; Job 9:7; see *HALOT*, s.v.

221 See W. Zimmerli, *Ezekiel* 1 (1979) 243–46 [*Ezechiel* (1969) 220–24].

222 On this whole subject see H.-P. Stähli, *Solare Elemente im Jahweglauben des Alten Testaments* (1985).

223 See E. von Nordheim, "Der Grosse Hymnus des Echnaton und Psalm 104: Gott und Menschen im Ägypten der Amarnazeit und in Israel," in *SAÄK* 7 (1979) 227–51.

224 The decisive passage in the Akhenaton hymn runs as follows (see ibid.):
(27) If you go down in the eastern light-land
  the earth is in darkness,
  in the condition of death.

therefore presume that the liturgical sequence was already laid down for DtIsa. That would explain the occurrence of particular catchwords and traditional phrases. The exodus from Egypt and the deliverance at the Reed Sea has always been recalled at the Feast of Passover, and celebrated as "a night of vigil for Yahweh." The ritual may be presupposed.[225]

The agreements—some of them word for word—between this DtIsa text and other texts in the OT are particularly striking. Examples are Nah 2:1-3 (1:15—2:2), compared with vv. 7-8 here, and Psalm 98, compared with v. 10. These texts—in themselves so different—are combined here. I believe that the most probable explanation is a common dependence on liturgical traditions. But it is what DtIsa makes of the existing traditions that is important. This will become clearer as we investigate the present text in greater detail.

■ **7** "How beautiful . . . are the feet. . . ." Beuken makes the appropriate point when he says that here beauty cannot be meant in the sense of a "beauty contest";[226] but, as will be seen, the statement in v. 7 can be understood in different ways, according to the context. Beuken rightly observes that a meaning along the lines of "desired, expected, at the right time" would fit the action best. As a derivation, a *Niphal* of אוה is proposed. The LXX rendering ὡς ὥρα already brings out the point that this is the appropriate time.[227] That could very well be what DtIsa means. But, as we see again and again, he loves to keep the different levels of meaning in play.

The same sentence can be found almost word for word in Nah 2:1 (1:15): "Look! On the mountains the feet of one who brings good tidings, who proclaims salvation/peace (שָׁלוֹם)!"[228] This does not necessarily imply any direct literary dependency. It may have been the way the feast-day liturgy began: "Look!" For in his oracle of salvation Nahum goes on: "Celebrate your festivals, Judah, fulfill your vows." That is his way of lending a contemporary reference. DtIsa has "See, it is I" in the previous verse as part of a Yahweh saying.

נָאווּ can also mean "beautiful, lovely." Thus one can derive it either from the root אוה or from נאה. The roots cannot be distinguished with any certainty, as the lexical discussion shows.[229] Perhaps DtIsa needs this meaning too for a quite different reason, one connected with the musical performance.

Psalm 147 is a hallelujah psalm. In the introduction a double reason for the praise is given (כִּי טוֹב): first, "for it is [or: should be?] good to play for our God" (זמר is

---

30 The sleepers [or: they sleep] in the chamber,
    their heads are covered,
    no eye sees the other.
    Their possessions are stolen from under
       their heads and they do not mark it.
    Every wild beast has come out of its lair.
    Every creeping thing stings.
35 The darkness is a grave,
    the earth lies in silence:
    their creator has gone down in his light land.
(Following J. Assmann's translation in *Ägyptische Hymnen und Gebete* [1975] no. 92).
    Psalm 104 reads (see von Nordheim, *SAÄK* 7 [1979] 230):
19 He makes the moon for the (festal) seasons,
    the sun knows its setting.
20 You create darkness, and it becomes night,
    when all the beasts of the forest slink round.
21 The young lions roar for prey,
    they demand their food from God.
22 When the sun rises they withdraw.
Cf. Psalm 121:
 4 See, he who keeps Israel does not sleep and
    does not slumber. . . .
 6 The sun does not strike you by day, nor the
    moon by night.
 7 Yahweh keeps you from all evil.

225 The plot in Attic drama is comparable: the writer can presuppose that the audience is familiar with it. It is the way the writer modifies the material that is of interest.
226 Beuken, 161 on this passage: "It is not a matter of the description or praise of beauty."
227 Cf. the quotation in Rom 10:15: ὡς ὡραῖοι. . . .
228 On the text and its problem see Jörg Jeremias, *Kultprophetie und Gerichtsverkündigung in der späten Königszeit Israels* (1970) 11–58, esp. 13ff.; C. A. Keller, "Die theologische Bewältigung der geschichtlichen Wirklichkeit in der Prophetie Nahums," *VT* 22 (1972) 399–419, esp. 400ff.; W. Rudolph, *Nahum* (1975) 158, 163; H. E. Spykerboer, *The Structure and Composition of Deutero-Isaiah* (1976) 174–75.
229 See *HALOT* on נאה, אוה; GB on אוה; E. Gerstenberger, "אוה *ʾwh* pi. to desire," *TLOT* 1:55–56 [*THAT* 1:74–76]; G. Mayer, "אָוָה *ʾāwāh*," *TDOT* 1:134–37 [*ThWAT* 1:145–48].

often used for instruments). Second: "Beautiful, lovely (נָעִים נָאוֶה) is [or: should be?] a song of praise."[230] Here the two Hebrew words for "beautiful, lovely" could be explaining one another mutually, or they could be used for emphasis, in the sense of "very lovely." The verse can be the beginning of the psalm. I suspect that directions for the performance are being given, as is often the case in the psalm headings. But at present we still know too little about this.

Starting from our own presuppositions, Psalm 147 is very close to DtIsa, and to the present text:

Yahweh builds up Jerusalem; the dispersed of Israel he gathers (v. 2).

Praise Yahweh, O Jerusalem! O Zion, boast of your God (v. 12).

For he secures the bars of your gates, blesses your sons in your midst (v. 13).[231]

In its performance instructions (vv. 1-3), Psalm 33 also talks about a "beautiful, lovely song of praise" (נָאוָה תְהִלָּה, v. 1), and this psalm goes on to name a whole series of instruments, ending: "Play skillfully with תְּרוּעָה." This can mean "rejoicing" in general, particularly also the signal with the shofar (Lev 25:9) or trumpets (Num 31:6; 2 Chr 13:12).[232] I suspect that "beautiful, lovely" in the present text is indicating the sound, comparable with our major and minor keys or modes.

"On [or better: 'over,' עַל] the mountains" also rouses the suspicion that it may simultaneously be an instruction about the pitch or register. In comparable hymnic passages in DtIsa, the sequence suggested the same thing: "sea, desert, tops of the mountains" (42:10-11); "heavens, depths of the earth, mountains" (44:23); "heavens, earth, mountains" (49:13). In these indications or instructions, height in the geographical sense would correspond to the musical pitch. "Over the mountains"

would then mean a relatively high register.

Finally, "feet" (the feet of a messenger) could be an indication of rhythm. A messenger runs quickly. The rhythm of his pace could be given by a drum, for example (or a sistrum, or castanets?). So a whole series of signals could be associated with the messenger. The messenger as figure remains curiously colorless. The text just says "a messenger"; the definite article is not used. We shall have to consider the reasons for this in what follows. First the musical levels require further consideration.

"One who lets be heard . . . one who reports/announces . . . one who lets be heard." These three are not, in my view, identical with the first messenger. They have a special function, the pair that in each case "makes heard" (מַשְׁמִיעַ) being distinguished from the one who "acts as messenger" (מְבַשֵּׂר). The different "voices" in 40:1-8 are comparable. There they act as a kind of stage direction.

But how can one hear "peace" and "help," and probably "good" too, or "let them be heard"? Curiously enough the commentators see no problem here. They generally pass on immediately to the last statement: "Your God reigns as king." But the text says explicitly "One . . . says to Zion" (cf. 40:6: "Voice of one who speaks"). If we wish to explain this sequence in the text we have to take into account the whole scene in vv. 7-10.

A key can be found in the Qumran War Scroll (1QM),[233] which includes a "rule for the trumpets" (1QM 2.15–3.11). There are "trumpets for giving the alarm for war," "trumpets to summon the soldiers when the gates of war are opened for the advance." The trumpets are designated and differentiated by their inscriptions. Of particular interest for the present scene in DtIsa is the text in 1QM 3.4–11:

230　תְהִלָּה according to *HALAT* is also a technical musical term for a song of praise. The article refers to Ps 145:1; Neh 12:46; 11:17 cj.; see also J. Blau, "*Nāwā thillā* (Ps. cxlvii 1): Lobpreisen," *VT* 4 (1954) 410–11.

231　Thus the English translation in H.-J. Kraus, *Psalms 60–150* (1989) [*Psalmen 60–150* [1978]]. Kraus expounds: "So far as the themes are concerned, Psalm 147 is dependent on the more ancient hymnic tradition; it is related to Psalm 33 and it has borrowed a number of individual figures of speech from Psalm 104. Worth noting in this context is also

the relation to Deutero-Isaiah (Isaiah 40–55) and to texts from Isaiah 56ff." (556 [1136]). He refers to Gunkel's comment on the text, and concludes about the date: "The statements in vv. 2 and 13 could permit the deduction that the psalm originated after the completion of the building of the walls by Nehemiah (cf. Neh 12:27ff.) at the end of the 5th century" (ibid.).

232　See *HALAT;* cf. Num 10:5-6; 29:1.

233　Translation following E. Lohse, ed., *Die Texte aus Qumran. Hebräisch und Deutsch* (4th ed. 1986) 177–225, esp. 184–87; see H. Seidel, "Horn und

(4) And on the trumpets of the camps (5) shall be written: the peace of God (שָׁלוֹם אֵל) in the camps of his saints. And on the trumpets for breaking camp shall be written: the mighty acts of God (גְּבוּרוֹת אֵל), for the scattering of the enemy and to put to flight all who (6) hate righteousness.

(10) And on the trumpets of withdrawal (11) from the battle against the enemy, in order to come to the congregation in Jerusalem, shall be written: Praise God on the fortunate return (גִּילוֹת אֵל בְּמַשׁוֹב שָׁלֵם).

The War Scroll presupposes an elaborate system of trumpet signals. The use of trumpets unquestionably goes back to ancient models. Clearest of all is the relation to Egypt, or to be more precise to the signal system of the pharaohs. H. Hickmann writes here:[234]

The Egyptian trumpet was . . . a signaling instrument on which the few notes that could be played were sounded in various rhythmical variations. The trumpeter is called the one who speaks through the trumpet, that is, who passes on the commands of the pharaoh or the general.[235]

In ancient Egypt, with only a few exceptions, two trumpeters are always depicted in each case. But they are never shown as playing together. . . . The Tutankhamen trumpets (are) separated in the scenes depicted, since the one counts as a war trumpet, and the other as a trumpet of peace.[236]

Trumpets are frequently assigned to sun deities, and it is quite possible that one of the instruments was blown at sunrise, the other one being sounded only in the evening.[237]

Hickmann says about the trumpets in Tutankhamen's tomb: "The two existing instruments give in each case a regular-pitch note and a higher note achieved by overblowing."[238]

For a comparison with DtIsa, the most important point is that in Egypt the presence of sovereignty was associated with the two trumpets. In Egypt the pharaoh as monarch is "the sun," whose sovereignty is shown in this way. For DtIsa it is clear that Yahweh alone is king. He is announced with trumpets.

A striking feature of v. 7 is that the signal "peace" is expressly mentioned, but not "war." "Sound signals" (תְּרוּעָה *t^erû^cāh*) were a feature of the so-called holy war. Here we have "help" (יְשׁוּעָה *y^ešû^cāh*) instead. The rhythm of the syllables and the vowels are the same, and thus probably the note that was sounded too. But it is *help* that is to be announced—and "Yahweh's arm" is help too, according to v. 10. DtIsa's tendency to "demilitarize" is still maintained here: protection, yes; but no aggression! With trumpets the signals "peace" and "help" can "let—be heard" (שׁמע *Hiphil*),[239] and one can "hear" (שׁמע) them.

The message of "good" (טוֹב), which has its place between the signals "peace" and "help," still requires explanation. Schilling writes about this passage: "The addition טוֹב is not adverbial and is by no means simply a qualifying nuance. It is the second element in the triad peace, salvation, deliverance. . . . In DtIsa מבשׂר is always related to Yahweh's victory and the dawn of salvation."[240] Höver-Johag agrees: "All three termini in the message point beyond present redemption to the announcement of God's kingdom."[241]

Here too one may ask whether the "message" can be assigned to an instrument. The horn or shofar (שׁוֹפָר) is a possibility.[242] In the OT this too is an instrument used for giving signals, both in war (Joshua 6; Judges 7; Amos 2:2; Zeph 1:16) and peace (e.g., the announcement of the feasts of the new moon, the New Year and the Day of Atonement). In the OT the horn is linked particularly

Trompete im alten Israel unter Berücksichtigung der 'Kriegsrolle' von Qumran," *Wissenschaftliche Zeitschrift der Karl-Marx-Universität Leipzig* (1956/57) 589–99.

234 H. Hickmann, *Ägypten* in *Musikgeschichte in Bildern*, vol. 2: *Musik des Altertums* (1961); see also H. Hickmann, "La trompette dans l'Égypte ancienne," *Annales du Service des Antiquités de l'Égypte* (Cahier no. 1, 1946).

235 Hickmann, *Ägypten*, 74, on pl. 43.

236 Ibid., 74, on pl. 44.

237 Ibid.

238 Ibid., 120, on pl. 88.

239 See H. Schult, "שׁמע *šm^c* to hear," *TLOT* 3:1375–80, esp. 1378 [*THAT* 2:974–82, esp. 979]: "The Chr[onicler's] history uses *šm^c* hi. as a technical term for making music (Neh 12:42; 1 Chron 15:16, 19, 28; 16:5, 42; 2 Chron 5:13)."

240 O. Schilling, "בשׂר *bśr*," *TDOT* 2:315–16 [*ThWAT* 1:848–49].

241 I. Höver-Johag, "טוב *ṭôb*," *TDOT* 5:296–317, esp. 306 [*ThWAT* 3:315–39, esp. 326].

242 See E. Davis, "Shofar," *EncJud* 14:1442–48; G. Wallis, "Horn," *BHH* 2:749.

with the theophany (see already Exod 19:16, 19). It is
used to proclaim "the release (דְּרוֹר) throughout the land
for all who dwell in it" (Lev 25:9-10), for example, on the
occasion of the sabbath year and the year of release. The
relatively dark, simple ô sound of טוֹב (ṭôb) could fit this
unsophisticated instrument.

The three instruments and their function would then
correspond to Ps 98:6: "With trumpets and the sound of
the horn (בַּחֲצֹצְרוֹת וְקוֹל שׁוֹפָר) give signals before the
king, Yahweh." Here Psalm 98 has preserved the specific
liturgical directive, whereas DtIsa, clearly more abstract,
presupposes and interprets the movement of the liturgy.

The last "messenger" in the series "speaks." He has a
factual message "for Zion": מָלַךְ אֱלֹהָיִךְ. This can be rendered: "your God has proved himself king" or "as king
reigns your God." There is no doubt that in the context
this sentence is connected with the formula יהוה מלך.[243]
It therefore involves the same difficulties: the problems
of translating the formula, of elucidating its link with
the feast-day cult, and of establishing the significance of
the concept of Yahweh's rule as king. In all three sectors
the present text has played an important part in the
scholarly discussion. But it is impossible to go into that
in detail here.

In my view the context is always important in DtIsa,
and especially at this point.[244] The verb is used, not the
title "king" (מֶלֶךְ). The perfect can therefore be translated: "he reigns as king" or "he is king." The verb is
placed at the beginning, the antecedent position thus
stressing the activity. The point in dispute here is not
that Yahweh is king unlike other gods (although this
theme is always implicitly present in DtIsa). What is at
issue in the whole of Act V is whether Yahweh still
acknowledges Zion/Jerusalem. "But Zion says: 'Yahweh
has forsaken me and my Lord has forgotten me'": that is

the first sentence in 49:14, and it is taken up again at the
close of the act. It is not Yahweh's kingdom in general
that must be restored; it is Zion/Jerusalem's position as
royal city that has to be endorsed. Jerusalem is the royal
city even if it no longer has an earthly king to reside
there. This also tells us something about the rank of the
city. Consequently what the messenger says is "news,"
new information "for Zion" (לְצִיּוֹן). That is why the messenger states the legal foundation by way of the covenant
formula "your God," to whom the phrase "his people"
(עַמּוֹ, v. 9) corresponds.[245] This explicitly relates the
covenant relationship to Zion/Jerusalem. Otherwise the
relationship is grounded on the exodus from Egypt,
where "signs and wonders" reveal Yahweh as sovereign.

"Yahweh's arm" was already mentioned in 51:9-11.
There the miracle at the Reed Sea, during the exodus, is
interpreted through the image of the victory over
"Rahab." According to 51:17-23, the victory is won
before Jerusalem rises from its deepest humiliation.
Under this aspect, what the message is saying is: "Your
God has proved himself as king." In 51:9 as in 52:10,
"Yahweh's arm" is manifested. Yahweh's sovereignty
extends down to the present and into the future too.
Thus the catchword "Yahweh's arm" (cf. 53:1) already
heralds the Servant of God text in 52:13—53:12. In the
wider context, the royal title ascribed to Yahweh is
related to "Jacob": in 41:21 in the dispute about the predictive capabilities of the foreign gods. In 43:15
Yahweh's sovereignty over Israel is justified by his acts in
creation. According to 44:6, as king of Israel Yahweh is
at the same time its redeemer. Now the royal rule of its
God acquires its new meaning, for Zion/Jerusalem too.

243 See the survey with lit. in J. A. Soggin, "מֶלֶךְ melek
     king," *TLOT* 2:767–80, esp. 677–79 [*THAT*
     1:908–20, esp. 914–18]; D. Michel, "Studien zu den
     sogenannten Thronbesteigungspsalmen," *VT* 6
     (1956) 40–68, esp. 68; Jörg Jeremias, *Das Königtum
     Gottes in den Psalmen* (1987), esp. 121–36; on the
     text see 127, 133–34; J. H. Ulrichsen, "*JHWH
     Mālāk*: Einige sprachliche Beobachtungen," *VT* 27
     (1977) 361–74, esp. 370–71; P. Welten,
     "Königsherrschaft Jahwes und Thronbesteigung,"
     VT 32 (1982) 297–310, esp. 307–8.

244 See W. H. Schmidt, *Königtum Gottes in Ugarit und
     Israel: Zur Herkunft der Königsprädikation Jahwes*

     (1963) 75: "The herald's cry 'Your God has become
     king!' (52:7) can be more readily explained as a
     modification of an already existing proclamation—
     'Yahweh has become king!'—than vice versa."

245 Cf. 40:1. Beuken has seen this correctly.

There are different spheres of rule, and regard must be paid to their special legitimation and the consequences of the claim in each given case. This will become clearer still in the verses that follow.

A comparison with messenger scenes in the literature of the ancient world makes clear that they are frequently the place where programmatic declarations are made. That is true of the present text too. The nature of the messenger always plays an important part as well. But in this text we at first sight learn almost nothing.

In the prologue (40:9-11) Yahweh's return is also depicted. The text can be compared with the present one, as a "mirror scene." There the (female) messenger (or messengers) is at least named: she is the personification of Zion/Jerusalem (40:9). Similar to the present scene, she is to climb up to a high mountain. The message is sent to "the cities of Judah" (v. 9). I am no longer sure that the messenger on the mountains in 52:7 is originally meant to be a human being, and is not also a personification. This remains an open question, apart from the doubt as to whom the messenger (masc. or fem.) represents in each case. Here we have to come back once more to the question, raised by Beuken, as to whether the beginning of v. 7 describes a kind of beauty contest ("how beautiful . . . are the feet"). Did a description of Venus as "beauteous morning star" once have its place here, in the earlier stages of the text? DtIsa says "a messenger." He does not name the stars in 40:26 either ("these . . ."). The messenger here is masculine, the Venus ascription being avoided. In 52:5, two verses back, we suspected that DtIsa was playing on *Helel*, the morning star, in a negative sense. But what remains (because it is necessary for the progress of the action) is the indication of time. If "the feet" (the heavenly figure of the morning star?) are "on the mountains," the sun is soon going to rise. In the words of v. 6 "that day" will begin.

The announcement of "peace" and "help," if these are trumpet calls, really allows us to expect authorized officeholders, and those of no mean rank. According to Num 10:1-10, this is the task of "the sons of Aaron, the priests" (v. 8). In DtIsa they are not named. Someone who blows the shofar is not mentioned either. Since this instrument was linked with the theophany, the sounding of it was bound to be a specially sacred activity. For the message that Yahweh reigns as king surely demanded a herald of high rank. But there is no mention of this either. "One who speaks" is sufficient!

All in all, I believe that we have to assume that there are five messengers, corresponding to the five activities. We see a tendency to describe them only according to what they do, not by way of their office, rank and dignity. But this is equally true of the Servant.

■ **8** The verse begins with a threefold, implicit stage direction, comparable to 40:1-8: (1) "Voice of your watchmen," (2) "they raise their voice," (3) "they rejoice together." "Lookouts, watchmen" (צפה, *Qal* participle) presuppose a raised standpoint—in the case of Jerusalem, the walls or a tower.

They see "eye to eye" (עַיִן בְּעַיִן). This may be a reference to the nearness of Yahweh,[246] like the phrase "face-to-face."[247] But that would normally presuppose nonhuman watchmen. Who is permitted to see Yahweh face-to-face? Or are earthly and heavenly watchmen associated in their "watching"? It seems to me more probable that, like the double "together" (יַחְדָּו) in vv. 8 and 9, the phrase expresses the shared activity of the watchmen.[248]

But what do the "watchmen, the lookouts" see? According to everything that has gone before, the expected answer would be: "Yahweh's coming." Then the end of v. 8 would have to be rendered: "They see the return (בְּשׁוּב) of Yahweh to Zion." That would correspond directly to the message to Zion: "As king your God reigns" (v. 7). So returning (שׁוּב) can be a way of describing the restoration of legitimate rule.

That applies to the earthly ruler in just the same way. When, after Absalom's rebellion, David is once again to be king over the whole of Israel and Judah, "the bringing back (לְהָשִׁיב) of the king to his house" (2 Sam 19:11-13 [10-12]) belongs to the restoration, which takes place in 19:31 (30); 20:3. The entry into the palace is the goal.

It is in similar terms that Ezekiel sees the return of Yahweh's glory, according to Ezekiel 43.[249] It enters the Temple from the east: "and the glory of Yahweh filled the house" (הַבַּיִת, v. 5). In DtIsa, however, there is no

---

246 Cf. Num 14:14; Jer 32:4.
247 Cf. Exod 33:11.
248 See Isa 52:8 LXX: ὀφθαλμοὶ πρὸς ὀφθαλμοὺς ὄψονται (plur.!).

249 Cf. Ezek 1:28; 3:23; 10:4, 18; 11:23; see K. Baltzer, "The Meaning of the Temple in the Lukan Writings," *HTR* 58 (1965) 263–77.

mention of either palace or temple. This is now all the more striking. Yahweh returns to Zion; the city is the place of his presence. The people are to raise the song of praise to the king. If even "the ruins of Jerusalem"[250] are to join in the jubilation, that is an adherence to reality, contrary to all false triumphalism.

But the text has also been read differently. The watchmen see "how Yahweh brings back Zion." As a translation this is disputed.[251] But Delitzsch already gave as reasons for this interpretation[252] the translation in LXX, Syriac and Jerome, the transitive use of the *Qal* of שׁוּב in Ps 85:2, 5 (1, 4), as well as the formulation שׁוּב שְׁבוּת, "bring back the prisoners, turn aside the misery," for which he cites Pss 14:7 and 126:1.[253]

The matter is complicated by the fact that in 52:2 DtIsa has already played on יָשַׁב, "sit, throne," and שְׁבִיָּה, "captive daughter Zion." Consequently I do not think it impossible that he is leaving both possibilities open here: Yahweh's return to Zion (omitting the more correct preposition לְ) and the bringing back of Zion—that is, the prisoners from afar.[254] But this latter return was already announced in the prologue in 40:9-11, in that case as a message to the cities of Judah.

---

250 חָרְבוֹת יְרוּשָׁלַם cf. Isa 5:17; 49:19; 51:3. Beuken on this passage (166) draws attention to the fact that although the root חרב means "lay waste," it also covers "to be dry, forsaken" in respect of the landscape. Melugin (*Int* 36 [1982] 179) points to the link with Isaiah 6, esp. v. 11.

251 Beuken on this passage, with lit. He writes: "A transitive interpretation of *běšûb yhwh ṣiyôn* . . . is lexigraphically untenable, however."

252 Delitzsch on this passage; see also Torrey [*Second Isaiah* (1928)] here.

253 On שׁוּב שְׁבוּת cf. Deut 30:3; Pss 53:7 (6); 85:2 (1), 5 (4); Jer 29:14; 30:3, 18; 31:23; 48:47; Ezek 16:53; Hos 6:11; Amos 9:14; Zeph 2:7; 3:20. E. Baumann already assumed a connection with debt slavery; see his "שׁוּב שְׁבוּת Eine exegetische Untersuchung," *ZAW* 47 (1929) 17–44.

254 Cf. Zech 8:3, 7-8.

The confessional formula in v. 9b states the reason for the rejoicing and also the content of the hymn. It is again introduced with the affirmatory "Yes, truly, indeed" (כִּי). These "brief formulas" can be spoken or cried out by everyone present (v. 9b), and this is in fact the intention: "Yes, Yahweh has comforted (נחם) his people, he has redeemed (גאל) Jerusalem." This formula binds together the whole of Israel's traditions as Yahweh's people, as well as the city traditions of Jerusalem. It is a program of unity in all the tensions brought about by history. It is a theological program, but a political one too. Jerusalem was the city of David, the city of the dynasty and the royal administration. It was the city of the temple and its priesthood. It was often caught up in the tension between its own interests and those of the surrounding countryside with its people, represented preeminently by the prophets.

If Yahweh is Zion's king, then Jerusalem can be the royal city even without the Davidic dynasty. Thus the text fits into the wider context of DtIsa's position. It reads like a replica of the end of Queen Athaliah's rule and Jehoash's ascent to the throne: then "all the people of the land (כָּל־עַם־הָאָרֶץ) rejoiced; and the city was quiet (וְהָעִיר שָׁקָטָה)" (2 Kgs 11:20; cf. 2 Chr 23:21). As distinct from this, even "the ruins of Jerusalem" are now supposed to break into rejoicing together. Outwardly only the ruins can be seen, but a new beginning has been made. That God "comforts" and "redeems" lends hope and lets human beings lighten the burden of others and liberate them in the light of their own experience. This is the correspondence of the "new day," and it also matches the situation premised in the scene in vv. 7-10.

■ **10** In v. 10 Yahweh is named for a third time in this text, following vv. 8 and 9. Yahweh's sovereignty extends over the whole world. It is embodied by way of his arm, which was probably originally meant as the sword arm, wielding the shining sword. But there is no talk of a battle. That is long since past (cf. 51:9-11). The sight of the sword is sufficient to secure peace. It is the reminder of the "signs and wonders" through which God delivered his people. The "help" (יְשׁוּעָה, v. 7) was first announced to Zion. Now it is help for "all the ends of the earth."[255]

The close of v. 10 echoes Ps 98:3 word for word: All the ends of the earth see the help of our God.[256] But the beginning of v. 10 is also close to Ps 98:1b and 2b. The psalm (vv. 1b-2) reads:

> His right hand and his holy arm have helped him.
> Yahweh has made known his help (יְשׁוּעָתוֹ),
> in the sight of the nations he has revealed his righteousness/
> justice (גִּלָּה צִדְקָתוֹ).

Verse 10a of our DtIsa passage corresponds (lit.):

> Yahweh has bared (חָשַׂף) his holy arm
> in the sight of all peoples.

In this case it is DtIsa who has the more concrete formulation. It is closer to the military sense of "baring *the arm*" in order to be able to fight better;[257] whereas "laying bare *his righteousness/justice*" in Ps 98:2 is used in the more abstract sense of "reveal." But in this text DtIsa is not talking about justice. He is talking about "help" (vv. 7 and 10). For him that is apparently the decisive point. It is typical of him once more to insert an "all (כָּל)" here—"in the sight of all peoples."

It seems to me most probable that both texts, Isa 52:10 and Psalm 98, are referring to the same cultic

---

255 See J. F. Sawyer, "ישע *yšʿ*," *TDOT* 6:441–63, esp. 457 [*ThWAT* 3:1035–59, esp. 1053]: "In the cultic hymn that praises God as king, when the news of God's intervention (*yᵉšûʿâ*) is announced in 52:7-10, the emphasis is on the completeness and finality of the action. The same applies to Jer. 31:7" [trans. altered].

256 On the text and the problem see H. L. Ginsberg, "The Arm of YHWH in Isaiah 51–63 and the Text of Isa 53:10-11," *JBL* 77 (1958) 152–56, esp. 154; Jörg Jeremias, *Das Königtum Gottes in den Psalmen* (1987) 131–36, esp. 133–34.

257 See F. J. Helfmeyer, "זרע *zᵉrôaʿ*," *TDOT* 4:131–40

[*ThWAT* 2:650–60], esp. II.1–II.3. On 52:10: "The expression is generally here too [for Isa 52:10, Ezek 4:7] presumed to refer to Yahweh's intervention as a warrior [Knobel, *Jesaia*, 426; Delitzsch, 300; K. Marti, *KHC* 10 [1900] 344; Kittel, *Jesaja*, 446; Eichrodt, *Ezekiel*, 85]. But Isa. 53:1 should caution against this interpretation, since here the bared arm of Yahweh cannot be taken exclusively as 'an allusion to the hidden judgment of Yahweh . . . imposed on the servants of Yahweh' [Kaiser, 96]; it does not refer to a warlike or (legally) punitive action on the part of Yahweh" (135–36 [655]) [trans. altered]. See also Beuken on this passage.

ritual, to which the royal proclamation for Yahweh belongs, as well as the music and rejoicing. "Yahweh's arm" is praised in hymnic form, and there is a connection here with Exodus 15, the miracle at the Reed Sea.[258] DtIsa is taking up the traditional phraseology and transforming it. The hymnic quotation: "All the ends of the earth shall see the help of our God,"[259] now becomes an effective conclusion to the act, even contrary to what was the traditional interpretation.[260] In the triumph too, God's undeserved commitment may be found.

---

258 Cf. also Exod 14:13, 31.

259 Melugin ("Isaiah 52:7-10," *Int* 36 [1982] 176–81) draws attention to the connection between the theme "seeing" and the prophet Isaiah's proclamation (179): "Not only will the deaf and blind Israel [cf. 42:16, 18-20; 43:8] be able to see, but *all* nations will be able to see and know Yahweh and his activity (40:5; 41:20; 42:6-7; 45:6, 14, 22-25; 49:26). When Yahweh returns to Zion before the eyes of all nations, they will 'see' the victory of God (52:10); therefore, the period of blindness and deafness inaugurated by Yahweh (6:10) is understood to be terminated with the coming of his kingdom."

260 For the reception of Isa 52:7-10 in Christian tradition see Rom 10:15; cf. Mark 16:15-16; Luke 2:29-32; Acts 10:36; Eph 6:15. See J. Fichtner, "Jesaja 52,7-10" in G. Eichholz, ed., *Herr, tue meine Lippen auf. Eine Predigthilfe,* vol. 5: *Die alttestamentlichen Perikopen* (2d ed. 1961) 197–212.

Act VI: 52:11–54:17

"This is the inheritance of Yahweh's servants and their righteousness before me, saying of Yahweh" (54:17)

A. 52:11-12
The New Exodus Procession with "the Vessels of Yahweh"

52

"Go out from there . . ." (52:11)

11 Depart! Depart! Go out from there!
You should not touch anything unclean!
Go out from the midst of her! Purify
    yourselves,
you who carry the vessels of Yahweh!

12 Truly, you should not go out in haste,
and should not go in flight.
Truly Yahweh goes before you,
and the God of Israel is your rearguard.

With 52:11-12 a new act begins.[1] The theme is once more the exodus.[2] It is developed on three different levels of understanding:

1. Remembrance of the exodus from Egypt.
2. Description of the new exodus from the Babylonian exile.
3. The topical reference to the situation of Zion/Jerusalem, now newly constituted.

The key to the text is the reference to "the vessels of Yahweh" (כְּלֵי יהוה), the mention of which links the three interpretive levels.

The text is announcing a procession.[3] Consequently two verses suffice for the beginning of the final act in the liturgical drama. The performance must have taken a considerable time. The text is a "mirror scene," corresponding to the procession of the idols in 46:1-2, at the beginning of Act IV. There it is followed by the deposition of Babylon (47:1-15); here the sequel is the coronation of Zion/Jerusalem (54:11-14).

The tone is itself solemn and measured. In these two verses the long $\hat{u}$ sound is used as many as twelve times.[4] The insistent repetitions are striking: "Depart, depart (סוּרוּ)," "Go out . . . go out (צְאוּ)," "Truly . . . truly (כִּי)," "Yahweh . . . Yahweh"; the last rises to a climax at the end: "the God of Israel." The verbs are verbs of movement that, as imperatives, are a call to action.

A first reference to the exodus from Egypt is probably the triple "go out" (יצא Qal) in the text. Since the word is a common one, it cannot be a definite formula. But its use in connection with Israel's "going out" from Egypt is

---

1 Volz already noted that a new section begins here. For a different view see, e.g., Muilenburg on this passage: "Coda: The New Exodus (52:11-12). The lines follow at once after vs. 10 and form an excellent close."

2 See B. W. Anderson, "Exodus Typology in Second Isaiah," in *Israel's Prophetic Heritage: FS J. Muilenburg* (1962) 177–95; B. J. van der Merwe, *Pentateuchtradisies in de Prediking van Deuterojesaja,* 157–64, §39c: "Die uittog uit Egipte en ander mosaiese tradisies in Jes 52,11"; D. Baltzer, *Ezechiel und Deuterojesaja* (1971) 12–26.

3 See Baltzer, *Ezechiel und Deuterojesaja* (1971) 17, 22–24. He refers to C. H. Ratschow, "Prozession,"

*RGG*³ 5:668–69; to M. Jastrow, *Die Religion Babyloniens und Assyriens* vols. 1–3 (1905–12) (see there the index) and, with particular reference to DtIsa, to F. Stummer, "Einige keilschriftliche Parallelen zu Jes 40–66," *JBL* 45 (1926) 172–73. See also Westermann, 252 [204]: "'Depart, depart, go out thence!' It would be quite wrong to regard [this command's] development in vv. 11f. as a literal description of the departure from Babylon. . . . In v. 11b there is a procession representing the journey of the Holy One. Here the figure is more important than the details."

4 Cf. 40:13-14.

by no means rare. H. D. Preuss counts about forty instances.[5] He writes: "The clear relationship of * yṣʾ* to the description of Yahweh's liberating activity begins with the book of Exodus. Yahweh sets his oppressed people free from their slavery in Egypt. Here, too, there is a striking similarity to military usage of *yṣʾ*. Yahweh acts as a warrior in order to liberate. Against the background of Ex. 11:4, v. 8, with three repetitions of *yṣʾ*, marks a first focal point. According to Ex. 12:31, Moses and Aaron are to give the command to depart, so that the people may serve Yahweh."[6]

In the present DtIsa text there is no sign of a warlike background. Moses and Aaron are not named. But DtIsa does specifically use *yāṣāʾ Qal* for the exodus from Babylon in 48:20. This has generally led to the conclusion that in the present text too Babylon is implicitly the point of departure ("from there").[7]

> What is meant by "exodus," however, is not quite as clear as would at first sight appear. It could be the case that here too, as otherwise in DtIsa, the exodus from Egypt and the exodus from Babylon are paralleled. Delitzsch already linked the first exodus with the second in connection with the command "do not touch anything unclean": "That is to say, <the people> should not line their pockets with the property of their now subjugated subjugators, as they did at the exodus from Egypt, Exod 12:36."[8] In view of the later polemic to which Exod 12:36 gave rise, this correction is conceivable.[9] But probably what is meant is the "uncleanness" of a place.[10] The description in Isaiah 46–47 would also be a sufficient reason for talking about the "uncleanness" of Babylon.

The admonition in v. 12: "not in (fearful) haste" is a clearer reference to the exodus from Egypt, and is at the same time a change of motif. The substantive חִפָּזוֹן is otherwise found in the OT only in Exod 12:11 and Deut 16:3. In Exod 12:11 it refers to the hasty eating of the Passover. In Deut 16:3 the unleavened mazzot is "the bread of oppression, of affliction" (עֹנִי). The reason given in Deuteronomy comes close to the present text: "because you came out (יָצָאתָ) of the land of Egypt in great haste." This time things will be different. There is no longer any pharaoh to pursue them![11]

That Yahweh should go ahead and should also form the rearguard is a reminder of "the angel of God"[12] (מַלְאַךְ הָאֱלֹהִים) at the miracle of the Reed Sea according to the Passover pericope, Exod 14:19. He protects Israel, in its departure, from the front and the rear. In the same passage this protection is set parallel to the pillars of cloud and fire.[13] According to Deut 1:30, Yahweh puts himself at the head of his people. It is he who points the way, in the pillars of cloud and fire (Deut 1:33). Other ways of representing the divine presence at the exodus are thereby excluded—the ark,[14] for example, which is not referred to here. It really is a new "exodus" and "the God of Israel" accompanies his people.[15]

The reception and the modification of tradition are signaled above all, however, by the use of the expression "the vessels of Yahweh" (כְּלֵי יהוה).[16] Vessels can be containers such as cups, pitchers and bowls; they can be tools for various purposes; and finally they can also be musical instruments. For use at the royal court or in the cult, they were frequently made of precious metal. In the description of the wanderings in the wilderness, according to Exodus 25—Numbers 10, vessels were manufactured for the cult according to divine instructions.[17] They all had to do with the tabernacle.[18] The holy tent dwelling,

---

5   H. D. Preuss, "יָצָא *yāṣāʾ*," *TDOT* 6:225–50, esp. 233–35, 244–46 [*ThWAT* 3:795–822, esp. 804–5, 816–17] (with lit.).

6   Ibid., 233 [804].

7   See North (224) on this passage: "Obviously Babylon (cf. xlviii.20). By some the 'there' has been taken to imply that the prophecy was composed outside Babylon: in Palestine (Mowinckel), in Egypt (Marti), or in the Lebanon (Duhm). Torrey takes 'there' to imply 'from this *modern* Egyptian bondage'. The simplest explanation is that the summons to leave Babylon is issued (ideally) from Jerusalem (so Volz), which is the *locus standi* of the preceding sections." See also Muilenburg here.

8   Delitzsch (510) on this passage (not included in the English translation).

9   Cf. also Ezra 1:5-6.

10   See Beuken here (174): "The chiastic arrangement of v. 11a shows sufficiently clearly that 'impure' (*ṭāmēʾ*) refers to a place, not to the possession of Babylon." He also refers to Hos 9:3 und Amos 7:17.

11   Cf. Exod 12:33, 39; and 14:9; Isa 48:20.

12   Cf. Exod 23:20; 32:34; Isa 63:9(?).

13   Cf. Num 14:14; Deut 1:30-33; Neh 9:12; Ps 78:14; 1 Cor 10:1.

14   Num 10:33-36; Josh 3:3-6.

15   North on this passage: "The meaning of 12b, therefore, is that Yahweh himself is to be both guide and protector of his people."

16   See K.-M. Beyse, "כְּלִי *keli*," *TDOT* 7:169–75 [*ThWAT* 4:179–85].

17   See Exodus 25–31; 35–40.

18   Exod 25:9.

the table for the shewbread, the seven-branched candlestick and the altars all had their proper "vessels."[19] In accordance with the concept of "the wandering people of God" whose sanctuary moved with them, the vessels were also portable. According to the version in Numbers, they were wrapped in purple and laid on a carrying frame (מוֹט, Num 4:10, 11). The Levites carried them (cf. Num 1:50; 3:1—4:49, esp. 3:8; 4:15, 19, 24, 31). So when the present DtIsa text talks about the people "who carry the vessels of Yahweh," the implication could be that these are the Levites. But according to 1 Chr 23:25-26 the Levites were relieved of their task as bearers by David, because "Yahweh, the God of Israel, has given rest to his people and resides in Jerusalem forever." Was this "rest" ended by the exile?[20] That would mean that, according to DtIsa, David's edict about the Levites is now set aside.

The account of the making of the vessels during the wanderings in the wilderness is in tension with the way they are given and made at the building of the temple by David and Solomon.[21] But the concern is to establish that their legitimation goes back to Moses.

The importance of the temple vessels for the exilic and postexilic period has been excellently worked out by P. R. Ackroyd.[22] He shows the amount of discussion that was waged on this subject, and the widely varying standpoints that were maintained.

2 Kgs 24:13 states that at the first deportation to Babylon by Nebuchadnezzar, all the golden vessels, at least the ones that Solomon had had made, were removed from the temple and broken up, because their metal was so valuable.[23] 2 Kgs 25:13-17 and Jer 52:17-23

suggest that when Jerusalem was destroyed in 587 B.C.E., the temple vessels may have been carried off to Babylon. In 27:16-22 and in 29:1-9 Jeremiah scouts false hopes for the preservation and return of the temple vessels (27:22): "They shall be carried to Babylon, and there they shall stay, until the day when I give attention to them, saying of Yahweh. Then I will bring them up and restore them to this place."[24]

The misuse of the temple vessels in Babylon is impressively described in the story about Belshazzar's feast in Daniel 5 (see vv. 3-4). 2 Chr 36:18 and Ezra 1:7-11 agree in saying that the vessels "large and small" were taken away, and were then fully restored by Cyrus, being returned to the temple in Jerusalem with Ezra.[25] The temple vessels symbolize the continuity of the cult in the Jerusalem temple before and after the exile, in spite of all the disruption.[26] Remembrance of the exodus from Egypt traces the line back to the era of the wanderings in the wilderness and the time of Moses. It is from these that the true legitimation derives. But I believe that the text has a number of undertones that should also be noted and that are connected with the contemporary situation. Why should those who "carry the vessels of Yahweh" *depart* "from there" and "from its midst"? What "uncleanness" is meant?

Neh 13:4-9 reports that the "chambers," an important part of the temple, have become impure.[27] These storerooms were used for keeping the grain offerings (הַמִּנְחָה), incense and "vessels" (וְהַכֵּלִים), as well as tithes and other contributions. In Nehemiah's absence, the priest Eliashib[28] put a large chamber at the disposal of Tobiah.

---

19   Exod 30:26-28; 31:7; 35:13-14; 37:16, 24; 38:31; 39:33-36, 40; 40:9.

20   For "rest" cf. Lev 26:34-35; 2 Chr 36:20-21.

21   See H. Utzschneider, *Das Heiligtum und das Gesetz. Studien zur Bedeutung der sinaitischen Heiligtumstexte (Ex 25–40; Lev 8–9)* (1988), esp. 270ff.

22   P. R. Ackroyd, "The Temple Vessels—A Continuity Theme," in *Studies in the Religion of Ancient Israel* (1972) 166–81.

23   Cf. 2 Chr 36:7, 10.

24   Cf. the commentaries on the text; also C. R. Seitz, *Theology in Conflict: Reactions to the Exile in the Book of Jeremiah* (1989) 184–89.

25   Cf. Ezra 5:14-15; 6:5; 7:19; 8:26-28, 33-34.

26   Ackroyd, "The Temple Vessels—A Continuity Theme," in *Studies in the Religion of Ancient Israel* (1972) 181: "The community which sought to reestablish itself after the exile, deeply conscious of its

ancestry in faith, but also aware of the problem of continuity with that faith, made use of the theme of the vessels, as it made use of other themes, to make good its claim to be the true successor (perhaps thereby to invalidate the claims of others), to be directly linked with those who stood on the other side of the exilic gulf. What they could see to be validated in spite of the historical break, their successors could see to be true also in later situations of distress. It is the same people of God which lives on in consciousness of its ancestry of faith."

27   On the text and the following passage see T. C. Eskenazi, *In an Age of Prose: A Literary Approach to Ezra-Nehemiah* (1988) 122–26; J. Blenkinsopp, *Ezra-Nehemiah: A Commentary* (1988) 352–57; A. H. J. Gunneweg, *Nehemiah* (1987) 164–67; H. G. M. Williamson, *Ezra, Nehemiah* (1985) 378–90.

28   Could it not perhaps be the high priest mentioned

This is the same Tobiah who, together with Sanballat and Geshem, formed a trio hostile to Nehemiah.[29] One of Nehemiah's measures was to abolish privileges of this kind in the temple. At the end we read (Neh 13:9): "Then I gave orders and they cleansed the chambers, and brought back the vessels of the house of God, with the grain offering and the frankincense" (וָאֹמְרָה ... וַיְטַהֲרוּ הַלְּשָׁכוֹת וָאָשִׁיבָה שָׁם כְּלֵי בֵּית הָאֱלֹהִים).

In the context, this passage is talking about provisions for the support of the Levites, so that they should be in a position to serve the temple once more (cf. vv. 10-14). This is in line with the obligation undertaken in Neh 10:39-40 (38-39) and there too the chambers with the sacred vessels (וְשָׁם כְּלֵי הַמִּקְדָּשׁ, v. 40) are mentioned. "Impurity" or "uncleanness" could therefore apply to the temple itself.[30] The Levites were not affected by this impurity. It was certain other sections of the priesthood with whom there was a conflict. In this context Numbers 4 is again of interest. There the rights of the Levites are diminished, over against those of "Aaron and his sons" (vv. 5, 15, 19, 27).[31] Direct access to the holy of holies is denied them. The covering of "all the utensils of the service that are used in the sanctuary" (v. 12) is also reserved solely for the family of Aaron (v. 15): "Thus Aaron and his sons shall completely cover the holy things and all the holy vessels when the camp sets out; only after that shall the Kohathites come to carry them, but *they must not touch the holy things*, or they will die (וְלֹא־יִגְּעוּ אֶל־הַקֹּדֶשׁ וָמֵתוּ)."

The present DtIsa text says the very contrary (v. 11a): "Go out from there, *touch no unclean thing!* (טָמֵא אַל־תִּגָּעוּ).

The text could therefore reflect a conflict between the descendants of Aaron and the Levites.[32] DtIsa does not mention Aaron, nor is the term "priest" ever used. If the people who carry "the vessels of Yahweh" are then told "to purify themselves, to keep themselves pure" (הִבָּרוּ),[33] this is reminiscent of another Nehemiah text. Before the dedication of the wall of Jerusalem (which was celebrated with a great procession) we are told (Neh 12:30): "And the priests and the Levites purified themselves (וַיִּטַּהֲרוּ); and they purified the people and the gates and the wall." T. C. Eskenazi has elicited the essential importance of this text.[34] According to her exposition, here the sanctity of the priests is transferred to the whole people. For DtIsa does not mention even the Levites explicitly. He talks about the people who "carry the vessels of Yahweh." It could be that for him too the whole sanctified assembly of God (cf. Neh 13:1) can participate in the procession—indeed, even has a share in the carrying of Yahweh's vessels. In a performance, this could also be acted out by a chorus, representing the people as a whole.

In the procession described in Nehemiah 12, "the scribe Ezra went in front of them (לִפְנֵיהֶם)" (12:36)—that is, in front of that half of the choir of thanksgiving that circled the city to the right. Nehemiah brought up the rear of those who went to the left (v. 38). In DtIsa it is Yahweh himself who goes in front (לִפְנֵיכֶם) and who also forms the rearguard (52:12). In the concept of his procession, God's presence is also manifest.

---

in 3:1, 20-21; 12:10-22, whose title is simply denied him here? The granting of rooms in the temple presupposes a prominent position. Blenkinsopp (*Ezra-Nehemiah*, 353) takes a different view of the passage.

29 For a discussion of the historical situation, see U. Kellermann, *Nehemia. Quellenüberlieferung und Geschichte* (1967), section IV: "Nehemias Feinde," 166ff.; on Tobiah, 167–70.

30 This could also explain the singular expression "vessels of Yahweh." The usual phrase is "the vessels of Yahweh's house" (כְּלֵי בֵית־יהוה); see, e.g., Jer 27:16; 28:3, 6; Ezra 1:7. It is significant that the text does not talk about "Yahweh's house" at all. The "vessels" belong directly to Yahweh.

31 On Num 3:1–4:49 see M. Noth, *Numbers* (1968) [*Numeri* (1966)]. On 4:1-33, ibid., 41 [39]: "Once more the theme is that of the duties of the individual groups of Levites. In contrast to ch. 3, however,

these duties are still further delimited in so far as reference is made simply to the striking of the camp and the further wanderings of Israel in the wilderness, in which circumstances the Levites had to dismantle the sanctuary and transport the various parts of it."

32 We cannot exclude the possibility that here the text is generalizing what was really the task of the Levites, a generalization that DtIsa achieves by omitting the name "Levites" altogether. See D. Baltzer, *Ezechiel und Deuterojesaja* (1971) 19.

33 See GKB s.v. ברר; V. Hamp, "בָּרַר *bārar*," *TDOT* 2:308–12 [*ThWAT* 1:841–45].

34 T. C. Eskenazi, *In an Age of Prose: A Literary Approach to Ezra-Nehemiah* (1988) 117–18: "The purification of all the people is especially important. It demonstrates that they are brought into the same ritual status as priests and Levites. They become a holy

Processions were an essential element in the public life of the ancient world.[35] On these occasions cultic objects of the most varied kind were frequently carried and displayed.[36] The entry and exit of the chorus were also a feature of the spectacle, in which the frontiers between play, cult and reality were fluid.

In the text, the indication of direction: "Go out from there," would have a point as an implicit stage direction if it were accompanied in the performance by a gesture. It could have to do with scenic convention;[37] and in view of the different levels on which the text can be understood, it is conceivable that for Jerusalem "from there" covers both the direction of Babylon and the direction of the temple. Something similar may be true of "out of its midst" (מִתּוֹכָהּ). The feminine suffix is related to Babylon, but there may also be a reference to the temple (הֵיכָל) and its forecourt (חָצֵר).[38]

For the present context it is again interesting that Nehemiah should have refused to enter "the innermost part of the temple" (אֶל־תּוֹךְ הַהֵיכָל) in order to save his life (Neh 6:10 [11]).[39] It is there, according to DtIsa, that the exodus and the new start are now beginning. Difficulties about the temple as an institution do not prevent DtIsa from holding fast to Zion and its election. But above all, for him Jerusalem is not just the place of the sanctuary; it is the holy city.

In the framework of the liturgical drama, it is worth considering how far the pillars of cloud and fire of the first exodus, or the presence of Yahweh in the festal procession, could have been symbolized by incense. This presence is interpreted (52:12b), if we take a slightly different translation:

Truly, the one who goes before you is Yahweh,
and he who brings up the rear is the God of Israel.

1QIsa^a follows "the God of Israel" with the acclamation: "he is called 'the God of the whole earth.'"

The acclamation is an appropriate conclusion to the procession. It leads over to 52:13—53:12, with its epiphany. But above all, the following Servant of God text IV provides an answer to the question: Is there an exodus without "Moses"?[40]

---

people. This amplifies the point made by the Israelite pedigrees: the sanctity of the people, not merely of clergy, matters."

35   See F. Bömer, "pompa (πομπή)," PW 21/2:1878–1994, esp. 1886: "The *pompa* is ἡ ἐν ταῖς τῶν θεῶν πανηγύρεσι πρόσοδος (Thom. Mag. under this heading), the festal procession put on by the *polis* or by a cultic community, with the deity, or aiming at an encounter with the deity."

36   See ibid., 1891–92, 1903–4; "Geräte" ("vessels"), 1910–11.

37   Cf. K. Joerden, "Exkurs II, Rechts und Links; die Bedeutung der Parodoi" in W. Jens, ed., *Die Bauformen der griechischen Tragödie* (1971) 409: "One thing, however, can be transferred from the special conditions of the Athenian theater to other places of dramatic representation too: in the awareness of the audience, above all the Athenian audience, who on the slopes of the Acropolis looked roughly south, the west—i.e., the right-hand side—was always 'proximity,' embodied through the city in its various forms—fields, harbor, city area—whereas east ('left') was always the road coming from afar."

38   Cf. GKC § 122 k, l.

39   For "the middle of the forecourt" (תּוֹךְ הֶחָצֵר) see 1 Kgs 8:64; 2 Chr 7:7.

40   Mark (chap. 1) links "the beginning of the gospel of Jesus Christ" with the first exodus (Exod 23:20) and with the second (Isa 40:3). It is in these categories that the events that follow have to be understood. John baptizes in the desert at the Jordan. "And there went out to him (ἐξεπορεύετο) all the country of Judea, and all the people of Jerusalem . . ." (Mark 1:5). It is the baptism of repentance. What follows is Jesus' baptism and with it his installation, with which the coming of "the Spirit" is associated.

B. 52:13—53:12
Servant of God Text IV
The Suffering Servant of God:
His Life,
His Death,
and His Exaltation
The Rehabilitation of the Servant of God
in a Heavenly Court

52:13	See, my Servant shall be "beatified.'"[a] He will rise and be carried up and be very high.
14	Just as many were dismayed over you[a]— so maltreated,[b] no longer human was his appearance, and his form not like the form of a human being—
15	so he shall sprinkle many peoples. Above/over him[a] kings will shut their mouths. Truly, what they had not been told they will have seen, and what they have never heard they will have understood.
53:1	Who has believed our revelation? And over whom has the arm of Yahweh been revealed?
2	But he grew up like a young shoot before him, and like a root out of dry land. He had no form and no beauty that we should have looked at him, and no appearance that we should have desired him.
3	He was despised, and forsook human beings, a man of suffering and familiar with sickness, and like one before whom one covers one's face, despised—so we held him to be of no account.
4	Truly he bore *our* sickness, and *our* sufferings—he took them upon himself. But we held him to be one who is (had been) touched, by the stroke[a] of a god and humiliated.
5	But he was <desecrated> for *our* "sin,"[a] smitten because of *our* "transgressions." The rebuke leading to *our* healing lay on him, and through his fellowship/invocation[b] *we* have received healing.
6	We all wander around like a herd of small cattle, each has taken his own way. But Yahweh has allowed to fall on him the "guilt" of all of *us*.
7	He was oppressed and he was bowed down and does not open his mouth— like a lamb that is led to the slaughter, and like a sheep that is dumb before his shearer,

52:13a On the translation see the comment below.

14a See below.

14b Instead of מָשְׁחַת the reading should perhaps be מוּשְׁחָת (as in one manuscript) or מְשֻׁחָת (as in the Babylonian tradition); cf. *BHS*.

15a Lit.: "are they over him (עָלָיו)." See below.

53:4a Read as מַכֵּה, thus to be pointed as a substantive.

5a MT has מְחֹלָל, "pierced," *Polel* participle of חלל II; it has been proposed that instead of this the reading should be מְחֻלָּל, "desecrated," *Pual* participle of חלל I; see below on this passage.

5b The traditional translation is "by his wounds/stripes (weals)" (sing.! cf. *HALOT* 1:285 [*HALAT* 1:274]): see below on the text.

8　　he does not open his mouth.
　　He has been taken away out of exclusion
　　　　and condemnation.
　　But who thinks about his generation?
　　Truly, he is cut off from the land of the living;
　　because of the "sins" of <his>ᵃ people a
　　　　blow has struck him.

9　　And he gaveᵃ him his grave among criminals
　　and his "place"ᵇ beside a rich man,
　　although he had not committed any act of
　　　　violence,
　　and there was no deceit in his mouth.

10　　But it had pleased Yahweh <to let him
　　　　become dust>.ᵃ
　　He had <desecrated> him.ᵇ
　　If he gives his life to wipe out debt
　　　　(guilt)/as an offering for sin (guilt),
　　he will see descendants and have a long
　　　　life [lit.: "he (Yahweh) will make
　　　　days long"]
　　and Yahweh's good pleasure/cause will
　　　　have success through his hand.

11　　After [or "because of"?] the trouble/anguish
　　　　of his life/soul he shall see <light>ᵃ
　　<and> be satisfied.
　　Through his knowledge [or: "experience"?]
　　　　he, the one who is just,
　　my Servant will make the many just [or:
　　　　"achieve justice for the many"?],
　　and their "debts" he will take them upon
　　　　himself.

12　　Therefore I will give him a share with the
　　　　many,
　　and with the powerful he will share "spoil,"ᵃ
　　because he surrendered his life to death,
　　and let himself be numbered among sinners.
　　He was the one who bore the crimes/
　　　　transgressions of many,
　　and he will intercedeᵇ for their sins.ᶜ

8ᵃ　Thus following 1QIsaᵃ (עמו) instead of עַמִּי, "my people."
9ᵃ　Thus following MT. 1QIsaᵃ has ויתנו: "they gave him." It would also be possible to read וַיֻתַּן ("and it was given") instead of וַיִּתֵּן ("and he gave").
9ᵇ　It has been proposed that בְּמֹתָיו "in his deaths" (cf. LXX [S, Vg]: ἀντὶ τοῦ θανάτου αὐτοῦ) should be corrected to בָּמָתוֹ or בּוֹמָתוֹ "his <high> place" (cf. 1QIsaᵃ). See below.
10ᵃ·ᵇ　See the comment below. MT can be rendered: "But it has pleased Yahweh to smite him. He let him become sick."
11ᵃ　Cf. 1QIsaᵃ·ᵇ and LXX; see below.
12ᵃ　For the translation see the comment below (with lit.).
12ᵇ　MT has the *Hiphil* (יַפְגִּיעַ). But I think *Qal* should be read, with 1QIsaᵃ (יפגע). The form in 1QIsaᵃ could be a defective writing for the *Hiphil*, but 1QIsaᵃ generally aims at *plene* writings rather than defective ones.
12ᶜ　Thus following 1QIsaᵃ·ᵇ and LXX. MT has וְלַפֹּשְׁעִים: "And he will intercede for the sinners."

The solemn procession in 52:11-12 moves toward an epiphany. In a scene in heaven, the exaltation (52:13) and the justification of the Servant by God, his Lord, are described (52:14—53:12). The importance and later history of this text are almost inexhaustible. Every generation must try to find an answer to the old questions with the presuppositions and instruments of its own time.[41]

Thus "the Ethiopian eunuch" already asked: "About whom, may I ask you, does the prophet say this, about himself or about someone else?" (Acts 8:34).

The following exegesis is determined by three premises:

1. The close correlation and interdependence of the four Servant of God texts. They help to interpret one

---

41　In the case of this fourth Servant text, it has proved impossible, in view of the restricted compass of the commentary, to enter into detailed discussion with previous literature. I can only point to the commentaries and to the summings-up mentioned at the close of this note. I should like instead to

another. They are stages in an "ideal biography."[42] The presupposition of the present text is that the Servant is dead (53:9).

2. The place of the text in the context of DtIsa's book as a whole must also be taken into account. This can be said of the content, but it is equally true of the form. The text is part of the liturgical drama. That explains its scenic structure. Elements of lament and thanksgiving are incorporated. An oracle of salvation is proclaimed at the beginning (52:14-15) and at the end (53:11-12). These genre elements have not gone unobserved, but it may be said more precisely that together they are built up into a scene in a court of law, in which the Servant is rehabilitated.

3. These observations provoke the question as to whether the addressees of the text could and should know that the subject is the "remembrance" (זִכָּרוֹן the *memoria*) of the Servant of God, "Moses." That this is indeed the subject is something that still has to be shown in detail; but one indication is the immediate context, 52:11-12, which sounds the theme of the exodus.

52:13
Appearance and Exaltation of the Servant of God

"See, my Servant shall be 'beatified.'
He will rise and be carried up and be very high" (52:13)

The literature on Isa 52:13—53:12 is immense, beyond the bounds of any survey; and yet v. 13 has never received the attention it deserves.[43] The verse contains essential clues for an understanding of the whole. "See" (הִנֵּה) should be understood in the same literal sense as in the presentation of the Servant in the first Servant of God text (42:1): there is something to be seen! The Servant appears. Since, with only a few exceptions, there are no stage directions in DtIsa, everything that happens is contained and indicated in the text.

■ **13a** The Servant will "understand, realize" or/and "be successful, succeed, have good fortune" (יַשְׂכִּיל).[44] The two meanings are closely related. The background is wisdom vocabulary. The opposite of "to be wise" is "to be foolish" (cf. Isa 44:25; Qoh 1:17). If one follows M. Sæbø, the following can be said:

> The main semantic stress, however, has now the resultative verbal meaning "to have come to perceive, to be understanding, wise" (cf. the parallelization of eye and heart in Isa 41:20; 44:18). In the effective sense, the one who has perception is skilful and understanding in what he does, but is then also successful. Such statements are made primarily about kings and other leaders of their people. . . . In the causative sense, a human being is then the object of the making-perceptive, of an instruction that can aim at someone's conduct, as a pointer or guide, . . . but it is frequently said to have come from God or his Spirit (cf. Ps 32:8; Dan 9:22; Neh 9:20; 1 Chr 28:19), just as "perception" in general is in the most varied ways dependent on God, or is related to him."[45]

That reads like a paraphrase of the present DtIsa text.

Two other passages deserve attention, in view of the tradition complex to which v. 13 belongs, for they tell

substantiate my own interpretation as fully as possible. I especially regret that it is impossible to consider more fully here the early Jewish and Christian interpretation of the text. This must be reserved for further interdisciplinary work. I hope that the consequences of my own approach will be evident.
K. Baltzer, "Jes 52:13: Die 'Erhöhung' des 'Gottesknechtes,'" in *Religious Propaganda and Missionary Competition in the New Testament World: FS D. Georgi* (1994) 45–56; D. J. A. Clines, *I, He, We and They: A Literary Approach to Isaiah 53* (1976); H. Haag, "Ebed Jahwe–Forschung 1948–1958," *BZ* n.s. 3 (1959) 174–204; B. Janowski, "Er trug unsere Sünden. Jesaja 53 und die Dramatik der Stellvertretung," *ZThK* 90 (1993) 1–24, reprinted with updated literature and corrigenda, in his *Gottes Gegenwart in Israel* (1993) 303–26, 37; R. N. Whybray, *Thanksgiving for a Liberated Prophet: An*

Interpretation of Isaiah Chapter 53 (1978). See now B. Janowski and P. Stuhlmacher, eds., *Der leidende Gottesknecht. Jesaja 53 und seine Wirkungsgeschichte* (FAT 14; 1996), with bibliography.

42 K. Baltzer, "Zur formgeschichtlichen Bestimmung der Texte vom Gottesknecht im Deuterojesaja Buch," in *Probleme biblischer Theologie. FS G. von Rad* (1971) 27–43; idem, *Die Biographie der Propheten* (1975) 171–77.

43 On the text see W. Richter, *Untersuchungen zur Valenz althebräischer Verben, 2. GBH, 'MQ. QSR II* (1986) 18–20. Richter's observation on v. 13 is important: "Syntactically too it does not point beyond itself" (18).

44 The Zurich translation (1931) renders it appropriately in the sense of: "See, my Servant will have good fortune."

45 M. Sæbø, "שׂכל *śkl* hi. to have insight," *TLOT*

how, before his death, Moses talks about success and perception: Deut 29:8 (9): "Therefore diligently observe the words of this covenant, in order that you may have success (תַּשְׂכִּ֫ילוּ) in everything that you do"; and Deut 32:29, in the Song of Moses: "O that they were wise and understood this (יַשְׂכִּ֫ילוּ), so that they might discern what their future time (לְאַחֲרִיתָם) would be."

The Servant is in this sense "discerning," when he gains access to the heavenly sphere, and he is able to make others "discerning" too (cf. 52:15; 53:11). I should like to go a step further and ask whether through the divine proclamation the Servant does not here become one of the "wise" of whom Dan 12:3 then writes: "The wise (וְהַמַּשְׂכִּלִים) shall shine like the brightness of the firmament and those who lead many to righteousness like the stars forever and ever." Perhaps this should be taken much more literally, in the light of the "ascension" of the Servant, which follows immediately in the text. In his exaltation the Servant of God finally finds ultimate perception and lasting "success." He is given a new status. I should like to describe this with the word "beatific." The Servant is counted among "the beatified."

The declaration "my Servant" already fully confirms him in his rights and duties. A word suffices! The outcome of the proceedings has already been anticipated. The Servant is a servant in life and in death. His Lord calls him to himself. What the Lord says comes to pass, and through his word he throws open the path to the heavenly sphere. It is there that the following judicial scene takes place.

■ **13b** The "exaltation" of the Servant is described with three verbs of movement. They should initially be taken literally, not interpreted in a transferred sense, to mean "honored." The exaltation takes place in three stages:[46] the ascent (רום), the being carried (נשא), the being very high (גָּבַהּ מְאֹד).

1. "He will rise" (יָרוּם *yārûm*): About this text, H.-P. Stähli observes: "Positively, the resultant meaning is qal '(to rise up=) to arrive at honor' (Isa 52:13 . . .)."[47] The

other texts that Stähli adduces—though in other stems—make this seem a possible meaning. Yet the active form is striking. Where is the Servant supposed to rise *to*?

A first indication of the sense in this connotation is that the participle רָם is used for the "highness" of mountains (Deut 12:2; Isa 2:14) and hills (Ezek 6:13; 20:28; 34:6). These references show that the root רום has a spatial, geographical meaning too. The same is true of the substantive. Here Stähli writes:

> *mārôm* "height" (primarily used poetically) is employed first in a concrete sense for the height of mountains (2 Kgs 19:23 = Isa 37:24a; Jer 31:12; Ezek 17:23; 20:40; 34:14—the concept of the mythic mountain of the gods may stand in the background here, according to Zimmerly [*Ezekiel*] 1:417 [BK XIII, 457] [comment on 20:40]) In general any high place can be meant (Isa 22:16; 26:5), so that sometimes the simple translation "upwards, on high" seems appropriate.[48]

In view of the other references in the text to the Moses tradition, down to his death and burial, the strange "he will ascend" is in my view a first signal pointing to Deuteronomy 34: "Then Moses went up (וַיַּעַל) from the plains of Moab to Mount Nebo, to the top of Pisgah, which is opposite Jericho, and Yahweh showed him the whole land (אֶת־כָּל־הָאָרֶץ)" (v. 1; cf. Deut 32:49-50). In this passage the word עלה is used for Moses' "ascent"—the same word that is used at Sinai. But perhaps this term could have been open to misunderstanding, since DtIsa uses it in more than one sense in 40:31, where it signifies both the "going up" to Egypt and Babylon, and the "rising up with wings like eagles." So here he constructs the term "ascend into the heights," and is sure of being still understood,[49] because everyone knows what the reference is. In the progress of the drama, the "exaltation" of the Servant Moses begins with his ascent. This ascent can thus be understood in a concrete sense, like the climbing of a mountain. In Deuteronomy 34 the connection is clear: Moses climbs a mountain, dies there, and is buried. But in DtIsa it is

3:1269–72, esp. 1270–71 [*THAT* 2:824–28, esp. 825].

46   Cf. P. E. Bonnard writes (270): "whose triumph is now accentuated by the accumulation of three synonyms."

47   See H.-P. Stähli, "רום *rûm* to be high," *TLOT* 3:1220–25, esp. 1222 [THAT 2:753–61, esp. 757].

48   Ibid., 1223 [757].

49   According to 40:9, the messenger Zion is supposed to climb up onto a high mountain, but at this particular point רום *Hiphil* is used for "to raise the voice." In 49:11 the highways are raised, and in 49:22 Yahweh is going to raise his signal. These findings show the wide variations in DtIsa's use of language. But I would also assume that DtIsa, like some of his addressees, has in mind Isa 6:1: "I saw

initially not clear whether the Servant's ascent takes place while he is still alive or only after his death. For an interpretation that starts from the present complex and sees the Servant's biography ending in the past with his death and burial, the command to the Servant to "rise" can mean that he rises from the underworld. For retrospectively he has already "departed/been cut off from the land of the living" (53:8).

2. "And he will be carried up" (וְנִשָּׂא):[50] This is the second stage in the "exaltation," and here the Servant is passive. Who or what carries him is not stated. It could be said that at the exodus Yahweh carried his people "as a man carries his child" (Deut 1:31), or that "as an eagle . . . he bears it aloft on his pinions" (Deut 32:11 cf. Exod 19:4). But it is unlikely that in the present text Yahweh is involved in the action in this way. We should more probably think of heavenly powers or angels, who carry out the commission.[51] It is a matter of surmounting the space between earth and heaven.[52] According to Deut 34:5, Moses died on Mount Nebo. But the frontier between life and death is not mentioned in the present text. The Servant is still the Servant of God, before his death and afterward.

3. "And he will be very high" (וְגָבַהּ מְאֹד):[53] This is the third and final stage in the exaltation. According to Isa 55:9, the heavens are "high above the earth" (גָּבְהוּ; cf. Ps 103:11). According to Ps 113:5, Yahweh is enthroned "in

the heights" (הַמַּגְבִּיהִי). The Servant is taken up into this presence of his Lord. The intensification "exalted very high" (וְגָבַהּ מְאֹד) suggests that in DtIsa's world picture God's throne is actually above the heavens.[54] Thus the Servant has arrived at the divine sphere, where the trial that is to rehabilitate him will take place. This is the highest honor that can be confered on him.

The text of 52:13 therefore describes in succinct form the "exaltation" of the Servant. I would assume that the text belongs to a wider tradition complex. It is a dispute about the death of Moses, according to the account in Deuteronomy 34. A comparison with other texts that have an "exaltation" as their subject is illuminating.[55]

Here the writing known as the *Testament of Moses* (*Assumptio Mosis*) is interesting because of its similarities and its differences.[56] In form, it is a "last will and testament." Moses is addressing Joshua, his successor, in a farewell speech that surveys Israel's past history and prophesies the future, down to the final judgment. In the following passage, the announcement of judgment is joined with the announcement of the "exaltation." But it is easy to detect the independence of the two elements. I believe that in 10:8ff. Moses originally prophesies his end and his future. It is really a divine saying that has been given to him ("Then *you* will be happy") and that he here passes on to Joshua.

---

the Lord sitting upon a throne, high and lofty (רָם וְנִשָּׂא)."

50 The same may be said of "carry" according to Beuken on this passage (200–201): "an important catchword"; he refers to 45:20; 46:7; 40:11; 46:3; 49:22. See also F. Stolz, "נשׂא *nś* to lift, bear," *TLOT* 2:769–74 [*THAT* 2:109–17].

51 Thus through "the hand of God" Ezekiel is seized by the spirit and carried between earth and heaven to Jerusalem (וַתִּשָּׂא אֹתִי רוּחַ, Ezek 8:3; 11:1; cf. 37:1; 40:1).

52 The comparison with Enoch (Gen 5:24) and Elijah (2 Kgs 2:9-12) is obvious.

53 H.-P. Stähli, "גבה *gbh* to be high," *TLOT* 1:296–99 [*THAT* 1:394–97]; R. Hentschke, "גָּבַהּ *gābhah*," *TDOT* 2:356–60 [*ThWAT* 1:890–95]; G. Bertram, "ὕψος," *TDNT* 8:602–20 [*ThWNT* 8:600–619].

54 See above on 40:22; 41:4. Here the role of the Servant of God and the Moses tradition for the development of christology requires renewed attention. There is a reminiscence of the brief formula of Isa 52:13, with its "highly raise/exalt" (וְגָבַהּ מְאֹד), in

Phil 2:9 (ὑπερύψωσεν); see also Eph 1:20 (ἐν τοῖς ἐπουρανίοις ὑπεράνω); Heb 1:3 (ἐν ὑψηλοῖς); 7:26 (ὑψηλότερος τῶν οὐρανῶν). Acts 2:33 says that Jesus has been exalted (ὑψωθείς) by the right hand of God. This is further expounded when Stephen, the first martyr, then witnesses to the identity between the earthly Jesus and the one exalted into heaven: "But filled with the Holy Spirit, he gazed into heaven and saw the glory of God (δόξαν θεοῦ) and Jesus standing at the right hand of God" (Acts 7:55).

55 See here esp. G. W. E. Nickelsburg, *Resurrection, Immortality, and Eternal Life in Intertestamental Judaism* (1972).

56 For the most part the translation follows J. H. Charlesworth, "Testament of Moses," in his *OTP*, 1:919–34 (1983), but is modified in the direction of E. Brandenburger's translation, "Himmelfahrt Moses" (1976) 57–84, esp. 77, and my own exegesis; see also the translation of R. H. Charles, *Apocrypha and Pseudepigrapha of the OT* (1913) 2:407–24. For the Latin text see C. Clemen, "Die Himmelfahrt des Mose," in H. Lietzmann, *Kleine Texte* 10 (1924).

7   For God Most High will surge forth, the Eternal
    One alone,
    In full view he will come to work vengeance on
    the nations.
    Yea, all their idols will he destroy.
8   Then you will be happy, O Israel!
    And you will mount up above the necks and the
    wings of an eagle.
    And they [the wings] shall be *filled.*[57]
9   And God will raise you to the heights.
    Yea, he will give you a firm place in the heaven
    of the stars,
    in the place of their habitations.
10 And you will behold from on high. . . .

The most important catchwords that correspond to
Isa 52:13 are recognizable in the Latin version too:
"be happy" ("tunc felix eris"). The three stages of the
"exaltation are (1) "go up, mount" ("ascendes"). Here
"going up" means climbing onto an eagle, as a means
of transport from earth to heaven. (2) But it is clear
that this is intended to be an "ascent into heaven" ("et
altavit te deus"). (3) In the *As. Mos.* the "being very
high" of Isa 52:13 is the "firm place in the heaven of
the stars" ("et faciet te herere caelo stellarum").

It is worth noting that in the text of *As. Mos.* the
second person singular ("you will") is understood in a
collective sense, the "you" being applied to "Israel"
(v. 8a)—a problem familiar to us from DtIsa. But

above all, it is clear in the *As. Mos.* that "the exalted
one" is originally Moses. In 10:12 Moses talks to
Joshua about "of <my> death, <my> assumption" ("a
morte receptione<m>").[58] In my view this refers to
the assumption or reception of Moses into the heavenly sphere. It is noticeable that this work links
Moses' "assumption" with the sepulchre tradition. In
the following chapter (11) the question about Moses'
burial place is discussed, and here again it is plain
that the text is an interpretation of Deuteronomy 34.
As. Mos. is still interpreting Deuteronomy 34 (and
with it the Moses tradition) when it makes Joshua say:
5   What place will receive you? ("quis locus recipit
    . . . te)
6   Or where will be the marker of your sepulchre?
    ("aut quod erit monumentum sepulturae")
The answer is:
8   The whole world is your sepulchre ("omnis orbis
    terrarum sepulcrum est tuum").

If the text of *As. Mos.* 10–11 is an exposition of
Deuteronomy 34 and a dispute with the Moses tradition, we may perhaps ask whether the same may not
be said of Isa 52:13—53:12.[59]

A further text describing the "exaltation" of Moses
is found in the *Exagoge* of Ezekiel the Tragedian
(68–89 c.e.).[60] This drama dates only from the
Hellenistic period, but it nevertheless deserves attention, because in its treatment of the theme of the

---

Text and commentary in E.-M. Laperrousaz, *Le
Testament de Moïse* (1970). The Latin text of the
Assumptio is extant in a palimpsest. The work was
probably originally written in Greek, but it may
possibly have had a Hebrew or Aramaic basis.
Brandenburger (57–84) assumes that the version
dates from "only a little later than the 6th century
a.d.,"; others, such as Laperrousaz, put it a little
later. Parts of the text have been poorly preserved.
It is as a whole a fragment. It is impossible to enter
here into the literary problems that it presents.

57   My italics. Brandenburger ("Himmelfahrt Moses")
     translates v. 8c in the sense of "and so they will have
     their end." He understands the statement as part of
     an announcement of judgment. In my view *et imple-
     buntur* (they shall be filled) should be related to the
     wings: they will fill like sails in the wind before the
     eagle flies up; cf. *Thesaurus Linguae Latinae*, VII 1
     (1934–64) under the heading *impleo* IA 1a αII (col.
     630, ll. 14–25) and βII (col. 631, ll. 7–11): see, e.g.,
     Virgil *Aeneid* 7.23 "Neptunus ventis implevit vela
     secundis" (LCL 64, 4–5: "Neptune filled their sails
     with favoring winds"); also Ovid *Amores* 2.11.38
     (LCL 41, 416–17), *Metamorphoses* 9.592 (LCL 43,
     44–45); Quintilian *Institutio Oratoria* 10.7.23 (LCL
     127, 144–45); see also Seneca *Naturales Quaestiones*
     5.8.1 (LCL 457, 84–85).

58   On the text see Brandenburger, "Himmelfahrt
     Moses," 77–78 n. 12a.

59   On the dispute about the interpretation of
     Deuteronomy 34 and Isaiah 52–53 in Jewish tradi-
     tion see esp. M. Rosenfeld, "Der Midrasch Deutero-
     nomium Rabba über den Tod des Mose verglichen
     mit der Assumptio Mosis" (1899). On the midrash
     on the death of Moses (פטירת משה; Jellinek 1.122)
     see the literature in E.-M. Laperrousaz, *Le Testament
     de Moïse* (1970) 26–28. Cf. also Pseudo-Philo *Lib.
     Ant. Bibl.*, esp. 19, 16; as G. Vermes has shown, his
     picture of Moses is particularly close to that of
     Deuteronomy, as well as to DtIsa. See G. Vermes,
     "Die Gestalt des Mose an der Wende der beiden
     Testamente," in H. Cazelles et al., *Moses* (1963)
     61–93 esp. 86, 93.

60   Cf. also M. Lafargue, "Orphica" in J. H. Charles-
     worth, ed. *OTP* 2:795–801. Further D. Georgi, *The
     Opponents of Paul in Second Corinthians* (1986)
     54–56; this book is an expanded translation of *Die
     Gegner des Paulus im 2. Korintherbrief. Studien zur
     religiösen Propaganda in der Spätantike* (1964); see
     there 54–56.

exodus it closely resembles DtIsa in form and content.[61] Its subject is a dream of Moses, and its interpretation by Reuel, Moses' father-in-law. In the dream, the "exaltation" is Moses' enthronement on the divine throne. The throne stands on the top of Sinai and reaches to heaven. Here the text may be taking up Exodus 24 and Ps 110:1, although the reading "Sinai" is not absolutely certain.[62] It is possible that the text speaks only about a "high throne" on a mountain peak.[63] In the interpretation of Moses' dream in the *Exagoge*, we are told that Moses will act as a judge and teacher of humanity,[64] and that he is able prophetically to survey the whole world[65] and the whole of time. This interpretation, again, is relevant for an understanding of the Servant of God text in DtIsa. God's sovereignty and the rule of his Servant are closely connected.

In what follows it will become clear why it is so important for the judicial proceedings to take place in the heavenly sphere and not in the underworld; for one of the points at issue is the dispute with the "gods" of the underworld and their power. With his exaltation, the Servant has arrived at the immediate presence of his Lord. The throne scene is a way of expressing God's sovereignty.[66] Its special point in this text is that the Ruler over the whole world helps a human being whose life has been at his service to arrive at the justice due to him.

52:14-15
Throne Scene:
Opening of the Proceedings with a Speech by the Divine Judge

"Above/over him kings will shut their mouths" (52:15)

Verse 13 establishes the place and time of the following scene, in a kind of trailer or preview. The place is the heavenly sphere. Yahweh must surely be imagined as

enthroned. Whether he is visible is another question—probably not. But his voice, at least, can be heard. The time assumed is after the death of the Servant—if it is Moses, at the latest at the beginning of the settlement of the land under Joshua, which follows on Deuteronomy 34, and which is described in the book of Joshua. This could explain why the final section of the fourth Servant text talks about a "portion" (חלק, Isa 53:12; cf. 54:17, "inheritance [נַחֲלָה] of the Servant of Yahweh").

The scene is set in a court of law, where a dispute about the view to be taken of a certain person is under consideration.[67] Those present are: the judge, the person in question, witnesses brought by the disputing parties, and listeners. The course of the proceedings is described quite precisely.

First of all the presiding judge speaks. What he says is given in vv. 14 and 15. He immediately comes to the point and presents the case, introducing each different point by a brief particle (lit.): "inasmuch as . . ." (כַּאֲשֶׁר). He argues precisely: "just as . . ." (כֵּן), "so . . ." (כֵּן), and closes emphatically: "truly . . ." (כִּי). This sequence is incidentally a slight indication that the texts are intended for listeners. The judge begins each of his four points with a כ (*k*). His verdict anticipates the outcome of the trial.[68] In pronouncing it he introduces the debate that follows, in which the pros and cons of the case are discussed. That the judge speaks does not per se exclude the possibility that his speech is accompanied by action.

■ **14** In v. 14a Yahweh first addresses the Servant directly.[69] That is a supreme honor,[70] if it is compared with the usual relationship between a ruler and his

61 H. Jacobson, *The Exagoge of Ezekiel* (1983): text, 54; commentary, 87–97; and notes, 199–203. Translation in *OTP* 2:811–12; E. Vogt, *Tragiker Ezechiel* (1983) 124–25.

62 See esp. Jacobson, *Exagoge*, 200–201 nn. 2 and 14.

63 The Samaritan tradition links Moses' throne with his death; see M. Gaster, *The Asatir* (1927) 317–19; also Jacobson, *Exagoge*, 201 nn. 14 and 18.

64 "[B]ecome a judge and leader of men" (καὶ αὐτὸς βραβεύσεις καὶ καθηγήσῃ βροτῶν); see *Exagoge* 86; Jacobson, *Exagoge*, 54/55.

65 Is this therefore interpreting אֶת־כָּל־הָאָרֶץ in Deut 34:1 as meaning "the whole world"?

66 Cf. among other passages Isaiah 6, Ezekiel 1–3, and Daniel 7.

67 Cf. Zechariah 3; Job 1. See also D. L. Page, *Select Papyri*, vol. 3: *Literary Papyri: Old Comedy, Κρατινος, Πλουτοι* (1970) 196–201. I am grateful to Thomas Krüger for this reference.

68 For the precision of the text as far as its genre is concerned, cf. T. Jacobsen's observation on Akkadian court proceedings, "An Ancient Mesopotamian Trial for Homicide," in *Studia Biblica et Orientalia* 3 (1959) 130–50, esp. 138: "The text, as is customary in Sumero-Akkadian court records, opens with a concise statement of the facts of the

servants. It confirms that the Servant has been received into the heavenly sphere, as the preceding verse, v. 13, has described. There is no need to emend "dismayed over you" (עָלֶיךָ) to "dismayed over him" (עָלָיו). The dismay of the many is registered and is vouched for to the Servant himself. The word שָׁמֵם has an overtone of the sinister, even the demonic.[71] This was indeed the case!

The second point takes up the arguments of "the many," although they are not actually addressed. The Servant did not match the normally held picture of a man (אִישׁ) or a human being in general (בְּנֵי־אָדָם *bᵉnê ʾādām*). The striking thing is only that among "the many" there is no talk of kings, as there is in conjunction with the phrase that follows about the "many peoples"; nor is there a mention of any other members of the ruling classes—priests, prophets, and so forth.[72]

My own supposition would be that "the many" are represented in the following proceedings, as a kind of chorus. Whether they are drawn exclusively from the people of Israel is left open, probably intentionally. There is no doubt that they have above all experienced the Servant's sufferings at firsthand.

■ **15** The third point in the judge's speech (v. 15a) is fraught with textual difficulties. Here too I would assume that representatives of "many peoples" and "kings" actually come forward.[73] What is said does not suggest that these people are meant to be interpreted in an unfavorable sense. The declarations may be connected with the entry of these groups. Contrary to the sequence in the text—the peoples are named first and then the kings—I should like to begin with the gesture by the kings: they "shut their mouths." The commentators explain this by saying that the kings are speechless in the face of what they experience. But there is such clear evidence that a gesture of this kind—the covering of the mouth—played a part in ceremonies at the Persian court that we may assume a connection here.[74] This gesture had its special place when someone was received in audience. The kings' gesture therefore signifies the highest honor: a distinction is here conferred on the Servant that is otherwise reserved for the Persian ruler.

This suggests a comparison with Isa 45:14-15, which is a mirror scene to this one. There the throne scene with Cyrus describes the homage paid to him by foreign peoples. A kind of stage direction says: "They pass above you" (עָלַיִךְ יַעֲבֹרוּ, 45:14). The "above" is used because Cyrus himself is seated on his throne. This could also explain the difficult "above him" (עָלָיו) in v. 15 of the present text. From the Masoretes down to modern commentators, it has been a matter of dispute whether the phrase belongs to the preceding "sprinkling" or to the following gesture by the kings. But in my view it is a separate, elliptical statement: they are "above him"—that is, "the many" or "the kings" are standing or walking,

---

case reported on. It is a characteristic of such statements that they do not, as might perhaps have been expected, present the facts as they appeared at the beginning of the trial but rather as they were eventually proved and as they underlie the verdict."

69   See already Delitzsch on this passage, contrary to most commentators: "The Servant of Yahweh is therefore addressed: just as his humiliation was the most profound of all, so he will be most highly glorified" [trans. altered].

70   Cf. Isa 6:8-9.

71   See F. Stolz, "שׁמם *šmm* to lie deserted," *TLOT* 3:1372–75 [*THAT* 2 (1976) 970–74]: "When the subjective aspect dominates, the qal of the verb means 'to be terrified.' The occasion is often another's misfortune: common par[allel] expressions include *šrq* qal 'to whistle' (1 Kgs 9:8 . . . ; cf. Noth, BK 9/1, 199: 'with the apotropeic purpose of averting demonic effects'; Jer 19:8; 49:17; 50:13)" (1372 [971]).

72   For "many" used as an indication of social status, see BAGD 688 [1365]: "*oἱ πολλοί* . . . a connotation of disapproval *most people, the crowd* (Socrat., Ep. 6,2. Dio Chrys. 15 [32], 8. Epict. 1,3, 4; 2,1, 22 al.; Plut., Mor. 33A; 470B; Plotinus, Enn. 2, 9, 9. Philo, Rer. Div. Her. 42) 2 Cor 2:17; Pol. 2:1. 7:2"; the Greek "*oἱ πολλοί*" is retained in just this sense in the English epithet "the hoi polloi."

73   Cf. the kings in the judgment of the dead in Ezek 28:17-18.

74   See H. Gabelmann, *Antike Audienz- und Tribunalszenen* (1984), esp. 7–16, and pl. 1,1.2, a relief from the reception court of the treasury in Persepolis: "The 'self-restraining' gesture (see Graeve) of the *hazarapt* in the audience relief in Persepolis should therefore certainly not be interpreted as a *proskynesis*, as Altheim wished to assume, but is rather meant to indicate the holding of the breath in the immediate proximity of the great king (P. J. Junge). The meaning of the gesture is apparently 'not to pollute the incense-filled aura of the great king' (Walser)" (15). See also the illustration in *ANEP*, p. 159, no. 463.

whereas the Servant is sitting. Three declarations are made, as they are in v. 14 too, about "the many." The number "three" continues to dominate the statements in chap. 53 as well.

But why is the comment "above him" (עָלָיו) so important? It implies that the Servant is now sitting on a throne.[75] But the comparison with 45:14 brings out the essential point. There we read: "and they fall before you" (וְאֵלַיִךְ יִשְׁתַּחֲווּ). That means: the representatives of the foreign countries prostrate themselves before Cyrus. This prostration was a characteristic mark of Persian rule, and it was not only the Greeks to whom it gave profound offense. As long as "the many peoples" and "the kings" are "above" the Servant, they do not prostrate themselves before him, and do not worship him. Nor is there any mention of their bringing with them the products of their countries, as in 45:14, or of their having to walk in chains. I agree with the commentators who see 52:15 rather as a friendly reception of foreigners; for peoples and kings are supposed to acquire discernment—and without compulsion!

From this point, we can look back and ask whether the "sprinkling of many peoples" by the Servant might not also have its place in the court ritual. "Sprinkling" (נזה *Hiphil*) is a well-attested reading. In view of the situation assumed, it is improbable that it is meant as a priestly purification. Is it a gesture, similar to the greeting with rose water still encountered in the East today? The LXX rendering θαυμάζειν, "be astonished," has probably been suggested by the context, and cannot provide the basis for an emendation.

Finally, one may ask whether v. 15a does not imply a subtle criticism of Persian rule. The rule of Cyrus and the "rule" of the Servant must not be confused. That was already the theme in 41:25-28, where Cyrus was expected and the Servant came. That subtleties of this kind become evident only when one really knows the texts tells us something about the political situation. The Persian peace is acknowledged, but it is not the peace of the Servant of God.

Since no other "actors" are named, we can assume that the statements in v. 15b point to the context. According to what is said here, peoples and kings "see"

what they had not previously been told. This seeing and hearing takes place when, in the following passage, the fate of the Servant is described and interpreted. The difficulty of the tenses in this part of the verse is again due to the shifts in the dramatic time. On the other hand "what they have not heard they will have understood" (וַאֲשֶׁר לֹא־שָׁמְעוּ הִתְבּוֹנָנוּ) can also refer to the many in Israel, when, for example, the "hardening of their hearts" that is part of the prophet Isaiah's call is revoked: "Go and say to this people: 'Keep listening but do not comprehend (שִׁמְעוּ שָׁמוֹעַ וְאַל־תָּבִינוּ). . . .' Harden the heart of this people and stop their ears" (6:9-10).[76]

The importance for DtIsa of the question of "understanding" or "discernment" is already shown earlier in the heralding of the fourth Servant text in 40:14: "He will show him a way of understanding."[77] But in 40:14 too it is impossible to decide whether the "he" who communicates discernment is Yahweh himself or his Servant. In the present text, 52:15, the double אֲשֶׁר is ambiguous. It can be rendered as a neuter: "what was not told them" and "what they never heard," or—related to the Servant as person—as "who had not been told them" and "whom they had never heard." The explanation about the kind of discernment that is meant is picked up again for all the participants in the following passage, 53:1ff. Consequently, in the simultaneity of the dramatic times, the audience is also able to see and hear the Servant's message—and to understand it. The reevaluation of all values in what happens to the Servant is relevant for peoples and kings, but it is relevant too and above all for "the many" at all times.

53:1
Double Question by the "Prosecuting Counsel"

"Who has believed our revelation? And over whom has the arm of Yahweh been revealed?" (53:1)

Of decisive importance for an understanding of the text in its context is the question: Who is it that says, "Who has believed our message/revelation (לִשְׁמֻעָתֵנוּ)?" It is obvious that this is not a continuation of the divine speech, because it talks about "the arm of Yahweh." The Servant does not speak at all throughout this whole text;

75   Cf. Isa 6:2; 1 Kgs 22:19.
76   Cf. Isa 42:18-20; 43:8-9.
77   K. Baltzer, "Jes 40,13-14—ein Schlüssel zur Einheit Deutero-Jesajas?" *BN* n.s. 37 (1987) 7-10.

and if it were the Servant, the plural "*our* message/revelation" would be strange. The other persons who have been mentioned do not come into question. "The many," like the audience, can do no more than enter sympathetically into what is said: "Who has believed," that is, who believes—even now. In this uncertainty one might think of a member of the heavenly household and lawcourt. This can be given credence by a comparison with two other lawcourt scenes in the OT, scenes that also contribute to an understanding of the rest of the Servant text.

Excursus: The Lawcourt Scenes in Zechariah 3 and Job 1

Zechariah 3

In Zechariah 3, Zechariah sees in a vision the heavenly investiture of Joshua, the first high priest of the postexilic community. Joshua's grandfather, Seraiah, had been executed by the Babylonians, so the line of legitimate "high priests" had for the time being been severed. Joshua's legitimation was disputed. It has now to be clarified in a heavenly trial: that is the meaning of the prophet Zechariah's vision. The text describes the court procedure in considerable detail. Zech 3:1 reads: "Then he [Yahweh] showed me the high priest Joshua standing before the angel of Yahweh (מַלְאַךְ יהוה), and the Accuser (הַשָּׂטָן) standing at his right hand to accuse him (לְשִׂטְנוֹ)."[78]

Two parties come before the court, the accuser and the defense. The "Satan's" function can be compared with that of a prosecuting counsel.[79] His speech is not reported, but the defending counsel says: "May Yahweh rebuke you, Satan! May Yahweh who has chosen Jerusalem rebuke you! Is not this man a brand plucked from the fire?" (Zech 3:2). The text can be paraphrased: Has this man not just escaped, and is his fate not a sufficient reason to legitimate him? The accused himself does not utter a single word during the whole case. Nor does he need to do so. Here, in Zechariah 3, we have to assume two speakers, who describe the same case from different points of view. The decision of the heavenly court is then that the

high priest's guilt—the blot on his legitimacy—will be set aside, and he will again be installed in the rights and duties of his office. This is made clear by the fact that he is given new robes. This, then, is an investiture. As endorsement, Yahweh's angel also gives him an oracle of salvation from Yahweh Sabaoth himself, an oracle that determines his future:

> If you will walk in my ways
> and if you observe my order,
> then you shall also administer my house[80]
> and have charge of my forecourts.
> Then I will give you "the right of access" (מַהְלְכִים)[81]
> among those who are standing here.
> (Zech 3:7)

As a priest, he is God's servant in the earthly and the heavenly world.

Job 1

Whereas Zechariah 3 is directly concerned with a judicial clarification, in Job 1 the court scene is more developed, in the literary sense. But the genre's basic elements are still detectable.

The prologue to the book of Job recounts: "One day, 'the sons of God' (בְּנֵי הָאֱלֹהִים) came in to present themselves before Yahweh,[82] and 'Satan' (הַשָּׂטָן) also came in among them" (Job 1:6). Here again, the scene takes place among the heavenly household. Yahweh and "Satan" are locked in a dispute. "Satan's" position can again be described as prosecuting counsel, but here he behaves more like a kind of sparring partner, who puts forward the counterarguments. The subject of the dispute is the person of Job and his conduct, and how they are to be judged: "And Yahweh said to 'Satan': Have you considered my servant Job . . ." (Job 1:8). Yahweh clearly expects a favorable answer; but Satan counters with two critical questions, both introduced by the interrogative particle: "Is it for nothing (הַחִנָּם) that Job fears God?" and: "Is it not you [הֲלֹא־אַתָּה—i.e., Yahweh] who has blessed him?" In the present literary context the response to these two questions is a presentation of Job's biography.

These two texts alone, Zechariah 3 and Job 1, show the wide range of the situations in which the sociomorpheme "legal proceedings" can be used. We may

---

78   See the commentaries on the text, esp. D. L. Petersen, *Haggai and Zechariah 1–8* (1984) 186–214; C. L. and E. M. Meyers, *Haggai, Zechariah 1–8* (1987) 178–227; R. Hanhart, *Sacharja* (1992) 166–240; H. Graf Reventlow, *Die Propheten Haggai, Sacharja und Maleachi* (1993) 51–56; on שָׂטָן, Satan, see *HALOT* 3:1317 [*HALAT* 4:1227–28] (with lit.).

79   Thus von Rad, Eichrodt, Koehler, and Rudolph; Horst and Fohrer see him as "opponent, antagonist,

adversary"; for detail see *HALOT* 3:1317 [*HALAT* 4:1228]; cf. also K. Nielsen, "שָׂטָן *śāṭān*," *ThWAT* 7:745–51, esp. 750 (on Zechariah 3) and 748–49 (on Job 1–2).

80   For the task given to Moses cf. Num 12:7.

81   Cf. here the vocalization proposed in the textual apparatus in *BHS*.

82   The Hebrew text again states that in the framework

assume that the author of the texts and the people to whom they were addressed were familiar enough with the genre and concepts for a few signals to suffice.

If we then turn back to Isa 52:13–53:12, the first conclusion that we may draw from this excursus is that the speaker in 53:1 must here too be thought of as "prosecuting counsel." He formulates the objections to the divine speech in 52:14-15. In the dramatic buildup, this is followed by a discussion about the view to be taken of the Servant, with the pros and cons. Two questions are put by "Satan," as they are in Job 1:9-10: "who . . . ?" (מִי) and "over whom . . . ?" (עַל־מִי). The first question, then, is: "Who has believed our report/revelation?" The rendering of שְׁמוּעָה is a matter of dispute among scholars. According to *HALAT*'s comment on 53:1 ("what we have heard"), the possibilities are: "α) what we reveal = revelation . . . β) proclamation . . . γ) report/tidings/intelligence or, to be more precise, 'our report/tidings.'"[83]

A key to the interpretation is offered in my view by K. van der Toorn's investigation of Isa 28:7-22.[84] On the basis of this text, he shows the connection between cults of the underworld and the conjuring up of the dead. Priests and prophets practiced techniques of this kind in order to receive divine messages with the help of spirits. They probably thought that this practice could be reconciled with belief in Yahweh—a view that the prophet Isaiah strictly rejects. The "revelations" were acquired in sessions held by circles of initiates, who were in a semiconscious state induced by sleep or alcohol. But the knowledge acquired through the invocation of the dead was by no means a merely private affair. It was used as an aid in making political decisions and as an instrument in exercising rule over the people. Isaiah brings out this connection (28:14-15a): "You boasters with your big sayings to [or: who rule over—מֹשְׁלֵי] this people in

Jerusalem, for you have said 'We have made a covenant with death, and with the underworld (שְׁאוֹל) we have brought about a vision (חֹזֶה).'"[85] According to 28:9, the "priests and prophets" claim against the prophet Isaiah: "Whom (אֶת־מִי) will he teach knowledge, and whom will he cause to understand the message/revelation (וְאֶת־מִי יָבִין שְׁמוּעָה?)"

It is precisely this that DtIsa takes up. His "message" or "revelation" (שְׁמוּעָה) becomes in this way almost uncomfortably sharp. The double "who" (מִי) is now a question put by "the Accuser." The revelation is public, according to 52:13-15, not esoteric. It is not given in the temple, and is not meant solely for priests and prophets. Its subject is the "exaltation" of the Servant; and he has been exalted for the sake of "the many," and even for "many peoples and kings." They are the ones who have not heard, and yet "discern" it or him (v. 15: לֹא־שָׁמְעוּ הִתְבּוֹנָנוּ). In what follows—in the heavenly sphere—the question, "And over whom has the arm of Yahweh been disclosed (i.e., revealed)?" receives an answer.

In his article, van der Toorn also puts forward another thesis: that according to the texts the message that the dead communicate after they have been conjured up can be compared with a birdsong, which is then interpreted.[86] This is the way van der Toorn explains the famous "ṣaw lāṣāw ṣaw lāṣāw qaw lāqāw qaw lāqāw" in 28:10, 13. He further points to 24:4; 19:3; 8:19; and 38:14, and sees a link with the Mesopotamian "birdcall text."[87] There too birdsong is rendered onomatopoeically, in rather the same way as our "cuckoo," except that the birdcall is given a meaning. The birds are assigned to particular deities.

With all due caution, I should like to point to the curious sequence of sounds in 52:11-15. It begins—at the

---

of the throne scene the sons of God stand "above Yahweh" (עַל־יהוה)!

83   *HALAT* 4:1439.

84   K. van der Toorn, "Echoes of Judaean Necromancy in Isaiah 28,7-22," *ZAW* 100 (1988) 199–217. Van der Toorn mentions our text only in passing (215), because he believes that "Isa 53,1 furnishes no evidence about the circumstances under which the message was received."

85   H. Wildberger (*Jesaja 28–39* [1982] 1064 on this passage) assumes that חֹזֶה is an abstract substantive (see *ZAW* 71 [1959] 55ff.), which is taken up again in 18 with חזות." If we accept this view, then in the

present context the rendering "vision" makes good sense (cf. שְׁמוּעָה, "tidings, revelation," in Isa 28:19). B. Duhm's interpretation (*Jesaja*, 174–75 [p. 200 in 5th ed. of 1968]) is then by no means so out of the question, in spite of Wildberger's critical view: "we have made a vision with Sheol means: we have ourselves summoned a dead person, or a god or goddess of death, and have entered into a contract with the appearance."

86   Van der Toorn, "Echoes of Judean Necromancy in Isaiah 28,7-22," *ZAW* 100 (1988) 209–12.

87   Van der Toorn refers to W. G. Lambert, "The Sultantepe Tablets IX: The Birdcall Text," in *AnSt*

beginning of act 6, according to the division we have made—with . . . צֵאוּ צְאוּ סוּרוּ סוּרוּ (sûrû sûrû ṣeʾû . . . ṣeʾû) and continues in vv. 14-15 with כֵּן . . . כֵּן . . . כַּאֲשֶׁר כִּי אֲשֶׁר . . . (kaʾašer . . . kēn . . . kēn . . . kî ʾašer). This gives four s and four k sounds, and that in a context which is probably casting back to 28:7-22 and which, according to 53:1, has to do with a dispute about divination! Is DtIsa making public what was otherwise an esoteric technique, and interpreting it in a new sense? But as if this were not enough: in the comment on 50:2, on the appearance of the Servant in the third Servant text, we already hazarded the guess that here a birdsong was being imitated. In the fourth Servant text the Servant again appears accompanied by similar signs. The texts could well contain signals that were thoroughly familiar both to Isaiah's listeners and to DtIsa's, but that certainly had an undertone of fear, as had everything that was connected with death and the underworld. Isa 52:11-12 does not sound like fear. "See my Servant" (52:13) introduces a message of good tidings. 53:1 asks, "Who has believed *our* revelation?" that is, not the revelation of those who conjure up the dead. According to 28:15 "the Lord" Yahweh himself promises: "The one who trusts will stand firm."[88]

■ **53:1b** The question, "And Yahweh's arm, over whom is it bared?" sums up what is about to follow. It is a question of the Servant's legitimation.

Talk about Yahweh's arm[89] originates in Yahweh's title as "warrior" (אִישׁ מִלְחָמָה Exod 15:3). It is especially associated with the exodus. According to the Song of Moses in Exodus 15, Yahweh acts with his mighty arm at the passage through the sea (Exod 15:16). In Deuteronomy especially, the formula "with a strong hand and an outstretched arm" is a reminder of the help given at the exodus (cf. Deut 4:34; 5:15; 7:19; 9:29; 11:2; 26:8). There it was the "signs and wonders" that Yahweh performed. According to the end of Moses' blessing, *"Jeshurun's* God"* offers protection and a refuge "underneath the everlasting arms" (Deut 33:27). According to Isa 63:12 it can be said that Yahweh "caused his glorious arm to march at the right hand of Moses." The latter text is interesting because it corrects the Passover pericope, Exodus 14: here it is not Moses who divides the waters—it is Yahweh himself. In my view we find something similar in Isa 53:1, which says that Yahweh's arm is "over" (עַל־מִי) a human being. Yahweh both guides and protects. This is reminiscent of the iconography in the area of Persian culture, where the personal tutelary god—frequently identified with Ahuramazda in the literature—is shown above the king.[90]

In DtIsa, גלה "uncover, unveil, reveal," refers to "the activity of God in history,"[91] but one may pin this down more closely and say that it is recalling the exodus from Egypt—with which the biography of Moses is closely interwoven. In what follows the text discusses how far

---

20 (1970) 111–17. Van der Toorn himself (211) offers examples for this group of texts. See also Lambert, *AnSt* 20 (1970) 112–13 (Sultantepe version 341.6): "The *suššuru* is the bird of Anšar. Its cry is, 'How he is desolated'." According to Lambert, *suššuru* is perhaps a kind of dove. In Akkadian its call is *kīkī muššur* (ibid., 112–13); cf. the text KAR 125,14). From an Assyrian text (KAR 125.12 and 19, Lambert, ibid., 114–15): "The partridge is the bird of Asakku. [Its cry is], 'Go away, Asakku! [Go away], Asakku!' . . . The *paʾû* is the bird of Tiāmat. [Its cry is], 'How (Akkad. *ke-ke-e*) [. . . ."

88   See the commentaries on this passage. The LXX has ὁ πιστεύων ἐπ᾽ αὐτῷ οὐ μὴ καταισχυνθῇ; cf. Rom 9:33; 10:11; 1 Pet 2:6; and 1QS 8.7-8.

89   F. J. Helfmeyer, זְרוֹעַ *zerôaʿ*," *TDOT* 4:131–40 [*ThWAT* 2:650–60]; I. L. Seeligmann, "A Psalm from Pre-Regal Times," *VT* 14 (1964) 75–82; H. L. Ginsberg, "The Arm of YHWH in Isaiah 51–63 and the Text of Isa 53:10-11," *JBL* 77 (1958) 152–56; P. D. Miller, *The Divine Warrior in Early Israel* (1973); J. K. Hoffmeier, "The Arm of God versus the Arm of Pharaoh in the Exodus Narratives," *Bib* 67 (1986) 378–87.

90   See P. Calmeyer, "Fortuna—Tyche—Khvarna," *JDAI* 94 (1979) 347–65; J. Duchesne-Guillemin, "Sonnenkönigtum und Mazdareligion, mit einem Exkurs von P. Lecoq: À propos du *F* 'mède,'" in H. Koch and D. N. Mackenzie, eds., *Kunst, Kultur und Geschichte der Achämenidenzeit und ihr Fortleben* (1983) 135–43; S. Dalley, "The God Šalmu and the Winged Disk," *Iraq* 48 (1986) 85–101; B. Jacobs, "Das Chvarnah—Zum Stand der Forschung," *MDOG* 119 (1987) 215–48. Cf. also Neh 2:18: "And I told them that the gracious hand of my God was over me"; also Ezra 8:22.

91   C. Westermann and R. Albertz, "גלה *glh* to uncover," *TLOT* 1:314–20, esp. 319 [*THAT* 1:418–26, esp. 425]; H.-J. Zobel, "גלה *gālāh*," *TDOT* 2:476–88 [*ThWAT* 1:1018–26].

the activity of God can be perceived in the abasement of God's Servant.

53:2-10
The Biography of the Servant of God and Its Interpretation
Pro and Contra—the Arguments of the Witnesses

"If he gives his life to wipe out debt (guilt)/as an offering for sin (guilt), he will see descendants . . ." (53:10)

In these verses we have a remembrance or memorial of the Servant's life and death. The special thing about this memorial is that his fate is described from two antithetical standpoints, as if this were a court case. On the one hand an account of the Servant's fate is given, seen from the outside (vv. 2-3 and 7-9). Then his life and sufferings are interpreted under the aspect of what he did for the community (vv. 4-6 and 10). The context shows that the action is still taking place in the heavenly sphere; for a divine speech once more follows in v. 11. The account talks about a collective ("that *we* should have looked at him," v. 2; "*we* held him of no account," v. 3); and the same is true of the interpretation ("*our* sickness," v. 4; "all *our* guilt," v. 6). We may therefore assume that it is a collective that is speaking. Since the two groups of utterances (description and interpretation) are so closely connected, it is conceivable that a double chorus was used in the dramatic performance. "The many" are perhaps the speakers, for in 52:14 they have already been introduced as the people who are "dismayed." They are in the heavenly sphere as well, so they too are already dead. They are witnesses of the Servant's life, and belong to his people.[92] They now "know." As will presently emerge, they are Moses' contemporaries, the people of the exodus. They represent Israel as a whole. A judgment on someone who is dead is taking place, but in the heavenly

sphere, not in the underworld. The time is the "eternity" that joins past and present. The listeners experience it now, and thus become for the future "those who discern." This is a public mystery.

■ **2-3** "Shoot/branch" (יוֹנֵק) and "root" (שֹׁרֶשׁ) associate this passage with the "messianic" prophecy in Isa 11:1-9, 10. It should be borne in mind here that in Isaiah to talk about "the root of Jesse" means first that the tree has been hewn down, that the Davidic dynasty has come to an end. The fulfillment of the promise to David must issue from the root. It is a continuity in discontinuity.[93] Other elements strengthen the impression that the text's premise is the expectation of a king:

1. "Appearance, stature" (תֹּאַר). David is "a fine figure of a man," "a man of good presence," according to the ideal description of the son of Jesse the Bethlehemite in 1 Sam 16:18.[94]

2. "Adornment, magnificence" (הָדָר). God is "glorious,"[95] but so is the king.[96] The term is used above all for the king's robes of state.[97] It is an essential component in the royal ideology.

3. "Looks, appearance, countenance" (מַרְאֶה) can be used in various different contexts. But this term too is applied to David in 1 Sam 17:42, when Goliath the Philistine looks him over—and despises him (וַיִּבְזֵהוּ).

If we take the semantic field of v. 2 into account, the text is establishing that the Servant is not kingly—not, at least, from a human point of view. He does not possess the beauty and perfection that belong to the picture of a sovereign. But then what is he? He is marked above all by the fact that he grows up "before him" (לְפָנָיו), that is, "before Yahweh."[98] The text can be understood in the quite general sense: "God does not look on the outward appearance."[99] But perhaps it takes on an extra perspective if it is read once more against the background of the

92 An indication of the performance practice may be offered by a textual variant in v. 8: whether the reading should be עַמִּי, "my people" (MT) or עמו, "his people" (cf. 1QIsaᵃ; 4QIsaᵈ; following F. J. Morrow, "The Text of Isaiah at Qumran" [1973] 142; the Syro-Palestinian translation presupposes this reading according to M. H. Gottstein, "Die Jesaja-Rolle im Lichte von Peschitta und Targum," *Bib* 35 [1954] 62). I myself think that the reading "his people" is the more probable. But if only one chorus leader is speaking at the performance, "my people" makes sense. A whole chorus of speakers would be an extravagant affair and cannot therefore

always be assumed.
93 Cf. Isa 55:3.
94 Cf. Judg 8:18; 1 Kgs 1:6.
95 Pss 96:6; 104:1; 111:3; Job 40:10 (40:5); 1 Chr 16:27; cf. Isa 35:2; Ezek 16:14; Mic 2:9; Pss 29:4; 90:16; 149:9.
96 Pss 21:6 (5); 45:4 (3), 5 (4).
97 Cf. Pss 104:1 and 110:3.
98 Cf. Deut 34:10.
99 Cf. 1 Sam 16:7.

Moses tradition. The relevant text is Exodus 2, which tells about the birth and marvelous rescue of the child Moses. But that his own mother should be permitted to feed him herself is another miracle. The root יָנַק, "suckle, breast-feed," is used four times in Exod 2:5-10. It is the same root found in the substantive יוֹנֵק, "shoot/branch," in Isa 53:2, but it can also be rendered "infant, child."[100] The implicit problem is probably detectable in Exod 2:10, in the comment: "But the child grew up, and she [his mother] brought him to Pharaoh's daughter, and she took him as her son, and she named him Moses; because, she said: 'I drew him out of the water.'" If Moses as Servant has grown up "before Yahweh," even his upbringing at Pharaoh's court can do him no harm. But we may also ask whether this comment does not imply *one* reason for avoiding Moses' name in talking about the Servant: the fact that his name was given him by Pharaoh's daughter.

The text says that (in the eyes of his mother) the little Moses was "beautiful, good" (טוֹב, Exod 2:2). Later tradition developed this theme further. According to Philo, the boy was "noble and well-made to look at" (εὐγενῆ καὶ ἀστεῖον ὀφθῆναι).[101] Josephus sounds the same note even more emphatically in describing the impression made by Moses' "comeliness."[102] When the child is presented to Pharaoh, he can then talk about his "divine stature,"[103] associating this with Moses' possible succes-

sion to the throne! In this light it is understandable that there may have been some reserve about royal "beauty." DtIsa is taking up a critical position toward an "Egyptian" ideal of what a ruler should look like.

"Like a root out of dry land." The phrase "dry land" (אֶרֶץ צִיָּה) is not used very often, but when it does occur, it is at significant points. The antithesis is "land where there are springs of water,"[104] as in Isa 41:18. "Dry land" is therefore also the land "that no one (לֹא אִישׁ) passes through and where no human being (אָדָם) lives."[105] Job's complaint (30:1-8) gives an impression of the way this land and its inhabitants were thought of. These are people who "gnaw the dry and desolate ground" (v. 3). Their food is "the roots of broom"[106] (שֹׁרֶשׁ רְתָמִים, v. 4). They are "a godless people, people without a name, who have been driven out of the land" (v. 8). All in all, the picture matches the one that the Egyptian Sinuhe[107] gives when, describing his flight through the eastern desert, he talks about the bedouin as the "sand wanderers," whose life contrasts so markedly with life at court.[108] In Jer 2:6 (cf. Ps 105:37-42), the desert through which Yahweh led Jacob/Israel at the Exodus from Egypt is described in a similar way. The historical survey in Psalm 78 also uses the catchword "parched land" when it is talking about the wanderings through the desert (בַּצִּיָּה, v. 17; cf. Ps 107:35).

---

100 Cf. Num 11:12; Deut 32:25; 1 Sam 15:3; 22:19; Isa 11:8; Jer 44:7; Ps 8:3 (2); Lam 2:11; 4:4. Used for "sucklings" or "infants at the breast" according to *HALOT* in Joel 2:16 and Cant 8:1.

101 Philo *Vit. Mos.* 1.18.

102 Josephus *Ant.* 2.9.6 (230-31): "When he was three years old, God gave wondrous increase to his stature; and none was so indifferent to beauty as not, on seeing Moses, to be amazed at his comeliness (τῆς εὐμορφίας). And it often happened that persons meeting him as he was borne along the highway turned, attracted by the child's appearance, and neglected their serious affairs to gaze at leisure upon him: indeed childish charm so perfect and pure as his held the beholders spell-bound" (καὶ τριετεῖ μὲν αὐτῷ γεγενημένῳ θαυμαστὸν ὁ θεὸς τὸ τῆς ἡλικίας ἐξῆρεν ἀνάστημα, πρὸς δὲ κάλλος οὐδεὶς ἀφιλότιμος ἦν οὕτως, ὡς Μωυσῆν θεασάμενος μὴ ἐκπλαγῆναι τῆς εὐμορφίας . . .)
See also the midrash on Exod 2:10 (according to A. Wünsche, *Der Midrasch Schemot Rabba* [1882, reprint 1967]); cited in Josephus *Ant.* 2.9.6 (231)

[LCL, p. 265 n. c]: "Pharaoh's daughter . . . let him no more leave the king's palace; because he was beautiful all wished to see him, and whoever saw him could not turn away from him."

103 Josephus *Ant.* 2.9.7 (232): παῖδα μορφῇ τε θεῖον καὶ φρονήματι γενναῖον.

104 Ezek 19:13; Hos 2:5 (3); Pss 63:2 (1); 107:35.

105 Jer 2:6; cf. Jer 51:43; Job 38:26-27.

106 On broom, *Retama raetam* (in a more recent conjecture *Lygos raetam*) see I. Löw, *Die Flora der Juden* (1924-34) 2:469ff.; J. Feliks, "Ginsterstrauch," *BHH* 1:573; M. Zohary, *Plants of the Bible* (1982), esp. 144 (and 34-35, 139).

107 *AOT* 55-61; *ANET* 18-22.

108 *ANET* 22: "Years were made to pass away from my body. I was plucked, and my hair was combed. A load (of dirt) was given to the desert, and my clothes (to) the Sand-Crossers. I was clad in fine linen and anointed with prime oil. I slept in a bed. I gave up the sand to them who are in it."

In Exodus 2–the text that, as we have said, offers the point of reference—vv. 11-22 describe the episode in Moses' life that compels him to flee from Egypt to Midian. In intervening on behalf of "a Hebrew, one of his kinsfolk," Moses strikes and kills an Egyptian (vv. 11-12). This evidently leaks out, for when two Hebrews are fighting and Moses interferes, "the evildoer" (רָשָׁע) rails at him: "Who made you a ruler (לְאִישׁ שַׂר) and judge (שֹׁפֵט) over us? Did you mean to kill me as you killed the Egyptian?" (v. 14). The pharaoh hears what Moses has done and threatens to kill him (v. 15). In later tradition the pros and cons of this episode were a theme of discussion. The present text Isa 53:2-3 picks it up by way of brief formulas.

"He grew up" (וַיַּעַל): This can refer both to a shoot from a root and to a child. Exod 2:11 says: "And Moses became great" (וַיִּגְדַּל; cf. v. 10). This could be open to misunderstanding, as meaning "important." But עלה, "go up," is a key word for the exodus[109] from Egypt—and from Babylon too. DtIsa uses it in the same sense and already played on the different meanings of the word in 40:31.[110] 53:2 can be saying that the "Servant Moses" "grew up," and at the same time, on another interpretive level, that he was the first to "go up"—out of Egypt. Then, as a shepherd in Midian, he received the revelation at the burning bush. That is "the parched land" in which broom grows.[111] Exod 2:14 makes clear the degree to which Moses was "despised."

Finally we have in v. 3a the declaration that can also be referring to Moses' biography as Exodus 2 gives it (v. 15): "leaving human beings" (חֲדַל אִישִׁים). The form probably requires this to be understood in the active sense,[112] not as meaning "forsaken by human beings." Moses was forced to flee, and to flee into the country that human beings do not generally pass through (Jer 2:6; Job 38:26-27).

If the different levels of interpretation are put together, we see that the Servant is someone who grows up as a desert dweller among the bedouin, who were despised by people who lived in the cultivated lands; and yet he is "before Yahweh." Moses is an example of just this. His message has its roots neither in Egypt nor in Babylon, but in the desert.

■ **3aβ** In a second step, three other declarations are made about the Servant. He is characterized by pain, by the "knowledge" of sickness, and by the rejection of his contemporaries. The conclusion here too is: "despised!" These are declarations such as we find in the prayers of lament in the Psalter especially. Here the most profound suffering to which the Servant is subjected is his severance from the society of other human beings. If we trace through his biography as a whole, we can again think of Moses as the *typos* of someone who suffers in an exemplary way. "Man/human being" (אִישׁ) is placed in the emphatic position, at the beginning of the sentence. It picks up the word "human beings" that precedes it, so in addition it is easy to remember. But if "shoot/branch" in v. 2 also has an echo of "child," then v. 3 signals that the Servant has come of age. His death and burial follow in vv. 8-9. When, instead of "the particulars of his office, profession and status,"[113] he is described as "a man of sorrows/sufferings," the contrast could hardly be greater. For, after all, "the man Moses" (Num 12:3, הָאִישׁ מֹשֶׁה [וְ]) is *the* "man of God" (אִישׁ [הָ]אֱלֹהִים; see esp. Deut 33:1; cf. Josh 14:6; Ps 90:1 [heading of the psalm in the English Bible]; Ezra 3:2; 1 Chr 23:14; 2 Chr 30:16). He is the "prophet" who blessed Israel before his death (Deut 33:1). That is the reason why the "contempt" has such grave consequences.

The text to which the three individual declarations refer is probably Exodus 3, Moses' installation. This text is the continuation of Exodus 2, Moses in Midian, which—in my view—plays a role as background for the preceding section of our DtIsa text, v. 2. This time the word "sorrow" (מַכְאֹב) in Exod 3:7 serves as the identifying signal. It is the only time that this word is used in the Pentateuch. It refers to the misery and affliction of

---

109 See G. Wehmeier, "עלה *ʿlh*, to go up" *TLOT* 2:883–96 [*THAT* 2:272–90, esp. 274]; *HALOT* 2:828 [*HALAT* 3:783] on עלה: "a) from Egypt to Palestine, with reference to the stopping-places on the way, or to the stages on the way there, Gen 13:1; 45:25; Ex 12:38; 13:18; Nu 32:11; Jud 11:13, 16; etc.; b) from Babylon to Palestine (the return of the exiles) Ezr 2:1, 59; 7:6, 7, 28; 8:1; Neh 7:5, 6, 61; 12:1."

110 See above on this passage.

111 Cf. Job 30:4 and, in the Elijah story, 1 Kgs 19:4-5.

112 Contrary to *HALOT*, s.v.

113 N. P. Bratsiotis, "אִישׁ *ʾish*," *TDOT* 1:222–35, esp. 223–34 [*ThWAT* 1:238–52, esp. 239–40].

God's people in Egypt (v. 7; cf. 2:23-25). Yahweh says to Moses: "I know their sorrows" (כִּי יָדַעְתִּי אֶת־מַכְאֹבָיו).

"Man of sorrows" can therefore be understood in several different ways. The sorrows are his sufferings,[114] and at the same time they are the sufferings of God's people,[115] from which they have been freed through Moses. For this purpose Moses has been commissioned by the God of his fathers.

Whereas in Exod 3:7 it is Yahweh who knows the sorrows or sufferings, in the present text the "knowing" (ידע) is said of the Servant. He is "acquainted with sickness"[116] (וִידוּעַ חֹלִי). "Sickness" is mentioned three times in Isaiah 53 (vv. 3, 4, 10). We may therefore assume that the term has special weight. In view of the semantic range of חלה as a verb and a substantive,[117] we have to ask whether any special nuances can be detected here. "To be sick, sickness" is a firm *topos* in the prayers of lament. As the book of Job shows, the question about the origin of illness exercised the minds of men and women at that time too. The Servant is familiar with sickness. But in the context of Exodus 3 sickness has a specific connotation. According to Exod 4:6-8, Moses' hand becomes leprous and is healed. It is a confirmatory sign of his commission (v. 8), and it is required because Moses is afraid: "They will not believe me or listen to me, for they will say, 'Yahweh did not appear to you'" (Exod 4:1).

Moses has experienced sickness personally, but the reason was the unbelief of his people. To this Exod 3:6 must at once be added. Moses behaved appropriately at the burning bush: "Moses hid his face, for he was afraid to look at God." The same gesture—the covering of the face—is used against the Servant, according to Isa 53:3.[118] It signifies the withdrawal of community, and is therefore also an element in the lament. An ironical aspect could also be implicit here, for listeners could have been expected to remember the shine on Moses' face after his encounter with God on the mountain (Exod 34:29-35). Then the gesture of covering the face on an encounter with the Servant would, again—involuntarily—be perfectly proper, since he is associated with the divine presence. But in Isa 53:1, in the framework of the heavenly trial, it was the question that triggers off the whole: "To whom has the arm of Yahweh been revealed?" In Moses the radiance on his face was the divine legitimation.

The verdict on what can be plainly seen is passed in the second section too (v. 3aβ): "he was despised."[119] But the summing up that follows—and that surely applies to all the declarations in vv. 2-3—is: "We held him to be of no account." After the individual points have been enumerated in the nominative form, the perfect-tense verb draws the final conclusion. This is in line with the verb's significance as Seybold gives it: "*ḥšb* carries the meaning of a technical and rational, calculating reckoning."[120] Among the spectators at a performance, the merchants could feel that with the "accounting" they were the target group, according to 46:6, provided they were present! In our language we are accustomed to say that something "is not worth it." This Servant is certainly of no account, that is, not worth anything—at least not according to the usual social criteria.

---

114 As a term in lamentation cf. Jer 45:3; Ps 69:27-30 (26-29); 2 Chr 6:28-30; see J. Scharbert, *Der Schmerz im Alten Testament* (1955).

115 Jer 30:15; Lam 1:12; 2 Chr 6:29: "from any individual or from all your people Israel."

116 Translation following *HALOT* 2:391 [*HALAT* 2:374] on ידע. For a different view see D. W. Thomas, "The Root ידע in Hebrew," *JTS* 35 (1934) 298–306; idem, "More Notes on the Root ידע in Hebrew," *JTS* 38 (1937) 404–5, and J. Barr, *Comparative Philology and the Text of the Old Testament* (1968) 19ff.; both derive the word from ידע II, "degrade, humiliate" and translate in the sense of "degraded through sickness." See also K. Seybold, "חָלָה *chālāh*," *TDOT* 4:405 [*ThWAT* 2:967].

117 Seybold, *TDOT* 4:399–409 [*ThWAT* 2:960–72]: "The semantic potential of both the verb and the nouns may be characterized by calling them general terms for a 'state of bodily weakness' [Scharbert], to be translated 'be or become weak', 'weakness.' This broad range can be limited through contextual determinatives to instances of physical or mental impotence, organic diseases, and injuries, so that in most cases 'be or become sick,' 'sickness' are accurate translations" (402) [964]; see also his comment on Isa 52:13—53:12.

118 See S. Wagner, "סָתַר *sātar*," *ThWAT* 5:967–77; Wagner cites Exod 3:6; Isa 50:6; 53:3 and writes: "To hide the face means to withdraw one's presence from another personal entity" (971). According to him, the form of סתר in 53:3 "is either the hiphil participle or a noun derived from that" (ibid.).

119 1QIsaᵃ has נבוזהו, but in the sequence נִבְזֶה is more likely.

120 K. Seybold, "חָשַׁב *ḥāšab*," *TDOT* 5:228–45, esp. 231 [*ThWAT* 3:243–61, esp. 247]; see also 230–31 [246].

■ 4-6 After the different episodes in the Servant's life and sufferings have been listed—episodes that were evident to every eye—a comprehensive interpretation of the whole follows. This interpretation is given from the standpoint of people who are stricken by the Servant's fate. The very sound makes this unmistakable. The darkly toned נוּ- (-nû), "we, our," is used twelve times in the final position, with the repeated, intensifying "we all" (כֻּלָּנוּ kullānû) at the beginning and end of v. 6. It is an admission of guilt in remembrance of the Servant. As Beuken has shown particularly clearly, the verses are constructed with complete regularity.[121] I should like to draw attention to the chain of argument. It begins with אָכֵן (ʾākēn), which as an "exclamation emphasizing the unexpected"[122] can be rendered "truly," but can also imply the strongly antithetical "yet."[123] This is followed by "But we . . ." or: "We, however . . ." (v. 4bα), then by "But he . . ." (v. 5aα) and finally by "We all . . ." (v. 6aα). This is the way an argument is presented in a court of law or a disputation. The catchwords "sickness," "sorrows/sufferings," "regard/hold as" also indicate that the points listed in vv. 2-3 are now about to be considered in detail. In this respect vv. 4-6 are the rejoinder—at greater length—to vv. 2-3.

■ 4 "Our sickness—he bore it": This does not necessarily mean that the Servant himself became ill. But what kind of sickness is meant? Verse 3 probably played on Moses' "leprosy" at the revelation at the burning bush. On the other hand v. 4 refers to v. 3. Is it the same sickness, leprosy? In the story of Moses' life as told in the Pentateuch, Num 10:11ff. describes the departure from Sinai: "They set out for the first time at the command of Yahweh through the hand of Moses" (v. 13). In chap. 11 the theme is "the murmuring of the people" and in chap. 12 Miriam's "leprosy." These texts can contribute

to an understanding of Isa 53:4. Miriam's leprosy acts as a signal for these texts. It is a story that anyone reasonably familiar with the biblical tradition could have been expected to know. A closer look at the text of Numbers 12 reminds us that v. 7 talks about "my servant Moses," while v. 8 goes on: "Why then were you not afraid to speak against my servant Moses?" The dispute with Aaron and Miriam is a conflict about Moses' authority. Aaron acknowledges to Moses: "We have sinned" (חָטָאנוּ, v. 11). He implores mercy for the leprous Miriam. Moses thereupon cries to Yahweh and she is healed (v. 13) and taken back again into the community of the people (v. 15). On the basis of the Numbers passage, the DtIsa text can be interpreted to mean that the Servant Moses bears the sickness as intercessor.

But in the context of Numbers 10–12 the catchword "bear" (נשא) also has its own special weight. When the people are murmuring (chap. 11), Moses expostulates with Yahweh (vv. 11-12, 14): "Why have you treated *your servant* so badly . . . so that you lay the burden (מַשָּׂא) of all this people on me? . . . that you should say to me: 'Carry them (שָׂאֵהוּ) in the skirts of your garment, as a nurse carries (יִשָּׂא) a sucking child,' to the land that you promised on oath to their ancestors? . . . I am not able to carry (לָשֵׂאת) all this people alone."

The announcement of the appointment of the seventy elders follows, the root "carry" still being used (נשא, 3 times in v. 17). It would seem conceivable that Moses was called "the one who carries" (נשא).[124] For in the fourth Servant text the catchword "carry" is also used, in a triple variation (in 52:13 and 53:12). In the present text, v. 4, the word sums up the era of the wanderings in the wilderness. This is underlined when, in the *parallelismus membrorum*, the Servant is described as "the bearer of sorrows." According to Exod 3:7—and hence probably

---

121 Beuken 214: "In this function the adverb ['yet' (ʾākēn)] orders the five lines [units of meaning]. . . . Two show the meaning of what has happened, seen from the standpoint of the 'We' figure (the first and the fourth lines [units of meaning]: vv. 4a, 5b). These two are followed by a line [unit of meaning] that gives the wrong interpretation of what has happened (the second and the fifth lines [units of meaning]: vv. 4b, 6a), whereas the third line [unit of meaning] (v. 5a) describes as bluntly from the Servant's own standpoint what he has experienced. . . ." The middle line [unit of meaning] touches precisely the heart of the tragic happening:

'Our sins/transgressions have prepared his downfall. . . .'"

122 See *HALOT* 1:47 [*HALAT* 1:46] following I. Eitan, "Hebrew and Semitic Particles," *AJSL* 45, 197–98, on Gen 28:16; Exod 2:14; 1 Sam 15:32; Isa 40:7; 45:15; Jer 3:23; 4:10; 8:8.

123 See *HALOT* 1:47 [*HALAT* 1:46] on Ps 66:19; following אָמַרְתִּי (in a divine speech): Isa 49:4; 53:4; Zeph 3:7; Pss 31:23 (22); 82:7; Job 32:8.

124 If we remember that "prince" (נָשִׂיא) is formed from the same root, a polemic directed against the expectation of a new David could play a part here (cf. Ezek 34:24; 37:25). Unlike other "princes," "Moses"

408

also according to Isa 53:3—"sorrows" (מַכְאֹב) meant the suffering of oppression in Egypt. There it was the people who were "the bearers of burdens," which is to say they were subjected to forced labor.[125] In a strange reversal, Moses is "the bearer of burdens" in the wilderness for the seemingly liberated people.

Once the fact of this reversal of situation has been established, the "many" who are involved are given the chance to say how they viewed the situation at that time: "We held him to be. . . ."[126] The admission of error is certainly meant to serve as instruction for the present.

I would assume that in view of what is said in vv. 2 and 3, v. 4b relates to the same context, and therefore refers to the same text as v. 4a.

Schwienhorst insists that the verb נָגַע should be rendered "touch."[127] According to the MT of v. 4b, two participles follow one another without a link: "Someone who has been touched" (passive participle), "someone who has been struck" (Hophal participle). Another curious point is that here the word "God" (אֱלֹהִים) is used, not Yahweh, as elsewhere in the text. The name for God is missing from the LXX, the identity therefore being left open.

It is not absolutely clear either whether this is a positive judgment. The difficulties can be solved, in my view, if the Hophal participle is pointed as a substantive, מֻכֵּה, and the phrase is rendered: "touched by the stroke of a god." In Jacob's encounter at the brook Jabbok in Genesis 32, it was not certain whether he had been touched by Yahweh or by a demon (v. 26).

Because of a denunciation, the prophet Jeremiah was supposed to be put in the stocks and the collar by the priest Zephaniah, who had been put in the temple "to control any madman (מְשֻׁגָּע) who in a state of ecstasy prophesies (מִתְנַבֵּא)" (Jer 29:26).

The reference text, Numbers 11–12, is also concerned with prophecy, the "prophecy" of Moses. The spirit given him is so powerful that it sends the seventy elders into a state of prophetic ecstasy (Num 11:24-30). In place of prophecy through visions and dreams (Num 12:6-8), Yahweh speaks to his servant Moses "mouth to mouth" (v. 8). That is the reason for the conflict with Aaron and Miriam. These are confusing phenomena, and it was at this very point that "the many"—Moses' contemporaries— failed to judge the situation correctly. In short, they thought that the Servant was mad. To apply the question in 53:1 to Numbers 11–12: to them "the arm of Yahweh over his servant" was *not* revealed! But with v. 4b DtIsa himself rejects an interpretation that claimed that Moses was "touched by the stroke of a god."

The final comment in v. 4, "humiliated" (מְעֻנֶּה) by God, was a misunderstanding too. Yet if we compare Num 12:3, we see that the description in one sense fits the facts: "The man Moses was very humble (עָנָו), more so than anyone else on the face of the earth," where the word עָנָו can carry the whole semantic range from "poor" to "devout."[128]

---

really "carried." According to *HALAT* the 130 instances of the title are very unevenly distributed. There are 62 instances in Numbers alone, 37 in Ezekiel, 13 in Joshua. All in all, 80 instances belong to the Priestly writing. See also A. D. H. Mayes, "Israel in the Pre-Monarchy Period," *VT* 23 (1973) 151–70, esp. 161–62.

125 D. Kellermann, "סָבַל *sābal*," *ThWAT* 5:744–48, esp. 747–48 on the noun *sōbel* (Isa 9:3 [4]; 10:27; 14:25); *sēbel* (Ps 81:7 [6]). "The word **sebālôt*, which is found only in the plural, occurs in Exod 1:11; 2:11; 5:4, 5; 6:6, 7 always in connection with the forced labor of the Israelites in Egypt" (747). But cf. Neh 4:4, 11!

126 K. Seybold, "חָשַׁב *ḥāšab*," *TDOT* 5:228–45, esp. 231 [*ThWAT* 3:243–61, esp. 246]: "But *ḥšb* goes beyond the meaning of reckoning with numbers and quantities, referring rather to values and factors in general: weighing, evaluating, calculating, rational

assignment of place and rank, the technical accounting of a merchant."

127 L. Schwienhorst, "נָגַע *nāgaʿ*," *ThWAT* 5:219–26, esp. 221: "However, *nāgaʿ* never means a violent blow. . . . In Gen 32:26, 33 too *nāgaʿ* should be translated 'touch.' This is not a violent blow on the hip joint but a 'magical touch' (C. Westermann, *Genesis 12–36* [1985] 517, 520 [*Genesis 2* (1981) 625, 630])." Schwienhorst (222) also points to "*nāgaʿ* as meaning 'touch' where God is the subject . . . in the genre of the theophany account (cf. Jörg Jeremias, *Theophanie* [2d ed. 1976] 160–62)" on Pss 104:32; 144:5; Amos 9:5. Cf. also K. Seybold, *Das Gebet des Kranken im Alten Testament* (1973) 25 on this passage.

128 See R. Martin-Achard, "ענה *ʿnh* II to be destitute," *TLOT* 2:931–37 [*THAT* 2:341–50], and on this pas-

■ **5** The whole verse is dominated by a note of lament.[129] The traditional translation and interpretation underline this: "pierced [the usual rendering] . . . smitten . . . chastisement . . . wounds." The picture is consistent in its presentation of a typical suffering leading to death. Yet there are still tensions in the text. Is it meant literally or in a transferred sense? What is the progression—that is, does "pierced" (the usual translation) not already imply death? If we take into account the immediate context in DtIsa, another interpretation seems possible. But could not the two levels of understanding be actually intentional, as is so often the case in DtIsa? We assumed that v. 4 is an allusion to the wanderings in the wilderness. Moses is "the one who carries." But perhaps he is meant in the confession of guilt in v. 5 too.

The MT does in fact point the word as a *Polal* participle from the root חלל II, "pierced through." But it has been suggested that the *Pual* participle of חלל I should be read instead: "profaned." This conjecture goes right back to Aquila, who translates βεβηλωμένος. In Hebrew the ear can hardly detect the difference between מְחֹלָל (*meḥolāl*) and מְחֻלָּל (*meḥullāl*). In Ezek 36:23 the form is used when the text says that Yahweh's name has been "profaned" (מְחֻלָּל)[130] by Israel before the gentile nations, but will be sanctified again by Yahweh (וְקִדַּשְׁתִּי) when he gathers his people (v. 28) from all the lands. To determine whether a person or a thing was "holy" or "profane" (חֹל) was one of the tasks of the priest.[131] So it is a provocation when the Servant is desacralized, declared to be "profaned."[132] This is even more the case if it is clear that here too it is Moses who is meant.

The verse contains a comprehensive confession and declaration of repentance. The suspension of fellowship with both God and neighbor is stated in weighty terms.[133] The people's own history is admitted to be a history of guilt.[134] The miracle of an individual's solidarity, even though he himself is guiltless, signifies the turn of events. Assuming that this too recapitulates the era of the wanderings in the wilderness, the text that comes into question is Numbers 14, which describes the rebellion of the Israelites after the spies have returned from the promised land. Num 14:18 is the only passage in the book of Numbers that mentions "crime" (פֶּשַׁע). It is linked with "iniquity, wrongness" (עָוֹן, two times in v. 18, also in vv. 19 and 34). But "blows" or "strokes" (נכה) are also mentioned twice in this chapter: the threat of plague is a "stroke" (v. 12) inflicted by Yahweh himself, and the end of the chapter (v. 45) tells that Israel was "struck down" because they did not follow Moses' advice. It is only through Yahweh's intervention that Moses and Aaron escape stoning (v. 10).

The people take up two different positions in opposition to Moses. One group is afraid of going up into the land, because of the rumors that "the country devours its inhabitants" (Num 13:30-33; 14:36-38). The other group wants to move up too quickly (Num 14:39-45). In both cases the consequences are severe. We may assume that on the return to the land after the exile, the story in Numbers 14 provided a highly topical theme.

---

sage, 934 [345]: "Of 21 passages with ʿānāw in the OT only Num 12:3 [*Qere*], the sole occurrence in the narrative literature, appears in the sg. (of Moses' 'humiliation,' probably a later addition; cf. J. Schildenberger, "Moses als Idealgestalt eines Armen Jahwes," *FS Gelin* [1961] 71–84). . . . ʿānāw is fundamentally indistinct from ʿānī in meaning: 'poor, lowly, bowed down, insignificant, humble,' also 'meek.'"

129 See esp. O. Kaiser, *Der königliche Knecht* (1959) 104–7.

130 Cf. Amos 2:7; Jer 34:16; Ezek 20:5-24.

131 Cf. Ezek 22:26; 42:20; 44:23.

132 See W. Zimmerli, *Ezekiel 2* (1983) 535 [*Ezechiel 2* (1969) 1223] on Ezek 48:15: "In the formula חֹל הוּא ('it is profane') can be discerned linguistically the form of the priest's declaratory judgment"; see also *Ezekiel 1* (1979) 376–77 [*Ezechiel 1* (1969) 398–99]

on Ezek 18:5-9.

133 We may follow R. Knierim, "פֶּשַׁע *pešaʿ* crime," *TLOT* 2:1036 [*THAT* 2:493], and differentiate: "Whoever commits *pešaʿ* [crimes] does not merely rebel or protest against Yahweh but breaks with him, takes from him what is his, robbing, embezzling and misappropriating it." And on "iniquity, wrongness" (ʿāwōn)" Knierim says in "עָוֹן *ʿāwôn* perversity," *TLOT* 2:964 [*THAT* 2:245]: "Given the basic meaning, a translation 'bend' (act and consequence)—'bent down, to be bent down' (destiny, punishment)—'twist, to be twisted' or 'wrongness, to be wrong' seems most consistent." See also R. Knierim, *Die Hauptbegriffe für Sünde im Alten Testament* (2d ed. 1967); K. Koch, "עָוֹן *ʿāwôn*," *ThWAT* 5:1160–77.

134 Cf. Ezra 9; Nehemiah 9; Daniel 9.

"Chastisement," "rebuke," or "correction" (מוּסָר) is a term in wisdom teaching. The basic meaning of the root יסר is probably "instruct."[135] Branson sums up: "The primary purpose of instruction (yāsar) is to communicate knowledge in order to shape specific conduct."[136] "The verb yāsar often appears with the meaning 'correct', i.e., instruct someone by using punishment to 'correct' what has been done."[137] The semantic field is relevant to the relationship between parents and children, and between teachers and pupils. As a sociomorpheme it is also used to describe the relationship to God.[138]

"Instruct" (יסר) is not found either as verb or as substantive in the book of Numbers, but it does occur five times in Deuteronomy, where it is used for human upbringing or discipline (Deut 21:18 and 22:18), but also for discipline imposed by God (4:36; 8:5 and 11:2). All three last-named passages are talking about the exodus from Egypt and the wanderings in the wilderness. The substantive מוּסָר used in Isa 53:5 is found only in Deut 11:2, where there is a recollection of the miracle at the Reed Sea and of "what he [Yahweh] did to Dathan and Abiram" (Deut 11:6). That is a pointer to Numbers 16–17. It is worth considering whether this is not also the reference text for Isa 53:5bα. G. Gerlemann doubts whether it is correct to translate שָׁלוֹם (šālôm) in v. 5 by "peace, salvation,"[139] and whether it is not connected with "requital in the negative sense, i.e., as punishment, revenge, retribution."[140] The sentence would then fit into the declarations of guilt, as the third element in the series. Indeed, Numbers 16–17 offers sufficient grounds for this. It is a story of murmuring or sullen discontent

that calls into question God's authority as well as the authority of Moses (and Aaron).[141] It is the history of a terrible catastrophe, in which the complete annihilation of people and community is averted only through Moses' intervention. Num 17:20 (17:5) sums up events in a divine speech addressed to Moses: "The staff of the man whom I choose shall sprout; thus for my own relief (וַהֲשִׁכֹּתִי מֵעָלַי) I will put a stop to the complaints of the Israelites that they continually make against you" (cf. v. 25 [v. 10]).[142]

It is especially noticeable at this point that DtIsa does not mention Aaron at all, although it is his staff that is meant in Num 17:20 (5). It could be that when DtIsa uses the substantive שָׁלוֹם he is hinting at the end of the incident as told in Num 17:20-28 (5-13). The Servant has taken the "retribution" on himself. It is only because of this that retribution can ultimately lead to "healing," "salvation."[143] The tension in the term מוּסָר between "correction" or "chastisement" and "instruction" therefore already prepares for the announcement of the Servant's death.

חֲבֻרָה means "wounds, stripes, weals," if the whole complex of meanings in Gen 4:23; Exod 21:25; Isa 1:6; Ps 38:6 (5); and Prov 20:30 is taken into account. But the derivation from the root חבר I is by no means as clear as one could wish.[144] According to the lexicons חבר II in Qal means "to join together, be fused, touch one another, charm." But it is not certain which meaning is the original one. The other stems and substantives correspond to the range of meaning of the root חבר I. As we have frequently observed, DtIsa works with the

---

135 See R. D. Branson and G. J. Botterweck, "יָסַר yāsar," TDOT 6:129 [ThWAT 3:689].

136 Ibid. [690].

137 Ibid., 129–30 [691].

138 See J. A. Sanders, Suffering as Divine Discipline in the Old Testament and Post-Biblical Judaism (1955).

139 G. Gerlemann, "שלם šlm to have enough," TLOT 3:1337–48 [THAT 2:919–35]: "Equally questionable is the usual interpretation of šālōm in Isa 53:5, where it refers to Yahweh's Servant. It is only with great difficulty that mûsar šᵉlômēnû ʿālāyw 'our šālōm-correction came on him' can be interpreted as a punishment that brings salvation. The reference is quite probably to 'the punishment we deserved as retribution'" (1345 [930]). For a contrary view see HALAT s.v. שלום, 4:1395–99 (with the lit. there cited); this article starts from the assumption that the verb שלם means "to remain whole, unscathed."

140 Gerlemann, TLOT 3:1345 [THAT 2:930].

141 Cf. Jer 7:28; 32:33; 35:13; Zeph 3:2; see also Branson and Botterweck, "יָסַר yāsar," TDOT 6:132 [ThWAT 3:694]: "In all four passages Yahweh or the prophet is rejected. The prophet's message is identified with the voice of Yahweh, so that rejection of the former means rejection of the latter also. The teaching of their message (mûsār) is rejected." The connection of the Moses tradition with the tradition of the prophets requires further investigation.

142 Translation following M. Noth, Numbers (1968) 120 [Numeri (1966) 107]; see also HALAT 4:1382 on this passage.

143 See below on Isa 54:10.

144 See HALOT, s.v.; H. Cazelles, "חבר chābhar," TDOT 4:193–97, esp. 193–94 [ThWAT 2:721–26, esp.

ambivalence, or rather multivalence, of words. The variety in the lexical findings suggests that this may very well be the case here too.

The supposition that the root חבר II means "cast a spell, charm" has been backed up by references to Deut 18:11; Ps 58:6 (5); and Sir 12:13. The sense can be pinned down more exactly here, since these passages are talking about snake charming.[145] Verse 5bβ could thus be rendered: "And through his (snake) charming (וּבַחֲבֻרָתוֹ) we received healing." In this form, the sentence could be a precise pointer to the reference text Num 21:4-9, with its story about the "bronze serpent." Again it is a story about the murmuring in the wilderness: "Seraph or fiery serpents . . . bit the people, so that many Israelites died" (Num 21:6).[146] Moses prays for the people (v. 7). He makes a serpent out of bronze and sets it on a pole: "And whenever a serpent bit someone, that person would look at the serpent of bronze and live" (Num 21:9).

Deut 8:15 also has the *topos* about the preservation from "seraph or fiery serpents and scorpions" during the period of the desert wanderings. When DtIsa picks it up here, close attention is required of the listener: through *his* (the Servant Moses') spells, and not through the spells of others, healing is possible.

According to DtIsa, "the many" (53:14) who took part in the wanderings in the desert testify that "God healed through Moses." This experience is expressly preserved in a kind of vow. In this respect too "the arm of Yahweh was revealed" over the Servant Moses (53:1). For DtIsa's contemporaries, the immediate occasion is the conflict with other kinds of sorcery. According to 47:9, 12, Babylon practices "sorcery" (חֶבֶר). In that passage the word is used parallel to "enchantment" (כֶּשֶׁף).

In the present DtIsa text the conflict probably has a particular reference to other cults of healing especially. Against the background of the fifth century B.C.E., one may think especially of cults such as the cult of Asclepius. His emblem was the serpent curled around a staff, an emblem still seen today in the Asclepius staff as symbol of physicians and pharmacists. Thus the end of v. 5 once more endorses what Exod 15:26 had already said: "I am Yahweh, your physician" (אֲנִי יהוה רֹפְאֶךָ).

Finally, the root חבר can mean "to join, be joined." From this are derived חֶבֶר as "community," חָבֵר, "companion" and חַבָּר, "fellow-guildsman." Verse 5bβ could therefore also be translated: "Through fellowship with him we received healing." In 44:11 DtIsa calls the artisans who manufacture idols "his [the idol's] comrades" (חֲבֵרָיו). They are to "assemble" (קבץ). In this way he is probably accurately characterizing the guild system that was developing at this time together with the towns and cities. To formulate the question boldly: Is "the community (חֶבְרָה) of the Servant" distinguished here both from the guilds, with the danger of foreign cults that went hand in hand with them, and from the religious unity represented by the temple, with its sacrificial cult?[147] Is a terminology developing here that makes it possible to say, along with Ps 119:63: "I am the comrade (חָבֵר אָנִי) of all who fear you and keep your precepts"? Is this "healing," according to 53:5?[148]

■ **6** The verse begins and ends "we all/us all" (כֻּלָּנוּ). It is the conclusion of the admission of guilt. The going astray of sheep is linked with the assumption of guilt. But how do these two declarations, which are so very different, fit together?

The semantic field indicated by "small cattle (צֹאן)—stray" can be expanded by "flocks/herd—shepherd/herdsman." In the social sphere, the relationship between people and ruler is described as being similar to that between the shepherd and his flock. At that time it was an image that was familiar to everyone. As a sociomorpheme it can also be applied to the relationship to God. Ezekiel 34 and Zechariah 10–11 show what a wide range of communication is possible with the help of this image. For example, a flock without a shepherd is scattered (Ezek 34:5, 6, 12). When sheep go astray and

---

721–22]; J. J. Finkelstein, "Hebrew חבר and Semitic *ḤBR," *JBL* 75 (1956) 328–31.

145 See *HALOT,* s.v.

146 For the translation and the text see Noth, *Numbers* (1968) [*Numeri* (1966)] on this passage.

147 See also Cazelles, "חָבֵר *chābhar*," *TDOT* 4:196 [*ThWAT* 2:724]: "The original religious notions, demythologized, appear with reference to the 'union' of the tribes about the sanctuary: 'the tabernacle shall be one whole (*'echādh*)' we read in Ex. 26:6. The qal participle appears twice (Ex. 28:7; 39:4) in connection with the ephod of the high priest as a symbol of the unity of the twelve tribes. . . . This positive use of the root to designate the unity of the chosen people could not carry the day in all cases."

get lost, this can be expressed in different ways (cf. Jer 50:17; Ezek 34:6; and Ps 119:176). The formula "like (the) sheep without a shepherd" is found in Num 27:17; 1 Kgs 22:17 par.; and 2 Chr 18:16.

Numbers 27 deserves attention as a text that can help toward an understanding of Isa 53:6. It is true that there is no mention of any shepherd in 53:6. DtIsa uses the title "shepherd" for Cyrus; he expects nothing in the way of shepherding from Israel's own kings—perhaps he is not so very far removed from 1 Kgs 22:17 in this respect. But Num 27:15-23 has to do with Moses' successor. Joshua is to be installed as "someone over the congregation" (אִישׁ עַל־הָעֵדָה, v. 16), "so that the congregation of Yahweh may not be like sheep without a shepherd" (v. 17). This would mean that we can once again detect a reference text from the era of the wanderings in the wilderness, this time as those wanderings reach their end. To say that "everyone" (אִישׁ) goes his own way is probably a topical interpretation of the formula about the shepherd and the sheep; this is indicated by a comparison with Trito-Isaiah (56:9-12; 57:12), where the greed of the upper class is particularly under attack.

But the text of Numbers 27 is of still further interest for the interpretation of 53:6. The reason why Joshua has to be appointed is given in Num 27:12-14 as Moses' death, which is now announced once more. Moses is not permitted to lead the people into the promised land, because of the events at Kadesh, "the waters of strife." This is a recollection of the somber story in Num 20:1-13. That too is a story about the people's murmurings. Again they have no water in the desert. Moses performs a miracle and makes water come out of the rock. As a result Moses and Aaron have to die before the promised land is entered. They have not "sanctified Yahweh before the eyes of the Israelites" (v. 12). The ancient interpreters already puzzled over this text. The conflict has the somber depths of a Greek tragedy. Moses has intervened for the sake of his people, and yet he is guilty in the eyes of God. He is told to "speak to" the rock (v. 8). He then strikes it twice (v. 11). Presumably the possibility that Moses might be confused with a miracle worker lies behind the conflict ("we will bring water for you out of this rock," v. 10). This infringes on God's holiness.

Here the understanding, or misunderstanding, of the people ("Why have you brought the assembly of Yahweh into this wilderness?" v. 4) coincides with Moses' own understanding or misunderstanding: it is the question about the point and significance of the period in the wilderness. The mystery of the Servant Moses' suffering could not be more succinctly summed up than in the words of 53:6: "But Yahweh allowed to fall on him the guilt of *us* all."

At the beginning we asked where the unity of v. 6 was to be found. This question now finds an answer through the comparison with Num 27:12-23. Succession and the announcement of the death of Moses are closely bound up with one another.

In retrospect we may say that Isa 53:4-6 is a summary of the desert era. The reference texts from Numbers (as far as I can see) show a clear sequence:

Numbers 11–12	The burden of the people and Miriam's leprosy
Numbers 13–14	The sending out of the spies and their return
Numbers 16	The rebellion of Dathan and Abiram
Numbers 21	The bronze serpent
(Numbers 20	At the waters of strife)
Numbers 27	Joshua as Moses' successor

It is noticeable that in this list only the story about "the waters of strife" in Numbers 20 is not in its proper place in the narrative sequence of the book of Numbers; it has been re-sited in accordance with its mention in Num 27:12-14. But in this way it constitutes the close and explanation of the whole as a confession of guilt, while at the same time preparing the way for the following verses, with their account of Moses' death, before he has reached the promised land. Num 20:12-13 and 27:14 make clear that the real sin was disregard of Yahweh's holiness. This also makes retrospectively evident the extent to which the Servant has been profaned (v. 5). "Holy" (קדשׁ) and "profaned" (מחלל) are antithetical concepts.

Isa 53:4-6 is also a reminder of part of Moses' life, beginning with the departure from Sinai-Horeb and ending with the arrival at the river Jordan. It is a history of suffering caused by his people. It is therefore fitting that in DtIsa this history should be recalled in the form of confession and repentance.

---

148 See H.-J. Kraus, *Psalms 60–150* (1989) [*Psalmen 2* (5th ed. 1978)] on this passage.

Here too a comparison with the drama of the ancient world can be of help. That drama expects a public well versed in the myths and hero sagas, and familiar with its Homer.[149] At the same time "strangers" without any previous knowledge of these things can still participate, because the dramas deal with general human problems. Verses 4-6 presuppose familiarity with biblical tradition. The high art of allusion is practiced in order to delineate the problems of the present. The matter can be put more precisely by saying: 52:11-12 already announces the theme of the exodus tradition. Then, with the remembrance of the Servant of God in the present text, recollection of the period in the wilderness has its proper place. By taking up the stories about the "murmurings" from the book of Numbers, this recollection acquires its critical potential, for the present day too.

■ **7-9** For the understanding of vv. 7-9 it is important to be clear that here the half-chorus of "the many" is again speaking. It tells about the Servant's life as this can be seen and evaluated from outside. This again takes up the style of vv. 2-3. There are three small units:

1. The Servant's sufferings (v. 7)
2. The Servant's death (v. 8)
3. The Servant's burial (v. 9).

■ **7** The witnesses have seen that the Servant was "oppressed" and "bowed down." Debts can oppress,[150] but guilt is a burden too. The term עָוֹן in itself contains an element of "being bowed down/bentness," according to Knierim.[151] This element is all the more pronounced if the guilt was the guilt of all, as v. 6 says. Even in the austere and matter-of-fact enumeration, the sympathy of the people who are speaking shines through. The Servant is not presented as a hero, even in his suffering: "He was bowed down!"

I suspect, however, that this comment also contains an indication of the Servant's age.[152] After "like a sucking child" ["like a shoot"] (v. 2), "a man" (v. 3), "he bore" (v. 4), the declaration "he was bowed down" touches on the fourth stage in the Servant's life, which lasts until his death and burial. The biographical thread is therefore also followed through to the end.

The only unusual thing about the Servant's behavior is his silence. The three statements about the Servant in v. 7a build up, so that they have an intensifying effect, especially in Hebrew. The statements increase in length, the main emphasis falling on: "and he does not open his mouth." This is interpreted by way of the double comparison and is repeated at the end. To eliminate the sentence, as has often been proposed, would be a grievous pity! Job 3 shows how a man at prayer could complain. As every concordance shows, the Psalms are full of the "cries" of petitioners who call upon God. Hebr[ew] has "more than twenty different roots available to indicate crying, groaning, complaining, etc.," writes R. Albertz.[153] Lamentation was a cultivated art that we have meanwhile lost, an art in which it is made entirely clear why someone is crying out, and how. In the complaint or lament, the cry (צעק) is addressed to both human beings and God. After all, Israel too "cried" to Yahweh (Exod 2:23, זעק; 14:10), as did Moses (Exod 8:8 [12]; 15:25; 17:4) .

If a petitioner "does not open his mouth," it is for a particular reason.[154] Lamentations 3 names hope (vv. 26-29), perhaps thinking of Jeremiah as a model.[155] But why is the Servant silent? A recollection of the Moses traditions can again provide an answer, and in this case the most probable passage is Deuteronomy's version of Israel's arrival in east Jordan in the neighborhood of Beth-Peor, and the installation of Joshua. The text corresponds to Num 27:12-23. According to Deut 3:23-29, Moses prays: "'Let me cross over to see the good land beyond the Jordan. . . .' But Yahweh was angry with me on your account and would not heed me. Yahweh said to

149 See G. Nagy, *Pindar's Homer: The Lyric Possession of an Epic Past* (1990).

150 For נגש see Deut 15:2-3; 2 Kgs 23:35; Isa 58:3; Dan 11:20; E. Lipiński, "נָגַשׂ *nāgaś*," *ThWAT* 5:230–32.

151 R. Knierim, "עָוֹן *ʿāwōn* perversity," *TLOT* 2:864 ["verkehrtheit," *THAT* 2:245].

152 Cf. Jer 51:22 and H. W. Wolff's comments in his *Anthropology of the Old Testament* (1973) 120 [*Anthropologie des Alten Testaments* (4th ed. 1984) 179].

153 R. Albertz, "צעק *ṣʿq* to cry out," *TLOT* 3:1088–93, esp. 1089 [*THAT* 2:568–75, esp. 570].

154 Cf. Psalm 38 (esp. v. 14 [13]); 39 (esp. vv. 3 [2], 10 [9]; but see v. 13 [12]).

155 See the commentaries on this passage, e.g., W. Rudolph, *Die Klagelieder* (1962).

me: 'That is enough! Never speak to me of this matter again!'"[156]

Moses' request is human. But when he holds his tongue he is obeying a definite command. He is obedient. It is moving when, on the silence of the Servant, DtIsa marks out the distance between the unknowing but foreboding silence of a lamb before it is slaughtered[157] and the knowledge of a ewe, who has surely often enough endured the shearing process. The Servant is silent before God and human beings.[158]

■ **8** Like v. 7, this verse begins[159] with a series of utterances that build in intensity. This is shown even externally by the length of the first three comments. מִן ("out of") is used four times: mē-... mi- and mē-... mi-, and in the middle of these two pairs a question is asked: מִי mi ("who?"). The tone fits the lament over the death.

To translate עֹצֶר as "oppression" is not wrong,[160] and is suggested by the train of thought in v. 7. The root עצר means "hold back, hold fast, close up." Exclusion from the community is characteristic in this connection, especially exclusion from the temple cult. Such an exclusion is reported by Jeremiah, for example (Jer 36:5); Nehemiah does not enter the temple with someone who

has been "shut out," even in order to save his own life (Neh 6:10). As regards "close," the "closing" of the womb should be mentioned (Gen 16:2; 20:18; 1 Sam 21:6 [5]; Isa 66:9; Prov 30:16; Sir 42:10) or the closing of the heavens (Deut 11:17; 1 Kgs 8:35; 2 Chr 6:26; 7:13). In order to link the aspect of "closing" with the relationship to community, I should like to render the substantive "exclusion."

Where the Servant Moses is concerned, the term is ambiguous. Has he been "shut out" by human beings or by God? Was Moses "shut out" from the cult of Baal of Peor, to which the Israelites "yoked themselves" (Num 25:3, 5; Ps 106:28)? Was he "shut out" from his people when they entered the promised land?

Equally ambiguous is the "judgment" (מִשְׁפָּט): "mišpāṭ as verdict can mean either deliverance or condemnation" (G. Liedke).[161] Once again, the interpretation can differ according to whether the viewpoint is that of human beings or of God.

"Exclusion (shut-outness) and condemnation" continued throughout the Servant's lifetime, until he "was taken away." The verb "take" (לקח) is used very frequently in the OT in widely different connections.[162]

156 Vv. 25-26, following G. von Rad, *Deuteronomium* (2d ed. 1968) [von Rad's translation not available in the OTL, which used RSV].

157 Note should be taken of V. Hamp's comment in his article, "טָבַח ṭābaḥ," *TDOT* 5:283–87 (284) [*ThWAT* 3:302–6 (303)]: "Only in the OT do we find the limitation of ṭbḥ to the ordinary nonreligious slaughter of domestic animals to provide for a banquet (Gen. 43:16; Ex. 21:37 [22:1] [Covenant Code]: Dt. 28:31; Prov. 9:2; cf. Mt. 22:4; Lk. 15:23)." This is in distinction from זבח and שחט. It is hence remarkable that no sacrificial terminology is used here in connection with the Servant. In Jer 11:19 the image is used somewhat differently, the point of the comparison there being the guilelessness.

158 Ibn Ezra (ed. M. Friedländer [1873, reprint 1965]) writes about this passage: "*Yet he opened not his mouth.* This requires no explanation; for this is the case with every Jew in exile." See also O. Kaiser, *Der königliche Knecht* (1959) 110: "'And he opened not his mouth' is reminiscent of the acknowledgment of trust by the sufferer, who affirms that he is not opening his mouth to accuse God, but awaits God's help (cf. Pss 38:14ff. [13ff.]; 39:10 [9]; 62:2 [1], 6 [5]; Lam 3:28; in contrast, Job 3:1ff.). The suffering Servant is therefore described as the one who is obedient, who enters upon the sacrificial road laid

down for him by God without rebellion."

159 The difficulty of this verse is formulated by E. Kutsch, *Sein Leiden und Tod–unser Heil* (1967) 26: "In v. 8 no less than four out of five substantives and verbs allow of different translations." Kutsch himself translates v. 8: "Out of imprisonment and judgment he was led away—but who of his contemporaries reflects upon it?—so that he is cut off from the land of the living, 'stricken' 'unto death' because of the wickedness of his 'people'" (13).

160 See *HALOT*, s.v.

161 G. Liedke, "שפט špṭ to judge," *TLOT* 3:1392–99, esp. 1396 [*THAT* 2:999–1009, esp. 1006]. For "deliverance" he cites Deut 32:4; Isa 4:4; 30:18; 51:4; 58:2; Jer 9:23 (24); 10:24; Pss 17:2; 33:5; 36:7 (6); 76:10 (9); 101:1; 111:7. For "condemnation, annihilation" Isa 34:5; Jer 48:21; 51:9; Ezek 23:24; 39:21; Mic 3:8; Zeph 3:8; Pss 9:17 (16); 48:12 (11); 97:8; Job 36:17. See also *HALAT* under שפט, esp. 4:1498.

162 See H. H. Schmid, "לקח lqḥ to take," *TLOT* 2:648–51 [*THAT* 1:875–79]; H. Seebass, "לָקַח lāqaḥ," *TDOT* 8:16–21 [*ThWAT* 4:588–94].

As far as the present text is concerned, two special uses of לקח have been introduced into the discussion: (1) "to take life," in the sense of "let die,"[163] and (2) to take a person away, in the sense of "translate."[164]

Yet again, I think it possible that the text intends to initiate precisely this discussion. For the verse is still part of the account of the Servant's fate. Through its mention of grave and burial, the following verse already excludes a "translation," as in the case of Enoch or Elijah. But that is not all. It is only Yahweh's verdict, according to vv. 11-12, that makes a decision possible. Then the special character of the Servant can be perceived. What human beings can see and tell becomes unequivocally clear only through the divine word.

The "taking away" also arouses concern[165] lest the Servant be forgotten. דור is a generation, as a period of time.[166] DtIsa thinks in terms of generations. There are the generations of the beginning (41:4), the primordial period (51:8-9). Here in v. 8, "his generation" means the Servant's generation. In the interweaving of dramatic time, this initially means the time and generation of Moses, the desert era. Judg 2:10 says that after the death of Joshua and his generation "another generation (דוֹר אַחֵר) grew up . . . who did not know Yahweh or the acts that he had performed for Israel." Deuteronomy 29 makes Moses in his farewell discourse remember salvation but also disaster, as admonition and instruction (cf. v. 28 [29]) for future generations (הַדּוֹר הָאַחֲרוֹן, v. 21 [22]). To render v. 8 of the present text as "his [the Servant's] fate" (instead of "his generation") falls short. The point is remembrance of the mutual relationship between Moses and his people, the experience of this generation. The rhetorical question: "Who thinks about his generation?" provokes the answer, "We do!" For precisely this has taken place in vv. 4-6, which is a meditation on the desert era, as "the time of murmuring." The breadth of meaning of שׂיח, "think about, speak, lament," is taken up here in its totality.[167]

In the dramatic simultaneity that links past and present "the many" are participants (v. 14; cf. Deut 29:21 [22]: "the future generation of your children who will rise up after you") as well as "many nations" (v. 15; cf. Deut 29:21 [22]: "the foreigner who comes from a distant country"). It is the interpretation of the commandment given at the institution of the Passover in Exodus 12: "a remembrance . . . a festival to Yahweh throughout your generations (לְדֹרֹתֵיכֶם) . . . as a perpetual ordinance" (v. 14; cf. vv. 17, 24). It is this that is taking place "now!" It may also be noted here that this indicates the *Sitz im Leben* of DtIsa's work: it has to do with the exodus and the Passover, or with the celebration of these events.

Verse 8b once more establishes the Servant's death[168] and its cause ("Truly," כִּי). This is merely a summing up of what has already been said. Whether the reading should be "my people" (עַמִּי) or "his people" (עַמּוֹ) depends on whether these sentences are spoken by an individual or by a chorus. Act and consequence correspond. The "sins" of the people become a "blow" for the Servant. In this way, the fellowship has been finally destroyed, from a human point of view.

163 E.g., 1 Kgs 19:4, 10, 14; Isa 57:13; Jer 15:15; Ezek 33:6; Jonah 4:3; Ps 31:14 (13).

164 Gen 5:24; 2 Kgs 2:3, 10; disputed for Pss 49:16 (15); 73:24. To be noted in this connection is the use of לקח for a prophet's change of place, when this is brought about by God's "hand" or "spirit"; see, e.g., Ezek 8:3. Cf. also 1 Kgs 18:12; 2 Kgs 2:16 (there linked with נשׂא), and the misunderstanding of the prophet's disciples).

165 See H. Seebass, "לָקַח lāqaḥ," *TDOT* 8:17 [*ThWAT* 4:590]: "Often lāqaḥ designates the initiative for subsequent action."

166 Cf. the summing up in *HALOT* 1:217–18 s.v. (*HALAT* 1:209): "from a man's birth until the birth of his first son; a person's adult contemporaries as a whole"; Noth, *Überl[ieferungsgeschichtliche] St[udien]* 21 [*The Deuteronomistic History* (2d ed. 1991) 37–38]; a period with particular events and people,

Ped[ersen,] *Isr[ael]* 1–2:490"; see also G. Gerlemann, "דוֹר dôr generation," *TLOT* 1:333–35 [*THAT* 1:443–45]; D. N. Freedman, J. Lundbom, and G. J. Botterweck, "דוֹר dôr," *TDOT* 3:169–81 [*ThWAT* 2:181–94].

167 See *HALOT* 3:1319–20 [*HALAT* 4:1230] on שׂיח II and on this passage (1320 [1231]) *Pilel* (with lit. and selected quotations).

168 On the semantic field of the root גזר, "cut," cf. *HALOT* 1:187 [*HALAT* 1:179–80]; see also Ezek 37:11cj.; Pss 31:23 (22); 88:6 (5); Lam 3:54; see further J. Bergman and M. Ottosson, "אֶרֶץ ʾerets," *TDOT* 1:388–405 [*ThWAT* 1:418–36]: "The earth is ʾerets chayyim, 'the land of the living' (or 'of life'), i.e., the earth as the place of human life is contrasted with the Underworld (Isa. 38:11; 53:8; Jer. 11:19; Ezek. 26:20; 32:23-27, 32; Ps. 27:13; 52:7 [5]; 116:9; 142:6 [5]; Job 28:13)" (399 [430]).

■ **9** This verse is also a fine example of the interweaving of past and present in the Servant of God, Moses. The last chapter of Deuteronomy (and hence of the Pentateuch) records Moses' death and burial in the following words (Deut 34:5-6): "And Moses, the Servant of Yahweh (עֶבֶד יהוה), died there in the land of Moab, at Yahweh's command (עַל־פִּי יהוה). And he buried him (וַיִּקְבֹּר אֹתוֹ) in the valley in the land of Moab, opposite Beth-peor, but no human being knows his burial place to this day."

The Deuteronomy text and the text in DtIsa share the same difficulty—which is not really a difficulty at all if the context in Deuteronomy is taken into account: The subject in "*He* buried him . . ." (Deut 34:6) is Yahweh, without mention of the circumstances in any detail. "*He* gave him his grave . . ." (Isa 53:9) says nothing different. In the case of both texts translations and commentators have continually tried to get rid of the stumbling block by translating the verb as a passive; but this is not in the texts. How can God's love for his Servant be more marvelously expressed?

What is a real stumbling block, however, is that the Servant's grave is "among criminals." "The wicked" (רָשָׁע *rāšaᶜ*) is the most extreme antithesis to "the righteous" (צַדִּיק *ṣaddîq*). What is "detrimental to the community" and what is "faithful to the community" (צַדִּיק *ṣaddîq*) is the subject of continually new reflection in the biblical texts. But no one wants to have his grave among "criminals"—which means in "unclean" land. Moses is buried opposite Beth-peor. That this is more than a piece of mere topographical information becomes clear if, in the light of Hos 9:10 (בַּעַל־פְּעוֹר *baᶜal-pᵉᶜôr*), one is aware of the "wickedness" that was associated with the name of Peor,[169] and that at all events included a foreign cult, sexual offenses, and the cult of the dead.

■ **9aβ** But who is meant by "a rich man"? I have the impression that for DtIsa's own time this was a topical allusion, Gesenius already noted that in the parallelism (53:2-10, p.16) the consonants of "wicked" (רשע *ršᶜ*, v. 9aα) and "rich man" (עשר *ᶜšr*, v. 9aβ) are the same, though their order is reversed. The particle אֵת is also common to both. Anyone who is aware of this reads silently "a wicked man" together with "a rich man."

But the next word is strange too, for the text that has come down to us in the Masoretic version reads: "He was beside a rich man in his deaths" (בְּמֹתָיו *bᵉmotâw*). This does not make much sense. Death has certainly already been mentioned in the context, and thus the interpretation that follows this reading is harmless. But perhaps—in accordance with the rule about preferring the more difficult reading (*lectio difficilior*)—we should read the text differently? It has continually been suggested that the reading should be "his burial place" (בָּמָתוֹ *bāmātô*), perhaps also in the form בּוֹמָתוֹ *bômātô*,[170] in the sense of tumulus or burial mound. But what is the problem about this? On the one hand בָּמָה *bāmāh* as "high place" is a technical term for Canaanite sanctuaries, or for sanctuaries that were at least suspect for the Yahweh faith. On the other hand, someone else might wish to make "his burial place" in association with[171] the Servant. But anyone who remembers Deuteronomy 34 is aware that no human being knows Moses' burial place—"to this day."

The text of v. 9 is probably intentionally mysterious. The variants are of interest for someone who can read and write. This is a deviation from DtIsa's usual practice, for the subtleties of his text are generally designed to be picked up by the ear. Ambiguous texts that have to be read between the lines are often indications of political pressure. It could be that the *topos* about Moses'

---

169 Cf. Num 23:28; 25:3, 5, 18; 31:16; Josh 22:17; Ps 106:28.

170 Thus esp. W. F. Albright in his lecture on במה: "The High Place in Ancient Palestine" in *Volume du Congrès: Strasbourg 1956* (1957) 242–58, esp. 244–45, on the basis of the Qumran form of the text (1QIsaª). Alonso-Schökel, Elliger, Soggin, and Thomas, among others, all follow him. For a view contrary to this solution cf. J. Lindblom, "Die Ebed-Jahwe Orakel in der neuentdeckten Jesajahandschrift (DSIa)," *ZAW* 63 (1951) 245–46; W. B. Barick, "The Funerary Character of 'High-Places' in Ancient Palestine: A Reassessment," *VT* 25 (1975)

565–95, esp. 580–86.

171 1QIsaª first wrote עם: "in the company of, together with, also with." This was then probably supposed to be corrected through a ת [sic] written over the top, in correspondence to the אֵת of the MT. The plural "rich men" (עשירים) has been erased again. So the plural in the LXX too is no doubt the easier reading. See the facsimile edition of the Isaiah scroll, J. C. Trever, *Scrolls from Qumrân Cave I. The Great Isaiah Scroll . . . From Photographs by J. C. Trever* (1972) 51.

unknown grave preserves a historical remembrance. For Martin Noth it was the starting point for his reconstruction of the figure of Moses.[172] I suspect that quite early on this *topos* was already an element in the dispute about the significance of Moses. If there is no grave, no reverence can be paid to it, and such reverence played an important role in the hero cults of the ancient world. Moses was no hero! The brief comment at the beginning of the Moses tradition (Exod 2:1-2) serves to make the same point: "A man from the house of Levi went and married a Levite woman. And the woman conceived and bore a son." Moses is not of divine descent! As R. Bartelmus has shown,[173] the question of hero worship played a part in the legitimation of the Davidic monarchy in Jerusalem. Heroes were frequently regarded as the founders of dynasties. The development of the cities from the fifth century B.C.E. onward probably went hand in hand with the renewed importance of hero cults.

Against this background, the fact that the precise place of Moses' grave is unknown could be significant, as well as the circumstance that reverence for the Servant's grave is inconceivable if the grave is "among criminals." The remembrance of "Moses—the Servant" has to be kept alive in a different way, and hence also his importance for the new constitution of Jerusalem: his legacy is his Torah. For a solution to the puzzle of Moses' grave, the topographical reference in Deuteronomy 34 should again be made the point of departure: Mount Nebo, opposite Jericho (v. 1), Beth-Peor, in the land of Moab (v. 6). Seen from Jerusalem, this means on the other side of the Jordan, at the northern end of the Dead Sea. In the Persian period this area probably belonged to the Ammonites.[174]

In Nehemiah, Tobiah is called "an Ammonite servant" (Neh 2:10, 19; 3:35 [4:3]). He was probably a higher-up Persian official.[175] His family then ruled over this country for several centuries.[176] He was one of Nehemiah's three opponents (the others being Sanballat the Horonite and Geshem the Arab); and we postulated that these three were also the addressees of DtIsa's polemic in another passage.[177] Neh 13:4-9 tells that the priest Eliashib gave Tobiah a chamber in the forecourt of the temple.[178] Nehemiah put an end to this, had the chamber cleaned, and brought back "the vessels of Yahweh's temple," together with the grain offering and the incense (Neh 13:8). But this was the very text that we assumed was the background of Isa 52:11-12 ("Go out from there, you should not touch anything unclean!").

Is this Tobiah the type of the "rich man" who is really "one of the wicked"? Moses was given a grave beside him, that is, in his country, not in the holy land. Why this was so remains a mystery.

From the human point of view it was a dishonorable burial for the Servant. Consequently it is explicitly stated in v. 9, at the close of the account, that the Servant was innocent, legally speaking. The witnesses confirm once more that he had not committed any political act of violence (חָמָס), nor was he guilty of fraud (מִרְמָה) in the criminal sense.

172 M. Noth, *History of Israel* (2d ed. 1960, reprint 1983) 136 n. 2 [*Geschichte Israels* (10th ed. 1986) 128 n. 2].

173 R. Bartelmus, *Heroentum in Israel und seiner Umwelt. Eine traditionsgeschichtliche Untersuchung zu Gen 6,1-4 und verwandten Texten im Alten Testament und der altorientalischen Literatur* (1979).

174 See A. Alt, "Judas Nachbarn zur Zeit Nehemias," in his *Kleine Schriften zur Geschichte des Volkes Israel,* vol. 2 (4th ed. 1978) 338–45: "But if the oases on the eastern side of the lower Jordan valley and the whole of the adjoining hills—once the area of dispute between Israel and Moab—were now added to the previously more restricted area of the Ammonites, the frontier between the province of Judah and this eastern neighbor described by Nehemiah touched just as directly as did the frontier to the province of Samaria to the north" (341–42).

175 See ibid., 338–45; U. Kellermann, *Nehemia: Quellen-überlieferung und Geschichte* (1967) 166–73: "Nehemias Feinde," esp. 167–70.

176 B. Mazar, "The Tobiads," *IEJ* 7 (1957) 137–45, 229–38; C. C. McCown, "The ʿAraq el-Emir and the Tobiads," *BA* 20 (1957) 63–76; J. H. Hayes and J. M. Miller, eds., *Israelite and Judaean History* (1977) 532, 545, 550, 565, 572–82 and also under Tobiads, Tobiah (with lit.). It is worth considering whether the Tobiads' claims are also connected with the tradition about Moses' grave.

177 See above on 49:7; 52:1 (cf. Neh 2:19; 4:1).

178 See here A. H. J. Gunneweg, *Nehemia* (1987) 166, with reference to Kellermann, *Nehemia: Quellen-überlieferung und Geschichte* (1967) 170: "A man with such connections and relations in the city will hardly have required it as a kind of second residence. We should rather think of its being used for

■ **10** This verse again reverts to an interpretation of the Servant's fate.[179] The connection with vv. 4-6 should therefore be noted. Verse 6 ended with a summing up of the period in the wilderness: "But Yahweh allowed to fall on him the 'guilt' of all of us." Guilt is the consequence of what "the many" have done. The direct experience of the burden of the guilt, indeed its tremendous force, is conveyed here. The question how that could be, and why it had to be, is again evoked by this death, and this burial, of the Servant (vv. 7-9).

■ **10aα** This line again speaks about the "striking" (דֻּכָּאוֹ) of the Servant (see v. 5, מְדֻכָּא; cf. v. 8, נגע) and dares to interpret it as having been permitted by Yahweh—indeed, as having actually been brought about by him. Yahweh acts as a ruler who is free to decide as he sees fit. But this means that the fate meted out to the Servant is not completely inexplicable. The mystery, which prompts Job's question too,[180] is no less great for that.

As the MT stands, the "stroke" that falls upon the Servant is understood as sickness.[181] There are various ways of explaining this. On the one hand, the text can again be taking up v. 3 ("familiar with sickness") and v. 4 ("he bore our sickness"). It could be a level of interpretation according to which the Servant was really ill—perhaps there is a topical reference here. Another possibility is to understand "sickness" (חֳלִי) in the widest sense, as a term for "infirmity of either body or mind."[182]

To me it seems more probable that this is a deliberate textual change. If we follow C. R. North's pointing,[183] 1QIsaᵃ reads וַיְחַלְּלֵהוּ: "And he [Yahweh] had profaned him." That is an outrageous statement: Yahweh is holy. How can he profane his Servant? But for that very reason 1QIsaᵃ may very well have preserved the original reading. For the tendency to avoid any statement about

the profanation of the Servant can already be observed in v. 5 ("pierced" instead of "profaned").

That would mean that we should have to reckon with two statements about the Servant in v. 10aα that are not completely covered by "stroke" and "become sick." It could be that here there is an interpretation of the immediately preceding statement about the "grave among criminals/the wicked" in v. 9. Consequently MT's formulation about "his being struck" (דַּכְּאוֹ Piel infinitive with suffix) again deserves attention. K. Elliger[184] has proposed pointing it as in nominal, instead of the verbal, form: דַּכְּאוֹ. This could then be rendered: "his being stricken" or "struck down." דַּכָּא I is according to HALOT also found in Isa 57:15; Ps 34:19 (18) in the sense of "crushed, humiliated." As a final occurrence HALOT gives Ps 90:3: "crushed matter = dust = ? land of the dead (see Gen 3:19)."[185] Ps 90:3 reads:

> You turn humankind back to dust (עַד־דַּכָּא)
> "and" say: "Come back, you mortal beings (בְּנֵי־אָדָם)."

In the case of v. 10aα, this would mean: "His 'crushing' [i.e., the crushing of the Servant] pleased Yahweh." That is, Yahweh decided that the Servant should once more become dust, which is the general fate of human beings after the Fall, according to Gen 3:19. And—in accord with Psalm 90—Moses is a human being, and remains so! דַּכָּא is a strange word for "dust," but for that very reason it is particularly well adapted as a signal pointing to the reference text, Psalm 90,[186] which (as will emerge) is helpful for an understanding of the following text. Several catchwords are common to both texts, but above all the heading to Psalm 90 runs: "A prayer of Moses, the man of God" (תְּפִלָּה לְמֹשֶׁה אִישׁ־הָאֱלֹהִים). The death and burial of the Servant Moses have been reported and are now interpreted with the help of this psalm.

It is a fact that the Servant of God has his grave in an

---

the purpose of official business, such as the collection of taxes and payments in kind, at the orders of Sanballat or the Persian authorities."

179 On the textual variants and the attempts to explain them see esp. North, 231–32; and B. Janowski, "Er trug unsere Sünden. Jesaja 53 und die Dramatik der Stellvertretung," in *Gottes Gegenwart in Israel* (1993) 317–18, n. 37 (with lit.).

180 Cf. Job 3:1-26 and his answers to his friends. The connection between DtIsa and Job has been stressed particularly by R. H. Pfeiffer, *Introduction to the OT* (1948) 462, 467–69.

181 According to MT, the form הֶחֱלִי is 3d person masc.

sing. perfect *Hiphil* from the root חלה: "he made him sick." LXX (καθαρίσαι αὐτὸν τῆς πληγῆς) already probably presupposes הֶחֳלִי, "the sickness"; see J. Ziegler, *Untersuchungen zur Septuaginta des Buches Isaias* (1934) 24–25.

182 F. Stolz, "חלה *ḥlh* to be sick," *TLOT* 1:426 [*THAT* 1:569].

183 North, 231.

184 K. Elliger, *Deuterojesaja in seinem Verhältnis zu Tritojesaja* (1933); also his "Jes 53:10: alte crux—neuer Vorschlag," *MIOF* 15 (1969) 228–33.

185 *HALOT* 1:221 [*HALAT* 1:212].

186 *BHK* still proposes in the textual apparatus to

"unclean" land. But the "becoming dust" and the "profanation of the Servant" were Yahweh's will and took place with his consent. Human beings alone could not bring this about. That is the interpretation of his fate, and "the many's" new insight.

■ **10aβ-γ** Whereas v. 10aα is related to the declaration about the burial (which has been mentioned immediately before), v. 10aβ names the presupposition for the promises that follow in v. 10aγ. This as yet says nothing about the temporal relation of events, seen in absolute terms. The phrase "it pleased Yahweh . . ." could also implicitly preface the word "if" (אִם). The chiastically inverted "But it had pleased Yahweh (וַיהוה חָפֵץ)"—"and Yahweh's good pleasure/cause . . ." (וְחֵפֶץ יהוה) frames this verse in any case, in a similar way to the double "he will not open his mouth" in v. 7. But why is there a condition (אִם) as premise for the blessing conferred on the Servant, the blessing whose content is descendants and a long life?

The difficulties of the text suggest that here again brief formulas are being used. But since we may assume that references are again being made to events in the life of the Servant of God, Moses (and to texts relating to those events), the search is not entirely hopeless. Are there any texts according to which Moses offers his life in pledge? (For the moment we shall leave to one side the interpretation "guilt offering.")

What comes into question is again Exodus 32, the story of the golden calf. Here 32:30-35 records Moses' petition: "Alas, this people has sinned a great sin (חֲטָאָה גְדֹלָה); they have made for themselves a god of gold. But now, if (אִם) you will only forgive their sin <it is well>—but if not (וְאִם־אַיִן), blot me out of the book that you have written" (vv. 31b-32). Here there is a double condition for the people's survival. Moses offers to take upon himself the consequences of the "great sin," on behalf of the people.[187] To be blotted out of "the book of life"—the list of citizens of heaven—means that his death

will be final.[188] The question is whether DtIsa's non-naming of the name of Moses in speaking about the Servant is also connected with this event on Sinai.

For an understanding of the present text, however, the version of the golden calf story transmitted by Deuteronomy (9:7-15) should also be taken into account. There it is the people, Israel, whose name will be blotted out (הָעָם הַזֶּה, v. 13). Moses is given the promise (v. 14): "I will make of you a more powerful and numerous nation than they" (לְגוֹי־עָצוּם וָרָב ; comp. Exod 1:9; Mic 4:3). That fits in with the promise given to the Servant in the DtIsa text—the promise of "seed/descendants." It is also worth noting that in the promise to Moses Deut 9:14 talks about גּוֹי (*gôy*),[189] which is the word normally used for foreign peoples. Finally, Isa 53:12 goes on to talk about "the powerful" (in numbers) (עֲצוּמִים). On the basis of Exodus 32 and Deuteronomy 9, we can say that Moses offered his life, taking upon himself the consequences of the "great sin" of the deviation into idolatry. In Isaiah 53 this act is related to the Servant. Since he bore the consequences, he will also receive the promise. The time is the past time of the Servant's life.

One of the text's subtleties must still be touched upon. As it stands the text reads: "If 'his life' (נַפְשׁוֹ) makes an offering for guilt." The active subject is accordingly "the *nepeš*." The emendation: "If he pledges (יָשִׂים) his life" (i.e., replacing the feminine imperfect form by the masculine imperfect תָּשִׂים) is too rash an intervention.[190] For the text leaves the matter open: is נַפְשׁוֹ a stressed reflexive ("himself") or does it mean "his life," so that here "his soul" could even be imagined as itself acting, independent of the part of the person that has become dust, according to the beginning of the verse.[191] The problem will have to be considered once more in v. 11a.

Psalm 90: "3b-b prb l (וַ)תֹּאמֶר דַּכָּא)." This would correspond precisely to the text of Isa 53:10! For the discussion about Psalm 90 see now T. Krüger, "Psalm 90 und die Vergänglichkeit des Menschen," *Bib* 75 (1994) 191–219.

187 Exod 32:35 talks about the stroke (וַיִּגֹּף) inflicted by Yahweh on the people.

188 Cf. Isa 4:3; Mal 3:16; Ps 69:29 (28); Dan 12:1; Luke 10:20; Heb 12:23; Rev 3:5; 13:8; 17:8; 20:12; 21:27;

see O. Eissfeldt, *Der Beutel der Lebendigen*, BVSAW.PH 105/6 (1960).

189 Also in the promise given to Abraham in Gen 12:2 that he will become "a great people" (לְגוֹי גָּדוֹל)!

190 Thus, e.g., RSV, which thereby corresponds to the Vulgate; see North, 232 on this passage.

191 C. Westermann, "נֶפֶשׁ *nepeš* soul," *TLOT* 2:743–59 [*THAT* 2:71–96] (with lit.).

The text can be understood without its being necessary to enter into the catchword "guilt offering" (אָשָׁם).[192] In this verse the catchword belongs to the interpretive elements; it serves an understanding of the Servant's death. Once the background in the Moses tradition is perceived, the whole connotation of אָשָׁם as R. Knierim formulates it[193] fits in very well: "It means an obligation resulting from a guilt incurred, the duty imposed by guilt, the obligation arising from guilt, being obligated by guilt or liability." Through his offer, Moses has made himself "liable" toward his God for the guilt of his people. In this situation he puts himself on their side, acting in solidarity with them to the uttermost, even though he himself is not guilty. The Servant has thus put his life in pledge so that the guilt might be "paid off."[194] A legal interpretation of this kind is consistent with the rest of the text.

But it is impossible to overlook the fact that אָשָׁם as "guilt offering" is a technical term for a special form of sacrifice. This is at least true for the postexilic period with which we have to do in DtIsa. Lev 5:14-26 (5:14–6:7) gathers together a whole number of regulations about guilt offerings.[195]

The sacrifice has to do with "trespass in matters of offerings," for example (5:14-16), or with restitution in the case of offenses against property (5:20-26 [6:1-7]). Lev 5:19 sums the matter up in the formula: "It is a guilt offering; you have incurred guilt before Yahweh." A priest makes the "atonement" (5:16, 18, 26 [6:7]). The sacrificial laws in Lev 7:1-7 stress that the guilt offering is particularly sacred.[196]

The priest makes the sacrifice on the altar in the form of a "burnt offering" (7:5). This is to "become his property" (לוֹ יִהְיֶה לַכֹּהֵן, 7:8). If these sacrificial regulations alone are taken into account, there could be no greater contrast. The Servant Moses is not a priest. He sacrifices himself, not a ram (Lev 5:15, 18) or any other animal.[197] It is not a burnt offering.

But above all: if Yahweh himself has profaned the Servant, then he is no longer "holy." This suggests that the present text is arguing against the theory and practice of guilt offerings. It is therefore in line with Isa 43:22-25 and 52:5.[198] In his work DtIsa makes no mention at all of the temple cult and its sacrifices at the restitution of Zion/Jerusalem; and this omission is too striking to be fortuitous. Another point worth considering is how far the polemic against blood sacrifice and burnt offerings was a feature of the discussion during the Persian period. In DtIsa it is only in this one important passage that a sacrificial term is definitely used. But the—true—guilt offering is the Servant Moses.[199] Was that also viewed as a model?

The interpretation in v. 10 allows the life of the Servant to be understood in a new way. But this is one

---

192 See D. Kellermann, "אָשָׁם ʾāshām," TDOT 1:429–37 with lit. [ThWAT 1:463–72]; on 53:10 see 435 [470]; see further R. Rendtorff, Studien zur Geschichte des Opfers im Alten Israel (1967).

193 R. Knierim, "אָשָׁם ʾāšām guilt," TLOT 1:191–95, esp. 193 [THAT 1:251–57, esp. 254].

194 For detail see here B. Janowski, "Er trug unsere Sünden. Jesaja 53 und die Dramatik der Stellvertretung," in Gottes Gegenwart in Israel (1993) 303–26, n. 37.

195 On the texts see K. Elliger, Leviticus (1966), as well as E. Gerstenberger, Leviticus (1996) [Das dritte Buch Mose/Leviticus (1993)].

196 הָאָשָׁם קֹדֶשׁ קָדָשִׁים הוּא, 7:1; cf. v. 6.

197 See K. Koch, "עָוֹן ʿāwōn," ThWAT 5:1160–77, esp. 1174: "In the case of severe transgressions in general, ḥaṭṭāʾt—and/or ʾāšām—animals are the efficacious means of removing ʿāwōn, disaster, from human beings and of expiating it through the death of an animal that is sent to its death in their stead (Lev 5:1-6, 17-19). Where kpr (כפר) is validly performed, the burden of an ʿāwōn is eliminated for ever (Lev 10:17)."

198 See above on these passages.

199 See D. Kellermann, "אָשָׁם ʾāshām," TDOT 1:429–37 [ThWAT 1:463–72], esp. 435 [470]): "The experiences that are intensified in times of great catastrophe, when sins and guilt severely strain the relationship between God and man, explain why the Jews in the postexilic period had such a lively interest in thinking about and reflecting on means of expiating sin. The literary remains from this period in the Priestly Code reveal the fervor with which the movement to guilt-offerings and sin-offerings was carried out." This is undoubtedly correct, but DtIsa also shows in what fundamental categories this discussion was carried on, with all its pros and cons. DtIsa stands for a noncultic solution, and is hence in the prophetic tradition.

reason for the difficulty of the time sequence in the text. The verse begins with a declaration about the death of the Servant. Moses died before the entry into "the promised land" because of the murmuring of his people. From this point the text goes back in time, in a kind of flashback. On Sinai-Horeb, because of the sin of the golden calf, Moses puts his life in pledge to save Israel. This whole stretch of time—the period in the desert—is recapitulated once more. The two events, Sinai-Horeb and Nebo-Pisgah, belong closely together. They are orientation points in Moses' life. Seen from the standpoint of Sinai-Horeb, the blessing, with its promise of descendants and long life, lies in the future.

"He will see seed/descendants." The promise of descendants is one of the fundamental elements in the stories about the patriarchs and matriarchs.[200] In the Moses tradition the promise is explicitly recalled in Moses' intercessory prayer when the people are threatened with annihilation because of the golden calf (Exod 32:13). The promise that follows Moses' offer to give his life for the people (32:32)—his "guilt offering," according to the interpretation in the present DtIsa text—renews the promise given to earlier generations. Explicitly, and in a form found only here,[201] this promise runs: "To your seed/descendants I will give it [the land]" (לְזַרְעֲךָ אֶתְּנֶנָּה; Exod 33:1).

This very same sentence, with its promise, is reiterated at Moses' death (Deut 34:4a). The Deuteronomy text goes on (34:4b-5): "I [Yahweh] have let you see it with your eyes, but you shall not cross over there. Then Moses, the servant of Yahweh, died there."

At this point DtIsa has left out the reference to the land and its part in the promise. The "seeing" therefore no longer refers to the land; it refers to Moses' descendants. But at the same time it is not said that these descendants will be the Servant's descendants in the physical sense. Already in the Exodus text, as then above all in Deuteronomy, the identity of "your seed" is left open. To put it concisely, the seed of Abraham, Isaac and Jacob is Moses' seed too. Deuteronomy stresses the unity of God's people in past, present and future.[202] DtIsa is concerned with the question: who belongs to the Servant's people? Is Yahweh's word not "sown" too?[203] This "seed" scattered by Moses continues to increase, even after his death.

For Moses, Sinai-Horeb and Nebo-Pisgah are connected in spatial terms by way of Exodus 32 and Deuteronomy 34. In the Servant, DtIsa links *the times*. The promise of long life stands in the same tension as the promise of "descendants." Seen from Sinai-Horeb, the life of Moses was future. According to Deut 34:7 he died at the age of 120. Against the background of Ps 90:10, it is clear that this was a great age: "The days of our years (יְמֵי־שְׁנוֹתֵינוּ), in them[204] (they are) seventy years, or eighty years at most." According to Ps 90:1 (the heading of the psalm in the English Bible), Moses himself said this. Then 120 years are forty years more than the utmost number—a very long life indeed.

Isa 53:10 establishes that for the Servant "he will . . . live long" (lit.: "He [Yahweh] will make days long" [יַאֲרִיךְ יָמִים]). The promise, and with it the blessing, had been fulfilled in him himself. That long life is a continuing hope if the divine commandments are fulfilled is already stated by the Decalogue (Exod 20:12; Deut 5:16), but elsewhere too, and above all by the Moses of Deuteronomy.[205]

In Isa 53:10a the "if" (אִם) clause is followed by two subordinate clauses or statements in the preformative conjugation with a future sense. In both cases it has proved useful to interpret them in the context of Moses'

---

200 Gen 12:7; 15:7, 13, 18; 16:10; 17:5-6, 16; 21:13; 24:7; 26:3-5; 28:13; see H. D. Preuss, "זָרַע zāraʿ," *TDOT* 4:143-62, with lit. [*ThWAT* 2:663-86]; also J. Scharbert, *Solidarität in Segen und Fluch im Alten Israel und in seiner Umwelt* (1958).

201 See H. D. Preuss, *TDOT* 4:154 [*ThWAT* 2:673]; cf. Gen 15:7.

202 See, e.g., Deut 5:3; 6:3; 26:9, 15; 27:3; 29:12-14 (13-15); 30:3, 6, 19; 31:20; cf. G. von Rad, "Das Gottesvolk im Deuteronomium" in his *Gesammelte Studien zum Alten Testament* 2 (1973) 9-108; see also N. Lohfink, "Beobachtungen zur Geschichte des Ausdrucks עַם יהוה," in *Probleme biblischer Theologie.*

FS G. von Rad (1971) 275-305.

203 Cf. Isa 55:10-11, and as a countertype, 40:24.

204 A whole series of emendations have been proposed (see *BHS* and the commentaries). But the very mention of "days" in Isa 53:10 warns us against too hasty and simplistic a solution. A discussion of the understanding of time, an understanding that may well seem alien to us, is really a first requirement.

205 Cf. Deut 4:26, 40; 4:33; 6:2; 11:9; 17:20; 22:7; 25:15; 30:18; 32:47.

life from Sinai until his death. The same approach should therefore be tried out in the case of the third statement in this verse too: "Through his hand it will succeed/have success" (בְּיָדוֹ יִצְלָח). When the people set out from Sinai, according to Num 10:11-36, the account says (v. 13): "They set out for the first time at the command of Yahweh through the hand of Moses" (עַל־פִּי יהוה בְּיַד־מֹשֶׁה). This is a legitimate departure, in contrast to the one in Num 14:40. There the people want to go up to the land on their own initiative. Moses warns them: "You transgress the command of Yahweh. That will not succeed." Here the same verb "succeed/have success" (צלח)[206] is used as in the verse we are considering, Isa 53:10. Success or nonsuccess depends on conformity with the will of God, and on his support. In this theological approach Num 10:13 and the present text agree. The approach acquires its rigor, or sting, once it is seen in the context of the expectations of happiness cherished in DtIsa's time. Confidence must not rest on good fortune and human achievement.[207] That is why the text puts the free decision (חפץ) of Yahweh ahead of the "success." At the beginning of the verse this decision meant the "willing" of disaster, now it means "the joy, the pleasure" over salvation. The chiasmus in the text (וְחֵפֶץ יהוה//וַיהוה חָפֵץ) is therefore more than just an external stylistic device.

The text takes up the summary formulation of the "first" (בָּרִאשֹׁנָה) departure in Num 10:13; but the same formulation fits the second departure too—the departure from exile. DtIsa continually talks about the things that happen as the first and the later things. It is scriptural proof in the deeper sense that links the first exodus with the second.[208] This means that the Servant Moses is not merely a figure belonging to the past. This final statement is a worthy conclusion to the dispute about the earthly life of the Servant in vv. 2-10, in which the account of what could be seen was contrasted with its interpretation. Two groups of witnesses have spoken in the heavenly court of justice. Expectation is therefore wholly directed toward the verdict that God himself will pronounce.

53:11
Judgment Pronounced by the Judge: Yahweh's Salvific Oracle for His Servant

"Because of the anguish of his soul he shall see <light> . . ." (53:11)

53:12
Departure of the Servant of God (Exit) and His New Task

"He was the one who bore the transgressions of many, and he will intercede for their sins" (53:12)

For an understanding of these verses it is important to remember that this is still the same scene as in 52:13-15. Its subject is the rehabilitation of the Servant in a heavenly trial. In 52:13 he is called "my Servant," and in 53:11 the endorsment is pronounced: "the just one, my Servant." He is this in truth: that is the real divine verdict. Further statements allow the setting to emerge. This is the place of God's presence, the heavenly throne room, where the Servant has been received.

"He shall see. . . ." Here the object is actually missing. But we should probably follow 1QIsa[a,b] and add "light" (אוֹר). LXX presupposes a corresponding text.[209] MT gives the impression that a kind of dogmatic correction has been made, as it was in v. 10a.[210] If he can see the "light," he has been judged worthy to enter into the immediate presence of God; he has been received into the company of the heavenly beings.

---

206 See *HALOT*, s.v.; M. Sæbø, "צלח *ṣlḥ* to succeed," *TLOT* 3:1077–80 [*THAT* 2:551–56]; also E. Puech, "Sur la racine *slḥ* en hébreu et en araméen," *Sem* 21 (1971) 5–19. Important for an understanding of the text is the occurrence of the root in Ps 1:3; Dan 8:12, 24-25; 11:27, 36; 3:30 (Aram.) and Neh 1:11; 2:20; cf. Isa 48:15; 54:17; 55:11.

207 See K. Baltzer, "The Polemic against the Gods and Its Relevance for Second Isaiah's Conception of the New Jerusalem," in *Second Temple Studies* (1994) 52–59 ["Stadt-Tyche oder Zion/Jerusalem? Die Auseinandersetzung mit den Göttern der Zeit bei Deuterojesaja," in *Alttestamentlicher Glaube und Biblische Theologie. FS H. D. Preuss* (1992) 114–19].

208 Cf. the interpretation in Mark 1:1-8.

209 See G. R. Driver, "Isaiah 52,13–53,12: the Servant of the Lord," in *In Memoriam P. Kahle* (1968) 90–105, esp. 97–98 (with lit.).

210 See D. Barthélemy, "Le grand rouleau d'Isaïe trouvé près de la Mer Morte," *RB* 57 (1950) 530–49, esp. 547. Also H. Haag, "Ebed-Jahwe Forschung 1948–1958," *BZ* n.s. 3 (1959) 174–204, esp. 180–81. Haag cites I. L. Seeligmann, *Tarbiz* 27 (1957/58) 127–41, who conversely assumes a correction in the

The text can best be illustrated by later texts such as *1 Enoch* 39:3-14; 92:3-5; and 108:10-15.[211] *1 Enoch* 92:3-4 runs:

> And the righteous one shall arise from sleep,
> [Shall arise] and walk in the paths of righteousness,
> And all his path and conversation shall be in eternal goodness and grace.
> He will be gracious to the righteous and give him eternal uprightness,
> And He will give him power so that he shall be (endowed) with goodness and righteousness,
> And he *shall walk in eternal light*.[212]

The individual *topoi* are certainly older than *1 Enoch*, however. Thus for Moses and the elders to ascend Mount Sinai is an essential feature of the meal of the covenant, according to Exod 24:9-11: "And when they had beheld God they ate and drank" (24:11). Other elements in the tradition acquire their special significance at a later period.[213]

But it should be noted that the very fact that basic elements of a throne scene can be reconstructed, in the present verses of DtIsa, makes the differences all the more striking. An unfavorable and a favorable verdict is frequently associated with a judicial hearing in the framework of a throne scene: the unjust are punished and the just rewarded. In the present text, Isa 52:13—53:12, there is no question of punishment. The favorable verdict on the Servant actually has as its purpose the "making righteous" of the many. They are to recognize their error (52:15). Here the proceedings include an element drawn from wisdom tradition, namely, the appeal. It appeals for understanding.[214] This is not a final judgment. There is still a chance.

Verses 11-12 are a divine speech throughout. In clos-ing, v. 10 names the name of Yahweh, for the fourth time in the fourth Servant text. The admission to the divine presence in v. 11 can be pronounced only by Yahweh himself.

The whole of the Servant's life as it has been recollected in vv. 2-10 is characterized by a single word: עָמָל (ʿāmāl, "trouble" or "anguish," v. 11). This corresponds to what Psalm 90 says about human life in general—that it means trouble and woe (עָמָל וָאָוֶן, v. 10; cf. v. 15).[215] In Isa 53:11 the phrase is often translated "because of (מִן) the anguish (trouble) of his soul." But it is more probable that מִן is used in its temporal sense: "after the trouble."[216] The catchword "his life" (נַפְשׁוֹ) in v. 11 is taken up from v. 10.

Further in our Dt.-Isaianic v. 11, the phrase "see and be satisfied" (in the sense of being sated or filled) announces the meal as an expression of the divine presence. Here the two statements can be given a transferred or abstract sense in a number of ways. We find this transference in prayers of lament and thanksgiving particularly. Again Psalm 90 offers an example: "Have compassion on your servants and satisfy us in the morning with your steadfast love (חַסְדֶּךָ)" (vv. 13b-14a), "Let your work be be manifested over your servants, your glory by their children" (v. 16).

In the present v. 11, the question is whether "satisfy" stands on its own as an absolute, or whether it belongs to the following phrase "through his knowledge" (בְּדַעְתּוֹ). The other possibility, again, is to see "through his knowledge" as an instrumental phrase governing the following "he will make just." Both options have been discussed.[217] I would assume that no final choice between the two is

---

Qumran text. For "to see light" Haag points particularly to Job 3:20; Pss 36:10 (9); 56:14 (13) (181 n. 26).

211 See here the still important study by G. W. E. Nickelsburg, *Resurrection, Immortality, and Eternal Life in Intertestamental Judaism* (1972).

212 Translation in R. H. Charles, *Apocrypha and Pseudepigrapha of the OT* 2 (1913) 261.

213 Cf. Dan 12:9; Wis 2:12-24; 5:1-6; 1QS 2.2-4; 1QSb 4.24-28; 1QH 4.21-25.

214 This is particularly clear in the interpretation of the text in the book of Wisdom; see D. Georgi, *Weisheit Salomos* (1980), esp. on Wisdom 2 and 5. See also M. J. Suggs, "Wisdom of Solomon 2:10–5: A Homily Based on the Fourth Servant Song," *JBL* 76 (1957) 26–33; further U. Schwenk-Bressler, *Sapientia*

Salomonis als ein Beispiel frühjüdischer Textauslegung (1993).

215 In Qohelet this is an important theme. Cf. Qoh 2:24; 3:13; 5:18 and other texts; see T. Krüger, "Theologische Gegenwartsdeutung im Kohelet-Buch" (1991).

216 See Beuken, 231 on this passage.

217 Aquila, Symmachus and Theodotion link the phrase with the previous "satisfy"; see North, 233, 244 on the text. Various emendations have also been proposed. By way of the accents, the MT establishes a link with the following phrase. 1QIsaᵃ reads unequivocally: "And (ו) through his knowledge." Unfortunately this is no longer registered in *BHS*, as it was earlier in *BHK*.

intended. At all events, the statement "through his [the Servant's] knowledge" (or experience) is strongly emphasized. It is twice implicit in this divine speech. The exalted Servant will receive the fulfillment of his hope. He is permitted to experience the presence of his God, and in such a way that he may "have his fill" of it.[218] This is his own individual knowledge. On the other hand, through "his knowledge" the Servant makes "the many" just. But what *is* "his knowledge" (דַּעְתּוֹ) in this context?

The fourth Servant text is heralded in 40:14:[219] "He will let him know (יוֹדִיעֶנּוּ) a way of understanding." Here whether "he" is the Servant or Yahweh himself is left open. It is a veiled revelation. This is taken up in 52:15. After this introduction "the many peoples . . . will have seen . . . and understood." What has been told them afresh is the subject of the hearing in 53:1-10: the life and death of Moses, the era of the wanderings in the desert, from the exodus until the arrival in the promised land, salvation and disaster, as the interpretation has explained. The result is the perception or knowledge that makes "many" just and that is mediated through "him."

The third and fourth Servant texts are linked by the fact that both have to do with the Moses of Deuteronomy. The third text is heralded in 40:14: "And he taught him knowledge (understanding)" (וַיְלַמְּדֵהוּ דַעַת). 50:4 refers to Deuteronomy as Moses' "teaching." Comparable is the whole scope of the term ידע: "perceive, experience, discern, learn, understand, know."[220] In this way too the fourth Servant text is portraying the Moses of Deuteronomy, as a glance at the concordance shows: "Today you shall know and take to heart that Yahweh is God; there is no other" (Deut 4:39); "You shall know that Yahweh your God alone is God, the faithful God, who keeps the covenant and faithfulness to those who love him and keep his commandments" (Deut 7:9).[221]

For the prophet Hosea, "knowledge of God" (דַּעַת אֱלֹהִים) comprehends both the divine history and the divine law for God's people.[222] The term can be employed critically toward priests and cultic prophets, and toward the whole people too. For DtIsa, "his knowledge" means the Servant's own knowledge, and thereby also the knowledge given to the Servant by his Lord ("my servant," עַבְדִּי).

It is the same approach as in the first Servant text, where in 42:4 "his law" (תּוֹרָתוֹ) is, as Moses' Torah, God's law.[223] The two texts are further linked by the fact that according to 42:4 "the islands" wait for "his law," whereas here "his knowledge (understanding)" makes the many just. In both cases foreigners are surely included. It is a supplicating testimony that reaches beyond the frontiers of Israel and is directed to sympathizers.

Verse 4 already stated that the Servant bore (סְבָלָם) the miseries of his people. But here v. 11 says that he "*will* (again and again) bear the transgressions" (יִסְבֹּל, preformative conjugation)! In the temporal sense, these statements in vv. 11 and 12 point to the future. This results in difficulty for the interpretation, but it probably has to do with the Servant's "exaltation." This will have to be discussed further in connection with the close in v. 12.

■ **12** The verse begins with a puzzle, and this is probably intentional. A whole series of questions require an answer, for example, how can the Servant give a share (חֵלֶק) if, being dead, he is in the heavenly sphere? As far as Moses is concerned the facts are clear. According to Numbers 26 (esp. vv. 1-4) he was commissioned to take a census of the Israelites: "To these the land shall be apportioned[224] according to the number of names. To a large tribe you shall give a large inheritance (לָרַב תַּרְבֶּה נַחֲלָתוֹ)" (Num 26:53-56).

Again Deuteronomy 9 should be drawn upon in

---

218 Cf. Exod 33:12-23, esp. Moses' plea: "Show me your glory, I pray!" (v. 18).

219 See K. Baltzer, "Jes. 40,13-14—ein Schlüssel zur Einheit Deutero-Jesajas?" in *BN* 37, *FS V. Hamp* (1987) 7–10.

220 See *HALOT*.

221 Cf. Deut 8:5-6; 9:3-6.

222 See H. W. Wolff, "'Wissen um Gott' bei Hosea als Urform von Theologie," in his *Gesammelte Studien zum Alten Testament* (2d ed. 1973) 182–205. Also McKenzie, 136; cf. Hos 4:1; 6:6; further 2:10-15 (8-

13); 4:6; 5:4; 8:1-3; 10:12; 11:3; 13:4-6.

223 Cf. N. Lohfink, "Das Deuteronomium. Jahwegesetz oder Mosegesetz?" *ThPh* 65 (1990) 387–91.

224 The MT (Num 26:53) reads תֵּחָלֵק, *Niphal* imperfect of חלק II, "to be distributed." It is proposed in the apparatus of *BHS* that the word be pointed as *Piel* imperfect, תְּחַלֵּק, "distribute, apportion." This would accord with the sense (cf. Num 26:54a) and with the stem in Isa 53:12.

addition. There Moses is promised: "I will make of you a nation more powerful, mightier, and more numerous (לְגוֹי־עָצוּם וָרָב) than they" (Deut 9:14). The story goes on to tell of Moses' intercession for the people and the land (נַחֲלָה, Deut 9:26, 29). Finally, according to Deut 31:7-8, Joshua, as Moses' successor, is supposed to "distribute" (תַּנְחִילֶנָּה) the land. It is the catchwords "give a share," "many," and "more powerful" that are striking in the texts mentioned, but also the theme of the apportioning of the land on the first entry. At that time the distribution was legitimated by Moses, in accordance with God's charge.

But what does "land, heritage" now mean for DtIsa? I suspect that the divine saying in v. 12a already forges the link with the following chap. 54. 54:17 is the final sentence in this scene, before the epilogue in chap. 55: "This is the heritage of the servants of Yahweh (נַחֲלַת עַבְדֵי יהוה) and their righteousness from me, saying of Yahweh." Here the heritage is the previous, and yet prevenient, promise of peace for Zion/Jerusalem. It could actually be the motto for the whole of DtIsa's text.

This would mean that in the present text the connection between the Moses and the Zion traditions is again established. It is a matter of the legacy of the Servant of God, Moses. But this now brings us up against a further difficulty in the text that may be summed up under the catchword "share the spoil" (חלק שָׁלָל). That is a somewhat different kind of "distribution." The verse plays on the double חלק. "Spoil" clearly belongs to the language of war.[225] But in DtIsa there is a tendency to suppress warlike elements. Thus Yahweh's triumphal procession in 40:9-11 is a shepherd's triumph, and is entirely peaceful. If the saying in 53:12a is translated in the sense that Luther, for example, gave it, the warlike tone is clear: "Therefore will I give him the many as spoil and he shall have strong men as booty."

But this translation is by no means indisputably correct. Perhaps it is just here that the "offense" of the text is to be found—that the Servant is not warlike at all. A translation that would fit the context could run roughly as follows: "Therefore I will give him a share among [or 'of'] the many, and with the powerful [in number][226] he will share spoil."[227] This sounds somewhat like a riddle, but it makes sense if the second half of the verse also refers to the restoration of Zion/Jerusalem, which follows in chap. 54. At the same time, the catchword "spoil" in part one of the book of Isaiah should be remembered here. There the prophet's son bears the strange name "Speed-*spoil*-hasten-plunder" (Isa 8:1-14).[228] In Isa 9:2 (3) the division of spoil is associated with rejoicing. According to 10:6, Assyria was charged "to take spoil and seize plunder" from Judah-Jerusalem. In its arrogance, Assyria exceeded its commission. According to 33:1-6, Zion turns to Yahweh in its distress over "the spoil-gatherers" (v. 4). If Isa 2:1-5 is read in this light,[229] it evidently describes the turn of events that brings salvation to Judah-Jerusalem. Instead of the onslaught of foreign armies there is a pilgrimage to the temple mount, to which "all the nations (כָּל־הַגּוֹיִם) stream" and "many peoples (עַמִּים רַבִּים) come" (vv. 2-3):[230] "For out of Zion shall go forth the law (תּוֹרָה), and Yahweh's word from Jerusalem." According to the sense of the present text, 53:12, that could be paraphrased as: this is the new "spoil," which the Servant Moses shares with many peoples.

But the promise in Isa 2:4, above all, is a reminder of "spoil" in the literal sense: "They shall beat their swords into plowshares and their spears into pruning hooks." Weapons are no longer a danger for Zion/Jerusalem. The smiths have something more important to do! In

---

225 See, e.g., Deut 2:35; 3:7; 13:17 (16); 20:14; Josh 7:21; 8:2, 27; 11:14; 2 Sam 12:30. For "dividing the spoil": Gen 49:27; Exod 15:9; Josh 22:8; Zech 14:1; Ps 68:13 (12); Prov 16:19; cf. H. J. Stoebe, "Raub und Beute" (1967) 340–54; H. Ringgren, "בזז *bzz* בַּז, שלל, שָׁלָל," *TDOT* 2:66–68 [*ThWAT* 1:585–88].

226 For the translation of עָצוּם as "powerful" cf. the different possibilities presented in *HALOT*: "(a) powerful in number (parallel with רַב) . . . , (b) powerful in strength" (*HALOT* 2:868 [*HALAT* 3:821]; see also on עצם I).

227 See J. W. Olley's careful study, "'The Many': How Is Isa 53:12a to Be Understood?" *Bib* 68 (1987) 330–56

(with a research report and lit.); see esp. 348 and 355. Cf. also E. Kutsch, *Sein Leiden und Tod–unser Heil, BibS(N)* 52 (1967) 37–38; H.-J. Hermisson, "Der Lohn des Knechtes," in *Die Botschaft und die Boten. FS H. W. Wolff* (1981) 269–87, esp. 284–87; also his "Israel und der Gottesknecht bei Deuterojesaja," *ZThK* 79 (1982) 1–24, esp. 21–24.

228 See H. Wildberger, *Isaiah 1–12* (1991) on these texts [*Jesaja 1–12* (2d ed. 1980)].

229 See K. Baltzer, E. Brandenburger and F. Merkel, "Jesaja 2,1-5 (Epiphanias)," *GPM* 58 (1969) 70–75.

230 The parallel text in Mic 4:1-5 should be compared in considering the terminology "many peoples"

this light Yahweh's promise at the end of chap. 54 is comprehensible: "I myself have created the smith. . . . No devices (weapon) formed against you will succeed" (vv. 16-17). It is the covenant of peace (54:10) that is promised.

The divine saying in 53:12 shows in a nutshell the link between the Moses and the Zion traditions. It is both claim and promise. In form it resembles an oracle, enigmatic yet at the same time disclosing the future. As a divine saying it comprehends past, present and future. It provokes the question about the fulfillment of the divine word: how and when will it be fulfilled?

The reason and justification for the divine saying is once again said to be the Servant's death and his readiness to be numbered among sinners. According to the traditional theology of the OT, this meant that the Servant had betaken himself to the uttermost distance from God. But the divine saying confirms that it is this very thing that means salvation. It is the most extreme paradox of this proclamation.

The final sentence of the fourth Servant text is an ultimate, enduring proclamation of the Servant by his Lord. In order to make the emphasis clear, the phrase can be translated, "as that one (וְהוּא) he bore. . . ." The two parts of the declaration can be understood in different ways, as can be seen from the early versions down to modern commentaries. The MT can be rendered:

> As that one he bore the transgressions of many
> and for the sinners he again and again made intercession.[231]

Since 1QIsaᵃ has shown itself to be a reliable source for this text in particular, I should like to follow that version here too, even if it is the more difficult one:

> As that one he bore the transgressions of many,
> and for their sins he will intercede.

In this latter version it is clear that it is "the many" as a collective that is meant. "Many" (רַבִּים) is used three times in the divine judgment in vv. 11-12. This corresponds to the three parts of the verdict. Twice the word is used with the definite article: ". . . My Servant will make the many just. Therefore I will give him a share with/among the many." At the end there is no definite article; the word embraces a wider circle, not a particular group—but not "all" either. A distinction is made at the beginning in 52:14, 15 between "many" and "many peoples." "Many" and the "multitude" are linked in v. 12, as the Servant's share. Now the text talks only about bearing the transgressions "of many."[232]

It is hence appropriate that in these two verses the most important terms for "sin" should be named once more:[233] "wrongness, guilt" (עָוֹן, v. 11), transgression (חֵטְא, v. 12) and "crime" (פֶּשַׁע; cf. v. 12). Each group of "the many" has its own particular way of breaching the relationship to God. But in each case the life of the community is thereby imperiled. The process of disaster takes its course, unless it is interrupted by forgiving.

In connection with another passage we already established that the phrase "who bears" characterizes the Servant in a special way.[234] Here it is the bearing of transgressions. The verb "bear" (נשׂא) is in the perfect conjugation. It therefore describes a completed act in the past. That fits in well enough with the remembrance of someone who is dead. But then how ought we understand the imperfect preformative conjugation tense of the last verb (יַפְגִּיעַ)?

The Hebrew preformative conjugation can indicate a continuous action—that is, according to the MT, the iterative "he continually intervened"; or it can announce a future event: "he will intervene." The former would be a glance back to the past acts of the Servant, the latter the announcement of a new task. It would not be the first time that DtIsa leaves open both possible interpretations.

(עַמִּים רַבִּים) and "many (foreign) nations" (גּוֹיִם עֲצֻמִים).

231 Contrary to Westermann on this passage (269 [217]): "This does not mean, as some editors imagine, that he made prayers of intercession for them, but that with his life, his suffering and his death, he took their place and underwent their punishment in their stead."

232 See Beuken, 237 on v. 12: "Thus the second divine speech ends with acknowledgment of the Servant: he had to bear in the same way the guilt of the world and that of faithless Israel."

233 See R. Knierim, *Die Hauptbegriffe für Sünde im Alten Testament*, and the corresponding article in *TLOT* [*THAT*]. Cf. the summing up in R. Knierim, "פֶּשַׁע *peša'* crime," *TLOT* 2:1036 [*THAT* 2:493–94]: "The interpretation of *peša'* put forward determines the relation of the word to the other major terms for 'sin.' *hṭ'* means 'to miss the mark.' It passes by the goal. *'wh* (*'āwōn*) means 'to bend, twist.' It contorts the course of things. *pš'* means 'to break (with).' It disengages from a social partner his property. The difference among the terms lies not in different psychologies but in their varied origins."

234 See above on 53:4.

It should also be noted that 1QIsaᵃ clearly uses the *Qal*, not the *Hiphil*, form of the verb. It is true that 53:6 has the *Hiphil*, "to allow something to happen to someone"; but DtIsa loves these fine nuances. According to *HALAT* the *Qal* can mean among other things: "meet someone . . . , fall upon someone . . . , go pleading to someone, press someone. . . ." Finally it has a spatial component: "the border touches. . . ."[235]

In the sense of "approach someone with a plea" it is used for the prophetic function of intercession. This is the case in two highly characteristic passages in the book of Jeremiah. In the framework of the temple speech, the prophet is told by his Lord Yahweh (Jer 7:16): "Do not bother me!" The reason why the intercession is rejected is the cult of foreign gods in the towns of Judah and in Jerusalem. According to Jer 27:18, Jeremiah exhorts his opponents "to approach Yahweh Sabaoth in intercession," so that the remainder of the vessels belonging to Yahweh's house may stay in Jerusalem. But these prophets have no authority.

In the context of DtIsa both themes are relevant. According to 52:11-12, the bearers of Yahweh's vessels are told to "go out." And chap. 54 is concerned with the restoration of Zion/Jerusalem. Jeremiah's threatening oracle has therefore implicitly been revoked.[236] The Servant is permitted to "approach his Lord in intercession," even though the sins of many have still to be perceived and noted. That is a fundamental change. Perhaps there is also a remembrance of what Jeremiah was forced to accept, according to Jer 15:1: "And Yahweh said to me: Though Moses or Samuel were to stand before me, yet I have no heart (אֵין נַפְשִׁי) for this people. Send 'them' out of my sight, and make them go away!"[237] A judgment speech over Jerusalem follows. So when in DtIsa the Servant as Moses is again permitted to act as intercessor, the turn of events is clearly manifest. In this way Moses has a prophetic function. This last statement therefore points to the future. We should also bear in mind the situation where the scene takes place.

The divine saying is pronounced over the exalted Servant. The beginning in 52:13 and the end in 53:12 correspond. Since for the future he will be "beatified" (יַשְׂכִּיל, 52:13), he will also "intercede" (יפגע, 1QIsaᵃ 53:12) before Yahweh.

I believe that this final saying in the Servant text may also contain an implicit stage direction. In order to fulfill his function, the Servant goes into the innermost domain "before Yahweh," who for the spectators is not visible. He must be imagined as an *orans*, a man with arms raised in prayer. As has been mentioned, פגע also has a spatial component, in the sense of "meet, encounter." Here we should remember in addition that it was Moses—not Aaron—who was allowed to enter "the tent of meeting"[238] (אֹהֶל מוֹעֵד). On his final exit, does the Servant enter a tent that in the drama represents the (heavenly) "tent of meeting"?

The sufferings and death of the Servant have thrown his way open. They have not cut him off from God. He becomes someone who can be the advocate for the many, with their sins. He can fulfill this function as one who in God's sight is just, and who is yet in solidarity with human beings. Intercession does not mean that the Lord has to decide in accordance with what the Servant proposes; but he will listen to him. The theme of guilt is not put aside. It is part of human life and human experience—in God's sight too. But the Servant's life has shown how disaster can become salvation, and that gives hope.

The preceding exegesis has proceeded from the assumption that the portrait of the Servant is molded by the Moses tradition. I have attempted to show this even down to points of detail. But at the end we still have to ask yet again why the name of Moses is never pronounced. The Servant's anonymity is also a means of abstraction. He becomes the "type." He is the just person who suffers for the sins of the many. But in the "type" that the role represents, an unmistakable individuality is preserved.

The Servant as model is a call to *imitatio*, for in him

---

235 *HALOT* 3:910 [*HALAT* 3:860–61].

236 Cf. Jer 22:24-30 and Hag 2:23; see K. Baltzer, "Das Ende des Staates Juda und die Messias-Frage," in *Studien zur Theologie der alttestamentlichen Überlieferung. FS G. von Rad* (1961) 33–43, esp. 38.

237 On the text and the translation see W. Rudolph, *Jeremia* (3d ed. 1968); W. L. Holladay, *Jeremiah 1–25* (1986). Holladay (439) points out that apart from

this passage in Jeremiah, Moses is mentioned explicitly only four times in the prophetic books: Isa 63:11, 12; Mic 6:4; Mal 3:22 (4:4).

238 See *HALOT*, s.v. For the significance of the "tent/tabernacle" in the postexilic period, see H. Utzschneider, *Das Heiligtum und das Gesetz. Studien zur Bedeutung der sinaitischen Heiligtumstexte (Ex 25–40; Lev 8–9)* (1988).

exemplary virtues can be perceived: the renunciation of outward renown, the readiness to bear misunderstanding and not to repay evil with evil, the avoidance of violence and deception, intervention for others to the point where life itself is surrendered. These are above all virtues that were seen to be lacking in the rulers of the time—but not in them only. That the special mark of the one who is just in God's eyes should actually be trouble and the experience of suffering—this is the astonishing message for a world that lauds its heroes for very different virtues.

Seen from this aspect, it is not by chance that the Servant can also be understood in a collective sense, even if this was not the original interpretation. It is not a question of hero worship. This is a remembrance that makes hope for one's own life possible.

Finally, the interpretation makes clear why the suffering Servant became in typology a foreshadowing of Jesus Christ. In the language of this text the Christian community could communicate its own experience. To pursue this through all the details of the interpretation's history would be a task of its own.

C. 54:1-17
The (Renewed) Marriage of Zion/Jerusalem

In the third and last scene of Act VI, the processional exit (52:11-12) and the legal dispute about the Servant of

God and his memorial (52:13—53:12) are followed by the "sacred marriage." Yahweh associates himself once more with his "spouse." Her name is no longer mentioned; it is replaced by the various epithets.[239] The context makes clear, however, that it is initially Zion/Jerusalem who is meant. Personified as a female, she was already the main character in Act V. There her investiture and enthronement were presented in 52:1-6. In 52:7 the message "as king reigns your God" was passed on to Zion, together with the announcement of Yahweh's return (52:8). What is still to come is the crowning of the personified city. That is the climax of the scene in 54:11-14a. These verses describe the mural crown, with its adornment of precious stones.[240]

The omission of the name is not, in my view, fortuitous. It permits a greater degree of abstraction and hence general applicability. The "spouse" to whom Yahweh joins himself is Zion/Jerusalem, and at the same time the representation of Israel as a whole. The reception of early traditions and their association with the tradition about Zion once more makes this identification possible. The association was already present in 51:1-2, through Abraham and Sarah. In 54:1 the general theme of the matriarch's barrenness can be detected. The sociomorpheme of the marriage between Yahweh and Israel has its place in the prophetic proclamation[241]—for us most readily available in the work of Hosea,[242] but

---

239 According to Grimm and Dittert, *Deuterojesaja: Deutung, Wirkung, Gegenwart–Ein Kommentar zu Jesaja 40–55* (1990), 436, there are seven in all: "barren" (v. 1), "left desolate" (v. 1), "forsaken" (v. 6), "afflicted in spirit" (v. 6), "wretched, storm-tossed, not comforted" (v. 11).

240 See K. Baltzer, "The Polemic against the Gods and its Relevance for Second Isaiah's Conception of the New Jerusalem," in T. C. Eskenazi and K. H. Richards, eds., *Second Temple Studies*, 2 (1994) 43–50 ["Stadt-Tyche oder Zion-Jerusalem? Die Auseinandersetzung mit den Göttern der Zeit bei Deuterojesaja," in *Alttestamentlicher Glaube und Biblische Theologie: FS H. D. Preuß* (1992) 114–19].

241 G. Hall, "Origin of the Marriage Metaphor," *HS* 23 (1982) 161–71; also O. H. Steck, "Zion als Gelände und Gestalt. Überlegungen zur Wahrnehmung Jerusalems als Stadt und Frau im Alten Testament," *ZThK* 86 (1989) 261–81 (with lit.).

242 See H. W. Wolff, *Hosea* (1974) [*Hosea* (3d ed. 1976)] on Hosea 1–3, esp. 14–16 [13–15]; Jörg Jeremias, *Der Prophet Hosea* (1983) on Hosea 1–3; H. Utz-

schneider, *Hosea: Prophet vor dem Ende* (1980). In describing Hosea 1–3, Utzschneider introduces the interesting term "figural speech" (54–58), following E. Auerbach, "Figura," in his *Gesammelte Aufsätze zur Romanischen Philologie* (1967) 55–92. Auerbach defines it as follows: "'*Figura*' is something real, historical, that represents and heralds something different that is also real and historical. The mutual relation of the two events can be recognized through their congruity or similarity" (65). Utzschneider observes in the Hosea text the "playful" character of the use of image (56). He thinks that "it is impossible to distinguish clearly between image and the thing imaged. The image and its object 'oscillate'" (56). Elements of this kind can be seen in DtIsa too. The term "sociomorpheme" as I am using it is intended to identify—functionally at first—the relationship between husband and wife as it is transferred to the relationship to God.

then also in Isaiah, Jeremiah and Ezekiel. We may therefore presume that it was familiar to Deutero-Isaiah's addressees. The specific transformation of the sociomorpheme in the present text is therefore all the more important.

It is not only catchwords[243] that link 52:13—53:12 with chap. 54; the way the language is used also shows that they belong together. In Isa 52:13—53:12 it is the sociomorpheme lord-servant that makes it possible to communicate the fate of the Servant of God. Here in chap. 54 it is the story of "the spouse of God." The "spouse" in her various aspects (e.g., "forsaken wife," "wife of <the man's> youth," v. 6) becomes—again—her lord's wife (v. 5). The renewed bond is presented as a marriage. In factual terms it is a legal act with the promise: "My 'grace/bond of affection' (וְחַסְדִּי) will not depart from you, and the covenant of my peace (וּבְרִית שְׁלוֹמִי) will not be shaken" (54:10).

Other elements define the sociomorpheme more precisely still. This is not just any relationship between husband and wife, nor is it some random marriage. The crown (vv. 11-12) already makes clear that this is the marriage of a king. The "spouse" is, or will be, queen. That makes the quality or rank of the events clear. Here heavenly and earthly events are linked in a way comparable with 52:13—53:12: Yahweh himself is speaking from 54:11 onward. It will be the task of the exegesis to show in detail how the language and concept of "marriage ceremony, marriage" have been taken up and transformed.[244]

The strict use of different forms of *parallelismus membrorum*[245] would itself be sufficient to show that chap. 54 is a poetical text.[246] The complicated use of chiasmus again speaks in favor of written composition, while series of similar-sounding consonants and vowels suggest

oral delivery.[247] It is noticeable, above all, how often the text calls for action: "Rejoice" (v. 1), "Make wide the site of your tent" (v. 2), "Do not be afraid" (v. 4), "Hold aloof from . . . it will surely not come near you" (v. 14b). Or action is described: "See, I am covering" (v. 11), "Anyone who attacks you will fall" (v. 15), "See, I myself have created the smith who blows" (v. 16). The dramatic structure is preserved throughout. The most important active characters are "the spouse" and Yahweh. These are joined by a speaker in 54:1-3 and by the messengers in 54:4-10.

In the text כִּי (*kî*), "for, indeed," is used twelve times, with varying nuances. It is an element used for its sound effect and also as an indication that explanations and reasons are important. The speech sections include both action and interpretation. Both what happens and what is said convey the same message, though on different levels.

Viewed as a whole, the scene of the "sacred marriage" in chap. 54 can be divided into three part-scenes:

1. Arrival of the "spouse" and her train
   Rejoicing, song, building of the tent (vv. 1-2)
2. Arrival of the messengers with the announcement of the Lord (vv. 4-10)

First messenger:	"Do not be afraid . . ."	(vv. 4-5)
Second messenger:	". . . [Yahweh], your God, has spoken"	(v. 6)
Third messenger:	". . . your (deliverer) redeemer Yahweh has said"	(vv. 7-8)
Fourth messenger:	". . . so I have sworn"	(v. 9)
Fifth messenger:	". . . Yahweh, who has compassion on you, has said"	(v. 10)

3. The "Lord's" arrival and crowning of the "spouse" (vv. 11-14a)

---

243 See Beuken, 242: "This connection can also be demonstrated. It finds expression in the themes 'seed' (53:10; 54:3), 'the many' (52:14-15; 53:11-12; 54:1), 'righteousness' (53:11; 54:14, 17) and 'peace' (53:5; 54:10, 13)." See also Bonnet, 54 on this passage.

244 See Muilenburg (633): "It is remarkable that the prophets were able to utilize the relationship which had been so corrupted in contemporary nature cults, purge it of all its debasing elements, and transform its significance into a profound expression of the holy and intimate relation between the covenant people with her covenant God. Israel is to

experience a new life and a new covenant devotion in which her Lord takes the initiative."

245 See the list in Grimm and Dittert, *Deuterojesaja*, 437: "We find the synonymous form (vv. 1a/b; 4; 6; 9e/f; 10a/b; 10c/d; 14b/c; 17), the synthetic form (vv. 1c/d; 5; 8; 15; 16b/c), the antithetical form (vv. 7; 8a/c; 10a-b/c-d), but also the parabolic form (v. 9), and in addition the climax built up of three consecutive terms (vv. 3; 11; 12; 13-14a)."

246 Westermann begins his interpretation as follows (270 [218]): "This poem is an exceptionally impressive example of Deutero-Isaiah's poetic art. Yet it is proclamation throughout, and what gives the utter-

But this structure—seemingly so simple—has other elements superimposed on it, for example, the interpretation in v. 3 and the determination of destinies in vv. 14b-17. The weight of the individual sections of the structure is thereby altered. As far as the action goes, the structure suggests that this is a marriage ceremony: the rejoicing—the woman's preparation of the tent—the announcement and arrival of the husband. But in content there is a tension in the text between marriage and remarriage.

The emblem of the mural crown establishes the association with the royal marriage. Marriage can certainly be conceived of as a festival. The elements "determination of destinies," assurance of protection and the averting of oppression/violence (vv. 14b-17) can belong to this level, "royal marriage," or to the level of the "sacred marriage." But even under this aspect, one can still observe tensions in the text. Why, for example, is there a reminder of the time of Noah (v. 9)? Or what is the significance of the children or builders (vv. 1, 13)? I suspect that older models have been used for the description of the "marriage" and that they are here being freshly molded and reinterpreted. For an understanding of the scene in its present form we should note that this is a marriage between the Deity and the representation of the city of Zion/Jerusalem. Thus the arrival of "the Lord" is an epiphany and the mural crown is an emblem of the city.

Under this aspect the scene has sometimes been compared with the "sacred marriage" familiar in the history of religion. The state of research into the theme of "the sacred marriage" as ἱερὸς γάμος is far from satisfactory.[248] No adequate differentiation is made between sexual cults and mythological presentation. There are sexual relationships between gods, and between gods and human beings, where it is impossible to talk about marriage ceremonies or marriage.[249]

Divine couples are frequently found—Dumuzi and Inanna, for example, or Isis and Osiris, or Baal and Anat, or Zeus and Hera. In these cases the nature of the bond can vary considerably. The connection between the ἱερὸς γάμος and the fertility of human beings, animals and land also requires more precise clarification. Since archaic ideas play a part in this sector, we must distinguish between original function and subsequent interpretation. Thus all that is left to us is to examine the particular nature of the different texts as precisely as possible.

The following exegesis assumes that the present text is taking up ancient cultic traditions. To reconstruct the passage in simplified form: we may say, first, that the text itself is describing a "remarriage." For this purpose, second, it uses elements of a marriage ceremony. Finally, it is probable that it does so in critical awareness of the forms of sacred marriage (ἱερὸς γάμος) that had been passed down in the civilizations of Israel's surrounding world. These three aspects could explain the difficulties and inherent tensions in the text, tensions that are often productive or lead to a new understanding.

---

ance its brilliant tone is the perfect unity achieved between poetry and proclamation."

247 See, e.g., vv. 7-8.

248 On ἱερὸς γάμος see C. H. Ratschow, "Ehe/Eherecht/Ehescheidung, I. Religionsgeschichtlich," *TRE* 9 (1982) 308-11; M. P. Nilsson, *Geschichte der griechischen Religion*, 1 (2d ed. 1955) 120-22, 431-33, 661-62 [*A History of Greek Religion* (2d ed. 1949) 33-44, 121-23, 294-95]; G. Freymuth, "Zum Hieros Gamos in den antiken Mysterien," *Museum Helveticum* 21 (1964) 86-95; H. Ringgren, "The Marriage Motif in Israelite Religion," in *Ancient Israelite Religion: FS F. M. Cross* (1987) 421-28.

249 See R. Bartelmus, *Heroentum in Israel und seiner Umwelt* (1979).

1   Rejoice, you barren one who has not borne!
Break out into joy, rejoice, you who had no
      labor pains!
For the descendants of the woman who has
      been left desolate are more
      numerous
than the descendants of the married woman,
Yahweh has said.

2   Make wide the site of your tent!
And let them spread out the coverings of
      your dwellings!
Do not be sparing!
Make the cords of your tent long
and make your stakes fast!

3   For you will spread out to the right and to
      the left,
and your descendants will inherit nations,
and they will settle deserted towns.

                  (1st messenger)
4   Do not be afraid, for you will not be put to
      shame,
and do not be ashamed, for you will not find
      yourself to be disgraced.
No, you can forget the shame of your youth,
and you need no longer remember the
      shame of your widowhood.
5   Yes, the one who weds you is your Creator
      <or: "it is your Lord, who made
      you">—
Yahweh Sabaoth is his name,
and he who redeems you is the Holy One of
      Israel—
he is called God of the whole earth.

                  (2nd messenger)
6   Yes, like a forsaken woman,
and one who is afflicted in spirit has
      Yahweh your God called you,
and (like) a wife of (a man's) youth who is
      cast off,
your God has said.

                  (3rd messenger)
7   For a little while I forsook you,
but in great compassion I will gather you.
8   In floods of anger for a while
I hid my face from you,
but in steadfast grace/bond of affection I
      have had compassion on you,
your redeemer Yahweh has said.

                  (4th messenger)
9   <As the days> [or: <like the waters>][a] of
      Noah is this for me:
As I swore that the waters of Noah should
      not again cover the earth,

9[a]   Either with a correction from כִּי־מֵי to כִּימֵי, "as the days," or
with a correction to כְּמֵי (cf. LXX); see below on this passage.

so I have sworn that I will not be angry
    with you and will not scold you.

(5th messenger)

10   The mountains may depart
and the hills may sway,
but my grace/bond of affection will not
    depart from you,
and the covenant of my peace will not be
    shaken,
*Yahweh, who has compassion on you,
    has said.*

54:1
Call for Joy

"Rejoice, you barren one who has not borne!" (54:1)

The verse begins with the call for rejoicing. It is probably uttered by the speaker. The formula at the end, "Yahweh has said" (אָמַר יהוה), identifies him. This makes clear that here, in the dramatic progression, Yahweh is not yet speaking directly; but he tells the speaker what he has to say. It is a threefold directive for action, specifying different modes of rejoicing. Unfortunately we are no longer able to identify these musically, but the performance of southwest Asian women singers at the present day may perhaps give a good impression of the sound and ryhthm, which to us generally sound strange.

According to *HALOT,* "the basic meaning of the root רנן is assumed to be a loud, resouding cry, which can embrace the sense of jubilation as well as that of a lament."[250] "*rnn* parallels verbs that indicate a loud cry, a raised voice, or expressions of a more musical nature."[251] Here a difference must be noted between the *Qal* form of the verb, as in the text, which expresses the individual shout of jubilation, and the *Piel,* which is used for a whole series.[252]

פָּצַח רִנָּה with the substantive means "to break into rejoicing" and occurs again in Isa 44:23; 49:13. According to *HALOT,* פצח has a "bright, cheerful, clear" sound.[253] צהל also means "rejoice," but it is used for the neighing of horses too, for example (Jer 5:8; 50:11).

This rejoicing terminology originates in the cult, and probably goes back to the Canaanite fertility cult.[254] For DtIsa פצח, "to be cheerful, happy," is characteristic (see 44:23; 49:13; 52:9; 55:12; cf. also Isa 14:7; Ps 98:4). It is noticeable that in the present text גיל *gîl* ("ecstatic cries," according to *HALAT*) is missing. In 41:16 it is used—critically, I believe—over against the Song of Miriam in Exodus 15.[255] Is DtIsa's avoidance of גיל again a rejection of any warlike note? This overture to the scene, with its rejoicing, must surely have taken some time. It heightens the listener's attention for what is to come.

F. Crüsemann has given an important pointer for an understanding of the present text.[256] He starts from "the imperative hymn," a form that he reconstructs. Within this group of hymns, drawing on a total of twelve texts[257] with shared characteristics, he discovers a separate form

---

250 See *HALOT,* s.v. רִנָּה I 2:1246–47 [*HALAT* 3:1163], with reference to N. E. Wagner, "רִנָּה in the Psalter," *VT* 10 (1960) 435–41, esp. 440.

251 Thus R. Ficker, "רנן *rnn* to rejoice," *TLOT* 3:1240–43, esp. 1240 [*THAT* 2:781–86, esp. 782]: "in Prov 1:20 and 8:3, *rnn* is the term used for appealing calls of Wisdom that arouse attention."

252 See *HALOT* 3:1248 [*HALAT* 4:1164], and E. Jenni, *Das hebräische Piʿel. Syntaktisch-semasiologische Untersuchung einer Verbalform im alten Testament* (1968) 155.

253 *HALOT* s.v. פצח I, 3:953 [*HALAT* 3:898].

254 See P. Humbert, "*Laetari et exultare* dans le vocabulaire religieux de l'Ancient Testament," *RHPhR* 22

(1942) 185–214; reprinted in his *Opuscules d'un hebraïsant* (Neuchâtel: Secrétariat de l'Université, 1958) 119–45; F. Crüsemann, *Studien zur Formgeschichte von Hymnus und Danklied in Israel* (1969) 64 with n. 1.

255 See above under 41:16.

256 Crüsemann, *Studien zur Formgeschichte von Hymnus und Danklied in Israel* (1969) 55–65.

257 Crüsemann's point of departure is an analysis of Isa 12:4-6 (cf. v. 6: "Rejoice and sing for joy, inhabitant of Zion, for great in your midst is the Holy One of Israel"). See also (following Crüsemann's sequence) Zeph 3:14-15; Zech 2:14 (10); 9:9-10; Lam 4:21; Isa

that can be described as a "call for joy—an assurance of salvation."[258]

At the beginning there is a statement that is a call to joy, rejoicing and jubilation, or to the opposite of this. It is generally addressed to an individual female figure. . . . A sentence follows that is frequently (Isa 12:6; Zech 2:14 [2:10]; Isa 14:29; 54:1; Joel 2:21, 23; Hos 9:1), but not regularly, introduced by כִּי, . . . which gives the reason for this joy. . . . It is only in the majority of cases that this sentence takes the form of an address to those who are called to joy. Generally it contains the promise of an act of Yahweh's for or with those addressed.[259]

Crüsemann thinks it probable "that the original *Sitz im Leben* . . . was an assurance of salvation in the sphere of the sexual and fertility cult. . . . This genre was then taken up by salvation prophecy and transferred to Israel or to Zion."[260] The texts are linked by way of their semantic field, concept and genre. It again becomes clear that DtIsa is building on a much broader tradition. This is the premise for the understanding, and is the only way in which the brevity of the references can be explained. But the modification of the form and content hence deserve all the more attention.[261]

The female person who is addressed is described as "barren, one who has not borne (עֲקָרָה ‘ᵃqārâ),"[262] a statement that seems at variance with the fact that the subject of the wider context in DtIsa is the reinstallation of "the spouse of God" in her original position.

If the statement "who has not borne" is taken just by itself, it may be assumed to describe a woman before her wedding. This has a point if—as the wording ("your lord," v. 5; "wife of [a man's] youth," v. 6; "covenant of my peace," v. 10) and the action suggest—chap. 54 has to do with wedding and marriage.

Finally another possibility should be considered: that "barren one who has not borne" is a reference to the "virginity" of a goddess. Athena has the cognomen Parthenos (virgin) or Pallas (girl). Anat, for example, remains a virgin even as Baal's beloved. The erotic undertones in vv. 1 and 2 suggest these reflections.[263] References of this kind would fit in with DtIsa's polemic against the gods.

The reason given in the second half of the verse ("for descendants are more numerous") puts forward another interpretation. This draws attention once more to the catchword "barren" (עֲקָרָה). It is no new recognition that this is intended as a reminder of Sarah and her story.[264] There is probably even a reference to a particular text, for in Gen 11:30, at the end of the primeval history and before the beginning of the stories about the patriarchs and matriarchs, the text reads: "Now Sarah was barren; she had no child." This is a very marked passage, in which the root עקר occurs for the first time in the book of Genesis.

Sarah's barrenness then plays a moving part in the rest of the history.[265] In spite of the errors of human beings who want to help on the divine promise, Sarah becomes the mother of nations. The link between Sarah and the Jerusalem tradition was already put forward in Isa 51:1-3, a fact that also speaks in favor of this interpretation of the present text. For the OT, the miracle that a

---

54:1; Joel 2:21-24; Hos 9:1; Isa 66:10; Jer 50:11; Mic 7:8; Isa 14:29.

258 See Crüsemann, *Studien zur Formgeschichte von Hymnus und Danklied in Israel* (1969) 55.

259 Ibid., 60.

260 Ibid., 65.

261 I would only take issue with Crüsemann when he states (ibid., 65 n. 2): "The reason why DtIsa takes over the topic is that his hymns are not really songs to be sung but, in the context of his proclamation, have the function of an oracle of salvation." In the framework of the liturgical drama, the imperatives are "stage directions," which supply directions for action. The text is not just theological literature.

262 This is one of the cases in which the text could also be heard in Greek: ἀκρεία is the title of Athena in her capacity as guardian of the city. In a bilingual text Athena is equated with Anat. It is an inscrip-

tion on an altar from Cyprus, dating from the end of the 4th c. B.C.E. (*KAI* 1:9–10; 2:59):

Ἀθηνᾶ Σωτείρᾳ Νίκη . . .

5 Ἀγα[θ]ῆ Τύχη.

לענת מעזחים . . . (5) [ל]מזל

The epiclesis of Athena is: "savior" (*sōteira*) and "victory" (*nikē*) . . . "for good fortune" (*tychē*); the epiclesis of Anat: "refuge of the living . . . for prosperity."

263 See above (n. 248) on the ἱερὸς γάμος ("sacred marriage").

264 See B. J. van der Merwe, *Pentateuchtradisies in de Prediking van Deuterojesaja* (1955) 139, 240; W. A. M. Beuken, "Isaiah LIV: The Multiple Identity of the Person Addressed," *OTS* 19 (1974) 29–70, esp. 37–42; J. Van Seters, "The Problem of Childlessness in Near Eastern Law and the Patriarchs of Israel," *JBL* 87 (1968) 401–8.

265 See Genesis 16; 17:15-19; 18:9-15; 21:1-13.

barren woman can have children becomes a fundamental experience that can be an illustration of the way in which God acts.[266]

Barrenness is a hard fate in a society where a woman's dignity is bound up with children.[267] Children, especially sons, guarantee the certainty of a legacy for the next generation. Since there is no social insurance, children are necessary as a provision for sickness and old age. Sons can appear for their mothers before a court of law. So when God enables the barren woman to become a mother, the miracle is of particular significance.

Conversely, barrenness could also be the consequence of a curse. In Hos 9:10-17 the prophet interprets childlessness in the context of Israel's cult of foreign gods. This text is interesting because in Hosea image and fact already merge, just as they do here in DtIsa. Because Israel has despised God's love, it has no longer any future; it will be lost among the foreign nations. DtIsa revokes a curse of this kind. If the barren woman has "many children," this also means that the new beginning is really an impossible possibility; to utter it can have a meaning only if the act is God's. In my opinion, therefore, the difficulty of explaining v. 1b is due to its subject and is intentional.

The reevaluation of experience is formulated through the Yahweh saying, as in an oracle that requires interpretation.

F. Stolz says of שׁמם: "The basic meaning of the root may be rendered by the expressions 'to be desolate, cut off from life.'"[268] The element always also has an element of the uncanny about it. In DtIsa, according to 49:18, 19, the land is "empty of people and desolate, devastated."[269] In the following 54:3 it is towns that are described in this way.[270] Human beings can "be appalled," as they are, for example, over the appearance

of the Servant of God in 52:14. For a woman שְׁמֵמָה can mean that she has been cut off from marital intercourse (cf. 2 Sam 13:20). The negative fate of land, town, and woman is summed up in this single term "desolate." It is worth considering whether the antithesis between "solitary" and "wife" is not implicitly a historical image too.[271] The preexilic Jerusalem and Israel were a "wife." With the exile they became "solitary, desolate." Here image and the thing imaged coincide. What appears in the present text as a brief formula is illustrated in Isa 62:1-5, also through the wedding image.[272]

The miracle is not merely that the solitary woman has children, but that they are "many" (רַבִּים), that is, these are probably again the nations, including Israel, who are addressed in the fourth Servant text.[273] Here the speaker turns to the listeners: "We are many," even if Jerusalem is as yet modest in appearance. But if a woman has a lord, in accordance with v. 5 (בְּעָלַיִךְ), she can also—again—be one who is married (בְּעוּלָה).

Rejoicing and the songs of women have a special place at a wedding, when the bridegroom is awaited. This has a point in the progress of the drama when, according to v. 1, there is jubilation and song at the lord's return.

54:2-3
The Building of the Tent

"Make wide the site of your tent!" (54:2)

■ 2 The second task given to "the woman" is to prepare her tent. Once again the text can be seen under different aspects.[274] The imperatives set off the action: there is something to see. This is all the more evident if one starts from a minor text-critical observation. MT has the plural: "Let them spread out (יַטּוּ) the coverings." 1QIsa^a as well as LXX, Syriac, Targum, and Vulgate read the

---

266 For עקר see Gen 25:21, Rebekah; 29:31, Rachel; Judg 13:2-3, Manoah's wife and Samson's mother; 1 Sam 2:5, Hannah; cf. Exod 23:26; Deut 7:14; Ps 113:9.

267 Job 24:21.

268 See F. Stolz, "שׁמם *šmm* to lie deserted," *TLOT* 3:1372–75, esp. 1372 [*THAT* 2:970–74, esp. 971].

269 Cf. Hos 5:9, 15; see Wolff, *Hosea* (1974) on this text [*Hosea* (3d ed. 1976)].

270 Cf. Amos 9:14; Ezek 36:35.

271 See Fohrer on this passage.

272 See T. D. Andersen, "Renaming and Wedding Imagery in Isaiah 62," *Bib* 67 (1986) 78–80.

273 See Beuken, 247 on this passage; cf. 52:14, 15; 53:11, 12 (bis).

274 In sound, "*your* tent" (אָהֳלֵךְ) begins the series of no less than thirty 2d person sing. fem. suffixes (with a *k* sound at the end, in combination with different vowels).

singular, so that the verb agrees with the imperative "make wide" addressed to "the woman." But MT is the more difficult reading and has a point. Anyone who has ever put up a tent single-handed knows how difficult it can be. Among nomads, erecting the tent is a job for the women. When preparations for a wedding are going forward, the bride is not alone but is accompanied by her "virgins." Even more does a queen have her household; it is this that signals her position. The text suggests that the woman's attendants have now entered—if indeed they did not already act as chorus in the rejoicing called for in v. 1.

In spite of the scene's realism, we must remember that what is now happening is the very opposite of what the house of Israel and the land have experienced, according to Jeremiah 10.[275] There, after the dispute about the "idols," the text reads (Jer 10:20):

> My tent is destroyed, all my cords are broken.
> My children have gone from me and are no longer there.
> There is no one to spread my tent any more, and to set up my tent coverings.[276]

The lament in Jeremiah 10 has now been turned into joy. The promise to Zion according to Isa 33:20-21aα has also been fulfilled:

> Look on Zion, the city of our festivals!
> Your eyes will see Jerusalem as a quiet pasture,
> as a tent which must not be taken down,
> whose stakes will never be pulled up,
> and none of whose ropes will break.
> For there [Yahweh] will be for us a glorious one.[277]

The tent[278] can be a tent set up for a festival, a tent of meeting. It is strange if a tent is set up for "the woman" as Zion/Jerusalem. The city's buildings take the form of house, palace, and temple. But this is probably once again an evocation of Israel's early tradition, when the people still "dwelt in tents."[279] If this is so, "tent" is a deliberate archaism. Anyone who knows the Scriptures will also remember here the name given to Jerusalem in Ezekiel: "Oholibah" (אָהֳלִיבָה), which contains the word for tent (אֹהֶל).[280] In Ezekiel 23 Oholibah and her sister "Oholah" (for Samaria) "play the whore," a caricatured version of the reason for the downfall. Now "the tent" is to be built once more. The tradition history of "dwelling" (מִשְׁכָּן) provides an image comparable with that of "tent" (אֹהֶל).[281]

But the text clearly has a topical reference too. Immediately after the action announced in v. 2, the site or "place" (מָקוֹם) of the tent is to be expanded. This is necessary if the number of people to be accommodated increases (cf. v. 1). Now, מָקוֹם can be any place. But as "the place that Yahweh chooses" the term was applied from Deuteronomy onward to Jerusalem and Zion.[282] The temple is the place where Yahweh lets his name dwell (1 Kgs 8:16-19, 29, 44, 48; 11:36).[283] In Zion theology, the temple and the Davidic dynasty can be closely linked (cf. 2 Samuel 7; Psalms 78 and 132). According to the pilgrimage song Ps 132:5, David vowed that he would search "until I find a place (מָקוֹם) for Yahweh, and a dwelling place (מִשְׁכָּנוֹת) for the Mighty One of Jacob." But the fact that the same catchwords are used as in the present text makes it all the more noticeable that in DtIsa king and kingship are talked about only when the kingship is Yahweh's. The expansion of the tent will hardly mean the extension of the temple. It is more

---

275 Bonnard particularly, commenting on this passage, has drawn attention to this and the following text of Isa 33:20-21a.

276 See Holladay, *Jeremiah 1–25* (1986) 342 on this text. He suspects a connection with P's description of the "tent" or "tabernacle" in Exod 35:18, and the temple.

277 Translation following H. Wildberger, *Jesaja 28–39* (1982) 1309.

278 See K. Koch, "אֹהֶל *ʾōhel*," *TDOT* 1:118-30 [*ThWAT* 1:128–41].

279 See D. Baltzer, *Ezechiel und Deuterojesaja* (1971) 170 on Isa 54:2: "v. 2 points to the nomadic situation and could be addressed to Sarah (Gen 18:1-16)"; see also Gen 24:67.

280 The meaning may perhaps be: "My (cultic) tent is in her"; see W. Zimmerli, *Ezekiel* 1 (1979) 483–84 [*Ezechiel* 1 (1969) 541–42].

281 See D. Kellermann, "מִשְׁכָּן *miškān*," *ThWAT* 5:62–69; on the plural *miškānôt*, 64. His summing up (66) is important: "It has become clear that *miškān* as human habitation is frequently associated in meaning with *ʾōhel*, but that in some passages it also means firm settlements and villages. Perhaps one could follow M. Görg (*Das Zelt der Begegnung. Untersuchung zur Gestalt der sakralen Zelttraditionen Altisraels* [1967] 106ff.) and could also consider whether *miškān* may characterize dwelling places where the legal right to permanent settlement is excluded—i.e., that it means not a permanent dwelling but only a temporary stay." Could the present text, therefore, also contain a reference to the pilgrimage to Jerusalem? Cf. also ibid., 67–68 and Pss 43:3; 132:7.

282 See Deut 12:5; 14:23-25; 1 Kgs 8:29; cf. H. Koester, "τόπος," *TDNT* 8:187–208 [*ThWNT* 8:187–208].

likely that the "place" for the city of Jerusalem is meant. Finally מָקוֹם could also mean the land,[284] especially when coupled with the explanation in v. 3.

■ **3** A tripartite oracle interprets the action. Here too traditional formulations are used. The promise to Jacob in Gen 28:14 comes closest in wording and meaning: "And your offspring shall be like the dust of the earth, and you shall spread abroad to the west and to the east and to the north and to the south, and all the families of the earth shall be blessed through you and through your offspring."[285]

In my view, however, the declarations about the future cannot be understood without the presuppositions of Isaiah 52–53. It is not clear whether "right and left" is intended as a piece of precise geographical information, or whether it simply means "on all sides," in the sense of the rhetorical figure that uses two contrasting points to indicate the whole. One can "break out/spread out"[286] if one is shut in from the outside—but also if one has shut oneself in on one's own initiative. Both political situations are conceivable.

Should the translation be "inherit from nations" or "inherit nations"? In the promises to the patriarchs, "inherit" generally has to do with land, but not here. In 53:10 "seed/descendants" probably does not mean descendants in the natural sense, any more than does the children/descendants of "the desolate one" in 54:1. Does "inherit nations" refer to what is in common with the nations, in a similar sense to 53:12? Is this a specific reference to the "pilgrimage of the nations to Zion," following Isaiah 2? That would be a new interpretation of

"inherit." "They will settle deserted/destroyed towns": here the שׁמם of v. 1 is taken up again. Anyone who settles or populates deserted towns is no conqueror.[287] The relationship between the *gōlâ* and the people who had remained in the country was a delicate one when property rights were in question. That could be the background of a formulation of this kind.[288] It is surely also a reassurance for neighbors with regard to any plans that might possibly be initiated in Jerusalem. If, as the present text says, there are "deserted towns," no one can have anything against their repopulation. This rules out the possibility of any dispute.

Destruction was an element in the curse, and in the same way the rebuilding of ruined towns was a theme in the expectation of salvation.[289] The essential point is that DtIsa can announce the fulfillment of promise now, in his own day.

54:4-10
The Heralding of the "Lord" (Five Messages)

"Do not be afraid, for you will not be put to shame . . ." (54:4)
"The covenant of my peace will not be shaken" (54:10)

■ **4-5** "Do not be afraid" begins the five messages to the "woman" that herald her "lord" (vv. 4-5, 6, 7-8, 9, 10). The commentators generally see no problem here, since they assume that these are individual sayings, especially if the text is assigned to the "priestly salvation oracles" in DtIsa.

If one starts from the assumption that here a wedding is acted out, "Do not be afraid . . . do not be ashamed

283 For terminology comparable to שׁכן, "dwell," see Deut 12:11; 14:23; 16:2, 6, 11; 26:2 and above all Neh 1:9. Cf. W. H. Schmidt, "מִשְׁכָּן als Ausdruck Jerusalemer Kultsprache," *ZAW* 75 (1963) 91–92.

284 Cf. Exod 3:8; Num 32:1; Judg 18:10.

285 Cf. Exod 1:12; 1 Chr 4:38; on the text see van der Merwe, *Pentateuchtradisies in . . . Deuterojesaja* (1955) 240.

286 It seems to me a striking fact that otherwise פרץ often has a negative connotation; see Exod 19:22; Judg 21:15; Hos 4:2, 10; Ps 106:29; see also Amos 4:3; 9:11.

287 "Deserted towns" are a danger, partly because they are uncanny. See *HALAT* s.v. שׁמם on *Qal* no. 3, *Niphal* no. 2, *Poel*, to the point of "desolating abomination (שִׁקּוּץ שֹׁמֵם) in Dan 12:11; 11:31 (LXX βδέλυγμα ἐρημώσεως, cf. 1 Macc 1:54; Mark 13:14),

Hiphil no. 2 and *Hitpoel* no. 1.

288 See under 49:18-21 above.

289 Cf. Amos 7:4 and esp. 9:14: "When I restore the fortunes of my people Israel, they shall rebuild the ruined cities and inhabit them." See H. W. Wolff, *Joel and Amos* (1977) on this passage, as well as on Amos 4:1 [*Joel und Amos* (3d ed. 1985)]. See also Wolff, *Hosea* (1974) 105 [on Hos 5:15] [*Hosea* (3d ed. 1976) 132, 134]. We also find the catchword שׁמם several times in the salvation oracle in Ezek 36:33-37: "On the day that I cleanse you from all your iniquities, I will cause the towns to be inhabited" (v. 33). "And they shall inhabit (יָשֵׁבוּ) the destroyed and desolate (הַנְשַׁמּוֹת) and ruined towns, <now once again> fortified" (v. 35).

. . ." could quite conceivably be addressed to a bride who has just arranged her bridal chamber. But we cannot disregard that in the text the "lord" who is announced (v. 5) and comes (v. 11) is Yahweh. The buildup in v. 4 corresponds to that of vv. 1, 2, and 3, where action is interpreted in each case, although here the levels of image and fact merge. Thus the speaker in v. 4 could be the same as the one in vv. 1-3; he would simply be continuing.

I would assume, however, that "Do not be afraid" is an internal signal in the text announcing new action. Here someone enters the scene in the face of whom fear is an appropriate reaction, that is, a heavenly messenger. That would correspond to 52:7, at the close of Act V: "How beautiful upon the mountains are the feet of the messenger." There, this introduces the announcement to Zion: "as king reigns your God," and Yahweh's return to Zion (52:8). In the present text too there are probably five messengers in all, of varying rank. The "Do not be afraid" would then belong to the passages in which "the original numinous character of the 'fear (of God)' is still clear."[290] More particularly, the comparable texts are the ones in which a divine messenger appears to a human being.[291]

When, according to Judg 6:11-24, Gideon meets "Yahweh's messenger" (מַלְאַךְ יהוה), he fears for his life: "But Yahweh said to him: 'Peace be to you; do not be afraid (אַל־תִּירָא), you shall not die'" (Judg 6:23).

When the birth of Samson is announced in Judges 13, Manoah's wife tells her husband: "A man of God came to me, and his appearance was like that of a messenger of God, very terrible" (נוֹרָא מְאֹד) (Judg 13:6).[292] This text is also interesting because here too one of the themes is the woman's inability to bear children.

Finally, it is one of the heavenly beings who expounds the future to Daniel (Daniel 10): "Do not be afraid, beloved of God! Peace be with you! Be strong, be strong" (Dan 10:19).

Against a background of this kind—the encounter with the divine—בּוֹשׁ acquires the sense of "being put to shame, being reduced to ignominy."[293] In the *parallelismus membrorum* the phrase corresponding to "Do not be afraid" is "do not be ashamed" (וְאַל־תִּכָּלְמִי). We find the closest parallel to כלם in the sense of "fear" in Ezra 9:5-6, the beginning of Ezra's prayer of repentance: "I fell on my knees, spread out my hands to Yahweh my God, and said: 'O my God, I will be disgraced (בֹשְׁתִּי) and *am ashamed* (וְנִכְלַמְתִּי) to lift my face to you, my God, for our guilt has risen higher than our heads'" (Ezra 9:5-6).

The phrases "Do not be afraid . . ." and "do not be ashamed . . ." already set the key in such a way that a message of salvation can be expected. In this sense it is correct to call this text a salvation oracle. It is the negation of disaster, and the turn to good.

The theme "shame, disgrace" is then given five variations. The concordance and the lexicon show how profoundly these terms are bound up with prophetic traditions. They have their function in the prophetic judgment speech. Social conduct is pilloried, and the foreign cult exposed. "Shame, disgrace" is the active and passive diminution of quality of life. It calls into question reputation, dignity, and honor. Since it is a matter of a person's standing within a social group, a distinction can be made between shame and guilt, even if the two cannot be separated from one another completely. DtIsa evidently finds it important to play on the different terms in such a way as to link everything that can be said on the subject with "the woman," as the representation of Jerusalem and Israel.

The first impression: v. 4a talks about a "bride," and this is sustained in the context and throughout the text. The promise stands, for a bride as well: "Do not be afraid" and "do not be ashamed" As far as the bridal imagery is concerned, the levels of action and understanding are consistent. But at the same time the choice

290 See H.-P. Stähli, "ירא *yrʾ* to fear," *TLOT* 2:568–78, esp. 571–72 (quotation on 572) [*THAT* 1:765–78, esp. 769–70 (quotation on 769)]; H. F. Fuhs, "יָרֵא *yārēʾ*\," *TDOT* 6:290–315, esp. 300–303 [*ThWAT* 3:869–93, esp. 879–83].

291 See R. Ficker, "מַלְאָךְ *malʾāk* messenger," *TLOT* 2:666–72 [*THAT* 1:900–908].

292 See the commentaries on the text.

293 See F. Stolz, "בּוֹשׁ *bôš* to be ashamed," *TLOT* 1:204–7, esp. 205 [*THAT* 1:269–72, esp. 270]: "The basic meaning in the qal may be assumed 'to be confounded,' and that in a double sense: on the one hand, objectively, establishing the fact ('to be annihilated') but, on the other, subjectively, the feeling by which the one annihilated is qualified ('feel ashamed')." See also, ibid., the list of "parallel expressions" for the verb's range of meaning.

of words implies more. This becomes clear through the declaration in v. 4b, which is already set aside by—or rather gathered up into—v. 4a. In the past there was "shame, disgrace" (בֹּשֶׁת, v. 4b, instead of לֹא תֵבוֹשִׁי, "you will not be put to shame," in v. 4a) and "ignominy" (חֶרְפַּת, v. 4b, instead of לֹא תַחְפִּירִי, "you will not find yourself to be disgraced," in v. 4a). The catchword "disgrace" (בֹּשֶׁת) can be a pointer to the tradition context. For Jeremiah "disgrace" (בֹּשֶׁת) is a code word for the foreign cult. It is the cult of the city gods—"For you have as many gods as you have towns, O Judah"[294]—but above all of the Baal cult. It is noticeable how much there is a play on the "marriage relationship" between Yahweh and Israel in Jeremiah too.[295] There is the reference to the time of youth in the book of Jeremiah (3:4, 24, 25): "But the disgrace (הַבֹּשֶׁת) has devoured all for which our fathers had labored from our youth up, their flocks and their herds, their sons and their daughters. Let us lie down in our disgrace (בְּבָשְׁתֵּנוּ), and cover ourselves with our ignominy (כְּלִמָּתֵנוּ)." Yahweh claims to be Lord himself: "for it is I who am your lord" (בָּעַלְתִּי בָכֶם, Jer 3:14).[296]

In Ezekiel the consistent portrayal of "disgrace" in the personification of Jerusalem is clearer still. She is Yahweh's unfaithful wife. According to Ezekiel 16, Yahweh has legally acquired Jerusalem as his property (Ezek 16:8). All that the city owns is thanks to him. The cult in the high places and the offerings to idols are termed "whoredom" (Ezek 16:16-17). This is explicitly formulated: "Be ashamed and bear your disgrace" (בּוֹשִׁי וּשְׂאִי כְלִמָּתֵךְ, Ezek 16:52).[297] The present text in Ezekiel is also familiar with the renewal of the covenant of Jerusalem's youth (Ezek 16:60, 62). But the text maintains: "In order that you may remember and be ashamed (וָבֹשְׁתְּ), and you will never open your mouth because of

your shame (מִפְּנֵי כְּלִמָּתֵךְ), when I allow you to expiate all that you have done" (Ezek 16:63). In this respect DtIsa explicitly goes beyond this saying of Ezekiel, when he can proclaim that "the disgrace" should no longer be remembered; it can be forgotten.

In Ezekiel 23 the reproach of "whoredom" refers to the relationship to the foreign peoples. No less drastic is the description of the "disgrace," in which Samaria and Jerusalem are involved, under the names of Oholah and Oholibah respectively. Compared with Ezekiel 16, the view that the whoredom has already begun in their youth—to be precise, ever since the sojourn in Egypt—is emphasized more strongly: "There were two women, the daughters of one mother; they played the whore in Egypt; they already played the whore in their youth (בִּנְעוּרֵיהֶן)" (Ezek 23:2-3; cf. also vv. 8, 19-20, 21). In his Ezekiel commentary, W. Zimmerli shows how greatly these chapters have been subjected to revision. From this we may conclude that this tradition, and the need to come to terms with it, retained their topical force.

For the present DtIsa text, one result is that it becomes clear why youth is a time that is viewed in unfavorable terms. The favorable era of the matriarchs lay further back. This is an implicit historical concept. The time of youth lasts from the captivity in Egypt until the present—until the exile and the destruction of Jerusalem. For Ezekiel, the turning point was still in the future; for DtIsa it is history.[298]

Against the background of the Jeremiah and Ezekiel traditions, the sentence in v. 4bα can be perhaps be rendered still more directly: "The disgrace (i.e., the Baal) of your youth you can forget"—but you will not forget

---

294   Cf. Jer 2:26-28; 11:13. Both texts have evidently been edited, as the LXX already shows. In Jer 11:13 the MT has parallel to each other "altars for shame" (לַבֹּשֶׁת) and "altars . . . for Baal" (לַבַּעַל i.p.). For בוֹשׁ in Jeremiah see also 6:15; 8:9-12; 10:14; 46:24; 48:1, 20; 50:2. Comparable too is the deliberate corruption in the OT of names in which Baal was originally an element, through the substitution of the element בֹּשֶׁת, "shame," e.g., in 2 Sam 2:8; 1 Chr 8:33: Ishbosheth instead of Ishbaal for Saul's son; see also 2 Sam 11:21. The name of the goddess Astarte is treated similarly: instead of עַשְׁתָּרוֹת (see Judg 2:13; 10:6; 1 Sam 7:3, 4; 12:10) עַשְׁתֹּרֶת is pro-

nounced (1 Kgs 11:5, 33; 2 Kgs 23:13), with the vowels of בֹּשֶׁת.

295   Cf. Jer 2:32-33, virgin (בְּתוּלָה), bride; Jer 3:1: "If a man (אִישׁ) sends away his wife (אֶת־אִשְׁתּוֹ)" (see also esp. vv. 6-11); Jer 3:20: "As a woman 'deceives' her lover."

296   Cf. Jer 31:32; but see, conversely, 2:8: "The prophets prophesied by Baal" (נִבְּאוּ בַבַּעַל).

297   Cf. Ezek 32:24-25, 30; 36:7; 44:13.

298   See Bonnard, 291–92; Fohrer, 170; R. Martin-Achard, "Esaïe liv et la nouvelle Jérusalem," in J. A. Emerton, ed., *Congress Volume: Vienna 1980* (VTSup 32; 1981) 238–62, esp. 250.

Yahweh. But what does "the disgrace of widowhood"[299] mean in this context? "In biblical Hebrew the word אלמנה has a completely negative nuance. It means a woman who has been divested of her male protector (husband, sons, often also brothers). As a person without living relative, money, or influence, the widow is often mentioned together with the orphan, . . . the sojourner, . . . the poor."[300]

The transferred sense in which Jerusalem is called a widow can be found at a prominent point at the beginning of the book of Lamentations (Lam 1:1): "How lonely sits the city that once was full of people! How like a widow (כְּאַלְמָנָה) she has become, she that was great among the nations! She that was a princess among the provinces has been reduced to forced labor."[301]

Jeremiah's oracle against Babylon includes the words (Jer 51:5a): "Israel and Judah shall not be widowed by their God, by Yahweh Sabaoth."[302] F. Delitzsch already wrote here: "It was not a true widowhood, only a seeming one (Jer 51:5), for Jerusalem's husband is still alive."[303] It is nevertheless striking that widowhood is not nearly so much a feature of the formalized language of the tradition as is the "disgrace of youth." But when the "forsakenness" of Zion/Jerusalem is the theme (see Lam 1:1; Isa 49:14; 54:6), the time since the city's destruction and the exile can be interpreted as "widowhood."

If the individual terms are not taken each for itself, the text and its context present an additional problem; for "the woman" cannot be unmarried, a widow, and forsaken at one and the same time. W. A. M. Beuken puts this point in a nutshell,[304] and assumes a process of abstraction. The ground shared by the epithets is that

they describe a status in which social protection is lacking.[305] The present distress is the "desolateness." An abstraction of this kind is typical of DtIsa, but the path leading to it can perhaps be traced more precisely.

I assume that this text too is part of the dispute with the "foreign" gods and their cult. "Virgin," "forsaken woman" and even "widow" can be united in a single person—the goddess Anat, for example. She was the goddess of war and love. She was well known in Egypt and especially in Ugarit. At a later period she became merged with Astarte.[306] In Hellenistic times she was worshiped as Atargatis. For the Romans she was the *Dea Syria*. Fragments of her myths have been preserved in different places.

Excursus: Anat

Anat's most important appellation in the Ugaritic texts is "virgin" (*btlt*). She is the consort of the god Baal. She is called Baal's sister (*ybmt limm*), but the god nevertheless sleeps with her and she conceives. M. Pope interprets the title *ybmt limm* (the meaning of which is disputed) as "widowed wife of the prince (Baal)."[307] If we follow him and others, this interpretation is connected with the mythical story of the Baal cycle.

At the invitation of the god Mot, Baal has betaken himself to the underworld. He dies there. The goddess Anat searches for him over the whole earth, until she finds his body and buries it on Mount Zaphon. It is also told that she searches for him or his shadow in the underworld and slays Mot. Finally when "the heavens rain oil and the brooks bubble with honey"[308] it is evident that Baal, the weather god, is alive again. He resumes his throne and his rule.[309]

---

299 In sound אַלְמְנוּתַיִךְ (ʾalmᵉnûtayik "widowhood") and עֲלוּמַיִךְ (ʾᵃlûmayik "youth") differ only slightly.

300 Thus H. A. Hoffner's definition in "אַלְמָנָה ʾalmānāh," *TDOT* 1:287–91, esp. 288 [*ThWAT* 1:308–13, esp. 309].

301 See also the commentaries on the text; cf. Lam 5:3.

302 Conversely in Isa 47:8-9 Babylon is threatened with widowhood and childlessness. But see above on this text.

303 Delitzsch, 2:344 [561] on this passage [trans. altered]. One might compare 2 Sam 20:3, where David's concubines, secured in the harem, are described as "living as if in widowhood during the lifetime (of their husband)."

304 Cf. Beuken, 250.

305 Cf. C. Cohen, "The 'Widowed' City," *JANESCU* 5

(1973) 75–81.

306 For Jerusalem see 1 Kgs 11:5, 33; 2 Kgs 23:13.

307 M. Pope, *El in the Ugaritic Texts* (1955); also his article "Anat" in *Wörterbuch der Mythologie*, 1 (1965) 235–41. On the various interpretations of the title *ybmt limm* for Anat, see also N. H. Walls, *The Goddess Anat in Ugaritic Myth* (1992) 78–107, 156.

308 For this image for fertility cf. Gen 27:28; Exod 3:8; Job 20:17; Ezek 32:14; Joel 4:18 (3:18).

309 For the more general recent discussion about Anat see also Walls, *The Goddess Anat in Ugaritic Myth* (1992) with more recent lit.; see esp. 186–206 and 217–24.

The background of the myth is probably the rhythm of the seasons.[310] In the summer drought Mot reigns; Baal's lordship shows itself in the life-giving rain. Anat is Baal's wife who—forsaken by him—searches for him, finds him and mourns him.

In Ugaritic the most important elements of the myth are quite recognizable. The gap in time between the Ugaritic and OT, as well as other texts enjoins caution about a direct transference. But essential motifs and themes from the myth can be found much later. These are associated with other gods too, as the myth about Isis and Osiris shows. The name of the goddess Anat is an element in a number of ancient names.

Although in Elephantine there is talk about an Anat-Bethel and an Anat-Yahweh, DtIsa testifies to the strict repudiation of any link of this kind. He does not mention Anat's name. But this very omission could mean that this is his way of entering into a dispute about the worship of a goddess, in addition to Yahweh. This possibility should again be considered in interpreting 54:11. The link in the myth between "virgin" and "widow" turns into a historical interpretation.[311] The positive era of "the matriarchs" precedes the era of "the virgin." The era of "the widow" is the exile. The text depicts the reinstallation of the wife in the original relationship with God. Now the new era is beginning. The whole can be compared with Luke 1:26-38, the annunciation to Mary. This text is in its own way also a dispute with the tradition reflected in Isa 54:4, for in Luke it is the angel Gabriel who says "Do not be afraid."

someone who knows the bridegroom: "Yes, the one who weds you is. . . ." The messenger is thus comparable with "the bridegroom's friend" presupposed in Isa 5:1 (cf. John 3:29). In the same tenor, the impression that this is a marriage is strengthened if the first word in the verse is rendered: "the one who weds you" (בֹּעֲלַיִךְ).[312] According to the Masoretic pointing, this is probably a *Qal* active participle of the verb בעל. The plural form of the suffix is explained as "the royal we" (see GKC § 124k). Other commentators (e.g., North) believe that it is an assimilation to the following "who has made you" (עֹשַׂיִךְ).[313] LXX, Syriac, and Targum are evidently assuming a simple "(your) lord" (בַּעַל). This too would still fit in with the wedding image.[314] But it is impossible to overlook that the text is preparing for a theophany and that—as the exegesis of v. 4 showed—the text belongs to the dispute with the foreign myth. "Baal" is a title for the weather god, a description has become a proper name. Baal is the counterpart to Anat. I therefore do not believe that it is just a Masoretic scribal peculiarity when a verb is used here instead of the substantive; this belongs to the original text, the purpose being to avoid confusion with the foreign god. It is certainly closely linked with the following "who has made you," the temporal sense of the participles being left open. Verses 6-10 will make clear that the subject is a "marriage," or a restoration of the marriage relationship as a relationship that is permanent. "The covenant of my peace" is God's covenant with his people.

In the Ezekiel text about Oholah and Oholibah (Ezekiel 23), to which there is probably a covert refer-

The announcement of "the lord" continues (v. 5) as he is presented to us with his name and titles. Through the endorsing "yes" (כִּי) the messenger legitimates himself as

---

310 See here J. C. de Moor, *The Seasonal Pattern in the Ugaritic Myth of Ba⁽lu* (1971).

311 This interpretation and its tradition have been finely developed by A. Neher, "Le symbolisme conjugal dans l'Ancien Testament," *RHPhR* 34 (1954) 30–49, esp. 49: "We believe that there is a certain legitimacy in recognizing in a conjugal symbolism in the OT a significance that is eminently historical, as distinct from the psychological import of the same symbolism among the Christian mystics."

312 According to *HALOT* 1:142 [*HALAT* 1:136], the verb בעל I means "possess, control." For the meaning "to take someone into possession as betrothed or wife, thus initiating the marriage," *HALOT* cites Deut 21:13; 24:1; Isa 62:5; Mal 2:11.

313 See *HALOT* 1:142 [*HALAT* 1:136, 137] s.v. בעל I and II on this passage; also North, 246.

314 I should like here to pass on a suspicion of my own. The curious בֹּעֲלַיִךְ (bō⁽ălayik) occurs in precisely this form only here in the OT. It can also be heard differently if a separation is made between bō and ⁽ālayik. bō would represent the *Qal* infinitive of בוא (bô᾽) "come," ⁽ālayik the preposition עַל (⁽al) with the 2d person sing. fem. suffix. The rendering would then have to be: "it comes over you" or "to you." עַל (⁽al) and בוא (bô᾽) as a covert reference to Baal are already presupposed in Hos 7:16 cj.; 11:2, 7, 9 (see the commentaries on those texts). I am grateful to Jörg Jeremias for drawing my attention to this. Even the curious form in 1QIsaᵃ בעלכי could be explained. Ps 116:7 offers an instance of עַל with 2d person sing. fem. suffix and the resulting form עָלָיְכִי . Why in chap. 54 1QIsaᵃ should—6 times in all—substitute כ for the suffix form ־ךְ is not clear to me.

ence in DtIsa 54:2,[315] the text says about Oholibah's foreign lovers (Ezek 23:24): "They will fall upon you" (וּבָאוּ עָלַיִךְ). In that passage this is meant in a hostile sense.[316]

But according to the present text too, this is not Baal arriving for a sexual adventure, as the myth relates. The one who is coming is "he who made you," and this bond is a bond purposing peace and permanence. Consequently the reading "who weds you" is in line with the present context and its dispute with the Baal–Anat myth. It would again be a dramatic hyperbole characteristic of DtIsa, in which seriousness and wit are closely knit.

Beuken, following Köhler, asks rightly: What is the subject and what is the predicate in the nominal clauses in v. 5?[317] His conclusion is that the sequence is predicate-subject: "He who marries you is your Creator." I agree that the weight of the reasoning lies on God's being as Creator. That Yahweh "has made" (עשׂה) Israel and Zion is a constant formula of faith in DtIsa (see 43:1-7; 51:13; 54:5; comp. 44:21-24). But we should also note the text's concern to point out that "husband," "Creator," and "Yahweh Sabaoth" are one and the same. Yahweh is the revealed name. In DtIsa צְבָאוֹת (sᵉbāʾôt) includes especially his lordship over the heavenly powers (cf. 40:26).

The second announcement made by the messenger who heralds his lord again contains a series of three identifying statements. It also begins with a verbal definition: "The one who redeems you" (וְגֹאֲלֵךְ).[318] It is parallel to "the one who weds you" in v. 5, as Beuken has shown. "Redemption," in the literal sense, is the declaration immediately touching on the present. It is the ninth time that the term "Redeemer" (גֹּאֵל) for Yahweh in a titular sense is used in DtIsa up to this point (41:14; 43:14; 44:6; 44:24; 47:4; 48:17; 49:7; 49:26; comp. 54:8. For further use of the term גאל gʾl in DtIsa see 43:1; 44:22-23; 48:20; 51:10; and 52:3, 8). With its help the sociomorpheme "lord-servant" can be linked with the sociomorpheme "husband-wife." In the case of lord-servant it was the "redemption" from slavery for debt, in the sense of the liberation from Egypt at the exodus. In the case of husband-wife it is used in the family-law sense to mean "the renewal of a previous order, the restoration of a lost unity."[319] The woman again receives her original status in relationship to her husband. In this way she is "whole," "redeemed"; this is the state of "wholeness," "salvation." The link between the two different sectors, slave law and family law, creates a new, more abstract conceptual level that can be rendered by the idea of "redemption" in the theological sense. Israel and Jerusalem, represented by "the woman," are "redeemed." Thus "the Holy One" too is not just some god or other; he is "the Holy One of Israel."[320] He secures his being as God from profanation, and sanctifies his people anew. Because his people are redeemed, they can partake of God's holiness, his saving power. What at first sounds exclusive—"the Holy One of Israel"—becomes inclusive in a third step. It is the furthest possible horizon: "the God of the whole earth." That is the name ascribed to the "Redeemer," and that is also the way he is to be invoked. This is the message of the first and most important messenger. Verse 5a

---

315 See above on this passage.

316 H. D. Preuss ("בוֹא bôʾ," TDOT 2:20-49 [ThWAT 1:536-68]) writes about this text (37 [554]): "Oholibah's former paramours will now come against her with hostility and warfare (23:24). It is clear that boʾ was selected here as a contrast to its meaning coire cum femina, 'have sexual relations with a woman.'" Cf. Gen 19:33, 34; 2 Sam 12:24; Esth 2:12, 15.

317 Beuken, 251 on this passage. In his article "Isaiah LIV," OTS 19 (1974) 44-45, he defines the alternative: "We can paraphrase this choice as follows: 'Your Maker is your husband, he marries you' and set it against the opposite interpretation: . . . 'Your husband is your Maker, he has created you'" (44); cf also A. Schoors, I Am God Your Saviour (1973) 83; Martin-Achard, "Esaïe liv et la nouvelle Jérusalem," in J. A. Emerton, ed., Congress Volume: Vienna 1980

(VTSup 32; 1981) 238-62; on the present passage, 250-51.

318 See on גאל J. J. Stamm, Erlösen und Vergeben im Alten Testament (1940), and his article "גאל gʾl to redeem," TLOT 1:288-96 [THAT 1:383-94]; also A. R. Johnson, "The Primary Meaning of גאל," in Congress Volume: Copenhagen 1953 (VTSup 1; 1953) 67-77; A. Jepsen, "Die Begriffe des 'Erlösens' im Alten Testament," in Solange es "Heute" heisst. FS R. Hermann (1957) 153-63; H. Ringgren, "גָּאַל gāʾal," TDOT 2:350-55 [ThWAT 1:884-90].

319 Stamm, "גאל gʾl to redeem," TLOT 1:291 [THAT 1:387], with reference to Jepsen, "Die Begriffe des 'Erlösens' im Alten Testament," 159; see also THAT 1:390-92 on DtIsa.

320 See H.-P. Müller, "קדשׁ qdš holy," TLOT 3:1103-18 [THAT 2:589-609].

embraces the heavenly sphere, v. 5b the earthly sphere of God's sovereignty. The divine predications in this verse are in the tradition of the call vision of the prophet Isaiah, according to Isaiah 6. The question raised by the dispute is: "Who is a God like this God?"

■ **6 -10** These verses contain four messages to "the woman." They thrice conclude with "your God (or Yahweh) . . . has said."[321] Verse 9 has a variation: "So I have sworn." From this concluding phrase it is possible to deduce the division into the smallest units: vv. 6, 7-8, 9, 10. Here Yahweh is not yet speaking himself, in direct speech, as he does from v. 11 on. The prophetic formula: "Thus says Yahweh" (כֹּה אָמַר יהוה) is not used. I would assume that the four messages also correspond to four different messengers. These messengers belong to "the heavenly one" who appeared in vv. 4-5.

Formally, the sequence of the messages is striking. Whereas v. 6 contains two statements, vv. 7-8 have four, v. 9 four, and v. 10 four too. This buildup matches the increased weight of the declarations. Thus v. 9 talks about a double oath sworn by Yahweh, v. 10 about "the covenant of my peace"—that is, a legal bond is at all events named. Tension is built up, pointing forward to the event that immediately follows. The text has been very carefully crafted. The *parallelismus membrorum* is precisely observed. There is chiasmus, with corresponding catchwords. The consonants, and probably the vowels too, form a chain of similar sound elements.

The fiction of a marriage-remarriage is retained. The text can be consistently understood on this level. The messengers pass on to "the woman" declarations made by "the lord," which can count as marriage vows. At the same time it is clear—and intentionally so—that here a message from the God of Israel is being proclaimed.

There is an awareness that with the help of a sociomorpheme something is being communicated that can be experienced by everyone: "Yes, *like* a woman" (כִּי־כְאִשָּׁה, v. 6). The text itself signals that this is a comparison. Important traditional terms are given fresh content.

Both strata, the level of the sociomorpheme and the level of the theological interpretation, will be developed in the exegesis below.

■ **6** "A forsaken woman" (אִשָּׁה עֲזוּבָה) belongs terminologically to the divorce sector.[322] In Isa 60:15 it is parallel to "hated" (שְׂנוּאָה). In marriage contracts, "to hate" is a technical term for divorce.[323] A woman can be sent away for unfaithfulness. That was the mode of argument in Hosea and in Ezekiel 16 and 23.

"Afflicted in spirit": The verb עצב means "to be sad, grieved, wounded." The different related substantives cover "injury, trouble, sorrow." It looks as if "afflicted" (עֲצוּבַת) has been chosen because of its similarity in sound to "forsaken" (עֲזוּבָה). Interesting, at all events, is Neh 8:10-11, because there the reaction of the people to the reading of the law is described by way of עצב *Niphal*: they are "troubled"; to this trouble the Levites respond by encouraging the people to rejoice before Yahweh on the feast day. Now, in our v. 6, is the woman's affliction of spirit a sign that she acknowledges that this is the consequence of what she has done? At all events there can no longer be any talk of "arrogance" (גָּאוֹן, Ezek 16:56). If after a divorce, whether it be de facto or de jure (in either case it is a civil law transaction), the man "calls" the woman, this is the first sign of a restoration of the original status. Anyone who "calls" someone else is

---

321 In v. 6 1QIsaᵃ should be followed: "Yahweh, your God."

322 For a different view see H.-P. Stähli, "עזב ʿzb to abandon," *TLOT* 2:867 [*THAT* 2:250]; E. Gerstenberger ("עָזַב ʿāzaḇ," *ThWAT* 5:1200–1208) formulates as follows (1206): "The multifarious use of ʿzb in the legal sector shows that the word means the departure from a relation of solidarity. The word itself is value free; the context determines the evaluation of the particular case."

323 Cf. Gen 29:31; Deut 21:15-17; 24:3; Judg 14:16; 2 Sam 13:15; Jer 12:8; Prov 30:23, with the comments in Y. Zakovitch, "The Woman's Rights in the Biblical Law of Divorce," *JLA* 4 (1981) 28–46; M. Fander, *Die Stellung der Frau im Markusevangelium*

(1989), esp. 209–47. As texts, cf. the marriage contracts from Elephantine in E. G. Kraeling, *The Brooklyn Museum Aramaic Papyri* (1953) 142–43: Papyrus 2 (Brooklyn 47.218.89), pl. XIX,1, l. 7. Kraeling writes here (148): שנאת: 'I divorce (literally 'hate, take a dislike to') my wife' is evidently fixed phraseology that must be used to make the thing legal. It is Babylonian, however, and not found in demotic or Greek marriage contracts. On this see San Nicolò, *OLZ* 30, 1927, 217f., and Paul Koschaker, 'Beiträge zum altbabylonischen Recht,' *ZA* 35, 1924, 200, according to whom the term originally refers to refusal of intercourse." See here Isa 60:15; see also Kraeling, *Aramaic Papyri*, 204–5: Papyrus 7 (Brooklyn 47.218.150), ll. 21-22.

issuing an invitation.[324] A comparison with Isa 62:1-5 suggests that what is meant is the calling by a new name (v. 2: וְקֹרָא לָךְ שֵׁם חָדָשׁ "You are called by a new name").

62:4 says: "They will no more call you 'Forsaken' (עֲזוּבָה) . . . but you shall be called 'My Delight is in Her' (כִּי לָךְ יִקָּרֵא חֶפְצִי־בָהּ)." The context makes clear that the marriage relationship has thereby been restored.

In marriage contracts too the calling by name of the two partners to the marriage is part of the fundamental acts that establish the marriage relationship.[325] Where the present text is concerned, the lord has been named (יִקָּרֵא) in the preceding 54:5. Verse 6 deals with the woman's name (קְרָאָךְ). The names are officially given only in 54:11 for the first time. But here in v. 6 the woman's status is already secured in the form of a comparison. She is and remains "the wife of [her husband's] youth" (אֵשֶׁת נְעוּרִים).[326] What has happened since cannot do away with this fundamental experience, either for the man or for the woman.

The text touches on the problem of remarriage with the previous husband.[327] Deut 24:1-4 specifically excludes this possibility. The reason is probably the feared "defilement" of the woman (cf. Lev 18:20; Num 5:13). This could have the effect of "polluting the land" (cf. Jer 3:1). Hosea hopes that it may be possible for a divorced woman to return to her husband.[328] Against the background of these discussions, that a remarriage is possible is for DtIsa a miracle of God's free grace and an outcome of his love. In this text, therefore, the seam joining the marriage image and the portrayal of Israel/Jerusalem's relationship to God is already detectable. The love even for "the one who has been forsaken" is the very opposite of "contempt" or "repudiation" (מָאַס, v. 6b).[329]

■ **7-8** The somber *u* sounds in v. 6 are taken up by vv. 7-8 (twice וְ, "but," at the beginning). Each of the four declarations in these verses begins with בְּ (*bᵉ*, "in, with"). But the keynote is sounded with the striking series of *e* sounds (*segol*, 8 times). Is the sound supposed to accord with the lament? At all events this is again a carefully composed unit.[330] The link with the language of the Psalms is obvious.[331] The terms used are emotional: "great compassion" and "floods of anger." "Steadfast grace/bond of affection" (חֶסֶד עוֹלָם) is a marriage vow reduced to a brief formula. Hosea already put it in similar terms:

I betroth you to me for ever (לְעוֹלָם).[332]
I betroth you to me in law and righteousness
and in goodness (וּבְחֶסֶד) and mercy (וּבְרַחֲמִים).
I betroth you to me in faithfulness
(Hos 2:21-22 [2:19-20]).[333]

Here tradition has already laid down the lines for a transition from the sociomorpheme "marriage" to an understanding of the relationship with God.

---

324 See C. J. Labuschagne, "קרא *qrʾ* to call," *TLOT* 3:1158–64, esp. 1161 [*THAT* 2:666–74, esp. 669–70]: "A frequent nuance is 'to call on' in the sense of 'to summon to oneself' or 'to invite.' It occurs particularly in cases involving the establishment of contact over some distance."

325 See, e.g., Kraeling, *The Brooklyn Museum Aramaic Papyri* (1953) 142–43: Papyrus 2, pl. XIX,1, ll. 1-4; cf. the Aramaic text, ll. 3-4:
. . . לתמת שׁמה זי אמתך לאנתו הי אנתתי
. . . ואנה בעלה מן יומא זנה ועד עלם.

326 According to *HALOT* 2:704 [*HALAT* 3:665]: "she who was married as a virgin (chaste, intact)"; cf. Mal 2:14-15; Prov 5:18; also Jer 2:2; Ezek 16:22, 43, 60; Hos 2:17 (15).

327 On the following see Fander, *Die Stellung der Frau im Markusevangelium* (1989) 210–13.

328 See esp. Hos 2:16-25 (14-23) and the commentary on the text in Jörg Jeremias, *Hosea* (1983); cf. Judges 19; 2 Sam 3:13-16.

329 See H. Wildberger, "מָאַס *mʾs* to reject," *TLOT* 2:651–60 [*THAT* 1:879–92]; S. Wagner and H.-J. Fabry, "מָאַס *māʾas*," *TDOT* 8:47–60 [*ThWAT* 4:618–33].

330 Westermann (274 [221]) writes about the text: "Here we have the heart of the matter, the basic factor in Deutero-Isaiah's proclamation—with God himself and in God himself the change has already taken place, and therefore everything must alter. A change has come over God. He ceases from wrath, and again shows Israel mercy. This makes everything all right again." Cf. also Zech 1:16-17; 8:3.

331 Cf. Pss 30:6-8 (5-7); 44:25 (24); 51:3 (1); 69:17 (16); 88:15 (14); 104:29; 106:45-46; 143:7.

332 Cf. the formulation in the Aramaic marriage contracts; see, e.g., Kraeling, *The Brooklyn Museum Aramaic Papyri* (1953) 142–43: Papyrus 2, pl. XIX,1, l. 4.

333 See H. J. Stoebe, "חֶסֶד *ḥesed* kindness," *TLOT* 2:449–64 [*THAT* 1:600–621]; on the Hosea text, 458–59 [614]: "The modes of behavior named are the bride-price paid by the man, since they are for the direct benefit of the woman, and are really his gift to her. The sequence of terms represents an inner logic: behavior in accordance with the norm, law and morality provide the framework, filled with

According to H.-J. Zobel, "there are three elements constitutive of the *ḥesed* concept: it is active, social, and enduring."[334] The rendering "goodness, graciousness, kindness" or "faithfulness, loyalty" roughly describes what is meant.

Here DtIsa employs the term with great precision. It is noticeable that it occurs only four times in all: in 40:6; 54:8, 10; and 55:3. Its use in 55:3—"the steadfast grace for David"—is clearly related to the dynastic promises. These are now to apply to the whole of Israel.[335] I believe that in the first chapter too, in 40:6-8, the "goodliness of the flower" (חַסְדּוֹ כְּצִיץ הַשָּׂדֶה, 40:6bβ) that fades refers to the dynasty. The people are "grass," as is explicitly stated in this parablelike comparison (40:7b).[336]

Here in 54:8 (as in v. 10) *ḥesed* is the personification of the unity of Jerusalem and Israel who, as "woman," is promised "grace, goodness, faithfulness, a bond of affection" by her "lord," in a new community with God.

The final formula "your redeemer Yahweh" (גֹּאֲלֵךְ יהוה) also links the family and the political spheres, gathering up both possibilities into the religious interpretation. A forsaken woman is in danger of shipwreck. There can be many reasons why she is forsaken. The biblical texts bring out the economic causes in particular (cf. the book of Ruth). A member of her family clan could "redeem" her. This would mean that the woman was no longer without rights or unprovided for. In a transferred sense, "one could also include the patriarchal period in the usage of *gᵓl* [redeem], and one could understand the exodus from Egypt as the return of the enslaved to their legitimate lord, as a reestablishment of their freedom."[337] For DtIsa the corresponding event would be the liberation from exile. It is therefore plain that right down to the individual concepts the historical dimension of the text continually emerges.

This may also be said, finally, of the term "while, for a time."[338] What first sounds completely personal—a man is angry with his wife and is estranged from her "for a while" (רֶגַע, v. 8)—becomes an explicit interpretation of the exilic-postexilic period. It is said of Yahweh: "For a little while (בְּרֶגַע קָטֹן) I forsook you."[339] A period of time that from the human point of view may be cruelly long is in God's eyes "a little while." The prayers of lament in the Psalter especially make this plain (see Pss 6:4; 79:5, 80:5). But this recognition also fosters the hope that help will soon come.

Who has actually forsaken whom, and why? It is striking that a text that initially talks in the categories of a patriarchal view of marriage should leave this open. There is evidently a play on the catchword "forsake" (עזב).[340] It is not only male virtues that are mentioned: at this point above all there is talk about "great mercy" (plur. בְּרַחֲמִים גְּדֹלִים *bᵉraḥᵃmîm gᵉdolîm*, v. 7b),[341] and the listeners are told: "I have had mercy on you" (רִחַמְתִּיךְ *riḥamtîk*, v. 8aγ). Here the word "mercy" (רחם *rḥm*) probably contains an echo of the word for "womb" (רֶחֶם *reḥem*). God's strength comes from his compassion.

■ **9** In the framework of the action, which depicts the preparations for a wedding, the man's promise to the woman has its special point: "So I have sworn that I will not be angry with you and will not scold you" (54:9b). The listeners could assent to this with all their hearts. Appeal can be made to a marriage vow of this kind! As oath (נִשְׁבַּעְתִּי), the man's promise is divinely sanctioned. But by way of the catchword "oath" (which is twice used) the message is at the same time transposed from everyday experience ("being angry and scolding" are destructive of a relationship) into theological conceptuality. This transference again takes place through a proof based on Scripture and tradition: the reminder of Noah.

ḥesed wᵉraḥᵃmîm, the bestowal of affection and mercy that exceeds the norm; *ᵓᵉmûnâ* 'faithfulness' underscores the steadfastness and reliability already implicit in 'forever.'" See also H.-J. Zobel, חֶסֶד *ḥesed*," *TDOT* 5:44–64, esp. 55–56 [*ThWAT* 3:48–71, esp. 61–62].

334 Zobel, "חֶסֶד *ḥesed*," *TDOT* 5:44–64, esp. 51 [*ThWAT* 3:48–71, esp. 56]. The German title of N. Glueck's pioneering study seems to me to be still helpful: *Das Wort ḥesed im alttestamentlichen Sprachgebrauch als menschliche und göttliche gemeinschaftsgemässe Verhaltensweise* (2d ed. 1961). (The title of the English trans. is simply *Ḥesed in the Bible* [1967].)

335 See below on this passage.

336 See above on this passge.

337 Stamm, "גאל *gᵓl* to redeem," *TLOT* 1:293 [*THAT* 1:390]; cf. also further on DtIsa, 390–92.

338 See *HALOT* s.v. רֶגַע.

339 Cf. Zech 1:15.

340 Cf. Isa 54:6 and 41:17; 42:16; 49:14; 55:7.

341 "In great compassion I will *gather* you" (אֲקַבְּצֵךְ, v. 7b) is strange. It may be a result of the collective understanding of "the woman." "Things" can be gathered—possessions, grain, or people. In

At the beginning of v. 9 the sounds or consonants do not permit a definite decision as to whether this is a reminder of "the days of Noah" or of "the waters of Noah." But the ambiguity may very well be intentional.

If read as "the days of Noah" (correctly the phrase would have to be written: כִּימֵי, "as the days") this could be a reminder of the beginning of the story of the flood as told in Genesis 6–9. According to Gen 6:4, "The giants (הַנְּפִלִים) were on the earth in those days" (בַּיָּמִים הָהֵם). They were the outcome of the union of the sons of God and the daughters of human beings. That is ἱερὸς γάμος in its mythological form. R. Bartelmus has shown how the motifs in Gen 6:1-4 are connected with Jerusalem, the dynasty and the hero cult.[342] The catastrophe of the flood is caused by the infringement of the borderline between the divine and the human.

On the other hand, v. 9a could be pointing to the end of the flood story when it says that "the waters of Noah should not again cover the earth." The verse begins: "As the waters of Noah" (כְּמֵי, v. 9aα; cf. LXX), and now "the waters of Noah" are stressed once more. The reason for this could lie in the immediate context of chap. 54, where the theme is the acute dispute with the deities Baal and Anat. Baal is the weather god, with whom Yahweh's activity in the history of the flood is contrasted. Against the background of the dispute with the Baal myth, "not to be angry" and "not to scold" in v. 9 no longer sound so innocuous. "Scolding" (גָּעַר, v. 9b) can reveal the deity as "a wild warrior who 'cries out' in his wrath, in order to drive away his enemies. . . . The addressees of the invective described through gāʿar are all the different opponents of Yahweh, everything that symbolizes chaos in nature and rebellion in history."[343]

The struggle is against water and sea (cf. Ps 18:16 [15] par. 2 Sam 22:16). In Ps 104:7 "scolding" (usually translated "rebuke") is set parallel to "thunder." These are *topoi* belonging to a God who rules over the weather. But the present text explains that this primordial power of "scolding" is to come to an end.

"Not again" (עוֹד) is the promise that already concluded the Yahwist's account of the flood: "I will never again (עוֹד) curse the earth because of humankind. . . . From henceforth (עֹד) all the days, as long as the earth endures, seedtime and harvest, cold and heat, summer and winter, day and night, shall not cease" (Gen 8:21-22). This promise makes obsolete a cult that is supposed to secure the rhythm of the seasons. Yet it is actually the alternation of the seasons that reflects the relationship between Baal and Anat. According to the myth, Anat seeks Baal in the underworld so that the fertility of the land should be ensured. But for Genesis as for DtIsa, it is Yahweh's promise that secures life. According to Isa 55:10-11, the rain "that waters the earth" is the correspondence to God's word. Water is a highly important theme for DtIsa, in its threatening character and as a gift that confers life. This probably also has to do with the character of the spring festival, for which the liturgical drama was composed.

■ **10** This last message is summed up by the key expression: "covenant of my peace" (בְּרִית שְׁלוֹמִי), as the conclusion of the whole. It once more links the two levels of the text: the marriage contract and the covenant with Noah. "Contract, covenant" (בְּרִית) can be used for a marriage contract.[344] The remarkable thing is that this is also the case in the context of Ezekiel 16, "the unfaithful wife"[345] (Jerusalem). Ezek 16:8 is a reminder of "the act of the divine choice to wed."[346] The history of the destruction of the relationship with God follows (Ezek 16:15-51). Ezek 16:59-63 defines the hope for the renewal of the covenant: "For so has Yahweh your God spoken: But I have done to you what you have done, you who have despised the oath, breaking the covenant (בְּרִית); yet I will remember my covenant (בְּרִיתִי) with you (which I made) in the days of your youth and I will renew for you an everlasting covenant (בְּרִית עוֹלָם)" (Ezek 16:59-60).[347]

For DtIsa to take up the catchword "covenant" in this connection shows that this is the interpretation of tradi-

---

Nehemiah it is a catchword for the "gathering" of the community: *Qal*, Neh 5:16; 7:5; 13:11; *Niphal*, Neh 4:14; *Piel*, Neh 1:9; for the banished see E. Sehmsdorf, "Studien zur Redaktionsgeschichte von Jesaja 56–66 (II)," *ZAW* 84 (1972) 547-48; cf. *HALOT* 3:1063 [*HALAT* 3:995].

342 See R. Bartelmus, *Heroentum in Israel und seiner Umwelt* (1979). See also above (on 52:13–53:12) the observation about the "antiheroic" presentation of

the Servant Moses.

343 A. Caquot, "גָּעַר gāʿar," TDOT 3:49-53, esp. 51 [*ThWAT* 2:51-56, esp. 53].

344 See Ezek 16:8; Mal 2:14; Prov 2:17; also the Damascus Document, CD 16.10-12.

345 W. Zimmerli, *Ezekiel 1* (1979) 342 [*Ezechiel* (3d ed. 1979) 331].

346 Ibid., 339-40, quote on 339 [350-51, quote on 350].

347 Cf. ibid. on the text.

446

tion. Hope is fulfilled. The promise is a marriage vow: "My grace/bond of affection (וְחַסְדִּי) will not depart from you" (54:10b). The marriage contracts show how this can be thought of in concrete terms. These contracts are mutual, but the partners do not always have to be equal. The mutual undertakings and obligations are laid down for the particular case in each instance. Thus the sociomorpheme "marriage" must be taken seriously here too.[348]

But the understanding of "the covenant of my peace" (בְּרִית שְׁלוֹמִי)[349] is not confined to the level of the marriage contract and the wedding. With this catchword the text is also referring to the Noachic covenant, as the Priestly writing has transmitted it, according to Gen 9:11-17:[350] "I renew my covenant with you (וַהֲקִמֹתִי אֶת־בְּרִיתִי) that never again (עוֹד) shall all flesh be cut off by the waters of the flood, and never again (עוֹד) shall there be a flood to destroy the earth" (Gen 9:11).[351] According to Gen 9:16 this is "an everlasting covenant" (בְּרִית עוֹלָם), and according to Gen 9:17 it applies to everything living on the earth. The end of the story of the flood in the Priestly writing, with the bow in the clouds as the sign of God's covenant (Gen 9:13), is undoubtedly very close to the DtIsa text.

A number of commentators see the point in common between the DtIsa text and the Noah tradition as being the notion of "the turn of the age." The Noachic covenant meant a new beginning after the catastrophe of the flood, and in the same way there can be a new beginning after the catastrophe of the exile. "The covenant of peace" is the divine promise. This interpretation is conceivable because in this way the level of "the woman" and the level of Israel's history can be linked. The new covenant is as sure and enduring as the covenant with Noah.

This last message concludes the proclamation to Zion/Jerusalem. The text should be consistently heard on the two levels. It contains "marriage vows" and at the same time talks about the renewal of the relationship with God in the broadest sense.

In conclusion, I should like to raise the question whether the text of vv. 6-10 is not also taking up a particular stance with regard to a topical question of its own time.

The marriage promises explicitly stress the permanence of the marriage relationship in both the emotional sphere and legally. The arc reaches from "the wife of your youth" by way of the "lasting grace/bond of affection" to "the covenant of my peace."

The example of the Noachic covenant is related to the whole of humanity, not just to Israel. Is the text a covert polemic against the dissolution of so-called mixed marriages? I believe that DtIsa supports Nehemiah's measures—with the exception of the laws about marriage. The building of the wall, and with that the elevation of Jerusalem, is again the subject of the immediately following text, 54:11-14. DtIsa also demands the liberation of slaves—the remission of debts. In the land of Israel the measures Ezra and Nehemiah introduced about the dissolution of marriages were based—for us problematically—on a particular rationale: a line drawn round Israel's own ethnic identity within the structure of the Persian Empire. The law of inheritance plays a part. But DtIsa appeals decidedly to the *gōlâ* too, to "the many." Could someone outside the country itself be in favor of a measure such as the dissolution of marriages? The marriage contracts of Elephantine in my view speak against this, as does DtIsa's position in general.

---

348 G. Gerlemann's comments in his article, "שלם *šlm* to have enough" (in the sense of "retaliation"), *TLOT* 3:1337–48 [*THAT* 2:919–35], must be read critically. But I can agree with his definition (1344 [928–29]): "If the main stress falls on the action, the means of satisfaction, *šālōm* can mean a contract, an agreement. . . . If more stress is laid on the condition brought about by the compensation, . . . the meaning of *šālōm* shifts toward 'peace,' i.e., a state that proceeds from actions or services performed on both sides."

349 On בְּרִית שָׁלוֹם, cf. Num 25:12; Ezek 34:25; 37:26.

350 Van der Merwe, *Pentateuchtradisies in de Prediking van Deuterojesaja* (1955) 74–81.

351 See C. Westermann, *Genesis 1–11* (1984) on the text [*Genesis 1–11* (3d ed. 1983)].

54

"See, I am covering your stones with
<turquoises> . . ." (54:11)
"In/Through righteousness you will be firmly
founded" (54:14a)

11	Wretched One, "Storm-Tossed," Not-Comforted!
	See, I am covering your stones with <turquoise>ᵃ
	and <your foundation walls>ᵇ with sapphires.
12	And I am making your pinnacles of rubies,
	and your doors of crystal,
	and all your surrounding wall of precious stones.
13	And all your descendants [or: "builders"]ᵃ have been taught by Yahweh,
	and great will be the peace/salvation of your descendants [or: "builders"]ᵇ.
14a	In/Through righteousness you will be firmly founded.

11ᵃ Thus with a correction from בַּפּוּך, "with mortar," to בְּנֹפֶך.

11ᵇ Thus with a correction from וִיסַדְתִּיך, "and I found you (on sapphires)," to וִיסֹדֹתַיִך (cf. 1QIsaᵃ, LXX).

13ᵃ·ᵇ Either בָּנַיִך, "your sons/descendants," or בֹּנַיִך, "your builders," depending on the pointing; see below.

"The Lord is coming!" That could be the description of what happens in the transition from v. 10 to v. 11.[352] This is a new scene. 54:1-10 describes the different stages in which the coming is prepared and heralded. Now "the lord" himself appears. He is perceived and identified by way of the unequivocal: "See, *I* . . ." (הִנֵּה אָנֹכִי). In whatever way we ought to imagine the performance, the dramatic tension builds up to this point. Here too elements of the wedding ("the bridegroom is coming") and the restoration of the woman's original status are intertwined, making something that is new. The female personification is not given a name. The mention of "pinnacles and gates" (v. 12) again suggests a city, hence Zion/Jerusalem. But since v. 13 talks about children (or descendants), it is not just the city alone that is meant. If one compares it here with the Servant of God, "the spouse of God" is also directly addressed by "the lord."[353]

■ **11 a** This verse begins by giving the woman three names: she is called "Wretched One, 'Storm-Tossed,' Not-Comforted." These are extremely curious descriptions, somewhat comparable with the names given by prophets to their children, as signs.[354] A man can give his wife a new name representing her significance, as when Adam called his wife "*ḥawwâ*" (Eve), "because she was the mother of all the living" (Gen 3:20; cf. 2:23).[355] But it is absurd for a bridegroom to address his bride as "Wretched One."[356] This must be a spur to listeners to reflect, and is surely intended as such. In my view, the very first word implies a distinct criticism of all sacred-marriage ideology.

In line with DtIsa's general thinking, Jerusalem is called in 51:21 "Wretched/poor one"[357] (עֲנִיָּה), this being the moment of profoundest humiliation for the personified city and her children. She is "drunk—but not with wine." Now, in 54:11-14, "the miserable one" is about to be crowned. This is therefore a kind of mirror scene.

According to *HALOT,* עָנִי "in a sociological sense

352 Cf. Matt 25:6; Heb 10:37; Rev 19:7; 22:17-20.

353 See in vv. 11-13 the series of seven 2d person fem. sing. suffixes, "your. . . ." The sound sequence is: *ʾăbānayik wîsōdōtayik . . . šimšōtayik ûšĕʿārayik . . . gĕbûlēk . . . bānayik . . . bānāyik.*

354 See Hos 1:3-5, 6-7, 8-9; Isa 8:1-4.

355 Cf. Westermann, *Genesis 1–11* (1984) on this passage [*Genesis 1–11* (3d ed. 1983)].

356 See also Isa 62:4.

357 Cf. also Lam 1:3, 7, 9 (substantive עָנִי in various forms).

[means] being without adequate land and therefore dependent on others,"[358] and then "in a general sense to be poor, wretched, in a needy condition, and therefore particularly dependent on God, esp. in Ps[alms]."[359] If one takes H.-J. Kraus's definition: "'Poor' are those who are denied justice, who possess no influence or status, who are at the mercy of opponents with unlimited power,"[360] this could be a precise definition of "Zion's" situation, when it comes forward for the first time at the beginning of Act V, in 49:14-21. There it is the wife who has been forsaken by her "lord" (אֲדֹנָי), and who appeals for judicial help to Yahweh as judge.[361] Now, at the close of Act VI, she is again publicly confirmed in her former status. The promise given there, "I will not forget you," is now fulfilled with the coming of her lord. The history that has led up to this point—the misery caused by guilt—is not forgotten, but it is now gathered up into the new commitment. This makes hope for the future possible.[362]

The naming of the woman as סֹעֲרָה is another difficulty. The meaning of the verb סער in the *Qal* is "storm."[363] The form used in the MT is explained as being the *Pual* perfect or participle, "blown away, driven away."[364] DtIsa uses the image of the storm or tempest that blows away the stubble (40:24) or chaff (41:16). In the OT, a tempest (סער and its derivatives) can be a sign of the epiphany.[365] This epiphany can have warlike features.[366] The struggle is directed against the enemy,[367]

but against Israel itself too.[368] It is possible to interpret the word "blown away" as referring to the fate of Zion/Jerusalem; but the interpretation remains unsatisfactory.

1QIsaᵃ offers another solution, reading סחורה instead of סֹעֲרָה. סחר probably originally means "to pass through," but is then a word used in commerce; thus סוֹחֵר is the dealer, trader (1 Kgs 10:28; Ezek 27:12, 16 and frequently). A noteworthy example is the song about Tyre in Ezekiel (Ezekiel 27),[369] where the word is used in different ways for trade. סחורה (passive participle) in Isa 54:11 would then be the woman who has been treated as a marketable commodity.[370]

Perhaps, however, it is on the face of it plausible enough for Jerusalem to be addressed as "driven by storm."[371] The city lies relatively high,[372] and is more exposed to variable winds than the sultry coastal plains or the Jordan Valley.

When the woman is called "she was not comforted" (לֹא נֻחָמָה, *Pual* perfect of נחם), this form of address takes up the "comfort" theme, which runs right through DtIsa.[373] In 51:3 it already refers to Zion, and in 51:19 to Jerusalem. The status of one who is "not comforted" is now to be transformed into the status of one who is "comforted." The very sound itself (*lōʾ nūḥāmâ*) perhaps

---

358 *HALOT* 2:856 [*HALAT* 3:810], with reference to Exod 22:24 (25); Lev 19:10; 23:22; Deut 15:11; 24:12, 14, 15; Isa 3:14, 15; 10:2; Jer 22:16.

359 *HALOT* 2:856 [*HALAT* 3:810], with reference to, among other passages, Pss 10:2, 9; 14:6; 22:25 (24); 34:7 (6); 68:11 (10); 72:12; 88:16 (15); 102:1 (heading); 140:13 (12).

360 H.-J. Kraus, *Theology of the Psalms* (1986) 150–54: "The Poor," esp. 152 [*Theologie der Psalmen* (1979) "Exkurs: 3. Die Armen," 188–93, esp. 190].

361 See above on this passage. In considering the connection of the two texts, further catchwords should be noted. In 49:17 "your children" (בָּנָיִךְ) are mentioned, as in 54:13. In both cases it may be asked whether the reading should be "your builder." In 49:18 "Zion" is compared with a bride who puts on her adornments; so the marriage image is present there too.

362 The term עני plur. for the miserable or wretched occurs in DtIsa in 41:17 and 49:13. Cf. also 48:10, "furnace of misery"; this term links the time in Egypt (Deut 4:20; Jer 11:4) with the exile. The LXX

renders עני by ταπεινή ("low, poor, humble"). In so doing it brings the passage into line with the sayings about the Servant of God in 53:4, 7 (*Pual* or *Niphal* of ענה).

363 E.g., in Jonah 1:11, 13 talking about the sea.

364 See *HALOT*, s.v.; cf. Hos 13:3; Job 15:30; Hab 3:14.

365 2 Kgs 2:1, 11; Ezek 1:4.

366 E.g., Isa 29:6; Zech 9:14.

367 Ps 83:16 (15); Isa 29:6.

368 Amos 1:14; Hos 13:2-3; Zech 7:14.

369 Cf. Isa 23:3, 18.

370 Cf. Isa 45:14, "the (trading) profit" (סְחַר) of Cush.

371 Chicago, for example, is called "the windy city." This accords with its position on Lake Michigan. But the epithet originally referred to the political circumstances.

372 In the northwest, 2,600 ft. (790 m.) above sea level. The Temple Mount in the southeast lies at a height of 2,350 to 2,400 ft. (720–740 m.).

373 Cf. 40:1; 49:13; 51:12; 52:9; see further 66:13: "As a mother comforts her child, so I will comfort you."

establishes an association with the name of Hosea's daughter "Without-Pity" (לֹא רֻחָמָה *lōʾ rūḥāmâ*).[374] The prophet Hosea used the name to proclaim disaster to the house of Israel (Hos 1:6-7). That disaster is now ended. Hosea 2:25 (23) promises pity for "Without-Pity." Here the context in Hosea (esp. 2:16-25 [14-23]) makes clear that what is meant is a new covenant and a renewed marriage relationship with Israel, as God's people. This interpretation again brings out the striking closeness between Hosea and DtIsa's theme. Here too scriptural interpretation is employed as a way of grasping the present.

But as a whole, the interpretation of v. 11a offered hitherto cannot be considered completely satisfactory. We have seen that the titular statements have their point in the framework of DtIsa's concept. But tensions remain, and these are all the more noticeable because of the prominent position given to the text, at the beginning of the theophany. In DtIsa, however, difficulties in the text have continually proved to be signals indicating different possible levels of understanding. Continuing what was worked out for 54:1-10, we may ask whether the dispute with the foreign cult (and the cult of the goddess Anat in particular) does not play a part in v. 11a too.

To render עֲנִיָּה as "wretched" easily obscures the fact that the scope and meaning of the Hebrew root ענה (*ʿnh*) is much disputed.[375] *HALAT* 3:805–8, for example, lists four different but homonymous roots. This provides an ideal opportunity for wordplay. If it is derived from ענה IV, עֲנִיָּה could theoretically also be translated "singing

one." Since the context is a wedding, this is not wholly out of the question. The interchangeability of ענה I, "respond" and ענה II, "to be miserable," offers a more serious possibility. If עֲנִיָּה is derived from ענה I, it could mean "the one who responds." "Respond" in the sense of "agreeing to follow" is used in Hos 2:17 (15) to express the restoration of the original relationship to God.[376] But even in Hosea, the interpretation "betrothal" and "marriage" has already been acquired in the course of the dispute with Canaanite cultic tradition.

I suspect that the three titular descriptions of "the woman" are references to three aspects of the goddess Anat:

1. "To respond," in the sense of "to react willingly (in the sexual sense)": this can be a way of describing her as goddess of love.[377]
2. "Storm-Tossed":[378] This epithet for Zion-Jerusalem may conceal a term for the goddess Anat. All that is necessary is to change the form, from *Pual*, "storm-driven, storm-tossed," to *Qal*, "storming one." Anat is depicted as a winged deity.[379] She is swift when she has to bring a message.[380] But her role as tutelary goddess of horses[381] could also play a part in a description of this kind.
3. "Not-Comforted": Here we should also have to assume a reversal of the expected epithet. As goddess of war, Anat does not "comfort," nor does she have mercy.[382]

Thus these three titles, disparate though they are, can be linked in a way that makes sense.[383] They are consistent

In contrast, cf. Lam 1:2, 9, 17, 21: "There is no one to comfort her."

374 See Beuken, 260 on this passage; H. J. Stoebe, "נחם *nḥm* pi. to comfort," *TLOT* 2:736, §b [*THAT* 2:63 §b]; Jörg Jeremias, *Hosea* (1983) 32–33, 46–52.

375 See C. J. Labuschagne, "ענה *ʿnh* I, to answer," *TLOT* 2:926–30, esp. 926 [*THAT* 2:335–41, esp. 335]: "The usual distinction presumed in the lexicons between four homonymous roots *ʿnh* I 'to answer,' *ʿnh* II 'to be bowed down,' *ʿnh* III 'to be occupied with' and *ʿnh* IV 'to sing' . . . is anything but uncontested" (with lit.).

376 On the text see H. W. Wolff, *Hosea* (1974) 30–31, 42–43 [*Hosea* (3d ed. 1976) 36–37, 52–53]; Jörg Jeremias, *Hosea* (1983) 48.

377 See here Labuschagne's thesis in "ענה *ʿnh* I, to answer," *TLOT* 2:927 [*THAT* 2:336]: "The name of the goddess *ʿanāt* is associated, in my view, with *ʿnh*

in the meaning 'sexually willing/responsive' (cf. Hos 2:17 [15]; Exod 21:10 . . .)." See also A. S. Kapelrud, *The Violent Goddess: Anat in the Ras Shamra Texts* (1969) 27–31. Also Walls, *The Goddess Anat in Ugaritic Myth* (1992) with more recent lit.

378 See also H.-J. Fabry, "סָעַר *sāʿar*," *ThWAT* 5:893–98, esp. 896.

379 Kapelrud, *Violent Goddess*, 108: text 10:II:10-12 (*UT* 76:II:10-12).

380 Kapelrud, *Violent Goddess*, 107, with reference to 3:D:55-56, *UT* ʿnt 4:55-56.

381 See W. Helck, "Anat, Ägypten," in H. W. Haussig, ed., *Wörterbuch der Mythologie*, vol. 1: *Götter und Mythen im Vorderen Orient* (1965) 333.

382 See M. H. Pope, "Anat, Syrien," in ibid., 1:238–39, with reference to the second column, V AB (Baal cycle).

383 See also Kapelrud, *The Violent Goddess: Anat in the*

with the background developed for an understanding of 54:1-10, in the dispute with the Baal-Anat cult.

Anat's different aspects are thus picked up and changed into titles. Nevertheless, their original meaning can still be reconstructed fairly easily. With the first word of this scene עֲנִיָּה (*ʿaniyyâ*), DtIsa ventures a breathtaking allusion. He takes up the goddess's attributes. But this does not make "the wife of God" a goddess. Israel-Zion/Jerusalem is a unity that remains a personification. It is a concrete abstraction that formulates the relationship between God, the city, and the people.

■ **11b-12** Since chap. 54 has to do with a new beginning for Zion/Jerusalem, it seems appropriate that one topic should be the rebuilding of the city walls. Walls make a city, because they ensure its safety and independence. The text contains a series of building terms. It enumerates explicitly: "Stones, foundation stones (or foundation walls), pinnacles, gates, enclosure." The splendor of the walls is emphasized by the precious stones, a whole list of which is also given. Some exegetes (following a suggestion of F. Stummer) have compared the text with Babylonian building inscriptions.[384] These suggest, among other things, that in the comparison with precious stones it is merely their color—perhaps the result of faience techniques—that provides the point of comparison.

But the subject of the text seems to me more complicated than that. There is a curious interweaving of image and fact, an interweaving typical of emblems. I should like to propose a solution that gives more weight to the immediate context.

In the text, the city is represented by a woman, "marriage" being the sociomorpheme. The dispute with other religious views and cults is pursued simultaneously. The object that Yahweh himself fashions—surely with artistry—could be a mural crown.[385] This would link the architectural elements listed in the text with the mural crown as ornament. Mural crowns are an essential identification mark for a city goddess, especially when she takes the form of Tyche.[386] They designate her as a tutelary goddess, who secures the city's good fortune. A number of deities wear the mural crown, the best known being Cybele and Astarte.[387] Representations of mural crowns may even date as far back as the Hittite period. An Assyrian example is the one worn by the queen Ashur-sharrat, Ashurbanipal's consort.[388] The wide distribution of this type of representation (the city goddess wearing the mural crown) has to do with the growth of cities in the Persian and Hellenistic periods, especially in Asia Minor and Syria.

Against this background it is notable that Yahweh himself should give the command to rebuild Jerusalem (44:26, 28; 45:13). Her walls are always "before him" (49:16). The text that immediately follows (54:15-17)

Ras Shamra Texts (1969) 105 on "5. The winged goddess": "The picture of Anat which Cassuto published [U. Cassuto, *The Goddess Anath: Canaanite Epics of the Patriarchal Age* (2d ed. 1953)] . . . shows the goddess as an attractive young lady, furnished with the attributes of the war goddess. This indicates that she was primarily seen as goddess of love and goddess of war, and that her usual shape was human." See also M. H. Pope, "Anat, Syrien," in Haussig, *Wörterbuch der Mythologie*, vol. 1, pl. III, 315; and the article "Anat, Syrien," 235–41; W. Helck, "Anat, Ägypten," in ibid., 333. Cf. also the reference to Anat in the Elephantine texts; cf. B. Porten, *Archives from Elephantine* (Berkeley, 1968) 149, 166, 170–73, 177–79.

384 F. Stummer, "Einige keilschriftliche Parallelen zu Jes 40–66," *JBL* 45 (1926) 171–89; Westermann, 291 [234]; Beuken, 244: "a building oracle (vv. 11-14a)"; cf. also 261–64; D. Baltzer, *Ezechiel und Deuterojesaja* (1971) 168 (with reference to S. Langdon, *Die neubabylonischen Königsinschriften* [1912], esp. I 53–II 5, 220–23).

385 See K. Baltzer, "The Polemic against the Gods and Its Relevance for Second Isaiah's Conception of the New Jerusalem," in T. C. Eskenazi and K. H. Richards, eds., *Second Temple Studies*, 2 (1994) 43–50 ["Stadt Tyche oder Zion-Jerusalem?" in *Alttestamentlicher Glaube und Biblische Theologie. FS H. D. Preuss* (1992) 114–19].

386 See W. Deonna, "Histoire d'un emblème. La couronne murale des villes et pays personnifiés," *Bulletin du Musée et d'Histoire de Genève* 18 (1940) 119–236; S. M. Paul, "Jerusalem—A City of Gold," *IEJ* 17 (1967) 259–63; M. Hörig, *Dea Syria: Studien zur religiösen Tradition der Fruchtbarkeitsgöttin in Vorderasien* (AOAT 208 [1979]) 129–97.

387 The closeness of Astarte and Anat is striking. In Atargatis they probably fuse into a single figure. This is of interest for the present text.

388 Following Hörig, *Dea Syria: Studien zur religiösen Tradition der Fruchtbarkeitsgöttin in Vorderasien* (1979) 191–92; *AOB*, pls. 148–49 (text: 50).

makes clear that Yahweh himself also protects the city.[389] But it is Yahweh who confers the crown on the woman representing Zion/Jerusalem. It remains her adornment. With that the city is simultaneously reinstalled in her rights by Yahweh.

Even if the catchword "crown" (עֲטָרָה) is not actually used, the description in vv. 11-12 is nonetheless correct. A "mural crown" quite realistically depicts a wall with pinnacles and gates. The specific building and defense technology can easily be gathered from the sculptures and coins that have been preserved. Unfortunately, in the present text some of the terms can no longer be identified with any certainty, especially where the precious stones are concerned.[390] How many speculative elements play a part in the description of the crown, the gems and the colors is difficult to decide.[391] According to v. 11b, the costly crown is fashioned by Yahweh himself; he is the "goldsmith."[392] Verse 11bα can be rendered: "I am one who permits a setting (מַרְבִּיץ) with פּוּךְ your stones." This would mean that פּוּךְ can be assumed to be "mortar."[393] That would fit, inasmuch as the setting of the stones is important (cf. 1 Chr 29:2). But if פּוּךְ is used as powder for eye makeup (2 Kgs 9:30: Jer 4:30; cf. Job 42:14; Ezek 23:40), then the word could have to do with the color, and this can either be black (*stibium*, antimony; the LXX has ἄνϑρακα, "coal") or red.[394]

Another possibility is to emend פּוּךְ to נֹפֶךְ, which according to *HALOT*, is a "green coloured, semi-precious stone, found in Sinai." It is identified as turquoise or malachite. This would provide a parallelism to the following סַפִּירִים. I myself think that turquoise is more probable because it is definitely an ornamental stone. The rendering would then be: "I am covering your stones with (a semiprecious stone)."

The usual practice now is to follow 1QIsa^a in emend-

ing to וִיסוֹדוֹתַיִךְ, "and your foundation walls." The סַפִּיר used for this corresponds in its semantic elements to the brilliant blue sapphire. But it is frequently presumed that what is really meant is lapis lazuli, a semiprecious stone that is also blue.[395]

The word כַּדְכֹד is generally supposed to mean the ruby.[396] The LXX has ἴασπις. The jasper is gray, and usually opaque.

On the basis of LXX τὰς ἐπάλξεις σου, שִׁמְשֹׁת is generally rendered "pinnacles." But *HALAT* contradicts this, believing that—because of the connection with שֶׁמֶשׁ, "sun"—it means "sunlike shields, such as are affixed to towers in the ancient East."[397] The mural crown would not speak against this, although there pinnacles are also a prominent feature.

HALOT gives "beryl" for אֶקְדָּח. Beryl is found in different forms, ranging from greenish yellow (the most common color) to blue in the aquamarine. The LXX κρυστάλλος is probably assuming קֶרַח as the Hebrew reading (cf. Ezek 1:22). The relatively large crystals of the rock would certainly be well suited for the gates, the more so when they are transparent.

When it occurs in a list of architectural features, גְּבוּל, "limit," means a border or rim of some kind.[398] In Ezek 43:13, 17, 20, for example, in the description of the altar, it means "rim, sill."[399] The term could be used here to designate the top or bottom border of the wall. It is set with "stones of joy, of pleasure," that is, with "costly gems."[400] What is at all events clear is the costliness and beauty of the mural crown, with its adornment of precious stones. To say that the mural crown was the emblem of Jerusalem does not mean that the topic is not also Jerusalem's real walls, and its existence as a city.[401]

---

389 Cf. Zech 2:8b-9.
390 The explanation put forward here follows for the most part D. Baltzer, *Ezechiel und Deuterojesaja* (1971) 166–68 and *HALOT*. The LXX is also of interest. See further *BHH* on "Edelstein," "Farben." For lists of precious stones cf. Exod 28:18; 39:11; Ezek 27:16; 28:13.
391 See Beuken, 261 with lit.
392 On צָרַף cf. 40:19; 41:7; 46:6.
393 See *HALOT*, s.v.
394 *HALOT*, s.v.; see also Pliny the Elder *Nat. Hist.* 33.33–34.
395 Cf. Exod 24:10; 28:18; Ezek 1:26; see also Pliny the

Elder *Nat. Hist.* 39.
396 Cf. Ezek 27:16; Rev 21:19.
397 *HALAT* points to pictures from Lachish; see *AOB*, pl. 141 (cf. pl. 133); *ANEP*, p. 130, nos. 372–73; see also Ezek 27:11; Cant 4:4. Delitzsch (2:349 [564]) proposed a different solution: "The שִׁמְשֹׁת, however, the pinnacles which stand out like rays of the sun . . . are red" [trans. altered].
398 LXX has τὸν περίβολόν ('border').
399 *HALOT*, s.v.
400 Cf. Sir 45:11 (Hebr.); 50:9 (Hebr.); 1QM 5; 6:9, 14; 12:12-13.
401 Cf. also Tob 13:16-17; Acts 21:10-21.

We must assume that the emblem of the crown would also evoke a long tradition, a tradition particularly evident in Ezekiel. According to Ezekiel 16, Yahweh himself adorned Jerusalem with the mark of a "glorious crown" (וַעֲטֶרֶת תִּפְאֶרֶת, v. 12). It is all the worse when, according to Ezek 32:42, the cities personified as Oholah and Oholibah allow "a glorious crown" to be placed on their heads by foreigners. The judgment on Jerusalem also means loss of the crown (Ezek 21:31 [26]). The city is condemned to be a heap of rubble (Ezek 21:32 [27]; cf. Lam 5:16-18). By saying that Yahweh himself is fashioning a new crown, Dtsa is showing that the prophecy of disaster has now been set aside. Salvation is also shown through the restoration of the city's original status and its dignity.[402]

■ **13-14a** It is strange that vv. 12 and 13 should be linked. "And all your children/descendants" (וְכָל־בָּנָיִךְ, v. 13) takes up "and all your surrounding wall" (וְכָל־גְּבוּלֵךְ, v. 12). In sound, "your stones" (אֲבָנָיִךְ ᵃbānayik, v. 11) and "your children/descendants" (בָּנַיִךְ bānayik, v. 13a) correspond.[403] But what does the mural crown have to do with the children/descendants? In my view, the connection is to be found in the symbolism of the city goddess of fortune or Tyche. This becomes clearer through a comparison with the mirror scene in 51:17-23. There the horn of plenty, or cornucopia, as the emblem of the city goddess Tyche, is parodied in "the cup of staggering." In that text too the "children" play an important part, making Jerusalem's misery plain (51:18, 20). But in Greek city iconography πλοῦτος, "wealth," is the city's "child," which the city goddess Tyche frequently carries in her arms or holds by the hand. A great number of children symbolizes wealth, in population or material riches. It is hence appropriate when now, in 54:13, "your children" manifest the city's new happiness. It is at this point that DtIsa's own interpretation begins. There can only be happiness if *all* the city's inhabitants have come to know Yahweh's commitment to them, and his commandments.[404] The catchword "teach, learn" (למד) picks up what the fourth Servant text in 50:4-11 proclaimed, following the Moses of Deuteronomy. The promise of 53:10 is thus also fulfilled—the promise that the Servant will see descendants, just as "the woman" now does too.

In the salvation saying the crowning is interpreted as Yahweh's "teaching." It is the knowledge conferred that creates life, not the marriage as such.

If *all* are instructed by Yahweh, this is in accordance with the ideal of the coming age. Simple-mindedness is never considered a virtue in Israel. Isaiah 55 will explicitly explain what the teaching is.

DtIsa goes on with his interpretation: The city and its economy are hoping for a favorable future, for the able and industrious especially. But it is not this fleeting good fortune that guarantees salvation. It is the "numerous, diverse, rich forms of peace" (רֹב שָׁלוֹם) that Yahweh confers. This expresses DtIsa's conviction that שָׁלוֹם is not a static concept, nor a mere negation (the absence of war). It is extremely active and means the harmonization of interests in justice and equity. This is the enduring meaning of שָׁלוֹם for "the descendants/children" too.

---

402   Cf. also for a similar approach under the catchword "crown," Isa 28:1-3, 5-6.

403   Beuken (262) suspects that the wordplay with בנה, "build," encapsulates a reference to the matriarchs Sarah und Rachel (Gen 16:2; 30:3); see also P. Marinković, "What Does Zechariah 1–8 Tell Us About the Second Temple?" in T. C. Eskenazi and K. H. Richards, eds., *Second Temple Studies*, 2 (1994) 88–103, esp. 98 with reference to Ruth 4:11 ("like Rachel and Leah, who together built up the house of Israel") and Deut 25:9 (levirate marriage) ["Was wissen wir über den zweiten Tempel aus Sach 1–8?" in *Konsequente Traditionsgeschichte. FS Klaus Baltzer* (1993) 281–95, esp. 290].

404   Cf. Neh 8:1-8, the reading of "the book of the law of Moses . . . which Yahweh had given to Israel" (8:1). It takes place "in the presence of the men and the women and all who could understand; and the ears of all the people (כָל־הָעָם) were attentive to the book of the law (אֶת־סֵפֶר הַתּוֹרָה)" (8:3). In W. Rudolph, *Esra und Nehemia samt 3. Esra* (1949) v. 8 reads (translated into English): "And they read from the book, from the law of God, translating from the page and (thereby) making it understandable, and so they understood the reading." The Nehemiah text is a good illustration of what could be meant by "all your children/descendants have been taught by Yahweh" (v. 13). This need not stand in contradiction to the tradition of Jer 24:7; 31:34; Ezek 36:26-27. See also Schoors, *I Am God Your Saviour* (1973) 142. In the NT the text is cited in John 6:45.

If Jerusalem is again the "mother city," or metropolis (Gk. μητρόπολις), then the country towns can be viewed as her children. DtIsa's program in 40:9 makes Zion/Jerusalem, the messenger (of joy), proclaim the return of the Lord Yahweh to the towns of Judah (לְעָרֵי יְהוּדָה, 40:10). He is their God too. That is a precise legal and theological assertion. The "rich peace" that 54:13 talks about is to exist between town and country, as well as among the different country towns. But it may be that this is also the beginning of a topical reference, one indication being the interpretation of "your children" (בָּנָיִךְ) as "your builders" (בוניכי), which is also the reading in 1QIsaᵃ.[405] A comparison with the situation as described in the book of Nehemiah once again shows that help in the rebuilding could involve practical problems that called the "peace" into question. The list of the people who rebuild the walls of Jerusalem (Neh 2:17; 3:1-32)[406] does not include only people belonging to all the different social classes in Jerusalem itself. It also includes people from the country towns: "And next the men of Jericho built next to him" (Neh 3:2).

Conflicts emerge: "And next to them the Tekoites made repairs; but their nobles would not put their shoulders to the work of their Lord" (Neh 3:5).[407] So there is no "peace" among the builders. Other places from which builders came are also named: Gibeon, Meronoth, Mizpah (Neh 3:7),[408] and Zanoah (3:13). In some cases

the administrative districts to which the country towns belonged are added, for example, Beth-zur (Neh 3:16) and Keilah (3:17). The note in Neh 3:38 (4:6) says: "So we rebuilt the wall; and (soon) all the wall was joined together to half its height; for the people had a mind to work."[409]

After the symbolic restitution of Zion/Jerusalem signaled by the mural crown, and the clarification of the relationship to the "children/descendants (or <builders>)," v. 14a once more reverts to a statement of principle: "In/through righteousness you will be firmly established." "You" means both the woman and the city; but at the same time it means the whole unity that the woman now represents. This raises yet again the question about the text's levels of abstraction, and the way in which it was dramatically presented. "Found, establish" (כּוּן Polel) belongs appropriately enough to the semantic field "city" (Hab 2:12; Pss 48:9; 87:5; 107:36). For DtIsa the word "establish" takes up the ancient divine predications and is associated with the creation and preservation of the earth (Isa 45:18; cf. Pss 24:2; 119:90). But in the present text the link between "establish" and "righteousness" (צְדָקָה) already suggests a more abstract interpretation. As so often in DtIsa, this is a brief formula. The background becomes clear if we compare the Trito-Isaiah text chaps. 60–62,[410] the group of texts that already proved helpful in explaining 52:7-10.

---

405 It should be said, more precisely, that in 1QIsaᵃ a ו has been subsequently added above the line, over the ב. The older commentators already considered whether בניך should be read instead of בָּנַיִך (thus Duhm, Grätz, Cheyne). The reason is probably the quotation from Isa 54:13 in b. Ber. 64a: "R. Eleazar says: 'Do not read "thy children" but "thy builders".'" J. Barr (Comparative Philology and the Text of the Old Testament [1968] 45–46) supposed that this was what is known as an al-tiqre (אל־תקרי) interpretation: "The interpreter may know perfectly well the general usage and reference of a word at the same time as he is producing an artificial analysis of it in quite another sense" (46). See also S. Talmon, "Aspects of the Textual Transmission of the Bible in the Light of Qumran Manuscripts," Textus 4 (1964) 95–132, reprinted in F. M. Cross and S. Talmon, eds., Qumran and the History of the Biblical Text (1975) 226–63, esp. 257–58. In my view, 1QIsaᵃ is generally a reliable text. DtIsa could be playing on בניך. In sound, the first "descendants/children" picks up "your stones" (אֲבָנַיִך), while the second "builders" with its ô sound

could match שָׁלוֹם. It is worth considering whether historical grounds do not also speak in favor of this solution (cf. also Isa 49:17). See also E. Tov, Textual Criticism of the Hebrew Bible (1992), esp. 59 n. 40.

406 Translations of the Nehemiah passages here follow Rudolph, Esra und Nehemia samt 3. Esra (1949).

407 Thus with A. H. J. Gunneweg, Nehemia (1987) 64–65 esp. n. 5c; he draws attention to the fact that אֲדֹנֵיהֶם can also be interpreted as a plural, "their lords."

408 In Neh 3:12 "daughters" are also mentioned in connection with the building—unless "daughter cities" are meant, as some commentators think. Cf. Rudolph, Esra und Nehemia, 117 on v. 12b.

409 In this connection Sanballat's mockery according to Neh 3:34 (4:2): "Will they revive the stones out of the heaps of rubbish?" brings to mind the link between "stones" in Isa 54:11 and "descendants/children" in Isa 54:13.

410 The relationship of the two groups of texts (DtIsa and TritoIsa) here requires further investigation.

In Isaiah 60 too, Zion is addressed as mother and city (see vv. 4, 9, 10-14). Verses 15-16 add the image of the woman who has been forsaken (cf. 62:4, 12). There are also concurrences in the semantic field "city," for example, walls/gates in 60:10-11, 18; 62:6, 10, 12. The catchword "righteous, righteousness" (צדקה) occurs in 60:17, 21; 61:3, 10, 11; 62:1, 2, where it means the righteousness conferred by Yahweh, as well as the righteous behavior of human beings that springs from that: "Your people shall all be righteous" (60:21; cf. 61:3, 10).

The decisive point, however, is the use of the sociomorpheme "marriage," in all its different nuances, to describe the relationship to God. In 62:2, 4 the new name is expressly given, in contrast to 54:11 (but cf. 54:1, 4). "Zion" is termed a "beautiful crown" (62:3, עֲטֶרֶת תִּפְאֶרֶת) in Yahweh's hand, and a "royal turban."

Apart from these coincidences and differences, the use of the root כון in this Trito-Isaiah text is of special interest for 54:14. According to 62:7, the sentinels on the walls of Jerusalem are to give Yahweh "no rest until he establishes (כון < יְכֹונֵן Polel) Jerusalem and makes it renowned throughout the earth." In this text "establishes" is used to proclaim the new foundation of Jerusalem. In spite of a textual difficulty,[411] I think it also probable that in the context of what is said about the marriage[412] in 61:10-11, כון Polel is once more being used for the placing of a headdress (פְּאֵר) on the bridegroom's head.[413]

This double use in 62:7 and 61:10, to found and to crown, could contribute to an understanding of 54:14a. The latter is a concluding statement: the new foundation comes about through "the righteousness" conferred by Yahweh. Like peace, it is something given to human beings, and something that can be lived by them.

At the same time, this statement could signal the close of the action in this scene. For—and this is a difficulty—the address to the woman in v. 11 and the description of the fashioning of the crown by Yahweh himself are not followed by an account of the actual crowning. According to what we have observed in DtIsa's work hitherto, vv. 13-14a are probably not a direct divine speech; they are the utterance of a "speaker." The reason for this conclusion is that Yahweh does not otherwise talk about himself by name (see v. 13: "taught by Yahweh"). It is conceivable that this is implicitly a stage direction introducing the entry of "the children/descendants" and "builders."

In reconstructing the staging, however, the presentation of the crown still presents a problem. At the investiture of Zion/Jerusalem (52:1-2) she puts on her robes herself. But if, as is probable, "Yahweh" himself is present in his voice, how ought we to imagine the crowning itself?

I should like to suggest the possibility that here "righteousness" may again have been personified.[414] She could have undertaken the crowning, at Yahweh's command.[415] That would have illustrated symbolically the declaration: "Through righteousness you will be firmly established." For the new community this would mean: "Unless righteousness is transferred into reality step by step, peace has no chance either."[416]

---

411 See the commentaries.

412 Beuken has described the use of the marriage metaphor in these texts particularly well. See on the present text Beuken, *Jesaja deel II A* (1979) 217: "'Bridegroom and bride and garden belong within a single metaphoric unit, as do the themes 'adorn oneself' and 'spring up.' The two *imagines* are related to one another as preparation and completion. They transfer this mutual relation to the two *res*. God has clothed the 'I' figure with righteousness, and in the same way he will let righteousness spring up, so that the nations can look upon it."

413 Ibid., 218: "Delitzsch (590 [Eng.: 2:433]) explains *yĕkahēn* as a denominative meaning 'to come forward as priest.' . . . But most [scholars] follow an early textual correction of Bredenkamp and read *yākîn* or *yĕkōnēn*: 'who fastens his headdress' (כון

Polel, HALAT 2:443; Duhm, Dillmann-Kittel, Torrey, Volz, Kissane, Muilenburg, Westermann), incidentally thus following LXX (*periethēke*) and Vg (*decoratum corona*)."

414 See under 45:8; cf. Isa 60:10, 17. We may also ask whether "peace" (שָׁלֹום) in v. 13 is not personified too. For the link between "righteousness" and "peace," Grimm/Dittert point to Isa 1:26-27; 9:5-6 (6-7); 32:17; 59:8-9; Pss 72:1-4, 7; 85:11 (10), 14 (13) and esp. to Gen 14:18 in connection with "Jerusalem" (see *Deuterojesaja . . . Ein Kommentar* [1990] 447 n. 39). Cf. also Rom 5:1; Eph 6:14-15; Phil 4:7; Col 3:15.

415 The iconography of "the coronation of the Virgin Mary" might be compared with this scene.

416 V. Wörl, "Die Utopie Gerechtigkeit," *Süddeutsche Zeitung* (Munich) 18–20 April 1992.

54

"Hold aloof from oppression—truly you must not
be afraid . . . !" (54:14b)

14b   Hold aloof from oppression—truly you must
              not be afraid!
       and from terror/ruin—he/it will surely not
              come near you.
15   *See,* anyone who makes an attack—I have
              not prompted it.
       Anyone who attacks you will fall before you.

16   *See,* I myself have created the smith,
       he blows the fire of coals
       and produces the devices for his work.
       And I myself have created the ravager to
              destroy.
17   No devices formed against you will succeed,
       ªand every tongue that rises against you in
              judgment, you will confute.ª

       ᵇThis is the inheritance of Yahweh's servants
       and their righteousness before me, saying of
              Yahweh.ᵇ

17ª⁻ª   This clause is missing in 1QIsa¹; see BHK.
17ᵇ⁻ᵇ According to MT, this is the last sentence of chap. 54 (see ס
        for Setuma). 1QIsaª puts it at the beginning of the text of
        chap. 55. See below on the passage.

These verses form a separate part-scene, but they are intimately connected with what has gone before. The direct divine speech is resumed, and continues until v. 17a. The concluding saying in v. 17b brings Act VI to an end. The alternating suffixes, or personal pronouns as the case may be (1st person sing. masc.—2nd person sing. fem.), also make clear that Yahweh is still conversing with "the woman." The theme is the assurance of protection for the bride and woman against numerous threats. This means that the assurance is also a promise: "That is the inheritance of Yahweh's servants" (v. 17b). Salvation and blessing for the mother are assured for her descendants too.[417]

The divine speech can also be understood as a stage direction,[418] and here it is important that the direction is given by the Lord himself. In the way in which it is directed toward the future, the action is prophecy, and in this respect it can be compared with the symbolic acts of the prophets.

That there is something to be seen is signaled by the repeated "see" (הן) in vv. 15 and 16.[419]

Examples of verbs of movement and action are "hold aloof" (רחק) and "come near" (קרב) in v. 14b, "fall" (נפל) in v. 15, "blow" (נפח) and "produce" (יצא) in v. 16, and "rise" (קום) in v. 17. What action actually takes place must be considered in each given case. In v. 14 state-

---

417 Westermann is therefore right in saying (278–79
     [224]) about the demarcation of the units in vv. 13b-
     17: "It is a promise of blessing, which elsewhere is
     made only to an individual. And it is a fixed form,
     which certainly had some particular act of worship
     as its basis. There are instances of it in Pss. 91 and
     121 and in Job 5.17-26. . . . [The assurance of bless-
     ing] promises God's constant presence, help, protec-
     tion and blessing."
418 This explains McKenzie's impression (140): "It

     seems that the level of expression and poetry falls
     in vss 15-17. They expand the statement of the secu-
     rity of the new Jerusalem, but the expansion is not
     impressive. The lines become prosy. . . ." Duhm
     (392) already considered the text to be "an addi-
     tion." These observations are correct in that the
     tension in this text proceeds not so much from the
     word as from the action.
419 I am here following 1QIsaª. MT has retained this
     reading in v. 16 in the *Qere.*

ments of action derive from the abstract terms "oppression" and "terror/ruin" in v. 14b, and from the personal descriptions "smith" and "destroyer" in vv. 16-17a. In the different sections of the text, explanations are given for these two pairs. Here the strict parallelism (sometimes with chiasmus) is striking.

These considerations make clear that the whole text, and with it the scene, falls into three parts: (a) vv. 14b-15; (b) vv. 16-17a; (c) v. 17b.

■ **14b-15** These verses are generally classed as "difficult." The views of the ancient textual traditions deviate widely, and the same may be said of modern commentators. It is therefore easy to understand A. Schoors's sigh of dejection, but also his comment: "The objection that vs. 15 disturbs the context is without any foundation. The verse is not easy to translate."[420] But perhaps here too the ambiguity is intentional. What is clear is that all forms of "oppression" (עֹשֶׁק) and "terror/ruin" (מְחִתָּה) are to be averted. This is visually presented. The warding off of oppression/violence implies the promise of protection by God himself, as the (actual) "lord." In the context "the marriage" destinies are thus proclaimed.

According to *HALOT*, עֹשֶׁק means "oppression, brutality, extortion." The very root עשק itself, says *HALOT*, means "oppress, exploit (a debtor unable to pay, the weaker party in a business contract)." A special theme is "to force down a wage." The texts cited read like a cross section of the OT's social message and its social criticism. DtIsa uses the same term for Assyria's oppression, in a series that begins with Egypt and ends with Babylon (52:4). In this way inward and outward violence are put on the same level.

מְחִתָּה means "terror" and then also "ruin."[421] The root חתת[422] ranges from the *Qal* "be shattered, to be filled with terror," by way of the *Niphal* "be broken to pieces" (but above all the most frequent use: "to be cast down, horrified") down to the *Piel* "discourage" and *Hiphil* "shatter."[423] The term with its derivations belongs evidently to the sphere of elemental experience. "Terror" can befall both individuals and communities. The psychological and physical results endanger the life of the whole person.[424]

DtIsa may well be using the same word in 51:6,[425] when he talks about God's justice not being "broken," and his help enduring. The two terms can be paraphrased in this sense. But they are not explained in the text. They are codes, whose familiarity is more or less presupposed. It is strange that in the text the terms are presented as if the reaction to them can be physical or "spatial" ("hold aloof from . . . not come near").[426] This suggests that these concepts, like others in DtIsa, should be thought of as personified in some form or other. They are evidently terrible in appearance ("you must not be afraid").

Verse 14b is the point when they enter the stage. They are not directly addressed, because they are not on a par with the other characters. The commands are addressed to the woman, but this also implies that the ill-disposed figures remain "far off." Limits are set for them. If they nevertheless attack,[427] the result is their annihilation. This, I believe, is the sense of v. 15. It presupposes that גּוֹר יָגוּר in v. 15a is initially derived from גור II *Qal*, "be

---

420 Schoors, *I Am God Your Saviour* (1973) 144. He gives a good survey of the variants and the state of research, as does Beuken, 265–67.

421 See *HALOT* 2:572 [*HALAT* 2:542]; cf. Jer 17:17; 48:39; Prov 10:14, 29; 13:3; 14:28; 18:7; 21:15.

422 *HALOT* 1:365 [*HALAT* 1:351].

423 See F. Maass, "חָתַת *ḥātat*," *TDOT* 5:277–83, esp. 278 [*ThWAT* 3:296–302, esp. 297]: "The basic meaning of the passive stems is 'be terrified,' that of the active stems, 'terrify.' Jenni goes into more detail: 'be filled with terror' (not simply 'be afraid') and piel, 'terrify (fill with terror)' (*Das hebräische Piʿel*, [1968] 67f.)."

424 A good impression of the social and psychological talk about "terror" (*scantu*) in popular Sicilian culture even today is given by E. Guggino, "Von Würmern und bösen Müttern: Magie und

Krankheit in der Sizilianischen Volkskultur," *Zibaldone* 5 (1988) 25: "The 'terror' is a fortuitous, natural event: arbitrary occurrences of various kinds and varying extent can evoke it, under particular circumstances. Sometimes extreme grief, stress or violent anger is judged as 'terror'. People who count as being in the nature of things weak are particularly exposed to it, such as women and children, or people who have been weakened by some earlier 'terror.'"

425 See above on the text and its dramatic presentation.

426 See J. Kühlewein, "קרב *qrb* to approach," *TLOT* 3:1164–69, esp. 1165 [*THAT* 2:674–81, esp. 675]: "In most passages, *qrb* indicates approach in the spatial sense."

427 For קרב cf. Exod 14:20; Deut 20:2, 10; Josh 8:5; Judg 20:24; 1 Sam 7:10; 17:48; 2 Sam 10:13.

hostile to, attack."[428] In correspondence to the *parallelismus membrorum*, the implicit complement would be: "Who is the one who attacks so violently?" The consequence would be: "That is the end of him, he is finished." אֶפֶס could thus mean "end, nothingness," as often in DtIsa (cf. 41:12, 24, 29; see also 40:17). From Yahweh's standpoint, or through his efficacy, the aggressor is "nothing." He has disappeared[429]—a good way of paraphrasing his exit.

The same may be said of the person who is indicated by way of the question, "Who is the one who attacks you?" (מִי־גָר אִתָּךְ):[430] "he will fall before you" (v. 15b). The assailant is done for, but the "fall" can also be understood practically as an exit. He collapses, or drops down out of sight.

Verses 14b-15 would thus be describing the entry and exit of two terrible beings. One may ask retrospectively whether anything more about their nature can be deduced from the text. A comparison with Isa 51:7-8 could offer a clue. In that passage we supposed that עָשׁ (ʿāš) and סָס (sās) represent two voracious monsters. Could גּוֹר (gôr) and גָּר (gār) in the present text not be a similar pair?[431] גּוֹר is "a young lion."[432] Do these two terrible beings have the form of lions, or are they wearing lion masks? The text could be rendered: "See, a young lion attacks, he will be destroyed by me, anyone who attacks you [i.e., a lion][433] will fall before you."

This would conclude the first, surely exciting part-scene, with the entry and exit of the symbolic figures. There will be no more danger from "oppression" and "terror," to the relief and joy of all. It is also possible,

however, that everything that takes place here in such visual terms also contains a topical political message for anyone who has ears to hear or eyes to read.

It is possible as well that DtIsa is still playing on the root גור. It is again one of the cases in which *HALOT* gives four homonymous roots. גור can mean:

I   to dwell as alien and dependent
II to attack
III to be afraid
IV * to hollow out

Hitherto we started from the meaning גור II, in the *parallelismus membrorum* too, though asking whether the double meaning of גּוֹר as infinitive absolute and as "young lion" was also deliberately intended. Some of the early translations—like a whole series of commentators—already attempted in different ways to arrive at a derivation from גור I, "to dwell as stranger."[434] The LXX version of v. 15a is along these lines: "proselytes will come to you" (προσήλωτοι προσελεύσονταί σοι). The LXX does not translate v. 15b at all, but a number of recensions render it as: "they will dwell among you as strangers" (παροικήσουσι[ν] σοι).[435] Ibn Ezra's explanation is interesting too, and I believe that it grasps the double meaning of v. 15b very well: "Anyone who lives *with* you as a stranger must fall in the struggle *against* you."[436] But who is meant by the stranger who does not keep the rules laid down for a "foreigner and protected citizen" (גֵּר), but is "against you" (עָלֶיךָ), hostile?

Isa 52:1 presents a similar problem: "Yes, an uncircumcised person and an unclean person shall no more enter you (יָבֹא־בָךְ)." Neh 4:1-5 (7-11) already led us to

---

428 See *HALOT* 1:184–85 [*HALAT* 1:177].

429 Instead of מְאוֹתִי as the accusative particle with suffix, the reading should probably be מֵאִתִּי, as in 1QIsᵃ; cf. LXX δι᾽ ἐμοῦ; see *HALOT* 1:101 [*HALAT* 1:98] (on "II אֵת: prep. with"): "4. with מִן: . . . out of, from, after verbs of removing . . . cj. מֵאִתִּי by my orders, Is 54:15." MT's rendering "not at my sign" (אוֹת with suffix) is also possible, cf. 44:25; 55:13 (see also the commentaries on 49:22). See further Young and Beuken on this passage.

430 Schoors, (*I Am God Your Saviour* [1973] 145) translates v. 15 : "If any one stirs up strife, it is not from me; whoever stirs up strife with you shall fall because of you." Schoors explains: "Here one regards *hēn* as a conditional particle, *mî* as an indefinite relative pronoun (cf. Is. 1,10), and one reads *mēʾittî* instead of *mēʾôtî*, and one translates *gûr* as 'to attack.'"

431 Cf. also רַהַב and תַּנִּין in 51:9 as well as יָם and מֵי תְּהוֹם רַבָּה in 51:10.

432 See *HALOT;* on גּוֹר see Jer 51:38; Nah 2:13. The normal form is גּוּר; see Gen 49:9; Deut 33:22; Ezek 19:2-3, 5.

433 For the doublet "young lion—lion" see Gen 49:9; Num 23:24; 24:9; Job 4:10-11; Isa 5:29; 31:4; Jer 51:38; Hos 5:14.

434 See the list in Schoors, *I Am God Your Saviour* (1973) 144–45; Beuken, 265–67.

435 The Hexaplaric recension B (Codex Vaticanus), the Lucian recension L and the catena group C, according to J. Ziegler, *Isaias* (Septuaginta, 14; 2d ed. 1967).

436 In M. Friedländer's translation (*Ibn Ezra,* 252): "I take גור יגור in its usual meaning and explain the verse thus: Can there dwell any stranger with thee in my land, except it be with my will; he who desires

suspect that what is meant is the incursion of enemies: "They all plotted together to come in (לְבוֹא) and fight against Jerusalem" (Neh 4:2 [8]). The people meant are Nehemiah's opponents, the Horonite Sanballat and Tobiah the Ammonite. They could be apostrophized not only as "uncircumcised" and "unclean," but now as (hostile) "foreigners" too.

To attack Yahweh leads to "nothing," and even hostility toward those in his protection results in defeat: that would be the hidden message.

■ **16-17a** If in looking at vv. 16-17a we also start from the action that is taking place, the following picture emerges. Here again a pair comes forward: "See. . . ." It is again a highly disparate pair, the smith (חָרָשׁ) and the destroyer (מַשְׁחִית). The trade or occupation of the latter still has to be discovered. But it is explicitly stated that both have been created by Yahweh himself.

Both we ourselves and the audience have already met the smith in 40:19 and 41:6-7. He is the "specialist for iron" (44:12).[437] Pyrotechnical devices would make him an effective theatrical figure—"He blows the fire of coals"—especially since it is supposed to be evening toward the end of the last act. It is not only children for whom the smith is a bogeyman! He is once more shown at work: "he fashions the implements (כְּלִי) for his work." The scene is again as lively as one of the clown scenes in Shakespeare.[438] But here too, just as in Shakespeare, the serious purpose should not be overlooked.

One indication of this purpose is the twice-mentioned "devices, implements" (כְּלִי). The formulation is curiously neutral. Translations and commentators waver as

to whether it should be rendered "tools" or "weapons." But that is precisely the question! If, as the declaration about the smith says in v. 17a, "no devices formed *against* you will succeed,"[439] then it is weapons that are meant; otherwise the devices are tools. This shows the horizon of the text, which is the same as that of Isa 2:1-5: swords into plowshares—that is the alternative open to the smith. But in the context, there is a more far-reaching decision: whether Zion is in danger of being attacked by foreign peoples, or whether it is the goal of the pilgrimage of the nations, since "out of Zion goes forth *torah*" (Isa 2:3). The Servant texts, especially Isaiah 53, have made clear that the latter is a true hope. The call: "house of Jacob, let us go and walk in the light of Yahweh" (2:5) still obtains. God's promise according to the present text is that the weapons will not prevail. This promise has its foundation in the mystery of creation. The smith need no longer fashion weapons—or idols either. His function is to make tools, plowshares, scythes, and pruning hooks—that is the way the text has to be understood in the light of its wider context.

The characteristic signs of the smith's activity and the resulting message are clear enough; but it is at first difficult to see what is meant by "the ravager."[440] If DtIsa's work is the basis for a Passover-Mazzot play, as I assume is the case, then the catchword "ravager" (מַשְׁחִית) once more brings into play the remembrance of the first Passover night in Egypt.[441] But the word is at the same time a dispute with this tradition. It is first of all specifically stated that the ravager was created by Yahweh, in just the same way as the smith. He is a person. He is not

---

to dwell with thee in my land, עָלַיִךְ יִפּוֹל *must surrender to thee*."

437 See V. Hamp, "חָרָשׁ *ḥārāš*," *TDOT* 5:220–23 [*ThWAT* 3:234–38].

438 Cf. the famous dialogue between Hamlet and the gravediggers in Act V Scene 1:
   HAMLET: I think it be thine indeed, for thou liest in 't.
   FIRST CLOWN: You lie out on 't, sir, and therefore 'tis not yours; for my part, I do not lie in 't, and yet it is mine.
   HAMLET: Thou dost lie in 't, to be in 't, and say it is thine. 'Tis for the dead, not for the quick; therefore thou liest.
   Here too the wordplay should be noted.

439 The two interpretations given in v. 17a are parallel. Both are introduced by "all, every" (כָּל־). The first

refers to the "smith," the second to the "ravager." For a different view see Ewald, 96–97; and Beuken, 351 n. 90 on this passage, also 267–68.

440 See *HALAT* 4:1363–65 on the root שׁחת (with lit.), and *HALOT* 2:644 [*HALAT* 2:609] מַשְׁחִית; D. Vetter, "שׁחת *šḥt* pi./hi. to ruin," *TLOT* 3:1317–19 [*THAT* 2:891–94].

441 See Exod 12:13, 23.

divine. He is not an independent power, let alone a counterforce. He can do only what Yahweh permits him. This is also true of his "destroying, annihilating" (חבל Piel).[442] Yahweh decides who is to be the object of the destruction. All this could be an interpretation of Exod 12:23. But as in the case of the smith, an explanation is added: "Every tongue that rises against you in judgment" (לְמִשְׁפָּט)."[443]

The commentators are largely at one in believing that what is meant here is the accusation before the court.[444] This will not succeed either; on the contrary: she—the woman as representing the whole—will declare the opposing party guilty. She will not be surrendered to "the ravager." But perhaps we can come closer still to what is meant by "legal case" (מִשְׁפָּט). Exod 12:13 promises that "the devastating stroke" (נֶגֶף לְמַשְׁחִית) will not fall on those who celebrate the Passover. But before that we are told that Yahweh will "execute judgment" (Exod 12:12): "And on all the gods of Egypt I will pass judgment (אֶעֱשֶׂה שְׁפָטִים), for I am Yahweh."

False charges before a court of law have been common practice from time immemorial. The plea that innocent persons who are accused should be assigned counsel is a continual theme in the prayers of complaint in the Psalter. But right down to the present day, the accusation of adhering to a false religion is a particularly dangerous indictment. Even in the ancient world, both Jews and Christians were accused of what the Greeks called asebeia, "godlessness," because they believed in the one God. The classic example is Daniel 3, the story of the three men in "the burning fiery furnace," because there the religious and the political charges are evidently inextricably intertwined. In that text too, denunciation plays an important part ("every tongue that rises against you in judgment"; cf. Dan 3:8-9). In the Daniel story, both

the personal integrity of the three friends and their loyalty to Nebuchadnezzar are emphasized. It is only the demand that they worship Nebuchadnezzar's image and his god that they reject. Here we have the genuine criteria for martyrdom. The three men experience the help of their God; "the fourth man" ("he looks as if he were a son of the gods," Dan 3:25) is beside them even in the furnace. It is not just by chance that this Daniel text probably dates from the Persian period. "Every tongue . . . you will declare and pronounce guilty (תַּרְשִׁיעִי)." Where, when and how this will happen is not stated here. Nor is it explained what the result of the verdict "guilty" will be. "You will destroy the false accuser" is never said. But injustice is to be given its proper name.

Anticipating, we may paraphrase the close of v. 17 as follows: to establish "their righteousness" is Yahweh's business. He will restore the order of law and make "peace" possible.

What "the ravager" looked like was surely familiar to DtIsa's audience; no doubt he was very like the devil of popular imagination throughout the ages. But at the end DtIsa records a new Passover experience. "Judgment" cannot be victorious any more than war. But probably a more extensive tradition must be presupposed here too. For if the catchwords "terror/ruin" (מְחִתָּה, v. 14b) and "ravager" (מַשְׁחִית, v. 16b) are taken as starting points, it emerges that the latter is used in Ezek 5:16 in connection with the justification for, and description of, the judgment on Jerusalem. It is Yahweh who "cuts down" (Ezek 5:11; see HALOT s.v. גרע and גדע), who draws the sword after them (5:1-2), who "looses arrows" (5:16), "arrows for destruction (לְמַשְׁחִית), which I will let loose to destroy you (לְשַׁחֶתְכֶם)."

Another announcement of the visitation of Jerusalem in Ezekiel (9:1-2) also talks about men sent by God with

---

442 See J. Gamberoni, "חָבַל chābhal III," TDOT 4:185–88, esp. 187 [ThWAT 2:712–16, esp. 715]: "In Isa. 54:16, the terminology is instructive: mashchîth recalls mechittāh (54:14), and takes us by way of hachittōthā (Isa. 9:3) to yechubbāl (Isa. 10:27 conj.), yēchath (Isa. 30:31), and shābhar (Isa 14:5). The word lechabbēl summarizes the effects of various destructive forces, all of which God has irresistibly at his disposal, like all creation. At least in Isa. 13:5 and 54:16, therefore, chābhal functions amid the tensions created by the paradox of the power of God, whose final purpose is salvation."

443 This clause (v. 17aβ) is missing in 1QIsaᵃ, perhaps

because it begins in the same way as v. 17aα (homoioarcton). This need not indicate that 1QIsaᵃ is unreliable (thus North, 251: "The omission of this whole sentence by Qᵃ is only one indication of the general unreliability of the ms.")

444 מִשְׁפָּט can also be "legal decision" or "legal dispute"; see HALOT, s.v.

445 Cf. Jer 22:7-8.

446 See F. M. Cross, "The Divine Warrior," in his Canaanite Myth and Hebrew Epic (1973) 91–111; P. D. Miller, The Divine Warrior in Early Israel (1973).

"destroying weapons" (כְּלִי מַשְׁחֵתוֹ). According to Ezek 9:2 these are "crushing tools" (מַפָּץ). Finally, a saying to Ammon (Ezek 21:36 [31]) talks about "smiths of destruction" (חָרָשֵׁי מַשְׁחִית).

Ezekiel by no means stands alone in this tradition. According to Jeremiah 51 Babylon is for Yahweh "a hammer" (or warclub?), "a weapon of battle" (Jer 51:20).[445] This text also already announces the reversal: Babylon, "the ravaging mountain that has ravaged the whole earth" (v. 25), will also be called to account.

All these declarations are based on the concept of Yahweh as warrior.[446] Here the idea that he himself is an armed warrior corresponds to the notion that heavenly[447] or earthly forces are his weapons. Ever since Amos it had become a conceivable idea for the prophetic tradition that God can also turn against his own people and land. The conviction that in war God was self-evidently "on our side" had perished on the rock of experience. The most extreme tension exists between the prophet Isaiah's view that Zion/Jerusalem is inviolable, and the proclamation of the downfall even of the temple by the prophets from Jeremiah[448] to Ezekiel. With all DtIsa's familiar brevity, the present text repeals the prophecy of disaster. Yahweh will again assume the protection of his city.[449] The premise is the affirmation that Yahweh is at work in all destiny. Yahweh has acted, even in disaster, and then especially: that is the enduring recognition. The testimony of Jeremiah and Ezekiel is in no way thereby diminished. Whatever has happened to Zion/Jerusalem in the way of disaster was the consequence of its own unjust actions. The paradoxical idea that even its enemies—"the ravager"—can do nothing unless it is God's will is the reason why peace and renewed salvation can be hoped for.

To this extent an understanding accessible to general experience can be reconstructed from the text of vv. 16-17a: this is a dramatic presentation of resistance against disaster, and an affirmation of faith in the face of war and judgment.

But the text probably also has a topical reference that links it with vv. 15 and 17b. Our assumption is that DtIsa and the book of Nehemiah are close in time, and related; and it is noticeable that in the account of the reconstitution of Jerusalem, with the building of the wall, the Nehemiah memorandum several times mentions military threats[450] and slander[451] by Nehemiah's opponents. But the attempt of Sanballat, Tobiah, and Geshem is unsuccessful. After Nehemiah has armed the defenders, he proclaims a "holy war" (Neh 4:8 [14]): "Do not be afraid of them, remember the Lord." But the attack never materializes. Nor are the slanderers able to frighten the people (Neh. 6:9, 13, 14; also 6:19). The miraculous preservation that DtIsa describes had also been the practical experience of his own day.[452] That does not diminish its permanent and general significance.

■ **17b** This part of the verse is clearly designated as a separate divine saying. The divine name Yahweh (יהוה) is used twice (cf. v. 13). The close takes up the time-honored prophetic formula "murmur/saying of Yahweh" (נְאֻם־יהוה). "This (is) . . ." (זאת) initially establishes the connection with the preceding text. To talk about "heritage" (נַחֲלָה) and "righteousness" (צְדָקָה) is to cite traditional concepts. But in what sense should they be understood here?

The plural "servants of Yahweh" (עַבְדֵי יהוה) is for DtIsa a new and unique usage.[453] Hitherto the community has always been described by way of a collective. Jacob/Israel is a "servant," Zion/Jerusalem is a "woman." The final sentence adds something new here: what applies collectively is to apply to individuals too.[454]

---

447 Cf. Judg 5:4-5, 19-22; Daniel 8; 10. On the heavenly weapon see also Gen 9:12-17.

448 Cf. Mic 3:12 and its citation in Jer 26:18.

449 Cf. Zech 2:4b-5 (8b-9).

450 See A. H. J. Gunneweg, *Nehemiah* (1987) [on 4:8-9]: "They all plotted together to come and fight against Jerusalem and to prepare confusion for it."

451 Cf. Neh 2:19: "Will you dare to rebel against the king?" Neh 6:2, 5-9; 6:13: "so that they could give me a bad name"; 6:19.

452 Cf. Aeschylus *Persians*. It was written in 472 B.C.E., only eight years after the battle of Salamis, and gives the recollection of the Persian war topical relevance, in light of contemporary events.

453 Cf. in TritoIsa 56:6; 60:12; 63:17; 65:8, 9, 13, 15; 66:14. On the following passage in the commentary see K. Baltzer, "Moses Servant of God and the Servants: Text and Tradition in the Prayer of Nehemiah (Neh 1:5-11)," in *The Future of Early Christianity: FS H. Koester* (1991) 121–30.

454 See Bonnard, 297: "It is not only the Servant Israel, seen as a whole, but rather every Israelite, personally Yahweh's servant, who enjoys the help of his God."

The different communities are determined by tradition, for good or evil: DtIsa has made this clear. But the individual lives in the present. It is characteristic of the Persian period that individuals should have to live for themselves, and should be able to do so, above all in the Diaspora. According to everything we know, neither the *gōlâ* nor those who had remained behind were a closed or homogeneous group. DtIsa's specific concern is certainly the unity of God's whole people. But it is a unity in belief in the one God. It is a believed unity in the experience of diversity, even of antithesis. All those who serve this God could be "servants of Yahweh" (עַבְדֵי יהוה). To put it in modern terms, what we see beginning here is a process of individualization and democratization. Israel has experienced the breakdown of collective institutions. The exile has called in question the legitimation of prophecy, monarchy, and temple cult. That will once more be the theme in the chapter that follows, chap. 55.

נַחֲלָה as "inalienable heritage"[455] is the land given to Israel, which it possesses as Yahweh's people. It is the fulfillment of the promise to the patriarchs and matriarchs, according to the picture in Deuteronomy. The land had been distributed to the tribes and families by Moses and Joshua, and was given to them for their responsible use. But the owner was still Yahweh. נַחֲלָה is a share in the land, and at the same time a share in salvation. The loss of the land through collapse and exile is the outcome of Israel's guilt: that is the opinion of the "confession" in the book of Nehemiah, for example (Neh 9:25, 35-37).

This means that in the present text the נַחֲלָה of "the servants of Yahweh" could mean a "share" in the unity of Zion/Jerusalem (as represented by "the woman")[456] and of people and land. The return to the land of the patriarchs is possible, according to DtIsa. He pleads for a new beginning. In the tradition of prophetic proclamation, this new beginning is for him bound up with social justice.[457]

"Share" can mean possession of a piece of land in the practical sense.[458] But in these changed economic conditions it is improbable that all the people living in the country towns were tillers of the soil, let alone all the inhabitants of Jerusalem. DtIsa mentions merchants and craftsmen.[459] If they lived in Jerusalem, it is conceivable that נַחֲלָה also included the ownership of a house, or the right to live there.

To this extent the text of v. 17b, with its unusual linking of the phrase "share in the heritage" with "righteousness," is comprehensible. But if "That is . . ." (זֹאת) is taken seriously as a pointer to the immediate context, it is worth asking whether this verse too, like vv. 14b-17a, does not contain a direct reference to the political situation.

In order to answer this question, we should consider once more the text of Neh 2:16-20. Neh 2:19 records the slanderous accusation of Sanballat, Tobiah, and Geshem, which finds its correspondence in Isa 54:17a. Nehemiah's answer, if we follow A. H. J. Gunneweg, is: But I replied to them and said: "The God of heaven himself will let us succeed (יַצְלִיחַ לָנוּ הוּא), for we, his servants, will set out and start building (וַאֲנַחְנוּ עֲבָדָיו נָקוּם). But you have no share (וְלָכֶם אֵין־חֵלֶק) or claim (וּצְדָקָה) or

---

DtIsa's message is addressed to the people of his time. What prompted this interest in peoples and nations, and in the individuation? The exilic period—and the Persian era above all—brought with it the experience of other peoples. The opportunity to travel undoubtedly played a part. We need only think of Nehemiah's biography, or of Herodotus. But more people also participated in this process of individual development.

The names mentioned in the Elephantine texts give us an impression here (see B. Porten, *Archives from Elephantine* [Berkeley and Los Angeles, 1968], index of personal names, 368–94).

For the Greek-speaking world, illuminating material can be found in Josef Hofstetter's study, *Griechen in Persien: Prosopographie der Griechen im persischen Reich vor Alexander* (AMI suppl. vol. 5; Berlin, 1978).

455   See *HALAT* 649; also G. Wanke, "נַחֲלָה *naḥ^alâ* possession," *TLOT* 2:731–34 [*THAT* 2:55–59]; E. Lipiński, "נָחַל *nāḥal*," *ThWAT* 5:342–60.
456   See Beuken, 270.
457   See K. Baltzer, "Liberation from Debt Slavery After the Exile in Second Isaiah and Nehemiah," in *Ancient Israelite Religion: FS F. M. Cross* (1987) 477–84.
458   Cf. Isa 47:6; 49:8.
459   For merchants see Isa 46:5-8; for craftsmen, 40:18-20; 44:12-13. Cf. the list of the people involved in building the wall in Neh 3:1-32. There perfumers, goldsmiths, and merchants are called to take part in the building (3:8, 31).
460   See among other passages Gen 31:14; Num 18:20; Deut 10:9; 12:12.
461   See Gunneweg, *Nehemia* (1987) 62, etc.

remembrance (וְזִכָּרוֹן) in Jerusalem." (Neh 2:20)

A whole series of terms in Neh 2:20 and Isa 54:17 correspond. Where "the God of heaven" lets succeed (יַצְלִיחַ יַצְלִחַ), the enemies fail. The servants of "the God of heaven" start out (נָקוּם, Neh 2:20), not the enemies (תָּקוּם, Isa 54:17); but "the servants" (plural!) are "Yahweh's servants." Instead of נַחֲלָה, "share," Neh 2:20 has חֵלֶק, "inherited share"; but, as the dictionaries show, the two terms are often used parallel to one another.[460] Both texts mention צְדָקָה and Neh 2:20 talks in addition about "remembrance." But the building of the wall, and Jerusalem as reference point, also link the two texts. These indications make it seem probable that the two texts are not unrelated. But what the precise relationship is still requires analysis.

Gunneweg has worked out a specific definition of the terms חֵלֶק and צְדָקָה as they are used in Neh 2:20: "Here one term interprets the other, and both state in the form of a negation that Sanballat is not permitted to exercise any administrative, governmental or judicial power in Jerusalem."[461]

Through the crowning of Zion/Jerusalem, DtIsa is also maintaining the city's independence. Politically he recognizes the Persian overlord, in the form of Cyrus. But by describing the inheritance of Yahweh's servants in positive terms, and by stating that their righteousness comes from Yahweh himself, he once more widens out the specific and topical reference. In this respect the texts of Neh and DtIsa also belong to very different genres. For we must not forget that in the Servant texts DtIsa has described the function of the Servant for the nations, and this function knows no frontiers.[462] But above all, when the text says: "Through his knowledge <or: 'experience'?> he, the one who is just, my Servant, will make the many just [or: 'achieve justice for the

many'?]" (יַצְדִּיק צַדִּיק, 53:11) and "Therefore I will give him a share (אֲחַלֶּק־לוֹ) among the many" (53:12), then here too the "righteousness" and "share" terminology is taken up. The wider community is made possible "because he has borne the transgression of many and continually intercedes for the sinners" (53:12). Here a wider reality is embraced, simply because the terms are more abstract.

"A share in the inheritance" is now the whole tradition for "the many" too.[463] To pick up Isaiah 2 once more, they come as sympathizers: "For out of Zion goes forth the torah, and Yahweh's word from Jerusalem" (Isa 2:3). There DtIsa could agree.[464] Up to this point the interpretation of v. 17b put forward here follows the traditional division, which is also supported by the Masoretic text when, at the end of v. 17b, it inserts the symbol ס (for Setuma) as the conclusion. This means that the demonstrative pronoun "this" (זֹאת) is used in a concluding sense. 1QIsaᵃ probably understands it as a distinct dividing mark in the margin. A wider space follows, a line having been partly left free.[465] The sentence is thus used as a heading for chap. 55. In the translation it could also be followed by a colon.

With regard to the interpretation, this could mean that pilgrimage and festival also count as participation in the "inheritance" (נַחֲלָה)—that is to say, in salvation and righteousness. They become the fulfillment of the promise.

As is so often the case in DtIsa, the two declarations represented by the text transmitted in 1QIsaᵃ and the Masora are not necessarily mutually exclusive. In this sense the statement, "This is the inheritance of Yahweh's servants and their righteousness; saying of Yahweh," could also serve as the signature for DtIsa's whole work, and indeed as its title.

---

462 Cf. the Servant texts: I, 42:1, 4; II, 49:6; III, 51:4-8; IV, 52:14; 53:11-12.

463 E. Lipiński ("נָחַל nāḥal," ThWAT 5:359–60) believes that in Isa 54:17 too an interpretation as "lot" or "destiny" should already be assumed (360): "Not only is the substantive naḥᵃlāh used here in the sense of 'lot, fate' (Isa 54:17; Job 20:29; 27:13; 31:2); the verb nḥl also governs objects that describe positive or negative values of a spiritual or moral kind."

For the use of the demonstrative pronoun as a conjoining element, cf. Deut 28:69. With the statement, "These are the words of the covenant" (אֵלֶּה דִּבְרֵי הַבְּרִית), the proclamation of the laws is

concluded. At the same time, it points to the following chapter, Deut 29, with Moses' festal address. The editions and commentaries differ correspondingly in the division. I am indebted to R. Achenbach for pointing this out.

464 On Torah as "inheritance" (נַחֲלָה) see M. Greenberg, "Three Conceptions of the Torah in Hebrew Scriptures," in Die Hebräische Bibel und ihre zweifache Nachgeschichte. FS R. Rendtorff (1990) 365–78.

465 See O. H. Steck, Die erste Jesajarolle von Qumran (1QIsaᵃ) (SBS 173; 1998), 1:100; 2:69.

"These are the things that I do and do not cease to do" (42:16)

A. 55:1-5
Promises

55

1   Ho!
     All who are thirsty—come to the water!
     And anyone who has no money—come, buy,
              eat!
     And come, buy[a] wine and milk, for no
              money and for a nonprice.[b]

2   Why do you weigh out your money for
              something that is not bread/
              nourishment,
     and the fruit of your labor for that which
              does not satisfy?
     Just listen to me and eat something good,
     so that your souls may feast on fat!

3a   Incline your ear and come to me!
     Listen, so that your souls may live!

3b   And I will make for you an everlasting
              <enduring> covenant—
     the steadfast graces of David.

4   *See,* I have installed him as a witness for
              nations,
     as one who makes known <or: "who has
              been made known">,
     as one who commands nations.

5   *See,* you call <or: "you shall call"> a people
              that you do not know,
     and a people that does not know you comes
              running to you <or: "shall come
              running to you">[a]
     because of Yahweh your God,
     and for the Holy One of Israel, for he has
              furnished you with glory.

1a   וְלְכוּ שִׁבְרוּ is missing in 1QIsa[a], LXX, and S.

1b   I cannot find any better translation. But בְּלוֹא־כֶסֶף and בְּלוֹא מְחִיר do not seem to mean "not for money" and "without any price." That would be לוא בכסף and לוא במחיר. For in v. 2 also, בְּלוֹא לֶחֶם does not mean "not for nourishment"; it means "for something that is not nourishment." Is the sense something along the lines of the phrase "for a song," or "it costs really nothing"—meaning that it costs almost nothing, or as good as nothing?

5a   Lit.: "and a nation (of people) who do not know you—they come running to you."

With the invitation to the banquet for everyone: "Come . . ." (v. 1), and with the exit "with joy" (v. 12), DtIsa concludes his work.[1] The most important themes are named once more: Yahweh is *your* God, the Holy One of Israel (v. 5). That is "an everlasting covenant" (v. 3b). But this message also has its relevance for the other peoples (v. 5). "Conversion"—the new beginning—is possible for human beings because God is merciful and "abundant in forgiving" (v. 7). Yahweh's "word" is efficacious and dependable (v. 11). He is the creator of the whole world, and guides it in his ways (vv. 8-11). But, as we shall see,

controversial themes are taken up again too: the David tradition for one, and also the meaning of the messianic promise, in the kingly sense (vv. 3b-4). If we apply the categories of classical theater, chap. 55 may be termed the epilogue, corresponding to chap. 40, the prologue. The two texts are intimately related, as the themes themselves show: forgiveness (40:2; 55:7); "exodus" (40:3, 4; 55:12); "Yahweh's glory shall unveil itself before all flesh" (40:5; cf. 55:5); the efficacy of God's word (40:8; 55:10-11). A closer examination will bring to light still further connections between the two texts. But the link

---

1   For a comparison with the close of the Attic tragedy see G. Kremer, "Die Struktur des Tragödien-schlusses," in W. Jens, ed., *Die Bauformen der griechi-* *schen Tragödie* (1971) 117–41, esp. 117: "In the basic pattern of the earliest Greek tragedy, as it can be hypothetically reconstructed, the close of the drama

with chap. 54 should be noted too. In its dramatic tension, this final act has elements of a genuine finale.[2]

Commentators see the structure of the chapter in different ways, with the appropriate justification. If one starts from the speakers (the presupposition being that Yahweh does not talk about himself in the third person), the structure may provisionally be described as follows:

A. 1. vv. 1-3a (*X* is speaking).
   2. vv. 3b-4 Yahweh speech "And *I* will make for you an everlasting covenant . . ."
   3. v. 5 Speaker "because of Yahweh, your God . . ."
B. 1. vv. 6-8 Speaker "seek Yahweh . . . , saying of Yahweh"
   2. vv. 9-11 Yahweh speech " . . . so <also> are my ways higher than your ways . . . So <also> shall my word be . . ."
   3. vv. 12-13 Speaker "and this shall come to pass for Yahweh <for a sign> . . ."

In its structure, with 2 × 3 very brief units, the text fits the scheme that we have observed elsewhere in DtIsa. The text of this epilogue is shorter than the prologue in chap. 40, for example.[3] Again, series of similar forms are a striking feature of the text. Thus vv. 1-3a contain twelve imperatives, with a corresponding number of *û* (וֹ) sounds. Running right through vv. 7-12 are six instances of כִּי,[4] in the exclamatory sense of "Yes!" or in the explanatory sense: "For." The commentators draw atten-

tion to several uses of chiasmus, which indicates the careful artistry of the text.

A. 1. 55:1-3a
Invitation to the Feast

"Incline your ear and come to me! Listen, so that your souls may live!" (55:3a)

Who is speaking in vv. 1-3a?[5] This is a difficult question but an important one. Various possible aspects have been clearly seen by commentators. The text begins afresh with the signal הוֹי (*hôy*),[6] a call to attention, and with the following invitation "to come and buy." Westermann thinks that the model for invitations of this kind might have been "the cries of the water-sellers and others who shouted their wares in the market—these certainly had a fixed form and were familiar to everyone."[7] This could explain the beginning of the text but, as Delitzsch already saw,[8] not the way it goes on up to v. 3a.

The link with everyday experience fits in well with another explanation of the text, proposed by J. Begrich

---

consists of the 'exit,' the ἔξοδος, of the chorus, which recites a poem in marching *anapaests* as it goes off. Aristotle expands the ἔξοδος in this original sense when he defines the final section of the Greek tragedy in general as *exodus*: for him the *exodus* is the part of the drama that is followed by no further choric song."

2 On the form and function cf. ibid., 121: "On the one hand, no question is to remain open at the end of the drama. On the other, the large number of those involved lends events on the stage a colorful variety and dramatic intensity that emphasises the solemn character of the final act particularly. A final group of minor characters act as the persons who as deus ex machina, or instead of a deus ex machina, unravel the plot and bring the drama to an end. One of their functions in Euripides (but in Sophocles' *Philoctetes* too) is to unveil the future, or it may be to explain an *aition* or cause. But one can again explain this with the poet's wish not to leave any question open and, in addition, to link the mythical happenings acted out in the drama with the present."

3 Is that because the "unofficial" part of the festival follows?

4 See *HALOT* 2:470 [*HALAT* 2:448]; Joüon and Muraoka, *Grammar of Biblical Herbrew* (1991) 617, § 164b; *ZAH* 1 (1988) 217; *ZAH* 5 (1992) 107; T. Muraoka, *Emphatic Words and Structures in Biblical Hebrew* (1985) 158–64; Y. Thorion, *Studien zur klassischen hebräischen Syntax* (1984) 3–36.

5 W. Brueggemann, "Poem of Summons (Is. 55:1-3)/Narrative of Resistance (Dan 1:1-21)," in *Schöpfung und Befreiung: FS C. Westermann* (1989) 126–36, with an account of the history of research and interpretation.

6 According to E. Jenni, "הוֹי *hôy* woe," *TLOT* 1:357 [*THAT* 1:475], in the present text it is an "agitated demand: 'up!'" (cf. Zech 2:10, 11 [6, 7]), not " a prophetic woe as an adaptation of the funeral lament" (358 [476]). Here the positive context can bring about a surprise effect.

7 Westermann, 282 [226–27].

8 Delitzsch, 2:353 [567–68]: "When Jehovah summons the thirsty ones of His people to come to the water, the summons must refer to something more than

especially.[9] According to this interpretation it is "Lady Wisdom" who is issuing the invitation to the banquet here. A comparison with Prov 9:1-12 suggests itself. There it is the maidservants who pass on their mistress's invitation, after the meal has been properly prepared:

> Wisdom has built her house. . . .
> She calls from the highest places in the town:
> "You that are simple, turn in here!"
> To those without sense she says:
> "Come, eat of my bread
> and drink of the wine I have mixed!"
> Leave those who are simple, then you shall live,
> and walk straight along the way of insight!"
>
>   Prov 9:1, 3-6[10]

Common to both texts is the transferred meaning of food. In both (true) life is the benefit gained from the banquet.[11]

It is noticeable, however, that in DtIsa the term "wisdom" (חָכְמָה) is only used in the negative sense of the wisdom and knowledge that has led Babylon astray (47:10).[12] It is therefore improbable that in the present text she appeared in personified form. All the same, the clue that Begrich offers is no bad one. For who else could give an invitation to the feast in this form?

H. C. Spykerboer has provided an answer to this question to which I can only assent: "In 55,1-5 reference is made to Jerusalem, the new and restored city of abundance where God reigns as a King."[13] Here his starting point is H. Eising's observation[14] that, if the Gihon spring in Jerusalem can be linked with the Gihon River in the paradisal map of the world in Gen 2:10-14, that would explain a whole series of texts[15] in which an abundance of water and food belongs to the expectation of a renewed Zion/Jerusalem, with Yahweh's presence.[16] Spykerboer's explanation certainly shows an excellent grasp of the tradition-history background of the present text. But the same traditional *topoi* could also reflect different positions. Whether the spring issues from the temple, for example (Ezek 47:1), or whether "living waters flow out from Jerusalem" (מַיִם־חַיִּים מִירוּשָׁלַ͏ִם, Zech 14:8) can make an essential difference when it is a question of the holiness of the temple or the city (see Zech 14:20). The exclusive holiness of the temple is in fact a matter of dispute. Here DtIsa deliberately avoids mentioning the temple. It is the waters of Jerusalem to which the people are invited.[17] He opts for the "holy city" and

---

the water to which the water carriers in Cairo and elsewhere invite with their call *yâ ʿaṣḥân môye* ('O thirsty ones, water!')" [trans. altered] (he refers to C. von Orelli, *Durch's Heilige Land: Tagebuchblätter* [2d ed. 1879] 49).

9   J. Begrich, *Studien zu Deuterojesaja* (1938, reprint 1963).

10   Translation following A. Meinhold, *Die Sprüche,* Part 1 (1991) 149. Meinhold asks what kind of building can be meant by "the house of Lady Wisdom," which lays on a banquet as a housewarming: "If it is a patrician house, she would appear to be a high-born lady or patroness (cf. 4:6, 8-9); if we are supposed to think of a palace, she might be thought of as a queen or perhaps even as a goddess." He points to the Ugaritic texts *CTA* 4 VI 35-38 = *KTU* 1.4 VI 35-58 and *CTA* 15 IV 2-28 = *KTU* 1.15 IV 2-28.

11   See Isa 55:3; cf. Prov 9:6, 11 as well as 8:32-35.

12   The verb חכם is also used for the production of idols in Isa 40:20 and 44:25. In DtIsa the Wisdom (חָכְמָה) that was beside God (Prov 8:30) has probably been replaced by the Torah (see above on 51:4).

13   H. C. Spykerboer, "Isaiah 55,1-5: The Climax of Deutero-Isaiah. An Invitation to Come to the New Jerusalem," in J. Vermeylen, ed., *The Book of Isaiah* (1989) 357-59.

14   H. Eising, "גִּיהוֹן *gîḥôn*," *TDOT* 2:466-68 [*ThWAT*

1:1008-11].

15   Gen 2:13; 1 Kgs 1:33-40; Isa 12:3; Ezek 47:1-12; Joel 4:18 (3:18); Zech 14:1-11; Psalms 46; 65:2 (1), 5 (4), 10 (9); 87:7; 110:7.

16   Cf. Ezek 47:1-12; Joel 4:18 (3:18); further Isa 33:20, 22; Zech 13:1; 14:8-9. See in Isaiah 12 the hymn of thanksgiving raised by the redeemed (at the close of Isaiah 1–11 and before chaps. 13–14, with the divine judgment on Babylon):

> 1 And you shall say on that day:
> I thank you, Yahweh, certainly you have been angry with me. . . .
> 2 For my power and my strength is Yah [Yahweh].
> Yes, he has been salvation for me.
> 3 So you will draw water with joy
> out of the wells of salvation (מִמַּעַיְנֵי הַיְשׁוּעָה). . . .
> 6 Rejoice and be glad, you townspeople of Zion (יוֹשֶׁבֶת צִיּוֹן),
> for great in your midst is the Holy One of Israel."

Translation in H. Wildberger, *Isaiah 1–12* (1991) 499–500 [*Jesaja 1–12* (1972)]; cf. also his commentary on the text.

17   Isa 41:17-20 is in this way received into DtIsa's composition. See also D. Kellermann, "צָמֵא *ṣāmēʾ*," *ThWAT* 6:1065–68, esp. 1067: "Thirst is also used as a term for absolute longing, e.g., for the proclamation of God's word (Amos 8:11), or the yearning

"for the Holy One of Israel, for he has furnished you with glory" (פֵּאֲרֵךְ, 55:5). In vv. 1-3a the gender of the speaker cannot be determined. But here at the end of v. 5 there is probably a feminine suffix.[18] It is the forsaken woman Zion/Jerusalem whom Yahweh has furnished with glory afresh. She is directly addressed. That is, in this final scene she is imagined as present.

But this also makes clear that chap. 54 should be taken into account as the context for interpreting vv. 1-3a. There the subject was the reinstallation of "the wife of (a man's) youth" (54:6) in her former rights. This is presented as a "sacred marriage." The climax is the woman's crowning in vv. 11-14a, with the promise of protection by Yahweh himself (vv. 14b-17). It would therefore seem reasonable to assume that in the text that follows, the speakers are the same. It is certainly the final scene, but no new characters are introduced. This means that v. 1 is either the beginning of Yahweh's speech, or that the speaker is Zion/Jerusalem. The question is made more difficult because from chap. 54 onward the name of Zion/Jerusalem is, for whatever reason, no longer mentioned;[19] so we should not expect to find it in 55:1 either.

Now, in my view, the postulate that vv. 1-3a are a divine speech can in all probability be excluded. W. A. M. Beuken has provided the decisive argument, for he has noticed that "coming to God" with the verb הלך (*hlk*) does not otherwise occur in the OT at all.[20] To assume that the present passage is an exception is problematical. Beuken also sees the parallel between v. 1: "come (or go) to the water" and v. 3: "come (or go) to me." I therefore think that the most probable solution is that in both cases Zion/Jerusalem is calling the people to come—that is, she is speaking throughout the whole unit vv. 1-3a. It is she, the woman as the representation of the city, who is giving the invitation to the banquet,[21] not Lady Wisdom or any goddess. She is thereby inviting the people to make a pilgrimage to Jerusalem: "Come to the water!" "Come to me!" But this will be clearer still in the text that follows.

The feast is open to all, which means that the poor can participate too ("Even those who have no money, come!"). The food is free.[22] Wine and milk are among the country's delicacies. There is bread enough. "Good" (טוֹב) can be a way of describing good things to eat and drink in general, but it may perhaps refer to special

---

desire for God himself (Ps 42:3 [2]: 'my soul thirsts for God'; cf. Ps 63:2 [1]; 143:6), or for salvation (Isa 55:1). In Isa 41:17 the torment of thirst is an image for the misery of the people of Israel (cf. Lam 4:4; Jer 2:25)."

18 See GKC § 58a and g under "rare forms." In Isa 60:9 the same form, "for he has furnished you with glory" (כִּי פֵּאֲרֵךְ), is, through the chapter's context, unequivocally related to "the city of Yahweh, the Zion of the Holy One of Israel" (v. 14); cf. also the suffix forms in 54:1-3.

19 For example, the demand "to go" to Jerusalem can very well be problematical if it is a return for political and economic reasons. Who willingly lets the experts go! Yet they constituted a large percentage of the *gōlâ*, as the lists of the exiles show. "To go" to Zion/Jerusalem on pilgrimage also meant strengthening the city. The pilgrimage, with its religious significance, can also trigger political and economic consequences, as the pilgrimage to Mecca shows down to the present day. So there can have been reasons for leaving the name of Zion/Jerusalem unmentioned (see also below on 55:13).

20 Beuken, 353 n. 20: "The standard lexicons and theological dictionaries fail to add an entry *hlk ʾel* + God under the heading *hlk*"; see also 282 on this passage. The sole exception could be Job 34:23, but

there the formulation is different.

21 See R. J. Clifford, "Isaiah 55: Invitation to a Feast," in *The Word of the Lord Shall Go Forth: FS D. N. Freedman* (1983) 27–35. According to J. A. Sanders, "Isaiah 55:1-9," *Int* 32 (1978) 291–95, esp. 292, this is the tradition of the invitation "to David's royal banquet." "At the new year of the king the common people ate to their heart's content the sort of food which the rest of the year only royalty and nobility could afford."

22 Or is it just the drinks? Are those who are well off supposed to buy "bread" for themselves and for others? Does that which is "not bread/not nourishment" and that which "does not satisfy" mean the food that is bought at other places and sanctuaries, thus being part of the polemic against idols, reiterated here once more at the end (cf. Amos 5:4-7)? These are questions that can hardly be answered. We should like to know more about the organization of a feast of this kind. A slight impression of the connection among feast, food, and proclamation is given by Neh 8:9-12, where the subject is the Feast of Booths.

23 See I. Höver-Johag, "טוֹב *ṭôb*," *TDOT* 5:296–317, esp. 299 [*ThWAT* 3 315–33, esp. 318]: "The element of sweetness appears in Arab. *ṭiyāb*, which is used by metonymy for a kind of date, as well as in Akk. *ṭābu*,

sweet dishes[23] (cakes, for example) of the kind that would be appropriate for a feast. The parallelism to "fat" could point in the same direction—sweet things baked or fried in fat. What kind of fat is not stated. It could be oil[24] or butter—hardly animal fat. It is noticeable that meat is not mentioned at all. But this could be connected with the special character of this feast. The explicit mention of milk would exclude the eating of meat, if the dietary law separating milk and meat dishes were observed: "You shall not boil a kid in its mother's milk."[25] Even if the rabbinic rule was not yet applicable, it remains curious that the "festive roast" is not mentioned. Were there other cultic reasons—or some conflict that was to be avoided—that prevented the enjoyment of meat from being mentioned? Milk for a whole festive group suggests a spring feast, during the season when animals have their young.[26] This is one of the points that leads me to ask whether this is not meant to be the celebration of a Passover feast without the slaughter of a Passover lamb. Perhaps it would be better to say: a pure Mazzot festival is to be celebrated in Jerusalem, in remembrance of the exodus. But this thesis must be discussed in a wider context.

The dishes that are offered at the feast are in themselves God's good gifts. Water, wine, milk, and bread: these are "good things," pointing to the goodness of God. But it is not just a question of "feasting your souls" (נַפְשְׁכֶם, v. 2b)—where "soul" means the physical life itself, with its thirst and hunger; for the life of "your souls"[27] (נַפְשְׁכֶם, v. 3aβ) "hearing" is required too.[28] In the course of the festival, celebrated from chap. 40 onward, there has certainly been plenty to listen to; but the conclusion of the drama that now follows is also commended to the attention of its listeners.[29]

A. 2. 55:3b-4
Divine Speech

"And I will make for you an everlasting <enduring> covenant—the steadfast graces of David" (55:3b)

Three times in vv. 2-3 "Zion/Jerusalem" is told to listen (שמע), a demand emphasized by "incline your ear!" (v. 3a). The purpose is "life for your souls." This demand is important in the immediate context too, since to all those who can hear, a divine saying is directly addressed in vv. 3b-4. In the same way, in 40:1-5 "all" could also witness to the resolve taken in the heavenly sphere.

'sweetmeat.'" Cf. our words "bonbon" and the old-fashioned "goody." See also Prov 24:13-14.

24 Cf. Judg 9:9: the oil of the olive tree.

25 Cf. Exod 23:19; Deut 14:21; see A. Caquot, "חָלָב chālābh," *TDOT* 4:386–91, esp. 386–87 and 388 on the dietary laws (*kashrut*) [*ThWAT* 2:945–51, esp. 946 and 947–48]. See also O. Keel, *Das Böcklein in der Milch seiner Mutter und Verwandtes. Im Lichte eines altorientalischen Bildmotivs* (1980); E. A. Knauf, "Zur Herkunft und Sozialgeschichte Israels. 'Das Böckchen in der Milch seiner Mutter,'" *Bib* 69 (1988) 153–69.

26 See G. Dalman, *Arbeit und Sitte in Palästina*, vol. 1: *Jahreslauf und Tageslauf* (1928; reprint 1964) 336–37, with reference to Ps 65:12-14 (11-13); Joel 4:18 (3:18); Exod 3:8; Cant 4:11; 5:1: "The animals enjoy the fresh spring greenery, which they have to do without for most of the year. . . . But human beings too are glad because the green fodder means that they again have milk (Arab. *ḥalīb*), curds (*leben*), fresh butter (*zibde*) and then cooking butter (*semne*) in plenty." Dalman quotes a proverb: "The one who marries in April [*nīsān*] eats meat and eggs, milk and vegetables!" (266).

27 See C. Westermann, "נֶפֶשׁ *nepeš* soul," *TLOT* 2:743–59, esp. 759 [*THAT* 2:71–96, esp. 95]: "The life that God saves and preserves, but also the desire

of the soul for God, is life in intentionality. . . . When human beings turn toward God, this corresponds to God's own commitment; *nepeš* is the selfhood of the human being in this mutual happening." Cf. H. Seebass, "נֶפֶשׁ *nepeš*," *ThWAT* 5:531–55.

28 Cf. the discourse on the Bread of Life in John 6:22-59. The invitation in Isa 55:1-3 is explicitly taken up in Rev 21:6 and 22:17. There it is "the Spirit and the bride" who invite: "And the Spirit and the bride say, 'Come.' And let everyone who hears say, 'Come.' And let everyone who is thirsty come. Let anyone who wishes take the water of life freely." But this Revelation text is linked with the DtIsa tradition very much more profoundly when Revelation 18–19 describe the downfall of Babylon, and chaps. 21–22 depict the descent of the new Jerusalem.

29 See G. Liedke, "אֹזֶן *'ōzen* ear," *TLOT* 1:71–73, esp. 71 [*THAT* 1:95–98, esp. 96]: "The wisdom teacher can call people to listen with the expression *nṭh* hi[phil] *'ōzen* 'to incline the ear' (Pss 78:1; Prov 4:20; 5:1, 13; 22:17; similarly Isa 55:3; Psa 45:11 [10] and 49:5 [4])."

The promise of an "everlasting covenant" for "you" (לָכֶם) is announced. The people addressed are the same as those in 55:1-3a—all who come and listen. The covenant is not only for "the people" in the collective sense; every individual is addressed too. The special point about the text is that Yahweh himself is speaking. This stresses the importance of the message.

But the command to listen exactly can also refer to the content of the message, and that content was a matter of dispute, a dispute reflected in the modern exegetical controversy.[30] The problem can initially be focused on the question of the translation of ḥasdê dāwid (הַסְדֵי דָוִד), "the graces of David." Should this be rendered as a *subjective* genitive ("David's demonstrations of grace") or as an *objective* genitive ("the demonstrations of grace to David")? The wording would allow either translation, and both have therefore been maintained with cogent reasoning in the history of the text's interpretation.

Another question is the understanding that results from the translation chosen. The faithfulness that David has shown (subjective genitive) could justify the restitution of the Davidic monarchy. The faults of his successors do not cancel out the merits of the dynasty's founder.

The other translation (objective genitive) stresses what God has done for David. This too could be understood in a messianic sense, as the expectation that the dynasty will be restored because of God's promise to David; but it does not have to be read in this way. The formula can also mean: Yahweh's faithfulness endures, but it is not bound to David and his dynasty; it can show itself in a new way. The enduring demonstrations of the bond between David and his God are transferred to the community, as a lasting covenant, put into force afresh for the benefit of "the people (of God)." So the phrase ḥasdê dāwid can be heard and applied in very different ways. I suspect that by citing this slogan DtIsa is designedly setting off a discussion exceeding the boundaries of his own work—and in this design he was successful!

About his own position there can surely be no doubt,[31] as the context shows. The first signal is the beginning of the text in v. 3b: "and I . . . for you. . . ." This is just as sudden and unprepared for as 40:1-2: "Comfort, comfort my people . . . speak to the heart of Jerusalem. . . ." There "people" (עַמִּי) and "Jerusalem" are the names for a collective. The person who talks about "you" here (in the plural) is restricting neither "covenant"[32] nor "demonstrations of grace"[33] to a particular ruler. The addressee is every man and every woman.[34] The permanent validity of covenant and promise can be maintained;[35] but the partners to whom the covenant is granted are now all the people belonging to the community that has been newly constituted. This is the "democratization" of the David tradition that

30 See the commentaries on this passage and particularly A. Caquot, "Les 'grâces de David.' A propos d'Isaïe 55:3b," *Sem* 15 (1965) 45–59; K. Seybold, *Das davidische Königtum im Zeugnis der Propheten* (1972), esp. 152–62; W. A. M. Beuken, "Isa 55,3-5: The Reinterpretation of David," *Bijdr* 35 (1974) 49–64; H. G. M. Williamson, "'The Sure Mercies of David': Subjective or Objective Genitive?" *JSS* 23 (1978) 31–49; R. J. Clifford, "Isaiah 55: Invitation to a Feast," in *The Word of the Lord Shall Go Forth: FS D. N. Freedman* (1983) 27–35; P. Bordreuil, "Les 'grâces de David' et 1 Maccabées II 57," *VT* 31 (1981) 73–75.

31 See above on 40:6-8. Perhaps there the word "flower" (צִיץ) is addressed to the rulers, if the people are "grass." But the "grace" of the ruler (חַסְדּוֹ, v. 6) passes away too.

32 For a survey of the meaning and the tradition of research see M. Weinfeld, "בְּרִית berîth," *TDOT* 2:253–79, on this text, 258 and 278 [*ThWAT* 1:781–808, on this text, 787 and 807]; K. Baltzer, *The Covenant Formulary* (1971), esp. 39–60; on the

renewal of the covenant, 89–93 [*Das Bundesformular* (2d ed. 1964), esp. 48–70; on the renewal of the covenant, 96–100]; E. Zenger, "Die Bundestheologie—ein derzeit vernachlässigtes Thema der Bibelwissenschaft und ein wichtiges Thema für das Verhältnis Israel–Kirche," in E. Zenger, ed., *Der Neue Bund im Alten* (1993) 13–49. E. Kutsch ("בְּרִית berît obligation," *TLOT* 1:256–66 [*THAT* 1:339-52]) adopts a different position. On DtIsa: Š. Porúbčan, *Il patto nuovo in Is. 40–66* (1958).

33 See H. J. Stoebe, "חֶסֶד ḥesed kindness," *TLOT* 2:449–64 [*THAT* 1:600–621]; H.-J. Zobel, "חֶסֶד ḥesed," *TDOT* 5:44–64 [*ThWAT* 3:48–71]; K. D. Sakenfeld, *The Meaning of Hesed in the Hebrew Bible: A New Inquiry* (1978).

34 Cf. 54:6-10.

35 See H.D. Preuss, "עוֹלָם ʿôlām," *ThWAT* 5:1144–59, esp. 1150 and 1152; A. Jepsen, "אָמַן ʾāman," *TDOT* 1:292–323, esp. 294–97 [*ThWAT* 1:313–48, esp. 317–18].

many scholars have assumed. A series of studies have shown that DtIsa is probably waging a dispute with particular traditions.

Important catchwords in the present text can thus be found in the so-called Nathan prophecy in 2 Samuel 7, the fundamental charter of the Davidic kingdom, according to the Deuteronomic history.[36] In 2 Sam 7:8-16 these catchwords are: the designation of David as prince (*nāgîd* נָגִיד v. 8; cf. 55:4); the promise of "demonstrations of grace" (וְחַסְדִּי, "my grace") for David (v. 15; cf. 55:3b);[37] and the promise that David's dynasty will endure forever (v. 16: וְנֶאֱמַן . . . עַד־עוֹלָם; cf. 55:3b). These catchwords point to a common conceptual complex, if they do not actually show that DtIsa was familiar with the text. But although the texts presumably drew on the same traditions, it was still possible to make different decisions about the standpoints to be assumed with regard to those traditions. A comparison with Psalm 89 shows this with particular clarity, as O. Eissfeldt already pointed out in his important study of our text.[38] The psalm talks about the promises of grace given to David (Ps 89:50 [49]) and laments their loss. It prays for the restoration of the dynasty, and its universal sovereignty (89:26-28 [25-27]). For DtIsa this expectation of a restored monarchy is inconceivable, as is evident from his immense stress on the kingship of Yahweh[39] and Yahweh's rule over the whole world as creator. He has

lent the Persian Cyrus sovereignty as his "anointed one" (מָשִׁיחַ, 45:1). In this light, the covenant and the promise to David take on a new meaning. This is not just a political question. The decision also affects the question about the validity of God's word, as the passage that immediately follows shows (cf. 55:11).[40]

David's significance is described in v. 4 with three terms, the striking point about them being that they are highly unspecific. They are not throne names, like the terms associated with the messianic hope in Isa 9:5-6 (6-7).[41] What they have in common, however, is that they express communicative activities.

David is "a witness" (עֵד). Now, no other text describes David in this way. How DtIsa sees the function of a witness can be deduced to some extent from 43:9-12. His function is to witness to earlier events (וְרִאשֹׁנוֹת, 43:9)—which can mean creation and salvation history—and also to the uniqueness of Yahweh (43:10)[42] and his help for his people (43:11, 12). According to the texts I have cited, this is Israel's task, on the grounds of its election (43:10). In the case of David, his historical acts could fall into this category, but so could his personal experiences as recorded in the Court History (2 Samuel [6] and 9–20; 1 Kings 1-2).[43] Here and in what follows I am assuming that F. Delitzsch is by no means wide of the mark in thinking that the statements could also refer to the David of "the psalms of David."[44]

36　On the connection with the present text see M. Tsevat, "Studies in the Book of Samuel, III: The Steadfast House: What Was David Promised in II Sam. 7:11b-16?" *HUCA* 34 (1963) 71–82. He translates חסד in 55:3 and 40:6 by "loyalty."

37　Cf. also 2 Chr 6:42.

38　O. Eissfeldt, "The Promises of Grace to David in Isaiah 55:1-5," in *Israel's Prophetic Heritage. FS J. Muilenburg* (1962) 196–207 ["Die Gnadenverheissungen an David in Jes 55,1-5," in O. Eissfeldt, *Kleine Schriften*, vol. 4 (1968) 44–52].

39　See Isa 41:21; 43:15; 44:6; 52:7.

40　Even the proponents of the counterposition, who pinned their hopes to a restitution of the monarchy, had to take account of scriptural interpretation. Thus Haggai explicitly withdraws the Jeremiah saying over Jehoiachin (Jer 22:24-27) so as to legitimate the dynastic claim of Zerubbabel, Jehoiachin's grandson (Hag 2:20-23, cf. also Zech 3:8; 4:6-10; 6:9-15); see K. Baltzer, "Das Ende des Staates Juda und die Messiasfrage" in *Studien zur Theologie der alttestamentlichen Überlieferung. FS G. von Rad* (1961)

33–43, esp. 38.

41　See G. von Rad, "The Royal Ritual in Judah," in *The Problem of the Hexateuch* (1966) 222-31 ["Das judäische Königsritual" (1947), in *Gesammelte Studien zum Alten Testament* (1958) 205–13]; H. Wildberger, *Isaiah 1–12* (1991) on this text [*Jesaja 1-12* (2d ed. 1980)].

42　Cf. Isa 44:8-9.

43　L. Rost, *The Succession to the Throne of David* (1982), trans. of *Die Überlieferung von der Thronnachfolge Davids* (1926), reprinted in his *Das kleine Credo und andere Studien zum Alten Testament* (1965) 119–253; R. N. Whybray, *The Succession Narrative. A Study of II Samuel 9–20; I Kings 1 and 2* (1968); T. Veijola, *Die Ewige Dynastie. David und die Entstehung seiner Dynastie nach der deuteronomistischen Darstellung* (1975); G. von Rad, "The Covenant with David in History," in his *Old Testament Theology*, 1 (1962) 308–17 ["Der Davidbund in der Geschichte," in *Theologie des AT*, 1 (8th ed. 1982) 320–31].

44　Delitzsch, 355–57 on this passage [569–70].

The text of 2 Samuel 7 refers explicitly to David as a *nāgîd* (נָגִיד), whose dynasty receives its legitimation through the prophet Nathan (2 Sam 7:8).[45] *Nāgîd* is therefore a traditional title. It is used for "the leader of Israel, appointed by Yahweh."[46] The precise translation of the title is disputed. G. F. Hasel now proposes the rendering "exalted one."[47] The title is not identical with kingship, but from Saul onward the person to whom the prophets give this title could be a king.

I am not certain, however, whether this titular use of the word is the only way of understanding its use in DtIsa. It could be that here there is yet again a deliberate ambiguity. For the description of David as "witness" we pointed to Isa 43:9-12. In that passage the many are "witnesses," and according to 48:20 they are also "to declare with a voice of joy (בְּקוֹל רִנָּה הַגִּידוּ): 'Yahweh has redeemed his servant Jacob.'"

Is David not only "the one proclaimed"[48] but also the one who proclaims? Is proclaiming, to make known (נגד *Hiphil*), now supposed to be the task of the whole of Israel too? Again we may think of the appropriation and transmission of "the psalms of David."[49]

The same may be said about the final description as well. Is David a "commander" (מְצַוֵּה), or has he passed on Yahweh's commandments, a task that now has to be fulfilled by Israel as a whole?[50]

David, then, has three functions: he is one "who is a witness," one who "proclaims" and one who "commands." But these functions are not restricted to Israel. They apply to "the nations," as is established by the

---

45   See also 1 Sam 13:14; 16:6(?); 25:30; 2 Sam 5:2 (= 1 Chr 11:2); 6:21; 7:8 (= 1 Chr 17:7); 1 Chr 5:2; 28:4; 2 Chr 6:5. This is the title most often given to David. For the discussion about the term נָגִיד see W. Richter, "Die nagid-Formel," *BZ* n.s. 9 (1965) 71–84; L. Schmidt, *Menschlicher Erfolg und Jahwes Initiative* (1970) 141–71; T. N. D. Mettinger, *King and Messiah: The Civil and Sacral Legitimation of the Israelite Kings* (1976) esp. 151–84.

46   See *HALOT* 2:668 [*HALAT* 2:631].

47   See G. F. Hasel, "נָגִיד *nāgîd*," *ThWAT* 5:203–19, esp. 205, 212–16.

48   Cf. A. Alt, "The Formation of the Israelite State in Palestine" in his *Essays on Old Testament History and Religion* (1967) 195 n. 54 ["Die Staatenbildung der Israeliten in Palästina" (1930), reprinted in his *Kleine Schriften zur Geschichte des Volkes Israel*, 2 (3d ed. 1964) 23 n. 2]: "The religious aura . . . suggests that *nāgîd* can be taken as a passive participle, signifying that the charismatic leader was 'designated' by Yahweh" (thus with some reservations by Alt himself!).

49   Cf. נגד *Hiphil* "declare" in "the psalms of David," e.g., Ps 51:1 (heading): "To the choir leader. A psalm of David"; v. 2 (heading): "When the prophet Nathan came to him, after he had gone in to Bathsheba"; v. 17 (15): "O Lord, open my lips, and my mouth will declare your praise" (וּפִי יַגִּיד); see also the following "psalms of David," in which נגד *Hiphil*, "declare," occurs: Psalm 22, esp. v. 32 (31); 38, esp. v. 19 (18); 40, esp. v. 6 (5); 64, esp. v. 10 (9); 142, esp. v. 3 (2); 145, esp. vv. 4-7. See here F. García-López, "נגד *ngd*," *ThWAT* 5:188–201, esp. 196, 199–200.

50   Cf. Ps 19:8-12 (7-11): v. 1 (heading): "A psalm of David"; v. 8 (7): "The law of Yahweh is perfect . . .

the testimony of Yahweh is sure"; v. 9 (8): "the precepts of Yahweh are right . . . the commandment of Yahweh (מִצְוַת יְהוָה) is clear"; on the text see H.-J. Kraus, *Psalms 1–59* (1987) 267–76 [*Psalmen 1–59* (5th ed. 1978) 297–307]. Particularly since the psalm consists of two parts, of which A: vv. 1-17 (heading-v. 16) "exhibits all the signs of great age, [while] Psalm 19B should probably not be dated before the time of Ezra" (Kraus, 269 [299]), it is all the more remarkable that in the text as we have it, praise of Yahweh's law should be linked with David (v. 1 [heading]). The contrast to DtIsa's position becomes particularly clear in comparison with Psalm 132. G. Liedke ("צוה *ṣwh* pi. to command," *TLOT* 2:1062–65 [*THAT* 2:530–36]) establishes (1063–64 [531]): "Superiors who give orders or commands are: kings . . ." (with extensive references to relevant passages); F. García López ("צוה *ṣwh*," *ThWAT* 6:936–59) observes (938): "David [as subject of the verb *ṣwh*] 11 times (7 times in 2 Samuel; twice in 1 Kings, all passages with a single exception belonging to the succession narrative; twice in 1 Chronicles)." But in Isa 55:4 it is precisely *not* the "succession" of David that is the point! According to García López (952), in this text "*ṣwh* [is used] in a peculiar way; here and here alone is the participle *piel* used to express a function." This means that the word could be rendered as the term for a function, not as a title: David is a "commander for nations." The real "commander" is Yahweh himself. See again Liedke (534): "Numerically, the use of the verb as term for the proclamation of Yahweh's commandment and law is preeminent."

archaically solemn term לְאֻמִּים, used for them.[51]

What this passage succeeds in doing is to reevaluate the values of the David tradition. The triumphalist standpoints of messianic expectation are thereby called in question. The promises to David acquire a new relevance when the community itself perceives its task and mission in the sense of the interpretation that is given authority by the divine saying. In its new definition and collective understanding, this approach corresponds in summary form to the approach that DtIsa developed for the Servant of God. Here a disputed question is decided by God's own casting a vote.[52]

A. 3. 55:5
Speaker

"See, you call a people that you do not know . . . , and a people that does not know you comes running to you . . ." **(55:5)**

This verse stands on its own as a separate unit. The direct divine speech is not continued. The text is the utterance of a speaker ("because of Yahweh, your God"). Nevertheless, the verse can be understood only in the light of its close connection with vv. 1-3a and vv. 3b-4.

The speaker interprets the divine saying (הֵן, "See . . ."). He says what is going to happen in the future (cf. the preformative conjugation of the verbs). That can also mean: "From now on. . . ." If foreigners are called and come, then it must again be for a pilgrimage and a festival. It is in this sense that witness and proclamation are understood here. "Zion is the city of David" (2 Sam 5:7). Here if anywhere the question about the relation between "the demonstrations of grace to David," the dynasty, and the city is acute; and here, too, the implicit decisions should be noted. It is not a question of the struggle between nations, the onslaught of enemies. Nor are the foreign peoples an object of vengeance, as they are in the Zion psalm, 149. The tradition about the pilgrimage of the peoples to Zion that we find in Isa 2:1-5[53] seems to be the tradition that is most closely related to this passage. In Isaiah 2 the reason for the pilgrimage is said to be: "For out of Zion goes forth *torah* and the word of Yahweh from Jerusalem" (Isa 2:3b). DtIsa makes unequivocally clear that the sole point is the divine sovereignty ("for Yahweh's sake," לְמַעַן יהוה). It is for this that Israel witnesses to the world.

One other subtlety in the text deserves attention. Foreigners are twice designated with the singular "people" (גּוֹי).[54] It is the interpretation of the double "nations" (לְאֻמִּים *le'ummîm*) in the divine saying in 55:4. Does it mean that all those who come from far away to Zion/Jerusalem for the pilgrimage and the feast are a single "people"? It is no longer the distinction according to ethnic criteria that is the most important thing; the essential point is that the people "hasten" in response to the call. The comparable passage of Isa 2:1-5, it may be noted, has only plurals for the foreigners (vv. 2-4), not plurals and singulars as here.

That DtIsa addresses his message to foreigners as well as to Israel there can be no doubt. In the figure of the Servant he makes this a program (cf. 49:1, 6; 51:4-5; 52:15; 53:12). In my view 51:7 ("the *torah* in the heart") suggests that "sympathizers" could already be meant. DtIsa was living at a time when intercultural exchange had become possible in the Persian Empire. That also served as a challenge to discover one's own standpoint. The beginning of this process is the growth of mutual knowledge. Verse 5 marvels at this: "A people that you do not know . . . a people that does not know you." Yet they come together! We may assume that at that time too relations with "foreigners" were a matter for dispute. But in the text "Gentile" (גּוֹי *gôy*) is not used contemptuously.

At the same time DtIsa stressed the unity given through the link between Israel as people and Zion/Jerusalem as city. This also goes back to the prologue in 40:1-2. "Your God" here (אֱלֹהֶיךָ) corresponds to "my people" there (עַמִּי, 40:1). Yahweh is the Holy One of Israel—holy not only in respect of the temple and the city. But at the same time it is said that "he has furnished *you* with glory" (כִּי פֵאֲרָךְ);[55] and a comparison

---

51 See *HALOT* 2:513 [*HALAT* 2:488]; H. D. Preuss, "לְאֹם *le'ōm*," *TDOT* 7:397–98 [*ThWAT* 4:411–13].

52 Beuken (288) sums up important positions in the interpretation of the text. He considers them to be untenable ("We should refrain from adopting"). I would agree.

53 Cf. also the reference to the smith in the previous chapter, 54:16 (and also 2:4); see above on the text.

54 See R. E. Clements and G. J. Botterweck, "גּוֹי *gôy*," *TDOT* 2:426–33 [*ThWAT* 1:965–73].

55 See J. Hausmann, "פאר *p'r*," *ThWAT* 6:494–99, esp. 496 and 498 on 4QDibHam 4:12 (cf. Hag 2:7-9).

with 60:7, 9, 13 showed that here Zion/Jerusalem is addressed (cf. also 40:2). In 52:1, at the investiture of Zion/Jerusalem, DtIsa shows in highly visual terms how Yahweh adorned the city with her "state robes." Is he intending that—in the sense of 55:3b-4—his listeners should add: it is not kings belonging to the house of David whom the city has to thank for her "glory," for the buildings of those kings have passed away; it is Yahweh alone?

6 Seek Yahweh when he can be found!
 Call upon him when he is near!
7 Let a wicked man forsake his way
 and a man of guilt his thoughts/plans,
 so that he may return to Yahweh, that he
  may have mercy upon him,
 and to our God, for he is abundant in
  forgiving.
8 Yes indeed, my thoughts/calculations/plans
  are not your
  thoughts/calculations/plans,
 and your ways are not my ways—saying of
  Yahweh.

9 Yes, the heavens are higher than the earth.[a]
 So (also) are my ways higher than your ways,
 and my thoughts/plans (higher) than your
  thoughts/plans.
10 For as the rain comes down
 and the snow from heaven
 and does not return there
 without having watered the earth,
 making it bring forth and sprout,
 giving seed to the sower and bread/
  nourishment to the eater,
11 so (also) shall my word be that goes forth[a]
  from my mouth:
 it will not return to me empty,
 without its having accomplished that which I
  desired,
 and having happily succeeded in that for
  which I sent it.

12 Truly, you shall go out with joy,
 and you shall be guided[a] in peace.
 The mountains and hills shall break out into
  joy before you,
 and all the trees of the fields shall clap their
  hands.
13 Instead of thorns, cypresses shall spring up,
 and instead of[a] nettles, myrtles shall spring
  up,
 and that shall come to pass for Yahweh <for
  a sign>,[b]
 for an everlasting <name>[b] that shall not be
  blotted out.

9[a] Thus following MT. Following the early versions, the reading could also be כְּגֹבַהּ instead of MT כִּי־גָבְהוּ (cf. 1QIsaᵃ כנובה). In that case the translation would be: "Just as the heaven is higher than the earth." If the text is rendered: "Yes, the heavens are higher," that would presuppose a worldview in which the heavens are a series of overarching spheres; cf. 1 Kgs 8:27; also Qoh 1:9.

11[a] Or, if יצא is vocalized as a perfect (cf. S), "has gone out."

12[a] 1QIsaᵃ תלכו "go" (cf. S).

13[a] Thus following the *Qere*, 1QIsaᵃ and numerous other manuscripts, as well as the early versions.

13[b,b] Thus the reversed order, "sign—name," in 1QIsaᵃ. Cf. *BHK* (3rd., reprint 1971). This reading is no longer noted in *BHS*; see below on the text.

B. 1. 55:6-8
Speaker: Conversion Is Possible Because God Is Rich in Forgiveness

"Yes indeed: my thoughts/calculations/plans are not your thoughts/calculations/plans . . ." (55:8)

In vv. 3b-5 the controversial subject of the relationship among the Davidic dynasty, the city of Zion/Jerusalem, the people of Israel, and the peoples and nations has again been raised in succinct form. The solution to the crux is legitimized by a divine saying: the dynasty is at an end, but the promise given to it is still valid; city and people are united in "the Holy One of Israel"; common ground is shared with people from far-off lands (aliens) when they too listen to Yahweh's "law and word," which—as Isa 2:2-5 said—proceeds from Zion/Jerusalem.

In the second part of chap. 55 (vv. 6-13), the pilgrimage theme is pursued further. Here, at the close of the drama, the liturgical elements are more clearly evident, in the form of terms taken from the language of the cult. In this way the congregation gathered together for the feast is drawn in.

The three units in part B of chap. 55 are also closely related by way of catchwords. The catchwords in part B.1 (vv. 6-8)—"ways" and "thoughts" in v. 7 and "thoughts and ways" in v. 8—are varied further in part B.2 (vv. 9-11). "Go forth" (יצא), referring to God's word (v. 11), is taken up again in part B.3 (vv. 12-13) with "go out (יצא) in v. 12. The division between the units vv. 6-8 and 9-11 can be grasped only in the light of the exegesis,[56] so in this case we shall start from the individual verses.

■ **6** The first saying in the unit: "Seek Yahweh!" (דִּרְשׁוּ יהוה) acts as a signal. Now, it is perfectly correct to say that "*drš* belongs primarily to the cognitive sphere: 'to inquire after something, ask about something, investigate.'"[57] In this way "*drš yhwh* became such a comprehensive designation for Yahweh worship that it often stands in antithesis to the worship of idols."[58] But important for the present passage is a special meaning that occurs in a limited but prominent group of texts. There "to seek Yahweh" is a term for pilgrimage.[59]

This is also the meaning in Deuteronomy 12, a passage that deals in principle with the place chosen by Yahweh: "You shall seek (תִדְרְשׁוּ) the place (הַמָּקוֹם) that Yahweh your God will choose out of all your tribes as his habitation to put his name there. You shall go there" (Deut 12:5). Instructions about offerings then follow. Verse 7 goes on: "And you shall eat there in the presence of Yahweh your God . . . rejoicing."[60]

Amos 5:4-15 passes on to the people Yahweh's command to make Jerusalem the goal of pilgrimage, and to reject the sanctuaries in Bethel and Gilgal: "Yes, thus says Yahweh to the house of Israel: Seek me (דִּרְשׁוּנִי) and you will live" (Amos 5:4).[61] The word "seek" (דרש) is then varied and interpreted several times in the course of the Amos text (vv. 5, 6, 14). The hymnal tradition is cited ("The one who made the Pleiades and Orion,"

v. 8). The ethical requirement is also emphasized (vv. 7, 10-11). Verse 14 ends: "Seek good (דִּרְשׁוּ־טוֹב) and not evil, that you may live; and so Yahweh, the God of Sabaoth, will be with you (אִתְּכֶם), just as you have said."

Finally, attention should be drawn to Jer 29:10-14. This is the famous prophecy about the seventy years of Babylonian exile. It begins: "When Babylon's seventy years are completed will I visit you, and will fulfill to you my goodly word, to bring you back to this place (לְהָשִׁיב)" (Jer 29:10).

The similarity between the semantic fields in this Jeremiah text and in Isaiah 55 is striking:

Jer 29:12: "You will call upon me (וּקְרָאתֶם) . . ." (cf. Isa 55:6)
Jer 29:13a: "You will search for me (וּבִקַּשְׁתֶּם) and find me;"
Jer 29:13b: "if you seek me with all your heart (כִּי תִדְרְשֻׁנִי)"
Jer 29:14: "I will let you find me (וְנִמְצֵאתִי) . . ." (cf. Isa 55:6).

The subject in each case is the return (שׁוּב, Isa 55:7, 10, 11; Jer 29:14).[62] But what is above all common to both texts is the question about the enduring validity of God's word (cf. Jer 29:10 and Isa 55:11), and of "God's thoughts" in contrast to the thoughts of human beings (מַחֲשָׁבוֹת, Jer 29:11, twice; cf. Isa 55:7, 8). Yet again, it is evident that by means of a few catchwords DtIsa is introducing whole complexes of tradition. It could even be that he is pointing to particular texts.

Like "All who are thirsty—come to the water" (v. 1), "Seek Yahweh" (v. 6) is an invitation to come to the sanctuary, an invitation to pilgrimage. Both texts take up 41:17: "The needy and the poor seek (בקש) water, but there is none. Their tongue is parched with thirst" (41:17a). Then, in this first act, Yahweh's decision is made: "I, Yahweh, will hear them, (I) the God of Israel will not forsake them" (41:17b).

"Come . . ." (v. 1), "seek . . ." (v. 6), and "go out with joy . . ." (v. 12) introduce units in the present text; but in the drama they are also stage directions. Thus after v. 6

---

56 For the translation and the structure of the text see F. Breukelman, "Uitleg en Verklaring van Jes. 55:6-11," *Om het Levende Woord Serie 1* (Dec. 1966) 17-27.

57 G. Gerlemann, "דרש *drš* to inquire after," *TLOT* 1:346-47, esp. 347 [*THAT* 1:460-62, 466-67, esp. 461]; see also C. Westermann, "Die Begriffe für Fragen und Suchen im AT," *KuD* 6 (1960) 2-30.

58 E. Ruprecht, "דרש *drš* to inquire after," *TLOT* 1:347-51, esp. 350 [*THAT* 1:462-66, esp. 466] with reference to Isa 65:1, 10; Jer 8:2; Zeph 1:6; Ezra 6:21; 2 Chr 15:12, 13; 17:3, 4; 34:3; further Ps 24:6; Ezra 4:2; 2 Chr 25:15, 20.

59 See also S. Wagner, "דרש *dārash*," *TDOT* 3:293-307,

esp. 294 [*ThWAT* 2:313-29, esp. 314]: "The element of movement as a presupposition for the process of seeking and asking seems to be more or less inherent in all OT examples, even when it is not explicitly mentioned but is clearly indicated by the context (e.g., in Isa. 11:10)." Cf. also his article "מָצָא *māṣā*," *TDOT* 8:465-83 [*ThWAT* 4:1043-63, esp. 1057-58].

60 Cf. Isa 55:12.

61 Cf. Amos 8:11-14.

62 See also Isa 62:12, where Zion is called "Sought Out" (דְּרוּשָׁה) and "A City No Longer Forsaken."

63 See above on 55:1 the quotation from G. Kremer,

the scene can fill with "people involved"[63] or, to be more exact, with "seekers of Yahweh," who now come on for the finale. Here "a single people" gathers.

■ **7** But then the admonition in v. 7 also has its place. No literary or textual operation is required. The function of this section of text also becomes clear if it is seen in the content of the pilgrimage tradition. What is being presented here is the *topos* of the entry liturgy at the opening of the gates. Starting from studies made by G. von Rad,[64] K. Koch has investigated the temple entry liturgies and decalogues.[65] Drawing on a series of texts, he describes the genre and function of these liturgies. Out of the question put to believers by the priests on their entry into the temple, the OT develops criteria for "the fundamental condition of a human being in the face of his holy God."[66] One particular observation of Koch is of special interest for the present text. He says about Psalm 24: "The gate liturgy that lies behind Ps 24 [was] also once shaped in such a way that it began with a brief but comprehensive description of upright—and hence cultically unexceptionable—conduct."[67] 55:7a could be just such a "description." More detailed comments "as to individual acts," such as would correspond to decalogues, are missing here. But Koch says about Psalms 15 and 24 and Isaiah 33: "*One* common feature (runs) through the phrases that have been taken over: everywhere a stand is taken *against any unjust pursuit of profit* and thus against economic and social injustice."[68] The same could be said of v. 7.

רשע rš‘, "to be wicked/guilty,"[69] is another term for "to be sinful, godless." "ʾāwen can take the form of different kinds of pernicious activity."[70] In the prophetic tradition, "unlawful legal manipulations and, in general, social injustice" could be described with this word. It could even be used in criticism of cult and sacrifice.[71] The special point about the present text is that "the wicked man" and "the unrighteous man" are told that repentance is still possible. That is by no means a matter of course. It presupposes Yahweh's "compassion." It is again moving that, at this point of all others, the speaker (and surely DtIsa too) should have included himself in the circle of the community by using the phrase: "to *our* God."

סלח slḥ, "forgive,"[72] is a term belonging to the language of the cult. There forgiveness is promised in association with expiatory and sacrificial regulations.[73] But in the present text there is no mention of either priest or sacrifice. Thus one must ask whether DtIsa is not here again taking up the tradition of the prophets, Jeremiah in particular. In the book of Jeremiah, in connection with the new covenant, Yahweh promises: "I will forgive their iniquity" (אֶסְלַח לַעֲוֺנָם, Jer 31:34bβ). Jer 33:8 is addressed particularly to Jerusalem: "I will cleanse them from all the guilt of their sin against me, and I will forgive (וְסָלַחְתִּי)."

The point at issue is Yahweh's own restoration of the divine relationship.[74] The confessions of sin in

---

"Die Struktur des Tragödienschlusses," in W. Jens, ed., *Die Bauformen der griechischen Tragödie* (1971) 121: "the large number of those involved lends events on the stage . . . a colorful variety and dramatic intensity."

64 See G. von Rad, "'Righteousness' and 'Life' in the Cultic Language of the Psalms," in *The Problem of the Hexateuch* (1966) 243–66 ["'Gerechtigkeit' und 'Leben' in der Kultsprache der Psalmen" in *FS A. Bertholet* (1950) 418–37, reprinted in his *Gesammelte Studien zum AT* (4th ed. 1971) 225–47]; also idem, "The Righteousness of Yahweh and of Israel" in his *Old Testament Theology,* vol. 1 (1962) 370–83 ["Jahwes und Israels Gerechtigkeit," in *Theologie des AT,* vol. 1 (7th ed. 1978) 382–95].

65 See K. Koch, "Tempeleinlassliturgien und Dekaloge," in *Studien zur Theologie der alttestamentlichen Überlieferungen: FS G. von Rad* (1961) 45–60.

66 See ibid., 60.

67 Ibid., 52.

68 Ibid., 59.

69 See C. van Leeuwen, "רשע rš‘ to be impious/guilty," *TLOT* 3:1261–65 [*THAT* 2:813–18].

70 See R. Knierim, "אָוֶן ʾāwen harm," *TLOT* 1:60–62, esp. 61 [*THAT* 1:81–84, esp. 82].

71 See K.-H. Bernhardt, "אָוֶן ʾāven," *TDOT* 1:140–47, esp. 143 [*ThWAT* 1:151–59, esp. 156].

72 See J. J. Stamm, "סלח slḥ to forgive," *TLOT* 2:797–803 [*THAT* 2:150–60].

73 See J. Hausmann, "סָלַח sālaḥ," *ThWAT* 5:859–67, esp. 861–62.

74 J. J. Stamm ("סלח slḥ to forgive," *TLOT* 2:803 [*THAT* 2:159]) points here to the connection between סלח and the NT ἀφιέναι/ἄφεσις: "Just like the Hebr. verb, the Gk. verb can also indicate God's forgiveness (e.g., Matt 6:12a, 14b; Mark 11:25; Luke 12:10; Acts 8:22). . . . Jesus has the authority during his lifetime to grant God's forgiveness (Mark 2:5ff. par.), and through his saving act

Nehemiah 9 and Daniel 9[75] point to the experience of "forgiveness/forgiving." With their catchwords "renewal of the covenant" (cf. Isa 55:3b) and remembrance of "God's proofs of his righteousness in prayer," these are all texts that are close to DtIsa.[76]

At this point I must once more stress that the text of vv. 6-7 can be understood even if "seek Yahweh" does not only mean the seeking of the sanctuary but covers the whole range of the term, in its full cognitive and emotional significance. The text's message can therefore also be developed in general terms. It is not least on these complex levels of understanding that the masterly quality of the text can be seen. Its climax comes in v. 8, which forms the end of the unit as well as the transition to the unit vv. 9-11.

■ **8** The beginning of v. 8 with its endorsing כִּי ("Yes, it is true: my thoughts are not your thoughts") indicates that even what is said in vv. 6-7 can be a point of controversy. Is Yahweh truly "near" (v. 6)? That is, what hour has struck? Can the wicked repent? Or is destruction their inevitable end (v. 7a)? Is there forgiveness without sacrifice (v. 7b)? Views different from those that DtIsa maintains were quite conceivable at that time—and not only then.

However graphically the statements in v. 8 are formulated, we should not fail to note their astonishing theological abstraction. An interpretation should therefore start from the concepts employed.

מַחֲשָׁבָה means: "1. thought, intent . . . ; 2. plan . . . ; 3. invention. . . ."[77] But these meanings cover only the spectrum of the root חשׁב, with "calculate, plan."[78] Both aspects are required for an understanding of vv. 7 and 8. Verse 7 requires "charge, settle accounts." The "calculation" made by the man whose acts are pernicious is certainly different from God's reckoning. But the relation goes beyond the one term and its modifications. The decisive point is that Yahweh "settles accounts" in a different way, when he permits repentance and has compassion. The theological problem becomes clearer through a comparison with other texts.

Here again attention should be drawn to Jeremiah 29, Jeremiah's letter to the people in Babylonian exile: "Yes, I know the 'thoughts' (הַמַּחֲשָׁבֹת) that I 'think' (חֹשֵׁב) about you, saying of Yahweh, 'thoughts' (מַחְשְׁבוֹת) of salvation (שָׁלוֹם) and not for your harm (לְרָעָה)" (Jer 29:11). At the period of this letter, it was also disputed whether there could still be "future and hope" after the exile. God himself brings about the return (Jer 29:14)!

A similar picture also emerges from the term "way" (דֶּרֶךְ). "In a highly general sense 'way,' meaning 'conduct, general state of affairs, custom, maner,' describes certain fundamental facts in the life of human beings or nature."[79] But it can also have the quite concrete meaning "enterprise, business."[80] The word can be used for both human and divine behavior.

Ezekiel 18 gives an impression of the discussion that

the community obtains forgiveness (Eph 1:7; Col 1:14), which it then offers or bestows through him (Matt 26:28; Luke 24:47; Acts 2:38; 10:43; 1 John 2:12; etc.)."

75 See סְלַ(י)חוֹת Dan 9:9; Neh 9:17; cf. Ps 130:4 and N. Lohfink's comments in "'Ich bin Jahwe, dein Arzt.' Gott, Gesellschaft und menschliche Gesundheit in der Theologie einer nachexilischen Pentateuch-bearbeitung (Ex 15,25b.26)," in H. Merklein and E. Zenger, eds., *"Ich will euer Gott werden." Beispiele biblischen Redens von Gott* (1981) 11–73.

76 See K. Baltzer, *The Covenant Formulary* (1971), part 1, chap. III: "The Covenant Formulary at the Renewal of the Covenant," 39–62, esp. 49–50 on 1QS 1:18–2:18 (*Manual of Discipline*) [*Das Bundes-formular* (2d ed. 1964) Abschnitt III: "Das Bundes-formular bei der Erneuerung des Bundes," 48–70, esp. 58–59].

77 See *HALOT* 2:572 [*HALAT* 2:542].

78 See K. Seybold, "חָשַׁב *ḥāšab*," *TDOT* 5:228–45, esp. 230 [*ThWAT* 3:243–61, esp. 245]: "The Hebrew verb *ḥšb* exhibits two basic semantic elements. The first

is the element of calculation, with its modifications 'account, compute, charge, settle (accounts)' thus 'count, value, calculate.' The second is the element of planning: 'think out, conceive, invent.' Both elements appear in the derived nouns, and can also be recognized in part in non-Hebrew cognates."

79 See G. Sauer, "דֶּרֶךְ *derek* way," *TLOT* 1:343–46, esp. 345 [*THAT* 1:456–60, esp. 458]. Cf. also J. Bergman, A. Haldar, H. Ringgren, and K. Koch, "דֶּרֶךְ *derekh*," *TDOT* 3:270–93 [*ThWAT* 2:288–312]. On the problems involved in rendering דֶּרֶךְ see Bergman, 270–73 [288–90]. See also Koch's important comments, 275–91 [293–310]; on DtIsa 289–90 [308–9].

80 See *HALOT* 1:232 [*HALAT* 1:222].

81 On the text see K. Baltzer, D. Georgi, and F. Merkel (Exegetisch-homiletische Arbeitsgemeinschaft), "Ezekiel 18:1-4, 21-24, 30-32," *GPM* 18 (1963/64) 233–38; also C. Westermann, "3. Sonntag nach Trinitatis—Hes 18,1-4.21-24.30-32," in H. Breit and C. Westermann, eds., *CPH*, vol. 2 (1963) 153–62.

raged over the guilt question in the exilic period, and the different views held.[81] In Ezekiel too (as in Isa 55:7) the point at issue is the guilt of individuals, not the guilt of the people as a whole. According to Ezek 18:23, God's decision is based on "his strong bias for the *life* of man."[82] "Have I really any pleasure <in> the death of the wicked (רָשָׁע), says the Lord Yahweh, and not rather that he should turn from his ways (מדרכו)[83] and live?" (Ezek 18:23).

Yet according to Ezek 18:29 the people react with indignation: "But the house of Israel says: 'The way of Yahweh is unfair (לֹא יִתָּכֵן)!' O house of Israel, are my ways unfair? Is it not your ways that are unfair?" "Unfair" here means "not right, confused and confusing."[84] It is actually God's *saving action* that gives offense. Yet that is the presupposition for the turn to life (Ezek 18:3-32).

Isa 55:8 sounds like a summing up, in a brief formula, of Jer 29:11 and Ezek 18:29. A comparison of the texts makes clear that what human beings find especially incomprehensible is God's will for salvation, his "compassion." That God is gracious can be a stumbling block for "the good people." This is one of the themes of the book of Jonah. The prophet is resentful because Nineveh repents. Jonah turns his own confession of faith against God: "For I knew that you are a gracious God and merciful, slow to anger, and abounding in steadfast love (רַב־חֶסֶד) and ready to relent from punishing" (Jonah 4:2).

A comparison with the way this formula is used elsewhere in the OT[85] shows that this was a matter of discussion: is God's forgiveness coupled with conditions ("Yet he does not leave unpunished"),[86] or does it rest solely on his free grace?[87] In maintaining that Yahweh's "thoughts and ways" are different from the thoughts and ways of human beings, DtIsa is passing on the experience that he is "abundant in forgiving" (v. 7).

I believe, however, that the relationship between v. 7 and v. 8 could imply a still further dispute about מַחֲשָׁב(וֹ)ת in the sense of "calculate, take into account," for the term has a special meaning in the context of priestly sacrificial terminology.[88] The priests' task was to approve and accept sacrifices.[89] This also meant that the priests decided whether there could be forgiveness (סְלִיחָה).[90] But if, as v. 7 maintains, "our God" is "abundant in forgiving" (יַרְבֶּה לִסְלוֹחַ), then, according to v. 8, the divine "calculations" (מַחֲשָׁבוֹת) can be different from human ones. This could be a very lofty but unequivocal criticism of "the priestly theory and practice of sacri-

82   See W. Zimmerli, *Ezekiel* 1 (1979) 385 on this passage [*Ezechiel* (2d ed. 1979) 413]; also on the text of Ezek 18:29.

83   *Qere*, LXX, S, Tg: מִדַּרְכּוֹ; *Ketib*: מִדְּרְכָיו, "from his ways."

84   Koch ("דֶּרֶךְ *derekh*," *TDOT* 3:289 [*ThWAT* 2:308]) writes about Ezekiel: "In no other OT book is the noun *derekh* [way] used so often (107 times)." And on the present Ezekiel text: "Ezk 18 . . . concludes with a discussion of the question whose *derekh* is reliable, the divine or the human (vv. 25ff.; 33:17-20). Part of the divine *derekh* is that it guarantees the functioning of the sphere of act and destiny within the movement of human life. . . . Return is again based on the concept of the *derekh*" [trans. altered].

85   See H. Spieckermann, "Barmherzig und gnädig ist der Herr . . . ," *ZAW* 102 (1990) 1–18, on Jonah esp. 15–16.

86   See Exod 34:6-7; Num 14:18; cf. Nah 1:2-3 and the Damascus Document, CD 2.3-5.

87   See Joel 2:13; Pss 86:15; 103:8; 145:8; Neh 9:17; Sir 2:11.

88   Cf. Lev 7:18; 17:4 (and Num 18:27, 30?).

89   See K. Seybold, "חָשַׁב *ḥāšaḇ*," *TDOT* 5:228–45, esp. 241–44 (with lit.) [*ThWAT* 3:243–61, esp. 256–59];

W. Schottroff, "חשׁב *ḥšb* to think," *TLOT* 2:479–82 [*THAT* 1:641–46]; E. Würthwein, "Amos 5,21-27," *ThLZ* 72 (1947) 143–52; also his "Kultpolemik oder Kultbescheid?" in *Tradition und Situation: Studien zur alttestamentlichen Prophetie. FS A. Weiser* (1963) 115–31; reprinted in E. Würthwein, *Wort und Existenz. Studien zum AT* (1970) 144–60; G. von Rad, "Faith Reckoned as Righteousness," in *The Problem of the Hexateuch* (1966) 125–30 ["Die Anrechnung des Glaubens zur Gerechtigkeit," *ThLZ* 76 (1951) 129–32; reprinted in his *Gesammelte Studien zum AT* (4th ed. 1971) 130–35]; R. Rendtorff, "Priesterliche Kulttheologie und prophetische Kultpolemik," *ThLZ* 81 (1956) 339–42; also his *Die Gesetze in der Priesterschrift. Eine gattungsgeschichtliche Untersuchung* (2d ed. 1963), esp. 74–76 on "declaratory formulations"; also his *Studien zur Geschichte des Opfers im alten Israel* (1967), esp. 253–60.

90   See Lev 4:20, 26, 31, 35; 5:10, 13, 16, 18, 26 (6:7); Num 15:25, 26, 28.

fice,"[91] a criticism that would follow the lines of the position adopted by DtIsa elsewhere too. For him, Yahweh's "plans for good" are not tied to sacrifice. The sacral "calculations" are not Yahweh's. He calculates differently (v. 8). DtIsa preaches the salvation, the peace of God, that comes from forgiveness. That is why "conversion" is possible[92] (see v. 7). So here, in closing, he puts forward a reason or cause (αἴτιον).

The weight and rank of what is expounded in vv. 6-8 become clear at the end through the phrase "saying of Yahweh" (נְאֻם יהוה), the age-old formula of prophetic tradition.[93] At the same time the phrase marks the end of the divine spokesman's address. In what follows God must again be understood as speaking directly, in the first person.

B. 2   55:9-11
Divine Speech: The Unity of the World
God Acts through His Word

"[My word] will not return to me empty, without its having accomplished that which I desired . . ." (55:11)

In form and content, this unit is a direct "revelatory speech." It can be heard by everyone; it is not restricted to the initiated. Verses 9 and 8 correspond almost word for word,[94] and for that very reason the differences

require particular attention. Common to both verses is the theme of the "ways and thoughts." Verse 8 is a summing up of vv. 6-7. The problem of the chargeability of guilt is solved with divine authority. Verse 9 is the heading for vv. 10-11, in the question about God's plan for his world. The differences lie in the nuances of the terms "ways" (דְּרָכִים) and "thoughts" (מַחֲשָׁבוֹת). This unit too begins with the endorsing כִּי, "Yes, indeed."[95] What follows is the argument.[96] The text is probably picking up critical questions again that were under discussion at the time. The subject is God's preeminence ("are higher," גָּבְהוּ). His "ways and thoughts" are truly "higher," when it is a matter of the rain that comes down from heaven, and the word from Yahweh's mouth.

■ **9** This verse makes the point clear with a reminder of the distance between heaven and earth.[97] This takes up again what was already the basis of the argument in 40:22, there in the form of a hymnal acknowledgment. God's throne is in heaven.[98] This means that he rules over the earth and its inhabitants. Here what is an element in the worldview becomes an instrument for a theological statement. The cosmological view can bring out the limits and inappropriateness of human thinking.[99] That is developed in what follows: the "ways" are illustrated by the way taken by water (v. 10), the "thoughts" by God's plan, which is implemented by his

---

91   It is worth considering how far this also reflects a dispute between different priesthoods in the temple, for example between Aaronites/Zakodites and Levites. An observation of K. Seybold ("חָשַׁב ḥāšab," TDOT 5:228–45 [ThWAT 3:243–61]) should at least be recorded: a whole series of proper names are formed with the root חשב in the OT. These are "confessional statements. . . . 'YH(WH) has calculated, planned' or '(YHWH) plans.'" "We can discover about 20 people in the OT who have names of this kind. By far the greatest number of them are clearly Levites (about two-thirds are explicitly so). About half of them belong to the time of Nehemiah" [trans. altered]. That would mean that these "thanksgiving" names belong to the period to which I should most readily assign DtIsa. He would accordingly here, at the close of his work, be picking up one of the key terms of Levite theology.
92   Cf. the argument in Mark 1:1-20.
93   See D. Vetter, "נְאֻם nᵉʾum utterance," TLOT 2:692–94 [THAT 2:1–3]; H. Eising, "נְאֻם nᵉʾum," ThWAT 5:119–23.
94   Consequently most commentators view this as a

single unit, unless their underlying assumption is that the unit is more extended, comprising vv. 6-11. For the "differing demarcation of the units" in Isa 55:6-13 "and the varying definition of their genres," see D. Baltzer, Ezechiel und Deuterojesaja (1971) 120–21. He perceives the relative independence of vv. 8, 9 and 10, and the close cohesion in vv. 9-10 (see ibid. and 122); see also his fine stichometric division (121; also Beuken's comments, 294–95).
95   See W. Schneider, Grammatik des Biblischen Hebräisch (5th ed.; 1982) § 53.3.1.c; also HALOT 2:470 [HALAT 2:448]; Joüon and Muraoka 617, § 164b; bibl. on ki: ZAH 1 (1988) 217; ZAH 5 (1992) 107; T. Muraoka, Emphatic Words and Structures in Biblical Hebrew (1985) 158–64; Y. Thorion, Studien zur klassischen hebräischen Syntax (1984) 3–36.
96   See the introduction, v. 10, with a further endorsing כִּי and a following "if not" (כִּי אִם, vv. 10 and 11). The conclusion is drawn twice: "accordingly, thus" (כֵּן, vv. 9, 11).
97   Cf. Gen 11:1-9.
98   Cf. Pss 33:13; 93; 103:19; Isa 33:5.
99   Cf. Job 22:12-13.

word (v. 11). The fundamental premise of the argument is the unity of the whole of creation.

■ **10** Taken on its own, detached from the comparison in v. 11, v. 10 describes the "way"[100] of rain and snow: "It comes down . . . it returns." The text suggests that the water cycle is the presupposition here. That possibility cannot be excluded. DtIsa no longer imagines the heavens as a "firmament" (רָקִיעַ) with a heavenly ocean above—the notion found in Genesis 1. For him the earth is firm, the heavens are "stretched out" (see 42:5; 51:13). Thus they can also vanish "like smoke" (51:6).[101]

Elsewhere too DtIsa carries into his work the most modern science of his time.[102] The period is more familiar to us as the era of the Ionic natural philosophers.[103] But with the Persian era an intensive exchange of knowledge about the world got under way. We have only the barest notion of the labor such apparently matter-of-course perceptions required.[104] The text does not describe *how* the water returns. It is mainly interested in the chain of cause and effect. An older, more distinctly mythological way of speaking is still recognizable—for example, when the rain makes the earth "give birth" (וְהוֹלִידָהּ). This is how the phrase is usually translated. One can see the development from concrete language ("procreation/birth") to the abstraction "rain/water" as

an element (comp. esp. Job 38:28-30).

Seed and bread are now the product of the rain. In its interest in the world of human beings, the text shows traces of the wisdom tradition.

The question is why DtIsa should take up the "rain" theme at this point. The reason could perhaps have to do with the calendar and liturgy of the feast days. Isaiah 54 reflected the dispute with the Baal/Anat cult, and this cult was closely associated with the cycle of the seasons, and the return of the autumn rains, with the fertility they brought. There could be no greater contrast than that between the sober rationality of the present text and the myth, with the explanation it offers. Since the text concerns Israel here, "rain" could speak in favor of a link with the autumn festival. But the problem is probably more complicated than that because in the exilic period the New Year was moved from autumn to spring.[105]

"Rain" (הַגֶּשֶׁם) could also be the late rains in March/April.[106] This would mean that a link with the Passover-Mazzot feast is not out of the question. The late rains are especially important for the sowing of the summer grain and for the resulting yield.[107]

---

100 On "way" (דֶּרֶךְ) as a generic term for different ways of proceeding cf. Prov 30:19-20.

101 See R. Bartelmus, "שָׁמַיִם šāmajim," *ThWAT* 8:204–39.

102 Cf. above on 40:12, 22.

103 Aristotle describes the water cycle in his *Meteorica* 346b, 359b-360a; cf. also E. F. Sutcliffe, "The Clouds as Water-Carriers in Hebrew Thought," *VT* 3 (1953) 99–103, esp. 101. In his view, "Knowledge is apt to increase with the passing of the centuries rather than to decrease"; but historical experience shows that scientific knowledge can be lost too.

104 For a formulation of the cycles in the earthly world ("under the sun") see Qohelet 1, esp. v. 7. Cf. Job 38:22-38; also Deut 28:24; Jer 14:22; Job 36:26-29.

105 Cf. the relationships among the Easter, Epiphany, and Christmas liturgies in the early church.

106 See H.-J. Zobel, "מָטָר māṭār," *TDOT* 8:350–65, esp. 355 [*ThWAT* 4:827–42, esp. 832]: "The latter [spring] rain is even more important for the land's yield [than the early rains]. . . . It is with this rain only that the plea in Zec. 10:1 is concerned. It 'refreshes, revives' the earth (Hos. 6:3 conj.; cf. Isa. 55:10), and 'moistens' it (Ps. 72:6). The latter rain is expected three months before the harvest (Am. 4:7 [there the word is הַגֶּשֶׁם]), i.e., after March/April"

(see also Jer 3:3; Ezek 34:25-30; Ps 105:32, 41, 43). Cf. G. Dalman, *Arbeit und Sitte in Palästina,* vol. 1: *Jahreslauf und Tageslauf* (1928; reprint 1964); P. Reymond, *L'eau, sa vie, et sa signification dans l'Ancien Testament* (1958). On גֶּשֶׁם as a term for rain in general see Isa 44:14; Jer 14:4; 1 Kgs 17:7, 14. In Isa 55:10 the text uses singular verbs throughout, thus taking no account of the double rain *and* snow. In Palestine, snow is most likely in January/February, but it is still possible in March/April too. For snow see Dalman, *Arbeit,* vol. 1 part 2: "Frühling und Sommer," 305; R. B. Y. Scott, "Meteorological Phenomena and Terminology in the OT," *ZAW* 64 (1952) 11–25, esp. 15.

107 זֶרַע is "seed, seed for sowing," but according to Gen 8:22 and Lev 26: 5 it can also mean "seedtime." The spring rains make it possible to sow the seed for the summer grain and they are essential for the year's harvest. See also Dalman, *Arbeit,* 1:291: "The winter rains can have filled the cisterns and watered the ground. But if the rains fail in the months of increasing warmth that follow the winter, a plentiful harvest is not to be expected, because the grain then dries up instead of developing rich ears" (see also 298–300). In its own poetic language, there-

In this text rain and snow are natural phenomena, as part of the water cycle or, to adhere more closely to the sense of the text, the water cycle is one of the "ways" created by God. But like the cycle as a whole, rain and snow remain God's creation. Even if a water ceremony formed part of the feast, rainmaking rites or magical invocations are not necessary here; nor would they have any point.

■ **11** G. von Rad wrote about vv. 10-11: "This is surely prophecy's most comprehensive statement about the word of Yahweh and its effects."[108] The text is certainly a fundamental contribution to the theme "theology of the Word."[109] But here too the significance of Yahweh's word (דָּבָר)[110] in the immediate context should be considered first of all. I myself think it problematical to describe the relationship of vv. 10 and 11 as image (v. 10) and fact (v. 11), in the framework of metaphorical speech.[111] The point is the correspondence of the two statements. They do not differ in their reality content. What is said about rain can be said about the word in

exactly the same way—hence the precise correspondence of the two verses.[112]

Both phenomena belong to the categories of "ways . . . and thoughts" (v. 9). Here the "word" can be better grasped through "my thoughts" (מַחְשְׁבֹתַי) if—in distinction from the nuance "calculate, charge" in vv. 6-8—"the element of planning"[113] is stressed.

One difference between "rain" and "Yahweh's word" could be that the word comes from a still higher sphere,[114] directly from the mouth of God. The word links the heavenly and the earthly world, God and human beings. The special point of the statement of this text at the end of DtIsa's work is that in his word the far-off God is also the one who is near.[115]

In order to fill out the formula "my word" fully, we should have again to go through all the passages in which DtIsa's concern is "Yahweh's word." The close in 55:11 clearly finds its correspondence in the beginning in 40:8: "but the word of our God shall stand forever!"

fore, the text could thus also be a precise description of the springtime situation.

108 See G. von Rad, "The Prophets' Conception of the Word of God," in *Old Testament Theology,* vol. 2 (1962) 80–98, esp. 93 ["Die Auffassung der Propheten von dem Wort Gottes," in *Theologie des Alten Testaments,* vol. 2 (8th ed. 1984) 93–111, esp. 102].

109 See W. Zimmerli, "Jahwes Wort bei Deuterojesaja," *VT* 32 (1982) 104–24, and esp. on 55:8-11: C. Stuhlmueller, *Creative Redemption in Deutero-Isaiah* (1970) 188–91.

110 See G. Gerlemann, "דָּבָר *dābār* word," *TLOT* 1:325–32 [*THAT* 1:433–43]; J. Bergman, H. Lutzmann, and W. H. Schmidt, "דָּבָר *dābhar*," *TDOT* 3:84–125 (with lit.); on the text, 123–25 [*ThWAT* 2:89–133, on the text, 131–33]. The following older books were of fundamental importance: O. Grether, *Name und Wort Gottes im AT* (1934); L. Dürr, *Die Wertung des göttlichen Wortes im Alten Testament und im antiken Orient* (1938).

111 See C. Westermann, 289: "comparison" [Gleichnis, "parable" [232]; D. Baltzer, *Ezechiel und Deuterojesaja* (1971) 124–29: "parable speech" with reference to E. Linnemann; J. Muilenburg (650) talks about "parable figure, interpretation."

112 See von Rad, *Old Testament Theology,* vol. 2 (1962) 93 [*Theologie des Alten Testaments,* vol. 2 (8th ed. 1982) 102]: "When the word of Yahweh is likened to rain and snow, what comes into a modern reader's mind are simply the laws of nature; ancient Israel, however, regarded both of these, the sending of the rain and the sending of the word, as contingent

events which took their origin from Yahweh alone (Ps. CXVII.15ff.)."

113 See K. Seybold, "חָשַׁב *ḥāšaḇ,* "*TDOT* 5:228–45, esp. 230 [*ThWAT* 3:243–61, esp. 245]. Cf. *HALOT* 1:360 [*HALAT* 1:346] under חשׁב 5; 2:572 [2:542] under מַחֲשָׁבָה 1 und 2. On this subject see W. Werner, *Studien zur alttestamentlichen Vorstellung vom Plan Jahwes* (1988).

114 See v. 9 on גָּבְהוּ. The Masoretic reading (*Qal* perfect 3d person plur.) could presuppose a genuine plural of "heaven" (שָׁמַיִם). 1QIsa^a has כנבה, "in accordance with [its] height"; cf. Isa 52:13. In that text (see above on the passage) the exaltation of the Servant into the sphere of God is announced with "He will be very high" (וְגָבַהּ מְאֹד). K. Koch ("דֶּרֶךְ *derekh,*" *TDOT* 3:275–93 [*ThWAT* 2:293–312]) disputes the spatial meaning in both instances (289–90 [309]). The distinction between two spheres can then also be found in Qohelet: "There is nothing new under the sun" (Qoh 1:9). What happens "under the sun" is what continually recurs (see the water cycle in Qoh 1:7). The implicit corollary would be "There is something new *above* the sun," i.e., where God is. DtIsa, at least, acknowledges that Yahweh creates what is new (Isa 43:19).

115 Here the reception of DtIsa in the NT would require further investigation; cf., e.g., J. V. Dahms, "Isaiah 55:11 and the Gospel of John," *EvQ* 53 (1981) 78–88. For the understanding of "the Word" (λόγος) cf. also John 1:1-18 and the commentaries.

There it is also maintained that the promise stands because "Yahweh's mouth has spoken it" (40:5).

It is a creative word (51:16); it is a prophetic word (44:26; cf. 46:10-11; 48:15). The word creates justice (45:13). It is "teaching" (50:4; cf. 42:16). It is public, not secret (45:19; 48:16). That God speaks—reveals himself— is his special characteristic (52:6). His word is reliable.[116] The word of God comprehends space and time, nature and history. Before the one God it is the one world.

The text casts back once more to the sociomorpheme "God as ruler," as the catchwords show. Like a king, he has his messenger. He sends him out (שְׁלַחְתִּיו). The messenger returns when he has carried out his task in the way his lord (חֶפְצְתִי) wishes.[117]

"In vain" ("empty," רֵיקָם)[118] or "happily completed" (וְהִצְלִיחַ) is the alternative on which the Lord can decide thanks to the energy and power of his word. Otherwise Tyche or other gods of fortune decide what will be happily completed. To invoke them cannot help. The end of his book shows once again how closely intertwined DtIsa's themes are.

The personalization or even hypostatization of the word (דָּבָר) in the present text has been the subject of continual research.[119] The personification of abstracts is a widespread phenomenon in the ancient Near East. Either deities or concepts can be presented as persons.

This had a long tradition in Egypt, particularly in the sphere of "word" too.[120] It plays a part in the Greek world, above all later in Hellenism.[121]

As far as the present text is concerned, it is again worth considering whether this personalization is connected with the genre. In the liturgical drama, "the word" could be presented as a messenger. The verbs of movement are noticeable in v. 11: "go out" (יצא) and "return" (שׁוּב). But the same is already true of v. 10: "come down" (ירד) and "return" (שׁוּב). We may once more ask whether "rain," "snow," and "word" came forward in a mime. Finally, vv. 10 and 11 have to do with "ways" and "plans" (v. 9). They could have been depicted in the form of movement, in steps or dance. In the ancient world concepts are recognizable from their attributes. That is true of both plastic representation and the theater. For the rain, water that was poured out or sprinkled would probably be enough.[122]

With regard to Yahweh's word a further theological reflection is necessary at this point. If, as has been said above, for DtIsa God's word is the *torah* and above all the prophetic word too,[123] then it could be presented emblematically as "the divine scripture," that is, as an actual scroll.[124] Through his interpretation of texts from the Torah, the Prophets, and the Psalms, DtIsa has shown the efficacy of God's word. It has therefore

---

116 See C. J. Labuschagne, "פֶּה *peh* mouth," *TLOT* 2:976–79, esp. 978 [*THAT* 2:406–11, esp. 409]: "The phrase 'to come forth from the mouth' with *yṣʾ* (Josh 6:10) is usually used as a technical expression in relation to a promise or vow (Num 30:3; 32:24; Judg 11:36; Jer 44:17; cf. Deut 23:24 [23]) and always refers to Yahweh (Deut 8:3 . . . ; Isa 45:23; 48:3; 55:11 . . .)."

117 Cf. 44:28; 46:10; 48:14. On the conflict between God's will and purpose and the earthly ruler, see G. J. Botterweck, "חָפֵץ *ḥāpēṣ*," *TDOT* 5:92–107, esp. 96 [*ThWAT* 3:100–116, esp. 105]: "We find a totally different problem when the king is the subject of *ḥāpēṣ*. In all such instances, the verb can become a term for the royal power and authority of the king, which, when exercised for the king's own pleasure or without check, can come into collision with the power of Yahweh, the universal king." Botterweck refers to 2 Sam 24:2-3; 1 Kgs 13:33; 1 Chr 28:9; Qoh 8:3.

118 The root ריק means "empty, pour out," hence the meaning of the adjective in the different forms: "empty, null and void, in vain"; see *HALOT*

3:1227–29 [*HALAT* 4:1145–46].

119 See W. H. Schmidt, "דָּבָר *dābhar*," *TDOT* 3:120–25 [*ThWAT* 2:128–33]: "IV.8. Beginnings of Hypostatization" (with lit.); P. Hänisch, *Personifikation und Hypostasen im AT und im Alten Orient* (1921); O. Grether, *Name und Wort Gottes im AT* (1934) 150–58; H. Ringgren, *Word and Wisdom. Studies in the Hypostatization of Divine Qualities and Functions in the Ancient Near East* (1947); G. Gerlemann, "Bemerkungen zum alttestamentlichen Sprachstil" in *Studia Biblica et Semitica. FS T. C. Vriezen* (1966) 108–14.

120 See J. Bergman's summing up (with lit.) "דָּבָר *dābhar*," *TDOT* 3:84–91: "1. Egypt" [*ThWAT* 2:92–98: "1. Ägypten"].

121 See L. Petersen, *Zur Geschichte der Personifikation in griechischer Dichtung und bildender Kunst* (1939).

122 Cf. the interpretation of 40:15 above.

123 See 48:3: "The earlier (happenings) I already told, and they went out of my mouth, and I caused them to be heard"; cf. 51:16.

124 Cf. Jeremiah 36, esp. vv. 1-2: "this word came to Jeremiah from Yahweh: Take a scroll and write on it

become clear for later eras too that the word does not return "empty, in vain." One only has to remember the importance of the Torah scrolls in the service of the synagogue, and the liturgical use of Holy Scripture in the churches.

B. 3.   55:12-13
Speaker:
Festal Procession in Peace (Exit)
Praise of Yahweh's Name
Soli Deo gloria

"And that shall come to pass for Yahweh <for a sign>, for an everlasting <name> that shall not be blotted out" (55:13)

In these two verses we can again see DtIsa's skill in allowing a text to speak on different levels. It is the great themes that are now named at the end: The exodus (v. 12a), the transformation of nature (vv. 12b-13a) and the *soli Deo gloria* (v. 13b): to the sole glory of God.

DtIsa sounds the keynote when he sets aside the normal word order and begins: "Truly, with joy . . . !" Then, accompaniment "in peace" (בְּשָׁלוֹם) takes up everything that has been said from chap. 40 onward about the many different ways of God and human beings, about the fears but also the protection and the consolation.[125] These are experiences that men and women have shared with these writings throughout the ages. These texts, says DtIsa, will be a perpetual "sign" or lodestone for human beings; and this prophecy has been fulfilled.

At the same time the text is the close of the liturgical drama. It therefore also contains the "dismissal." Even today, church services often end: "Go in the peace of the Lord . . ." or "Ite missa est. . . ." "You shall go out!" (תֵּצֵאוּ) is intended literally. In the drama it announces the end, with the exit of the chorus and all the players. The people who now go out represent the exodus. As DtIsa has continually shown, that means the Exodus from Egypt and the exodus from Babylon in one. Both are remembered. At the same time it is the exodus of God's people into a new beginning *now*.

The use of the name of Yahweh in v. 13 again shows that these verses were pronounced by the speaker.

■ **12** All DtIsa's wit comes into play again too. For v. 12a can also be taken as "exit with joy" but please: "in peace!"[126] The people who go out are to be escorted, as in a procession.[127] Verse 12b may perhaps also contain covert stage directions. "Breaking out into joy (יִפְצְחוּ . . . רִנָּה) before you" (i.e., the people who are physically going out) refers to the whole festal assembly. As with DtIsa's other hymns,[128] we may ask whether mountains-hills-fields also indicate the particular pitch or voices required (women or men).

But above all v. 12b calls for the clapping appropriate for the end of a play.[129] "All the trees": are these participants in the feast who were adorned with greenery?[130] We may suspect that the plants described in v. 13a also refer to different groups of people.

■ **13a** יַעֲלֶה is ambiguous.[131] It can be rendered "spring up," because of the plants.[132] But since עלה is a stock

---

all the words that I have spoken to you against Israel and Judah and all the nations." See also Nehemiah 8, esp. v. 1: "to bring the book (scroll) of the law of Moses, which Yahweh had given/commanded Israel" (לְהָבִיא אֶת־סֵפֶר תּוֹרַת מֹשֶׁה אֲשֶׁר־צִוָּה יהוה אֶת־יִשְׂרָאֵל); cf. v. 8.

125 "You shall be guided in peace" (v. 12) is surely an explicit reference back to Isa 40:11 (Yahweh as shepherd leading the flock). See already Duhm (417) on the passage: "תובלון the solemn saying (will be slowly guided, like the flock) in solemn archaic language." This is probably again simultaneously a stage direction; see below.

126 1QIsaᵃ's version: "you shall go" (תלכו) instead of MT: "you shall be guided" (תּוּבָלוּן) would also be a more distinct command to the players to form a proper procession. The dangers of emotionalization in religious plays must also be seen! There are examples enough, from ancient Egypt down to the Christian passion plays.

127 Cf. Jer 31:9; Pss 45:15-16 (14-15); 60:11 (9); 108:11 (10); Job 21:32; see H. A. Hoffner, "יבל *ybl*," *TDOT* 5:364–67, esp. 365 [*ThWAT* 3:390–93, esp. 391]: "In the OT, the verb *hôbîl* and its pass. *hûbal* are used for the escorting of important persons, often in ceremonial contexts."

128 Cf. Isa 42:10-13; 44:23; 49:13.

129 For "clapping the hands" as an element in the rejoicing over Yahweh as king, see Ps 98:6-8; cf. 2 Kgs 11:12; Ps 47:2-3 (1-2); also J. S. Rogers, "An Allusion to Coronation in Isaiah 2:6," *CBQ* 51 (1989) 232–36.

130 Cf. Matt 21:8: at Jesus' entry into Jerusalem branches from the trees are strewn on the road.

131 Cf. *HALOT* 2:828–30 [*HALAT* 3:783–85]; G. Wehmeier, "עלה *ʿlh* to go up," *TLOT* 2:833–96 [*THAT* 2:272–90]; H. F. Fuhs, "עָלָה *ʿālāh*," *ThWAT* 6:84–105.

132 Cf. Gen 40:10; Isa 5:6; 32:13; 34:13 (on the growing up of thorns and thistles).

expression for the "going up" from Egypt,[133] it will doubtless be used here as a formula for the return home of the exiles from Babylon.[134] עלה means the going up to Jerusalem,[135] and ultimately the pilgrimage to the sanctuary.[136] Even to the present day, עֲלִיָּה is the term used for the pilgrimage to Jerusalem.[137] But right at the beginning, in 40:31, DtIsa already played on the term עלה, as he does here: "To rise up with wings like eagles" (see above on this passage). Here, at the end, the comparison is taken from the plant world, with fablelike "distancing" or "defamiliarization."

The word for thornbush (נַעֲצוּץ)[138] is otherwise found only in Isa 7:19. But various kinds of thorns are used in the OT as a pictorial way of describing particular groups and people.[139] This suggests that what the text is saying is that not only will nature again become a paradise, as 41:17-20 describes; human beings too—even hostile neighbors and opponents—will be transformed: "thornbushes" into "cypresses."[140]

For nettles[141] to be changed into myrtles[142] is certainly a marvel, but here too it could well be that the text specifically has the exodus in view. There could be a play on the words הֲדַס, "myrtle," and חֲדָשָׁה for אִשָּׁה חֲדָשָׁה. The latter is "the bride, the young wife."[143] In the ancient world the bride's wreath was made of myrtle.[144] "Nettles" will "go up" as "young wives." That is a feature of the feast!

The text in v. 13a can be compared with the artisan scene in the prologue, 40:18-20.[145] Its purpose is to amuse also at the end.

■ **13b** The final unit contains yet one more textual problem, and here the decision also affects the understanding of the text. 1QIsa[a] differs from the MT, reversing the order of "for a name" (לְשֵׁם) and "for a sign" (לְאוֹת). Both readings can be defended. I incline to the view that, once again, 1QIsa[a]'s version is the original reading. The link with the accompanying verbs is easier: "and it will be (וְהָיָה) for Yahweh for a sign"[146] and "for an everlasting

---

133 See Gen 13:1; 45:25; Exod 1:10; 12:38; 13:18; Num 32:11; Judg 11:13, 16; 19:30; 1 Sam 15:2, 6; 1 Kgs 9:16; Isa 11:16; Hos 2:17 (15). It is unmistakable even without any topographical indication; cf. among other passages Gen 44:17, 24, 33, 34; 45:9; 50:5-7, 9, 14.

134 See Ezra 2:1, 59; 7:6, 7, 28; 8:1; Neh 7:5, 6, 61; 12:1.

135 1 Kgs 12:27, 28; Zech 14:16-18.

136 Exod 34:24; Jer 31:6; Ps 122:4.

137 Cf. the "going up" of Jesus and his disciples to Jerusalem for the Passover, Matt 20:17-19; Mark 10:32-34; Luke 9:51; 18:31; 19:28; John 12:1, 12, 20.

138 It is explained as "camel thorn" (*alhagi camelorum Fisch*) (Löw, *Die Flora der Juden*, 2:416–17). According to *HALOT* 2:706 [*HALAT* 3:667] the verb נעץ means "to stick into."

139 Num 33:55: The inhabitants of the country who have been left behind will be "barbs (שֵׂךְ) in your eyes and thorns (צֵן) in your side." In Jotham's fable the thornbush (אָטָד) sets itself up to become king over the trees (see Judg 9:14). Comparable—also as fable—are 2 Kgs 14:9; 2 Chr 25:18; in these texts חוֹחַ is the thornbush growing in Lebanon. According to 2 Sam 23:6, in his last words David describes his opponents as "worthless people like thorns" (וּבְלִיַּעַל כְּקוֹץ), which have to be destroyed by fire. In Isa 33:12 it is peoples who will be "burnt in the fire" "like thorns cut down" (קוֹצִים כְּסוּחִים). In Ezek 2:6 Ezekiel's opponents, Israelites of the "rebellious house," are termed "thorns" (סַלּוֹן; see W. Zimmerli, *Ezechiel* 1 (1979) on this passage [*Ezechiel* 1 (1969)]). In Ezek 28:24 the hostile neighbors are "thorns"

(סִלּוֹן) and "briars" (קוֹץ). Complaining about the ruling class ("the prince," "the judge," and "the mighty"), Mic 7:4 says that the best of them is like "a briar" (כְּחֵדֶק).

140 Or junipers (*juniperus phoenicea*); see 41:19 above.

141 See *HALOT* 2:770 [*HALAT* 3:727] on סִרְפָּד. LXX has κόνυξα, "redshank"; Vg *urtica*, "stinging nettle."

142 הֲדַס, *myrtus communis*.

143 *HALOT* 1:294 [*HALAT* 1:282] s.v., with reference to Deut 24:5: "When a man has taken a new wife, he shall not go out (לֹא יֵצֵא) with the army. . . . He shall be free for his family one year, to rejoice in the wife he has taken." On the connection between "myrtle" and "bride" (cf. Esth 2:7 on Esther's name הֲדַסָּה Hadassah, J. Lewy ("The Feast of the 14th Day of Adar," *HUCA* 14 [1939] 129) writes: "הדסה is an Aramaized form of Akkadian *ḥadašatu* 'bride' and equals the aforementioned Babylonian word *kallātu*, the frequent epithet of various *Ištar* goddesses. In other words, הדסה was originally not a proper name meaning 'myrtle'"; see also *HALOT* 1:234 [*HALAT* 1:229] under הֲדַסָּה. It could well be that the text thus once again conceals a subtle scribal play, in the alternation between ס (*s*) and שׁ (*š*). Cf. also the "shibboleth" of Judg 12:5-6.

144 See Pindar 1.3.88.

145 See above on this text.

146 Cf. Isa 19:20: "it will be a sign and a witness for Yahweh" (וְהָיָה לְאוֹת לְעֵד לַיהוה)."

name that shall not be blotted out (לֹא יִכָּרֵת)."[147] There are several examples of the phrase "blot out the name" (כרת שֵׁם) in the OT, but as far as I know "blot out the sign" does not occur anywhere else. The blotting out of a human name is an explicit theme in Isa 48:19 (לֹא יִכָּרֵת וְלֹא־יִשָּׁמֵד שְׁמוֹ מִלְּפָנָי, "his name would not have been wiped out and not destroyed before me").[148] Zech 13:2 shows that "cutting off" or "blotting out" the name was a feature of the dispute with foreign gods. The summing up at the end, and the link with DtIsa's work as a whole, can be grasped more precisely through the text offered by 1QIsa^a.

> For the term אוֹת ʾôt, "sign," F. Stolz's summary is helpful:[149] "The term ʾôt acquires an essentially theological meaning in classical prophecy, in [Deuteronomistic] theology, and in the [Priestly] document."[150] He points to the connection in classical prophecy between the sign as a "symbolic act" and the prophetic word. For Deuteronomistic theology "not only are the 'plagues' described as ʾôt but so is the whole divine history in Egypt, i.e., the basic datum of [Deuteronomistic] theology; ʾôt is, then, the form of Yahweh's revelation that is to be understood in the present."[151] Finally, for the Priestly writing: "Here ʾôt signifies the appearance of a comprehensive divine order encompassing nature and time, taking shape in Israel's history, and finally reaching completion in the cult."[152]

This clearly shows the degree to which DtIsa is involved in the discussion with the traditions of prophecy, Deuteronomistic theology and the Priestly writing.

This is true, not least, of the summing up in 55:6-13.[153] God's word is the subject of 55:11, 55:12 has to do with the exodus tradition, while the unity of the world in nature and history is a fundamental theme in chap. 55 as a whole. If the cult does not have to be a sacrificial cult, then for DtIsa it means the pilgrimage to the Holy City and the remembrance of Yahweh's "signs and wonders."[154]

DtIsa's very last sentence praises Yahweh's everlasting name, which will not be cut off; and this is the quintessence of his testimony to the one God—and the one world.

> Looking back, it is possible to detect the play within the play, and the role that "the name" plays in it.[155] The name that has been blotted out is the name of Moses, the Servant of God. It has been "blotted out" because of the sins of the people.[156]
>
> The name of Jacob (22 times)[157] is mentioned for the first time in 40:27 and finally in 49:26, while the name of Israel (42 times) can be found throughout, from chap. 40 to chap. 55; it is only in chaps. 50, 51 and 53 that it is not mentioned. By contrast, the name of Judah occurs only three times (48:1; "the

---

147 On the blotting out of the name cf. in the *Niphal* Isa 48:19; 56:5; Ruth 4:10; 1 Sam 20:16 cj.; in the *Hiphil* Josh 7:9; Zeph 1:4; Zech 13:2, cf. 1 Sam 24:22. On the phenomenon of the blotting out of the name see E. Brunner-Traut, "Namenstilgung und -verfolgung," *LÄ* 4:338–41. For the *damnatio memoriae* in the Roman sphere, see S. Brassloff, "Damnatio memoriae," PW 4/2 (1958) 2059–62; T. Mayer-Maly, "Damnatio memoriae," *KP* 1:1374.

148 See above on this passage.

149 See F. Stolz, "אוֹת ʾôt sign," *TLOT* 1:67–70 [*THAT* 1:91–95]; also F. J. Helfmeyer, "אוֹת ʾôth," *TDOT* 1:167–88 [*ThWAT* 1:182–205].

150 Stolz, *TLOT* 1:69 [1:93].

151 Ibid., 70 [94]. For the "Deuteronomic theology" Stolz points to the formula for the deliverance from Egypt, Deut 4:34; 6:22; 7:19; 11:2-3; 26:8; 29:2 (3); 34:11; see also B. S. Childs, "Deuteronomic Formulae of the Exodus Traditions," in *Hebräische Wortforschung. FS W. Baumgartner* (1967) 30–39. Also important is the reference to the Passover haggadah in Exod 13:9, where the "sign . . . and remembrance/reminder" (לְאוֹת וּלְזִכָּרוֹן . . .) are

linked with the eating of the maṣṣot; see F. J. Helfmeyer, "אוֹת ʾôth," *TDOT* 1:179–80 [*ThWAT* 1:195–96].

152 Stolz, *TLOT* 1:70 [94–95].

153 On these themes see Beuken, 297–98.

154 See Childs, "Deuteronomic Formulae of the Exodus Traditions," in *Hebräische Wortforschung. FS W. Baumgartner* (1967) 30–39; W. Brueggemann, "Isaiah 55 and Deuteronomic Theology," *ZAW* 80 (1968) 191–203.

155 See K. Baltzer, "Namenglaube: II. Im AT," *RGG*³, 4:1302–4; see also ibid., "Name Gottes," "Namenglaube." Particularly instructive as regards the theological usage is A. S. van der Woude, "שֵׁם šēm name," *TLOT* 3:1348–67, on this text, 1364 [*THAT* 2:935–63, on this text, 958–59].

156 See 48:19: "His name would not have been wiped out . . . [lit.] from before me (לֹא־יִכָּרֵת . . . שְׁמוֹ מִלְּפָנָי)"; see above on that text.

157 Figures for the name references follow E. Talstra, F. Postma and H. A. van Zwet, *Deuterojesaja. Proeve van automatische tekstverwerking ten dienste van de exegese* (2d ed. 1981).

cities of Judah" in 40:9; 44:26). David's name is mentioned only once (55:3). The name of Cyrus is three times suppressed (in 40:13; 41:1-5, 25-27), before it is given in 44:28 and 45:1, only to disappear again.[158] Zion (11 times) and Jerusalem (10 times) are mentioned in the second part of DtIsa's work especially, from 49:14 onward. But from 52:11 onward the city too is nameless.

No name is mentioned as frequently as the name of God—126 times in all. This is the name that is above every name. To that name the writer whom we call Deutero-Isaiah has placed his testimony at the end of his work, a testimony that is to be echoed in the "hallelujah" of the people's song of praise.

---

158 Thus, Cyrus's name is not mentioned in three passages where he is obviously the person referred to: 45:11-17, 46:9-11 and 48:14-15; see K. Baltzer, "Jes 40,13-14—ein Schlüssel zur Einheit Deutero-Jesajas?" *BN* 37 (1987) 7-10.

Bibliography
Index

The bibliography to this commentary is unusually extensive, although completeness can never be the aim. The present list remains my personal selection, developed throughout the years of my work on the commentary. My concern has been to draw attention to the wealth of the different interpretive traditions and to incorporate it. Works cited in the footnotes only by author's name and with page number (without title) refer to commentaries.

1. Commentaries on Deutero-Isaiah

Beuken, W. A. M.
Jesaja deel II A (POT 21/1; Nijkcrk: Callenbach, 1979).

Beuken, W. A. M.
Jesaja deel II B (POT 21/2; Nijkerk: Callenbach, 1983).

Bonnard, P.-E.
Le Second Isaïe: Son disciple et leurs éditeurs Isaïe 40–66 (Ebib; Paris: Gabalda, 1972).

Bonora, A.
Isaia 40–66. Israele: servo di Dio, popolo liberato (LoBAT 19; Brescia, 1988).

Cheyne, T. K.
The Book of Isaiah: Chronologically arranged. An amended version with historical and critical introductions and explanatory notes (London: Macmillan, 1870).

Clifford, R. J.
Fair Spoken and Persuading: An Interpretation of Second Isaiah (New York and Toronto: Paulist, 1984).

Delitzsch, F.
Biblical Commentary on the Prophecies of Isaiah, trans. J. Martin, 2 vols. (Grand Rapids: Eerdmans, 1954) [ET of *Commentar über das Buch Jesaja* (BC 3.1; 4th ed.; Leipzig: Dörffling & Franke, 1889)].

Dillmann, A.
Der Prophet Jesaja (KEH 5; 6th ed.; rev. and ed. R. Kittel; Leipzig: Hirzel, 1898).

Duhm, B.
Das Buch Jesaja, übersetzt und erklärt (1892; 4th ed.; Göttingen: Vandenhoeck & Ruprecht, 1922).

Ekman, J. A.
Likheter mellan Esaias Kapp. 40–66 och Jeremias. Betraktade med hänsyn till fraagan om de foerras ursprung (Uppsala: Essais Edquists Boktryckeri, 1877).

Elliger, K.
Deuterojesaja (BKAT XI/1; Neukirchen-Vluyn: Neukirchener, 1978).

Ezra, Ibn
The Commentary on Isaiah, vol. 1 (trans. and rev. M. Friedländer; 1873; reprint New York: Feldheim, 1965).

Fischer, J.
Das Buch Isaias (HSAT VII; Bonn: Hanstein, 1937).

Fohrer, G.
Das Buch Jesaja, vol. 3 (ZBK 10/3; Zurich and Stuttgart: Zwingli, 1964).

Frey, H.
Das Buch der Weltpolitik Gottes: Kapitel 40–55 des Buches Jesaja (2d ed.; Stuttgart: Calwer, 1938).

Grimm, W., and K. Dittert
Deuterojesaja: Deutung–Wirkung–Gegenwart. Ein Kommentar zu Jesaja 40–55 (Stuttgart: Calwer, 1990).

Grimm, W., and K. Dittert
Das Trostbuch Gottes: Jesaja 40–55 (Stuttgart: Calwer, 1990).

Grotius, H.
Annotationes in Vetus Testamentum, vol. 2 (erweiterte Auflage von G. J. L. Vogel, ed. J. C. Doederlein; Halle, 1776).

Holmgren, F.
With Wings as Eagles: Isaiah 40–55, an Interpretation (Chappaqua, N.Y.: Biblical Scholars Press, 1973).

Jones, D. R.
Isaiah 56–66 and Joel: Introduction and Commentary (TBC 11; London: SCM, 1964).

Kissane, E. J.
The Book of Isaiah: Translated from a Critically Revised Hebrew Text with Commentary (2 vols.; Dublin: Browne and Nolan, vol. 1 [cc. 1–39], 1941, rev. ed. 1960; vol. 2 [cc. 40–66], 1943).

Knight, G. A. F.
Deutero-Isaiah: A Theological Commentary on Isaiah 40–55 (New York and Nashville: Abingdon, 1965).

Knight, G. A. F.
Servant Theology: A Commentary on the Book of Isaiah 40–55 (International Theological Commentary; Edinburgh: Hansel; Grand Rapids: Eerdmans, 1984).

König, E.
Das Buch Jesaja: Eingeleitet, übersetzt und erklärt (Gütersloh: Bertelsmann, 1926).

Kraus, H.-J.
Das Evangelium des unbekannten Propheten: Jesaja 40–66 (Neukirchen-Vluyn: Neukirchener, 1990).

Lamparter, H.
Jesaja II: Kapitel 40–66 des Buches Jesaja (Stuttgart: Quell, 1958).

Marti, K.
Das Buch Jesaja (KHC X; Tübingen: Mohr, 1900).

McKenzie, J. L.
Second Isaiah: Introduction, Translation, and Notes (AB 20; Garden City, N.Y.: Doubleday, 1968).

Muilenburg, J.
"The Book of Isaiah: Chapters 40–66, Introduction and Exegesis" (*IB* 5; New York and Nashville: Abingdon, 1956).

Naegelsbach, C. W. E.
  Isaiah. Commentary on the Holy Scriptures, ed.
  J. P. Lange; trans. P. Schaff, vol. 11 (Grand Rapids:
  Zondervan, n.d.) [ET of *Der Prophet Jesaja* (Biele-
  feld: von Velhagen; Leipzig: Klasing, 1877)].
North, C. R.
  *The Second Isaiah: Introduction, Translation and Com-
  mentary to Chapters XL–LV* (Oxford: Clarendon,
  1964).
North, C. R.
  Isaiah 40–55: Introduction and Commentary (TBC
  10; London: SCM, 1952).
Porúbčan, Š.
  Il patto nuovo in Is. 40–66 (AnBib 8; Rome: Pontifi-
  cal Biblical Institute, 1958).
Schoors, A.
  Jesaja II: uit de grondtekst vertaald en uitgelegd
  (BOT 9B; Roermond: Romen & Zonen-Uitgevers,
  1973).
Simon, U. E.
  *A Theology of Salvation: A Commentary on Isaiah
  40–55* (London: SPCK, 1953).
Smart, J. D.
  *History and Theology in Second Isaiah: A Com-
  mentary on Isaiah 35, 40–66* (London: Epworth,
  1967).
Thexton, S.
  Isaiah 40–66 (Epworth Preacher's Commentaries;
  London: Epworth, 1959).
Torrey, C. C.
  The Second Isaiah: A New Interpretation (New York:
  Scribner, 1928).
Volz, P.
  *Jesaia: Zweite Hälfte Kapitel 40–66 übersetzt und
  erklärt* (Leipzig: Deichert, 1932; reprint Hildesheim
  and New York: Olms, 1974).
Watts, J. D. W.
  Isaiah 34–66 (WBC 25; Waco: Word, 1987).
Westermann, C.
  Isaiah 40–66, trans. D. M. G. Stalker (OTL;
  Philadelphia: Westminster, 1969) [Eng. trans. of
  Das Buch Jesaja Kap. 40–66: Übersetzt und erklärt
  (ATD 19; Göttingen: Vandenhoeck & Ruprecht,
  1966)].
Wildberger, H.
  Isaiah: A Commentary, trans. T. H. Trapp, 2 vols.
  (Minneapolis: Fortress, 1991–98) [Eng. trans. of
  Jesaja (BKAT X/1-2; Neukirchen-Vluyn: Neu-
  kirchener, 1972–1982)].
Young, E. J.
  *The Book of Isaiah: The English Text, with Introduc-
  tion, Exposition and Notes,* vol. 3: *Chapters 40–66*
  (Grand Rapids: Eerdmans, 1972).

2. Select Monographs and Articles

Ackroyd, P. R.
  *Exile and Restoration: A Study of Hebrew Thought of
  the Sixth Century B.C.* (OTL; Philadelphia: West-
  minster, 1968).
Ackroyd, P. R.
  Israel under Babylon and Persia (Oxford: Oxford
  Univ. Press, 1970).
Ackroyd, P. R.
  "The Temple Vessels—A Continuity Theme," in
  Studies in the Religion of Ancient Israel (VTSup 23;
  Leiden: Brill, 1972) 166–81.
Ackroyd, P. R.
  "Recent Foreign Old Testament Literature," *ExpT*
  93 (1982) 136–39.
Adinolfi, M.
  "De Mariologicis Lyrani Postillis in Prophetas'
  Medii Aevi Exegeseos Lumine Perpensis," *SBFLA*
  9 (1958/59) 199–250.
Adna, J.
  "Herrens tjener i Jesaja 53 skildret som triumfer-
  ende Messias, Profet-targumens giengivelse og
  tolkning av Jes 52,13–53,12," *TTK* 63 (1992)
  81–94.
Adrados, F. R.
  *Festival, Comedy and Tragedy. The Greek Origins of
  Theatre* (trans. C. Holme; Leiden: Brill, 1975).
Aeschylus
  The Persians, in *Aeschylus I* (LCL; trans. and rev.
  H. W. Smyth; Cambridge, Mass.: Harvard Univ.
  Press; London: Heinemann, 1922; reprint 1973)
  108–207.
Aeschylus
  Prometheus Bound, in *Aeschylus I* (LCL; trans. and
  rev. H. W. Smyth; Cambridge, Mass.: Harvard
  Univ. Press; London: Heinemann, 1922; reprint
  1973) 211–315.
Aeschylus
  Tragödien und Fragmente (trans. and ed. O. Werner;
  4th ed.; Munich: Artemis, 1988).
Ahuviah, A.
  "*ʾêkâ yāšbâ bādād hāʿîr rabbātî ʿām* (Lam 1:1)," *Beth
  Mikra* 24 (1979) 423–25.
Aichele, K.
  "Das Epeisodion," in W. Jens, ed., *Die Bauformen
  der griechischen Tragödie* (Munich: Fink, 1971) 48–
  83.
Aistleitner, J.
  Wörterbuch der ugaritischen Sprache (3d ed.; Berlin:
  Akademie, 1967).
Albertz, R.
  *A History of Israelite Religion in the Old Testament
  Period,* trans. J. Bowden, 2 vols. (OTL; Louisville:
  Westminster/John Knox, 1994) [Eng. trans. of *Reli-
  gionsgeschichte Israels* (GAT 8; Göttingen: Vanden-
  hoeck & Ruprecht, 1992)].
Albrecht, K.
  "Das Geschlecht der hebräischen Hauptwörter,"
  ZAW 16 (1896) 41–121.
Albright, W. F.
  "The Oracles of Balaam," *JBL* 63 (1944) 207–33.
Albright, W. F.
  "The High Place in Ancient Palestine," in *Volume
  du Congrès: Strasbourg 1956* (VTSup 4; Leiden:
  Brill, 1957) 242–58.

Albright, W. F.
"The Role of the Canaanites in the History of Civilization," in G. E. Wright, ed., *The Bible and the Ancient Near East: Essays in Honor of W. F. Albright* (Garden City, N.Y.: Doubleday, 1961) 328–62.

Alfonso, L. J.
"Netherworld," *EncJud* 12 (1971) 996–97.

Allegro, J. M.
"A Possible Mesopotamian Background to the Joseph Blessing of Genesis 49," *ZAW* 64 (1952) 249–51.

Allen, L. C.
"Isaiah 53:2 Again," *VT* 21 (1971) 490.

Alt, A.
Essays on Old Testament History and Religion, trans. R. A. Wilson (Garden City, N.Y.: Doubleday, 1967) [selections from the essays published in *Kleine Schriften zur Geschichte des Volkes Israel* (3 vols.; Munich: Beck, 1953–59)].

Alt, A.
Kleine Schriften zur Geschichte des Volkes Israel (3 vols.; Munich: Beck, 1953–59; 4th ed. 1978).

Altenmüller, H.
"Denkmal memphistischer Theologie," *LÄ* I (1975) 1065–69.

Altenmüller, H.
"Dramatischer Ramesseumspapyrus," *LÄ* I (1975) 1132–40.

Althann, R.
"*Yōm*, 'Time' and Some Texts in Isaiah," *JNSL* 11 (1983) 3–8.

Althann, R.
"Isaiah 42:10 and KRT 77–78 (KTU 1.14: II: 24–25)," *JNSL* 13 (1987) 3–9.

Amsler, S.
"Les prophètes et la communication par les actes," in R. Albertz, et al., eds., *Werden und Wirken des Alten Testaments: FS C. Westermann* (Göttingen: Vandenhoeck & Ruprecht; Neukirchen-Vluyn: Neukirchener, 1980) 194–201.

Andersen, T. D.
"Renaming and Wedding Imagery in Isaiah 62," *Bib* 67 (1986) 78–80.

Anderson, B. W.
"Exodus Typology in Second Isaiah," in B. W. Anderson and W. Harrelson, eds., *Israel's Prophetic Heritage: Essays in Honor of James Muilenburg* (New York: Harper, 1962) 177–95.

André, G.
"Deuterojesaja och Jobsboken. En jämförande studie (Deutero-Isaiah and Job: A Comparative Study)," *SEÅ* 54 (1989) 33–42.

Andresen, C., ed.
Lexikon der Alten Welt (Tübingen and Zurich: Artemis, 1965).

Ap-Thomas, D. R.
"Two Notes on Isaiah," in *Essays in Honour of G. W. Thatcher* (Sydney, 1967) 45-61.

Archer, G. L.
In the Shadow of the Cross: Insights into the Meaning of Calvary, Drawn from the Hebrew Text of Isaiah 53 (Grand Rapids: Zondervan, 1957).

Aristotle
Athenaion Politeia–Staat der Athener, übersetzt und erläutert von Mortimer Chambers (Berlin: Akademie, 1990).

Aristotle
The Athenian Constitution, in *Aristotle* XX (LCL; trans. and rev. H. Rackham; Cambridge, Mass.: Harvard Univ. Press; London: Heinemann, 1935; reprint 1971) 1–188.

Arnecke, F.-J.
"Krisen und Krisenbewältigung bei Deuterojesaja und 4 Esra: Versuch einer Analyse von Texten mit Hilfe dissonanztheoretischer Methoden" (Baccalaureatsschrift, Ev.-theol. Fakultät der Universität Munich, 1979).

Assmann, J.
Ägyptische Hymnen und Gebete (Zurich and Munich: Artemis, 1975).

Assmann, J.
"Hymnus," *LÄ* 3 (1980) 103–10.

Assmann, J.
"Das ägyptische Prozessionsfest," in J. Assmann and T. Sundermeier, eds., *Das Fest und das Heilige: Religiöse Kontrapunkte zur Alltagswelt* (Gütersloh: Mohn, 1991) 105–22.

Assmann, J.
Das kulturelle Gedächtnis: Schrift, Erinnerung und politische Identität in frühen Hochkulturen (Munich: Beck, 1992).

Aston, F. A.
The Challenge of the Ages (Cambridge, Mass.: Harvard Univ. Press, 1963).

Atkinson, K. M. T.
"The Legitimacy of Cambysos and Darius as Kings of Egypt," *JAOS* 76 (1956) 167–77.

Auerbach, E.
Mimesis: The Representation of Reality in Western Literature, trans. W. R. Trask (Princeton: Princeton Univ. Press, 1953; reprint New York: Doubleday Anchor Books, 1957) [Eng. trans. of *Mimesis: Dargestellte Wirklichkeit in der Abendländischen Literatur* (1946; 3d ed.; Berlin: Franke, 1964)].

Auerbach, E.
"Figura," in *Gesammelte Aufsätze zur Romanischen Philologie* (Bern and Munich, 1967) 55–92.

Auvray, P.
"Cyrus, instrument du Dieu unique," *BVC* 50 (1963) 17–23.

Avishur, Y.
"*Mî baʿal mišpāṭî yiggaš ʾēlāy* (Isa 50:8)—A Stylistical Figure or a Calque from Akkadian," *Leš* 52 (1987–88) 18–25.

Ayton, R. A.
"The Servant of the Lord in the Targum," *JTS* 23 (1922) 172–80.

Bacher, W.

"שֵׁרוּן‎," *ZAW* 5 (1885) 161–63.

Balsdon, J. D.

"Die 'Göttlichkeit' Alexanders," in A. Wlosok, ed., *Römischer Kaiserkult* (Darmstadt: Wissenschaftliche Buchgesellschaft, 1978) 254-90.

Baltzer, D.

Ezechiel und Deuterojesaja: Berührungen in der Heilserwartung der beiden großen Exilspropheten (BZAW 121; Berlin and New York: de Gruyter, 1971).

Baltzer, K.

"Namenglaube II," *RGG* 4 (3d ed.; 1960) 1302–4.

Baltzer, K.

"Das Ende des Staates Juda und die Messias-Frage," in R. Rendtorff and K. Koch, eds., *Studien zur Theologie der alttestamentlichen Überlieferung. FS G. von Rad* (Neukirchen-Vluyn: Neukirchener, 1961) 33–43.

Baltzer, K.

"The Meaning of the Temple in the Lukan Writings," *HTR* 58 (1965) 263–77.

Baltzer, K.

"Zur formgeschichtlichen Bestimmung der Texte vom Gottesknecht im Deuterojesaja-Buch," in H. W. Wolff, ed., *Probleme biblischer Theologie. FS G. von Rad* (Munich: Kaiser, 1971) 27–43.

Baltzer, K.

The Covenant Formulary, trans. D. E. Green (Philadelphia: Fortress, 1971) [Eng. trans. of *Das Bundesformular* (WMANT 4; 2d ed.; Neukirchen-Vluyn: Neukirchener, 1964)].

Baltzer, K.

Die Biographie der Propheten (Neukirchen-Vluyn: Neukirchener, 1975).

Baltzer, K.

"Jes 40,13-14—sein Schlüssel zur Einheit Deutero-Jesajas?" in M. Görg, ed., *FS V. Hamp, BN* n.s. 37 (1987) 7–10.

Baltzer, K.

"Liberation from Debt Slavery After the Exile in Second Isaiah and Nehemiah," in P. D. Miller Jr., P. D. Hanson and S. D. McBride, eds., *Ancient Israelite Religion: Essays in Honor of Frank Moore Cross* (Philadelphia: Fortress, 1987) 477–84.

Baltzer, K.

"Schriftauslegung bei Deuterojesaja?—Jes 43,22-28 als Beispiel," in M. Görg, ed., *Die Väter Israels: Beiträge zur Theologie der Patriarchenüberlieferung im Alten Testament. FS J. Scharbert* (Stuttgart: Katholisches Bibelwerk, 1989) 11–16.

Baltzer, K.

"Moses Servant of God and the Servants: Text and Tradition in the Prayer of Nehemiah (Neh 1:5-11)," in B. A. Pearson with A. T. Kraabel, G. W. E. Nickelsburg, N. R. Peterson, eds., *The Future of Early Christianity. FS Helmut Koester* (Minneapolis: Fortress, 1991) 121–30.

Baltzer, K.

"Stadt-Tyche oder Zion-Jerusalem? Die Ausein-

andersetzung mit den Göttern der Zeit bei Deuterojesaja," in J. Hausmann and H.-J. Zobel, eds., *Alttestamentlicher Glaube und Biblische Theologie. FS H. D. Preuss* (Stuttgart: Kohlhammer, 1992) 114–19.

Baltzer, K.

"Jes 52:13: Die 'Erhöhung' des 'Gottesknechtes'," in L. Bormann, K. Del Tredici, and A. Standhartinger, eds., *Religious Propaganda and Missionary Competition in the New Testament World. FS Dieter Georgi* (Leiden: Brill, 1994) 45–56.

Baltzer, K.

"The Polemic against the Gods and its Relevance for Second Isaiah's Conception of the New Jerusalem," in T. C. Eskenazi and K. H. Richards, eds., *Second Temple Studies,* vol. 2: *Temple and Community in the Persian Period* (JSOTSup 175; Sheffield: JSOT Press, 1994) 52–59.

Baltzer, K., D. Georgi, and F. Merkel (Exegetisch-homiletische Arbeitsgemeinschaft)

"Jesaja 52,13–53,12," *GPM* 16 (Göttingen: Vandenhoeck & Ruprecht, 1961/62) 154–59.

Baltzer, K., D. Georgi, and F. Merkel (Exegetisch-homiletische Arbeitsgemeinschaft)

"Ezechiel 18,1-4, 21-24, 30-32," *GPM* 18 (Göttingen: Vandenhoeck & Ruprecht, 1963/64) 233–38.

Baltzer, K., D. Georgi, and F. Merkel (Exegetisch-homiletische Arbeitsgemeinschaft)

"Jesaja 5,1-7," *GPM* 18 (Göttingen: Vandenhoeck & Ruprecht, 1963/64) 391–95.

Baltzer, K., and Th. Krüger

"Die Erfahrungen Hiobs. 'Konnektive' und 'distributive' Gerechtigkeit nach dem Hiob-Buch," in H. T. C. Sun and K. L. Eades, eds., *Problems in Biblical Theology. FS R. Knierim* (Grand Rapids: Eerdmans, 1997) 27–37.

Bardtke, H.

"Die Parascheneinteilung der Jesajarolle I von Qumran," in H. Kusch, ed., *FS F. Dornseiff* (Leipzig: VEB Bibliographisches Institut, 1953) 33–75.

Barick, W. B.

"The Funerary Character of 'High-Places' in Ancient Palestine: A Reassessment," *VT* 25 (1975) 565–95.

Barr, J.

Comparative Philology and the Text of the Old Testament (Oxford: Clarendon, 1968).

Barr, J.

"Some Semantic Notes on the Covenant," in H. Donner, R. Hanhart, and R. Smend, eds., *Beiträge zur alttestamentlichen Theologie. FS W. Zimmerli* (Göttingen: Vandenhoeck & Ruprecht, 1977) 23–38.

Barré, M. L.

"The Meaning of *l'šybnw* in Amos 1:3–2:6," *JBL* 105 (1986) 611–31.

Barstad, H. M.

"Tjenersangene hos Deuterojesaja: Et Eksegetisk villspor," *NTT* 83 (1982) 235–44.

Barstad, H. M.
"Lebte Deuterojesaja in Judäa?" *NTT* 83 (1982) 77–87.

Barstad, H. M.
"On the So-called Babylonian Literary Influence in Second Isaiah," *JSOT* 2 (1987) 90–110.

Barta, W.
"Der Epilog der Götterlehre von Memphis," *MDAIK* 28 (1972) 79–84.

Bartel, D.
Handbuch der musikalischen Figurenlehre (Laaber: Laaber, 1985).

Bartelmus, R.
Einführung in das biblische Hebräisch: Mit einem Anhang Biblisches Aramäisch (Zurich: Theologischer Verlag, 1994).

Bartelmus, R.
Heroentum in Israel und seiner Umwelt: Eine traditionsgeschichtliche Untersuchung zu Gen 6,1-4 und verwandten Texten im Alten Testament und der altorientalischen Literatur (AThANT 65; Zurich: Theologischer Verlag, 1979).

Bartelmus, R.
HYH: Bedeutung und Funktion eines hebräischen 'Allerweltswortes'–zugleich ein Beitrag zur Frage des hebräischen Tempussystems (ATSAT 17; Munich: St. Ottilien, 1982).

Bartelmus, R.
"Textkritik, Literarkritik und Syntax: Anmerkungen zur neueren Diskussion um Ez 37:11," *BN* n.s. 25 (1984) 55–64.

Bartelmus, R.
"Ez 37,1-14, die Verbform *w^eqatal* und die Anfänge der Auferstehungshoffnung," *ZAW* 97 (1985) 366–89.

Barth, C.
"Die Antwort Israels," in H. W. Wolff, ed., *Probleme biblischer Theologie. FS G. von Rad* (Munich: Kaiser, 1971) 44–56.

Barthélemy, D.
"Le grand rouleau d'Isaïe trouvé près de la Mer Morte," *RB* 57 (1950) 530–49.

Battenfield, J. R.
"Isaiah LIII 10: Taking an 'If' out of the Sacrifice of the Servant," *VT* 32 (1982) 485.

Batto, B. F.
"The Covenant of Peace: A Neglected Near Eastern Motif," *CBQ* 49 (1987) 187–211.

Bauer, W.
A Greek-English Lexicon of the New Testament and Other Early Christian Literature, trans. W. F. Arndt, F. W. Gingrich, and F. W. Danker (2d ed.; Chicago: University of Chicago Press, 1979) [Eng. trans. of *Griechisch-Deutsches Wörterbuch zu den Schriften des Neuen Testaments und der übrigen urchristlichen Literatur* (5th ed.; Berlin: Töpelmann, 1959)].

Baumann, E.
"שוב שבות Eine exegetische Untersuchung," *ZAW* 47 (1929) 17–44.

Beaucamp, E.
"'Chant nouveau du retour' (Is 42:10-17). Un monstre de l'exégèse moderne," *RevScRel* 56 (1982) 145–58.

Beaucamp, E.
"Le IIe Isaïe (Is 40:1—49:13)—Problème de l'unité du livre," *RevScRel* 62 (1988) 218–26.

Beauchamp, P.
Le Deutéro-Isaïe dans le cadre de l'Alliance (Lyon: Faculté de Théologie de Fourvière, 1970).

Becker, D.
"Fragments from Karaite Philological Commentaries to the Books of Leviticus and Isaiah," *Leš* 51 (1986/87) 131–68.

Beckerath, J. von
Abriß der Geschichte des Alten Ägypten (Darmstadt: Wissenschaftliche Buchgesellschaft, 1971).

Beegle, D. M.
"Ligatures with Waw and Yodh in the Dead Sea Isaiah Scroll," *BASOR* 129 (1953) 11–14.

Begg, C.
"Zedekiah and the Servant," *EThL* 62 (1986) 393–98.

Begrich, J.
"Das priesterliche Heilsorakel," *ZAW* n.s. 11 (1934) 81–92; reprint in J. Begrich, *Gesammelte Studien zum Alten Testament* (ThBü 21; Munich: Kaiser, 1964) 217–31.

Begrich, J.
Studien zu Deuterojesaja (BWANT 4/25; Stuttgart: Kohlhammer, 1938 ; reprint ThBü 20; Munich: Kaiser, 1963).

Bengtson, H.
Griechische Geschichte: Von den Anfängen bis in die römische Kaiserzeit (IIAW 3/4; 4th ed.; Munich: Beck, 1969).

Bentzen, A.
"On the Ideas of 'the Old' and 'the New' in Deutero-Isaiah," *StTh* 1 (1948) 183–87.

Ben-Zvi, I.
Sefer Hashomronim (The Book of the Samaritans) (rev. ed.; Jerusalem, 1970, 1977).

Berger, K.
Das Buch der Jubiläen (JSHRZ 2/3; Gütersloh: Mohn, 1981).

Berges, U.
Das Buch Jesaja: Composition und Endgestalt (Biblische Studien; Freiburg: Herder, 1998).

Berlin, A.
"Isaiah 40:4: Etymological and Poetic Considerations," *HAR* 3 (1979) 1–6.

Berlin, A.
"Motif and Creativity in Biblical Poetry," *Prooftexts* 3 (1983) 231–41.

Berlin, A.
"Lexical Cohesion and Biblical Interpretation," *Hebrew Studies* 30 (1989) 29–40.

Bernhardt, K.-H.
  Gott und Bild (Berlin: Evangelische Verlagsanstalt, 1956).
Bertram, G.
  "ὕψος," *TDNT* 8 (1972) 602–20 [Eng. trans. of *ThWNT* 8 (1969) 600–19].
Bertram, G.
  Zur begrifflichen Prägung des Schöpferglaubens im Griechischen Alten Testament (FB 1; Würzburg: Echter, 1972) 21–30.
Bertram, G.
  "ὠδίν, ὠδίνω," *TDNT* 9 (1974) 667–74 [Eng. trans. of *ThWNT* 9 (1973) 668–75].
Bertram, R. W.
  "A Baptismal Crossing, Isaiah 42:1-9," *CurTM* 9 (1982) 344–53.
Beuken, W. A. M.
  "Mišpāt. The First Servant Song and Its Context," *VT* 22 (1972) 1–30.
Beuken, W. A. M.
  "The Confession of God's Exclusivity by all Mankind," *Bijdr* 35 (1974) 336–56.
Beuken, W. A. M.
  "Isa 55,3-5: The Reinterpretation of David," *Bijdr* 35 (1974) 49–64.
Beuken, W. A. M.
  "Isaiah LIV: The Multiple Identity of the Person Addressed," *OTS* 19 (1974) 29–70.
Bews, J. W.
  The World's Grasses: Their Differentation, Distribution, Economics and Ecology (London: Longmans, Green, 1929).
Beyerlin, W., ed.
  Near Eastern Religious Texts Relating to the Old Testament, trans. J. Bowden (OTL; Philadelphia: Westminster, 1978) [Eng. trans. of *Religionsgeschichtliches Textbuch zum Alten Testament* (Göttingen: Vandenhoeck & Ruprecht, 1975)].
Bickerman, E. J.
  "The Edict of Cyrus in Ezra 1," *JBL* 65 (1946) 249–75.
Bickerman, E. J.
  "A propos d'un passage de Charès de Mytilène," *ParPass* 91 (1963) 241–55.
Bickerman, E. J.
  From Ezra to the Last of the Maccabees. Foundations of Post-biblical Judaism (4th ed.; New York: Schocken, 1970).
Birch, B. C.
  "Tradition, Canon and Biblical Theology," *HBT* 2 (1980) 113–25.
Bizeul Y., and L. Ganzevoort
  "Créateur et aménagement de l'espace dans l'hymne du louange d'Ésaïe 40,12-31," *CBFV* 25 (1986) 42–51.
Bjørndalen, A. J.
  "Zu den Zeitstufen der Zitatformel . . . כה אמר im Botenverkehr," *ZAW* 86 (1974) 393–403.
Blank, S. H.
  "Studies in Deutero-Isaiah," *HUCA* 15 (1940) 1–46.

Blau, J.
  "Nāwā ṯhillā (Ps cxlvii 1): Lobpreisen," *VT* 4 (1954) 410–11.
Bleeker, J. C.
  Egyptian Festivals: Enactments of Religious Renewals (SHR 13; Leiden: Brill, 1987).
Blenkinsopp, J.
  "Absicht und Sinn der Exodustradition in Deuterojesaja (Is 40–55)," *Concilium* 2 (1966) 762–67.
Blenkinsopp, J.
  Ezra-Nehemiah: A Commentary (OTL; Philadelphia: Westminster, 1988).
Blenkinsopp, J.
  "Second Isaiah—Prophet of Universalism," *JSOT* 41 (1988) 83–103.
Blenkinsopp, J.
  "A Jewish Sect of the Persian Period," *CBQ* 52 (1990) 5–20.
Blum, H.
  "Daniel 9 und die chronistische Geschichtsdarstellung," *ThGl* 72 (1982) 450–60.
Blythin, I.
  "A Note on Isaiah 49:16-17," *VT* 16 (1966) 229–30.
Boadt, L.
  "Isaiah 41:8-13: Notes on Poetic Structure and Style," *CBQ* 35 (1973) 20–34.
Boadt, L.
  "Intentional Alliteration in Second Isaiah," *CBQ* 45 (1983) 353–61.
Boccaccio, P. P.
  "I termini contrari come espressioni della totalità in Ebraico," *Bib* 33 (1952) 173–90.
Bodenheimer, F. S.
  Animal and Man in Bible Lands (Collection de Travaux de l'Academie Internationale d'Histoire des Sciences 10; Leiden: Brill, 1960).
Boecker, H. J.
  Redeformen des Rechtslebens im Alten Testament (2d ed.; Neukirchen-Vluyn: Neukirchener, 1970).
Boecker, H. J.
  Law and the Administration of Justice in the Old Testament and Ancient East, trans. J. Moiser (Minneapolis: Augsburg, 1980).
Boehl, F. M. T.
  "Prophetentum und stellvertretendes Leiden in Assyrien und Israel," in *Opera Minora: Studies en bijdragen op assyriologisch en oudtestamentisch terrein* (Groningen-Djakarta: Wolters, 1953) 63–80.
Boer, P. A. H. de
  Second-Isaiah's Message (OTS 11; Leiden: Brill, 1956).
Boesinger, R.
  Horizonte des Heils: Sieben Texte des Zweiten Jesajas gepredigt von Rudolf Boesinger (Lahr: Moritz Schauenburg, 1964).
Bogaert, M.
  "Les suffixes verbaux non accusatifs dans le sémitique nord-occidental et particulièrement en hébreu," *Bib* 45 (1964) 220–47.

Bohren, R.
Prophet in dürftiger Zeit–Auslegung von Jesaja 56–66 (Bibliothek der Lesepredigten 2; Neukirchen-Vluyn: Neukirchener, 1969).

Bömer, F.
"Pompa (πομπή)," PW 21/2 (1952) 1878–1994.

Bonnet, H.
Die Waffen der Völker des Alten Orients (Leipzig: Hinrichs, 1926).

Bonnet, H.
Reallexikon der ägyptischen Religionsgeschichte (Berlin: de Gruyter, 1952).

Booij, Th.
"Negation in Isaiah 43,22-24," *ZAW* 94 (1982) 390–400.

Bordreuil, P.
"Les 'grâces de David' et l Maccabées II 57," *VT* 31 (1981) 73–75.

Borger, R.
"Gott Marduk und Gott-König Šulgi als Propheten: Zwei prophetische Texte," *BiOr* 28 (1971) 3–24.

Boskoop, J.
De opstandige der regtveerdige, 's heeren gunstgenooten, . . . voorgehouden in een lykrede over Jesaja XXVI, 19. Ter Nagedagtenis van den Wet Eerwarden en Godtzalingen Heere Johann Temmink . . . Uitgesproken in de Nieuwe Kerk, op Zondag Avond den 6. November 1768 (3d ed.; Amsterdam: Nicolaas Byl, 1768).

Bottéro, J., and A. Finet
Répertoire analytique des tomes I à V des Archives Royales de Mari XV (Paris: Imprimerie Nationale, 1954).

Botterweck, J. G.
"Hirte und Herde im Alten Testament und im alten Orient," in W. Corsten, A. Frotz, and P. Linden, eds., *Die Kirche und ihre Ämter und Stände. FS J. Kardinal Frings* (Cologne: Bachem, 1960) 339–52.

Botterweck, J. G.
"Die Frohbotschaft vom Kommen Jahwes (Jes. 40:1-11)," *BibLeb* 15 (1974) 227–34.

Botterweck, J. G., et al., eds.
Theological Dictionary of the Old Testament, trans. J. T. Willis et al. (8 vols.; Grand Rapids: Eerdmans, 1974–1997) [Eng. trans. of vols. 1–4 of *Theologisches Wörterbuch zum Alten Testament* (8 vols.; Stuttgart: Kohlhammer, 1973–95)].

Boyce, R. N.
"Isaiah 55:6-13," *Int* 44 (1990) 56–60.

Brandenburger, E.
Adam und Christus (WMANT 7; Neukirchen-Vluyn: Neukirchener, 1962).

Brandenburger, E.
Fleisch und Geist: Paulus und die dualistische Weisheit (WMANT 29; Neukirchen-Vluyn: Neukirchener, 1968).

Brandenburger, E.
"Himmelfahrt Moses," *JSHRZ* 5/2 (1976) 57–84.

Brandenburger, E.
Das Recht des Weltenrichters. Untersuchung zu Matthäus 25,31-46 (SBS 99; Stuttgart: Katholisches Bibelwerk, 1980).

Brandenburger, E.
"Gericht Gottes III. Neues Testament," *TRE* 12 (1984) 469–83.

Brandenburger, E.
"Pistis und Soteria. Zum Verstehenshorizont von 'Glaube' im Urchristentum," *ZThK* 85 (1988) 165–98.

Brandenburger, E.
"Gerichtskonzeptionen im Urchristentum und ihre Voraussetzungen," *SNTU* 16 (1991) 5–54.

Brandenburger, E., K. Baltzer, and F. Merkel
"Jesaja 2,1-5 (Epiphanias)," *GPM* 58 (1969) 70–75.

Brandenstein, W., and M. Mayrhofer
Handbuch des Altpersischen (Wiesbaden: Harrassowitz, 1964).

Brandt, H.
"Das leidende Volk in Brasilien als Träger des missionarischen Auftrags—am Beispiel einer kontextuellen Auslegung der Gottesknechtslieder," *JbMiss* 19 (1987) 87–102.

Brassloff, S.
"Damnatio memoriae," PW 4/2 (1958) 2059–62.

Bräuninger, F.
"Persephone," PW 19/1 (1937) 944–72.

Brayley, I. F. M.
"Yahweh is the Guardian of His Plantation: A Note on Is 60:21," *Bib* 41 (1960) 275–86.

Breasted, J. H.
"The Philosophy of a Memphite Priest," *ZÄS* 39 (1901) 39–54.

Bresciani, E.
"The Persian Occupation of Egypt," in I. Gershevitch, ed., *The Cambridge History of Iran*, vol. 2 (Cambridge: Cambridge Univ. Press, 1985) 502–28.

Bresciani, E.
"Oracles d'Égypte et prophéties bibliques," *MoBi* 45 (1986) 44–45.

Breslauer, S. D.
"Power, Compassion and the Servant of the Lord in Second Isaiah," *Encounter* 48 (1987) 163–78.

Breton, S.
"Image, schème, concept (Esquisse d'une théorie thomiste du schématisme)," *ScEc* 15 (1963) 7–20.

Breukelman, F.
"Uitleg en Verklaring van Jes. 55:6-11," *Om het Levende Woord Serie* 1 (1966) 17–27.

Bright, J.
"Faith and Destiny: The Meaning of History in Deutero-Isaiah," *Int* 5 (1951) 3–26.

Broek, R. van den
The Myth of the Phoenix According to Classical and Early Christian Traditions (Leiden: Brill, 1972).

Brongers, H. A.
De Scheppingstradities bij de Profeten (Amsterdam: Paris, 1945).

Brongers, H. A.
"Der Zornesbecher," *OTS* 15 (1969) 177–92.

497

Bronznick, N.M.
"'Metathetic Parallelism'—An Unrecognized Subtype of Synonymous Parallelism," *HAR* 3 (1979) 25–39.

Brossier, F.
"Isaïe et le messianisme: 2. Un roi idéal pour le futur," *MoBi* 49 (1987) 42.

Brownlee, W. H.
"The Servant of the Lord in the Qumran Scrolls I," *BASOR* 132 (1953) 8–15.

Brownlee, W. H.
"The Servant of the Lord in the Qumran Scrolls II," *BASOR* 135 (1954) 33–38.

Brownlee, W. H., and J. Reider
"On *MŠḤTY* in the Qumran Scrolls," *BASOR* 134 (1954) 27–28.

Brueckner, M.
"Die Komposition des Buches Jesaja cc. 28–33" (Th.D. diss., Leipzig, 1897).

Brueggemann, W.
"Isaiah 55 and Deuteronomic Theology," *ZAW* 80 (1968) 191–203.

Brueggemann, W.
"From Dust to Kingship," *ZAW* 84 (1972) 1–18.

Brueggemann, W.
"Psalms and Life of Faith: A Suggested Typology of Function," *JSOT* 17 (1980) 3–32.

Brueggemann, W.
"Unity and Dynamic in the Isaiah Tradition," *JSOT* 29 (1984) 89–107.

Brueggemann, W.
"A Poem of Summons (Is. 55:1-3) / A Narrative of Resistance (Dan 1:1-21)," in R. Albertz, F. W. Golka, and J. Kegler, eds., *Schöpfung und Befreiung. FS C. Westermann* (Stuttgart: Calwer, 1989) 126–36.

Brunner, H.
"Lehre des Cheti," *LÄ* 3 (1980) 977–78.

Brunner, H.
Die Lehre des Cheti, Sohn des Duauf (ÄF 13; Glückstadt and Hamburg: Augustin, 1944).

Brunner-Traut, E.
"Mythos im Alltag. Zum Loskalender im Alten Ägypten," in M. Eliade and E. Jünger, eds., *Antaios* 12 (Stuttgart: Klett, 1971) 332–47.

Brunner-Traut, E.
"Namenstilgung und -verfolgung," *LÄ* 4 (1982) 338–41.

Buber, M.
Bücher der Kündung (Cologne and Olten: Hegner, 1956).

Burden, J. J.
"Poetic Texts," in F. E. Deist and W. S. Vorster, eds., *Words from Afar* (Cape Town: Tafelberg, 1986).

Buri, F.
Vom Sinn des Leidens: Eine Auslegung des Liedes vom leidenden Gottesknecht (Basel: Reinhardt, 1963).

Burkert, W.
"Greek Tragedy and Sacrificial Ritual," *GRBS* 7 (1966) 89–121.

Burkert, W.
Homo Necans: The Anthropology of Ancient Greek Sacrificial Ritual and Myth, trans. P. Bing (Berkeley: University of California Press, 1983) [Eng. trans. of *Homo Necans. Interpretation altgriechischer Opferriten und Mythen* (Berlin and New York: de Gruyter, 1972)].

Burkert, W.
Greek Religion, trans. J. Raffan (Cambridge: Harvard Univ. Press, 1985) [Eng. trans. of *Griechische Religion der archaischen und klassischen Epoche* (RM 15; Stuttgart: Kohlhammer, 1977)].

Burn, A. R.
"Persia and the Greeks," in I. Gershevitch, ed., *The Cambridge History of Iran*, vol. 2 (Cambridge: Cambridge Univ. Press, 1985) 292–391.

Burrows, M.
"The Origin of the Term 'Gospel,'" *JBL* 44 (1925) 21–33.

Buttrick, G. A., ed.
Interpreter's Dictionary of the Bible: An Illustrated Encyclopedia (4 vols.; Nashville and New York: Abingdon, 1962).

Calmeyer, P.
"Fortuna–Tyche–Khvarna," *JDAI* 94 (1979) 347–65.

Calmeyer, P.
"Die 'Statistische Landcharte' des Perserreiches I, II," *AMI* 15 (1982) 109–87 and *AMI* 16 (1983) 141–222.

Calvin, J.
Sermons on Isaiah's Prophecies of the Death and Passion of Christ (trans. and ed. T. H. L. Parker; London: Clarke, 1956).

Campbell, A. F.
The Study Companion to Old Testament Literature: An Approach to the Writings of Pre-Exilic and Exilic Israel (OTStudies 2; Wilmington, Del.: Glazier, 1989).

Cangh, J.-M. van
"Nouveaux fragments Hexaplaires. Commentaire sur Isaïe d'Eusèbe de Césarée (Cod. Laur., Plut., XI, 4)," *RB* 78 (1971) 384–90.

Caquot, A.
"Les 'graces de David'. A propos d'Isaïe 55:3b," *Sem* 15 (1965) 45–59.

Carmignac, J.
"Six passages d'Isaïe éclairés par Qumran (Isaïe 14:11; 21:10; 22:5; 25:4; 26:3; 50:6)," in S. Wagner, ed., *Bibel und Qumran: Beiträge zur Erforschung der Beziehungen zwischen Bibel- und Qumranwissenschaft. FS H. Bardtke* (Berlin: Evangelische Hauptbibelgesellschaft, 1968) 37–46.

Carpenter, L. L.
Primitive Christian Application of the Doctrine of the Servant (Durham, N.C.: Duke Univ. Press, 1929).

Carroll, R. P.
"The Aniconic God and the Cult of Images," *StTh* 31 (1977) 51–64.

Carroll, R. P.
"Second Isaiah and the Failure of Prophecy," *StTh* 32 (1978) 119–31.

Caspari, W.
Heils- und Gottessprüche der Rückwanderer (Jes 40–55) (BZAW 65; Giessen: Töpelmann, 1934).

Caspi, M.
"I Have *qnh* a Man with the Lord," *Beth Mikra* 33 (1987/88) 29–35.

Cassuto, U.
The Goddess Anath: Canaanite Epics of the Patriarchal Age (trans. I. Abrahams; 2d ed.; Jerusalem: Magnes, 1953).

Cazelles, H.
"Les poèmes du Serviteur. Leur place, leur structure, leur théologie," *RSR* 43 (1955) 5–55.

Ceresko, A. C.
"The Rhetorical Strategy of the Fourth Servant Song (Isaiah 52:13–53:12): Poetry and the Exodus–New Exodus," *CBQ* 56 (1994) 42–55.

Charles, R. H.
Apocrypha and Pseudepigrapha of the OT (2 vols.; Oxford: Clarendon, 1913).

Charlesworth, J. H.
The Pseudepigrapha and Modern Research (SBLSCS 7; Missoula: Scholars Press, 1976).

Charlesworth, J. H., ed.
The Old Testament Pseudepigrapha (2 vols.; Garden City, N.Y.: Doubleday, 1983–85).

Chiesa, B.
"Ritorno dall'esilio e conversione a dio (Is 55)," *BeO* 14 (1972) 167–80.

Childs, B. S.
"Deuteronomic Formulae of the Exodus Traditions," in B. Hartmann et al., eds., *Hebräische Wortforschung. FS W. Baumgartner zum 80. Geburtstag* (VTSup 16; Leiden: Brill, 1967) 30–39.

Childs, B. S.
The Book of Exodus (OTL; Philadelphia: Westminster, 1974).

Childs, B. S.
Review of *Biblical Interpretation in Ancient Israel*, by Michael Fishbane, *JBL* 106 (1987) 511–13.

Chirichigno, G. C.
Debt-Slavery in Israel and the Ancient Near East (JSOTSup 141; Sheffield: JSOT Press, 1993).

Clark, D. J.
"The Influence of the Dead Sea Scrolls on Modern Translations of Isaiah," *BT* 35 (1984) 122–30.

Clemen, C.
Die Himmelfahrt des Mose (KlT 10; Bonn: Marcus und Weber, 1924).

Clements, R. E.
"The Unity of the Book of Isaiah," *Int* 36 (1982) 117–29.

Clements, R. E.
"Beyond Tradition-History: Deutero-Isaianic Development of First Isaiah's Themes," *JSOT* 31 (1985) 95–113.

Clements, R. E.
"Isaiah 45:20-25," *Int* 40 (1986) 392–97.

Clifford, R. J.
Fair Spoken and Persuading (New York: Paulist, 1984).

Clifford, R. J.
"The Use of *HÔY* in the Prophets," *CBQ* 28 (1966) 458–64.

Clifford, R. J.
"The Tent of El and the Israelite Tent of Meeting," *CBQ* 33 (1971) 221–27.

Clifford, R. J.
The Cosmic Mountain in Canaan and the Old Testament (HSM 4; Cambridge: Harvard Univ. Press, 1972).

Clifford, R. J.
"Rhetorical Criticism in the Exegesis of Hebrew Poetry," *SBLASP* 19 (1980) 17–28.

Clifford, R. J.
"The Function of Idol Passages in Second Isaiah," *CBQ* 42 (1980) 450–64.

Clifford, R. J.
"Isaiah 55: Invitation to a Feast," in C. L. Meyers and M. O'Connor, eds., *The Word of the Lord Shall Go Forth: FS D. N. Freedman* (Winona Lake: Eisenbrauns, 1983) 27–35.

Clifford, R. J.
"Cosmogonies in the Ugaritic Texts and in the Bible," *Or* 53 (1984) 183–201.

Clines, D. J. A.
I, He, We and They: A Literary Approach to Isaiah 53 (JSOTSup 1; Sheffield: JSOT Press, 1976).

Clines, D. J. A.
"The Parallelism of Greater Precision: Notes from Isaiah 40 for a Theory of Hebrew Poetry," *JSOT* 40 (1987) 77–100.

Cogan, M.
"Chronology," *ABD* 1 (1992) 1002–11.

Coggins, R. J.
"Recent Continental Old Testament Literature," *ExpT* 100 (1989) 413–17.

Cohen, C.
"The 'Widowed' City," *JANESCU* 5 (1973) 75–81.

Cohen, D.
"But His Father Called Him Benjamin," *Beth Mikra* 23 (1978) 239–41.

Cohen, M. E.
The Cultic Calendars of the Ancient Near East (Bethesda: CDL, 1993).

Conrad, E. W.
"Second Isaiah and the Priestly Oracle of Salvation," *ZAW* 93 (1981) 234–46.

Conrad, E. W.
"The 'Fear Not' Oracles in Second Isaiah," *VT* 34 (1984) 129–52.

Conrad, E. W.
"The Royal Narratives and the Structure of the Book of Isaiah," *JSOT* 41 (1988) 67–81.

Conrad, E. W., and E. G. Newing, eds.
Perspectives on Language and Text: Essays and Poems in Honor of Francis I. Andersen's Sixtieth Birthday, July 28, 1985 (Winona Lake: Eisenbrauns, 1987).

Coppens, J.
"Les origines littéraires des Poèmes du Serviteur de Yahvé," *Bib* 40 (1959) 248–58.

Coppens, J.
"Le Serviteur de Yahvé: Vers la solution d'une énigme," in J. Coppens et al., eds., *Sacra Pagina: Miscellanea Biblica. Congressus Internationalis Catholica de Re Biblica* (BEThL 12–13; Gembloux: Duculot, 1959) 1:434–54.

Corney, R. W.
"Isaiah L 10," *VT* 26 (1976) 497–98.

Corré, A. D.
" *ʾēlle, hēmma = sic,*" *Bib* 54 (1973) 263–64.

Couroyer, B.
"Isaïe, XL,12," *RB* 73 (1966) 186–96.

Couroyer, B.
"Note sur II Sam, I:22 et Is, LV:10-11," *RB* 88 (1981) 505–14.

Cowley, A., ed.
Aramaic Papyri of the Fifth Century B.C. (1923; reprint Osnabrück: Zeller, 1967).

Crenshaw, J. L.
"YHWH Ṣᵉbaʾôt Šᵉmô: A Form-Critical Analysis," *ZAW* 81 (1969) 156–75.

Crenshaw, J. L.
"A Liturgy of Wasted Opportunity (Am 4:6-12; Isa 9:7-10; 45: 25-29)," *Semitics* 1 (1970) 27–37.

Cross, F. M.
"Aspects of Samaritan and Jewish History in Late Persian and Hellenistic Times," *HTR* 59 (1966) 201–11.

Cross, F. M.
"The Council of Yahweh in Second Isaiah," *JNES* 12 (1953) 274–78.

Cross, F. M.
"The Divine Warrior in Israel's Early Cult," in A. Altmann, ed., *Biblical Motifs* (Cambridge: Harvard Univ. Press, 1966) 11–27.

Cross, F. M.
Canaanite Myth and Hebrew Epic: Essays in the History of the Religion of Israel (Cambridge: Harvard Univ. Press, 1973).

Cross, F. M.
"The Priestly Tabernacle in the Light of Recent Research," in A. Biran, ed., *Temples and High Places in Biblical Times* (Jerusalem: Hebrew Union College–Jewish Institute of Religion, 1981) 169–80.

Cross, F. M.
"The Redemption of Nature," *PSB* 10 (1988) 94–104.

Cross, F. M., and D. N. Freedman
Early Hebrew Orthography (AOS 36; New Haven: American Oriental Society, 1952).

Cross, N.
"Those Poor Misquoted Scriptures," *HPR* 84 (1986) 57–60.

Crüsemann, F.
Studien zur Formgeschichte von Hymnus und Danklied in Israel (WMANT 32; Neukirchen-Vluyn: Neukirchener, 1969).

Crüsemann, F.
"Kritik an Amos im deuteronomistischen Geschichtswerk. Erwägungen zu 2. Könige 14:27," in H. W. Wolff, ed., *Probleme biblischer Theologie. FS G. von Rad* (Munich: Kaiser, 1971) 57–63.

Crüsemann, F.
"Jahwes Gerechtigkeit im Alten Testament," *EvTh* 36 (1976) 427–50.

Crüsemann, F.
"Zwei alttestamentliche Witze. I Sam 21,11-15 und II Sam 6,16. 20-23 als Beispiele einer biblischen Gattung," *ZAW* 92 (1980) 215–27.

Crüsemann, F.
Bewahrung der Freiheit. Das Thema des Dekalogs in sozialgeschichtlicher Perspektive (Munich: Kaiser, 1983).

Crüsemann, F.
The Torah: Theology and Social History of Old Testament Law, trans. A. W. Mahnke (Minneapolis: Fortress, 1996) [Eng. trans. of *Die Tora: Theologie und Sozialgeschichte des alttestamentlichen Gesetzes* (Munich: Kaiser, 1992)].

Cryer, F. H.
Divination in Ancient Israel and Its Near Eastern Environment, (JSOTSup 142; Sheffield: JSOT Press, 1994).

Dahms, J. V.
"Isaiah 55:11 and the Gospel of John," *EvQ* 53 (1981) 78–88.

Dahood, M.
"The Linguistic Position of Ugaritic in the Light of Recent Discoveries," in J. Coppens et al., eds., *Sacra Pagina: Miscellanea Biblica. Congressus Internationalis Catholica de Re Biblica* (BEThL 12–13; Gembloux: Duculot, 1959) 1:266–79.

Dahood, M.
"חֲדֵל 'Cessation' in Isaiah 38:11," *Bib* 52 (1971) 215–16.

Dahood, M.
"Phoenician Elements in Isaiah 52:13—53:12," in H. Goedicke, ed., *Near Eastern Studies: Essays in Honor of William Foxwell Albright* (Baltimore: Johns Hopkins Univ. Press, 1971) 63–73.

Dahood, M.
"The Breakup of Two Composite Phrases in Isaiah 40:13," *Bib* 54 (1973) 537–38.

Dahood, M.
"Isaiah 51:19 and Sefire III 22," *Bib* 56 (1975) 94–95.

Dahood, M.
"Yiphil Imperative yaṭṭî in Isaiah 54:2," *Or* 46 (1977) 383–84.

Dahood, M.
"The Conjunction *wn* and the Negative *ʾî* in Hebrew," *UF* 14 (1982) 51–54.

Dahood, M.
"Isaiah 53:8-12 and Masoretic Misconstructions," *Bib* 63 (1982) 566–70.

Dahood, M.
"The Divine Designation *hû'* in Eblaite and the Old Testament," *Annali del' Istituto Universitario Napoli Orientale* 43 (1983) 193–99.

Dalley, S.
"The God Šalmu and the Winged Disk," *Iraq* 48 (1986) 85–101.

Dalman, G.
Arbeit und Sitte in Palästina (5 vols.; 1928–39; reprint Hildesheim: Olms, 1964).

Dandamaev, M. A., and V. G. Lukonin
The Culture and Social Institutions of Ancient Iran (Eng. ed. by P. L. Kohl with the assistance of D. J. Dadson; Cambridge: Cambridge Univ. Press, 1989).

Danell, G. A.
Studies in the Name Israel in the Old Testament (Uppsala: Appelbergs, 1946).

Darr, K. P.
"Like Warrior, Like Woman: Destruction and Deliverance in Isaiah 42:10-17," *CBQ* 49 (1987) 560–71.

Davies, G. H.
"Psalm 95," *ZAW* 85 (1973) 183–95.

Davies, N. de Garis
The Tomb of Rekh-mi-Re at Thebes (Publications of the Metropolitan Museum of Art XI; New York: Metropolitan Museum, 1943; reprint 1973).

Davis, E.
"Shofar," *EncJud* 14 (1971) 1442–48.

Day, J.
"*Daʿat* 'Humiliation' in Isaiah liii 11 in the Light of Isaiah liii 3 and Dan xii 4, and the Oldest Known Interpretation of the Suffering Servant," *VT* 30 (1980) 97–103.

Deist, F. E.
"Reflections on Reinterpretation in and of Isaiah 53," *OTE* 3 (1985) 1–11.

Delekat, L.
Asylie und Schutzorakel am Zionsheiligtum: Eine Untersuchung zu den privaten Feindpsalmen mit zwei Exkursen (Leiden: Brill, 1967).

Delekat, L.
"Zum hebräischen Wörterbuch," *VT* 14 (1964) 35–39.

Deller, K.
"Neuassyrisches aus Sultantepe," *Or* 34 (1965) 457–77.

Delling, G.
"Alexander der Große als Bekenner des jüdischen Gottesglaubens," *JSJ* 12 (1981) 1–51.

Deonna, S. W.
"Histoire d'un emblème. La couronne murale des villes et pays personnifiés," *Bulletin du Musée et d'Histoire de Genève* 18 (1940) 119–236.

Derchain, P.
"Kultspiele," *LÄ* 3 (1980) 856–59.

Derchain-Urtel, M. T.
"Thronbesteigung," *LÄ* 6 (1986) 529–32.

Derousseaux, L., ed.
La création dans l'orient ancien (LD 127; Paris: Cerf, 1987).

Derret, J. D. M.
"'Every Valley Shall Be Exalted': Borrowings from Isaiah in Ancient India?" *ZRGG* 24 (1972) 153–55.

Dick, M. B.
"Prophetic *Poiēsis* and the Verbal Icon," *CBQ* 46 (1984) 226–46.

Dicks, D. R.
"Astrology and Astronomy in Horace," *Hermes* 91 (1963) 60–73.

Diebner, B. J.
"Wozu betreiben wir im akademischen Unterricht Textkritik?" *DBAT* 16 (1982) 49–67.

Diels, H.
Die Fragmente der Vorsokratiker, vol. 1, ed. W. Kranz (6th ed.; Berlin: Weidmann, 1951).

Dihl, A.
"Herakles," *RGG*[3] 3:227–28.

Dijk, H. J. van
"Consolamini, consulamini, popule meus? Observationes exegeticae ad Is 40:1-2," *VD* 45 (1967) 342–46.

Dijkstra, M.
"Zur Deutung von Jes 45,15ff," *ZAW* 89 (1977) 215–22.

Dijkstra, M.
Gods Voorstelling: Predikatieve expressie van zelfopenbaring in Oudoosterse teksten Deutero-Jesaja (DNL 2; Kampen: Kok, 1980).

Dion, P.-E.
"Le genre littéraire sumérien de l'hymne à soi-même et quelques passages du Deutéro-Isaïe," *RB* 74 (1967) 215–34.

Dion, P. E.
"The Patriarchal Traditions and the Literary Form of the 'Oracle of Salvation,'" *CBQ* 29 (1967) 198–206.

Dion, P.-E.
"Les chants du Serviteur de Yahweh et quelques passages apparentés d'Is 40–55. Un essai sur leurs limites précises et sur leur origines respectives," *Bib* 51 (1970) 17–38.

Dion, P.-E.
"The 'Fear Not' Formula and the Holy War," *CBQ* 32 (1970) 565–70.

Dion, P.-E.
"L'universalisme religieux dans les différentes couches rédactionelles d'Isaïe 40–55," *Bib* 51 (1970) 161–82.

Dohmen, C.
"Ein kanaanäischer Schmiedeterminus (*NSK*)," *UF* 15 (1983) 39–42.

Dohmen, C.
Das Bilderverbot. Seine Entstehung und seine Entwicklung im Alten Testament (BBB 62; 1985; 2d ed.; Bonn: Hanstein, 1987).

Donner, H., and W. Röllig, eds.
Kanaanäische und Aramäische Inschriften [*KAI*]
(Wiesbaden: Harrassowitz); vol. 1, 3d ed., 1971;
vol. 2, 2d ed., 1968.

Dossin, G., et al., eds.
Archives royales de Mari XIII: Textes divers (Paris:
Librairie Orientaliste Geuthner, 1964).

Drioton, E.
Le théatre égyptien (Cairo: Editions de la Revue du
Caire, 1942).

Driver, G. R.
"Studies in the Vocabulary of the Old Testament
V," *JTS* 34 (1933) 33–44.

Driver, G. R.
"Linguistic and Textual Problems: Isaiah XL–
LXVI," *JTS* 36 (1935) 396–406.

Driver, G. R.
"Hebrew Poetic Diction," in *Congress Volume:
Copenhagen 1953* (VTSup 1; Leiden: Brill, 1953)
26–41.

Driver, G. R.
"Birds in the Old Testament: I. Birds in Law," *PEQ*
87 (1955) 5–20.

Driver, G. R.
"Isaianic Problems," in G. Wiessner, ed., *FS W.
Eilers* (Wiesbaden: Harrassowitz, 1967) 43–57.

Driver, G. R.
"Isaiah 52:13–53:12: The Servant of the Lord," in
M. Black and G. Fohrer, eds., *In Memoriam P. Kahle*
(BZAW 103; Berlin: Töpelmann, 1968) 90–105.

Dubarle, A. M.
Judith. Formes et sens des diverses traditions (AnBib
24; Rome: Biblical Institute, 1966).

Duchesne-Guillemin, J.
"Sonnenkönigtum und Mazdareligion mit einem
Exkurs zu Farnah von P. Lecoq: À propos du *F
'mède'*," in H. Koch and D. N. Mackenzie, eds.,
*Kunst, Kultur und Geschichte der Achämenidenzeit und
ihr Fortleben* (AMI Ergänzungsband 10; Berlin:
Reiner, 1983) 135–44.

Dumbrell, W.
"The Role of the Servant in Isaiah 40–55," *RTR* 48
(1989) 105–13.

Dupont-Sommer, A.
The Essene Writings from Qumran, trans. G. Vermes
(Oxford: Basil Blackwell, 1961; New York: Meridi-
an Books, 1962).

Dürr, L.
*Die Wertung des göttlichen Wortes im Alten Testament
und im Antiken Orient* (MVAG 42/1; Leipzig: Hinrichs, 1938).

Eakins, J. K.
"Anthropomorphisms in Isaiah 40–55," *Hebrew
Studies* 20/21 (1979–80) 47–50.

Eaton, J. H.
"The Origin of the Book of Isaiah," *VT* 9 (1959)
138–57.

Eaton, J. H.
Festal Drama in Deutero-Isaiah (London: SPCK,
1979).

Ebeling, E.
"Ein Preislied auf Babylon," *OLZ* 19 (1916)
132–33.

Ebeling, E.
Quellen zur Kenntnis der babylonischen Religion I
(Leipzig: Hinrichs, 1918).

Ebeling, E.
*Keilschrifttexte aus Assur religiösen Inhalts; Erster
Band: Autobiographien* (Leipzig: Hinrichs, 1919).

Ebeling, E.
*Bruchstücke eines politischen Propagandagedichtes aus
einer assyrischen Kanzlei* (MAOG XII/2; Leipzig:
Harrassowitz, 1938).

Edzard, D. O.
"Mari und Aramäer?" *ZA* 56 (1964) 142–49.

Edzard, D. O.
"Gilgameš und Huwawa A. I. Teil," *ZA* 80 (1990)
165–203; "II. Teil," *ZA* 81 (1991) 165–233.

Edzard, D. O.
*Gilgameš und Huwawa: Zwei Versionen der
sumerischen Zedernwaldepisode nebst einer Edition von
Version "BC."* (Bayerische Akademie der Wissen-
schaften, Philosophisch-Historische Klasse,
Sitzungsberichte, Jahrgang 1993, Heft 4; Munich:
Beck, 1993).

Eggebrecht, H. H.
Heinrich Schütz, Musicus poeticus (2d ed.; Wilhelms-
hafen: Heinrichshofen's, 1984).

Ehrlich, A. B.
Randglossen zur hebräischen Bibel IV (Leipzig: Hinrichs, 1912).

Eichhorn, D.
*Gott als Fels, Berg und Zuflucht: Eine Untersuchung
zum Gebet des Mittlers in den Psalmen* (EHS.T 4;
Bern: Lang, 1972).

Eichhorn, J. G.
Einleitung in das Alte Testament, vol. 3 (1782; 3d ed.;
Leipzig: Weidmann, 1803).

Eilers, W.
"Kyros," *Beiträge zur Namenforschung* 15 (1964)
180–236.

Einheitsübersetzung, die Bibel
(Stuttgart: Katholische Bibelanstalt; Stuttgart:
Deutsche Bibelgesellschaft; Klosterneuburg: Öster-
reichisches Katholisches Bibelwerk, 1980).

Eissfeldt, O.
Ras Schamra und Sanchunjaton (BRGA 4; Halle:
Niemeyer, 1939).

Eissfeldt, O.
"Neue Forschungen zum Ebed Jahwe-Problem,"
ThLZ 68 (1943) 273–80.

Eissfeldt, O.
Sanchunjaton von Berut und Ilumilka von Ugarit
(Halle: Niemeyer, 1952).

Eissfeldt, O.
*Der Beutel der Lebendigen. Alttestamentliche Erzäh-
lungs- und Dichtungsmotive im Lichte neuer Nuzi-Texte*
(BVSAW.PH 105/6; Berlin: Akademischer Verlag,
1960).

Eissfeldt, O.
"The Promises of Grace to David in Isaiah 55:1-5,"
in B. W. Anderson and W. Harrelson, eds., *Israel's
Prophetic Heritage: Essays in Honor of James Muilenburg* (New York: Harper, 1962) 196–207.

Eissfeldt, O.
The Old Testament: An Introduction, trans. P. R.
Ackroyd (Oxford: Basil Blackwell; New York:
Harper & Row, 1965) [Eng. trans of *Einleitung in
das Alte Testament unter Einschluss der Apokryphen
und Pseudepigraphen sowie der apokryphen und
pseudepigraphischen Qumranschriften. Entstehungsgeschichte des AT* (3d ed.; Tübingen: Mohr, 1964)].

Eitrem, S.
The Necromancy in the Persai of Aischylos (SO 4;
Oslo, 1928).

Elayi, J.
"Les cités phéniciennes et l'empire Assyrien à
l'époque d'Assurbanipal," *RA* 77 (1983) 45–58.

Elayi, J., and H. G. Elayi
"Trésors de monnaies phéniciennes et circulation
monétaire (Vᵉ–IVᵉ siècles avant J.C.)," *Transeuphratène Suppl.* 1 (1993) 322ff.

Ellenbogen, M.
*Foreign Words in the Old Testament: Their Origin and
Etymology* (London: Luzac, 1962).

Elliger, K.
Die Einheit des Tritojesaja (Jesaja 56–66) (BWANT
45; Stuttgart: Kohlhammer, 1928).

Elliger, K.
Deuterojesaja in seinem Verhältnis zu Tritojesaja
(BWANT 63; Stuttgart: Kohlhammer, 1933).

Elliger, K.
"Der Begriff 'Geschichte' bei Deuterojesaja," in
Kleine Schriften zum Alten Testament (ThBü 32;
Munich: Kaiser, 1966) 199–210.

Elliger, K.
"Ich bin der Herr euer Gott," in *Kleine Schriften
zum Alten Testament* (ThBü 32; Munich: Kaiser,
1966) 211–31.

Elliger, K.
Leviticus (HAT 1/4 ; Tübingen: Mohr, 1966).

Elliger, K.
"Jes 53:10: alte Crux–neuer Vorschlag," in *FS R.
Meyer MIOF* 15 (1969) 228–33.

Elliger, K.
"Textkritisches zu Deuterojesaja," in H. Goedicke,
ed., *Near Eastern Studies: Essays in Honor of William
Foxwell Albright* (Baltimore: Johns Hopkins Univ.
Press, 1971) 113–19.

Elliger, K.
"Nochmals Textkritisches zu Jes 53," in J.
Schreiner ed., *Wort, Lied und Gottesspruch. Beiträge
zu Psalmen und Propheten. FS J. Ziegler* (FB 2;
Würzburg: Echter, 1972) 137–44.

Elliger, K.
"Dubletten im Bibeltext," in H. N. Bream, R. D.
Heim and C. A. Moore, eds., *A Light into My Path:
FS J. M. Myers* (GTS 4; Philadelphia: Temple Univ.
Press, 1974) 131–40.

Ellis, R. R.
"The Remarkable Suffering Servant of Isaiah
40–55," *SWJT* 34 (1991) 20–30.

Emerton, J. A.
"A Note on Isaiah 35:9-10," *VT* 22 (1977) 488–89.

Epstein, I., ed.
The Babylonian Talmud, vol. 3 (London: Soncino
Press, 1932).

Erlandsson, S.
The Burden of Babylon: A Study of Isaiah 13:2—14:23
(ConBOT 4; Lund: Gleerup, 1970).

Erman, A.
Life in Ancient Egypt, trans. H. M. Tirard (New
York: Macmillan, 1894) [Eng. trans. of *Ägypten und
ägyptisches Leben im Altertum* (2d ed; H. Ranke, ed.;
Tübingen: Mohr, 1923)].

Erman, A.
"Ein Denkmal memphitischer Theologie, " SPAW
43 (1911) 916–50.

Eskenazi, T. C.
*In an Age of Prose: A Literary Approach to Ezra-
Nehemiah* (SBLMS 36; Atlanta: Scholars Press,
1988).

Eslinger, L., and G. Taylor, eds.
*Ascribe to the Lord: Biblical and Other Studies in
Memory of Peter C. Craigie* (JSOTSup 67; Sheffield:
JSOT Press, 1988).

Etheridge, J. W.
*The Targums of Onkelos and Jonathan Ben Uzziel on
the Pentateuch with the Fragments of the Jerusalem
Targum: From the Chaldee* (London: Longman and
Green, 1862–1865; reprint New York: Ktav, 1968).

Euripides
Hippolytus, in *Euripides IV* (LCL; trans. and rev.
A. S. Way; Cambridge: Harvard Univ. Press; Lon-
don: Heinemann, 1912, reprint 1971) 157–277.

Eusebius,
De Praeparatio Evangelica (Eusebius Werke 8/1; ed.
K. Mras; GCS 43/1; Berlin: Akademie, 1954).

Fairman, H. W., ed.
*The Triumph of Horus: An Ancient Egyptian Sacred
Drama* (London: Batsford, 1974).

Falk, Z. W.
"Gestures Expressing Affirmation," *JSS* 3 (1958)
268–69.

Falkenstein, A., and W. von Soden
Sumerische und Akkadische Hymnen und Gebete
(Zurich and Stuttgart: Artemis, 1953).

Fander, M.
*Die Stellung der Frau im Markusevangelium: Unter
besonderer Berücksichtigung kultur- und religionsgeschichtlicher Hintergründe* (MThA 8; Allenberge:
Telos, 1989).

Fascher, E.
Jesaja 53 in christlicher und jüdischer Sicht (AVTRW
4; Berlin: Evangelische Verlagsanstalt, 1958).

Faur, J.
"The Third Person in Semitic Grammatical
Theory and General Linguistics," *LB* 46 (1979)
106–13.

Fenton, T. L.
"Questions Related to Ugaritic Evidence Pertaining to the Biblical Vocabulary," *Leš* 44 (1980) 268–80.

Feuillet, A.
"Le messianisme du livre d'Isaïe: Ses rapports avec l'histoire et les traditions d'Israël," *RSR* (1949) 182–228.

Feuillet, A.
"La religion d'Israel, préparation de celle du Christ. Les poèmes du serviteur de la seconde partie du livre d'Isaïe," *Div.* 37 (1993) 215–24.

Fichtner, J.
"Jesaja 52,7-10," in G. Eichholz, ed., *Herr, tue meine Lippen auf: Eine Predigthilfe*, vol. 5: *Die alttestamentlichen Perikopen* (2d ed.; Wuppertal-Barmen: E. Müller, 1961) 197–212.

Finet, A., and J. Bottéro
Répertoire Analytique des Tomes I à V des Archives Royales de Mari XV (Paris: Imprimerie Nationale, 1954).

Finkelstein, J. J.
"Hebrew הבר and Semitic *ḤBR*," *JBL* 75 (1956) 328–31.

Fischel, H. A.
"Die deuterojesajanischen Gottesknechtslieder in der juedischen Auslegung," *HUCA* 18 (1944) 53–76.

Fischer, G.
"Die Redewendung דבר על־לב im Alten Testament—Ein Beitrag zum Verständnis von Jes 40:2," *Bib* 65 (1984) 244–50.

Fischer, I.
Tora für Israel–Tora für die Völker: Das Konzept des Jesajabuches (SBS 164; Stuttgart: Katholisches Bibelwerk, 1995).

Fischer, J.
Isaias 40–55 und die Perikopen vom Gottesknecht: Eine kritisch-exegetische Studie (AtAbh 6/4-5; Münster: Aschendorff, 1916).

Fischer, J.
Wer ist der EBED in den Perikopen Jes 42:1-7; 49:1-9a; 50:4-9; 52:13–53:12? Eine exegetische Studie (AtAbh 8/5; Münster: Aschendorff, 1922).

Fischer, J.
"Das Problem des neuen Exodus in Isaias 40–55," *ThQ* 110 (1929) 111–30.

Fishbane, M.
Biblical Interpretation in Ancient Israel (Oxford: Clarendon, 1985).

Fisher, J.
"The Herald of Good News in Second Isaiah," in J. J. Jackson and M. Kessler, eds., *Rhetorical Criticism: Essays in Honor of J. Muilenburg* (PTMS 1; Pittsburgh: Pickwick, 1974) 117–32.

Fitzgerald, A.
"The Mythological Background for the Presentation of Jerusalem as Queen and False Worship as Adultery in the OT," *CBQ* 34 (1972) 403–16.

Fitzgerald, A.
"*BTWLT* and *BT* as Titles for Capital Cities," *CBQ* 37 (1975) 167–83.

Fitzgerald, A.
"The Interchange of *L, N,* and *R* in Biblical Hebrew," *JBL* 97 (1978) 481–88.

Fitzgerald, A.
"The Technology of Isaiah 40:19-20 + 41:6-7," *CBQ* 51 (1989) 426–46.

Flusser, D.
"The Text of Isa 49:17 in the DSS," *Textus* 2 (1962) 140–42.

Fohrer, G.
"Deutero- und Tritojesaja," *ThR* n.s. 19 (1951) 298–305.

Fohrer, G.
"Über den Kurzvers," *ZAW* 66 (1954) 199–236.

Fohrer, G.
"Zum Text von Jes. xli 8-13," *VT* 5 (1955) 239–49.

Fohrer, G.
"Umkehr und Erlösung beim Propheten Hosea," *ThZ* 11 (1955) 161–85; reprint in *Studien zur alttestamentlichen Prophetie (1949–1965)* (BZAW 99; Berlin: de Gruyter, 1967) 22–41.

Fohrer, G.
"Zehn Jahre Literatur zur alttestamentlichen Prophetie (1951–1960), VI, Deuterojesaja (Jes 40–66)," *ThR* n.s. 28 (1962) 235–49.

Fohrer, G.
Das Buch Hiob (KAT 16; Gütersloh: Mohn, 1963).

Fohrer, G.
Neue Studien zu Deuterojesaja (BWANT 4/25; 1938; reprint Munich: Kaiser, 1965).

Fohrer, G.
"Stellvertretung und Schuldopfer in Jesaja 52:13–53:12 vor dem Hintergrund des Alten Testaments und des Alten Orients," in P. Rieger, ed., *Das Kreuz Jesu: Theologische Überlegungen* (Göttingen: Vandenhoeck & Ruprecht, 1969) 7–31.

Fokkelman, J.
"Stylistic Analysis of Isaiah 40:1-11," *OTS* 21 (1981) 68–90.

Follis, E. R., ed.
Directions in Biblical Hebrew Poetry (JSOTSup 40; Sheffield: JSOT Press, 1987).

Forbes, R. J.
Metallurgy in Antiquity (Leiden: Brill, 1950).

Forbes, R. J.
Studies in Ancient Technology 8 (Leiden: Brill, 1964).

Frankfort, H.
"Studia Mariana: Publiés sous la direction de André Parrot," *BiOr* 8 (1951) 181–83.

Fredriksson, H.
Jahwe als Krieger: Studien zum alttestamentlichen Gottesbild (Lund: Ohlssons, 1945).

Freedman, D. N.
"The Slave of Yahweh," *Western Watch* 10 (1959) 1–19.

Freedman, D. N.
"Isaiah 42:13," *CBQ* 30 (1968) 225–26.

Freedman, D. N.
"A Note on Isaiah 47:7," *Bib* 51 (1970) 538.

Freedman, D. N.
"Divine Names and Titles in Early Hebrew Poetry," in F. M. Cross, W. E. Lemke, and P. D. Miller, Jr., eds., *Magnalia Dei: The Mighty Acts of God. Essays on the Bible and Archaeology in Memory of G. E. Wright* (Garden City, N.Y.: Doubleday, 1976) 55–107.

Freedman, D. N.
"The Spelling of the Name 'David' in the Hebrew Bible," *HAR* 7 (1983) 89–104.

Freedman, D.N.
"The Structure of Isaiah 40:1-11," in E. W. Conrad and E. G. Newing, eds., *Perspectives on Language and Text: Essays and Poems in Honor of Francis I. Andersen* (Winona Lake, Ind.: Eisenbrauns, 1987) 167–93.

Freedy, K. S., and D. B. Redford
"The Dates in Ezekiel in Relation to Biblical, Babylonian and Egyptian Sources," *JAOS* 90 (1970) 462–85.

Frei, P., and K. Koch
Reichsidee und Reichsorganisation im Perserreich (OBO 55; Freiburg: Universitätsverlag; Göttingen: Vandenhoeck & Ruprecht, 1984; 2d ed., 1996).

Frerichs, E. S.
"The Torah Canon of Judaism and the Interpretation of Hebrew Scriptures," *HBT* 9 (1987) 13–25.

Freud, S.
Moses and Monotheism, trans. K. Jones (New York: Vintage, 1939) [Eng. trans. of *Der Mann Moses und die monotheistische Religion: Schriften über die Religion* (reprint Frankfurt: Fischer, 1975).

Freund, Y.
"'Depart, Depart, Go Out Thence . . .' (Isa 52:11), The Prophet and His Public," *Beth Mikra* 34 (1988/89) 50–58.

Freymuth, G.
"Zum Hieros Gamos in den antiken Mysterien," *Museum Helveticum* 21 (1964) 86–95.

Friedländer, M., trans. and ed.,
The Commentary of Ibn Ezra on Isaiah, 1 (London, 1873; reprint New York: Feldheim, 1965).

Friedman, T.
"Wĕrûaḥ ʾĕlōhîm mĕraḥepet ʿal pĕnê hammāyim (Gen 1:2)," *Beth Mikra* 25 (1980) 309–12.

Friedrich, G.
"εὐαγγελίζομαι," *TDNT* 2 (1964) 707–21 [Eng. trans. of *ThWNT* 2 (1935) 705–7].

Fritz, K. v.
"Das Prooemium der Hesiodischen Theogonie," in *FS B. Snell* (Munich: Beck, 1956) 29–45.

Frye, R. N.
The History of Ancient Iran (HAW 3/7; Munich: Beck, 1983).

Füglister, N.
"Kirche als Knecht Gottes und der Menschen: Israel bei Deuterojesaja," *BK* 39 (1984) 109–22.

Gabelmann, H.
Antike Audienz- und Tribunalszenen (Darmstadt: Wissenschaftliche Buchgesellschaft, 1984).

Gabriel, J.
"Die Kainitengenealogie," *Bib* 40 (1959) 409–27.

Gabrion, H.
"L'interprétation de l'Écriture dans la littérature de Qumran," in W. Haase, ed., *ANRW* II/19/1: *Principat. Religion (Judentum: Allgemeines; Palästinisches Judentum)* (Berlin and New York: de Gruyter, 1979) 779–848.

Galbiati, G.
"'Nel deserto preparate la via . . .' (Isaia 40,3 e sue citazioni)," *RBR* 15 (1981) 7–46.

Galling, K.
"Weltanschauung und Gottesglaube im 'Prediger,'" in O. Eissfeldt, ed., *Theologische Gegenwartsfragen* (Halle: Gebauer-Schwetschke, 1940) 36–46.

Galling, K.
Bagoas und Esra: Studien zur Geschichte Israels im persischen Zeitalter (Tübingen: Mohr, 1964) 149–84.

Galling, K.
"Ziegel," *BRL* (2d ed. 1977) 364.

Galling, K., ed.
Biblisches Reallexikon (HAT I,1; 2d ed.; Tübingen: Mohr, 1977)

Galling, K., ed.,
Textbuch zur Geschichte Israels (Tübingen: Mohr, 1950).

Galling, K., et al., eds.
Religion in Geschichte und Gegenwart (6 vols.; 3d ed.; Tübingen: Mohr, 1957–70).

Gammie, J. G.
"On the Intention and Sources of Daniel I–VI," *VT* 31 (1981) 282–92.

Garbini, G.
"Gli Ebrei in Palestina: Yahvismo e religione fenicia," in *Forme di Contatto e Processi di Trasformazione nelle Società Antiche* (Pisa and Rome: École Française de Rome, 1983) 899–910.

Garbini, G.
"Universalismo iranico e Israele," *Henoch* 6 (1984) 293–312.

Gardiner, A. H.
Ancient Egyptian Onomastica, 2 vols. (London: Oxford Univ. Press, 1947).

Gardiner, A. H.
The Ramesseum Papyri (Oxford: Oxford Univ. Press, 1955).

Garofalo, S.
"Preparare la strada al Signore," *RevB* 6 (1958) 131–34.

Gaster, M., ed.
The Asatir: The Samaritan Book of the 'Secrets of Moses', together with the Pitron or Samaritan Commentary and the Samaritan Story of the Death of Moses (London: Royal Asiatic Society, 1927).

Gaster, T. H.
 Thespis: Ritual, Myth and Drama in the Ancient Near East (1950; 2d ed. New York: Harper & Row, 1966).
Geller, S. A.
 "Were the Prophets Poets?" *Prooftexts* 3 (1983) 211–21.
Geller, S. A.
 "A Poetic Analysis of Isaiah 40:1-2," *HTR* 77 (1984) 413–24.
Gelston, A.
 "The Missionary Message of Second Isaiah," *SJT* 18 (1965) 308–18.
Gelston, A.
 "A Note on יהוה מלך," *VT* 16 (1966) 507–12.
Gelston, A.
 "Some Notes on Second Isaiah," *VT* 21 (1971) 517–27.
Gemser, B.
 "The *rîb-* or controversy-pattern in Hebrew mentality," in M. Noth and D. W. Thomas, eds., *Wisdom in Israel and in the Ancient Near East. FS H. H. Rowley* (VTSup 3; Leiden: Brill, 1955) 120–37.
Gemser, B.
 Sprüche Salomos (HAT 16; 2d ed.; Tübingen: Mohr, 1963).
Georgi, D.
 The Opponents of Paul in Second Corinthians, trans. H. Attridge et al. (Philadelphia: Fortress, 1986) [Eng. trans. of *Die Gegner des Paulus im 2. Korintherbrief. Studien zur religiösen Propaganda in der Spätantike* (WMANT 11; Neukirchen-Vluyn: Neukirchener, 1964)].
Georgi, D.
 "Die Visionen vom himmlischen Jerusalem in Apk. 21 und 22," in D. Lührmann and G. Strecker, eds., *Kirche. FS G. Bornkamm* (Tübingen: Mohr, 1980) 35–72.
Georgi, D.
 Weisheit Salomos (JSHRZ 3/4; Gütersloh: Mohn, 1980).
Georgi, D.
 "Who Is the True Prophet?" in G. W. E. Nickelsburg and G. MacRae, eds., *Christians among Jews and Gentiles: FS K. Stendahl* (Philadelphia: Fortress, 1986) 100–126.
Gerke, F.
 Spätantike und frühes Christentum (Baden-Baden: Holle, 1967).
Gerlemann, G.
 "Bemerkungen zum alttestamentlichen Sprachstil," in *Studia Biblica et Semitica. FS Th. Chr. Vriezen* (Wageningen: Veeneman, 1966) 108–14.
Gershevitch, I., ed.
 Cambridge History of Iran, vol. 2: *The Median and Achaemenian Periods* (Cambridge: Cambridge Univ. Press, 1985).
Gerstenberger, E.
 "Woe-Oracles of the Prophets," *JBL* 81 (1962) 249–63.

Gerstenberger, E.
 Leviticus, trans. D. W. Stott (OTL; Louisville: Westminister/John Knox, 1996) [Eng. trans. of *Das dritte Buch Mose: Leviticus* (ATD 6; Göttingen: Vandenhoeck & Ruprecht, 1993)].
Gertner, M.
 "The Masorah and the Levites," *VT* 10 (1960) 241–84.
Geus, J. K. de
 "Die Gesellschaftskritik der Propheten und die Archäologie," *ZDPV* 98 (1982) 50–57.
Gevirtz, S.
 Patterns in the Early Poetry of Israel (Chicago: University of Chicago Press, 1963).
Geyer, J.
 "קצות הארץ—Hellenistic?," *VT* 20 (1970) 87–90.
Giblin, C. H.
 "A Note on the Composition of Isaiah 49:1-6 (9a)," *CBQ* 21 (1959) 207–12.
Gigon, O., and K. Schubert
 "Hades," *LAW* 2 (1965) 1180.
Ginsberg, H. L.
 "Some Emendations in Isaiah," *JBL* 69 (1950) 51–60.
Ginsberg, H. L.
 "The Oldest Interpretation of the Suffering Servant," *VT* 3 (1953) 400–404.
Ginsberg, H. L.
 "The Arm of YHWH in Isaiah 51–63 and the Text of Isa 53:10-11," *JBL* 77 (1958) 152–56.
Gitay, Y.
 "Deutero-Isaiah: Oral or Written?" *JBL* 99 (1980) 185–97.
Gitay, Y.
 Prophecy and Persuasion: A Study of Isaiah 40–48 (FThL 14; Bonn: Linguistica Biblica, 1981).
Glueck, N.
 Ḥesed in the Bible, trans. A. Gottschalk (Cincinnati: Hebrew Union College Press, 1967) [Eng. trans. of *Das Wort ḥesed im alttestamentlichen Sprachgebrauch als menschliche und göttliche gemeinschaftsgemässe Verhaltensweise* (BZAW 47; 2d ed.; Berlin: Töpelmann, 1961).
Goedicke, H.
 Die Darstellung des Horus: Ein Mysterienspiel in Peri-lae unter Ptolemäus VIII (BWZKM 11; Wien, 1982).
Goitein, S. D.
 "*YHWH* the Passionate: The Monotheistic Meaning and Origin of the Name *YHWH*," *VT* 6 (1956) 1–9.
Goldingay, J.
 "The Arrangement of Isaiah XLI–XLV," *VT* 29 (1979) 289–99.
Golebiewski, M.
 "Le sens de la Parole divine chez le Deutéro-Isaïe," *CoTh* 49 (special edition, 1979) 47–56.
Golebiewski, M.
 "L'alliance éternelle en Is 54–55 en comparaison avec d'autres textes prophétiques," *CoTh* 50 (special edition, 1980) 89–102.

Golebiewski, M.
"Is 51:17–52:2 nella struttura generale dei cc. 51-52 e il suo significatio teologico," *CoTh* 53 (special edition, 1983) 147-60.

Goodenough, E. R.
By Light, Light: The Mystic Gospel of Hellenistic Judaism (1935; reprint Amsterdam: Philo, 1969).

Goodenough, E. R.
Jewish Symbols in the Greco-Roman Period, vol. 11: *Symbolism in the Dura Synagogue* (New York: Pantheon, 1964).

Gordis, R.
"More on *mrḥm bn bṭnh* (Isa 49:15)," *Tarbiz* 53 (1983/84) 137-38.

Gordon, R. P.
"Isaiah LIII 2," *VT* 20 (1970) 491-92.

Görg, M.
Das Zelt der Begegnung: Untersuchung zur Gestalt der sakralen Zelttraditionen Altisraels (BBB 27; Bonn: Hanstein, 1967)

Goshen-Gottstein, M. H.
"Theory and Practice of Textual Criticism," *Textus* 3 (1963) 130-58.

Gosse, B.
"Isaïe 52,13–53,12 et Isaïe 6," *RB* 98 (1991) 537-43.

Gossel, A. A.
Das Evangelium von der Herrlichkeit der Kirchen Christi im Neuen Bunde in dem vier und funffzigsten Capitel Jesaiae durch einige über dasselbe angestellete Betrachtungen angewiesen, Nothdürfftig erkläret und erläutert, und nach seinem Zwecke angewandt (Bremen: Saurmann, 1736).

Gottstein, M. H.
"Die Jesaja-Rolle im Lichte von Peschitta und Targum," *Bib* 35 (1954) 51-71.

Gottstein, M. H.
"Die Jesaja-Rolle und das Problem der hebräischen Bibelhandschriften," *Bib* 35 (1954) 429-42.

Goudoever, J. van
"The Celebration of the Torah in the Second Isaiah," in J. Vermeylen ed., *The Book of Isaiah* (BEThL 81; Leuven: Leuven Univ. Press and Peeters, 1989) 313-17.

Goyon, J.-C.
"Dramatische Texte," *LÄ* 1 (1975) 1140-44.

Gozzo, P. S. M.
La dottrina teologica del libro di Isaia (BPAA 11; Rome: PAA, 1962).

Graesser, C.
"Righteousness, Human and Divine," *CurTM* 10 (1983) 134-41.

Gray, G. B.
Sacrifice in the OT: Its Theory and Practice (Oxford: Clarendon, 1925; reprint New York: Ktav, 1971).

Greenberg, M.
"Three Conceptions of the Torah in Hebrew Scriptures," in E. Blum, Chr. Macholz, and E. Stegemann, eds., *Die Hebräische Bibel und ihre zweifache Nachgeschichte. FS R. Rendtorff* (Neukirchen-Vluyn: Neukirchener, 1990) 365-78.

Greenfield, J. C.
"Adi balṭu—Care for the Elderly and Its Rewards," in H. Hirsch and H. Hunger, eds., *Vorträge gehalten auf der 28. Rencontre Assyriologique Internationale* (*AfO* Beiheft 19; Horn: Berger, 1982) 309-16.

Greenwood, D.
"Rhetorical Criticism and Formgeschichte: Some Methodological Considerations," *JBL* 89 (1970) 418-26.

Grelot, P.
"Un parallèle Babylonien d'Isaïe lx et du Psaume lxxii," *VT* 7 (1957) 319-21.

Grese, W. C.
"'Unless One Is Born Again': The Use of a Heavenly Journey in John 3," *JBL* 107 (1988) 677-93.

Gressmann, H.
Altorientalische Bilder zum Alten Testament (Tübingen, 1909; 2d ed.; Berlin and Leipzig: de Gruyter, 1927).

Gressmann, H.
"Die literarische Analyse Deuterojesajas," *ZAW* 34 (1914) 254-97.

Gressmann, H.
"Ἡ κοινονία τῶν δαιμονίων," *ZNW* 20 (1921) 224-30.

Gressmann, H.
Altorientalische Texte zum Alten Testament (Tübingen, 1909; 2d ed.; Berlin and Leipzig: de Gruyter, 1926).

Grether, O.
Name und Wort Gottes im AT (BZAW 64; Giessen: Töpelmann, 1934).

Griffiths, J. W.
"The Egyptian Derivation of the Name Moses," *JNES* 12 (1953) 225-31.

Grimm, W.
Weil ich dich liebe: Die Verkündigung Jesu und Deuterojesaja (Bern and Frankfurt: Lang, 1976).

Grimm, W.
"Weil ich dich lieb habe; Der Einfluß der deuterojesajanischen Prophetie auf die Botschaft Jesu," *ThLZ* 101 (1976) 153-55.

Grimm, W.
Fürchte dich nicht: Ein exegetischer Zugang zum Seelsorgepotential einer deuterojesajanischen Gattung (EHS.T 298; Frankfurt: Lang, 1986).

Grözinger, K. E.
"Middat Ha-Din und Middat Ha-Rahamim: Die sogenannten Gottesattribute 'Gerechtigkeit' und 'Barmherzigkeit' in der rabbinischen Literatur," *FJB* 8 (1980) 95-114.

Gruber, M. I.
"Can a Woman Forget Her Sucking Child . . . ?" *Tarbiz* 51 (1981/82) 491-92.

Gruber, M. I.
"The Motherhood of God in Second Isaiah," *RB* 90 (1983) 351-59.

Guggino, E.
"Von Würmern und bösen Müttern: Magie und Krankheit in der Sizilianischen Volkskultur," *Zibaldone* 5 (1988) 25–35.

Guillaume, A.
"Isaiah 53:5 in the Light of the Elephantine Papyri," *ExpT* 32 (1920/21) 377–79.

Guillaume, A.
"Isaiah XLIII.14," *JTS* 49 (1948) 54–55.

Guillet, J.
"Le thème de la Marche au désert dans l'Ancien et le Nouveau Testament," *RSR* 36 (1949) 161–81.

Guillet, J.
"La polémique contre les idoles et le Serviteur de Yahvé," *Bib* 40 (1959) 428–34.

Gundel, H., and R. Böker
"Zodiakos," PW 10 A (1972) 462–709.

Gunkel, H.
The Folktale in the Old Testament, trans. M. D. Rutter (Sheffield: Almond, 1987) [Eng. trans. of *Das Märchen im Alten Testament* (RV II,23/26; 1917; 2d ed.; Tübingen: Mohr, 1921)].

Gunkel, H., and J. Begrich
Einleitung in die Psalmen (Göttingen: Vandenhoeck & Ruprecht, 1933).

Gunn, D. M.
"Deutero-Isaiah and the Flood," *JBL* 94 (1975) 493–508.

Gunnel, A.
"Deuterojesaja och Jobsboken. En Jämförande Studie," *SEÅ* 54 (1989) 33–42.

Gunneweg, A. H. J.
Nehemia: Mit einer Zeittafel von A. Jepsen und einem Exkurs zur Topographie und Archäologie Jerusalems von M. Oeming (KAT 19/2; Gütersloh: Mohn, 1987).

Güterbock, H. G.
The Song of Ullikummi (New Haven: American Schools of Oriental Research, 1952).

Güterbock, H. G.
"Hittite Mythology," in S. N. Kramer, ed., *Mythologies of the Ancient World* (Garden City, N.Y.: Doubleday, 1961) 139–79.

Gutmann, J.
"The 'Second Commandment' and the Image in Judaism," in J. Gutmann, ed., *No Graven Images: Studies in Art and the Hebrew Bible* (New York: Ktav, 1971) 3–14.

Gyllenberg, R.
"Till julevangeliets exeges," *SEÅ* 5 (1940) 83–94.

Haag, E.
"Gott als Schöpfer und Erlöser in der Prophetie des Deuterojesaja," *TThZ* 85 (1976) 193–204.

Haag, E.
"Das Opfer des Gottesknechts (Is 53:10)," *TThZ* 86 (1977) 81–98.

Haag, E., ed.
Gott, der Einzige: Zur Entstehung des Monotheismus in Israel (QD 104; Freiburg: Herder, 1985).

Haag, H.
"Ebed Jahwe—Forschung 1948–1958," *BZ* n.s. 3 (1959) 174–204.

Haag, H.
"'Ich mache Heil und erschaffe Unheil' (Jes 45,7)," in J. Schreiner, ed., *Wort, Lied und Gottesspruch. Beiträge zu Psalmen und Propheten. FS J. Ziegler* (FB 2; Würzburg: Echter, 1972) 179–85.

Haag, H.
"Bund für das Volk und Licht für die Heiden (Jes 42:6)," *Didaskalia* 7 (1977) 3–14.

Haag, H.
Der Gottesknecht bei Deuterojesaja (EdF 233; Darmstadt: Wissenschaftliche Buchgesellschaft, 1985).

Haag, H.
"Der 'Gottesknecht' bei Deuterojesaja im Verständnis des Judentums," *Judaica* 41 (1985) 23–36.

Habel, N. C.
"The Form and Significance of the Call Narratives," *ZAW* 77 (1965) 297–323.

Habel, N. C.
"He Who Stretches out the Heavens," *CBQ* 34 (1972) 417–30.

Habel, N. C.
"Yahweh, Maker of Heaven and Earth: A Study in Tradition Criticism," *JBL* 91 (1972) 321–37.

Habel, N. C.
"Appeal to Ancient Tradition as a Literary Form," *ZAW* 88 (1976) 253–72.

Haenchen, E.
The Acts of the Apostles, trans. B. Noble et al. (Philadelphia: Westminster, 1971) [Eng. trans. of *Die Apostelgeschichte* (KEK 3; 12th ed.; Göttingen: Vandenhoeck & Ruprecht, 1959)].

Haldar, A.
The Notion of the Desert in Sumero-Accadian and West-Semitic Religions (UUÅ; Uppsala: Lundequist, 1950).

Hall, G.
"Origin of the Marriage Metaphor," *HS* 23 (1982) 161–71.

Haller, M.
"Die Kyros-Lieder Deuterojesajas," in H. Schmidt, ed., *Eucharistērion I: Studien zur Religion und Literatur des Alten und Neuen Testaments. FS H. Gunkel* (Göttingen: Vandenhoeck & Ruprecht, 1923) 261–77.

Halperin, S.
"Tragedy in the Bible," *Semitics* 7 (1980) 28–39.

Hamlin, J. E.
"The Meaning of 'Mountains and Hills' in Isa 41:14-16," *JNES* 13 (1954) 185–90.

Hammer, R., trans. and ed.
Sifre: A Tannaitic Commentary on the Book of Deuteronomy (YJS 24; New Haven: Yale Univ. Press, 1986).

Hamp, V.
"Das Hirtenmotiv im Alten Testament," in Professorenkollegium der Philosophisch-theologischen

Hochschule Freising, ed., *FS J. Kardinal Faulhaber* (Munich: Pfeiffer, 1949) 7–20.

Hanhart, R.
Text und Textgeschichte des Buches Judith (AAWG 109; Göttingen: Vandenhoeck & Ruprecht, 1979).

Hanhart, R.
Sacharja (BKAT XIV/7/3; Neukirchen-Vluyn: Neukirchener, 1992).

Hanson, P. D.
"Isaiah 52:7-10," *Int* 33 (1979) 389–94.

Hanson, P. D.
"War and Peace in the Hebrew Bible," *Int* 38 (1984) 341–62.

Haran, M.
Between Former Prophecies and New Prophecies: A Literary-Historical Study in the Group of Prophecies Isaiah XL–XLVIII (Jerusalem: Magnes, 1963) (Hebrew).

Haran, M.
"The Literary Structure and Chronical Framework of the Prophecies in Is XL–XLVIII," in *Congress Volume: Bonn 1962* (VTSup 9; Leiden: Brill, 1963) 127–55.

Haran, M.
"The Graded Numerical Sequence and the Phenomenon of 'Automatism' in Biblical Poetry," in *Congress Volume: Uppsala 1971* (VTSup 22; Leiden: Brill, 1971) 238-67.

Hardmeier, C.
"'Geschwiegen habe ich seit langem . . . wie die Gebärende schreie ich jetzt.' Zur Komposition und Geschichtstheologie von Jes 42,14–44,23," *WuD* n.s. 20 (1989) 155-79.

Hardmeier, C.
Prophetie im Streit vor dem Untergang Judas: erzählkommunikative Studien zur Entstehungssituation der Jesaja- und Jeremiaerzählungen in II Reg 18–20 und Jer 37–40 (BZAW 187; Berlin and New York: de Gruyter, 1990).

Harner, P. B.
"Creation Faith in Deutero-Isaiah," *VT* 17 (1967) 298–306.

Harner, P. B.
"The Salvation Oracle in Second Isaiah," *JBL* 88 (1969) 418-34.

Harner, P. B.
Grace and Law in Second Isaiah: "I Am the Lord" (ANETS 2; Lewiston, N.Y.: Mellen, 1988).

Harvey, J.
"La typologie de l'Exode dans les Psaumes," *ScEc* 15 (1963) 383–405.

Haughton, R.
"Prophecy in Exile," *Cross Currents* 39 (1989) 420-30.

Hausmann, J.
Israels Rest: Studien zum Selbstverständnis der nachexilischen Gemeinde (BWANT 124; Stuttgart: Kohlhammer, 1987).

Haussig, H. W., ed.,
Wörterbuch der Mythologie, vol. 1: *Götter und Mythen im Vorderen Orient* (Stuttgart: Klett, 1965).

Hayes, J. H.
"The Usage of Oracles Against Foreign Nations in Ancient Israel," *JBL* 87 (1968) 81–92.

Hayes, J. H., and J. M. Miller, eds.
Israelite and Judaean History (OTL; Philadelphia: Westminster, 1977).

Heichelheim, F. M.
Wirtschaftsgeschichte des Altertums: Vom Paläolithikum bis zur Völkerwanderung der Germanen, Slaven und Araber, 1 (Leiden: Sijthoff's Uitgeversmaatschappij, 1938).

Heidel, A.
The Gilgamesh Epic and Old Testament Parallels (2d ed.; Chicago: University of Chicago Press, 1949; reprint 1967).

Heinisch, P.
Personifikation und Hypostasen im AT und im Alten Orient (1921).

Heintz, J.-G.
"De l'absence de la statue divine au 'Dieu qui se cache' (Esaïe, 45/15): Aux origines d'un thème biblique," *RHPhR* 59 (1979) 427–37.

Helck, W.
"Bemerkungen zum Ritual des dramatische Ramesseumspapyrus," *Or* 23 (1954) 383–411.

Helck, W.
"Wenamun," *LÄ* 6 (1986) 1215–17.

Helck, W., ed.
Die Lehre des Dwj-Ḥtjj, Part 1 (KÄT; Wiesbaden: Harrassowitz, 1970).

Helck, W., E. Otto and W. Westendorf, eds.
Lexikon der Ägyptologie (7 vols.; Wiesbaden: Harrassowitz, 1975–92).

Held, M.
"Studies in Biblical Lexicography in Light of Akkadian," *ErIsr* 16 (1982) 76–85.

Henry, M.-L.
Glaubenskrise und Glaubensbewahrung in den Dichtungen der Jesaajaapokalypse: Versuch einer Deutung der literarischen Komposition von Jes 24–27 aus dem Zusammenhang ihrer religiösen Motivbildungen (BWANT 86; Stuttgart: Kohlhammer, 1966).

Hentschke, R.
Die Stellung der vorexilischen Propheten zum Kultus (BZAW 75; Berlin: Töpelmann, 1957).

Hentschke, R.
"Opfer II im Alten Testament," *RGG* 4 (3d ed., 1960) 1641–47.

Hermann, W.
"Das Aufleben des Mythos unter den Judäern während des babylonischen Zeitalters," *BN* 40 n.s. (1987) 97–129.

Hermisson, H.-J.
"Diskussionsworte bei Deuterojesaja," *EvTh* 31 (1971) 665–80.

Hermisson, H.-J.
"Jeremias Worte über Jojachin," in R. Albertz and H.-P. Müller, eds., *Werden und Wirken des Alten Testaments. FS C. Westermann* (Göttingen: Vanden

hoeck & Ruprecht; Neukirchen-Vluyn: Neukirchener, 1980) 252–70.

Hermisson, H.-J.
"Der Lohn des Knechtes," in J. Jeremias and L. Perlitt, eds., *Die Botschaft und die Boten. FS H. W. Wolff* (Neukirchen-Vluyn: Neukirchener, 1981) 269–87.

Hermisson, H.-J.
"Israel und der Gottesknecht bei Deuterojesaja," *ZThK* 79 (1982) 1–24.

Hermisson, H.-J.
"Voreiliger Abschied von den Gottesknechts-liedern," *ThR* 49 (1984) 209–22.

Hermisson, H.-J.
"Deuterojesaja-Probleme," *VF* 31 (1986) 53–84.

Hermisson, H.-J.
"Einheit und Komplexität Deuterojesajas. Probleme der Redaktionsgeschichte von Jes 40–55," in J. Vermeylen ed., *The Book of Isaiah* (BEThL 81; Leuven: Leuven Univ. Press and Peeters, 1989) 287–312.

Herntrich, V.
"Gottes Knecht und Gottes Reich nach Jesaja 40–55," *ZSTh* 16 (1939) 132–70.

Herodotus
Historien: Griechisch-deutsch. vol. 1: Books I–V (ed. J. Feix; 4th ed.; Munich and Zurich: Artemis, 1988).

Herodotus
Historia I–II (LCL; trans. and rev. A. D. Godley; Cambridge: Harvard Univ. Press; London: Heinemann, 1931, reprint 1996).

Herrmann, S.
Gesammelte Studien zur Geschichte und Theologie des Alten Testaments (ThBü 75; Munich: Kaiser, 1986).

Hertzberg, H. W.
"Die prophetische Kritik am Kult," *ThLZ* 75 (1950) 219–26; reprint in *Beiträge zur Traditionsgeschichte und Theologie des Alten Testament* (Göttingen: Vandenhoeck & Ruprecht, 1962) 81–90.

Herzog-Hauser, G.
"Tyche 1," PW 7 A2 (1948) 1643–89.

Hesiod
Theogony, trans. M. L. West (Oxford: Clarendon, 1966).

Hesiod
Theogony, in *Hesiod, the Homeric Hymns and Homerica* (LCL; trans. and rev. H. G. Evelyn-White; Cambridge: Harvard Univ. Press; London: Heinemann, 1914, reprint 1977) 78–155.

Hess, J. J.
"Beduinisches zum Alten und Neuen Testament," *ZAW* 35 (1915) 120–36.

Hessler, E.
"Gott der Schöpfer: Ein Beitrag zur Komposition und Theologie Deuterojesajas" (Th.D. diss.; Greifswald, 1960).

Hessler, E.
"Die Struktur der Bilder bei Deuterojesaja," *EvTh* 25 (1965) 349–69.

Hessler, E.
Das Heilsdrama: Der Weg zur Weltherrschaft Jahwes (Jes. 40–55) (RWTS 2; Hildesheim: Olms, 1988).

Hickman, R. M.
Ghostly Etiquette on the Classical Stage (ISCP 7; Iowa City: The Torch, 1938).

Hickmann, H. R. M.
"La trompette dans l'Égypte ancienne," *Annales du Service des antiquités de l'Égypte. Supplement* 1 (Le Caîre: Inst. franç. d'arch. orient., 1946).

Hickman, H. R. M.
Musikgeschichte in Bildern, vol. II/1: *Ägypten* (ed. H. Besseler and M. Schneider; Leipzig: VEB Deutscher Verlag für Musik, 1961).

Hillers, D. R.
"*Bĕrît ʿām*: 'Emancipation of the People,'" *JBL* 97 (1978) 175–82.

Hillyer, N.
"The Servant of God," *EvQ* 40 (1963) 143–60.

Himmelfarb, M.
"Heavenly Ascent and the Relationship of the Apocalypses and the *Hekhalot* Literature," *HUCA* 59 (1988) 73–100.

Hinz, W.
Darius und die Perser. Eine Kulturgeschichte der Achämeniden, 2 (Baden-Baden: Holle, 1979).

Hocherman, Y.
"Etymological Studies in Biblical Language," *Beth Mikra* 31 (1985/86) 220–26.

Hörig, M.
Dea Syria: Studien zur religiösen Tradition der Fruchtbarkeitsgöttin in Vorderasien (AOAT 208; Neukirchen-Vluyn: Neukirchener, 1979).

Hoffman, Y.
"The Root QRB as a Legal Term," *JNSL* (1982) 67–73.

Hoffman, Y.
"Prophetic Call and Prophetic Consciousness," *Tarbiz* 53 (1983/84) 169–86.

Hoffmann, A.
"Jahwe schleift Ringmauern—Jes 45:2aβ," in J. Schreiner, ed., *Wort, Lied und Gottesspruch,* vol. 2: *Beiträge zu Psalmen und Propheten. FS J. Ziegler* (FB 2; Würzburg: Echter, 1972) 187–95.

Hoffmeier, J. K.
"The Arm of God Versus the Arm of Pharaoh in the Exodus Narratives," *Bib* 67 (1986) 378–87.

Hofstetter, J.
Griechen in Persien: Prosopographie der griechen im persischen Reich vor Alexander (AMI Suppl. vol. 5; Berlin: Reimer, 1978).

Holladay, C. R., ed.
Fragments from Hellenistic Jewish Authors, vol. 2: *Poets, Ezekiel the Tragedian* (SBLTT 30; Atlanta: Scholars Press, 1989).

Holladay, W. L.
The Root Šûbh in the Old Testament: With Particular Reference to Its Usages in Covenantal Contexts (Leiden: Brill, 1958).

Holladay, W. L.
"Form and Word-Play in David's Lament over Saul and Jonathan," *VT* 20 (1970) 153–89.

Holladay, W. L.
Jeremiah: A Commentary on the Book of the Prophet Jeremiah (2 vols.; Hermeneia; Philadelphia and Minneapolis: Fortress, 1986–89).

Hollenberg, D. E.
"Nationalism and 'the Nations' in Isaiah XL–LV," *VT* 19 (1969) 23–36.

Holm-Nielsen, S.
"Religiöse Poesie des Spätjudentums," in W. Haase, ed. *ANRW* II/19/1. *Principat. Religion (Judentum: Allgemeines; Palästinisches Judentum)* (Berlin and New York: de Gruyter, 1979) 152–86.

Holmes, I. V.
"Study on Translation of Isaiah XL, 6-8," *ExpT* 75 (1963) 317–18.

Holmgren, F.
The Significance of the Word דבר *in the Theology of Second Isaiah* (Chappaqua, N.Y.: Biblical Scholars Press, 1957).

Holmgren, F.
"The Concept of Yahweh as *Goʾel* in Second Isaiah" (Th.D. diss., Union Theological Seminary, New York, 1963).

Holmgren, F.
"Chiastic Structure in Isaiah LI,1-11," *VT* 19 (1969) 196–201.

Hölscher, G.
Das Buch Hiob (HAT 17; 2d ed.; Tübingen: Mohr, 1952).

Homer
The Odyssey I (LCL; trans. and rev. A. T. Murray; Cambridge: Harvard Univ. Press; London: Heinemann, 1919; reprint 1976).

Homer
The Iliad I (LCL; trans. and rev. A. T. Murray; Cambridge: Harvard Univ. Press; London: Heinemann, 1924; reprint 1971).

Hoonacker, A. van
"Questions de critique littéraire et d'exégèse touchant les chapitres XL ss. d'Isaïe," *RB* 7 (1910) 557–72.

Hoppe, L. J.
"The School of Isaiah," *TBT* 23 (1985) 85–89.

Hoppe, L. J.
"Israel and the Nations," *TBT* 25 (1987) 289–90.

Hornung, E.
Geschichte als Fest: Zwei Vorträge als Geschichtsbild der frühen Menschheit. Sonderausgabe (Darmstadt: Wissenschaftliche Buchgesellschaft, 1966).

Hornung, E.
Ägyptische Unterweltsbücher (Zurich and Munich: Artemis, 1972).

Hornung, E.
"Jenseitsführer," *LÄ* 3 (1980) 246–49.

Horst, F.
"Die Visionsschilderungen der alttestamentlichen Propheten," *EvTh* 20 (1960) 193–205.

Hossfeld, F.-L.
Der Dekalog: Seine späten Fassungen, die originale Komposition und seine Vorstufen (OBO 45; Göttingen: Vandenhoeck & Ruprecht, 1982).

Hossfeld, F.-L.
"Du sollst dir kein Bild machen!" *TThZ* 98 (1989) 81–94.

Huey, F. B.
"Great Themes in Isaiah 40–66," *SWJT* 11 (1968) 45–58.

Humbach. H.
Die Gathas des Zarathustra, vol. 1 (Heidelberg: Carl Winter Universitätsverlag, 1959).

Humbert, P.
"À propos du 'serpent' (*bšn*) du mythe de Môt et Aleïn," *AfO* 11 (1936/37) 235–37.

Humbert, P.
"*Laetari et exultare* dans le vocabulaire religieux de l'Ancient Testament," *RHPhR* 22 (1942) 185–214.

Humbert, P.
La "Terouʿâ," Analyse d'un rite biblique (Neuchâtel: Secrétariat de l'Université, 1946).

Humbert, P.
"Le substantif *toʿēbā* et le verbe *tʿb* dans l'Ancien Testament," *ZAW* 72 (1960) 217–37.

Humbert, P.
"L'étymologie du substantif *toʿēbā*," in A. Kuschke, ed., *Verbannung und Heimkehr: Beiträge zur Geschichte und Theologie Israels im 6. und 5. Jahrhundert v. Chr. FS W. Rudolph* (Tübingen: Mohr, 1961) 157–60.

Humbert, P.
"Dieu fait sortir," *ThZ* 18 (1962) 357–61 and 433–36.

Humbert, P.
"Emploi et portée bibliques du verbe *yāṣar* et de ses dérivés substantifs," in J. Hempel and L. Rost, eds., *Von Ugarit nach Qumran: Beiträge zur alttestamentlichen und altorientalischen Forschung. FS O. Eissfeldt* (BZAW 77; 2d ed.; Berlin: Töpelmann, 1967) 82–88.

Hurvitz, A.
"The History of a Legal Formula cxv 6: *kōl ʾašer-ḥāpēṣ ʿaśāh* (Psalms cxv 3, cxxxv 6)," *VT* 32 (1982) 257–67.

Hyatt, J. P.
The Prophetic Criticism of Israelite Worship (Cincinnati: Hebrew Union College, 1963).

Ihromi
"Die Häufung der Verben des Jubelns in Zephanja iii 14f.,16-18: *rnn, rwʿ, śmḥ, ʿlz, śwś* und *gîl*," *VT* 33 (1983) 106–9.

Isbell, C. D.
"Initial *ʾalef-yod* Interchange and Selected Biblical Passages," *JNES* 37 (1978) 227–36.

Ishikawa, R.
"Der Hymnus im Alten Testament und seine kritische Funktion" (Th.D. diss., Munich, 1996).

Isser, S.
"Studies of Ancient Jewish Messianism: Scholarship and Apologetics," *JES* 25 (1988) 56–73.

Iwry, S.
"The Qumrân Isaiah and the End of the Dial of Ahaz," *BASOR* 147 (1957) 27–33.

Jacobs, B.
"Das Chvarnah—zum Stand der Forschung," MDOG 119 (1987) 215–48.

Jacobsen, T.
"An Ancient Mesopotamian Trial for Homicide," *Studia Biblica et Orientalia* 3 (1959) 130–50.

Jacobsen, T.
"Religious Drama in Ancient Mesopotamia," in H. Goedicke and J. J. M. Roberts, eds., *Unity and Diversity: Essays in the History, Literature and Religion of the Ancient Near East* (Baltimore: Johns Hopkins Univ. Press, 1975) 65–97.

Jacobson, H.
The Exagoge of Ezekiel (Cambridge: Cambridge Univ. Press, 1983).

Jahnow, H.
Das hebräische Leichenlied im Rahmen der Völkerdichtung (Giessen: Töpelmann, 1923).

Jakovljević, R.
"The Sense of Ebed Yahweh's Suffering," *CV* 30 (1987) 59–62.

Janowski, B.
Rettungsgewißheit und Epiphanie des Heils: Das Motiv der Hilfe Gottes 'am Morgen' im Alten Orient und im Alten Testament, vol. 1: *Alter Orient* (WMANT 59; Neukirchen-Vluyn: Neukirchener, 1989).

Janowski, B.
Sühne als Heilsgeschehen: Studien zur Sühnetheologie der Priesterschrift und zur Wurzel KPR im Alten Orient und im Alten Testament (WMANT 55; Neukirchen-Vluyn: Neukirchener, 1982).

Janowski, B.
"Er trug unsere Sünden. Jesaja 53 und die Dramatik der Stellvertretung," *ZThK* 90 (1993) 1–24; reprint (with updated literature and corrigenda) in B. Janowski, *Gottes Gegenwart in Israel* (Neukirchen-Vluyn: Neukirchener, 1993) 303–26, 337.

Janowski, B.
"JHWH der Richter—ein rettender Gott. Psalm 7 und das Motiv des Gottesgerichts," in *JBTh* 9: *Sünde und Gericht* (Neukirchen-Vluyn: Neukirchener, 1994) 53–85.

Janowski, B., and P. Stuhlmacher, eds.
Der leidende Gottesknecht: Jesaja 53 und seine Wirkungsgeschichte (FAT 14; Tübingen: Mohr, 1996).

Janzen, J. G.
"Another Look at *yaḥălîpû kōaḥ* in Isaiah xli 1," *VT* 33 (1983) 428–34.

Janzen, J. G.
"Rivers in the Desert of Abraham and Sarah and Zion (Isaiah 51:1-3)," *HAR* 10 (1986) 139–55.

Janzen, J. G.
"An Echo of the Shema in Isaiah 51:1-3," *JSOT* 43 (1989) 69–82.

Jastrow, M.
The Religion of Babylonia and Assyria (Boston: Athenaeum, 1898).

Jean, J. F., and J. Hoftijzer
Dictionnaire des inscriptions sémitiques de l'ouest (Leiden: Brill, 1965).

Jenni, E.
"Das Wort *ʿōlām* im Alten Testament," *ZAW* 64 (1953) 197–248; 65 (1953) 1–35.

Jenni, E.
"Die Rolle des Kyros bei Deuterojesaja," *ThZ* 10 (1954) 241–56.

Jenni, E.
Die politischen Voraussagen der Propheten (Zurich: Zwingli, 1956).

Jenni, E.
Das hebräische Piʿel: Syntaktisch-semasiologische Untersuchung einer Verbalform im Alten Testament (Zurich: EVZ, 1968).

Jenni, E.
"'Kommen' im theologischen Sprachgebrauch des Alten Testaments," in E. Jenni, J. J. Stamm and H. J. Stoebe, eds., *Wort–Gebot–Glaube: Beiträge zur Theologie des Alten Testaments. FS W. Eichrodt* (AThANT 59; Zurich: Zwingli, 1970) 251–61.

Jenni, E., and C. Westermann, eds.
Theologisches Handwörterbuch zum Alten Testament (2 vols.; 2d ed.; Munich: Kaiser; Zurich: Theologischer Verlag, 1971–76) [Eng. trans. *Theological Lexicon of the Old Testament,* trans. Mark E. Biddle (3 vols.; Peabody: Hendrickson, 1997)].

Jens, W., ed.
Die Bauformen der griechischen Tragödie (Beiheft zu Poetica 6; Munich: Fink, 1971).

Jensen, J.
"Yahweh's Plan in Isaiah and in the Rest of the Old Testament," *CBQ* 48 (1986) 443–55.

Jeppesen, K.
"The Cornerstone (Isa. 28:16) in Deutero-Isaianic Rereading of the Message of Isaiah," *StTh* 38 (1984) 93–99.

Jeppesen, K.
"From 'You, My Servant' to 'the Hand of the Lord Is with My Servants'. A Discussion of Is 40–66," *SJOT* 4/1 (1990) 113–29.

Jepsen, A.
"Die Begriffe des 'Erlösens' im Alten Testament," in *"Solange es 'Heute' heisst." FS R. Hermann* (Berlin: Evangelische Verlagsanstalt, 1957) 153–63.

Jepsen, A.
"צדק und צדקה im Alten Testament," in H. Graf Reventlow, ed., *Gottes Wort und Gottes Land. FS H.-W. Hertzberg* (Göttingen: Vandenhoeck & Ruprecht, 1965) 78–89.

Jepsen, A.
"Warum? Eine lexikalische und theologische Studie," in F. Maass, ed., *Das ferne und das nahe*

Wort. FS L. Rost (BZAW 105; Berlin: Töpelmann, 1967) 106–13.

Jeremias, Joachim
"ποιμήν," TDNT 6 (1968) 485–502 [Eng. trans. ThWNT 6 (1959) 484–501].

Jeremias, Jörg
Kultprophetie und Gerichtsverkündigung in der späten Königszeit Israels (WMANT 35; Neukirchen-Vluyn: Neukirchener, 1970).

Jeremias, Jörg
"Lade und Zion. Zur Entstehung der Ziontradition," in H. W. Wolff, ed., Probleme biblischer Theologie. FS G. von Rad (Munich: Kaiser, 1971) 183–98.

Jeremias, Jörg
"mišpāṭ im ersten Gottesknechtslied (Jes. xlii 1-4)," VT 22 (1972) 31–42.

Jeremias, Jörg
Die Reue Gottes: Aspekte alttestamentlicher Gottesvorstellung (BibS[N] 65; Neukirchen-Vluyn: Neukirchener, 1975).

Jeremias, Jörg
Theophanie: Zur Geschichte einer alttestamentlichen Gattung (WMANT 10; 2d ed.; Neukirchen-Vluyn: Neukirchener, 1976).

Jeremias, Jörg
"Zur Eschatologie des Hoseabuches," in J. Jeremias and L. Perlitt, eds., Die Botschaft und die Boten. FS H.W. Wolff (Neukirchen-Vluyn: Neukirchener, 1981) 217–33.

Jeremias, Jörg
Der Prophet Hosea (ATD 24/1; Göttingen: Vandenhoeck & Ruprecht, 1983).

Jeremias, Jörg
Das Königtum Gottes in den Psalmen (FRLANT 141; Göttingen: Vandenhoeck & Ruprecht, 1987).

Jerusalemer Bibel, die Heilige Schrift des alten und neuen Bundes
(ed. A. Arenhoevel, A. Deissler and A. Vögtle; Freiburg: Herder, 1968).

Joerden, K.
"Exkurs II, Rechts und links: Die Bedeutung der Parodoi," in W. Jens, ed., Die Bauformen der griechischen Tragödie (Beiheft zu Poetica 6; Munich: Fink, 1971) 409–10.

Joerden, K.
"Zur Bedeutung des Ausser- und Hinterszenischen," in W. Jens, ed., Die Bauformen der griechischen Tragödie (Beiheft zu Poetica 6; Munich: Fink, 1971) 369–407.

Jogeling, B.
"Lākēn dans l'Ancien Testament," OTS 21 (1981) 190–200.

Johns, A. F.
"A Note on Isaiah 45:9," AUSS 1 (1963) 62–64.

Johnson, A. R.
"The Primary Meaning of √‏נאל‏," in Congress Volume: Copenhagen 1953 (VTSup 1; Leiden Brill, 1953) 67–77.

Jones, G. H.
"Abraham and Cyrus: Type and Anti-Type?" VT 22 (1972) 304–19.

Josephus, F.
Antiquitates I–VI, in Josephus vol. IV–IX (LCL; trans. and rev. H. St. J. Thackeray, R. Marcus, A. Wikgren, and L. H. Feldman; Cambridge: Harvard Univ. Press; London: Heinemann, 1930, reprint 1967).

Joüon, P., and T. Muraoka
A Grammar of Biblical Hebrew, vol. 2: Part Three: Syntax (SubBi 14/II; Rome: Pontifical Biblical Institute, 1991).

Junge, F.
"Zur Fehldatierung des sogenannten Denkmals memphitischer Theologie oder: Der Beitrag der ägyptischen Theologie zur Geistesgeschichte der Spätzeit," MDAIK 29/2 (1973) 195–204.

Junker, H.
"Der Sinn der sogenannten Ebed-Jahwe-Stücke," TThZ 79 (1970) 1–12.

Jürgens, H.
Pompa Diaboli: Die lateinischen Kirchenväter und das antike Theater (TBAW 46; Stuttgart: Kohlhammer, 1972).

Kahmann, J.
"Die Heilszukunft in ihrer Beziehung zur Heilsgeschichte nach Isaiah 40–55," Bib 32 (1951) 65–172.

Kaiser, O.
Der königliche Knecht: Eine Traditionsgeschichtlich-exegetische Studie über die Ebed-Jahwe-Lieder bei Deuterojesaja (FRLANT 70; Göttingen: Vandenhoeck & Ruprecht, 1959).

Kaiser, O.
Die mythische Bedeutung des Meeres in Ägypten, Ugarit und Israel (BZAW 78; 3d ed.; Berlin: Töpelmann, 1962).

Kaiser, O.
Isaiah 13–39, trans. R. A. Wilson (OTL; Philadelphia: Westminster, 1974) [Eng. trans. of Der Prophet Jesaja: Kapitel 13–39 (ATD 18; Göttingen: Vandenhoeck & Ruprecht, 1973)].

Kaiser, O.
Introduction to the Old Testament, trans. J. Sturdy (Minneapolis: Augsburg, 1975) [Eng. trans. of Einleitung in das Alte Testament (4th ed.; Gütersloh: Mohn, 1974)].

Kaiser, O.
"Der geknickte Rohrstab: Zum geschichtlichen Hintergrund der Überlieferung und Weiterbildung der prophetischen Ägyptensprüche im 5. Jahrhundert," in Von der Gegenwartsbedeutung des Alten Testaments: Gesammelte Studien (ed. V. Fritz et al.; Göttingen: Vandenhoeck & Ruprecht, 1984) 181–88.

Kaiser, O.
"Zwischen den Fronten: Palästina in der Auseinandersetzung zwischen Perserreich und Ägypten in der ersten Hälfte des 4. Jahrhunderts," in Von der

Gegenwartsbedeutung des Alten Testament: Gesammelte Studien (ed. V. Fritz et al.; Göttingen: Vandenhoeck & Ruprecht, 1984) 189–98.

Kaiser, O., ed.
Texte aus der Umwelt des Alten Testaments (vols. 1–3; Gütersloh: Mohn, 1982–97).

Kaiser, O., and E. Lohse
Death and Life, trans. J. E. Steely (Nashville: Abingdon, 1981) [Eng. trans. of *Tod und Leben* (Stuttgart: Kohlhammer, 1977)].

Kaiser, W. C.
"The Promise to David in Psalm 16 and Its Application in Acts 2:25-33 and 13:32-37," *JETS* 23 (1980) 219–29.

Kaiser, W. C.
"The Unfailing Kindnesses Promised to David: Isaiah 55:3," *JSOT* 45 (1989) 91–98.

Kapelrud, A. S.
"Levde Deuterojesaja i Judea?" *NTT* 61 (1960) 23–27.

Kapelrud, A. S.
Et folk paa hjemford: 'Troestprofeten'–den annen Jesaja–og hans budskap (Oslo: Universitetsforlaget, 1964).

Kapelrud, A. S.
The Violent Goddess: Anat in the Ras Shamra Texts (Scandinavian University Books; Oslo: Universitätsverlag, 1969)

Kapelrud, A. S.
"The Identity of the Suffering Servant," in H. Goedicke, ed., *Near Eastern Studies in Honor of W. F. Albright* (Baltimore: Johns Hopkins Univ. Press, 1971) 307–14.

Kapelrud, A. S.
"Second Isaiah and the Suffering Servant," in J. Amusin et al., eds., *Hommages à A. Dupont-Sommer* (Paris: Maisonneuve, 1971) 297–303.

Kapelrud, A. S.
"The Main Concern of Second Isaiah," *VT* 32 (1982) 50–58.

Kapolny, P.
"Demotische Chronik," *LÄ* 1 (1975) 1056–60.

Kautzsch, E., ed.
Gesenius' Hebrew Grammar, trans. A. E. Cowley (2d ed.; Oxford: Clarendon, 1910) [Eng. trans. of *Wilhelm Gesenius' Hebräische Grammatik* (26th rev. ed.; Leipzig: Vogel, 1896)].

Kautzsch, E.
Die Apokryphen und Pseudepigraphen des Alten Testament (1900; reprint Tübingen: Mohr, 1921).

Keane, D. P.
"Creation Faith in Second Isaiah," *DunRev* 11 (1971) 40–76.

Kedar, B.
"Netherworld," *EncJud* 12 (1971) 997–98.

Kedar-Klopfstein, B.
"Divergent Hebrew Readings in Jerome's Isaiah," *Textus* 4 (1964) 176–210.

Keel, O.
The Symbolism of the Biblical World, trans. T. J. Hal-lett (New York: Seabury, 1978) [Eng. trans. of *Die Welt der altorientalischen Bildsymbolik und das Alte Testament: Am Beispiel der Psalmen* (2d ed.; Zurich and Cologne: Benziger; Neukirchen-Vluyn: Neukirchener, 1977).

Keel, O.
Das Böcklein in der Milch seiner Mutter und Verwandtes: Im Lichte eines altorientalischen Bildmotivs (OBO 33; Fribourg: Universitätsverlag; Göttingen: Vandenhoeck & Ruprecht, 1980).

Keel, O.
"Jahwe in der Rolle der Muttergottheit," *Orientierung* 53 (1989) 89–92.

Keel, O., ed.
Monotheismus im Alten Israel und seiner Umwelt (Fribourg: Schweizer Katholisches Bibelwerk, 1980).

Keel, O., and C. Uehlinger
Gods, Goddesses, and Images of God in Ancient Israel (Minneapolis: Fortress, 1998) [Eng. trans. of *Göttinnen, Götter und Gottessymbole: Neue Erkenntnisse zur Religionsgeschichte Kanaans und Israels aufgrund bislang unerschlossener ikonographischer Quellen* (QD 134; Freiburg i. Br.: Herder, 1992)].

Kees, H.
Totenglauben und Jenseitsvorstellungen der Alten Ägypter (Leipzig: Hinrich, 1926).

Keller, C. A.
"Die theologische Bewältigung der geschichtlichen Wirklichkeit in der Prophetie Nahums," *VT* 22 (1972) 399–419.

Kellermann, D.
"ʾāšām in Ugarit?" *ZAW* 76 (1964) 319–22.

Kellermann, U.
Nehemia: Quellenüberlieferung und Geschichte (BZAW 102; Berlin: Töpelmann, 1967).

Kellermann, U.
"Zum traditionsgeschichtlichen Problem des stellvertretenden Sühnetodes in 2 Makk 7:37f," *BN* 13 (1980) 63–83.

Kelso, J. L.
The Ceramic Vocabulary of the Old Testament (New Haven: American Schools of Oriental Research, 1948).

Kennedy, J. M.
"The Social Background of Early Israel's Rejection of Cultic Images: A Proposal," *BTB* 17 (1987) 138–44.

Kern, O.
"Demeter," *PW* 4/2 (1958) 2713–64.

Kerrn-Lillesø, E.
"Stirnband und Diademe," *LÄ* 6 (1986) 45–49.

Kessler, R.
"Das hebräische Schuldenwesen; Terminologie und Metaphorik," *WuD* n.s. 20 (1989) 181–95.

Kessler, W.
"Zur Auslegung von Jesaja 56–66," *ThLZ* 81 (1956) 336–38.

Kida, K.
"Second Isaiah and the Suffering Servant—A New Proposal for a Solution," *AJBI* 5 (1979) 45–66.

Kida, K.
"The Prophet, the Servant and Cyrus in the Prophecies of Second Isaiah," *AJBI* 16 (1990) 3–29.

Kiesow, K.
Exodusgesetze im Jesajabuch. Literarkritische und motivgeschichtliche Analysen (OBO 24; Fribourg: Universitätsverlag; Göttingen: Vandenhoeck & Ruprecht, 1979) 4–15.

Kiesow, K.
"Die Gottesknechtlieder—Israels Auftrag für die Menschheit," *BLit* 63 (1990) 156–59.

Kilian, R.
"Ps 22 und das priesterliche Heilsorakel," *BZ* n.s. 12 (1968) 172–85.

Kim, J. C.
"Das Verhältnis Jahwes zu den anderen Göttern in Deuterojesaja" (Th.D. diss., Heidelberg, 1962).

Kirchschläger, W.
"Die Schöpfungstheologie des Deuterojesaja," *BLit* 49 (1976) 407–22.

Kirk, G. S., J. E. Raven, and M. Schofield
The Presocratic Philosophers: A Critical History with a Selection of Texts (2d. ed.; Cambridge: Cambridge Univ. Press, 1983).

Kisch, G.
Pseudo-Philo's Liber Antiquitatum Biblicarum (Notre Dame, Ind.: Univ. of Notre Dame Press, 1949).

Kittel, G., and G. Friedrich, eds.
Theological Dictionary of the New Testament, trans. G. W. Bromiley (10 vols.; Grand Rapids: Eerdmans, 1964–76) [Eng. trans. of *Theologisches Wörterbuch zum Neuen Testament* (9 vols.; Stuttgart: Kohlhammer, 1933–73)].

Kittel, R.
"Cyrus und Deuterojesaja," *ZAW* 18 (1898) 149–62.

Kittel, R.
"εἰκών," *TDNT* 2 (1964) 381–97 [Eng. trans. of *ThWNT* 2 (1960) 378–96].

Klein, H.
"Der Beweis der Einzigkeit Jahwes bei Deuterojesaja," *VT* 35 (1985) 267–73.

Klein, M.
Targumic Manuscripts in the Cambridge Genizah Collections (CULGS 8; Cambridge: Cambridge Univ. Press, 1992).

Klein, R. W.
"Going Home—A Theology of Second Isaiah," *CurTM* 5 (1978) 198–210.

Kleinig, J. W.
The Lord's Song: The Basis, Function and Significance of Choral Music in Chronicles (JSOTSup 156; Sheffield: JSOT Press, 1993).

Klopfenstein, M. A.
Die Lüge nach dem Alten Testament: Ihr Begriff, ihre Bedeutung und ihre Beurteilung (Zurich and Frankfurt: Gotthelf, 1964).

Klopfenstein, M. A.
Scham und Schande nach dem Alten Testament. Eine begriffsgeschichtliche Untersuchung zu den hebräischen Wurzeln bôš, klm und ḥpr (AThANT 62; Zurich: Theologischer Verlag, 1972).

Klopfenstein, M. A.
"Alttestamentliche Themen in der neueren Forschung," *ThR* 53 (1988) 332–53.

Kloppers, M. H. O.
"Die rol en funksie van die 'vreemdeling' (*gēr*) in die latere profete (Skrifprofete)," *NGTT* 30 (1989) 367–75.

Knauf, E. A.
Ismael: Untersuchungen zur Geschichte Palästinas und Nordarabiens im 1. Jahrtausend v. Chr. (ADPV; Wiesbaden: Harrassowitz, 1985; 2d ed., 1989).

Knauf, E. A.
"Zur Herkunft und Sozialgeschichte Israels: Das Böckchen in der Milch seiner Mutter," *Bib* 69 (1988) 153–69.

Knauf, E. A.
Midian: Untersuchungen zur Geschichte Palastinas und Nordarabiens am Ende des 2. Jahrtausend v. Chr. (ADPV; Wiesbaden: Harrassowitz, 1988).

Knierim, R.
Die Hauptbegriffe für Sünde im Alten Testament (Gütersloh: Mohn, 1965; 2d ed., 1967).

Knight, G. A. F.
Exile and After: Studies in Isaiah 40–55 (WCB 3/55; London: United Society for Christian Literature, Lutterworth, 1966).

Kniper, K.
"De Ezechiele poeta Judaeo," *Mnemosyne* 28 (1900) 237–80.

Koch, H.
Die religiösen Verhältnisse der Dareioszeit: Untersuchungen anhand der Elamitischen Persepolis-täfelchen, Göttinger Orientforschungen III. Series: Iranica, vol. 4 (Wiesbaden: Harrassowitz, 1977).

Koch, K.
"Zur Geschichte der Erwählungsvorstellung in Israel," *ZAW* 67 (1956) 205–26.

Koch, K.
"Tempeleinlassliturgien und Dekaloge," in R. Rendtorff and K. Koch, eds., *Studien zur Theologie der alttestamentlichen Überlieferungen. FS G. von Rad* (Neukirchen-Vluyn: Neukirchener, 1961) 45–60.

Koch, K.
"Messias und Sündenvergebung in Jesaja 53—Targum. Ein Beitrag zur Praxis der aramäischen Bibelübersetzung," *JSJ* 3 (1972) 117–48.

Koch, K.
"Die Stellung des Kyros im Geschichtsbild Deuterojesajas und ihre überlieferungsgeschichtliche Verankerung," *ZAW* 84 (1972) 352–56.

Koch, K.
"Šaddaj: Zum Verhältnis zwischen israelitischer Monolatrie und nordwest-semitischem Polytheismus," *VT* 26 (1976) 299–332.

Koch, K.
"Weltordnung und Reichsidee im alten Iran," in P.

Frei and K. Koch, *Reichsidee und Reichsorganisation im Perserreich* (OBO 55; Freiburg: Universitätsverlag; Göttingen: Vandenhoeck & Ruprecht, 2d expanded ed., 1996) 133–325.

Koch, K.
"Wind und Zeit als Konstituenten des Kosmos in phönikischer Mythologie und spätalttestamentlichen Texten," in M. Dietrich and O. Loretz, eds., *Mesopotamica–Ugaritica–Biblica. FS K. Bergerhof* (AOAT 232; Kevelaer: Butzon und Bercker; Neukirchen-Vluyn: Neukirchener, 1993).

Koenen, K.
"Zur Aktualisierung eines Deuterojesajawortes in Jes 58,8," *BZ* 33 (1989) 255–9.

Koenig, J.
"L'allusion inexpliquée au roseau et à la mèche (Isaïe 42:3)," *VT* 18 (1968) 159–72.

Koenig, J.
"Réouverture du débat sur la Première Main rédactionelle du rouleau ancien d'Isaïe de Qumrân (I Q Isᵃ) en 40:7-8," *RevQ* 11 (1983) 219–37.

Koester, H.
"*ΝΟΜΟΣ ΦΥΣΕΟΣ*: The Concept of Natural Law in Greek Thought," in J. Neusner, ed., *Religions in Antiquity: FS E. Goodenough* (SHR 14; Leiden: Brill, 1968) 521–41.

Koester, H.
"τόπος," *TDNT* 8 (1972) 187–208 [Eng. trans. of *ThWNT* 8 (1969) 187–208].

Koester, H.
Introduction to the New Testament, vol. 1: *History, Culture, and Religion of the Hellenistic Age;* vol. 2: *History and Literature of Early Christianity* (Hermeneia: Foundations and Facets; Philadelphia: Fortress, 1982; vol. 1, 2d ed.; New York: de Gruyter, 1995) [Eng. trans. of *Einführung in das NT* (Berlin and New York: de Gruyter, 1980)].

Koester, H.
Ancient Christian Gospels: Their History and Development (Philadelphia: Trinity Press International, 1990).

Köhler, L.
"Die Offenbarungsformel 'Fürchte dich nicht' im Alten Testament," *SThZ* 36 (1919) 33–39.

Köhler, L.
Deuterojesaja (Jes 40–55) stilkritisch untersucht (BZAW 37; Giessen: Töpelmann, 1923).

Köhler, L.
"Hebräische Vokabeln I," *ZAW* 54 (1936) 287–93.

Köhler, L.
"Hebräische Vokabeln II," *ZAW* 55 (1937) 163–74.

Köhler, L.
"Alttestamentliche Wortforschung Schᵉʾōl," *ThZ* 2 (1946) 71–74.

Köhler, L.
"Justice in the Gate," in *Hebrew Man,* trans. P. R. Ackroyd (New York: Abingdon, 1956) 127–50 [Eng. trans. of "Die hebräische Rechtsgemeinde," in *Der hebräische Mensch. Eine Skizze. Mit einem*

Anhang: Die hebräische Rechtsgemeinde (Tübingen: Mohr, 1953) 143–71].

Köhler, L.
"Problems in the Study of the Language of the Old Testament," *JSS* 1 (1956) 3–24, esp. 9 and 19–20.

Köhler, L., et al.
The Hebrew and Aramaic Lexicon of the Old Testament, trans. and ed. M. E. J. Richardson et al. (3 vols. New York: Brill, 1994) [Eng. trans. of *Hebräisches und aramäisches Lexikon zum Alten Testament* (3d ed.; 5 vols. plus supp.; Leiden: Brill, 1967–96)].

Köhne, J.
"Die Schrift Tertullians 'Über die Schauspiele' in kultur- und religionsgeschichtlicher Beleuchtung" (Th.D. diss., Breslau, 1929).

König, F. E.
Historisch-Kritisches Lehrgebäude der hebräischen Sprache (3 vols.; Leipzig: Hinrichs, 1881–97).

Kooij, A. van der
Die alten Textzeugen des Jesajabuches: Ein Beitrag zur Textgeschichte des Alten Testaments (OBO 35; Göttingen: Vandenhoeck & Ruprecht, 1981).

Koole, J. L.
"Zu Jes 45:9ff," *Studia Semitica Neerlandica* 16 (1974) 170–75.

Koran, Der
(trans. R. Paret; Stuttgart: Kohlhammer, 1962).

Koran, Der: arabisch-deutsch
(6 vols.; Übersetzung und wissenschaftlicher Kommentar 5; trans. and ed. A. Th. Khoury; Gütersloh: Mohn, 1994).

Kosmala, H.
"Form and Structure in Ancient Hebrew Poetry (A New Approach)," *VT* 14 (1964) 423–45.

Kosmala, H.
"Form and Structure in Ancient Hebrew Poetry (Continued)," *VT* 16 (1966) 152–80.

Kraeling, E. G.
The Brooklyn Museum Aramaic Papyri: New Documents of the Fifth Century B.C. from the Jewish Colony at Elephantine (New Haven: Yale Univ. Press, 1953).

Kraft, R. A.
"Barnabas' Isaiah Text and the 'Testimony Book' Hypothesis," *JBL* 79 (1960) 336–50.

Kratz, R. G.
Kyros im Deuterojesaja-Buch. Redaktionsgeschichtliche Untersuchungen zu Entstehung und Theologie von Jes 40–55 (FAT 1; Tübingen: Mohr, 1991).

Kraus, G., and G. Müller, eds.
Theologische Realenzyklopädie (24 vols.; Berlin and New York: de Gruyter, 1977–1994).

Kraus, H.-J.
Die Klagelieder (BKAT 20; Neukirchen-Vluyn: Neukirchener, 1968).

Kraus, H.-J.
"Hören und Sehen in der althebräischen Tradition," *StGen* 19 (1966) 115–23; reprint in H.-J. Kraus, *Biblisch-theologische Aufsätze* (Neukirchen-Vluyn: Neukirchener, 1972) 84–101.

Kraus, H.-J.
Psalms 1–59 and *Psalms 60–150,* trans. H. C. Oswald (Continental Commentary; Minneapolis: Augsburg, 1988–89) [Eng. trans. of *Psalmen* (BKAT 15/1-2; 5th ed.; Neukirchen-Vluyn: Neukirchener, 1978)].

Kraus, H.-J.
Theology of the Psalms, trans. K. Crim (Continental Commentary; Minneapolis: Augsburg, 1986) [Eng. trans. of *Theologie der Psalmen* (BKAT 15/3; Neukirchen-Vluyn: Neukirchener, 1979)].

Kremer, G.
"Die Struktur des Tragödienschlusses," in W. Jens, ed., *Die Bauformen der griechischen Tragödie* (Beiheft zu Poetica 6; Munich: Fink, 1971) 117–41.

Krinetzki, L.
"Zur Stilistik von Jes 40:1-8," *BZ* n.s. 16 (1972) 54–69.

Krüger, T.
Geschichtskonzepte im Ezechielbuch (BZAW 180; Berlin and New York: de Gruyter, 1989).

Krüger, T.
"Theologische Gegenwartsdeutung im Kohelet-Buch" (diss., Munich, 1991).

Krüger, T.
"Psalm 90 und die Vergänglichkeit des Menschen," *Bib* 75 (1994) 191–219.

Kselman, J. S.
"The ABCD Pattern: Further Examples," *VT* 32 (1982) 224–29.

Kugel, J.
The Idea of Biblical Poetry: Parallelism and Its History (New Haven and London: Yale Univ. Press, 1981).

Kuhl, C.
"Schreibereigentümlichkeiten; Bemerkungen zur Jesajarolle (DSIa)," *VT* 2 (1952) 307–33.

Kuhrt, A.
"The Cyrus Cylinder and Achaemenid Imperial Policy," *JSOT* 25 (1983) 83–97.

Kuschke, A.
"Tempel," *BRL* (HAT 1/1; 2d ed., 1977) 333–42.

Kutsch, E.
Salbung als Rechtsakt im Alten Testament und im Alten Orient (BZAW 87; Berlin: Töpelmann, 1963).

Kutsch, E.
Sein Leiden und Tod–unser Heil: Eine Auslegung von Jesaja 52,13–53,12, (BibS[N] 52; Neukirchen-Vluyn: Neukirchener, 1967).

Kutsch, E.
"Ich will meinen Geist ausgiessen auf deine Kinder," in R. Riess and D. Stollberg, eds., *Das Wort, das weiter wirkt. FS K. Frör* (Munich: Kaiser, 1970) 122–33.

Kutscher, E. Y.
The Language and Linguistic Background of the Isaiah Scroll (1QIsaᵃ) (STDJ 6; Leiden: Brill, 1974).

Kuyper, L. J.
"The Meaning of חסדו Isa. XL 6," *VT* 13 (1963) 489–92.

Laato, A.
"The Composition of Isaiah 40–55," *JBL* 109 (1990) 207–28.

Laato, A.
The Servant of YHWH and Cyrus: A Reinterpretation of the Exilic Messianic Programme in Isaiah 40–55 (ConBOT 35; Stockholm: Almqvist & Wiksell International, 1992).

Labuschagne, C. J.
The Incomparability of Yahweh in the Old Testament (POS 5; Leiden: Brill, 1966).

Labuschagne, C. J.
"The Particles הֵן and הִנֵּה," in *Syntax and Meaning: Studies in Hebrew Syntax and Biblical Exegesis,* OTS 15 (1973) 1–14.

Lack, R.
"La strutturazione di Isaia 40–55," *ScC* 101 (1973) 43–58.

Lack, R.
La symbolique du livre d'Isaïe: Essai sur l'image littéraire comme élément de structuration (AnBib 59; Rome: Biblical Institute Press, 1973).

Lambert, W. G.
"Lier et délier: L'expression de la totalité par l'opposition de deux contraires," *VivPen* 3 (1943/44) 91–103.

Lambert, W. G.
"Le Livre d'Isaïe parle-t-il des Chinois?" *NRTh* 85 (1953) 965–72.

Lambert, W. G.
Babylonian Wisdom Literature (Oxford: Clarendon, 1960).

Lambert, W. G.
"The Sultantepe Tablets IX: The Birdcall Text," *AnSt* 20 (1970) 111–17.

Lambert, W. G., and P. Walcot
"A New Babylonian Theogony and Hesiod," *Kadmos* 4 (1965) 64–72.

Lampl, P.
Cities and Planning in the Ancient Near East (Planning and Cities 2; New York: Braziller, 1968).

Landy, F.
"The Construction of the Subject and the Symbolic Order: A Reading of the Last Three Suffering Servant Songs," in P. R. Davies and D. J. A. Clines, eds., *Among the Prophets* (JSOTSup 144; Sheffield: JSOT Press, 1993) 60–71.

Lang, B.
"Die Geburt der jüdischen Hoffnungstheologie," *BK* 33 (1978) 74–78.

Lang, B.
"Glaubensbekenntnisse im Alten und Neuen Testament," *Concilium* (German ed.) 14 (1978) 499–503.

Lang, B., ed.
Der einzige Gott: Die Geburt des biblischen Monotheismus (Munich: Kösel, 1981).

Lang, B.
"Jahwe allein! Ursprung und Gestalt des biblischen Monotheismus," *Concilium* (German ed.) 21/1 (1985) 30–35.

Langdon, S.
Die neubabylonischen Königsinschriften (trans. R. Zehnpfund; Leipzig: Hinrichs, 1912).

Lapointe, R.
"The Divine Monologue as a Channel of Revelation," *CBQ* 32 (1970) 161–81.

Laperroussaz, E.-M.
Le Testament de Moïse (Semitica 19; Paris: Adrien-Maisonneuve, 1970).

Lasch, R.
"Pfeifen und Dämonenglaube," *ARW* 18 (1915) 589–92.

Latacz, J.
Einführung in die griechische Tragödie (Göttingen: Vandenhoeck & Ruprecht, 1993).

Lauffer, S.
Alexander der Große: Mit einem Literaturnachtrag von K. Brodersen (3d ed.; Munich: DeutscherTaschenbuch Verlag, 1993).

Lauha, A.
"Der Bund des Volkes: Ein Aspekt der deuterojesajanischen Missionstheologie," in H. Donner, R. Hanhart, and R. Smend, eds., *Beiträge zur alttestamentlichen Theologie. FS W. Zimmerli* (Göttingen: Vandenhoeck & Ruprecht, 1977) 257–61.

Leclant, J.
"Shabaka," *LÄ* 5 (1984) 495–513.

Leene, H.
"Juda en de heilige stad in Jesaja 48:1-2: Verkenningen in een stroomgebied," in M. Boertien, ed., *Proeven van oudtestamentisch onderzoek: ter gelegenheid van het afscheid van Prof. Dr. M. A. Beek* (Amsterdam: Univ. of Amsterdam, 1974) 80–92.

Leene, H.
"Universalism or Nationalism? Isaiah XLV 9-13 and its Context," *BTFT* 35 (1974) 309–34.

Leene, H.
"Isaiah 46:8—Summons to be Human?" *JSOT* 30 (1984) 111–21.

Leene, H.
De Vroegere en de Nieuwe Dingen bij Deuterojesaja: The Former and the New Things in Deutero-Isaiah (Amsterdam: Free Univ. Press, 1987).

Lesky, A.
A History of Greek Literature, trans. J. Willis (London: Methuen, 1966) and with C. de Heer (New York: Thomas Y. Crowell, 1966) [Eng. trans. of the 2d ed. of *Geschichte der griechischen Literatur* (3d ed.; Bern and Munich: Franke, 1971)].

Levenson, J. D.
Creation and the Persistence of Evil (San Francisco: Harper & Row, 1988).

Levine, B. A.
"The Descriptive Tabernacle Texts of the Pentateuch," *JAOS* 85 (1965) 307–18.

Lewy, J.
"The Feast of the 14th Day of Adar," *HUCA* 14 (1939) 127–51.

Lichtenstein, A.
"The Cyrus Cylinder and Isaiah 40–50," *DD* 16 (1987/88) 164–69.

Liedke, G.
Gestalt und Bezeichnung alttestamentlicher Rechtssätze: Eine formgeschichtlich-terminologische Studie (WMANT 39; Neukirchen-Vluyn: Neukirchener, 1971).

Limburg, J.
"Isaiah 40:1-11," *Int* 29 (1975) 406–11.

Lind, M. C.
"Monotheism, Power, and Justice: A Study in Isaiah 40–55," *CBQ* 46 (1984) 432–46.

Lindars, B.
"Good Tidings to Zion: Interpreting Deutero-Isaiah Today," *BJRL* 68 (1986) 473–97.

Lindblom, J.
"Die Ebed-Jahwe Orakel in der neuentdeckten Jesajahandschrift (DSIa)," *ZAW* 63 (1951) 235–48.

Lindblom, J.
The Servant Songs in Deutero-Isaiah: A New Attempt to Solve an Old Problem (LUÅ 47/5; Lund: Gleerup, 1951).

Lindsey, F. D.
"The Call of the Servant in Isaiah 42:1-9," *BSac* 139 (1982) 12–31.

Lindsey, F. D.
"The Career of the Servant in Isaiah 52:13—53:12," *BSac* 139 (1982) 312–29.

Lindsey, F. D.
"The Career of the Servant in Isaiah 52:13—53:12 (Concluded)," *BSac* 140 (1983) 21–39.

Lipiński, E.
La royauté de Jahwé dans la poésie et le culte de l'Ancien Israël (Brussels: Palais des Academiëns, 1965).

Lipiński, E.
"On the Comparison in Isaiah lv 10," *VT* 23 (1973) 246–47.

Lipiński, E.
"*skn* et *sgn* dans le sémitique occidental du nord," *UF* 5 (1973) 191–207.

Littmann, E.
Über die Abfassungszeit des Tritojesaja (Freiburg, Leipzig, and Tübingen: Mohr, 1899).

Litwak, K. D.
"The Use of Quotations from Isaiah 52:13—53:12 in the New Testament," *JETS* 26 (1983) 385–94.

Liverani, M.
"Contrasti e confluenze di concezioni politice nell'età di El-Amarna," *RA* 1 (1967) 1–18.

Loewenstamm, S. E.
"The Hebrew root חרש in the light of the Ugarit texts," *JJS* 10 (1959) 63–65.

Lohfink, N.
"Die deuteronomistische Darstellung des Übergangs der Führung Israels von Mose auf Josua: Ein Beitrag zur alttestamentlichen Theologie des Amtes," *Schol.* 37 (1962) 32–44.

Lohfink, N.
Das Hauptgebot: Eine Untersuchung literarischer Ein-leitungsfragen zu Dtn 5–11 (AnBib 20; Rome: Pontifical Biblical Institute, 1963).

Lohfink, N.
Die Landverheißung als Eid: Eine Studie zu Gen. 15 (SBS 28; Stuttgart: Katholisches Bibelwerk, 1967).

Lohfink, N.
"Beobachtungen zur Geschichte des Ausdrucks עם יהוה," in H. W. Wolff, ed., *Probleme biblischer Theologie: FS G. von Rad* (Munich: Kaiser, 1971) 275–305.

Lohfink, N.
"'Israel' in Jes 49:3," in J. Schreiner, ed., *Wort, Lied und Gottesspruch: Beiträge zu Psalmen und Propheten. FS J. Ziegler* (FB 2; Würzburg: Echter, 1972) 217–29.

Lohfink, N.
"'Ich bin Jahwe, dein Arzt': Gott, Gesellschaft und menschliche Gesundheit in der Theologie einer nachexilischen Pentateuchbearbeitung (Ex 15,25b.26)," in H. Merklein and E. Zenger, eds., *"Ich will euer Gott werden": Beispiele biblischen Redens von Gott* (SBS 100; Stuttgart: Katholisches Bibelwerk, 1981) 11–73.

Lohfink, N.
"Das Deuteronomium: Jahwegesetz oder Mosegesetz?" *ThPh* 65 (1990) 387–91.

Löhr, M.
Räucheropfer im Alten Testament (SKG.G 4/4; Halle: Niemeyer, 1927).

Lohse, E., ed.
Die Texte aus Qumran: Hebräisch und Deutsch mit masoretischer Punktation, Übersetzung, Einführung und Anmerkungen (Darmstadt: Wissenschaftliche Buchgesellschaft, 1964).

Lohse, E., and O. Kaiser
Death and Life, trans. J. E. Steely (Nashville: Abingdon, 1981) [Eng. trans. of *Tod und Leben* (Stuttgart: Kohlhammer, 1977)].

Loretz, O.
"Die Sprecher der Götterversammlung in Jes 40,1-8," *UF* 6 (1974) 489–91.

Loretz, O.
"Mesopotamische und ugaritisch-kanaanäische Elemente im Prolog des Buches Deuterojesaja (Jes 40:1-11)," *Or* 53 (1984) 284–96.

Loretz, O.
"Die Gattung des Prologs zum Buch Deuterojesaja (Jes 40:1-11)," *ZAW* 96 (1984) 210–20.

Lourenço, J. D.
"A 'Humilhação-Exaltação' do Servo de Is 53 no Targum e na Literatura Rabiníca," *Itin.* 121–22 (1985) 302–47.

Lourenço, J. D.
"Targum de Is 52,13–53,12. Pressupostos históricos e processos literários," *Did(L)* 20 (1990) 155–66.

Löw, I.
Die Flora der Juden (4 vols.; Vienna and Leipzig: 1924–1934; reprint Hildesheim: Olms, 1967).

Ludwig, O.
Die Stadt in der Jesaja-Apokalypse: Zur Datierung von Jes 24–27 (Cologne: Kleikamp, 1961).

Ludwig, T. M.
"The Traditions of the Establishing of the Earth in Deutero-Isaiah," *JBL* 92 (1973) 345–57.

Lührmann, D.
"Biographie des Gerechten als Evangelium; Vorstellungen zu einem Markus-Kommentar," *WuD* n.s. 14 (1977) 25–50.

Lupieri, E.
Il cielo e il mio trono (Temi e testi 28; Rome: Edizioni di Storia e Letteratura, 1980).

Luther, M.
Der Knecht Gottes: Luthers Auslegung zu Jesaja 53 (trans. and rev. H. Robscheit; Berlin: Evangelische Verlagsanstalt, 1957).

Luther, M.
Die gantze Heilige Schrifft Deutsch: Auffs neu zugericht. Wittenberg 1545 (2 vols.; ed. H. Volz; Munich: Rogner & Bernhard, 1972).

Maag, V.
"Der Hirte Israels (Eine Skizze von Wesen und Bedeutung der Väterreligion)," in V. Maag, *Kultur, Kulturkontakt und Religion: Gesammelte Studien zur allgemeinen und alttestamentlichen Religionsgeschichte* (ed. H. H. Schmid and O. H. Steck; Göttingen: Vandenhoeck & Ruprecht, 1980) 111–44.

Maalstad, K.
"Einige Erwägungen zu Jes 53:4," *VT* 16 (1966) 512–14.

Maass, F.
"'Tritojesaja'?" in F. Maass, ed., *Das ferne und das nahe Wort. FS L. Rost* (BZAW 105; Berlin: Töpelmann, 1967) 153–63.

Machinist, P.
"Assyrians on Assyria in the First Millennium B.C.," in K. Raaflaub, ed., *Anfänge politischen Denkens in der Antike: Die nahöstlichen Kulturen und die Griechen* (Munich: Oldenbourg, 1993) 77–104.

Maisler, B.
"Canaan and the Canaanites," *BASOR* 102 (1946) 7–12.

Malamat, A.
"Prophetic Revelations in New Documents from Mari and the Bible," in *Volume du Congrès: Genève 1965* (VTSup 15; Leiden: Brill, 1966) 207–27.

Malchow, B. V.
"The Prophetic Contribution to Dialogue," *BTB* 16 (1986) 127–31.

Mallowan, M. E. L.
"Cyrus the Great (558–529 B.C.)," in I. Gershevitch, ed., *The Cambridge History of Iran,* vol. 2 (Cambridge: Cambridge Univ. Press, 1985) 392–419

Marcus, R.
"The 'Plain Meaning' of Isaiah 42:1-4," *HTR* 30 (1937) 249–59.

Marg, W.
Hesiod: Sämtliche Gedichte (BAW.GR; Zurich and Stuttgart: Artemis, 1970).

Marinković, P.
"What Does Zechariah 1–8 Tell Us about the Second Temple?" in T. C. Eskenazi and K. H. Richards, eds., *Second Temple Studies*, vol. 2: *Temple and Community in the Persian Period* (JSOTSup 175; Sheffield: JSOT Press, 1994) 88–103. [ET of "Was wissen wir über den zweiten Tempel aus Sach 1–8?" in R. Bartelmus, T. Krüger and H. Utzschneider, eds., *Konsequente Traditionsgeschichte: FS K. Baltzer* (OBO 126; Freiburg: Universitätsverlag; Göttingen: Vandenhoeck & Ruprecht, 1993) 281–95.]

Marinković, P.
"'Geh in Frieden' (2 Kön 5,19). Sonderformen legitimer JHWHverehrung durch 'Heiden' in 'heidnischer' Mitwelt," in R. Feldmeier and U. Heckel, eds., *Die Heiden: Juden, Christen und das Problem des Fremden* (WUNT 70; Tübingen: Mohr, 1994) 3–21.

Marinković, P.
"Stadt ohne Mauern: Die Neukonstitution Jerusalems nach Sacharja 1–8" (Th.D. diss., Munich, 1996).

Marney, C.
The Suffering Servant: A Holy Week Exposition of Isaiah 52:13–53:12 (New York: Abingdon, 1965).

Martin, W. C.
"An Exegesis of Isaiah 51:9-11," *RestQ* 3 (1966) 151–59.

Martin-Achard, R.
Actualité d'Abraham (Neuchâtel: Delachaux et Niestlé, 1969).

Martin-Achard, R.
"Esaïe liv et la nouvelle Jérusalem," in J. A. Emerton, ed., *Congress Volume: Vienna 1980* (VTSup 32; Leiden: Brill, 1981) 238–62.

Martin-Achard, R.
"Trois études sur Esaïe 53," *RThPh* 114 (1982) 159-70.

Martinez, F. G.
"Le livre d'Isaïe à Qumran," *MoBi* 49 (1987) 43–44.

Mason, R.
"Continuity and Newness," *ExpT* 95 (1983) 103–6.

Matheus, F.
"Jesaja XLIV 9-20: das Spottgedicht gegen die Götzen und seine Stellung im Kontext," *VT* 37 (1987) 312–26.

Matheus, F.
Singet dem Herrn ein neues Lied: Die Hymnen Deuterojesajas (SBS 141; Stuttgart: Katholisches Bibelwerk, 1990).

May, H. G.
"The Righteous Servant in Second Isaiah's Songs," *ZAW* 25 (1954) 236–44.

May, H. G.
"The King in the Garden of Eden: A Study of Ezekiel 28:12-19," in B.W. Anderson and W. Harrelson, eds., *Israel's Prophetic Heritage: Essays in Honor of James Muilenburg* (New York: Harper, 1962) 166–76.

Mayer-Maly, T.
"Damnatio memoriae," *KP* 1 (1964) 1374.

Mayes, A. D. H.
"Israel in the Pre-monarchy Period," *VT* 23 (1973) 151–70.

Mazar, B.
"The Tobiads," *IEJ* 7 (1957) 137–45, 229–38.

Mazar, B.
"En-Gedi," in D.W. Thomas, ed., *Archaeology and Old Testament Study* (Oxford: Clarendon, 1967) 222–30.

McCarthy, D. J.
"Vox *bśr* praeparat vocem 'evangelium'," *VD* 42 (1964) 26–33.

McConville, J. G.
"Statement of Assurance in Psalms of Lament," *IBS* 8 (1986) 64–75.

McCown, C. C.
"The ʿAraq el-Emir and the Tobiads," *BA* 20 (1957) 63–76.

McEleney, N. J.
"The Translation of Isaias 41:27," *CBQ* 19 (1957) 441–43.

McGee, D. B.
"The Servant Songs in Isaiah," *Bib* 15 (1988) 26–29.

McGowan, J.
"Reflections on Isaiah 40–55: The Prophetic Minority within the Unreformed Community," *TBT* 30 (1967) 2121–36.

McKane, W.
Prophets and Wise Men (SBT 1/44; London: SCM, 1965).

McKane, W.
Proverbs: A New Approach (OTL; Philadelphia: Westminster, 1970).

McNeese, A.
"The God of No Respect (Isaiah 40:12-31)," *RestQ* 28 (1985/86) 79–85.

Meek, T. J.
"Some Passages Bearing on the Date of Second Isaiah," *HUCA* 23/1 (1950/51) 173–84.

Mees, G.
Het droevige Ongeluk Op de MAES: Voorgevallen op den 30. May 1680. Met alle omstandigheden en Geestelycke bedenckingen daer over voor-gestelt, aen de Gemeynte des Heeren tot Rotterdam, in twee Predicatien over Jesaias 43, vers 2 (Rotterdam: Barent van Santbergen, 1680).

Meinhold, A.
Die Sprüche, Part 1 (ZBK 16/1; Zurich: Theologischer Verlag, 1991).

Melugin, R. F.
"The Structure of Deutero-Isaiah" (Th.D. diss., Yale, 1968).

Melugin, R. F.
"Deutero-Isaiah and Form Criticism," *VT* 21 (1971) 326–37.

Melugin, R. F.
The Formation of Isaiah 40–55 (BZAW 141; Berlin and New York: de Gruyter, 1976).

Melugin, R. F.
"Isaiah 52:7-10," *Int* 36 (1982) 176–81.

Mendecki, N.
"Die zehnte Bitte des Achtzehngebets," *CoTh* 53 (special edition, 1983) 161–66.

Mendecki, N.
"Deuterojesajanischer und ezechielischer Einfluß auf Sach 10,8.10," *Kairos* n.s. 27 (1985) 340–44.

Mendenhall, G. E.
"Puppy and Lettuce in Northwest-Semitic Covenant Making," *BASOR* 133 (1954) 26–30.

Mendenhall, G. E.
"Election," *IDB* 2 (1962) 76–82.

Menes, A.
"A New World and a New Man: Utopias in the Era of the Babylonian Exile and the Return to Zion," *DD* 11 (1983) 249–57.

Menken, M. J. J.
"The Quotation from Isa 40,3 in John 1,23," *Bib* 66 (1985) 190–205.

Menken, M. J. J.
"The Old Testament Quotation in John 6,45: Source and Redaction," *EThL* 64 (1988) 164–72.

Merendino, R. P.
"Literarkritisches, Gattungskritisches und Exegetisches zu Jes 41,8-16," *Bib* 53 (1972) 1–42.

Merendino, R. P.
"Jes 49:1-6: ein Gottesknechtslied?" *ZAW* 92 (1980) 236–48.

Merendino, R. P.
Der Erste und der Letzte: Eine Untersuchung von Jes 40–48 (VTSup 31; Leiden: Brill, 1981).

Merendino, R. P.
"Jes 49:7-13: Jahwes Bekenntnis zu Israels Land," *Henoch* 4 (1982) 295–329.

Merendino, R. P.
"Jes 49:14-26: Jahwes Bekenntnis zu Sion und die neue Heilszeit," *RB* 89 (1982) 321–69.

Merendino, R. P.
"Jes 50:1-3 (9b.11): Jahwes immerwährende Huld zum erprobten Volk," *BZ* 29 (1985) 221–44.

Merendino, R. P.
"Allein und einzig Gottes prophetisches Wort: Israels Erbe und Auftrag für alle Zukunft (Jesaja 50:4-9a.10)," *ZAW* 97 (1985) 344–66.

Merendino, R. P.
"Les chants du Serviteur, une relecture du Deutéro-Isaïe," *SIDIC* 19 (1986) 11–15.

Merendino, R. P.
"Is 40:1-2. Un analisi del materiale documentario," *RivB* 37 (1989) 1–64.

Merkelbach, R.
"Gefesselte Götter," in M. Eliade and E. Jünger, eds., *Antaios* 12 (Stuttgart: Klett, 1971) 549–65.

Merrill, E. H.
"Isaiah 40–55 as Anti-Babylonian Polemic," *GTJ* 8 (1987) 3–18.

Merrill, E. H.
"The Literary Character of Isaiah 40–55, Part 1: Survey of a Century of Studies on Isaiah 40–55," *BSac* 144 (1987) 24–43.

Merrill, E. H.
"The Literary Character of Isaiah 40–55, Part 2: Literary Genres in Isaiah 40–55," *BSac* 144 (1987) 144–56.

Merwe, B. J. van der
Pentateuchtradisies in de Prediking van Deuterojesaja (Groningen: J. B. Wolters, 1955).

Merwe, B. J. van der
"'Actualizing Eschatology' in Isaiah 40–55," *ThEv (SA)* 1 (1968) 16–19.

Mesters, C.
Die Botschaft des leidendes Volkes (Neukirchen-Vluyn: Neukirchener, 1982).

Mettinger, T. N. D.
"The Elimination of A Crux? A Syntactic and Semantic Study of Isaiah XL 18-20," in *Studies on Prophecy: A Collection of Twelve Papers* (VTSup 26; Leiden: Brill, 1974) 77–83.

Mettinger, T. N. D.
King and Messiah: The Civil and Sacral Legitimation of the Israelite Kings (ConBOT 8; Lund: Gleerup, 1976).

Mettinger, T. N. D.
"Die Ebed-Jahwe-Lieder: Ein fragwürdiges Axiom," *ASTI* 11 (1977/78) 68–76.

Mettinger, T. N. D.
"The Veto on Images and the Aniconic God in Ancient Israel," in H. Biezais, ed., *Religious Symbols and Their Functions* (Stockholm: Alquist & Wiksell, 1979) 15–29.

Mettinger, T. N. D.
A Farewell to the Servant Songs: A Critical Examination of an Exegetical Axiom (Scripta minora 3; Lund: Gleerup, 1983).

Mettinger, T. N. D.
"In Search of the Hidden Structure: JHWH as King in Isaiah 40–55," *SEÅ* 51–52 (1986–87) 148–57.

Mettinger, T. N. D.
In Search of God: The Meaning and Message of the Everlasting Names (trans. and rev. F. H. Cryer; Philadelphia: Fortress, 1988).

Meuli, K.
"Die gefesselten Götter," in *Gesammelte Schriften*, vol. 2 (ed. T. Gelzer; Basel and Stuttgart: Schwabe, 1975) 1035–81.

Meyers, C. L., and E. M. Meyers
Haggai, Zechariah 1–8: A New Translation with Introduction and Commentary (AB 25B; Garden City: Doubleday, 1987).

Michel, D.
"Studien zu den sogenannten Thronbesteigungspsalmen," *VT* 6 (1956) 40–68.

Michel, D.

"Zur Eigenart Tritojesajas," *ThViat* 10 (1966) 213–30.

Michel, D.

"Deuterojesaja," *TRE* 8 (1981) 510–30.

Michelini, A. N.

Tradition and Dramatic Form in the Persians of Aischylus (Cincinnati Classical Studies 4; Leiden: Brill, 1982).

Miegge, G.

"Autour d'une exégèse orthodoxe d'Esaïe 40:6," in *maqqél shâqédh: La branche d'amandier. Hommage à Wilhelm Vischer* (Montpellier: Causse, Graille, Castelnau, 1960) 165–70.

Mihelic, J. L.

"The Concept of God in Deutero-Isaiah," *BR* 11 (1966) 29–41.

Millard, A., and I. R. Snook

"Isaiah 40:20: Towards a Solution," *TynBul* 14 (1964) 12–13.

Millard, M.

Die Komposition des Psalters: Ein formgeschichtlicher Ansatz (FAT 9; Tübingen: Mohr, 1994).

Miller, J. M.

"The Concept of Covenant in Deutero-Isaiah: Its Forms and Sources" (Th.D. diss., Boston, 1971).

Miller, J. W.

"Prophetic Conflict in Second Isaiah: The Servant Songs in the Light of Their Context," in E. Jenni, J. J. Stamm and H. J. Stoebe, eds., *Wort–Gebot–Glaube. FS W. Eichrodt* (AThANT 59; Zurich: Zwingli, 1970) 77–85.

Miller, P. D. Jr.

"The Divine Council and the Prophetic Call to War," *VT* 18 (1968) 100–107.

Miller, P. D. Jr.

The Divine Warrior in Early Israel (HSM 5; Cambridge: Harvard Univ. Press, 1973, reprint 1975).

Miller, P. D. Jr.

"Studies in Hebrew Word Patterns," *HTR* 73 (1980) 79–89.

Miller, P. D. Jr.

"Moses My Servant: The Deuteronomic Portrait of Moses," *Int* 41 (1987) 245–55.

Miller, P. D. Jr., P. D. Hanson, and S. D. McBride, eds.

Ancient Israelite Religion: Essays in Honor of Frank Moore Cross (Philadelphia: Fortress, 1987).

Monloubou, L.

"Le Serviteur de Iahvé selon Isaïe," *BLE* 83 (1982) 288–93.

Moor, J. C. de

The Seasonal Pattern in the Ugaritic Myth of Baʿlu (AOAT 16; Neukirchen-Vluyn: Neukirchener, 1971).

Moran, W. L.

"Some Remarks on the Song of Moses," *Bib* 43 (1962) 317–27.

Moran, W. L.

"The Ancient Near Eastern Background of the Love of God in Deuteronomy," *CBQ* 25 (1963) 77–87.

Morenz, S.

"Ägyptischen und davidische Königs-titulaten," *ZÄS* 79 (1954) 73–74; reprint in idem, *Religion und Geschichte der alten Ägypten,* ed. B. Blumenthal and S. Herrmann (Cologne and Vienna: Böhlen Verlag, 1975) 401–2.

Morgenstern, J.

"Isaiah 42:10-13," in R. M. Pierson, ed., *To Do and to Teach: FS C. L. Pyatt* (Lexington: College of the Bible, 1953) 27–38.

Morgenstern, J.

"The Message of Deutero-Isaiah in Its Sequential Unfolding," *HUCA* 30 (1959) 1–102.

Morgenstern, J.

"'The Oppressor' of Isa 51:13—Who was He?" *JBL* 81 (1962) 25–34.

Morgenstern, J.

"Two Additional Notes to 'The Suffering Servant—a New Solution,'" *VT* 13 (1963) 321–32.

Morgenstern, J.

"The Cultic Setting of the 'Enthronement Psalms'," *HUCA* 35 (1964) 1–42.

Moriarty, F. L.

"Word as Power in the Ancient Near East," in H. N. Bream, R. D. Heim, and C. A. Moore, eds., *A Light into My Path: Old Testament Studies in Honor of J. M. Myers* (GTS 4; Philadelphia: Temple Univ. Press, 1974) 345–62.

Moriarty, F. L.

"Preacher and Prophet," *Way* 20 (1980) 3–14.

Morrow, F. J.

"The Text of Isaiah at Qumran" (Th.D. diss., Catholic University of America, 1973).

Mowinckel, S.

"Die Komposition des deuterojesajanischen Buches," *ZAW* 49 (1931) 87–112 and 242–60.

Mowinckel, S.

"Hat es ein israelitisches Nationalepos gegeben?" *ZAW* 53 (1935) 130–52.

Mowinckel, S.

"Neuere Forschungen zu Deuterojesaja, Tritojesaja und dem Ebed-Jahwe-Problem," *AcOr* 16 (1937/38) 1–40.

Moye, J. E. L.

"Israel and the Nations in Isaiah 40–66" (Th.D. diss., Southern Baptist Theological Seminary, 1972).

Müller, D.

"Der gute Hirte. Ein Beitrag zur Geschichte ägyptischer Bildreden," *ZÄS* 86 (1961) 126–44.

Müller, H.-P.

"Magisch-mantische Weisheit und die Gestalt Daniels," *UF* 1 (1969) 79–94.

Müller, H.-P.

"Ein Vorschlag zu Jes 53:10f," *ZAW* 81 (1969) 377–80.

Müller, H.-P.
"Altes und Neues zum Buch Hiob," *EvTh* 37 (1977) 284–304.

Müller, H.-P.
"Die weisheitliche Lehrerzählung im Alten Testament und seiner Umwelt," *WO* 9/1 (1977) 77–98.

Müller, H.-P.
Das Hiobproblem: Seine Stellung und Entstehung im Alten Orient und im Alten Testament (EdF 84; Darmstadt: Wissenschaftliche Buchgesellschaft, 1978).

Müller, H.-P.
"Das Bedeutungspotential der Afformativkonjugation—Zum sprachgeschichtlichen Hintergrund des Althebräischen," *ZAH* 1 (1988) 74–98, 159–90.

Müller, H.-P.
"*wa-*, *ha-* und das Imperfectum consecutivum," *ZAH* 4 (1991) 144–60.

Müller, K.-F.
"Das assyrische Ritual Teil I. Texte zum assyrischen Königsritual," *MVAG* 41/3 (1937) 1–89.

Muilenburg, J.
"A Study in Hebrew Rhetoric: Repetition and Style," in *Congress Volume: Copenhagen 1953* (VTSup 1; Leiden: Brill, 1953) 97–111.

Muilenburg, J.
"Fragments of Another Qumran Isaiah Scroll," *BASOR* 135 (1954) 28–32.

Muilenburg, J.
"The Speech of Theophany," *HDSB* 28 (1963–64) 35–47.

Muilenburg, J.
"Form Criticism and Beyond," *JBL* 88 (1969) 1–18.

Muraoka, T.
Emphatic Words and Structures in Biblical Hebrew (Jerusalem: Magnes; Leiden: Brill, 1985).

Murphy, R. T.
"Second Isaias: The Literary Problem," *CBQ* 9 (1947) 170–78.

Murray, D. F.
"The Rhetoric of Disputation: Re-examination of a Prophetic Genre," *JSOT* 38 (1987) 95–121.

Myer, C. F.
"The Prophet—A Heavenly Messenger," *RestQ* 9 (1966) 290–94.

Nagy, G.
Pindar's Homer: The Lyric Possession of an Epic Past (Baltimore: Johns Hopkins Univ. Press, 1990).

Naidoff, B. D.
"The Rhetoric of Encouragement in Isaiah 40:12-31: A Form-Critical Study," *ZAW* 93 (1981) 62–76.

Naidoff, B. D.
"The Two-fold Structure of Isaiah xlv 9-13," *VT* 31 (1981) 180–85.

Nápole, G. M.
"Mi Salvation por siempre sera y mi Justicia no caera," *RevBib* 50 (1988) 143–69.

Navarro, E. F.
El Desierto Transformando (Rome: Pontifical Biblical Institute, 1992).

Neher, A.
"Le symbolisme conjugal dans l'Ancien Testament," *RHPhR* 34 (1954) 30–49.

Neubauer, A.
The Fifty-Third Chapter of Isaiah: According to the Jewish Interpreters (New York: Ktav, 1969).

Newing, E. G., and E. W. Conrad, eds.
Perspectives on Language and Text: Essays and Poems in Honor of F. I. Andersen's Sixtieth Birthday, July 28, 1985 (Winona Lake, Ind.: Eisenbrauns, 1987).

Nickelsburg, G. W. E.
Resurrection, Immortality, and Eternal Life in Intertestamental Judaism (HTS 26; Cambridge: Harvard Univ. Press, 1972).

Nida, E. A.
"Establishing Translation Principles and Procedures," *BT* 33 (1982) 208–13.

Niebuhr, U. M.
"Glory," *BTB* 14 (1984) 49–53.

Niehr, H.
Rechtsprechung in Israel (SBS 130; Stuttgart: Katholisches Bibelwerk, 1987).

Nielsen, E.
"Deuterojesaja; Erwägungen zur Formkritik, Traditions- und Redaktionsgeschichte," *VT* 20 (1970) 190–205.

Nilsson, M. P.
A History of Greek Religion (2d ed., 1949) [ET of *Geschichte der griechischen Religion* (2 vols.; Munich: Beck, 1941–50)].

Nilsson, M. P.
"Demeter," in *Griechische Feste von religiöser Bedeutung: Mit Ausschluß der Attischen* (Leipzig: Teubner, 1906; reprint Milano: Cisalpino-Goliardica, 1975) 311–54.

Nordheim, E. von
"Der große Hymnus des Echnaton und Psalm 104. Gott und Menschen im Ägypten der Amarnazeit und in Israel," *Studien zur altägyptischen Kultur* 7 (1979) 227–51.

North, C. R.
"The Former Things and the New Things in Deutero-Isaiah," in H. H. Rowley, ed., *Studies in Old Testament Prophecy: Presented to T. H. Robinson* (Edinburgh: T. & T. Clark, 1950) 111–26.

North, C. R.
Isaiah 40–55: The Suffering Servant of God (2d ed.; London: SCM, 1956).

North, C. R.
"The Essence of Idolatry," in J. Hempel and L. Rost, eds., *Von Ugarit nach Qumran: Beiträge zur Forschung. FS O. Eissfeldt* (BZAW 77; Berlin: Töpelmann, 1958) 151–60.

Noth, M.
The Old Testament World, trans. V. I. Gruhn (Philadelphia: Fortress, 1966) [Eng. trans. of *Die Welt des Alten Testaments. Einführung in die Grenzgebiete der alttestamentlichen Wissenschaft* (STö 3/2; 4th ed.; Berlin: Töpelmann, 1962)].

Noth, M.
Die israelitischen Personennamen im Rahmen der Gemeinsemitischen Namensgebung (1928; reprint Hildesheim: Olms, 1966).

Noth, M.
Das System der zwölf Stämme Israels (1930; reprint Darmstadt: Wissenschaftliche Buchgesellschaft, 1966).

Noth, M.
A History of Pentateuchal Traditions, trans. B. W. Anderson (Englewood Cliffs, N.J..: Prentice-Hall, 1972) [Eng. trans. of *Überlieferungsgeschichte des Pentateuch* (1948; reprint Darmstadt: Wissenschaftliche Buchgesellschaft, 1960)].

Noth, M.
The Deuteronomistic History, trans. J. Dossall et al. (JSOTSup 15; 2d ed.; Sheffield: Sheffield Academic Press, 1991) [Eng. trans. of *Überlieferungsgeschichtliche Studien* (1943; reprint Darmstadt: Wissenschaftliche Buchgesellschaft, 1957) 1–110].

Noth, M.
The Chronicler's History, trans. H. G. M. Williamson (JSOTSup 50; Sheffield: Sheffield Academic Press, 1987) [Eng. trans. of *Überlieferungsgeschichtliche Studien* (1943; reprint Darmstadt: Wissenschaftliche Buchgesellschaft, 1957) 110–217].

Noth, M.
The History of Israel, trans. P. R. Ackroyd (2d ed.; London: SCM, 1960) [Eng. trans. of *Die Geschichte Israels* (Göttingen: Vandenhoeck & Ruprecht, 1954)].

Noth, M.
Die Ursprünge des alten Israel im Lichte neuer Quellen (VAFLNW.G 94; Cologne and Opladen: Westdeutscher Verlag, 1961).

Noth, M.
Numbers, trans. J. T. Martin (OTL; London: Westminster, 1968) [Eng. trans. of *Das vierte Buch Mose, Numeri* (ATD 7; Göttingen: Vandenhoeck & Ruprecht, 1966)].

Noth, M.
Könige 1–16 (BKAT 9/1; Neukirchen-Vluyn: Neukirchener, 1968).

Notopoulos, J. A.
"Homer, Hesiod and the Achaean Heritage of Oral Poetry," *Hesperia* 29 (1960) 177–97.

Oberholzer, J. P.
"'Die Kneg van Jahwe' in Deuterojesaja," *HTS* 26 (1971) 11–37.

O'Callaghan, R. T.
"Ritual, Myth and Drama in Ancient Literature," *Or* 22 (1953) 418–25.

O'Connor, M.
Hebrew Verse Structure (Winona Lake, Ind.: Eisenbrauns, 1980).

Odeberg, H.
Trito-Isaiah (Isaiah 56–66): A Literary and Linguistic Analysis (Lund: Gleerup, 1931).

Oeming, M.
"Exkurs zur Topographie und Archäologie Jerusalems," in A. H. J. Gunneweg, *Nehemia* (KAT 19/2; Gütersloh: Mohn, 1987) 180–94.

Oexinger, F.
"Beschneidung," *TRE* 5 (1980) 714–24.

Ogden, G. S.
"Moses and Cyrus: Literary Affinities between the Priestly Presentation of Moses in Exodus VI–VIII and the Cyrus Song in Isaiah XLIV 24—XLV 13," *VT* 28 (1978) 195–263.

Ollenburger, B. C.
Zion, the City of the Great King: A Theological Symbol of the Jerusalem Cult (JSOTSup 41; Sheffield: JSOT Press, 1987).

Olley, J. W.
"Notes on Isaiah xxxii 1, xlv 19, 23 and lxiii 1," *VT* 33 (1983) 446–53.

Olley, J. W.
"'The Many': How Is Is 53:12a to Be Understood?" *Bib* 68 (1987) 330–56.

Oosterhoff, B. J.
"Tot een Licht der Volken," in *De Knecht: Studies rondom Deutero-Jesaja. FS J. L. Koole* (Kampen: Kok, 1978) 157–72.

Oppenheim, L.
"Zur keilschriftlichen Omenliteratur," *Or* 5 (1936) 199–228.

Orelli, C. von
Durch's Heilige Land: Tagebuchblätter (2d ed.; Basel: Spittler, 1879).

Orlinsky, H. M.
The So-Called "Suffering Servant" in Isaiah 53 (Cincinnati: Hebrew Union College Press, 1964).

Orlinsky, H. M.
"The So-Called 'Servant of the Lord' and 'Suffering Servant' in Second Isaiah," in H. M. Orlinsky and N. H. Snaith, *Studies in the Second Part of the Book of Isaiah* (VTSup 14; Leiden: Brill, 1967) 1–133.

Ortloph, A.
"Ueber den Begriff von קדוש, und den wurzelverwandten Wörtern im zweiten Theile des Propheten Jesaja," *ZLThK* 21 (1860) 401–26.

Oswalt, J. N.
"The Myth of the Dragon and Old Testament Faith," *EvQ* 49 (1977) 163–72.

Otten, H.
Mythen vom Gotte Kumarbi (Deutsche Akademie der Wissenschaften 3; Berlin: Institut für Orientforschung, 1950).

Otten, H.
"Das Hethiterreich," in H. Schmökel, ed., *Kulturgeschichte des Alten Orients* (Stuttgart: Kröner, 1961) 313–446.

Otto, Eberhard
Die biographischen Inschriften der ägyptischen Spätzeit: Ihre geistesgeschichtliche und literarische Bedeutung (Probleme der Ägyptologie 2; Leiden: Brill, 1954).

Otto, Eckart
Das Mazzotfest in Gilgal (BWANT 107; Stuttgart: Kohlhammer, 1975).

Otto, Eckart
"Schöpfung als Kategorie der Vermittlung von Gott und Welt in Biblischer Theologie," in H. G. Geyer et al., eds., *"Wenn nicht jetzt, wann dann?" FS H.-J. Kraus* (Neukirchen-Vluyn: Neukirchener, 1983) 53–68.

Otto, Eckart
Theologische Ethik des Alten Testaments (ThW 3/2; Stuttgart: Kohlhammer, 1994).

Otto, Eckart
"Zivile Funktionen des Stadttores in Palästina und Mesopotamien," in M. Weippert et al., eds., *Meilenstein. FS H. Donner* (ÄAT 30; Wiesbaden: Harrassowitz, 1995) 188–97.

Page, D. L.
Select Papyri, vol. 3: *Literary Papyri: Old Comedy, Κρατινος, Πλουτοι* (LCL; Cambridge: Harvard Univ. Press, 1970).

Palache, J. L.
The Ebed-Jahveh Enigma in Pseudo-Isaiah: A New Point of View (Amsterdam: Hertzberger, 1934).

Paolantonio, M.
"God as Husband," *TBT* 27 (1989) 299–303.

Parrot, A.
"Cérémonie de la main et réinvestiture," in A. Parrot, ed., *Studia Mariana* (Leiden: Brill, 1950) 37–40.

Pastor-Ramos, F.
"Murió por nuestros pecados (1 Cor 15,3; Gál 1,4). Observaciones sobre el origen de esta fórmula en Is 53," *EstEcl* 61 (1986) 385–93.

Paton-Williams, D., and P. Wilcox
"The Servant Songs in Deutero-Isaiah," *JSOT* 42 (1988) 79–102.

Patrick, D. A.
"Epiphanic Imagery in Second Isaiah's Portrayal of a New Exodus," *HAR* 8 (1984) 125–41.

Paul, S. M.
"Jerusalem—A City of Gold," *IEJ* 17 (1967) 259–69.

Paul, S. M.
"Deutero-Isaiah and Cuneiform Royal Inscriptions," *JAOS* 88 (1968) 180–86.

Paul, S. M.
"Literary and Ideological Echoes of Jeremiah in Deutero-Isaiah," in P. Peli, ed., *Proceedings of the Fifth World Congress of Jewish Studies* (Jerusalem: World Union of Jewish Studies, 1969) 102–20.

Pausanias
Description of Greece I–V (LCL; trans. and rev. W. H. S. Jones, H. A. Ormerod and R. E. Wycherley; Cambridge: Harvard Univ. Press; London: Heinemann, 1918–1935, reprint 1965–69).

Payne, D. F.
"The Servant of the Lord: Language and Interpretation," *EvQ* 42/43 (1970/1971) 131–43.

Payne, J. B.
"Eighth Century Israelitish Background of Isaiah 40–66," *WTJ* 30 (1967) 50–58, 185–203.

Pedersen, J.
Israel: Its Life and Culture (4 vols.; vol. 1 and 2:

1926; vol. 3 and 4: 1940; reprint London: Cumberlege and Copenhagen: Branner, 1946–47).

Perlitt, L.
"Die Verborgenheit Gottes," in H.W. Wolff, ed., *Probleme biblischer Theologie. FS G. von Rad* (Munich: Kaiser, 1971) 367–82.

Petersen, D. L.
Haggai and Zechariah 1–8 (OTL; Philadelphia: Westminster, 1984).

Petersen, L.
Zur Geschichte der Personifikation in griechischer Dichtung und bildender Kunst (Würzburg-Aumühle: Triltsch, 1939).

Pfeifer, G.
"Amos und Deuterojesaja denkformenanalytisch verglichen," *ZAW* 93 (1981) 439–43.

Pfeiffer, R. H.
Introduction to the Old Testament (2d ed.; New York: Harper, 1948).

Pfisterer Darr, K.
"Like Warrior, Like Woman: Destruction and Deliverance in Isaiah 42:10-17," *CBQ* 49 (1987) 560–71.

Philipp, W.
"Der Name Gottes," *RGG* 4 (3d ed.; 1960) 1298–1300.

Philipps, M. L.
"Divine Self-Predication in Deutero-Isaiah," *BR* 16 (1971) 32–51.

Phillips, A.
"The Servant-Symbol of Divine Powerlessness," *ExpT* 90 (1979) 370–74.

Phillips, A.
"'Double for All Her Sins,'" *ZAW* 94 (1982) 130–32.

Philo
Quod deo mittantur Somnia, in *Philo V* (LCL; trans. and rev. F. H. Colson; Cambridge: Harvard Univ. Press, 1966) 285–579.

Philo
De Vita Mosis, in *Philo VI* (LCL; trans. and rev. F. H. Colson; Cambridge: Harvard Univ. Press; London: Heinemann, 1935, reprint 1966) 274–595.

Pickard-Cambridge, A. W.
The Theatre of Dionysus in Athens (Oxford: Clarendon, 1946).

Pickard-Cambridge, A. W.
The Dramatic Festivals of Athens (2d ed.; Oxford: Clarendon, 1968).

Pipal, B.
"The Lord's Ebed in the Exile," *CV* 13 (1970) 177–80.

Plamondon, P.-H.
"Sur le chemin du salut avec le IIe Isaïe," *NRTh* 104 (1982) 241–66.

Plamondon, P.-H.
"Le Deutéro-Isaïe: de la multipicité de genres littéraires à l'unité d'un discours," *LavTP* 39 (1983) 171–93.

Plato
    Timaeus (LCL 234; trans. R. G. Bury; Cambridge: Harvard Univ. Press, 1929; reprint 1975).
Pliny
    Naturgeschichte (trans. and rev. C. F. L. Strack and M. E. D. L. Strack; 1853–55; reprint Darmstadt: Wissenschaftliche Buchgesellschaft, 1968).
Ploeg, J. van der
    "*Šāpaṭ* et *Mišpaṭ*," *OTS* 2 (1943) 144–55.
Plöger, O.
    "Siebzig Jahre," in L. Rost, ed., *FS F. Baumgärtel* (EdF 10; Erlangen: Universitätsbund Erlangen, 1959) 124–30.
Plöger, O.
    Das Buch Daniel (KAT 18; Gütersloh: Mohn, 1965).
Plöger, O.
    "Zusätze zu Daniel," in H. Bardtke and O. Plöger, *Historische und legendarische Erzählungen* (JSHRZ 1/1; Gütersloh: Mohn, 1973), 63–86.
Plutarch
    Solon: Übersetzung von K. Ziegler und W. Wuhrmann (Zurich: Artemis, 1954; reprint Munich: Deutscher Taschenbuch Verlag, 1979).
Plutarch,
    "Solon," in *Plutarch's Lives I* (LCL; trans. and rev. B. Perrin; Cambridge: Harvard Univ. Press; London: Heinemann, 1914; reprint 1967) 403–99.
Pohl, A.
    "Die Klage Marduks über Babylon im Irra-Epos," *HUCA* 23 (1968) 405–09.
Pongratz-Leisten, B.
    INA ŠULMI ĪRUB: Die Kulttopographische und ideologische Programmatik der akītu-Prozession in Babylon und Assyrien im 1. Jahrtausend v. Chr. (Baghdader Forschungen 16; Mainz: von Zabern, 1994).
Pope, M. H.
    "Isaiah 34 in Relation to Isaiah 35, 40–66," *JBL* 71 (1952) 235–43.
Pope, M. H.
    El in the Ugaritic Texts (VTSup 2; Leiden: Brill, 1955).
Pope, M. H.
    "Anat," in *Wörterbuch der Mythologie,* vol. 1, ed. H. W. Haussig (Stuttgart: E. Klett, 1965) 235–41.
Porten, B.
    Archives from Elephantine: The Life of an Ancient Jewish Military Colony (Berkeley and Los Angeles: Univ. of California Press, 1968).
Porten, B.
    Jews of Elephantine and Arameans of Syene: Aramaic Texts with Hebrew and English Translation (Jerusalem: Hebrew Univ. Press, 1980).
Porten, B., and A. Yardeni, eds.
    Textbook of Aramaic Documents from Ancient Egypt: Newly Copied, Edited and Translated into Hebrew and English; vol. 1: *Letters;* vol. 2: *Contracts* (Jerusalem: Hebrew Univ. Press, distributed by Winona Lake, Ind.: Eisenbrauns, 1989).

Porteous, N. W.
    "Jerusalem-Zion: The Growth of a Symbol," in A. Kuschke, ed., *Verbannung und Heimkehr. FS W. Rudolph* (Tübingen: Mohr, 1961) 235–52.
Preuss, H. D.
    ". . . ich will mit dir sein!" *ZAW* 80 (1968) 139–73.
Preuss, H. D.
    Verspottung fremder Religionen im Alten Testament (BWANT 92; Stuttgart: Kohlhammer, 1971).
Preuss, H. D.
    Deuterojesaja: Eine Einführung in seine Botschaft (Neukirchen-Vluyn: Neukirchener, 1976).
Preuss, R.
    "Das Ordal im alten Israel II," *ZAW* 51 (1933) 227–55.
Prijs, L.
    "Ein 'Waw der Bekräftigung'?" *BZ* n.s. 8 (1964) 105–9.
Pritchard, J. B., ed.
    Ancient Near East in Pictures Relating to the Old Testament (Princeton: Princeton Univ. Press, 1954).
Pritchard, J. B., ed.
    Ancient Near East: Supplementary Texts and Pictures Relating to the Old Testament (Princeton: Princeton Univ. Press, 1969).
Pritchard, J. B., ed.
    Ancient Near Eastern Texts Relating to the Old Testament (Princeton: Princeton Univ. Press, 1950).
Pseudo-Philo
    Antiquitates Biblicae (ed. C. Dietzfelbinger; JSHRZ 2/2; Gütersloh: Mohn, 1975).
Puech, E.
    "Sur la racine *slh* en hébreu et en araméen," *Sem* 21 (1971) 5–19.
Qimron, E.
    "More Regarding *mrḥm* = Woman, Mother," *Tarbiz* 52 (1982/83) 509 (in Hebrew).
Quintilian
    Institutio Oratoria (4 vols.; LCL; Cambridge: Harvard Univ. Press, 1920–22).
Raabe, P. R.
    "The Effect of Repetition in the Suffering Servant Song," *JBL* 103 (1984) 77–81.
Raaflaub, K., and E. Müller-Luckner, eds.
    Anfänge politischen Denkens in der Antike: Die nahöstlichen Kulturen und die Griechen (Munich: Oldenbourg, 1993).
Rabinowitz, J.
    "A Note on Isa 46:4," *JBL* 73 (1954) 237.
Rad, G. von
    "The Royal Ritual in Judah," in *The Problem of the Hexateuch and Other Essays,* trans. E. W. T. Dicken (New York: McGraw-Hill, 1966) 222–31 [Eng. trans. of "Das jüdische Königsritual," *ThLZ* 72 (1947) 211–16, reprint in *Gesammelte Studien zum Alten Testament,* vol. 1 (ThBü 8; Munich: Kaiser, 1965) 205–13].
Rad, G. von
    "'Righteousness' and 'Life' in the Cultic Language of the Psalms," in *The Problem of the Hexateuch and*

Other Essays, trans. E. W. T. Dicken (New York: McGraw-Hill, 1966) 243–66 [Eng. trans. of "'Gerechtigkeit' und 'Leben' in der Kultsprache der Psalmen," in W. Baumgartner et al., eds., *FS A. Bertholet zum 80. Geburtstag* (Tübingen: Mohr, 1950) 418–37].

Rad, G. von
"Faith Reckoned as Righteousness," in *The Problem of the Hexateuch and Other Essays,* trans. E. W. T. Dicken (New York: McGraw-Hill, 1966) 125–30 [Eng. trans. of "Die Anrechnung des Glaubens zur Gerechtigkeit," *ThLZ* 76 (1951) 129–32].

Rad, G. von
"Job xxxviii and Ancient Egyptian Wisdom," in *The Problem of the Hexateuch and Other Essays,* trans. E. W. T. Dicken (New York: McGraw-Hill, 1966) 281–91 [Eng. trans. of "Hiob xxxviii und die alt-ägyptische Weisheit," in M. Noth and D. W. Thomas, eds. *Wisdom in Israel and in the Ancient Near East. FS H. H. Rowley* (VTSup 3; Leiden: Brill, 1955) 293–301].

Rad, G. von
Old Testament Theology, trans. D. M. G. Stalker (2 vols.; New York: Harper & Row, 1962–65) [Eng. trans. of *Theologie des Alten Testaments* (2 vols.; Munich: Kaiser, 1957–60; 8th ed., 1982–1984)].

Rad, G. von
Gesammelte Studien zum Alten Testament (2 vols.; ThBü 8 and 48; 3d ed.; Munich: Kaiser, 1965–73).

Rad, G. von
"כִּפְלַיִם in Jes 40:2 = Äquivalent?" *ZAW* 79 (1967) 80–82.

Rad, G. von
Deuteronomy, trans. D. Barton (OTL; Philadelphia: Westminster, 1966) [Eng. trans. of *Das fünfte Buch Mose. Deuteronomium* (ATD 5; 2d ed.; Göttingen: Vandenhoeck & Ruprecht, 1968)].

Rad, G. von
Holy War in Ancient Israel, trans. M. J. Dawn (Grand Rapids: Eerdmans, 1991) [Eng. trans. of *Der Heilige Krieg im alten Israel* (1951; 5th ed.; Göttingen: Vandenhoeck & Ruprecht, 1969)].

Rad, G. von
Wisdom in Israel, trans. J. D. Martin (Nashville: Abingdon, 1972) [Eng. trans. of *Weisheit in Israel* (Neukirchen-Vluyn: Neukirchener, 1970)].

Radday, Y. T.
"Two Computerized Statistical-Linguistic Tests Concerning the Unity of Isaiah," *JBL* 89 (1970) 319–24.

Radday, Y. T.
"Eccentricities of the Vocabulary and Unity of the Book of Isaiah," *Tarbiz* 39 (1970) 323–28.

Ratschow, C. H.
"Prozession," *RGG* 5 (3d ed.; 1961) 668–69.

Ratschow, C. H.
"Ehe/Eherecht/Ehescheidung, I. Religions-geschichtlich," *TRE* 9 (1982) 308–11.

Ratzhabi, Y.
"R. Saadia Gaon's Commentary on the Servant of the Lord Passage (Isa 52:13–53:12)," *Tarbiz* 57 (1987/88) 327–47 (in Hebrew).

Ravenna, A.
"Isaia 43:14," *RevBib* 12 (1964) 293–96.

Reardon, P. H.
"Second Isaiah and the Creative Word," *TBT* 96 (1978) 1614–21.

Redford, D. B., and K. S. Freedy
"The Dates in Ezekiel in Relation to Biblical, Babylonian and Egyptian Sources," *JAOS* 90 (1970) 462–85.

Reed, W. L.
"Nabonidus, Babylonian Reformer or Renegade?" *Lexington Theological Quarterly* 12 (1977) 21–30.

Reicke, B.
"Namensglaube III. Im NT," *RGG* 4 (3d ed.; 1960) 1304–6.

Reicke, B.
"The Knowledge of the Suffering Servant," in F. Maass, ed., *Das ferne und das nahe Wort. FS L. Rost* (BZAW 105; Berlin: Töpelmann, 1964) 186–92.

Reicke, B.
"πᾶς, ἅπας: 3. πᾶς in the World of Greek and Hellenistic Thought [with Greek texts]; 4. πᾶς in the NT [lit.]," *TDNT* 5 (1967) 892–96 [*ThWNT* 5 (1966) 890–95].

Reicke, B.
"Der Gottesknecht im Alten und Neuen Testament," *ThZ* 35 (1979) 342–50.

Reicke, B., and L. Rost, eds.
Biblisch-historisches Handwörterbuch (4 vols.; Göttingen: Vandenhoeck & Ruprecht, 1962–1979).

Reider, J.
"Etymological Studies in Biblical Hebrew," *VT* 2 (1952) 113–30.

Reider, J., and W. H. Brownlee
"On *MŚḤTY* in the Qumran Scrolls," *BASOR* 134 (1954) 27–28.

Reinhardt, K.
"Vorschläge zum neuen Aischylos," *Hermes* 85 (1957) 1–17.

Reinhardt, K.
"Personifikation und Allegorie," in C. Becker, ed., *Vermächtnis der Antike* (2d ed.; Göttingen: Vandenhoeck & Ruprecht, 1966) 7–40.

Reinwald, G.
Cyrus im zweiten Teil des Buches Isaias: Kap. 40–55 (Bamberg: Selbstverlag, 1956).

Rembaum, J. E.
"The Development of a Jewish Exegetical Tradition Regarding Isaiah 53," *HTR* 75:3 (1982) 289–311.

Rendsburg, G.
"Hebrew *rḥm* = 'RAIN,'" *VT* 33 (1983) 357–61.

Rendtorff, R.
Canon and Theology (trans. M. Kohl; Minneapolis: Fortress, 1993).

Rendtorff, R.
"Die theologische Stellung des Schöpfungsglaubens bei Deuterojesaja," *ZThK* 51 (1954) 3–13.

Rendtorff, R.
"Priesterliche Kulttheologie und prophetische
Kultpolemik," *ThLZ* 81 (1956) 339–42.

Rendtorff, R.
"The Concept of Revelation in Ancient Israel," in
W. Pannenberg, ed., *Revelation in History,* trans. D.
Granskou (New York: Macmillan, 1968) 23–53
[Eng. trans. of "Die Offenbarungsvorstellungen im
Alten Israel," in W. Pannenberg, ed., *Offenbarung
als Geschichte* (Göttingen: Vandenhoeck &
Ruprecht, 1961) 21–41].

Rendtorff, R.
*Die Gesetze in der Priesterschrift: Eine gattungs-
geschichtliche Untersuchung* (FRLANT 62; 2d
ed.; Göttingen: Vandenhoeck & Ruprecht,
1963).

Rendtorff, R.
Studien zur Geschichte des Opfers im Alten Israel
(WMANT 24; Neukirchen-Vluyn: Neukirchener,
1967).

Rendtorff, R.
"Jes 6 im Rahmen der Komposition des Jesajabuches," in J. Vermeylen, ed., *The Book of Isaiah*
(BEThL 81; Leuven: Leuven Univ. Press, 1989)
73–82.

Renkema, J.
*'Misschien is er Hoop . . .' De Theologische Vooronder-
stellingen van het boek Klaagliederen* (Franeker:
Wever, 1983).

Reventlow, H. Graf
Die Propheten Haggai, Sacharja und Maleachi (ATD
25/2; Göttingen: Vandenhoeck & Ruprecht,
1993).

Reymond, P.
*L'eau: Sa vie et sa signification dans l'Ancien Testa-
ment* (VTSup 6; Leiden: Brill, 1958).

Rice, E. E.
The Grand Procession of Ptolemy Philadelphus
(Oxford: Oxford Univ. Press, 1983).

Richardson, H. N.
"Some Notes on לִיץ and Its Derivatives," *VT* 5
(1955) 163–79.

Richter, A.
"Hauptlinien der Deuterojesaja-Forschung von
1964–1979," in C. Westermann, ed., *Sprache und
Struktur der Prophetie Deuterojesajas* (CTM 11;
Stuttgart: Calwer, 1981) 89–123.

Richter, W.
"Die nagid-Formel," *BZ* n.s. 9 (1965) 71–84.

Richter, W.
"Beobachtungen zur theologischen Systembildung
in der alttestamentlichen Literatur anhand des
'kleinen geschichtlichen Credo,'" in L. Scheffczyk,
W. Dettloff, and R. Heinzmann, eds., *Wahrheit
und Verkündigung. FS M. Schmaus,* vol. 1 (Pader-
born, Munich and Vienna: Schöningh, 1967)
175–212.

Richter, W.
*Untersuchungen zur Valenz althebräischer Verben, 2.
GBH, ʿMQ. QṢR II* (ATSAT 25; St. Ottilien: EOS,
1986).

Ridderbos, N. H.
"עָפָר als Staub des Totenortes," *OTS* 5 (1948)
174–78.

Rignell, L. G.
A Study of Isaiah cc. 40–55 (LUÅ; Lund: Gleerup,
1956).

Ringgren, H.
*Word and Wisdom: Studies in the Hypostatization of
Divine Qualities and Functions in the Ancient Near
East* (Lund: H. Ohlssons, 1947).

Ringgren, H.
"Gottesurteil, Ordal," *BHH* 1 (1962) 600.

Ringgren, H.
Israelite Religion, trans. D. E. Green (Philadelphia:
Fortress, 1966) [Eng. trans. of *Israelitische Religion*
(Die Religionen der Menschheit 26; Stuttgart:
Kohlhammer, 1963)].

Ringgren, H.
"Deuterojesaja och kultspråket," *TAik* 72 (1967)
166–76.

Ringgren, H.
"Die Funktion des Schöpfungsmythos in Jesaja
51," in K.-H. Bernhardt, ed., *Schalom. FS A. Jepsen*
(Stuttgart: Calwer, 1971) 38–40.

Ringgren, H.
"Zur Komposition von Jesaja 49–55," in H. Donner, R. Hanhart, and R. Smend, eds., *Beiträge zur
alttestamentlichen Theologie. FS W. Zimmerli* (Göttingen: Vandenhoeck & Ruprecht, 1977) 371–76.

Ringgren, H.
"The Marriage Motif in Israelite Religion," in P. D.
Miller Jr., P. D. Hanson and S. D. McBride, eds.,
Ancient Israelite Religion. FS Frank Moore Cross
(Philadelphia: Fortress, 1987) 421–28.

Roaf, M.
"The Subject Peoples on the Base of the Statue of
Darius," *Cahiers de la délégation archéologique
Française en Iran* 4 (1974) 73–160.

Robert, P. de
*Le berger d'Israël. Essai sur le thème pastoral dans l'An-
cien Testament* (CTh 57; Neuchâtel: Delachaux et
Niestlé, 1968).

Roberts, B. J.
"The Second Isaiah Scroll from Qumrân (IQIs[b]),"
BJRL 42 (1959/60) 132–44.

Roberts, J. J. M.
*The Earliest Semitic Pantheon: A Study of the Semitic
Deities Attested in Mesopotamia before Ur III* (Balti-
more: Johns Hopkins Univ. Press, 1972).

Roberts, J. J. M.
"The Davidic Origin of the Zion Tradition," *JBL*
92 (1973) 329–44.

Roberts, J. J. M.
"Isaiah in Old Testament Theology," *Int* 36 (1982)
130–43.

Robinson, G.
"The meaning of יָד in Isaiah 56:5," *ZAW* 88 (1976) 282–84.

Robinson, T. H.
"Hebrew Poetic Form: The English Tradition," in *Congress Volume: Copenhagen 1953* (VTSup 1; Leiden: Brill, 1953) 128–49.

Roche, M. de
"Yahweh's *rib* Against Israel: A Reassessment of the So-Called 'Prophetic Lawsuit' in the Preexilic Prophets," *JBL* 102 (1983) 563–74.

Rode, J.
"Das Chorlied," in W. Jens, ed., *Die Bauformen der griechischen Tragödie* (Beiheft zu Poetica 6; Munich: Fink, 1971) 93–116.

Rodriguez, E. Z.
"Filologia y critica textual en Is. 40–55," *Burgense* 11 (1970) 81–116.

Roeder, G.
Kulte, Orakel und Naturverehrung im Alten Ägypten (Zurich and Stuttgart: Artemis, 1960).

Rössler-Köhler, U.
"Jenseitsvorstellungen," *LÄ* 3 (1980) 252–67.

Rogers, J. S.
"An Allusion to Coronation in Isaiah 2:6," *CBQ* 51 (1989) 232–36.

Roloff, K.-H.
"Demeter," *LAW* (1965) 708–10.

Roloff, K.-H.
"Persephone," *LAW* (1965) 2260.

Roscher, W. H., ed.
Ausführliches Lexicon der griechischen und römischen Mythologie (7 vols.; Leipzig 1884–1937; reprint Hildesheim: Olms, 1965).

Rosenfeld, M.
"Der Midrasch Deuteronomium Rabba über den Tod des Mose verglichen mit der Assumptio Mosis" (Th.D. diss., Berlin and Bern, 1899).

Rost, L.
The Succession to the Throne of Daivd, trans. M. D. Rutter and D. M. Gunn (Sheffield: Almond Press, 1982) [Eng. trans. of *Die Überlieferung von der Thronnachfolge Davids* (BWANT 3/6; Stuttgart: Kohlhammer, 1926); reprint in *Das kleine Credo und andere Studien zum Alten Testament* (Heidelberg: Quelle & Meyer, 1965) 119–253].

Rost, L.
"Erwägungen zum Kyroserlaß," in A. Kuschke, ed., *Verbannung und Heimkehr. FS W. Rudolph* (Tübingen: Mohr, 1961) 300–307.

Roth, W. M. W.
"The Anonymity of the Suffering Servant," *JBL* 83 (1964) 171–79.

Roth, W. M. W.
"For Life, He Appeals to Death (Wis. 13:18): A Study of OT Idol Parodies," *CBQ* 37 (1975) 21–47.

Rothkoff, A.
"Sacrifice: Second Temple Period," *EncJud* 14 (1971) 607–10.

Rottenberg, M.
"Towards the Meaning of *kayyôm* in Eight of Its Biblical Occurrences," *Leš* 48-49 (1983–85) 60–62 (in Hebrew).

Routtenberg, H.
"Jerusalem in the Bible and Talmud: Part I," *DD* 14 (1985/86) 119–23.

Rowley, H. H.
The Biblical Doctrine of Election (London: Lutterworth, 1950).

Rowley, H. H.
"The Suffering Servant and the Davidic Messiah," in *The Servant of the Lord and Other Essays on the Old Testament* (2d ed.; Oxford: Blackwell, 1965) 61–93.

Rowley, H. H.
"The Marriage of Ruth," in *The Servant of the Lord and Other Essays on the Old Testament* (2d ed.; Oxford: Blackwell, 1965) 171–94.

Rubinstein, A.
"The Theological Aspect of Some Variant Readings in the Isaiah Scroll," *JSS* 6 (1955) 187–200.

Rudolph, W.
Esra und Nehemia samt 3. Esra (HAT I/20/1; Tübingen: Mohr, 1949).

Rudolph, W.
Die Klagelieder (KAT 17; Gütersloh: Mohn, 1962).

Rudolph, W.
Jeremia (HAT I/12; 1947; 3d ed.; Tübingen: Mohr, 1968).

Rudolph, W.
Nahum (KAT 13/3; Gütersloh: Mohn, 1975).

Rudolph, W.
"Zu Jes 62:9," *ZAW* 88 (1976) 282–84.

Rüger, H. P.
"Das Tyrusorakel Ez 27" (Th.D. diss., Tübingen, 1961).

Rüterswörden, U.
"Erwägungen zur Metaphorik des Wassers in Jes 40ff," *JSOT* 2 (1989) 1–22.

Ruffenach, F.
"'Rorate, caeli, desuper et nubes pluant iustum (Is. 45,8)," *VD* 12 (1932) 353–56.

Ruhl, L.
"Tyche," *ALGM* 5 (1965) 1309–57.

Ruiz, G.
"Ambivalencia de las preposiciones en Is 40–66," in A. Vargas-Machuca and G. Ruiz, eds., *Palabra y vida: Homenaje a José Alonso Díaz en su 70 cumpleanos* (Madrid: UPCM, 1984) 87–99.

Ruppert, L.
"Das Heil der Völker (Heilsuniversalismus) in Deutero- und 'Trito'-Jesaja," *MThZ* 45 (1994) 137–59.

Ruprecht, E.
"Die Auslegungsgeschichte zu den sogenannten Gottesknechtliedern im Buch Deuterojesaja unter methodischen Gesichtspunkten bis zu Bernhard Duhm" (Th.D. diss., Heidelberg, 1972).

Rusch, A.
"Phoinix," *PW* 20/1 (1941) 414–23.

Sacon, K. K.
"Isaiah 40:1-11: A Rhetorical-Critical Study," in J. Jackson and M. Kessler, eds., *Rhetorical Criticism: Essays in Honor of J. Muilenburg* (PTMS 1; Pittsburgh: Pickwick, 1974) 99–116.

Saggs, H. W. F.
"A Lexical Consideration for the Date of Deutero-Isaiah," *JTS* 9 (1958) 84–87.

Sakenfeld, K. D.
The Meaning of Hesed in the Hebrew Bible: A New Inquiry (HSM 17; Missoula: Scholars, 1978).

Sanders, J. A.
Suffering As Divine Discipline in the Old Testament and Post-Biblical Judaism (Colgate Rochester Divinity School Bulletin, special issue 28; Rochester, N.Y.: Colgate Rochester Divinity School, 1955).

Sanders, J. A.
"Isaiah 55:1-9," *Int* 32 (1978) 291–95.

Sasson, J. M.
"Circumcision in the Ancient Near East," *JBL* 85 (1966) 473–76.

Sasson, J. M.
"Isaiah lxvi 3-4a," *VT* 26 (1976) 199–207.

Sauer, G.
"Deuterojesaja und die Lieder vom Gottesknecht," in G. Fitzer, ed., *Geschichtsmächtigkeit und Geduld. FS der Evangelisch-theologischen Fakultät der Universität Wien* (EvTh-Sonderheft; Munich: Kaiser, 1972) 58–66.

Sawyer, J.
"What Was a mošiaᶜ?" *VT* 15 (1965) 475–86.

Sawyer, J. F. A.
"Daughter of Zion and Servant of the Lord in Isaiah: A Comparison," *JSOT* 44 (1989) 89–107.

Sawyer, J. F. A.
"Christian Interpretations of Isaiah 45:8," *BEThL* 81 (1989) 319-23.

Saydon, P. P.
"The Use of Tenses in Deutero-Isaiah," *Bib* 40 (1959) 290–301.

Schadewaldt, W.
Griechisches Theater. Aischylos: Die Perser; Die sieben gegen Theben; König Ödipus; Elektra. Aristophanes: Die Vögel; Lysistrata. Menander: Das Schiedsgericht (Frankfurt: Suhrkamp, 1964).

Schalit, A.
"Elephantine," *EncJud* 6 (1971) 604–10.

Scharbert, J.
Der Schmerz im Alten Testament (BBB 8; Bonn: Hanstein, 1955).

Scharbert, J.
Solidarität in Segen und Fluch im Alten Israel und in seiner Umwelt (BBB 14; Bonn: Hanstein, 1958).

Scharbert, J.
"Stellvertretendes Sühneleiden in den Ebed-Jahwe-Liedern und in altorientalischen Ritualtexten," *BZ* n.s. 2 (1958) 190–213.

Scharbert, J.
"'Erwählung' im Alten Testament im Licht von Gen 12,1-3," in *Dynamik im Wort. FS aus Anlass des 50-jährigen Bestehens des Katholischen Bibelwerkes in Deutschland* (Stuttgart: Katholisches Bibelwerk, 1983) 13–33.

Scharbert, J.
"Das 'Wir' in den Psalmen auf dem Hintergrund altorientalischen Betens," in E. Haag and F. L. Hossfeld, eds., *Freude an der Weisung des Herrn: Beiträge zur Theologie der Psalmen. FS H. Gross* (SBB 13; Stuttgart: Katholisches Bibelwerk, 1986) 297–324.

Schart, A.
Mose und Israel im Konflikt: Eine redaktionsgeschichtliche Studie zu den Wüstenerzählungen (OBO 98; Freiburg: Universitätsverlag; Göttingen: Vandenhoeck & Ruprecht, 1990).

Scheiber, A.
"Der Zeitpunkt des Auftretens von Deuterojesaja," *ZAW* 84 (1972) 242–43.

Schenk, W.
"Was ist ein Kommentar?," *BZ* n.s. 24 (1980) 1–20.

Schian, M.
Die Ebed-Jahwe-Lieder in Jes. 40–66: Ein literarkritisch Versuch (Inaugural diss., Halle an der Saale: J. Krause, 1895).

Schildenberger, J.
"Moses als Idealgestalt eines Armen Jahwes," in *À la rencontre de Dieu. FS A. Gelin* (Le Puy: Mappus, 1961) 71–84.

Schlier, H.
"ἀνατολή," *TDNT* 1 (1964) 352–53 [Eng. trans. of *ThWNT* I (1933) 354–55].

Schlögl, H.
"Schauspieler," *LÄ* 5 (1984) 545–46.

Schlumberger, D.
"L'argent grec dans l'empire achéménide," *MDAFA* 14 (1953) 55–57.

Schmid, H. H.
Wesen und Geschichte der Weisheit: Eine Untersuchung zur altorientalischen und israelitischen Weisheitsliteratur (BZAW 101; Berlin: Töpelmann, 1966).

Schmid, H. H.
Gerechtigkeit als Weltordnung: Hintergrund und Geschichte des alttestamentlichen Gerechtigkeitsbegriffs (BHTh 40; Tübingen: Mohr, 1968).

Schmidt, H.
Das Gebet des Angeklagten im Alten Testament (BZAW 49; Giessen: Töpelmann, 1928).

Schmidt, H. W.
"Die Struktur des Eingangs," in W. Jens, ed., *Die Bauformen der griechischen Tragödie* (Beiheft zu Poetica 6; Munich: Fink, 1971) 1–46.

Schmidt, J.-U.
"Überlegungen zur Interpretation der Antigone des Sophokles," *WuD* n.s. 14 (1977) 165-83.

Schmidt, L.
Menschlicher Erfolg und Jahwes Initiative (WMANT 38; Neukirchen-Vluyn: Neukirchener, 1970).

Schmidt, L.
"König und Charisma im Alten Testament. Beobachtungen zur Struktur des Königtums im alten Israel," *KD* 28 (1982) 73–87.

Schmidt, M.
"Dionysien," *Antike Kunst* 10 (1967) 70–81.

Schmidt, W. H.
"מִשְׁכָּן als Ausdruck Jerusalemer Kultsprache," *ZAW* 75 (1963) 91–92.

Schmidt, W. H.
Königtum Gottes in Ugarit und Israel: Zur Herkunft der Königsprädikation Jahwes (BZAW 80; 2d ed.; Berlin: Töpelmann, 1966).

Schmidt, W. H.
"Mythos im Alten Testament," *EvTh* 27 (1967) 237–54.

Schmidt, W. H.
"Ausprägungen des Bilderverbots? Zur Sichtbarkeit und Vorstellbarkeit Gottes im Alten Testament," in H. Balz and S. Schulz, eds., *Das Wort und die Wörter. FS G. Friedrich* (Stuttgart: Kohlhammer, 1973) 25–34.

Schmidt, W. H.
"Monotheismus," *TRE* 23 (1994) 233–62.

Schmitt, A.
Entrückung–Aufnahme–Himmelfahrt: Untersuchungen zu einem Vorstellungsbereich im Alten Testament (Stuttgart: Katholisches Bibelwerk, 1973).

Schmitt, H.-C.
"Prophetie und Schultheologie im Deuterojesajabuch: Beobachtungen zur Redaktionsgeschichte von Jes 40–55," *ZAW* 91 (1979) 43–61.

Schmitt, J. J.
"The Motherhood of God and Zion as Mother," *RB* 92 (1985) 557–69.

Schmitt, J. J.
"The Wife of God in Hosea 2," *BR* 34 (1989) 5–18.

Schmitt, R.
Exodus und Passah: Ihr Zusammenhang im Alten Testament (OBO 7; 2d ed.; Göttingen: Vandenhoeck & Ruprecht, 1982).

Schmitz, C. A.
"Namensglaube I. Religionsgeschichtlich," *RGG* 4 (3d ed. 1960) 1301–12.

Schneider, W.
Grammatik des Biblischen Hebräisch (5th ed.; Munich: Claudius, 1982).

Schnutenhaus, F.
"Das Kommen und Erscheinen Gottes im Alten Testament," *ZAW* 76 (1964) 1–21.

Schoors, A.
"Les choses antérieures et les choses nouvelles dans les oracles Deutéro-Isaïens," *EThL* 40 (1964) 19–47.

Schoors, A.
"L'Eschatologie dans les prophéties du Deutéro-Isaïe," *RechBib* 8 (1962) 107–28.

Schoors, A.
"The Rîb-Pattern in Isaiah, XL–LV," *Bijdr.* 30 (1969) 25–38.

Schoors, A.
"גלות דנא שבי" in Is. XL–LV: Historical Background," in P. Peli, ed., *Proceedings of the Fifth World Congress of Jewish Studies* (Jerusalem: World Union of Jewish Studies, 1969) 90–101.

Schoors, A.
"Two Notes on Isaiah XL–LV," *VT* 21 (1971) 501–5.

Schoors, A.
"Arrière-fonds historique et critique d'authenticité des textes deutéro-isaïens," *OLP* 2 (1971) 105–35.

Schoors, A.
I Am God Your Saviour: A Form-Critical Study of the Main Genres in Is. 40–55 (VTSup 24; Leiden: Brill, 1973).

Schott, S.
Mythe und Mythenbildung im Alten Ägypten (UGAÄ 15; Hildesheim: Olms, 1964).

Schottroff, W.
'Gedenken' im Alten Orient und im Alten Testament: Die Wurzel zākar im semitischen Sprachkreis (WMANT 15; 2d ed.; Neukirchen-Vluyn: Neukirchener, 1967).

Schreiner, J.
"Hören auf Gott und sein Wort in der Sicht des Deuteronomiums," *EThSt* 12 (1962) 27–47.

Schubert, K., and O. Gigon
"Hades," *LAW* (1965) 1180.

Schüpphaus, J.
"Stellung und Funktion der sogenannten Heilsankündigung bei Deuterojesaja," *ThZ* 27 (1971) 161–81.

Schürer, E.
The History of the Jewish People in the Age of Jesus Christ, vol. 1, rev. and ed. G. Vermes et al. (Edinburgh: Clark, 1973) [Eng. trans. and ed. of *Geschichte des jüdischen Volkes*, vol. 1 (Leipzig: Hinrichs, 1901)].

Schwabl, H.
"Zur 'Theogonie' bei Parmenides und Empedokles," *Wiener Studien: Zeitschrift für klassische Philologie und Patristik* 70 (1957) 278–89.

Schwabl, H.
"Die griechischen Theogonien und der Orient," in *Éléments orientaux dans la religion grecque ancienne: Colloque de Strasbourg 22–24 mai 1958* (Paris: Presses Universitaires de France, 1960) 39–56.

Schwabl, H.
"Aufbau und Struktur des Prooimions der Hesiodischen Theogonie," *Hermes* 91 (1963) 385–415.

Schwarz, E.
Identität durch Abgrenzung: Abgrenzungsprozesse in Israel im 2. vorchristlichen Jahrhundert und ihre traditionsgeschichtlichen Voraussetzungen. Zugleich ein Beitrag zur Erforschung des Jubiläenbuches (EHS.T 162; Frankfurt and Bern: Lang, 1982).

Schwarz, G.
"'(. . .) zum Bund des Volkes' (. . .)?—Eine Emendation," *ZAW* 82 (1970) 279–81.

Schwarz, G.
"'Keine Waffe' (Jes 54,17a)?" *BZ* n.s. 15 (1971) 254–55.

Schwarz, G.
"'. . . wie ein Reis vor ihm'?" *ZAW* 83 (1971) 255–56.

Schwarz, G.
"'(. . .) sieht er wird er satt' (. . .)?—Eine Emendation," *ZAW* 84 (1972) 356–58.

Schwarzenbach, A.
Die geographische Terminologie im Hebräischen des Alten Testaments (Leiden: Brill, 1954).

Schweizer, H.
"Prädikationen und Leerstellen im 1. Gottesknechtslied (Jes 42:1-4)," *BZ* n.s. 26 (1982) 251–58.

Schwenk-Bressler, U.
Sapientia Salomonis als ein Beispiel frühjüdischer Textauslegung (BEAT 32; Frankfurt: Lang, 1993).

Scott, R. B. Y.
"Meteorological Phenomena and Terminology in the OT," *ZAW* 64 (1952) 11–25.

Scullion, J. J.
"ṣedeq-ṣedaqah in Isaiah cc. 40–66," *UF* 3 (1971) 335–48.

Seale, D.
Vision and Stagecraft in Sophocles (Chicago: Univ. of Chicago Press, 1982).

Seebass, H.
"Noch einmal bḥr im alttestamentlichen Schrifttum," *ZAW* 90 (1978) 105–6.

Seebass, H.
"Opfer II. Altes Testament," *TRE* 25 (1996) 258–67.

Seeber, C
"Jenseitsgericht," *LÄ* 3 (1980) 249–52.

Seeligmann, I. L.
The Septuagint Version of Isaiah (Leiden: Brill, 1948).

Seeligmann, I. L.
"A Psalm from Pre-regal Times," *VT* 14 (1964) 75–92.

Seeligmann, I. L.
"Zur Terminologie für das Gerichtsverfahren im Wortschatz des biblischen Hebräisch," in B. Hartmann et al., eds., *Hebräische Wortforschung. FS W. Baumgartner* (VTSup 16; Leiden: Brill, 1967) 251–78.

Segal, J. B.
The Hebrew Passover from the Earliest Times to A.D. 70 (LOS 12; London: SCM, 1963).

Sehmsdorf, E.
"Studien zur Redaktionsgeschichte von Jesaja 56–66 (II)," *ZAW* 84 (1972) 547–48.

Seidel, H.
"Horn und Trompete im alten Israel unter Berücksichtigung der 'Kriegsrolle' von Qumran," *Wissenschaftliche Zeitschrift der Karl-Marx-Universität Leipzig* 6 (1956/57) 589–99.

Seidel, H.
Musik in Altisrael: Untersuchungen zur Musik-geschichte und Musikpraxis Altisraels anhand biblischer und außerbiblischer Texte (BEAT 12; Frankfurt: Lang, 1989).

Seidl, T.
"Jahwe der Krieger—Jahwe der Tröster. Kritik und Neuinterpretation der Schöpfungsvorstellungen in Jesaja 51,9-16," *BN* n.s. 21 (1983) 116–34.

Seitz, C. R.
"The Prophet Moses and the Canonical Shape of Jeremiah," *ZAW* 101 (1989) 3–27.

Seitz, C. R.
Theology in Conflict: Reactions to the Exile in the Book of Jeremiah (BZAW 176; Berlin and New York: de Gruyter, 1989).

Seitz, C. R.
"The Divine Council: Temporal Transition and New Prophecy in the Book of Isaiah," *JBL* 109 (1990) 229–47.

Seitz, C. R.
Zion's Final Destiny: The Development of the Book of Isaiah: A Reassessment of Isaiah 36–39 (Minneapolis: Fortress, 1991).

Seitz, C. R., ed.
Reading and Preaching the Book of Isaiah (Philadelphia: Fortress, 1988).

Sekine, M.
"Das Problem der Kultpolemik bei den Propheten," *EvTh* 28 (1968) 605–9.

Sekine, S.
"A Sketch of the Redaction History of the Second Isaiah," *Seishogaku Ronshu* 13 (1978) 32–69.

Sekine, S.
"Die Theodizee des Leidens im deuterojesajanischen Buch—unter redaktionsgeschichtlichem Gesichtspunkt," *AJBI* 8 (1982) 50–112.

Sekine, S.
Die tritojesajanische Sammlung (Jes 56–66) redaktionsgeschichtlich untersucht (BZAW 175; Berlin and New York: de Gruyter, 1989).

Sellin, E.
Studien zur Entstehungsgeschichte der jüdischen Gemeinde nach dem babylonischen Exil I: Der Knecht Gottes bei Deuterojesaja (Leipzig: Deichert, 1901).

Sellin, E.
Mose und seine Bedeutung für die israelitisch-jüdische Religionsgeschichte (Leipzig and Erlangen: Deichert, 1922).

Sellin, E.
Geschichte des israelitisch-jüdischen Volkes (Leipzig: Quelle & Meyer, 1924–32).

Seneca
Naturales Questiones (2 vols.; LCL; Cambridge: Harvard Univ. Press, 1971–72).

Seters, A. Van
"Isaiah 40:1-11," *Int* 35 (1981) 401–4.

Seters, J. Van
"The Problem of Childlessness in Near Eastern Law and the Patriarchs of Israel," *JBL* 87 (1968) 401–8.

Seters, J. Van
"The Religion of the Patriarchs in Genesis," *Bib* 61 (1980) 220–33.

Sethe, K.
Dramatische Texte zu altägyptischen Mysterienspielen II. Der dramatische Ramesseumspapyrus: Ein Spiel zur Thronbesteigung des Königs (UGAÄ 10; Leipzig: Hinrichs, 1928).

Seux, M. J.
Épithètes royales akkadiennes et sumériennes (Paris: Letouzey et Ané, 1967).

Seybold, K.
Das davidische Königtum im Zeugnis der Propheten (FRLANT 107; Göttingen: Vandenhoeck & Ruprecht, 1972).

Seybold, K.
Das Gebet des Kranken im Alten Testament (BWANT 99; Stuttgart: Kohlhammer, 1973).

Seybold, K.
"Thesen zur Entstehung der Lieder vom Gottesknecht," *BN* n.s. 3 (1977) 33–34.

Shaki, M.
"Universal Homage to Cyrus the Great," *ArOr* 45 (1977) 259–63.

Sichtermann, H.
"Heracles," in *LAW* (Zurich: Artemis, 1965) cols. 1258–62.

Sievi, J.
"Der unbekannte Prophet: Buch und Botschaft des Deuterojesaja," *BK* 24 (1969) 122–41.

Simian-Yofre, H.
"Exodo en Deuteroisaias," *Bib* 61 (1980) 530–53.

Simian-Yofre, H.
"La teodicea del Deuteroisaias," *Bib* 62 (1981) 55–72.

Simon, E.
The Ancient Theatre, trans. C. E. Vafopoulou-Richardson (New York: Methuen, 1982) [Eng. trans. of *Das Antike Theater* (Heidelberg: Kerle, 1972)].

Simon, E.
Festivals of Attica: An Archaeological Commentary (Wisconsin Studies in Classics; Madison: Univ. of Wisconsin Press, 1983).

Simon, N. E.
"König Cyrus und die Typologie," *Judaica* 11 (1955) 83–89.

Skehan, P. W.
"Some Textual Problems in Isaiah," *CBQ* 22 (1960) 47–55.

Sklba, R. J.
"The Redeemer of Israel," *CBQ* 34 (1972) 1–18.

Smend, R.
Die Bundesformel (ThSt[B] 68; Zurich: EVZ, 1963).

Smend, R.
Yahweh War and Tribal Confederation, trans. M. G. Rogers (Nashville: Abingdon, 1970) [Eng. trans. of *Jahwekrieg und Stämmebund* (FRLANT 84; 2d ed.; Göttingen: Vandenhoeck & Ruprecht, 1966)].

Smith, Mark S.
"*Běrît ʿam/Běrît ʿôlām:* A New Proposal for the Crux of Isa 42:6," *JBL* 100 (1981) 241–43.

Smith, Morton
"II Isaiah and the Persians," *JAOS* 83 (1963) 415–21.

Smith, S.
Isaiah Chapters XL–LV: Literary Criticism and History (Schweich Lectures on Biblical Archaeology 1940; London: Oxford Univ. Press, 1944).

Smyth, F.
"Les espaces du IIᵉ Esaie," *CBFV* 85 (1986) 31–41.

Snaith, N. H.
"The Exegesis of Isaiah XL 5–6," *ExpT* 52 (1940/41) 394–96.

Snaith, N. H.
"The Servant of the Lord in Deutero-Isaiah," in H. H. Rowley, ed., *Studies in Old Testament Prophecy. FS T. H. Robinson* (Edinburgh: Clark, 1950) 187–200.

Snaith, N. H.
"The Hebrew Root *gʾl*," *ALUOS* 3 (1961/62) 60–67.

Snaith, N. H.
"The Meaning of the Hebrew אַף," *VT* 14 (1964) 221–25.

Snaith, N. H.
"Isaiah 40–66: A Study of the Teaching of the Second Isaiah and Its Consequences," in H. M. Orlinsky and N. H. Snaith, *Studies in the Second Part of the Book of Isaiah* (VTSup 14; Leiden: Brill, 1967) 135–264.

Snaith, N. H.
"Psalm i 1 and Isaiah xl 31," *VT* 29 (1979) 363–64.

Snell, B.
The Discovery of the Mind: The Greek Origins of European Thought, trans. T. G. Rosenmeyer (New York: Harper Torchbooks, 1960) [Eng. trans. of *Entdeckung des Geistes. Mythos und Wirklichkeit in der griechischen Tragödie* (3d ed.; Hamburg: Klasen und Goverts, 1955; 7th ed.; Göttingen: Vandenhoeck & Ruprecht, 1993)].

Snell, B., ed.
Tragicorum Graecorum Fragmenta, 1 (Göttingen: Vandenhoeck & Ruprecht, 1971).

Snijders, L. A.
"The Meaning of זָר in the OT," *OTS* 10 (1954) 1–154.

Soden, W. von
"Hymne. B: Nach akkadischen Quellen," *RLA* 4 (1972–5) 544–48.

Soden, W. von
Akkadisches Handwörterbuch (3 vols.; Wiesbaden: Harrassowitz, 1965–81).

Soden, W. von, and A. Falkenstein
Sumerische und akkadische Hymnen und Gebete (Zurich and Stuttgart: Artemis, 1953).

Soggin, J. A.
"Tod und Auferstehung des leidenden Gottesknechtes Jesaja 53:8-10," *ZAW* 87 (1975) 346–55.

Sollberger, E.
"Graeco-Babylonica," *Iraq* 24 (1962) 63–72.

Sorg, T.
"Stellvertretung (Jes 52,13—53,12)," *ThBei* 16 (1985) 251–55.

Southwood, C. H.
"The Problematic *hᵃdūrîm* of Isaiah XLV 2," *VT* 25 (1975) 801–2.

Spieckermann, H.
"Barmherzig und gnädig ist der Herr . . . ," *ZAW* 102 (1990) 1–18.

Spiegel, J.
"Göttergeschichten, Erzählungen, Märchen, Fabeln," in *Ägyptologie. Literatur* (B. Spuler, ed., *Handbuch der Orientalistik* I/1 sec. 2 [2d ed.; Leiden: Brill, 1970]) 147–68.

Spiegelberg, W., ed.
Die sogenannte demotische Chronik des Pap. 215 der Bibliothèque Nationale zu Paris (Leipzig: J. C. Hinrichs'sche, 1914).

Spiro, S. J.
"Who Was the *Ḥaber*? A New Approach to an Ancient Institution," *JSJ* 11 (1980) 186–216.

Spykerboer, H. C.
The Structure and Composition of Deutero-Isaiah (Meppel: Krips Repro, 1976).

Spykerboer, H. C.
"Isaiah 55,1-5: The Climax of Deutero-Isaiah. An Invitation to Come to the New Jerusalem," in J. Vermeylen, ed., *The Book of Isaiah* (BEThL 81; Leuven: Leuven Univ. Press and Peeters, 1989) 357–59.

Staats, R.
"Auferstehung II/2. Alte Kirche," *TRE* 4 (1979) 513–29.

Stachowiak, L.
"Das Problem der Eschatologie im Buch Jesaja," *CoTh* 53 (special edition, 1983) 133–45.

Stachowiak, L.
"Druga Pieśń o Słudze Jahwe (IZ 49,1-15)," *RTK* 31 (1984) 31–42.

Stadelmann, L. I. J.
The Hebrew Conception of the World: A Philological and Literary Study (AnBib 39; Rome: Pontifical Biblical Institute, 1970).

Stadelmann, R.
"Prozessionen," *LÄ* 4 (1982) 1160–64.

Staerk, W.
Soter: Die biblische Erlösererwartung als religionsgeschichtliches Problem I: Der biblische Christus (BFCTh 31; Gütersloh: Bertelsmann, 1933).

Stähli, H.-P.
Knabe, Jüngling, Knecht: Untersuchungen zum Begriff נער *im Alten Testament* (BET 7; Frankfurt: Lang, 1978).

Stähli, H.-P.
Solare Elemente im Jahweglauben des Alten Testaments (OBO 66; Göttingen: Vandenhoeck & Ruprecht, 1985).

Stamm, J. J.
Erlösen und Vergeben im Alten Testament (Bern: Francke, 1940).

Stamm, J. J.
"Ein Vierteljahrhundert Psalmenforschung," *ThR* n.s. 23 (1955) 1–68.

Stamm, J. J.
"*Berît ᶜam* bei Deuterojesaja," in H. W. Wolff, ed., *Probleme biblischer Theologie: FS G. von Rad* (Munich: Kaiser, 1971) 510–24.

Steck, O. H.
"Aspekte des Gottesknechts in Deuterojesajas 'Ebed-Jahwe-Liedern'," *ZAW* 96 (1984) 372–90.

Steck, O. H.
"Aspekte des Gottesknechtes in Jes 52:13—53:12," *ZAW* 97 (1985) 36–58.

Steck, O. H.
"Heimkehr auf der Schulter oder/und auf der Hüfte: Jes 49:22b/60:4b," *ZAW* 98 (1986) 275–77.

Steck, O. H.
"Zur literarischen Schichtung in Jesaja 51," *BN* n.s. 44 (1988) 74–86.

Steck, O. H.
"Beobachtungen zu den Zion-Texten in Jesaja 51–54. Ein redaktionsgeschichtlicher Versuch," *BN* 46 (1989) 58–90.

Steck, O. H.
"Zion als Gelände und Gestalt. Überlegungen zur Wahrnehmung Jerusalems als Stadt und Frau im Alten Testament," *ZThK* 86 (1989) 261–81.

Steck, O. H.
"Zions Tröstung. Beobachtungen und Fragen zu Jesaja 51,1-11," in E. Blum and C. Macholz, eds., *Die Hebräische Bibel und ihre zweifache Nachgeschichte. FS R. Rendtorff zum 65. Geburtstag* (Neukirchen-Vluyn: Neukirchener, 1990) 257–76.

Steck, O. H.
Der Abschluß der Prophetie im Alten Testament: Ein Versuch zur Frage der Vorgeschichte des Kanons (BThSt 17; Neukirchen-Vluyn: Neukirchener, 1991).

Steck, O. H.
Gottesknecht und Zion: Gesammelte Aufsätze zu Deuterojesaja (FAT 4; Tübingen: Mohr, 1992).

Steck, O. H.
"Gottesvolk und Gottesknecht in Jes 40–66," *Jahrbuch für biblische Theologie* 7 (1992) 51–75.

Steck, O. H.
Die erste Jesajarolle von Qumran (2 vols.; SBS; Stuttgart, 1998).

Stein, N.
"'A Drop of a Bucket,' Delving into an Enigmatic Verse," *DD* 17 (1988/89) 199–200.

Steiner, R. C.
"The Aramaic Text in Demotic Script: The Liturgy of a New Year's Festival Imported from Bethel to Syene by Exiles from Rash," *JAOS* 111 (1991) 362–63.

Steiner, R. C.
"The Aramaic Text in Demotic Script (1.99)," in William W. Hallo and K. Lawson Younger, Jr., eds.,

The Context of Scripture, vol. 1: *Canonical Compositions from the Biblical World* (Leiden: Brill, 1997) 309–27.

Steinmann, J.
Le livre de la consolation d'Israël et les prophètes du retour de l'exil (Paris: Cerf, 1960).

Stockmans, A.
Redenvoering van den hyligen geest, gedaen in den hemel, met her begin des Nieuwen Testaments, tot de hemelsche gemeente der aertsvaderen, welke geestelyk genaemt word Sara en Jerusalem; beschreeven in het LIVste hooftstuk van Jesais (Amsterdam: Isaac Stokmans, 1736).

Stockmans, A.
Het vier en vyftigste hooftstuk der godspraeken van Jesaias, verklaert door Aegidius Stockmans: Twede uytgaeve. Waer by komt een brief ter verdediging van het gevoelen des schryvers (Amsterdam: Hendrik Vieroot, 1743).

Stoebe, H. J.
"Zu Jesaja 40,6," *WuD* n.s. 2 (1950) 122–28.

Stoebe, H. J.
"Raub und Beute," in *Hebräische Wortforschung. FS W. Baumgartner* (VTSup 16; Leiden: Brill, 1967) 340–54.

Stoebe, H. J.
Das erste Buch Samuelis (KAT 8/1; Gütersloh: Mohn, 1973).

Stoebe, H. J.
"Überlegungen zu Jesaja 40:1-11," *ThZ* 40 (1984) 104–13.

Stolper, M. W.
Entrepreneurs and Empire: The Murašu Archive, the Murašu Firm, and Persian Rule in Babylonia (Nederlands Historisch-Archäologisch Instituut te Istanbul 54; Leiden: Brill, 1985).

Stolz, F.
Jahwes und Israels Kriege: Kriegstheorien und Kriegserfahrungen im Glauben des Alten Israel (AThANT 60; Zurich: TVZ, 1972).

Stolz, F.
"Jahwes Unvergleichlichkeit und Unergründlichkeit; Aspekte der Entwicklung zum alttestamentlichen Monotheismus," *WuD* n.s. 14 (1977) 9–24.

Stolz, F.
Einführung in den biblischen Monotheismus (Darmstadt: Wissenschaftliche Buchgesellschaft, 1996).

Stone, M. E.
"Reactions to Destructions of the Second Temple: Theology, Perception and Conversion," *JSJ* 12 (1981) 195–204.

Störk, L.
"Nilpferd," *LÄ* 4 (1982) 501–6.

Stuhlmueller, C.
"The Theology of Creation in Second Isaias," *CBQ* 21 (1959) 429–67.

Stuhlmueller, C.
"Yahweh-King and Deutero-Isaiah," *BR* 11 (1966) 32–45.

Stuhlmueller, C.
"'First and Last' and 'Yahweh-Creator' in Deutero-Isaiah," *CBQ* 29 (1967) 189–205.

Stuhlmueller, C.
"Deutero-Isaiah," *JBC* 1 (1968) 366–86.

Stuhlmueller, C.
"'Oh Comfort My People'—The Commission of Second Isaiah Today," *TBT* 39 (1968) 2709–14.

Stuhlmueller, C.
"Quid Deutero-Isaia in capitibus 40–55 de redemptione creatrice doceat," *VD* 47 (1969) 170–76.

Stuhlmueller, C.
Creative Redemption in Deutero-Isaiah (AnBib 43; Rome: Biblical Institute Press, 1970).

Stuhlmueller, C.
"Deutero-Isaiah (cc. 40–55): Major Transitions in the Prophet's Theology and in Contemporary Scholarship," *CBQ* 42 (1980) 1–29.

Stummer, F.
"Einige keilschriftliche Parallelen zu Jes 40–66," *JBL* 45 (1926) 171–89.

Suggs, M. J.
"Wisdom of Solomon 2:10–5: A Homily Based on the Fourth Servant Song," *JBL* 76 (1957) 26–33.

Sutcliffe, E. F.
"The Clouds as Water-Carriers in Hebrew Thought," *VT* 3 (1953) 99–103.

Syrén, R.
"Targum Isaiah 52:13–53:12 and Christian Interpretation," *JJS* 15 (1989) 201–12.

Tabor, J. D.
"'Returning to the Divinity': Josephus's Portrayal of the Disappearances of Enoch, Elijah, and Moses," *JBL* 108 (1989) 225–38.

Talmon, S.
"Aspects of the Textual Transmission of the Bible in the Light of Qumran Manuscripts," *Textus* 4 (1964) 95–132; reprint in F. M. Cross and S. Talmon, eds., *Qumran and the History of the Biblical Text* (Cambridge: Harvard Univ. Press, 1975) 226–63.

Talmon, S.
"The 'Desert Motif' in the Bible and in Qumran Literature," in A. Altmann, ed., *Biblical Motifs, Origins and Transformations* (Cambridge: Harvard Univ. Press, 1966) 31–63.

Talmon, S.
"*Yād wāšēm* : An Idiomatic Phrase in Biblical Literature and Its Variations," *Hebrew Studies* 25 (1984) 8–17.

Talstra, E., F. Postma, and H. A. van Zwet
Deuterojesaja: Proeve van automatische tekstverwerking ten dienste van de exegese (2d ed.; Amsterdam: Vrije Universiteit Boekhandel/Uitgeverij, 1981).

Tångberg, A.
"Nehemia/Nehemiabuch," *TRE* 24 (1994) 242–46.

Taplin, O.
The Stagecraft of Aeschylus (Oxford: Clarendon, 1977).

Taplin, O.
Greek Tragedy in Action (Cambridge: Cambridge Univ. Press, 1978).

Terian, A.
"The Hunting Imagery in Isaiah li 20a," *VT* 41 (1991) 462–71.

Terrien, S.
"Quelques remarques sur les affinités de Job avec le Deutéro-Esaïe," in *Volume du Congrès: Géneve 1965* (VTSup 15; Leiden: Brill, 1966) 295–310.

Tertullian
"De Corona," in *Tertulliani Opera pars II: Opera Montanistica II* (CChrSL II; Turnhout: Brepols, 1954) 1037–65.

Texier, R.
"Le Dieu caché de Pascal et du Second Isaïe," *NRTh* 111 (1989) 3–23.

Thomas, D. W.
"The Root ידע in Hebrew," *JTS* 35 (1934) 298–306.

Thomas, D. W.
"'A Drop of a Bucket'? Some Observations on the Hebrew Text of Isaiah 40:15," in M. Black and G. Fohrer, eds., *In Memoriam P. Kahle* (BZAW 103; Berlin: Töpelmann, 1968) 214–21.

Thomas, D. W.
"Isaiah XLIV,9-20: A Translation and Commentary," in J. Amusin et al., eds., *Hommage à André Dupont-Sommer* (Paris: Libr. d'Amérique et d'Orient, 1971) 319–30.

Thomson, J. G. S. S.
"The Shepherd-Ruler Concept in the OT and Its Application in the NT," *SJT* 8 (1955) 406–18.

Thorion, Y.
Studien zur klassischen hebräischen Syntax, MSAA.As 6 (1984) 3–36.

Thorion-Vardi, T.
"A Note on I Q Hodayot IX 5," *RevQ* 11 (1983) 429–30.

Thureau-Dangin, F.
Rituels accadiens (Paris: Ernest Leroux, 1921).

Tidwell, N. L.
"My Servant Jacob, Is. XLII 1," in *Studies on Prophecy: A Collection of Twelve Papers* (VTSup 26; Leiden: Brill, 1974) 84–91.

Tidwell, N. L.
"M.T. Isa. 40,10 בְּחָזָק: An approach to a textual problem via rhetorical criticism," *Semitics* 6 (1978) 15–27.

Tiede, D. L.
"Expository Article: Luke 6:17-26," *Int* 40 (1986) 63–68.

Tom, W.
"Welke is de Zin van het 'Dubbel Ontvangen' uit Jesaja 40:2?" *GThT* 59 (1959) 122–23.

Toorn, K. van der
"Echoes of Judaean Necromancy in Isaiah 28,7-22," *ZAW* 100 (1988) 199–217.

Toperoff, S. P.
"The Fox in Bible and Midrash," *DD* 16 (1987/88) 112–15.

Torrey, C. C.
"Isaiah 41," *HTR* 44 (1951) 121–36.

Tov, E.
"The Representation of the Causative Aspects of the *Hiph⁽il* in the LXX: A Study in Translation Technique," *Bib* 63 (1982) 417–24.

Tov, E.
Textual Criticism of the Hebrew Bible (Minneapolis: Fortress, 1992).

Trever, J. C.
Scrolls from Qumrân Cave I: The Great Isaiah Scroll, the Order of the Community, the Pesher to Habakkuk (London: Clowes & Son, 1972).

Treves, M.
"Isaiah LIII," *VT* 24 (1974) 98–108.

Treves, M.
The Dates of the Psalms (Pisa: Giardini Stampatori, 1988).

Tromp, N. J.
Primitive Conceptions of Death and the Nether World in the Old Testament (BibOr 21; Rome: Pontifical Biblical Institute, 1969).

Trudinger, P.
"To Whom Then Will You Liken God?" (A Note on the Interpretation of Isaiah XL 18-20)," *VT* 17 (1967) 220–25.

Tsevat, M.
"Studies in the Book of Samuel III. The Steadfast House: What Was David Promised in II Sam. 7:11b-16?" *HUCA* 34 (1963) 71–82.

Tsumura, D. T.
"tōhû in Isaiah xlv 19," *VT* 38 (1988) 361–64.

Tucker, G. M., David L. Petersen, and Robert R. Wilson, eds.
Canon, Theology and Old Testament Interpretation: Essays in Honor of B.S. Childs (Philadelphia: Fortress, 1988).

Tuplin, C.
"The Administration of the Achaemenid Empire," in I. Carradice, ed., *Coinage and Administration in the Athenian and Persian Empires* (British Archeological Reports, International Series 343; Oxford: B.A.R., 1987) 109–66.

Uchelen, N. A. van
"Abraham als Felsen (Jes 51,1)," *ZAW* 80 (1968) 183–91.

Uehlinger, C.
"'Zeichne eine Stadt . . . und belagere sie!' Bild und Wort einer Zeichenhandlung Ezechiels gegen Jerusalem (Ez 4f)," in M. Küchler and C. Uehlinger, eds., *Jerusalem. Texte–Bilder–Steine, zum 100 Geburtstag von H. und O. Keel-Leu* (NTOA 6; Freiburg: Universitätsverlag; Göttingen: Vandenhoeck & Ruprecht, 1987).

Uffenheimer, B.
"Aspects of the Spiritual Image of Deutero-Isaiah," *Imm.* 12 (1981) 9–20.

Uhlig, S.
Das ätheiopische Henochbuch (JSHRZ 5/6; Gütersloh: Mohn, 1984).

Ulrichsen, J. H.
"*JHWH mālak:* Einige sprachliche Beobacht-ungen," *VT* 27 (1977) 361–74.

Ungnad, A.
"Der Gottesbrief als Form assyrischer Kriegs-berichterstattung," *OLZ* 21 (1918) 72–75.

Urbrock, W. J.
"Samson: A Play for Voices," in E. R. Follis ed., *Directions in Biblical Hebrew Poetry* (JSOTSup 40; Sheffield: JSOT Press, 1987) 233–37.

Utzschneider, H.
Hosea: Prophet vor dem Ende (OBO 31; Göttingen: Vandenhoeck & Ruprecht, 1980).

Utzschneider, H.
Das Heiligtum und das Gesetz: Studien zur Bedeutung der sinaitischen Heiligtumstexte (Ex 25–40; Lev 8–9) (OBO 77; Göttingen: Vandenhoeck & Ruprecht, 1988).

Utzschneider, H.
Künder oder Schreiber? Eine These zum Problem der 'Schriftprophetie' auf Grund von Maleachi 1,6–2,9 (BEAT 19; Frankfurt: Lang, 1989).

Utzschneider, H.
Gottes langer Atem: Die Exoduserzählung (Ex 1–14) in ästhetischer und historischer Sicht (SBS 166; Stuttgart: Katholisches Bibelwerk, 1996).

Utzschneider, H.
"Michas Reise in die Zeit. Ein Werkstattbericht," in W. Sommer, ed., *Zeitenwende–Zeitenende* (Theolo-gische Akzente 2; Stuttgart: Kohlhammer, 1997) 11–40.

Vaccari, A.
"I carmi del 'Servo di Jahve'. Ultime risonanze e discussioni," *SPIB* 22 (1934) 216–44.

Valbelle, D.
Les Neuf Arcs: L'égyptien et les étrangers de la préhistoire à la conquête d'Alexandrie (Paris: Colin, 1990).

Vanderkam, J. C.
"Calendars," *ABD* 1 (1992) 810–20.

Vanoni, G.
"Anspielungen und Zitate innerhalb der hebräi-schen Bibel. Am Beispiel von Dtn 4,29; Dtn 30,3 und Jes 29,13-14," in W. Gross, ed., *Jeremia und die "deuteronomistische Bewegung"* (BBB 98; Weinheim: Beltz Athenäum, 1995) 383–95.

Vattoni, F.
Ecclesiastico: Testo ebraico con apparato critico e ver-sioni greca, latina e siriaca (Publicazioni del Semi-nario di Semitica, Testi 1; Naples: Istituto Orientale, 1968).

Veijola, T.
Die Ewige Dynastie: David und die Entstehung seiner Dynastie nach der deuteronomistischen Darstellung (AASF B 193; Helsinki: Suomaleinen Tiedeakatemia, 1975).

Vergil
Aeneis, lateinisch-deutsch (Sammlung Tusculum; 8th ed.; Munich: Artemis & Winkler, 1994).

Vermes, G.
"Die Gestalt des Mose an der Wende der beiden Testamente," in H. Cazelles et al., eds., *Moses* (Düs-seldorf: Patmos, 1963) 61–93.

Vermes, G.
The Dead Sea Scrolls in English (2d ed.; Harmonds-worth: Penguin, 1984).

Vermeylen, J.
"Le motif de la création dans le Deutéro-Isaïe," in *La création dans l'Orient ancien* (LD 127; Paris: Cerf, 1987) 183–240.

Vernant, J. P., et al.
Divination et rationalité (Paris: du Seuil, 1974).

Versnel, H. S.
Triumphus: An Inquiry into the Origin, Development and Meaning of the Roman Triumph (Leiden: Brill, 1970).

Vesco, J.-L.
"Abraham: Actualisation et Relectures," *RSPhTh* 55 (1971) 33–80.

Vetter, D.
"Untersuchung zum Seherspruch im Alten Testa-ment" (Th.D. diss.; Heidelberg, 1963).

Vetter, D.
Seherspruch und Segensschilderung. Ausdrucksabsicht-en und sprachliche Verwirklichungen in den Bileam-Sprüchen von Numeri 23 und 24 (CTM 4; Stuttgart: Calwer, 1974).

Vischer, W.
Valeur de l'Ancien Testament: Commentaires des livres de Job, Esther, l'Ecclésiaste, le second Esaïe, précédés d'une introduction (Geneva: Labor et Fides, 1958).

Voget, A.
De luyster van de kerk des nieuwen testaments naa haar laatst verval: vertoont in schriftmaatige opening van de LVIIIste, LIXste en LXste hoofdstukken der godspraaken van den propheet Jesajas (Utrecht: Johannes Evelt, 1741).

Vogt, E.
"Vox *bᵉrît* concrete adhibita illustratur," *Bib* 36 (1955) 565–66.

Vogt, E.
"Einige hebräische Wortbedeutungen," *Bib* 48 (1967) 57–74.

Vogt, E.
Tragiker Ezechiel (JSHRZ 4; Gütersloh: Mohn, 1983).

Vogt, E.
"Das Mosesdrama des Ezechiel und die attische Tragödie," in A. Bierl, P. von Möllendorff, and E. Vogt, eds., *Orchestra–Drama Mythos Bühne. FS H. Flashar* (Stuttgart and Leipzig: B.G. Teubner, 1994) 151–60.

Vogt, H. C. M.
Studie zur nachexilischen Gemeinde in Esra-Nehemia (Werl: Coelde, 1966).

Vriezen, Th. C.
Die Erwählung Israels nach dem Alten Testament (AThANT 24; Zurich: Zwingli, 1953).

Vriezen, Th. C.
"Bubers Auslegung des Liebesgebotes, Lev 19,18b," *ThZ* 22 (1966) 4–7.

Wachsmuth, D.
"Unterwelt," *KP* 5 (1975) 1053–56.

Wächter, L.
"Israel und Jeschurun," in K.-H. Bernhardt, ed., *Schalom. FS A. Jepsen* (Stuttgart: Calwer, 1971) 58–64.

Wada, M.
"Reconsideration of *Mišpāṭ* in Isaiah 42:1-4," *Seishogaku Ronshu* 16 (1981) 46–79.

Waerden, B. L. van der
Die Astronomie der Griechen (Darmstadt: Wissenschaftliche Buchgesellschaft, 1988).

Wagner, G.
"Le scandale de la croix expliqué par le chant du serviteur d'Esaïe 53. Réflexion sur Philippiens 2/6-11," *EThR* 61 (1986) 177–87.

Wagner, N. E.
"רָנָה in the Psalter," *VT* 10 (1960) 435–41.

Wagner, S. M.
Die lexikalischen und grammatikalischen Aramaismen im alttestamentlichen Hebräisch (BZAW 96; Berlin: Töpelmann, 1966).

Walcot, P., and W. G. Lambert
"A New Babylonian Theogony and Hesiod," *Kadmos* 4 (1965) 64–72.

Waldow, H. E. von
"Anlass und Hintergrund der Verkündigung des Deuterojesaja" (Th.D. diss., Bonn, 1953).

Waldow, H. E. von
Denn ich erlöse dich: Eine Auslegung von Jes 43 (BibS[N] 29; Neukirchen-Vluyn: Neukirchener, 1960).

Waldow, H. E. von
"The Message of Deutero-Isaiah," *Int* 22 (1968) 259–87.

Waldow, H. E. von
"Der Gottesknecht bei Deuterojesaja. Israel, die Juden und die Kirche Jesu Christi," *ThZ* 41 (1985) 201–19.

Walker, N.
"Concerning hûʾ and ʾanî hûʾ," *ZAW* 74 (1962) 205–6.

Walla, M. L.
Der Vogel Phönix in der antiken Literatur und der Dichtung des Laktanz (Phil. diss. 291; Vienna: Universität Wien, 1969).

Wallis, G.
"Horn," *BHH* 2 (1964) 749.

Wallis, G.
"Jeschurun," *BHH* 2 (1964) 858.

Wallis, G.
"Musik," *BHH* 2 (1964) 1258–62.

Walls, N. H.
The Goddess Anat in Ugaritic Myth (SBLDS 135; Atlanta: Scholars Press, 1992).

Walser, G.
Die Völkerschaften auf den Reliefs von Persepolis: Historische Studien über die sogenannten Tributzüge an der Apadanatreppe (Berlin: Gebrüder Mann, 1966).

Walsh, J. T.
"The Case for the Prosecution. Isaiah 41.21–42.17," in E. R. Follis ed., *Directions in Biblical Hebrew Poetry* (JSOTSup 40; Sheffield: JSOT Press, 1987) 101–18.

Walton, J. H.
"New Observations on the Date of Isaiah," *JETS* 28 (1985) 129–32.

Wanke, G.
"אוֹי und הוֹי," *ZAW* 78 (1966) 215–18.

Waschke, E.-J.
"Das Verhältnis alttestamentlicher Überlieferungen im Schnittpunkt der Dynastiezusage und die Dynastiezusage im Spiegel alttestamentlicher Überlieferungen," *ZAW* 99 (1987) 157–79.

Waser, O.
"Tyche in bildlicher Darstellung," *ALGM* 5 (1965) 1357–83.

Watson, W. G. E.
"Fixed Pairs in Ugaritic and Isaiah," *VT* 22 (1972) 460–67.

Webster, E. C.
"A Rhetorical Study of Isaiah 66," *JSOT* 34 (1986) 93–108.

Webster, T. B. L.
The Greek Chorus (London: Methuen, 1970).

Weinberg, J.
The Citizen-Temple Community (JSOTSup 151; Sheffield: JSOT Press, 1992).

Weinberg, S. S.
"Post-Exilic Palestine: An Archaeological Report," *PIASH* 4 (1969) 78–97.

Weinberg, W.
"Language Consciousness in the OT," *ZAW* 92 (1980) 185–204.

Weinfeld, M.
"Ancient Near Eastern Patterns in Prophetic Literature," *VT* 27 (1977) 178–95.

Weinfeld, M.
"God the Creator in Gen I and the Prophecy of Second Isaiah," *Tarbiz* 37/2 (1968) 105–32 (in Hebrew).

Weippert, H.
"Panzer," *BRL* (1977) 248.

Weippert, M.
"'Heiliger Krieg' in Israel und Assyrien," *ZAW* 84 (1972) 461–93.

Weippert, M.
"Erwägungen zu Jesaja 44,24-28," *DBAT* 21 (1985) 121–32.

Weippert, M. H. E.
"De herkomst von het heilsorakel voor Israel bij Deutero-Jesaja," *NedThT* 36 (1982) 1–11.

Weiss, M.
"Methodologisches über die Behandlung der Metapher—dargelegt an Am 1:2," *ThZ* 23 (1967) 1–25.

Weissbach, F. H., ed.
Die Inschriften Nebukadnezars II im Wâdī Brîssā und am Nahr el-Kelb (WVDOG 5, 1906; reprint; Osnabrück: Zeller, 1978).

Welte, M.
"Trostbotschaft: Gedanken zu Jes 40:1-8," *GuL* 49 (1976) 469–72.

Welten, P.
"Bilder II, AT," *TRE* 6 (1980) 517–21.

Welten, P.
"Königsherrschaft Jahwes und Thronbesteigung. Bemerkungen zu unerledigten Fragen," *VT* 32 (1982) 297–310.

Wenin, A.
Le poème dit du 'Serviteur souffrant' (Is 52,13–53,12). Proposition de lecture," *La Foi et le temps* 24 (1993) 493–507.

Wentzel, G.
"Acheron," PW 1/1 (1893) 217–19.

Wernberg-Møller, P.
"Studies in the Defective Spellings in the Isaiah-Scrolls of St. Mark's Monastery," *JSS* 3 (1958) 244–64.

Wernberg-Møller, P.
"Observations on the Hebrew Participle," *ZAW* 71 (1959) 54–67.

Werner, W.
Studien zur alttestamentlichen Vorstellung vom Plan Jahwes (BZAW 173; Berlin and New York: de Gruyter, 1988).

Westermann, C.
"Die Begriffe für Fragen und Suchen im AT," *KD* 6 (1960) 2–30.

Westermann, C.
The Praise of God in the Psalms, trans. K. R. Crim (Richmond: John Knox, 1966) [Eng. trans. of *Das Loben Gottes in den Psalmen* (3d ed.; Göttingen: Vandenhoeck & Ruprecht, 1963)].

Westermann, C.
"3. Sonntag nach Trinitatis—Hes 18,1-4.21-24.30-32," *CPH* 2 (1963) 153–62.

Westermann, C.
Forschung am Alten Testament: Gesammelte Studien (2 vols.; ThBü 24 and 55; Munich: Kaiser, 1964 and 1974).

Westermann, C.
"Das Heilswort bei Deuterojesaja," *EvTh* 24 (1964) 355–73.

Westermann, C.
"Sprache und Struktur der Prophetie Deuterojesajas," in idem, *Forschung am Alten Testament: Gesammelte Studien,* vol. 1 (ThBü 24; Munich: Kaiser, 1964) 92–170; reprint in idem, *Sprache und Struktur der Prophetie Deuterojesajas: Mit einer Literaturübersicht "Hauptlinien der Deuterojesajaforschung von 1964–1979" zusammengestellt und kommentiert v. A. Richter* (CTM 11; Stuttgart: Calwer, 1981) 9–87.

Westermann, C.
"Jesaja 48 und die 'Bezeugung gegen Israel'," in W. C. van Unnik and A. S. van der Woude, eds., *Studia Biblica et Semitica. FS Th. C. Vriezen* (Wageningen: H. Veenmann en Zonen N.V., 1966) 356–66.

Westermann, C.
Basic Forms of Prophetic Speech, trans. H. C. White (1967; reprint Louisville: John Knox, 1991) [Eng. trans. of *Grundformen prophetischer Rede* (BEvTh 31; 4th ed.; Munich: Kaiser, 1971)].

Westermann, C.
Genesis 1–11 (EdF 7; Darmstadt: Wissenschaftliche Buchgesellschaft, 1972).

Westermann, C.
Genesis (BKAT I/1-3; Neukirchen-Vluyn: Neukirchener, 1974–82).

Westermann, C.
Genesis 1–11 and *Genesis 12–36,* trans. J. J. Scullion (Continental Commentary; Minneapolis: Augsburg, 1984–85) [Eng. trans. of *Genesis* (BKAT I/1 and I/2; Neukirchen-Vluyn: Neukirchener, 1974–81)].

Westermann, C.
Praise and Lament in the Psalms, trans. K. R. Crim and R. N. Soulen (Atlanta: John Knox, 1981) [Eng. trans. of *Lob und Klage in den Psalmen* (5th ed.; Göttingen: Vandenhoeck & Ruprecht, 1977)].

Westermann, C.
"Zur Erforschung und zum Verständnis der prophetischen Heilsworte," *ZAW* 98 (1986) 1–13.

Whitehouse, O. C.
"The Historical Background of the Deutero-Isaiah," *Exp.* ser. 8, vol. 25 (1923) 241–59, 321–44, 405–26.

Whitley, C. F.
"A Note on Isa. XLI,27," *JSS* 2 (1957) 327–28.

Whitley, C. F.
"Textual Notes on Deutero-Isaiah," *VT* 11 (1961) 457–61.

Whitley, C. F.
"Deutero-Isaiah's Interpretation of ṣedeq," *VT* 22 (1972) 469–75.

Whitley, C. F.
"Further Notes on the Text of Deutero-Isaiah," *VT* 25 (1975) 683–87.

Whitley, C. F.
"The Semantic Range of Ḥesed," *Bib* 62 (1981) 519–26.

Whybray, R. N.
The Succession Narrative: A Study of II Samuel 9–20; I Kings 1 and 2 (SBT 2/9; London: SCM, 1968).

Whybray, R. N.
The Heavenly Counsellor in Isaiah xl 13-14. A Study of the Sources of the Theology of Deutero-Isaiah (SOTSMS 1; Cambridge: Cambridge Univ. Press, 1971).

Whybray, R. N.
Thanksgiving for a Liberated Prophet: An Interpretation of Isaiah Chapter 53 (JSOTSup 4; Sheffield: JSOT Press, 1978).

Whybray, R.N.
"Two Recent Studies on Second Isaiah," *JSOT* 34 (1986) 109–17.

Widengren, G.
"The Sacral Kingship of Iran," in *The Sacral Kingship: Contributions to the Central Theme of the VIIIth International Congress for the History of Religions (Rome, April 1955)* (SHR 4; Leiden: Brill, 1959) 242–57.

Widengren, G.
Die Religionen Irans (Stuttgart: Kohlhammer, 1965).

Widengren, G.
"Yahweh's Gathering of the Dispersed," in W. B. Barrick and J. R. Spencer, eds., *In the Shelter of Elyon: Essays on Ancient Palestinian Life and Literature in Honor of G. W. Ahlström* (JSOTSup 31; Sheffield: JSOT Press, 1984) 227–45.

Wieringen, A. van
"Jesaja 40,1-11: eine drama-linguistische Lesung von Jesaja 6 her," *BN* n.s. 49 (1989) 82–93.

Wieringen, A. van
Analogies in Isaiah, vol. A: *Computerized Analysis of Parallel Text between Isaiah 56–66 and Isaiah 40–66;* vol. B: *Computerized Concordance of Analogies between Isaiah 56–66 and Isaiah 40–66* (Amsterdam: Free Univ. Press, 1993).

Wigoder, G., ed.
Encyclopaedia Judaica (16 vols.; Jerusalem: Keter, 1971–72).

Wijngaards, J.
"הוציא and העלה, a twofold approach to the Exodus," *VT* 15 (1965) 91–102.

Wilcke, C.
"Hymne. A. Nach sumerischen Quellen," *RLA* 4 (1972–75) 539–44.

Wilcox, P., and D. Paton-Williams
"The Servant Songs in Deutero-Isaiah," *JSOT* 42 (1988) 79–102.

Wildberger, H.
"Die Neuinterpretation des Erwählungsglaubens Israels in der Krise der Exilszeit," in E. Jenni, J. J. Stamm and H. J. Stoebe, eds., *Wort–Gebot–Glaube: Beiträge zur Theologie des Alten Testaments. FS W. Eichrodt* (AThANT 59; Zurich: Zwingli, 1970) 307–24.

Wildberger, H.
"Der Monotheismus Deuterojesajas," in *Jahwe und sein Volk: Gesammelte Aufsätze zum AT* (ThBü 66; Munich: Kaiser, 1979) 249–73.

Wilkie, J. M.
"Nabonidus and the Later Jewish Exiles," *JTS* 11 (1951) 36–45.

Will, E.
"Théâtres sacrés de la Syrie et de l'empire," *MUSJ* 37/10 (1961) 207–19.

Willers, D.
"Athene," *LAW* 1 (1965) 382–85.

Williamson, H. G. M.
"'The Sure Mercies of David': Subjective or Objective Genitive?" *JSS* 23 (1978) 31–49.

Williamson, H. G. M.
"DA'AT in Isaiah LIII 11," *VT* 28 (1978) 118–22.

Williamson, H. G. M.
"Word Order in Isaiah XLIII.12," *JTS* 30 (1979) 499–502.

Williamson, H. G. M.
Ezra, Nehemia (WBC 16; Waco: Word, 1985).

Williamson, H. G. M.
"Isaiah 40:20–A Case of Not Seeing the Wood for the Trees," *Bib* 67 (1986) 1–20.

Willis, J. T.
"Alternating (ABA'B') Parallelism in the Old Testament Psalms and Prophetic Literature," in E. R. Follis, ed., *Directions in Biblical Hebrew Poetry* (JSOTSup 40; Sheffield: JSOT Press, 1987) 49–76.

Willmes, B.
"Gott erlöst sein Volk. Gedanken zum Gottesbild Deuterojesajas nach Jes 43:1-7," *BN* n.s. 51 (1990) 61–93.

Wilshire, L. E.
"The Servant-City: A New Interpretation of the 'Servant of the Lord' in the Servant Songs of Deutero-Isaiah," *JBL* 94 (1975) 356–67.

Wilson, R. R.
"Israel's Judicial System in the Preexilic Period," *JQR* 74 (1983) 229–48.

Winkle, D. W. van
"The Relationship of the Nations to Yahweh and to Israel in Isaiah xl–lv," *VT* 35 (1985) 446–58.

Wiseman, D. J.
The Vassal-Treaties of Esarhaddon (Iraq 20; London: British School of Archaeology in Iraq, 1958).

Wissowa, G., et al., eds.
Paulys Realencyclopädie der classischen Altertumswissenschaft (24 vols.; Stuttgart: Druckmüller, 1893–1964).

Wolf, E. F. H.
De lijdende knecht des Heeren: Het drieenvijftigste hoofdstuk van Jezaja, eene messiaansche prophetie, verklaard (Amsterdam: Hoeveker & Zoon, 1872).

Wolff, H. W.
Jesaja 53 im Urchristentum: Die Geschichte der Prophetie "Siehe, es siegt mein Knecht" bis zu Justin (Bielefeld: Buchdruckerei der Anstalt Bethel, 1942).

Wolff, H. W.
Amos, the Prophet: The Man and His Background, trans. F. R. McCurley (Philadelphia: Fortress, 1973) [Eng. trans. of *Amos' geistige Heimat* (Neukirchen-Vluyn: Neukirchener, 1964)].

Wolff, H. W.
Joel and Amos, trans. W. Janzen (Hermeneia; Philadelphia: Fortress, 1977) [Eng. trans. of *Dodekapropheton 2: Joel und Amos* (BKAT XIV/2; Neukirchen-Vluyn: Neukirchener, 1969)].

Wolff, H. W.
Gesammelte Studien zum Alten Testament (ThBü 22; 2d ed.; Munich: Kaiser, 1973).

Wolff, H. W.
Hosea, trans. G. Stansel (Hermeneia; Philadelphia: Fortress, 1974) [Eng. trans. of *Dodekapropheton 1:*

Hosea (BKAT XIV/1; 3d ed.; Neukirchen-Vluyn: Neukirchener, 1976)].

Wolff, H. W.
Anthropology of the Old Testament, trans. M. Kohl (Philadelphia: Fortress, 1974) [Eng. trans. of *Anthropologie des Alten Testaments* (4th ed.; Munich: Kaiser, 1984)].

Wörl, V.
"Die Utopie Gerechtigkeit," *Süddeutsche Zeitung, Ausgabe vom 18.-20. April 1992* (Munich: Süddeutscher Verlag, 1992).

Woude, A. S. van der
Micha (POT; Nijkerk: Callenbach, 1976).

Woude, A. S. van der
"Hoe de Here naar Sion wederkeert. Traditio-historische overwegingen bij Jesaja 52:7-8," in *De Knecht: Studies rondom Deutero-Jesaja. FS J. L. Koole* (Kampen: Kok, 1978).

Woude, A. S. van der
Zacharia (POT; Nijkerk: Callenbach, 1984).

Wright, G. E.
The Old Testament against Its Enviroment (London: SCM, 1950).

Wright, G. E.
"The Lawsuit of God: A Form-Critical Study of Deuteronomy 32," in B. W. Anderson and W. Harrelson, eds., *Israel's Prophetic Heritage: Essays in Honor of J. Muilenburg* (New York: Harper, 1962) 26–67.

Wünsche, A.
Der Midrasch Schemot Rabba: Das ist die allegorische Auslegung des zweiten Buches Mose (Bibliotheca Rabbinica III; 1882; reprint Hildesheim: Olms, 1967).

Würthwein, E.
"Amos 5,21-27," *ThLZ* 72 (1947) 143–52.

Würthwein, E.
"Kultpolemik oder Kultbescheid?" in E. Würthwein and O. Kaiser, eds., *Tradition und Situation: Studien zur alttestamentlichen Prophetie. FS A. Weiser* (Göttingen: Vandenhoeck & Ruprecht, 1963) 115–31.

Wyatt, N.
"Atonement Theology in Ugarit and Israel," *UF* 8 (1976) 415–30.

Xenophon
Anabasis, in *Xenophon III* (LCL; trans. and rev. C. L. Brownson; Cambridge: Harvard Univ. Press; London: Heinemann, 1922; reprint 1968).

Xenophon
Cyropaedia I and II, in *Xenophon V and VI* (LCL; trans. and rev. W. Miller; Cambridge: Harvard Univ. Press; London: Heinemann, 1914; reprint 1968).

Yadin, Y.
The Finds from Bar Kokhba Period in the Cave of Letters (Jerusalem: Israel Exploration Society, 1963).

Yeivin, S.
"Philological Notes, XVI," *Leš* 42 (1978) 307 (in Hebrew).

Zakovitch, Y.
"The Woman's Rights in the Biblical Law of Divorce," *JLA* 4 (1981) 28–46.

Zenger, E.
"Jahwe und die Götter: Die Frühgeschichte der Religion Israels als eine theologische Wertung nichtisraelitischer Religionen," *ThPh* 43 (1968) 338–59.

Zenger, E.
"Was wird anders bei kanonischer Psalmenauslegung," in F.V. Reiterer, ed., *Ein Gott–eine Offenbarung. Beiträge zur biblischen Exegese, Theologie und Spiritualität. FS N. Füglister* (Würzburg: Echter, 1991) 397–413.

Zenger, E.
"Die Bundestheologie—ein derzeit vernachlässigtes Thema der Bibelwissenschaft und ein wichtiges Thema für das Verhältnis Israel–Kirche," in E. Zenger, ed., *Der neue Bund im alten: Studien zur Bundestheologie der beiden Testamente* (QD 146; Freiburg: Herder, 1993) 13–49.

Ziegler, J.
Untersuchungen zur Septuaginta des Buches Isaias (ATAbh XII/3; Münster: Aschendorff, 1934).

Ziegler, J.
"Die Hilfe Gottes 'am Morgen'," in H. Junker and J. Botterweck, eds., *Alttestamentliche Studien. FS F. Nötscher* (Bonn: Hanstein, 1950) 281–88.

Ziegler, J.
"Die Vorlage der Isaias-Septuaginta (LXX) und die erste Isaias-Rolle von Qumran (1QIsaᵃ)," *JBL* 78 (1959) 34–59; reprint in F. M. Cross and S. Talmon, eds., *Qumran and the History of the Biblical Text* (Cambridge: Harvard Univ. Press, 1975) 90–115.

Ziegler, J., ed.
Isaias: Septuaginta. Vetus Testamentum Graecum vol. XIV (Auctoritate Academiae Litterarum Gottingensis editum; 2d ed.; Göttingen: Vandenhoeck & Ruprecht, 1967).

Ziegler, K., and W. Sontheimer, eds.
Der kleine Pauly. Lexikon der Antike (5 vols.; Stuttgart: Deutsche Taschenbuch Verlag, 1962–75).

Zimmerli, W.
"Knowledge of God According to the Book of Ezekiel," in *I Am Yahweh,* trans. D. W. Stott; ed. W. Brueggemann (Atlanta: John Knox, 1982) 29–98, 143–54 [Eng. trans. of *Erkenntnis Gottes nach dem Buch Ezechiel* (AThANT 27; Zurich: Zwingli, 1954)].

Zimmerli, W.
"Ich bin Jahwe," in G. Ebeling, ed., *Geschichte und Altes Testament. FS A. Alt* (Tübingen: Mohr 1953) 179–209.

Zimmerli, W.
"παῖς θεοῦ, AT," *TDNT* 5 (1967) 654–77 [Eng. trans. of *ThWNT* 5 (1954) 653–76].

Zimmerli, W.
Ezekiel [Eng. trans. of *Ezechiel* (BKAT 13/1-2; Neukirchen-Vluyn: Neukirchener, 1969)] vol. 1,

trans. R. E. Clements; vol. 2, trans. J. D. Martin (Hermeneia; Philadelphia: Fortress, 1979–83).

Zimmerli, W.
Gottes Offenbarung: Gesammelte Aufsätze zum Alten Testament (ThBü 19; Munich: Kaiser, 1963).

Zimmerli, W.
"Der Wahrheitserweis Jahwes nach der Botschaft der beiden Exilspropheten," in E. Würthwein and O. Kaiser, eds., *Tradition und Situation: Studien zur alttestamentlichen Prophetie. FS A. Weiser* (Göttingen: Vandenhoeck & Ruprecht, 1963) 133–51.

Zimmerli, W.
"Zur Vorgeschichte von Jes LIII," in *Congress Volume: Rome 1968* (VTSup 17; Leiden: Brill, 1969) 236–44.

Zimmerli, W.
"Jahwes Wort bei Deuterojesaja," *VT* 32 (1982) 104–24.

Zimmern, H.
Akkadische Fremdwörter als Beweis für vabylonischen Kultureinfluß (2d ed.; Leipzig: Hinrich, 1917).

Zohary, M.
Pflanzen in der Bibel (Stuttgart: Calwer, 1983).

Züricher Bibel: Die Heilige Schrift des Alten und des Neuen Testaments
(Zurich: Verlag der Zürcher Bibel, 1931; 3d ed. 1971).

3. Articles from *TDOT (TWAT)* and *TLOT (THAT)*

All quotations from *THAT* in the text have been translated directly from the German edition. The English translation is now available as *TLOT* (Peabody: Hendrickson, 1997), and those citations are included below as well.

Aalen, S.
"אוֹר *ʾôr*," *TDOT* 1 (1974) 147–67 [Eng. trans. of *TWAT* 1 (1973) 160–82].

Albertz, R.
"צעק *ṣʿq* to cry out," *TLOT* 3 (1997) 1088–93 [*THAT* 2 (1976) 568–75].

Albertz, R. and Westermann, C.
"גלה *glh* to uncover," *TLOT* 1 (1997) 314–20 [*THAT* 1 (1971) 418–26].

Amsler, S.
"צמח *ṣmḥ* to sprout," *TLOT* 3 (1997) 1085–87 [*THAT* 2 (1976) 563–66].

André, G.
"טמא *ṭāmēʾ*," *TDOT* 5 (1986) 330–42 [Eng. trans. of *TWAT* 3 (1982) 352–66].

André, G.
"כָּשַׁף *kāšap*," *TDOT* 7 (1995) 360–66 [*TWAT* 4 (1984) 375–81].

Bartelmus, R.
"שָׁמַיִם *šāmajim*," *TWAT* 8 (1996) 204–39.

Baumann, A.
"דָּמָה *dāmāh*," *TDOT* 3 (1978) 260–65 [Eng. trans. of *TWAT* 2 (1977) 277–83].

Bergman, J., and M. Ottosson
"אֶרֶץ *ʾereṣ*," *TDOT* 1 (1974) 388–405 [Eng. trans. of *TWAT* 1 (1971) 418–36].

Bergman, J., H. Ringgren, and H. Seebass
"בָּחַר *bāḥar*," *TDOT* 2 (1975) 73–87 [Eng. trans. of *TWAT* 1 (1973) 592–608].

Bergman, J., H. Ringgren, and M. Tsevat
"בְּתוּלָה *bᵉthûlāh*," *TDOT* 2 (1975) 338–43 [Eng. trans. of *TWAT* 1 (1973) 872–77].

Bergmann, J., H. Lutzmann, and W. H. Schmidt
"דבר *dābhar*," *TDOT* 3 (1978) 84–125 [Eng. trans. of *TWAT* 2 (1977) 89–133].

Bergman, J., A. Haldar, H. Ringgren, and K. Koch
"דֶּרֶךְ *derek*," *TDOT* 3 (1978) 270–93 [Eng. trans. of *TWAT* 2 (1977) 288–312].

Bernhardt, K.-H.
"אָוֶן *ʾāven*," *TDOT* 1 (1974) 140–47 [Eng. trans. of *TWAT* 1 (1973) 151–59].

Beyse, K.-M.
"כְּלִי *kᵉlî*," *TDOT* 7 (1995) 169–75 [*TWAT* 4 (1984) 179–85].

Botterweck, G. J.
"אֶבְיוֹן *ʾebhyôn*," *TDOT* 1 (1974) 27–41 [Eng. trans. of *TWAT* 1 (1973) 28–43].

Botterweck, J. G.
"חָפֵץ *ḥāpēṣ*," *TDOT* 5 (1986) 92–107 [Eng. trans. of *TWAT* 3 (1982) 100–16].

Branson, R. D., and G. J. Botterweck
"יָסַר *yāsar*," *TDOT* 6 (1990) 127–34 [Eng. trans. of *TWAT* 3 (1982) 689–97].

Bratsiotis, N. P.
"אִישׁ *ʾîsh*," *TDOT* 1 (1974) 222–35 [Eng. trans. of *TWAT* 1 (1973) 238–52].

Brekelmans, C.
"חֵרֶם *ḥērem* ban," *TLOT* 2 (1997) 474–77 [*THAT* 1 (1971) 635–39].

Caquot, A.
"גָּעַר *gāʿar*," *TDOT* 3 (1978) 49–53 [Eng. trans. of *TWAT* 2 (1977) 51–56].

Caquot, A
"חָלָב *chālābh*," *TDOT* 4 (1980) 386–91 [Eng. trans. of *TWAT* 2 (1977) 945–51].

Cazelles, H.
"חָבַר *chabhar*," *TDOT* 4 (1980) 193–97 [Eng. trans. of *TWAT* 2 (1977) 721–26].

Clements, R. E., and G. J. Botterweck
"גּוֹי *gôy*," *TDOT* 2 (1975) 426–33 [Eng. trans. of *TWAT* 1 (1973) 965–73].

Delcor, M., and E. Jenni
"שלח *šlḥ* to send," *TLOT* 3 (1997) 1330–34 [*THAT* 2 (1976) 909–16].

Dohmen, C.
"פסל *psl*," *TWAT* 6 (1989) 688–97.

Dohmen, C., and P. Stenman
"כָּבֵד *kābēd*," *TDOT* 7 (1995) 13–22 [*TWAT* 4 (1984) 13–23].

Eising, H.
"גִּיחוֹן *gîchôn*," *TDOT* 2 (1978) 466–68 [Eng. trans. of *TWAT* 2 (1973) 1008–11].

Eising, H.
"זָכַר zākhar," TDOT 4 (1980) 64–82 [Eng. trans. of TWAT 1 (1977) 571–93].

Eising, H.
"נְאֻם nᵉʾum," TWAT 5 (1986) 119–23.

Eissfeldt, O.
"אָדוֹן ʾādhôn ," TDOT 1 (1974) 59–72 [Eng. trans. of TWAT 1 (1973) 62–78].

Erlandsson, S.
"בָּגַד bāghadh," TDOT 1 (1974) 470–73 [Eng. trans. of TWAT 1 (1973) 507–11].

Erlandsson, S.
"הַוָּה havvāh," TDOT 3 (1978) 356–58 [Eng. trans. of TWAT 2 (1977) 379–81].

Fabry, H.-J.
"סָעַר sāʿar," TWAT 5 (1986) 893–98.

Fabry, H.-J.
"צוּר ṣūr I and II," TWAT 6 (1989) 973–83.

Ficker, R.
"מַלְאָךְ malʾāk messenger," TLOT 2 (1997) 666–72 [THAT 1 (1971) 900–908.

Ficker, R.
"רנן rnn to rejoice," TLOT 3 (1997) 1240–43 [THAT 2 (1976) 781–86].

Freedman, D. N., J. Lundbom, and G. J. Botterweck
"דּוֹר dôr," TDOT 3 (1978) 169–81 [Eng. trans. of TWAT 2 (1977) 181–94].

Fuhs, H. F.
"יָרֵא yārēʾ," TDOT 6 (1990) 290–315 [Eng. trans. of TWAT 3 (1982) 869–93].

Fuhs, H. F.
"עָלָה ʿālāh," TWAT 6 (1989) 84–105.

Gamberoni, J.
"חָבַל chābhal III," TDOT 4 (1980) 185–88 [Eng. trans. of TWAT 2 (1977) 712–16].

Gamberoni, J.
"קוּם qûm," TWAT 6 (1989) 1252–74.

García López, F.
"נגד ngd," TWAT 5 (1986) 188–201

García López, F.
"פֶּה peh," TWAT 6 (1984) 522–38.

García López, F.
"צוה ṣwh," TWAT 6 (1989) 936–59.

Gerlemann, G.
"בקשׁ bqš pi. to seek," TLOT 1 (1997) 251–53 [THAT 1 (1971) 333–36].

Gerlemann, G.
"דָּבָר dābār word" TLOT 1 (1997) 325–32 [THAT 1 (1971) 433–43].

Gerlemann, G.
"דּוֹר dôr generation," TLOT 1 (1997) 333–35 [THAT 1 (1971) 443–45].

Gerlemann, G.
"חפץ ḥpṣ to be pleased" TLOT 2 (1997) 466–67 [THAT 1 (1971) 623–26].

Gerlemann, G
" רצה rṣh to be pleased with," TLOT 3 (1997) 1259–61 [THAT 2 (1976) 810–3].

Gerlemann, G.
"שְׁאוֹל šᵉʾōl realm of the dead," TLOT 3 (1997) 1279–82 [THAT 2 (1976) 837–41].

Gerlemann, G.
"שׁלום šlm to have enough," TLOT 3 (1997) 1337–48 [THAT 2 (1976) 919–35].

Gerlemann, G., and E. Ruprecht
"דרשׁ drš to inquire after," TLOT 1 (1997) 346–51 [THAT 1 (1971) 460–67].

Gerstenberger, E.
"אבה ʾbh to want," TLOT 1 (1997) 15–19 [THAT 1 (1971) 20–25].

Gerstenberger, E.
"אוה ʾwh pi. to desire," TLOT 1 (1997) 55–56 [THAT 1 (1971) 74–76].

Gerstenberger, E.
"בטח bṭḥ to trust," TLOT 1 (1997) 226–30 [THAT 1 (1971) 300–305].

Gerstenberger, E.
"כון, kūn ni. to stand firm," TLOT 2 (1997) 602–6 [THAT 1 (1971) 812–17].

Gerstenberger, E.
"תעב tᶜb pi. to abhor," TLOT 3 (1997) 1428–31 [THAT 2 (1976) 1051–55].

Gerstenberger, E. S.
"עָזַב ʿāzab," TWAT 5 (1986) 1200–1208.

Gerstenberger, E. S.
"פלל pll," TWAT 6 (1989) 606–17.

Görg, M.
"בָּזָה bāzāh," TDOT 2 (1975) 60–65 [Eng. trans. of TWAT 1 (1973) 581–85].

Hamp, V.
"אפס ʾps," TDOT 1 (1974) 361–62 [Eng. trans. of TWAT 1 (1973) 389–91].

Hamp, V.
"בָּרַר bārār," TDOT 2 (1975) 308–12 [Eng. trans. of TWAT 1 (1973) 841–45].

Hamp, V.
"חָרַשׁ ḥāraš I," TDOT 5 (1986) 220–23 [Eng. trans. of TWAT 3 (1982) 234–38].

Hamp, V.
"טָבַח ṭābaḥ," TDOT 5 (1986) 283–87 [Eng. trans. of TWAT 3 (1982) 302–6].

Hasel, G. F.
"נָגִיד nāḡîd," TWAT 5 (1986) 203–19.

Hasel, G. F.
"פלט pālaṭ," TWAT 6 (1989) 589–606.

Hausmann, J.
"סָלַח sālaḥ," TWAT 5 (1986) 859–67.

Hausmann, J.
"פאר pʾr," TWAT 6 (1989) 494–99.

Helfmeyer, F. J.
"אוֹת ʾôth," TDOT 1 (1974) 167–88 [Eng. trans. of TWAT 1 (1973) 182–205].

Helfmeyer, F. J.
"זְרוֹעַ zᵉrôaᶜ," TDOT 4 (1986) 131–40 [Eng. trans. of TWAT 2 (1977) 650–59].

Hentschke, R.
"גָּבַהּ gābhah," TDOT 2 (1975) 356–60 [Eng. trans. of TWAT 1 (1973) 890–95].

Hoffner, H. A.
"אַלְמָנָה ʾalmānāh," TDOT 1 (1974) 287–91 [Eng. trans. of TWAT 1 (1973) 308–13].

Hoffner, H. A.
"יבל ybl," TDOT 5 (1986) 364–67 [Eng. trans. of TWAT 3 (1982) 390–93].

Höver-Johag, I.
"טוֹב ṭôḇ," TDOT 5 (1986) 296–317 [Eng. trans. of TWAT 3 (1982) 315–39].

Hulst, A. R.
"גּוֹי/עַם ʿam/ gôy people," TLOT 2 (1997) 896–919 [THAT 2 (1976) 290–325].

Illmann, K.-J.
"פָּעַל pāʿal," TWAT 6 (1989) 697–703.

Jenni, E.
"אהב ʾhb to love," TLOT 1 (1997) 45–54 [THAT 1 (1971) 60–73].

Jenni, E.
"אחר ʾḥr after," TLOT 1 (1997) 83–88 [THAT 1 (1971) 110–18].

Jenni, E.
"גָּדוֹל gāḏôl great," TLOT 1 (1997) 302–7 [THAT 1 (1971) 402–9].

Jenni, E.
"הוֹי hôy woe," TLOT 1 (1997) 357–58 [THAT 1 (1971) 474–77.

Jenni, E.
"יצא yṣʾ to go out," TLOT 2 (1997) 561–66 [THAT 1 (1972) 755–61].

Jenni, E.
"למד lmd to learn," TLOT 2 (1997) 646–48 [THAT 1 (1971) 872–75].

Jenni, E.
"עוֹלָם ʿôlām eternity," TLOT 2 (1997) 852–62 [THAT 2 (1976) 228–43].

Jenni, E.
"עָנָן ʿānān cloud," TLOT 2 (1997) 937–39 [THAT 2 (1976) 351–53].

Jepsen, A.
"אָמַן ʾāman," TDOT 1 (1974) 292–323 [Eng. trans. of TWAT 1 (1973) 313–48].

Kapelrud, A. S.
"אָבִיר ʾabhîr ," TDOT 1 (1974) 42–44 [Eng. trans. of TWAT 1 (1973) 43–46].

Kapelrud, A. S.
"לָמַד lāmaḏ," TDOT 8 (1997) 4–10 [TWAT 4 (1989) 576–82].

Kedar-Kopfstein, B.
"לָשׁוֹן lāšôn," TDOT 8 (1997) 8–33 [TWAT 4 (1984) 595–605].

Kedar-Kopfstein, B.
"קוֹל qôl," TWAT 6 (1989) 1237–52.

Keller, C. A.
"אָלָה ʾālâ curse," TLOT 1 (1997) 113–15.

Keller, C. A
"שבע šbʿ ni. to swear," TLOT 3 (1997) 1292–97 [THAT 2 (1976) 855–63].

Kellermann, D.
"אָשָׁם ʾāšhām," TDOT 1 (1974) 429–37 [Eng. trans. of TWAT 1 (1973) 463–72].

Kellermann, D.
"מִשְׁכָּן miškān," TWAT 5 (1986) 62–69.

Kellermann, D.
"סָבָל sāḇāl," TWAT 5 (1986) 744–48.

Kellermann, D.
"צָמֵא ṣāmeʾ," TWAT 6 (1989) 1065–68.

Klopfenstein, M. A.
"בגד bgd to act faithlessly," TLOT 1 (1997) 198–200 [THAT 1 (1971) 261–64].

Klopfenstein, M. A.
"שקר šqr to deceive," TLOT 3 (1997) 1399–1405 [THAT 2 (1976) 1010–19].

Knierim, R.
"אָוֶן ʾāwæn to harm," TLOT 1 (1997) 60–62 [THAT 1 (1971) 81–84].

Knierim, R.
"אָשָׁם ʾāšām guilt," TLOT 1 (1997) 191–95 [THAT 1 (1971) 251–57].

Knierim, R.
"חטא ḥṭʾ to miss," TLOT 1 (1997) 406–11 [THAT 1 (1971) 541–49].

Knierim, R.
"עָוֹן ʿāwôn perversity," TLOT 2 (1997) 862–66 [THAT 2 (1976) 243–49].

Knierim, R.
"פֶּשַׁע pešaʿ crime," TLOT 2 (1997) 1033–37 [THAT 2 (1976) 488–95].

Koch, K.
"אֹהֶל ʾōhel," TDOT 1 (1974) 118–30 [Eng. trans. of TWAT 1 (1973) 128–41].

Koch, K.
"צדק ṣdq to be communally faithful, beneficial," TLOT 2 (1997) 1046–62 [THAT 2 (1977) 507–30].

Koch, K.
"חָטָא ḥāṭāʾ," TDOT 4 (1980) 309–19 [Eng. trans. of TWAT 2 (1977) 857–70].

Koch, K.
"כון kûn," TDOT 7 (1995) 89–101 [TWAT 4 (1984) 95–107].

Koch, K.
"עָוֹן ʿāwôn," TWAT 5 (1986) 1160–77.

Kornfeld, W., and H. Ringgren
"קדש qdš," TWAT 6 (1989) 1179–1204.

Kühlewein, J.
"גבר gbr to be superior," TLOT 1 (1997) 299–302 [THAT 1 (1971) 398–402].

Kühlewein, J.
"קרב qrb to approach," TLOT 3 (1997) 1164–69 [THAT 2 (1976) 674–81].

Kühlewein, J.
"רֵעַ rēaʿ companion," TLOT 3 (1997) 1243–46 [THAT 2 (1976) 786–91].

Kutsch, E.
"בְּרִית bᵉrît obligation," TLOT 1 (1997) 256–66 [THAT 1 (1971) 339–52].

Labuschagne, C. J.
"ענה ʿnh I, to answer" TLOT 2 (1997) 926–30 [THAT 2 (1976) 335–41].

Labuschagne, C. J.
"פֶּה peh mouth," *TLOT* 2 (1997) 976–79 [*THAT* 2 (1976) 406–11].

Labuschagne, C. J.
"קרא qrʾ to call," *TLOT* 3 (1997) 1158–64 [*THAT* 2 (1976) 666–74].

Lang, B.
"כִּפֶּר kipper," *TDOT* 7 (1995) 288–303 [*TWAT* 4 (1984) 303–18].

Leeuwen, C. v.
"רשע ršʿ to be impious, guilty," *TLOT* 3 (1997) 1261–65 [*THAT* 2 (1976) 813–18].

Liedke, G.
"אֹזֶן ʾōzen ear," *TLOT* 1 (1997) 71–73 [*THAT* 1 (1971) 95–98.

Liedke, G.
"ישר yšr to be straight, right," *TLOT* 2 (1997) 588–90 [*THAT* 1 (1971) 790–94].

Liedke, G.
"צוה ṣwh pi. to command," *TLOT* 2 (1997) 1062–65 [*THAT* 2 (1976) 530–56].

Liedke, G.
"שפט špṭ to judge," *TLOT* 3 (1997) 1392–99 [*THAT* 2 (1976) 999–1009.

Lipiński, E.
"נגש nāḡaś," *TWAT* 5 (1986) 230–32.

Lipiński, E.
"נחל nāḥal,," *TWAT* 5 (1986) 342–60.

Lohfink, N.
"חרם ḥāram," *TDOT* 5 (1986) 180–99 [Eng. trans. of *TWAT* 3 (1982) 192–213].

Maass, F.
"טמא ṭāmēʾ to be unclean," *TLOT* 2 (1997) 495–97 [*THAT* 1 (1971) 664–67].

Maass, F.
"חתת ḥātat," *TDOT* 5 (1986) 277–83 [Eng. trans. of *TWAT* 3 (1982) 296–302].

Martin-Achard, R.
"ענה ʿnh II to be destitute," *TLOT* 2 (1997) 931–37 [*THAT* 2 (1976) 341–50].

Mayer, G.
"אוה ʾāvāh," *TDOT* 1 (1974) 134–37 [Eng. trans. of *TWAT* 1 (1973) 145–48].

Mayer, G.
"ירד yārad," *TDOT* 6 (1990) 315–22 [Eng. trans. of *TWAT* 3 (1982) 894–901].

Mayer, W., L. Alonso-Schökel, and H. Ringgren
"ישר yāšar," *TDOT* 6 (1990) 463–72 [Eng. trans. of *THAT* 3 (1982) 1059–70].

Müller, H.-P.
"קדש qdš holy," *TLOT* 3 (1997) 1103–18 [*THAT* 2 (1976) 589–609].

Müller, H.-P.
"ראש rōš head," *TLOT* 3 (1997) 1184–94 [*THAT* 2 (1976) 701–15].

Müller, H.-P.
"פחד pāḥad," *TWAT* 6 (1989) 552–62.

Mulder, M. J.
"ישרון yešurûn," *TDOT* 6 (1990) 472–77 [*TWAT* 3 (1982) 1070–75].

Niehr, H.
"ערב ʿæræb," *TWAT* 6 (1989) 359–66.

Nielsen, K.
"שטן śāṭān," *TWAT* 7 (1993) 745–51.

Otzen, B.
"בליעל belîyaʿal ," *TDOT* 2 (1975) 131–36 [Eng. trans. of *TWAT* 1 (1973) 654–58].

Preuss, H. D.
"בוא bôʾ," *TDOT* 2 (1975) 20–49 [Eng. trans. of *TWAT* 1 (1973) 536–68].

Preuss, H. D.
"דמה dāmāh," *TDOT* 3 (1978) 250–60 [Eng. trans. of *TWAT* 2 (1977) 266–77].

Preuss, H. D.
"זרע zāraʿ," *TDOT* 4 (1980) 143–62 [Eng. trans. of *TWAT* 2 (1977) 663–86].

Preuss, H. D.
"יעל yʿl," *TDOT* 6 (1990) 144–47 [Eng. trans. of *TWAT* 3 (1982) 705–10].

Preuss, H. D.
"יצא yāṣāʾ," *TDOT* 6 (1990) 225–50 [Eng. trans. of *TWAT* 3 (1982) 795–822].

Preuss, H. D.
"לאם leʾōm," *TDOT* 7 (1995) 397–98 [*TWAT* 4 (1984) 411–13].

Preuss, H. D.
"עולם ʿôlām," *TWAT* 5 (1986) 1144–59.

Ringgren, H.
"אב ʾābh," *TDOT* 1 (1974) 1–19 [Eng. trans. of *TWAT* 1 (1973) 1–19].

Ringgren, H.
"בזז bzz," *TDOT* 2 (1975) 66–68 [Eng. trans. of *TWAT* 1 (1973) 585–88].

Ringgren, H.
"גאל gāʾal," *TDOT* 2 (1975) 350–55 [Eng. trans. of *TWAT* 1 (1973) 884–90].

Ringgren, H.
"הלל hll I and II," *TDOT* 3 (1978) 404–10 [Eng. trans. of *TWAT* 2 (1977) 433–41].

Ringgren, H.
"זרח zāraḥ," *TDOT* 4 (1980) 141–43 [Eng. trans. of *TWAT* 2 (1977) 661–63].

Ringgren, H., and H. Seebass
"פשע pāšaʾ," *TWAT* 6 (1989) 791–810.

Ringgren, H., K. Seybold, and H.-J. Fabry
"מלך melek," *TDOT* 8 (1997) 345–75 [*TWAT* 4 (1984) 926–57].

Ruprecht, E.
"פלט plṭ pi. to save," *TLOT* 2 (1997) 986–90 [*THAT* 2 (1976) 420–27].

Saebø, M.
"אור ʾôr light," *TLOT* 1 (1997) 63–67 [*THAT* 1 (1971) 84–90].

Saebø, M.
"יעל yʿl hi. to be of use," *TLOT* 2 (1997) 554–56 [*THAT* 1 (1971) 746–48].

Saebø, M.
"צלח ṣlḥ to succeed," *TLOT* 3 (1997) 1077–80 [*THAT* 2 (1976) 551–56].

Saebø, M.
"שׂכל śkl hi. to have insight," *TLOT* 3 (1997) 1269–72 [*THAT* 2 (1976) 824–28].

Sauer, G.
"דֶּרֶךְ *derek* way," *TLOT* 1 (1997) 343–46 [*THAT* 1 (1971) 456–60].

Sauer, G.
"נצר *nṣr* to guard," *TLOT* 2 (1997) 762–63 [*THAT* 2 (1976) 99–101].

Sauer, G.
"נקם *nqm* to avenge," *TLOT* 2 (1997) 767–69 [*THAT* 2 (1976) 106–9].

Sawyer, J. F. A.
"קבץ *qbṣ* to assemble," *TLOT* 3 (1997) 1099–1101 [*THAT* 2 (1976) 583–86].

Sawyer, J. F. A.
"ישׁע *yšʿ*," *TDOT* 6 (1990) 441–63 [Eng. trans. of *TWAT* 3 (1982) 1035–59].

Scharbert, J.
"ברך *brk*," *TDOT* 2 (1975) 279–308 [Eng. trans. of *TWAT* 1 (1973) 808–41].

Schilling, O.
"בשׂר *bśr*," *TDOT* 2 (1975) 313–16 [Eng. trans. of *TWAT* 1 (1973) 845–49].

Schmid, H. H.
"בין *bîn* to understand," *TLOT* 1 (1997) 230–32 [*THAT* 1 (1971) 305–8].

Schmid, H. H.
"לקח *lqḥ* to take," *TLOT* 2 (1997) 648–51 [*THAT* 1 (1971) 875–79].

Schmidt, W. H.
"אל *ʾēl* God," *TLOT* 1 (1997) 107–12 [*THAT* 1 (1972) 142–49].

Schottroff, W.
"זכר *zkr* to remember," *TLOT* 1 (1997) 381–88 [*THAT* 1 (1971) 507–18].

Schottroff, W.
"חשׁב *ḥšb* to think," *TLOT* 2 (1997) 479–82 [*THAT* 1 (1971) 641–46].

Schottroff, W.
"ידע *ydʿ* to perceive, know," *TLOT* 2 (1997) 508–21 [*THAT* 1 (1971) 682–701].

Schottroff, W.
"קשׁב *qšb* hi. to pay attention" *TLOT* 3 (1997) 1171–74 [*THAT* 2 (1976) 684–89].

Schottroff, W.
"שׁכח *škḥ* to forget," *TLOT* 3 (1997) 1322–26 [*THAT* 2 (1976) 898–904].

Schreiner, J.
"אמץ *ʾāmats*," *TDOT* 1 (1974) 323–27 [Eng. trans. of *TWAT* 1 (1973) 348–52].

Schreiner, J., and G. J. Botterweck
"יָלַד *yālaḏ*," *TDOT* 6 (1990) 76–81 [Eng. trans. of *TWAT* 3 (1977) 633–39].

Schreiner, J.
"עור *ʿwr*," *TWAT* 5 (1986) 1184–90.

Schult, H.
"שׁמע *šmʿ* to hear," *TLOT* 3 (1997) 1375–80 [*THAT* 2 (1976) 974–82].

Schwertner, S.
"סור *sûr* to deviate," *TLOT* 2 (1997) 796–97 [*THAT* 2 (1976) 148–50].

Schwienhorst, L.
"נָגַע *nāḡaʿ*," *TWAT* 5 (1986) 219–26.

Seebass, H.
"בּוֹשׁ *bôsh*," *TDOT* 2 (1975) 50–60 [Eng. trans. of *TWAT* 1 (1973) 568–80].

Seebass, H.
"לְקַח *lāqaḥ*," *TDOT* 8 (1997) 16–21 [*TWAT* 4 (1984) 588–94].

Seebass, H.
"נֶפֶשׁ *nepeš*," *TWAT* 5 (1986) 531–55.

Seybold, K.
"חוּג *chugh*," *TDOT* 4 (1980) 244–47 [Eng. trans of *TWAT* 2 (1977) 780–84].

Seybold, K.
"חָלָה *chālāh* ," *TDOT* 4 (1980) 399–409 [Eng. trans. of *TWAT* 2 (1977) 960–72].

Seybold, K.
"חָשַׁב *ḥāšaḇ*," *TDOT* 5 (1986) 228–45 [Eng. trans. of *TWAT* 3 (1982) 243–61].

Seybold, K.
"מָשַׁח *māšaḥ*," *TWAT* 5 (1985) 46–59.

Soggin, J. A.
"מֶלֶךְ *melek* king," *TLOT* 2 (1997) 672–80 [*THAT* 1 (1971) 908–20].

Soggin, J. A.
"משׁל *mšl* to rule," *TLOT* 2 (1997) 689–91 [*THAT* 1 (1971) 930–33].

Soggin, J. A.
"רעה *rʿh* to tend," *TLOT* 3 (1997) 1246–48 [*THAT* 2 (1976) 791–94].

Soggin, J. A.
"שׁוב *šûb* to return," *TLOT* 3 (1997) 1312–17 [*THAT* 2 (1976) 884–91].

Stähli, H.-P.
"גבה *gbh* to be high," *TLOT* 1 (1997) 296–99 [*THAT* 1 (1971) 394–97].

Stähli, H.-P.
"ירא *yrʾ* to fear," *TLOT* 2 (1997) 568–78 [*THAT* 1 (1971) 765–78].

Stähli, H.-P.
"עזב *ʿzb* to abandon," *TLOT* 2 (1997) 866–68 [*THAT* 2 (1976) 249–52].

Stähli, H.-P.
"פחד *pḥd* to shake," *TLOT* 2 (1997) 979–81 [*THAT* 2 (1976) 411–13].

Stähli, H.-P.
"פלל *pll* hitp. to pray," *TLOT* 2 (1997) 991–94 [*THAT* 2 (1976) 427–32].

Stähli, H.-P.
"רום *rûm* to be high," *TLOT* 3 (1997) 1220–25 [*THAT* 2 (1976) 753–61].

Stamm, J. J.
"גאל *gʾl* to redeem," *TLOT* 1 (1997) 288–96 [*THAT* 1 (1971) 383–94].

Stamm, J. J.
"סלח slḥ to forgive," *TLOT* 2 (1997) 797–803
[*THAT* 2 (1976) 150–60].

Stamm, J. J.
"פדה pdh to redeem, liberate," *TLOT* 2 (1997)
964–76 [*THAT* 2 (1976) 389–406].

Stoebe, H. J.
"חֶסֶד ḥesed kindness," *TLOT* 2 (1997) 449–64 [*THAT*
1 (1971) 600–621].

Stoebe, H. J.
"נחם nḥm pi. to comfort," *TLOT* 2 (1997) 734–39
[*THAT* 2 (1976) 59–66].

Stolz, F.
"אוֹת ʾôt sign," *TLOT* 1 (1997) 67–70 [*THAT* 1
(1971) 91–95].

Stolz, F.
"בוש bôš to be ashamed," *TLOT* 1 (1997) 204–7
[*THAT* 1 (1971) 269–72].

Stolz, F.
"חלה ḥlh to be sick," *TLOT* 1 (1997) 425–27 [*THAT*
1 (1971) 567–70].

Stolz, F.
"נשא nśʾ to lift, bear," *TLOT* 2 (1997) 69–74 [*THAT*
2 (1976) 109–17].

Stolz, F.
"שמם šmm to be deserted," *TLOT* 3 (1997) 769–74
[*THAT* 2 (1976) 970–74].

Vetter, D.
"הִנֵּה hinnēh behold," *TLOT* 1 (1997) 379–80 [*THAT*
1 (1971) 504–7].

Vetter, D.
"חזה ḥzh to see," *TLOT* 1 (1997) 400–403 [*THAT* 1
(1971) 533–37].

Vetter, D.
"נְאֻם nᵉʾum utterance," *TLOT* 2 (1997) 692–94
[*THAT* 2 (1976) 1–3].

Vetter, D.
"פאר pʾr pi. to glorify," *TLOT* 2 (1997) 963–64
[*THAT* 2 (1977) 387–89].

Vetter, D.
"ראה rʾh to see," *TLOT* 3 (1997) 1176–83 [*THAT* 2
(1976) 692–701].

Vetter, D.
"שחת šḥt pi./hi. to ruin," *TLOT* 3 (1997) 1317–19
[*THAT* 2 (1976) 891–94].

Vollmer, J.
"פעל pʿl to make, do," *TLOT* 2 (1997) 1014–18
[*THAT* 2 (1976) 461–66].

Wagner, S.
"בִּקֵּשׁ biqqesh," *TDOT* 2 (1975) 229–41 [Eng. trans.
of *TWAT* 1 (1973) 754–69].

Wagner, S.
"דָּרַשׁ dārash," *TDOT* 3 (1978) 293–307 [Eng. trans.
of *TWAT* 2 (1977) 313–29].

Wagner, S., and H.-J. Fabry
"מָאַס māʾas," *TDOT* 8 (1997) 47–60 [*TWAT* 4 (1984)
618–33].

Wagner, S.
"מָצָא māṣāʾ," *TDOT* 8 (1997) 465–83 [*TWAT* 4
(1984) 1043–63].

Wagner, S.
"סָתַר sātar," *TWAT* 5 (1986) 967–77.

Wanke, G.
"נַחֲלָה naḥᵃlâ possession," *TLOT* 2 (1997) 731–34
[*THAT* 2 (1976) 55–59].

Wanke, G.
"עָפָר ʿāpār dust," *TLOT* 2 (1997) 939–41 [*THAT* 2
(1976) 353–56].

Warmuth, M.
"הָדָר hādhār," *TDOT* 3 (1978) 335–41 [Eng. trans.
of *TWAT* 2 (1977) 357–63].

Wehmeier, G.
"סתר str hi. to hide," *TLOT* 2 (1997) 813–19 [*THAT*
2 (1976) 173–81].

Wehmeier, G.
"עלה ʿlh to go up," *TLOT* 2 (1997) 883–96 [*THAT* 2
(1976) 272–90].

Weinfeld, M.
"בְּרִית bᵉrîth," *TDOT* 2 (1975) 253–79 [Eng. trans. of
TWAT 1 (1973) 781–808.].

Weinfeld, M.
"כָּבוֹד kābôd," *TDOT* 7 (1995) 22–38 [*TWAT* 4
(1984) 23–40].

Westermann, C.
"אָדָם ʾādām person," *TLOT* 1 (1997) 31–42 [*THAT*
1 (1971) 41–57].

Westermann, C., and R. Albertz
"גלה glh to uncover," *TLOT* 1 (1997) 314–20 [*THAT*
1 (1971) 418–26].

Westermann, C.
"הלל hll pi. to praise," *TLOT* 1 (1997) 371–76
[*THAT* 1 (1971) 493–502].

Westermann, C.
"כבד kbd to be heavy," *TLOT* 2 (1997) 590–602
[*THAT* 1 (1971) 794–811].

Westermann, C.
"נגד ngd hi. to communicate," *TLOT* 2 (1997)
714–18 [*THAT* 2 (1976) 31–37].

Westermann, C.
"נֶפֶשׁ nepeš soul," *TLOT* 2 (1997) 743–59 [*THAT* 2
(1976) 71–96].

Wildberger, H.
"אמן ʾmn to be secure," *TLOT* 1 (1997) 134–57
[*THAT* 1 (1971) 177–204].

Wildberger, H.
"בחר bḥr to choose," *TLOT* 1 (1997) 209–26 [*THAT*
1 (1971) 275–300].

Wildberger, H.
"מאס mʾs to reject," *TLOT* 2 (1997) 651–60 [*THAT*
1 (1971) 879–92].

Wildberger, H.
"שאר šʾr to remain," *TLOT* 3 (1997) 1284–92
[*THAT* 2 (1976) 844–55].

Woude, A. S. van der
"אמץ ʾmṣ to be strong," *TLOT* 1 (1997) 157–59
[*THAT* 1 (1971) 209–11].

Woude, A. S. van der
"זְרוֹעַ zᵉrôaʿ arm," *TLOT* 1 (1997) 392–93 [*THAT* 1
(1971) 522–24].

Woude, A. S. van der
"יָד *yād* hand," *TLOT* 2 (1997) 497–502 [*THAT* 1 (1971) 667–74].

Woude, A. S. van der
"עזז *ʿzz* to be strong," *TLOT* 2 (1997) 868–72 [*THAT* 2 (1977) 252–56].

Woude, A. S. van der
"צבא *ṣābāʾ* army," *TLOT* 2 (1997) 1039–46 [*THAT* 2 (1976) 498–507].

Woude, A. S. van der
"צוּר *ṣûr* rock," *TLOT* 2 (1997) 1067–71 [*THAT* 2 (1976) 538–43].

Woude, A. S. van der
"שֵׁם *šēm* name," *TLOT* 3 (1997) 1348–67 [*THAT* 2 (1976) 935–63].

Zobel, H.-J.
"גָּלָה *gālāh*," *TDOT* 2 (1975) 476–88 [Eng. trans. of *TWAT* 1 (1973) 1018–31].

Zobel, H.-J.
"חֶסֶד *ḥesed*," *TDOT* 5 (1986) 44–64 [Eng. trans. of *TWAT* 3 (1982) 48–71].

Zobel, H.-J.
"יְהוּדָה *yᵉhûdâ*," *TDOT* 5 (1986) 482–99 [Eng. trans. of *TWAT* 3 (1982) 512–33].

Zobel, H.-J.
"מָטָר *māṭār*," *TDOT* 8 (1997) 350–65 [*TWAT* 4 (1984) 827–42].

Genesis (*continued*)

28:13	102, 165[140], 422[200]
28:14	437
28:15	165[140]
28:16	408[122]
28:17	165[140]
28:18	310[230]
28:19	165[140]
29:15	63, 180[223], 373[195]
29:18	180[223]
29:20	180[223]
29:27	180[223]
29:30	180[223]
29:31	435[266], 443[323]
30–32	182
30:26	180[223]
30:27	100[73]
30:29	180[223]
30:30	100[73]
30:32–33	63
30:32	180
30:37	181
31:1	180
31:6	180[223]
31:9	335[52]
31:14	462[460]
31:36	287[157]
31:41	180, 180[223]
31:42	180, 287[157]
31:54	178[206], 181
32	409
32:5	180[223]
32:13	299[184]
32:14	178[207], 181[227]
32:19	178[207], 180[223], 181[227]
32:21–22	178[207]
32:21	159[97], 180[223], 181[227]
32:22	181[227]
32:23–33	157[82], 251[284]
32:26	409[127]
32:27–28	100[73]
32:32	377[220]
32:33	285
33:5	180[223]
33:10	178[207], 181[227]
33:11	100[73]
33:13	63[89]
33:14	63, 63[89], 180[223]
33:18	182[235]
34:3	51[19], 93[24]
35:20	310[230]
37:10	241[217]
37:35	271[85]
40:5	118[187]
40:8	118[187]
40:10	484[132]
40:12	118[187]
40:18	118[187]
41	214[39]
41:11	118[187]
41:24–25	117[177]
41:24	118[187]
41:38	118[179]
41:52	287[157]
42:6	241[217]
43:16	415[157]
43:18	373
43:26	241[217]
43:28	241[217]
44:17	485[133]
44:24	485[133]
44:33	485[133]
44:34	485[133]
45:8	150[47]
45:9	485[133]
45:25	406[109], 485[133]
45:26	150[47]
47:19	246[247]
48:8–9	100[73]
49:9	256, 458[432], 458[433]
49:15	260[41]
49:18	85
49:24	265, 333
49:27	426[225]
50:5–7	485[133]
50:9	485[133]
50:14	485[133]
50:18	241[217]
50:21	51[19]

Exodus

1–12	91[15]
1:9	420
1:10	485[133]
1:11	409[125]
1:12	437[285]
2	406
2:1–2	418
2:2	405
2:5–10	405
2:10	405, 406
2:11–12	406
2:11	129, 409[125]
2:13–14	132[262]
2:13	98[59]
2:14	406, 408[122]
2:15	406
2:23–7:7	129[245]
2:23–25	407
2:23	414
3	20, 127, 133, 294, 375
3:1–4	133[266]
3:1	140, 302
3:2	42[205]
3:4	307
3:6	96, 407, 407[118]
3:7	133[266], 277, 287[157], 406, 407, 408
3:8	437[284], 440[308], 469[26]
3:10	20, 127
3:11	20
3:12	20, 98[57]
3:13–15	293
3:13	20, 21
3:14	20, 134
3:15	20
3:17	287[157]
3:21–22	127[238]

553

10:7	158[89]
10:10	110[141]
10:13	110[141], 406[109], 485[133]
11:16	406[109], 485[133]
11:29	127
11:36	483[116]
12:5–6	485[143]
12:6	215[55], 332[42]
13	438
13:2–3	435[266]
13:6	438
14:12	117[177]
14:16	443[323]
16:2	377[219]
16:23	105
17:2	331, 373
17:4	92
18:9	144[3]
18:10	437[284]
19	444[328]
19:3	51[19]
19:26	377[219]
19:30	485[133]
20:15–16	84[178]
20:24	457[427]
20:28	141[308]
21:15	437[286]

Ruth
1:14	93[24]
2:23	93[24]
4:1–8	185
4:10	299, 486[147]
4:22	235[175]

1 Samuel
1:10	241[217]
1:12	241[217]
1:26	241[217]
2:2	346[99]
2:4	332
2:5	332, 435[266]
2:7	54[43]
2:10	249[273]
2:36	241[217]

3:20	313
5	256[13]
5:1–5	91[15], 93[28]
5:3–4	93[23]
6:6	105[109]
6:19	203
7:3	439[294]
7:4	439[294]
7:10	457[427]
8:3	237[195]
8:8	110[141]
8:20	127[236], 141[308]
9:17	222[94]
10:24	222[94]
10:27	178[207]
11:6–7	127[236]
11:6	127
11:7	195[298]
12:3	129[248], 225[116]
12:4	129[248]
12:7	250[278]
12:8–15	158
12:10	110[141], 439[294]
13:5	122[220]
13:13	215[48]
13:14	472[45]
13:19	92
13:20	198[321]
14:23	122[220]
15	183[244]
15:2	485[133]
15:3	405[100]
15:6	485[133]
15:23	214[43]
15:32	408[122]
16:1–13	225[116]
16:6	472[45]
16:7	277, 404[99]
16:12	222[94]
16:13–14	127
16:18	404
17:20	141[311]
17:35	335[52]
17:42	404
17:48	457[427]
17:52	141[311], 207[400]

18:4	370[179]
18:5	215[52]
18:6	66
18:15	215[52]
18:22	152[57]
18:30	127[236], 141[308]
20:16	486[147]
21:6	415
21:14	214[45]
22:2	334[48]
22:19	405[100]
24:3	84[178]
24:6–7	225[116]
24:9	241[217]
24:10	225[116]
24:22	486[147]
25:30	472[45]
26:9	225[116]
26:11	225[116]
26:16	225[116]
26:23	225[116]
27:11	117[177]
28	136
28:9	118[181]
28:13	271[87]
28:14	241[217]
28:15	118[181]
31:9	61[74]

2 Samuel
1:14	225[116]
1:20	61[74]
1:22	147[33]
2:4	225[116]
2:8	204[372], 439[294]
3:13–16	444[328]
5:2	219[84], 219[86], 472[45]
5:3	225[116]
5:11	92
5:24	127[236], 141[309]
6	471
6:2	213
6:12	105
6:17	213
6:21	472[45]

21:9	93[28], 255
21:10	93[28]
21:16	139[296], 141[305]
22:13	332
22:16	395
22:24	131[254]
23:3	449[369]
23:17	226[126]
23:18	226[126], 240[213], 449[369]
24–27	14[84]
24:2	334[48]
24:4	402
24:10	246[246]
24:16	286[148]
24:18	290[160]
24:19	93
24:23	1[7], 1[9]
25:7–8	325
25:11	54[43]
26:1	358[136]
26:5	271[86], 395
26:21	141[309]
27:13	370[177]
28:1–3	453[402]
28:1	57[64], 366[159]
28:5–6	453[402]
28:7–22	402, 403
28:7	366[159]
28:10	402
28:13	402
28:14–15	402
28:14	151[47], 374
28:15	403
28:16	1[7]
28:21	141[310]
28:24	230[141]
28:28	70[124]
29:4	271[87], 337
29:6	449[366], 449[367]
29:9	366[159]
29:16	233[160], 234[162]
29:19	1[8]
29:22	100[83]
29:23	1[8]
30:2	156[73]
30:9	151[55]
30:11	1[8]
30:12	1[8], 277[117]
30:15	1[8], 277[117]
30:17	330[28]
30:18	415[161]
30:31	460[442]
31:1	1[8], 85
31:3	73
31:4	1[7], 141[310], 458[433]
32:1	1[9]
32:13	484[132]
32:17	455[414]
33:1–6	426
33:1	286[148]
33:5	480[98]
33:14	195[298]
33:15	237[195], 247[260]
33:17	1[9]
33:20–21	436, 436[275]
33:20	467[16]
33:22	1[9]
34–35	1, 1[9], 14[84]
34:1	131[254]
34:2	183[244]
34:5	415[161]
34:8–15	109[136]
34:11	246[246]
34:12	374[202]
34:13	174[190], 484[132]
34:17	226[126]
35	372
35:2	71[127], 404[95]
35:6	109[139]
35:7	145[19]
35:8	371
35:10	1[7], 355[124], 358[138], 371
	371[192]
36–39	
36–37	1, 371, 372, 373, 374
36	355[124]
36:1–2	372
36:2	374
36:6	129[247]
37:4	373
37:14–20	192[277]
37:23	1[8]
37:24	395
37:33	372
38:10	272[97]
38:11	246[251], 416[168]
38:14	337, 402
40–66	1
40–55	1, 1[9], 2, 48
40–48	4, 6[40], 48
40–46	73
40	1, 6, 56[54], 69[115], 466
40:1–31	47
40:1–11	47, 47[2], 131
40:1–8	49, 382
40:1–6	48
40:1–5	469
40:1–2	5, 16, 32, 33, 47, 61, 138, 470, 473
40:1	33, 34, 49, 58, 62, 152, 163[123], 316, 319, 361, 381[245], 473
40:2	48[6], 59, 216, 319, 361, 465, 474
40:3–5	47, 53, 61, 297
40:3	53, 175[196], 391[40], 465
40:4	55, 186, 465
40:5	53, 111[156], 210, 229[141], 385[259], 465, 483
40:6–8	16, 22, 30, 47, 48, 57, 250, 445, 470[31]
40:6–7	57

Reference	Pages
41:2-3	222
41:2	88, 121[210], 135, 164[128], 223[97], 227, 229, 263
41:3	30[153], 227[129]
41:4	296, 396[54], 416
41:5-7	17[97], 32, 91
41:5	38, 71[126], 101, 311[235]
41:6-7	4[30], 13[72], 91, 92, 459
41:6	32, 91, 91[16], 92, 92[18], 97[52]
41:7	74[143], 92, 266, 452[392]
41:8-16	125, 126, 188
41:8-13	16, 25[129], 95, 96, 97, 101, 102[95], 103, 156[77], 165
41:8-9	122
41:8	4[30], 44[211], 82[169], 95, 118[187], 125, 165[138], 308
41:9-13	99, 110
41:9	92, 101, 165[138], 308, 311[235], 347
41:10	91[16], 185[248], 201[354], 229
41:11-13	98
41:11-12	95, 98
41:11	332
41:12-29	122
41:12-13	118[187]
41:12	374[202], 458
41:13-14	185[248]
41:13	91[16], 92, 97[52], 101[88]
41:14-20	25[128]
41:14-16	26[132], 96, 103
41:14	1[8], 34, 37[181], 81, 82[169], 97[52], 99[72], 101, 103, 105, 159[92], 212[27], 288, 297[174], 442
41:15-20	122
41:15-16	18[103], 104, 112, 113, 122, 308
41:15	91[16], 118[187], 125
41:16	37[181], 40[195], 41[200], 297[174], 318, 433[255], 449
41:17-20	25[129], 107, 107[118], 174[190], 467[17], 485
41:17-19	107[119]
41:17	18, 40[195], 107, 108, 109, 112, 113, 302[195], 445[340], 449[362], 468[17], 476
41:18-20	112
41:18-19	109, 110
41:18	40[195], 54[39], 55[48], 112, 145[16], 145[19], 405
41:19	4[30], 111
41:20	4[30], 37[181], 109, 215[50], 297[174], 385[259], 394
41:21-29	6[39], 16[88], 17[92], 17[94], 35, 122, 123, 124, 134, 163, 176, 227
41:21-26	210[10]
41:21-24	116
41:21-22	188[262]
41:21	1[9], 34, 35, 115, 126, 229[139], 242[226], 381, 471[39]
41:22-24	117, 120
41:22	111[155], 118[182], 164, 264[56]
41:23	35, 97, 227[129], 236[187]
41:24	35, 165[138], 458
41:25-29	88, 116, 120
41:25-28	400
41:25-27	124, 487
41:25-26	135, 169
41:25	30[153], 32, 40, 79, 121[205], 222, 263
41:26-27	122
41:27-28	122
41:27	61[75], 82, 122
41:28	124, 125
41:29	40[195], 72[129], 122, 194[290], 194[291], 374[202], 458
42:1-9	15, 16, 19, 20, 21, 42, 57, 96, 123, 124, 126, 132, 135, 137, 188, 314
42:1-7	156[78]
42:1-4	212
42:1	20, 40[195], 44, 69[119], 69[120], 70, 98[55], 100, 124, 128, 136, 205[382], 293, 295, 463[462]
42:2-4	128, 137
42:2	138, 139, 237[192]

51:9–10	356, 370	51:17–20	366, 367, 368	52:5	22, 30, 32, 35, 38, 63[93], 150, 373[195], 382, 421
51:9	51, 141, 198[324], 339[70], 355, 356, 367, 367[170], 370, 377, 458[431]	51:17–18	122		
		51:17	53, 61[76], 335, 339[70], 360, 361, 363, 369	52:6	40, 375, 377, 430, 483
				52:7–11	24
51:10–16	4[30]	51:18	63[91], 101[88], 453	52:7–10	2, 18[102], 18[103], 34, 156[75], 369, 374[209], 376, 377, 378, 379, 380, 381, 382, 383, 384[255], 385, 385[260], 454
51:10–11	30	51:19	53, 449		
51:10	26[132], 34, 40[195], 139[295], 145[17], 159[92], 159[94], 218, 355, 442, 458[431]	51:20	453		
		51:21–23	367		
		51:21–22	368		
		51:21	361, 448		
		51:22	29[146], 365		
51:11	4[30], 25[129], 207[399], 356, 357, 360, 371	51:23–27	122	52:7–8	122, 430
		51:23	368	52:7	1[7], 22, 24, 32, 61[75], 122, 227[129], 339[70], 376, 378, 381[244], 382, 429, 438, 471[39]
		52–53	397, 437		
51:12–16	14, 43, 25[128], 360, 361	52:1–6	16, 26[132], 369, 371, 375, 376, 429		
51:12–14	51				
51:12	335, 355, 361, 362	52:1–3	36[173]	52:8	207[399], 369, 371, 382, 429, 438, 442
51:13–14	30, 33, 355, 361, 362	52:1–2	61[76], 122, 281, 370, 371, 372, 455		
51:13	40[194], 213[31], 290[159], 442, 481	52:1	1[7], 30[155], 32, 37[182], 339[70], 358, 367, 367[170], 370[177], 372, 418[177], 458, 474	52:9–10	384
				52:9	18[100], 34, 51, 159[94], 207[399], 302, 316, 361, 369, 384, 430, 433
51:14	146[20], 373				
51:15–16	363, 364	52:2	360, 377, 383		
51:15	21, 40, 139[295], 188[263], 362, 363	52:3–6	370		
		52:3–5	372, 373, 374, 375	52:10	1[7], 198[324], 249[273], 319, 350[110], 381, 384, 384[257], 385[259], 430
51:16	1[7], 40[194], 43, 213[31], 290[159], 319, 348, 360, 363, 364, 368, 483[123]	52:3	32, 159[94], 237[197], 369, 372, 373[195], 375, 442		
		52:4–6	4[30]	52:11–54:17	387
		52:4–5	430	52:11–15	402
51:17–52:10	365	52:4	25[129], 26, 29[146], 362, 372, 373, 374, 374[202], 457	52:11–14	430
51:17–23	32, 36[173], 365, 367, 368, 369, 381, 453			52:11–12	15, 18, 32[160], 330, 387, 387[1], 388, 389, 390,
51:17–21	320				

Reference	Pages	Reference	Pages	Reference	Pages
54:6-10	441, 443, 470[34]		449[361], 454[405], 454[409], 461	55:3	49, 50, 58, 58[66], 125, 445, 467[11], 469[29], 471, 478, 487
54:6-7	30	54:14-17	2[16], 17, 26[132], 30[155], 431, 456		
54:6	40[195], 156[75], 321[5], 430, 434, 440, 443, 444, 445[340], 468	54:14-15	332, 457, 458, 459	55:4	471, 472[50], 473
54:7-8	26[133], 156[75], 431[247], 444, 445	54:14	229, 362, 430, 430[243], 448, 455, 456, 460[442]	55:5	1[8], 37[181], 297[174], 465, 466, 468, 473, 474
54:7	36, 63[93]			55:6-13	475
54:8	34, 58[66], 104[104], 159[92], 159[94], 442, 445	54:15-17	451, 456[418]	55:6-8	466, 476, 480
		54:15	430, 458[429]	55:6-7	478
54:9-10	156[75]	54:16-17	427, 457, 459, 460	55:6	476
54:9	40[195], 125, 218, 431, 445, 446	54:16	32, 41, 92, 430, 456[419], 460[442], 473[53]	55:7	36[175], 445[340], 465, 476, 477, 479
54:10	50, 58[66], 93, 150[43], 227[129], 260, 427, 430, 430[243], 434, 445, 446, 447	54:17	44, 229, 387, 398, 423[206], 426, 430[243], 457, 461, 462, 463, 463[463]	55:8	40[194], 476, 478, 479, 480
				55:9-11	466, 476, 478, 480
54:11-14	17, 30, 36, 36[173], 208[407], 271, 368, 370[185], 387, 429, 447, 448, 449, 450	55	6, 24, 37, 426, 456	55:9	396, 480, 482[114]
		55:1-13	465	55:10-11	40[195], 58, 250, 422[203], 446, 465
54:11-12	24, 32, 217, 366, 430, 451, 452, 453	55:1-5	22, 32, 132[260], 465, 467	55:10	22, 58, 174[190], 202[358], 228, 230[141], 476, 480[96], 481, 481[106], 482
54:11	51, 367[168], 438, 441, 443, 448, 449, 450, 454[409], 455	55:1-3	44, 345[94], 466, 467, 468, 469, 469[28], 470, 473	55:11	6, 33, 210, 228, 263, 423[206], 471, 476, 480[96], 482, 483, 483[116]
		55:1-2	22		
54:13-17	456[417]	55:1	23, 109[139], 287, 302, 332, 468, 468[17], 476, 476[58], 476[63]	55:12-13	112, 330, 466, 476
54:13-14	32, 453, 454, 455	55:2	270[83]	55:12	18, 18[100], 174[190], 207[399], 207[404], 227[129],
54:13	32, 323, 339, 340, 367[166], 430[243], 431,	55:3-4	466, 469, 470, 471, 472, 473, 474		

Jeremiah (*continued*)

19:9	332
19:15	285
20:7–18	19[107]
20:7–13	339[73]
20:10	99[65], 99[67], 117[177], 340
20:11	215[52], 331[35], 340
20:12	99[64], 340
20:13	340
20:14–18	234, 339[73]
20:20	272[93]
21:5	63[90]
22:3	150[47], 332[40]
22:5	250[275]
22:7–8	460[445]
22:9	110[141]
22:13	373[195]
22:16	108[128], 449[358]
22:24–30	428[236]
22:24–27	471[40]
23:1–2	219[85]
23:1	219[84]
23:3–6	219[85]
23:4	219[86]
23:5	215[52]
23:7–8	218
23:29	92
23:33–40	254
23:35	92[18]
24:7	49[11], 453[404]
24:12–13	121
25:9	183[244], 225
25:11	27[141]
25:14–15	366
25:23–24	139[296], 141[305]
25:27	366[163]
25:33	308
25:34–38	219[85]
25:37	273[101]
26	19[107], 372
26:7–19	16
26:9	302
26:18	25[129], 461[448]
27:6	225
27:9	278
27:16	390[30]
27:18	428
27:21–22	121[202]
27:22	389
28:3	390[30]
28:6	390[30]
29	348
29:1–23	39
29:1–9	389
29:6	235[174], 326
29:10–14	476
29:10–11	121
29:10	27[141], 326
29:11	478, 479
29:14	383[253], 478
29:24–32	39
29:26	409
30:3	383[253]
30:15	407[115]
30:18	383[253]
30:22	50[11]
31	63[91]
31:5	183[241]
31:6	485[136]
31:7	384[255]
31:9	160[106], 484[127]
31:12	395
31:15–16	63[86]
31:23	370[177], 383[253]
31:27–38	206[389]
31:31–34	43[208], 50[14], 132[259]
31:32	222, 439[296]
31:33	50, 50[11], 152[58]
31:34	92[18], 453[404], 477
31:35	363
31:37	101[93], 290[160]
32:4	382[246]
32:8	185
32:18	331[35]
32:21	355
32:33	411[141]
32:36–44	50[14]
32:38	50[11], 50[14]
33:8	477
33:9	195[298]
33:10	246[247]
33:11	17[98]
33:23–26	100[83], 101[91]
33:25	227[129]
33:26	100[83]
34:8–27	246[248]
34:8–22	135[272], 362, 363
34:14	187
34:16	410[130]
34:17	92[18]
34:22	187, 246[248]
36:1–2	483[124]
36:5	415
36:16	195[298]
36:22	199[330]
36:24	195[298]
38:22	147[33]
39:13	256[15]
40:2–3	50
40:12	160[105]
43	213[33]
43:8	213[33]
43:10	225
44	284
44:2	284
44:6	284
44:7	405[100]
44:15–19	36[174]
44:15	153
44:17	483[116]
44:22–23	284
44:26	284
44:28	248[264]
45:3	407[114]
46:5	147[33]
46:24	439[294]
47:5	273[101]
48:1	439[294]
48:15	84[178]
48:20	439[294]
48:21	415[161]
48:30	214[42]

33:24	100[83]	43:17	452	4:15–16	118[188], 119[188]
34	63[91], 412	43:20	452	4:17	216[61]
34:1–10	219[85]	44:13	439[297]	4:21	119[188]
34:5	412	44:23	410[131]	4:32	234[168]
34:6	395, 412, 413	45:8	332[40]	4:35	227[129]
34:14	395	46:18	332[40]	5:1–6:1	374[201]
34:23–24	30, 219[85]	47	347	5:3–4	389
34:23	219[84]	47:1–12	112, 467[15], 467[16]	5:7–8	119[188]
34:24	408[124]	47:1	467	5:8	118[188]
34:25–30	481[106]	47:7	111[154]	5:12	118[188], 119[188]
34:25	447[349]	47:12	111[154]	5:15–17	119[188]
35–36	217[65]	48:15	410[132]	5:16	118[188]
35:8	54[40]			5:25–28	374[201]
35:9	216[65]	**Daniel**		5:26	119[188]
35:10	216[65]	1–6	29[149], 196	7	72, 80, 120, 218[69], 350, 357, 398[66]
35:12	216[65]	1	214[39]		
35:15	217[65]	1:4	202[363]		
36	50[14]	1:17	202[363], 215[50]	7:2–3	357
36:2	216[65], 242[224]	1:21	219[82]	7:9–10	214[39]
36:4	54[40]	2	117, 214[39], 279	7:9	163[119]
36:7	439[297]	2:2	278, 291	7:12	357
36:26–27	453[404]	2:4–7	118[188]	7:16	119[188]
36:26	50[14]	2:4	291	7:25	119
36:28	50[11]	2:7	118[188]	7:28	119[193]
36:29–38	112	2:9	118[188]	8	119[192], 461[447]
36:35	217, 435[270]	2:10	117[178]	8:11–14	375
37:1–14	290	2:16	118[188]	8:12	423[206]
37:1–4	186	2:24–26	118[188]	8:23	202[363]
37:1	396[51]	2:30	118[188]	8:24–25	423[206]
37:10–11	290	2:34	54[41]	8:26	165[132]
37:11	416[168]	2:35	54[41]	9	43, 121, 153[66], 183[239], 410[134], 478
37:15–27	50[14]	2:36	118[188]		
37:23	50[14]	2:45	118[188]		
37:24–25	30	3	29[147], 157, 191[268]	9:2–3	27[141], 119[192]
37:25	408[124]			9:2	121[204], 215[57]
37:26	50[14], 132[259], 447[349]	3:8–9	460	9:9	478[75]
37:27	50[11], 50[14]	3:16–18	157	9:11	121[204], 126[232], 131[253]
38:4	172[179]	3:25	460		
39:18–19	332	3:26	157	9:13	42[205], 131[253], 215[49]
39:21	415[161]	3:28	157		
40:1	396[51]	3:30	423[206]	9:15	121[204]
42:20	410[131]	4–5	214[39]	9:20	370[177]
43:1–4	24[125]	4:3–4	118[188]	9:21–23	121[204]
43:5	382	4:6	119[188]	9:22	119[192], 215[51], 394
43:13	452			9:24–27	121

Zephaniah (continued)

3:14	207[399]
3:15	188[262]
3:17	331[35]
3:20	383[253]

Haggai

2:6	302[197]
2:7–9	473[55]
2:20–23	30, 471[40]
2:23	428[236]

Zechariah

1–8	370[177]
1:4	299
1:8	217[68]
1:15	367[169], 445[339]
1:16–17	444[330]
2:4–5	461[449]
2:8–9	452[389]
2:10–13	367[169]
2:10	466[6]
2:11	466[6]
2:14	207[399], 433[257], 434
2:17	370[177]
3	30, 398[67], 401, 402
3:1–7	183[242], 370
3:1	401
3:2	401
3:7	401
3:8	471[40]
4:1–14	30
4:1	339[70]
4:6–10	471[40]
4:7	54[41]
4:14	225[118]
5:4	284[139]
6:9–15	471[40]
7:10	108[130]
7:11	299
7:12	152[58]
7:14	246[247], 449[368]
8:3	370[177], 383[254], 444[330]
8:7–8	383[254]
8:8	50[11]
8:12	186[252]
9:9–10	433[257]
9:10	249[273]
9:13–14	141[310]
9:14	449[366]
10–11	412
10:8	254
10:11	217[68]
11:1–2	71[127]
13:1	467[16]
13:2	486, 486[147]
13:9	92, 286[151], 286[152]
14:1–11	467[15]
14:1	426[225]
14:3	56, 141[309]
14:4	54[40]
14:8–9	467[16]
14:8	467
14:16–18	485[135]
14:20–21	370[177]
14:20	467
14:21	187[257]

Malachi

1:6	160[106]
2:10	235[178], 286[150]
2:11	120[198], 168[152], 441[312]
2:14–15	444[326]
2:14	446[344]
3:1	55
3:5	284[139]
3:16	420[188]
3:20	226[126], 377, 377[220]
3:21	332
3:22	42[205], 126[232], 130[253], 428[237]

b / New Testament

Matthew

2:1–12	24
3:17	127[234]
6:12	477[74]
6:14	477[74]
7:25	261[45]
8:12	291[165]
12:18–21	125[222]
12:42	249[273]
13:42	291[165]
13:50	291[165]
15:14	151[50]
16:1–4	204[373]
16:18	272[97]
17:5	127[234]
20:17–19	485[137]
21:8	484[130]
22:1–14	17[98]
22:4	415[157]
22:13	291[165]
24:51	291[165]
25:1–13	17[98]
25:6	448[352]
25:30	291[165]
26:28	478[74]

Mark

1:1–20	480[92]
1:1–8	423[208]
1:2–3	55
1:2	175[196]
1:3	175[196]
1:5	391[40]
1:6	156[74]
1:11	127[234]
1:15	175[196]
1:45	249[273]
2:5	477[74]
9:7	127[234]
10:32–34	485[137]
11:25	477[74]
13:14	437[287]
13:27	249[273]
16:15–16	385[260]

In the design of the visual aspects of *Hermeneia,* consideration has been given to relating the form to the content by symbolic means.

The letters of the logotype *Hermeneia* are a fusion of forms alluding simultaneously to Hebrew (dotted vowel markings) and Greek (geometric round shapes) letter forms. In their modern treatment they remind us of the electronic age as well, the vantage point from which this investigation of the past begins.

The Lion of Judah used as visual identification for the series is based on the Seal of Shema. The version for *Hermeneia* is again a fusion of Hebrew calligraphic forms, especially the legs of the lion, and Greek elements characterized by the geometric. In the sequence of arcs, which can be understood as scroll-like images, the first is the lion's mouth. It is reasserted and accelerated in the whorl and returns in the aggressively arched tail: tradition is passed from one age to the next, rediscovered and re-formed.

"Who is worthy to open the scroll and break its seals. . . ."
Then one of the elders said to me
"weep not; lo, the Lion of the tribe of David,
the Root of David, has conquered,
so that he can open the scroll and
its seven seals."
Rev. 5:2, 5

To celebrate the signal achievement in biblical scholarship which *Hermeneia* represents, the entire series will by its color constitute a signal on the theologian's bookshelf: the Old Testament will be bound in yellow and the New Testament in red, traceable to a commonly used color coding for synagogue and church in medieval painting; in pure color terms, varying degrees of intensity of the warm segment of the color spectrum. The colors interpenetrate when the binding color for the Old Testament is used to imprint volumes from the New and vice versa.

Wherever possible, a photograph of the oldest extant manuscript, or a historically significant document pertaining to the biblical sources, will be displayed on the end papers of each volume to give a feel for the tangible reality and beauty of the source material.

The title-page motifs are expressive derivations from the Hermeneia logotype, repeated seven times to form a matrix and debossed on the cover of each volume. These sifted-out elements will be seen to be in their exact positions within the parent matrix.

Horizontal markings at gradated levels on the spine will assist in grouping the volumes according to these conventional categories.

The type has been set with unjustified right margins so as to preserve the internal consistency of word spacing. This is a major factor in both legibility and aesthetic quality; the resultant uneven line endings are only slight impairments to legibility by comparison. In this respect the type resembles the handwritten manuscripts where the quality of the calligraphic writing is dependent on establishing and holding to integral spacing patterns.

All of the type faces in common use today have been designed between AD 1500 and the present. For the biblical text a face was chosen which does not arbitrarily date the text, but rather one which is uncompromisingly modern and unembellished so that its feel is of the universal. The type style is Univers 65 by Adrian Frutiger.

The expository texts and footnotes are set in Baskerville, chosen for its compatibility with the many brief Greek and Hebrew insertions. The double-column format and the shorter line length facilitate speed reading and the wide margins to the left of footnotes provide for the scholar's own notations.

Kenneth Hiebert